Traditional
FRENCH
Cooking

LAROUSSE

Traditional
FRENCH
Cooking

CURNONSKY

DOUBLEDAY
New York   London   Toronto   Sydney   Auckland

Published by Doubleday, a division of
Bantam Doubleday Dell Publishing Group, Inc.
666 Fifth Avenue, New York, New York 10103

Library of Congress Cataloging-in-Publication Data
Curnonsky, 1872–1956.
[Cuisine et vins de France. English]
Larousse, traditional French cooking/Curnonsky. — 1st ed.
p.   cm.
Translation of: Cuisine et vins de France.
Includes index.
ISBN 0–385–28532–8:
1. Cookery (French)   2. Wine and wine making—
France. I. Title.

TX719.C8513 1989
841.5944 — dc19
89–1164
CIP

English language edition edited by
Jeni Wright.
Assisted by Helen Dore, Helen Southall,
Danielle Lawrence-de Froidmont, Felicity Jackson.
American editor: Norma MacMillan
Wine editor: Andrew Jefford
Translation by Rosetta Translations

Typeset in England by
Chapterhouse Typesetting Ltd., Formby L37 3PX

French edition, *Curnonsky: Cuisine et Vins de France*,
first published in 1987 by Librairie Larousse
Translation © 1989 The National Magazine Company Limited

Text and photographs © Librairie Larousse, 1987
Photos: Daniel Czap

All Rights Reserved

Printed and bound in Italy by
New Interlitho, S.p.a., Milan

October 1989
First edition

CONTENTS

FOREWORD

'Make it simple . . . and let things taste of what they are.' These words of Curnonsky, prince of gastronomes, became famous during the years when he was criss-crossing France as an investigative 'gastronomad' and discovering the culinary riches of his native land. How many chefs there must be who would love to claim these words as their own! The collection of recipes presented here in *Traditional French Cookery* by Curnonsky, nourished as it was by the experience of hundreds of masters of the art of eating well, is offered by way of delicious illustration. And you have only to leaf through this chefs' anthology with all its many facets to find it full of flavours and aromas more alluring than a tale from *A Thousand and One Nights*. Haute cuisine, plain bourgeois fare, regional and impromptu cooking, are the four aspects of the culinary art that together make up a book in which the text is supported by equally enticing photographs.

For us, the Troisgros, cooking has been our destiny. Our cuisine is one of family traditions and regional produce, but it is also open to other influences, sometimes from the far ends of the earth. Marrying tradition and modernity seems to me to be the ambition of today's chefs, who sometimes venture some original combinations, but always favour a return to first sources, the rediscovery of simple – some would say rustic – ingredients, produced as they are with painstaking diligence. This is the view that my brother Jean and I have held from the start, and which I am maintaining with my son Michel. Salmon steak with sorrel is the best-known example: it was no accident that this was chosen by Valéry Giscard d'Estaing on the occasion of the presentation of the 'Légion d'honneur' medal to Paul Bocuse.

Like many chefs who worked with Fernand Point, I have always put the emphasis on the quality of the ingredients used. Only this allows the inspiration that brings about a happy blend of the elements involved. Cooking is an art that needs to evolve and change on the basis of its methods and materials, its organization – and even of the whole concept of the role of the chef.

Meals, however, should always be celebrations. A chef should be a generous gourmand, open and welcoming. It is this craftsman's privilege, surely, to have at his table a variety of people he would never otherwise have occasion to meet. 'We are the last of the seigneurs,' said my father, Jean-Baptiste, the son of burgundian winegrowers. I like the food I prepare for my guests to be light, readily digestible, pure and wholesome, particularly in a country that has such wonders as Isigny butter, olive oil from the Alpilles, Chalan duck and Charolais beef – not to mention its marvellous store of wines.

There are many epicurean ways of drawing on this monumental compendium of recipes. You could start by reading it like a novel, for example, working up an appetite as you let your imagination wander from dish to dish. But above all else, do not let yourself be intimidated by the lists of ingredients or the recipes, which can sometimes seem complicated.

A recipe is not a straitjacket. Take an idea here, a combination there – what a range of resources there are in, for example, the chapters on chicken or sole. Make yourself an inventory of those recipes that match your own level of proficiency.

You should also pay particular heed to the suggestions regarding wine, which in their diversity offer an ingenious tour through the rich resources of the French vineyards, from Burgundy to Bordeaux, from the Côtes du Rhône to the Loire valley.

An inexhaustible source of culinary discovery, *Traditional French Cookery*, inspired by true French gastronomy, will more than satisfy you through the seasons, combining as it does the great classics and regional specialities.

Constantly updated, French cuisine has a unique history. Its traditions, its class, its reputation and, too, its heart, its warmth and its allure all speak to both eye and palate. With his compendium, Curnonsky wrote a succulent chapter of this history. Just start to read it, recipe by recipe, and your mouth will begin to water . . .

Pierre Troisgros

CURNONSKY

One morning in July 1956, in the Square de Laborde, Paris, a man fell from a third-floor window on to the pavement below: a tragic end to a life largely devoted to good cheer and all the riches of gastronomy. It was Maurice Edmond Sailland, better known by his pseudonym Curnonsky.

Born in Angers in 1872, he went to Paris to begin his literary studies, but soon turned towards journalism and resolved to live by his pen. On the advice of Alphonse Allais, the young man decided to choose a pen-name. It was a time of Franco-Russian friendship, so Why-Not (in Latin *Cur-Non*)-Sky? His Parisian literary and journalistic career began with the thankless task of ghost writing for Willy, Colette's first husband. With his friend Toulet he then published several successful works and made the acquaintance of Raoul Ponchon, Léon Daudet and Franc-Nohain, of Forain, Pierre Louÿs and Debussy.

Soon known to all Paris for his openness, and as a good trencherman, he signed the first piece in '*le Journal*' under the 'gastronomade' heading. This neologism – gastro-nomad – was his own. Henceforth Curnonsky was to put his talent, his experience as a writer and his sturdy appetite to the service of gastronomy. In 1921, with his friend Marcel Rouff, he embarked upon the project '*la France gastronomique*', an impressive good food guide to France published in 28 pamphlets.

When in 1927 the review *Le Bon Gîte et la Bonne Table* organized a referendum to choose the 'prince of gastronomes', the crown went – with 1823 votes out of 3388 – to this unique and eclectic bard of good eating and drinking. 'Prince Cur' now divided his time between dinners and enthronements, sponsorships and wine tastings. Yet he still found time to continue his work as a writer on gastronomy: *les Recettes des provinces de France*, *le Trésor gastronomique de la France* (edited in collaboration with Austin de Croze), and *les Fines Gueules de France* (with P. Andrieu) were his, not forgetting *la Table et l'Amour*, a witty account of aphrodisiac recipes.

Founder and first president of the 'Académie des gastronomes' in 1930, he at once became the defender of 'good cooking, characterized by honesty and simplicity, which serves things tasting of what they are'. During the Second World War Curnonsky took refuge in Riec-sur-Belon, in Mélanie Rouat's little hotel-restaurant – one of his discoveries, which he had made famous – and there he went on with his writing.

In 1947, back in Paris, he founded the review *Cuisine et Vins de France*. In 1952 he received a resounding tribute from the restaurateurs who owed him so much. On the initiative of *Cuisine et Vins de France* and R. Courtine, eighty Parisian and Île-de-France restaurants were involved in putting up a brass plaque in his honour:

CETTE PLACE EST CELLE DE

MAURICE EDMOND SAILLAND CURNONSKY

PRINCE ÉLU DES GASTRONOMES

DÉFENSEUR ET ILLUSTRATEUR

DE LA CUISINE FRANÇAISE

HÔTE D'HONNEUR DE CETTE MAISON.

THE ART
OF THE TABLE

With its decorations, its cutlery, glass and china, its food and its rituals, a well-laid table appears as an aesthetic form indicative of a certain culture, a certain civilization. The creative aspect of the culinary arts is based on the processing of raw ingredients to the point where they finally make their appearance on the plate or in the serving dish. For the art of the table is the arranging of items of food and serving them according to certain social forms, which vary in time and space; but it is also the choosing and buying of produce, the working out of the menu and, of course, the cooking techniques themselves. This art has its own place among the other arts – painting, literature or music – to the extent that its affinity with nature is most intense and direct, and also in so far as it responds – even in forms that are sometimes very sophisticated – to what is a vital function; and it also has the advantage of being a popular art, shared by the greatest number of participants.

Nevertheless, the art of the table goes beyond the mere putting of recipes into practice; it embraces good manners, the balance of the menu, the skills of being a host, and of best organizing that privileged moment when a meal is shared with guests or family. 'A meal is good cheer and rejoicing. It is also the framework within which the family celebrates its mutual understanding; the privileged moment when it takes its most important decisions. In the most ancient of the world's civilizations, in Mesopotamia, the table was already an important aspect of life.' So wrote J. Bottéro in *l'Histoire, 5000 ans de gastronomie*.

For as long as men have lived in society and taken their meals in company, certain rules have been applied – differing of course according to the country, and indeed the very soil, and the time: variations that reveal the way in which manners and tastes have evolved. Belching, which today in the West is considered coarse in the extreme, was a sign of good manners among the Romans – as it still is in the Middle East. The art of putting together a menu is quite different in Europe and in Asia. In China the order of courses traditionally begins with several cold dishes, followed by hot dishes and then finally a light soup – although perhaps a few small delicacies may still be eaten after that. In Japanese cuisine it is rather the alternation of textures, flavours and colours, according to season, that determines the menu.

Even in such closely neighbouring countries as France, Italy, Great Britain and Germany, a sense of strangeness may proceed from quite different ideas of the art of the table. Such details as dessert before the cheese in Britain; the place of the salad in Italy; or the frequent absence of hors-d'œuvre in Germany. As for the actual methods, cooking utensils and produce, these naturally influence the way in which meals are conceived and served. The microwave oven, frozen food and steaming, for example, are now creating a style of cuisine and gastronomy far removed from those huge joints of meat with their elaborate garnishes and accompaniments, served to guests on great showpiece plates in the past. As a result, notions of decorating both table and dishes have undergone significant changes.

Quite early, deportment at table inspired a number of works aimed at codifying the rules of decorum, the art of being a host or a guest and being conversant with all the subtleties of receiving or being received. One of the first manuals was written by Robert de Blois, after chivalric custom had developed the ceremonial of the table and the courtesies of welcome. Washing hands before and after a meal was obligatory: you have to remember that many diners used the same bowl and goblet, and that the fork did not yet exist. Even in the time of Louis XIV the use of this item, although quite widespread in Italy, was still rare in France. You took the food on the point of your knife, or in your fingers – but politeness required you to use no more than three. In a small work entitled *Convenance de la table* (*convenance* means propriety, decorum, convention), dating from the 12th century, the following recommendations can be read: 'throw the bones under the table, but always without harming any person'; or 'always eat all you can; if you are at a friend's house, this will flatter him, if at an enemy's it will upset him . . .'.

As far as glasses are concerned, it was only after the French Revolution that guests were entitled to one each. Until then bottles and glasses or goblets were set out on a small side table. The guest would signal to a servant, who brought the filled glass to him on a serving plate and cleared it away again afterwards. In 1526 the philosopher Erasmus applied his great mind to these more mundane questions of good manners and stated a number of precepts: 'do not drink until the second course, after the soup, and you should always wipe your lips with a handkerchief beforehand . . . putting food you have already chewed back on your plate is dirty . . . sticking your fingers in the sauces is gross' – these rules make us smile now, but they have to be seen in their own context. Domestic animals used to haunt the public rooms and hearths of inns, attracted there by the scraps of food which the manuals of good manners, right up to the 18th century, were recommending should be thrown on the floor or into corners, rather than put back on the plate. In the days of the 'Grand Siècle' at the court of Louis XIV (1643–1715), a nobleman was considered quite odd for recommending special spoons to serve ragoûts and sauces.

However, despite the apparent lack of sophistication, there had been a decisive turning point in good manners and table etiquette at the beginning of the 17th century, indicating the efforts of a well-to-do and enlightened society that was particularly open to Italian influences, to fashion a true art of polished, elegant living. This concern with refinement was reflected in the vocabulary: this was the period when 'soupe' became 'potage'. Things then veered towards affectation in France in the following century, with its 'petits soupers en ambigu' (cold buffets in which meat and fruit were served together) and its 'médianoches' (late night suppers). Manners, however, are always slow to evolve: it was not until the mid-19th century that people gave up using their hands to toss the salad, and that a good hostess's dinner service included a leg of mutton holder.

It was only in the 19th century that architects began to create a specific area in private hotels that was set aside for meals – a dining room. This rather late phenomenon resulted from a profound change in social relationships that was also reflected in table manners. Previously, tables had been 'set up' rather than 'set', often close to the area where the food was prepared and where there was available space – trestle tables would be put up in the nearest big room and to them would be brought the 'covers'. The term still had its literal meaning then, for the plates would be carried from the kitchen with covers on so as to keep them hot for as long as possible – and also to prevent anyone poisoning the food. Afterwards the table would be taken down and removed. Once an area specifically for meals had been organized, social interaction was improved, acquiring nuances and subtleties that varied according to the social environment. Henceforth

the table often moved to a central place in the dining room, so that both the piece of furniture itself and the act that was played out around it were given due significance. Increasingly the organization of the meal became ritualized, taking on the quality of a performance – an effect heightened by the candlesticks, the candelabras, the glasses and the centrepieces. At the same time the serving of the food changed radically. The French style of serving, with guests offered a great variety of dishes at the same time, began to be replaced around 1850 by what was termed the 'Russian style'. This had several distinct sequences and a distribution of the food that, although simplified, remains in practice today (even if certain restaurants now extol a system that sometimes seems to be a return to the old French style). From that time on, the order (in France) was: soup, fish, poultry, roast, salad, *entremets*, cheese, dessert; with everything, including scraps and crumbs, cleared away before serving the dessert.

All through the 'Ancien Régime', it had been the showy French style that had prevailed. Numerous dishes were served simultaneously – hot and cold, salt and sweet – and replenished, and arranged almost geometrically according to a given order on the table in a manner reminiscent of a buffet. Faced with this array, guests served themselves in any order they wished, calling on servants to bring them any items beyond their reach. Without doubt this allowed sumptuous decorative effects to be composed, with the china, the 'pièces montées' (elaborate tiered pâtisserie), the pyramids of fruit, the flower arrangements and the treasures of the gold- and silversmith's art playing leading roles in this display of luxury. If a royal banquet might easily include more than 150 dishes, then the order of precedence meant that most of the guests either had to eat the food cold, or not eat at all. The customary five courses offered to Louis XIV in 1656 by Madame de La Chancellière at her Château de Pontchartrain totalled 168 dishes or accompaniments, excluding desserts. In 1808 the *Manuel des amphitryons* suggested a score of menus, each comprising two soups, two *relevés*, eight *entrées*, two large 'pièces' (large dishes of fish, poultry or other meat), two roasts and eight desserts. However, the great Carême, 'prince of chefs and chef of princes', considered that the number of dishes might properly be reduced and, above all, served 'one after the other, so that they would be hotter and better'. It was then that the Russian style of serving made its appearance, 'launched' by the Tsar's ambassador to Paris, Prince A. B. Kurakin, in the mid-19th century. The dishes were served in sequence, there were fewer of them, and no course was brought on until the guests had finished the preceding one. The taste for ostentatious display in tableware and decoration did not, however, disappear – far from it. But a new code was established, a new circulation of dishes in the dining room. This 'service à la russe' divided the number of guests into groups of eight, ten or twelve, each group being served by a maître d'hôtel, with guests indicating in advance which of them he should serve first. Dishes were served from the left of the seated person and the plate placed or withdrawn from the right. Wine was served from the right, in the same order as the courses, but only after the first drops had been poured into the host's glass. At an informal meal it was the latter who carved and served the meat, passing round the plates in order, starting with the person on his right.

The most recent manifestation with regard to serving food, and all the arts of the table associated with this, made its appearance in the 1970s. This was service on the plate, currently practised in restaurants and beginning to spread to private dinners. The Troisgros brothers, chefs and restaurateurs at Roanne, were the originators of this new practice; they saw that carving in the dining room, on a small table beside the guest, did not produce the desired aesthetic effect, that there was waste, and that the food got rather cold. When he arranges the food on each individual plate, the chef remains in sole charge, without the head waiter being involved either in the final effect or the serving. Service on the plate allows an exact measuring of portions, and a particular aesthetic arrangement with regard to the garnish and accompaniments, the sauce, and the decoration – but above all the retention of heat and ease of presentation at the table. This method is less easy for a hostess, but is nevertheless to be recommended for first courses, mixed salads and certain desserts.

Evolution and change in social customs and ways of life have over the centuries influenced interior architecture and the arrangement of furniture; in particular, the appearance of very modest-sized rooms and 'integrated' kitchens has paralleled changes in the position of women.

But the fact remains that the social rituals that have grown up around and because of the table and the food presented there, and the manner of its serving, retain all their force. The etiquette that determines the positioning of guests at a table has long been rather obscure. Among the Greeks the position of honour belonged by right to any stranger invited to share the meal. During the whole of the Middle Ages, and for as long as banquets were accompanied by entertainments, the master of the house would invite the most notable guest to sit beside him, so as to profit from his company at leisure. It was this guest, too, who was accorded the honour of carving the great roast. The sometimes complex conventions that still quite often hold force today did not really take shape until the 18th century. We will not go into details here of the protocol that accords to politicians, churchmen and others their respective positions around the table, but remember the general principle is that title goes before age and, where social rank is equal, age takes precedence. Beyond this, the custom is to honour the person invited for the first time by seating him or her to the right of the host or hostess.

More decisive when it comes to the prized conviviality of a successful dinner, however, is the menu itself, to which the host or hostess should give all their attention. There are theories on the subject; and the recommendation is to pay due heed to both variety and harmony: a principle easier to state than to practise, above all when restraint within elegance has to be shown. Down the centuries gourmets and gastronomes have not been lacking in formulating advice: during the course of a meal, never serve dishes with the same kind of sauce – both fish and chicken 'à la crème', for example; do not overdo the luxury – such as following foie gras with fillet steak Rossini; do not serve a tart or anything else in pastry as a dessert if you have had a quiche, vol-au-vent or flaky pastry as a hot first course; do not follow ice-cold food with something boiling hot, or vice versa, thus avoiding contrasts that are too great. But these negative principles are often of limited help to the hostess. Putting together a menu is neither a matter of a secret code known only to initiates, nor a game of arbitrary chance. The first principle is variation, in the sense that in a well-thought-out menu nothing should appear twice: thus there should not be chicken in a mixed salad or as a first course and then again as the main dish. Heed should also be paid to the accompanying vegetables (especially the ever-present potato) and, indeed, to the method of cooking (avoid having two lots of fried ingredients, in the first course and dessert for example, or two poached dishes). Finally, the balance of a menu depends also on variations in the shapes, consistencies and colours of the food served.

The second principle is that of a 'grading' system: there should always be an ascending order of flavours, starting with mild, delicate items, the colour of which would also tend to place them here: egg dishes, creamed soups, asparagus, vegetable casseroles, fish mousses, etc. Then you come to the stage of the meal that could consist of, for example, game, marinated and roasted meat, a fish stew or braised salmon or a chicken flambé. This system of grading holds good for choosing the wines and making up the cheese board. Sequence and grading are thus two principles that enable you to put together a menu without any obvious errors. It goes without saying that an inspired chef may not 'respect' these theories, but nevertheless knows how to create culinary symphonies fit to enrapture the gourmet.

A sequence of three dishes is necessary to justify the term 'menu'. However, this reduction to a strict minimum – first course, main dish with vegetables, then dessert – is not enough for a meal of any consequence and, of course, is quite inadequate for a reception. In his *Vie à table à la fin du XIXᵉ siècle*, Châtillon-Plessis describes with great zest the 'plan for big dining room manœuvres', following a pattern that has not really altered much down to our own times, apart from the *relevés*:

'Soup, piping hot and velvety. This is what starts the march, clears the ground and rids the tongue of any taste alien to the gourmet, replacing it with the first of the nourishing essences . . . the *relevés*, large pieces of fish or meat, are for satisfying the first urgings of keen appetites . . . the hot or cold *entrées* bring an appreciation of the delicacy of the culinary art in content and form . . . then follows the roast, which is for the epicure what the *entrée* is for the gourmet: a more solid, less delicate, source of pleasure. Welcome now to the salads, the sharpness of which quickens nerves deadened by fare too delicate! Here now is the end of the procession with vegetable *entremets* . . . then,

suddenly, the gendarmes who bring up the rear of the parade, assuring all is in good gustatory order: the cheeses. Now the décor has been changed with the covers. Here are the pastries and the creams, the ices, petits fours and fruit . . . Not forgetting the bread, without which no good, honest feast, no meal, is possible!'

Nowadays a formula that is relatively simple, but worked out none the less both in terms of concept and in the time it takes to eat, is imposed on formal dinners. The menu starts with a cold *entrée*, or a mixed salad. A hot *entrée* then follows, or a soup, then a light fish dish. A sorbet sprinkled with alcohol (without a fruit sauce) may be brought in here to act like a 'trou normand' in reactivating the appetite for the main course of poultry, meat or game. After a short interval, a selection of cheeses is served, then a dessert, pâtisserie, ice cream or fruit. Finally coffee is served – with a few chocolates and petits fours – then liqueurs and spirits. It is easy, of course, to imagine a shorter menu based on this, leaving out, for example, the cold or hot *entrées* or the fish, leaving out the cheese and serving the sorbet as a dessert, etc.

A menu, however, is not an abstract exercise. Its composition is based on whatever shopping has been done. A chef or a housewife with an eye for the quality of produce does not shop according to preconceived ideas, after first listing the ingredients needed for some arbitrarily chosen recipe. It is undoubtedly useful, however, to have some general plan in mind for the meal (meat rather than fish, mixed salad rather than a hot *entrée*, individual steaks rather than one large roast, and so on). But at the shops it is sight, smell and touch, and a little practical experience, that determine the final choice when selecting vegetables or fruit in season, the freshest fish, the most appetizing poultry, etc. It is through knowing your tradesmen, building up mutual confidence – but going from shop to shop as well – that you will be able to make your choice judiciously and in peace. All the great chefs and 'cordons-bleus' confirm the obvious advantage of 'cuisine du marché' (cooking according to the market), which gives preference to seasonal or early produce and allows the best relationship between quality and price (always a difficult point in household economy). Over and against this, ingredients such as caviar, foie gras, truffles and smoked salmon allow no substitutes. Better to do without rather than choose a cheap alternative or a poor-quality product. Care should also be taken over ingredients that are hard to find and are replaced by others thought to be similar. There is some risk here, for creative cooking is never an easy matter: one product cannot be automatically replaced by another merely on the basis of analogy.

It is the balance of colours and flavours among the dishes, their accompaniments and sauces, the variety of textures among the items, refraining from gratuitous ostentation, that make a meal a success.

'And above all, make it simple!', was Curnonsky's recommendation to the chefs he met: a precept sometimes rather forgotten, but one that should always guide you when working out a menu.

Here are some dinners arranged for the centenary in 1972 of the birth of the 'prince of gastronomes':

The 'Académie des gastronomes' celebrated its founder with the following menu at Maxim's:
SUPRÊME DE SAINT-PIERRE
SAUCE MIREILLE
POULE FAISANE RÔTIE SUR CANAPÉ
POMMES MAXIM'S
PURÉE DE CÉLERI
SALADE LORETTE
FROMAGES
MILLE-FEUILLE AUX FRAMBOISES
FRIANDISES

Jacques Manière prepared the following dinner at Le Pactole restaurant, Paris:
TOURIN BLANCHI
HOMARD À LA NAGE SAUCE MANIÈRE
GRANITÉ AU CHAMPAGNE ROSÉ
POULET PÈRE LATHUILE
DAUBE FROIDE DE JOUE DE BŒUF
SALADE À L'HUILE DE NOIX
FROMAGES DE FRANCE
ÎLE FLOTTANTE AUX PRALINES ROSES
BRIOCHE MOUSSELINE TIÈDE

Pierre Laporte, of the Café de Paris, Biarritz, suggested:
FOIE DE CANARD FRAIS EN TERRINE
ESCALOPE DE LOUVINE BRAISÉE AU VIN ROUGE
PERDREAUX RÔTIS SUR CANAPÉ
FROMAGES
TIMBALE ÉLYSÉE (DE RENÉ LASSERRE)

The Hôtel du Rhône, Geneva, took the initiative in honouring Curnonsky, placing the first International Gastronomy Congress under his patronage and arranging the following dinner:
FEUILLETÉ AUX CHAMPIGNONS DU JURA
FILETS D'OMBLE DU LAC
AU BEURRE BLANC
MIGNON DE VEAU À LA BROCHE
FEUILLES D'ÉPINARDS AUX LARDONS
FROMAGES
BISCUIT GLACÉ À L'EAU-DE-VIE DU VALAIS

The 'gastronomadism' so valued by Curnonsky is beautifully illustrated in the menus composed today by the 'grandes toques' (top chefs) of French gastronomy, each one reflecting the personality of its creator. Here are twelve examples.

– CLASSICISM –

Point, Restaurant de la Pyramide, Vienna

MOUSSE DE FOIE EN BRIOCHE
DÉLICE DE SAINT-JACQUES
TURBOT BRAISÉ AU VERMOUTH
POULARDE DE BRESSE ALBUFÉRA
GRATIN DAUPHINOIS
PLATEAU DE FROMAGES
SORBET À L'EAU-DE-VIE DE POIRES
SUCCÈS PRALINÉ
CORBEILLE DE FRUITS

– HARMONIOUS SIMPLICITY –

Charles Barrier, Tours

TERRINE DE LÉGUMES
AU COULIS DE TOMATES
SANDRE GILLÉ AU BEURRE D'ÉCREVISSES
FRICASSÉE DE POULET AU VINAIGRE DE
FRAMBOISES
NOUILLES FRAÎCHES
LES FROMAGES AVEC PAIN AUX NOIX
FEUILLETÉ DE POIRES AU BOURGUEIL

– TRADITION REVIVED –

Auberge du Père Bise, Talloires

PÂTÉ DE CANARD AUX PISTACHES
GRATIN DE QUEUES D'ÉCREVISSES
POULET DE BRESSE GRILLÉ
SAUCE DIABLE
PLATEAU DE FROMAGES
VACHERIN GLACÉ

– VITALITY AND GENEROSITY –

Bocuse, Collonges-au-Mont-d'Or

SOUPE DE TRUFFES
LOUP EN CROÛTE DE LA MÉDITERRANÉE,
SAUCE CHORON
PIÈCE DE BŒUF DU CHAROLAIS À L'ÉCHALOTE
PLATEAU DE FROMAGES
LES DESSERTS DE PAUL BOCUSE
ET PETITS FOURS

– IMAGINATIVE AND INVENTIVE RECIPES –

Alain Chapel, Mionnay

FOIE GRAS DE CANARD POÊLÉ
COURGETTES À LA FLEUR, JEUNES AUBERGINES
ET PETITS OIGNONS FANES, EN AIGRE-DOUX
RIS, CERVELLE ET AMOURETTES D'AGNEAU AUX
FÈVES DE PRINTEMPS
SUPRÊME DE TURBOT DE LIGNE
CLOUTÉ D'ANCHOIS RÔTI AU PERSIL
ET BAIGNÉ D'UNE SAUCE AU CHAMPAGNE
QUELQUES FROMAGES FERMIERS
DESSERTS GLACÉS, MIGNARDISES
PRALINES, CANDIS ET CHOCOLATS
PÂTISSERIE MAISON

– SUBTLETIES OF TASTE AND FLAVOURS –

Michel Guérard, Eugénie-les-Bains

SOUPE AUX ÉCREVISSES DE RIVIÈRE
FEUILLETÉ DE TRUFFES AU VIN DE GRAVES
COQUILLES SAINT-JACQUES À LA COQUE
NAVARIN DE FAISAN AUX PIEDS DE COCHON
TARTE FINE CHAUDE AUX POMMES ACIDULÉES

– THE STRENGTH OF TRADITION –

The Haeberlin Family, Auberge de l'Ill

BOUDIN DE CAILLE ET DE RIS DE VEAU
AU FOIE GRAS FRAIS
BLANC DE TURBOT AU CHAMPAGNE ROSÉ
FILET DE BŒUF AU POIVRE VERT
ET AUX CONCOMBRES
FROMAGES
PÊCHE POCHÉE, GLACE PISTACHE
SABAYON AU CHAMPAGNE

– CLASSICISM AND A DELIGHT FOR THE EYES –

Louis Outhier, L'Oasis, La Napoule

SOUPE DE POISSONS
FILET DE SAINT-PIERRE AU NOILLY
SORBET WILLIAMS
SUPRÊMES DE PIGEON MARIE-LOUISE
SALADE DE MESCLUN
LES FROMAGES DE LA FERME
COUPE OASIS, MIGNARDISES

– A SPREAD OF INDEPENDENT CREATIONS –

Jacques Pic, Valence

SALADE DES PÊCHEURS AU XÉRÈS
CHAUSSONS AUX TRUFFES
FILET DE LOUP AU CAVIAR
POULARDE DE BRESSE EN VESSIE
SOUFFLÉ GLACÉ A L'ORANGE

– EPICUREAN DELIGHTS –

Thuilier, L'Oustau de Baumanières, Baux-de-Provence

ŒUF EN SURPRISE
LOUP À LA MOUSSELINE DE POISSON
POULARDE AUX ÉCREVISSES
GIGOT D'AGNEAU EN CROÛTE
MOUSSELINE D'ARTICHAUTS
GÂTEAU LE FRAISIER

– NATIVE FLAVOURS –

The Troisgros brothers, Roanne

TERRINE DE LÉGUMES
SALADE NOUVELLE
COQUILLES SAINT-JACQUES BOULEZ
ESCALOPES DE SAUMON À L'OSEILLE
AIGUILLETTES DE COL-VERT
AUX MOUSSERONS DES PRÉS
CÔTE DE BŒUF AU FLEURIE
PAMÉLAS

– EXUBERANT ORIGINALITY –

Roger Vergé, Moulin de Mougins

TERRINE DE RASCASSE AU CITRON
AVEC LES CONCOMBRES À LA CRÈME
GRATIN DE QUEUES D'ÉCREVISSES
AUX ÉPINARDS, SAUCE CHAMPAGNE
GRANITÉ DE PAMPLEMOUSSE AU VERMOUTH
AIGUILLETTES DE SELLE D'AGNEAU
DE SISTERON AVEC LA SAUCE ESTRAGON
ET LA GARNITURE BONNE BOUCHE
VACHERIN GLACÉ AU MIEL DES ALPES
AVEC LA FONDUE D'ABRICOTS

The first factor in putting together a menu is the season. With its particular produce and style of cooking, the season provides the keynote for the whole meal. A number of examples are suggested here for autumn, winter, spring and summer.

Lunch and dinner menus are given both for everyday meals and for entertaining. All of the recipes can be found in this book; refer to the French index (*page 695*) for page numbers.

AUTUMN

Lunch

QUENELLES DE BROCHET
FAISAN AU CHOU
BEIGNETS VIENNOIS ET
OMELETTE À LA CONFITURE

Lunch

TOASTS DES GOURMETS
JARRET DE PORC AUX POIRES
ENDIVES À LA CRÈME
POIRES IMPÉRATRICE

Sunday lunch

GÂTEAU DE FOIES BLONDS
DE POULARDES DE BRESSE
CAILLES À LA BROCHE
EN FEUILLES DE VIGNE
CÈPES À LA BORDELAISE
CHARLOTTE AUX POMMES

Dinner

SOUPE À L'OIGNON GRATINÉE
COQUILLES SAINT-JACQUES AU CURRY
SALADE À LA VIGNERONNE
PUDDING AUX AMANDES

Dinner party

PETITS BERLUGANS
FOIES DE CANARD AUX RAISINS
TRUITE SAUMONÉE BRAISÉE AU VIN ROUGE
GÂTEAU DE COURGE
CRÈME DE CALVILLES EN SUÉDOISE

Dinner party

POTAGE AUX CHAMPIGNONS
ÉCREVISSES À L'ANETH EN SALADE
SALMIS DE CANARD SAUVAGE
GÂTEAU AUX FRUITS CONFITS ET AU RHUM

WINTER

Lunch

PAIN DE POISSON
CÔTES DE PORC À LA FLAMANDE
POIREAUX À LA CHAPELURE
PLATEAU DE FROMAGES
MOUSSE AUX POMMES À LA GÂTINAISE

Lunch

SOUFFLÉ AU BLEU D'AUVERGNE
CASSOULET AU MOUTON
PRUNEAUX À LA MODE D'AGEN

Sunday lunch

PÂTÉ BOURBONNAIS
OMELETTE AU BOUDIN
FILETS DE MORUE SAUTÉS À LA LYONNAISE
SALADE DE PISSENLITS AUX NOIX
BEIGNETS DE BANANES

Dinner

CRÈME DE POIREAUX AU CURRY
SALADE D'HUÎTRES MARINÉES AUX ŒUFS DURS
TOURNEDOS BÉARNAISE
SALADE VERTE
SOUFFLÉ À LA LIQUEUR

Dinner party

SALADE BEAUCERONNE
CRÈME DE CÉLÉRI
ŒUFS POCHÉS PÉRIGUEUX
GOUJONS DE SOLE AU PAPRIKA
POULET AU CHAMPAGNE
ANANAS À LA MERINGUE SUR SON BISCUIT

Dinner party

SOUPE AUX HUÎTRES À L'AMÉRICAINE
MOUSSE FROIDE DE SAUMON
ROGNONS DE VEAU À LA MAÎTRE D'HÔTEL
ÉPINARDS EN VERDURE À L'ANCIENNE
BAVAROIS AU KIRSCH

SPRING	SUMMER

Lunch

SALADE TOURANGELLE
MORILLES FARCIES À LA FORESTIÈRE
RÂBLES DE LAPIN À L'ESTRAGON
FLAN MERINGUÉ

Lunch

MOULES À L'OSEILLE
CÔTELETTES D'AGNEAU DE LAIT MONTROUGE
CONCOMBRES PERSILLÉS
TARTE À LA FRANGIPANE

Sunday lunch

ASPERGES À LA FLAMANDE
CANETON BRAISÉ AUX PETITS POIS
NOUVEAUX
PETITS GÂTEAUX DE CAROTTES
FROMAGES
MOUSSE GLACÉE AUX FRUITS

Dinner

CRÈME DE CONCOMBRE
CRÊPES SOUFFLÉES AUX BOUQUETS
TRANCHES DE LOTTE AU FOUR
GÂTEAU À L'ANISETTE ET À LA PISTACHE

Dinner

VELOUTÉ D'ASPERGES À LA CRÈME
CUISSES DE GRENOUILLES AUX FINES HERBES
FRICANDEAU DE VEAU À LA PROVENÇALE
SALADE VERTE
ŒUFS À LA NEIGE

Dinner party

POTAGE DE L'OCÉAN AUX FILETS DE SOLE
VOL-AU-VENT DE POULET
RIS DE VEAU À LA CRÈME
FROMAGE FRAIS
MELON À LA SOUVAROFF

Lunch

SALADE DE RIZ AUX LANGOUSTINES
MOUSSAKA
FROMAGES
SORBET AU MELON

Lunch

PISSALADIÈRE
LOUP GRILLÉ AU FENOUIL
TOMATES FRITES
TOURTEAU FROMAGÉ

Sunday lunch

ARTICHAUTS À LA BARIGOULE
ROUGETS AUX MOUSSERONS
CURRY D'AUBERGINES
COMPOTE DE FRUITS FRAIS AUX FROMAGES DE
FONTAINEBLEAU

Dinner

ŒUFS FARCIS AUX ANCHOIS
LOTTE À LA PROVENÇALE
HARICOTS VERTS TOMATÉS
POIRES SURPRISE D'ÉTÉ

Dinner

GNOCCHI À LA ROMAINE
CÔTES DE VEAU À LA GELÉE
SALADE VERTE
GÂTEAU AUX FRAISES

Dinner party

POTAGE GLACÉ À L'OSEILLE
PETITS CRABES GRATINEÉS AU FOUR
FOIE DE VEAU À LA VÉNITIENNE
PÊCHES FLAMBÉES

One of the most elegant ways for a hostess to express her personality lies in stimulating the appetite of her guests through a nicely laid table and carefully thought out presentation of the food. Gone for ever are the ostentatious days of the reign of Louis XIV when dishes were carried in on the shoulders of liveried servants, parading peacocks with tails spread before the admiring guests. Gone, too, is an era closer to our own when Horace Raisson, in his *Code gourmand* (1829), described down to the last detail the staging of a successful dinner at which, for example, the 'hors-d'œuvre were served passively, as it were, remaining on the table until the third course was served, lying there to whet our appetites . . .' The evolution of manners and customs has now gone so far that sometimes, what with fondues and raclettes, guests share in a form of hospitality where the cooking is done in the dining room. It is still accepted, nevertheless, that tables should be set with some style – indeed, with a certain studied elegance in the choice of colours and materials, shapes and decorations (paisley tablecloths, hexagonal plates, special lighting, coloured candles, etc), but avoiding ostentatious luxury or over-sophistication. The ease and comfort of guests remains the basic rule.

The cloth is laid over a table felt, which muffles noise. Place settings laid directly on the wood or marble surface of a table are for less formal, family meals. In contrast, the French 'assiette de présentation' is a special refinement. Very shallow and in gilded silver, silver, or silver plate, it is slightly larger than the dinner plate it has to go under and it stays in place on the table for each course up to the cheese. The rules of etiquette require that no plate should be placed on top of another, except, of course, on the 'assiette de présentation'. French tables are set with dinner plates in place; these are replaced when the guests are seated by those used for the first course (soup plates for consommé or soup). This practice is, of course, the rule in restaurants, where plates and cutlery have to be changed after each course. It is applied less strictly in the home; but a change of plates is always necessary after a fish course, and for the cheese. Providing warmed plates for food that has to be eaten hot is

to be recommended. A full dinner service comprises, in descending order of size, dinner plates, soup plates or bowls, and plates for cheese, dessert, fruit and bread. It is supplemented by various dishes suitable for serving particular kinds of food: those for snails, for oysters (by the dozen or half dozen), for avocados, and a compartmented one for fondues, etc.

Each guest should have enough space to move easily and without feeling at all cramped (60–70 cm/23½–27½ inches). Place settings are arranged symmetrically: the fork to the left of the plate (traditionally in France with the points downwards, as crests or monograms were on the back of the handle), soup spoon (convex side up) and dinner knife (cutting edge inwards) to the right and next to the plate. Fish knives and oyster forks, when required, are also placed on the right. Knife rests, which are tending to go out of fashion, implying as they do that the cutlery does not change with the courses, should not be set for grand occasions: these homely gadgets were devised to reduce soiling of the tablecloth.

A maximum of three glasses for the wines are placed in front of each plate, in descending order of size (not including champagne, which requires tall flutes), and for fresh water, which is always provided in a carafe. Quite often, however, it is preferable to have just two glasses: a large one for water and a small balloon or tulip-shaped one for the wine, burgundy or bordeaux – with possibly a change when you go from white to red, or from one red *cru* to another. Coloured glasses are not included in any classic service. The natural colour of the wine should be shown to advantage in pure crystal or another perfectly transparent glass.

Glasses should never be completely filled; and their shape should allow the nose to be introduced when the lips are touching the rim – the pleasure of a good wine lies equally in its flavour as in its aroma. To avoid clutter you should refrain from placing spoons for the dessert, cheese knives or cutlery for the fruit in their position in front of the glasses at the start of the meal. Napkins, folded as simply as possible, are placed on the plate (already on the table in French-style settings). Sometimes they will hold a bread roll tucked into a fold; but this may go on a small plate instead, if you prefer.

Individual napkins came into use during the Renaissance, when the fashionable large lace ruffs made them indispensable. At first they were placed on the shoulders, later around the neck. Today you place them on your knees, partly unfolded, but never tuck them into your collar. Do not fold them up again on leaving the table: this would indicate that you are expecting to be invited back.

Traditionally, when a meal begins with soup, it is served in very hot plates just before the guests take their places at table – but this practice (introduced into etiquette during the period of the Empire by Émilie Comtat, a comedienne) is debatable and can easily be bypassed. Salt cellars and carafes are placed here and there along the table – or in the centre if it is round. The wine, opened in advance, stays in its original bottle; but, in the case of a *vieux* red wine, it may be decanted into a crystal carafe. The practice of laying the bottle in a basket is now rather outmoded and only justified for very old wines that have a sediment and which you want to disturb as little as possible and therefore do not decant. It is always a good idea to bring the wine up from the cellar beforehand, long enough before the start of the meal to uncork it and to see whether or not it needs decanting.

Avoid bulky centrepieces that obstruct the guests' views of one another, and also strongly scented flowers, ashtrays and unnecessary odds and ends. The colour and texture of the tablecloth and napkins are, of course, a matter of taste, but white damask is always an elegant solution. Contrasting colours, flowered prints or lace on a pastel background can produce some most attractive and original tables, always so long as they harmonize with the dinner service and the glasses both in terms of style and material. 'To invite someone is to take upon yourself the responsibility for his happiness all the time he is under your roof', said Brillat Savarin. This precept remains as true today as it was then. Respecting social conventions is never a simple reflex action governed by etiquette. After all, it requires paying attention to other people, a form of respect which is quite incompatible with the hypocrisy of pure appearance, a sign of true and genuine feeling rather than mere politeness.

Sylvie Girard

USEFUL INFORMATION

Metric, Imperial and American measures are shown in separate columns in this book. The original French recipes were written using metric measures; the Imperial and American measures are the nearest equivalents. Only one set of measures should therefore be followed; they are not interchangeable.

American equivalents of ingredients and terminology are given in parentheses.

All spoon measures are level unless otherwise stated. Flour is plain (all purpose) unless otherwise stated.

Words printed in *italics* are explained in the Glossary or in The French Cook's Larder.

An asterisk following a recipe title denotes that the recipe is illustrated.

The French Cook's Larder gives information on French ingredients which may be unfamiliar.

Oven temperatures are not given in the recipes in this book. The following table is a helpful guide to the descriptions of oven heat given in the recipes.

	°Celsius Scale	*Electric Scale °F*	*Gas Oven Marks*
low (very slow)	110°C	225°F	¼
low (very slow)	130	250	½
low (very slow)	140	275	1
low (slow)	150	300	2
low (slow) to moderate	170	325	3
moderate	180	350	4
moderately hot	190	375	5
hot	200	400	6
hot	220	425	7
very hot	230	450	8
very hot	240	475	9

As a general rule, all recipes serve 8 people. If this is not the case, this will be apparent in individual recipes.

THE FRENCH
COOK'S LARDER

Amourettes: this is spinal bone marrow, usually from veal but also from beef and mutton, that has been cleaned and poached briefly in *court bouillon*.

anchovy: small sea fish (maximum length 20 cm/8 inches) with silver sides and belly and a greenish-black back. Available fresh, but most often sold salted or preserved in oil (or in a sauce), both whole and filleted. Well-dried salted anchovies should be soaked in several changes of water for some hours before use; if not overly dry, they can be soaked in milk for just 20 minutes and then rinsed well. Canned anchovy fillets can be desalted by soaking briefly in milk, rinsing and patting dry with paper towels.

andouillette: a type of pork sausage using pork intestines as the casing, these are 10–15 cm/4–6 inches long and sold ready-cooked. There are several varieties, from different regions of France. They are fried or grilled (broiled) before eating, usually with mustard.

apples: the varieties specified in recipes in this book are firm, tart apples which keep their shape when cooked. The French do not use cooking- or baking-type apples that disintegrate when cooked. The most commonly used variety is reinette, a medium to large apple with a golden yellow skin and crisp, juicy, sweet flesh. Reinette grise is similar to the English russet apple, having a reddish-brown matt skin and tart-sweet flesh. Another variety mentioned is calville, a large apple with a bright yellow skin and juicy, tart-sweet flesh. If the apples specified in a recipe are not available where you live, you can substitute a local variety such as Cox's Orange Pippin, Rome Beauty, York Imperial, Granny Smith or even Golden Delicious.

bacon: French bacon is very fatty, and may be salted or smoked. Both unsmoked and smoked British streaky bacon and American sliced or slab bacon can be substituted; however, British bacon is generally stronger in flavour than French bacon, so it is a good idea to blanch it in boiling water for 1–2 minutes before use in delicately-seasoned dishes.

biscotte: this is a rusk made commercially from slices of sweetened bread rebaked in the oven until golden and crumbly in texture. Biscottes are available in packets in Britain and the United States (where they are often called 'zwieback'). One can also buy the less sweet oblong slices called 'French toasts'. Biscottes are eaten in France at breakfast and for snacks, and are widely used in cookery.

boudin blanc: a white pudding or sausage made from a finely-textured, spiced mixture of white meat (poultry, rabbit, veal or pork) and fat plus binding ingredients such as cream, eggs, milk and breadcrumbs or flour. The boudin, in its intestine casing, may be poached, fried gently, baked or cooked in buttered paper.

boudin noir: a black pudding or blood sausage made basically from seasoned pig's blood and fat, in an intestine casing. Other ingredients such as onions, herbs, milk or cream and bread may be added, according to the individual butcher's whim and traditional regional French recipes.

bread: In France, a housewife will rarely bake her own bread but will instead buy it fresh each day from the local bakery. In particular, she would never consider making a baguette, the familiar long loaf of what we call 'French bread', with its soft crumb and crisp crust. This is because it is virtually impossible to produce even a passable imitation of a baguette in a domestic oven. For recipes in this book that specify using slices from a baguette, buy the best French bread you can find. In recipes that call for canapés, croûtons and breadcrumbs, etc, make these from coarse but firm-textured bread, not from the type of sliced soft bread that compresses into a solid ball when squeezed.

butter: French cooks use both unsalted (sweet) and slightly salted butter, but never butter that is heavily salted. Most recipes specify the kind of butter to be used. For sweet dishes in particular, be sure to use the best quality unsalted butter (from Normandy if possible), because the flavour and richness are important for a successful result.

caul: the thin fatty membrane from the stomach of animals such as pigs, used in French cookery to wrap around savoury preparations (sausagemeat mixtures, stuffed cabbage leaves, and so on) to hold them together and add moistness during cooking. Most butchers can supply caul, although it may have to be ordered in advance. Some caul is dry salted to preserve it, and needs to be soaked for about 30 minutes in lukewarm water, to which a little lemon juice or vinegar has been added; it then needs to be rinsed before use.

cheese: most of the cheeses specified in recipes will be familiar, and available in large supermarkets or speciality cheese shops. Three fresh cow's milk cheeses are mentioned – fromage blanc, demi-sel (lightly salted fromage blanc) and petit-suisse (unsalted fromage blanc beaten with cream). Petit-suisse is the most widely obtainable, and may be substituted for the other two (adding a little extra salt to the recipe when demi-sel is called for). Fontainebleau is the brand name of a factory-made, creamy fromage blanc.

cornichon: this is a small gherkin pickled in unsweetened vinegar.

cream: several different types of cream are called for in the recipes in this book. Single (light) cream, whipping cream and double (heavy) cream are all easily obtainable, but crème fraîche and crème fleurette may be more difficult to find. Crème fraîche, which is widely used in French cookery, is a lightly cultured cream that has a sharp, slightly soured flavour. If you cannot buy crème fraîche, you can make it at home: heat two part double (heavy) cream with one part live buttermilk or plain live yogurt (check the label – the buttermilk or yogurt must contain the live lactic bacteria) until lukewarm, then half cover and leave at room temperature for at least 6 hours. The longer you leave the cream, the thicker and sharper it will become. Crème fraîche will keep well in the refrigerator. Crème fleurette is a semi-liquid, light cream (only 12–15% butterfat). If you cannot find it, you can substitute half cream (half-and-half) or single (light) cream.

demoiselle de Cherbourg: this is a name sometimes given to 'langoustine', the small cousin of the lobster. The langoustine is variously called Dublin Bay prawn, Norway lobster and scampi in English.

flageolet: this is a small pale green bean that is harvested in August and September, before it is fully matured. Flageolets are rarely sold fresh, but instead are usually dried or canned. Even if you do see them still in their pods, they will probably be 'demi-sec' (semi-dried) as they will have already dried out a little before being picked. (If demi-sec, they do not need to be soaked before cooking.) Small beans such as the British haricot and American baby lima can be substituted for flageolets, if necessary.

foie gras: this is the liver from a specially fattened goose or duck. In France, foie gras is available 'cru' (raw) and 'frais' (freshly cooked) from delicatessens; semi-cooked and pasteurized 'mi-cuit pasteurisé' (pasteurized) in cans. 'Foie gras de conserve' (preserved foie gras) is available in jars. Semi-cooked pure whole livers in cans used to be labelled 'au naturel', and this term is used in some of the recipes in this book. Today such livers are labelled 'foie gras d'oie entier' (whole goose liver) or 'foie gras de canard entier' (whole duck liver). Be sure not to confuse foie gras with 'parfait de foie gras' or 'pâté de foie gras'. Another preparation used in this book is 'purée de foie gras', which contains 50–75% finely pounded goose liver; it is available in cans.

gum arabic: a sticky, translucent substance secreted from acacia trees grown in Egypt and Sudan. In confectionery, it is used as a glaze, and is the main ingredient in chewing gum and marshmallow. **Gum tragacanth** is a thick, sticky, translucent substance exuded from shrubs of the genus *Astragalus*. It is used in the preparation of ice cream and jam to prevent crystallization. Guar gum can be substituted. Gum arabic and tragacanth are available in specialist food shops, particularly those stocking confectionery and cake decorating supplies.

ham: every region in France has its own tradition for curing hams, and it is often the case that many of the so-called 'country' or 'mountain' hams are not found out-side the region in which they are produced. Those designated 'jambon cru' (raw ham) are, of course, cured in some way, and they may also be smoked. In the recipes in this book, you will find 'raw ham', 'raw country ham', 'air-dried ham' and 'raw mountain ham' called for. All of these will have been cured by rubbing with salt repeatedly throughout their maturing period, and the 'mountain' and 'country' hams may also have been injected with brine. Morvan ham is a raw ham that is lightly smoked. Any good-quality raw French ham – such as Bayonne ham, specified in some recipes and widely obtainable in Britain and the United States – may be used, or even the Italian prosciutto.

herbs: wherever possible, French cooks like to use fresh herbs in cooking. A classic mixture, used in many of the recipes in this book, is **fines herbes**. This consists of chopped parsley, chervil, chives and tarragon, in varying proportions but going easy on the tarragon (or omitting it). Another mixture is **herbes à tortue**, comprising basil, marjoram, chervil, savory and fennel. It is used mainly for turtle soup, but may also flavour dishes of offal (variety meat) such as ox tongue and calf's head.

marmelade: this is a thick sweet purée made from fruit that has been macerated in a sugar syrup and then stewed for a long time. Do not confuse it with marmalade, the jam-like preserve.

marrons glacés: these are chestnuts (marrons) that have been poached in a vanilla-flavoured sugar syrup for 48 hours and then glazed with liquid sugar.

mignonette pepper (mignonnette): this is simply coarsely ground pepper, more likely to be from white peppercorns than black.

mushroom: many recipes in this book call for 'Paris mushrooms' (champignons de Paris). These are, in fact, cultivated mushrooms (called Paris mushrooms because they are extensively cultivated around that city). In France, you can find two varieties of Paris mushroom – 'blanc' (white) and 'blond' or 'bistre' (golden), with the 'bistre' variety having more flavour. Ordinary button mushrooms can be used when Paris mushrooms are called for. Field mushrooms are specified in some recipes. These are wild mushrooms belonging to the genus *Agaricus* (which also includes cultivated varieties) that grow in meadows and fields in France, and in Britain. Any fresh wild mushroom can be substituted, or even cultivated mushrooms with a few dried wild mushrooms added to enhance the flavour.

mustard: three main types of mustard are used in French cookery – strong or Dijon mustard, mild or Bordeaux mustard and whole-grain or Meaux mustard. Dijon mustard is familiar to cooks all over the world and is widely available, as is Meaux, but Bordeaux may be more difficult to find. What the British call 'French' mustard

In France, butchers cut up animals differently from the way they are butchered in Britain and the United States, therefore it is impossible to give exact equivalents for French cuts of meat in the recipes in this book. However, the nearest equivalents have been given and they will work successfully for British and American cooks. T[...] names of the original French cuts are given in the cha[...] here, numbered to correspond with the drawings [...] show the part of the animal from which they come. T[...] suggested British and American cuts are given alongsi[...]

Lamb and Mutton

	FRENCH	BRITISH	AMERICAN
1	collier	neck	neck
2	carré	best end of neck	rack or rib roast
3	côtelette	cutlet	rib chop
4	filet	loin	loin
5	côte	loin chop	loin chop
6	noisette	noisette	noisette
7	selle	saddle	saddle
8	gigot	leg	leg
9	baron	baron	baron
10	poitrine	breast	breast
11	épaule	shoulder	shoulder

Beef

	FRENCH	BRITISH	AMERICAN
1	collier	neck	chuck
2	entrecôte	entrecote steak	boneless rib steak
3	faux-filet	boneless sirloin joint	boneless sirloin roast
4	filet	fillet	tenderloin
5	tournedos	tournedos steak	filet mignon
6	bavette	skirt	skirt
7	contre-filet	boneless sirloin joint	boneless sirloin roast
8	romsteck	rump (steak)	top round (steak)
9	pointe de culotte (aiguillette de romsteck)	top rump	sirloin tip roast
10	tranche	topside	top round
11	gîte à la noix	silverside	bottom round
12	gîte	shin	shank
13	flanchet	thick flank	flank
14	poitrine	breast	short plate
15	tendron	brisket	brisket
16	macreuse	clod	chuck blade
17	gîte-gîte	neck	chuck arm
18	jumeau	neck	chuck arm

Veal

	FRENCH	BRITISH	AMERICAN
1	carré	best end of neck	rib roast
2	côtelette	cutlet	rib chop
3	longe	loin	loin with sirloi[...]
4	rognonnade	loin with kidney	loin with kidn[...]
5	filet	loin	loin
6	côte	loin chop	loin chop
7	grenadin	medallion	medallion
8	quasi, cul de veau	joint cut from top of leg, such as chump end of loin	roast cut from top of leg, suc[...] as rump roast
9	noix, sous-noix, noix pâtissière	topside (fillet end of leg)	round (top of [...]
10	escalope	escalope	cutlet, scallopi[...]
11	jarret	shin or knuckle	shank
12	flanchet	breast	breast
13	tendron	middle neck	blade
14	poitrine	breast	breast
15	épaule	shoulder	shoulder

Pork

	FRENCH	BRITISH	AMERICAN
1	échine	spare rib or chine	blade or Bosto[...] roast
2	carré de côtes	fore loin	blade loin
3	côte	chop	chop
4	filet	loin	loin
5	noisette	noisette	noisette
6	milieu de filet, côtes de filet	hind loin	sirloin, centre loin
7	pointe de filet	fillet end of leg	loin end of leg [...]
8	gigue, cuissot	haunch	haunch
9	cuissot de porcelet	haunch of sucking pig	haunch of suckling pig
10	jambon frais	leg	fresh ham (leg)[...]
11	jambonneau	ham knuckle joint	ham roast, sha[...] end
12	jarret	knuckle	shank or hock
13	poitrine	belly	bacon, fresh p[...] sides
14	travers	spareribs	spareribs
15	épaule	shoulder or hand	picnic shoulde[...]
16	palette	shoulder	arm or picnic

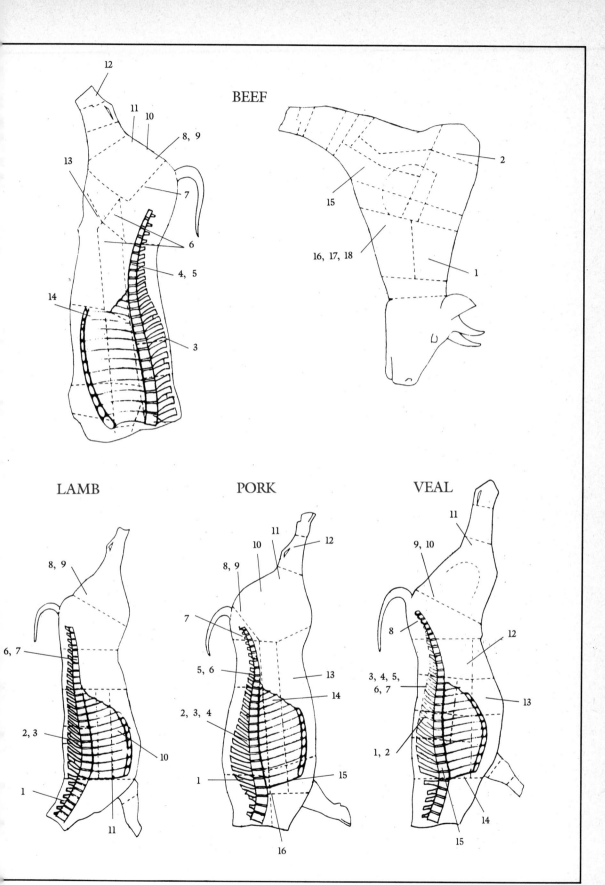

BEEF

LAMB

PORK

VEAL

can be substituted for Bordeaux; American cooks can use spicy brown mustard or a German-type mustard. If a recipe just says 'mustard', use Dijon.

orgeat: this is a syrup made from sweetened almond milk, flavoured with orange-flower water. It is mostly used in cocktails, but is also used as a flavouring in cooking.

pralines: these are almonds coated with several layers of caramelized sugar. The last layer is coloured red or beige, or brown if the pralines are flavoured with chocolate or coffee. Pralines are a popular sweet, and are also used as a decoration for desserts and cakes.

prune: several varieties of red and purple plums are dried and processed to make prunes in France, but the finest is considered to be the Agen or Ente (literally 'grafted') plum. The large Touraine damson and the Catherine are also considered to be good.

quatre-épices: a mixture of four spices – usually grated nutmeg, ground cloves, ground pepper and ground cinnamon or ginger – sold in jars and packets in France. If you cannot buy this spice mixture, you can make your own, using an equal quantity of each spice.

rillettes: a preparation of meat, usually pork, or sometimes poultry (rabbit or goose) cooked in lard or its own fat until very tender, then pounded to a smooth paste and packed into pots or jars. Rillettes are served cold as an hors-d'œuvre with toast, or as a sandwich filling. Rillettes are also prepared from fish such as sardines, tuna, eel and salmon, cooked in butter.

rillons: a preparation of pork made from pieces of shoulder or belly (fresh pork sides), sprinkled with salt and then cooked in lard until well browned and caramelized. The pieces are left whole and not pounded like rillettes (*above*), and may be served hot or cold.

sausage: in France there are two main types: saucisse, a small fresh sausage that is sometimes lightly smoked and is usually grilled (broiled), fried or boiled before eating; and saucisson, a large smoked sausage that is dried (saucisson sec) or otherwise preserved and ready to eat.

sausagemeat: called 'chair à saucisse', in France this is 100% pork, in equal parts of lean meat and fat, with no seasonings or cereals added. Check the label when buying sausagemeat to be sure it is pure pork, or make your own by mincing (grinding) lean pork and pork fat or working them in a food processor.

spirits and eaux-de-vie: several kinds of alcoholic beverages are used in the recipes in this book. In addition to cognac, you will come across two other brandies – armagnac and calvados. Armagnac is made from wine produced in a specified area in Gascony. Calvados is distilled from cider in the Auge region of France; that designated '*vieux*' has been aged for 3 years. Another strong spirit used is marc, which is distilled from the resi-

due (skin, seeds, stalks, etc) left after the final pressing of grapes for wine. The term 'eau-de-vie' (water of life) is used generally for strong spirits such as brandies and 'marc', but more particularly is applied to colourless spirits distilled from fruits or herbs which are kept in glass rather than being aged in wooden casks, and are not sweetened. Poire William (pear), kirsch (cherry), framboise (raspberry) and mirabelle (plum) are some examples. The aniseed-flavoured drink pastis is used in some regional recipes, particularly those from the South of France. 'Ricard' and 'Berger' are two well-known brands. An aniseed liqueur called anisette, is also used.

sugar: French granulated sugar is finer than British granulated, so British cooks should use caster sugar when 'sugar' is specified. Cooks in the United States can use American granulated sugar, which is finer than British granulated, in most recipes; superfine sugar is specified for meringues and preparations where the sugar must dissolve quickly. Lump sugar, which is made by moulding moistened hot granulated sugar and then drying it so the crystals fuse together, is called for in some recipes. In France it is available in cubes, tablets and irregular chunks. If you cannot find lump sugar, you can use granulated. Another type of French sugar is 'sucre crystalisé' (coarse-grained sugar crystals), which is similar to British granulated sugar; crushed lump sugar can be used as a substitute. Lemon and orange sugars are flavoured with the oil (or zest) from the skin of these fruits. To make these sugars, rub sugar lumps over the skin so that the sugar becomes coloured and impregnated.

truffle: this much-prized fungus is found in chalky soil or clay, near oak, chestnut, hazel and beech trees, growing just underground among the tree roots. In France, the black or Périgord truffle is the most highly esteemed. Because of deforestation and pollution, the production of truffles in France has greatly declined, and they are now very expensive and used much more sparingly than they once were. One can buy them fresh in season as well as preserved whole in cans and jars. Less expensive are truffle peelings, liquid, essence and juice, sold in cans.

vanilla: in addition to the familiar vanilla pods (beans) and essence (extract), vanilla is used in two other forms in recipes in this book. One is vanilla sugar, which is sold in small sachets. You can make your own vanilla sugar by crushing and pounding a vanilla pod (bean) with 225 g/8 oz lump sugar in a mortar or using a food processor, then sieving it. For a more subtle vanilla flavour, keep a vanilla pod (bean) in a covered jar of sugar. French cooks also use powdered vanilla in pâtisserie and confectionery. This is a dark brown powder made from ground dried vanilla pods (beans) and is available outside France at specialist shops; vanilla essence (extract) may be substituted.

SOUPS

ORIGINALLY, A SOUP CONSISTED OF A LARGE slice of bread on to which stock was poured, hence the expression 'tremper la soupe' – to pour soup on to bread. Today, soup still retains its rustic, homely character.

Flavoursome and smooth, a soup is, in the words of the Marquis de Cussy, 'a few handfuls of good soil thrown on to the ground on which you are going to scatter seeds'. It calms hunger pangs, soothes the day's stress, and can immediately be followed by a little wine, that excellent 'coup du médecin' (doctor's drink) which 'chasse la maladie' (drives out illness), as they say in the country.

Potage, a refined version of soup, allows the chef a full range of subtle variations and elegant creations. According to Grimod de la Reynière, it is to a dinner 'what a peristyle is to a building'. Today, soups are still 'a long game of patience', as Curnonsky used to say. The prince of gourmets collected, both from gourmand folklore and from various chefs, more than 500 different recipes for soups, sub-divided according to type, into cream, thickened and puréed soups, bisques, veloutés, consommés and broths, not to mention the classic regional recipes such as garbure, tourin, bouillabaisse, cotriade, and so on.

CRAYFISH BISQUE

Preparation 2 hours • Cooking about 45 minutes

US	Ingredients	Met/Imp
1	carrot	1
1	large onion	1
a few	parsley sprigs	a few
a few	thyme sprigs	a few
1	bay leaf	1
14 tbsp	butter	200 g/7 oz
24, each weighing 3½–4 oz	live crayfish	24, each weighing 90–100 g/3½–4 oz
¼ cup	cognac	50 ml/2 fl oz
scant 1 cup	white wine	200 ml/7 fl oz
scant 1 cup	light Fish Fumet (page 57)	200 ml/7 fl oz
	salt and pepper	
1½ cups	long grain rice	260 g/9 oz
2 quarts	chicken consommé	2 litres/3½ pints
½ cup	crème fraîche	100 ml/4 fl oz
¾–1 cup	fish stuffing (see Forcemeat Stuffing on page 54)	150 g/5 oz

Crayfish should always be gutted, no matter how they are to be cooked. This consists of removing the intestine, the end of which may be found at the small opening under the middle tail phalanx.

Make a fine Mirepoix (*page 50*) with the carrot, onion, parsley and thyme sprigs and the bay leaf, then brown lightly in one-third of the butter. Add the crayfish, which have been rinsed in water and gutted, and sauté them over a high heat for about 15 minutes or until the shells are nicely red. Pour in three-quarters of the cognac, the white wine and the fish fumet, add salt and pepper, cover and cook for 10–12 minutes, according to the size of the crayfish.

Meanwhile, cook the rice in the boiling consommé for about 12 minutes or until very soft. Drain well, reserving the consommé.

Remove the crayfish from the cooking liquid. Shell them, reserving all of the tail shells and heads. Set aside 12 of the heads with the crayfish tails for the garnish.

Pound the tail shells and remaining heads with the rice and the mirepoix, keeping the cooking liquid to one side.

Add the cooking liquid to the pounded mixture, then work through a sieve lined with cheesecloth. Mix this purée with enough of the reserved consommé to give the desired consistency and bring to the boil.

Just before serving, add three-quarters of the crème fraîche and the remaining cognac and butter.

Garnish the bisque with crayfish heads, filled with fish stuffing mixed with the remaining crème fraîche, and with the crayfish tails, diced.

BOUILLABAISSE*

Preparation 1 hour • Cooking 15 minutes

US	Ingredients	Met/Imp
9 lb	various fish (see method)	4 kg/9 lb
1¼ cups	olive oil	300 ml/½ pint
2	onions	2
4	tomatoes	4
10	garlic cloves	10
a few	parsley sprigs	a few
1	bay leaf	1
4	fennel sprigs	4
1	small orange, rind of	1
	salt and pepper	
2 quarts	mussels (optional)	2 litres/3½ pints
1 pinch	saffron	1 pinch
6 tbsp	flour	50 g/2 oz
8	slices French bread (baguette), toasted	8

Bouillabaisse has acquired its reputation amongst gourmets by adhering to a few vital rules:

First, the fish must be extremely fresh. Use wrasse, scorpion fish, gurnard, conger eel, monkfish, spider crabs, John Dory, etc. Pour some good olive oil into a wide, flat casserole and lightly fry the chopped onions and tomatoes, most of the garlic, chopped, the parsley, bay leaf, fennel and orange rind. Add a pinch of saffron. Put in the prepared fish and mussels, if using, both well seasoned. Add just enough boiling water to cover, bring to the boil and boil rapidly.

Cook over a high heat for 15 minutes, then take out the whole fish and mussels, put them on a heated serving dish and keep warm. Mix the flour with enough olive oil to make a paste, then use to thicken the soup. Boil for a few minutes, then check the seasoning. Rub the toast with the remaining cut cloves of garlic, then place in a tureen. Work the soup through a sieve lined with cheesecloth on to the toast. Serve the fish and soup separately so that each person can combine them both in his or her own bowl.

US	Ingredients	Met/Imp
	leftover roast chicken meat	
½ cup	finely chopped blanched almonds	50 g/2 oz
3	egg yolks, hard-boiled	3
about 1 quart	chicken consommé	about 1 litre/1¾ pints
½ cup	crème fraîche	100 ml/4 fl oz
5 oz	biscottes	150 g/5 oz
1 stick	butter	100 g/4 oz
2	large onions	2
	salt and pepper	
2	parsley sprigs	2
2	thyme sprigs	2
½	bay leaf	½
2	fennel sprigs	2
1	marjoram sprig	1
1	chervil sprig	1
2 lb	potatoes	1 kg/2 lb
4½ lb	various fish (see method)	2 kg/4½ lb
	slices French bread (baguette)	
2 cups	wine vinegar	500 ml/18 fl oz
3	heads celery	3
1 stick	butter	100 g/4 oz
2 quarts	water	2 litres/3½ pints
	salt	
3	potatoes	3
½ cup	milk	100 ml/4 fl oz
3	egg yolks	3
½ cup	crème fraîche	100 ml/4 fl oz
3 cups	firm-textured bread, finely diced	100 g/4 oz

CHICKEN CONSOMMÉ WITH ALMONDS

Preparation 40 minutes • Cooking 15 minutes

Pound the chicken in a mortar and pestle (preferably marble) with the almonds and hard-boiled egg yolks. Stir in a little consommé, then work the mixture through a sieve lined with cheesecloth. Add the crème fraîche and heat in a *bain-marie*.

Simmer the biscottes in the remaining consommé. Just before serving, add the mixture from the bain-marie, making sure there is enough liquid for 8 people.

COTRIADE BRETONNE

BRETON BOUILLABAISSE

Preparation 15 minutes • Cooking about 30 minutes

Melt the butter in a saucepan and cook the chopped onions over a very high heat for about 10 minutes or until brown. Pour in enough water to make soup for 8 people, then add some salt and the parsley sprigs, thyme, bay leaf, fennel, marjoram and chervil. Add the peeled and sliced potatoes and continue cooking for about another 10 minutes or until the potatoes are nearly cooked. Add the fish (whiting, garfish, mackerel, smelt), cut into sections if necessary. Boil the soup vigorously for about 8 minutes, but do not overcook the fish.

Put the bread slices in the bottom of a heated tureen and pour two-thirds of the stock over them. Put the fish in a shallow heated serving dish with the potatoes. Add plenty of salt to the remaining stock and sprinkle it on the fish.

First eat the potatoes and fish, dipping each piece in well-seasoned vinegar, then serve the well-seasoned soup, which will have had time to cool down.

CRÈME DE CÉLERI

CREAM OF CELERY SOUP

Preparation 40 minutes • Cooking 2 hours

Trim and wash the celery, then blanch it in boiling water. Drain and cool in cold water, then wipe dry. Cut into large pieces and sweat in half of the butter. Add the water, some salt and the peeled and sliced potatoes and simmer over a low heat for 1½ hours.

Work the soup through a fine sieve. Add some milk if the soup is too thick and bring to the boil. Stir in the egg yolks whisked with the crème fraîche to thicken the soup, and heat gently without boiling. Fry the bread cubes in the remaining butter and sprinkle these croûtons over the soup just before serving.

CREAM OF CUCUMBER SOUP

Preparation 30 minutes • Cooking 1 hour

US	Ingredients	Met/Imp
2 lb	cucumbers	1 kg/2 lb
1¾ lb	potatoes	800 g/1¾ lb
	salt and pepper	
1 stick	butter	100 g/4 oz
6 tbsp	flour	50 g/2 oz
½ cup	crème fraîche	100 ml/4 fl oz

Peel the cucumbers, remove the seeds and dice the flesh. Place in a saucepan of boiling water with the peeled and diced potatoes, salt and pepper.

Simmer gently for about 1 hour, then strain through a sieve. Thicken with *beurre manié* made by combining the butter and flour. Put the crème fraîche in a heated tureen and gently pour in the soup. Stir well and serve immediately.

CRÈME DE HARICOTS BLANCS AUX PETITS LÉGUMES

CREAM OF WHITE BEAN SOUP WITH YOUNG VEGETABLES

Preparation 2 hours • Cooking 1½ hours • Makes about 2 litres/3½ pints

US	Ingredients	Met/Imp
1½ lb (about 3½ cups)	fresh white beans (see page 528)	750 g/1½ lb
2½ quarts	water	2.5 litres/ 4½ pints
	salt	
1	parsley sprig	1
2 cups	milk	500 ml/18 fl oz
2	carrots	2
2	turnips	2
6 tbsp	butter	75 g/3 oz
⅔ cup	shelled peas	100 g/4 oz
¼ lb	French (fine green) beans	100 g/4 oz
2	egg yolks	2
scant 1 cup	crème fraîche	200 ml/7 fl oz
1 tsp	chopped chervil	5 ml/1 tsp

Put the beans in a large saucepan with the water, salt and parsley. Cook until tender.

As soon as the beans are cooked, drain them (reserving the cooking liquid) and vigorously work them through a sieve into a saucepan. Mix in 500 ml/18 fl oz (2 cups) of the bean cooking liquid and the boiled milk and bring to the boil, stirring. Cook gently over a low heat for 15–20 minutes, removing the scum from time to time.

For the garnish, use a round melon baller to make about 20 small carrot balls (about the size of a large pearl) and the same number of turnip balls. (If a melon baller is unavailable, simply cut the carrots and turnips into 5 mm/¼ inch dice.) In view of the small quantity of each, cook them together with a little of the remaining cooking water from the beans and a piece of butter.

Cook the peas and the French (green) beans, cut into small diamond shapes, in boiling salted water, then drain well. This garnish must be prepared in advance.

A few minutes before serving, whisk together the egg yolks and crème fraîche and stir into the soup to thicken it. Heat through without boiling. Remove from the heat and add the remaining butter. Pour the soup into a heated tureen through a fine sieve. Finally, add the carrots, turnips, peas, French (fine green) beans and chervil.

US	Ingredients	Met/Imp
1¼ cups	large grain pearl barley	250 g/8 oz
2½ quarts	white stock	2.5 litres/ 4½ pints
1	celery heart	1
½ cup	Crayfish Butter (page 51)	125 g/4½ oz
½ cup	Forcemeat Stuffing (page 54)	100 g/4 oz
½ cup	fine grain pearl barley.	100 g/4 oz
3	egg yolks	3
½ cup	crème fraîche	100 ml/4 fl oz
	salt	

CREAM OF BARLEY SOUP WITH CRAYFISH BUTTER

Preparation 1 hour • Cooking 3 hours

A soup of this type (with a butter liaison) should only be completed at the very last minute.

Wash the large grain pearl barley several times in lukewarm water. Put it in a saucepan with 1.5 litres/2½ pints (1½ quarts) of the stock and the thinly sliced celery heart.

Bring to the boil and carefully remove the scum, then cook gently for 3 hours.

Prepare a very red crayfish butter and mix about one-quarter of it with the poultry stuffing. Shape this mixture into about 20 small *quenelles* about the size of beans and arrange on a buttered tray. Set aside.

About 1 hour before serving, put the fine grain pearl barley in a saucepan with 500 ml/18 fl oz (2 cups) of the remaining white stock. Bring to the boil and simmer gently. About 15 minutes before serving, poach the prepared quenelles in simmering water, then drain.

Meanwhile, when the large grain pearl barley is cooked, first drain it and crush it in a mortar and pestle, then work it through a sieve lined with cheesecloth into a saucepan. Stir in the remaining stock and bring to the boil, then add the egg yolks whisked together with the crème fraîche. Heat without boiling until thickened, then remove from the heat and add the crayfish butter. Pour the soup into a heated tureen and add the drained fine grain pearl barley and the drained quenelles. Add salt to taste.

CURRIED CREAM OF LEEK SOUP

Preparation 1 hour • Cooking 1 hour

US	Ingredients	Met/Imp
¾ lb	leeks, white part only	300 g/10 oz
1 stick	butter	100 g/4 oz
1 cup	rice	200 g/7 oz
1 quart	white stock	1 litre/1¾ pints
1 tsp	curry powder	5 ml/1 tsp
	salt	
1 glass	milk	1 glass
2	egg yolks	2
½ cup	crème fraîche	100 ml/4 fl oz
	a little cooked rice, to garnish	

Blanch the leeks in boiling water for 8–10 minutes, then drain and press them to remove all the excess water. Chop them and dry them out by frying them in half of the butter. Add the rice, pour in three-quarters of the stock and add the curry powder and salt. Cover and cook slowly for 45 minutes–1 hour.

Work the rice and leek mixture through a fine sieve, then thin it with the remaining stock and a little milk, to obtain a creamy consistency. Bring to the boil, taste and season well with salt. Stir in the egg yolks whisked with the crème fraîche and heat gently without boiling, stirring, until thick and smooth. Mix in the remaining butter and sprinkle with a little cooked rice.

'A true gastronome should always be ready to eat, just as a soldier should always be ready to fight . . . I have forgotten the menu, but a delicate memory of a chicken "au blanc" remains with me . . .'(Charles Monselet, Lettres gourmandes)

'... You should have elbow room, and not be cramped, with the ability to gesticula
while you talk if you wish. Food nibbled at in a confined space is indigestible!' (Jean
Richepin, À Table)

'A brace of pheasants, and goodness knows what else besides, awaits you at dinner
(. . .). Come then, let us enjoy ourselves without respite and hold off old age, the spy
of death.' (Letter from Aretino to Titian, Venice, December 1547)

'White linen enhances the whole setting, heightening and accentuating the table decoration; it looks fresh and appetizing . . . It is the foundation of the whole decor and covers the table two-thirds of the way to the floor.' (Eugène Briffault, Paris à table, 1846)

'Rooms can be used for all sorts of occasions, for banquets, for plays, for weddings and
other such diversions.' (*Andrea Palladio*, The Four Books of Architecture,
1570, Book I, Chapter XXI)

'The dining room should be luxuriously lit, the table set with particular care and neatness . . . The number of guests should not exceed twelve, so that the conversation can remain general. . . . The dishes should be choice, but limited in number, and the wines of the first quality, each in its own way . . . The pace of the meal should be easy . . .' (Brillat-Savarin, Physiologie du goût, Méditation XIV)

'I declare that it is not so much necessary to consider what you are eating, rather what
you are eating it with . . . There is for me no dish so pleasant, no sauce so appetizing,
as that taken in company.' (Montaigne)

BÉARNAISE GARBURE WITH PRESERVED GOOSE

Preparation 1 hour • Cooking 1½ hours

Garbure is not, as is sometimes said, a purée of fresh and dried vegetables. It is a flavoured broth based on goose fat and preserved goose and garnished with a *macédoine* of carrots, turnips, peas, French (fine green) beans, white or broad (lima or fava) beans, potatoes, cabbage, leeks and onions.

Put the water in a large saucepan with the parsley, bay leaf and plenty of thyme. Add a macédoine of white or broad (lima or fava) beans, sliced French (fine green) beans, chopped potatoes, some salt and the preserved goose. Bring to the boil and add the sliced carrots and leeks, chopped turnips and onion, and the peas, all of which have been fried in goose fat until soft but not brown. Cook over a high heat for about 1 hour.

About 30 minutes before serving, remove the preserved goose from the pan and reserve. Add the chopped cabbage. Serve the garbure with no garnish other than perhaps a few croûtons. Serve the preserved goose afterwards, accompanied by potatoes or green vegetables.

US	Ingredients	Met/Imp
3 quarts	water	3 litres/5¼ pints
a few	parsley sprigs	a few
I	bay leaf	I
a few	thyme sprigs	a few
I cup	fresh white beans (see page 528) or broad beans (fresh lima or fava beans)	150 g/5 oz
2 oz	French (fine green) beans	50 g/2 oz
½ lb	potatoes	250 g/8 oz
	salt	
1½ lb	Preserved Goose (page 297)	750 g/1½ lb
¼ lb	carrots	100 g/4 oz
2	leeks	2
2 oz	turnips	50 g/2 oz
I	onion	I
⅓ cup	shelled peas	50 g/2 oz
½ cup	goose fat	100 g/4 oz
I	cabbage	I
	croûtons, to garnish (optional)	

ONION SOUP AU GRATIN WITH ROQUEFORT CHEESE

Preparation 25 minutes • Cooking 15 minutes

Thinly slice the onions and fry them in the butter for about 5 minutes or until they are nicely translucent without having changed colour too much. Pour the boiling water on to the onions and cook for a further 10 minutes. Add salt and pepper, a little nutmeg and the cognac.

Put the bread slices in the bottom of 8 small, individual ovenproof soup bowls and cover them with crumbled Roquefort. Pour in the onion soup to fill the bowls three-quarters full, sprinkle with the grated cheese and brown in a hot oven for 10 minutes. Serve immediately.

US	Ingredients	Met/Imp
1½ lb	onions	750 g/1½ lb
I stick	butter	100 g/4 oz
2 quarts	boiling water	2 litres/3½ pints
	salt and pepper	
	nutmeg	
I tbsp	cognac	15 ml/I tbsp
a few	thin slices French bread (baguette)	a few
¼ lb	Roquefort cheese	100 g/4 oz
a little	Gruyère cheese, grated	a little

US	Ingredients	Met/Imp
2	large onions	2
2 bottles	cider	2 bottles
4½ lb	various fish (see method)	2 kg/4½ lb
a few	parsley sprigs	a few
a few	thyme sprigs	a few
1	bay leaf	1
	salt and pepper	
2 cups	crème fraîche	500 ml/18 fl oz
1 tbsp	chopped parsley	15 ml/1 tbsp

FISH SOUP
WITH CREAM AND ONIONS

Preparation 45 minutes • Cooking 8 minutes

Thinly slice the onions and put them in a saucepan with the cider. Cook over a high heat until reduced to about a quarter. Put the pieces of firm-fleshed sea fish (brill, gurnard, bream, etc) into the saucepan. Add the herbs and a little salt and pepper, cover and boil over a high heat for 8 minutes or until the fish is tender. Remove the fish from the pan and continue boiling the cooking liquid until it is almost dry. Return the fish to the pan and reheat gently.

To serve, cover the fish with the crème fraîche and bring just to the boil. Remove from the heat. Take the fish out of the sauce and arrange in a large heated vegetable dish or tureen. Whip the cooking liquid to a creamy consistency, check the seasoning, then coat the fish with it. Sprinkle with chopped parsley.

VARIATION
Add 1 litre/1¾ pints (1 quart) mussels to the soup, if liked.

US	Ingredients	Met/Imp
1	boiling fowl (stewing chicken)	1
1, about 1.5 kg/3 lb	small knuckle (hock) ham	1, about 1.5 kg/3 lb
1 lb	leg (shank) of beef	500 g/1 lb
2	carrots	2
2	turnips	2
2	leeks	2
1	onion	1
1	clove	1
a few	parsley sprigs	a few
1	bay leaf	1
a few	thyme sprigs	a few
3 quarts	water	3 litres/5¼ pints
	salt	
1 tsp	saffron	5 ml/1 tsp
½ lb	firm-textured bread slices	250 g/8 oz

SAFFRON SOUP

Preparation 1 hour • Cooking 1 hour

Mourtayrol is a saffron-flavoured soup from the Rouergue.

First prepare an excellent stock with the boiling fowl (stewing chicken), ham and beef, the chopped vegetables, onion spiked with the clove, herbs, water, salt and saffron. Strain the stock, reserving the meats and vegetables.

Put the bread slices in an ovenproof terrine and pour hot stock over them until they are completely soaked, then simmer for 30 minutes in a low oven, adding more hot stock from time to time.

Serve the mourtayrol from the terrine. Serve the soup first, followed by the reserved meats and vegetables.

PETITE MARMITE DE VOLAILLE À LA MOELLE

CHICKEN SOUP
—— WITH VEAL AND BEEF MARROW ——

Preparation 1 hour • Cooking 1¾ hours

Blanch the knuckle (shank) of veal and the chicken giblets in boiling water, then drain.

Cut the carrots, turnips, leeks and celery into large sticks. Blanch in boiling water, then refresh in cold water and drain.

Put the veal, giblets and vegetables in a large saucepan and pour in the consommé. Bring to the boil, cover and cook for 1½ hours. About 10 minutes before the end of the cooking time, add the vermicelli.

Remove the veal and the giblets from the pan and cut the meat into thin slices, discarding the bones. Pour the soup into heatproof soup bowls and add the meat. Add 2 croûtons to each bowl and top with thin slices of poached marrow with salt and pepper added. Flash the bowls under the grill (broiler) just before serving. Hand the grated cheese in a separate bowl so that guests can help themselves.

US	Ingredients	Met/Imp
2 lb	shin or knuckle (shank) of veal	1 kg/2 lb
2 sets	chicken giblets (wings, gizzards and necks)	2 sets
2	carrots	2
2	turnips	2
2	leeks, white part only	2
1	head celery	1
3 quarts	chicken consommé	3 litres/5¼ pints
½ lb	vermicelli	250 g/8 oz
16	French bread (baguette) croûtons	16
1 lb	beef marrow, poached	500 g/1 lb
	salt and pepper	
1 cup	Parmesan or Gruyère cheese, grated, to serve	100 g/4 oz

POTAGE DE CÉLERI AUX PETITS CROÛTONS

CELERIAC SOUP
——— WITH SMALL CROÛTONS ———

Preparation 30 minutes • Cooking 1 hour

Thinly slice the vegetables and put them in a saucepan with about one-quarter of the butter. Sweat over a low heat for 15 minutes.

Add the water and some salt, bring to the boil and cook gently for 35–40 minutes.

Drain the vegetables, reserving the cooking liquid. Work the vegetables through a sieve and return the purée to the saucepan.

Mix in the reserved cooking liquid and the boiled milk.

Bring to the boil, stirring, then remove from the heat and add the remaining butter. Stir until melted.

Pour into a heated tureen and sprinkle with the fried croûtons and chopped chervil.

US	Ingredients	Met/Imp
14 oz	celeriac	400 g/14 oz
5	celery stalks	5
1	large onion	1
10 tbsp	butter	150 g/5 oz
2 quarts	water	2 litres/3½ pints
	salt	
2 cups	milk	500 ml/18 fl oz
2 cups	small fried croûtons	100 g/4 oz
1 tbsp	chopped fresh chervil	15 ml/1 tbsp

US	Ingredients	Met/Imp
½ lb	mushrooms	250 g/8 oz
I stick	butter	100 g/4 oz
½ cup	flour	75 g/3 oz
I quart	milk	I litre/1¾ pints
I quart	chicken consommé	I litre/1¾ pints
	salt and pepper	
½ cup	crème fraîche	100 ml/4 fl oz
2	egg yolks	2

MUSHROOM SOUP

Preparation 30 minutes • Cooking 15 minutes

The flavour of this soup is, of course, better if field or wild mushrooms are used.

Peel and wash the mushrooms and chop them finely.

Make a blond roux (*page 50*) with the butter and flour and gradually stir in the hot milk to make a fairly thick white sauce.

Add the consommé, then the chopped mushrooms and some salt and pepper. Cook for about 10 minutes, then add three-quarters of the crème fraîche. If the soup is too thick, add a little more hot milk. Adjust the seasoning.

Whisk the egg yolks with the remaining crème fraîche in a heated tureen. Pour in the soup and serve.

US	Ingredients	Met/Imp
1½ lb	pumpkin flesh	750 g/1½ lb
¼ lb	tomatoes	100 g/4 oz
⅓ cup	onion	40 g/1½ oz
I tsp	salt	5 ml/1 tsp
I pinch	sugar	I pinch
3 cups	milk	750 ml/1¼ pints
4 tbsp	butter	50 g/2 oz
2	egg yolks	2
	small croûtons, to garnish (optional)	

POTAGE À LA CRÈME DE POTIRON

CREAM OF PUMPKIN SOUP

Preparation 5 minutes • Cooking about 1 hour

Cut the pumpkin into 5 cm/2 inch cubes. Halve the tomatoes and squeeze them gently to remove the juice and seeds. Cut the onion into thin slices. Put all the vegetables in a flameproof casserole and cover them closely with a sheet of foil. Do not add any liquid and put the lid on the casserole. Cook in a moderate oven for 1 hour. Transfer the contents of the casserole to a blender or food processor and blend to a purée, then work through a sieve into a saucepan. Add salt and sugar, then place over a low heat and gradually stir in the milk. Cook for 2 minutes, stirring constantly, then cover and keep warm. Heat a tureen by rinsing it with boiling water. Put the diced butter and the egg yolks in the heated tureen and mix them rapidly with a wooden spoon. Gradually stir in the very hot soup. Serve immediately, with a garnish of small croûtons, if liked.

US	Ingredients	Met/Imp
2 quarts	milk	2 litres/3½ pints
a few	slices French bread (baguette)	a few
I stick	butter	100 g/4 oz
a few	chervil sprigs	a few
I	bunch watercress	I
2	egg yolks	2
	salt	

POTAGE DE CRESSON

WATERCRESS SOUP

Preparation 10 minutes • Cooking 5 minutes

Heat the milk in a saucepan. Meanwhile, fry the bread slices in the butter, arrange them in a heated tureen and sprinkle them with very finely chopped chervil and watercress. Gradually thicken the milk (which should be hot, but not boiling, to avoid cooking the eggs) by whisking in the egg yolks. Add salt and pour on to the bread slices in the tureen. Serve immediately.

— CHILLED CREAM OF SORREL SOUP —

Preparation 30 minutes • Cooking 20 minutes

US	Ingredients	Met/Imp
5 oz (about 3 cups)	sorrel	150 g/5 oz
1 quart	chicken stock	1 litre/1¾ pints
2	egg yolks	2
2 tbsp	crème fraîche	30 ml/2 tbsp
	salt and pepper	

Prepare some sorrel purée. Wash the sorrel and put it in a saucepan with a little water. Cover, bring to the boil and cook for 5–10 minutes or until tender and reduced in volume. Work through a fine sieve. Return the purée to the saucepan and heat gently until dry.

Bring the stock to the boil in a separate saucepan. Meanwhile, in a bowl, beat together the egg yolks, crème fraîche, salt and pepper. Gradually beat one-quarter of the boiling stock into the egg mixture, then pour the mixture back into the stock in the pan. Heat until almost boiling, then add the very dry sorrel purée.

Pour into cold soup bowls and leave to cool. Serve chilled.

SPRING VEGETABLE BROTH

Preparation 50 minutes • Cooking 45 minutes

US	Ingredients	Met/Imp
¼ lb	young carrots	100 g/4 oz
¼ lb	young turnips	100 g/4 oz
3	young leeks	3
1	small onion	1
	salt and pepper	
1 pinch	sugar	1 pinch
1 stick	butter	100 g/4 oz
2½ quarts	Veal Stock (*page 56*)	2.5 litres/ 4½ pints
3 oz	firm cabbage	75 g/3 oz
6	sorrel leaves	6
8	lettuce leaves	8
1 tbsp	cooked peas	15 ml/1 tbsp
1 tsp	chopped fresh chervil	5 ml/1 tsp

Cut the carrots, turnips and leeks into small, even-sized strips and thinly slice the onion. Mix the vegetables in a bowl and add some salt and the sugar. Sweat them gently in the butter in a saucepan for 15–20 minutes, without letting them change colour. Pour in enough of the veal stock to cover the vegetables.

Add the cabbage, cut into strips, and continue cooking gently until all the vegetables are tender. Remember to remove the scum frequently.

About 10 minutes before serving, add the remaining veal stock to the broth, then, just before serving, add a *chiffonnade* of sorrel and lettuce, the cooked peas and the chervil.

— LETTUCE SOUP —

Preparation 20 minutes • Cooking 15 minutes

US	Ingredients	Met/Imp
4	lettuces	4
	salt and pepper	
10 tbsp	butter	150 g/5 oz
2 quarts	milk	2 litres/3½ pints

This soup may also be sieved and thickened with egg yolks.

Blanch the lettuces in boiling salted water, then drain them and chop them finely. Sweat in half of the butter in a saucepan. Pour in the boiling milk and add salt and pepper. Boil for 5 minutes, then add the remaining butter and serve.

US	Ingredients	Met/Imp
2	leeks	2
1	small cabbage	1
1 lb	potatoes	500 g/1 lb
4 tbsp	butter	50 g/2 oz
3 quarts	stock	3 litres/5¼ pints
⅔ cup	long grain rice	100 g/4 oz
½ cup	Parmesan cheese, grated	50 g/2 oz

– VEGETABLE BROTH FROM PIEDMONT –

Preparation 30 minutes • Cooking 50 minutes

Thinly slice the vegetables and sweat for 10 minutes in the butter in a saucepan. Pour in the stock and cook for 40 minutes, adding the rice about halfway through the cooking time.

To serve, pour the broth into a heated tureen and sprinkle with the grated cheese.

VARIATION

If liked, 15 ml/1 tbsp tomato paste and 100 g/4 oz (⅔ cup) fresh white beans may be added to this soup.

US	Ingredients	Met/Imp
1, weighing 400 g/14 oz	sole	1, weighing 400 g/14 oz
2	small gurnard	2
2	weever	2
2	medium whiting	2
2½ quarts	water	2.5 litres/ 4½ pints
2 cups	white wine	500 ml/18 fl oz
	salt and pepper	
1	carrot	1
1	onion	1
1	leek	1
a few	parsley sprigs	a few
1	thyme sprig	1
14 tbsp	butter	200 g/7 oz
½ cup	flour	75 g/3 oz
¼ lb	white mushrooms	100 g/4 oz
4	egg yolks	4
scant 1 cup	*crème fraîche*	200 ml/7 fl oz

SEAFOOD SOUP
WITH FILLETS OF SOLE

Preparation 1 hour • Cooking 1 hour

This soup can be made without the sole, in which case some fish stock must be prepared for the basic velouté.

Make the fish stock. Fillet the sole and set the fillets aside. Break the bones into small pieces and put them in a saucepan with the other fish which have been cleaned and halved. Add the water, wine, some salt, the carrot, sliced onion and a bouquet of the leek, parsley and thyme. Bring to the boil, remove the scum, then boil gently for 30 minutes.

Meanwhile, prepare the fillets of sole to garnish the soup. Put them on a buttered ovenproof dish, sprinkle with a little salt and add small pieces of butter. Cover with buttered foil and cook in a moderate oven for about 10 minutes or until tender. Wrap the fillets in a fine cloth and leave them to cool under a light weight.

Make the velouté. Melt 75 g/3 oz (6 tbsp) of the butter in a saucepan and mix in the flour. Cook over a low heat until the roux has turned slightly blond. Strain the fish stock through a sieve lined with cheesecloth, then add gradually to the roux. Bring to the boil, stirring constantly. Leave to boil gently, removing the scum fairly frequently.

Clean the mushrooms and chop them very finely or work them through a metal sieve. Add to the velouté immediately and cook for 10–12 minutes.

A few minutes before serving, cut the fillets of sole into a fine *julienne*. Whisk the egg yolks with the crème fraîche and stir into the soup. Heat very gently for another 2 minutes, without letting it boil. Remove from the heat, mix in the remaining butter and adjust the seasoning.

Pour the soup into a heated tureen through a fine sieve and add the sole julienne.

— PETITS POIS SOUP WITH CHICKEN —

Preparation 1 hour • Cooking 1¼ hours

US	Ingredients	Met/Imp
1, weighing 1 kg/2 lb	chicken	1, weighing 1kg/2 lb
1	carrot	1
1	small onion	1
1	celery stalk	1
1	leek	1
1 quart	shelled petits pois	1 litre/2 pints
14 tbsp	butter	200 g/7 oz
1	large onion	1
2	lettuces	2
about 20	young spinach leaves	about 20
a few	parsley and chervil sprigs	a few
5 tsp	sugar	20 g/¾ oz
	salt	
2 cups	water	500 ml/18 fl oz
4	egg yolks	4
scant 1 cup	crème fraîche	200 ml/7 fl oz
	GARNISH	
½ cup	shelled petits pois	100 ml/4 fl oz
1 tbsp	chopped fresh chervil	15 ml/1 tbsp

The addition of spinach does not contribute to the flavour of the dish; it simply brightens the colour of the pea purée and gives a light green tinge to the soup.

Cook a nice tender chicken in boiling water flavoured with the chopped carrot, small onion, celery and leek until tender. Drain, reserving the stock.

Put the petits pois in a saucepan with half of the butter. Add the finely sliced large onion, the lettuces (cut into *julienne*), the spinach leaves, a small bouquet of parsley and chervil, the sugar, some salt and the water. Cover, bring to the boil and cook fairly rapidly for about 5 minutes.

Meanwhile, cook the petits pois for the garnish in boiling salted water so that they are ready just in time to be served. Drain well and set aside.

As soon as the pea and lettuce mixture is cooked, remove the peas from the liquid with a slotted spoon and crush to a purée in a mortar and pestle. Work through a sieve lined with cheesecloth into a saucepan and mix with 1 litre/1¾ pints (1 quart) of the chicken stock. Bring to the boil, stirring, then leave to boil gently over a low heat.

Detach 100 g/4 oz meat from the breast of the chicken and put it aside. Pound all the remaining meat to a purée in a mortar and pestle, then thin it down with 45–60 ml/3–4 tbsp stock. Work this purée immediately through a sieve into a heated tureen. Cut the reserved chicken breast into fine julienne and keep hot between 2 plates.

About 6 minutes before serving, whisk together the egg yolks and crème fraîche and whisk into the soup. Continue to simmer the soup gently over a low heat for 5–6 seconds, then remove from the heat and mix in the remaining butter. Finally, pour the soup gradually into the tureen, stirring it with a whisk to ensure it mixes completely with the puréed chicken. Add the julienne of chicken, then garnish with the well-drained petits pois and the chervil. Serve immediately.

US	Ingredients	Met/Imp
2	middle sections of oxtail	2
1½ lb	gelatinous ox bones	750 g/1½ lb
1½ lb	leg (shank) of beef	750 g/1½ lb
4 quarts	water	4 litres/7 pints
	salt	
2	carrots	2
1	onion	1
2	cloves	2
3	leeks	3
a few	parsley sprigs	a few
½	celery stalk	½
1	thyme sprig	1
¼	bay leaf	¼
1 tsp	*herbes à tortue*	5 ml/1 tsp
¼ cup	madeira	50 ml/2 fl oz
8 small glasses	sherry	8 small glasses
	BRUNOISE	
¼ lb	carrots	100 g/4 oz
¼ lb	turnips	100 g/4 oz
2	leeks, white part only	2
2 oz	celery heart	50 g/2 oz
3 tbsp	butter	40 g/1½ oz
1¼ cups	beef stock	300 ml/½ pint
	CLARIFICATION	
1 lb	lean boneless beef such as silverside (round)	500 g/1 lb
½	carrot	½
1	leek, white part only	1
2	egg whites	2

OXTAIL BROTH WITH MADEIRA

Preparation 5¾ hours • Cooking 4¾–5 hours

Cut the oxtails at the joints into 8 chunks. Soak them in cold, preferably running, water for 3–4 hours to remove the impurities and blood.

Drain the oxtails and wrap in cheesecloth. Put in a large saucepan with the gelatinous ox bones, the leg (shank) of beef, and three-quarters of the water. Add some salt and bring to the boil. Remove any scum that appears and add the carrots, onion spiked with the cloves and a bouquet of leeks, parsley, celery, thyme and bay leaf. Cook gently and evenly for 4 hours.

Meanwhile, prepare the brunoise. Cut the carrots, turnips, leeks and celery into 1 cm/½ inch cubes. Place in a saucepan with the butter and sweat over a low heat for 30 minutes. Pour in the stock and continue cooking until all the vegetables are tender. (This is what is called a large brunoise.) Keep warm.

After the oxtails have been cooking for 4 hours, remove them from the pan, unwrap them and keep them warm in a little of the stock. Strain the stock left in the saucepan and remove the grease from it.

Make the clarification. Finely mince (grind) the beef and put it in a saucepan with the finely diced carrot and leek and the egg whites. Mix well, then gradually stir in the strained oxtail stock. Put the saucepan over a low heat and boil very gently for 45 minutes–1 hour. The purpose of this 'clarification' is to obtain a clear stock by the action of the egg whites, which have a clarifying effect, and to make the broth tastier by adding beef.

Strain the stock through a piece of cheesecloth which has been soaked in lukewarm water, then wrung out. Infuse the herbs in the madeira for 2 minutes and add them to the broth. Pour into a heated tureen, add the oxtail sections and the brunoise and serve immediately.

Flavour each portion individually with a small glass of sherry.

US	Ingredients	Met/Imp

——— CREAM OF TOMATO SOUP ———

Preparation 10 minutes • Cooking about 1 hour

US	Ingredients	Met/Imp
2 lb	plump tomatoes	1 kg/2 lb
5 tbsp	butter	60 g/2½ oz
1½ quarts	hot water	1.5 litres/2½ pints
1 tbsp	salt	15 g/½ oz
1 pinch	pepper	1 pinch
1	garlic clove	1
¼ cup	tapioca	60 ml/4 tbsp
2	egg yolks	2
3 tbsp	crème fleurette	45 ml/3 tbsp

Cut the tomatoes in half and squeeze them gently to remove the juice and seeds. Put them in a large heavy-based saucepan. Add the butter, cover and cook gently for 30 minutes. Pour in the hot water and add the salt, pepper and the unpeeled garlic clove. Cook for another 15 minutes. Remove the garlic clove and sieve the soup into a bowl, then return it to the rinsed-out saucepan. Bring to the boil and sprinkle immediately with the tapioca. Cover the saucepan and simmer for a further 20 minutes or until the tapioca is cooked. Put the egg yolks in a heated tureen and whisk in the crème fleurette. Gradually pour in the soup, stirring well. Check the seasoning and serve immediately.

——— BASQUE SOUP (ELZEKARIA) ———

Preparation 30 minutes • Soaking overnight • Cooking 3 hours

US	Ingredients	Met/Imp
¼ lb	onions	100 g/4 oz
6 tbsp	lard	75 g/3 oz
1	white cabbage	1
½ lb (1⅓ cups)	dried white haricot beans (Great Northern or navy beans)	250 g/8 oz
2	garlic cloves	2
3 quarts	water	3 litres/5¼ pints
	salt and pepper	

In the Basque country, a drop of wine is added to the steaming elzekaria.
  Fry the thinly sliced onions in the lard in a large saucepan. Add the cabbage leaves, cut into strips, the beans, which have been soaked overnight and drained, and the crushed garlic. Pour in the boiling water and add salt and plenty of pepper. Cover and cook for 3 hours, then serve.

——— CRAB SOUP ———

Preparation 40 minutes • Cooking 40 minutes

US	Ingredients	Met/Imp
3	leeks, white part only	3
1	onion	1
½ lb	potatoes	200 g/7 oz
½ cup	oil	100 ml/4 fl oz
24	small crabs	24
a few	fish heads	a few
2½ quarts	water	2.5 litres/4½ pints
1 glass	white wine	1 glass
2	garlic cloves	2
1	bouquet garni	1
2	fennel leaves	2
	salt and pepper	
3–4	saffron threads	3–4
	or	
1 pinch	ground saffron	1 pinch
½ lb	vermicelli	250 g/8 oz

Fry the chopped leeks, onion and potatoes in the oil in a large saucepan for about 10 minutes or until soft. Add the well-washed crabs and the fish heads and pour in the water and wine. Add the crushed garlic, bouquet garni, fennel, salt, pepper and saffron. Boil for 20 minutes, then work through a metal sieve, firmly crushing the crabs and fish heads. Return to the saucepan and bring to the boil once more. Add the vermicelli and cook for a further 10 minutes or until the vermicelli is cooked. Serve at once.

US	Ingredients	Met/Imp
48	flat oysters	48
about 4½ pints	water	about 2.25 litres/4 pints
2 cups	crème fraîche	500 ml/18 fl oz
6 tbsp	butter	75 g/3 oz
	pepper	

——— OYSTER SOUP AMÉRICAINE ———

Preparation 25 minutes • Cooking 10 minutes

Open the oysters, trim them and keep to one side in a saucepan. Add enough water to the oyster juice to make it up to 2.25 litres/4 pints (4½ pints) and boil gently for 10 minutes with the oyster trimmings. Work through a fine sieve, mix with the oysters and poach gently, without boiling, for 1 minute. Add the very hot crème fraîche, the butter and pepper to taste and serve immediately.

US	Ingredients	Met/Imp
2	medium onions	2
3	parsley sprigs	3
1	bay leaf	1
2	thyme sprigs	2
2	garlic cloves	2
¾ bottle	dry white wine	¾ bottle
2 cups	water	500 ml/18 fl oz
3 quarts	mussels	3 litres/5¼ pints
	salt and pepper	
6 tbsp	flour	50 g/2 oz
1	lemon, juice of	1
½ cup	crème fraîche	125 ml/4½ fl oz

——— MUSSEL SOUP ———

Preparation 40 minutes • Cooking 20 minutes • Serves 6

Put the roughly chopped onions in a large saucepan with the parsley, bay leaf, thyme and halved garlic cloves. Add the white wine and water. Bring to the boil, then cover and cook over a low heat for 10–15 minutes.

While the court bouillon is cooking, carefully clean the mussels. Trim away their 'beards' and, if necessary, scrape the shells to remove any barnacles. Scrub the mussels under cold running water, then quickly wash them in plenty of cold water 2–3 times. Drain well.

Strain the court bouillon through a fine sieve; discard the flavouring ingredients. Rinse out the saucepan and pour in 250 ml/9 fl oz (1 cup) of the court bouillon and 250 ml/9 fl oz (1 cup) cold water. Set the remaining court bouillon aside. Add the mussels to the liquid in the pan, cover and place over a low heat. Boil until the mussels open, shaking the pan from time to time to make sure all the mussels come into contact with the heat at the bottom of the saucepan and open at the same time. The mussels should have opened after 4–5 minutes; longer cooking makes them tough. Discard any mussels that do not open.

Remove the mussels from the saucepan with a slotted spoon. Set a few large mussels (6–8 per portion) aside to use as a garnish. Remove the shells from the remaining mussels, then place the mussel meat in a bowl with the reserved court bouillon.

Pour the cooking liquid from the mussels through a sieve lined with cheesecloth into a bowl. Pour the liquid out very carefully through the sieve so as not to disturb any sand which should stay at the bottom of the saucepan. Rinse out the saucepan and return the strained cooking liquid to it.

Pour the mussels and some of the court bouillon into a vegetable mill fitted with the fine grill. Put the mussels through the mill. Alternatively, purée the mussels with a little court bouillon in a blender or food processor. Add the purée to the strained cooking liquid, then stir in the remaining court bouillon and heat gently.

Meanwhile, mix the flour with a little cold water. Sieve this paste into the saucepan of soup, stirring with a wooden spoon. Bring gently to the boil and simmer for a few moments.

Add the strained lemon juice. Slowly add the crème fraîche and heat for a few moments, stirring constantly, until thick. Check the seasoning and add salt and pepper, if necessary. Complete the dish with the reserved mussels.

Serve in heated soup bowls. If desired, a few cubes of bread may be toasted under the grill (broiler) and served with the soup.

SOUPE À L'OIGNON GRATINÉE

ONION SOUP AU GRATIN*

Preparation 15 minutes • Cooking 30 minutes

US	Ingredients	Met/Imp
½ lb	onions	250 g/8 oz
5 tbsp	butter	60 g/2½ oz
3 tbsp	flour	25 g/scant 1 oz
2 quarts	water, mixed with 12.5 ml/2½ tsp sea salt or 200 ml/7 fl oz (scant 1 cup) light meat stock	2 litres/3½ pints
	salt and pepper	
1 cup	Comté cheese, grated	100 g/4 oz
1 cup	Emmenthal cheese, grated	100 g/4 oz
1	loaf French bread (baguette)	1
1 cup	Gruyère cheese, grated	100 g/4 oz

Skin and finely slice the onions. Melt the butter in a heavy-based saucepan and fry the onions over a low heat for about 10 minutes or until uniformly golden. Stir in the flour and cook, stirring, until lightly browned.

Pour in a little of the salted water or water and stock. Stir thoroughly, then add the remaining water or stock. Add salt, if necessary, and pepper and bring to the boil. Cover and cook gently for 20–30 minutes. Meanwhile, mix the Comté and Emmenthal cheeses together.

The onion soup may be served just as it is, or it may be worked through a sieve to remove any stringy pieces of onion.

Put 2–3 thin slices of toasted baguette in the bottom of each of 8 individual ovenproof soup bowls. Sprinkle with the grated Comté and Emmenthal cheeses and pour over the onion soup, sieved or otherwise. Float a few thin slices of baguette on top of the soup, sprinkle with a thin layer of grated Gruyère cheese and brown in a very hot oven or under the grill (broiler). Serve immediately.

US	Ingredients	Met/Imp
1½ lb	various fish (see method)	750 g/1½ lb
scant 1 cup	olive oil	200 ml/7 fl oz
4	shallots	4
1	bouquet garni	1
2	leeks	2
1	onion	1
1 bottle	dry white bordeaux wine (eg Graves)	1 bottle
1 quart	water	1 litre/1¾ pints
	salt and pepper	
scant ½ lb	firm-textured bread, sliced	200 g/7 oz
1 pinch	saffron	1 pinch
3	egg yolks (optional)	3
1	lemon, juice of (optional)	1

FISH SOUP BORDELAISE

Preparation 50 minutes • Cooking 30 minutes

Cut the fish (whiting, plaice, conger eel) into pieces and put it in a saucepan with a glass of olive oil. Add the thinly sliced shallots, the bouquet garni, the sliced leeks and thinly sliced onion.

Pour in the wine and water and add salt and pepper. Cook over a low heat for 30 minutes.

Meanwhile, quickly fry the bread slices in the remaining olive oil in a frying pan. Put them in a heated tureen. Strain the fish stock and pour it over the fried bread croûtons. Just before serving, add a large pinch of saffron.

If liked, the soup may be thickened by adding the egg yolks whisked with the lemon juice to the strained hot stock and heating gently, stirring, until thickened. Pour over the croûtons and serve as above.

US	Ingredients	Met/Imp
4	tomatoes	4
1	large onion	1
2	leeks, white part only	2
½ cup	oil	100 ml/4 fl oz
2	garlic cloves	2
3 quarts	water	3 litres/5¼ pints
	salt and pepper	
1	bouquet garni	1
2 lb	various fish (see method)	1 kg/2 lb
4	small crabs	4
1 pint	mussels	500 ml/18 fl oz
¾ lb	large vermicelli	300 g/10 oz

FISH SOUP FROM LA ROCHELLE

Preparation 1½ hours • Cooking 1 hour

Halve the tomatoes and squeeze gently to remove the juice and seeds. Roughly chop the flesh. Fry the thinly sliced onion and leeks in the oil, add the chopped tomatoes and the crushed garlic and fry gently for a few moments. Pour in the water and add salt and pepper. Bring to the boil, add the bouquet garni, the fish (weever, gurnard, whiting, conger eel) cut into pieces, the crabs and the steamed and shelled mussels.

Cook over a high heat for 20 minutes, then work through a sieve, lightly pressing the fish to extract all the juice. Collect the stock in a saucepan and bring to the boil once more. Sprinkle in the vermicelli and poach gently for 25 minutes. Serve immediately.

US	Ingredients	Met/Imp
4	tomatoes	4
2	onions	2
½ cup	olive oil	100 ml/4 fl oz
2	garlic cloves	2
4	leeks, white part only	4
1 quart	white wine	1 litre/1¾ pints
2 cups	water	500 ml/18 fl oz
	salt and pepper	
1	small piece pimiento	1
2	crabs	2
1	small crawfish (rock lobster)	1
4–4½ lb	various white fish (see method)	1.8–2 kg/ 4–4½ lb
¾ lb	large vermicelli	300 g/10 oz

SOUP FROM SÈTE

Preparation 50 minutes • Cooking crabs and crawfish 25 minutes, white fish 12 minutes

Sète is a town on the Mediterranean coast in the Hérault region of south-west France. Traditionally this soup is made with freshly caught crabs and crawfish (rock lobster), which are cut up live at the last moment.

Skin, chop and de-seed the tomatoes. Chop the onions and brown them lightly in the oil. Add the tomatoes, crushed garlic and sliced leeks. Pour in the wine and water and add salt, plenty of pepper and the piece of pimiento.

As soon as the mixture comes to the boil, add the crabs and the crawfish. Bring back to the boil, cover and boil gently for 12 minutes. Add the white fish (bass, whiting, dab, mullet, scorpion fish, sole) and continue cooking for another 12 minutes.

Part-cook the vermicelli in boiling, slightly salted water and drain as soon as it has swollen.

Remove the fish from the court bouillon, add the vermicelli and cook for 10 minutes. Return the fish to the soup and serve very hot.

TOURIN À L'AIL ET AU VERMICELLE

— GARLIC AND VERMICELLI TOURIN —

Preparation 10 minutes • Cooking 45–50 minutes • Serves 4

US	Ingredients	Met/Imp
4 tsp	olive oil	20 ml/4 tsp
20	garlic cloves	20
2 tsp	flour	10 ml/2 tsp
about 5 cups	water or green bean cooking water	about 5 cups
	salt and pepper	
3 oz	vermicelli	75 g/3 oz
1	egg	1
1 tsp	wine vinegar	5 ml/1 tsp

Heat the oil gently in a saucepan. Add the garlic cloves and cook for about 5 minutes or until only slightly golden. The garlic must not turn brown or it will become bitter. Stir in the flour with a wooden spoon and cook for 2–3 minutes.

Pour in a little of the water, stirring well until smooth, then add the remaining liquid. Add a moderate amount of salt. (If you are using bean stock, remember that it is already salted.)

Cover and simmer gently for 20–30 minutes. Boiled in this way, for a long time, garlic is very digestible and does not have any of the usual disadvantages. Add the vermicelli and cook for about 8 minutes.

Separate the egg. Put the egg white into the soup when it is just simmering and poach for 2–3 minutes. Remove the egg white with a slotted spoon and put it in the heated tureen (to stop it cooking any more, which would harden it).

Mix the egg yolk with the wine vinegar and stir in a little of the hot stock. Remove the soup from the heat and add this egg mixture. The soup will instantly turn white. Return to the heat and bring to the boil, stirring constantly. Boil for 1–2 minutes or until thickened. The presence of the flour will prevent the egg yolk from curdling.

Remove the soup from the heat, add salt, if necessary, and a little pepper. Pour on to the poached egg white in the tureen. Serve very hot.

VARIATIONS
Omit the vermicelli and place thin slices of toast in the bottom of the tureen before pouring in the soup.

For a thicker, creamier soup, use 2 eggs and omit both vermicelli and bread.

If a thin soup is preferred, the egg need not be added.

US	Ingredients	Met/Imp
1 stick	butter	100 g/4 oz
1 cup	flour	150 g/5 oz
3 quarts	chicken stock	3 litres/5¼ pints
1 lb	white asparagus	500 g/1 lb
	salt	
scant ½ lb	green asparagus tips	200 g/7 oz
	LIAISON	
3	egg yolks	3
scant 1 cup	crème fraîche	200 ml/7 fl oz
1 stick	butter	100 g/4 oz

– ASPARAGUS VELOUTÉ WITH CREAM* –

Preparation 1 hour • Cooking 1 hour

Make the velouté. Melt the butter in a saucepan and mix in the flour. Stir over a low heat until a light blond colour. Gradually mix in the stock, bring to the boil, stirring constantly, and cook gently on a low heat until thickened, skimming off the fat.

Peel the white asparagus and cut it into sections. Put it in a saucepan of lightly salted boiling water and cook quickly for 8 minutes or until just tender. Drain, mix with the velouté and continue cooking for 50 minutes.

Break the stems of the green asparagus at the point where they are no longer flexible and cut them into 1 cm/½ inch sections. Rinse in cold water, then put into a saucepan of boiling salted water. Cook rapidly until tender but still a little firm. Drain thoroughly and set aside.

Work the velouté and asparagus through a sieve lined with cheesecloth and return the purée to the rinsed-out saucepan. Heat, stirring constantly, until almost boiling. Add the egg yolks whisked with the crème fraîche and cook gently for 5–6 seconds, stirring constantly, until thickened.

Finally, remove from the heat and add the butter. Pour the soup into a heated tureen through a fine sieve. Add the green asparagus tips and serve immediately.

BASIC RECIPES
&
SAUCES

'SAUCES ARE THE JEWELS AND THE HONOUR OF French cuisine,' Curnonsky would say. 'They have helped to earn and maintain its superiority, or rather, as they used to say in the 16th century, its undisputed pre-eminence.' All gourmets remember the words of Talleyrand, who was as much a perfect gastronome and magnificent host as he was a great diplomat: 'In England there are three sauces and 360 religions; in France there are three religions and 360 sauces.'

There are, in fact, many uses for sauces: dressing a salad; contributing to the elaboration of a dish (au gratin, salmis, seafood timbale, etc; accompanying a hot or cold side dish; or forming part of it (ragoût, stew, coq au vin, blanquette, etc). It is not surprising that the sauce chef is such a great craftsman in a kitchen team.

A distinction must first be made between cold sauces (vinaigrette, ravigote (herb), mayonnaise, rémoulade, etc), which are relatively easy to prepare by making a simple mixture or emulsion, and hot sauces, which are by far the most numerous and often require an elaborate technique. These sauces may be divided into: 'mother' sauces (or basic sauces) – Espagnole, demi-glaze and tomato sauce among the brown sauces; – béchamel and velouté among the white sauces – and 'compound' sauces, made from one or more mother sauces with various other ingredients added according to the nature of the dish concerned. The equipment for sauce-making is very important. You will need a variety of saucepans of different sizes with high sides (for a *bain-marie*) and made of thick metal (to ensure heat is evenly distributed). A whisk (for beating the sauces), a fine mesh sieve, an ordinary sieve and cheesecloth (for straining them) are also needed. Ideally, you should have enough equipment to be able to carry out these operations simultaneously.

To keep sauces hot until they are needed, they must be put in a bain-marie, which is not too hot, and stirred with a spatula while they cool. The final addition of butter must only be made at the very last moment.

For ease of presentation we have included stocks, *fumets*, aspics, liaisons, butters and marinades in this chapter, in addition to sauces.

BASES, BEURRES MANIÉS ET ROUX

BASIC RECIPES, KNEADED BUTTER AND ROUX

BEURRE MANIÉ

—————— KNEADED BUTTER ——————

Preparation 5 minutes

To thicken 600 ml/1 pint (2½ cups) liquid, put 50 g/2 oz (4 tbsp) butter in a bowl, beat until very soft and add 20 g/¾ oz (2 tbsp) flour. Mix together thoroughly with a fork or small whisk until a creamy paste is formed. Beurre manié is used when there is not enough time to make a roux (two completely different things). Roux must be cooked for a long time, whereas beurre manié, once it has been added to the cooking liquid, must be removed from the heat as soon as the liquid boils.

In home cooking, beurre manié is often used for quick liaisons or improvised sauces. It is also used in haute cuisine, but more rarely.

Spices, herbs and essences may all be added to beurre manié. As we will see later, there are numerous variations of this butter preparation.

BLANC

—————— WHITE COURT BOUILLON ——————

Preparation 5 minutes • Cooking 3 minutes

US	Ingredients	Met/Imp
3 tbsp	flour	30 g/1 oz
I quart	salted water	I litre/1¾ pints
½	lemon, juice of	½

This is a court bouillon or clear stock, in which poultry giblets, mushrooms and certain other vegetables such as cardoons, salsify and Chinese cabbage, are cooked.

Blend the flour with a little of the cold salted water, stirring until smooth. Add the remaining water and the lemon juice. Boil the court bouillon for about 3 minutes before cooking anything in it.

DUXELLES SÈCHE

—————— DRY DUXELLES ——————

Preparation 20 minutes • Cooking 15 minutes

US	Ingredients	Met/Imp
½ lb	mushroom trimmings	250 g/8 oz
2 oz (⅓ cup)	onions and shallots	50 g/2 oz
2 tbsp	oil	30 ml/2 tbsp
2 tbsp	butter	30 g/1 oz
	salt and pepper	
I pinch	chopped fresh parsley	I pinch

Chop the mushroom trimmings very finely, put them in a clean cloth and twist tightly to extract all moisture.

Heat the chopped onions and shallots with the oil and butter. Add the mushroom trimmings and fry for about 10 minutes or until brown. Add salt, pepper and parsley.

US	ingredients	Met/Imp
¼ lb	carrots	125 g/4½ oz
¼ lb	onions	125 g/4½ oz
2 oz (½ cup)	celery	50 g/2 oz
¼ lb	raw ham	100 g/4 oz
4 tbsp	butter	50 g/2 oz
I	thyme sprig	I
I	bay leaf	I
¼ cup	madeira	50 ml/2 fl oz

VEGETABLE GARNISH

Preparation 30 minutes • Cooking 15 minutes

Dice the vegetables and ham and sweat in the butter with the thyme and bay leaf for about 15 minutes or until tender. Deglaze with madeira.

US	ingredients	Met/Imp
¼ lb	fresh fat belly (side) of pork	100 g/4 oz
scant ½ lb	carrots	200 g/7 oz
¼ lb	onions	100 g/4 oz
I	bouquet thyme flowers	I
2	bay leaves	2
I glass	dry white wine	I glass

MIREPOIX

Preparation 30 minutes • Cooking 15 minutes

Finely dice the pork, carrots and onions. Heat the pork in a pan until the fat runs, then add the vegetables, thyme and bay leaves. Cook for about 15 minutes or until brown, then drain off the fat and pour the vegetables into the desired sauce or soup, having first removed the thyme and bay leaves. Deglaze the pan with the white wine and reduce by half.

ROUX

Preparation 10 minutes • Cooking 1 hour

Roux are made by combining a fatty substance (butter or margarine) with flour; they are the basis for the liaison of sauces. There are 3 types – brown, blond or white – according to the degree of cooking. However surprising it may seem, a roux of whatever kind should be very well cooked. The longer a roux is cooked, the clearer, smoother and shinier the sauce will be. If time is limited, it is better to make a *beurre manié*.

For roux, the proportions per 1 litre/1¾ pints (1 quart) of liquid are: 75 g/3 oz (6 tbsp) butter and 75 g/3 oz (½ cup) flour. Allowing for reduction during 1 hour's cooking, this will make enough to serve eight.

Brown roux Mix the clarified butter or margarine in a saucepan with the flour. Cook this mixture over a very low heat, stirring frequently, until it has turned a dark russet colour, or even slightly brown. Transfer to a small bowl, cover with greaseproof or parchment paper when it has completely cooled and keep until needed.

White roux Mix butter and flour as above, but cook quickly for about 5 minutes only, stirring constantly, so that the roux remains white.

BEURRES COMPOSÉS

COMPOUND BUTTERS

BEURRE D'AIL

GARLIC BUTTER

Preparation 15 minutes • Cooking 5 minutes

US	Ingredients	Met/Imp
¼ lb	garlic cloves	100 g/4 oz
10 tbsp	butter, softened	150 g/5 oz
	salt	

Skin and blanch garlic, dip in cold water, then crush in a mortar and pestle with the butter. Add salt and work through a fine sieve.

BEURRE D'ANCHOIS

ANCHOVY BUTTER

Preparation 10 minutes

US	Ingredients	Met/Imp
3 oz	canned anchovy fillets, soaked in milk	75 g/3 oz
14 tbsp	butter, softened	200 g/7 oz

Rinse and dry the anchovies. Pound in a mortar and pestle with the butter, then work through a fine sieve.

BEURRE D'ÉCHALOTE

SHALLOT BUTTER

Preparation 10 minutes • Cooking 5 minutes

Blanch a chopped shallot in boiling salted water. Drain and twist tightly in a clean cloth. Pound in a mortar and pestle with the same weight of softened butter. Work through a sieve lined with cheesecloth.

BEURRE D'ÉCREVISSES, DE HOMARD OU DE LANGOUSTE

CRAYFISH, LOBSTER OR CRAWFISH BUTTER

Preparation 1 hour • Cooking 15 minutes

US	Ingredients	Met/Imp
15	crayfish	15
	butter and Mirepoix (left)	
1	bouquet garni (not including garlic, tarragon or chervil)	1
¼ cup	cognac	50 ml/2 fl oz
½ cup	white wine	100 ml/4 fl oz
½ cup	Fish Fumet (page 57)	100 ml/4 fl oz
1 tsp	tomato paste	5 ml/1 tsp
4 tbsp	butter, softened	50 g/2 oz
	salt and pepper	

Sauté the crayfish in butter and mirepoix. Add the bouquet garni. Pour in the cognac (but do not flambé) and white wine. Reduce to two-thirds, then add the fish fumet, tomato paste and a little salt and pepper.

Shell the crayfish. Keep the tails and pound the scraps, pincers, body and eggs in a mortar and pestle. When they are well ground, return them to the pan and cook in the stock until reduced. Squeeze in a cloth and collect the juice in a bowl. There will only be a few spoonfuls.

Grind the crayfish tails with the softened butter, add the juice extracted from the scraps to this paste and work through a fine nylon sieve. Proceed in the same way for lobster or crawfish.

SNAIL BUTTER

(FOR SNAILS À LA BOURGUIGNONNE)

Preparation 15 minutes

For 100 fair-sized snails. Beat 100 g/4 oz (1 stick) softened butter with 75 g/3 oz (½ cup) finely chopped shallot, 2 garlic cloves, ground to a paste, and 30 ml/2 tbsp chopped fresh parsley. Add 25 g/scant 1 oz (1½ tbsp) salt and 5 ml/1 tsp pepper.

BEURRE D'ESTRAGON

TARRAGON BUTTER

Preparation 15 minutes • Cooking 2 minutes

Blanch 125 g/4½ oz tarragon leaves for 2 minutes in boiling salted water. Drain, dip in cold water and dry. Grind the leaves with 200 g/7 oz (14 tbsp) softened butter in a mortar and pestle. Work through a fine sieve.

BEURRE À LA MAÎTRE D'HÔTEL

MAÎTRE D'HÔTEL BUTTER

Preparation 5 minutes

Using a spoon, mix together 200 g/7 oz (14 tbsp) softened butter, 15 ml/1 tbsp chopped fresh parsley, 5 ml/1 tsp salt, a pinch of freshly ground pepper and a drop of lemon juice until a paste is formed.

This butter may either be served melted as a separate sauce, or put on hot food in small pieces just before serving.

BEURRE DE MONTPELLIER

MONTPELLIER BUTTER

Preparation 30 minutes • Cooking 3 minutes

In a saucepan of rapidly boiling water, blanch 50 g/2 oz mixed watercress, parsley, chervil, chives and tarragon with 15 g/½ oz spinach leaves. Drain, dip in cold water, drain again and press well to remove moisture. Put in a mortar and pestle and grind with a medium *cornichon*, 5 ml/1 tsp drained capers, a little garlic and 2 canned anchovy fillets. Add 250 g/8 oz (2 sticks) softened butter, 1 hard-boiled egg yolk and 1 raw egg yolk, then, while still gently grinding with the pestle, pour in 50 ml/2 fl oz (¼ cup) each oil and vinegar, a little at a time. Add salt and pepper. Finally, work the butter mixture through a fine nylon sieve.

'BLACK' BUTTER

Burnt butter is wasted butter; so make sure it does not become too dark.

This is butter cooked in a frying pan until it turns brown. After cooking the butter, add a dash of vinegar to the hot frying pan and heat before stirring it into the butter just before serving.

NOISETTE BUTTER

Cooking 2 minutes

Generally, noisette butter is butter which has been melted and cooked until it has turned the colour of hazelnuts. It may be served on sole, trout or fish cooked *à la meunière*. Lemon juice and chopped parsley should, of course, be put on the fish before pouring over the butter. However, a butter can also be made using ground hazelnuts (filberts): this is *real* nut butter.

PAPRIKA BUTTER

Cooking 3 minutes

Cook ½ onion, chopped, in butter and add a shake of paprika. The amount of paprika used depends on its quality. When the onions have cooled, mix in 125 g/4½ oz (1 stick) softened butter, then work through a sieve.

An alternative method is simply to beat the butter with paprika.

HOT RED CHILLI BUTTER

Preparation 10 minutes

Pound 1 hot red chilli with 125 g/4½ oz (1 stick) butter. Add a little salt and work through a fine sieve.

STUFFINGS

GRATIN STUFFING FOR CANAPÉS AND CROÛTONS

Preparation 30 minutes • Cooking 10 minutes

US	Ingredients	Met/Imp
5 oz	bacon	150 g/5 oz
10 oz	trimmed chicken livers	300 g/10 oz
1½ tbsp	thinly sliced shallot	15 g/½ oz
3 tbsp	mushroom trimmings	20 g/¾ oz
1	thyme sprig	1
½	bay leaf	½
	salt and pepper	
1 pinch	quatre-épices	1 pinch

Heat the finely chopped bacon in a pan. When it is hot, add the livers and all the other ingredients. Quickly sauté to seal the livers, then leave to cool. Grind in a mortar and pestle, and then work through a sieve. Keep the stuffing in a bowl covered with a piece of buttered greaseproof or parchment paper.

FORCEMEAT STUFFING (GODIVEAU) TO MAKE INTO QUENELLES

US	Ingredients	Met/Imp
	salt and pepper	
1 lb	butter	500 g/1 lb
1 cup	flour	150 g/5 oz
1 lb	boneless chicken breast or veal fillet (tenderloin)	500 g/1 lb
3	whole eggs	3
3	egg yolks	3

The following 2 stuffings are interchangeable, but the second recipe produces a richer and more delicate result. The same ingredients and proportions can be used for FISH STUFFING, substituting in order of preference: lobster, pike, John Dory, sole, whiting, salmon, for the meat.

First recipe

Preparation 1 hour

Prepare a PASTRY PANADA as follows: pour 600 ml/1 pint (2½ cups) water into a saucepan and add a little salt. Add the butter and bring to the boil. Add the flour, mix and beat with a spatula over the heat, as if making choux pastry. Cook until thoroughly dry, then spread the dough on a dish and leave to cool.

Meanwhile, pound the meat in a mortar and pestle with salt and pepper. Add the pastry panada and continue to pound. Add the whole eggs and the extra yolks, one at a time, making sure each egg is completely amalgamated before adding the next. Work through a fine sieve. Pound once more while cold. The stuffing should be very smooth.

Second recipe

Preparation 1 hour

Finely dice the chicken or veal and add salt and pepper. Pound vigorously in a mortar and pestle until a paste starts to form. Add the egg whites, one by one, continuing to pound so that each egg white is absorbed before the next is added. Work through a very fine metal sieve.

Put the mixture in a pan resting on crushed ice. Work with a spatula and incorporate the crème fraîche into the meat, spoon by spoon. If, however – as sometimes happens – the crème fraîche is too fatty, dilute it with a little cold milk. If it were too rich it would turn into butter and the stuffing (or quenelles) would disintegrate while poaching. (Before putting in all the crème fraîche, do a trial run by poaching a little paste in a small saucepan of boiling water.) The quenelles must be smooth but firm. Depending on what they are intended for, the stuffing or the quenelles may be garnished with finely diced or chopped truffles or any other condiment.

US	Ingredients	Met/Imp
I lb	boneless chicken breast or veal fillet (tenderloin)	500 g/I lb
	salt and pepper	
5	egg whites	5
1¼ cups	chilled *crème fraîche*	300 ml/½ pint

GARNITURE À LA FINANCIÈRE

'FINANCIÈRE' GARNISH

Preparation 1 hour • Cooking 10 minutes

Make the stuffing into 24 quenelles with either a forcing (pastry) bag or a teaspoon and poach them in boiling salted water. Combine the quenelles with the mushroom caps, cocks' combs and kidneys, truffles and sweetbreads. Bind with the demi-glaze and truffle juice and arrange around the dish to be garnished. If the garnish is intended for a piece of meat, then a few stoned (pitted) and blanched green olives may be added.

This garnish may, like so many others, be interpreted in various ways. It may be made with olives, foie gras, chicken livers, etc. However, the basic ingredients are always the same: quenelles, mushrooms, cocks' combs, kidneys and truffles.

US	Ingredients	Met/Imp
	Forcemeat Stuffing (*left or above*)	
16–20	small mushroom caps, sweated in butter	16–20
5 oz	cocks' combs and kidneys cooked in a White Court Bouillon (*page 49*)	150 g/5 oz
¼ lb	truffles, cut into strips or even beads	100 g/4 oz
10 oz	lamb sweetbreads, sweated in butter	300 g/10 oz
scant I cup	excellent, well-flavoured Demi-Glaze with madeira (*page 56*)	200 ml/7 fl oz
	truffle juice	

STOCKS AND FUMETS

FOND OU JUS DE VEAU BRUN (DEMI-GLACE ET GLACE)

BROWN VEAL STOCK OR JUICE —— (DEMI-GLAZE AND MEAT GLAZE) ——

Preparation 40 minutes • Cooking 2½ hours

US	Ingredients	Met/Imp
4½ lb	crushed veal bones	2 kg/4½ lb
2 lb	knuckle (shank) of veal, tied with string	1 kg/2 lb
¼ lb	carrots	100 g/4 oz
¼ lb	onions	100 g/4 oz
I	bouquet garni	I
9½ cups	water	2.3 litres/4 pints
1–1½ tbsp	salt	15–25 g/½–1 oz
½ cup	white wine or madeira	100 ml/4 fl oz
	potato flour	

Roast the veal bones and knuckle (shank) in the oven until browned. Put the carrots, thinly sliced onions and bouquet garni in a large high-sided, heavy-based saucepan. Put the bones and the knuckle (shank) on top of the vegetables and add 100 ml/4 fl oz (½ cup) water. Bring to the boil and cook until reduced and lightly coloured. Pour in the remaining water. Bring to the boil again, remove any scum and add the salt, allowing for the reduction.

Cook for 2–2½ hours, then strain through a damp cloth and leave to cool. Before the stock solidifies, put it through the cloth once more to remove all the fat.

When using this stock, take the necessary amount and reduce it, allowing it to colour and thicken, then add, depending on what it is intended for, some mushroom trimmings or tomato paste.

In order to give more flavour to the stock, or rather the sauce, reduce the white wine or madeira and add the reduced stock. Thicken with potato flour. When the stock is mixed with wine or madeira, it is thickened VEAL JUICE; when reduced until almost dry, it is known as DEMI-GLAZE or MEAT GLAZE.

FOND BLANC

WHITE STOCK ——

Preparation 1 hour • Cooking 4½ hours

US	Ingredients	Met/Imp
3¼ lb	shoulder of veal	1.5 kg/3¼ lb
3¼ lb	knuckle (shank) of veal	1.5 kg/3¼ lb
4½ lb	chicken giblets	2 kg/4½ lb
4½ lb	chicken carcass	2 kg/4½ lb
7 quarts	water	7 litres/12 pints
½ lb	carrots	250 g/8 oz
scant ½ lb	onions	200 g/7 oz
5 oz	leeks	150 g/5 oz
5 oz	celery	150 g/5 oz
5 tsp	salt	30 g/1 oz
I	bouquet garni	I

Bone the veal and break the bones into small pieces. Put them in a large saucepan with the meats, giblets and carcass, add the cold water and bring to the boil. Remove any scum. Add the vegetables, salt and bouquet garni and simmer for 4–4½ hours. Skim off the fat, strain through cheesecloth and continue cooking over a high heat until reduced. Strain once more and keep until needed.

	US	Ingredients	Met/Imp

FOND DE GIBIER

GAME STOCK

Preparation 1 hour • Cooking 3 hours

US	Ingredients	Met/Imp
6½ lb	neck, breast, bones and leftovers of game	3 kg/6½ lb
½ lb	carrots	200 g/7 oz
½ lb	onions	200 g/7 oz
I	sage sprig	I
10	juniper berries	10
I	bouquet garni	I
2 cups	dry white wine	500 ml/18 fl oz
2 quarts	water	2 litres/3½ pints

Brown the game pieces in the oven, then put the thinly sliced vegetables and the herbs in a large saucepan and put the game leftovers on top. Reduce the juice from the deglazed oven tray and pour into the pan. Add the white wine and water. Bring to the boil and cook gently for about 3 hours. Remove any scum. When reduced, this stock is known as GLACE DE GIBIER or GAME GLAZE.

FUMET DE POISSON

FISH FUMET

Preparation 30 minutes • Cooking 10–15 minutes

US	Ingredients	Met/Imp
I	onion	I
I	shallot	I
	parsley sprigs	
	thyme sprig	
	butter	
	fish bones and heads	
2 cups	white wine	500 ml/18 fl oz
2 cups	water	500 ml/18 fl oz
	salt	
	mushroom trimmings	

Put the sliced onion and shallot, the parsley, thyme and a little very good quality butter in a large saucepan with the fish bones and heads. (Use sole, whiting, turbot, brill, etc, according to what is to hand.) Sweat over a low heat for a few minutes, then pour in the white wine and the water with a very little salt. Add some mushroom trimmings (indispensable for a good fumet). Bring to the boil and boil continuously for 10–15 minutes. Work immediately through a fine sieve into a porcelain or stoneware bowl.

When needed, reduce the required amount, or cook fish in it and then use it as the basis for the sauce. When very reduced, it is known as GLACE DE POISSON or FISH GLAZE.

VELOUTÉ POUR SAUCE DE POISSON (SAUCE ALLEMANDE)

FISH VELOUTÉ (ALLEMANDE SAUCE)

Preparation 30 minutes • Cooking 2 hours

US	Ingredients	Met/Imp
1½ sticks	butter	175 g/6 oz
¾ cup	flour	100 g/4 oz
I quart	Fish Fumet (*page 57*)	I litre/1¾ pints
I quart	White Court Bouillon (*page 49*)	I litre/1¾ pints
½ cup	mushroom trimmings	50 g/2 oz
I	bouquet garni	I
½ cup	*crème fraîche*	100 ml/4 fl oz
2	egg yolks	2
	salt and pepper	

Make a roux. Melt two-thirds of the butter in a saucepan and stir in the flour. Add the fish fumet, court bouillon, mushroom trimmings and bouquet garni and cook for about 2 hours.

Finally, stir in the crème fraîche, egg yolks, remaining butter and salt and pepper. Work through a sieve lined with cheesecloth.

VELOUTÉ DE VOLAILLE

CHICKEN VELOUTÉ

Preparation 30 minutes • Cooking 2 hours

US	Ingredients	Met/Imp
10 tbsp	butter	150 g/5 oz
I cup	flour	150 g/5 oz
2 quarts	White Stock, preferably chicken (*left*)	2 litres/3½ pints
I cup	mushroom trimmings	100 g/4 oz
I cup	double (heavy) cream	250 ml/8 fl oz
6 tbsp	extra butter (optional)	75 g/3 oz
¼ cup	Veal Juice (*left*)	60 ml/4 tbsp

Make a white roux (*page 50*), then proceed according to the instructions for Fish Velouté (*above*). When thickened with the cream, added gradually, and the extra butter, this becomes SUPRÊME SAUCE. If the veal juice is added, it becomes IVOIRE SAUCE.

ASPIC

US	Ingredients	Met/Imp
2 lb	knuckle (shank) of veal and, if possible, chicken giblets	1 kg/2 lb
2	calf's feet, boned and blanched	2
4½ lb	veal bones	2 kg/4½ lb
½ lb	bacon rind	200 g/7 oz
3 quarts	water	3 litres/5¼ pints
	salt	
2	carrots	2
1	onion	1
1	clove	1
1	bouquet garni with 2 leeks (white part), 1 small celery stalk and 4–5 peppercorns	1
2–3	sheets gelatine, if needed,	2–3
	or	
½–¾ envelope	powdered (unflavoured) gelatine	7.5–10 ml/ 1½–2 tsp
5 oz	lean minced (ground) beef	150 g/5 oz
2	tarragon sprigs	2
2	chervil sprigs	2
2	egg whites	2
½ cup	port, sherry or cognac	100 ml/4 fl oz

GELÉE ORDINAIRE

PLAIN ASPIC

Preparation 1 hour • Cooking 5 hours • Clarification 1 hour

Put the meat, bones and bacon rind in a large saucepan with the cold water and salt and bring to a gentle boil. When the stock is frothy, add the carrots, onion spiked with the clove, and bouquet garni. Remove the knuckle (shank) when it is cooked, but continue to cook the bones, calf's feet and rind so that they give up all their taste and their gelatine. After 5 hours of cooking, strain the stock through a clean damp tea-towel, then leave to cool. While the stock is still liquid, sieve it through the cloth once more to remove all the fat. (Do not wait until it has cooled completely before sieving it again.)

At the end of the cooking time, there will only be about two-thirds of the liquid left and, after the clarification, only about one-quarter. Before clarifying, check that the stock is thick enough by putting a little in the refrigerator to set. If the cooking has been successful, it will be just right. If not, add the gelatine to be on the safe side, especially in the summer.

Clarify the stock 1 hour before it is needed by mixing the minced (ground) beef, herbs and lightly beaten egg whites with a ladleful of the stock, so that the beef can give up its blood while cold and thus help the clarification. Put the stock back on the heat and add the beef mixture. Bring to the boil, stirring with a whisk or spatula to prevent it sticking to the bottom of the saucepan. Place over a low heat so that it is hardly simmering, then leave for 30–45 minutes. Strain through a clean tea-towel. Wait until almost cold before adding the port, sherry or cognac.

9	leaves gelatine	9
	or	
2½ envelopes (2½ tbsp)	powdered (unflavoured) gelatine	37.5 ml/2½ tbsp
a few	scraps raw fish	a few
2 cups	Fish Fumet (page 57)	500 ml/18 fl oz
4	egg whites	4
a few	parsley, chervil and tarragon sprigs	a few
¼ cup	mushroom trimmings	25 g/scant 1 oz
½	lemon, juice of	½

GELÉE DE POISSON

FISH ASPIC

Preparation 10 minutes • Cooking 15 minutes

This fish aspic needs to be set with gelatine, as meat is not being used. A few moments before clarifying the aspic, put the gelatine in cold water to soak. Chop some raw fish scraps and put them in a large heavy-based saucepan with the fumet. Add the lightly beaten egg whites, the sprigs of parsley, chervil and tarragon, mushroom trimmings, lemon juice and the softened or melted gelatine. Stir with a spatula until boiling. After 15 minutes cooking, strain immediately through a clean, damp tea-towel into an earthenware or porcelain bowl. Taste to check the seasoning.

MARINADES

MARINADE CRUE

—————— UNCOOKED MARINADE ——————

Preparation 5 minutes

US	Ingredients	Met/Imp
scant 1 cup	oil	200 ml/7 fl oz
scant 1 cup	wine vinegar	200 ml/7 fl oz
1 quart	white wine	1 litre/1¾ pints
½ cup	madeira	100 ml/4 fl oz
1	sage sprig	1
1	basil sprig	1
1	garlic clove	1
10	juniper berries	10
2	cloves	2
10	peppercorns	10
2	shelled walnuts (green if possible)	2
	salt	

It is better not to use vinegar except for larger game, especially if it is no longer very young. For pieces of meat, use an uncooked marinade with only a little liquid: white wine, a little cognac and oil, herbs and spices. Always use wine vinegar. The marinade may be flavoured with sprigs of rosemary, marjoram, savory, basil, juniper berries or coriander seeds.

Before using this marinade, always remember first to pour the oil on to the food to be marinated, and never put water on it. Mix together the remaining ingredients and pour on to the food. Turn the food in the marinade every 24 hours, but do *not* use your hands. A young animal will need less time in the marinade than an older one. A hare, for example, does not necessarily need marinating; only a little liquid is required – 100 ml/4 fl oz (½ cup) cognac, 200 ml/7 fl oz (scant 1 cup) oil and a few herbs and spices are enough. Always keep foods to be marinated in a cool place.

MARINADE CUITE

—————— COOKED MARINADE ——————

Preparation 10 minutes • Cooking 1 hour

US	Ingredients	Met/Imp
2 oz	carrots	50 g/2 oz
2 oz	onions	50 g/2 oz
1½ oz	shallots	40 g/1½ oz
1	bouquet garni with a small celery stalk	1
1	garlic clove	1
½ cup	oil	100 ml/4 fl oz
2 cups	water	500 ml/18 fl oz

For large game birds or animals, marinades may be made with red wine. The difference will be evident in the type of sauce used to accompany the dish, as it is necessary to incorporate some of the marinade in the sauce. Sometimes, when there is insufficient time for marinating, the operation can be speeded up by pouring on hot marinade, but only if absolutely necessary. However, when tough game, such as stag or wild boar, is to be cooked, boiling marinade must be poured on to them several times while marinating. This is as much to tenderize the meat as to remove, or lessen, the strong taste.

Sweat the carrots, the thinly sliced onions and shallots, the bouquet garni and the crushed garlic in the oil in a saucepan. Add the amount of white wine and vinegar used for Uncooked Marinade. Add a few peppercorns and 2 cloves. Cook slowly without a lid for 1 hour, then leave to cool. When cold, pour on to the food to be marinated. As when using uncooked marinade, pour oil on to the food first to isolate it completely from the air. Cover with a clean cloth or some greaseproof or wax paper.

SAUCES

———— AÏOLI (GARLIC SAUCE) ————

Preparation 15 minutes

US	Ingredients	Met/Imp
1¼ cups	extra-virgin olive oil	300 ml/½ pint
	bread without crusts (the size of an egg)	
5	garlic cloves	5
2	shelled sweet almonds	2
2	egg yolks	2
	salt and pepper	
1	lemon, juice of	1

The oil should be at room temperature, not cold.

Soak the bread in water, press and pound it in a mortar and pestle with the garlic cloves and sweet almonds. Add the egg yolks and a little salt, mix well with a whisk and, while still stirring, pour in a thin trickle of olive oil. Add freshly ground pepper. Finally, add the lemon juice.

When beating the aïoli, take care that the sauce does not become too thick, because it can easily separate. If the sauce does separate, add a few drops of water and beat vigorously.

———— AMÉRICAINE SAUCE ————

Preparation 40 minutes • Cooking 25 minutes

US	Ingredients	Met/Imp
2 lb	fresh lobsters (1 large or 2 small)	1 kg/2 lb
	salt and pepper	
½ cup	olive oil	100 ml/4 fl oz
about 2 sticks	butter	200–250 g/7–8 oz
1 bottle	white wine	1 bottle
½ cup	cognac	100 ml/4 fl oz
1 tbsp	chopped shallot	15 ml/1 tbsp
1 pinch	crushed garlic	1 pinch
6	fresh tomatoes	6
1 tbsp	tomato paste	15 ml/1 tbsp
1 tbsp	Meat Glaze (page 56)	15 ml/1 tbsp
1¾ cups	Fish Fumet (page 57)	400 ml/14 fl oz
1	bouquet garni with chervil and tarragon	1
1 tsp	potato flour	5 ml/1 tsp

Shellfish form the basis of this sauce, and lobsters or crawfish give it its characteristic flavour. Cut the lobster into sections. Crush the pincers and legs. Collect the broken pieces, intestines and coral in a bowl. Remove the gritty substance near the head. Sprinkle the pieces of lobster with salt and pepper. Put the pieces in a saucepan containing the hot olive oil and about one-quarter of the butter and fry until nicely browned. Pour in the white wine and cognac (but do not flambé). Continue cooking until reduced by half. Add the chopped shallot, garlic, crushed fresh tomatoes, tomato paste, meat glaze, fish fumet and bouquet garni. Cook for 20 minutes or until substantially reduced. Drain the lobster pieces and remove the meat from the tail and the claws. Grind the meat finely in a mortar and pestle. Chop the liver and grind with an egg-sized piece of butter and the potato flour. Stir this and the lobster meat back into the sauce, then work through a fine sieve. Finish by blending in the remaining butter.

It is better not to flambé the cognac because, if it burns the lobster pieces even just a little, it can produce an unpleasant taste. Also, it is better to use ordinary white pepper than cayenne because the latter completely changes the flavour.

AURORE SAUCE

Preparation 30 minutes • Cooking 20 minutes

US	Ingredients	Met/Imp
I	medium onion	I
2 tbsp	butter	30 ml/2 tbsp
2 tbsp	flour	30 ml/2 tbsp
2 cups	milk	500 ml/18 fl oz
I	bouquet garni	I
I–2 tsp	tomato paste	5–10 ml/I–2 tsp
	salt and pepper	
	nutmeg	

Skin the onion and chop into large pieces. Melt the butter in a saucepan, add the onion and sweat for about 5 minutes without letting it change colour. Sprinkle in the flour and cook for 2 minutes, stirring with a spatula. Pour in all the cold milk at once. Bring to the boil, stirring constantly, and add the bouquet garni. Simmer gently without a lid for about 20 minutes. Work through a fine sieve, then return to the pan and add the tomato paste. Add salt, pepper and nutmeg and mix well.

BÂTARDE SAUCE

Preparation 30 minutes • Cooking 15 minutes

US	Ingredients	Met/Imp
10 tbsp	butter	150 g/5 oz
⅓ cup	flour	45 g/1¾ oz
2 cups	boiling salted water	500 ml/18 fl oz
3	egg yolks	3
1¾ cups	crème fraîche	400 ml/14 fl oz
I	lemon, juice of	I

Using half of the butter and all of the flour, make a very blond roux (*page 50*) which is very hot. Stir in the water, bring to the boil, then remove from the heat and continue beating until smooth. Add the egg yolks, crème fraîche and lemon juice, strain through a sieve lined with cheesecloth and beat in the remaining butter in small pieces.

BÉARNAISE SAUCE

Preparation 10 minutes • Cooking 15 minutes

US	Ingredients	Met/Imp
¼ cup	dry white wine	60 ml/4 tbsp
¼ cup	wine vinegar, if possible flavoured with tarragon	60 ml/4 tbsp
6	white peppercorns	6
1½ tbsp	chopped shallot	15 g/½ oz
I	chervil sprig	I
I	tarragon sprig	I
3	egg yolks	3
1½ sticks	butter	175 g/6 oz
I tsp	chopped fresh tarragon	5 ml/I tsp
I tsp	chopped fresh chervil	5 ml/I tsp

Put the wine, wine vinegar, peppercorns and chopped shallot into a small saucepan (enamelled, flameproof china or stainless steel).

Add the chervil and tarragon sprigs, cut into small pieces, then boil gently until the liquid has reduced to about one-third.

Strain the reduction through a nylon sieve, pressing the herbs to extract all the flavour. Leave to cool.

Carefully remove any small dark flecks from the egg yolks. Cut the butter into nut-sized pieces. Put the cooled reduction and the yolks into a heavy-based, stainless steel saucepan. Break the yolks with the rounded edge of a wooden spoon, add the salt and mix.

Prepare a hot, but not boiling, *bain-marie*. Add a piece of butter to the sauce, put the pan in the bain-marie and mix well. The butter will become incorporated and the sauce will thicken. Remove from the bain-marie.

Add the pieces of butter, one by one, returning the pan to the heat after each addition until each piece of butter mixes in well with the rest of the sauce. The sauce will thicken and no lumps should form.

Add the chopped herbs and transfer to a warm sauce boat.

US	Ingredients	Met/Imp
I	onion	I
6 tbsp	butter	75 g/3 oz
½ cup	flour	75 g/3 oz
I quart	milk	I litre/1¾ pints
	salt	
I pinch	nutmeg	I pinch
I	clove	I
I	sugar cube	I
I	bouquet garni	I

BÉCHAMEL SAUCE

Preparation 20 minutes • Cooking 2 hours

Sweat the chopped onion in the butter. Stir in the flour. Cook this blond roux for 35 minutes over a low heat. Add the milk, salt, nutmeg, clove, sugar cube and bouquet garni. Continue to cook for at least 1½ hours.

Strain the cooked sauce through a sieve lined with cheesecloth into an earthenware or porcelain container. Lay a piece of buttered greaseproof or wax paper over the surface of the sauce to prevent a skin forming.

Béchamel, like velouté, has several uses, ie it may form the basis of several other sauces. However, it is sufficient to add a little crème fraîche and a little stock from the food for which it is intended; thicken with egg yolks, reduce for a few minutes and add butter.

US	Ingredients	Met/Imp
I tbsp	chopped shallot	15 ml/1 tbsp
½ cup	white wine	100 ml/4 fl oz
½ cup	Fish Fumet (*page 57*)	100 ml/4 fl oz
1¼ cups	Fish Velouté (*page 57*)	300 ml/½ pint
4 tbsp	butter	50 g/2 oz
I tsp	chopped fresh parsley	5 ml/1 tsp

SAUCE BERCY (MAIGRE)

BERCY SAUCE (BASED ON FISH STOCK)

Preparation 15 minutes • Cooking 15 minutes

Cook the shallot in the white wine and fish fumet until reduced by one-third. Add the velouté, bring to the boil and stir in the butter and parsley.

US	Ingredients	Met/Imp
½ cup	vinegar	100 ml/4 fl oz
2	shallots	2
14 tbsp	butter	200 g/7 oz
	salt and pepper	

SAUCE BEURRE BLANC NANTAIS

WHITE BUTTER SAUCE NANTAIS

First recipe

Preparation 10 minutes • Cooking 10 minutes

Cook the vinegar with the chopped shallots until reduced by two-thirds, the put on a low heat and gently beat in the butter in small pieces. Add salt and pepper.

Second recipe

Preparation 10 minutes • Cooking 10 minutes

US	Ingredients	Met/Imp
½ cup	dry white wine	100 ml/4 fl oz
3	shallots	3
14 tbsp	butter	200 g/7 oz
	salt and pepper	
	vinegar	

Cook the wine with the very finely chopped shallots until well reduced. Leave to cool.

Beat the softened butter (preferably slightly salted) into a cream. Gradually stir the butter into the reduction with a whisk over a low heat. Do not beat the sauce: this will keep it creamier. Add salt and pepper and a few drops of vinegar if necessary. This sauce is delicate and should be served fairly spicy. It may be used as an accompaniment to fish.

BORDELAISE SAUCE WITH WHITE WINE

Preparation 25 minutes • Cooking 40 minutes

This sauce may be prepared in advance, but the butter and herbs should be added at the last moment.

Cook the white wine with the chopped shallots, mushroom trimmings, bouquet garni and mignonette pepper until reduced to one-third. Add the demi-glaze and cook for 40 minutes, skimming off the scum and grease. Keep the sauce flavoursome and thick. Remove from the heat, work through a fine sieve and add enough butter to make the sauce creamy. Add the chopped herbs.

US	Ingredients	Met/Imp
1¼ cups	white wine (bordeaux)	300 ml/½ pint
3	shallots	3
3 tbsp	mushroom trimmings	20 g/¾ oz
1	bouquet garni	1
1 pinch	*mignonette pepper*	1 pinch
1¼ cups	Demi-Glaze (*page 56*)	300 ml/½ pint
4–5 tbsp	butter	50–60 g/ 2–2½ oz
1 tbsp	chopped fresh parsley and tarragon	15 ml/1 tbsp

SAUCE BORDELAISE AU VIN ROUGE

BORDELAISE SAUCE WITH RED WINE

Preparation 25 minutes • Cooking 1 hour

Brown the shallot in one-third of the butter. Pour in the wine and cook until reduced to about one-quarter. Add the demi-glaze and continue cooking at least 1 hour. Work the sauce through a fine sieve and add the remaining butter.

Dice the marrow, poach it lightly and add it to the sauce. Add the chopped parsley if desired.

US	Ingredients	Met/Imp
1 tbsp	chopped shallot	15 ml/1 tbsp
6 tbsp	butter	75 g/3 oz
3 cups	very good bordeaux red wine	750 ml/1¼ pints
1¾ cups	Demi-Glaze (*page 56*)	400 ml/14 fl oz
5 oz	bone marrow	150 g/5 oz
1 tbsp	chopped fresh parsley (optional)	15 ml/1 tbsp

SAUCE BOURGUIGNONNE AU VIN ROUGE

BOURGUIGNON SAUCE WITH RED WINE

Preparation 10 minutes • Cooking 30 minutes

Fry the finely chopped onions in the butter until transparent. Pour in the red wine and add salt and pepper and the bouquet garni. Cook until reduced by two-thirds. Add the brown sauce.

US	Ingredients	Met/Imp
2	onions	2
10 tbsp	butter	150 g/5 oz
2 cups	good red wine	500 ml/18 fl oz
	salt and pepper	
1	bouquet garni	1
1¼ cups	Brown Sauce (*page 64*)	300 ml/½ pint

SAUCE AU BRESSE BLEU

BRESSE BLEU CHEESE SAUCE

Preparation 10 minutes

Mix the cheese with the cream and work through a fine sieve. Add the cayenne and store in a cool place.
This sauce is excellent with cold fish.

US	Ingredients	Met/Imp
1	small Bresse Bleu cheese	1
2 cups	cream	500 ml/18 fl oz
1 pinch	cayenne	1 pinch

BROWN OR ESPAGNOLE 'SPANISH' SAUCE

Preparation 40 minutes • Simplified recipe 3 hours • Haute cuisine recipe 7 hours
Makes 3 litres/5¼ pints (3 quarts)

It may seem strange that one of the main sauces in French cuisine is called 'Spanish', since that might suggest a foreign origin.

The explanation given for this, which seems to hold some truth, is as follows: according to certain historians, this sauce was imported into France by Spanish cooks who were conscripted to the royal kitchens of Louis XIV. However, the 'sauce espagnole' imported at that time was merely a very thick brown purée containing large amounts of tomatoes, poultry and game fumet, and whose sole basic spice was pimento. Contemporary authors referred to an identical sauce in their works, which the cooks of the period called sauce brûlée or 'burnt sauce', made by frying veal, poultry, ham and vegetables in butter. These ingredients were all sprinkled with plenty of flour then browned in the oven before water, instead of veal juice, was added.

This is indeed the basic principle of sauce brune or 'brown sauce', which later underwent certain improvements until it became one of our main sauces. The name 'espagnole' remained.

US	Ingredients	Met/Imp
¼ lb	carrots	100 g/4 oz
1	medium onion	1
2 oz	raw ham or hard fat (pure bacon fat)	50 g/2 oz
	fat	
¾ cup	flour	100 g/4 oz
3 quarts	Veal Juice or Stock (*page 56*)	3 litres/5¼ pints
1	bouquet garni	1
4–5	tomatoes	4–5

Simplified recipe

This recipe is a simplified version of the haute cuisine recipe (*right*), which is more or less impracticable to make in a domestic kitchen. In any case, in contemporary cooking, espagnole sauce is often replaced, thankfully, by 'thickened juices'.

Dice the carrots, onion and raw ham or hard fat. Brown everything lightly in some good fat. Butter may readily be used because the grease will later be skimmed off the sauce. Add the flour and cook on a low heat or in a cool oven until it has taken on a red-brown tinge.

Stir in the juice or stock and bring to the boil, stirring constantly. Add the bouquet garni and the fresh chopped tomatoes (or 45 ml/3 tbsp tomato paste). Put on a low heat and continue to boil gently for 2½–3 hours.

While the sauce is boiling, frequently skim off the grease and impurities brought to the surface. This operation, which, in fact, purifies the sauce, is made easier by adding a few tablespoonfuls of cold liquid (veal juice or stock) from time to time.

At the end of the cooking time, work the sauce through a fine sieve and leave until required, stirring frequently to prevent a skin forming.

Onion Soup au Gratin
It is the toast with grated cheese floating in the onion soup which transforms it into a 'gratinée': a comforting and heart-warming first course. (Recipe on page 43.)

Bouillabaisse

All the fragrance of the cooking of Provence engulfs the table when a steaming bouillabaisse of locally caught fish and crustaceans of the utmost freshness, is served. The saffron-coloured bouillon and the garlic-flavoured croûtons add their delicious flavours to the dish. Like a soufflé, a bouillabaisse should be served as soon as it is ready. (Recipe on page 29.)

Asparagus Velouté with Cream
A delicate soup, velouté owes its name to its smooth and creamy appearance. The sma firm, green asparagus tips add a tempting touch of colour. (Recipe on page 46.)

US	Ingredients	Met/Imp
6½ lb	ox and veal bones	3 kg/6½ lb
3¼ cups	water	800 ml/1⅓ pints
2 lb	knuckle (shank) of veal	1 kg/2 lb
	salt	
4	carrots	4
2	onions	2
1	clove	1
1	bouquet garni	1
scant ½ lb	pork fat	200 g/7 oz
1 cup	flour	150 g/5 oz
¼ lb	*Bayonne ham*	100 g/4 oz
	parsley stalks	
2	thyme sprigs	2
¼ cup	bay leaf	¼
2	garlic cloves	2
	Veal Juice or Stock (*page 56*)	
4–5	tomatoes	4–5
½ cup	mushroom trimmings	50 g/2 oz
a few	peppercorns	a few

Brown the ox and veal bones in the oven, then put them in a saucepan and pour in the water. Bring to the boil, add the knuckle (shank) of veal and a very little salt and bring to the boil. Add 2 roughly chopped carrots, 1 onion spiked with the clove, and the bouquet garni. Cook for 3 hours.

Meanwhile, make a roux with three-quarters of the pork fat (do not use butter) and the flour. Cook until very brown.

After 3 hours, when the brown stock is very well cooked, strain it through a sieve lined with cheesecloth (this is important) and pour it on to the roux.

Bring the sauce to the boil and continue cooking over a low heat. Thinly slice the remaining carrots and onion and the Bayonne ham. Brown in a frying pan with the remaining pork fat, adding the parsley, thyme, bay leaf and garlic. Add this mixture to the sauce. Continue to cook for 3 hours, then work through a nylon sieve.

Next day, return the sauce to the heat and add a little juice or stock, the chopped tomatoes (or 45 ml/3 tbsp tomato paste), the mushroom trimmings and peppercorns. Cook for 1 hour, skimming off grease and impurities as they rise to the surface. It is this cooking that rids the espagnole of its impurities and initial ugly appearance and makes it more attractive and appetizing. In order to make this sauce a demi-glaze, reduce it with white wine, red wine, madeira, port or sherry, or even with fish fumet, according to the flavour you require.

Always sieve juices or stock through linen or cheesecloth. This will make them shinier and more attractive.

SAUCE CARDINAL

CARDINAL SAUCE

Preparation 30 minutes • Cooking 15 minutes

US	Ingredients	Met/Imp
2 cups	Fish Velouté (*page 57*) or Béchamel Sauce (*page 62*)	500 ml/18 fl oz
½ cup	*crème fraîche*	100 ml/4 fl oz
½ cup	Fish Fumet (*page 57*)	100 ml/4 fl oz
½ cup	Lobster Butter (*page 51*)	100 g/4 oz
	truffle juice (optional)	

Cook the velouté or (preferably) the béchamel with the crème fraîche and the fish fumet until reduced. Remove from the heat and add the lobster butter. If desired, add a thimbleful of truffle juice.

US	Ingredients	Met/Imp
2 tbsp	chopped shallot	30 ml/2 tbsp
2 tbsp	chopped mushrooms	30 ml/2 tbsp
6 tbsp	butter	75 g/3 oz
I glass	white wine	I glass
½ cup	Tomato Sauce (page 80)	100 ml/4 fl oz
¼ cup	Demi-Glaze (page 56)	50 ml/2 fl oz
I tsp	chopped fresh chervil and tarragon	5 ml/I tsp

CHASSEUR SAUCE

Preparation 15 minutes • Cooking 40 minutes

Brown the chopped shallot and mushrooms in one-third of the butter and pour in the wine. Cook for about 35 minutes or until reduced by half.

Add the tomato sauce and the demi-glaze and boil for 5 minutes.
Finally, add the remaining butter and the chervil and tarragon.

US	Ingredients	Met/Imp
I stick	butter	120 g/4½ oz
¾ cup	flour	100 g/4 oz
4–5 quarts	chicken stock	4–5 litres/7–9 pints
½ cup	mushroom trimmings	50 g/2 oz
I	bouquet garni	I
2	egg yolks	2
scant I cup	Plain Aspic (page 58)	200 ml/7 fl oz
½ cup	crème fraîche	100 ml/4 fl oz

WHITE CHAUD-FROID SAUCE

Preparation 1 hour • Cooking 1½ hours

Melt the butter in a saucepan and stir in the flour. Cook the roux for 30 minutes over a low heat until blond. Gradually mix in the stock.

Bring to the boil, stirring constantly, then add the mushroom trimmings and the bouquet garni. Continue cooking gently for 1 hour, remembering to skim off the grease and impurities frequently.

Pour the sauce through a sieve into a clean saucepan, add the egg yolks and stir with a spatula over a high heat. Add the (melted) aspic and the crème fraîche, a few spoonfuls at a time.

When the aspic and cream have been mixed in, continue to cook the sauce, stirring, until it has reduced to about half. Strain through a sieve lined with cheesecloth.

US	Ingredients	Met/Imp
⅓	carrot	⅓
I	medium onion	I
3	shallots	3
I oz	lean *raw ham*	30 g/I oz
½ cup	olive oil	100 ml/4 fl oz
	parsley, thyme, bay leaf	
4–5 tbsp	vinegar	60–75 ml/ 4–5 tbsp
2 glasses	Cooked Marinade (page 59)	2 glasses
2½ cups	Brown Sauce (page 64)	600 ml/I pint
3	juniper berries	3
5–6	peppercorns	5–6
	TO FINISH	
	red wine	
	Cooked Marinade (page 59)	
I pinch	cayenne	I pinch
I pinch	sugar	I pinch
3 tbsp	butter	40 g/I½ oz

VENISON SAUCE

Preparation 35 minutes • Cooking about 2 hours

This sauce is characterized by the inclusion of the reduced marinade, in which the venison to be cooked has been soaked, plus the animal's blood, if there is any.

Put the finely diced carrot, onion, shallots and lean, raw ham into the hot oil. Add a few parsley stalks, broken into small pieces, a thyme sprig and a fragment of bay leaf. Fry until lightly browned, then pour in the vinegar and a glass of the marinade. Cook until reduced to 60 ml/4 tbsp, then add the brown sauce and the remaining glass of marinade. Bring to the boil, reduce the heat and boil gently for 45 minutes. After 35 minutes, add the juniper berries and the crushed peppercorns. (For these spices, 10 minutes in the sauce is sufficient.) Work the sauce through a fine sieve, pressing with a spoon to extract the flavours from the herbs and spices.

To finish, return the sauce to the pan and bring to the boil, adding ½ glass of red wine, the same amount of marinade, the cayenne and the sugar. Continue to cook gently for 35 minutes, frequently skimming off grease and impurities, each time adding a spoonful of wine and a spoonful of marinade to help the skimming process. Continue to cook the sauce, stirring, on a high heat until it has reduced to 600 ml/1 pint (2½ cups). Work through the fine sieve once more and finish by adding the butter.

SAUCE CHORON

CHORON SAUCE

This is a Béarnaise Sauce (*page 61*), without tarragon but with tomato paste added.

SAUCE CRÈME

CREAM SAUCE

Preparation 15 minutes • Cooking 15 minutes

US	Ingredients	Met/Imp
2 cups	Béchamel Sauce (*page 62*)	500 ml/18 fl oz
scant 1 cup	single (light) cream	200 ml/7 fl oz
scant 1 cup	double (heavy) cream	200 ml/7 fl oz
½	lemon, juice of	½

Mix the béchamel and single (light) cream and cook over a high heat for about 15 minutes or until reduced. Strain through a sieve lined with cheesecloth and add the double (heavy) cream. Finish by adding the lemon juice.

SAUCE CREVETTES

PRAWN SAUCE

Preparation 50 minutes • Cooking 20 minutes

US	Ingredients	Met/Imp
5 oz	cooked prawns or shrimp	150 g/5 oz
2 tbsp	cognac	30 ml/2 tbsp
4 tbsp	butter	50 g/2 oz
2 cups	Fish Velouté (*page 57*)	500 ml/18 fl oz
	cooking liquid from the fish to be served	
½ cup	crème fraîche	100 ml/4 fl oz
2	egg yolks	2
	salt and pepper	

This sauce should have a clear, pale pink tinge.

Peel the prawns, mix with the cognac and keep warm.

Pound the prawn shells with the butter in a mortar and pestle, then work through a sieve. Put to one side. Strain the velouté and add the cooking liquid from the fish to be served. Cook for about 20 minutes or until reduced, then add the crème fraîche and the egg yolks. Add salt and pepper, if necessary. Remove from the heat and add the prawn butter. Add the prawns as a garnish.

67 • SAUCES

US	Ingredients	Met/Imp
½ cup	vinegar	100 ml/4 fl oz
	pepper	
2	shallots	2
½ cup	white wine	100 ml/4 fl oz
1½ cups	Demi-Glaze (page 56)	300 ml/½ pint

DEVIL SAUCE

Preparation 10–15 minutes • Cooking 35 minutes

This is a well-seasoned sauce.

Cook the vinegar with the ground pepper and the chopped shallots until reduced by two-thirds. Add the white wine and continue cooking until reduced by half. Add the demi-glaze. Strain through a sieve lined with cheesecloth.

US	Ingredients	Met/Imp
½ cup	white wine	100 ml/4 fl oz
½ cup	cooking liquid from duxelles (see below)	100 ml/4 fl oz
3	shallots	3
1 cup	Demi-Glaze (page 56)	200 ml/7 fl oz
1 tbsp	Tomato Sauce (page 80)	15 ml/1 tbsp
4 cups	Dry Duxelles (page 49)	300 g/10 oz
	salt and pepper	
1 tbsp	chopped parsley	15 ml/1 tbsp

SAUCE DUXELLES

DUXELLES SAUCE

Preparation 40 minutes • Cooking 20 minutes

Put the white wine, the cooking liquid from the duxelles and the chopped shallots in a small saucepan. Cook until reduced by two-thirds, then add the demi-glaze, tomato sauce and duxelles. Boil for a few minutes, then add salt and pepper.

If this sauce is intended for something that is to be cooked au gratin, keep it fairly thick; if it is intended to accompany meat, make it lighter, ie with the same consistency as an ordinary sauce, and add the chopped parsley at the last minute.

If some cooked tongue or lean ham, cut into a *brunoise*, is added to duxelles sauce, it is called ITALIAN SAUCE.

SAUCE ENRAGÉE

FIERY EGG SAUCE

Preparation 15 minutes

This is the sort of egg purée in which the flavour of cayenne must be predominant.

Pound some hard-boiled egg yolks in a mortar, adding oil from time to time. Add salt, pepper, cayenne and saffron, then work this mixture through a sieve lined with cheesecloth.

SAUCE FOYOT

FOYOT SAUCE

This is Béarnaise Sauce (*page 61*) with 30 ml/2 tbsp Meat Glaze (*page 56*) added at the end.

	US	Ingredients	Met/Imp

'COLD' SAUCE

Preparation 30 minutes • Cooking 10 minutes

	US	Ingredients	Met/Imp
	a few	parsley, chervil and tarragon sprigs	a few
	¼ lb	spinach leaves	100 g/4 oz
	2 cups	crème fraîche	500 ml/18 fl oz
		salt and cayenne	
	I	lemon, juice of	I

Pound together the parsley, chervil, tarragon and spinach in a mortar and pestle. Extract the juices by squeezing in a cloth. Put the juice into a small saucepan, preferably a copper one, and put on a high heat until it boils. Remove immediately from the heat and pour on to a clean cloth placed over a small bowl. As you pour, a green, flavoursome paste will be left on the cloth. Whip some crème fraîche as if for a *chantilly*, then mix it into the green paste. Add the lemon juice and salt and cayenne to taste.

SAUCE GENEVOISE

GENEVOISE SAUCE

Preparation 50 minutes • Cooking 2 hours

	US	Ingredients	Met/Imp
	2	carrots	2
	I	large onion	I
	2	small garlic cloves	2
	2	shallots	2
	1½ sticks	butter	175 g/6 oz
	2	bouquets garnis	2
	2 cups	Fish Fumet (*page 57*)	500 ml/18 fl oz
	½ bottle	red wine	½ bottle
	I quart	Demi-Glaze (*page 56*)	I litre/1¾ pints
	I tsp	anchovy essence	5 ml/I tsp

Thinly slice the carrots, onion, garlic and shallots and brown them all in one-third of the butter with the bouquets garnis. Drain off the butter, add the fish fumet and cook until reduced. Pour in the red wine, cook to reduce again by half, then add the demi-glaze. Continue cooking for a long time, skimming off the impurities, then strain through a sieve lined with cheesecloth.

Return the sauce to the heat and continue cooking until it is thick and light and a nice golden-brown colour. Strain through the cheesecloth once more. Finish by adding the anchovy essence and the remaining butter.

SAUCE GRAND VENEUR

BROWN SAUCE FOR GAME

As when making a stew, add about 100 ml/4 fl oz (½ cup) hare's blood and 30 ml/2 tbsp redcurrant jelly to a light Pepper Sauce for Game (*page 76*).

Nowadays, cream is much used and abused in sauces; it should not be added automatically because, although it makes a sauce milder, it also lessens its characteristic flavour. It should not be used in this sauce.

US	Ingredients	Met/Imp
2	shallots	2
½ cup	white wine	100 ml/4 fl oz
	cooking liquid from the fish to be served	
scant 1 cup	Dry Duxelles (page 49)	200 ml/7 fl oz
1¾ cups	Fish Velouté (page 57)	400 ml/14 fl oz
1 stick	butter	100 g/4 oz
	salt and pepper	
½ cup	fresh breadcrumbs	25 g/scant 1 oz
¼ cup	Gruyère cheese, grated	25 g/scant 1 oz

SAUCE GRATIN (MAIGRE)

GRATIN SAUCE (BASED ON FISH STOCK)

Preparation 35 minutes • Cooking 20 minutes

Put the chopped shallots in the white wine and fish cooking liquid and cook for about 20 minutes or until reduced by half. Add the duxelles and the velouté. Finish by adding the butter and salt and pepper. Sprinkle with the fine breadcrumbs and grated cheese.

US	Ingredients	Met/Imp
4	hard-boiled egg yolks	4
1 tbsp	mustard	15 ml/1 tbsp
1¼ cups	oil	300 ml/½ pint
2½ cups	vinegar	600 ml/1 pint
	salt and pepper	
2 tbsp	chopped *cornichons*	20 g/¾ oz
2 tbsp	chopped capers	20 g/¾ oz
2 each	parsley, tarragon and chervil sprigs, all chopped	2 each

SAUCE GRIBICHE

GRIBICHE SAUCE

Preparation 20 minutes • Cooking the eggs 10 minutes

This is a highly flavoured sauce.

Work the egg yolks and mustard together with a whisk. Add the oil, then the vinegar and all the remaining ingredients.

US	Ingredients	Met/Imp
2 tbsp	vinegar	30 ml/2 tbsp
1 pinch	salt	1 pinch
1 pinch	pepper	1 pinch
1 pinch	*mignonette pepper*	1 pinch
¼ cup	water	50 ml/2 fl oz
4	egg yolks	4
1½ sticks	butter	175 g/6 oz
1	lemon, juice of	1

SAUCE HOLLANDAISE

HOLLANDAISE SAUCE

Preparation and Cooking 25 minutes

Put the vinegar, salt and peppers in a high-sided saucepan, perferably in a *bain-marie*. Cook until reduced to about 5 ml/1 tsp, then leave to cool a little.

Add the cold water, the egg yolks (having removed any dark specks) and 2–3 small pieces of butter. Return the saucepan or bain-marie to a low heat (in a bain-marie the temperature remains constant). Stir with a spoon or small whisk until the sauce starts to thicken (which shows that the yolks are cooking), then gradually add the remaining butter in very small pieces, allowing each piece to be absorbed into the sauce before adding the next. Add a spoonful of cold water with each addition of butter, to help prevent the sauce separating. Finally, strain the sauce through a sieve lined with cheesecloth and add lemon juice to taste. Keep the sauce in the bain-marie right up until the moment it is needed, but do not forget that if it gets in the least bit too hot, it could separate. To keep the sauce at an even temperature, cool it with a few drops of cold water or reheat it with a very little boiling water.

If the juice of blood oranges is added to Hollandaise sauce, it becomes MALTAISE SAUCE.

LOBSTER SAUCE

SAUCE HOMARD

Preparation 30 minutes • Cooking 15 minutes

Cook the velouté with the crème fraîche and the fish fumet for about 15 minutes or until reduced. Pound the butter with the lobster coral, lobster eggs and the anchovy fillet. Work the reduced sauce through a sieve and add the lobster butter. To finish, add some diced lobster and a trickle of cognac.

US	Ingredients	Met/Imp
2 cups	Fish Velouté (*page 56*)	500 ml/18 fl oz
scant 1 cup	crème fraîche	200 ml/7 fl oz
scant ½ cup	Fish Fumet (*page 57*)	100 ml/3½ fl oz
1 stick	butter	100 g/4 oz
	lobster coral and lobster egg	
1	canned anchovy fillet	1
	TO FINISH	
	diced lobster meat	
	cognac	

HUNGARIAN SAUCE

SAUCE HONGROISE

Preparation 15 minutes • Cooking 15 minutes

This sauce should have a gentle pink colour, produced by the paprika alone. It makes an excellent accompaniment for noisettes of lamb or veal, for poultry, fish or eggs.

Fry the very finely chopped onions in about one-quarter of the butter until translucent, then add the salt and paprika. Pour in the white wine and add the bouqet garni. Cook until reduced by two-thirds, then remove the bouquet garni. Finally, add the velouté and keep boiling gently for 5 minutes. Strain the sauce through a sieve lined with cheesecloth and finish by adding the remaining butter.

US	Ingredients	Met/Imp
2	large onions	2
10 tbsp	butter	150 g/5 oz
1 pinch	salt	1 pinch
1 tbsp	paprika	15 ml/1 tbsp
scant 1 cup	white wine	200 ml/7 fl oz
1	bouquet garni	1
2 cups	Fish or Chicken Velouté (*page 57*)	500 ml/18 fl oz

JOINVILLE SAUCE

SAUCE JOINVILLE

Preparation 1 hour • Cooking 12 minutes

The mixture of crayfish and prawns gives a great flavour to this sauce.

When the crayfish are cooked, shell them and set aside the shells and meat. Mix the crayfish cooking liquid with the Bordelaise sauce and cook until reduced. Meanwhile, pound the crayfish shells and most of the prawns in a mortar and pestle with the butter. Reserve the remaining prawns. Work the butter mixture through a fine sieve, then add to the reduced sauce. Finish by adding the crème fraîche, the diced crayfish meat and reserved peeled prawns. Flavour with cognac.

US	Ingredients	Met/Imp
12	Crayfish Bordelaise (*page 239*)	12
2 cups	Bordelaise Sauce with White Wine (*page 63*)	500 ml/18 fl oz
2 oz	cooked prawns or shrimp, in their shells	50 g/2 oz
1 stick	butter	100 g/4 oz
scant ½ cup	crème fraîche	100 ml/4 fl oz
¼ cup	cognac	50 ml/2 fl oz

US	Ingredients	Met/Imp
scant 1 cup	Veal Stock (*page 56*)	200 ml/7 fl oz
½ cup	mushroom trimmings	50 g/2 oz
2½ cups	Brown Sauce (*page 64*)	600 ml/1 pint
4 tbsp	butter	50 g/2 oz
½ cup	madeira	100 ml/4 fl oz

MADEIRA SAUCE

Preparation 30 minutes • Cooking 50 minutes

Add the veal stock and mushroom trimmings to the brown sauce. Cook over a high heat for about 50 minutes or until reduced, stirring constantly with a spatula. When the sauce is thick enough to coat the spoon, work it through a fine sieve. Add the butter in pieces, and the madeira. This returns the sauce to the correct consistency without further cooking, and the madeira thus retains its flavour.

US	Ingredients	Met/Imp
4	egg yolks	4
1 tbsp	mustard	15 ml/1 tbsp
	salt and pepper	
about ¼ cup	vinegar	about 50 ml/ 2 fl oz
2 cups	oil	500 ml/18 fl oz

MAYONNAISE

Preparation 10 minutes

The best flavoured mayonnaise is made with extra-virgin olive oil; a highly flavoured mustard is also an advantage.

The required conditions for successful mayonnaise are: a bowl at room temperature, boiling vinegar, and oil at a moderate temperature. The only other requirement is a wire whisk.

There is no professional secret for successful mayonnaise, yet many people are reluctant to try their hand at it. It is one of the easiest and quickest of sauces to make, since a quantity for 8 people can be made in as little as 10 minutes.

Mayonnaise should be protected from cold rather than heat. It curdles more often in winter than in summer and this is caused by using oil that is too cold or which has almost set. This is why the oil should be at room temperature or even warmed slightly. This precaution is, of course, unnecessary in summer. Another reason why mayonnaise curdles is if the oil is added too quickly to begin with.

Put the yolks, mustard, salt, pepper and a trickle of boiling vinegar in a bowl. Mix with a whisk, then add a little oil, drop by drop, until an emulsion is formed by the complete absorption of the oil into the yolks.

Continue adding the oil in a continuous thin trickle, stirring vigorously – whether this is done clockwise or anticlockwise is unimportant. From time to time, as the sauce starts to thicken, add a few drops of vinegar to thin it.

If the mayonnaise should curdle, ie if the oil separates from the yolks and the sauce goes lumpy, start again by putting a little mustard (if there is only a small amount of sauce) in a bowl and gradually beating in the curdled sauce. If making a larger quantity of mayonnaise, start again using an extra egg yolk.

Mayonnaise may be kept for several days. In the winter, care should be taken to keep it at an even temperature. Just before serving mayonnaise made the day before, or a few days previously, a few drops of vinegar or boiling water should be beaten in to thin it slightly.

SAUCE MAYONNAISE LIÉE À LA GELÉE
MAYONNAISE
THICKENED WITH ASPIC

Add 200 ml/7 fl oz (scant 1 cup) reduced, runny, almost cold Plain Aspic (*page 58*) to 500 ml/18 fl oz (2 cups) mayonnaise (*left*). Use immediately to cover food as this sauce sets very quickly.

SAUCE MAYONNAISE À LA MENTHE
MAYONNAISE WITH MINT

Make an infusion of mint, with 30 ml/2 tbsp vinegar and 15 ml/1 tbsp water. Use this (cold) infusion, instead of ordinary vinegar, to make the mayonnaise.

SAUCE MAZOT
MAZOT (MUSTARD) SAUCE

Preparation 20 minutes • Cooking 20 minutes

Put the butter, beef marrow, finely diced ham and mustard in a frying pan and simmer for 5 minutes. Add salt, pepper, the juice from a piece of meat cooked under the grill (broiler), the ketchup, Worcestershire sauce and finally the crème fraîche beaten into a *chantilly*. Simmer the sauce for 10 minutes, stirring with a whisk. Add the chopped fines herbes, pour on to the meat and serve at once.

US	Ingredients	Met/Imp
4 tbsp	butter	50 g/2 oz
2 oz	beef marrow	50 g/2 oz
2½ oz	cooked ham	60 g/2½ oz
2 tbsp	mustard	30 ml/2 tbsp
	salt and pepper	
	meat juice	
1 tbsp	tomato ketchup	15 ml/1 tsbp
1 tsp	Worcestershire sauce	5 ml/1 tsp
	crème fraîche	
	fines herbes	

SAUCE MORNAY
MORNAY SAUCE

Preparation 35 minutes • Cooking 20 minutes

Combine the egg yolks with the grated cheese and add to the boiling béchamel. Stir in the very reduced fish fumet or the fish cooking liquid, the crème fraîche and butter.

US	Ingredients	Met/Imp
2	egg yolks	2
½ cup	Parmesan or Gruyère cheese, grated	50 g/2 oz
2 cups	Béchamel Sauce (*page 62*)	500 ml/18 fl oz
2 cups	Fish Fumet (*page 57*) or the cooking liquid from the fish to be served	500 ml/18 fl oz
½ cup	crème fraîche	100 ml/4 fl oz
4 tbsp	butter	50 g/2 oz

US	Ingredients	Met/Imp
1½ cups	Pepper Sauce for Game (page 76)	300 ml/½ pint
½ cup	Malaga wine	100 ml/4 fl oz
½ cup	pine nuts	50 g/2 oz
⅓ cup	currants	50 g/2 oz

MUSCOVITE SAUCE

Preparation 30 minutes • Cooking 10 minutes

This sauce is like a Romaine sauce, which also contains pine nuts and currants.

Put the pepper sauce in a saucepan and cook for about 10 minutes or until reduced by about one-third. Remove from the heat and stir in the wine, which will restore the sauce to its original consistency. Add toasted pine nuts (or, if unavailable, use split almonds) and currants which have been washed, then soaked in Malaga wine until plump.

MOUSSELINE SAUCE

Preparation 10 minutes

Add 100 ml/4 fl oz (½ cup) whipped *crème fraîche* to 300 ml/½ pint (1½ cups) Hollandaise Sauce (*page 70*). This sauce is very light and creamy. Whip to make it frothy.

US	Ingredients	Met/Imp
1¼ cups	Hollandaise Sauce (page 70)	300 ml/½ pint
1 tbsp	strong mustard	15 ml/1 tbsp

MUSTARD SAUCE

Preparation 5 minutes

Stir the mustard into the Hollandaise sauce just before serving.
The Hollandaise may be replaced by Cream Sauce (*page 67*), using the same amount of mustard. If the sauce has to be left standing for a few minutes, keep it in a *bain-marie*.

US	Ingredients	Met/Imp
2 cups	Béchamel Sauce (page 62)	500 ml/18 fl oz
scant 1 cup	crème fraîche	200 ml/7 fl oz
a little	butter	a little
½ cup	Crayfish Butter (page 51)	100 g/4 oz

NANTUA SAUCE

Preparation 20 minutes • Cooking 15 minutes

Cook the béchamel with the crème fraîche for about 15 minutes or until reduced. Strain through a sieve lined with cheesecloth. Add the butter, then the crayfish butter. If liked, garnish with 24 cooked crayfish tails.

US	Ingredients	Met/Imp
2	sweet red peppers	2
2 tbsp	tomato paste	30 ml/2 tbsp
a few	tarragon leaves	a few
2 cups	Mayonnaise (page 72)	500 ml/18 fl oz

NIÇOISE SAUCE

Preparation 30 minutes

Peel the sweet red peppers, add the tomato paste and the tarragon and pound together in a mortar and pestle. Work through a nylon sieve and add to the mayonnaise.

SAUCE NOIRE ENRAGÉE

──── FIERY BLACK SAUCE ────

Preparation 20 minutes • Cooking 2 hours

US	Ingredients	Met/Imp
½ glass	red wine vinegar	½ glass
2	ducks, blood and livers of	2
6 tbsp	butter	75 g/3 oz
½ cup	flour	75 g/3 oz
1 quart	stock	1 litre/1¾ pints
15	garlic cloves	15
¼ cup	hard fat (pure bacon fat)	50 g/2 oz
	salt and pepper	

Add the red wine vinegar to the blood from the 2 ducks.

Make a roux (*page 50*) with the butter and flour and pour in the stock. Chop the garlic cloves with the fat and the duck livers and add to the sauce. Add salt and pepper and bring to the boil. Cover and cook for 1 hour, then add the blood and vinegar mixture. Cook for a further 30 minutes, then work the sauce through a sieve. Check the seasoning.

SAUCE NORMANDE

──── NORMANDY SAUCE ────

Preparation 20 minutes • Cooking 20 minutes

US	Ingredients	Met/Imp
1¾ cups	Fish Velouté (*page 57*)	400 ml/14 fl oz
scant 1 cup	Fish Fumet (*page 57*)	200 ml/7 fl oz
scant 1 cup	cooking liquid from mushrooms	200 ml/7 fl oz
3	egg yolks	3
½ cup	crème fraîche	100 ml/4 fl oz
4 tbsp	butter	50 g/2 oz

Mix the velouté, fish fumet and the mushroom cooking liquid in a saucepan. Add the egg yolks, mixed with the crème fraîche. Cook over a high heat for about 20 minutes or until reduced by one-third. Add the butter and work through a fine sieve.

SAUCE PÉRIGUEUX

──── PÉRIGUEUX SAUCE ────

Preparation 15 minutes • Cooking 30 minutes

US	Ingredients	Met/Imp
½ cup	madeira	100 ml/4 fl oz
2 cups	Demi-Glaze (*page 56*)	500 ml/18 fl oz
3 tbsp	butter	40 g/1½ oz
3 oz	truffles	75 g/3 oz

Boil the madeira over a high heat for about 25 minutes or until reduced by half. Add the demi-glaze. Leave on the heat for a few minutes, then remove and work through a sieve lined with cheesecloth. Add the butter in small pieces, a trickle of extra madeira and the finely diced truffles.

SAUCE PIQUANTE

──── PIQUANT SAUCE ────

Preparation 15 minutes • Cooking 1 hour

US	Ingredients	Met/Imp
2 tbsp	butter	30 g/1 oz
3 tbsp	flour	30 g/1 oz
2	onions	2
	thyme, bay leaf	
	shallots, parsley	
1	garlic clove	1
	vinegar	
	salt and pepper	
3–4 small	cornichons	100 g/4 oz

Melt the butter in a saucepan, add the flour and make a brown roux (*page 50*). Add the finely chopped onions, thyme, bay leaf, shallots, parsley and garlic. Pour in a little water and a trickle of vinegar and cook over a very low heat. Add salt and pepper, work through a sieve, then add the sliced cornichons.

US	Ingredients	Met/Imp
2	carrots	2
1	large onion	1
2	shallots	2
	parsley	
1	thyme sprig	1
1	bay leaf	1
2 tbsp	butter	25 g/scant 1 oz
¼ cup	oil	50 ml/2 fl oz
	scraps of game	
scant ½ cup	white wine	100 ml/4 fl oz
scant ½ cup	vinegar	100 ml/4 fl oz
	Marinade (page 59) or game stock	
6	peppercorns	6
2 cups	Demi-Glaze (page 56)	500 ml/18 fl oz
	OPTIONAL	
1 tbsp	redcurrant jelly	15 ml/1 tbsp
4 tbsp	butter	50 g/2 oz

PEPPER SAUCE FOR GAME

Preparation 30 minutes • Cooking 2 hours

Brown the thinly sliced vegetables and the herbs in the butter and oil and make them into a Mirepoix (*page 50*). Add the scraps of game. Pour in the white wine and vinegar, one-third of the marinade, 6 crushed peppercorns and the demi-glaze. As the sauce reduces, gradually add the remaining marinade, or game stock if possible. Add plenty of salt and pepper. Strain through a sieve lined with cheesecloth. If desired, add the redcurrant jelly and butter.

US	Ingredients	Met/Imp
½ cup	cooking liquid from 8–10 very fresh and very white mushrooms cooked in White Court Bouillon (page 49)	100 ml/4 fl oz
1 quart	Chicken Velouté (page 57)	1 litre/1¾ pints
4	egg yolks	4
½ cup	crème fraîche	100 ml/4 fl oz
6 tbsp	butter	75 g/3 oz
1	small lemon, juice of	1

POULETTE SAUCE

Preparation 45 minutes • Cooking 20 minutes

Put the mushroom cooking liquid in a saucepan and boil until reduced to about 30 ml/2 tbsp.

Add the velouté and boil for 5–6 minutes, then add the egg yolks mixed with the crème fraîche. Cook over a high heat, stirring constantly.

Remove from heat and add the butter and lemon juice. Serve immediately, without further boiling.

US	Ingredients	Met/Imp
4	garlic cloves	4
4½ lb	tomatoes	2 kg/4½ lb
½ cup	olive oil	100 ml/4 fl oz
½ cup	white wine	100 ml/4 fl oz
	salt and pepper	
1 tbsp	crushed parsley	15 ml/1 tbsp
1½ tbsp	butter	20 g/¾ oz

PROVENÇAL SAUCE

Preparation 20 minutes • Cooking 20 minutes

Chop the garlic and the hulled and de-seeded tomatoes. Cook in hot oil until reduced to a thick purée. Add the white wine to thin it. Add salt and pepper and, when the sauce has boiled for 20 minutes, remove from the heat. Strain through a sieve lined with cheesecloth, then add the parsley and butter.

COLD RAVIGOTE SAUCE

Preparation 10 minutes

US	Ingredients	Met/Imp
scant 1 cup	oil	200 ml/7 fl oz
¼ cup	vinegar	50 ml/2 fl oz
	salt and pepper	
1 tbsp	capers	15 ml/1 tbsp
2 each	parsley, tarragon, chervil and chive sprigs	2 each
1	small onion	1
	OPTIONAL	
1	hard-boiled egg, finely chopped	1
a few drops	Worcestershire sauce	a few drops

This sauce is mainly used for offal (variety meats) such as calf's head, calf's and sheep's feet, etc. If it is to be served with fish, the onion should be omitted.

Put the oil, vinegar, a large pinch of salt, a little pepper, the capers and the chopped parsley, tarragon, chervil and chives in a bowl. Chop the onion as finely as possible, wash it in cold water and squeeze it in a clean cloth to extract the water and bitter juices. Add the onion to the bowl and mix well. If liked, add the chopped hard-boiled egg and Worcestershire sauce.

RÉGENCE SAUCE

Preparation 35 minutes • Cooking 4 hours in all (including making the stock)

US	Ingredients	Met/Imp
2 lb	calf's bones	1 kg/2 lb
2 lb	knuckle (shank) of veal	1 kg/2 lb
3 quarts	water	3 litres/5¼ pints
	salt	
2	carrots	2
1	onion	1
1	clove	1
1	bouquet garni	1
	ROUX	
1 stick	butter	100 g/4 oz
½ cup	flour	75 g/3 oz
	TO FINISH	
	mushroom cooking liquid and trimmings	
½ cup	crème fraîche	100 ml/4 fl oz
1 stick	butter	100 g/4 oz
	salt and pepper	
	port, cognac or truffle essence	

Make the white stock. Put the calf's bones and knuckle (shank) of veal in a large saucepan, add the water and a little salt and bring to the boil. Add the roughly chopped carrots, the onion spiked with the clove, and the bouquet garni. Cover and cook for 2 hours. Skim and strain through cheesecloth.

Prepare a fairly light roux (*page 50*) with the butter and flour and stir in about two-thirds of the white stock. Cook for 2 hours.

Just before serving, stir the mushroom cooking liquid and trimmings into the sauce, followed by the crème fraîche. Strain through a sieve lined with cheesecloth. Finally, add the butter and salt and pepper, if necessary. Flavour the sauce with port, cognac or truffle essence, depending on the food it is to accompany. If reduced mushroom cooking liquid is added, this sauce becomes a rich SUPRÊME SAUCE.

RÉMOULADE SAUCE

First recipe

Preparation 20 minutes

US	Ingredients	Met/Imp
3 tbsp	capers	25 g/scant 1 oz
1–2 small	cornichons	25 g/scant 1 oz
a few	parsley, chervil and tarragon sprigs	a few
1 tsp	mustard	5 ml/1 tsp
1 tsp	anchovy essence	5 ml/1 tsp
scant 1 cup	Mayonnaise (page 72)	200 ml/7 fl oz

Chop the capers, cornichons, parsley, chervil and tarragon and mix with the mustard, anchovy essence and mayonnaise.

Second recipe

Preparation 10 minutes

US	Ingredients	Met/Imp
1 small	cornichon	20 g/¾ oz
a few	tarragon, parsley and chervil sprigs	a few
a few	chive stems	a few
2 tbsp	capers	20 g/¾ oz
2 cups	Mayonnaise (page 72)	500 ml/18 fl oz
1 tsp	mustard	5 ml/1 tsp
1 tbsp	Worcestershire sauce	15 ml/1 tbsp

The cornichon should be chopped and squeezed in a clean cloth to remove the liquid before adding it to the sauce.

Chop the herbs and capers and stir into the mayonnaise with the mustard. Add the cornichon and Worcestershire sauce.

US	Ingredients	Met/Imp
I	large onion	I
	butter	
scant I cup	white wine	200 ml/7 fl oz
I¼ cups	Demi-Glaze (page 56)	300 ml/½ pint
I	bouquet garni	I
I tbsp	Meat Glaze (page 56)	15 ml/1 tbsp
I tbsp	strong mustard	15 ml/1 tbsp
I pinch	sugar	I pinch

ROBERT SAUCE

Preparation 40 minutes • Cooking 35 minutes

This sauce is particularly good with grilled (broiled) pork.

Lightly brown the finely chopped onion in butter. Add the white wine and cook until reduced by half. Add the demi-glaze, bouquet garni and meat glaze, then, at the last minute, stir in the mustard and sugar.

US	Ingredients	Met/Imp
½ bottle	very good red wine (Gevrey-Chambertin or Gigondas)	½ bottle
I tsp	chopped shallot	5 ml/1 tsp
scant I cup	good Demi-Glaze (page 56)	200 ml/7 fl oz
I	duckling liver	I
I stick	good butter	100 g/4 oz
	duckling cooking juices	

SAUCE ROUENNAISE POUR LE CANETON

ROUENNAISE SAUCE FOR DUCKLING

Preparation 30 minutes • Cooking 20 minutes

Put the wine and shallot in a saucepan. Cook until reduced by two-thirds, then add the demi-glaze. Boil for 2 minutes, then remove from the heat and stir in the raw duckling liver, which has been sieved or chopped as finely as possible. The heat of the sauce alone is enough to cook the liver and it must not be allowed to boil once it has been added.

Strain the sauce through cheesecloth or a very fine sieve, add the butter and stir in the cooking juice from the duckling.

SAUCE RUSSE

RUSSIAN SAUCE

Work some caviar and the creamy parts (coral, etc) of a lobster through a fine sieve. Mix with Mayonnaise (*page 72*), and a little mustard.

US	Ingredients	Met/Imp
7 tbsp	butter	90 g/3½ oz
6 tbsp	flour	50 g/2 oz
I¾ cups	Fish Fumet (page 57)	400 ml/14 fl oz
	white pepper	
4	shallots	4
I glass	white wine	I glass
3	canned anchovy fillets or	3
½ tsp	anchovy essence	2.5 ml/½ tsp
I–2 tsp	mustard	5–10 ml/1–2 tsp

SAUCE SAINT-MALO

SAINT-MALO SAUCE

Preparation 1 hour • Cooking 45 minutes

Melt 50 g/2 oz (4 tbsp) of the butter in a saucepan, stir in the flour and cook until very light blond. Stir the fish fumet into this roux, add a little pepper and bring to the boil, stirring constantly. Continue to boil gently.

Meanwhile, put the chopped shallots and the white wine in a small saucepan and cook until completely reduced. Add the desalted anchovy fillets which have been crushed with the remaining butter. Mix well, sieve and set aside.

Just before serving, remove the sauce from the heat and mix in the shallot and anchovy butter and the mustard, making sure the seasoning is fairly strong. If canned anchovy fillets are unavailable, complete the sauce with the shallot butter, anchovy essence and mustard.

SALMI SAUCE FOR GAME

Preparation 1 hour • Cooking 2 hours

US	Ingredients	Met/Imp
I	carrots	I
I	large onion	I
2	shallots	2
I	bouquet garni	I
2 oz	*raw ham*	50 g/2 oz
	game giblets	
2 cups	wine or water	500 ml/18 fl oz
4–5	mushrooms	4–5
I quart	strong Demi-Glaze (*page 56*)	I litre/1¾ pints
1½ tbsp	butter	20 g/¾ oz
I tbsp	foie gras purée	15 ml/I tbsp
	freshly ground pepper	
	cognac, *truffle essence* or madeira	
¾ cup	flour	100 g/4 oz
	heart-shaped croûtons	

Although this may appear rather unorthodox, there are several principles involved in making salmi sauces.

Let us forget large game, such as roe-deer, stag, young wild boar, chamois and izard, which are treated like venison. What we are interested in is feathered game, such as partridge, pheasant and woodcock.

For all feathered game, the procedure is the same; only the liquid used in the stock is different. This can be white or red wine or even water, because it does not affect the flavour of the game.

1st recipe. Make a Mirepoix (*page 50*) with the carrot, onion, shallots, bouquet garni and diced raw ham, all well browned. Add the game giblets, drain off the fat, then pour in white or red wine, according to preference. Cook slowly for about 2 hours, then add the mushrooms and demi-glaze. Strain through a sieve lined with cheesecloth—the stock should be smooth, thick and shiny. At the last minute, add the butter, in pieces, the foie gras purée and some pepper. If desired, flavour with a little cognac, truffle essence or madeira.

2nd recipe (for real salmi lovers). Make the mirepoix as above, add the flour and brown. Add water and more game giblets than in the first recipe (for a more concentrated flavour). Cook slowly for about 2 hours, then skim off any fat and impurities. Strain through a sieve lined with cheesecloth. Just before serving, carve the game and put it on a dish. Break up the carcasses and squeeze them in a cloth to extract all the juices. Add this to the sauce, having first added the butter. Surround the dish with heart-shaped croûtons fried in butter.

VARIATIONS

If desired, cultivated mushrooms or morels may also be added. Of course, the sauce can also be thickened with the livers from the game. Work them through a fine sieve before adding them to the stock.

US	Ingredients	Met/Imp
4	large onions	4
	salt and pepper	
	butter	
2 cups	Béchamel Sauce (*page 62*)	500 ml/18 fl oz
scant 1 cup	*crème fraîche*	200 ml/7 fl oz

SOUBISE (ONION) SAUCE

Preparation 40 minutes • Cooking 50 minutes

Soubise may be used as a garnish as well as a sauce. Make it thicker or thinner according to its intended use.

Blanch the thinly sliced onions in boiling salted water, drain them thoroughly, then sweat them in butter until translucent. Mix with the béchamel, add the crème fraîche and check the seasoning, which should be fairly pronounced.

US	Ingredients	Met/Imp
4	hard-boiled egg yolks	4
1	raw egg yolk	1
	salt and pepper	
1 tsp	mustard	5 ml/1 tsp
¼ cup	vinegar	50 ml/2 fl oz
1¾ cups	oil	400 ml/14 fl oz
1 tbsp	snipped chives	15 ml/1 tbsp
2 tbsp	Mayonnaise (*page 72*), optional	30 ml/2 tbsp
1 tbsp	Worcestershire sauce	15 ml/1 tbsp

TARTARE SAUCE

Preparation 20 minutes • Cooking the eggs 10 minutes

Crush the hard-boiled egg yolks and mix with the raw egg yolk. Add salt, pepper, mustard and vinegar, then beat in the oil in the same way as for mayonnaise (*page 72*). Add the chives. For a thick tartare sauce, add the mayonnaise. Finally, add the Worcestershire sauce.

This sauce must be made at the last minute because it separates quickly, since cooked egg is not as resistant as raw egg yolk. If absolutely necessary, use 1 raw egg yolk with 3 cooked yolks to help preserve it briefly, but this means it is no longer a true tartare sauce.

US	Ingredients	Met/Imp
1 cup	Mirepoix (*page 50*)	150 g/5 oz
4 tbsp	butter	50 g/2 oz
¼ lb	fresh fat belly (side) of pork	100 g/4 oz
6 tbsp	flour	50 g/2 oz
4½ lb	tomatoes	2 kg/4½ lb
	salt and pepper	
1 pinch	sugar	1 pinch
1	bouquet garni	1
3–4 cloves	garlic	10 g/scant ½ oz
1 quart	stock	1 litre/1¾ pints

TOMATO SAUCE

Preparation 30 minutes • Cooking 2 hours

Fry the mirepoix in the butter with the finely diced pork until the fat runs. Stir in the flour and cook until browned, then add the crushed or puréed tomatoes, the salt, pepper, sugar, bouquet garni, crushed garlic and stock. Cook very gently for about 2 hours. Work through a fine sieve and keep until needed.

VENETIAN SAUCE

Preparation 30 minutes • Cooking 4 minutes

US	Ingredients	Met/Imp
a few	parsley, tarragon and chervil sprigs	a few
¼ lb	spinach	100 g/4 oz
	salt	
1 stick	butter	100 g/4 oz
½ cup	vinegar	100 ml/4 fl oz
2	shallots	2
2 cups	Bercy Sauce (*page 62*)	500 ml/18 fl oz

Blanch the herbs and spinach in boiling salted water for just a few minutes. Drain and press to remove all moisture, then pound with the butter in a mortar and pestle. Work through a fine sieve.

Put the vinegar and chopped shallots in a saucepan and cook until reduced. Add the Bercy sauce, remove from the heat and add the herb butter, which will give the sauce the desired colour.

GREEN HERB MAYONNAISE

Preparation 30 minutes • Cooking 5 minutes

US	Ingredients	Met/Imp
5 oz	mixed watercress, spinach, tarragon, parsley, chervil and chives	150 g/5 oz
	salt	
3 tbsp	capers	25 g/scant 1 oz
1–2 small	*cornichons*	25 g/scant 1 oz
1	canned anchovy fillet	1
2 cups	Mayonnaise (*page 72*)	500 ml/18 fl oz

Blanch the greens in boiling salted water for 5 minutes. Drain, dip in cold water, then squeeze in a cloth to remove all moisture. Add the capers, cornichons and anchovy fillet. Pound together in a mortar and pestle, then work through a nylon sieve. Mix this purée with the mayonnaise.

VILLEROY SAUCE

Reduce 200 ml/7 fl oz (scant 1 cup) Allemande Sauce (*page 57*) thinned with 400 ml/14 fl oz (1¾ cups) White Stock (*page 56*). Strain through cheesecloth, then leave to cool, stirring constantly. Use the sauce lukewarm, it should coat the food without running off.

VINAIGRETTE DRESSING

Preparation 10 minutes

Ingredients
salt
white wine vinegar with tarragon or shallot
oil – sunflower, olive or flavoured with *fines herbes*
freshly ground pepper

To dress a green salad, make vinaigrette dressing in the proportions of about 1 part vinegar to 3 parts oil.

Put a few pinches of salt in a bowl and pour on the vinegar, stirring with a wooden spoon. When the salt has completely dissolved, pour in the oil and stir, without beating too much. Add pepper to taste. The vinegar may be replaced by lemon juice.

There are numerous secondary ingredients that may be added to this basic dressing, such as finely chopped shallots; a little grated garlic; snipped chives; chopped parsley or chervil; strong or mild mustard; anchovy essence; chopped hard-boiled egg; chopped *cornichons*, etc. Walnut or hazelnut oils, which have a very fruity taste, are not suitable for all green salads. Sherry vinegar, cider vinegar or raspberry-flavoured vinegar also produce a particular effect which is best suited to the ingredients of some mixed salads (with fruit, poultry, fish, etc).

VINCENT SAUCE

Preparation 30 minutes

US	Ingredients	Met/Imp
¼ lb	mixed chervil, tarragon, chives, burnet and sorrel (in equal amounts)	100 g/4 oz
1 oz (about 30 sprigs)	parsley	30 g/1 oz
2 oz	spinach	50 g/2 oz
	salt and pepper	
2	hard-boiled egg yolks	2
2 cups	Mayonnaise (*page 72*)	500 ml/18 fl oz
1 tsp	Worcestershire sauce	5 ml/1 tsp

Blanch all the greens briefly in boiling salted water. Dip them in cold water, then squeeze in a cloth to remove all the water. Pound them in a mortar and pestle with the hard-boiled egg yolks, then work through a fine sieve. Add this purée to the mayonnaise and stir in the Worcestershire sauce. Check the seasoning.

HORS-D'ŒUVRE
&
HOT AND COLD ENTRÉES

THE HORS-D'ŒUVRE (OR ENTRÉE) PLAYS A major role in the modern meal. Its aim is to whet the appetite without completely satisfying it, but, even in high-class cooking, it also performs the secondary function of using up leftovers (poultry, fish, cheese and also meat) which could not properly be served at the table. The presentation of hors-d'œuvre is just as important as their composition. They must be pleasing to the eye before they satisfy the palate.

A distinction must first be made between hot and cold hors-d'œuvre (or entrées). The latter include, for example, marinated vegetables or fish, Italian style antipasti, various cold meats, mixed salads, seafood cocktails, stuffed avocados, cold vegetables prepared and seasoned in various ways, etc. Hot hors-d'œuvre include vol-au-vents, croquettes, fritters, cheese straws, stuffed crêpes, savoury pies and quiches, rissoles and meat patties, etc.

We have placed the egg recipes after the hors-d'œuvre because they are often served as entrées. Other ideas may be found in the chapter on shellfish or in the cheese chapter.

	US		Ingredients		Met/Imp

CHEESE STRAWS

Preparation 10 minutes • Cooking 5 minutes

US	Ingredients	Met/Imp
2	eggs	2
	salt and pepper	
14 oz	Gruyère cheese	400 g/14 oz
	flour	
	day-old white breadcrumbs	
	oil for deep frying	

Comté or Beaufort Savoyard cheese may be used instead of Swiss Gruyère.

Beat the eggs and add salt and pepper. Cut the cheese into slices about 5 mm/¼ inch thick and 2.5 cm/1 inch wide. Coat the cheese slices in flour, then dip into the beaten eggs. Finally, coat with breadcrumbs. Drop into very hot oil and fry for about 5 minutes or until golden, then drain on paper towels. Serve piping hot.

AMUSE-GUEULE AUX SAUCISSES, ANCHOIS ET JAMBON

SAUSAGE, ANCHOVY AND HAM SNACKS

Preparation 15 minutes • Cooking 15–20 minutes

US	Ingredients	Met/Imp
1	can long anchovies in oil	1
¼ lb	sliced cooked ham	125 g/4½ oz
1 lb	Puff Pastry (page 579)	500 g/1 lb
20	chipolata or canned 'cocktail' sausages	20
1	beaten egg, to glaze	1

Put the anchovies between 2 pieces of paper towel to soak up the oil. Cut the ham into 2 cm/¾ inch cubes.

Roll out the pastry to 5 mm/¼ inch thick. Cut a strip of pastry wide enough to roll around one anchovy. Lay an anchovy on the strip, roll up and seal with water. Repeat for the remaining anchovies.

Cut 20 strips of pastry 2 cm/¾ inch wide and long enough to wrap around the sausages. Wrap 1 strip around each sausage, then seal with water. If using canned sausages, simmer them in water first for 5 minutes.

Cut the remaining pastry into rectangles about 6×3 cm/2¼×1¼ inches. Put a ham cube on each rectangle, fold over and seal with water.

Place the anchovy rolls, the little sausages and the ham pastries on a baking sheet and brush with beaten egg to glaze. Cook in a hot oven.

Before serving, cut the anchovy rolls into bite-sized pieces. Serve with an apéritif, for a buffet or as an hors-d'œuvre.

ASPERGES EN TOMATES

ASPARAGUS WITH TOMATOES

Preparation 30 minutes • Cooking 40 minutes

US	Ingredients	Met/Imp
2 lb	asparagus	1 kg/2 lb
	salt	
4	hard-boiled eggs	4
	Mayonnaise (page 72)	
3 small	cornichons	50 g/2 oz
1 lb	firm tomatoes	500 g/1 lb
	Vinaigrette Dressing (page 81)	

Trim and scrape the asparagus and cook in plenty of boiling salted water for 40 minutes. Drain and arrange in small heaps on a large round serving dish. Halve the eggs lengthways, remove the yolks and stuff with a mixture of mayonnaise and chopped cornichons reserving a little mayonnaise for garnish.

Place the stuffed eggs and the tomatoes, cut into thin slices, on the dish with the asparagus. Sprinkle with vinaigrette and garnish with the reserved mayonnaise. Serve very cold.

If liked, 100 g/4 oz peeled cooked peeled prawns or shrimp can be used instead of the cornichons.

US	Ingredients	Met/Imp
32–40	large raw peeled prawns or shrimp	32–40
	Fritter Batter (page 580)	
	oil for deep frying	
	Tomato Sauce (page 80)	

PRAWN FRITTERS*

Preparation 20 minutes • Cooking 5 minutes

Dip the prawns or shrimp into the batter a few at a time, then cook in batches in very hot oil until crisp and golden. Drain well and serve with the tomato sauce.

US	Ingredients	Met/Imp
4⅔ cups	buckwheat flour	450 g/1 lb
1 pinch	dried yeast	1 pinch
	beer	
3	egg yolks	3
1 pinch	salt	1 pinch
1 tbsp	oil	15 ml/1 tbsp
about ½ cup	lukewarm water or milk	about 100 ml/4 fl oz
4	egg whites	4

BLINIS

Preparation 1 hour • (Dough to be made the day before) • Cooking 8 minutes

In Russia it was customary to serve blinis every day during Lent, expecially during 'carnival' week. From the greatest palace to the most humble cottage, everyone ate blinis, the variations of which are numerous. Their history is quite similar to that of quiche lorraine. Without going into the various recipes for blinis, it is useful to define the general principles involved in their preparation.

Since you are unlikely to have any ready-made yeast dough at home, it has to be prepared the day before. Make a soft dough with 150 g/5 oz (1½ cups) of the buckwheat flour (if unavailable, use wheat flour) and a pinch of yeast soaked in a little beer. Put a few drops of oil on the dough to stop a crust forming. Cover with cling-wrap or a cloth and leave to rise in a warm place overnight.

The next day, a few hours before making the blinis, put the remaining flour in a bowl and add the egg yolks, salt, oil and lukewarm water or milk. Add all the liquid at once and mix to a thick crêpe batter. Add a little more liquid if necessary. Add the yeast dough prepared the day before. Beat the egg whites until stiff and add them to the mixture.

If possible, cook blinis in special blini pans. These are small, flat pans (10 cm/4 inches in diameter) without handles. Alternatively, cook in a small frying pan. Heat a little oil in the pan and add enough batter to make blinis twice as thick as crêpes. Cook for 4 minutes on each side, until golden. Serve at once with butter and *crème fraîche*, or as an accompaniment to caviar and smoked salmon.

PUFF PASTRY VOL-AU-VENTS WITH FOIE GRAS AND TONGUE

Preparation 1½ hours • Cooking 15 minutes

US	Ingredients	Met/Imp
½ lb	Puff Pastry (page 579)	250 g/8 oz
I	egg, to glaze	I
	FILLING	
3 oz	foie gras	75 g/3 oz
2½ oz	very red cooked tongue	60 g/2½ oz
2½ oz	mushrooms, cooked	60 g/2½ oz
I oz	truffles	30 g/I oz
1¼ cups	Madeira Sauce (page 72)	300 ml/½ pint

Vol-au-vent cases can be prepared in advance and reheated just before serving; the filling may also be prepared in advance and kept warm in a *bain-marie*. Once the filling has been put in the cases, however, they should be served immediately.

Make the vol-au-vent cases. Roll out the pastry to 1 cm/½ inch thick. Using a 7.5 cm/3 inch square fluted pastry cutter, cut out 15 squares from the pastry. The square shape is peculiar to this sort of vol-au-vent. However, if a square pastry cutter is unavailable, use the 7.5 cm/3 inch round fluted cutter normally used for chicken vol-au-vents (patty shells).

Place the pastry squares on a slightly moistened baking sheet, brush with beaten egg and, with the tip of a small knife, make lines about 1 cm/¼ inch in from each edge to mark the position of the lid. Bake in a hot oven for about 15 minutes.

As soon as the vol-au-vents are cooked, lift off the lids and remove the soft dough from inside each one. Make the filling. Cut the foie gras, tongue, cooked mushrooms and truffles into cubes. Put everything in a saucepan with the madeira sauce and simmer for a few minutes. Use to fill the vol-au-vents and replace the lids. Put the vol-au-vents on a napkin-lined plate and serve immediately.

ROQUEFORT BALLS WITH PAPRIKA

Preparation 15 minutes

US	Ingredients	Met/Imp
½ lb	Roquefort cheese	250 g/8 oz
I tbsp	finely chopped celery	15 ml/I tbsp
I tbsp	snipped chives	15 ml/I tbsp
I tbsp	paprika	15 ml/I tbsp

In France, these cheese balls are usually made with a blue-veined cheese called Fourme d'Ambert instead of Roquefort.

Mix the sieved cheese, celery and chives together thoroughly and form into balls. Sprinkle with paprika.

US	Ingredients	Met/Imp
I	head Chinese (or napa) cabbage	I
2	celery stalks	2
½ lb	pig's liver	200 g/7 oz
¼ lb	pig's heart	100 g/4 oz
1½ lb	fatty pork such as shoulder, or neck and part of hand	700 g/1½ lb
4	garlic cloves	4
	salt and pepper	
I pinch	dried basil	I pinch
½ tsp	dried thyme	2.5 ml/½ tsp
I pinch	quatre-épices	I pinch
½ lb	pig's caul	200 g/7 oz
½ lb	lard	250 g/8 oz

— CAILLETTES FROM THE ARDÈCHE —

Preparation 25 minutes • (Vegetables to be prepared the day before) • Cooking 40 minutes • Makes 12

Prepare the vegetables the day before to ensure they are well drained. Wash the Chinese cabbage (both the ribs and the green) and celery and cut into large pieces. Blanch for 15 minutes in boiling salted water. Drain, rinse under cold water and drain once more. Chop very finely in a food processor and put in a cloth which should be knotted and hung up overnight so that the chopped vegetables can drain.

The next day, cut the liver, heart and pork into large pieces and mince (grind) with the garlic. Mix the chopped vegetables and meat together and add salt, pepper, herbs and spice. Using your hands, shape the mixture into 12 balls. Wrap each caillette in a piece of caul.

Grease a baking sheet with lard and arrange the caillettes on it. Using a spatula, spread the remaining lard on top of the caillettes. Cook in a moderate oven for 25 minutes.

Caillettes can be eaten either hot or cold and may be kept for up to 2 weeks in a stoneware pot full of lard.

US	Ingredients	Met/Imp
3 lb	fresh belly (side) of pork	1.5 kg/3 lb
⅓ cup	salt	90 g/3½ oz
I tsp	pepper	5 ml/I tsp
½ tsp	quatre-épices	2.5 ml/½ tsp
3 oz	dark truffles	75 g/3 oz
¼ cup	shelled pistachios	30 g/I oz
I tbsp	madeira	15 ml/I tbsp
	ox's intestines (sausage casings)	
	BRIOCHE	
7 cups	flour	I kg/2.2 lb
3 tbsp	dried yeast	20 g/¾ oz
1½ tbsp	salt	30 g/I oz
¼ cup	sugar	50 g/2 oz
12	eggs	12
1¼ lb (5 sticks)	butter	600 g/I lb 5 oz

SAVELOY WITH TRUFFLES IN A BRIOCHE*

Preparation 2 hours • (To be prepared 24–48 hours in advance) • Cooking 2 hours

Remove the skin and soft fat from the pork. Cut into small pieces and add the salt, pepper and spice. Mix well and mince (grind) finely.

Cut the truffles into 5 mm/¼ inch cubes and add to the mixture with the pistachios. Flavour with the madeira. Mix well and pack into ox's intestines (sausage casings).

Hang the saveloys in a cool, dry room and leave to dry out for 24–48 hours, depending on the time of year.

Weigh the saveloys and cook in water at about 90°C/195°F for 30 minutes per 500 g/1 lb. Take them out of the hot water, remove the skin by cutting it and leave to cool.

Make the brioche dough. Sift 250 g/8 oz (1¾ cups) of the flour into a bowl, make a well in the centre and add the yeast and little lukewarm water. Mix to a fairly soft dough. Cover and leave in a warm place until the dough has doubled in size.

Sift the remaining flour into a bowl, make a well in the centre and add the salt, sugar and eggs. Mix with the softened butter. Knead the dough several times and then spread it out. Add the yeast mixture and mix well, kneading the dough on a board. Put the dough in the bowl and leave in a warm place for 4–6 hours. Knock back the dough, then keep it cool until it is required.

Roll out the brioche dough to 1 cm/½ inch thick, wrap the saveloy in it and seal securely. Wrap in several layers of well buttered greaseproof or baking parchment paper so as to form a sheath attached to both ends and wider than twice the width of the brioche. Leave to rise in a warm place for 1–2 hours, then cook in a hot oven for about 30 minutes or until golden.

COQUILLES DE POISSON À LA PHOCÉENNE

——— FISH IN SCALLOP SHELLS ———

Preparation 25 minutes • Makes 8

US	Ingredients	Met/Imp
1	garlic clove	1
1¼ lb	leftover cooked fish	600 g/1¼ lb
	extra-virgin olive oil	
	salt	
	cayenne	
8	scallop shells	8

The fish filling can equally well be used in baked tartlet cases or on croûtons of fried bread.

This is a pleasant way to use up leftover fish. Crush the garlic and mash to a paste with the skinned fish and a little olive oil. Add salt and cayenne. Serve in the scallop shells.

CRÈMES FRITES AU FROMAGE

——— CHEESE FRITTERS ———

Preparation 30–40 minutes • Cooking 15–20 minutes • Makes about 12

US	Ingredients	Met/Imp
¼ lb	Comté cheese	125 g/4½ oz
2 cups	milk	500 ml/18 fl oz
¾ cup	flour	100 g/4 oz
6 tbsp	rice flour	50 g/2 oz
2	egg yolks	2
3	whole eggs	3
	salt	
1 pinch	cayenne	1 pinch
	nutmeg	
	breadcrumbs	
	oil for deep frying	

Finely grate the cheese and set aside.

Bring the milk to the boil. Meanwhile, put the flours, egg yolks and 2 of the whole eggs in a terrine or bowl and mix carefully. Add salt, cayenne and a little grated nutmeg. Stir in the hot milk, then transfer the mixture to a saucepan. Bring to the boil and boil for 5 minutes, stirring constantly. Reserve 25 g/1 oz (¼ cup) of the grated cheese and add the rest to the mixture. Stir until melted.

Spread the mixture to a thickness of 1.5–2 cm/½–¾ inch on a lightly greased baking sheet. Leave until completely cold. Cut into strips, then into about 12 lozenge-shapes.

Lightly beat the remaining egg. Dip each lozenge into the beaten egg, then into the reserved cheese and finally into the breadcrumbs. Put one-third of the lozenges into the basket of a deep-fat fryer and cook in very hot oil for about 5 minutes or until the fritters rise to the surface, are golden brown and slightly souffléed. Remove from the oil and leave to drain on paper towels for about 2 minutes. Repeat for the remaining fritters.

Serve lukewarm – they will be firmer in the middle and their flavour will be more appreciated than if they are eaten as soon as they come out of the hot oil.

US	Ingredients	Met/Imp
4	egg yolks	4
3 cups	very thick Béchamel Sauce (page 62)	750 ml/1¼ pints
2 cups	grated cheese (half Parmesan, half Beaufort)	250 g/8 oz
	cayenne	
	breadcrumbs	
	oil	
	parsley sprigs	

CHEESE FONDUE CROQUETTES

Preparation 1 hour • Cooking 10 minutes

Add the egg yolks to the béchamel with the grated cheese and a little cayenne. Spread the sauce on a tray and leave to cool.

Shape the mixture into croquettes and coat with breadcrumbs. Fry in batches in very hot oil until crisp and golden. Serve on folded napkins with a parsley garnish.

US	Ingredients	Met/Imp
6 tbsp	flour	50 g/2 oz
10 tbsp	butter	150 g/5 oz
scant ½ cup	cold milk	100 ml/4 fl oz
	nutmeg	
8	small, long brioches	8
1 cup	thick crème fraîche	250 ml/9 fl oz
½ lb	cooked York ham	200 g/7 oz
1¾ cups	Comté cheese	200 g/7 oz
	salt and pepper	

BRIOCHE CROUSTADES WITH CHEESE

Preparation 10 minutes • Cooking 15 minutes

Put the flour and 100 g/4 oz (1 stick or 8 tbsp) of the butter in a saucepan. Heat gently until the butter has just melted and combined with the flour, then remove from the heat and add the cold milk. Mix well and heat gently, stirring, until thickened. Flavour with nutmeg.

Meanwhile, cut the brioches in half lengthways. Remove the excess crumb and brown the brioche halves in the remaining butter in a flameproof gratin dish.

Combine the crème fraîche with the sauce, then add the chopped ham and grated cheese. Add salt and pepper and spread the mixture on the brioche halves. Cook in a hot oven for about 15 minutes.

US	Ingredients	Met/Imp
1½ lb	day-old bread	750 g/1½ lb
4 tbsp	butter	50 g/2 oz
1 lb	poached beef marrow	500 g/1 lb
scant ½ cup	Bordelaise Sauce (page 63)	100 ml/4 fl oz
	salt and pepper	
	fried parsley sprigs	

CROUSTADES WITH BEEF MARROW

Preparation 30 minutes • Poaching 6 minutes

Cut the bread into 16 lozenge-shaped croûtons about 3 cm/1¼ inches thick and the same in diameter. Use a knife to make shallow cuts to mark a lid on one side of each lozenge.

Fry the croûtons in butter until golden. Drain well, then take off the lids and remove the bread from inside. Mix the diced beef marrow into the Bordelaise sauce and add salt and pepper. Use to fill the croustades. Replace the lids. Serve on napkins, garnished with fried parsley.

CROUSTADES AUX MOUSSERONS

—— FIELD MUSHROOM CROUSTADES ——

Preparation 1 hour • Cooking 30 minutes

Roll out the pastry and use to line 8 round or oval tartlet tins. Bake blind in a hot oven until almost cooked.

Melt the butter in a saucepan and add the thinly sliced mushrooms and the chopped onion or shallots. Add salt, pepper and a reduced tomato sauce with thickened veal stock added. Cover and cook slowly for 20 minutes or until reduced and thick enough to use as a filling.

Fill the baked tartlet cases with the mushroom mixture and coat with the béchamel to which a hint of tomato paste has been added. Sprinkle with the cheese and heat briefly under a hot grill (broiler) to melt the cheese before serving.

US	Ingredients	Met/Imp
1 lb	Puff Pastry (*page 579*)	500 g/1 lb
1 stick	butter	100 g/4 oz
2 lb	field or other wild mushrooms	1 kg/2.2 lb
1	onion	1
	or	
4	shallots	4
	salt and pepper	
scant 1 cup	thick Tomato Sauce (*page 80*)	200 ml/7 fl oz
	Veal Stock (*page 56*)	
½ cup	Béchamel Sauce (*page 62*)	100 ml/4 fl oz
	tomato paste	
¼ cup	Gruyère cheese, grated	25 g/scant 1 oz

CROÛTE À VOL-AU-VENT

———— VOL-AU-VENT CASE ————

Preparation 40 minutes • Cooking 15 minutes

Roll out the pastry to 2 cm/¾ inch thick. Cut out a round piece of the size required for the vol-au-vent and place on a dampened baking sheet. Using the tip of a knife, mark a second smaller circle 1 cm/½ inch in from the edge of the larger one, cutting only about halfway through the pastry. This inner circle will form a 'lid' that can be removed so that undercooked pastry can be scooped out, forming a hollow to accommodate some sort of filling.

Brush the vol-au-vent with egg yolk and bake in a hot oven for about 15 minutes or until golden brown. Remove the 'lid' and scoop out any undercooked pastry inside.

Fill the vol-au-vent with a mixture such as a *blanquette* of poultry or fish with béchamel, veal or poultry escalopes, etc. Replace the lid before serving.

US	Ingredients	Met/Imp
1 lb	Puff Pastry (*page 579*)	500 g/1 lb
1	egg yolk, to glaze	1

US	Ingredients	Met/Imp
1½ lb	day-old bread	750 g/1½ lb
	clarified butter for frying	
1 lb	fresh beef marrow	500 g/1 lb
scant 1 cup	red wine	200 ml/7 fl oz
2–3	shallots	2–3
2 tbsp	Veal Stock (page 56)	30 ml/2 tbsp
1 stick	butter	100 g/4 oz
1 tbsp	chopped fresh parsley, to serve	15 ml/1 tbsp

CROÛTES À LA MOELLE

BEEF MARROW CROÛTES

Preparation 30 minutes • Cooking 25 minutes

Cut the bread into 8 rectangles measuring 7 cm/2¾ inches long, 5 cm/2 inches wide and 1 cm/½ inch thick. Cut off the corners and trim around the edges to form neat oval shapes.

Using the tip of a knife, mark a smaller oval 5 mm/¼ inch inside the outer edge of each oval, cutting only halfway through the bread. Fry the ovals in clarified butter, then remove the small ovals marked out by the knife and take out the bread inside each one, leaving little oval boxes.

Dice the beef marrow and poach it in salted water for 8 minutes, then drain thoroughly. Put the red wine and finely chopped shallots in a saucepan and reduce the wine to about 30 ml/2 tbsp. Add the veal stock and butter and cook until melted.

Mix the beef marrow into the sauce and use to fill the fried bread boxes. Place them on an ovenproof serving dish and put them in a hot oven for a few moments or until the sauce 'shimmers'. Sprinkle with chopped parsley before serving.

US	Ingredients	Met/Imp
16	fresh herring fillets	16
	salt and pepper	
1 lb	very ripe tomatoes	500 g/1 lb
1	sugar cube	1
1 tbsp	vinegar	15 ml/1 tbsp
1	lemon, to serve	1

FILETS DE HARENGS AUX TOMATES

HERRING FILLETS WITH TOMATOES

Preparation 6½ hours • Cooking 10 minutes

Place the herring fillets in a dish which has been sprinkled with salt and sprinkle more salt on top. Leave for 6 hours.

Rinse the fish fillets to remove excess salt and place them in a flame-proof dish. Skin, de-seed and crush the tomatoes.

Put the sugar cube and vinegar in a saucepan and add pepper. Heat until the sugar starts to become coloured. Add the tomatoes and bring to the boil.

Bring the herring fillets to the boil for just 1 second, then pour over the tomato mixture. Leave to cool. Serve cold with slices of well-peeled lemon.

US	Ingredients	Met/Imp
2	egg yolks	2
½ lb	peeled shrimps	250 g/8 oz
1½ cups	thick Béchamel Sauce (page 62)	350 ml/12 fl oz
	pig's caul	
	Fritter Batter (page 580)	
	oil for frying	

FRITOTS DE CREVETTES

SHRIMP FRITTERS

Preparation 35 minutes • Cooking 5 minutes

Mix the egg yolks and shrimps into the cool béchamel.

Spread the pig's caul out on a work surface and cut it into squares. Put 15 ml/1 tbsp of the shrimp mixture on each square and wrap up well. Dip into the batter a few at a time, then cook in batches in very hot oil until crisp and golden. Drain well before serving.

CHEESE GOUGÈRES

Preparation 15 minutes • Cooking 30 minutes • Makes 20

US	Ingredients	Met/Imp
scant ½ lb	Gruyère or Comté cheese	200 g/7 oz
2 cups	milk	500 ml/18 fl oz
1 tsp	salt	5 ml/1 tsp
1 pinch	pepper	1 pinch
1 stick	butter	120 g/4 oz
1¾ cups	flour	250 g/8 oz
8	eggs	8
2 tbsp	double (heavy) cream	30 ml/2 tbsp
1	beaten egg, to glaze	1

Cut the cheese into small cubes.

Put the milk, salt, pepper and butter into a saucepan and bring to the boil. Remove from the heat and add the flour. Stir briskly with a wooden spoon. Return to the heat for 1–2 minutes to 'dry' the pastry until it stops sticking to the saucepan.

Remove the pan from the heat and add the eggs, stirring continuously. The eggs should be added one at a time and each one should be completely absorbed before the next is added.

Add just over half of the diced cheese and mix in thoroughly, then stir in the cream. Spoon the pastry in small mounds on to a greased baking sheet. Brush with beaten egg, then stick a few of the remaining cubes of cheese on to the surface of each pie.

Bake in a moderate oven for about 20 minutes or until the gougères are crisp and golden brown but still have soft, fondant-like centres. They may be eaten hot or cold, but they should always be freshly made. In Burgundy, they are particularly appreciated with wine.

MOUSSE DE JAMBON

HAM MOUSSE

Preparation 3 hours • Cooking 20 minutes

US	Ingredients	Met/Imp
¾ lb	lean cooked ham	350 g/12 oz
scant 1 cup	very thick Béchamel Sauce (*page 62*)	200 ml/7 fl oz
	red food colouring (optional)	
	salt and pepper	
scant 1 cup	Plain Aspic (*page 58*) made with madeira	200 ml/7 fl oz
scant 1 cup	*crème fraîche*	200 ml/7 fl oz

The cooked ham should be lean and red (with no pieces of fat in it). Cut it into large cubes, reserving 8 for the garnish. Crush the remaining ham in a mortar and pestle until it is reduced to a fine paste. Gradually add the béchamel, which should be cold. (If the ham is not very red, the colour can be improved by adding a few drops of red food colouring, but this should be done with great care.) Work the ham mixture through a sieve into a shallow dish. Cover and leave to stand in a cool place for 20 minutes.

Work the ham purée with a spatula until smooth. Add salt and pepper, bearing in mind the saltiness of the ham and the fact that the effect of the seasoning will be lessened when the cream is added. Gradually add some of the aspic jelly to the paste, then add the thick crème fraîche, whipped as usual.

Transfer the mousse to a mould lined with aspic jelly or a glass serving dish. Smooth the surface and use the reserved 8 cubes of ham to make a rosette in the centre. Pour several layers of cold runny aspic jelly on to the surface, allowing each one to set before adding the next, so that a thin transparent veil forms over it. Garnish as liked. Keep the mousse on ice or in a cool place until set.

US	Ingredients	Met/Imp
3½ cups	flour	500 g/1 lb
2 tsp	salt	10 ml/2 tsp
3 sticks less 2 tbsp	butter	300 g/10 oz
1	egg	1
½ cup	water	100 ml/4 fl oz
1 lb	potatoes	500 g/1 lb
	fresh *fines herbes*	
	salt and pepper	
1	beaten egg, to glaze	1
scant 1 cup	*crème fraîche*	200 ml/7 fl oz

—— BOURBON PIE ——

Preparation 50 minutes • Cooking 1 hour

Put the flour in a bowl, make a well in the centre and add salt, butter and 1 egg. Mix together and add enough water to form a thick dough. Leave for 20 minutes.

Roll out half of the pastry into the shape of a tart, place on an oven-proof plate and cover with several layers of thinly sliced potatoes, leaving a 2 cm/¾ inch border around the edge. Sprinkle fresh fines herbes between each layer. Add salt and pepper and a little fresh or clarified butter. Roll out the remaining pastry and use to cover the pie. Fold over the edges like a hem, make a hole in the middle and brush with beaten egg. Cook in a fairly hot oven for about 1 hour.

On removal from the oven, add enough crème fraîche to moisten the potatoes, either by pouring it through the hole made in the middle of the crust or by cutting the crust very close to the hem. Ensure that the crème fraîche is spread evenly, then immediately re-cover the pie. Eat hot or cold.

US	Ingredients	Met/Imp
1½ lb	foie gras	750 g/1½ lb
½ lb	fresh fat belly (sides) of pork	250 g/8 oz
½ lb	pork suet	250 g/8 oz
1	piece of larding bacon	1
1	bay leaf	1
	salt and pepper	
1	clove	1
1 pinch	nutmeg	1 pinch
	truffles (optional)	

—— COUNTRY FOIE GRAS PÂTÉ ——

Preparation 1 hour • Cooking 45 minutes

Finely chop all the ingredients, adding whole or chopped truffles, if liked. Spoon into a terrine, filling it only three-quarters full, and cook in a moderate oven for 45 minutes.

US	Ingredients	Met/Imp
1¾ cups	sifted flour	250 g/8 oz
6 tbsp	butter	75 g/3 oz
1 pinch	salt	1 pinch
1 cup	water	250 ml/9 fl oz
1	egg, to glaze	1
	FILLING	
scant ¾ lb	pork fillet (tenderloin)	300 g/10 oz
scant ¾ lb	veal fillet	300 g/10 oz
2	shallots	2
	parsley	
	salt and pepper	
scant ½ glass	cognac	scant ½ glass
1 glass	white wine	1 glass
1	bay leaf	1
1	thyme sprig	1
scant ½ lb	sausagemeat	200 g/7 oz

—— PANTIN PIE ——

Start the day before • Preparation 2¼ hours • Cooking 1 hour

First make the filling. Cut the meat into slices and then into 2 cm/¾ inch cubes. Mix the meat with the chopped shallots and parsley in a large bowl and add salt and pepper. Add the cognac and wine, mix well and put in a terrine. Put the bay leaf and thyme on top, cover and leave in a cool place for 24 hours.

Make the pastry. Put the flour, softened butter, salt and water in a bowl. Mix well, using the fingertips. Shape the pastry into a ball and knead with the palms of the hands. Repeat this operation twice more. Make into a ball again and leave for 2 hours in an airtight container.

Remove the thyme and the bay leaf from the meat, add the sausagemeat and knead well.

Roll out two-thirds of the pastry into an oval shape. Put on a greased baking sheet and put the meat mixture in the centre of it. Dampen the edges of the pastry with water. Bring up the 2 long sides to that they overlap over the meat, then bring up the 2 ends in the same way. Roll the remaining pastry into a rectangle to make the lid and place it on the pie, dampening the edges to seal. Beat the egg and brush the top with it.

Using the tip of a knife, criss-cross the top of the pie with lines, without pushing too hard. Make a chimney from a tube of white cardboard and push it in so that it reaches the meat in the centre. Cook in a hot oven for about 1 hour. Pantin pie should be eaten lukewarm. The pie may be left overnight in a cold place before cooking. In this case, do not put on the pastry lid until just before the pie goes in to the oven.

PÂTÉ DE PÂQUES BERRICHON

EASTER PIE FROM BERRY

Preparation 35 minutes • Cooking about 1¼ hours

Make the pastry. Put the flour into a bowl and add the butter (cut into small pieces), the lard, salt and egg. Mix to a smooth dough, roll into a ball and set aside.

Make the filling. Hard-boil 2 eggs in boiling salted water for 9 minutes. Meanwhile, wash and dry the parsley, cut the onion into quarters, and dice the meats.

Put the parsley, onion and meats through a fine mincer (grinder) or food processor. Separate the remaining egg. Add the white to the filling and keep the yolk somewhere cool. Add salt, pepper and spice to the filling and pour in the cognac. Mix well.

Roll out two-thirds of the pastry and place on a sheet of foil on a baking sheet. Put half of the filling in the centre of the pastry, leaving a wide margin of pastry all round. Shell the hard-boiled eggs, place them on top, end to end, then cover with the remaining filling.

Roll out the remaining pastry and place on top of the filling. Turn up the edges and seal securely with water. Mark the top of the pie with a fork and brush with the leftover egg yolk beaten with a little water. Make a small hole in the top of the pie and insert a rolled-up piece of card to form a small chimney through which steam can escape. Cook in a moderate oven for 1 hour. Remove the chimney and serve the pie hot.

US	Ingredients	Met/Imp
1½ cups	flour	200 g/7 oz
4 tbsp	butter	50 g/2 oz
4 tbsp	lard	50 g/2 oz
1 pinch	salt	1 pinch
1	egg	1
	FILLING	
3	eggs	3
	parsley sprigs	
1	onion	1
5 oz	fresh fat belly (sides) of pork	150 g/5 oz
7 oz	shoulder of veal	200 g/7 oz
7 oz	pork fillet (tenderloin)	200 g/7 oz
	salt and pepper	
1 pinch	quatre-épices	1 pinch
2 tbsp	cognac	30 ml/2 tbsp

US	Ingredients	Met/Imp
1	large, round, firm cabbage	1
½ lb	onions	250 g/8 oz
⅔ cup	olive oil	150 ml/¼ pint
scant ½ lb	sausagemeat	200 g/7 oz
scant ½ lb	boned loin of veal	200 g/7 oz
scant ½ lb	boned loin of pork	200 g/7 oz
3	eggs	3
3 tbsp	chopped fresh parsley	45 ml/3 tbsp
1 cup	Parmesan cheese, grated	100 g/4 oz
1 pinch	ground bay leaf	1 pinch
1	dried thyme sprig	1
	salt and pepper	
½ cup	thick *crème fraîche*	100 ml/4 fl oz
1 cup	Gruyère cheese, grated	100 g/4 oz
	lettuce leaves, to serve	

PETITS BERLUGANS

STUFFED CABBAGE PARCELS

Preparation 35 minutes • Cooking 25 minutes • Serves 6

Blanch the whole cabbage in boiling water for about 10 minutes or until cooked but not too soft. Drain. Slice the onions and cook in half of the olive oil for about 5 minutes or until soft but not brown. Leave to cool.

Meanwhile, mix together the sausagemeat and minced (ground) veal and pork. Add the eggs, chopped parsley, Parmesan, ground bay leaf, thyme (crushed by hand), salt and pepper. Mix well.

When the onions are cool, add them to the stuffing. Pour in all but 30 ml/2 tbsp of the remaining oil and mix well. Separate the cabbage leaves and spread them out on the work surface. Put 15 ml/1 tbsp stuffing on each leaf. Wrap the stuffing in the cabbage leaves and shape into little cabbages with the hands.

Put the remaining olive oil in an ovenproof serving dish and add the petits berlugans. Put 5 ml/1 tsp crème fraîche on each berlugan, sprinkle with Gruyère and add a little pepper. Cook in a moderate oven for about 15 minutes or until the berlugans are nicely browned. Serve lukewarm or cold on lettuce leaves.

US	Ingredients	Met/Imp
½ lb	Puff Pastry (page 579)	250 g/8 oz
1	beaten egg yolk, to glaze	
	BÉCHAMEL SAUCE	
1 stick	butter	100 g/4 oz
6 tbsp	flour	50 g/2 oz
	salt and pepper	
1 pinch	nutmeg	1 pinch
scant 1 cup	milk or chicken stock	200 ml/7 fl oz
2 cups	*crème fraîche*	500 ml/18 fl oz
	FILLING	
½ lb	cooked boneless chicken breast	200 g/7 oz
¼ lb	asparagus tips	100 g/4 oz
	salt and pepper	
2 tbsp	butter	25 g/scant 1 oz
¾ oz	truffle gills	20 g/¾ oz

PETITS FEUILLETÉS À LA VOLAILLE ET AUX POINTES D'ASPERGE

LITTLE CHICKEN AND ASPARAGUS TIP PASTRIES

Preparation 1 hour • Cooking 20 minutes

Since these are so small, it is better to do 2 pastries per person. If leftover cooked chicken is used, béchamel sauce is called for. With fresh chicken, it is better to make a Suprême Sauce (*page 57*) with the stock from the chicken.

These pastries are different from chicken vol-au-vents (bouchées à la reine) and other similar pastries in that they are smaller but taller.

Make the béchamel according to the instructions on page 62 and add the crème fraîche at the end. Roll out the puff pastry to about 1 cm/½ inch thick and cut out 16 circles using a 5 cm/2 inch round fluted pastry cutter. Turn pastry circles over and arrange on a slightly moistened baking sheet. Brush with beaten egg yolk and mark a circle on the top of each one with the tip of a small knife. Cook in a hot oven.

Take the pastry rounds out of the oven, remove the inner circles and take out the soft dough inside.

Finely chop the cooked chicken breast and mix with the béchamel. Cook the asparagus quickly in boiling salted water, but stop while they are still fairly firm. Drain thoroughly, then sauté over a high heat to evaporate any excess moisture. Add salt, pepper and the butter.

Put a few asparagus tips in the bottom of each pastry and fill with the chopped chicken and sauce. Top with a thin slice of truffle cut with a 2.5 cm/1 inch cutter.

Prawn Fritters
Choose large, chunky peeled prawns or shrimps to make these fritters. Crisp yet melt-in-the-mouth, they are accompanied by a well-flavoured sauce. (Recipe on page 86.)

Saveloy with Truffles in a Brioche
The pure pork 'saveloy' attractively studded with both pistachio nuts and truffles, is a speciality of the charcuteries of Lyon. Wrapped in a soft casing of brioche pastry, it makes a warm first course of the highest gastronomic quality. It may be accompanied by a salad of curly endive. (Recipe on page 88.)

Huguette Salad
Asparagus tips, beans and artichoke bottoms: these are the ingredients of this summer salad. Garnished with lettuce and sieved hard-boiled eggs, this version is served with mayonnaise, although a vinaigrette dressing can equally well be used. (Recipe on page 106.)

Japanese Salad
It was Alexandre Dumas fils who, in his play 'Francillon' in 1887, gave the recipe for this salad, which has now become a classic. The white wine of the vinaigrette plays a most important part in it. (Recipe on page 107.)

Beauceronne Salad
The basic ingredients of this salad – apple, chicory (Belgian endive), celery, celeriac and beetroot (beet) – automatically define it as a winter dish. Garnished with slivers of ham, thinly sliced potatoes and mushrooms, it is a generous first course which is further enhanced by a dressing of mayonnaise. (Recipe on page 105.)

Wine Grower's Salad
*This colourful combination of corn salad (lamb's lettuce) and dandelion leaves,
beetroot (beet) and fried diced bacon is served with a walnut oil vinaigrette.
(Recipe on page 109.)*

LITTLE PUFF PASTRY PIES WITH CHIVES

Preparation 1 hour • Cooking 20 minutes

US	Ingredients	Met/Imp
14 oz	Forcemeat Stuffing (*page 54*)	400 g/14 oz
2 tbsp	finely snipped chives	30 ml/2 tbsp
1 lb	Puff Pastry (*page 579*)	500 g/1 lb
1	beaten egg yolk, to glaze	1

Prepare the forcemeat stuffing and mix in the chives.

Roll out the pastry to about 1 cm/½ inch thick and cut out 8 circles using a 7.5 cm/3 inch plain or fluted pastry cutter. Re-roll the trimmings to only 5 mm/¼ inch thick and cut out 8 more circles.

Arrange the 8 thinner pastry circles on a slightly moistened baking sheet and put a little forcemeat in the middle of each one. Dampen the edges and cover with the remaining pastry circles. Press the middle of the pies with the back of a 5 cm/2 inch round pastry cutter. Brush with egg yolk and cook in a hot oven.

PISSALADIÈRE

ANCHOVY 'PIZZA' FROM NICE

Preparation 50 minutes • Cooking 40 minutes

US	Ingredients	Met/Imp
2 lb	onions	1 kg/2 lb
3 tbsp	olive oil	45 ml/3 tbsp
	salt and pepper	
2 cups	flour	300 g/10 oz
1½ sticks	butter	180 g/6 oz
2 tbsp	water	30 ml/2 tbsp
about 15	canned anchovy fillets	about 15
a few	black olives	a few

The original pissaladière recipe, like the Italian pizza, used bread dough rather than pastry for the base. However, we prefer to give a recipe that uses pastry, which is lighter and can be more quickly made at home. This is, in any case, how pissaladière is now made in the Nice region.

Slice the onions, but not too finely. Heat the olive oil in a frying pan and cook the onions gently for about 15 minutes or until tender but not brown. Add a little salt and pepper.

Meanwhile, make shortcrust (pie) pastry according to the instructions on page 577 with the flour, butter, a good pinch of salt and the water.

Grease a flan or tart tin. Roll out the pastry to 5 mm/¼ inch thick and use to line the tin. Roll out the pastry trimmings, cut into long strips 1 cm/½ inch wide and reserve.

Keep 3–4 anchovy fillets to one side for the final garnish and arrange the remainder in a star formation on the pastry. Spread the onions on top of the anchovies. Arrange the reserved strips of pastry in a criss-cross design on the pissaladière. Push the black olives into the onion purée and complete the decoration with the reserved anchovy fillets cut into little squares. Cook in a moderate oven for 20–25 minutes or until golden brown. Serve lukewarm or cold.

US	Ingredients	Met/Imp
½ lb	belly (side) of pork	200 g/7 oz
¼ lb	lean cooked ham	100 g/4 oz
4	eggs	4
2 cups	*crème fraîche*	500 ml/18 fl oz
	salt and pepper	
generous ½ lb	rich Shortcrust Pastry, for lining (*page 577*)	250 g/8 oz
1 stick	butter	100 g/4 oz

QUICHE LORRAINE

Preparation 1 hour • Cooking 30 minutes

In the days when most people made their own bread, quiche Lorraine, which is called 'fouée' in Burgundy and elsewhere, consisted simply of a lightly buttered case of bread dough, with turned back edges, topped with cream, egg yolks, salt and pepper, and a few small pieces of butter. Like everything else, however, it has since been modified and even transformed.

Remove any rind from the pork and cut the pork into 2.5 cm/1 inch cubes. Blanch in boiling water for 7–8 minutes, then drain.

Finely chop the cooked lean ham. Break the eggs into a bowl, beat them as for an omelette and mix in the crème fraîche. Add salt and pepper and the chopped ham.

Roll out the pastry and use to line a 20.5 cm/8 inch flan or quiche dish, taking care to make the pastry slightly overlap the edges. Scatter small pieces of butter over the bottom, then put in the cubes of pork. Finally, add the cream and ham mixture. Cook in a fairly hot oven for about 30 minutes or until golden. The quiche should be eaten lukewarm.

	PASTRY	
3 ½ cups	flour	500 g/1 lb
2	eggs	2
14 tbsp	butter	200 g/7 oz
	FILLING	
scant ½ lb	*rillettes* (potted meat made from pork or poultry)	200 g/7 oz
1 lb	*rillons* (chopped pork cooked in lard)	500 g/1 lb
1 tbsp	chopped parsley	15 ml/1 tbsp
4	eggs	4
	salt and pepper	
1 cup	milk	250 ml/9 fl oz
scant ½ cup	*crème fraîche*	100 ml/4 fl oz

TOURAINE QUICHE

Preparation 1 hour • Cooking 15 minutes

Make the pastry. Put the flour on a work surface and make a well in the centre. Break the eggs into the well and add the softened butter. Work the ingredients together to produce a fairly firm pastry. Leave for 1 hour, then roll out and use to line a flan or quiche dish.

Make the filling. Spread the rillettes in the bottom of the pastry case, add the boned, diced rillons and sprinkle with the parsley.

Beat the eggs in a bowl, add salt and pepper and stir in the boiling milk and crème fraîche. Pour into the pastry case so that it comes up to the brim. Cook in a hot oven for about 15 minutes or until golden brown. Serve lukewarm.

RAVIOLI

Preparation 1 hour • Cooking 25 minutes

US	Ingredients	Met/Imp
	PASTA	
1 ¾ cups	flour	250 g/8 oz
2	eggs	2
1	egg white	1
1 tsp	salt	5 ml/1 tsp
1 tbsp	olive oil	15 ml/1 tbsp
	FILLING	
2	onions	2
4 tbsp	butter	60 g/2½ oz
½ lb	minced (ground) veal	250 g/8 oz
5 oz	minced (ground) beef	150 g/5 oz
	salt and pepper	
	dried rosemary sprig	
1 cup	Parmesan cheese, grated	100 g/4 oz
	nutmeg	
1	egg	1
1	egg yolk	1

Make the pasta. Put the flour in a bowl and make a well in the centre. Add the whole eggs, the additional egg white and the salt and combine all together. Pour in the oil and mix carefully with a wooden spoon.

When the mixture is no longer sticky, turn it on to a work surface and knead, using the palms of your hands, for 10–15 minutes or until the pasta becomes shiny. Wrap in foil and leave in a cool place.

Prepare the filling. Cook the finely chopped onions in the butter for 5 minutes or until soft but not coloured. Add the meats, stir well and add salt and pepper. Crumble in the rosemary and continue cooking for about 10 minutes. If the meat produces a little water, cook for a little longer, so that the filling is soft but not moist. At the end of cooking, add about half of the cheese and a little nutmeg and mix well.

Turn the pasta on to a lightly floured surface and separate into 2 pieces. Roll out each piece until it is very thin. This is a fairly long operation and requires a certain amount of energy, as the rolled-out sheets of pasta should be only about 1 mm/¹⁄₁₆ inch thick.

Add the whole egg and the egg yolk to the filling mixture and stir well. Place small, evenly-sized mounds of filling in rows on one of the sheets of pasta. Dip a brush in water and use it to dampen the pasta between the mounds of filling. Put the second sheet of pasta on top of the first and press down between the rows of filling (a ruler may be helpful). Separate the ravioli using a pastry wheel or knife. The ravioli may be kept in the refrigerator for 24 hours before being cooked.

Drop the ravioli into a large saucepan of boiling salted water and cook for about 10 minutes. Drain carefully.

The ravioli may either be served immediately with melted butter and Parmesan or it may be cooked briefly au gratin in the oven with butter, Parmesan and tomato sauce.

RAVIOLIS AU PERSIL ET AU FROMAGE

CHEESE AND PARSLEY RAVIOLI

Preparation 30 minutes • Cooking 3 minutes

US	Ingredients	Met/Imp
1 quart	chicken stock	1 litre/1¾ pints
½ cup	Parmesan cheese, grated, to serve	50 g/2 oz
	PASTA	
1 ¾ cups	flour	250 g/8 oz
2	eggs	2
	salt	
1 stick	butter	100 g/4 oz
	lukewarm water	
	FILLING	
½ cup	parsley, cooked in butter	50 g/2 oz
2 ¾ cups	Beaufort cheese, grated	300 g/10 oz
2 oz	goat's milk *fromage blanc*, drained	50 g/2 oz
2	eggs	2
2 tbsp	butter	25 g/scant 1 oz

First make the pasta. Put the flour in a bowl and make a well in the centre. Add the eggs, salt and melted butter and work the ingredients together, adding enough lukewarm water to make a firm dough. Knead and leave for 1 hour. Mix together the filling ingredients.

Roll out the pasta very thinly and cut into strips about 2.5–4 cm/1–1½ inches wide. Using a piping (pastry) bag, put small mounds of the filling down one side of the pasta strips at 2 cm/¾ inch intervals. Fold the pasta over to seal, then cut between the mounds of filling.

Poach the ravioli in the salted chicken stock for about 3 minutes. Drain thoroughly, and serve with a little grated Parmesan, allowing about 6 ravioli per person.

US	Ingredients	Met/Imp
14 oz	sausagemeat	400 g/14 oz
½ cup	flour	75 g/3 oz
1½ sticks	butter	150 g/5 oz
1¼ cups	rice	225 g/8 oz
2 cups	hot stock	500 ml/18 fl oz
4	lettuces	4
	salt and pepper	
3	onions	3
1 cup	Gruyère cheese, grated	100 g/4 oz

RICE WITH MEATBALLS

Preparation 1 hour • Cooking 40 minutes

To avoid overcooking the rice, 'easy-cook' long grain rice may be used.

Make small balls with the sausagemeat and roll them in the flour. Melt two-thirds of the butter in a frying pan and fry the meatballs until brown. Drain and keep warm.

Wipe the rice in a dry cloth (without washing it). Melt the remaining butter in a large saucepan and cook the rice until golden. As soon as it has slightly changed colour, pour in the hot stock. Thoroughly wash the lettuces, separate the leaves (cutting large ones in half) and add to the rice and stock along with salt, pepper and the chopped onions. Finally, put the meatballs on top, cover the saucepan and cook for 25–30 minutes, or until the rice is tender, adding more stock if necessary.

Remove the meatballs from the pan and add the cheese to the rice. Stir well, then pour the rice into a warm serving dish. Top with the meatballs and serve immediately.

US	Ingredients	Met/Imp
	PASTRY	
1½ cups	flour	200 g/7 oz
1 stick	butter	120 g/4½ oz
	salt	
3 tbsp	water	45 ml/3 tbsp
	FILLING	
1 lb	onions	500 g/1 lb
5 tbsp	butter	60 g/2½ oz
7 tbsp	flour	60 g/2½ oz
scant 1 cup	thick *crème fraîche*	200 ml/7 fl oz
4	eggs	4
1 tsp	salt	5 ml/1 tsp
	pepper	
	nutmeg	
⅔ cup	milk	150 ml/¼ pint

ONION QUICHE

Preparation 1 hour • Cooking 1 hour • Serves 6

Make the pastry. Put the flour in a bowl and make a well in the centre. Cut the butter (which should be taken out of the refrigerator 1 hour before so that it is malleable) into large pieces and put it in the well with the salt and water. Quickly mix the butter and water into the flour with the tips of your fingers, forming a smooth dough.

When the pastry is smooth, form it into a ball without pressing too hard. If it is a little sticky, sprinkle in a little extra flour and work the pastry rapidly to mix it all in. Put the pastry on a plate and cover with a bowl or wrap it in foil and put in the bottom of the refrigerator (the least cold part) while preparing the filling.

Make the filling. Chop the onions into strips about 3 mm/⅛ inch wide and 2 cm/¾ inch long. Alternatively, mince (grind) or process them coarsely (they should not be reduced to a purée).

Melt the butter in a frying pan over a moderate heat. When it is hot but not browned, add the chopped onions and stir thoroughly with a wooden spatula. Cook over a low heat for 15 minutes or until the onions are soft but not brown, stirring from time to time. When the onions are cooked, pour them on to a plate and leave them to cool.

Grease a large flan or quiche dish. Roll out the pastry on a lightly floured surface and use to line the flan dish. Put the flour in a bowl and gently pour in the crème fraîche. Stir carefully with a fork. Mix in the eggs, one by one. Add the salt, a little pepper and a little nutmeg. Stir in the onions and then the milk. Pour the filling into the pastry case and cook in a moderately hot oven for 40 minutes.

Remove the flan from the dish and serve hot or lukewarm.

TARTLETS WITH TWO CHEESES

Preparation 15 minutes • Cooking 25 minutes

US	Ingredients	Met/Imp
about 1 lb	Puff Pastry (*page 579*)	about 450 g/1 lb
	FILLING	
3½ tbsp	flour	30 g/1 oz
2	eggs	2
	salt and pepper	
2 cups	*crème fraîche*	500 ml/18 fl oz
1 cup	grated cheese (equal parts of Comté and Parmesan)	100 g/4 oz
¼ lb	Comté cheese	100 g/4 oz

Divide the puff pastry in half and roll out each piece to a thickness of about 3 mm/⅛ inch. Thoroughly grease eight 9 cm/3½ inch tartlet tins and line them with the pastry. Trim the pastry about 5 mm/¼ inch above the edges of the tins. Prick the bottom of each tartlet with a fork.

Make the filling. Put the flour and eggs in a small bowl. Mix until a smooth paste is obtained. Add a little salt (the cheese is salty in any case) and pepper and gradually add the crème fraîche, stirring constantly. Rub through a fine sieve. Set 30 ml/2 tbsp of the grated cheese aside. Put an equal amount of the remaining grated cheese in the bottom of each tartlet. Pour the cream into the tartlets so that they are three-quarters full and sprinkle them with the reserved grated cheese.

Cut the Comté cheese into fine strips and use them to make triangles with rounded bases. Arrange these small pieces of cheese in star patterns on the surface of each tartlet with the points in the middle. Cook in a hot oven for 20–25 minutes or until golden brown and souffléed. Quickly take the tartlets out of their tins and serve immediately.

CHEESE TARTLETS

Preparation 20 minutes • Cooking 20 minutes

US	Ingredients	Met/Imp
1½ cups	thick Béchamel Sauce (*page 62*)	325 ml/11 fl oz
scant ½ cup	chopped bacon	200 g/7 oz
scant ½ lb	Gruyère cheese, diced	200 g/7 oz
8	tartlets made with rich Shortcrust Pastry (*page 577*), baked blind	8
¼ cup	Gruyère cheese, grated	50 g/2 oz

Mix the béchamel with a *julienne* of the bacon and the diced Gruyère. Spoon into the tartlets. Sprinkle with the grated Gruyère and brown in a hot oven.

US	Ingredients	Met/Imp
1 lb	beef marrow	500 g/1 lb
	salt and pepper	
10 tbsp	butter	150 g/5 oz
½ cup	flour	75 g/3 oz
2 cups	consommé or Veal Stock (page 56)	500 ml/18 fl oz
scant ½ cup	madeira	100 ml/4 fl oz
¼ lb	truffles	100 g/4 oz
8	12.5 cm/5 inch tartlets made with 250 g/8 oz Puff Pastry (page 579), baked blind	8

BEEF MARROW TARTLETS FROM PÉRIGORD

Preparation 50 minutes • Cooking 8 minutes

Poach the beef marrow in salted water until tender.

Meanwhile, make a Périgueux sauce in the following way. Melt the butter in a saucepan and stir in the flour to make a roux. Remove from the heat and gradually stir in the consommé or stock and three-quarters of the madeira. Add salt and pepper. Return to the heat and cook, stirring, until thickened.

Add the finely chopped truffles, reserving a few slices for garnish. Use fresh truffles if possible, but if unavailable use frozen or canned. Add the remaining madeira at the last moment to flavour the sauce.

Drain and slice the beef marrow and put 4–5 slices into each tartlet. Pour over the Périgueux sauce and garnish with the reserved truffle slices. Serve hot.

US	Ingredients	Met/Imp
1 lb	rich Shortcrust Pastry, for lining (page 577)	500 g/1 lb
¼ lb	small button mushrooms	125 g/4½ oz
1 stick	butter	100 g/4 oz
6 tbsp	flour	50 g/2 oz
⅔ cup	madeira	150 ml/¼ pint
scant 1 cup	stock or consommé	200 ml/7 fl oz
	salt and pepper	
1	bouquet garni	1
2	cooked lambs' brains	2
½ lb	cooked lambs' sweetbreads	250 g/8 oz
½ lb	Forcemeat Stuffing (page 54), made into quenelles	250 g/8 oz
12	slices truffle	12

'FINANCIÈRE' TIMBALE

Preparation 2 hours • Cooking 45 minutes

Roll out the pastry, use to line a deep cake tin and bake blind.

Prepare a *financière* filling in the following way. Fry the mushrooms in the butter, then remove from the pan with a slotted spoon and set aside. Stir the flour into the butter remaining in the pan and heat until browned. Pour in three-quarters of the madeira and the stock or consommé. Add salt and pepper and the bouquet garni, mix well and cook for 20 minutes. Strain the sauce, set aside and keep warm.

Add the following to the pan: the lambs' brains (already cooked in a vinegar *court bouillon*); the lambs' sweetbreads (cooked in a white court bouillon); the poached quenelles; the mushrooms fried in butter and 12 thin slices of truffle. Add the remaining madeira, heat well and add the sauce. Simmer, without stirring.

Pour the hot filling into the timbale crust and place the latter on a dish covered by a folded napkin.

If liked, a few stoned and blanched green olives may be added, as well as some cocks' combs and kidneys (cooked in the same way as the lambs' sweetbreads).

GOURMET TOASTS

Preparation 25 minutes • Cooking 25 minutes

US	Ingredients	Met/Imp
½ lb	lean *Bayonne* ham	200 g/7 oz
½ lb	button mushrooms	200 g/7 oz
½ cup	double (heavy) cream	100 ml/4 fl oz
1 stick	butter	100 g/4 oz
1 glass	Velouté Sauce (page 57)	1 glass
8	square slices firm-textured bread	8
1 liqueur glass	kirsch	1 liqueur glass
1 cup	cheese, grated	100 g/4 oz

Cook the diced ham, diced mushrooms and cream in some of the butter without colouring. Add the velouté sauce; keep fairly thick.

Brown the bread in the remaining butter, sprinkle with the kirsch and spread with the ham and mushroom mixture. Add the cheese and put under the grill (broiler) for 5 minutes. Serve immediately.

CÉVENNES PIE

Preparation 2 hours • Cooking 40 minutes

US	Ingredients	Met/Imp
1¾ cups	flour	250 g/8 oz
1 stick	butter	125 g/4½ oz
2	eggs	2
	salt	
scant ½ cup	water	100 ml/4 fl oz
1	egg yolk, to glaze	1
	FILLING	
¾ lb	peeled chestnuts	300 g/10 oz
	salt and pepper	
1	thyme sprig	1
1	bay leaf	1
¾ lb	pork fillet (tenderloin)	300 g/10 oz
¾ lb	*reinette* or other dessert apples	300 g/10 oz
2	eggs, beaten	2

Two hours in advance, make the pastry with the flour, butter, eggs, salt and water. The dough should be neither too hard nor over-kneaded. Roll out two-thirds of the pastry thinly and use to line a pie dish.

Cook the chestnuts for the filling in boiling salted water flavoured with the thyme and bay leaf. Cool, then layer in the pie dish with the sliced pork and apples. Add one of the beaten eggs halfway through and the other at the end.

Roll out the remaining pastry and use to cover the pie. Carefully seal the edges and make a cut in the centre. Decorate the top with pastry trimmings and brush with egg yolk. Cook in a moderate oven for about 40 minutes.

LYON PIE

Preparation 50 minues • Cooking 40 minutes

US	Ingredients	Met/Imp
4½ lb	potatoes	2 kg/4½ lb
½ lb	raw French cooking sausage	250 g/8 oz
	salt and pepper	
10 tbsp	butter	150 g/5 oz
1	onion	1
1 lb	Puff Pastry (page 579)	500 g/1 lb
½ cup	Gruyère cheese, grated	50 g/2 oz
	TO GLAZE	
1	egg yolk, beaten	1
1 tbsp	water	15 ml/1 tbsp

Peel the potatoes and cut into thin shreds as for potato straws. Remove the sausage skin and cut the sausage into shreds also. Add salt and pepper.

Melt the butter in a frying pan and cook the finely chopped onion until brown. Add the potatoes and sausage and cook over a high heat for 5–10 minutes, stirring with a fork. Make sure that the potato is cooked, then turn the mixture out into a round dish and spread with a fork to fill the dish. Leave to cool.

Roll out one-third of the pastry thinly so that it is a little larger than the size of the dish; place on a baking sheet. Slide the potato and sausage mixture on to the pastry and sprinkle with cheese. Dampen the edges of the pastry and cover with the remaining rolled-out pastry. Press the 2 pieces of pastry firmly together. Brush the top of the pie with the egg yolk mixed with the water. Cook in a fairly hot oven for about 30 minutes or until risen and golden. Serve lukewarm.

US	Ingredients	Met/Imp
I lb	veal fillet	500 g/I lb
I lb	pork fillet (tenderloin)	500 g/I lb
6	shallots	6
	salt and pepper	
I pinch	quatre-épices	I pinch
	thyme	
I	small bay leaf	I
6 tbsp	cognac	90 ml/6 tbsp
½ cup	white wine	100 ml/4 fl oz
½ lb	Puff Pastry (page 579)	250 g/8 oz
½ cup	crème fraîche	100 ml/4 fl oz
2	egg yolks	2

TOURTE DE VIANDE À LA LORRAINE

LORRAINE MEAT PIE

Preparation 1½ hours • Marinating 24 hours • Cooking 50 minutes

Cut the veal and pork into strips. In a large bowl, mix together the chopped shallots, salt, pepper, spice, thyme, bay leaf, cognac and white wine. Add the meat and leave to marinate for 24 hours.

Roll out half of the pastry to a circle and place on a baking sheet. Drain the meat well, reserving the marinade. Put the meat in the centre of the pastry circle and cover with another circle of rolled-out pastry. Make a hole in the centre of the lid. Seal the edges of the pie well. Bake in a fairly hot oven for 40 minutes.

Mix the reserved marinade with the crème fraîche and 1 egg yolk. Pour into the hole in the centre of the pie and brush the lid with the remaining egg yolk. Return to the oven for a further 10 minutes. Serve hot.

US	Ingredients	Met/Imp
2	chicken livers	2
4 tbsp	butter	50 g/2 oz
3	shallots	3
I tbsp	chopped fresh parsley	15 ml/I tbsp
½ lb	good-quality minced (ground) pork	250 g/8 oz
½ lb	leftover boneless chicken (optional)	250 g/8 oz
¼ lb	mushrooms	100 g/4 oz
	salt and pepper	
I	egg	I
¼ cup	cognac	50 ml/2 fl oz
I lb	Puff Pastry (page 579)	500 g/I lb
I	egg yolk, to glaze	I

TOURTE DE VOLAILLE AUX CHAMPS

COUNTRY CHICKEN PIE

Preparation 1 hour • Cooking 40 minutes

Cut the chicken livers into very small cubes, sauté in the butter, then drain and sprinkle with finely chopped shallots and parsley.

Chop the pork, chicken (if using) and mushrooms together, but not too finely. Add the chicken livers and salt and pepper. Bind the mixture with the whole egg and flavour with the cognac.

Roll out one-third of the pastry and use to line a pie dish. Fill with the meat mixture. Roll out the remaining pastry and cover the pie. Turn up the edges, seal well and brush with beaten egg yolk.

Cook in a moderate oven for about 40 minutes. Serve hot.

SALADES COMPOSÉES

MIXED SALADS

THERE ARE NO HARD AND FAST RULES FOR MIXED SALADS. IT is possible, as a rule, to omit or add ingredients as it suits you without violating the laws of cooking, although it is advisable to respect the basic elements of a recipe. Ultimately, however, your choice of ingredients will depend on the time of year and what is available.

SALADE BEAUCERONNE

BEAUCERONNE SALAD*

Preparation 1 hour

Remove the dark green and stringy parts from the celery. Scrub the celery stalks and cut into thin shreds. Peel the celeriac and cut into very thin shreds. Cut the ham in the same way. Separate the chicory (endive) heads into leaves. Slice the mushrooms, and peel, core and slice the apples.

Add salt and pepper to each of the following ingredients separately: celery, chicory and mushrooms. Sprinkle the apple slices with lemon juice to prevent them turning brown. Thinly slice the beetroot and potatoes into rings of the same diameter.

Arrange the vegetables and apple together in a salad bowl, forming a dome in the centre and making a border around the base with alternating slices of potato and beetroot. Sprinkle the shreds of ham and herbs on top. Add the mayonnaise to the finished salad at the last moment.

US	Ingredients	Met/Imp
2	heads celery	2
1	medium celeriac	1
½ lb	lean ham, cooked or cured	250 g/8 oz
6	heads chicory (Belgian endive)	6
½ lb	button mushrooms	250 g/8 oz
3	apples	3
	salt and pepper	
1	lemon, juice of	1
1	cooked beetroot (beet)	1
3	boiled potatoes	3
	fresh chervil	
	fresh tarragon	
½ cup	Mayonnaise (*page 72*)	100 ml/4 fl oz

SALADE COMPOSÉE AU POISSON

MIXED SALAD WITH FISH

Preparation 40 minutes

Put the fish, potatoes and beetroot in a bowl. Add a dressing made from the oil, vinegar and mustard and mix everything thoroughly but gently. Pile on a bed of lettuce leaves, sprinkle with fines herbes and garnish with slices of well-peeled lemon.

The salad may also be dressed with Mayonnaise (*page 72*) and individually served, topping the lettuce leaves with the salad at the last moment.

	Ingredients	
about 2 lb	fish cooked in a *court bouillon*	about 1 kg/2 lb
½ lb	boiled potatoes	250 g/8 oz
¾ cup	diced cooked beetroot (beet)	150 g/5 oz
½ cup	oil	100 ml/4 fl oz
¼ cup	vinegar	50 ml/2 fl oz
1 tsp	mustard	5 ml/1 tsp
3	lettuces	3
	chopped *fines herbes* (parsley, chervil, tarragon)	
1	lemon, to garnish	1

US	Ingredients	Met/Imp
12	small, waxy new potatoes	12
	salt and pepper	
I small pinch	*quatre-épices*	I small pinch
I	small onion	I
½	garlic clove	½
I tbsp	chopped fresh chervil	15 ml/1 tbsp
I, about 2 oz	truffle	I, about 50 g/2 oz
½ cup	Chablis white wine	100 ml/4 fl oz
¼ cup	madeira	50 ml/2 fl oz
2 tbsp	truffle juice	30 ml/2 tbsp
¼ cup	olive oil	50 ml/2 fl oz
2 tbsp	wine vinegar	30 ml/2 tbsp
2	truffles, cut into thin shreds	2
4	artichoke bottoms	4
I quart	White Court Bouillon (page 49)	I litre/1¾ pints
½ lb	asparagus	250 g/8 oz
	salt and pepper	
½ lb	French (fine green) beans	250 g/8 oz
2	lettuce hearts	2
3	hard-boiled eggs	3
	fresh chervil	
scant I cup	Mayonnaise (page 72)	200 ml/7 fl oz

—— THE GONCOURTS' SALAD ——

Preparation 1 hour

Cook the potatoes in boiling salted water, then drain and peel them while they are still hot. Slice them finely, put them in a warm bowl with the spice and salt and pepper and keep them covered. Add the onion (chopped, washed and spun-dry), the garlic, chervil and chopped truffle and pour in the white wine, madeira and truffle juice.

When the liquid has been absorbed by the hot potatoes, add the oil and vinegar and mix gently. Put the salad in a glass bowl and sprinkle with the shredded truffle. Add more salt and lots of freshly ground white pepper.

SALADE HUGUETTE

—— HUGUETTE SALAD* ——

Preparation 1 hour • Cooking 30 minutes

All mixed salads should be well seasoned in advance and dressed at the last moment.

Cook the artichoke bottoms in the white court bouillon. Drain.

Trim and scrape the asparagus and dice, but leave 2.5 cm/1 inch at the tips. Tie the tips into a bundle. Blanch the asparagus in boiling salted water. Trim the French beans, cutting the ends on the diagonal. Blanch in salted water, in a copper casserole if possible.

Remove the chokes from the cooked artichoke bottoms and slice them. Combine with the blanched French beans (which have been cooled) and the diced asparagus stems. Put in a salad bowl and add salt and pepper.

Just before serving the salad, drain off any liquid, mix well and form into a dome shape in a bowl. Arrange lettuce leaves (reserving 1 small heart) around the base of the salad, then sprinkle with the hard-boiled eggs, shelled and sieved. Crown the dome with the asparagus tips and place the small lettuce heart and chervil on top. Serve with the mayonnaise mixed with chervil.

SALADE JAPONAISE DITE FRANCILLON

JAPANESE SALAD
—— ALSO KNOWN AS 'FRANCILLON'* ——

Preparation 30 minutes • Cooking potatoes 25 minutes • Cooking mussels 8–10 minutes

US	Ingredients	Met/Imp
1½ lb	new potatoes	750 g/1½ lb
	salt and pepper	
scant 1 cup	Chablis white wine	200 ml/7 fl oz
¼ cup	olive oil	60 ml/4 tbsp
scant 3 tbsp	vinegar	40 ml/scant 3 tbsp
2 quarts	mussels	2 litres/3½ pints
1	celery stalk	1
½	garlic clove, crushed	½
	GARNISH	
	raw truffles	
	celery leaves	

Cook the potatoes in boiling salted water for 25 minutes, then peel and slice them while still hot. Dress with a vinaigrette made from a little Chablis, oil, vinegar, salt and pepper. Keep the potatoes warm so that they fully absorb the dressing.

Put the thoroughly cleaned mussels in a saucepan with pepper (no salt), sliced celery, garlic and remaining wine. Cook them for a little longer than usual, then remove the shells and add the mussels to the potatoes. Strain part of their stock through a cloth, then boil rapidly to reduce it. Add to the vinaigrette, to enhance its taste in an unusual way.

Serve the salad in a salad bowl or, better still, in a crystal dish. Sprinkle with diced truffles and celery leaves.

SALADE DE PÂTES AUX NOISETTES

—— PASTA SALAD WITH NUTS ——

Preparation 1 hour • Cooking 30 minutes • Serves 4–6

US	Ingredients	Met/Imp
¼ lb	short-cut macaroni	125 g/4½ oz
	salt and pepper	
1 tbsp	olive oil	15 ml/1 tbsp
½ cup	shelled hazelnuts	1 teacup
scant ¼ lb	Mimolette (a type of Dutch cheese), cut into small sticks	100 g/4 oz
1 cup	chopped celery	2 teacups
1	small white onion	1
	SAUCE	
½ cup	Mayonnaise (page 72)	1 teacup
1 tsp	strong mustard	5 ml/1 tsp
½ tsp	paprika	2.5 ml/½ tsp
1	lemon, juice of	1
	GARNISH	
	lettuce leaves	
	onion rings	
	shelled hazelnuts	

Put the macaroni in a large saucepan of boiling salted water and boil rapidly for 10 minutes. Drain as soon as it is cooked and mix with the olive oil while it is still hot.

Make the sauce. Prepare a well-seasoned mayonnaise, adding the mustard, paprika and lemon juice. When the macaroni has cooled, mix in the sauce along with the chopped hazelnuts, the small sticks of Mimolette, the celery and chopped onion. Add salt and pepper.

Just before serving, arrange lettuce leaves side by side around the inside of a salad bowl and pour the macaroni salad on to them. Garnish with the onion rings and some whole hazelnuts.

SALADE DE PISSENLITS AUX NOIX

— DANDELION SALAD WITH WALNUTS —

Preparation 45 minutes

US	Ingredients	Met/Imp
2½ cups	shelled walnuts	250 g/8 oz
2	garlic cloves	2
	salt and pepper	
½ cup	walnut oil	100 ml/4 fl oz
¼ cup	vinegar	50 ml/2 fl oz
1½ lb	light green dandelion leaves	750 g/1½ lb

Unlike other green salads, this one is improved by being dressed a little in advance.

Brown the walnuts in a dry shallow casserole in the oven. Grind them vigorously in a mortar and pestle with the peeled garlic cloves and salt and pepper to form a paste.

Put the paste in a salad bowl and gradually add the walnut oil and vinegar, stirring constantly with a whisk or wooden spoon. Gently mix the dandelion leaves into this mixture.

US	Ingredients	Met/Imp
I	onion	I
I	carrot	I
2	bunches parsley	2
I tbsp	cooking salt	15 ml/I tbsp
5	black peppercorns	5
I	thyme sprig	I
I	bay leaf	I
2 lb	langoustines	I kg/2 lb
3–4	sweet red peppers	3–4
I ½ cups	long grain rice	250 g/8 oz
I ½ cups	stoned (pitted) green olives	250 g/8 oz
I	egg yolk	I
½ tsp	strong mustard	2.5 ml/½ tsp
	olive oil	
I	lemon, juice of	I
	table salt	
	ground white pepper	

— RICE SALAD WITH LANGOUSTINES —

Preparation 45 minutes • Cooking 30 minutes

Cut the onion and carrot into rings. Wash the parsley. Fill a large saucepan with water and add the cooking salt, black peppercorns, thyme, bay leaf, parsley, onion and carrot. Cover and bring to the boil. Turn down the heat and let the *court bouillon* bubble for 15 minutes.

Put the langoustines into the court bouillon. Turn up the heat to high until boiling again. Reduce the heat, cover and leave to simmer for 10–15 minutes. Drain the langoustines, collecting the court bouillon in a bowl. Shell the langoustine tails and cut into 2–3 pieces. Leave on one side in a bowl.

Remove the stems from the peppers, cut them in half and take out all the seeds. Wash the peppers, cut them into thin strips, then into small pieces. Put the rice in a sieve and rinse it under the cold tap. Tip it into a saucepan and add 750 ml/1¼ pints (3 cups) of the court bouillon from the langoustines. Add the pieces of pepper. Do not add any more salt. Bring to the boil, then cover and cook over a low heat for 15 minutes. Remove from the heat and leave the rice to dry out for a few minutes. Fluff up the grains with a fork, then tip the rice into a bowl and stir in the langoustines and the olives cut in four. Leave to cool.

Meanwhile, make a thick Mayonnaise (*page 72*) with the egg yolk, mustard, some oil, lemon juice, a little salt and white pepper to taste.

When the rice mixture has cooled, dress it with the mayonnaise and pour into a salad bowl.

US	Ingredients	Met/Imp
¼ lb	carrots	100 g/4 oz
¼ lb	turnips	100 g/4 oz
¼ lb	French (fine green) beans	100 g/4 oz
¼ lb (about ⅔ cup)	shelled petits pois	100 g/4 oz
½ lb	flageolets	100 g/4 oz
I	small piece of cauliflower (the size of an egg)	I
	salt and pepper	
¼ cup	vinegar	50 ml/2 fl oz
½ cup	olive oil	100 ml/4 fl oz
¼ lb	large *cornichons*	100 g/4 oz
¼ lb	raw truffles	100 g/4 oz
¼ lb	lean cooked ham	100 g/4 oz
⅓ cup	capers	50 g/2 oz
½ cup	Mayonnaise (*page 72*)	100 ml/4 fl oz

RUSSIAN SALAD

Preparation 1 hour • Cooking variable

Cut the carrots and turnips as if for a *jardinière*, ie into small sticks. Cut the French beans into small cubes or lozenges. Cook all these vegetables and the peas, flageolets and cauliflower separately in boiling salted water.

When all the vegetables are cooked, drain them thoroughly and leave to cool. Season each vegetable separately in a bowl with salt, pepper, vinegar and a very little olive oil. This should be done a little in advance.

In a fruit or salad bowl, arrange bouquets of the vegetables into a dome shape. Separate each bouquet with cornichons, truffles and ham, each of them cut into thin shreds, as for a *julienne*. Place the cauliflower, covered with a little mayonnaise, at the top of the dome. Sprinkle with capers.

Dress lightly with mayonnaise just before serving.

	US	Ingredients	Met/Imp

SALADE TOURANGELLE

TOURAINE SALAD

Preparation 30 minutes • Cooking 30 minutes

US	Ingredients	Met/Imp
1 lb	French (fine green) beans	500 g/1 lb
1 lb	new potatoes, peeled	500 g/1 lb
½ cup	crème fraîche	100 ml/4 fl oz
2 tbsp	chopped fresh tarragon	30 ml/2 tbsp

Cut the French beans and potatoes into thin shreds, and cook separately in boiling salted water. Drain and cool. Mix together equal amounts of French beans and potatoes. Dress with a little crème fraîche and sprinkle with chopped tarragon.

SALADE À LA VIGNERONNE

WINE GROWER'S SALAD*

Preparation 45 minutes

US	Ingredients	Met/Imp
scant ½ lb	cooked beetroot (beet)	200 g/7 oz
5 oz	dandelion leaves	150 g/5 oz
5 oz	corn salad (lamb's or field lettuce)	150 g/5 oz
scant ½ lb	diced lean bacon	200 g/7 oz
½ cup	walnut oil	100 ml/4 fl oz
¼ cup	vinegar	50 ml/2 fl oz
	salt and pepper	

Cut the beetroot into thin shreds, as for a *julienne*. Put the dandelion leaves and corn salad into a salad bowl. Fry the diced bacon in the walnut oil. When it has just turned brown and before it goes dry, tip it into the salad with the oil from the pan. (If, however, there is too much oil remaining, keep some of it back.)

Put the vinegar in the hot frying pan and swirl it around. Do not leave it in the pan long enough for it to reduce. Pour the vinegar over the salad, add salt and pepper and serve at once.

EGGS

THE EGG IS A COMPLETE, WELL-BALANCED and nourishing food. It provides relatively few calories and is easily digested as long as it is not cooked with too much fat. Above all, it can be used in an extraordinary variety of dishes because of the many different ways in which it can be cooked and which transform it endlessly: in water for a greater or shorter length of time, with the shell (hard-boiled or soft-boiled) or without it (poached); in fat over a high heat (fried egg or omelette); or in the oven in a cocotte or ramekin.

The variety of garnishes and ingredients which may be used with eggs – cheese, ham, *fines herbes*, spring vegetables, prawns or shrimp, anchovies, onions, mushrooms – gives us immense freedom to invent a whole range of possible recipes.

When eggs are served on their own, they should be large and you should generally allow two per person. For scrambled eggs and omelettes, small eggs may be used and you need allow only one and a half per person.

Curnonsky was amused by 'oeufs monstrueux' (monstrous eggs), the recipe for which he gave as follows: 'First break three or four dozen eggs and separate the yolks from the whites. Take a carefully washed pig's bladder, pour the yolks into it and tie the top of the bladder securely so that it is completely airtight. Hang the bladder in a large pan of boiling water and leave until the yolks have formed a compact mass and have solidified in this *bain-marie*. Then cut open the bladder and take out the massive yolk. Next pour the egg whites into a larger bladder along with the enormous yolk, which because of its specific gravity, will stay in the middle of the gelatinous mass. Tie up the top of the second bladder and hang it in a pan of boiling water. Leave until the whites are completely hard. Cut open the bladder and you will find a huge egg. Remove the 'egg' from the bladder and serve on a bed of vegetables or with an appropriate poultry or game stuffing. For this recipe to succeed in producing a dish that is the exact shape of an egg, you will need to ensure that the volume of egg yolks and whites exactly fits the capacity of each bladder. Since you can use a mixture of chicken, duck, goose and lapwing eggs, you can have fun with your guests by making them guess from what sort of bird they came. This remarkable two-hundred-year-old recipe,' concluded Curnonsky, 'dates from a time when eggs used to cost only a few sous per dozen'.

EGG FRITTERS 'EN SURPRISE'

Preparation 1 hour • Cooking 10 minutes

Shell the eggs, halve them lengthways and remove the yolks. In a saucepan over a low heat, mash the yolks with the milk, breadcrumbs, butter, grated cheese and salt and pepper until a thick paste is formed. Use this paste to fill the hollow in each egg half. Make a fairly thick batter, dip the egg halves into it a few at a time, then deep fry in batches in very hot oil until golden brown. Drain and serve on a napkin.

White wines: Alsace Sylvaner, Côtes de Provence, Mâcon-Villages, Saumur.

US	Ingredients	Met/Imp
8	eggs, hard-boiled	8
¼ cup	milk	50 ml/2 fl oz
2 cups	fresh white breadcrumbs	100 g/4 oz
4 tbsp	butter	50 g/2 oz
½ cup	Gruyère cheese, grated	50 g/2 oz
	salt and pepper	
2 cups	Fritter Batter (*page 580*)	500 ml/18 fl oz
	oil for deep frying	

EGG CASSOLETTES WITH TRUFFLES

Preparation 30 minutes • Cooking 5 minutes

Generously butter 16 small dariole (baba) moulds and sprinkle them with salt and pepper and the finely chopped truffle trimmings. Break a very fresh egg into each mould and poach in a *bain-marie* or in a half-covered shallow saucepan for about 5 minutes. Watch the eggs carefully because they cook very quickly and the yolks should stay soft.

Remove the eggs from the moulds and place them in the pastry tartlets on top of a filling of chopped mushrooms and truffles, mixed with the demi-glaze.

Just before serving, coat the eggs with a sauce made of the veal juice which has been reduced and whipped with the butter.

White wines: Alsace Sylvaner, Saumur, Arbois.

US	Ingredients	Met/Imp
	salt and pepper	
	truffle trimmings	
16	eggs	16
16	small round tartlets, made with 400 g/14 oz Puff Pastry (*page 579*)	16
scant ½ lb	mushrooms	200 g/7 oz
¼ lb	truffles	100 g/4 oz
scant ½ cup	Demi-Glaze (*page 56*)	100 ml/4 fl oz
2 cups	Brown Veal Juice (*page 56*)	500 ml/18 fl oz
6 tbsp	butter	75 g/3 oz

US	Ingredients	Met/Imp
16	eggs	16
	salt	
½ cup	double (heavy) cream	100 ml/4 fl oz

ARDENNES EGGS

Preparation 45 minutes • Cooking 12 minutes

Separate the eggs and put the yolks in a bowl, being careful to keep them whole. Beat the egg whites until stiff, adding a little salt and the cream. Pour into a well-buttered flameproof serving dish.

Place the yolks one by one on top of the beaten whites then put the dish over a low heat, cover and cook for about 12 minutes. Serve as soon as the eggs have coloured slightly.

White wines: Graves, Chablis, Pouilly-Fuissé, Sancerre, Quincy.

ŒUFS À LA BOURGUIGNONNE

BURGUNDY EGGS

Preparation 40 minutes • Cooking: poached or soft-boiled, 8 minutes; hard-boiled 10 minutes

US	Ingredients	Met/Imp
16	eggs	16
1 quart	red wine	1 litre/1¾ pints
1	onion	1
2	shallots	2
⅓ cup	mushroom trimmings	25 g/scant 1 oz
a few	parsley sprigs	a few
1	thyme sprig	1
⅓	bay leaf	⅓
	salt and pepper	
6 tbsp	Kneaded Butter (*page 49*)	75 g/3 oz
4 tbsp	butter	50 g/2 oz
16	thin slices white bread, rubbed with garlic, toasted and buttered	16

This recipe works equally well with poached, soft-boiled or hard-boiled eggs.

According to local tradition, if the eggs are poached, this should be done in the wine which is then used for the sauce.

Pour the red wine into a saucepan and add the chopped onion and shallots, the mushroom trimmings, parsley and thyme sprigs, piece of bay leaf and salt and pepper.

Boil rapidly until the wine has reduced by half, then add the kneaded butter, divided into pieces. Stir with a whisk until well blended. Boil for a few more seconds, then remove the sauce from the heat and add the plain butter. Stir until melted, then work the sauce through a fine sieve.

If the eggs are poached, put them on the slices of toasted and buttered bread.

If they are soft-boiled, cut the toasted bread slices into round croûtons and put a shelled egg on each.

If they are hard-boiled, cut the shelled eggs in half and put them in a small serving bowl.

Whatever the case, cover the eggs with the sauce.

Red wines: as a rule, serve the same wine as the one used for the sauce. Good choices include Beaujolais-Villages, Bourgogne-Passetoutgrains or Côte de Nuits-Villages.

SCRAMBLED EGGS

Preparation 10 minutes • Cooking 20 minutes • Serves 3

US	Ingredients	Met/Imp
7 tbsp	butter	90 g/3½ oz
6	large eggs	6
	salt and pepper	

For a creamier result, reduce the amount of butter to 60 g/2½ oz (5 tbsp) and add 30 ml/2 tbsp *crème fraîche*.

Spread half of the butter over the bottom and sides of a heavy-based saucepan. Cut the other half into small pieces.

Break the eggs, one by one, into a bowl and add salt and pepper. Beat lightly with a balloon whisk, but not for too long, so that the eggs do not become frothy.

Pour the mixture through a sieve into the buttered saucepan, off the heat.

Put the saucepan over a very low heat and cook, stirring constantly, so that as the egg starts to set it is mixed back into the uncooked egg.

Gradually add the pieces of butter, removing the saucepan from the heat now and then, in order to heat the egg as slowly as possible. If you are using only butter and no cream, reserve a piece of the butter to be added at the last moment.

When the mixture has become creamy, remove it from the heat and add either the crème fraîche or the reserved butter. Mix thoroughly, pour into a heated serving dish and serve immediately

White wines: Mâcon-Villages, Saint-Véran, Arbois or Côtes du Jura.
Red wines: Gamay de Touraine, Bourgueil, Chinon, Saumur-Champigny.

SCRAMBLED EGGS WITH SHRIMPS*

Preparation 45 minutes • Cooking 10 minutes

US	Ingredients	Met/Imp
scant ½ lb	cooked shrimps	200 g/7 oz
14 tbsp	butter	200 g/7 oz
½ cup	Velouté Sauce (page 57)	100 ml/4 fl oz
16	eggs	16
	salt and pepper	
½ cup	crème fraîche	100 ml/4 fl oz

Carefully peel the shrimps. Pound the shrimp shells with a little of the butter, work through a sieve, then mix with the velouté sauce.

Scramble the eggs in the remaining butter with salt and pepper, as in the recipe above. Stir in the peeled shrimps and the crème fraîche at the last moment. Trickle the sauce over the scrambled eggs just before serving.

Dry white wines: dry Graves, Chablis, Muscadet, Sancerre.

US	Ingredients	Met/Imp
1	veal kidney	1
	salt and pepper	
1 stick	butter	100 g/4 oz
½ cup	Brown Sauce (page 64)	100 ml/4 fl oz
¼ cup	madeira	50 ml/2 fl oz
16	eggs	16
½ cup	very reduced Tomato Sauce (page 80)	100 ml/4 fl oz
1 tbsp	chopped fresh parsley	15 ml/1 tbsp

ŒUFS BROUILLÉS AU ROGNON DE VEAU

SCRAMBLED EGGS WITH VEAL KIDNEY*

Preparation 30 minutes • Cooking 6 minutes

Cut the kidney into 5 mm/¼ inch cubes, taking care to remove all the fat. Season with salt and pepper and sauté in about one-quarter of the butter over a high heat until firm. Add the brown sauce, a piece of the remaining butter and the madeira and keep warm without allowing the mixture to boil. (The slightest boiling will toughen the kidney.)

Beat the eggs lightly in a bowl, just long enough to mix the yolks with the whites. Add salt and pepper. Heat about half of the remaining butter in a heavy-based saucepan, then add the eggs. Stir over a very low heat, so that the eggs do not coagulate too rapidly, which would cause lumps to form. As the eggs start to cook, gradually add the tomato sauce and the remaining butter in small pieces. When the eggs are cooked to the required consistency, the mixture should have the appearance of a thick, smooth cream. Immediately pour the eggs into a well heated serving dish, arrange the kidney in the centre and sprinkle with chopped parsley.

White wines: Graves, Chablis, Meursault, Pouilly-Fuissé, Alsace Riesling or Sylvaner, Arbois, Vouvray, Saumur.

US	Ingredients	Met/Imp
14 tbsp	butter	200 g/7 oz
2	truffles	2
1	garlic clove	1
16	eggs	16
3	egg yolks	3
	salt and pepper	
½ cup	crème fraîche	100 ml/4 fl oz

ŒUFS BROUILLÉS AUX TRUFFES

— SCRAMBLED EGGS WITH TRUFFLES —

Preparation 15 minutes • Cooking 10 minutes

The extra egg yolks in this recipe allow more butter to be added, resulting in richer, creamier scrambled eggs.

Heat half of the butter in a heavy-based saucepan. Cut the truffles into strips. As soon as the butter is hot, put them in the hot butter and cook for 2 minutes.

Cut the garlic clove in half and rub it over the surface of the bowl in which the eggs are to be beaten. (The flavour of garlic used in this way is not noticeable but it brings out the flavour of the truffles.) Lightly beat the eggs and egg yolks in the bowl until just mixed. Add salt and pepper.

Add the beaten eggs to the truffles and continue as for Scrambled Eggs with Veal Kidney (above). Finally, add the crème fraîche and the remaining butter in small pieces. Serve in a heated serving dish.

White wines: Graves, Meursault, Alsace Gewürztraminer, Vouvray, Coteaux du Layon.

EGGS IN COCOTTES

Preparation 15 minutes • Cooking 5 minutes

US	Ingredients	Met/Imp
scant 1 cup	light *crème fraîche* or Veal Juice (*page 56*)	200 ml/7 fl oz
16	eggs	16
	salt	
4 tbsp	butter	50 g/2 oz

There are a number of ways of making eggs in cocottes, such as by lining the cocottes with a layer of stuffing or finely minced (ground) meat, but the 2 main types are based on the use of either crème fraîche or veal juice.

With crème fraîche: to ensure that the eggs cook evenly, it is advisable to heat the cocotte dishes in advance. There are 2 types of cocotte, some with small feet and others with flat bases. The latter are preferable. If you do not have traditional cocottes, use ramekin dishes.

Put a spoonful of boiling light crème fraîche in each of the heated cocottes and break an egg in on top. Add a little salt. Put the cocottes in a shallow pan and add enough water to come halfway up the sides of the dishes. Put a small piece of butter on either side of each yolk, cover and cook in a fairly hot oven for about 5 minutes or until the whites of the eggs have slightly solidified and the yolks have reached the same point as the yolk of a fried egg.

With veal juice: make as above, replacing the crème fraîche with the same amount of excellent, boiling braised veal juice.

White wines: Chablis, Mâcon-Villages, Arbois, Saumur, Muscadet.

ŒUFS À LA COQUE AU FUMET DE TRUFFES

TRUFFLE-FLAVOURED BOILED EGGS

Preparation 24 hours in advance • Cooking 3 minutes

US	Ingredients	Met/Imp
16	eggs	16
5 oz	truffles	150 g/5 oz

Put the very fresh whole eggs (first making sure that no shells are broken) in an airtight container with the cleaned truffles. Leave for at least 24 hours.

Boil the eggs as usual, for 2–3 minutes, and serve with toast and butter. The eggs will have a truffle flavour, because egg shells are porous and easily absorb the aroma of the truffles.

VARIATIONS

Replace the truffles with fresh tarragon or curry leaves.

White wines: Alsace Sylvaner, Vouvray, Côtes de Provence.

US	Ingredients	Met/Imp
16	eggs, hard-boiled	16
6½ cups (loosely packed)	fresh bread cubes, without the crust	200 g/7 oz
scant 1 cup	crème fraîche	200 ml/7 fl oz
10 tbsp	butter	150 g/5 oz
6	parsley sprigs	6
	salt and pepper	
1 cup	thick Tomato Sauce (page 80)	250 ml/9 fl oz

AURORA EGGS

Preparation 30 minutes • Cooking 20 minutes

Shell the eggs, halve them lengthways and remove the yolks. Mash the egg yolks in a mortar and pestle, mixing in the bread soaked in the crème fraîche, the butter, the chopped parsley and salt and pepper. Fill the egg whites with some of this stuffing.

Grease the bottom of a flameproof serving dish with butter, spread the remaining stuffing in the dish and arrange the stuffed eggs on top. Cover and place over a low heat for about 20 minutes or until well coloured. Trickle the tomato sauce over the eggs just before serving.

White wines: Graves, Chablis, Pouilly-Fuissé, Muscadet, Sancerre, Arbois, Gaillac.
Rosé wines: Cabernet d'Anjou, Tavel, Côtes de Provence, Arbois.

HARD-BOILED EGGS WITH MUSHROOM STUFFING

US	Ingredients	Met/Imp
8	large eggs	8
10 tbsp	butter	150 g/5 oz
2½–3 cups	Dry Duxelles (page 49)	200 g/7 oz
1 pinch	nutmeg	1 pinch
1 tsp	chopped *fines herbes*	5 ml/1 tsp
	salt and pepper	
1¾ cups	Mornay Sauce (page 73)	400 ml/14 fl oz
½ cup	Gruyère cheese, grated	50 g/2 oz

Preparation 1 hour • Cooking 10 minutes

Hard-boil the eggs and cool them in cold water. Shell the eggs, halve them lengthways and remove the yolks. Mash the yolks in a mortar and pestle, adding about one-quarter of the butter. (If a mortar and pestle is unavailable, crush the yolks in a bowl and beat them into the butter.) Mix in the duxelles and add the nutmeg, fines herbes and salt and pepper to taste.

Fill the egg whites with this mixture and, using the blade of a knife, smooth it into a dome shape covering all the egg white. Put a few spoonfuls of the Mornay sauce in the bottom of a shallow ovenproof dish, place the stuffed egg halves on it and cover with the remaining sauce. Sprinkle with grated cheese, add the remaining butter, melted, and brown in a very hot oven. Serve immediately.

White wines: Quincy, Alsace Riesling.

HARD-BOILED EGGS 'AU GRATIN'

US	Ingredients	Met/Imp
12	eggs	12
2 cups	Soubise (Onion) Sauce (page 80)	500 ml/18 fl oz
1 cup	mixed Gruyère and Parmesan cheeses, grated	100 g/4 oz

Preparation 1 hour • Cooking 10 minutes

Hard-boil the eggs, shell them and slice them crossways. Arrange in 8 well-buttered fairly large scallop shells or cocottes. Cover the egg slices with the sauce and sprinkle with grated cheese. Brown in a very hot oven for about 10 minutes. Serve immediately.

White wines: dry Vouvray, Saumur.

EGGS ROYALE

Preparation 35 minutes • Cooking eggs 10 minutes

US	Ingredients	Met/Imp
8	eggs, hard-boiled	8
scant ½ cup	very rich and concentrated Tomato Sauce (*page 80*)	100 ml/4 fl oz
2 cups	Béchamel or Mornay Sauce (*pages 62 or 73*)	500 ml/18 fl oz

Shell the eggs, halve them lengthways and remove the yolks.

Arrange the egg whites in a ring on a shallow serving dish, with their hollow sides upwards. Put the yolks in the centre of the ring. Heat the tomato sauce and fill the egg whites with it. Pour the hot béchamel or Mornay sauce on to the yolks and serve immediately.

White wines: Alsace Riesling, Mâcon-Villages, Arbois, Saumur.

EGG AND CRAWFISH GRATIN

Preparation 40 minutes • Cooking 10 minutes

US	Ingredients	Met/Imp
8	eggs, hard-boiled	8
½ lb	cooked crawfish (rock lobster) meat	250 g/8 oz
1 stick	butter	100 g/4 oz
3 tbsp	flour	30 g/1 oz
½ cup	milk	100 ml/4 fl oz
½ cup	crème fraîche	100 ml/4 fl oz
	salt and pepper	
1 cup	Gruyère cheese, grated	100 g/4 oz

Shell the eggs and cut them into thick slices crossways. Remove the yolks and mash them. Pound the crawfish in a mortar and pestle with the butter, then work through a sieve. Add the mashed yolks and the flour. Gradually mix in the milk, then add the crème fraîche and salt and pepper. Put the egg white rings in the bottom of a shallow ovenproof dish. Cover with the crawfish mixture and add the grated cheese. Brown in a very hot oven.

White wines: Graves, Meursault, Cassis, Sancerre, Quincy.

EGGS WITH SPINACH AND YORK HAM

Preparation 40 minutes • Cooking: spinach 15 minutes; eggs 6 minutes

US	Ingredients	Met/Imp
2 lb	spinach	1 kg/2 lb
	salt	
10 tbsp	butter	150 g/5 oz
1 pinch	nutmeg	1 pinch
¼ lb	lean cooked ham	100 g/4 oz
8	small slices York ham	8
16	eggs	16

Cook the spinach in boiling salted water until very tender. As soon as it is cooked, drain and cool it, then squeeze it between your hands to extract the water. Work the spinach through a coarse sieve, then put it in a small high-sided frying pan with a little less than half of the butter. Add a pinch of salt and nutmeg and braise for about 15 minutes. Stir over a high heat until a thick purée is formed. Remove from the heat and stir in almost all of the remaining butter and the lean ham, very finely diced. Keep warm.

Grease 8 small ovenproof dishes with some of the remaining butter. Put a thin slice of York ham in the bottom of each one and break 2 eggs on top. Sprinkle a little salt on the egg white and put a few drops of the remaining butter, melted, on the yolks. Cook in the oven for about 6 minutes or until the egg whites have set and the yolks are 'glistening'. (A thin white veil should form over the yolks.)

Put the warm spinach in a piping (pastry) bag fitted with a vegetable nozzle (flattened slit-like tube) and pipe a border around each pair of eggs, filling the gap between the eggs and the edge of the dish.

White wines: Quincy, Saumur, Arbois.

US	Ingredients	Met/Imp
8	eggs	8
16	salted whole anchovies	16
1 stick	butter	100 g/4 oz
	salt and pepper	
2 cups	Mayonnaise (page 72)	500 ml/18 fl oz
	lemon juice	
2	parsley sprigs	2
	chervil	
	tarragon	
3	lettuce hearts	3

─ EGGS STUFFED WITH ANCHOVIES ─

Preparation 1 hour • Cooking 10 minutes

First, hard-boil the eggs for 10 minutes. Shell them while they are still hot, halve them lengthways and remove the yolks. Set aside.

The anchovies should be soaked to desalt them and trimmed, ie the head, tail, bones and fins should be removed. Crush the anchovies in a mortar and pestle until reduced to a purée. Add the butter and the egg yolks, while still warm, and pound everything in the mortar until a smooth paste is formed. Add a little pepper, but no salt, since the anchovies are already very salty.

Use this anchovy stuffing to fill the hollow in each egg half. The excess stuffing may be spread over the surface of the egg whites.

Make the mayonnaise slightly tart with lemon juice, add a little salt and pepper and flavour with finely chopped parsley, chervil and tarragon. Arrange the stuffed egg halves on lettuce leaves and cover them with mayonnaise. Serve chilled.

VARIATION

In this excellent hors-d'œuvre, the anchovies may be replaced by poutargue (a sort of caviar made from mullet roe), or cooked or smoked cod's roe or marinated tuna, but always take care to crush finely. Serve very cold.

White wine: Côtes de Provence, Picpoul de Pinet, La Clape.

US	Ingredients	Met/Imp
12	eggs	12
14 oz	sorrel	400 g/14 oz
1½ tbsp	butter	20 g/¾ oz
	salt and pepper	
1¼ cups	thick *crème fraîche*	300 ml/½ pint
1½ lb	tomatoes	750 g/1½ lb
1	bouquet of parsley, chervil, tarragon, chives, rosemary, thyme and sage	1

─ EGGS STUFFED WITH SORREL AND TOMATO ─

Preparation 25 minutes • Cooking 20 minutes • Serves 6

Hard-boil the eggs for no more than 8–10 minutes. Put the eggs in cold water as soon as they are cooked, so that it is easier to shell them. Shell the eggs, halve them lengthways and remove the yolks. Put half of the yolks in one bowl and the remaining yolks in another. Lightly mash both lots of egg yolk with a fork.

Wash the sorrel and remove the stalks. Roughly chop the leaves and fry them gently in the butter. Add salt and pepper and continue cooking over a low heat for 4–5 minutes. Drain the sorrel and work it through the fine grill of a vegetable mill, or a fine sieve.

Add the sorrel purée to one bowl of egg yolk and mix thoroughly. Add 30 ml/2 tbsp of the crème fraîche and adjust the seasoning. Fill half of the egg whites with the sorrel filling, smoothing it into a dome shape with a knife.

Blanch the tomatoes in a saucepan of boiling water for 1 minute. Drain and skin them. Cut the tomatoes into large pieces and put them in a saucepan with 30 ml/2 tbsp water, salt, pepper and the bouquet of herbs.

Cover and cook for several minutes, then, when the tomatoes are boiling well, remove the lid so that they can reduce to a thick purée. Take out the bouquet of herbs and work the purée through the fine grill of a vegetable mill, or a fine sieve.

Mix the tomato purée thoroughly with the egg yolks in the second bowl. Add salt and pepper if necessary and fill the remaining egg whites with this stuffing. Reserve 60 ml/4 tbsp of the crème fraîche and pour the remainder into a large, long ovenproof dish. Place the stuffed eggs in the dish and put about 2.5 ml/½ tsp crème fraîche on top of each egg half. Cook in a hot oven for 5–6 minutes.

Just before serving, put the dish briefly under the grill (broiler) to brown the stuffing lightly. Serve hot.

Dry white wines: Alsace Sylvaner, Muscadet, dry Vourvray, Sauvignon de Touraine, Entre-Deux-Mers, Coteaux du Languedoc, Picpoul de Pinet.

ŒUFS FOURRÉS À LA PROVENÇALE

STUFFED EGGS PROVENÇAL

Preparation 45 minutes • Cooking eggs 7 minutes

US	Ingredients	Met/Imp
16	eggs	16
4 oz	canned anchovy fillets	100 g/4 oz
2	egg yolks	2
1	small garlic clove, crushed	1
1 quart	Fritter Batter (*page 580*)	1 litre/1¾ pints
	oil for deep frying	
1 handful	parsley, fried	1 handful

Soft-boil the whole eggs for about 7 minutes. Shell the eggs, take off the tops and remove the half-set yolks. Mix these yolks with a thick purée formed by pounding the anchovy fillets with the 2 raw egg yolks in a mortar and pestle. Add the garlic.

Fill each egg white with the anchovy purée. Make some thick fritter batter and dip the eggs into it so that they are completely coated. Deep fry in oil and serve on a napkin, garnished with fried parsley.

White wines: Côtes de Provence, Cassis, Gaillac.
Rosé: Coteaux de Pierrevert.

US	Ingredients	Met/Imp
	oil for frying	
16	eggs	16
	salt and pepper	
16	bacon slices	16
8	tomatoes	8
	parsley sprigs, fried	

AMERICAN-STYLE FRIED EGGS

Preparation 35 minutes • Cooking 6 minutes

The eggs are fried one at a time.

Heat about a glassful of oil in a frying pan. When it is hot, pour in an egg, which has already been broken into a cup and seasoned with salt and pepper. Using a wooden spoon, push the edges of the egg white, which have set on contact with the hot oil, on to the yolk, in order to seal it. Turn the egg over and cook for a few seconds, then, while the yolk is still soft, remove it from the pan and drain it on a clean cloth. Keep it somewhere warm. Grill (broil) the bacon and tomatoes, cut in half. Arrange the eggs and bacon alternately in a circle, overlapping them slightly. Put the tomato halves on top and a bouquet of fried parsley in the centre.

White wines: Côtes de Provence, Mâcon-Villages.
Rosé: Tavel.

US	Ingredients	Met/Imp
16	eggs	16
1½ cups	flour	200 g/7 oz
4	eggs, beaten	4
2 tbsp	oil	30 ml/2 tbsp
about 8 cups	fresh breadcrumbs	500 g/1 lb
about 2 cups	carrot-based Mirepoix (*page 50*)	250 g/8 oz
	oil for deep frying	
1 quart	thick Tomato Sauce (*page 80*), to serve	1 litre/1¾ pints

FRIED EGGS AURORA

Preparation 45 minutes • Cooking eggs 6 minutes

Soft-boil the eggs for about 6 minutes. Shell them, dip them into the flour, then into the beaten eggs thinned with the oil. Finally, coat them with a mixture of breadcrumbs and mirepoix (in which carrot must predominate). Fry in hot oil for a few seconds. Serve with the thick tomato sauce on the side.

White wines: Graves, Chablis, Pouilly-Fuissé, Sancerre.

US	Ingredients	Met/Imp
16	eggs	16
1	onion, chopped	1
4	courgettes (zucchini), diced and floured	4
6	tomatoes, hulled, de-seeded and crushed	6
3	sweet peppers, seeded and diced	3
scant 1 cup	oil	200 ml/7 fl oz
	salt and pepper	
1	garlic clove, crushed	1

FRIED EGGS BASQUAISE*

Preparation 1 hour • Cooking garnish 12 minutes; eggs 6 minutes

Fry the eggs for about 6 minutes, drain and serve with a garnish consisting of onion, courgettes (zucchini), tomatoes and peppers, all sautéed in oil and seasoned with salt, pepper and garlic.

White wines: Béarn, Pacherenc du Vic-Bilh, Côtes de Provence.

FRIED STUFFED EGGS

Preparation 35 minutes • Cooking 20 minutes • Serves 3–6

US	Ingredients	Met/Imp
6	eggs, hard-boiled	6
1 lb	spinach, cooked	500 g/1 lb
2 tbsp	thick Béchamel Sauce (page 62)	30 ml/2 tbsp
	salt and pepper	
	oil for deep frying	
1	egg	1
1 tbsp	oil	15 ml/1 tbsp
	fresh breadcrumbs	

These stuffed eggs make an excellent garnish for roast chicken, but they may also be served as an entrée (2 eggs per person) with tomato sauce, tartare sauce, etc. All sorts of stuffings can be used, including meat, minced fish, mushrooms, etc. The main thing is that the stuffing should have a very fine, dry texture. The sauce, if there is any, should be chosen to harmonize with the stuffing.

Shell the hard-boiled eggs carefully. They should have been cooked in boiling salted water for 10 minutes so as to be completely hard. Take care that the eggs do not crack during cooking.

Remove the yolk from each egg. Hold the egg upright, clasped firmly in the hand with the pointed end downwards. Take off a small cone about 2.5 cm/1 inch in diameter and 2 cm/¾ inch deep from the rounded end. In this way, a small hat-shaped piece of the egg white is removed along with a small piece of yolk. Remove the remaining yolk gently, using the handle of a teaspoon, all the while holding the egg firmly in your hand to avoid splitting the white. Your hand must come exactly up to the height of the opening. When a little yolk has been taken out, press gently with the fingers on the body of the egg to loosen the yolk which can then be removed more easily.

Use a fork to mash the egg yolks and the small pieces of egg white that were removed. Add the well-drained and finely chopped spinach and work into a fine, dry stuffing. The quantity of spinach added should be approximately equal in volume to that of the yolks. Add the béchamel (hot or cold) and a little salt and pepper and stuff the eggs with this mixture. It is a good idea to use a piping (pastry) bag fitted with a fairly narrow nozzle that will fit inside the eggs. As the egg fills you will be able to feel the pressure of the stuffing pushing the nozzle up. Make sure that the stuffing is tightly packed inside the eggs; there must be no air inside. Fill the eggs generously; the stuffing may stick out slightly on top of the egg. All this may be done in advance.

At the last moment, heat the eggs for a few minutes in a low oven. At the same time, heat the oil for frying. Beat the egg, oil and salt and pepper together with a fork. Put the breadcrumbs in a bowl. First dip the stuffed eggs in the egg and oil mixture, then in the breadcrumbs.

Put the coated eggs into the hot, but not smoking, oil and fry for about 3 minutes or until golden brown. Drain and serve hot and crispy.

Dry white wines: Mâcon-Villages, Saint-Véran.
Dry white wine or red wine from the Champagne region.
Red wines: Alsace Pinot Noir, Sancerre.

US	Ingredients	Met/Imp
4	aubergines (eggplants)	4
	salt and pepper	
2 lb	tomatoes, hulled, de-seeded, crushed and lightly fried in half oil and half butter	1 kg/2 lb
1	garlic clove, crushed	1
½ cup	oil	100 ml/4 fl oz
16	eggs	16
8	slices *Bayonne ham*, brushed with butter and cut into strips	8
2 tbsp	chopped fresh parsley	30 ml/2 tbsp

ŒUFS FRITS À LA GASCONNE

GASCONY FRIED EGGS

Preparation 12 minutes • Cooking: tomatoes 12 minutes; aubergines 13 minutes; eggs 6 minutes

Peel the aubergines (eggplants) and cut them into slices 1 cm/½ inch thick. Sprinkle with salt and leave for 1 hour. Meanwhile, work the cooked tomatoes to a purée through a sieve, adding plenty of garlic.

Rinse and drain the aubergine (eggplant) slices. Brush them lightly with oil, then grill (broil) them, at the same time as frying the eggs and the strips of Bayonne ham in the oil. Drain the eggs and place them on the aubergine (eggplant) slices in a heated serving dish. Put the ham strips on top and cover with the puréed tomatoes. Sprinkle with the chopped parsley and serve on hot plates.

White wines: Jurançon sec, Tursan, Pacherenc du Vic-Bilh.

16	eggs	16
4½ lb	spinach, washed and blanched	2 kg/4½ lb
½ lb	pickled ox tongue	200 g/7 oz
3	tarragon sprigs	3
14 tbsp	butter	200 g/7 oz
	salt and pepper	

ŒUFS FRITS À LA GISMONDA

GISMONDA FRIED EGGS

Preparation 1 hour • Cooking: spinach 12 minutes; eggs 6 minutes

Fry the eggs and arrange them in a circle on a large serving platter. Put the spinach, which has been roughly chopped and lightly fried in butter, in the centre. Quickly add a coarsely cut *julienne* of pickled tongue, a touch of tarragon, and the remaining butter cooked until nut-brown (*page 53*). Sprinkle with salt and pepper and serve immediately.

White wines: Clairette du Languedoc, Graves.

8	eggs	8
8	small aubergines (eggplants)	8
	oil for frying	
8	artichoke bottoms	8
¾ cup	flour	100 g/4 oz
	Fritter Batter (*page 580*)	
2 cups	Tomato Sauce (*page 80*)	500 ml/18 fl oz

ŒUFS FRITS À LA MONTALBANAISE

FRIED EGGS MONTAUBAN

Preparation 1 hour • Cooking: garnish 20 minutes; eggs 6 minutes

Fry the eggs and arrange them in a circle on a large serving platter, alternating them with little fans made from slices of aubergine (eggplant), fried in oil. Dip the artichoke bottoms in flour, then in the batter. Deep fry, then drain and place in the centre of the platter. Serve with the tomato sauce on the side.

White wines: Gaillac, Côtes de Saint-Mont.

VIROFLAY FRIED EGGS

Preparation 30 minutes • Cooking: garnish 1 hour; eggs 6 minutes

US	Ingredients	Met/Imp
1 lb	salsify (oyster plant)	500 g/1 lb
	White Court Bouillon (page 49)	
10 tbsp	butter	150 g/5 oz
about 1 cup	Fritter Batter (page 580)	250 ml/9 fl oz
1 cup	blanched almonds, flaked (sliced)	150 g/5 oz
	oil for deep frying	
8	eggs	8
8	mushrooms	8
1 quart	Tomato Sauce (page 80)	1 litre/1¾ pints
2	tarragon sprigs	2

Cook the salsify in the court bouillon, drain thoroughly and fry lightly in butter. Drain and leave until lukewarm, then dip the salsify in a little batter mixed with the almonds. Deep fry them in hot oil, then drain thoroughly. Fry the eggs and arrange them in a circle on a serving platter. Fill the centre of the dish with salsify fritters. Place small, grilled (broiled) mushrooms on the eggs and serve with tomato sauce flavoured with chopped tarragon.

White wines: Alsace Sylvaner, Pinot Blanc or Pinot Gris, Arbois, Chablis.

COLD EGGS MARINETTE

Preparation 1½ hours • Cooking: eggs 5 minutes; tomatoes 12 minutes

US	Ingredients	Met/Imp
3 lb	nicely ripe tomatoes	1.5 kg/3 lb
2½	large onions	2½
4 tbsp	butter	50 g/2 oz
	salt and pepper	
1 pinch	sugar	1 pinch
1	small garlic clove	1
1	bouquet garni	1
2 quarts	liquid Plain Aspic (page 58)	2 litres/3½ pints
16	eggs	16
16	chervil sprigs	16
2 tsp	chopped fresh chervil	10 ml/2 tsp
	Vinaigrette Dressing (page 81)	

Set aside one-third of the tomatoes for garnish. Chop and fry 2 of the onions briefly in the butter, without letting them brown. Add the remaining tomatoes, which should first be hulled, de-seeded, chopped and pressed to remove all of their juice. Add a little salt, pepper, sugar, the crushed garlic and bouquet garni and cook slowly for about 12 minutes or until a purée is formed. Work through a fine sieve into a shallow frying pan and stir over a high heat. When the purée has become very thick, add 200 ml/7 fl oz (scant 1 cup) of the aspic jelly, a spoonful at a time. Continue to cook the sauce until it has reduced to no more than about 400 ml/14 fl oz (1¾ cups). Pour this sauce into a piece of cheesecloth, twist, then leave to cool. Do not allow it to set.

Poach the eggs for about 5 minutes, drain and leave to cool. Neaten the whites of the eggs by trimming the edges, then place them on a large flat plate, having first carefully wiped them. Coat them with a little tomato sauce, which should be cold but still runny. Coat the eggs twice more at 5–6 minute intervals, so that they are covered with a fairly thick layer of tomato. Place a sprig of chervil in the middle of each egg and pour several layers of cold liquid aspic jelly on top. Leave in a cool place to set.

Peel, de-seed and chop the reserved tomatoes, then press them to remove all of their juice. Put them into a bowl, add the remaining ½ onion (finely chopped, rinsed in cold water and squeezed dry in a cloth) and the chopped chervil. Mix well together. Dress this salad just before serving with a few spoonfuls of highly seasoned vinaigrette.

Remove any excess sauce from the base of the eggs with the blade of a small knife and place them on a ring of chopped set aspic jelly on a serving dish. Arrange the tomato salad in the centre.

Rosé wines: Arbois or Tavel.

US	Ingredients	Met/Imp
a few spoonfuls	good-quality port wine or Banyuls (a sweet red wine)	a few spoonfuls
2 cups	liquid Plain Aspic (page 58)	500 ml/18 fl oz
a few	tarragon leaves	a few
4	eggs, soft-boiled or poached	4
2	small slices cooked, lightly smoked ham (York or Milan)	2
	GARNISH	
	lettuce	
	tomatoes	

EGGS IN ASPIC*

Preparation 3 hours (including setting) • Cooking 6 minutes • Serves 4

Add the port or Banyuls wine to the aspic jelly while it is still lukewarm.

Rinse 4 dariole moulds or ramekin dishes in cold water. Drain them quickly but do not dry them. Pour a little lukewarm aspic jelly into the bottom of each mould to make a layer about 5 mm/¼ inch thick. Put the moulds in the coldest part of the refrigerator to make the jelly set quickly. Blanch the tarragon leaves in boiling water for 1 minute, then drain.

Take the moulds out of the refrigerator. Decorate the aspic with tarragon leaves, add a little more jelly and return to the refrigerator.

Carefully shell the eggs, if necessary, then put them in the moulds. Place a piece of ham, trimmed to fit, over and around each egg, then fill the moulds by pouring aspic jelly under and over the ham so that it sticks firmly to the eggs. Return to the refrigerator.

Wash the lettuce and use to line a serving plate. Remove the eggs from the moulds, dipping the latter for a few moments into lukewarm water. Turn the eggs out on to the lettuce and complete the garnish with a few whole tomatoes.

Fine full-bodied red wines: Gevrey-Chambertin, Vosne Romanée, Mercurey, Hermitage.
Rosé or light red wines: Tavel, Médoc, young Graves.

US	Ingredients	Met/Imp
8	eggs, hard-boiled	8
12	artichoke bottoms	12
⅔ cup	chopped truffles	50 g/2 oz
	salt and pepper	
	nutmeg	
	White Court Bouillon (page 49)	
14 tbsp	butter	200 g/7 oz
2 cups	Mornay Sauce (page 73)	500 ml/18 fl oz
½ cup	Parmesan cheese, grated	50 g/2 oz
about 2 cups	truffle ragoût	300 g/10 oz

EGGS 'AU GRATIN' ELIZABETH

Preparation 1 hour • Cooking: artichoke bottoms 40 minutes; eggs 10 minutes

Recipe by Claude Terrail, la Tour d'Argent, Paris

Cut the tip off each end of the shelled hard-boiled eggs, so that they look like small barrels. Hollow them out, without breaking the whites, then work the yolks through a fine sieve. Mix these yolks with a fairly thick purée made from 4 of the artichoke bottoms and about one-quarter of the chopped truffles. Add salt, pepper and nutmeg. Stuff the eggs with this mixture and smooth the tops into dome shapes.

Put each egg into an artichoke bottom, which has already been cooked in white court bouillon and sweated in butter. Cover with Mornay sauce. Sprinkle with grated Parmesan cheese and cook au gratin.

Arrange the artichoke bottoms in a ring on a serving plate and garnish the centre with truffle ragoût (thickly sliced or diced truffles flavoured with Demi-Glaze [page 56] and madeira).

Fine white wines: Pouilly-Fuissé, Meursault, Corton-Charlemagne.

US	Ingredients	Met/Imp
8	eggs	8
1 pinch	salt	1 pinch
¾ cup	Gruyère cheese, grated	75 g/3 oz
2 tbsp	butter	25 g/scant 1 oz

EGGS IN THEIR NESTS

Preparation 20 minutes • Cooking 20 minutes

Separate the eggs and set the yolks aside. Beat the whites with the salt until stiff, then add the grated cheese. Shape the whites into 8 'nests' in a buttered ovenproof dish. Put an egg yolk in the centre of each nest and cook in a moderate oven for 20 minutes. Serve immediately.

White wines: Graves, Meursault, Chablis.

US	Ingredients	Met/Imp
1 stick	butter	100 g/4 oz
16	thin truffle slices	16
16	eggs	16
	salt	
16	round croûtons made from bread without crusts	16
2 spoonfuls	reduced Veal Stock (*page 56*)	2 spoonfuls
	chopped fresh parsley	
1¼ cups	Maître d'Hôtel Butter (*page 52*)	300 g/10 oz

PALAIS-ROYAL EGGS

Preparation 30 minutes • Cooking 6 minutes

Grease 16 small dariole (baba) moulds generously with butter. In the bottom of each one, place a slice of truffle about 2.5 cm (1 inch) in diameter, trimmed with a fluted round cutter.

Break an egg into each mould and add a little salt. Put the moulds in a shallow baking tin and pour in enough water to come two-thirds of the way up the moulds. Cook in a fairly hot oven for about 6 minutes or until the egg whites have set but the yolks are still soft.

Fry the croûtons in butter. They should be 4.5 cm/1¾ inches in diameter and 5 mm/¼ inch thick. Blend the veal stock and chopped parsley into the maître d'hôtel butter. Beat until very soft.

Turn the eggs out on to the croûtons and arrange them in a ring on a round serving plate. Coat each one with a spoonful of maître d'hôtel butter.

VARIATION
Use 16 small puff pastry tartlets instead of bread croûtons. Instead of maître d'hôtel butter, beat the reduced veal stock with plain butter.

White wines: Quincy, Savennières, Saumur, Muscadet.

US	Ingredients	Met/Imp
1 lb	tomatoes	500 g/1 lb
½ lb	sweet peppers	250 g/8 oz
2 oz	bacon	50 g/2 oz
	oil	
1	small red chili (chili pepper)	1
	salt and pepper	
3	garlic cloves	3
	sweet red vermouth	
8	eggs	8

PIPÉRADE EGGS

Preparation 30 minutes • Cooking 20 minutes • Serves 4

Blanch the tomatoes in boiling water for 10 seconds, then drain, peel and remove the hard cores. Cut the tomatoes in half and squeeze to remove the seeds, then cut into large pieces.

Grill (broil) the peppers to char them, then remove their skins. Halve them, remove the cores and seeds, then slice thinly.

Cut the bacon into thin strips. Heat plenty of oil in a high-sided copper frying pan (or, if unavailable, an ordinary frying pan). When the oil is hot, add the bacon, tomatoes, peppers, chilli, salt, pepper and crushed garlic. Mix with a wooden spoon and cook for 5–6 minutes over a high heat, until all the liquid has evaporated and a very thick purée is obtained. Just before removing from the heat, add a drop of sweet vermouth (to neutralize the acidity). This purée may be prepared in advance and then reheated.

Break 2 of the eggs into a bowl and add about 45 ml/3 tbsp of the pepper mixture. Stir well and adjust the seasoning, then beat vigorously with a fork. Heat a little oil in a small flameproof gratin dish. When the oil is really hot, pour in the mixture and cook in a fairly hot oven, or under the grill (broiler), for about 3 minutes or until set. The pipérade should be only slightly coloured. Serve immediately. Repeat with the remaining eggs and mixture to make 4 individual pipérades.

VARIATION

If preferred, it is possible to prepare this dish for several people, but individual pipérades stay softer and have more flavour.

Dry white wines from the south-west: Pacherenc du Vic-Bihl, Tursan.
Rosé wines or light red wines: Bordeaux Clairet, Irouléguy, Béarn.
Full-bodied red wines from the south-west: Madiran, Tursan, Cahors.

US	Ingredients	Met/Imp
16	thin slices fatty bacon	16
4 tbsp	butter	50 g/2 oz
½ cup	full-flavoured Veal Juice (page 56)	100 ml/4 fl oz
16	eggs	16
	salt and pepper	

FRIED EGGS WITH BACON

Preparation 20 minutes • Cooking 7 minutes

Cook the bacon in a frying pan with the butter. When it is cooked, transfer it to an ovenproof dish and mix in the meat juice. Break the eggs on top, sprinkle with a little salt and some pepper, then cook in a low oven for about 7 minutes or until the eggs are set but still soft.

White or red wines: Alsace Riesling, Saumur, Gaillac, Bourgogne-Passetoutgrains, Côtes du Rhône.

Fried Eggs Basquaise
The fried eggs for this dish are always cooked at the last minute: as soon as they are slipped into the hot oil the whites set instantly while the yolks remain runny. (Recipe on page 122.)

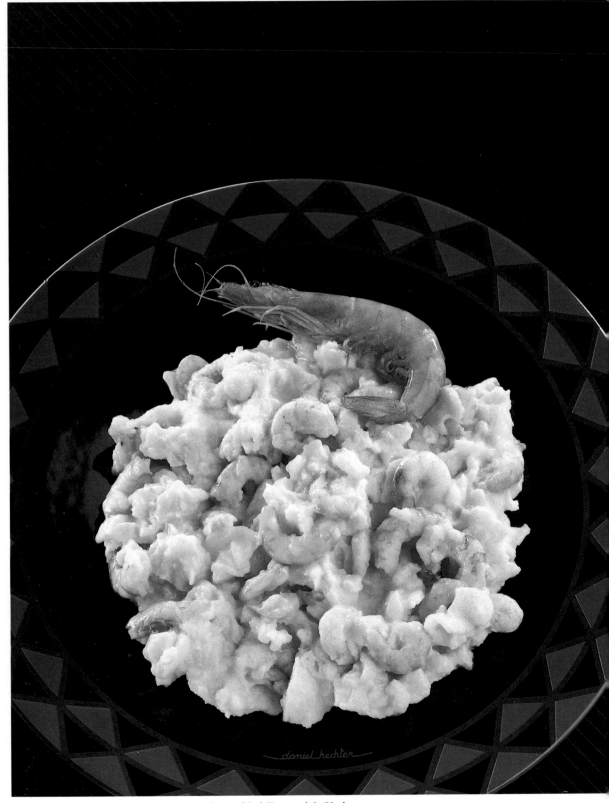

Scrambled Eggs with Shrimps
The secret of successful scrambled eggs is to cook them over a very low heat, stirring all the time with a wooden spoon; add salt carefully because of the shrimps.
(*Recipe on page 115.*)

Scrambled Eggs with Veal Kidney
The diced veal kidney, fried in madeira, is cooked separately from the scrambled eggs to which tomato sauce has been added. The two are combined at the last minute and the kidney is sprinkled with parsley. (Recipe on page 116.)

Eggs in Aspic
Soft-boiled or poached eggs are set in a port-wine-based aspic and garnished with har
and tarragon. This is a decorative first course which is easy to prepare in advance.
(Recipe on page 126.)

LORRAINE FRIED EGGS

Preparation 20 minutes • Cooking 7 minutes

US	Ingredients	Met/Imp
6 tbsp	butter	75 g/3 oz
16	small pieces fresh fat belly (side) of pork	16
¼ lb	Gruyère cheese	100 g/4 oz
16	eggs	16
	salt	
scant 1 cup	cream	200 ml/7 fl oz

Do not put salt on the egg yolks or the grains of salt will form little dots on the surface during cooking.

Grease the bottoms of 8 individual ovenproof dishes with plenty of butter. Put 2 pieces of fat pork, that have been blanched and lightly grilled (broiled) or browned in butter, and a few thin strips of cheese in each dish. Break 2 eggs into each dish, sprinkle a little salt on the egg white, surround the yolks with cream and cook in a fairly hot oven for about 7 minutes or until the whites set and the yolks start to glisten (a thin white veil should form over them).

White or red wines: Graves, Meursault, Mâcon-Villages, Mercurey, Givry.

ŒUFS POCHÉS PÉRIGUEUX

POACHED EGGS PÉRIGUEUX

Preparation 1 hour • Cooking 6 minutes

US	Ingredients	Met/Imp
8	eggs	8
	salt and pepper	
¼ cup	vinegar	50 ml/2 fl oz
8	slices bread, without crusts	8
6 tbsp	butter	75 g/3 oz
2 cups	Veal Stock (page 56)	500 ml/18 fl oz
6 tbsp	flour	50 g/2 oz
2 oz	truffles	50 g/2 oz
½ cup	madeira or Muscadet de Frontignan wine	100 ml/4 fl oz

Poach the eggs in boiling water with the salt and vinegar. Meanwhile, cut the slices of bread into oval croûtons and fry in one-third of the butter. Drain the eggs and arrange on the croûtons. Cover them with a Périgueux sauce prepared in the following way: pour some veal stock on to a brown roux made from 15 ml (1 tbsp) of the butter and the flour. Add salt and pepper and cook for 25 minutes. Fry the diced truffles in a shallow saucepan for a few moments in the remaining butter, then sprinkle with the madeira or wine. Strain the sauce through a fine sieve on to the truffles.

White wines: Bergerac sec, Côtes de Duras, Gaillac.

ŒUFS POCHÉS À LA PURÉE DE VOLAILLE TRUFFÉE

POACHED EGGS WITH CHICKEN AND TRUFFLE PURÉE

Preparation 1 hour • Cooking eggs 6 minutes

US	Ingredients	Met/Imp
¼ lb	cooked chicken breast meat	100 g/4 oz
2 cups	Chicken Velouté (page 57)	500 ml/18 fl oz
	salt and pepper	
⅓ cup	diced truffles	30 g/1 oz
8	slices white bread	8
14 tbsp	butter	200 g/7 oz
8	poached eggs	8
scant ½ cup	mushroom cooking juices	100 ml/4 fl oz
8	thin truffle slices	8

Mince (grind) the chicken and mix in a little of the velouté. Heat this purée gently, then work through a sieve lined with cheesecloth into a saucepan. Add salt and pepper and stir in the cooked, diced truffles. Cut the slices of bread into oval shapes and fry in butter. Form a slight hollow in the centre of each one and fill with the chicken purée.

Arrange the filled croûtes in a circle on a serving dish. Put a poached egg on each one, then cover the eggs with the remaining velouté which has first been reduced with the mushroom juices and a little butter.

On each egg, place a thin slice of truffle, cut with a fluted round cutter.

White wines: Vouvray, Coteaux du Layon, Meursault.

POACHED EGGS WITH WINE FROM THE BERRY REGION

Preparation 30 minutes • Cooking 50 minutes • Serves 4

US	Ingredients	Met/Imp
2	onions, chopped	2
14 tbsp	butter	200 g/7 oz
1 bottle	red wine	1 bottle
1	small garlic clove	1
	salt and pepper	
a few	parsley sprigs	a few
8	eggs	8
scant ½ lb	small mushrooms	200 g/7 oz
5 oz	slightly salted bacon, cut into *lardons*	150 g/5 oz
about 10	small onions	about 10
1 tbsp	flour	15 ml/1 tbsp
8	large fried croûtons	8

Brown the chopped onions in a little butter in a saucepan over a high heat. Pour the red wine on to the onions and bring to the boil. As soon as the wine is boiling, remove the pan from the heat and flambé the hot wine. Return the pan to a low heat and add the chopped garlic, a pinch of pepper and the parsley, chopped. Do not add salt at this stage. Leave to simmer gently.

Break the eggs, one by one, into the wine. Poach them for 3–4 minutes or until set but still soft. Remove the eggs with a slotted spoon, put them on a serving dish and keep them warm. Let the wine continue boiling for 15-20 minutes to remove the acidity and to reduce it.

Cook the mushrooms (whole or chopped) in a little water with a piece of butter for about 10 minutes. Drain and add the stock from the mushrooms to the reduced wine: there should be a total of about 400 ml/14 fl oz (1¾ cups) liquid. If necessary, reduce further by boiling.

Boil the bacon lardons for a few minutes in water, then drain and brown in a little butter with the mushrooms and small onions. Add some *beurre manié* (made by mixing the flour and a good nut of butter together with a fork).

Strain the boiling wine into the pan through a fine sieve. Mix everything gently together to obtain a thick, smooth sauce.

Finally, add the remaining butter, in small pieces, to the sauce, taste and adjust the seasoning.

Pour the sauce on to the poached eggs. Garnish the dish with fried croûtons, lightly rubbed with garlic.

Red wines: as a general rule, serve the same wine as the one used for cooking. Good choices include beaujolais or Sancerre served cool, or Morgan, Brouilly or Fleurie served at room temperature.

EGGS WITH ONION SAUCE

Preparation 1 hour • Cooking eggs 10 minutes

US	Ingredients	Met/Imp
3	large onions	3
1 stick	butter	100 g/4 oz
6 tbsp	flour	50 g/2 oz
1 quart	boiling milk	1 litre/1¾ pints
	salt and pepper	
1 pinch	nutmeg	1 pinch
12	eggs	12

As a rule, 'œufs à la tripe' are served with a sauce that contains sliced onions, as in the recipe here. However, if you prefer, you can work the onions and the sauce through a sieve, heat the resulting purée and then serve the eggs as described.

Slice the onions very thinly and blanch them for 7–8 minutes in boiling water to remove the acrid juice they contain, especially in the late autumn. Blanching is unnecessary if the onions are new and have not reached complete maturity. Drain the onions, refresh under cold running water, drain again and dry thoroughly with a cloth. Put the onions in a saucepan with the butter and sweat them over a very low heat for 20–25 minutes without letting them change colour. Mix in the flour and stir over the heat for a few minutes. Mix in the milk and add a generous pinch of salt, a pinch of pepper and the nutmeg. Bring to the boil, stirring constantly, and cook gently for 25 minutes (onion béchamel).

Put the eggs in a large sieve and plunge them into boiling water. For large eggs, allow 10 minutes cooking time, counted from the moment the water starts boiling again. Drain the eggs, cool and shell them and keep warm. Five minutes before serving, cut the eggs into thick slices and mix them into the onion sauce.

White wines: Graves, Mâcon-Villages, Arbois, Saumur.
Red wines: Côtes du Forez, Saint-Pourçain.

OMELETTE AU BOUDIN

——— BLACK PUDDING OMELETTE ———

Preparation 1 hour • Cooking 40 minutes

Grill (broil) the boudin, then remove the skin. Separate the eggs and mix the yolks with the boudin. Add the crème fraîche, the stiffly whisked egg whites and salt and pepper. Cook an omelette in butter until half set and, without folding it, slide it into a shallow dish. Make a purée of the mashed potatoes and milk, then spread it over the omelette. Scatter small pieces of butter on top and brown in the oven.

White wines: Alsace Sylvaner, Pinot Blanc or Pinot Gris.

US	Ingredients	Met/Imp
14 oz	boudin (French black pudding or blood sausage)	400 g/14 oz
8	eggs	8
½ cup	crème fraîche	100 ml/4 fl oz
	salt and pepper	
1 stick	butter	100 g/4 oz
1½ cups	mashed potatoes	300 g/10 oz
½ cup	milk	100 ml/4 fl oz

OMELETTE AU CRABE

——— CRAB OMELETTE ———

Preparation 40 minutes • Cooking crab 30 minutes; omelette 6 minutes

Put the crab in a saucepan with the carrot, onion, bouquet garni, vinegar and salt and pepper. Cover with boiling water and cook for 30 minutes. Drain and remove the crab meat from the centre of the shell. Scrape out the crab from inside the shell, place in a bowl and crush thoroughly to a paste. Beat the eggs and mix in the paste and crab meat. Melt the butter in a pan and make the omelette as usual.

White wines: Muscadet, Gros Plant du Pays Nantais.
Cider.

US	Ingredients	Met/Imp
14 oz	live crab	400 g/14 oz
1	carrot	1
1	onion	1
1	bouquet garni	1
¼ cup	vinegar	50 ml/2 fl oz
	salt and pepper	
16	eggs	16
6 tbsp	butter	75 g/3 oz

US	Ingredients	Met/Imp
5 oz	washed spinach	150 g/5 oz
	salt and pepper	
6 tbsp	butter	75 g/3 oz
1 pinch	nutmeg	1 pinch
2 oz	cooked lean ham	50 g/2 oz
8	eggs	8
1 tbsp	chopped parsley	15 ml/1 tbsp

OMELETTE AUX ÉPINARDS

SPINACH OMELETTE

Preparation 30 minutes • Cooking: spinach 20 minutes; omelette 6 minutes

Cook the spinach for 8 minutes in boiling salted water, drain thoroughly and press to remove excess water without cooling. Shred the spinach with a sharp knife, then sweat it in one-third of the butter for 10–12 minutes, having first seasoned it with salt, pepper and nutmeg. Mix in the cubed ham.

Beat the eggs. Brown the remaining butter until nut-coloured, then make the omelette as usual. Put the ham and spinach in the centre of the omelette and roll up, taking care to enclose the filling. Put the omelette on a long serving dish, pour plenty of slightly salted, melted butter over it and sprinkle with finely chopped parsley.

White and rosé wines: Mâcon-Villages, Arbois, Tavel.

US	Ingredients	Met/Imp
a few	clusters acacia flowers	a few
8	eggs	8
4 tbsp	butter	50 g/2 oz
	pepper or kirsch	

OMELETTE AUX FLEURS D'ACACIA

ACACIA FLOWER OMELETTE

Preparation 30 minutes • Cooking 8 minutes

Pull the petals off the acacias, chop them and use them to fill an omelette made in the usual way with beaten eggs and butter. For a savoury omelette, add plenty of pepper. If, on the other hand, you prefer a sweet omelette, add a little kirsch to bring out the scent of the flowers.

For a savoury omelette, white wines: Graves, Chablis, Mersault, Pouilly-Fuissé, Sancerre, Quincy, Alsace Riesling or Sylvaner, Arbois.
For a sweet omelette, white wines: Vouvray, Sauternes, Barsac, Monbazillac, Alsace Gewürztraminer.

US	Ingredients	Met/Imp
8	eggs	8
1 stick	butter	100 g/4 oz
1 tsp	salt	5 ml/1 tsp
1 pinch	pepper	1 pinch
	FILLING	
2	sheep's brains	2
1 quart	salted water	1 litre/1¾ pints
1	lemon, juice of	1
1	onion	1
1	clove	1

OMELETTE FONDANTE À LA CERVELLE DE MOUTON

BRAIN OMELETTE

Preparation 25 minutes • Cooking: filling 10 minutes; omelette 5 minutes

First make the filling. Clean the sheep's brains and cook them for 10 minutes in boiling salted water, to which the lemon juice, the thinly sliced onion and the clove have been added. Drain and put into cold water to make them firm, then dice them. Make the omelette in the usual way with the eggs, butter, salt and pepper. When it is just cooked, add the brains, fold over the omelette and place on a hot serving dish.

White wines: Graves, Meursault, Alsace Gewürztraminer.

SEAFOOD OMELETTE

Preparation 40 minutes • Cooking: filling 12 minutes; omelette 6 minutes

US	Ingredients	Met/Imp
1 cup	mussels	250 ml/9 fl oz
	or	
12	oysters	12
	or	
4	scallops	4
18	eggs	18
	salt and pepper	
4 tbsp	butter	50 g/2 oz

Any kind of shellfish may be used. If you choose cockles, mussels or scallops, just open them over the heat, remove the meat from the shells and keep warm in a bowl. Oysters should be poached in their own water; scallops should be blanched in a *court bouillon* and diced. When adding salt to the beaten eggs, take into account the kind of shellfish you have chosen, which may already be salty.

Add the seafood meat to the beaten eggs with salt and pepper. Cook the omelette in the usual way in butter over a high heat for about 6 minutes, taking care to keep the omelette runny.

White wines: Muscadet, Gros Plant du Pays Nantais, Coteaux d'Ancenis.
Cider.

OMELETTE GRATINÉE AUX CHAMPIGNONS

MUSHROOM OMELETTE 'AU GRATIN'

Preparation 30 minutes • First cooking 10 minutes; second cooking 8 minutes

US	Ingredients	Met/Imp
8	eggs	8
	salt and pepper	
1 tbsp	chopped fresh parsley	15 ml/1 tbsp
1 cup	Dry Duxelles (page 49)	75 g/3 oz
¼ cup	Gruyère cheese, grated	30 g/1 oz
¼ cup	milk	50 ml/2 fl oz
¼ cup	crème fraîche	50 ml/2 fl oz
6 tbsp	butter	75 g/3 oz

Beat the eggs as for an ordinary omelette, with salt, pepper and parsley. Keep the mushroom duxelles warm.

Melt the cheese, then stir in the milk and crème fraîche to make a paste. Keep warm.

Cook the omelette as usual in butter for 10 minutes. Fill with the duxelles, fold over both sides and place on an ovenproof dish. Spread the cheese paste on top of the omelette and brown in a hot oven for 8 minutes. Serve immediately.

White wines: Mâcon-Villages, Arbois, Saumur.

US	Ingredients	Met/Imp
scant ½ lb	asparagus tips	200 g/7 oz
2 oz	mushrooms	50 g/2 oz
¼ lb	truffles	100 g/4 oz
5 oz	foie gras, diced	150 g/5 oz
6 tbsp	butter	75 g/3 oz
16	eggs	16
	salt and pepper	
	Demi-Glaze (page 56)	
½ cup	thickened Brown Veal Juice (page 56)	100 ml/4 fl oz

MONSELET'S OMELETTE

Preparation 35 minutes • Cooking: omelette 6 minutes; filling 12 minutes

Monselet (1825–1888) was not only a refined and charming poet but also an enlightened connoisseur of the art of cooking. He brought the 'Almanach gourmand' back to life for a few years, and his 'Lettres gourmandes', published by the journal 'l'Evénement', was a great success. Moreover, almost all the great chefs of his time wanted to dedicate one of their creations to him. This recipe, which is a little complicated, and very rich and fanciful, has only been included by way of an anecdote.

Set aside 8 asparagus tips, about 4 cm/1½ inches long, and tie them into a bunch. Chop the remainder into little pieces. Set aside 8 mushrooms and 8 slices of truffle; chop the remainder into *julienne*.

Cook all of the asparagus (including the bunch) rapidly in boiling salted water, then drain as thoroughly as possible.

Put the foie gras in a small saucepan, crush it into a purée and heat without letting it boil. Mix in the mushroom and truffle julienne and the cooked chopped asparagus.

Heat some butter until it is a nut-brown colour, add the beaten eggs with salt and pepper and cook the omelette in the usual way for about 6 minutes. When the eggs have firmly coagulated, add the vegetable and truffle filling and roll up the omelette so that the filling is well enclosed. Put the omelette on a dish and put the bunch of asparagus tips in a hole cut in the centre. Garnish each side with the reserved 8 mushrooms, cooked, and the reserved 8 truffle slices, coated in demi-glaze. Surround the omelette with a few spoonfuls of thickened veal juice with the remaining butter added.

White wines: Pouilly-Fuissé, Meursault, Montrachet.
Rosé: Tavel.

OMELETTE AUX MORILLES

US	Ingredients	Met/Imp
3 oz	fresh morels	75 g/3 oz
4 tbsp	butter	50 g/2 oz
1	shallot	1
1 tbsp	chopped fresh parsley	15 ml/1 tbsp
8	eggs	8
	salt and pepper	
	thickened Veal Juice (page 56)	

MOREL OMELETTE

Preparation 25 minutes • Cooking: morels 15 minutes; omelette 6 minutes

In the collection of recipes suitable for morels, we must include the omelette, which can be made in 2 ways. For the first method, the morels are sautéed in butter in a frying pan, sprinkled with a little shallot and very finely chopped parsley, then mixed into the beaten eggs with salt and pepper. For the second method, they are sautéed as above, but in a saucepan, then mixed with a few spoonfuls of thickened veal juice and placed inside the omelette before it is rolled.

White wines: Alsace Pinot Gris, Arbois, Chablis.

- MUSSEL AND MUSHROOM OMELETTE -

Preparation 15 minutes • Cooking: mussels 5 minutes; omelette 10 minutes

US	Ingredients	Met/Imp
1 pint	Mussels 'Marinière' (*page 268*)	500 ml/18 fl oz
8	eggs	8
	salt and pepper	
⅔ cup	white mushrooms, sliced	50 g/2 oz
4 tbsp	butter	50 g/2 oz

Cook the mussels as usual; the flesh should be well trimmed and wiped. Beat the eggs with salt and pepper and mix in the mussels and mushrooms. Make the omelette in the usual way in butter, cooking it for about 10 minutes (it should still be runny).

White wines: Alsace Riesling, Muscadet, Jasnières.

——— SORREL OMELETTE ———

Preparation 40 minutes • Cooking: sorrel 10 minutes; omelette 6 minutes

US	Ingredients	Met/Imp
scant ½ lb	sorrel	200 g/7 oz
1 stick	butter	100 g/4 oz
8	eggs	8
½ cup	milk	100 ml/4 fl oz
	salt and pepper	
	oil	
¼ cup	thick *crème fraîche*	50 ml/2 fl oz

Chop the sorrel into large pieces and cook it in butter in a frying pan for about 10 minutes. Transfer the sorrel to a bowl and mix it with the beaten eggs, milk and salt and pepper. Beat thoroughly with a fork. Add a drop of oil to the butter in the frying pan to stop it becoming too brown. Cook the omelette in the usual way for about 6 minutes.

When the omelette is ready and served up on the dish, cut it in the centre and pour in the thick crème fraîche.

White wines: Graves, Meursault, Chablis, Sancerre.

——— FRIED BREAD OMELETTE ———

Preparation 15 minutes • Cooking 20 minutes

US	Ingredients	Met/Imp
scant 1 cup	oil	200 ml/7 fl oz
16	slices stale white bread	16
	salt and pepper	
8	eggs	8
1 stick	butter	100 g/4 oz

Heat some oil in a frying pan, add the slices of bread and brown on both sides, then remove from the pan.

Dip the fried bread into the salted beaten eggs. Fry the slices once more in butter and oil over a high heat.

VARIATION
Chopped York ham or ordinary cooked ham may be added to the fried bread, producing an excellent and nourishing omelette requiring half the quantity of eggs as a normal one.

White wines: Quincy, Jasnières, Sancerre.

US	Ingredients	Met/Imp
I lb	tomatoes, skinned and de-seeded	500 g/I lb
2	garlic cloves	2
2	tarragon sprigs	
	parsley and basil	
⅔ cup	onions, finely chopped	150 g/5 oz
¼ cup	olive oil	50 ml/2 fl oz
8	eggs	8
	salt and pepper	
3 tbsp	butter	40 g/I½ oz

—— PROVENÇAL OMELETTE ——

Preparation 15 minutes • Cooking: omelette 6 minutes; filling 10 minutes

Chop the tomatoes, garlic, tarragon, parsley and basil and cook with the onions in the oil in a frying pan for about 10 minutes or until reduced.

Beat the eggs, add salt and pepper and cook the omelette as usual in the butter in another frying pan, adding the tomato mixture at the start of cooking. Stir well to mix thoroughly. Cook for about 6 minutes. Serve the omelette runny, preferably, but above all very hot.

White or rosé wines: Côtes de Provence, Coteaux d'Aix-en-Provence.

US	Ingredients	Met/Imp
I	veal kidney	I
4 tbsp	butter	50 g/2 oz
8	eggs	8
	salt and pepper	
¼ cup	thickened Veal Stock (page 56)	50 ml/2 fl oz

OMELETTE AU ROGNON

—— KIDNEY OMELETTE ——

Preparation 25 minutes • Cooking: kidney 8 minutes; omelette 6 minutes

Trim the kidney, reserving a small piece of the fat, and finely dice the kidney or cut it into thin strips. Melt half of the butter in a frying pan and add the kidney with the reserved fat. Cook for about 8 minutes.

Break the eggs into a bowl and add salt and pepper and the remaining butter, cut into small pieces. Beat with a fork for just 1 minute.

When the kidney is hot, quickly pour the beaten eggs into the frying pan and cook the omelette in the usual way for about 6 minutes. When the eggs have set sufficiently, fold the omelette over like a turnover and slide it on to a heated oval serving dish. Pour hot veal stock around the omelette and serve immediately.

White or rosé wines: Pouilly-Fumé, Sancerre or Cabernet d'Anjou.
Red wines: Beaune, Mercurey, Beaujolais-Villages.

US	Ingredients	Met/Imp
8	eggs	8
¼ cup	crème fraîche	60 ml/4 tbsp
2 oz	Beaufort cheese	50 g/2 oz
	salt and pepper	
10 tbsp	butter	150 g/5 oz
¼ lb	small potatoes	100 g/4 oz
2	chervil sprigs	2
2	tarragon sprigs	2

OMELETTE SAVOYARDE

—— SAVOY OMELETTE ——

Preparation 20 minutes • Cooking: potatoes 25 minutes; omelette 8 minutes

Beat the eggs and, while still beating, add the crème fraîche, the cheese cut into very thin strips, and the salt and pepper. Heat the butter in a frying pan and, as soon as it has turned golden, pour in the egg mixture. When the omelette is starting to set, add the very thinly sliced potatoes, which have already been sautéed in butter. Sprinkle quickly with a pinch of chopped chervil and tarragon, roll up the omelette and serve immediately.

White wines from Savoy: Seyssel, Crépy, Vin de Savoie Ripaille.

	US	Ingredients	Met/Imp

——— TRUFFLE OMELETTE ———

Preparation 10 minutes • Cooking 5 minutes

US	Ingredients	Met/Imp
8	eggs	8
	salt and pepper	
3 oz	truffles	75 g/3 oz
4 tsp	madeira	20 ml/4 tsp
3 tbsp	butter	40 g/1½ oz

Beat the eggs with salt and pepper. Cut the truffles into thin slices and add to the eggs with the madeira and a large piece of almost melted butter. Stir the eggs with a fork, without beating them too much. Heat the remaining butter in a frying pan until it is nut-brown coloured. Pour in the eggs and cook, stirring constantly, for about 5 minutes or until just set.

White wines: Arbois, Puligny Montrachet, Graves.

POMMES DE TERRE FARCIES AUX ŒUFS POCHÉS

POTATOES STUFFED WITH POACHED EGGS ———

Preparation 1½ hours • Cooking 35 minutes

US	Ingredients	Met/Imp
8	potatoes	8
2 tbsp	butter	25 g/scant 1 oz
¼ cup	crème fraîche	60 ml/4 tbsp
	salt	
	nutmeg	
1 small bowl	Mornay Sauce (*page 73*)	1 small bowl
5 oz	cooked ham	150 g/5 oz
8	poached eggs	8
	breadcrumbs	
	Parmesan cheese, grated	

Select 8 large, evenly shaped potatoes and bake them in the oven. Using the tip of a knife, cut a cross in each one and open them up. Hollow out about two-thirds of the pulp with a spoon, collect it in a bowl and mash with about half of the butter, the crème fraîche, the salt and grated nutmeg. Mix well with a fork and use to refill the potatoes, leaving a hollow in the centre of each one.

Put about 5 ml/1 tsp Mornay sauce and 5 ml/1 tsp chopped lean ham in each hollow and top with a hot and well-drained poached egg. Finish with another 5 ml/1 tsp Mornay sauce. Sprinkle a mixture of half breadcrumbs and half grated Parmesan over the potatoes and sprinkle with melted butter. Brown in a hot oven and serve.

White wines: Vouvray, Rully, Crozes-Hermitage.

SOUFFLÉ AUX ŒUFS POCHÉS

——— SOUFFLÉ WITH POACHED EGGS ———

Preparation 1½ hours • Cooking: lobster à l'Américaine 25 minutes; soufflé 15 minutes; eggs 6 minutes

US	Ingredients	Met/Imp
	cheese soufflé, made with salt, pepper, 1 pinch of nutmeg, 500 ml/18 fl oz (2 cups) milk, 75 g/3 oz (6 tbsp) butter, 100 g/4 oz (¾ cup) flour, 6 eggs separated, 100 g/4 oz (1 cup) grated Parmesan cheese, 100 ml/4 fl oz (½ cup) cream	
8	poached eggs	8
	Américaine Sauce (*page 60*)	
1, about 10 oz	lobster, cooked	1, about 300 g/10 oz
2 oz	truffles, cooked	50 g/2 oz

Make a very creamy soufflé mixture with the Parmesan and cook in a moderate oven for about 15 minutes. Just before serving, lift up the browned top and place the lightly cooked poached eggs inside. Serve with an Américaine sauce which has had a little cream added to it and been worked through a sieve lined with cheesecloth. Add the chopped lobster and truffles to the sauce.

White wines: Pouilly-Fuissé, Graves, Hermitage.

US	Ingredients	Met/Imp
8	eggs	8
1 cup	Gruyère cheese, grated	125 g/4½ oz
	salt and pepper	
	oil for deep frying	
	GARNISH	
	fried parsley	
16	slices bread, without crusts	16

—— FRIED 'SNOW EGGS' ON TOAST ——

Preparation 45 minutes • Cooking 6 minutes

Separate the eggs and add the grated cheese to the yolks with some salt and pepper. Beat vigorously until a paste is formed. Cut the bread slices, which should be about 5 mm/¼ inch thick, into rounds with the help of a wineglass. Put a little yolk paste on each piece of bread.

Add a little salt to the egg whites and beat until they are as stiff as possible. Cover the pieces of bread with a layer of egg white.

Heat the oil in a deep fat fryer. Place the pieces of bread gently on the surface of the oil with a fork, as when making fritters. Cook for about 6 minutes or until the bread is nicely browned, then remove the slices from the pan. The egg white, having stayed out of the oil, should have cooked without changing colour. Serve with a garnish of fried parsley.

White wines: Graves, Meursault, Chablis.

US	Ingredients	Met/Imp
14 oz	tomatoes	400 g/14 oz
4 tbsp	butter	50 g/2 oz
½ cup	onion, chopped	75 g/3 oz
1 pinch	thyme	1 pinch
	salt and pepper	
8	eggs	8
4	slices chorizo sausage	4
4	small slices salted ham	4
6 tbsp	crème fraîche	75 g/3 oz
2 oz	Gruyère cheese	50 g/2 oz
	paprika	

—— TORTILLA FROM THE MOUNTAINS ——

Preparation 40 minutes • Cooking 30 minutes • Serves 4

Remove the stalks from the tomatoes and drop them into boiling water for a few moments. Cool them in cold water and then peel them. Remove the seeds and dice the flesh. Melt a piece of butter in a saucepan and, when it is hot, add the chopped onion. Fry until translucent, then add the tomatoes. Mix in the thyme, add salt and pepper and cook over a moderate heat for 5–8 minutes or until the liquid has evaporated, stirring constantly. Remove from the heat and keep warm.

Break the eggs into a bowl and add salt and pepper (not too much, since the tomatoes, chorizo and ham are already salted). Beat lightly with a fork. Melt 30 g/1 oz (2 tbsp) of the remaining butter in a frying pan and pour in the eggs. Half-cook the omelette, then shake the frying pan vigorously so that the omelette becomes detached.

Set aside 15 ml/1 tbsp of the tomato mixture and keep warm. Mix the remaining tomatoes with the eggs which are still very soft, then add the slices of chorizo and ham, placing them alternately in the omelette. Toss the omelette to turn it over like a pancake. Leave it on the heat for a few minutes more to brown the other side. Spread the remaining butter on a flameproof serving dish. Slide the omelette on to the dish (with the ham and chorizo underneath). Coat with crème fraîche and garnish the surface with thin lozenge-shaped pieces of cheese. Brown quickly under the grill (broiler). Garnish the middle of the tortilla with the remaining tomato mixture. Sprinkle with a pinch of paprika and serve hot.

Red wines: Madiran, Tursan, Gaillac, Cahors, Côtes de Buzet.

FISH

FISH IS OF CONSIDERABLE NUTRITIONAL value: an excellent source of protein, phosphorus and vitamins. Although some fish such as turbot or John Dory are expensive, others (sardine, herring, hake, cod) make excellent economical dishes. Besides, the price of certain fish does not only reflect how much of a delicacy they are, but also how they will look on the table at a grand occasion: this is true of turbot, salmon, pike, etc. The percentage of waste is also an important factor: there is almost twice as much waste on a gilt-head bream or John Dory as there is on a dab or a mackerel, for example.

Fish may be subdivided into two main types: those whose habitat is the sea, and which are more numerous and varied (dogfish, sardine, ray, sole, brill, conger eel, monkfish, etc.), and those that live in rivers (some of which also live in the sea, such as the eel and the salmon). Fish may also be classed as either lean (bass, pike, cod, gilt-head bream, dab, whiting, ray, sole, trout) or fatty (eel and conger eel, herring, lamprey, mackerel, sardine, salmon, tuna), the latter type being less easy to digest, but no more difficult than mutton or pork. Freshness is the most important quality in fish. Signs of freshness are rigidity of body, firmness of flesh, shininess of scales, near-transparency of the eye and bright red colour of the branchiae under the gills; fish, shellfish and crustaceans should not smell of ammonia.

As a general rule, when gutting the largest fish (ray, pike, salmon, turbot, etc), an incision is made in the stomach, whereas smaller ones (trout, herring, whiting, etc) are gutted through the gills. To braise a large fish, small incisions are made on its back and it is cut lengthways along the bone. The soft roe and the eggs are left in place, in particular in the case of the herring. As for the mullet, it is not gutted at all.

There are five classic methods of cooking fish: poaching in an often highly flavoured *court bouillon*; grilling (broiling); braising; frying; and cooking in a *matelote* sauce. We must also mention steaming, cooking in foil (in the oven or over charcoal) and marinating with lemon juice. Leftovers from fish which have been poached or braised may be served cold as an entrée or used in salads, gratins, *en coquilles*, etc.

One of the techniques which probably demands the greatest skill in the preparation of flat or round fish is removing the fillets. If you get the fishmonger to do this for you, you should ask him for the trimmings and the bones, which are indispensable for flavouring the Fish Fumet (*page 57*) in which the fish will be cooked.

Care must always be taken not to overcook fish without, however, making the opposite mistake of undercooking it. The bone but not the flesh should have a pinkish hue when the fish is just cooked. Recognizing the ideal degree of doneness is quite a subtle point and is acquired with experience. If this degree of doneness is missed, the flesh becomes either dry or hard, or soft and watery.

Boiled potatoes are not the obligatory accompanying vegetable for fish. Many vegetables may happily be served with it – spinach, broccoli, ratatouille, cabbage, leeks or chicory (Belgian endive) and, indeed, rice or fresh pasta. Curnonsky, who readily declared himself to be piscivorous, liked to quote, by way of example, 'his dear Brittany', which glories in its 300 fish recipes. 'One thousand million people live on almost nothing but fish, and,' he would add, 'I would gladly be counted amongst them.'

ALOSE

SHAD

SHAD IS IN FACT A MIGRATORY FISH WHICH LIVES IN THE SEA and swims up river in the spring to lay its eggs. The Loire shad is especially renowned, but this fish is also caught in the Garonne and the Adour. Its flesh is of very high quality, but riddled with bones.

ALOSE DE LA LOIRE À L'OSEILLE

—— LOIRE SHAD WITH SORREL ——

Preparation 5 minutes • Cooking 25 minutes

US	Ingredients	Met/Imp
I, about 3 lb	shad	I, about 1.5 kg/3 lb
	salt and pepper	
½ cup	oil	100 ml/4 fl oz
2 lb	sorrel, puréed	I kg/2 lb
4 tbsp	butter	50 g/2 oz
I	lemon, juice of	I
	GARNISH	
4	hard-boiled eggs	4
I	lemon, slices of	I

Using a sharp knife, make small incisions along the back of the shad. Season with salt and pepper. Pour over the oil and cook under a hot grill (broiler) for 5 minutes, turning and basting once. Finish cooking in a moderately hot oven, on a bed of sorrel purée, dotted with the diced butter sprinkled with the lemon juice, for a further 20 minutes. The acidity of the sorrel should make the shad's small bones disappear.

Serve hot with the sorrel purée, garnished with wedges of hard-boiled egg and lemon slices.

The shad could also be stuffed with sorrel purée.

Dry white wines: Saumur, Sancerre, Muscadet, Chablis.

ALOSE À LA PROVENÇALE

—— SHAD PROVENÇAL ——

Preparation 10 minutes • Cooking 7 hours

US	Ingredients	Met/Imp
	cut garlic cloves	
2 lb	sorrel	I kg/2 lb
20	button (pearl) onions	20
I, about 3 lb	shad	I, about 1.5 kg/3 lb
	chopped fresh thyme	
½ cup	olive oil	100 ml/4 fl oz
¼ cup	*marc from Provence*	60 ml/4 tbsp
	salt and pepper	

A large, close-fitting pan is required for this dish. Rub the pan well with garlic and then put a layer of sorrel and chopped onions in it. Put some slices of shad on this bed, then cover them with another layer of vegetables. Make another layer of shad and top with a final layer of vegetables. Sprinkle with thyme, pour in the oil and marc and season with salt and pepper.

Cook over very low heat for 7 hours, weighting the lid down if necessary to make sure none of the flavour escapes. When the lid is removed, the vegetables will perhaps have lost their flavour, but the flesh of the shad, from which all the bones will have miraculously disappeared, will be a real treat.

White wines: Cassis, Bellet, Côtes de Provence, Hermitage.

SHAD WITH TOMATOES
AND WHITE WINE

Preparation 10 minutes • Cooking 25–30 minutes

US	Ingredients	Met/Imp
10 tbsp	butter	150 g/5 oz
6	tomatoes	6
1	garlic clove	1
1, about 3 lb	shad	1, about 1.5 kg/3 lb
	salt and pepper	
	quatre-épices	
2	onions	2
¼ lb	mushrooms	100 g/4 oz
1 wineglass	dry white wine	1 wineglass

Put about one-third of the butter, diced, 3 skinned, de-seeded and chopped tomatoes and the chopped garlic in the bottom of a flameproof casserole. Put the shad on the bed of tomatoes, add salt, pepper, a good pinch of spice and the finely chopped onions, then cover with the remaining chopped tomato flesh and the chopped mushrooms. Pour on the wine and the remaining butter, melted. Cook for a few minutes, covered, on top of the stove, then finish cooking in a moderately hot oven for a further 20–25 minutes.

Dry white wines: Saumur, Sancerre, Quincy, Muscadet, Chablis, Mâcon-Villages.

ANGUILLE

EEL

AN EEL CAUGHT IN RUNNING WATER MAY BE IDENTIFIED BY its light brown skin, with shades of green on the back and silver on the stomach. It is preferable to eels from stagnant waters, which always have muddy-tasting flesh and which are distinguished by their dark brown backs and dirty yellow stomachs.

As far as possible, eels should always be bought alive and killed just before cooking. Their flesh goes off very quickly.

Preparation: Kill the eel and, using a sharp knife, make a small circular incision at the base of the head. Turn back the skin slightly, grasp it with a cloth and pull it off in one go. This may be easier if the eel is tied around the head and hung from a nail. Cut the barbs off the back and the stomach with scissors and then open the eel slightly to gut it.

Smoked eel, cut into thin slices, may also be served as an hors-d'oeuvre.

ANGUILLE BOUILLIE À LA MINUTE

BOILED EEL

Preparation 20 minutes • Cooking 15 minutes

US	Ingredients	Met/Imp
1, about 3 lb	eel	1, about 1.5 kg/3 lb
	salt	
1	lemon, juice of	1
	Maître d'Hôtel Butter, to serve (page 52)	

Skin, gut and wash the eel. Cut it into sections and cook in salted water for about 15 minutes. Place the eel on a heated serving dish. Serve sprinkled with the lemon juice and surrounded with celery purée, accompanied by hot maître d'hôtel butter.

Dry white wines: Meursault, Pouilly-Fuissé, Mâcon-Viré.

ANGUILLE À LA BROCHE

EEL ON SKEWERS

Preparation 30 minutes • Marinating 1 hour • Cooking 45 minutes

US	Ingredients	Met/Imp
1, about 3½ lb	eel	1, about 1.6 kg/3½ lb
½ cup	extra-virgin olive oil	100 ml/4 fl oz
1	bouquet garni	1
2	chive stems	2
	salt and pepper	
1 pinch	quatre-épices	1 pinch

Skin, gut and wash the eel. Cut it into sections and marinate for at least 1 hour in the oil with the bouquet garni, chives, salt, pepper and spice.

Push the eel pieces on to skewers and roast them in the oven, turning and basting with marinade from time to time. Serve accompanied by a peppery sauce.

Dry white wines: Chablis, Mâcon-Viré, Arbois.
Dry rosé wines: Cabernet d'Anjou, Tavel, Côtes de Provence.

US	Ingredients	Met/Imp
3 lb	medium eels	1.5 kg/3 lb
½ cup	olive oil	100 ml/4 fl oz
2	parsley sprigs	2
1	garlic clove	1
6 tbsp	flour	50 g/2 oz
3 cups	dry white wine	750 ml/1¼ pints
	salt and pepper	
1	bouquet garni	1
2	dried hot red chillies (chili peppers)	2

ANGUILLE À LA CATALANE

EEL CATALAN STYLE

Preparation 20 minutes • Cooking 25 minutes

Skin, gut and wash the eels. Cut them into sections and place in a saucepan with the oil, chopped parsley and garlic. Fry gently for about 5 minutes, then sprinkle with the flour, pour in the wine and season with plenty of salt and pepper. Add the bouquet garni and chillies and leave to cook for about 20 minutes. The sauce may be thickened with a little Aïoli (*page 60*) just before serving.

White wines: Chablis, Mâcon-Villages, Côtes de Provence.

US	Ingredients	Met/Imp
1, about 4 lb	eel	1, about 1.8 kg/4 lb
½ cup	oil	100 ml/4 fl oz
¼ cup	vinegar	50 ml/2 fl oz
2	carrots	2
1	onion	1
2	shallots	2
	salt and pepper	
7 oz	pork or bacon fat	200 g/7 oz
10 tbsp	butter	150 g/5 oz

ANGUILLE RÔTIE

ROAST EEL

Preparation 30 minutes • Marinating several hours • Cooking 30 minutes

Skin the eel, trim it and leave to marinate for several hours in the oil, vinegar, chopped vegetables and seasoning.

Roll up the eel and stick a skewer through the layers so that it cannot unroll. Thread it with the fat cut into *lardons* and roast it on a rotisserie spit, or in a roasting pan in the oven turning it over several times, for 30 minutes. Baste it with the melted butter and serve hot with a spicy sauce.

White wines: Arbois, Savennières.

US	Ingredients	Met/Imp
about 3½ lb	medium eels	about 1.6 kg/3½ lb
	salt and pepper	
½ cup	walnut oil	100 ml/4 fl oz
20	button (pearl) onions	20
6 tbsp	flour	50 g/2 oz
1 bottle	dry white wine from Anjou or red from Poitou	1 bottle
1	bouquet garni	1
½ cup	crème fraîche	100 ml/4 fl oz

BOUILLETURE D'ANGUILLES À L'ANGEVINE

ANJOU EEL STEW

Preparation 30 minutes • Cooking 1 hour 20 minutes

Skin, gut and wash the eels. Cut them into sections 4–5 cm/1½–2 inches long. Season with salt and pepper and sauté in the hot walnut oil with the onions. When it is all nicely browned, add the flour and pour in the wine. Add the bouquet garni and cook slowly for about 1 hour 20 minutes. Mix in the crème fraîche just before serving.

Wines: as a general rule, serve the same wine as the one used for cooking.

EELS STEWED IN WHITE WINE

Preparation 40 minutes • Cooking about 2 hours

US	Ingredients	Met/Imp
about 3½ lb	medium eels	about 1.6 kg/3½ lb
¾ cup	flour	100 g/4 oz
½ lb (2 sticks)	butter	250 g/8 oz
20	button (pearl) onions	20
1	garlic clove	1
2	shallots	2
¼ cup	cognac	50 ml/2 fl oz
½ cup	dry white wine	100 ml/4 fl oz
½ cup	Fish Fumet (*page 57*) salt and pepper	100 ml/4 fl oz

Skin, gut and wash the eels. Cut eels into sections, coat them with some of the flour and then brown them in butter in a frying pan along with the onions. When it is all a nice golden colour, add the finely chopped garlic and shallots. Flambé with cognac, then pour in the wine and the fish fumet, season and cook for 15–20 minutes. Remove the eel and onions and keep warm. Make a light roux with half of the remaining butter and the flour and pour in the eel stock. Leave this sauce to simmer for 1 hour. Arrange the sections of eel in an ovenproof dish, garnish with the onions and cover with the sauce. Brown in a hot oven with the remaining butter.

Wines: as a general rule, serve the same wine as the one used for cooking.

EELS STEWED IN RED WINE

Preparation 40 minutes • Cooking about 2 hours

US	Ingredients	Met/Imp
1½ sticks	butter	175 g/6 oz
2	carrots	2
1	leek (white part)	1
1	onion	1
2	shallots	2
2 bottles	good red wine	2 bottles
1	thyme sprig	1
2	parsley sprigs	2
½	bay leaf	½
1	clove	1
20	button (pearl) onions	20
3 lb	small eels	1.5 kg/3 lb
	nutmeg	
	salt and pepper	
¼ cup	cognac	50 ml/2 fl oz
6 tbsp	flour	50 g/2 oz
3	garlic cloves	3
	GARNISH	
	fried croûtons	
	chopped parsley	

Put one-third of the butter, the sliced carrots, leek, onion and shallots into a large saucepan. Fry until golden, then add the wine, thyme, parsley, bay leaf and clove. Boil over a moderate heat for 1 hour, then set aside to cool.

Fry the button (pearl) onions in half of the remaining butter until golden-brown. Pour in some of the wine sauce and continue cooking until the onions are just tender.

Skin, gut and wash the eels. Slice them into pieces the length of a little finger and put them in a shallow flameproof casserole. Strain the lukewarm sauce on to the eel through a fine sieve. Grate on a little nutmeg and add salt to taste. Add the cognac, bring to the boil, then poach for 20 minutes.

Make a blond roux with the remaining butter and the flour.

Take the eels out of their cooking liquid and put them into a frying pan. Strain the eel stock into the roux through a fine sieve. Add some of the juice from the onions and whisk the sauce until thickened.

Put the onions on top of the eel in the frying pan. Add the finely chopped garlic to the sauce. Season, then boil gently for 30 minutes. Pour the sauce through a fine sieve on to the eel and onions. Bring to the boil.

Arrange the sections of eel on a heated serving dish. Surround them with the onions. Garnish with croûtons and parsley.

Wines: as a general rule, serve the same wine as the one used for cooking.

BASS

CALLED 'LOUP' IN THE MEDITERRANEAN AND 'LOUBINE' OR 'louvine' in the Bay of Biscay, the bass is one of the finest fish. Its flesh is delicate, firm and dense, but smooth. If it weighs less than 500 g/1 lb, it is grilled (or broiled), flavoured with fennel, or cooked 'à la meunière'; if it is large, it is poached in a *court bouillon* (taking care not to overcook) or braised. The bass should be gutted through the gills and through a small incision in the belly. It should only be scaled (taking care not to tear the skin) if it is going to be braised or grilled. Remember to wipe it thoroughly.

BAR À LA FINANCIÈRE

BASS IN WHITE WINE WITH MUSHROOMS AND TRUFFLES

Preparation 35 minutes • Cooking 35 minutes

US	Ingredients	Met/Imp
I, about 3 lb	bass	I, about 1.5 kg/3 lb
14 tbsp	butter	200 g/7 oz
¾ cup	flour	100 g/4 oz
	chicken stock	
¼ lb	mushrooms	100 g/4 oz
3 oz	truffles	75 g/3 oz
about ½ lb	Forcemeat Stuffing (*page 54*), made into quenelles	200 g/7 oz
	COURT BOUILLON	
2	carrots, sliced	2
I	onion, sliced	I
I	bouquet garni	I
I quart	water	I litre/1¾ pints
3 cups	dry white wine	750 ml/1¼ pints
	salt and pepper	

Gut, trim and scale the bass. Wipe it thoroughly. Place the fish in a pan, cover it with a piece of cheesecloth and add the ingredients for the court bouillon. Poach over a low heat for about 20 minutes. Remove the bass from the liquid and keep warm.

For the sauce, make a roux with the butter and flour and stir in equal quantities of chicken stock and bass cooking liquid to give a coating consistency; the sauce must remain straw-coloured. Add the mushrooms, truffles and quenelles and heat through. Just before serving, remove the cheesecloth that is protecting the fish, drain well and place on a heated serving dish. Coat with the sauce.

White wines: dry Graves, Chablis, Alsace Riesling, Meursault, Pouilly-Fuissé.

LOUP GRILLÉ AU FENOUIL

——— GRILLED BASS WITH FENNEL ———

Preparation 15 minutes • Cooking 30 minutes

US	Ingredients	Met/Imp
I, about 3 lb	bass	I, about 1.5 kg/3 lb
	olive oil	
a few	fennel leaves and seeds	a few
	thyme sprigs	
	salt	
I small glass	aniseed spirit (pastis, ouzo, etc)	I small glass
I stick	butter	100 g/4 oz

Gut, trim and scale the bass. Wipe it thoroughly. Make incisions in each side. Brush it all over with olive oil and put the fennel leaves inside. Put the seeds in the incisions with a few sprigs of thyme and a little salt.

Grill (or broil) the bass for 10–15 minutes on each side. Just before serving, flambé with the spirit. Serve just as it is, with a dish of fresh butter.

Wines: fine white wines from the south of France: Cassis, Bellet, Châteauneuf-du-Pape.

LOUP AU FOUR À LA BOLOGNAISE

——— BAKED BASS BOLOGNAISE ———

Preparation 15 minutes • Cooking 15 minutes

US	Ingredients	Met/Imp
I, about 4 lb	bass	I, about 1.8 kg/4 lb
I stick	butter	100 g/4 oz
a few	parsley sprigs	a few
2	garlic cloves	2
½ cup	olive oil	100 ml/4 fl oz
½ cup	Marsala wine	100 ml/4 fl oz
	salt and pepper	

Gut, trim and scale the bass. Wipe it thoroughly. Spread some butter, chopped parsley and garlic in a flameproof dish and lay the bass on top. Pour in the olive oil and Marsala. Season with salt and pepper. Cover the dish and cook on top of the stove for 5 minutes, then finish cooking in a moderately hot oven for about 10 minutes. Serve hot.

Dry white wines: Chablis, Mâcon-Viré, Cassis.

LOUP AU FOUR À LA MARSEILLAISE

——— BASS MARSEILLAISE ———

Preparation 15 minutes • Cooking 15 minutes

US	Ingredients	Met/Imp
I, about 3 lb	bass	I, about 1.5 kg/3 lb
½ cup	olive oil	100 ml/4 fl oz
½ cup	dry white wine	100 ml/4 fl oz
I	bouquet garni	I
I	fennel bulb	I
2	garlic cloves	2
2 cups	Fish Fumet (*page 57*)	500 ml/18 fl oz
¼ lb	mushrooms	100 g/4 oz
I	lemon, juice of	I
15	button (pearl) onions	15
I lb	firm waxy potatoes	500 g/1 lb
	salt and pepper	
I stick	butter	100 g/4 oz
2	parsley sprigs	2
	Aïoli (*page 60*)	

Gut, trim and scale the bass. Wipe it thoroughly. Put it into an oval flameproof dish with the oil and wine. Add the bouquet garni, chopped fennel and garlic, the fish fumet, the quartered mushrooms sprinkled with the lemon juice, the blanched onions and the potatoes sliced 5 mm/¼ inch thick. Season with salt and pepper and cover with oiled greaseproof (wax) paper or foil.

Cook the bass in a hot oven for about 30 minutes, basting frequently. When cooked, drain off the cooking liquid into a frying pan and boil with the butter to obtain a light liaison, then season with salt and pepper. Pour over the bass and simmer for a few moments. Serve immediately, garnished with the parsley. Serve the aïoli on the side.

Dry white wines: Côtes de Provence, Vins du Pays des Sables du Golfe du Lion.

BARBUE

BRILL

A FLAT FISH LIKE TURBOT, BRILL HAS FINE, LEAN, WHITE and nutritious flesh, which is particularly tasty. It is gutted by making a transverse incision beneath the head near where the skin is dark. It should then be scaled on both sides and trimmed.

Brill cooked whole should be cut lengthways down the middle on the dark side and the bone should be broken so that the fish does not become deformed by the effect of the heat in cooking. The recipes given for brill – grilled (or broiled), poached, roasted or braised, with wine, champagne or even cider – are suitable for many flat fish (particularly sole and turbot) as well as for most sea fish. When garnished with prawns, shrimp, mussels or crayfish, brill can be made into a really high-class dish.

BARBUE FOURRÉE AU FOIE GRAS ET AUX CHAMPIGNONS

BRILL STUFFED WITH FOIE GRAS AND MUSHROOMS

Preparation 30 minutes • Cooking 30 minutes

US	Ingredients	Met/Imp
1, about 4½ lb	brill	1, about 2 kg/4½ lb
	butter for greasing	
2 cups	dry white wine	500 ml/18 fl oz
2	lemons, juice of	2
¼ cup	madeira	50 ml/2 fl oz
½ cup	Fish Fumet (page 57)	100 ml/4 fl oz
14 oz	mushrooms	400 g/14 oz
½ cup	crème fraîche	100 ml/4 fl oz
1 lb	foie gras	500 g/1 lb
1 lb	Lobster Butter (page 51)	500 g/1 lb
1 tbsp	tomato paste	15 ml/1 tbsp
	salt and pepper	
1 tsp	paprika	5 ml/1 tsp

Gut, scale and trim the brill. Put it on the ridged bottom of a turbotière (a diamond-shaped dish for cooking flat fish in) or in a flameproof dish which has been generously greased with butter and pour in the white wine, lemon juice, madeira and fish fumet. Cook on top of the stove for 5 minutes, then finish cooking in the oven (about 20 minutes) with the turbotière or dish covered.

When the brill is cooked, take it out and cut it lengthways on the dark side. Carefully lift up the fillets and remove the backbone. Spread a stuffing, made from 350 g/12 oz of the mushrooms puréed with a little of the crème fraîche and mixed with the foie gras, all over the inside of the fish. Reshape the brill, remove the dark skin and keep warm.

Reduce the brill cooking liquid, remove from the heat and mix in some well-flavoured lobster butter and the remaining crème fraîche, the tomato paste, salt, pepper and paprika. Add the remaining mushrooms, blanched and thinly sliced. Pour this sauce over the reshaped brill and glaze in a hot oven.

Dry white wines: Alsace Pinot Gris, Côtes de Provence, Gaillac.

BRILL IN WHITE WINE*

Preparation 15 minutes • Cooking 30 minutes

US	Ingredients	Met/Imp
I, about 5 lb	brill	I, about 2.3 kg/5 lb
2½ sticks	butter	300 g/10 oz
	salt and pepper	
2 cups	dry white wine	500 ml/18 fl oz

This recipe may be used for all flat fish (sole, dab, etc). The white wine may be replaced by mussel stock, mushroom stock, *court bouillon* or by a concentrated onion and shallot stock. Whichever stock is used, it should be highly concentrated. Cooking the fish in a dish without a rim is recommended, so that it cooks uniformly, with a nice light golden colour achieved by frequent basting.

Gut, scale and trim the brill. Cut it along its entire length on the dark side, so as to separate the fillets, then put in a large piece of butter and some salt and pepper. Reshape the brill. Grease a flat ovenproof dish generously with butter. Put the fish in it, dark side down, pour in the wine and coat the white surface of the fish with some of the remaining butter, slightly melted. Season with salt and pepper. Cook uncovered in a moderately hot oven, basting often, until cooked (about 25 minutes). At this point, gradually whisk the remaining butter into the cooking liquid, so as to blend in completely and not to form an oily mixture. In this way, a very tasty stock is obtained.

Wines: as a general rule, serve the same wine as the one used for cooking.

FILETS DE BARBUE AU CHABLIS

BRILL FILLETS WITH CHABLIS

Preparation 10 minutes • Cooking 25 minutes

US	Ingredients	Met/Imp
I, about 4½ lb	brill	I, about 2 kg/4½ lb
2 cups	Chablis	500 ml/18 fl oz
¼ cup	truffle liquid	50 ml/2 fl oz
½ lb	mushrooms	250 g/8 oz
scant I cup	Fish Fumet (*page 57*)	200 ml/7 fl oz
	salt	
	paprika	
3	egg yolks	3
½ lb (2 sticks)	butter	250 g/8 oz
¼ cup	cognac	50 ml/2 fl oz
2 tbsp	*crème fraîche*	30 ml/2 tbsp
I	lemon, juice of	I
3 oz	truffles	75 g/3 oz
2	sweet peppers	2

Fillet the brill and poach in the Chablis with the truffle liquid and the thinly sliced mushrooms for about 10 minutes. When the brill fillets are cooked, drain and keep warm with the mushrooms. Add the fish fumet to the cooking liquid and reduce over high heat. Put the reduced stock in a saucepan, along with the cooked mushrooms, a pinch of salt and paprika, the egg yolks and just under half of the butter, cut into pieces.

Stir over a low heat. As soon as the sauce begins to thicken, gradually add the remaining butter, the cognac, crème fraîche and lemon juice.

When the sauce is ready, put in a truffle *julienne* and the blanched, sliced peppers and pour over the brill fillets. Glaze in a hot oven, then serve.

Wines: as a general rule, serve the same wine as the one used for cooking.

US	Ingredients	Met/Imp
I, about 4½ lb	brill	I, about 2 kg/4½ lb
1½ pints	mussels	750 ml/1¼ pints
¼ lb	cooked prawns or shrimp	125 g/4½ oz
½ lb	mushrooms, lightly poached	200 g/7 oz
6 tbsp	flour	50 g/2 oz
14 tbsp	butter	200 g/7 oz
1¼ cups	Fish Fumet (page 57)	300 ml/½ pint
	pepper	
	nutmeg	
I	bouquet garni	I
½ cup	dry white wine	100 ml/4 fl oz
2	egg yolks	2

BRILL FILLETS DIEPPOISE

Preparation 40 minutes • Cooking 40 minutes

Fillet the brill and skin the fillets by sliding a sharp thin knife between the skin and the flesh. Cut the fillets into diagonal slices. Flatten them slightly with a moistened cutlet bat (meat mallet or pounder) and put them into a buttered flameproof dish. Cover with buttered greaseproof (wax) paper and keep in a cool place. Steam the mussels open, discarding any that do not open, and discard the shells. Pour off and reserve the liquid. Peel the prawns or shrimp, and thinly slice the lightly poached mushrooms (reserve the cooking liquid).

Make a blond roux with the flour and 50 g/2 oz (4 tbsp) butter. Mix the fish fumet into the roux, season with pepper and a hint of nutmeg, then bring to the boil, stirring. Add the bouquet garni and some pieces of mushroom skin and boil gently for 25 minutes, occasionally skimming off any scum or impurities from the surface.

Twenty minutes before serving, uncover the brill fillets and pour over the wine, 60 ml/4 tbsp of the reserved mussel liquid and the same amount of the mushroom cooking liquid. Add 50 g/2 oz (4 tbsp) of the remaining butter, cut into pieces. Bring to the boil on top of the stove. Cover the fillets again with the greaseproof (wax) paper and simmer very gently until the fish is cooked and the flesh feels firm to the touch (about 10 minutes). Drain the fillets, arrange them on a heated serving dish and surround them with the mussels, mushrooms and prawns or shrimp. Cover and keep warm.

Reduce the brill cooking liquid to about 45 ml/3 tbsp. Sieve the prepared sauce into a clean pan. Add the egg yolks mixed with 30 ml/2 tbsp of the mushroom cooking liquid and the brill cooking liquid. Stir over a brisk heat for several minutes, then remove and whisk in the remaining butter. Pour the sauce on to the fillets (but first drain off the liquid which has accumulated on the dish) and put immediately into the top of a hot oven to glaze, so that a thin golden layer forms on the surface. Serve immediately.

Dry and medium dry white wines: Graves, Chablis, Alsace Riesling or Gewürztraminer, Vouvray, Meursault.

US	Ingredients	Met/Imp
I, about 4½ lb	brill	I, about 2 kg/4½ lb
2	onions	2
4	tomatoes	4
2 tbsp	chopped parsley	30 ml/2 tbsp
	salt and pepper	
½ cup	dry white wine	100 ml/4 fl oz
heaping ½ cup	tomato paste	150 g/5 oz
½ cup	Kneaded Butter (page 49)	100 g/4 oz
2 cups	fresh breadcrumbs	100 g/4 oz
	GARNISH	
	truffle strips	

BRILL FILLETS DUGLÉRÉ

Preparation 20 minutes • Cooking 20 minutes

Fillet the brill. Put the sliced onions, skinned, de-seeded and chopped tomatoes and parsley in an ovenproof dish. Put in the brill fillets, season, pour in the wine and cook in a moderate oven for 10–15 minutes. Take out the fillets and keep warm.

Reduce the liquid the fish was cooked in, then mix in the tomato paste and the kneaded butter. Pour over the brill fillets, sprinkle with breadcrumbs and brown quickly in a hot oven. Garnish with truffle strips.

Dry white wines: Arbois, Sancerre, Alsace Sylvaner.

BRILL FILLETS FLORENTINE

Preparation 50 minutes • Cooking 20 minutes

US	Ingredients	Met/Imp
¾ lb	spinach	350 g/12 oz
	salt and pepper	
1 pinch	nutmeg	1 pinch
½ lb (2 sticks)	butter	250 g/8 oz
1, about 4½ lb	brill	1, about 2 kg/4½ lb
½ cup	dry white wine	100 ml/4 fl oz
½ cup	Fish Fumet (page 57)	100 ml/4 fl oz
	Mornay Sauce (page 73)	
¼ cup	Gruyère or Parmesan cheese, grated	25 g/scant 1 oz

Put the spinach into a pan of boiling salted water, boil rapidly for 10 minutes and drain as thoroughly as possible (normally the leaves are left whole, but it is preferable to cut them criss-cross fashion rather than to chop them).

Put the spinach in a frying pan with a pinch of salt, a little pepper, the nutmeg and 25 g/scant 1 oz (2 tbsp) of the butter. Heat through gently.

Fillet the brill and skin the fillets by sliding a sharp knife between the skin and the flesh. Cut each large fillet into 3 diagonal slices and each small fillet into 2 slices. Flatten them slightly with a moistened cutlet bat (meat mallet or pounder) and put them into a buttered flameproof dish. Season with salt and pepper and cover with buttered greaseproof (wax) paper.

Fifteen minutes before serving, pour the wine and fish fumet on to the fish fillets. Add about half of the remaining butter, cut into pieces, bring to the boil on top of the stove, then finish cooking in a moderately hot oven until the fish is white and firm to the touch (about 15 minutes).

Spread out the spinach on a flameproof serving dish and arrange the brill fillets on top. Reduce the cooking liquid rapidly to 30–45 ml/2–3 tbsp at the most and add the Mornay sauce. Cover the fillets with this sauce, sprinkle with grated cheese and the remaining butter, melted, then glaze in a hot oven.

Dry white wines: Arbois, Alsace Pinot Blanc, Montagny, Crozes-Hermitage.

BRILL FILLETS IN ASPIC

Preparation 30 minutes • Cooking 10 minutes • Serves 6

US	Ingredients	Met/Imp
1, about 2 lb	brill	1, about 1 kg/2 lb
	dry white wine	
2	shallots	2
	chopped parsley	
	salt and pepper	
a few	peppercorns	a few
3	tomatoes	3
	Fish Aspic (page 58)	
	GARNISH	
	lemon slices	

Fillet the brill, wash and trim the fillets. Marinate them for a few minutes in a flameproof dish with wine to cover, the chopped shallots, plenty of parsley, salt and a few crushed peppercorns. Bring to the boil, then simmer for about 10 minutes.

Cut the tomatoes in half, season with salt and pepper and leave them to drain on a cloth while the fish is cooking.

As soon as the brill fillets are cooked, drain them carefully and place a tomato half on each fillet. Leave to cool, then coat with aspic jelly. Leave in a cool place to set. Serve surrounded by lemon slices.

White wine: Alsace Gewürztraminer, Pacherenc du Vic-Bihl, dry Graves.

BROCHET

PIKE

THIS RENOWNED FRESHWATER FISH, WHICH GRIMOD DE LA Reynière called the 'Attila of the rivers', is particularly prized for its tasty, firm white flesh. Apart from the classic recipe for Brochet au Beurre Blanc (*below*), fish weighing 1–2 kg/2–4½ lb may be prepared with white wine, 'à la meunière', 'à la juive' or roasted. Small pike may be fried or cooked *au bleu* (sealed in vinegar). Quenelles, mousses and pâtés are possible ways of using the flesh of this fish, which has many bones and, if old, may be a little tough.

BROCHET À LA CANOTIÈRE

PIKE CANOTIÈRE

Preparation 10 minutes • Cooking 40 minutes

US	Ingredients	Met/Imp
1, about 2½ lb	pike	1, about 1.1 kg/2½ lb
3 quarts	court bouillon	3 litres/5¼ pints
1 stick	butter	100 g/4 oz
¾ cup	flour	100 g/4 oz
¼ cup	crème fraîche	50 ml/2 fl oz
	paprika	

Carefully scale the pike, wipe it and put it into the lukewarm court bouillon. Bring to simmering point over a moderate heat, then leave to simmer for a further 25 minutes. Drain and serve whole and hot, with a canotière sauce prepared as follows:

Take half the court bouillon and reduce it by three-quarters over a high heat. Make some *beurre manié* in a saucepan, mixing the cold butter with the flour. Gradually add the hot concentrated court bouillon over a moderate heat, stirring constantly. Leave to boil gently for 10 minutes. Remove from the heat and stir in the crème fraîche and paprika to taste. Stir well until the sauce has a creamy consistency.

White wine: Jasnières.
Red wine: Beaujolais-Villages.

BROCHET DE LA LOIRE AU BEURRE BLANC

LOIRE PIKE WITH BEURRE BLANC

Preparation 10 minutes • Cooking 30 minutes

US	Ingredients	Met/Imp
1, about 4½ lb	pike	1, about 2 kg/4½ lb
	court bouillon	
2 wineglasses	white wine vinegar	2 wineglasses
8	shallots	8
1 lb (4 sticks)	slightly salted butter	500 g/1 lb
	pepper	
	GARNISH	
2	lemons, slices of	2
	parsley sprigs	

Scale and wipe the pike, then poach it in court bouillon for 10 minutes. Reduce the vinegar and finely chopped shallots until all the liquid has evaporated. Add to the pike cooking liquid and finish cooking in a *bain-marie* in a moderately hot oven (about 10 minutes). Remove the pike and whisk the soft butter into the liquid, adding it in small pieces, until the mixture is creamy. Season with pepper. This sauce is to be served on the side at the last moment.

Place the whole pike on a long silver dish. Garnish with lemon slices and parsley sprigs.

Dry white wines: Muscadet, Gros Plant du Pays Nantais, Pouilly-Fumé

BROCHET 'MEURETTE DE SAILLAND'

—— 'MEURETTE DE SAILLAND' PIKE ——

Preparation 10 minutes • Cooking 1 hour 20 minutes

Cut the fish into equal pieces and remove the gills; remove and reserve the heads.

In a deep, heavy saucepan brown the onions in the fat with the bouquet garni. Make a roux with the butter and flour and pour in the wine and stock. Cook the fish heads in this sauce for 40 minutes. Take out the heads and put in the pieces of fish and the finely chopped garlic. Simmer for 30 minutes and serve hot, surrounded by croûtons.

Red wines: Chinon, Bourgueil.

US	Ingredients	Met/Imp
1, about 2 lb	pike	1, about 1 kg/2 lb
2, each about 7 oz	tench	2, each about 200 g/7 oz
1, about 1¼ lb	eel	1, about 600 g/1¼ lb
15	button (pearl) onions	15
¼ lb	pork or bacon fat	100 g/4 oz
1	bouquet garni	1
1 stick	butter	100 g/4 oz
6 tbsp	flour	50 g/2 oz
2 cups	red wine	500 ml/18 fl oz
2 cups	stock	500 ml/18 fl oz
8	garlic cloves	8
8	croûtons	8

BROCHETON À LA SÉNONAISE

—— SMALL PIKE FROM SENS ——

Preparation 20 minutes • Cooking 1 hour 5 minutes

First, make the court bouillon with the wine, water, carrots, onion and shallots, all finely chopped, the bouquet garni and salt. Bring to the boil and boil gently for 25–30 minutes, then strain. Meanwhile, brown the chopped onions and shallots in a little of the butter. Cut the barbels, fins and tail off the pike. Rinse it and make a lengthways cut into the fillet flesh on both sides.

Cover the bottom of a narrow flameproof dish with the cooked onion and shallot. Lay the pike on top, add the court bouillon and a little of the remaining butter, cut into small pieces. Bring to the boil, then cook in a moderately hot oven for 35 minutes.

Drain the pike and place it on a long dish. Rub a little of the remaining butter over it to make it shiny and surround it with parsley. Keep warm. Strain the cooking liquid through a fine sieve, pressing the mixture to make an onion and shallot purée. Reduce rapidly to 300 ml/½ pint (1¼ cups), then add the tomato paste and walnut butter, made by grinding walnuts finely, adding the remaining butter and pressing through a sieve. Stir well, season and serve on the side.

Dry white wines: Mâcon-Villages, Alsace Sylvaner, Rully, Pouilly-Fuissé.

US	Ingredients	Met/Imp
2	medium onions	2
4	shallots	4
10 tbsp	butter	150 g/5 oz
1, about 3 lb	pike	1, about 1.5 kg/3 lb
1 handful	parsley sprigs	1 handful
1 tbsp	tomato paste	15 ml/1 tbsp
¼ cup	shelled walnuts	25 g/scant 1 oz
	COURT BOUILLON	
2 cups	dry white wine	500 ml/18 fl oz
½ cup	water	100 ml/4 fl oz
a few	carrots	a few
1	small onion	1
3	shallots	3
1	small bouquet garni	1
1 pinch	salt	1 pinch

US	Ingredients	Met/Imp
½ lb	eel flesh	250 g/8 oz
	butter	
2 tbsp	sweet green pepper, diced	20 g/¾ oz
14 oz	sole fillets	400 g/14 oz
14 oz	scallop coral (roe) or diced salmon fillet	400 g/14 oz
14 oz	blanched crayfish tails	400 g/14 oz
2 oz	truffles	50 g/2 oz
7 oz	fresh, raw foie gras	200 g/7 oz
4 tbsp	butter, melted	50 g/2 oz
½ cup	white breadcrumbs	30 g/1 oz
	MOUSSELINE STUFFING	
1½ lb	pike fillets	750 g/1½ lb
4	egg whites	4
4½ cups	double (heavy) cream	1.1 litres/2 pints
	salt and pepper	
	cayenne	
	nutmeg	
	chopped parsley and chervil	

CURNONSKY'S PIKE SAVELOY

Preparation 1 hour • Cooking about 35 minutes

Although this recipe is perhaps a little fanciful and not very easy to put into practice, we thought that reading it might not be without its attractions. Dreaming is not prohibited!

First make the mousseline stuffing. Reduce the pike flesh to a purée, add the egg whites and mix well, then add the cream in several batches, beating constantly. Season with salt, pepper, cayenne, nutmeg and herbs to taste. Keep this stuffing firm in a cool place.

Brown the diced eel flesh in butter with the green pepper, sole, scallop coral and crayfish tails. Mix with the truffles and foie gras and season carefully, then mix in the mousseline stuffing gradually and put the mixture into intestine casings (sausage casings) of the sort used for 'boudin blanc' (fresh white sausage). Divide into sections about 15 cm/6 inches long. Poach for 15 minutes, without allowing to boil.

Let the saveloys cool, then skin them and cover with the melted butter and breadcrumbs. Cook gently in butter for about 10 minutes, without letting them brown, and serve very hot with a creamy leek purée on the side.

Leek purée: Take the white parts of some leeks, which have been blanched and steamed in butter, without browning, until cooked. Purée them carefully, then beat in some cream. Season with salt.

White wines: Saumur, Pouilly-Fumé.

US	Ingredients	Met/Imp
1, about 5½ lb	pike	1, about 2.5 kg/5½ lb
7 oz	pork or bacon fat	200 g/7 oz
6	shallots	6
2–3	bouquets garnis	2–3
	salt and pepper	
¼ cup	cognac	50 ml/2 fl oz
¼ cup	madeira	50 ml/2 fl oz
2 cups	dry white wine	500 ml/18 fl oz
14 tbsp	butter	200 g/7 oz
¼ lb	mushrooms	100 g/4 oz
½ cup	crème fraîche	100 ml/4 fl oz

PIKE FILLET DIJONNAISE

Preparation 30 minutes • Marinating 1–2 days • Cooking 20 minutes

Fillet and skin the pike. Lard the pike fillets with the fat, as for fillet (tenderloin) of beef. Marinate them for one day, or two at the most, with the very finely chopped shallots, the bouquets garnis, salt, pepper, cognac, madeira and white wine.

Grease an ovenproof dish very generously with about half of the butter and put the pike fillets in it, surrounded by the sliced mushrooms. Pour in the marinade and cook for about 20 minutes in a moderately hot oven, basting often, until nicely browned. Add the crème fraîche and remaining butter, cut into pieces, and serve.

Dry white wines: Sancerre, Pouilly-Fumé, Mâcon-Villages, Coteaux Champenois.

RIVER FISH MATELOTE BOURGUIGNON

Preparation 30 minutes • Cooking 1¾ hours

Cut the heads off the fish. Prepare a *court bouillon* with three-quarters of the wine and a reduced fish stock made by cooking the fish heads with the remaining white wine, bouquet garni, chopped large onions and half of the garlic. Strain, pressing hard to extract as much flavour as possible.

Cut the fish into pieces and poach them for 15 minutes in the court bouillon. Pour in the marc and flambé.

Make a white roux with the butter and flour, strain in the fish cooking liquid and add the button (pearl) onions, the pork belly (leaf lard), cut into cubes and blanched, and the remaining garlic, crushed or finely chopped. Cook for about 4 hours. Add the crème fraîche, season and pour the sauce over the fish, arranged in a dish. Garnish with croûtons, fried in butter and rubbed with garlic.

Dry white wines: Mâcon-Viré, Bourgogne-Aligoté, Rully, Pouilly-Fuissé.

US	Ingredients	Met/Imp
about 4½ lb	mixed freshwater fish such as pike, perch, tench, eel	about 2 kg/4½ lb
1½ quarts	dry white wine	1.5 litres/2½ pints
1	bouquet garni	1
4	large onions	4
8	garlic cloves	8
4 tsp	mature *marc*	20 ml/4 tsp
10 tbsp	butter	150 g/5 oz
½ cup	flour	75 g/3 oz
20	button (pearl) onions	20
½ lb	fat belly of pork (fresh leaf lard)	250 g/8 oz
2 cups	*crème fraîche*	500 ml/18 fl oz
	salt and pepper	
	GARNISH	
16	heart-shaped croûtons	16

QUENELLES DE BROCHET

PIKE QUENELLES

Preparation 45 minutes • Cooking 10 minutes

Skin the pike fillets. Pound the flesh and set aside in a dish. Pound the kidney fat, working in the butter towards the end. Set aside. Pound the panada and gradually mix in the kidney fat, pike, eggs and nutmeg to taste. Season and pound for a further 10 minutes.

Press the mixture through a sieve. Shape into quenelles, dusting lightly with flour. Put them in a saucepan full of water and bring to the boil, then drain and arrange on a flameproof dish. Cover them with some Nantua sauce, let them simmer for a few minutes and serve very hot. A finely chopped truffle may be added as a garnish.

White wine: Arbois.

US	Ingredients	Met/Imp
10 oz	pike fillets	300 g/10 oz
10 oz	veal kidney fat	300 g/10 oz
14 tbsp	butter	200 g/7 oz
10 oz	Pastry Panada (page 54)	300 g/10 oz
6	eggs	6
	nutmeg	
	salt and pepper	
	nutmeg	
	Nantua Sauce	

CABILLAUD

COD

'CABILLAUD' IS THE USUAL NAME FOR FRESH COD IN FRANCE. Its white, flaky flesh is suitable for many recipes. Large cod are sold in fillets, steaks or cutlets. The cod is the classic example of lean fish, available all the year round and easy to use. When cooking it in a *court bouillon*, put it in the cold liquid and bring to the boil; remove from the heat when it is two-thirds cooked and leave to continue cooking in the liquid while it is cooling down.

CABILLAUD À LA HOLLANDAISE

FRESH COD WITH HOLLANDAISE

Preparation 35 minutes • Cooking 15 minutes

US	Ingredients	Met/Imp
1, about 4½ lb	cod	1, about 2 kg/4½ lb
	court bouillon made with 2 carrots, 2 onions, some peppercorns, salt and a bouquet garni	
2 lb	small potatoes	about 1 kg/2 lb
1 handful	parsley sprigs	1 handful
	Hollandaise Sauce, to serve (page 70)	

Cook the cod for about 15 minutes in the court bouillon. Serve surrounded with steamed potatoes and parsley sprigs, with a Hollandaise sauce on the side.

Dry white wines: Saumur, Sancerre, Quincy, Chablis, Mâcon-Viré, Cassis, Pouilly-Fuissé.

CABILLAUD À LA TOMATE ET AUX FINES HERBES

FRESH COD WITH TOMATO AND FINES HERBES

Preparation 20 minutes • Cooking 30 minutes • Serves 6

US	Ingredients	Met/Imp
5–6	shallots	5–6
5 tbsp	butter	60 g/2½ oz
4	tomatoes	4
1 pinch	dried thyme	1 pinch
½	bay leaf	½
6, each about 6 oz	cod steaks	6, each about 175 g/6 oz
1 bottle	dry white wine	1 bottle
	salt and pepper	
2 tbsp	crème fraîche	30 ml/2 tbsp
¼ cup	fines herbes (parsley, chervil, tarragon, chives)	60 ml/4 tbsp
1	lemon, juice of	1

Peel the shallots and slice them thinly. Fry them gently in the butter in a small saucepan until transparent, then pour into a large ovenproof dish. Spread out the shallot and put the skinned, de-seeded and chopped tomatoes on top. Add the thyme and bay leaf. Place the cod steaks on top, in a single layer. Pour on the white wine and season with salt and pepper. Put into a hot oven. When the liquid starts to boil, turn off the oven and leave the dish inside for a further 6–7 minutes.

Take the dish out of the oven, remove the cod steaks and keep warm. Pour the fish cooking liquid into a saucepan and reduce by half over a high heat, then strain through a fine sieve, pressing hard. Put the cod steaks back in the dish, mix the crème fraîche with the sauce and pour over the fish. Heat in the oven, then sprinkle with plenty of fines herbes, add the lemon juice and serve immediately.

Wines: as a general rule, serve the same wine as the one used for cooking.

CARPE

CARP

THE CARP LIVES IN RIVERS AND PONDS AND CAN GROW UP TO a weight of 8 kg/18 lb. Carp from ponds has a muddy taste which may be removed either by keeping the fish alive in running water for about 10 days or by making it absorb a glass of vinegar as soon as it has been caught. When gutting carp, the gall bladder situated at the base of the head should be removed, since this would give the fish a bad taste. Fleshy, well-rounded carp are to be preferred and the fish may be roasted, stuffed (particularly 'à la juive'—*page 158*), grilled (or broiled), or braised in wine or beer. Carp is the favourite fish of the Chinese.

CARPE FARCIE

———————— STUFFED CARP ————————

Preparation 1 hour 30 minutes • Cooking 35 minutes

Clean and skin the carp. Lard it with the fat. Make a stuffing with the fish fillets, egg whites, chopped parsley, mushrooms and chopped shallots steamed in butter. Season with salt, pepper, paprika and thyme.

Add some crème fraîche to the stuffing, then fill the carp with it. Place the fish in a well-buttered ovenproof dish, on a bed of sliced carrots, onion and celery. Add a little thyme, the bouquet garni and peppercorns. Braise in a moderatly hot oven until the carp is lightly coloured (about 20 minutes), then pour in the wine and fish fumet. Continue to cook, basting often, for about 15 minutes. As soon as the carp is cooked, take it out of the oven, place it on a dish and keep warm. Add the remaining crème fraîche and the fish velouté to the fish cooking liquid. Reduce and season, then beat in the remaining butter cut into small pieces. Strain through a piece of cheesecloth and coat the fish with the sauce.

White wines: Montrachet, Meursault, Graves, Hermitage.

US	Ingredients	Met/Imp
1, about 6½ lb	carp	1, about 3 kg/6½ lb
¼ lb	pork or bacon fat	100 g/4 oz
2 cups	crème fraîche	500 ml/18 fl oz
14 tbsp	butter	200 g/7 oz
2	carrots	2
1	onion	1
1	celery stalk	1
	dried thyme	
1	bouquet garni	1
4	peppercorns	4
1 quart	dry white wine	1 litre/1¾ pints
1 quart	Fish Fumet (page 57)	1 litre/1¾ pints
½ cup	Fish Velouté (page 57)	100 ml/4 fl oz
	STUFFING	
10 oz	pike or whiting fillets	300 g/10 oz
2–3	egg whites	2–3
2	parsley sprigs	2
2 oz	mushrooms	50 g/2 oz
3	shallots	3
	salt and pepper	
1 tsp	paprika	5 ml/1 tsp
1 pinch	dried thyme	1 pinch

US	Ingredients	Met/Imp
I, about 3 lb	carp	I, about 1.5 kg/3 lb
3 tbsp	olive oil	45 ml/3 tbsp
3 oz	shallots or onions	75 g/3 oz
2	garlic cloves	2
I tbsp	flour	15 ml/I tbsp
3 tbsp	chopped parsley	45 ml/3 tbsp
	salt and pepper	

CARP IN THE JEWISH STYLE

Preparation 20 minutes • Cooking 50 minutes • Serves 4

Scale and wash the fish. Cut into slices 2 cm/¾ inch thick. If there is any soft roe in the carp, keep it to one side. Heat the oil in a flameproof casserole and gently fry the chopped shallots for several minutes until they are transparent. Add the finely chopped garlic and then the flour. Mix carefully and cook for a few moments over a low heat, without browning. Add 15 ml/1 tbsp parsley and put in the carp slices.

Pour in some hot water (or half water, half white wine; or half water, half fish stock), without completely covering the pieces of carp, which must nevertheless be swimming in a considerable amount of liquid. Add salt and pepper (not too much salt if you are using a fish stock which is already salted). Cover and simmer gently for about 30 minutes. Add the soft roe, if used, 10 minutes before the cooking is finished.

When the carp is cooked, add another 15 ml/1 tbsp parsley and turn off the heat. Lift out the carp slices and arrange them on a heated serving dish so as to reshape the fish. Arrange the soft roe, if used, around the carp. Put the casserole back on the heat and boil rapidly to reduce by half (about 10 minutes).

Cover the carp with the sauce and pour the rest into a sauce boat. Sprinkle the carp with the remaining parsley and leave until cold and the sauce has set to a jelly.

White wines: Alsace Riesling, Bourgogne-Aligoté, Mâcon-Villages, Côtes du Rhône, Côtes de Provence, Anjou-Coteaux de la Loire, Vouvray, Sancerre.
Light red wines, non-tannic, served cooled: Touraine, Anjou, Bordeaux Clairet.

US	Ingredients	Met/Imp
4, each about I lb	carp	4, each about 500 g/I lb
I¼ cups	water	300 ml/½ pint
	salt and pepper	
4 tbsp	butter	50 g/2 oz
I cup	flour	150 g/5 oz
6	eggs	6
½ cup	crème fraîche	100 ml/4 fl oz
	nutmeg	
	Nantua Sauce (page 74)	

CARP LOAF

Preparation 40 minutes • Cooking 40 minutes

Carefully fillet and skin the carp. Make a pastry panada according to the instructions on page 54 with the water, a pinch of salt, the butter and flour. Put the carp flesh and the panada into a food processor and process until smooth. Press the mixture through a fine sieve, add the whole eggs, one by one, then the crème fraîche, salt, pepper and a hint of nutmeg.

Generously butter a soufflé mould and put a piece of buttered grease-proof (wax) paper in the base. Fill the mould with the carp mixture and cook in a *bain-marie* in a moderately hot oven for 40 minutes.

Unmould carefully and remove the paper. Serve hot with a Nantua sauce.

White wines: Montrachet, Meursault, Hermitage.

COLIN

HAKE

HAKE IS KNOWN AS 'COLIN' IN THE MARKET PLACE IN FRANCE. It is highly regarded for its white flesh, which is firm, without being hard, and for the numerous recipes for which it is suitable, both hot (with a Mousseline Sauce [*page 74*], au gratin or with a Tomato Sauce [*page 80*]) and cold (with Mayonnaise [*page 72*] or Green Herb Mayonnaise [*page 81*]). It is also a very lean fish with very few bones. Hake goes off more quickly than other fish and must be eaten while it is still very fresh. When served cold, it must be allowed to cool in its *court bouillon*, then placed on a rack so that it drains completely. Recipes given for cod are in general also suitable for hake, as well as for haddock and coley.

COLIN FROID SAUCE TARTARE

— COLD HAKE WITH TARTARE SAUCE —

Preparation 30 minutes • Cooking 15 minutes

Cook the hake in a court bouillon for about 15 minutes, then leave it to cool in the liquid. Drain well, trim and place on a serving dish. Cover with tartare sauce and garnish to taste.

Serve the remaining tartare sauce on the side in a sauce boat.

Dry white wines: Quincy, Cheverny, Meursault.

US	Ingredients	Met/Imp
I, about 3 lb	hake	I, about 1.5 kg/3 lb
	court bouillon	
	salt and pepper	
2 cups	Tartare Sauce (page 80)	500 ml/18 fl oz
	GARNISH	
	hard-boiled eggs	
	tomatoes	
	cornichons	

COLIN À LA TOMATE ET AU VIN BLANC

HAKE WITH TOMATO AND WHITE WINE

Preparation 25 minutes • Cooking 30–40 minutes

Cut the hake into slices 2 cm/¾ inch thick. Fry the thinly sliced onions in the oil, then brown the hake in it. Take out the fish and replace it with the de-seeded and sieved tomatoes. Mix in the flour, stir and add the wine to thin the sauce. Put in the hake and simmer without boiling for 20–30 minutes. Put the hake on a heated serving dish and strain the sauce on to it through a sieve, having first checked the seasoning.

White wines: Côtes de Provence, Coteaux d'Aix-en-Provence, Cassis.
Rosé wines: Cassis, Bandol, Tavel.

US	Ingredients	Met/Imp
I, about 3 lb	hake	I, about 1.5 kg/3 lb
2	onions	2
½ cup	olive oil	100 ml/4 fl oz
10	tomatoes	10
I tbsp	flour	15 ml/I tbsp
2 cups	dry white wine	500 ml/18 fl oz
	salt and pepper	

US	Ingredients	Met/Imp
I, about 3 lb	hake	I, about 1.5 kg/3 lb
	salt and pepper	
I	lemon, juice of	I
I stick	butter	100 g/4 oz
I	onion	I
½ cup	Tomato Sauce (page 80)	100 ml/4 fl oz
I	bouquet garni	I
1½–2 cups	Pilau Rice (page 563)	250 g/8 oz

HAKE CREOLE

Preparation 30 minutes • Cooking 20 minutes

Cut the hake into 8 pieces and put them into cold salted water with the lemon juice.

Put the butter in a saucepan and fry the thinly sliced onion until golden. Add the rinsed hake, pour in enough hot water just to cover, add the tomato sauce and bouquet garni and simmer for 15–20 minutes over a low heat. Check the seasoning.

A dish of pilau rice should already have been prepared in such a way that the grains are still firm. Put the pieces of hake on the rice and serve the sauce from the pan on the side. If liked, a little pepper, 10 ml/2 tsp curry powder and some slices of aubergine (eggplant) may be added during the cooking.

Dry white wines: Saumur, Alsace Pinot Blanc, Sancerre, Quincy, dry Graves, Chablis.

DARNES DE COLIN 'COMME À BIRIATOU'

8, each about 7 oz	hake steaks	8, each about 200 g/7 oz
3	eggs	3
	flour for coating	
	frying oil	
	Creole Rice (page 563)	
2 cups	Tomato Sauce (page 80)	500 ml/18 fl oz
2	sweet peppers	2
3	onions	3
	salt and pepper	

HAKE STEAKS 'AS AT BIRIATOU'*

Preparation 40 minutes. • Cooking 12 minutes

Dip each hake steak into the beaten eggs, coat with flour and fry in the oil for about 6 minutes on each side. Place on a bed of Creole rice and garnish with a purée of tomato sauce, steamed peppers and fried onion rings. Season well.

Dry white wines: Saumur, Sancerre, Quincy, Pouilly-Fumé, Chablis, Montagny.

TRANCHES DE COLIN À LA PROVENÇALE

2	leeks	2
2	large onions	2
I	small fennel bulb	I
scant I cup	olive oil	200 ml/7 fl oz
2	garlic cloves	2
4	tomatoes	4
I tbsp	flour	15 ml/1 tbsp
I tsp	saffron	5 ml/1 tsp
I	bouquet garni	I
I quart	cooked mussels, with liquid reserved	1 litre/2 pints
2, each about 7 oz	hake steaks	2, each about 200 g/7 oz
	salt and pepper	
8	croûtons	8

HAKE STEAKS PROVENÇAL

Preparation 30 minutes • Cooking 20–30 minutes

Cut the leeks, onions and fennel into *julienne* and sweat them in a pan with the olive oil, crushed garlic and skinned, de-seeded and chopped tomatoes. When everything is cooked, sprinkle in the flour.

Add the saffron, bouquet garni and the mussel cooking liquid. Pour this liquid on to the hake steaks, season with salt and pepper and cook them for 10 minutes.

Serve garnished with the mussels and croûtons, which should be toasted in the oven and rubbed with garlic.

Dry white wines: Cassis, Côtes de Provence.

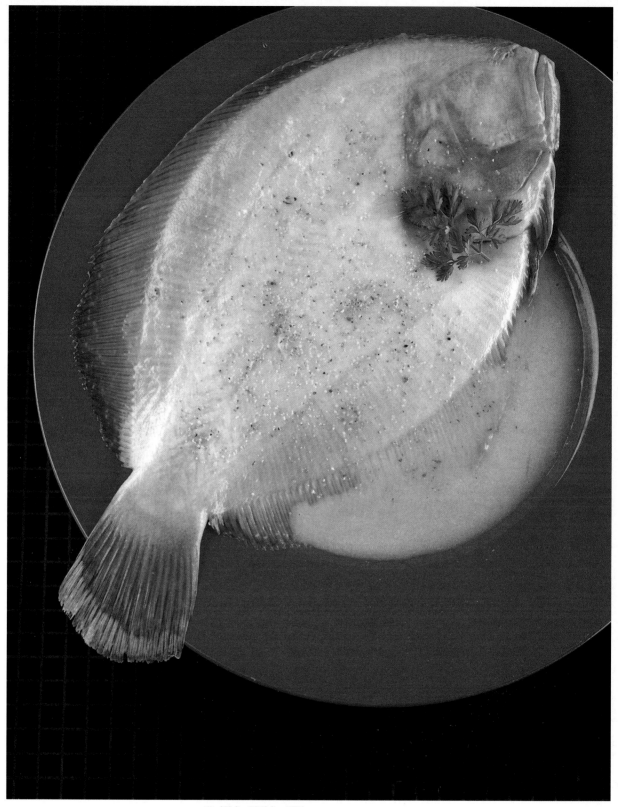

Brill in White Wine
Brill remains very tender when it is basted frequently. The cooking juices of butter and white wine are concentrated to provide a delicious sauce. (Recipe on page 149.)

Gilt-Head Stuffed with Spinach
Since its spine is so easy to remove, even when raw, the gilt-head is often stuffed: with fennel, mushrooms and onions, or with spinach and herbs. On the other hand, removing the scales of this delicious fish is rather difficult, and the operation is therefore best entrusted to one's fishmonger. (Recipe on page 162.)

Skate with Noisette Butter
Poached, drained and then skinned, the wing of the skate is sprinkled with capers, then moistened with noisette butter; be careful not to let the butter burn. (Recipe on page 190.)

Sole with Champagne
The sole is the fish with the largest number of recipes. Cooked whole, it is always more delicious than when filleted, and cooking it in champagne provides a delicate sauce. (Recipe on page 211.)

Grilled Salmon Steaks with Anchovy Butter
Grilled (or broiled) fish is often presented with a fairly strong tasting accompaniment. These fresh salmon steaks, first marinated, then cooked under the grill (broiler), blend perfectly with anchovy fillets pounded with butter. Lemon wedges and sprigs of parsley are the classic garnish; lime wedges can be added for extra colour. (Recipe on page 204.)

Red Mullet with Field Mushrooms
Tender, plump field or other wild mushrooms with a delicate flavour are an unusual accompaniment for red mullet. Although full of bones, this fish is a feast for the gourmet. (Recipe on page 193.)

CONGRE

CONGER

IN FRENCH, THE CONGER IS CALLED BOTH 'CONGRE' (CONGER eel) and 'anguille de mer' (sea eel), because of its shape. Its flesh is fairly hard and relatively bland. It is advisable to avoid the tail piece, which is full of long thin bones. Recipes for hake may also be used for conger eel, with a slightly increased cooking time, but conger is mostly used in soups and *matelotes*.

CONGRE GRATINÉ À L'ITALIENNE

ITALIAN-STYLE CONGER EEL 'AU GRATIN'

Preparation 50 minutes • Cooking 1¼ hours

Make a well-seasoned court bouillon with water and the listed ingredients. Cook it for 45 minutes, then add the wine and strain.

Put the eel into the court bouillon. Cook for about 25 minutes, then take it out, remove the skin and the bones and cut the flesh into thin slices.

Make a thick béchamel sauce with most of the butter, the flour and 450 ml/¾ pint (2 cups) court bouillon. Put the eel in an ovenproof dish between 2 layers of sauce, sprinkle with the grated cheese, add a little butter and brown in the oven.

Any excess court bouillon, thinned with hot water and supplemented by potatoes, carrots and leeks, makes an excellent fish soup.

Dry white wines: Saumur, Sancerre, Quincy, Pouilly-Fumé, Muscadet, Chablis.

US	Ingredients	Met/Imp
I wineglass	dry white wine	I wineglass
I, about 3 lb	conger eel	I, about 1.5 kg/3 lb
14 tbsp	butter	200 g/7 oz
¾ cup	flour	100 g/4 oz
⅓ cup	Parmesan cheese, grated	40 g/1½ oz
	COURT BOUILLON	
8	shallots	8
I	garlic clove	I
I	clove	I
a few	peppercorns	a few
I	thyme sprig	I
I	bay leaf	I
I	tarragon sprig	I

DORADE

GILT-HEAD

THERE ARE SEVERAL VARIETIES OF GILT-HEAD, BUT THE Mediterranean one known as the gilt-head bream is incontestably the best, with its fine, dense, soft skin. The grey gilt-head and the pink gilt-head are a little less delicate but are nevertheless tasty and cheaper. However, the proportion of waste is high, which always makes it a fairly expensive fish. It may be grilled (or broiled), roasted, poached or steamed, and when it is stuffed and cooked in the oven with an aromatic garnish or with slices of lemon, it is a rare delicacy. It is extremely fresh gilt-head that the Japanese use raw for sashimi.

DORADE BERCY

GILT-HEAD BERCY

Preparation 15 minutes • Cooking 25 minutes

US	Ingredients	Met/Imp
I, about 2 lb	gilt-head bream	I, about 1 kg/2 lb
	salt and pepper	
4	shallots	4
	parsley	
¼ lb	mushrooms	100 g/4 oz
6 tbsp	butter	75 g/3 oz
1¼ cups	dry white wine	300 ml/½ pint
	flour	
	TO SERVE	
	fried onions	

Scale, gut and trim the gilt-head and make shallow incisions in its back. Add a little salt and pepper. Put a layer of chopped shallots, parsley and mushrooms in an ovenproof dish greased with butter and lay the fish in it. Pour in the wine, add about one-third of the butter cut into small pieces and cook in the oven for 25 minutes, basting often.

Put the gilt-head on a heated serving dish. Add the remaining butter, with flour worked into it, to the fish cooking liquid. Check the seasoning and pour this over the fish. Serve with fried onions.

White wines: Mâcon-Viré, Pouilly-Fuissé, Chablis, Rully.

DORADE FARCIE AUX ÉPINARDS

GILT-HEAD STUFFED WITH SPINACH*

Preparation 20 minutes • Cooking 45 minutes • Serves 4

US	Ingredients	Met/Imp
3	shallots	3
9 tbsp	butter	125 g/4½ oz
I lb	spinach	500 g/1 lb
I cup	fresh white breadcrumbs	50 g/2 oz
¼ cup	crème fraîche	50 ml/2 fl oz
	salt and pepper	
I, about 3 lb	gilt-head bream	I, about 1.5 kg/3 lb
1–2 wineglasses	dry white wine	1–2 wineglasses
½	lemon, juice of	½
	GARNISH	
	parsley sprigs	
	lemon slices	

The silvery gilt-head bream with bluish-grey backs from the south of France have a finer flavour than the pink gilt-heads, but their skin is less thick and can be less solid when cooking.

Fry the chopped shallots in about one-quarter of the butter for 2–3 minutes. When golden, add the blanched, drained and chopped spinach, and cook for 10 minutes. Remove from the heat and mix with the breadcrumbs and crème fraîche. Season and set aside.

Wash and carefully dry the scaled and gutted gilt-head. Put it on a flat surface. Open up its stomach completely and detach the flesh from the main bone, using a very sharp knife.

Carry out the same operation on the other side of the fish. Cut the bone at the tail and along the dorsal fin, on the inside. The bone can then be removed very easily.

Fill the inside of the fish with the spinach stuffing. Sew up the stomach with a trussing needle and a strong thread. Do not sew too close to the edge or the skin, although fairly thick, may tear while the fish is cooking.

Grease an ovenproof dish with butter, put the gilt-head into it, add a glass of wine and dot the fish with small pieces of butter, reserving one large piece for the sauce. Cook in a moderate oven for 25–30 minutes, basting from time to time and adding another glass of wine if necessary.

Slide the fish on to a heated serving dish. Reduce the cooking liquid and add the reserved butter at the last minute, along with the lemon juice. Serve the gilt-head with this sauce, garnished with parsley sprigs and lemon slices.

Dry white wines: Bourgogne, Meursault, Chablis, Montagny, Hermitage, Châteauneuf-du-Pape, Cassis.

DORADE FARCIE À LA FORESTIÈRE

— STUFFED GILT-HEAD 'FORESTIÈRE' —

Preparation 30 minutes • Cooking 50 minutes

Scale the gilt-head, gut it through its gills, wash it and sponge it dry. Open it along the back on either side of the main bone. Cut the bone at the head and tail and carefully pull it out. Sprinkle salt and pepper inside the fish.

Chop the onions and shallot. Add the chopped parsley, the chanterelles, thoroughly cleaned and chopped into large pieces, and the cultivated mushrooms, thinly sliced with lemon juice added. Mix these ingredients and fry them gently in the butter, uncovered, until all the liquid has evaporated. Mix in the breadcrumbs, beaten egg and sultanas (raisins) and season with salt and pepper. Put this stuffing inside the gilt-head and tie it up, but not too tightly. Put the gilt-head in an ovenproof dish, pour over the oil and bake in a moderately hot oven for 30–35 minutes, basting several times. When the fish is a nice golden colour, carefully untie it and serve it straight from the dish, perhaps garnished with small boiled potatoes and parsley or with grilled (broiled) tomato halves and a little garlic.

White wines: Alsace Riesling or Pinot Gris, Meursault, Chablis, Pouilly-Fuissé, dry Graves, Savennières.

US	Ingredients	Met/Imp
1, about 3 lb	gilt-head bream	1, about 1.5 kg/3 lb
	salt and pepper	
2	onions	2
1	shallot	1
2 tbsp	parsley	30 ml/2 tbsp
¼ lb	chanterelle mushrooms	100 g/4 oz
¼ lb	cultivated mushrooms	100 g/4 oz
1	lemon, juice of	1
2 tbsp	butter	25 g/scant 1 oz
2 tbsp	fresh white breadcrumbs	30 ml/2 tbsp
1	egg	1
1 tbsp	sultanas (golden raisins)	15 ml/1 tbsp
2 tbsp	corn oil	30 ml/2 tbsp

US	Ingredients	Met/Imp
4, each about 14 oz	gilt-head breams	4, each about 400 g/14 oz
	salt and pepper	
½ cup	olive oil	100 ml/4 fl oz
	fennel stalks	
	thyme and rosemary sprigs	
scant 1 cup	Rémoulade Sauce (*page 77*)	200 ml/7 fl oz

GILT-HEAD BARBECUED MARSEILLE STYLE

Preparation 10 minutes • Cooking 25 minutes

This method may be used for other Mediterranean fish such as bass, couch's sea bream, white bream, pandora, etc.

Scale and gut the gilt-head. Make a few cuts on each side, season with salt and pepper and leave to marinate in a dish with the oil. Make a good wood fire (preferably with vine cuttings) or, if not possible, a charcoal one. Put 3–4 fennel stalks on the barbecue grill and place the gilt-head on top. Cook for about 25 minutes, depending on size. During cooking, sprinkle with the marinade oil and thyme and rosemary. Serve with a Rémoulade sauce.

Dry white wine: Côtes de Provence.

US	Ingredients	Met/Imp
20	oysters	20
20	mussels	20
	soft roe from 6 herrings	
2	large onions	2
14 oz (3½ sticks)	butter	400 g/14 oz
2, each about 2 lb	gilt-head breams	2, each about 1 kg/2 lb
	salt and pepper	
3 cups	red wine	750 ml/1¼ pints
1	bouquet garni	1
3 tbsp	flour	30 g/1 oz
	cayenne	

GILT-HEAD FROM LA ROCHELLE

Preparation 1 hour • Cooking 1 hour

Open the oysters and poach them in their own liquid until they become stiff. Cook and open the mussels also. Poach the herring roes. Fry the finely chopped onions in 50 g/2 oz (4 tbsp) of the butter until transparent.

Gut and scale the gilt-heads and remove the fins. Dip them in water and sponge them. Make small incisions in the flesh on both sides.

Lay the gilt-heads in a greased flameproof oval dish on a bed of cooked onion. Season with salt and pepper, add the wine, 200 ml/7 fl oz (scant 1 cup) of the mussel cooking liquid, 100 g/4 oz (1 stick) of the butter cut into small pieces and the bouquet garni. Bring to the boil on top of the stove, then continue cooking in a moderately hot oven for 35 minutes, basting from time to time.

Drain the gilt-heads, put them on a heated serving dish and surround them with the soft roe divided into two and with the oysters and mussels. Keep warm.

Pour the fish cooking liquid into a saucepan and add some kneaded butter (*page 49*) made with 50 g/2 oz (4 tbsp) of the butter and the flour, in small pieces, stirring constantly. Bring to the boil and boil for just a few seconds. Remove from the heat and add the remaining butter and a touch of cayenne. Pour this sauce over the fish and its garnish and place in a very hot oven for a few minutes to glaze the surface of the sauce.

Dry white wines: Sancerre, Quincy, Pouilly-Fumé, Muscadet, Gros Plant du Pays Nantais.

ESTURGEON

STURGEON

THIS FATTY FISH IS DISAPPEARING IN FRANCE AND IS NOW mostly found in the Black Sea and the Caspian Sea, where it is fished above all for its eggs – caviar – and its spinal cord which, when it is dried, is used as 'vesiga' in Russian cooking. Smoked sturgeon is served as an hors-d'oeuvre, cut into thin slices. Fresh sturgeon is prepared in the same way as veal: larded *fricandeau*, cut into slices and fried or grilled (broiled), or in a *matelote*.

DARNES D'ESTURGEON À LA BORDELAISE

—— STURGEON STEAKS BORDELAISE ——

Preparation 15 minutes • Cooking 30 minutes

Fry the sturgeon in a tin-plated copper saucepan with the oil, some of the butter, the chopped onions and shallots. When the fish starts to brown, add the skinned, de-seeded and chopped tomatoes, the wine, meat juice, salt, pepper, chopped thyme and bay leaf. Cover the pan and braise for 30 minutes over a low heat.

Take out the sturgeon steaks and put them on a heated serving dish. Reduce the cooking liquid and add the mushrooms, cooked in butter. Coat the sturgeon with the sauce and sprinkle with chopped parsley.

Dry white wines: Arbois, Alsace Riesling, dry Graves.

US	Ingredients	Met/Imp
8, each about 6 oz	sturgeon steaks	8, each about 175 g/6 oz
¼ cup	olive oil	60 ml/4 tbsp
½ lb (2 sticks)	butter	250 g/8 oz
2	onions	2
4	shallots	4
8	tomatoes	8
3 cups	dry white wine	750 ml/1¼ pints
1 wineglass	meat juice or consommé	1 wineglass
	salt and pepper	
1	thyme sprig	1
1	bay leaf	1
5 oz	mushrooms	150 g/5 oz
a few	parsley sprigs	a few

DACE

DACE IS FISHED MOSTLY IN THE SWISS LAKES, PARTICULARLY in Lake Geneva, but it is becoming very rare. When it is dying, it takes on all the colours of the rainbow, one by one. Its flesh, which is fine and delicate, has only very few bones, but it is very fragile.

US	Ingredients	Met/Imp
10 oz	whiting fillets	300 g/10 oz
4 slices	white bread, crusts removed	100 g/4 oz
½ cup	milk	100 ml/4 fl oz
1	lemon, rind and juice of	1
	chervil, parsley, chives	
½ cup	double (heavy) cream	100 ml/4 fl oz
2	eggs	2
	salt and pepper	
2, each about 1¼ lb	dace	2, each about 600 g/1¼ lb
6	shallots	6
14 tbsp	butter	200 g/7 oz
	white wine (Swiss Fendant or Crépy from French Savoy)	
	Bercy Sauce (page 62)	

FÉRA FARCIE

STUFFED DACE

Preparation 15 minutes • Cooking 30 minutes

Make the stuffing. Pound the whiting; soak the bread in the milk and squeeze dry; chop the lemon rind; chop the chervil, parsley and chives. Mix half of the chopped herbs with the pounded whiting, bread and lemon rind. Add the cream and one of the eggs and season with salt and pepper.

Stuff the dace which has been gutted through the gills. Roll in the chopped shallots, remaining chopped herbs and salt and pepper. Place in an ovenproof dish greased with butter. Add the butter cut into small pieces, a little white wine and the lemon juice. Cook for about 30 minutes in a moderately hot oven, basting from time to time. Serve Bercy sauce on the side.

Wines: serve the same wine as the one used for cooking, or another dry white wine.

FLÉTAN

HALIBUT

A FLAT FISH LIVING IN COLD AND DEEP WATERS, THE HALIBUT can grow up to about 2 metres/2 yards in length and weigh more than 150 kg/330 lb. Its very lean flesh is, according to its devotees, just as good as that of the turbot. It is greatly appreciated in the Nordic countries, but much rarer in the markets of France. It is prepared like brill.

FLÉTAN FROID SAUCE ROUGAIL AU BRESSE BLEU

COLD HALIBUT WITH TOMATO AND BRESSE BLEU SAUCE

Preparation 1 hour • Cooking 15 minutes

Prepare the court bouillon with water, the thinly sliced vegetables and the other listed ingredients. Cool completely, then put in the fish and bring very slowly to the boil. Simmer for 5 minutes, then remove from the heat and leave the halibut to cool completely in the court bouillon. Drain the fish, put it on a work surface (with the grey skin underneath) and carefully remove the white skin. This is not obligatory; the fish may also be served and garnished with its skin.

Prepare the garnish. Put the halibut on a serving dish. Cut the green parts of the leeks into strips which will represent the stems of a bouquet. Decorate the fish with the leek leaves and the tarragon leaves. Make flowers with small pieces of tomato and lemon rind. Complete the garnish by surrounding the fish with lettuce leaves, lemon slices, wedges of hard-boiled egg, tomato and parsley sprigs.

For the sauce (which must be prepared several hours in advance), put the tomatoes into a saucepan of boiling water for 1 minute, then drain and skin them. Cut each tomato in half and press to remove the seeds and juice.

Put the tomato flesh through a vegetable mill. Collect the purée in a piece of cheesecloth and hang it up so that the excess liquid drains off. Keep the juice which will perhaps be necessary for perfecting the sauce. Chill the tomato purée and juice in the refrigerator for 2–3 hours (the juice will set to a jelly). Crush the cheese with a fork and reduce it to a fine purée. Add the mustard to the cheese, then gradually and carefully mix in the cream.

Mix in the tomato purée and season with salt and pepper. If the mixture seems too thick, add a little of the tomato jelly. Chill the sauce in the refrigerator until ready to serve.

White wines: Chablis, Meursault, Montrachet, Pouilly-Fuissé, Savennières, dry Vouvray, dry Graves.

US	Ingredients	Met/Imp
1, about 5½ lb	halibut	1, about 2.5 kg/5½ lb
	COURT BOUILLON	
1	tomato	1
2	carrots	2
2	large onions	2
½	head garlic	½
2	thyme sprigs	2
2	bay leaves	2
	parsley stalks	
½ wineglass	wine vinegar	½ wineglass
	salt and pepper	
	GARNISH	
	a few leek and tarragon leaves	
2	tomatoes	2
2	lemons, rind and slices of	2
1	small lettuce	1
1	hard-boiled egg	1
	parsley sprigs	
	SAUCE	
3 lb	tomatoes	1.5 kg/3 lb
2 oz	Bresse Bleu cheese	50 g/2 oz
1 tbsp	strong mustard	15 ml/1 tbsp
½ cup	double (heavy) cream	100 ml/4 fl oz

GOUJON

GUDGEON

THIS IS THE MOST PRIZED OF THE SMALL RIVER FISH AND frying is practically the only way it is cooked. It is enough to gut it and wipe it without washing it. By extension, 'goujonettes' is the name given to the small strips of fried fillets of sole which are served – like gudgeons – as an entrée with sliced lemon, or as a garnish to a fish dish in sauce.

FRITURE DE GOUJONS

FRIED GUDGEON

Preparation 15 minutes • Cooking 5 minutes

US	Ingredients	Met/Imp
3 lb	gudgeons	1.5 kg/3 lb
2 cups	salted cold milk	500 ml/18 fl oz
¾ cup	seasoned flour	100 g/4 oz
	oil for frying	
	GARNISH	
	lemon slices	
	fried parsley	

When you have gutted the gudgeons, dip them in the salted milk, then roll them in flour. Put them into the oil when it is smoking hot, so that they will be well sealed, and fry until crispy. Serve on a paper doiley garnished with lemon slices and fried parsley. Be sure that the parsley stays green and is not greasy.

Dry white wines: Sancerre, Pouilly-Fumé, Saint-Pourçain.

GRONDIN

GURNARD

GURNARD IS THE NAME GIVEN TO SEVERAL VERY COMMON FISH characterized by their striking colours: the yellow gurnard, the red gurnard, the piper, etc. Their lean flesh is white and firm, but there is a fairly high proportion of waste. The gurnard is generally cooked in a *court bouillon* before being used in a variety of different ways. It is used in many fish soups.

FILETS DE GRONDIN AU RIZ

— FILLETS OF GURNARD WITH RICE —

Preparation 40 minutes • Cooking 50 minutes

US	Ingredients	Met/Imp
4½ lb	gurnard	2 kg/4½ lb
I quart	dry white wine	I litre/1¾ pints
I	onion	I
I	bouquet garni	I
2	garlic cloves	2
I cup	rice	200 g/7 oz
I tsp	saffron	5 ml/I tsp
I	lemon, juice of	I
	cayenne	

Fillet the gurnard. Cook the heads and bones in the wine with the onion, bouquet garni and garlic. Strain this stock and use it to poach the fillets in. Arrange them on a dish and keep warm. Boil the rice in the same stock with the saffron.

Put the rice on a dish and arrange the gurnard fillets on top. Make a sauce with a little of the stock, some lemon juice and cayenne. Pour this over the dish and serve.

Wines: as a general rule, serve the same wine as the one used for cooking.

SMOKED HADDOCK

THE FRENCH WORD 'HADDOCK' REFERS TO THE FISH FROM the northern seas when its head has been removed and it has been opened up into two and slowly smoked ('aiglefin' refers to non-smoked haddock).

Smoked haddock is characterized by its orange colour, its flavoursome taste and its smooth texture. It is generally gently poached in milk (which should diminish any bitter taste it may have acquired by being smoked), and is served just with melted butter, boiled potatoes or *crème fraîche*. Curnonsky refined this method by crowning the piece of poached haddock with a poached egg, 'whose dazzlingly yellow yolk lent still more suavity to the dish'. Poached smoked haddock also makes a pleasant addition to a variety of salads, especially with lukewarm sliced potatoes with olive oil or even with young and tender spinach.

PUDDING DE HADDOCK À L'AMÉRICAINE

SMOKED HADDOCK PUDDING AMÉRICAINE

Preparation 30 minutes • Cooking 2¼–2¾ hours

US	Ingredients	Met/Imp
2 lb	smoked haddock (finnan haddie)	1 kg/2 lb
	salt and pepper	
a little	butter	a little
5	egg yolks	5
2 cups	mashed potatoes	about 500 g/1 lb
2 cups	crème fraîche	500 ml/18 fl oz
	TO SERVE	
	Béchamel Sauce (page 62)	
⅓ cup	capers	50 g/2 oz

Take a piece of smoked haddock which has been cooked in a *court bouillon* and trim it. Pound the flesh to a pulp and cook over a gentle heat for 10 minutes with the salt and pepper, butter and the egg yolks, stirring well. Add a quantity of mashed potatoes which is equal to the amount of fish, then add the crème fraîche by spoonfuls, vigorously stirring the mixture all the time.

Put the mixture in a buttered mould and cook for 2–2½ hours in a *bain-marie* in a low oven. Serve with a béchamel sauce flavoured with the capers.

Dry or medium dry white wines: Graves, Alsace Gewürztraminer, Vouvray, Anjou.

HARENG

HERRING

AN INEXPENSIVE BASIC FOOD, HERRING IS TRADITIONAL IN all the countries of northern Europe and is available in various forms, fresh or smoked. Fresh herring should be cut along the back so that the bone can be removed before cooking. It should be gutted through the gills, with the soft roe or eggs left in place, and washed and wiped. The main ways of preparing it are grilling (or broiling), frying or cooking in a marinade. Onion goes well with it. Its aromatic flesh is rich in fats, especially when the fish is pregnant, and the shinier it is the better. As for smoked herring, it must be soaked for 12–48 hours, depending on how salty it is. This herring has various traditional names which are often picturesque and correspond to particular preparations: gendarme, bouffi (smoked and not put in a herring barrel); bloater (smoked herring); kipper (opened up before being smoked), etc. Herring salad with potatoes and oil is a dish typically served in a bar, whereas rollmops, another herring classic, are marinated with vinegar and seasonings and rolled around *cornichons*.

HARENGS GRILLÉS À LA MOUTARDE

– GRILLED HERRINGS WITH MUSTARD –

Preparation 40 minutes • Cooking 12 minutes

Scale and bone the herrings, season with salt and pepper, brush them with oil and grill (broil).

Meanwhile, prepare the sauce. Gently melt the butter in a saucepan. Add the flour to make a blond roux and gradually stir in the boiling milk. Season and cook for 10 minutes, stirring. Remove from heat and mix in the mustard, egg yolks and crème fraîche. Mix well and serve with the herrings.

Dry white wines: Saumur, Sancerre, Quincy, Muscadet, Sauvignon de Saint-Bris.

US	Ingredients	Met/Imp
8	herrings	8
	salt and pepper	
½ cup	oil	100 ml/4 fl oz
	SAUCE	
4 tbsp	butter	50 g/2 oz
6 tbsp	flour	50 g/2 oz
2 cups	boiling milk	500 ml/18 fl oz
1 tbsp	mustard	15 ml/1 tbsp
2	egg yolks	2
¼ cup	crème fraîche	50 ml/2 fl oz

US	Ingredients	Met/Imp
8	herrings with roe	8
scant 2 cups	dry white wine	500 ml/18 fl oz
1 cup	white wine vinegar	250 ml/9 fl oz
1	large carrot	1
3	onions	3
3	garlic cloves	3
2	cloves	2
	thyme sprigs	
	bay leaf	
1	small bouquet flat-leaved parsley	1
1 tbsp	coriander seeds	15 ml/1 tbsp
10	peppercorns	10

HERRINGS MARINATED IN WHITE WINE

Preparation 30 minutes • Cooking 1 hour

Clean and gut the herrings, cut off the heads, replace the soft roe inside the fish and arrange them head-to-tail in a fairly deep flameproof dish.

Pour the wine and vinegar into a saucepan and add the thinly sliced carrot and onions, the garlic cloves, peeled but whole, the cloves, thyme, bay leaf, parsley, coriander and peppercorns. Bring to the boil, then reduce the heat and continue to cook gently for 30–35 minutes. Pour the boiling marinade on to the herrings. Remove the thyme and bay leaf. Put the dish over the heat and bring to boiling point, then poach for about 12 minutes. Allow to cool completely, then chill in the refrigerator. Serve cold.

Wines: as a general rule, serve the same wine as the one used for cooking.

US	Ingredients	Met/Imp
6–8	herrings	6–8
	salt and pepper	
	flour for coating	
3	onions	3
9 tbsp	butter	120 g/4½ oz
	parsley	
2 tbsp	white wine vinegar	30 ml/2 tbsp

HARENGS SAUTÉS À LA LYONNAISE

SAUTÉED HERRINGS LYONNAISE

Preparation 15 minutes • Cooking about 30 minutes

Clean and trim the herrings. Season with salt and pepper and coat in flour. Peel and thinly slice the onions. Heat half of the butter in a frying pan and gently fry the herrings until golden on both sides.

Meanwhile, gently fry the onions in the remaining butter in another frying pan. Turn the herrings over and add the onions. Cook for a further 10 minutes. Put the fried herrings on a heated serving dish, pour the onions on top and sprinkle with chopped parsley. Keep warm.

Deglaze the frying pan with the vinegar, stir over a high heat for a few moments, then pour over the herrings and onions. Serve immediately.

Dry white wines: Alsace Pinot Gris, Bourgogne, Bourgogne-Aligoté, Mâcon-Villages, Côtes de Provence, Jasnières, dry Bergerac, Entre-Deux-Mers.

LAMPROIE

LAMPREY

THIS SEA FISH SWIMS UPSTREAM TO SPAWN AND, LIKE THE shad, is fished in the spring. It is a great delicacy but difficult to prepare. The lamprey should not be skinned; it should be thrown into boiling water while still alive, cleaned in cold water and hung up by the mouth to bleed, taking care to collect the blood in a bowl with some red wine, which is then traditionally used for making the sauce to serve with the fish. The main tendon should then be removed and the flesh cut into sections and marinated in good red wine. It may be cooked like eel.

LAMPROIE À LA BORDELAISE

—————— LAMPREYS BORDELAISE ——————

Preparation 45 minutes • Marinating and making sauce 3 hours • Cooking 35 minutes

Clean, bleed and slice the lampreys, removing and reserving the heads and tails. (If liked, the blood can be mixed with some of the red wine and reserved to thicken the sauce before serving the fish.) Cover the lampreys in red wine and leave to marinate while making the sauce.

Finely chop the onions, shallots, garlic, carrots, celery, leftover ham and the outer leaves of the leeks. Fry in half of the oil until lightly browned, then add the flour. Pour in the remaining red wine, add the skinned, de-seeded and chopped tomatoes, the reserved lamprey heads and tails, the bouquet garni, salt and pepper, the clove, nutmeg and sugar cubes. Cook in a low oven for 3 hours.

Strain this sauce and reserve. Brown the white parts of the leeks, the mushrooms and diced Bayonne ham in the remaining oil and the butter. Put the lampreys on top of this mixture, add the sauce and stir over a gentle heat until it boils; allow to boil for a few minutes. Put the lampreys into another flameproof dish and flambé them with the armagnac. Reduce the sauce to the required consistency, adding the blood and red wine if using. Put the lampreys back into the sauce and simmer until completely cooked. Before serving, a little butter may be added, but this is optional. Check the seasoning.

Red wines: Saint-Émilion, Pomerol, Médoc.

US	Ingredients	Met/Imp
4½ lb	lampreys	2 kg/4½ lb
2 bottles	full-bodied red bordeaux wine	2 bottles
2	onions	2
6	shallots	6
7	garlic cloves	7
2	carrots	2
½	head (bunch) celery	½
½ lb	cooked leftover ham	250 g/8 oz
12	leeks	12
½ cup	oil	100 ml/4 fl oz
1 tbsp	flour	15 ml/1 tbsp
6	tomatoes	6
1	bouquet garni	1
	salt and peppr	
1	clove	1
1 pinch	nutmeg	1 pinch
4	sugar cubes	4
¼ lb	mushrooms	125 g/4½ oz
¼ lb	lean *Bayonne* ham	100 g/4 oz
1 stick	butter	100 g/4 oz
¼ cup	armagnac	50 ml/2 fl oz

LAVARET

POLLAN

THIS DELICATE AND FRAGILE FISH IS FOUND ALMOST exclusively in the Lac du Bourget. It is cooked like dace or trout.

POLLAN GÂTEAU
WITH CRAYFISH RAGOÛT

Preparation 1 hour • Cooking 1 hour

US	Ingredients	Met/Imp
2 lb	pollan	1 kg/2 lb
2	cloves	2
	salt and pepper	
6	eggs	6
1 quart	crème fraîche	1 litre/1¾ pints
1	onion	1
4	shallots	4
5	garlic cloves	5
1	thyme sprig	1
1	parsley sprig	1
3 cups	dry white wine	750 ml/1¼ pints
	cayenne	
20	crayfish	20
½ lb (2 sticks)	butter	250 g/8 oz
1 tbsp	flour	10 g/½ oz

Scale, gut and wash the pollan. Wipe them carefully, then fillet and skin them. Work the fillets through a sieve. Using a mortar and pestle, crush 1 clove with some salt and pepper. Work the pollan flesh and the seasonings with the pestle until a smooth, frothy paste is obtained. Whisk the eggs into the paste, one at a time, and stir without beating until the paste is completely smooth. Lastly, add enough crème fraîche for the mixture to look like a smooth cream.

Pour the mixture into a large mould, or individual moulds, well greased with butter. Cook in a *bain-marie* in a hot oven for 20–30 minutes. Unmould and coat with a ragoût of crayfish tails, which is made as follows:

Put the thinly sliced onion, shallots and garlic into a tin-plated copper bowl or pan. Add the thyme, parsley and remaining clove. Pour over the white wine and cook over a high heat until reduced by half. Season with salt and 2 shakes of cayenne. Put the crayfish into the bowl, bring to the boil over a high heat, then cover and cook for 4 minutes. Stir the crayfish, cover the bowl or pan again and cook for a further 4 minutes or until the crayfish have become a uniform red colour: a total cooking time of 8 minutes should produce this result; otherwise cook for a few minutes more, depending on the level of heat.

When the crayfish are cooked, pour them into a clean bowl with their cooking liquid. Cover and leave to stand for 1 hour, stirring often so that they absorb the flavour and aroma of the liquid. Strain and shell the crayfish, reserving the liquid. Put the butter into a wide saucepan over a high heat. When a nut-brown colour, gradually add the crayfish tails, stirring constantly. Reduce the heat to moderate. When all of the liquid has evaporated and the butter has clarified, add the flour, stirring well, and cook gently for 3 minutes. Pour in half of the cooking liquid, bring to the boil, stirring constantly, then simmer for 10 minutes. Add the remaining crème fraîche and bring back to the boil. Taste, and add a little more cooking liquid if required. Boil for a further 3 minutes. Serve with the pollan gâteau.

Dry white wines: Arbois, Sancerre, Quincy, Pouilly-Fuissé, Condrieu.

MONKFISH OR BURBOT

A DISTINCTION MUST BE MADE BETWEEN FRESHWATER 'lotte' (burbot in English), which is becoming increasingly rare and is cooked like eel, and sea 'lotte' or 'baudroie' (monkfish in English), which is always sold under the name 'queue de lotte' (monkfish tail), without the head, which is enormous and monstrous.

The flesh of the monkfish is very white, finely textured and firm. It is cooked a little like meat, in an Américaine sauce, sautéed, roasted, or grilled (or broiled) on a skewer. 'Gigot de lotte' refers to a section of monkfish which has been trimmed and tied up, and it is usually braised with tomatoes and white wine.

BOURRIDE MARSEILLAISE

FISH SOUP MARSEILLAISE

Preparation 50 minutes • Cooking 1 hour

Poach the sliced monkfish in the court bouillon (predominantly flavoured with fennel from Provence) for about 15 minutes.

Make a creamy béchamel sauce (*page 62*) with the butter, flour and court bouillon from the fish, to which a few spoonfuls of aïoli will be added just before serving. Pour this on to the slices of bread in a tureen. Put the poached monkfish on a dish and surround it with the cooked carrots, potatoes and beans.

To serve, put the slices of fish and slices of bread dipped in the sauce in each individual bowl and serve the vegetables and aïoli on small side plates.

Côtes de Provence wines: white, rosé or red.

US	Ingredients	Met/Imp
5 lb	monkfish tail	2.3 kg/5 lb
7 cups	well-seasoned *court bouillon*	2 litres/3½ pints
14 tbsp	butter	200 g/7 oz
¾ cup	flour	100 g/4 oz
1¾ cups	Aïoli (*page 60*)	400 ml/14 fl oz
16	small thin slices bread, browned in the oven	16
14 oz	carrots, cooked	400 g/14 oz
1½ lb	potatoes, cooked	750 g/1½ lb
1¼ lb	French (fine green) beans, cooked	600 g/1¼ lb

US	Ingredients	Met/Imp
about 2 lb	monkfish tail	about 1 kg/2 lb
1 stick	butter	100 g/4 oz
½ lb	puff pastry	250 g/8 oz
¼ lb	mushrooms	100 g/4 oz
1½ oz	truffles	40 g/1½ oz
¼ cup	madeira	50 ml/2 fl oz
	salt and pepper	
	oil for frying	
	TO SERVE	
	fried parsley	
	Devil Sauce	
	(page 68)	

MONKFISH TURNOVERS

Preparation 40 minutes • Cooking 10 minutes

Cut the monkfish into 8 rectangular fillets, about 8×4 cm/3×1½ inches. Fry them in most of the butter until slightly stiffened. Cut the puff pastry into 8 circles, each large enough for a fillet. Prepare a mixture of chopped mushrooms sautéed in the remaining butter and chopped cooked truffles, all slightly moistened with madeira. Surround each fillet on its pastry circle with some of this mixture and season with salt and pepper.

Make turnovers, carefully sealing the edges with a little water. Make a hole in the top of each, for the steam to escape during cooking. Fry in fairly hot oil. Place on napkins, garnish with fried parsley and serve the Devil sauce on the side.

Dry white wines: Saumur, Sancerre, Quincy, Muscadet.

US	Ingredients	Met/Imp
3 lb	monkfish tail	1.5 kg/3 lb
	salt and pepper	
1 cup	flour	150 g/5 oz
½ cup	olive oil	100 ml/4 fl oz
1	onion	1
6 tbsp	Tomato Sauce	90 ml/6 tbsp
	(page 80)	
1	garlic clove	1
½ cup	dry white wine	100 ml/4 fl oz
2 cups	fresh white breadcrumbs	100 g/4 oz

LOTTE À LA PROVENÇALE

MONKFISH PROVENÇAL

Preparation 10 minutes • Cooking 15 minutes

Cut the monkfish into slices of equal thickness. Season these slices with salt and pepper and coat in the flour. Cook them in all but a little of the oil in a frying pan, until they are well browned on both sides. Remove, then add the chopped onion to the oil and fry until golden.

Put the monkfish on a bed of fried onion in an ovenproof dish. Pour the tomato sauce, with the crushed garlic added, on to the fish, add the white wine and season well. Sprinkle the fish with the breadcrumbs and the remaining little oil. Put in a hot oven for 10 minutes.

Dry white wines: Côtes de Provence, Bellet, Cassis.

US	Ingredients	Met/Imp
4½ lb	monkfish tail	2 kg/4½ lb
8	shallots	8
5 oz	mushrooms	150 g/5 oz
	salt and pepper	
a few	parsley sprigs	a few
½ lb (2 sticks)	butter	250 g/8 oz
scant 1 cup	dry white wine	200 ml/7 fl oz
2 cups	fresh white breadcrumbs	100 g/4 oz

TRANCHES DE LOTTE AU FOUR

BAKED MONKFISH

Preparation 15 minutes • Cooking 15 minutes

This method may also be used for the preparation of sole, whiting, etc.

Remove the dark skin and gelatinous part from the monkfish. Wash the fish and slice thickly. Cover the bottom of an ovenproof dish with most of the finely chopped shallots and thinly sliced mushrooms. Arrange the monkfish on top and season with salt and pepper, adding a little more shallot, chopped mushrooms, parsley, large pieces of butter and the wine. Cover with breadcrumbs.

Cook in a very hot oven for about 15 minutes until the top is slightly browned and the sauce is reduced to a light syrup.

Wines: as a general rule, serve the same wine as the one used for cooking.

MACKEREL

THOUGH IT IS OILY, MACKEREL FLESH IS MUCH APPRECIATED for its strong, fine flavour. It is traditionally combined with gooseberries, but may also be prepared in a variety of ways, often with mustard or spices: grilled (or broiled), stuffed, in a sauce or soup, etc. The best mackerel (called 'lisettes') are of average size and come from Dieppe; they must be firm to the touch, stiff and very shiny. Mackerel caught on a line are always preferable to trawled ones, which spend a longer time in ice.

COTRIADE DE MAQUEREAUX

COTRIADE OF MACKEREL

Preparation 25 minutes • Cooking 15 minutes

Brown the leeks in the oil and butter. Add the flour and pour in the water and wine. Cut the mackerel into pieces, remove the bones and cut off the heads. Cook the heads in the wine mixture for 15 minutes, then take them out and replace them with the mackerel pieces, adding the chopped garlic, the bay leaf, saffron, salt, pepper and lemon juice. Cook over a high heat until reduced by one-third.

To serve, arrange the bread slices (2 per person) in heated soup plates and pour over the soup. Put the pieces of mackerel, sprinkled with a little chopped parsley, on to another heated dish.

Dry white wines: Arbois, Alsace Riesling, Cassis, Pouilly-Fuissé, Bourgogne-Aligoté, Muscadet.

US	Ingredients	Met/Imp
6	leeks (white part)	6
¼ cup	oil	50 ml/2 fl oz
2 tbsp	butter	25 g/scant 1 oz
1 tbsp	flour	15 ml/1 tbsp
2 cups	water	500 ml/18 fl oz
2 cups	dry white wine	500 ml/18 fl oz
2 lb	small mackerel	1 kg/2 lb
2	garlic cloves	2
½	bay leaf	½
1 tsp	saffron	5 ml/1 tsp
	salt and pepper	
1	lemon, juice of	1
	TO SERVE	
16	slices firm-textured bread	16
2	parsley sprigs	2

US	Ingredients	Met/Imp
2 lb	mackerel	1 kg/2 lb
2 cups	milk	500 ml/18 fl oz
¾ cup	flour	100 g/4 oz
4 tbsp	butter	50 g/2 oz
	oil for frying	
½ lb	lean bacon slices	250 g/8 oz
	salt and pepper	

—— FRIED MACKEREL AMÉRICAINE ——

Preparation 20 minutes • Cooking 15 minutes

Split each mackerel in half. Dip into the milk, then into the flour. Fry them in the butter and oil, then divide each piece into four. Fry the bacon in the remaining butter and oil.

Arrange the pieces of mackerel and bacon alternately on a heated serving dish. Sprinkle with salt and pepper and serve immediately.

Dry white wines: Saumur, Quincy, Sancerre, Pouilly-Fumé.
Red wines: Beaujolais-Villages, Chinon, Bourgueil.

US	Ingredients	Met/Imp
3 lb	mackerel	1.5 kg/3 lb
3 tbsp	mustard	45 ml/3 tbsp
¾ cup	flour	100 g/4 oz
	salt and pepper	
1 lb (about 3 cups)	redcurrants	500 g/1 lb
1 stick	butter	100 g/4 oz

MAQUEREAUX AUX GROSEILLES

—— MACKEREL WITH REDCURRANTS* ——

Preparation 20 minutes • Cooking 12 minutes

Mackerel is traditionally served with gooseberries, called 'groseilles à maquereaux' in French. This recipe for 'maquereaux aux groseilles' uses redcurrants and is equally delicious.

Gut the mackerel and make shallow incisions on their backs. Brush the insides with mustard. Dip them in the flour, season and grill (broil) them. Sauté the redcurrants in the butter and pour over the mackerel.

Dry white wines: Muscadet, Quincy.
Red wines: Saumur-Champigny, Saint-Nicolas de Bourgueil.

MERLAN

WHITING

THE WHITING IS RELATED TO THE COD. WHITING FROM THE Channel and the Ocean are smaller and better than those from the Mediterranean. The flesh of the whiting is tender, delicate, easily digested, fine and puffy. Care should be taken when cooking, because whiting disintegrates easily. It may be fried, grilled (or broiled), cooked in breadcrumbs, stuffed or cooked in paupiettes (rolled-up fillets), and it may also be used in a stuffing or mousse.

MERLAN BERTHOMMIER

WHITING BERTHOMMIER

Preparation 20 minutes • Cooking 4–5 minutes • Serves 1

US	Ingredients	Met/Imp
1	whiting	1
6–8 tbsp	butter	75–100 g/ 3–4 oz
	salt and pepper	
1	large shallot	1
a few	parsley sprigs	a few
½ wineglass	dry white wine	½ wineglass
3 tbsp	fine white breadcrumbs	45 ml/3 tbsp

Using a knife with a flexible blade, cut the whiting along the backbone, cutting right through the flesh and scraping along the bone. Turn the fish over and make a similar cut on the other side of the bone. Cut the bone at the tail and pull it up to the head – it should come away very easily. Cut the bone off at the head. Grease an ovenproof dish with butter. Add salt and pepper. Chop the shallot and parsley separately. Sprinkle first the shallot and then the parsley into the dish. Pour in the white wine, then put in the opened fish, skin side down.

Season the whiting lightly and sprinkle it all over with the breadcrumbs. Melt the remaining butter and pour it over the whiting so that it is soaked up by the breadcrumbs. Cook in a hot oven for 4–5 minutes. If the fish is not sufficiently browned, put it under the grill (broiler) for a few minutes. Slide the fish on to a hot plate to serve.

White wines: Muscadet, Savennières, Sancerre, dry Graves, Entre-Deux-Mers, dry Bergerac.

MERLANS À L'ESTRAGON

WHITING WITH TARRAGON

Preparation 45 minutes • Cooking 20 minutes

US	Ingredients	Met/Imp
8	whiting	8
	salt and pepper	
	blanched tarragon leaves	
	Maître d'Hôtel Butter (*page 52*)	
1	lemon, wedges of	1
	Fish Glaze (*page 57*)	

Clean and trim the whiting, put them into salted cold water and bring to the boil. As soon as the water boils, remove from the heat and leave for 10 minutes. Arrange the whiting on a dish. Add chopped tarragon to the maître d'hôtel butter; garnish with whole tarragon leaves, lemon wedges, and pour a ribbon of fish glaze all around.

Dry white wines: Pouilly-Fumé, Muscadet, Chablis.

US	Ingredients	Met/Imp
8	whiting	8
2 oz	mushrooms	50 g/2 oz
2 tbsp	butter	30 g/1 oz
1	shallot	1
2	parsley sprigs	2
2	tarragon sprigs	2
4	tomatoes	4
1 quart	Mornay Sauce (page 73)	1 litre/1 ¾ pints
	Fish Fumet (page 57)	
¼ cup	Gruyère cheese, grated	25 g/scant 1 oz

STUFFED WHITING

Preparation 45 minutes • Cooking 15 minutes

Remove the bones from the whiting. Stuff the fish with mushrooms, chopped into large pieces and lightly fried in butter, and with the chopped shallot, parsley, tarragon and the skinned, de-seeded and chopped tomatoes, mixed with a little of the Mornay sauce. Close the whiting, tie them with string to keep the stuffing in place and poach them in the fish fumet for about 10 minutes. Drain and arrange on a dish. Cover with the remaining Mornay sauce, sprinkle with grated cheese and brown in a hot oven for about 5 minutes.

Dry white wines: Pouilly-Fuissé, Chablis, dry Graves, Alsace Pinot Blanc.

US	Ingredients	Met/Imp
1 ¾ lb	whiting fillets	800 g/1 ¾ lb
5 slices	fresh bread, crusts removed	150 g/5 oz
scant 1 cup	milk	200 ml/7 fl oz
	salt and pepper	
4	egg whites	4
2 cups	*crème fraîche*	500 ml/18 fl oz
	CHOICE OF SAUCES TO SERVE	
	Nantua Sauce (page 74), sauce for Lobster Newburg (page 249), or sauce for Sole Dieppoise (page 211)	

MOUSSE DE MERLAN

WHITING MOUSSE

Preparation 1 hour • Cooking 35 minutes

Pound the whiting with the bread which has been soaked in milk and then squeezed dry. Season and gradually work in the egg whites. Sieve the mixture, put it in a bowl placed on ice and gradually mix in the crème fraîche with a spatula. Pour into a buttered ring mould and poach in a *bain-marie* for about 35 minutes, until set. Serve hot with the sauce of your choice.
Chopped truffles may be added to the mousse mixture.

Dry or medium dry white wines: Graves, Alsace Gewürztraminer.

US	Ingredients	Met/Imp
8	whiting	8
	salt and pepper	
	Fish Stuffing (page 54)	
10 tbsp	butter	150 g/5 oz
	Fish Fumet (page 57)	
½ cup	dry white wine	100 ml/4 fl oz

PAUPIETTES DE MERLAN FARCIES AU VIN BLANC

STUFFED PAUPIETTES OF WHITING WITH WHITE WINE

Preparation 1 hour • Cooking 15 minutes

Gut, clean and fillet the whiting. Season the fillets with salt and pepper. Spread them with fish stuffing on the skin side and roll up into paupiettes. Wrap them in a piece of buttered greaseproof or baking parchment paper and tie them up with string. Place in a buttered dish and poach in fish fumet and wine in a moderate oven for about 15 minutes.

When the paupiettes are cooked, untie them and place them on a heated serving dish. Reduce the liquid, add the remaining butter and pour over the paupiettes.

Wines: as a general rule, serve the same wine as the one used for cooking.

MORUE

SALT COD

SALT COD EXISTS IN VARIOUS FORMS: IN A TAIL OR WRAPPED up, in pieces or in fillets (boned, blanched and rolled), etc. It must always be very carefully desalted before being used for cooking.

To desalt and poach salt cod: put the cod into cold water (with the skin downwards, to allow the salt to be removed) and change the water several times. Drain the cod, then place in a saucepan of tepid water over a high heat. As soon as it has started to boil, turn the heat down to very low and poach for 15 minutes without letting it boil again.

There are many recipes for salt cod because it was a basic food in France and throughout the Mediterranean for several centuries: hot or cold, in salads, au gratin, in croquettes, in tomato sauce, with onion, with cream, etc.

BEIGNETS DE MORUE À LA SAUCE TOMATE

SALT COD FRITTERS WITH TOMATO SAUCE

Preparation 1 hour • Cooking 20 minutes

Desalt and poach the cod according to the instructions above. Mix with the duchesse potatoes and shape into balls the size of a cork. Coat with breadcrumbs, dip in the beaten eggs and oil, season with salt, pepper and nutmeg, then coat with more breadcrumbs. Sauté in the butter. Garnish with fried parsley and serve the tomato sauce on the side.

Dry white wines: Saumur, Pouilly-Fumé, Muscadet, Mâcon-Viré, Chablis, Montagny.

US	Ingredients	Met/Imp
3 lb	salt cod	1.5 kg/3 lb
2 cups	Duchesse Potatoes (page 551)	500 g/1 lb
8 cups	fresh white breadcrumbs	500 g/1 lb
6	eggs	6
¼ cup	oil	50 ml/2 fl oz
	salt and pepper	
1 pinch	nutmeg	1 pinch
14 tbsp	butter	200 g/7 oz
	TO SERVE	
1	bunch fried parsley	1
1 quart	Tomato Sauce (page 80)	1 litre/1¾ pints

US	Ingredients	Met/Imp
2¾ lb	salt cod	1.25 kg/2¾ lb
2 cups	olive oil	500 ml/18 fl oz
	pepper	
8	thin triangular croûtons	8
2 tsp	butter	10 g/½ oz
½ cup	milk	100 ml/4 fl oz
1	lemon, juice of	1
1	boiled potato	1
	capers	
	truffles	

BRANDADE OF SALT COD

Preparation 1 hour • Cooking 25 minutes

Brandade can be made in three ways. Whichever method you choose, it is essential that it is cooked over a low heat:

1) Desalt the cod for 24 hours and poach it for 10 minutes, according to the instructions on page 181. Remove the skin and bones and break up the flesh. Put the flesh into a saucepan with a little of the oil and heat. Stir gently and constantly, gradually pouring in more oil until a smooth paste is formed. Season with pepper. Garnish the brandade with the croûtons fried in the butter and serve on a dish or in a vol-au-vent case.

2) The same as method 1, but gradually add the milk with the oil and add the lemon juice just before serving.

3) The same as method 1, but crush a floury boiled potato with the cod and add capers and chopped truffles.

The true brandade, which comes from Nîmes, does not contain garlic.

Dry or medium dry white wines: Graves, Alsace Gewürztraminer, Vouvray, Anjou, Pacherenc du Vic-Bilh.

US	Ingredients	Met/Imp
2½ lb	salt cod	1.1 kg/2½ lb
1 quart	very thick Béchamel Sauce (page 62)	1 litre/1¾ pints
1¼ cups	grated cheese	160 g/5 oz
⅔ cup	flour	75 g/3 oz
4	eggs	4
8 cups	fresh white breadcrumbs	500 g/1 lb
¼ cup	oil	50 ml/2 fl oz
10 tbsp	butter	150 g/5 oz
	GARNISH	
1 handful	parsley sprigs	1 handful

CROQUETTES DE MORUE AU FROMAGE

SALT COD CROQUETTES WITH CHEESE

Preparation 1 hour • Cooking 20 minutes

Desalt and poach the cod according to the instructions on page 181. Remove the bones and skin, then dice the flesh or flake it into small pieces. Mix it with the béchamel sauce and grated cheese. Spread out on a dish and leave to cool.

Shape the mixture into small balls, roll them in flour, then dip them in the beaten eggs and coat with breadcrumbs. Fry them in the oil and butter, arrange on a napkin and garnish with fried parsley.

Dry white wines: Saumur, Sancerre, Pouilly-Fumé, Muscadet, Quincy, Picpoul de Pinet.

	US	Ingredients	Met/Imp

—— SALT COD FILLETS 'ANGEVINE' ——

Preparation 25 minutes • Cooking 15 minutes

	US	Ingredients	Met/Imp
	8, each about 5 oz	salt cod fillets	8, each about 150 g/5 oz
		butter	
	2 lb	sorrel	1 kg/2 lb
	1	onion	1
	2	hard-boiled eggs	2
		parsley	
	1 pinch	dried thyme	1 pinch
	½ cup	crème fraîche	100 ml/4 fl oz
	1 lb	boiled new potatoes	500 g/1 lb

Desalt and poach the cod according to the instructions on page 181. Grease the bottom of an ovenproof dish with butter; cover it with half of the washed raw sorrel cut into thin strips, a little chopped onion, half of the chopped hard-boiled eggs, some chopped parsley and thyme.

Put the fillets of cod on this bed of ingredients and cover with another layer of sorrel, onion, egg and herbs. Cook in a moderate oven for 15 minutes.

Remove the cod and reduce the cooking liquid. Pour over the cod and top with the crème fraîche. Serve immediately, with the boiled new potatoes on the side.

Dry white wines: Saumur, Chablis, Pouilly-Fumé, Muscadet, Jasnières, Gros Plant du Pays Nantais.

SAUTÉED FILLETS OF SALT COD LYONNAISE ——

Preparation 40 minutes • Cooking 20 minutes

	US	Ingredients	Met/Imp
	2½ lb	salt cod	1.1 kg/2½ lb
	4	large onions	4
	10 tbsp	butter	150 g/5 oz
	½ cup	oil	100 ml/4 fl oz
	1 lb	boiled potatoes	500 g/1 lb
	1 tbsp	chopped parsley	15 ml/1 tbsp

Desalt and poach the cod according to the instructions on page 181. Fry the thinly sliced onions in the butter and oil until golden. Remove with a slotted spoon and reserve. Sauté the potatoes in the same pan and, before they are completely browned, add the flaked cod, the fried onions and the parsley.

Dry white wines: Mâcon-Viré, Bourgogne-Aligoté, Pouilly-Fumé.

—— SALT COD TONGUES IN A RING ——

Preparation 50 minutes • Cooking 20 minutes

	US	Ingredients	Met/Imp
	2½ lb	salt cod tongues	1.1 kg/2½ lb
	1 stick	butter	100 g/4 oz
	6 tbsp	flour	50 g/2 oz
	1 quart	milk	1 litre/1¾ pints
	3	egg yolks	3
		salt and pepper	
	1	bouquet garni	1
	¼ cup	grated cheese	25 g/scant 1 oz
		or	
	1 tbsp	fresh white breadcrumbs	15 ml/1 tbsp

If you can get hold of some cod tongues, here is a recipe for an entrée worthy of being on the menu of the grandest dinner.

Carefully wash the tongues, first in hot water, then in cold. Remove their coarse covering and wash them again. Blanch them, drain and keep warm. Prepare a fairly thick sauce with the butter, flour, milk, egg yolks and seasoning. Cook the cod tongues in the sauce for about 20 minutes, together with the bouquet garni. Pour the mixture into a buttered ring mould, sprinkle with grated cheese or breadcrumbs and brown in a hot oven. Serve as an entrée on a hot dish.

White wines: Arbois, Alsace Sylvaner, Sauternes, Graves, Anjou, Monbazillac.

US	Ingredients	Met/Imp

—— SALT COD WITH AÏOLI* ——

Preparation 45 minutes • Cooking 55 minutes

US	Ingredients	Met/Imp
8, each about 5 oz	salt cod fillets	8, each about 150 g/5 oz
1¾ lb	carrots	800 g/1¾ lb
½ lb	French (fine green) beans	200 g/7 oz
1 lb	cauliflower	500 g/1 lb
8	artichoke bottoms	8
1 lb	potatoes	500 g/1 lb
4	hard-boiled eggs	4
	Aïoli (page 60)	

Desalt and poach the cod according to the instructions on page 181. Serve cold with the boiled vegetables and hard-boiled eggs. Accompany by the aïoli in a sauce boat. Or serve with snails (which have been cooked in salted water), fennel and Jerusalem artichokes.

Dry white wines: Côtes de Provence, Cassis.
Rosé wines: Tavel, Cassis or Bandol.
Red wines: Bandol, Coteaux des Baux-de-Provence.

—— SALT COD WITH CREAM ——

Preparation 40 minutes • Cooking 20 minutes

US	Ingredients	Met/Imp
3½ lb	thick salt cod	1.6 kg/3½ lb
¼ cup	wine vinegar	50 ml/2 fl oz
1 stick	butter	100 g/4 oz
6 tbsp	flour	50 g/2 oz
3	egg yolks	3
scant 1 cup	crème fraîche	200 ml/7 fl oz
½	lemon, juice of	½
	GARNISH	
1 lb	boiled potatoes	500 g/1 lb

Cut the salt cod into 8 pieces. Desalt and poach it for 20 minutes according to the instructions on page 181, with the vinegar in the water. Make a white roux with the butter and flour in a heavy saucepan. Stir in the cod cooking liquid to make a thick sauce; boil for a few minutes.

Just before serving, mix the egg yolks, crème fraîche and lemon juice into the sauce and pour over the cod. Garnish with the boiled potatoes.

Dry white wines: Saumur, Pouilly-Fuissé, dry Graves, Chablis, Mâcon-Villages.

—— SALT COD PROVENÇAL ——

Preparation 30 minutes • Cooking 30 minutes

US	Ingredients	Met/Imp
2½ lb	salt cod	1.1 kg/2½ lb
1	large onion	1
4	tomatoes	4
⅔ cup	oil	150 ml/¼ pint
½	garlic clove	½
1 tbsp	chopped parsley	15 ml/1 tbsp
⅓ cup	capers	50 g/2 oz
1⅓ cups	black olives	250 g/8 oz
	salt and pepper	

Desalt and poach the cod according to the instructions on page 181. Sauté the chopped onion and the skinned, de-seeded and chopped tomatoes in the oil. Add the crushed garlic, parsley, capers, olives, a little salt and pepper and the cod. Simmer for 10 minutes.

Dry white wines: Cassis, Côtes de Provence, Bellet, Coteaux d'Aix-en-Provence.

—— SALT COD FROM TOULON ——

Preparation 40 minutes • Cooking 20 minutes

US	Ingredients	Met/Imp
2½ lb	salt cod	1.1 kg/2½ lb
1 quart	Tomato Sauce (page 80)	1 litre/1¾ pints
	salt and pepper	
1⅓ cups	Pilau Rice (page 563)	250 g/8 oz
4 tbsp	butter	50 g/2 oz

Desalt and poach the cod according to the instructions on page 181. Remove the skin and bones and heat the flesh through in the tomato sauce. Season. Serve with the pilau rice forked with the butter.

Dry white wines: Cassis, Côtes de Provence, Bellet, Coteaux d'Aix-en-Provence.

SALT COD MOUSSE AND
FRIANDISES WITH ANCHOVIES

Preparation 1 hour • Cooking 20 minutes

US	Ingredients	Met/Imp
1 lb	salt cod	500 g/1 lb
2 cups	thick Béchamel Sauce (page 62)	500 ml/18 fl oz
1 stick	butter	100 g/4 oz
6	anchovies	6
1 quart	Fish Aspic (page 58)	1 litre/1¾ pints
	truffles	

Traditionally, anchovies from Collioure (on the Mediterranean side of the Pyrenees) are used for this dish. The mousse balls may be covered in chopped, skinned and de-seeded tomatoes instead of the truffles.

Desalt and poach the cod according to the instructions on page 181. Press the flesh through a sieve or mince it in a mincer or food processor. Add the béchamel sauce, the softened butter and the sieved anchovies. Mix everything together well with a spatula to make a fairly thick mousse.

Using a forcing (pastry) bag with a star nozzle, fill some dariole moulds, which have first been coated with decorated fish aspic, with about three-quarters of the mousse; cover with more aspic and chill until set.

Meanwhile, shape the remaining mousse into small balls and roll them in chopped truffles. Brush with fish aspic to make them shiny.

Just before serving, unmould the mousses and garnish with the balls.

Dry white wines: Pouilly-Fumé, Picpoul de Pinet.

STUFFED POTATOES WITH SALT COD

Preparation 1 hour • Cooking about 1 hour

US	Ingredients	Met/Imp
2 lb	salt cod fillets	1 kg/2 lb
4	large firm potatoes	4
4	sweet peppers	4
2	large onions	2
10 tbsp	butter	150 g/5 oz
	salt and pepper	
6 tbsp	flour	50 g/2 oz
2 cups	milk	500 ml/18 fl oz
¼ cup	Gruyère cheese, grated	25 g/scant 1 oz

Desalt and poach the cod according to the instructions on page 181.

Scrub the potatoes. Prick them lightly and bake in a hot oven until cooked. Meanwhile cut the cod into 8 pieces the same length as the potatoes. Cut the de-seeded sweet peppers and the well-blanched onions into thin slices.

When the potatoes are cooked, cut them in half lengthways. Remove the flesh with a spoon, taking care not to pierce the skins. Put the potato pulp in a bowl and mash with a fork, adding about two-thirds of the butter and a very little salt and some pepper. Refill the potato halves. Put a well-drained fillet of cod on each one and sprinkle peppers and onions on top.

Make a fairly thick béchamel sauce with the remaining butter, flour and the milk and carefully pour it on to the potatoes. Sprinkle a little grated cheese on top and brown in a hot oven. Serve very hot.

Dry white wines: Muscadet, Sancerre, Pouilly-Fumé.

ROCKLING

THE ROCKLING IS A MEDITERRANEAN FISH WITH FINE, LEAN flesh. It is prepared like whiting.

MOTELLE AUX NONATS

ROCKLING WITH NONATS

Preparation 45 minutes • Cooking 12 minutes

US	Ingredients	Met/Imp
4, each about 7 oz	rocklings	4, each about 200 g/7 oz
½ lb (2 sticks)	butter	250 g/8 oz
3	shallots	3
1	bouquet garni	1
	salt and pepper	
2 cups	Chablis	500 ml/18 fl oz
½ cup	Fish Fumet (*page 57*)	100 ml/4 fl oz
	TO SERVE	
8	small tomatoes stewed in butter	8
1 lb	deep-fried nonats	500 g/1 lb
8	puff pastry *fleurons*	8

Nonats are a tiny Mediterranean fish. Whitebait can be used as a substitute.

Cut the rocklings open along their backs and remove the bones. Put the fish on a well-buttered dish with the chopped shallots and a small bouquet garni. Season with salt and pepper and pour in the wine and fish fumet. Cook in a moderately hot oven for about 8–10 minutes, basting frequently. When the rocklings are cooked, take them out and set aside.

Reduce the fish cooking liquid, then beat in most of the butter. Check the seasoning, then strain through cheesecloth. Cover the fish with the mixture and glaze in the oven.

To serve, arrange the small tomatoes around the fish, alternately with small bouquets of nonats. Garnish with fleurons.

Wines: as a general rule, serve the same wine as the one used for cooking.

OMBLE

CHAR

THIS FISH, WHICH LIVES IN COLD LAKES, IS BECOMING MORE and more rare, which is a pity because its very delicate pink flesh has earned it the name of 'king of freshwater fish'. It is cooked in the same way as sea trout.

OMBLE CHEVALIER À LA CRÈME ET AU CRÉPY BLANC

CHAR WITH CREAM AND WHITE CRÉPY WINE

Preparation 30 minutes • Cooking 10 minutes

Open up the char like gondolas (cut the fish open along the back and remove the bone, thus giving the fish the appearance of a boat). Put them on a buttered dish and sprinkle with the chopped shallots. Season, pour in the wine and fish fumet and cook in a moderately hot oven for about 10 minutes. Take out the fish and keep it warm.

Strain the fish cooking liquid and reduce it. Add the cream, check the seasoning and reduce to make a creamy sauce (without thickening it).

Cover the fish with the sauce and garnish with fine slices of truffle just before serving. Serve very hot.

Wines: as a general rule, serve the same wine as the one used for cooking.

US	Ingredients	Met/Imp
4	char	4
14 tbsp	butter	200 g/7 oz
4	shallots	4
	salt and pepper	
2 cups	white wine (Crépy from French Savoy)	500 ml/18 fl oz
½ cup	Fish Fumet (page 57)	100 ml/4 fl oz
2 cups	double (heavy) cream	500 ml/18 fl oz
	GARNISH	
8, each about ¾ oz	truffle slices	8, each about 20 g/¾ oz

OMBLE CHEVALIER DU LAC 'À MA FAÇON'

CHAR FROM THE LAKE 'DONE MY WAY'

Preparation 1 hour • Cooking 10 minutes

Bone the char. Season them with salt and a very little pepper. Prepare a *julienne* of mushrooms and truffles, not cut too fine. Lightly fry in butter in a frying pan, then mix in most of the crème fraîche and the egg yolks and leave to cool.

Pour this mixture over the char, tied with thread to keep their shape. Cook in a moderately hot oven in a well-buttered ovenproof dish, covered with buttered greaseproof (wax) paper.

Deglaze the frying pan with port and mix in the remaining crème fraîche. Serve with the fish.

Dry white wines: Sancerre, Pouilly-Fuissé, Hermitage, Crépy.

US	Ingredients	Met/Imp
4	char	4
	salt and pepper	
½ lb	mushrooms	250 g/8 oz
3 oz	truffles	75 g/3 oz
½ lb (2 sticks)	butter	250 g/8 oz
2 cups	crème fraîche	500 ml/18 fl oz
3	egg yolks	3
½ cup	port wine	100 ml/4 fl oz

PERCH

AN EXCELLENT FRESHWATER FISH, THE PERCH IS NEVER-theless difficult to handle because of the needles on its dorsal fin. Small perch are fried. Larger ones may be prepared 'à la meunière', or in a *matelote*; they may also be stuffed.

PERCHES SAUCE SUCHET

PERCH WITH SUCHET SAUCE

Preparation 35 minutes • Cooking 15 minutes

US	Ingredients	Met/Imp
¼ lb	carrots	100 g/4 oz
2–3	celery stalks	100 g/4 oz
	parsley stalks	
14 tbsp	butter	200 g/7 oz
3 cups	dry white wine	750 ml/1¼ pints
2 cups	water	500 ml/18 fl oz
	salt	
8, each about 5 oz	perch	8, each about 150 g/5 oz
6 tbsp	flour	50 g/2 oz

Cut the carrots, celery and parsley stalks into a fine *julienne*. Sweat this julienne with about one-third of the butter and, when it has softened, pour in 450 ml/¾ pint (2 cups) of the wine and the water. Season with a pinch of salt and boil gently until the julienne is tender.

Gut and trim the perch. Cut off the back and stomach fins and the tail, wash and place in an ovenproof dish. Strain in the boiling *court bouillon*, reserving the julienne for the sauce.

Cover the perch and cook in a moderately hot oven for about 15 minutes, keeping the liquid just at a simmer. As soon as the perch are cooked, drain and reserve the cooking liquid. Arrange the perch on a heated serving dish and keep warm.

Prepare the suchet sauce with the remaining butter and flour, reduced cooking liquid and the reserved vegetable julienne mixed with the remaining wine. Pour this sauce over the perch and serve.

Dry white wines: Quincy, Alsace Sylvaner, Coteaux Champenois.

RAIE

SKATE

UNLIKE OTHER FISH, WHICH MUST BE FRESH, SKATE MUST BE left to decompose a little in the cool before it is used (24–48 hours) otherwise its flesh is tough. It is advisable to choose thornback skate, which is the tastiest. Skate is a lean, thin fish with no bones and its cartilaginous support may be taken out easily. The skin should always be removed. The skate's liver is highly prized, as are the 'cheeks'.

CARBONNADE DE RAIE

SKATE CARBONNADE

Preparation 45 minutes • Cooking 15 minutes

Cook the skate in court bouillon. Trim it and cut into large pieces. Add salt, pepper and the lemon juice. Quickly fry the pieces of skate in most of the butter, then dip into the beaten egg and coat with the bread-crumbs. Place in an ovenproof dish with the remaining butter, then cook in a hot oven for 15 minutes. Serve immediately, with the Hollandaise sauce on the side.

Dry white wines: Quincy, Saumur, dry Graves, Alsace Pinot Blanc, Clairette de Die.

US	Ingredients	Met/Imp
3 lb	skate wings	1.5 kg/3 lb
	court bouillon	
	salt and pepper	
I	lemon, juice of	I
I stick	butter	100 g/4 oz
I	egg	I
5 cups	fresh white breadcrumbs	300 g/10 oz
	TO SERVE	
	Hollandaise Sauce (*page 70*)	

FILETS DE RAIE À LA POULETTE

SKATE POULETTE

Preparation 40 minutes • Cooking 40 minutes

Cook the skate in court bouillon. Trim it and cut it into 16 thin slices. Put the slices in a dish, sprinkle with a little lemon juice, season with salt and pepper and cover with the sliced onions. Leave to stand for 30 minutes.

Remove the onion. Quickly fry the skate slices in the butter, then roll up and secure with wooden cocktail sticks. Quickly fry again in butter, coat with flour and place in an ovenproof dish. Cook in a moderate oven for 20 minutes, then remove the cocktail sticks.

Slice the hard-boiled eggs and arrange around the skate on a heated serving dish. Accompany with béchamel sauce.

Dry white wines: Saumur, Alsace Pinot Blanc, Coteaux Champenois, Mâcon-Viré, Cheverny.

US	Ingredients	Met/Imp
2½ lb	skate wings	1.1 kg/2½ lb
	court bouillon	
I,	lemon, juice of	I
	salt and pepper	
2	large onions	2
I stick	butter	100 g/4 oz
⅔ cup	flour	75 g/3 oz
3	hard-boiled eggs	3
	TO SERVE	
I quart	Béchamel Sauce (*page 62*)	I litre/1¾ pints

US	Ingredients	Met/Imp
2½ lb	skate wings	1.1 kg/2½ lb
	court bouillon	
	salt and pepper	
⅓ cup	capers	50 g/2 oz
1 tbsp	chopped parsley	15 ml/1 tbsp
1 stick	butter	100 g/4 oz
¼ cup	white wine vinegar	50 ml/2 fl oz
	TO SERVE	
1 lb	boiled potatoes	500 g/1 lb

SKATE WITH NOISETTE BUTTER*

Preparation 20 minutes • Cooking 15 minutes

This is the most common way of cooking skate. Noisette butter may be quite a deep brown, but it should never be black.

Cook the pieces of skate in court bouillon, just at a simmer, then drain and pat dry. Arrange on a heated serving dish, season with salt and pepper and sprinkle with the capers and parsley. Pour on the butter, heated with the vinegar in a frying pan until nut-brown. Serve boiled potatoes on the side.

Dry white wines: Quincy, dry Graves, Alsace Riesling.

US	Ingredients	Met/Imp
3 lb	skate wings	1.5 kg/3 lb
	salt and pepper	
¼ cup	white wine vinegar	100 ml/4 fl oz
2	onions	2
1	bouquet garni	1
3	leeks (white parts)	3
1 stick	butter	100 g/4 oz
3 tbsp	flour	30 g/1 oz
2 cups	hot milk	500 ml/18 fl oz
1 pinch	nutmeg	1 pinch
	chopped parsley	
½ cup	fresh white breadcrumbs	25 g/scant 1 oz
¼ cup	grated cheese	25 g/scant 1 oz

RAIE À LA SAINT-CAST

GRATIN OF SKATE FROM SAINT-CAST

Preparation 30 minutes • Cooking 35 minutes

Take the skate wings, dip into cold water, then brush to remove the viscous coating. Cut off the flat edge of the wings, which is completely composed of cartilage, and cut the wings into pieces along the grain.

Put the skate pieces in a shallow pan, cover with cold water and add 15 ml/1 tbsp salt, the vinegar, sliced onions and bouquet garni. Bring to the boil, then cook gently for 15 minutes.

Meanwhile, prepare the sauce. Thinly slice the leeks and sweat them with three-quarters of the butter until they are nearly cooked. Mix in the flour and cook for a few minutes. Add the milk, a pinch each of salt and pepper and the nutmeg. Bring to the boil, stirring. Add the parsley and cook gently for 25 minutes.

Drain the pieces of skate on a tea-towel. Scrape off the skin from both sides and arrange the skate in the shape of a wing in an ovenproof dish. Place in a hot oven for 5–6 minutes to evaporate the remaining moisture in the flesh. Cover with the sauce and sprinkle with the breadcrumbs mixed with the grated cheese. Pour on the remaining butter, melted, and brown in the hot oven.

Dry white wines: Muscadet, Sancerre, Quincy, Pouilly-Fumé.

ROUGET

RED MULLET

THE SURMULLET AND THE SAND (OR MUD) MULLET ARE NOW grouped together as 'rouget barbet' (red mullet). La Reynière called them sea woodcocks, because it is recommended not to gut them (mainly the small ones); it is also possible to wait for a day before cooking them. Their taste is original and exquisite. They have only one fault: their thin and curved bones. The small Mediterranean red mullet are considered to be the best. Grilled (or broiled), fried, cooked in the oven, *en papillotes* (buttered paper), or with olive oil, they provide delicate and tasty dishes.

ROUGETS À LA BORDELAISE

——— RED MULLET BORDELAISE ———

Preparation 30 minutes • Cooking 15–20 minutes

US	Ingredients	Met/Imp
8, each about 5 oz	red mullet	8, each about 150 g/5 oz
	salt and pepper	
10 tbsp	butter	150 g/5 oz
2 cups	dry white wine	500 ml/18 fl oz
4	shallots	4
6 tbsp	flour	50 g/2 oz
	Tomato Sauce (*page 80*)	
2	tarragon sprigs	2

Trim and season the mullet, then cook them gently in half of the butter in a frying pan. Pour in the wine and add the finely chopped shallots. Bring to the boil, cover and simmer for 12 minutes. Take out the fish, drain them and reserve the cooking liquid. Keep the fish warm.

Mix the flour and a little tomato sauce with half of the remaining butter and cook to make a brown roux. Strain in the reserved mullet cooking liquid, then strain again through a fine sieve and reduce to a syrupy consistency. Remove from the heat and add the remaining butter and chopped tarragon. Check the seasoning and serve with the mullet.

Dry white wines: Graves, Bergerac, Entre-Deux-Mers, Alsace Sylvaner.

ROUGETS FROIDS À L'ORIENTALE

- COLD RED MULLET ORIENTAL STYLE -

Preparation 10 minutes • Cooking about 15 minutes

US	Ingredients	Met/Imp
8, each about 5 oz	red mullet	8, each about 150 g/5 oz
	olive oil	
½ cup	dry white wine	100 ml/4 fl oz
	salt and pepper	
6	tomatoes	6
2	parsley stalks	2
1	thyme sprig	1
¼	bay leaf	¼
6	coriander seeds	6
1 tsp	saffron	5 ml/1 tsp
1	lemon, slices of	1

Arrange the mullet in a lightly oiled flameproof dish. Cover with the wine and add salt and pepper, the skinned, de-seeded and chopped tomatoes, parsley stalks, thyme, bay leaf, coriander and saffron. Cover with greaseproof (wax) paper, bring to the boil, then cook for 10 minutes over a low heat. Remove and allow to cool, then serve in the cooking liquid, with a slice of lemon on each fish.

Dry white wines: Cassis, Côtes de Provence, Clairette du Languedoc, Muscadet.

US	Ingredients	Met/Imp
8, each about 5 oz	red mullet	8, each about 150 g/5 oz
2 cups	dry white wine	500 ml/18 fl oz
scant 1 cup	water	200 ml/7 fl oz
1	bouquet garni	1
2 tsp	salt	10 ml/2 tsp
	pepper	
1	shallot	10 g/½ oz
10 sprigs	parsley	10 g/½ oz
1 stick	butter	100 g/4 oz
¼ cup	double (heavy) cream	60 ml/4 tbsp
4	egg yolks	4
1	lemon, juice of	1

ROUGETS FROIDS POCHÉS À L'ÉCHALOTE

COLD POACHED RED MULLET WITH SHALLOT

Preparation 20 minutes • Cooking 15–20 minutes

Small mullet may be gutted or not, according to taste. Poach the mullet in the wine and water with the bouquet garni, salt and pepper for about 10 minutes. Take out the fish, drain them and reserve the cooking liquid.

Fry the chopped shallot and parsley in a little of the butter until soft, then strain in the reserved cooking liquid. Reduce, then mix in the cream and egg yolks. Add the remaining butter and lemon juice. Strain on to the mullet and chill.

Wines: as a general rule, serve the same wine as the one used for cooking.

US	Ingredients	Met/Imp
8, each about 6 oz	red mullet	8, each about 175 g/6 oz
3 oz	mushrooms	75 g/3 oz
½ cup	dry white wine	100 ml/4 fl oz
	salt and pepper	
	Duxelles Sauce (page 68)	
½ cup	fresh white breadcrumbs	25 g/scant 1 oz
4 tbsp	butter	50 g/2 oz
	TO SERVE	
1	lemon, juice of	1
1 tbsp	chopped parsley	15 ml/1 tbsp

ROUGETS GRATINÉS

RED MULLET AU GRATIN

Preparation 45 minutes • Cooking 12 minutes

Put the mullet on a buttered ovenproof dish, surround with thinly sliced raw mushrooms, pour over the wine, season with salt and pepper and cover completely with Duxelles sauce. Sprinkle with the breadcrumbs and the melted butter. Cook in a moderate oven for 12 minutes and serve sprinkled with lemon juice and parsley.

Dry white wines: Saumur, Sancerre, Quincy, Graves, Alsace Sylvaner or Riesling, Cassis, Pouilly-Fuissé.

US	Ingredients	Met/Imp
8, each about 6 oz	red mullet	8, each about 175 g/6 oz
4 tbsp	butter	50 g/2 oz
3 tbsp	flour	30 g/1 oz
½ cup	oil	100 ml/4 fl oz
3	shallots	3
1 tbsp	*fines herbes*	15 ml/1 tbsp
3 oz	mushrooms	75 g/3 oz
½ cup	dry white wine	100 ml/4 fl oz
	salt and pepper	
	GARNISH	
1	lemon, slices of	1

ROUGETS GRILLÉS

GRILLED RED MULLET

Preparation 20 minutes • Cooking 15 minutes

Grill the fish, preferably wrapped in oiled greaseproof or baking parchment or foil. Serve with a sauce made as follows:

Make a blond roux with most of the butter and the flour. Add a little oil, the chopped shallots, fines herbes and mushrooms, then the wine and seasoning. Cook for 15 minutes, then strain and add the remaining butter. Serve hot with the mullet, garnished with lemon slices.

Dry white wines: Saumur, Sancerre, Côtes de Provence, Chablis, Bellet, Cassis.

Hake Steaks 'as at Biriatou'
Biriatou is a tiny village in the mountains a few kilometres from Hendaye, evocative of all the scents of the Basque coast: tomatoes, sweet peppers and fried onion echo them. (Recipe on page 160.)

Salt Cod with Aïoli
*In this dish, in which Frédéric Mistral saw 'the warmth, strength and happiness of
the Provençal sun' concentrated, it is the aïoli, the famous mayonnaise with oil and
garlic, which takes the starring role. It is a festive dish with numerous players, who
form a chorus around the poached salt cod: boiled vegetables, olives, hard-boiled eggs,
and sometimes even snails. (Recipe on page 184.)*

Mackerel with Redcurrants

Mackerel is usually served with 'groseilles à maquereaux' (gooseberries), which enhance the fish with their delicious juice, crisp texture and sour taste. Redcurrants give a similar effect. (Recipe on page 178.)

Trout 'au Bleu'
This is a fisherman's recipe because as soon as the trout have been caught they must be wiped and gutted, then plunged immediately into a vinegary court-bouillon. (Recipe on page 217.)

Turbot with Chambertin Wine
'King of Lent', as it has been called over the years, this magnificent fish with fine white flesh well deserves a wine as luxurious as Chambertin for its preparation. The strength and smoothness of this grand cru burgundy, the subtlety of its bouquet as well as the firmness of its structure recommend it as the wine to accompany this top-class dish. (Recipe on page 222.)

Sardines with Spinach
Arranged on a bed of spinach, the sardines are moistened with a trickle of olive oil and dusted with breadcrumbs so that they become golden in the oven. An extremely simple dish, and one that is a guaranteed success. (Recipe on page 199.)

— MARINATED GRILLED RED MULLET —

Preparation 25 minutes • Marinating 1 hour • Cooking 15 minutes

US	Ingredients	Met/Imp
8, each about 6 oz	red mullet	8, each about 175 g/6 oz
½ cup	olive oil	100 ml/4 fl oz
½ cup	white wine vinegar	50 ml/2 fl oz
	salt	
6	peppercorns	6
1	large onion	1
1	lemon, juice of	1
2	tarragon sprigs	2
1 tsp	mustard	5 ml/1 tsp

Trim the mullet and marinate them for 1 hour in the oil, vinegar, salt, peppercorns, sliced onion and lemon juice. Grill (or broil) them, basting with the marinade and turning once. Serve with the remaining marinade, strained, heated and seasoned with the chopped tarragon and mustard.

Dry white wines: Chablis, Arbois, Alsace Sylvaner, Sancerre, Muscadet, Quincy, Gros Plant du Pays Nantais.

RED MULLET WITH FIELD MUSHROOMS*

Preparation 15 minutes • Cooking 15–20 minutes

US	Ingredients	Met/Imp
8, each about 5 oz	red mullet	8, each about 150 g/5 oz
1 stick	butter	100 g/4 oz
	salt and pepper	
1 tbsp	chopped parsley	15 ml/1 tbsp
5 oz	field or other wild mushrooms	150 g/5 oz
½ cup	dry white wine	100 ml/4 fl oz
1	bouquet garni	1

Trim the mullet. Put them in a flameproof casserole with three-quarters of the butter, salt, pepper and parsley. Cover and cook over a gentle heat.

Meanwhile, cook the mushrooms with the wine, bouquet garni and remaining butter. Pour all of this into the casserole when the mullet are nearly cooked. The liquid must cover them completely. Reduce for a few moments, then serve hot.

Dry white wines: Quincy, Graves, Chablis, Alsace Riesling, Coteaux Champenois.

RED MULLET NANTAISE

Preparation 30 minutes • Cooking 15 minutes

US	Ingredients	Met/Imp
8, each about 5 oz	red mullet	8, each about 150 g/5 oz
	salt and pepper	
½ cup	oil	100 ml/4 fl oz
1	shallot	1
½ cup	dry white wine	100 ml/4 fl oz
2 tbsp	Meat Glaze (page 56)	30 ml/2 tbsp
1 stick	butter	100 g/4 oz
1 tsp	chopped parsley	5 ml/1 tsp

Simply remove the gills from the mullet; mullet is not always gutted. Wipe the fish with a cloth but do not wash them. Slash them on both sides to prevent them bursting while cooking. Season with salt and pepper, sprinkle with the oil and put them on a preheated grill (broiler) pan. Cook them gently for 15 minutes.

Meanwhile, put the shallot, chopped as finely as possible, and the white wine in a small saucepan. Boil until the wine has evaporated completely, then add the melted meat glaze, the butter, a pinch of salt and pepper and the parsley. Mix everything together until the butter is just softened, as for Maître d'Hôtel Butter (*page 52*).

When the mullet are cooked, remove their livers. Crush these on a plate and stir into the butter mixture. Spread on a heated serving dish and arrange the mullet on top.

Dry white wines: Pouilly-Fumé, Muscadet, Quincy, Sauvignon de Touraine.

US	Ingredients	Met/Imp
1, about 10 oz	red mullet	1, about 300 g/10 oz
	salt and pepper	
1 tbsp	flour	15 ml/1 tbsp
2½ tbsp	olive oil	37.5 ml/ 2½ tbsp
3	tomatoes	3
1 tsp	tomato paste (optional)	5 ml/1 tsp
1	garlic clove, crushed	1
1 tsp	chopped shallot	5 ml/1 tsp
6	black olives	6
6	green olives	6
	GARNISH	
6	anchovy fillets in oil	6
2 tsp	butter	20 g/¾ oz
1	lemon slice	1
	parsley	

ROUGET À LA NIÇOISE

RED MULLET NIÇOISE

Preparation 25 minutes • Cooking 30 minutes • Serves 1

Scale, gut, wash and wipe the mullet. Season with salt and pepper and coat with the flour. Heat 30 ml/2 tbsp of the oil in a frying pan until very hot. Brown the mullet on both sides in the oil, then cook over a moderate heat for 10–15 minutes. Keep warm.

Hull the tomatoes and drop them into a pan of boiling water. After a few seconds, take them out of the water and skin them. Cut the tomatoes in half and press them to extract the seeds and juice. Chop the tomato flesh into large pieces and put in a small saucepan. Add salt, pepper and the remaining oil, and the tomato paste if using. Reduce over moderate heat for 5–6 minutes until the liquid has evaporated and a purée is obtained. Add the garlic, shallot and the stoned (pitted) olives. Stir well to mix. Place the mullet in an ovenproof serving dish and cover with the tomato mixture. Put in a hot oven for 5–6 minutes.

Make the garnish. Work 2 anchovy fillets through a sieve with the help of a pestle, then mix them with the butter. Cut the lemon slice so that it has a crinkled edge. Garnish the dish with 4 anchovy fillets criss-crossing each other, a pat of anchovy butter, the lemon slice and a little parsley.

Wines: preferably white or rosé Bellet, Cassis, Palette or rosé Tavel.

PAPILLOTE OF RED MULLET
DOGARESSE

Preparation 1½ hours • Cooking 40 minutes • Serves 1

US	Ingredients	Met/Imp
2	scallops in shell	2
1 cup	*court bouillon* made with dry white wine, water, salt, pepper, bouquet garni, 1 thinly sliced carrot and 1 thinly sliced onion	250 ml/9 fl oz
6	large mussels	6
5	langoustines	5
1	red mullet	1
	salt and pepper	
2 tbsp	flour	30 ml/2 tbsp
2 tbsp	oil	30 ml/2 tbsp
3 tbsp	butter	40 g/1½ oz
1 tbsp	chopped parsley	15 ml/1 tbsp
1 tsp	lemon juice	5 ml/1 tsp
	beaten egg	
3	small boiled potatoes	3

Open the scallops and take out the meat. Keep only the white and orange parts, remove the scraps and wash under cold running water.

Put the scallops in a small saucepan and cover with the lukewarm court bouillon. Simmer gently for about 15 minutes, then set aside, off the heat. Scrub the mussels and wash them in several changes of water, then make them open in a saucepan over high heat. Remove the shells and reserve the mussel meat. Shell the langoustines and remove their heads: break the tail carapace by bending it and slide the shell along the meat. Reserve the tails.

Gut the mullet, remove the gills and wash it. Cut off the fins and scale the fish. Wipe it and add salt on both sides. Coat in the flour.

Heat the oil in a frying pan until hot but not smoking and brown the mullet in it. Cook for a good 5 minutes on each side, basting often with the oil. Add the butter, keep the frying pan on a low heat, then add the langoustine tails and sprinkle with salt. Cook slowly, basting constantly with the cooking juices.

Drain the scallops from the court bouillon. Add them to the pan with the mussels, chopped parsley and lemon juice. Check the seasoning and keep warm.

Preheat the oven to very hot. Meanwhile, prepare the papillote. Brush a 5 cm/2 inch border of beaten egg around the edges of a sheet of grease-proof or baking parchment paper. Put the mullet on one half of the sheet and surround it with its seafood garnish and the potatoes. Sprinkle with the cooking juices. Fold the paper over the fish and press to seal the edges. Brush the 3 sides that are stuck together with more beaten egg. Fold the double edge once more, forming small overlapping folds to ensure a tight seal.

Put the papillote on an ovenproof serving dish in the preheated oven for 5 minutes. While in the oven, the papillote will swell up a lot, almost without browning. The mullet will become impregnated with the aroma of the garnish and will stay soft. It is of course possible to put several mullet and their garnishes into one papillote.

Fine white wines: Bellet, Cassis, Graves, Châteauneuf-du-Pape, Hermitage, Savennières-Coulée de Serrant, Chablis Grand Cru, Meursault, Corton-Charlemagne, Montrachet.

SAINT-PIERRE

JOHN DORY

THE FIRM, WHITE FLESH OF THIS HIGH-QUALITY FISH FORMS four fillets which have no bones and are easy to remove. The John Dory ('Saint-Pierre' or 'dorée' in French) is particularly appreciated by the English. Its enormous head and its viscera do mean there is up to 70 per cent waste, but its delicacy makes it one of the best sea fish for braising, sautéeing, grilling (or broiling) or cooking *en papillote*.

FILETS DE SAINT-PIERRE À LA CRÈME

– FILLETS OF JOHN DORY WITH CREAM –

Preparation 40 minutes • Cooking about 45 minutes

US	Ingredients	Met/Imp
2½ lb	John Dory fillets, trimmings reserved	1.1 kg/2½ lb
	salt and pepper	
14 tbsp	butter	200 g/7 oz
1	lemon, juice of	1
1	large onion	1
1	thyme sprig	1
½	bay leaf	½
2	parsley sprigs	2
½ cup	dry white wine	100 ml/4 fl oz
¼ cup	Kneaded Butter (*page 49*)	50 g/2 oz
2	egg yolks	2
½ cup	crème fraîche	100 ml/4 fl oz

Put the John Dory fillets on a buttered baking tray and season with salt and pepper. Dot with small pieces of butter and sprinkle with a little lemon juice. Cover with buttered greaseproof or baking parchment paper and cook in the oven for 10–12 minutes. Keep warm.

Meanwhile, make the sauce. Put the fish bones and trimmings into a saucepan. Add the thinly sliced onion, thyme, bay leaf, parsley and salt and pepper; pour in the wine and simmer for 25 minutes. Strain through a fine sieve. Boil this fish stock and thicken with the kneaded butter. Cook for a few minutes.

Add the juice produced by the John Dory fillets. Cook for a few moments to reduce, then thicken with the egg yolks mixed with the crème fraîche. Pour this sauce, which must be very creamy, on to the well-drained John Dory fillets.

White wines: Alsace Gewürztraminer, or Pinot Gris, Vouvray, Anjou, Graves, Barsac.

FISH LOAF

Preparation 30 minutes • Cooking 30 minutes • Serves 4

US	Ingredients	Met/Imp
scant 1 cup	milk	200 ml/7 fl oz
5 tbsp	butter	65 g/2½ oz
3 tbsp	flour	25 g/scant 1 oz
	salt and pepper	
1¼ lb	John Dory fillets, trimmings reserved	600 g/1¼ lb
3 tbsp	crème fraîche	45 ml/3 tbsp
2	whole eggs	2
1	egg yolk	1

Prepare a béchamel sauce. Heat the milk to boiling point. In another saucepan, melt 50 g/2 oz (4 tbsp) of the butter. When it is melted, add the flour. Mix well to obtain a thick paste. Add the boiling milk. Stir. Cook gently for a few minutes, stirring constantly. Add salt and pepper. Leave the sauce – which should be thick – to cool.

Skin the John Dory fillets. Cut the flesh into small pieces, then pound in a mortar and pestle. Alternatively, work in a food processor and complete the operation by crushing the purée with a fork. When the fish purée is really smooth, gradually add the cold béchamel to it. Mix thoroughly. In the same way, add the (unbeaten) crème fraîche, the whole eggs, egg yolk, salt and pepper.

Put the fish purée through a vegetable mill, using the very fine blade, or work it through a sieve, using a pestle.

Butter a charlotte mould. Pour the mixture into the mould and place in a *bain-marie* in a moderate oven to cook for 30 minutes. Remove from the oven and take the mould out of the bain-marie to allow the fish loaf to cool for a few minutes. It will detach itself from the mould.

Turn out on to a hot dish. Coat with a few spoonfuls of the accompanying sauce of your choice (*pages 60–82*). Serve the remaining sauce on the side.

White wines: Muscadet, Savennières, Bourgogne, Rully, Montagny, Pouilly-Fuissé, Saint-Véran, Crozes-Hermitage, Côtes de Provence.

JOHN DORY WITH COURGETTES AND LEMON

Preparation 10 minutes • Cooking about 15 minutes

US	Ingredients	Met/Imp
6 tbsp	butter	75 g/3 oz
6, each about 5 oz	John Dory fillets	6, each about 150 g/5 oz
6	thin-skinned courgettes (zucchini)	6
2	lemons	2
scant 1 cup	crème fraîche	200 ml/7 fl oz
	salt and pepper	
1 tbsp	chopped basil	15 ml/1 tbsp

Melt the butter in a large frying pan. Fry the John Dory fillets gently in it for 5–6 minutes on each side. Take them out and keep warm. Add the courgettes (zucchini), washed and very thinly sliced, to the pan. Sweat them in the same butter for 5 minutes, then add the grated rind of 1 lemon and its juice. Stir, then thicken with the crème fraîche. Add salt, pepper and the basil. Arrange the John Dory fillets on a heated serving dish, surround with the garnish of courgettes (zucchini) and cream and finish with the second lemon, cut into small cubes.

White wines: Alsace Riesling or Pinot Gris, Chablis, Meursault, Pouilly-Fuissé, Condrieu, Châteauneuf-du-Pape, dry Graves.

PIKE-PERCH

THE PIKE-PERCH INHABITS THE WATERWAYS OF CENTRAL and eastern Europe and its flesh is greatly prized. It has been introduced into the Doubs, the Rhine and the Saône, but is also bred in lakes. With its delicate white flesh, this fish may be prepared like pike or perch, and is especially good with cream.

SANDRE À LA BIÈRE

PIKE-PERCH WITH BEER

Preparation 40 minutes • Cooking 25 minutes

US	Ingredients	Met/Imp
3	onions	3
2	celery stalks	2
6 tbsp	butter	75 g/3 oz
2 tbsp	flour	30 ml/2 tbsp
I large glass	beer	I large glass
	fresh ginger root	
I	bouquet garni	I
3 tbsp	oil	45 ml/3 tbsp
I, about 3 lb	pike-perch	I, about 1.5 kg/3 lb
I tbsp	strong mustard	15 ml/I tbsp
	salt and pepper	
	parsley	

Finely chop the onions and celery and fry them in half of the butter until they are transparent. Sprinkle them with the flour and brown them. Stir in the beer. Season, add a little grated ginger and the bouquet garni and cook gently for 15 minutes.

Heat most of the remaining butter and the oil in a cocotte. Fry the fish in it on both sides. Pour in the strained sauce and simmer until cooked.

Put the pike-perch on a heated serving dish. Mix a little butter and mustard with the sauce, season with salt and pepper, then use to coat the fish. Sprinkle with chopped parsley.

Wines: Alsace Pinot Gris or Gewürztraminer, Arbois.

SARDINE

SARDINE

THIS POPULAR FISH IS ALWAYS BETTER WHEN EATEN AT THE seaside, because it should always be completely fresh: stiff body, very shiny eyes and no blood at the gills. The sardines known as 'royans' are particularly appreciated. The sardine is essentially a spring and summer fish and is at its best in June and July – fat, tasty and perfect for grilling. It is suitable for both soups and bouillabaisses and may also be prepared in the oven or the frying pan, 'en escabèche' (fried, marinated and served cold) or in a terrine, etc.

SARDINES WITH SPINACH*

Preparation 40 minutes • Cooking 12 minutes

US	Ingredients	Met/Imp
4½ lb	spinach	2 kg/4½ lb
	salt	
2 tsp	milk	10 ml/2 tsp
24	sardines	24
½ cup	fresh white breadcrumbs	25 g/scant 1 oz
½ cup	olive oil	100 ml/4 fl oz

Blanch the well-washed spinach, then drain, chop and season with salt. Mix in the milk, then spread out on the bottom of an ovenproof dish.

Scale and gut the sardines . Wash and dry them, then flatten them out and arrange them on the spinach. Sprinkle with breadcrumbs, a pinch of salt and the olive oil, then bake until browned in a moderately hot oven.

Dry white wines: Côtes de Provence, Cassis, Clairette du Languedoc, Clairette de Die.
Rosé wines: Bandol, Cassis.

SARDINES MAÎTRE D'HÔTEL

Preparation 20 minutes • Cooking 10 minutes

US	Ingredients	Met/Imp
24	sardines	24
½ cup	olive oil	100 ml/4 fl oz
	salt	
4	lemons, quarters of	4
	fried parsley	
	Maître d'Hôtel Butter (*page 52*)	

Scale the sardines without damaging the skin. Gut them through the gills. Brush them with the oil and grill (broil) them for 5 minutes under a very high heat (close to the source). Turn them over and finish cooking. Add salt and serve garnished with lemon quarters and fried parsley. Serve the maître d'hôtel butter in a sauce boat.

Dry white wines: Chablis, Sancerre, Muscadet, Quincy.

TOMATOES STUFFED WITH SARDINES

Preparation 30 minutes • Cooking 10 minutes

US	Ingredients	Met/Imp
8	tomatoes	8
	salt and pepper	
16	sardines	16
2 cups	oil	500 ml/18 fl oz
½ cup	Maître d'Hôtel Butter (*page 52*)	100 g/4 oz
8	croûtons	8

Cut a slice from the top of each tomato, remove the flesh and seeds, push back the flesh, season the inside and cook the tomatoes in a low oven. Take the tomatoes out and drain off the liquid inside. Brush the sardines with the oil and grill (broil) them. Remove the fillets, reserving the heads.

Divide each fillet into 2–3 pieces and mash with the maître d'hôtel butter. Fill the tomatoes with the mixture and heat through in the oven. Place the sardine heads on top of the tomatoes and serve with croûtons fried in butter.

Dry white wines: Saumur, Sancerre, Quincy, Muscadet.

SAUMON

SALMON

THIS MIGRANT SEA FISH SWIMS UP RIVER TO SPAWN, SOMETIMES leaping over high weirs. In France, salmon still sometimes come up the Loire and the Adour, but they are much rarer than they used to be. Norway, Canada and Scotland are now the most important suppliers to France. The firm pink flesh of this renowned fish is greatly appreciated by lovers of fine seafood. It is prepared whole (in which case, a fish kettle is indispensable) or cut into steaks or slices. It may be cooked in a *court bouillon* and served with a highly seasoned sauce, or braised or baked in the oven with herbs and spices. Steaks or fillets are the most convenient way of preparing salmon and they may be poached, grilled (or broiled) or sautéed. The recipes given here are only for fresh salmon; smoked salmon should be used for cold entrées or hors-d'œuvre.

COQUILLES DE SAUMON

SALMON SCALLOPS

Preparation 50 minutes • Cooking 12 minutes

US	Ingredients	Met/Imp
3 oz	leftover salmon, per scallop	75 g/3 oz
	sauce of choice (pages 60–82)	

These scallops are made with different sauces. Cover the bottom of scallop shells (silver or porcelain ones, or empty coquilles Saint-Jacques) with a spoonful of the chosen sauce. Fill with leftover salmon with all the bones and fragments of skin removed, cover with more sauce and glaze or cook au gratin in a moderately hot oven.

With white wine: fill the scallop shells and cover with Bordelaise Sauce (*page 63*) made with white wine and butter; glaze well.

À la Mornay: fill the scallop shells and cover with Mornay Sauce (*page 73*). Sprinkle with grated cheese and melted butter and brown in the oven.

Sauce crevettes: add cooked prawns or shrimp to the salmon and cover with Prawn Sauce (*page 67*).

Au gratin: fill the scallop shells and cover with Duxelles Sauce (*page 68*). Sprinkle with fine breadcrumbs and melted butter and brown in the oven. On removing from the oven, sprinkle with lemon and a little chopped parsley.

Cold: fill the bottom of the scallop shells with a small *macédoine* of seasoned vegetables or a fine *julienne* of lettuce. Add the salmon and cover with Mayonnaise (*page 72*) or Green Herb Mayonnaise (*page 81*). Surround with a narrow border of chopped hard-boiled egg (white and yolk) mixed with chopped parsley.

Dry white wines: Saumur, Sancerre, Pouilly-Fumé, Muscadet, dry Graves, Chablis, Hermitage.

——— POACHED SALMON ———

Preparation 25 minutes • Cooking 12 minutes

US	Ingredients	Met/Imp
	court bouillon	
1, about 2½ lb	thick salmon steak	1, about 1.1 kg/2½ lb
	salt and pepper	
1 handful	parsley	1 handful
1 lb	boiled potatoes	500 g/1 lb
	TO SERVE	
	Béarnaise Sauce (*page 61*) or Hollandaise Sauce (*page 70*)	

Prepare an adequate amount of court bouillon without vinegar, as its acidity would spoil the beautiful colour of the salmon. Put the salmon in it, bring to the boil, then poach over a gentle heat for about 30 minutes, or according to the thickness.

Season with salt and pepper, then serve garnished with parsley sprigs, accompanied by boiled potatoes and the sauce of your choice.

Dry or medium dry white wines: Vouvray, Anjou, Côtes de Montravel, Graves.

——— HOT SALMON MOUSSE ———

Preparation 1 hour • Cooking 45 minutes

US	Ingredients	Met/Imp
1¾ lb	filleted salmon	800 g/1¾ lb
	salt and pepper	
6	egg whites	6
scant 1 cup	crème fraîche	200 ml/7 fl oz
2 tbsp	butter	30 g/1 oz

Pound the salmon flesh in a mortar and pestle with salt, a little pepper, and 2 egg whites added gradually.

Sieve into a bowl, work for a few moments with a spoon, then keep on ice for 1 hour.

Using a spatula, mix in the crème fraîche and remaining egg whites, beaten until stiff. Put the mixture into a well-buttered ring mould and poach in a *bain-marie* for 40–45 minutes, until firm and springy to the touch. Remove the mould from the bain-marie and leave to stand for 7–8 minutes, to allow it to settle a little.

Serve the mousse hot with one of the sauces that go particularly well with salmon: Bordelaise Sauce (*page 63*); a good Béchamel Sauce (*page 62*) with 100 ml/4 fl oz (½ cup) crème fraîche added; Genevoise Sauce (*page 69*) with plenty of butter; Américaine Sauce (*page 60*). Cover the mousse with some of the chosen sauce and serve the rest on the side in a sauce boat.

Wines: with a white wine sauce, Coteaux Champenois, Vouvray, Anjou; with Américaine Sauce, Saumur, Quincy, Sancerre, Pouilly-Fumé, Muscadet, Chablis.

US	Ingredients	Met/Imp
I lb	salmon	500 g/I lb
¼ cup	olive oil	60 ml/4 tbsp
I	lemon, juice of	I
I tbsp	paprika	15 ml/I tbsp
	cayenne	
I cup	crème fraîche	250 ml/9 fl oz
3 tbsp	iced water	45 ml/3 tbsp
	COURT BOUILLON	
I quart	water	I litre/1¾ pints
2 cups	dry white wine	500 ml/18 fl oz
5 oz	carrots	150 g/5 oz
¼ lb	onions	100 g/4 oz
6	parsley stalks	6
I	thyme sprig	I
I	bay leaf	I
I½ tbsp	salt	25 g/scant I oz
6	peppercorns	6

COLD SALMON MOUSSE

Preparation 1 hour • Cooking 45 minutes

First prepare the court bouillon. Mix the water and wine with the sliced carrots, thinly sliced onions, parsley stalks, thyme and bay leaf. Add the salt (do not add the peppercorns to the court bouillon until the last few minutes of cooking) and simmer for 30 minutes, then strain and allow to cool.

Cook the salmon in the court bouillon for 10 minutes at a temperature where it is just simmering and not boiling. Drain the salmon, remove the skin and bones and pound the flesh finely in a mortar and pestle, gradually adding the oil, lemon juice, paprika and cayenne. Leave to cool.

Beat the crème fraîche and the iced water into a firm *chantilly*. Mix with the salmon purée. Pour into a mould and chill until set.

Wine: Champagne.

PIÈCE DE SAUMON BRAISÉ ET PURÉE D'OSEILLE

BRAISED SALMON WITH SORREL PURÉE

US	Ingredients	Met/Imp
3 lb	trimmed tail end of salmon	1.5 kg/3 lb
scant ½ lb	hard pork or bacon fat	200 g/7 oz
2	carrots	2
2	onions	2
I	bay leaf	I
I pat	butter	I knob
	salt and pepper	
2 cups	water	500 ml/18 fl oz
3 cups	dry white wine	750 ml/1¼ pints
6½ lb	sorrel	3 kg/6½ lb
½ cup	crème fraîche	100 ml/4 fl oz
3	egg yolks	3

Preparation 1 hour • Cooking 1 hour

Skin the salmon, then lard it with the fat like a fillet (tenderloin) of beef. Put it into a saucepan with the sliced carrots and onions, bay leaf, butter and salt and pepper. Add the water and wine so that the liquid just covers the fish. Bring to the boil, then cook very gently for 45 minutes.

Meanwhile, prepare a purée with the sorrel, crème fraîche and egg yolks. Put it in a hot dish and put the well-drained salmon on top. Reduce some of the salmon cooking liquid and pour over the sorrel.

The sorrel may be replaced by spinach. Tuna may be prepared in the same way.

Dry white wines: dry Graves, Arbois, Alsace Riesling, Chablis, Meursault, Pouilly-Fuissé, Sancerre.

— SALMON WITH BOILED POTATOES —

Preparation 35 minutes • Cooking 12 minutes

Poach the salmon in court bouillon for about 12 minutes or until cooked. Season, then serve covered with a napkin, accompanied by a fried parsley garnish and boiled potatoes.

Accompany the salmon with a sauce of your choice – Hollandaise (*page 70*), Prawn (*page 67*) or Venetian (*page 81*). Two sauces are usually served with large pieces of salmon.

White wines: Montrachet, Meursault, Condrieu, Graves.

US	Ingredients	Met/Imp
I, about 2½ lb	salmon piece	I, about 1.1 kg/2½ lb
	court bouillon	
	salt and pepper	
	fried parsley	
I lb	boiled new potatoes	500 g/I lb

SALMON WITH WHITE WINE SAUCE, — TRUFFLES AND MADERIA —

Preparation 50 minutes • Cooking 20 minutes

Take a very pink small salmon. Gut, trim and braise it gently in some dry white Sancerre wine, with a mirepoix of vegetables and herbs as listed, for 15–20 minutes, or until cooked.

When the fish is cooked, skin it carefully and keep it warm.

Reduce the salmon cooking liquid until it has the consistency of a sauce, then add the fish fumet, butter and crème fraîche.

Add plenty of lemon juice, season and cover the salmon with this sauce. Just before serving, sprinkle with fresh truffles, which have first been lightly poached in madeira.

White wines: Sancerre, Pouilly-Fumé, Quincy, Savennières.

US	Ingredients	Met/Imp
I	small salmon	I
I quart	white Sancerre wine	I litre/1¾ pints
	Mirepoix (*page 50*) made with carrot, onion, shallot, bay leaf, thyme, parsley and celery	
scant I cup	Fish Fumet (*page 57*)	200 ml/7 fl oz
14 tbsp	butter	200 g/7 oz
scant I cup	crème fraîche	200 ml/7 fl oz
I	lemon, juice of	I
	salt and pepper	
2 oz	truffles	50 g/2 oz
¼ cup	madeira	50 ml/2 fl oz

US	Ingredients	Met/Imp
8, each about 6 oz	salmon steaks	8, each about 175 g/6 oz
	salt and pepper	
I	onion	I
a few	parsley stalks	a few
¼ cup	oil	50 ml/2 fl oz
	melted butter	
⅔ cup	Anchovy Butter (page 51)	150 g/5 oz
8	canned anchovy fillets	8

GRILLED SALMON STEAKS WITH ANCHOVY BUTTER*

Preparation 25 minutes • Marinating 30 minutes • Cooking 15 minutes

The anchovy butter may also be served in a sauce boat, in which case serve the salmon steaks on a napkin with a parsley garnish.

Season the salmon steaks with salt and pepper. Put them on a dish and sprinkle with the finely chopped onion and the parsley stalks broken into small pieces. Pour on the oil and leave to marinate for 30 minutes, turning the steaks over from time to time.

Drain the steaks and brush them with melted butter. Cook under a hot grill (broiler) for about 15 minutes, turning them over after a few minutes. When both sides have browned, turn down the heat.

Spread some anchovy butter on a heated serving dish and arrange the salmon steaks on top. Using the tip of a small knife, remove the piece of bone from the middle of each steak and insert an anchovy fillet into each one. Garnish with the remaining anchovy butter.

Dry white wines: Sancerre, Pouilly-Fumé, dry Graves, Crozes-Hermitage.

US	Ingredients	Met/Imp
8, each about 5 oz	salmon steaks	8, each about 150 g/5 oz
	court bouillon made with I onion, 2 carrots, I bouquet garni, salt, pepper and 500 ml/18 fl oz (2 cups) each dry white wine and water	
I tsp	curry powder	5 ml/I tsp
I cup	Pilau Rice (page 563)	200 g/7 oz
4	hard-boiled eggs, to garnish	4
	SAUCE	
10 tbsp	butter	150 g/5 oz
6 tbsp	flour	50 g/2 oz
2	egg yolks	2
½ cup	crème fraîche	100 ml/4 fl oz

– SALMON STEAKS WITH CURRIED RICE –

Preparation 30 minutes • Cooking 15 minutes

Poach the salmon steaks in the court bouillon.

Make the sauce with the butter, flour and some of the salmon cooking liquid, then stir in the egg yolks and crème fraîche.

Stir the curry powder into the rice and put it in the middle of a serving dish. Arrange the salmon steaks around it and cover with the sauce. Garnish with the sliced hard-boiled eggs.

Dry or medium dry white wines: Saumur, Vouvray, Sancerre, Pouilly-Fumé.

SOLE

SOLE

SOLE IS A COMMON SEA FISH EVERYWHERE, WHETHER IT BE true sole (especially the delicate lined sole, which is exquisite, firm and smooth), the variegated sole, the 'séteau' from Vendée, or sole from Dakar or Senegal, which is much less tasty. Sole caught in cold water is reputedly better than those caught in warm seas. Whether whole or in fillets, this fish is most suitable for a very wide range of culinary preparations according to size: deep-fried, shallow-fried ('à la meunière'), grilled (broiled), poached or braised, not to mention rolled paupiettes or 'turbans de filet'. The *fumet* obtained from sole bones and trimmings has an unequalled flavour. Before preparing a sole, the fins on both sides of the fish, which are full of small bones, must be removed, as must the grey skin. The sole must then be carefully washed and wiped.

CASSOLETTES DE FILETS DE SOLE LASSERRE

FILLETS OF SOLE AND ASPARAGUS IN PUFF PASTRY TARTLETS

Preparation 1 hour • Cooking 30 minutes

Recipe created by the Lasserre restaurant in Paris

US	Ingredients	Met/Imp
I lb	Puff Pastry (*page 579*)	500 g/I lb
4, each about I lb, divided into fillets	sole	4, each about 500 g/I lb, divided into fillets
2½ sticks	butter	300 g/10 oz
3	shallots	3
	salt and pepper	
scant I cup	Chablis wine	200 ml/7 fl oz
scant I cup	Fish Fumet (*page 57*)	200 ml/7 fl oz
6 tbsp	Fish Velouté (*page 57*)	90 ml/6 tbsp
8 tbsp	Dry Duxelles (*page 49*)	120 ml/8 tbsp
24	asparagus tips	24
⅓ cup	Parmesan cheese, grated	40 g/1½ oz
I	truffle, to garnish	I

Roll out the pastry and use to line 8 fairly deep tartlet tins. Use the pastry trimmings to make 'saucepan handles' for each tartlet, then bake blind.

Trim, flatten and fold the fillets of sole and cook them for about 10 minutes in a deep frying pan with 30 g/1 oz (2 tbsp) of the butter and the finely chopped shallots. Add salt and pepper, the Chablis and fish fumet made with the sole trimmings.

When the fillets are cooked, remove them and keep them warm. Reduce the cooking liquid by three-quarters. Add the fish velouté to this reduced liquid, boil for a few minutes, then beat in 200 g/7 oz (14 tbsp) of the butter. Check the seasoning and strain through cheesecloth.

In the bottom of each tartlet, put a little of this sauce, 15 ml/1 tbsp duxelles and 3 asparagus tips lightly fried in the remaining butter. Add a little more sauce, then put in 2 strips of sole fillet. Cover with plenty of sauce, but without overflowing. Sprinkle with the cheese and glaze in a hot oven. Garnish each tartlet with a shiny thin slice of truffle before serving.

White wines: Beaune, Meursault, Champagne.

US	Ingredients	Met/Imp
4, each about 14 oz	sole	4, each about 400 g/14 oz
2 cups	Riesling wine from Alsace	500 ml/18 fl oz
3	shallots	3
½ cup	crème fraîche	100 ml/4 fl oz
1 stick	butter	100 g/4 oz
½ cup	Hollandaise Sauce (page 70)	100 ml/4 fl oz
	salt and pepper	
½ lb	fresh pasta	250 g/8 oz
4	aubergines (eggplants)	4
½ cup	olive oil	100 ml/4 fl oz
4	tomatoes	4
2	shallots	2
2	chervil sprigs	2
	salt and pepper	
4, each about ¾ lb	sole	4, each about 350 g/12 oz
½ cup	dry white wine	100 ml/4 fl oz
½ cup	Fish Fumet (page 57)	100 ml/4 fl oz
¼ cup	crème fraîche	50 ml/2 fl oz
½ cup	fresh white breadcrumbs	25 g/scant 1 oz
4 tbsp	butter	50 g/2 oz

—— FILLETS OF SOLE ALSACIENNE ——

Preparation 1 hour • Cooking 12 minutes

Poach the sole fillets in the wine for about 10 minutes or until cooked. Remove and keep warm. Add the chopped shallots to the cooking liquid, then reduce and mix in the crème fraîche and 75 g/3 oz (6 tbsp) of the butter. Add the Hollandaise sauce and check the seasoning.

Cook the pasta and toss with the remaining butter. Arrange the sole fillets on a bed of pasta, coat with the sauce and glaze in a low oven.

Dry white wines from Alsace: Riesling, Sylvaner, Pinot Blanc, Pinot Gris, Gewürztraminer.

FILETS DE SOLE AUX AUBERGINES

— FILLETS OF SOLE WITH AUBERGINES —

Preparation 1 hour • Cooking about 50 minutes

Cut the aubergines (eggplants) in half lengthways, sprinkle with the oil and cook in a moderately hot oven until tender (about 40 minutes). Scoop out the pulp, making sure you do not pierce the shells, and chop it very finely with the skinned, de-seeded tomatoes, the shallots and chervil. Season with salt and pepper and set aside.

Fillet the sole. Poach the fillets in the wine and fish fumet made with the sole trimmings for about 10 minutes, until cooked. Remove the fillets and keep warm. Reduce the cooking liquid until it is fairly thick, then add the crème fraîche and the chopped aubergine (eggplant) mixture. Put a little of this mixture in the bottom of the aubergine (eggplant) shells, put the fillets of sole on top and add a little more mixture. Sprinkle with the breadcrumbs and dot with the butter; brown quickly in the oven.

Dry white wines: Saumur, Quincy, dry Graves, Chablis, Mâcon-Villages, Coteaux Champenois.

FILLETS OF SOLE IN A CREAM, TOMATO AND WHITE WINE SAUCE

Preparation 25 minutes • Cooking 12 minutes

Fillet the sole. Make small cuts on both sides of the fillets and season them with a little salt and pepper. Put about half of the butter in a flame-proof fish dish, preferably one with a lid, otherwise use a well-buttered flameproof gratin dish. Put the sole fillets in the dish. Add a thin layer of skinned, de-seeded and finely chopped tomatoes, the finely chopped onion and shallots and the parsley. Add the wine. Cover with a piece of well-buttered greaseproof or baking parchment paper, then with the lid. Bring to the boil on top of the stove, then finish cooking in a very hot oven.

Arrange the sole fillets on a dish. Reduce the liquid slightly and stir in the remaining butter and the crème fraîche. Check the seasoning and pour over the fillets of sole.

Dry white wines: Saumur, Sancerre, Chablis, Rully.

US	Ingredients	Met/Imp
4, each about 14 oz	sole	4, each about 400 g/14 oz
	salt and pepper	
10 tbsp	butter	150 g/5 oz
3	tomatoes	3
1	onion	1
2	shallots	2
1 tbsp	chopped parsley	15 ml/1 tbsp
½ cup	dry white wine	100 ml/4 fl oz
½ cup	crème fraîche	100 ml/4 fl oz

FILLETS OF SOLE CURNONSKY

Preparation 2 hours • Cooking 35 minutes

Fillet the sole. Flatten the fillets and poach them in a fish fumet (*page 57*) made from the bones and trimmings, the wine and bouquet garni. Prepare the lobster according to the recipe for Lobster Américaine (*page 244*).

Add the sole cooking liquid to the reduced Américaine sauce and reduce still further. Add a Hollandaise Sauce (*page 70*) made with the egg yolks and butter. Thicken with the crème fraîche and season well with salt, pepper and paprika.

Arrange the sole fillets on a dish and flank them with small quenelles. Put a medallion of lobster on each fillet and coat everything with the sauce. Glaze quickly in a hot oven.

Dry white wines: Meursault, Montrachet, Montagny, Coteaux Champenois.

US	Ingredients	Met/Imp
2, each about 1 lb	sole	2, each about 500 g/1 lb
½ cup	dry white wine	100 ml/4 fl oz
1	bouquet garni	1
1, about 1 lb	lobster	1, about 500 g/1 lb
2	egg yolks	2
1 stick	butter	100 g/4 oz
½ cup	crème fraîche	100 ml/4 fl oz
	salt and pepper	
	paprika	
	Forcemeat Stuffing (page 54), made into quenelles	

SOLE GOUJONS

Preparation 30 minutes • Cooking 8 minutes

Cut the fillets of sole into 'gudgeon' shapes (*page 168*). Dip them in a light batter, deep-fry them and pile on to a heated serving dish. Garnish with fried parsley and quarters of lemon. Serve on a napkin.

Dry white wines: Saumur, Sancerre, Pouilly-Fumé, dry Graves, Chablis.

US	Ingredients	Met/Imp
2½ lb	sole fillets	1.1 kg/2½ lb
	salt	
	Fritter Batter (page 580)	
	oil for deep frying	
	GARNISH	
1 handful	parsley sprigs	1 handful
4	lemons, quarters of	4

US	Ingredients	Met/Imp
2, each about 1¼ lb	sole	2, each about 600 g/1¼ lb
I quart	dry white wine	I litre/1¾ pints
I quart	mussels	I litre/1¾ pints
½ lb	peeled cooked prawns or shrimp	250 g/8 oz
I quart	Bordelaise Sauce (page 63)	I litre/1¾ pints
	puff pastry *fleurons*	

FILLETS OF SOLE MARGUERY

Preparation 30 minutes • Cooking 30 minutes

This recipe is named after the 19th century Parisian restaurant, Marguery.

Fillet the sole. Poach the fillets in the wine. Steam the mussels open and add to the sole with the prawns, reserving a few of the best prawns for the garnish. Arrange on an ovenproof serving dish and coat with the Bordelaise sauce made with white wine and plenty of butter. Brown in a hot oven. Garnish with fleurons and the reserved prawns.

Dry or medium dry white wines: Coteaux Champenois, Montrachet, Meursault, Graves, Vouvray, Montlouis.

US	Ingredients	Met/Imp
4, each about 14 oz	sole	4, each about 400 g/14 oz
I quart	dry white wine	I litre/1¾ pints
I quart	mussels, cooked and liquid reserved	I litre/1¾ pints
scant ½ lb	cooked mushrooms	200 g/7 oz
2	egg yolks	2
½ cup	crème fraîche	100 ml/4 fl oz
14 tbsp	butter	200 g/7 oz
½ lb	peeled cooked prawns or shrimp	250 g/8 oz
¼ lb	truffles	100 g/4 oz
16	fried smelts	16
8	puff pastry *fleurons*	8
8	Crayfish Bordelaise (page 239)	8
8	Lobster Américaine (page 244)	8

FILLETS OF SOLE NORMANDE

Preparation 2 hours • Cooking 35 minutes

Fillet the sole. Roll the fillets into *paupiettes* and poach them gently in the wine. Make a good Normandy Sauce (*page 75*) with the cooking liquid from the mussels and the mushrooms and thicken it with the egg yolks and crème fraîche. Add the sole cooking liquid reduced to a glaze. Remove from the heat and add the butter.

Surround the paupiettes with the mussels, prawns and mushrooms. Coat with the sauce and garnish with the truffles, fried smelts, fleurons, crayfish and lobster.

Dry white wines: Sancerre, Quincy, Pouilly-Fumé, Muscadet.

US	Ingredients	Met/Imp
4, each about 5 oz	sole fillets	4, each about 150 g/5 oz
2	eggs	2
	salt and pepper	
	flour for coating	
I cup	fresh white breadcrumbs	50 g/2 oz
I stick	butter	125 g/4½ oz
2 tbsp	oil	30 ml/2 tbsp
½ lb	peeled cooked prawns or shrimp	200 g/7 oz
3	lemons	3

FILLETS OF SOLE IN BREADCRUMBS

Preparation 30 minutes • Cooking 10 minutes • Serves 4

Wash the sole fillets under the cold tap and dry them with paper towels. Put the eggs into a bowl with salt and pepper and beat with a fork.

Coat the fillets in the flour, shake off any excess, then coat with the beaten egg and finally with the breadcrumbs spread out on a plate. Leave for a moment.

Melt a little of the butter and the oil until hot. Fry the fillets in it, allowing about 3 minutes on each side. When they are a nice golden colour, put them into a heated serving dish.

Put the remaining butter into the frying pan and fry the prawns for a few minutes to heat through. Add the juice of one of the lemons.

Pour the cooking juices in the frying pan on to the sole fillets. Garnish with the prawns and serrated half slices of lemon. Serve lemon halves on the side.

Dry white wines: Muscadet, Gros Plant du Pays Nantais, Jasnières.

	US	Ingredients	Met/Imp

SOLE PAPILLOTES

Preparation 20 minutes • Cooking 5 minutes • Serves 6

	US	Ingredients	Met/Imp
		chervil and tarragon	
	6, each about ¼ lb	sole fillets	6, each about 100 g/4 oz
	1 stick	butter	100 g/4 oz
		salt and pepper	
	2	lemons	2

Chop the herbs finely. Cut 6 pieces of foil. Place a sole fillet on each piece, with the shiny side inside. Brush with the melted butter, sprinkle with the chopped herbs and add a little salt and pepper and a little lemon juice. Seal the papillotes and cook under a hot grill (broiler) for about 5 minutes. Serve in the papillotes with lemon quarters.

Dry white wines: Muscadet, Gros Plant du Pays Nantais, Sauvignon de Saint-Bris.

FILLETS OF SOLE WITH PRAWN SAUCE

Preparation 2 hours • Cooking 25 minutes

	US	Ingredients	Met/Imp
	2 tbsp	finely chopped shallot	50 g/2 oz
	1 stick	butter	125 g/4½ oz
	1 lb	mushrooms	500 g/1 lb
	¼ cup	Joinville Sauce (*page 71*)	60 ml/4 tbsp
	4, each about 14 oz	sole	4, each about 400 g/14 oz
	1 quart	dry white wine	1 litre/1¾ pints
	2 cups	Prawn Sauce (*page 67*)	500 ml/18 fl oz

First make a mushroom purée. Lightly fry the finely chopped shallot in butter; add the chopped mushrooms. Cook until softened, then purée in a food processor or blender. Reduce the purée over a fairly high heat and mix in the Joinville sauce.

Fillet the sole. Fold each fillet into a 'V' shape and fill the inside with some of the mushroom purée. Poach in the wine, arrange on the remaining mushroom purée and coat with prawn sauce.

Dry white wines: Saumur, Chablis, Bourgogne-Aligoté.

FILLETS OF SOLE WITH WHITE WINE

Preparation 25 minutes • Cooking 20 minutes

	US	Ingredients	Met/Imp
	4, each about 14 oz	sole	4, each about 400 g/14 oz
	2	shallots	2
	5 oz	mushrooms	150 g/5 oz
	4	tomatoes	4
		salt and pepper	
	½ cup	dry white wine	100 ml/4 fl oz
	1 tbsp	butter	15 g/½ oz
	½ cup	crème fraîche	100 ml/4 fl oz
	2 tbsp	Hollandaise Sauce (*page 70*)	30 ml/2 tbsp

Fillet the sole. Put the finely chopped shallots, thinly sliced mushrooms and the skinned, de-seeded and chopped tomatoes in a shallow heavy-based saucepan. Add the sole fillets, season with salt and pepper, then add the wine and butter and poach for 12 minutes. Take out the fillets and keep them warm.

Reduce the cooking liquid, add the crème fraîche and then stir in the Hollandaise sauce. Coat the fillets with this sauce and glaze in a very hot oven.

White wines: Anjou, Vouvray, Montlouis, Graves.

US	Ingredients	Met/Imp

FILLETS OF SOLE WITH WHISKY
—— ON A BED OF FIELD MUSHROOMS ——

Preparation 1¼ hours • Cooking 1 hour

US	Ingredients	Met/Imp
2, each about 1 lb	sole	2, each about 500 g/1 lb
scant 1 cup	dry white wine	200 ml/7 fl oz
scant 1 cup	water	200 ml/7 fl oz
2	onions	2
1	thyme sprig	1
1	bay leaf	1
¼ lb	field or other wild mushrooms	100 g/4 oz
	salt and pepper	
½ cup	crème fraîche	100 ml/4 fl oz
1 glass	whisky	1 glass
4 tbsp	butter	50 g/2 oz

Fillet the sole. Cook the trimmings with half of the wine, the water, onions and herbs for 45 minutes, to make a Fish Fumet (*page 57*).

Make a bed of field mushrooms in a buttered flameproof dish. Put the sole fillets on top. Season with salt and pepper and pour in the fish fumet and remaining wine. Cook on top of the stove for 10 minutes.

Drain off the liquid into a saucepan. Add the crème fraîche and whisky to the liquid, then reduce it until thick. Stir in the butter, check the seasoning and coat the fillets of sole with the sauce.

Wines: as a general rule, serve the same wine as the one used for cooking.

—— SOLE GOUJONS WITH PAPRIKA ——

Preparation 20 minutes • Cooking 10 minutes

US	Ingredients	Met/Imp
4, each about 14 oz	sole	4, each about 400 g/14 oz
	salt and pepper	
1 tbsp	paprika	15 ml/1 tbsp
10 tbsp	butter	150 g/5 oz
1	lemon	1

Fillet the sole. Cut the fillets into 'gudgeon' shapes (*page 168*). Season them with salt and pepper, roll them in paprika and fry them in some of the butter. Serve with the remaining butter made into a Noisette Butter (*page 53*) with the lemon juice added.

Dry white wines: Pouilly-Fumé, Chablis, Mâcon-Viré, Arbois, Alsace Sylvaner.

—— SOLE MATELOTE NORMANDE ——

Preparation 20 minutes • Cooking 10 minutes

US	Ingredients	Met/Imp
4, each about 1 lb	sole	4, each about 500 g/1 lb
2	large onions	2
10 tbsp	butter	150 g/5 oz
¼ lb	mushrooms	100 g/4 oz
2 cups	dry (hard) cider	500 ml/18 fl oz
¼ cup	calvados	50 ml/2 fl oz
24	oysters	24
1 pint	mussels	500 ml/18 fl oz
½ cup	dry white wine	100 ml/4 fl oz
2 cups	crème fraîche	500 ml/18 fl oz
	salt and pepper	
8	heart-shaped croûtons fried in butter	8
8	crayfish	8
	court bouillon	

Cut the sole into equal-sized pieces. Fry the chopped onions in half of the butter in a frying pan until they are translucent, then put in the pieces of sole and cook for a few minutes. Add the sliced mushrooms. Pour in the cider and calvados. Cook over a fairly high heat, covered, for 8–10 minutes. Drain the sole, arrange them in a round, deep dish and garnish with the poached oysters, the shelled mussels cooked in white wine and the mushrooms.

Reduce the cooking liquid, then add the crème fraîche to it. Heat through for a few moments, then work through a fine sieve and add the remaining butter. Season with salt and pepper.

Coat the fish with this sauce; garnish with the croûtons, and the crayfish cooked in the court bouillon.

Cider or dry white wines: Saumur, Sancerre, Quincy.

ALBERT SOLE

Preparation 30 minutes • Cooking 12 minutes • Serves 3–4

US	Ingredients	Met/Imp
1, about 1½ lb	sole	1, about 750 g/1½ lb
	salt and pepper	
1 stick	butter	125 g/4½ oz
1¼ cups	fresh white breadcrumbs	60 g/2½ oz
2	shallots	2
1 tbsp	chopped parsley	15 ml/1 tbsp
½ cup	dry white vermouth	100 ml/4 fl oz

Skin the sole and make a shallow cut along the backbone. Season the sole with salt and pepper, brush it with about half of the butter, melted, and sprinkle the upper side with the breadcrumbs.

Lay the sole in a buttered oven dish on a bed of chopped shallots and parsley; pour in the vermouth. Cook in a moderately hot oven for about 12 minutes, or until browned.

When the sole is cooked, pour the cooking liquid into a saucepan and reduce it almost completely. Meanwhile, remove the barbels from the sole, put the fish on a heated serving dish and keep warm. Remove the cooking liquid from the heat and add the remaining butter. Surround the fish with a ring of sauce and serve immediately, with the remaining sauce handed separately in a sauce boat.

Dry white wines: Saumur, Sancerre, Quincy, Alsace Pinot Blanc, Meursault, Pouilly-Fuissé.

SOLE WITH CHAMPAGNE*

Preparation 25 minutes • Cooking 15 minutes

US	Ingredients	Met/Imp
8, each about ½ lb	sole	8, each about 250 g/8 oz
½ bottle	champagne	½ bottle
½	onion	½
14 tbsp	butter	200 g/7 oz
	salt and pepper	
4	egg yolks	4
½ cup	crème fraîche	100 ml/4 fl oz

Put the gutted sole in a saucepan, pour in the champagne and add the finely chopped onion, a small piece of the butter and some salt and pepper. Cook gently until the ends of the fillets become slightly detached, then drain.

Skin the sole and arrange on a heated serving dish. Beat the egg yolks with the crème fraîche and the remaining butter, melted. Add a little of the sole cooking liquid, some salt and pepper, then pour over the sole.

Wine: Champagne.

SOLE DIEPPOISE

Preparation 40 minutes • Cooking 12 minutes

US	Ingredients	Met/Imp
4, each about ¾ lb	sole	4, each about 350 g/12 oz
½ cup	dry white wine	100 ml/4 fl oz
½ cup	Fish Fumet (page 57)	100 ml/4 fl oz
⅓ cup	peeled cooked prawns (small shrimp)	40 g/1½ oz
1 pint	shelled cooked mussels	500 ml/18 fl oz
½ lb	mushrooms, cooked	250 g/8 oz
14 tbsp	butter	200 g/7 oz
7 tbsp	flour	60 g/2½ oz
2	egg yolks	2
½ cup	crème fraîche	100 ml/4 fl oz
	salt and pepper	

Poach the gutted sole in the wine and fish fumet for about 12 minutes. Arrange on a heated dish with the prawns (shrimp), mussels and mushrooms.

For the sauce, make a roux with the butter and flour and pour in the cooking liquid from the sole, mussels and mushrooms. Mix in the egg yolks and crème fraîche. Season with salt and pepper, then pour over the sole. Serve immediately.

Dry white wines: Muscadet, Sancerre, Sauvignon de Touraine, Quincy.

US	Ingredients	Met/Imp
4, each about ¾ lb	sole	4, each about 350 g/12 oz
	mushroom and truffle Duxelles (page 49) made with 100 g/4 oz mushrooms and 40 g/1½ oz truffles	
10 oz	skinned sole fillets	300 g/10 oz
2	egg whites	2
	salt and pepper	
2 cups	crème fraîche	500 ml/18 fl oz
	Fish Fumet (page 57)	
2 cups	wine from Meursault	500 ml/18 fl oz
3	shallots	3
1	truffle, to garnish	1
a little	Fish Velouté (page 57)	a little
4	egg yolks	4
1	lemon, juice of	1
1 tbsp	butter	15 g/½ oz

STUFFED SOLE WITH MEURSAULT FUMET

Preparation 45 minutes • Chilling 1 hour • Cooking 18 minutes

Recipe created at the Hôtel de la Poste, Avallon

Clean and skin the sole and cut them along the top. Loosen the fillets, but do not take them out.

Using a forcing (pastry) bag, introduce into the opening thus made the mushroom and truffle duxelles fried in butter and mixed with a fish stuffing prepared as follows: finely pound the skinned sole fillets in a mortar, sieve them, then pound in the mortar again with the egg whites. Season with salt and pepper. Put this stuffing in a container on ice for 1 hour. Stir with a spatula from time to time and gradually mix in some of the crème fraîche.

Just before serving, poach the sole in fish fumet with the wine and chopped shallots with salt and pepper added, for about 12 minutes. When the sole are cooked, remove the barbels, place the fish on a heated serving dish and garnish with a few slices of truffle. Coat with the following sauce: reduce the sole cooking liquid, add a little fish velouté and thicken with the remaining crème fraîche and egg yolks. Add lemon juice to taste and stir in the butter.

Dry white wines: Meursault, Montrachet, Corton, Chablis, Pouilly-Fuissé.

GRATIN OF SOLE FROM GASCONY

Preparation 40 minutes • Cooking 18 minutes

US	Ingredients	Met/Imp
8, each about 7 oz	sole	8, each about 200 g/7 oz
	salt and pepper	
	chives	
4	shallots	4
	parsley	
2 cups	dry white wine from Graves	500 ml/18 fl oz
1 stick	butter	100 g/4 oz
1 tbsp	bordeaux mustard	15 ml/1 tbsp
	tarragon	
¼ cup	white wine vinegar	50 ml/2 fl oz
½	garlic clove	½
¼ cup	tomato paste	60 ml/4 tbsp
3	egg yolks	3
½ cup	fresh white breadcrumbs	25 g/scant 1 oz
1	lemon, juice of	1

Split the sole lengthways and season the inside with salt, pepper and snipped chives. Put the sole in a buttered shallow baking dish sprinkled with half of the chopped shallots and some parsley.

Put the wine and butter into a saucepan. Add the mustard with chopped tarragon, salt, pepper, the vinegar, chopped parsley and the remaining shallots, the crushed garlic and tomato paste. Pour the mixture on to the sole. Start cooking on top of the stove, then finish cooking in a moderately hot oven, basting from time to time (about 10 minutes). When the sole are cooked, drain them and put them in an ovenproof serving dish, the bottom of which is covered with a few spoonfuls of the cooking liquid.

Reduce the remaining cooking liquid, thicken it with the egg yolks and coat the sole with it. Sprinkle with the breadcrumbs mixed with snipped chives and brown in the oven. Sprinkle with more chopped parsley and lemon juice and serve in the oven dish.

Wines: as a general rule, serve the same wine as the one used for cooking.

GRATIN OF SOLE PROVENÇAL

Preparation 45 minutes • Cooking 18 minutes

Split the sole in half lengthways. Season them inside with salt and pepper, then arrange them on a buttered dish sprinkled with the chopped shallots, parsley and garlic.

Cover the sole with a *salpicon* of chopped mushrooms and onion, 3 of the tomatoes, skinned, de-seeded and chopped, the butter, wine, lemon juice, fish fumet and saffron. This last spice must be hardly detectable.

Start cooking on top of the stove (about 5 minutes) and finish in the oven, basting often (about 10 minutes). When the sole are cooked, drain them and arrange them on a glazed earthenware dish, the bottom of which has been covered with a little of the sole cooking liquid. Reduce the remaining cooking liquid, stir in the crème fraîche, check the seasoning and add more lemon juice if necessary, then mix in the strongly-flavoured lobster butter. Cover the sole with this sauce and sprinkle with the breadcrumbs mixed with the cheese. Slice the remaining tomatoes and place a slice in the middle of each sole. Brown in the oven. Before serving, sprinkle with chopped parsley and chives.

Dry white wines: Côtes de Provence, Bellet, Cassis, Coteaux d'Aix-en-Provence.

US	Ingredients	Met/Imp
8, each about 7 oz	sole	8, each about 200 g/7 oz
	salt and pepper	
3	shallots	3
2	parsley sprigs	2
½	garlic clove	½
3 oz	mushrooms	75 g/3 oz
1	onion	1
5	tomatoes	5
1 stick	butter	100 g/4 oz
½ cup	dry white wine	100 ml/4 fl oz
½	lemon, juice of	½
½ cup	Fish Fumet (page 57)	100 ml/4 fl oz
1 pinch	saffron	1 pinch
½ cup	crème fraîche	100 ml/4 fl oz
¼ cup	Lobster Butter (page 51)	50 g/2 oz
½ cup	fresh white breadcrumbs	25 g/scant 1 oz
¼ cup	Parmesan cheese, grated	25 g/scant 1 oz
1 tbsp	chopped parsley and chives, to garnish	15 ml/1 tbsp

SOLES AU VIN ROUGE

SOLE IN RED WINE

Preparation 45 minutes • Cooking 30 minutes

Trim and gut the sole. Wash them carefully. Grease a baking dish with plenty of butter. Put the fish in the dish head to tail, with the black skin facing downwards. Dot half of the butter over the surface. Season with salt and pepper, pour in the wine and bake in a hot oven for 15 minutes.

Pour the sole cooking liquid into a saucepan and keep the dish containing the sole warm. Boil the cooking liquid for 10 minutes to reduce it by half. Thicken with a small piece of the remaining butter kneaded with the flour.

Let it boil slightly, then remove from the heat and add a little lemon juice and the remaining butter. Coat the fish with this sauce.

Wines: as a general rule, serve the same wine as the one used for cooking. A Saumur-Champigny would be a good choice.

US	Ingredients	Met/Imp
2, each about 1 lb	sole	2, each about 500 g/1 lb
1 stick	butter	100 g/4 oz
	salt and pepper	
2 cups	red wine	500 ml/18 fl oz
5 tsp	flour	15 g/½ oz
1	lemon, juice of	1

US	Ingredients	Met/Imp
3 cups	crème fraîche	750 ml/1¼ pints
2 tbsp	groundnut (peanut) oil	30 ml/2 tbsp
24	sole fillets	24
	salt and pepper	
2½ lb	pike or whiting fillets	1.1 kg/2½ lb
½ tsp	nutmeg	2.5 ml/½ tsp
I	bunch chives	I
I	bunch chervil	I
	TO SERVE	
I	bunch tarragon	I
1¼ cups	Plain Aspic (page 58)	300 ml/½ pint
	Mayonnaise (page 72)	
5–6 tbsp	tomato paste	75–90 ml/ 5–6 tbsp

— TURBANS OF SOLE FILLETS IN ASPIC —

Preparation 1½ hours • Cooling and chilling 2 hours • Cooking 20–30 minutes

Chill the crème fraîche in the refrigerator until it is needed. Lightly oil 3 savarin moulds with an exterior diameter of 18 cm/7 inches, or 2 considerably larger moulds.

Carefully flatten the fillets of sole and slash the surface of each fillet lightly so that they do not lose their shape during cooking. Season with salt and line the prepared moulds with them, skinned side against the sides of the moulds. Arrange the fillets slightly diagonally, overlapping each other a little, and allow the ends of the fillets to protrude over the edges of the moulds.

Carefully remove all the bones from the fillets of pike or whiting and pound the flesh in a mortar or mince in a food processor. Put it through a fine sieve and place in a terrine kept on ice. Gradually add the chilled crème fraîche, working the mixture with a spatula, still over the ice. Add salt, pepper, nutmeg, the roughly snipped chives and the chopped chervil.

Fill the moulds with the mixture, press down lightly and fold back the ends of the sole fillets over it. Lightly oil 2–3 pieces of greaseproof or baking parchment paper, put them on the moulds, then cover the latter with lids or heatproof plates.

Put the moulds in 2–3 saucepans and pour in boiling water to come three-quarters of the way up their sides. Simmer for 20 minutes. If the water evaporates from the *bain-marie*, maintain the level by adding more hot water. Remove the moulds from the water, take off the lids and leave to cool completely.

Turn the moulds upside down on to a rack over a hollow dish, to allow the cooking juices to drain off. Turn them carefully the right way up again and keep them cool for 1 hour.

Turn the moulds out on to a round dish and garnish the tops with washed tarragon leaves, outlining each sole fillet. Coat all with a thin layer of syrupy aspic jelly, which is just on the point of setting. Chill in the refrigerator for 1 hour.

Serve the turbans with a well-seasoned, thick mayonnaise to which the tomato paste has been added.

White wines: Muscadet, Gros Plant du Pays Nantais, Tursan, Pacherenc du Vic-Bilh du Pays.

TANCHE

TENCH

THE TENCH LIKES THE MUD AT THE BOTTOM OF RIVERS AND ponds and therefore has a muddy taste. To lessen this, it must be kept in clear running water for about 1 week. It is used in *matelotes* but may also be deep- or shallow-fried.

TANCHE AU KIRSCH

TENCH WITH KIRSCH

Preparation 45 minutes • Cooking 15 minutes

Take some live tench and kill them by placing them in vinegar; plunge them quickly into boiling water, scale but do not skin them and put them into an ovenproof dish. Put a mixture of chopped garlic, shallots, parsley and tarragon on top and add salt, pepper and the butter, diced. Cook for about 15 minutes, sprinkling from time to time with the kirsch. As soon as the tench are cooked, sprinkle them with more kirsch and flambé them.

Dry white wines from Alsace: Riesling, Sylvaner, Gewürztraminer.

US	Ingredients	Met/Imp
8, each about ½ lb	tench	8, each about 250 g/8 oz
½ cup	white wine vinegar	100 ml/4 fl oz
1	garlic clove	1
4	shallots	4
6	parsley sprigs	6
2	tarragon sprigs	2
	salt and pepper	
1 stick	butter	100 g/4 oz
½ cup	kirsch	100 ml/4 fl oz

THON

TUNA

FIVE RELATED SPECIES ARE REFERRED TO AS TUNA. THE albacore, a very firm and tasty fish, is mostly destined for the canning factory, but it is sold fresh in the summer for braising, grilling (or broiling); the bluefin tuna is almost always sold fresh (it is better a little stale) and is mainly braised or cooked in a stew; the skipjack and the yellowfin tuna are mostly caught for canning, and the bigeye is sold fresh, but is less tasty than the albacore which it resembles. Tuna flesh is relatively fatty and dense, and a little heavy, but it has considerable nutritional value. In the days when people regularly abstained from meat on Fridays, the tuna was known as 'veau des chartreux' or 'veal of the Carthusians'.

DARNE DE THON À LA PROVENÇALE

—— TUNA STEAK PROVENÇAL ——

Preparation 1½ hours • Cooking 1 hour

US	Ingredients	Met/Imp
1, about 2 lb	tuna steak	1, about 1 kg/2 lb
½ cup	olive oil	100 ml/4 fl oz
1	onion	1
1 lb	tomatoes	500 g/1 lb
3	garlic cloves	3
1	basil sprig	1
1	bouquet garni	1
3 cups	white wine	750 ml/1¼ pints
3 cups	red wine	750 ml/1¼ pints
	salt	
a few	peppercorns	a few
1 stick	butter	100 g/4 oz
3 tbsp	flour	30 g/1 oz
6	anchovy fillets	6
1	lemon, juice of	1
2 tbsp	capers	20 g/¾ oz
1 tbsp	chopped parsley	15 ml/1 tbsp

Fry the tuna gently in the oil. Add the chopped onion, chopped tomatoes, crushed garlic, basil and bouquet garni. Pour in the white and red wines, so that the liquid comes halfway up the fish, then add salt and peppercorns. Cover and cook in a moderate oven for 1 hour.

Take out the tuna and put it on to a heated serving dish. Strain the cooking liquid and skim off the fat. Reduce a little, then thicken with *beurre manié* made with the butter and flour and the anchovies, puréed. Add the lemon juice, capers and parsley. Coat the tuna with the sauce.

Côtes de Provence wines: white, rosé or red.

TRANCHES DE THON BRAISÉES AU VIN BLANC

—— TUNA IN WHITE WINE ——

Preparation 2¼ hours • Marinating 1 hour • Cooking 1 hour 20 minutes • Serves 3

US	Ingredients	Met/Imp
3, each 5 oz	tuna slices	3, each 150 g/5 oz
1	lemon, juice of	1
½ cup	oil	100 ml/4 fl oz
	salt and pepper	
1 pinch	quatre-épices	1 pinch
15	button (pearl) onions	15
6	shallots	6
½ lb	mushrooms	250 g/8 oz
½ cup	white wine	100 ml/4 fl oz
½ cup	water	100 ml/4 fl oz
1 stick	butter	100 g/4 oz
3 tbsp	flour	30 g/1 oz

A good hour beforehand, marinate the tuna slices with the lemon juice, most of the oil, salt, pepper and spice.

Drain and sponge the tuna, then gently fry them in a little oil with the onions, chopped shallots and sliced mushrooms. Cook gently for 20 minutes, then pour in the wine and water. Braise for 1 hour.

Thicken with *beurre manié* made with the butter and flour. Serve hot.

Dry white wines: Sancerre, Pouilly-Fumé, Mâcon-Villages.

TRUITE

TROUT

THE FLESH OF THE WILD TROUT (FARIO) – WHITE, PINK OR orange – is fine and delicate. This gourmet fish lives in swiftly flowing cold rivers. Freshly caught trout should be killed at the very moment of cooking, especially for the excellent *au bleu* (sealing with vinegar) preparation, so that it is absolutely fresh. Like the brook trout or sea trout (often called salmon trout), the wild trout is fished by permit and reserved for private consumption. In restaurants, only farmed trout (rainbow) are found, which are much less tasty. The repertoire of trout recipes abounds in regional variations, with herbs, *crème fraîche*, *lardons* or mushrooms. Smoked trout fillets are served as an hors-d'oeuvre.

TRUITES BELLE MEUNIÈRE

——— TROUT BELLE MEUNIÈRE ———

Preparation 25 minutes • Cooking 12 minutes

US	Ingredients	Met/Imp
8, each about 6 oz	trout	8, each about 175 g/6 oz
6 tbsp	flour	50 g/2 oz
	salt	
10 tbsp	butter	150 g/5 oz
1	lemon, juice of	1
½ cup	crème fraîche	100 ml/4 fl oz

Coat the trout in the flour, and season with salt, then fry in the butter for about 10 minutes. Once they are cooked, arrange them on a heated serving dish. Add the lemon juice and crème fraîche to the butter remaining in the frying pan. Heat through just a little, then pour on to the trout. Serve immediately.

Dry or medium dry white wines: Vouvray, Hermitage, Alsace Pinot Gris.

TRUITES AU BLEU

——— TROUT 'AU BLEU'* ———

Preparation 10 minutes • Cooking 5 minutes

US	Ingredients	Met/Imp
8	trout	8
	court bouillon made with 400 ml/14 fl oz (1¾ cups) white wine vinegar instead of 100 ml/4 fl oz (½ cup)	
4 tbsp	butter	50 g/2 oz
	GARNISH	
	lemon slices	
	parsley sprigs	

Small pike or carp may be prepared in the same way.

Kill and gut the trout. Do not wash them and, most important of all, do not wipe them because they are coated with a special alluvium which gives them their blue colour when cooked.

Put the trout in the boiling court bouillon for 5 minutes. Serve accompanied by the butter, melted, and garnished with lemon and parsley.

White wines: Alsace Riesling, Crépy, Muscadet, Pouilly-Fumé.

US	Ingredients	Met/Imp
8, each about 6 oz	trout	8, each about 175 g/6 oz
1 bottle	Coteaux Champenois	1 bottle
	salt and pepper	
4	shallots	4
4	egg yolks	4
14 tbsp	butter	200 g/7 oz
½ cup	Fish Velouté (page 57)	100 ml/4 fl oz
½ cup	crème fraîche	100 ml/4 fl oz
1	lemon, juice of	1

——— TROUT IN CHAMPAGNE ———

Preparation 30 minutes • Cooking 12 minutes

Gut and clean the trout. Poach them in the champagne, seasoned with salt and pepper, for about 10 minutes, until cooked.

Reduce some of the poaching liquid with the finely chopped shallot. When reduced, allow to cool, then add the egg yolks. Cook over a very low heat, whisking vigorously, then remove from the heat and whisk in the butter. Add the fish velouté and crème fraîche. Check the seasoning, add a little lemon juice and keep warm.

Skin the trout, arrange them on a serving dish and coat them with the champagne sauce.

Wines: as a general rule, serve the same Champagne as the one used for cooking.

US	Ingredients	Met/Imp
8, each about 6 oz	trout	8, each about 175 g/6 oz
2 cups	milk	500 ml/18 fl oz
¾ cup	flour	100 g/4 oz
	salt and pepper	
10 tbsp	butter	150 g/5 oz
2 cups	Pouilly-Fuissé	500 ml/18 fl oz
2	shallots	2
2 cups	crème fraîche	500 ml/18 fl oz
3 oz	cooked mushrooms	75 g/3 oz
¼ cup	truffle juice	50 ml/2 fl oz
½	lemon, juice of	½
	GARNISH	
1 tbsp	chopped parsley	15 ml/1 tbsp
8	thin slices truffle	8
8	mushroom caps	8

TRUITES À L'ÉCLUSIÈRE

TROUT WITH MUSHROOMS ——— AND TRUFFLES ———

Preparation 30 minutes • Cooking 15 minutes

Sponge the trout carefully and gut them, then dip them in the milk and flour and put salt and pepper inside them. Fry gently in the butter in a flameproof dish until golden. Take them out of the dish, cover with buttered greaseproof or baking parchment paper and keep warm. Deglaze the dish with the wine, add the finely chopped shallots and reduce.

Turn the heat under the dish to very low. Pour in the crème fraîche, add the sliced mushrooms with some of their cooking liquid, the truffle and lemon juices.

Return the trout to the dish; let them simmer in the sauce until it has reached the desired consistency. Taste and adjust the seasoning.

Serve garnished with chopped parsley, thin slices of truffle and scalloped mushrooms.

Wine: Pouilly-Fuissé or other white burgundy.

STUFFED TROUT

TRUITES FARCIES

Preparation 1 hour • Cooking 20 minutes • Serves 4

US	Ingredients	Met/Imp
2, each about 1½ lb	trout	2, each about 750 g/1½ lb
1 cup	fresh white breadcrumbs	50 g/2 oz
5 oz	mushrooms	150 g/5 oz
	parsley	
4	shallots	4
10 tbsp	butter	150 g/5 oz
½ cup	crème fraîche	100 ml/4 fl oz
	salt and pepper	
2	tomatoes	2
½ cup	dry white wine	100 ml/4 fl oz

Gut the trout through their heads, without cutting open the stomachs; wash them. Prepare a stuffing by mixing together the breadcrumbs, chopped mushrooms, chopped parsley and half of the chopped shallots. Cook this mixture lightly in the butter until it is dry, remove from the heat and add 45 ml/3 tbsp crème fraîche and salt and pepper to taste.

Stuff this mixture through the gills into the stomachs of the trout. Place the trout in a buttered baking dish with the skinned, de-seeded and chopped tomatoes and the remaining chopped shallots. Cook in a hot oven for about 20 minutes until the trout are cooked, then add the wine and the remaining crème fraîche to the sauce.

Dry or medium dry white wines: Graves, Alsace Gewürztraminer, Saint-Péray, Coteaux Champenois, Vouvray, Anjou.

TRUITES EN GELÉE AU VIN ROUGE

TROUT IN ASPIC WITH RED WINE

Preparation 2 hours • Cooking 25 minutes

US	Ingredients	Met/Imp
8, each about 6 oz	trout	8, each about 175 g/6 oz
	Mirepoix (page 50) made with carrots, onions, celeriac, parsley stalks, garlic, thyme, bay leaf	
	a little butter	
scant 1 cup	Fish Fumet (page 57)	200 ml/7 fl oz
1 bottle	red Mâcon wine	1 bottle
	salt and pepper	
6	peppercorns	6
16	mushroom caps	16
4	egg whites	4
8	sheets gelatine or	8
2 envelopes	powdered unflavoured gelatine	30 ml/2 tbsp
¼ cup	cognac	50 ml/2 fl oz
	TO SERVE	
½ cup	Mayonnaise (page 72)	100 ml/4 fl oz
½ cup	whipping cream	100 ml/4 fl oz

Gut the trout and put them in iced water for 1 hour. Gently fry the mirepoix in butter, pour in the fish fumet and wine. Season with salt and the peppercorns. Simmer for 30 minutes with a few mushroom peelings, press the liquid through a sieve. Leave to cool.

Season the trout with salt and pepper and put them in a fish dish with the mushroom caps. Pour the mirepoix liquid on to the trout and poach gently for about 10 minutes or until cooked. Allow to cool in the liquid.

Drain and carefully wipe the trout and mushrooms and arrange them on a serving dish. Skim the fat off the liquid, *clarify* it with the egg whites and check the seasoning. Dissolve the gelatine in it, add the cognac, then chill until beginning to set. Coat the trout and leave to set completely.

Serve chilled with the mayonnaise lightened with the whipped cream on the side.

White wine: Mâcon-Villages.
Red wines: Beaujolais, Mâcon, Bourgogne Passetoutgrains.

219 • FISH

US	Ingredients	Met/Imp
8, each about 7 oz	trout	8, each about 200 g/7 oz
	salt and pepper	
14 tbsp	butter	200 g/7 oz
2 cups	dry white wine	500 ml/18 fl oz
2	carrots	2
1	bouquet garni	1
½ cup	Fish Fumet (page 57)	100 ml/4 fl oz
6 tbsp	flour	50 g/2 oz
12	peppercorns	12
3	shallots	3
4	egg yolks	4
½ cup	double (heavy) cream	100 ml/4 fl oz
15	sorrel leaves	15

ROAST TROUT 'AS IN MEDIEVAL TIMES'

Preparation 40 minutes • Cooking 15 minutes

Season the trout with salt and pepper and smear with the butter. Braise them in half of the wine with the carrots and bouquet garni for about 15 minutes or until cooked. Keep warm.

Deglaze with 1 glass of the wine and the fish fumet and use this to make a velouté sauce, thickening it with the flour.

Crush the peppercorns; boil with the chopped shallots and remaining wine; reduce to about 30 ml/2 tbsp. When the reduction is cold, add the egg yolks and cream. Whisk and keep warm in a *bain-marie*.

Add the velouté; strain through a cheesecloth and finish the sauce by adding the chopped sorrel leaves lightly fried in butter. Arrange the trout on a heated serving dish and cover them with the sauce before serving.

Dry white wines: Arbois, Alsace Sylvaner, Pouilly-Fuissé.

US	Ingredients	Met/Imp
1, about 3 lb	sea or salmon trout	1, about 1.5 kg/3 lb
	salt and pepper	
2	strips pork or bacon fat	2
2	carrots	2
2	onions	2
4	shallots	4
1	bouquet garni	1
1 quart	red bordeaux wine	1 litre/1¾ pints
2 cups	Fish Fumet (page 57)	500 ml/18 fl oz
2 oz	canned anchovy fillets	50 g/2 oz
14 tbsp	butter	200 g/7 oz
	Kneaded Butter (page 49)	

SEA TROUT BRAISED IN RED WINE

Preparation 45 minutes • Cooking 35 minutes

The sauce for this dish is a variation of Genevoise Sauce (*page 69*); it must be light and flavoursome with a good colour and a pure taste.

Season the trout with salt and pepper and lard with the pork fat. Put it on a well-buttered, long ovenproof dish and start cooking in a moderately hot oven (about 15 minutes). When it is half cooked, add the thickly sliced carrots, onions and shallots and the bouquet garni. When the vegetables have coloured, pour in half of the wine. Baste often so that the fish remains moist. Remove the pork fat and add a good fish fumet (made from the trout head and bones) mixed with the remaining wine. Make sure that the fish stays soft and highly flavoured.

When the trout is cooked, transfer to a heated serving dish. Strain the cooking liquid through cheesecloth. Skim off the fat and add the anchovy fillets, soaked in milk, drained and pounded in a mortar, with 50 g/2 oz (4 tbsp) of the plain butter. Thicken the sauce with kneaded butter, remove from the heat and whisk in the remaining plain butter. Pour over the trout to serve.

Wines: as a general rule, serve the same wine as the one used for cooking.

TURBOT

IF YOU ARE INTENDING TO COOK A WHOLE TURBOT, YOU WILL need a specially shaped fish kettle or 'turbotière', which is adapted to its rhomboid shape. To clean this highly-valued sea fish, remove the grey skin, taking care not to touch the white skin which is smooth and nutritious. Its firm, white, flaky, tender flesh, which has no bones and is easy to divide into fillets, makes it a choice fish, but it is also quite expensive. Whether it is poached, braised, grilled (or broiled) or fried, turbot should be cooked very carefully, because it loses its smoothness if overcooked. Despite the numerous and lavish ways in which chefs, past and present, have prepared it, simple poaching (with a little milk to keep the flesh white) is often considered the best to bring out the full flavour of turbot.

FILETS DE TURBOT À LA PORTAISE

FILLETS OF TURBOT WITH SCALLOPS AND CREAM

Preparation 1 hour • Cooking 45 minutes

US	Ingredients	Met/Imp
1, about 5½ lb	turbot	1, about 2.5 kg/5½ lb
1 bottle	dry white wine	1 bottle
4	shallots	4
	parsley	
1	bouquet garni	1
	salt and pepper	
8	scallops	8
14 tbsp	butter	200 g/7 oz
3 oz	mushrooms	75 g/3 oz
1	lemon, juice of	1
½ cup	crème fraîche	100 ml/4 fl oz

Detach the fillets from the turbot in order to remove the backbone. Remove the head, fins and tail. Use these trimmings to make a stock with the wine, chopped shallots, plenty of parsley, bouquet garni, salt and pepper; cook for a good 30 minutes. Pound it all and strain through a fine sieve.

Poach the shelled scallops in this reduction for 5–10 minutes. Take them out and set aside.

Meanwhile, put the turbot fillets into an ovenproof dish. Pour over the reduced fish stock and add most of the butter, cut into dice. Bake in a moderately hot oven for about 30 minutes.

Meanwhile, sweat the sliced mushrooms in the remaining butter, with a little lemon juice sprinkled on them to keep them white. This only takes a few minutes. Drain the mushrooms in a sieve to remove their water.

Put the mushrooms and scallops in the dish around the turbot fillets, after the first 30 minutes cooking. Add the crème fraîche, the remaining lemon juice, salt and pepper. Finish cooking in the oven (10 minutes at the most). (If crème fraîche is unavailable, make a liaison with beaten egg yolk just before serving.) Serve immediately.

Dry white wines: Hermitage, Coteaux Champenois, Pouilly-Fuissé.

US	Ingredients	Met/Imp
I, about 4½ lb	turbot	I, about 2 kg/4½ lb
3	shallots	3
	thyme sprigs	
I	bay leaf	I
I	lemon, juice of	I
	salt and pepper	
½ lb	mushrooms	250 g/8 oz
I stick	butter	125 g/4½ oz
½ cup	dry white vermouth	100 ml/4 fl oz
2 cups	crème fraîche	500 ml/18 fl oz

— FILETS OF TURBOT IN VERMOUTH —

Preparation 50 minutes • Cooking 30 minutes

Trim, gut and wash the turbot, then fillet it. Put the bones and trimmings into a saucepan with a chopped shallot, some thyme, the bay leaf and lemon juice. Add salt and pepper, cover with cold water and bring to the boil. Simmer for 20 minutes to obtain a Fish Fumet (*page 57*). Strain.

Meanwhile, sweat the sliced mushrooms in half of the butter for 10 minutes. In a third saucepan, gently fry the remaining chopped shallots in the remaining butter until they are transparent, then pour in the vermouth and 50 ml/2 fl oz (¼ cup) of the fish fumet. Add the mushrooms, crème fraîche, salt and pepper. Simmer for 5 minutes. Strain the remaining fumet into a deep frying pan and poach the turbot fillets in it for 8 minutes. Drain them, remove the skin and put them on a heated serving dish. Coat with the sauce.

White wines: Sauternes, Vouvray,
or chilled dry vermouth.

US	Ingredients	Met/Imp
I, about 5½ lb	turbot	I, about 2.5 kg/5½ lb
	salt and pepper	
½ cup	olive oil	100 ml/4 fl oz
10	button (pearl) onions	10
2	shallots	2
I	garlic clove	I
I	bouquet garni	I
I tsp	tomato paste	5 ml/1 tsp
I bottle	Chambertin	I bottle
2 oz	raw country ham	50 g/2 oz
10 tbsp	butter	150 g/5 oz
I cup	fresh white breadcrumbs	50 g/2 oz
½ cup	crème fraîche	100 ml/4 fl oz
	GARNISH	
	chopped thyme	

— TURBOT WITH CHAMBERTIN WINE* —

Preparation 40 minutes • Cooking 1 hour 20 minutes

Trim the turbot, rinse it well, then wipe dry. Put it in a buttered oven-proof dish and season with salt and pepper. Set aside.

Put the olive oil in a cocotte over heat and add the onions, the chopped shallots, crushed garlic, bouquet garni and tomato paste. Mix well. Pour in the Chambertin wine and cook for 20 minutes.

Take a good slice of country ham, both lean and fat, dice it very finely and brown it. Sprinkle some of the ham over the turbot, the remainder over the prepared sauce. Dot the fish with the butter cut into small pieces and sprinkle with the breadcrumbs. Cover with buttered grease-proof paper or baking parchment and bake in a moderately hot oven for about 1 hour.

Thicken the sauce with the crème fraîche, then reheat in the oven for a few minutes. Serve very hot in the cocotte, garnished with thyme.

Wines: Chambertin or Gevrey-Chambertin.

— TURBOT WITH HERBS AND PASTIS —

Preparation 30 minutes • Cooking 25 minutes • Serves 4–5

US	Ingredients	Met/Imp
1, about 4½ lb	turbot	1, about 2 kg/4½ lb
2½ sticks	butter	300 g/10 oz
	salt and pepper	
2 tsp	pastis	10 ml/2 tsp
2 tsp	chopped tarragon	10 ml/2 tsp
1 tsp	chopped chervil	5 ml/1 tsp
1 tsp	snipped chives	5 ml/1 tsp
	TO SERVE	
	puff pastry *fleurons*	
	boiled potatoes	

Cut the turbot into pieces and remove the black skin. Turn over the pieces and, if necessary, remove the white skin. Detach the fillets from the bone using a filleting knife. Put the pieces into a moistened deep frying pan and add 200 g/7 oz (14 tbsp) of the butter, cut into pieces, and a little salt and pepper.

Put the pan in a moderate oven or over a low heat, covered, for 10–15 minutes. Pour the pastis into a separate, small saucepan, add the remaining butter, cut into pieces, and the herbs.

Drain the pieces of turbot and keep them warm on a heated serving dish. Strain the turbot cooking liquid into the herb mixture through a fine sieve. Boil the sauce until it thickens, taking care not to allow the butter to separate and spoil the sauce. Quickly coat the fillets with the sauce. Garnish with fleurons and serve with boiled potatoes.

Dry white wines: Chablis Grand Cru or Premier Cru, Corton, Meursault, Chassagne-Montrachet, Hermitage, Châteauneuf-du-Pape.

——— STUFFED TURBOT 'ADMIRAL' ———

Preparation 1½ hours • Cooking 40 minutes

US	Ingredients	Met/Imp
1, about 4½ lb	turbot	1, about 2 kg/4½ lb
10 oz	Fish Stuffing made with lobster (*page 54*)	300 g/10 oz
2 tbsp	Tomato Sauce (*page 80*)	30 ml/2 tbsp
1 bottle	champagne	1 bottle
3 cups	Fish Fumet (*page 57*)	750 ml/1¼ pints
½ cup	Américaine Sauce (*page 60*)	100 ml/4 fl oz
3	tarragon sprigs	3
	salt and pepper	

Make a cut from head to tail along the back of the fish, as deep as the bone. Detach the fillets from the bone to form a pocket and fill this with the lobster mousseline stuffing, with raw lobster coral and the highly reduced tomato sauce. Push the fillets together again so that the stuffing is enclosed.

Turn the turbot over and lay it in a very well buttered deep ovenproof dish. Pour in the champagne and fish fumet. Cook in a low oven for about 40 minutes, basting often.

Put the turbot on a heated serving dish. Reduce the cooking liquid by half and add an equal amount of Américaine sauce with chopped tarragon added. Check the seasoning.

Coat the turbot with some of this sauce and serve the remainder on the side.

Dry white wines: Mâcon-Viré, Arbois, Alsace Sylvaner, Pouilly-Fuissé.

US	Ingredients	Met/Imp
6	shallots	6
4 tbsp	butter	50 g/2 oz
I glass	dry white wine	I glass
½ lb	mushrooms	250 g/8 oz
I, about 3 lb	turbot	I, about 1.5 kg/3 lb
	salt and pepper	
I quart	Béchamel Sauce (page 62)	I litre/1¾ pints
	Bresse Bleu cheese	
I tsp	strong mustard	5 ml/I tsp
I cup	grated cheese	100 g/4 oz

STUFFED TURBOT CHARLES RIGOULOT

Preparation 40 minutes • Cooking 25 minutes

This recipe was created by the chef Max Maupuy for his friend Charles Rigoulot – the strongest man in the world in the 1920s.

Chop the shallots and fry them gently in the butter. Add the wine and reduce completely. Add the mushrooms and cook until softened, stirring frequently.

Prepare the turbot by removing the black skin and opening it up down the middle, from head to tail, in order to remove the bone without breaking up the fillets. Add salt and pepper. Pour shallots and mushrooms mixed with 60 ml/4 tbsp of the béchamel into this opening. Push back the fillets and cook in the oven for 15–20 minutes.

Completely cover the turbot with the remaining béchamel mixed with the Bresse Bleu and mustard. Sprinkle over the grated cheese and glaze in a hot oven before serving.

White wines: Vouvray , Jasnières, Pouilly-Fumé.

US	Ingredients	Met/Imp
I, about 5½ lb	turbot	I, about 2.5 kg/5½ lb
½ cup	milk	100 ml/4 fl oz
	salt	
I	lemon	I
I handful	parsley sprigs	I handful
2 tbsp	butter	25 g/I oz
	TO SERVE	
I lb	boiled potatoes	500 g/I lb
	sauce of your choice (pages 60–82)	

POACHED TURBOT

Preparation 50 minutes • Cooking 15–20 minutes

Prepare the turbot ready for cooking, then make a fairly deep cut along the backbone (on the dark side). Put the turbot on the rack in a turbotière (*page 221*). Cover it with cold water and the boiled milk and add salt and a few slices of peeled, de-seeded lemon. Bring to the boil slowly, then reduce the heat so that the liquid is simmering gently. Faster boiling will in no way advance the cooking; it will merely break up the fish. The time required to poach the turbot is between 15 and 20 minutes, according to the thickness of the fish.

Slide the turbot gently on to a heated serving dish covered with a napkin and surround it with parsley. Brush the fish with the butter to make it shiny. Serve hot with boiled potatoes and one of the following sauces: Hollandaise, mousseline, prawn, lobster, Venetian, Béarnaise, white wine, Américaine. Melted butter or maître d'hôtel butter (*page 52*) can also be served with hot turbot.

Dry white wines: Saumur, Sancerre, Quincy, Pouilly-Fumé, Muscadet, Hermitage, Coteaux Champenois.

To serve the turbot cold, it should be glazed and garnished with mayonnaise, Hollandaise or mousseline sauce, or melted butter or maître d'hôtel butter.

Cold turbot should be served with medium dry white wines: Jurançon, Vouvray, Anjou, Graves; or with sweet white wines: Sauternes, Barsac, Monbazillac.

CRUSTACEANS, MOLLUSCS

&

SHELLFISH

GROUPED UNDER THE GENERAL HEADING OF 'shellfish', molluscs, crustaceans and other small marine creatures provide an interesting source of material for both the cook and the gastronome. The category includes, of course, those choice delicacies, the lobster and the crawfish (rock lobster). Edible snails, frogs and freshwater crayfish are also traditionally dealt with under the same heading.

Oysters and scallops are served with cooked dressings, but there are also more modest types of small shellfish which are well worth trying, and these are often eaten raw, in the most natural state possible. Winkles and periwinkles, for example, are very common around the North Sea, Channel and Atlantic coasts. They are simply boiled in well-seasoned water. They can be eaten on their own, using a pin to extract the flesh, or in an omelette, with scrambled eggs or in a salad. Clams, which are much appreciated by connoisseurs, were first brought over from the United States, to Charentes, in 1911. These are mainly eaten raw, but can also be cooked with vegetables or herbs; clam chowder, for example, is a most highly esteemed soup. In France, large quantities of shellfish and crustaceans are consumed, raw and in various cooked dishes. In order to protect the consumer, there are strict laws governing the quality of this type of produce. Shellfish must come from areas recognized as clean by the Institut Scientifique et Technique des Pêches Maritimes, which issues special labels confirming the wholesomeness of the produce, to be attached to the containers in which they will be transported and sold, and also displayed in the fishing areas themselves.

CALMAR

SQUID

A MARINE MOLLUSC SIMILAR TO CUTTLEFISH, SQUID IS particularly esteemed in Mediterranean countries, where it is eaten stuffed, cooked in a sauce or white wine, served in salads or fried. But the classic way of preparing it 'en su tinta' or in its own ink, is a Spanish one. Squid should be well-seasoned and not overcooked, so that it remains tender.

RIZ AUX CALMARS

RICE WITH SQUID

Preparation 1 hour • Cooking about 1 hour

Clean and wash the squid. Remove the skin and cut the flesh into small pieces; place the flesh in a frying pan with a small amount of olive oil and cook over a brisk heat for about 10 minutes; season with salt and pepper.

Place half of the tomato sauce in a sauté pan; add the wine, bay leaf and a good pinch of chilli powder. (This dish should be quite spicy.) Add the fried squid, moisten with the fish fumet and cook gently for about 45 minutes. Strain, reserving the liquid.

Put the butter into another sauté pan and add the remaining tomato sauce and the rice. Let the rice cook for 2–3 minutes, stirring so that it does not stick, then gradually add the squid cooking liquid (do not submerge the rice). Cook for about 20 minutes, until the rice is tender. Two or three minutes before it is ready, add the squid. Serve with grated cheese handed separately.

Wines: as a general rule, serve the same wine as the one used for cooking.

US	Ingredients	Met/Imp
16	small squid	16
½ cup	olive oil	100 ml/4 fl oz
	salt and pepper	
1 quart	Tomato Sauce (*page 80*)	1 litre/1¾ pints
2 cups	good dry white wine	500 ml/18 fl oz
1	bay leaf	1
	chilli powder	
2 quarts	Fish Fumet (*page 57*)	2 litres/3½ pints
1 large piece	butter	1 large knob
2¾ cups	long-grain rice	500 g/1 lb
1¾ cups	Parmesan cheese, grated	200 g/7 oz

COQUILLE SAINT-JACQUES

SCALLOP

THIS MOLLUSC, KNOWN AS 'RICARDEAU' IN BRITTANY AND 'gofiche' in Normandy, is also called 'peigne' or 'pèlerine'. There are several species of scallop, depending on whether they come from the English Channel, the Atlantic or the Mediterranean. The white meat, which is highly prized, is usually eaten cooked (American-style, au gratin, sautéed, *en brochette*, etc, or cold in salads), but it can also be very lightly poached and used in more elaborate salads, or else marinated and eaten raw. Only the meat (which is white and firm) and the coral (pale pink or bright orange) are used. The beards have an excellent flavour, but it is very difficult to rid them of sand; therefore, they are usually discarded when the scallop is trimmed. It is essential to choose scallops that are tightly closed, as this is a sign of freshness. In order to open them, heat them on top of the stove for a few minutes.

The scallop owes its name 'pèlerine Saint-Jacques' to the 'pèlerins' (pilgrims) who visited Santiago de Compostela in Spain wearing the symbol of the scallop shell on their hats and staffs.

BROCHETTES DE COQUILLES SAINT-JACQUES

SCALLOP BROCHETTES

Preparation 30 minutes • Cooking 12 minutes

US	Ingredients	Met/Imp
20	scallops	20
4 tbsp	butter	50 g/2 oz
4, each about 2 oz	slices smoked belly of pork (thick bacon)	4, each about 50 g/2 oz
I	garlic clove	I
	salt and pepper	
	nutmeg	
2–3 tbsp	olive oil	30–45 ml/ 2–3 tbsp
	parsley sprigs	
	Béarnaise Sauce (*page 61*), to serve	

Insert a knife blade between the 2 halves of each scallop shell; detach the flesh first from the lid, then from the hollow lower shell. Take the flesh in your right hand, keeping hold of the black part with your right thumb. Pull the flesh with your left hand. Remove and discard the beards; keep only the tongue-like coral and the white meat. Wash the meat and coral several times in clean water to remove the sand; dry them with a cloth and slit the white meat in half horizontally.

As raw scallops disintegrate easily, they should be fried for a moment in the butter, along with the coral, to prevent the brochette skewers from tearing the flesh. Grill (broil) the sliced belly of pork (bacon) quickly on both sides, then cut into 2.5 cm/1 inch squares.

Push each skewer through the garlic clove, in order to flavour them very slightly. Season the scallops with salt, pepper and nutmeg; thread each skewer with alternate pieces of scallop, pork and coral, until all the skewers are full. Brush the brochettes with oil and cook under the grill (broiler) for 8–10 minutes, turning from time to time so that they brown on all sides. Serve piping hot, on a heated serving dish garnished with parsley. Hand the Béarnaise sauce separately.

Rosé wines: Tavel, Bandol, Côtes de Provence, Coteaux-d'Aix-en-Provence.
Red wines: Côtes de Provence, Coteaux du Languedoc, Alsace Pinot Noir.

COQUILLES SAINT-JACQUES AU BEURRE BLANC

—— SCALLOPS WITH BEURRE BLANC ——

Preparation 25 minutes • Cooking 10 minutes

US	Ingredients	Met/Imp
24	scallops	24
	salt and pepper	
6 tbsp	flour	50 g/2 oz
6 tbsp	butter	75 g/3 oz
⅔ cup	White Butter Sauce Nantais (page 62)	150 ml/¼ pint

Shell the scallops, keeping only the white meat and the coral. Wash them carefully and pat dry, then season with salt and pepper. Dip them in flour, then fry in the very hot butter. Pour over the butter sauce just before serving.

Dry white wines: Muscadet, Saumur, Sancerre, Pouilly-Fumé.

COQUILLES SAINT-JACQUES À LA BORDELAISE

—— SCALLOPS BORDELAISE ——

Preparation 25 minutes • Cooking 12 minutes

US	Ingredients	Met/Imp
	Mirepoix (page 50), made with 2 carrots, 1 onion, 2 shallots, 1 bouquet garni, 1 garlic sliver	
10 tbsp	butter	150 g/5 oz
24	scallops	24
3 tbsp	cognac	40 ml/1½ fl oz
½ cup	white wine	100 ml/4 fl oz
3	tomatoes	3
	salt and pepper	

Fry the mirepoix in half of the butter; add the scallop meat and coral; sweat, then flambé with the cognac. Add the wine and the skinned, de-seeded and chopped tomatoes and cook for 10 minutes. Remove the scallop meat and coral and keep warm. Reduce the cooking juices and stir in the remaining butter; put back the scallops and coral and season to taste.

Dry white wines: dry Graves, Entre-Deux-Mers, Quincy, Sancerre, Pouilly-Fumé.

COQUILLES SAINT-JACQUES AU CURRY

—— CURRIED SCALLOPS ——

Preparation 30 minutes • Cooking 12 minutes

US	Ingredients	Met/Imp
24	scallops	24
10 tbsp	butter	150 g/5 oz
2–3	onions	2–3
½ cup	white wine	100 ml/4 fl oz
1	bouquet garni	1
1 tbsp	curry powder	15 ml/1 tbsp
½ cup	*crème fraîche*	100 ml/4 fl oz
	salt and pepper	
½ cup	Creole Rice (page 562)	125 g/4½ oz

Sweat the scallop meat and coral in butter with the chopped onions. Add the wine, bouquet garni and curry powder to taste; cook for 12 minutes. Remove the scallop meat and coral and keep warm. Reduce the cooking juices, then strain and add the crème fraîche. Season to taste. Serve the rice separately.

Dry white wines: Saumur, Quincy, Sancerre, Pouilly-Fumé, Muscadet, dry Graves, Mâcon-Viré, Chablis, Alsace Sylvaner or Riesling.

US	Ingredients	Met/Imp
24	scallops	24
	salt and pepper	
½ cup	flour	75 g/3 oz
1 stick	butter	100 g/4 oz
½ cup	oil	100 ml/4 fl oz
2	large onions	2
1 handful	parsley sprigs	1 handful
6	tomatoes, skinned and de-seeded	6
1	lemon	1

SCALLOPS 'GOURMET'

Preparation 40 minutes • Cooking 15 minutes

Attractive presentation is essential to this dish.

Cut the scallop meat into round slices no more than 1 cm/½ inch thick; season these and the coral with salt and pepper. Dip them in the flour and brown on both sides in 75 g/3 oz (6 tbsp) of the butter and a little of the oil (the latter stops the butter from burning). Use a good-sized frying pan, as the scallop meat must be fried in a single layer in order to cook quickly. Remove and set aside on a heated serving dish or gratin dish.

The garnish for this dish consists of onion slices and parsley deep-fried in the remaining oil and the tomatoes, grilled (broiled) or baked and well seasoned. Heat the remaining butter in the frying pan, until very frothy; add the juice of a freshly squeezed lemon; pour this over the scallops just before serving, season and sprinkle with a touch of chopped parsley. Serve very hot.

Dry white wines: Saumur, dry Vouvray, Quincy, Sancerre, Alsace Sylvaner, Pouilly-Fuissé.

US	Ingredients	Met/Imp
24	scallops	24
10 tbsp	butter	150 g/5 oz
1	onion	1
2	shallots	2
½ cup	white wine	100 ml/4 fl oz
1 tbsp	chopped parsley	15 ml/1 tbsp
2 cups	fresh white breadcrumbs	100 g/4 oz
1	bouquet garni	1

SCALLOPS AU GRATIN BRETON

Preparation 25 minutes • Cooking 12 minutes

Slice the scallop meat and coral and brown in half of the butter together with the chopped onion and shallots in a flameproof gratin dish. Add the wine, a little parsley, half of the breadcrumbs and the bouquet garni. Simmer for 8–10 minutes, until the cooking liquid has the consistency of a light sauce.

Remove the pan from the heat and add the remaining butter. Remove the bouquet garni. Sprinkle with the remaining breadcrumbs and brown under the grill (broiler).

Cider: medium or dry.
Dry white wines: Muscadet, Gros Plant du Pays Nantais, Saumur, dry Vouvray, Quincy, Sancerre, Pouilly-Fumé.

SCALLOPS AU GRATIN WITH MUSHROOMS

Preparation 40 minutes • Cooking 12 minutes

US	Ingredients	Met/Imp
24	scallops	24
10 tbsp	butter	150 g/5 oz
1 cup	Dry Duxelles (*page 49*)	250 ml/9 fl oz
2 cups	Mornay Sauce (*page 73*)	500 ml/18 fl oz
½ cup	Gruyère cheese, grated	50 g/2 oz
	salt and pepper	

Open the scallops with a knife and clean them. Keep the meat and coral; cook these for a few minutes in butter, then slice the scallop meat in half through the centre. Butter the scallop shells well and place a little of the duxelles in each; add the scallops and coral; cover with Mornay sauce and sprinkle with grated cheese. Season, pour over a little melted butter and brown in a hot oven.

White wines: Montrachet, Meursault, Graves, Vouvray.

SCALLOPS WITH MUSSELS NANTAISE*

Preparation 30 minutes • Cooking 25–30 minutes

US	Ingredients	Met/Imp
5 oz	mushrooms	150 g/5 oz
2 sticks	butter	250 g/8 oz
1 quart	mussels	1 litre/2 pints
16	scallops	16
	salt and pepper	
2 cups	white wine	500 ml/18 fl oz
6 tbsp	flour	50 g/2 oz

Clean and cook the mushrooms in a little of the butter. Open the mussels by warming them through on top of the stove; strain the cooking juice and reserve.

Clean and open the scallops, take out the meat and blanch. Slice the meat fairly thickly and cut the coral into small pieces. Place in a saucepan. Add a large pinch of salt and a pinch of white pepper, the wine and the cooking juices from the mushrooms. Cook gently for 12 minutes, then drain thoroughly and add the cooked, sliced mushrooms.

Make the sauce. Prepare a roux (*page 50*) using 150 g/5 oz (10 tbsp) of the remaining butter and the flour, and add the cooking juices from the scallops, with 100 ml/4 fl oz (½ cup) of the cooking juices from the mussels. Bring to the boil, stirring, and simmer for 7–8 minutes. Remove from the heat and add the remaining butter.

Take the scallop shells and spread a spoonful of the sauce in the bottom of each; add some scallops and mushrooms and, finally, 6 shelled mussels. Cover with more sauce. Arrange the shells on a dish and put them in a very hot oven for a few minutes to glaze the surface of the sauce. Serve at once.

Dry white wines: Muscadet, Gros Plant du Pays Nantais, Saumur, Sancerre, dry Graves, Chablis, Mâcon-Viré, Arbois, Alsace Riesling or Sylvaner.

US	Ingredients	Met/Imp
24	scallops	24
2 cups	dry white wine	500 ml/18 fl oz
2 cups	milk	500 ml/18 fl oz
4	carrots	4
2	onions	2
2	cloves	2
1	bouquet garni	1
	Rémoulade Sauce (page 77)	

COQUILLES SAINT-JACQUES À LA NAGE

SCALLOPS 'IN THE SWIM'

Preparation 25 minutes • Cooking 10 minutes

Open the scallops, remove and trim the meat and coral. Wash carefully and drain.

Prepare a *court bouillon* using 3 litres/5¼ pints (3 quarts) water, the wine and the boiled milk. Add the sliced carrots, onions spiked with the cloves and the bouquet garni. Bring to the boil, add the scallops, simmer for 5 minutes, then drain.

Serve the scallops hot in a little of the court bouillon, with rémoulade sauce on the side.

White wine: young Chablis.

US	Ingredients	Met/Imp
24	scallops	24
	salt and pepper	
¾ cup	flour	100 g/4 oz
14 tbsp	butter	200 g/7 oz
1	garlic clove	1
2 tbsp	chopped parsley	30 ml/2 tbsp
1	lemon	1

COQUILLES SAINT-JACQUES À LA PROVENÇALE

SCALLOPS PROVENÇAL

Preparation 20 minutes • Cooking 10 minutes

Clean the scallops thoroughly and discard the beards, keeping only the meat and coral. Wipe them dry and season with salt and freshly milled pepper. Roll them in the flour, dusting off the excess with your hands. Heat about half of the butter in a frying pan until sizzling, then add the scallops. Fry until well-browned on 1 side, then turn them carefully and brown on the other side. When cooked, take some of the washed, hollow shells (1 per person) and place some of the scallops in each.

Chop the garlic very finely and mix with the parsley. Sprinkle some over each shell. Add a little lemon juice. Put a large piece of butter into the frying pan and heat until nut-brown and frothy, then pour over the scallops. (Do not drown the scallops in butter, use just as much as is necessary.) Cover the shells with their lids and serve very hot.

Dry white wines: Côtes de Provence, Cassis, Sancerre, Pouilly-Fumé, Chablis.

SCALLOPS IN WHITE WINE

Preparation 1 hour • Cooking 20 minutes

US	Ingredients	Met/Imp
24	scallops	24
1 stick	butter	100 g/4 oz
	salt and pepper	
2	shallots	2
1 tbsp	chopped parsley	15 ml/1 tbsp
½ cup	dry white wine	100 ml/4 fl oz

Choose very fresh scallops. Remove them from their shells and keep only the meat and coral. Wash several times in clean water; cut into 2–3 slices. Place them in a heavy saucepan, together with the butter, salt and pepper, the chopped shallots and parsley and the wine. Cook for about 20 minutes over a moderate heat until the sauce is syrupy and ivory in colour.

Dry white wines: Saumur, dry Vouvray, Quincy, Sancerre.

SCALLOP SOUFFLÉ AU GRATIN

Preparation 45 minutes • Cooking 30 minutes

US	Ingredients	Met/Imp
3 tbsp	butter	40 g/1½ oz
3 tbsp	flour	30 g/1 oz
3 cups	milk	750 ml/1¼ pints
16	scallops	16
⅔ cup	dry white wine	150 ml/¼ pint
1	thyme sprig	1
3	eggs, separated	3
1 tbsp	paprika	15 ml/1 tbsp
	cayenne pepper	
	salt and pepper	

Melt 30 g/1 oz (2 tbsp) of the butter in a saucepan; stir in the flour, to make a *roux*, then gradually add the milk and cook for 10 minutes, stirring constantly. Remove from the heat.

Clean the scallops, keeping only the meat and coral. Pour the wine and an equal amount of water into a clean saucepan; add the thyme and bring to the boil. Turn the heat down and put the scallops in this liquid to simmer for 10 minutes; drain and discard the cooking liquid.

Mix the egg yolks with the white sauce, adding the paprika, a dash of cayenne and some salt and pepper. Beat the egg whites until stiff, then fold them gently into the sauce.

Butter a gratin dish and pour in half of this mixture. Cut the scallops into thin slices and arrange on top. Cover with the remaining sauce. Dot the surface with the remaining butter. Bake in a hot oven for 10 minutes. Serve at once.

White wines: Meursault, Puligny-Montrachet, Chassagne-Montrachet.

CRABE

CRAB

CRAB IS THE COLLECTIVE NAME GIVEN TO SEVERAL SPECIES OF edible crustacean, including the little swimming crab, the spider crab with its spiny shell and the big 'tourteau'. Choose a very heavy, full crab. Freshness is not enough; it should still be alive. The crab gives choice, delicate meat, but the shelling process is long and fiddly. The liver and creamy brown meat are exquisite spread on rye bread as an accompaniment to the plain, cooked white crabmeat. Only the tourteau crab can be stuffed; small crabs are suitable for soups and bisques.

CRABES AU BOUILLON À LA FAÇON DES PÊCHEURS

CRAB PÊCHEUR

Preparation 1 hour • Cooking 30 minutes

US	Ingredients	Met/Imp
2	large crabs	2
	salt and pepper	
	court bouillon made with 500 ml/18 fl oz (2 cups) each white wine and water	
1	garlic clove	1
3	egg yolks	3
scant 1 cup	olive oil	200 ml/7 fl oz
1 tbsp	mustard	15 ml/1 tbsp
1	fennel sprig	1
¼ cup	wine vinegar	50 ml/2 fl oz
1	lemon, juice of	1

Cook the crabs (1 female and 1 male if possible) for 30 minutes in the well-seasoned court bouillon. Drain the crabs and remove the roe or coral from the female, and the brown meat. Pound these in a mortar and pestle, together with the garlic, egg yolks and oil. Add the mustard, the chopped fennel, the vinegar and lemon juice. Crack the crabs slightly and remove the white meat. Serve lukewarm, with the sauce.

Dry white wines: Cassis, Bellet, Côteaux d'Aix-en-Provence.
Dry rosé wine: Côtes de Provence.

PETITS CRABES GRATINÉS AU FOUR

SMALL CRABS AU GRATIN

Preparation 1 hour • Cooking 15 minutes

US	Ingredients	Met/Imp
16	small crabs	16
	court bouillon	
1	onion	1
5 oz	mushrooms	150 g/5 oz
1 stick	butter	100 g/4 oz
¼ cup	cognac	50 ml/2 fl oz
3 tbsp	tomato paste	45 ml/3 tbsp
	salt	
1 tsp	curry powder	5 ml/1 tsp
½ cup	fresh white breadcrumbs	25 g/scant 1 oz
1¼ cups	cheese, grated	150 g/5 oz

Cook the small crabs in the court bouillon for 10–15 minutes. Shell them and reserve the meat; this will be served in the shells, which should be cleaned, inside and out. Chop the onion and mushrooms and fry in butter, together with the cognac, tomato paste, a pinch of salt and the curry powder. Add the crabmeat and mix well. Put the mixture back into the shells; sprinkle with the breadcrumbs mixed with the grated cheese and brown in a hot oven or under the grill (broiler) before serving.

Dry white wines: Muscadet, Gros Plant du Pays Nantais, Saumur, Pouilly-Fumé, Sancerre.

CRAB PILAU WITH MUSSELS PONT-AVEN

Preparation 1 hour • Cooking about 50 minutes

US	Ingredients	Met/Imp
2	large crabs	2
	court bouillon	
¼ cup	oil	50 ml/2 fl oz
2	onions	2
1 cup	long-grain rice	175 g/6 oz
4	tomatoes	4
	salt and pepper	
1 tsp	saffron	5 ml/1 tsp
2 quarts	mussels, shelled	2 litres/3½ pints

Cook the crabs in court bouillon to cover for 30 minutes. Heat the oil in a saucepan and lightly brown the chopped onions, then add the rice and stir well. Gradually add the hot court bouillon from cooking the crabs so that the rice absorbs it without becoming sticky; stir frequently. Add the skinned, de-seeded and chopped tomatoes. Season, then add the saffron and cooked mussels. Turn the mixture on to a heated serving dish and arrange the crabs on top. Alternatively, shell the crabs and mix the meat in with the pilau a few minutes before serving.

Dry white wines: Muscadet, Gros Plant du Pays Nantais.

CRAB TOASTS WITH PAPRIKA

Preparation 1 hour • Cooking 10 minutes

US	Ingredients	Met/Imp
1 stick	butter	100 g/4 oz
1 lb	crabmeat	500 g/1 lb
½ cup	crème fraîche	100 ml/4 fl oz
½ cup	Béchamel Sauce (page 62)	100 ml/4 fl oz
1 tbsp	paprika	15 ml/1 tbsp
2 cups	fresh white breadcrumbs	100 g/4 oz
4	egg yolks	4
16	rounds toasted French bread (baguette)	16
	TO FINISH	
1 tbsp	grated cheese	15 ml/1 tbsp
1 tbsp	fresh white breadcrumbs	15 ml/1 tbsp

Heat the butter until frothy and fry the crabmeat lightly; add the crème fraîche, béchamel, paprika, breadcrumbs and egg yolks. Pour the mixture on to the toasts; sprinkle with the grated cheese mixed with the breadcrumbs and heat through in a hot oven for 1 minute before serving.

Dry white wines: Muscadet, Saumur, Pouilly-Fumé, Alsace Riesling.

CRAB ESCOFFIER AU GRATIN WITH PAPRIKA*

Preparation 1 hour • Cooking 35 minutes

Recipe by August Escoffier (1846–1935), who devoted his life to French cuisine for over 60 years

US	Ingredients	Met/Imp
4	large crabs	4
	court bouillon or white wine	
1	bouquet garni	1
2	onions	2
4	shallots	4
½ lb	mushrooms	250 g/8 oz
	salt	
a few	peppercorns	a few
10 tbsp	butter	150 g/5 oz
1 tsp	curry powder	5 ml/1 tsp
1 tbsp	paprika	15 ml/1 tbsp
6 tbsp	flour	50 g/2 oz
3	egg yolks	3
½ cup	crème fraîche	100 ml/4 fl oz
½ cup	cheese, grated	50 g/2 oz

Cook the crabs for about 30 minutes in court bouillon or wine, together with the bouquet garni, the chopped onions and shallots, a little salt and the peppercorns.

Leave the crabs to cool, then remove the meat from the shells, taking care not to break them. Sauté the diced mushrooms in half of the butter, sprinkle with curry powder and paprika and mix in the crabmeat.

Strain the crab cooking liquid and use 500 ml/18 fl oz (2 cups) of it to make a very thick Béchamel Sauce (*page 62*) with the remaining butter, the flour, egg yolks and crème fraîche. Mix with the crab mixture and fill the crab shells. Sprinkle with grated cheese and brown in a hot oven.

Dry white wine: Pouilly-Fumé.

US	Ingredients	Met/Imp
4½ lb	large crabs, 1 of which should have a very attractive shell	2 kg/4½ lb
	salt	
¼ cup	wine vinegar	50 ml/2 fl oz
¼ cup	olive oil	50 ml/2 fl oz
2 tbsp	English mustard	30 ml/2 tbsp
	cayenne	
	TO FINISH	
4	hard-boiled eggs	4
2 oz (about ¼ cup)	lobster coral	50 g/2 oz
	parsley	
2 cups	Mayonnaise (page 72)	500 ml/18 fl oz

COLD TOURTEAUX WITH MAYONNAISE

Preparation 1 hour • Cooking 30 minutes

Cook the crabs in boiling salted water for 30 minutes, drain and leave to cool. Remove the legs and claws, take out the meat, including the liver, from the body shell. Mix the liver with the vinegar, oil, mustard, salt and cayenne. Flake the crabmeat with 2 forks and add to this mixture.

Wash and dry the nicest-looking crab shell and fill with the seasoned crabmeat; smooth with a knife, then garnish with the sieved hard-boiled eggs, the chopped lobster coral and parsley. Place the claws back in position, arrange on a table napkin and garnish with parsley sprigs. Hand the mayonnaise separately, in a sauce boat.

White wines: Muscadet, Gros Plant du Pays Nantais, Saumur, Pouilly-Fumé, Sancerre.

CREVETTE

SHRIMP AND PRAWN

BESIDES THE 'CREVETTES GRISES' (SHRIMPS) FROM THE ENGLISH Channel and the North Sea (which are also called 'boucauds' and considered the tastiest kind), there are 'crevettes roses' (prawns), also called 'bouquets', and 'chevrettes'. In addition to these there is the 'gamba' (large prawn) and the Senegalese prawn. Shrimps and prawns are served as hors-d'œuvre in salads and cocktails, in aspic and mousses, or plain, and are also used extensively in cooking (for sauces, *beurres composés*, broths, etc), and in many fish garnishes. Note that the usable part constitutes less than half the total weight, ie 100 g/4 oz shrimps or prawns will give 40 g/1½ oz meat when peeled.

SHRIMPS OR PRAWNS IN ASPIC WITH TRUFFLES

Preparation 2 hours

US	Ingredients	Met/Imp
10 oz	peeled cooked shrimps or prawns, diced	300 g/10 oz
2 cups	Mayonnaise (*page 72*)	500 ml/18 fl oz
1 quart	liquid Fish Aspic (*page 58*)	1 litre/1¾ pints
	small black truffles	
	extra peeled cooked prawns (large shrimp), for decoration	

Bind the diced shrimps or prawns with some mayonnaise and aspic; form this mixture into small balls and arrange on a dish. Chill until firm.

Line a mould with aspic. Decorate the bottom as you like, pour in a small quantity of aspic and chill until set, then add another layer of aspic and chill again. Arrange the seafood balls on top of the jelly, alternating them with truffles. Place a whole prawn (large shrimp) between each, turning it over on its back so that when the mould is turned out the prawn (large shrimp) will be the right way up. Fill up the rest of the mould with layers of seafood balls, truffles, prawns (large shrimp) and aspic.

Chill until set and turn out just before serving.

Dry white wines: Coteaux Champenois, Montrachet, Meursault, Graves.
Sweet wine wines: Sauternes, Barsac, Anjou, Vouvray, Monbazillac.

CRÊPES STUFFED WITH PRAWNS

Preparation 1 hour • Cooking 10 minutes

US	Ingredients	Met/Imp
scant ½ lb	peeled cooked prawns or shrimps	200 g/7 oz
	pepper	
2 cups	Fish Velouté (*page 57*)	500 ml/18 fl oz
2	egg yolks	2
6	egg whites	6
16	small unsweetened crêpes	16

Pound the prawns in a mortar and pestle; season them with pepper, then work through a sieve. Mix in a little velouté sauce and the egg yolks. Fold in the stiffly beaten egg whites.

Spread this mixture on to the very thin crêpes; roll up and heat through in a moderate oven for 10 minutes. Serve at once.

White wines: Coteaux Champenois, Montrachet, Saint-Péray, Vouvray, Anjou, Monbazillac.

SHRIMP OR PRAWN CROQUETTES

Preparation 1 hour • Cooking 5 minutes

US	Ingredients	Met/Imp
2 lb	uncooked shrimps or prawns	1 kg/2 lb
1 quart	Béchamel Sauce (*page 62*)	1 litre/1¾ pints
3	eggs	3
a little	oil	a little
	salt and pepper	
8 cups	fresh white breadcrumbs	500 g/1 lb
	oil for deep frying	
	deep-fried parsley, to garnish	

Peel the shrimps or prawns. Mix with the thick béchamel and cook over a gentle heat for 15 minutes, stirring. Leave to cool, then shape into croquettes. Dip in the eggs beaten with the oil and salt and pepper, then coat with the breadcrumbs and deep-fry until golden. Serve garnished with deep-fried parsley.

White wines: Muscadet, Vouvray, Sancerre, Pouilly-Fumé, Chablis, Mâcon-Villages.

ÉCREVISSE

FRESHWATER CRAYFISH

THIS HIGHLY ESTEEMED CRUSTACEAN IS NOW RARE IN FRENCH rivers. There are several types: the red-clawed crayfish found in the Auvergne is considered the most delicate, then there is the white-clawed variety, found in the mountains, and the type that lives in fast running water, in Morvan and Alsace. Those most commonly sold nowadays are imported from central Europe.

When preparing freshwater crayfish, the gut should be removed, as this would give the dish a bitter flavour. In fact the only part eaten is the tail, which constitutes one-fifth of the total weight. The crayfish can be kept alive for about a week by putting them in a salad shaker in water with some fresh nettles, which should be changed frequently. These crustaceans are the main ingredient in a number of the choicest regional dishes, especially those from the Jura, Alsace and Lyon, and are also used in haute cuisine, in bisques, gratins and sauces, and particularly in recipes bearing the name Nantua.

ÉCREVISSES À L'ANETH EN SALADE

——— CRAYFISH AND DILL SALAD ———

Preparation 45 minutes • Cooking 20 minutes

US	Ingredients	Met/Imp
2 cups	dry white wine	500 ml/18 fl oz
1	large onion	1
1	carrot	1
	salt and pepper	
	parsley, thyme, dill sprigs	
	a few peppercorns	
	cayenne	
36	freshwater crayfish	36
1	lemon, juice of	1
1¼ cups	crème fraîche	300 ml/½ pint
1	lettuce	1

Make a *court bouillon*, using the wine, an equal amount of water, the onion and carrot sliced into rings, some salt and herbs. Boil for 20 minutes, then add the peppercorns and a pinch of cayenne.

Add the crayfish, from which the gut should have been removed, to the court bouillon (in 2 batches if necessary). Cover the pan and cook for 8–10 minutes, then drain. Shell the crayfish and leave in a little of the court bouillon to cool. Pound 5 of the shells at a time in a mortar and pestle, mince (grind) them, then work them through a fine sieve.

Chop a handful of dill leaves finely and mix with salt and the lemon juice. Add the crème fraîche and sieved shells; adjust the seasoning. Mix the crayfish with the sauce and serve very fresh, garnished with shredded lettuce.

White wines: Sancerre, Pouilly-Fumé, Quincy.

CRAYFISH BORDELAISE

Preparation 45 minutes • Cooking about 40 minutes

US	Ingredients	Met/Imp
10 tbsp	butter	150 g/5 oz
24	freshwater crayfish	24
5 tbsp	cognac	80 ml/3 fl oz
2 cups	good dry white wine	500 ml/18 fl oz
2 tbsp	tomato paste	30 ml/2 tbsp
I pinch	cayenne	I pinch
	salt and pepper	
scant ½ cup	Fish Velouté (*page 57*)	100 ml/4 fl oz
I tbsp	chopped parsley, to finish	15 ml/I tbsp
	MIREPOIX	
2 oz (½ cup)	carrots	50 g/2 oz
2 oz (¼ cup)	onions	50 g/2 oz
2	shallots	2
I	parsley stalk	I
I	garlic clove	I
I pinch	ground bay	I pinch
I pinch	dried thyme	I pinch
I stick	butter	100 g/4 oz

First prepare the mirepoix. Chop as finely as possible the carrots, onions, shallots and parsley stalk. Add a piece of crushed garlic the size of a pea, together with the bay and thyme. Put these ingredients in a saucepan with the butter and cook until softened. This mirepoix can, and in fact should, be made in advance.

Reserve one-third of the butter. Put the remainder in a sauté pan and add the washed crayfish, from which the gut should have been removed; sauté over a brisk heat until the shells are a definite red colour. Add the cognac; remove from the heat and flambé, taking care not to burn the tentacles, as this would give the sauce a bitter flavour. (The cognac may be flambéed in advance.) Return to the heat and add the wine, tomato paste, cayenne, a pinch of salt and the mirepoix.

Cover and cook for 10–12 minutes, tossing the crayfish from time to time.

Remove the crayfish and arrange on a heated serving dish. Reduce the sauce to 300 ml/½ pint (1¼ cups) and add the velouté sauce and reserved butter. Taste and adjust the seasoning.

Pour this sauce over the crayfish and sprinkle with a little parsley.

Dry rosé wine: Tavel.
Dry white wines: dry Graves, Muscadet, Sancerre, Pouilly-Fumé, Chablis, Mâcon-Villages.

CRAYFISH CASSEROLE WITH WHISKY

Preparation 25 minutes • Cooking 45 minutes

US	Ingredients	Met/Imp
14 tbsp	butter	200 g/7 oz
	Mirepoix (*page 50*), made with I carrot, I large onion and 3 shallots	
I	bouquet garni	I
24	freshwater crayfish	24
	salt and pepper	
¼ cup	cognac	50 ml/2 fl oz
I cup	dry white wine	200 ml/7 fl oz
I cup	double (heavy) cream	200 ml/7 fl oz
I tsp	tomato paste	5 ml/I tsp
I tbsp	Kneaded Butter (*page 49*)	15 ml/I tbsp
¼ cup	whisky	50 ml/2 fl oz

Melt the butter in a sauté pan, but do not allow to brown. Fry the very finely chopped mirepoix ingredients for about 30 minutes, with the bouquet garni.

Remove the mirepoix and bouquet garni with a slotted spoon, leaving the butter in the pan; reserve the mirepoix. Put the pan back over a brisk heat and quickly add the crayfish from which the gut has been removed. Fry until browned, season and cook briefly (for 5 minutes only) in a fairly hot oven.

Remove from the oven and flambé immediately with good-quality cognac. Add the wine and cream, the tomato paste and the mirepoix. Cover and cook for 15 minutes. Thicken the sauce slightly with the kneaded butter and stir in the whisky just before serving.

Dry white wines: Sancerre, Pouilly-Fumé.

US	Ingredients	Met/Imp
	Mirepoix (page 50), made with 1 carrot, 1 onion and 3 shallots	
1 stick	butter	100 g/4 oz
24	freshwater crayfish	24
	salt and pepper	
	cayenne	
¼ cup	brandy	50 ml/2 fl oz
½ cup	white wine	100 ml/4 fl oz
1 cup	Fish Fumet (page 57)	200 ml/7 fl oz
3	tomatoes	3
1	bouquet garni	1
1 tbsp	Kneaded Butter (page 49)	15 ml/1 tbsp
1 cup	thick crème fraîche	200 ml/7 fl oz

ÉCREVISSES À LA CRÈME

CRAYFISH WITH CREAM

Preparation 35 minutes • Cooking 12 minutes

Chop the mirepoix ingredients very finely and cook in the butter until soft but not browned. Add the crayfish, from which the gut has been removed, salt, pepper and a very small pinch of cayenne. Sauté over a brisk heat until the crayfish are browned on all sides. Flambé with the brandy; add the wine and fish fumet, together with the skinned and chopped tomatoes and the bouquet garni. Cook for 10 minutes.

Remove the crayfish with a slotted spoon and place on a heated serving dish. Keep warm. Reduce the cooking juices by two-thirds; thicken with the kneaded butter and stir in the crème fraîche. Bring to the boil and adjust the seasoning. (The sauce should have a pink hue and be highly seasoned.) Strain through a conical sieve, pressing down well, over the crayfish. Serve very hot.

Dry white wines: Pouilly-Fumé, Saint-Joseph, Hermitage.

US	Ingredients	Met/Imp
24	freshwater crayfish	24
14 tbsp	butter	200 g/7 oz
½ cup	cognac	100 ml/4 fl oz
3	shallots	3
	bouquet garni with tarragon	
½ cup	crème fraîche	100 ml/4 fl oz
	salt and pepper	
¼ cup	Crayfish Butter (page 51)	50 g/2 oz

ÉCREVISSES FLAMBÉES AU COGNAC

CRAYFISH FLAMBÉED IN COGNAC

Preparation 20 minutes • Cooking 12 minutes

Remove the gut from the crayfish. Heat a small amount of the butter in a sauté pan and add the crayfish; flambé with the cognac; add the chopped shallots, bouquet garni and crème fraîche and season. Cover and cook as quickly as possible (this dish does not require prolonged cooking).

Remove the crayfish to a heated serving dish. Strain the sauce through a sieve and stir in the remaining butter. Add the crayfish butter and serve.

Dry white wines: Pouilly-Fuissé, Arbois, Coteaux Champenois, Château-Chalon.

US	Ingredients	Met/Imp
1	onion	1
1	carrot	1
10 tbsp	butter	150 g/5 oz
24	freshwater crayfish	24
6 tbsp	pure malt whisky	80 ml/3 fl oz
½ cup	white wine	100 ml/4 fl oz
1	bouquet garni with tarragon	1
	salt and pepper	
4	egg yolks	4
½ cup	crème fraîche	100 ml/4 fl oz

ÉCREVISSES FLAMBÉES AU WHISKY

CRAYFISH FLAMBÉED IN WHISKY

Preparation 35 minutes • Cooking 12 minutes

Dice the onion and carrot; fry in the butter in a saucepan but do not brown. Add the crayfish from which the gut has been removed and cook until they turn bright red; flambé with the whisky. Add the wine, bouquet garni, salt and pepper; cook over a brisk heat for 12 minutes.

When the crayfish are cooked, remove them from the pan, place in a heated flameproof dish and keep warm.

Strain the cooking juices, then bring to the boil in a saucepan; reduce the heat and add the egg yolks mixed with the crème fraîche. Finish off with a pinch of cayenne, pour the sauce over the crayfish and heat through gently. Do not allow to boil.

Dry white wine: Coteaux Champenois.

CRAYFISH WITH YORK HAM

Preparation 50 minutes • Cooking 12 minutes

US	Ingredients	Met/Imp
24	freshwater crayfish	24
2 quarts	well-seasoned court bouillon	2 litres/3½ pints
¼ cup	Kneaded Butter (page 49)	50 g/2 oz
1 stick	butter	100 g/4 oz
3	shallots	3
½ lb	York ham, fat removed	250 g/8 oz
6 tbsp	cognac	80 ml/3 fl oz
2 cups	crème fraîche	500 ml/18 fl oz
	salt and pepper	

Cook the crayfish from which the gut has been removed in court bouillon. Remove the crayfish, reduce the court bouillon by half, and thicken with the kneaded butter. Sauté the crayfish in butter in a sauté pan, together with the finely chopped shallots and York ham. Flambé with the cognac and cover with the crème fraîche mixed with the court bouillon. Simmer for a few minutes, check the seasoning and serve at once.

White wines: Vouvray, Coteaux du Layon, Hermitage, Coteaux Champenois.

CRAYFISH MORVANDELLE

Preparation 35 minutes • Cooking 12 minutes

US	Ingredients	Met/Imp
	Mirepoix (page 50), made with 2 carrots, 1 large onion, 4 shallots, 1 crushed garlic clove	
1 stick	butter	100 g/4 oz
1	bouquet garni	1
24	freshwater crayfish	24
¼ cup	marc from Burgundy	50 ml/2 fl oz
½ cup	double (heavy) cream	100 ml/4 fl oz
3 tbsp	tomato paste	45 ml/3 tbsp
1 cup	Veal Stock (page 56)	200 ml/7 fl oz
	salt	

Sweat the finely chopped mirepoix vegetables in half of the butter in a sauté pan; add the bouquet garni. Add the crayfish from which the gut has been removed and cook until red, then flambé with the marc. Add the cream, tomato paste, veal stock and salt; simmer until reduced. Add the remaining butter just before serving.

Dry white wines: Chablis, Mâcon-Clessé, -Lugny or -Viré.

CRAYFISH AU GRATIN 'ROUERGATE'

Preparation 1 hour • Cooking 15 minutes

US	Ingredients	Met/Imp
48	freshwater crayfish	48
	well-seasoned court bouillon	
2 sticks	butter	250 g/8 oz
2 cups	crème fraîche	500 ml/18 fl oz
¼ lb	truffles	100 g/4 oz
½ lb	mushrooms	250 g/8 oz
	salt and pepper	
½ cup	Gruyère cheese, grated	50 g/2 oz

Cook the crayfish, from which the gut has been removed, in the court bouillon. Shell them and set the tail meat aside. Make a Crayfish Butter (*page 51*) with the butter, shells and roes. Mix with the crème fraîche, stirring in the truffles and the mushrooms which have been previously sautéed in butter. Place in gratin dishes with the crayfish, sprinkle with salt and pepper and grated cheese and brown in the oven. Serve piping hot.

Dry white wines: Pouilly-Fuissé, Pouilly-Loché, Coteaux Champenois.

US	Ingredients	Met/Imp
40	freshwater crayfish	40
6 tbsp	Crayfish Butter (page 51)	75 g/3 oz
2 tbsp	cognac	30 ml/2 tbsp
scant ½ lb	Paris mushrooms	200 g/7 oz
2½ oz	truffles	60 g/2½ oz
1¼ cups	Béchamel Sauce (page 62)	300 ml/½ pint
2½ cups	crème fraîche	600 ml/1 pint
	salt and pepper	
	cayenne	

CRAYFISH TAILS AU GRATIN NANTUA

Preparation 1 hour • Cooking 15 minutes

Poach the crayfish, from which the gut has been removed, and shell them. Brown in the crayfish butter over a brisk heat; flambé with most of the cognac, then remove the sauté pan from the heat and add the diced mushrooms and truffles. Pour over the béchamel mixed with the crème fraîche and cook slowly, amalgamating the sauce with the crayfish butter until the mixture is emulsified and the aroma and colour are as required.

Add the juice from the truffles and a dash of cognac; season with salt, pepper and a pinch of cayenne. Turn the contents of the pan into a gratin dish and brown in a hot oven.

White wines: Jurançon, Anjou, Vouvray, Barsac, Sauternes.

RAGOÛT D'ÉCREVISSES À LA HONGROISE

HUNGARIAN CRAYFISH RAGOÛT

Preparation 45 minutes • Cooking 25 minutes

US	Ingredients	Met/Imp
¼ lb	onions	125 g/4½ oz
4 tbsp	lard	50 g/2 oz
24	freshwater crayfish	24
1	thyme sprig	1
1	bay leaf	1
½ cup	dry white wine	100 ml/4 fl oz
	salt and pepper	
	paprika	
1 cup	crème fraîche	200 ml/7 fl oz
4 tbsp	butter	50 g/2 oz

Peel and chop the onions finely; place in a sauté pan with the lard and brown over a gentle heat.

Wash the crayfish and remove the gut. Add them to the sauté pan, together with the thyme and bay. Cook over a brisk heat for 5 minutes, turning the crayfish constantly; add the wine and season with salt and pepper. Cover the pan and leave to simmer for 5 minutes.

Take out the crayfish and arrange on a heated serving dish. Add the paprika to the pan and reduce for 6 minutes; add the crème fraîche and diced butter. Remove the sauce from the heat as soon as it reaches boiling point, pour over the crayfish and serve.

White wines: Arbois, Meursault, Corton-Charlemagne.

HOMARD ET LANGOUSTE

LOBSTER AND CRAWFISH

LOBSTERS AND CRAWFISH (SPINY OR ROCK LOBSTERS) ARE THE largest, most delicate and most sought after of the crustaceans. Breton lobster enjoys a reputation for excellence that is recognized by all gourmets and cooks, but it is rare, and so Norwegian or American lobster is often used instead. Only very heavy lobsters give the dense white flesh that can be cut into pieces and used in haute cuisine. For most recipes, it is necessary to plunge the lobsters live into the cooking liquid, in which they turn red (hence the expression 'cardinalize' which the French use to describe cooking a lobster until it turns red like a cardinal's hat). Lobsters and crawfish that are to be served cold are often tied to a small board, so that they will maintain a perfect shape when cold. If cooking them in a *court bouillon*, use a copper or enamel saucepan for preference. When cutting up a live lobster*, take a cleaver and separate the head or body from the tail with one blow. If it is to be cut in half lengthways, begin by slicing the head between the eyes. Take care to remove the bag of grit situated in the head. Note that the female is often heavier than the male, and is therefore meatier and more useful in recipes. The smaller male has less meat, but it is considered superior in that its flavour is more delicate.

*Editor's note: if you prefer, you can kill the lobster first by dropping it into boiling water, weighting down the pan lid and simmering it gently. Allow 15 minutes for the first 500 g/1 lb and 10 minutes for each 500 g/1 lb after that.

COQUILLES DE HOMARD AU GRATIN 'COMME À SAINT-CAST'

— LOBSTER AU GRATIN SAINT-CAST —

Preparation 1 hour • Cooking 25 minutes

Cook the lobsters in a court bouillon made with the listed ingredients and 200 ml/7 fl oz (scant 1 cup) water. When cooked, remove from the pan and shell. Reserve all the meat suitable for slicing into escalopes; pound the rest carefully, then work through a fine sieve, moistening with a small amount of the cooking liquid and the madeira. Next add the duxelles thickened with the egg yolks; season. Fill each lobster shell with a little of this *salpicon* and divide the sliced lobster equally between them. Place some more salpicon on top, pour over the melted butter and glaze in a hot oven. Serve piping hot.

Dry white wine: Muscadet, Saumur, Chablis, Mâcon-Villages.

US	Ingredients	Met/Imp
4½ lb	live lobsters	2 kg/4½ lb
¼ cup	madeira	50 ml/2 fl oz
1 cup	Dry Duxelles (page 49)	250 ml/9 fl oz
3	egg yolks	3
5 tbsp	butter, melted	60 g/2½ oz
	COURT BOUILLON	
1 quart	dry white wine	1 litre/1¾ pints
1	onion	1
2	carrots	2
2	shallots	2
1	garlic clove	1
1	bouquet garni	1
	salt	
	peppercorns	

US	Ingredients	Met/Imp
8, each about 10 oz	live small lobsters (*demoiselles de Cherbourg*)	8, each about 300 g/10 oz
¼ cup	cognac	50 ml/2 fl oz
I tbsp	chopped parsley, to garnish	15 ml/I tbsp
	COURT BOUILLON	
I bottle	white wine	I bottle
I	onion	I
I	carrot	I
I	bouquet garni	I
	salt	
	peppercorns	
I pinch	cayenne	I pinch
4, each about 1¼ lb	live lobsters	4, each about 600 g/1¼ lb
	SAUCE	
	chervil, tarragon, chives and parsley	
4	hard-boiled egg yolks	4
	salt and pepper	
	oil	
	vinegar	
I tsp	English mustard	5 ml/I tsp
I tsp	Worcestershire sauce	5 ml/Itsp
I tbsp	madeira	15 ml/I tbsp
	COURT BOUILLON	
I quart	white wine	I litre/1¾ pints
scant ½ cup	wine vinegar	100 ml/4 fl oz
2	carrots	2
2	onions	2
	salt	
	peppercorns	
I	bouquet garni	I
5½ lb	live lobsters	2.5 kg/5½ lb
	salt and pepper	
14 tbsp	butter	200 g/7 oz
scant ½ cup	oil	100 ml/4 fl oz
4	shallots	4
I	garlic sliver	I
5 tbsp	cognac	80 ml/3 fl oz
2 cups	white wine	500 ml/18 fl oz
6	tomatoes	6
	or	
3 tbsp	tomato paste	45 ml/3 tbsp
2 tbsp	chopped parsley	30 ml/2 tbsp
I pinch	cayenne	I pinch
I	bouquet garni	I

SMALL LOBSTERS 'IN THE SWIM'

Preparation 1 hour • Cooking 15 minutes

Prepare a court bouillon with the listed ingredients, then add lobsters and boil for 15 minutes. Serve the lobsters hot in the cooking liquid, with the cognac added. Sprinkle with parsley.

Dry white wines: Muscadet, Gros Plant du Pays Nantais.

HOMARD ALEXANDRE

LOBSTER ALEXANDER

Preparation 1 hour • Cooking 25 minutes

Recipe by Claude Terrail, Tour d'Argent, Paris

Simmer the lobsters for about 20 minutes in a court bouillon made with the listed ingredients and 500 ml/18 fl oz (2 cups) water.

Cut the lobster tails in half lengthways and remove the white meat from the shell; slice the meat into escalopes and place on a cold plate.

Prepare the sauce. Chop the herbs finely. Mash the hard-boiled egg yolks with a fork; mix with the herbs, then treat as for a *rémoulade*, ie mix with salt, pepper, oil, vinegar, mustard and Worcestershire sauce. Add the madeira. Spoon this sauce between the lobster escalopes.

Dry white wines: Pouilly-Fuissé, Pouilly-Vinzelles, Coteaux Champenois.

HOMARD À L'AMÉRICAINE

LOBSTER AMÉRICAINE

Preparation 50 minutes • Cooking 25 minutes

Cut the lobster tails into even slices, following the marks of the joints to avoid splintering. Detach the legs and break the casing of the claws, so that it will be easier to extract the meat after cooking. Slice the carcass in half and set aside. Remove the bags from the head, which contains grit; set the liver and coral aside to thicken the sauce in the final stages of cooking. Season the pieces of lobster with salt and pepper. Heat half of the butter and the oil in a sauté pan, add the lobster and sauté until bright red.

Pour the fat from the sauté pan; sprinkle the lobster with the shallot and add the garlic, crushed. Add the cognac and flambé; then add the wine, the skinned, de-seeded and chopped tomatoes or the tomato paste and half of the parsley. Season with the cayenne and add the bouquet garni. Cover the pan and cook for 20 minutes.

Remove the lobster from the pan. Extract the meat from the tails and claws. Arrange in a heated serving dish and place the reserved carcass shells on top; keep warm while you finish cooking the sauce. Reduce the cooking liquid and add the reserved lobster liver and coral (both chopped) together with a spoonful of butter. Cook for a few moments, then remove from the heat and add the remaining butter, diced. Pour this sauce over the lobsters and sprinkle with the remaining parsley.

Dry white wine: Pouilly-Fuissé, Pouilly-Vinzelles, Coteaux Champenois.

HOMARD AU CHAMBERTIN

—— LOBSTER IN CHAMBERTIN WINE ——

Preparation 1 hour • Cooking about 45 minutes

Cut up the lobsters as for Lobster Américaine (*left*). Remove the coral (if any) and set aside. Fry the lobster pieces together with the blanched mirepoix in some of the butter and the oil. Flambé with good-quality marc, then moisten with the wine and fish fumet.

Season with salt and pepper and a small pinch of nutmeg; cook for 15 minutes. Remove the pieces of lobster from the pan and keep warm. Thicken the sauce with *beurre manié* made from the coral and remaining butter. Arrange the pieces of lobster on a heated serving dish and serve very hot, with the Creole rice and croûtons served separately.

Red wines: Chambertin or other wines from the Côte de Nuits, Châteauneuf-du-Pape.

US	Ingredients	Met/Imp
4, each 1–1¼ lb	live lobsters	4, each 500–600 g/1–1¼ lb
	Mirepoix (*page 50*), made with 1 carrot, 1 onion, 2 shallots, 1 garlic clove, 1 canned anchovy fillet, 1 bouquet garni	
10 tbsp	butter	150 g/5 oz
½ cup	oil	100 ml/4 fl oz
¼ cup	*marc* from Burgundy	50 ml/2 fl oz
1 bottle	Chambertin	1 bottle
½ cup	Fish Fumet (*page 57*)	100 ml/4 fl oz
	salt and pepper	
	nutmeg	
	GARNISH	
scant 1 cup	Creole Rice (*page 562*)	175 g/6 oz
16	toasted croûtons	16

HOMARD EN CHEMISE

—— LOBSTER 'EN CHEMISE' ——

Preparation 1¼ hours • Cooking 55 minutes

Tie up the lobsters. Bring a large saucepan of water containing a small handful of coarse salt to the boil. Plunge the lobsters quickly into the boiling water; remove and drain after 2 minutes; wipe dry.

Brush 2 sheets of greaseproof or parchment paper with oil. Smear the lobsters all over with butter, then season well with salt and pepper. Place each lobster on a sheet of greased paper; wrap up and tie. Bake in a hot oven for 50 minutes.

Serve the lobsters in their paper. Accompany with a sauce of your choice such as Béarnaise, Bordelaise or Américaine, or with a Vinaigrette Dressing (*page 81*) flavoured with herbs.

White wines: Graves, Vouvray, Coteaux du Layon.

US	Ingredients	Met/Imp
2, each about 1¼ lb	live lobsters	2, each about 600 g/1¼ lb
	coarse sea salt	
	oil	
	butter	
	pepper	
	sauce of your choice, to serve (*pages 60–82*)	

US	Ingredients	Met/Imp
4, each 1–1¼ lb	lobsters	4, each 500–600 g/1–1¼ lb
	salt and pepper	
scant 1 cup	Maître d'Hôtel Butter (page 52)	200 g/7 oz
1 tbsp	good-quality mustard	15 ml/1 tbsp
2 cups	fresh white breadcrumbs	100 g/4 oz
	butter	

DEVILLED LOBSTER

Preparation 35 minutes • Cooking 25 minutes

Split the lobsters in half lengthways and remove the bag of grit from the head. Place in a roasting tin. Season with salt and pepper. Melt the maître d'hôtel butter and mix it with mustard. Pour over the lobsters, sprinkle with breadcrumbs and bake in a fairly hot oven for about 20 minutes.

Take care to crack the claws of the lobsters before serving. The creamy meat should be mixed with some butter and served separately.

Dry white wines: Quincy, Sancerre, Pouilly-Fumé, dry Graves, Chablis.

US	Ingredients	Met/Imp
3, each 1¼ lb	live lobsters	3, each 600 g/1¼ lb
2 sticks	butter	250 g/8 oz
5 tbsp	cognac	80 ml/3 fl oz
2 cups	dry white wine	500 ml/18 fl oz
¼ lb	button mushrooms	100 g/4 oz
	salt and pepper	
scant 1 cup	crème fraîche	200 ml/7 fl oz
8	egg yolks	8
1 tbsp	chopped parsley and chervil	15 ml/1 tbsp

LOBSTER WITH MUSHROOMS

Preparation 1 hour • Cooking 20 minutes

Cut the lobsters into at least 4 small pieces, removing the bag of grit in the head. Sauté briskly in half of the butter. When red, flambé with the cognac; add the wine, a few small mushrooms and some salt and pepper. Cover and cook for 15 minutes, then add the crème fraîche; cook for a further 5 minutes. Remove the lobster pieces and place them in a heated deep serving dish. Reduce the cooking juices and thicken with the egg yolks and the remaining butter.

Add the parsley and chervil just before serving.

Dry white wines: Savennières, Jasnières, Coteaux Champenois.

US	Ingredients	Met/Imp
4, each 1–1¼ lb	live lobsters (including at least 1 female with coral)	4, each 500–600 g/1–1¼ lb
10 tbsp	butter	50 g/5 oz
6 tbsp	cognac	80 ml/3 fl oz
½ bottle	dry white wine	½ bottle
2	tomatoes	2
1	bouquet garni	1
1	onion	1
2	shallots	2
2	carrots	2
⅔ cup	Dry Duxelles (page 49)	150 ml/¼ pint
	salt and pepper	
½ cup	crème fraîche	100 ml/4 fl oz
¼ lb	peeled cooked shrimps or prawns	100 g/4 oz

LOBSTER AU GRATIN DUNKIRK

Preparation 50 minutes • Cooking 30 minutes

Cut the lobsters in half lengthways; remove the bag of grit in the head and reserve the coral. Fry the lobster halves in some butter until the shells are red and the meat is firm, then flambé with the cognac. Add the wine, the crushed tomatoes, the bouquet garni and the chopped onion, shallots and carrots.

When cooked, remove the lobsters from the pan and keep warm. Reduce the cooking liquid. Meanwhile, crack the claws, remove the meat and place the meat inside the body and tail shells. Strain the cooking liquid and mix in the duxelles; season carefully and add the crème fraîche. Finish the sauce by thickening it with the reserved coral mixed to a *beurre manié* with butter.

Add the shrimps or prawns. Pour the sauce over the lobster halves and brown in a hot oven.

Dry white wines: Muscadet, Sancerre, Chablis, Alsace Sylvaner or Pinot Blanc.

GRILLED LOBSTER*

Preparation 45 minutes • Cooking 30 minutes

US	Ingredients	Met/Imp
4, each 1–1¼ lb	live lobsters	4, each 500–600 g/1–1¼ lb
	salt and pepper	
½ cup	oil	100 ml/4 fl oz
2 tbsp	chopped shallot	30 ml/2 tbsp
1 cup	port wine	200 ml/7 fl oz
1 cup	crème fraîche	200 ml/7 fl oz
6	egg yolks	6
	cayenne	

Cut the lobsters in half lengthways and remove the bag of grit from the heads. Season the meat with salt and pepper and coat lightly with oil. Place under the grill (broiler) and cook, first on the shell side, then on the meat side (about 30 minutes for a 500 g/1 lb lobster).

Meanwhile, put the shallot into a saucepan, add the port and boil until completely reduced. Place the crème fraîche in another saucepan and reduce slightly; mix in the egg yolks and season with salt and cayenne. Add this mixture to the reduced port, then strain through a conical sieve.

Arrange the lobsters on a serving dish and coat the meat with some of the sauce. Hand the rest separately in a sauce boat.

Dry white wines: Savennières, Sancerre, Chablis, Meursault.

HUNGARIAN-STYLE LOBSTER

Preparation 35 minutes • Cooking about 15 minutes

US	Ingredients	Met/Imp
4, each about 1½ lb	live lobsters	4, each about 750 g/1½ lb
1 tbsp	paprika	15 ml/1 tbsp
1 stick	butter	100 g/4 oz
½ cup	crème fraîche	100 ml/4 fl oz
1 tbsp	finely chopped parsley, chervil and tarragon	15 ml/1 tbsp
	salt and pepper	
	COURT BOUILLON	
2	onions	2
2	carrots	2
4	shallots	4
½	head garlic	½
1	bouquet garni	1
2 tbsp	black peppercorns	30 ml/2 tbsp
¼ tsp	cayenne	1.25 ml/¼ tsp
	coarse sea salt	
1 glass	wine vinegar	1 glass
2 cups	dry white wine	500 ml/18 fl oz

Prepare a *court bouillon* with the listed ingredients. Boil for 10 minutes, then add the lobsters and cook for a further 10 minutes. Take the lobsters out of the pan and split them in half lengthways; remove the bag of grit from the heads. Place the halves on a long ovenproof dish. Sprinkle the meat with very good quality paprika, place a few pieces of fine-quality butter on top and bake in a very hot oven for about 5 minutes.

During this time, mix the crème fraîche with the herbs, a little salt and freshly milled pepper. Work these ingredients together thoroughly. Take the lobsters out of the oven and pour the mixture over them. Put them back into the oven immediately and bake until the surface is glazed. Serve piping hot, taking care not to remove the meat from the shell until guests are ready to eat.

Dry white wines: Muscadet, Sancerre, Chablis, Chassagne-Montrachet.

US	Ingredients	Met/Imp
5½ lb	live lobsters	2.5 kg/5½ lb
½ cup	olive oil	100 ml/4 fl oz
2	onions	2
4	shallots	4
	salt and pepper	
½ cup	good-quality cognac	100 ml/4 fl oz
2 tbsp	parsley, chervil and tarragon	30 ml/2 tbsp
I tsp	mustard	5 ml/I tsp
I tbsp	tomato paste	15 ml/I tbsp
	cayenne	
I	lemon, juice of	I
2 tbsp	Worcestershire sauce	30 ml/2 tbsp
	MAYONNAISE	
4	egg yolks	4
2 cups	oil	500 ml/18 fl oz

LOBSTER HOUSSINE

Preparation 2 hours • Cooking 30 minutes

For this recipe the lobsters are cut up and fried as for Lobster Américaine (*page 244*), then coated with mayonnaise and baked.

Stretch the lobsters out on a board in order to cut them; remove the claws and cut the tail meat into 5–6 slices, following the marks of the joints to avoid splintering. Slice the carcass in half lengthways. Remove the bag of grit from the head; crack the claws open with the flat of the cleaver in order to make it easier to extract the meat; detach the pincers. Reserve the liver and coral (if any), which will later be pounded together with the meat from the claws.

As soon as you have cut up the lobsters, put a sauté pan over a brisk heat, heat up the olive oil and brown the finely chopped onions and shallots. Add the pieces of lobster, seasoned with salt and pepper. Fry, turning from time to time, until the meat is firm and the shells are a nice red colour. Drain off the oil thoroughly, add the cognac and flambé;

Have ready the following ingredients on a plate: the herbs, mustard, tomato paste, a pinch each of cayenne pepper, salt and white pepper, and the lobster liver and coral, pounded together with the meat from the claws.

Make the mayonnaise with the egg yolks, bowl and oil at room temperature, as described on page 72. When the mayonnaise is thick, gradually mix in the ingredients from the plate. Finish with the lemon juice and Worcestershire sauce; season to taste with salt and pepper. The sauce is ready when you can stand a spoon up in it.

Arrange the pieces of lobster in an ovenproof dish; coat with the mayonnaise sauce and bake in a very hot oven until the mayonnaise sauce is liquid. Serve at once.

White wines: Vouvray, Montlouis, Jasnières, Coteaux Champenois.

LOBSTER 'IN THE SWIM' WITH FRENCH BEANS

Preparation 55 minutes • Cooking 30 minutes

US	Ingredients	Met/Imp
1 lb	French (fine green) beans	500 g/1 lb
1 per person, each 10 oz	live lobsters	1 per person, each 300 g/10 oz
	Hollandaise Sauce (*page 70*), to serve	
	COURT BOUILLON	
4	carrots	4
4	turnips	4
2	celery stalks	2
2	large onions	2
2	cloves	2
	thyme and parsley sprigs	
	salt and pepper	
	peppercorns	
½ bottle	dry sherry	½ bottle

Prepare the court bouillon. Peel and wash the carrots and turnips; cut into thick strips lengthways. Wash and brush the celery stalks; cut widthways into thick strips. Spike the onions with the cloves and place all these ingredients in a flameproof casserole together with some thyme, parsley, salt and a few peppercorns. Add the sherry and 1 litre/1¾ pints (1 quart) water. Bring to the boil and cook for 15 minutes.

Trim and wash the French (green) beans. Cook until al dente by boiling gently for 10 minutes in salted water, in an uncovered saucepan. Drain. Plunge the lobsters into the court bouillon and leave for about 12 minutes. Remove them from the pan, cut in half lengthways and crack the claws. Strain the court bouillon.

Serve in deep dishes, placing some green beans, some court bouillon and the lobster halves in each. Pour over some Hollandaise sauce mixed with a little of the court bouillon.

White wines: Coteaux Champenois, Alsace Pinot Blanc or Pinot Gris, Crémant d'Alsace.

LOBSTER NEWBURG

Preparation 40 minutes • Cooking 25 minutes

US	Ingredients	Met/Imp
5½ lb	live lobsters	2.5 kg/5½ lb
	salt and pepper	
2 sticks	butter	250 g/8 oz
1¼ cups	very dry madeira	300 ml/½ pint
1¼ cups	very dry sherry	300 ml/½ pint
1	bouquet garni	1
1¼ cups	*crème fraîche*	300 ml/½ pint
8	egg yolks	8
1 tbsp	Kneaded Butter (*page 49*)	15 ml/1 tbsp
1 cup	Creole Rice (*page 562*)	200 g/7 oz

Cut up the lobsters, removing the bag of grit in the head and reserving the coral (if any), then season. Reserve 50 g/2 oz (4 tbsp) of the butter, put the remainder in a sauté pan and heat until smoking, then add the lobster. Pour over the madeira and sherry, add the bouquet garni, cover and cook for 20 minutes. When cooked, shell the lobster pieces and keep warm.

Thicken the cooking liquid with the crème fraîche, egg yolks and the kneaded butter mixed with the lobster coral; do not allow to boil. Place the lobster meat in the sauce and add the reserved butter. Mix all the ingredients together carefully. Serve hot, accompanied by Creole rice.

Dry white wines: Vouvray, Sancerre, Pouilly-Fumé, Arbois, Alsace Riesling, Coteaux Champenois, Brut Champagne.

US	Ingredients	Met/Imp
2	carrots	2
I	onion	I
4	shallots	4
2	leeks, white part only	2
10 tbsp	butter	150 g/5 oz
5 tbsp	cognac	80 ml/3 fl oz
2 cups	Muscadet	500 ml/18 fl oz
I	bouquet garni	I
I tsp	curry powder	5 ml/I tsp
	salt and pepper	
4, each 1–1¼ lb	live lobsters	4, each 500–600 g/1–1¼ lb
2 cups	crème fraîche	500 ml/18 fl oz
I tbsp	flour	15 ml/I tbsp
I tbsp	chopped parsley, to garnish	15 ml/I tbsp

LOBSTER PALUDIÈRE

Preparation 1 hour • Cooking 25 minutes

Chop the carrots, onion, shallots and leeks finely. Cook slowly in one-third of the butter in a covered saucepan; do not allow to brown. Pour in the cognac and flambé; add the Muscadet, bouquet garni, curry powder and plenty of freshly milled pepper. Cook until reduced by half. Add the lobster, cut into pieces (reserve the corals and livers), and 400 ml/14 fl oz (1¾ cups) of the crème fraîche. Cook gently for 20 minutes, tossing the lobster pieces a number of times. Remove from the pan and place in a heated serving dish. Add the corals and livers with the remaining crème fraîche and the flour to the sauce; boil gently, then season lightly with salt. Strain the sauce over the lobster through a fine sieve and sprinkle with chopped parsley.

Dry white wines: Muscadet, Pouilly-Fumé, Chablis, Rully, Pouilly-Fuissé.

2, each about 1¼ lb	live lobsters	2, each about 600 g/1¼ lb
¼ cup	olive oil	60 ml/4 tbsp
	salt and pepper	
6 tbsp	butter	75 g/3 oz
3 tbsp	flour	30 g/I oz
1⅓ cups	milk	350 ml/12 fl oz
scant ½ cup	crème fraîche	100 ml/4 fl oz
I tbsp	strong mustard	15 ml/I tbsp
½ cup	Parmesan cheese, grated (optional)	50 g/2 oz

LOBSTER THERMIDOR

Preparation 15 minutes • Cooking 20 minutes

Cut the lobsters in half lengthways. To do this, place them upright on a board and plant a sharp, pointed knife between the eyes; bring the whole length of the blade down with a sharp blow along the back, from the head right down to the tail. Remove the bag of grit from the heads. Arrange the halves on a dish, pour some oil over them and season lightly with salt and pepper. Bake in a moderate oven for 15 minutes.

Meanwhile, prepare a béchamel sauce. Melt one-third of the butter in a saucepan over a low heat. Add the flour to make a *roux* and stir for 3 minutes; do not brown. Gradually add the milk and salt and pepper and stir until the sauce reaches boiling point. Leave to simmer for 10 minutes.

Take the lobsters out of the oven and remove the meat from the tails. Cut the meat crossways into thick slices.

Remove the sauce from the heat and stir in the crème fraîche, then the mustard. Spoon some of the sauce inside each lobster shell and place some of the lobster meat on top; pour over the remaining sauce. Melt the remaining butter over a low heat and pour it over the lobster halves. Sprinkle with grated cheese if liked. Crack the lobster claws with nutcrackers so that the meat can be removed more easily; brown under a hot grill (broiler) for 5 minutes. Arrange the lobsters on a heated serving dish and serve at once.

White wines: Chablis, Meursault, Pouilly-Fuissé, Vouvray, Savennières, Châteauneuf-du-Pape. Rosé Champagne.

CRAWFISH STEW

Preparation 45 minutes • Cooking 25 minutes

Peel and chop the onions and brown them in the oil in a sauté pan.

Stretch out the crawfish (remove the roe or coral if it is a female) and cut it into pieces; add to the pan and brown on both sides. Add the armagnac and flambé, then add the Banyuls.

Chop the shallots, garlic and parsley. Add to the pan, together with the thyme sprig and bay leaf. Season with salt and pepper, cover and cook for 15 minutes.

Take the pieces of crawfish out of the pan and keep warm. Stir the flour into the cooking juices and bring to the boil. Add the crawfish roe, if any, and the diced butter. Pour this sauce over the crawfish and serve.

White wines: Cassis, Bellet, Côtes de Provence.
Rosé wines: Tavel.

US	Ingredients	Met/Imp
2	onions	2
3 tbsp	extra-virgin olive oil	45 ml/3 tbsp
1, about 4 lb	live crawfish (rock lobster)	1, about 1.75 kg/4 lb
⅔ cup	armagnac	150 ml/¼ pint
1 bottle	Banyuls (sweet red wine)	1 bottle
6	shallots	6
3	garlic cloves	3
2	parsley sprigs	2
1	thyme sprig	1
1	bay leaf	1
	salt and pepper	
1 tsp	flour	5 ml/1 tsp
4 tbsp	butter	50 g/2 oz

CRAWFISH BIARROTE

Preparation 50 minutes • Cooking 25 minutes

Cut the crawfish in half lengthways, discard the gut and remove the coral (if any). Season them with salt, pepper and paprika and fry in the oil until firm; remove and drain. Fry the mirepoix vegetables in the cooking juices. Add the wine and cognac, then the pieces of crawfish. Simmer until cooked, then remove the crawfish and add the velouté sauce and cream. Mix the sauce well, pour over the crawfish and glaze with the butter in a hot oven.

Dry white wines: Muscadet, Saumur, dry Vouvray, Quincy, Sancerre, Pouilly-Fumé, dry Graves, Chablis, Bourgogne-Aligoté.

US	Ingredients	Met/Imp
4, each 1 lb	live crawfish (rock lobsters)	4, each 500 g/1 lb
	salt and pepper	
	paprika	
½ cup	oil	100 ml/3½ fl oz
	Mirepoix (page 50), made with 2 carrots, 1 onion, 4 shallots, 4 chopped tomatoes, 1 garlic clove, 1 bouquet garni	
1 quart	white wine	1 litre/1¾ pints
¼ cup	cognac	60 ml/4 tbsp
½ cup	Fish Velouté (page 57)	100 ml/3½ fl oz
scant 1 cup	double (heavy) cream	200 ml/7 fl oz
5 tbsp	butter	60 g/2½ oz

US	Ingredients	Met/Imp
2, each 2 lb	live crawfish (rock lobsters)	2, each 1 kg/2 lb
1 large piece	butter	1 large knob
2	onions	2
2	carrots	2
	salt and pepper	
1 quart	crème fraîche	1 litre/1¾ pints
¼ cup	Kneaded Butter, (page 49)	50 g/2 oz
½ cup	sherry	100 ml/4 fl oz

CRAWFISH WITH CREAM

Preparation 45 minutes • Cooking 25 minutes

Cut the crawfish into pieces, discarding the gut. Put the butter and the sliced onions and carrots into a sauté pan over a brisk heat. Add the pieces of crawfish and fry lightly. Season with salt and pepper, turn the pieces over and season again. Add the crème fraîche and cook for 25 minutes.

Remove the crawfish from the sauce and arrange on a heated serving dish. Finish the sauce by whisking in the kneaded butter. Stir well and adjust the seasoning to taste. Add the sherry, strain the sauce through a conical sieve, pour over the crawfish and serve.

White wines: Bonnezeaux, Coteaux du Layon, Monbazillac, Jurançon, Sauternes.

US	Ingredients	Met/Imp
4, each about 1 lb	live crawfish (rock lobsters)	4, each about 500 g/1 lb
	court bouillon	
½ lb	mushrooms	250 g/8 oz
10 tbsp	butter	150 g/5 oz
1 cup	stoned green olives	200 g/7 oz
	parsley, chervil and tarragon sprigs	
2 tbsp	fresh white breadcrumbs	30 ml/2 tbsp
5 cups	Béchamel Sauce (page 62)	1.2 litres /2 pints
¼ cup	cognac	50 ml/2 fl oz
	salt and pepper	

STUFFED CRAWFISH AU GRATIN

Preparation 1 hour • Cooking 25 minutes

Cook the crawfish in court bouillon and leave to cool. Cut the crawfish in half lengthways and remove the gut. Remove the meat from the tails and the body shells, without detaching the head from the tail.

Cut the meat from the tail into round slices or medallions; chop the meat from inside the body shell separately, and mix with the chopped mushrooms cooked in butter, the chopped olives and herbs, breadcrumbs and 1 litre/1¾ pints (1 quart) of the béchamel. Line the insides of the body and tail shells with this stuffing and brown in a hot oven for a few minutes. Take them out and place the tail meat on top of the stuffing; sprinkle with the cognac and cover with the remaining béchamel, well seasoned, with a few small pieces of butter added. Brown for a moment in the oven, then serve.

Dry white wines: Sauvignon de Touraine, Sauvignon de Saint-Bris, Gaillac, Hermitage, Coteaux Champenois.

GRILLED CRAWFISH

Preparation 45 minutes • Cooking 25 minutes

US	Ingredients	Met/Imp
4, each about 1 lb	live crawfish (rock lobsters)	4, each about 500 g/1 lb
2 sticks	butter	250 g/8 oz
1	shallot	1
	tarragon and chervil sprigs	
½ cup	wine vinegar	100 ml/4 fl oz
	peppercorns	
4	egg yolks	4
½ cup	oil	100 ml/4 fl oz
¼ cup	cognac	50 ml/2 fl oz
	salt and pepper	
1 cup	Creole Rice (page 562)	200 g/7 oz

Cut the crawfish in half lengthways. Remove the gut and set the coral (if any) aside; season the meat; coat with about 50 g/2 oz (4 tbsp) of the butter and grill (broil) in the usual way – see the recipe for Grilled Lobster (*page 247*).

Place the chopped shallot and herbs in a saucepan with the vinegar and peppercorns and reduce. Use this mixture with the egg yolks, remaining butter and the oil to make a Béarnaise Sauce (*page 61*).

Cook the crawfish coral in the cognac; sieve and reduce, then add to the sauce. Adjust the seasoning to taste. Serve the sauce with the crawfish, accompanied by the Creole rice.

Dry white wines: Muscadet, Sancerre, Pouilly-Fumé, Cassis.

CRAWFISH WITH MORELS

Preparation 1 hour • Cooking 25 minutes

US	Ingredients	Met/Imp
2, each about 1¾ lb	live crawfish (rock lobsters)	2, each about 800 g/1¾ lb
	oil	
	dry white wine	
¼ lb	shallots	100 g/4 oz
	salt and pepper	
a little	Meat Glaze (page 56)	a little
¼ cup	cognac	50 ml/2 fl oz
	Fish Fumet (page 57)	
1 tbsp	flour	15 ml/1 tbsp
14 tbsp	butter	200 g/7 oz
scant ½ lb	morels	200 g/7 oz
¼ cup	double (heavy) cream	60 ml/4 tbsp

Cut the crawfish in half lengthways and remove the gut; set the coral (if any) aside to thicken the sauce later. Sauté the unsalted crawfish halves, cut sides down, in oil, in a large sauté pan over a brisk heat, turning them over once. Add some wine and the finely chopped shallots; season with salt and pepper. Add a small amount of melted meat glaze and cook for about 15 minutes. Drain the crawfish, remove the meat from the tails and place in a bowl with the cognac. Keep warm.

Deglaze the sauté pan with a little fish fumet, then add the lightly pounded crawfish claws and shells to this reduced liquid. Mix the coral with the flour and a small amount of butter. Bring the sauce to the boil and thicken with the coral (the sauce should be amber coloured or quite golden), then sieve.

Remove the stalks from the morels. Wash the morels several times in running water, to remove any traces of sand, then drain and sweat in butter over a fairly brisk heat. Season with salt and pepper and add the cream.

Place the crawfish tail meat in the centre of a heated oval serving dish and pour over the crawfish sauce. Arrange the morels in the cream around the outside, so that you have 2 different coloured and flavoured sauces. Serve at once.

Wines: Coteaux Champenois, Montrachet.

US	Ingredients	Met/Imp
1, about 3¼ lb	live crawfish (rock lobster)	1, about 1.5 kg/3¼ lb
	court bouillon	
3 oz	truffles	75 g/3 oz
1 quart	liquid Fish Aspic (page 58)	1 litre/1¾ pints
1	wedge firm-textured bread	1
8	blanched artichoke bottoms	8
	Russian Salad (page 108)	
1 quart	Mayonnaise (page 72)	1 litre/1¾ pints
8	hard-boiled eggs	8
4	lettuces	4

CRAWFISH PARISIENNE

Preparation 3 hours • Cooking 40 minutes

Lay the crawfish flat on a small board in order to keep the tail stretched out; tie tightly, then cook in a court bouillon and leave to cool. Detach the membrane on the underside of the tail and remove the meat, taking care not to damage the shell as this will be used later. Discard the gut.

Extract what meat there is from inside the body shell, and also the creamy meat. Cut the tail meat into medallions of equal thickness; decorate each of these with pieces of truffle, and glaze thickly with aspic jelly. Place the shell, convex side upwards, on the wedge of bread and press down firmly. Arrange the crawfish medallions on top of the shell, propping them up slightly.

Fill the artichokes with the salad mixed with some mayonnaise and aspic jelly and the meat from inside the crawfish body shells, diced. Shape into smooth domes. Cut the hard-boiled eggs in half lengthways and remove the yolks. Chop the yolks and remaining truffles and bind together with aspic jelly. Fill the egg whites with this mixture. Arrange the artichokes and eggs around the crawfish on a bed of shredded lettuce and serve the remaining mayonnaise separately. Decorate the edges of the dish with chopped aspic jelly.

Dry white wines: Muscadet, Saumur, dry Vouvray, Quincy, Sancerre, Pouilly-Fumé, dry Graves, Chablis.

US	Ingredients	Met/Imp
4, each about 1¼ lb	live crawfish (rock lobsters)	4, each about 600 g/1¼ lb
10 oz	mushrooms	300 g/10 oz
¼ cup	cognac	50 ml/2 fl oz
14 tbsp	butter	200 g/7 oz
1 cup	crème fraîche	200 ml/7 fl oz
4	egg yolks	4
6	egg whites	6
	salt and pepper	

CRAWFISH SOUFFLÉ GASTRONOME

Preparation 2 hours • Cooking 25 minutes

Cook the crawfish as for Lobster Américaine (*page 244*); they should be split in half lengthways, taking care to keep the shells intact, as they will be used in the presentation of the dish.

Remove and drain the crawfish halves when cooked, then finish the Américaine sauce by reducing it as much as possible, which will concentrate the flavour. Dice the mushrooms, then sweat them in a saucepan with the cognac and some butter. Add the meat from the halved crawfish tails, sliced into medallions, plus about half of the Américaine sauce and the crème fraîche; simmer for a few moments. The sauce is ready when it reaches an oily consistency.

Add the egg yolks to the remaining Américaine sauce, then fold in stiffly beaten egg whites to make a soufflé mixture. Fill the halved crawfish shells with the crawfish mixture, then cover with the soufflé sauce, which should be about 2.5 cm/1 inch thick. Place briefly in a hot oven, until the soufflé is set and risen, then serve at once.

Dry white wines: Sancerre, Pouilly-Fumé, dry Graves, Chablis, Meursault, Pouilly-Fuissé.

CRAWFISH MEDALLIONS WITH CAVIAR

Preparation 3 hours • Cooking 40 minutes

Wash and scrub the crawfish; stretch it out on a small board and tie tightly; plunge into an oval saucepanful of boiling water with 15 ml/1 tbsp of salt and 45 ml/3 tbsp vinegar per litre/1¾ pints (quart) added. Add the parsley stalks, thyme sprig and bay leaf. The crawfish should be completely submerged in this *court bouillon*. Cook for 40 minutes, leave to cool in the court bouillon, then drain. When completely cold, detach the tail, remove the membrane underneath and take out the meat in 1 piece; discard the gut. Slice the tail meat crossways to form medallions about 7.5 cm/3 inches thick. Trim neatly. Extract the meat from the claws and body shell and dice finely, along with the trimmings from the medallions; set aside.

Reduce 200 ml/7 fl oz (scant 1 cup) of the aspic jelly by half, then mix with 500 ml/18 fl oz (2 cups) of the mayonnaise. Leave until beginning to thicken, then dip in the medallions until they are thickly coated. Arrange them on a serving dish as you work, placing a slice of truffle on each. Place a small chervil sprig on top of the truffle. When the sauce has almost set, moisten the medallions several times with cold, liquid aspic jelly. Add the remaining mayonnaise and the remaining aspic jelly to the Russian salad, then mix in the reserved diced crawfish meat. Put this salad into an oiled mould and leave in the refrigerator until it is time to serve.

Turn the salad out on to a cold round dish. Trim the edges of the medallions with a sharp knife, to remove any sauce that has spilled over. Arrange them around the edge of the salad overlapping them slightly, and surround with fluted paper petit four cases (the height of a thimble) filled with the caviar. Place chopped aspic jelly in between.

Dry white wines: Sancerre, Pouilly-Fumé, Meursault, Hermitage, fine dry Graves, Coteaux Champenois.

US	Ingredients	Met/Imp
1, about 3¼ lb	live crawfish (rock lobster)	1, about 1.5 kg/3¼ lb
	salt	
	wine vinegar	
	parsley stalks	
1	thyme sprig	1
1	bay leaf	1
1 quart	liquid Fish Aspic (*page 58*)	1 litre/1¾ pints
1 quart	Mayonnaise (*page 72*)	1 litre/1¾ pints
	truffles	
	chervil	
1 lb (about 3 cups)	*jardinière* of Russian salad vegetables (carrots, turnips, petits pois, green beans, *flageolets*)	500 g/1 lb
10 oz	caviar	300 g/10 oz

CRAWFISH MEDALLIONS IN ASPIC MONÉGASQUE

Preparation 3 hours • Cooking 25 minutes

Prepare a *court bouillon* with the wine, sherry, port and some water. Add the sliced carrots and onions, the bouquet garni and salt and pepper, then the crawfish. Cook for 25 minutes.

Leave the crawfish in the court bouillon to cool, then shell it and cut the tail meat into medallions. Arrange these on the bread, coat with aspic jelly and leave to set; decorate with the hard-boiled eggs, lettuce hearts, tomatoes and mayonnaise.

Dry white wines: Chablis, Sancerre, Arbois, Alsace Sylvaner.

US	Ingredients	Met/Imp
1 bottle	white wine	1 bottle
½ cup	sherry	100 ml/4 fl oz
½ cup	port wine	100 ml/4 fl oz
2	carrots	2
2	onions	2
1	bouquet garni	1
	salt and pepper	
1, about 2½ lb	live crawfish (rock lobster)	1, about 1.2 kg/2½ lb
1	wedge firm-textured bread	1
1¼ cups	liquid Fish Aspic (*page 58*)	300 ml/½ pint
8	hard-boiled eggs	8
8	lettuce hearts	8
8	tomatoes	8
	Mayonnaise (*page 72*)	

ESCARGOT

SNAIL

THERE ARE TWO SORTS OF EDIBLE SNAIL: THE BURGUNDY snail, which is the larger variety, is also to be found in Savoy and Franche-Comté, while the 'petit-gris', with its delicate, fruity flesh, is mostly found in Provence and Gascony. Snails captured live should be starved before cooking. Some delicatessens and fish shops sell freshly cooked snails; you may also buy canned snails, which are used in numerous different recipes.

The large snails found in winter are much appreciated by snail lovers, but June snails, although much thinner, are also popular. Connoisseurs always eat the 'tortillon', the part attaching the snail to the shell, which is extremely nourishing. The classic way to prepare snails is to stuff them with butter mixed with garlic and herbs.

BEIGNETS D'ESCARGOTS

SNAIL FRITTERS

Preparation 1 hour 35 minutes including marinating • Cooking 8 minutes

US	Ingredients	Met/Imp
60	Burgundy snails	60
	or	
100	petits-gris snails (canned or freshly cooked)	100
	oil for frying	
	parsley sprigs, to garnish	
	BATTER	
2	eggs, separated	2
1½ cups	flour	200 g/7 oz
2 tbsp	olive oil	30 ml/2 tbsp
	salt and pepper	
	MARINADE	
1 tbsp	olive oil	15 ml/1 tbsp
	herbs	

First make the batter. Mix the egg yolks with the flour and olive oil. Add a little warm water to give a smooth, creamy consistency. Season and leave to stand. Just before using, gently fold in the stiffly beaten egg whites.

Drain the snails and marinate for 1 hour in the olive oil and chopped herbs (parsley, tarragon, chives and chervil).

Drop the snails into the batter by the handful, then remove them one by one and drop into the hot frying oil (2 at a time in the case of petits-gris); fry until golden brown, then drain on paper towels. Serve garnished with fried parsley.

White wines: Cassis, Coteaux d'Aix-en-Provence, Saint-Joseph.

Scallops with Mussels Nantaise
Shelled mussels and scallops simmered together with mushrooms: this mixture is bound together with white wine sauce. They may be in scallop shells, or on a dish as a ragoût. (Recipe on page 231.)

Crab Escoffier au Gratin with Paprika
Crab is cooked and the meat removed; this is then seasoned with curry powder and paprika and put back in the shell with a rich and creamy béchamel. It is then sprinkled with cheese and browned until crisp on top. (Recipe on page 235.)

Mussels au Gratin from La Rochelle
This recipe is ideal for plump mussels. The flavour is sealed beneath a light coating of crisp breadcrumbs and enhanced by the white wine in which the mussels were cooked.
(Recipe on page 268.)

Grilled Lobster

Cut in half lengthways, lobsters need a bare half-hour under the grill (broiler). They are then served hot with a smooth sauce of crème fraîche enriched with egg yolks, flavoured with a reduction of port wine and shallots. (Recipe on page 247.)

Devilled Oysters
A recipe is termed 'à la diable', or devilled, when it is hot or highly seasoned. Here, a béchamel sauce seasoned with pepper, nutmeg and paprika is used to coat oysters which have been poached. (Recipe on page 263.)

Stewed Octopus with Onions
This octopus stew is simmered for a long time until aromatic with garlic and cloves. *I may be served hot with saffron rice, or cold with a salad. (Recipe on page 272.)*

	US	Ingredients	Met/Imp

CAGOUILLES EN OMELETTE

SNAIL OMELETTE

Preparation 15 minutes • Cooking 1 hour

	US	Ingredients	Met/Imp
	50	petits-gris snails	50
		salt and pepper	
		fennel	
	1	dried fig leaf	1
	6	eggs, separated	6

Starve the snails and clean them well. Cook them for 1 hour in boiling water with added salt, fennel and a fig leaf; drain and remove them from their shells.

Prepare an omelette mixture. Beat the egg yolks and fold in the stiffly beaten whites. Make an omelette in the usual way and fill with the snails.

Wine: red or white Haut-Poitou, Anjou or Touraine.

ESCARGOTS À LA BOURGUIGNONNE

SNAILS BOURGUIGNONNE

Preparation 15 minutes • Cooking 15 minutes

	US	Ingredients	Met/Imp
	24	large *Paris mushrooms*	24
		salt and pepper	
	½ cup	oil	100 ml/4 fl oz
	about 100	canned Burgundy snails	about 100
	½ cup	Snail Butter (*page 52*)	100 g/4 oz

Remove the stalks from the mushrooms.

Season the mushroom caps with salt, pour the oil over them and sweat them in the oven. Take the mushroom caps out and place 4–5 snails in each one. Cover with snail butter and heat in the oven just before serving, exactly as you would snails in their shells.

Dry white wines: Quincy, Pouilly-Fumé, Bourgogne-Aligoté.
Red wines: Saint-Émilion, Chinon, Bourgueil, Rully, Beaujolais-Villages.

ESCARGOTS À LA CAUDÉRAN

SNAILS CAUDÉRAN

Preparation 1 hour • Cooking 1 hour

	US	Ingredients	Met/Imp
	6 tbsp	lard	75 g/3 oz
	3 oz	*raw country ham*	75 g/3 oz
	10	shallots	10
		fresh white breadcrumbs	
	¼ cup	dry white bordeaux	60 ml/4 tbsp
		chicken stock	
		salt and pepper	
	1	bouquet garni	1
	100	petits-gris snails	100

Melt the lard in a sauté pan and brown the ham and chopped shallots; add a small amount of breadcrumbs soaked in the wine. Moisten with stock and season with salt and pepper. Add the bouquet garni and cook for 20 minutes.

Add the starved and well-washed snails. Cook over a low heat for 40 minutes, turning often.

Red wines: Bordeaux from the Côtes de Bourg or Blaye, Blayais or Premières Côtes de Blaye.

US	Ingredients	Met/Imp
48	Burgundy snails	48
	court bouillon	
4	shallots	4
	chives	
¾ cup	white Mâcon wine	150 ml/¼ pint
24	frogs' legs	24
½ cup	milk	100 ml/4 fl oz
	flour	
4 tbsp	butter	50 g/2 oz
	salt and pepper	
	chopped parsley, to garnish	

ESCARGOTS AUX GRENOUILLES

——— SNAILS WITH FROGS' LEGS ———

Preparation 1½ hours • Cooking 1¼ hours

Cook the snails in advance in a court bouillon, then remove them from their shells. Chop them, together with the peeled shallots and a small bunch of well-washed chives. Place these ingredients in a saucepan with the wine, cover and simmer for 1 hour.

Meanwhile, soak the frogs' legs in the milk for 1 hour. Drain them, then roll in flour and sauté in the butter in a frying pan over a brisk heat for 10 minutes. Add the snails, together with their cooking juices, and season with salt and pepper. Turn up the heat and cook for a further 5 minutes.

Sprinkle with chopped parsley and serve.

White wines: Mâcon-Clessé, -Lugny, -Viré or -Igé, Hermitage, Crépy.

US	Ingredients	Met/Imp
1 lb (4 sticks)	butter	500 g/1 lb
½ cup	parsley, chopped	30 g/1 oz
1 tbsp	crushed garlic	15 ml/1 tbsp
3 tbsp	shallots, chopped	30 g/1 oz
12	canned anchovy fillets	12
1 tbsp	salt	15 ml/1 tbsp
1 tsp	pepper	5 ml/1 tsp
1 tbsp	quatre-épices	15 ml/1 tbsp
100	canned snails	100
½ cup	white wine (optional)	100 ml/4 fl oz
2 cups	fresh white breadcrumbs	100 g/4 oz

ESCARGOTS À LA MÉNÉTREL

——— SNAILS MÉNÉTREL ———

Preparation 25 minutes • Cooking 8 minutes

Make snail butter by working the butter with a mixture of chopped parsley, garlic, shallots and anchovy fillets. Season with the salt, pepper and spice, then work through a fine sieve.

Place a piece of butter the size of a bean inside each snail shell. Add the snail, then close up the shell with some more butter, pressing it down firmly.

Arrange the snails on a dish and moisten with the wine if liked. Sprinkle with the breadcrumbs and bake in a hot oven for 8 minutes.

Dry white wines: Mâcon-Viré, Bourgogne-Aligoté, Rully, Pouilly-Fuissé.

US	Ingredients	Met/Imp
100	snails	100
	vinegar	
2	thyme sprigs	2
½	bay leaf	½
1	basil sprig	1
1 piece	pared orange peel	1 piece
scant ½ lb	pork rind	200 g/7 oz
½ cup	olive oil	100 ml/4 fl oz
½ lb	fatty bacon	250 g/8 oz
6	shelled walnuts, ground	6
4	canned anchovy fillets	4
3	garlic cloves	3
	salt and pepper	
3 tbsp	flour	30 g/1 oz
6½ lb	spinach leaves, trimmed and served whole	3 kg/6½ lb

ESCARGOTS À LÀ SOMMEROISE

——— SNAILS SOMMEROISE ———

Preparation 3 hours • Cooking 2½ hours

Starve the snails for at least 8 days, then wash them in several changes of water until clean. Rinse with vinegar, then drain.

Place the snails in a saucepan of boiling water with the thyme, bay leaf, basil, orange peel and pork rind. When the snails are almost cooked, drain them and remove them from their shells.

Brown the snails in olive oil with the fatty bacon, very finely chopped, the ground walnuts, anchovy fillets, crushed garlic and salt and pepper. thicken the mixture with the flour, then serve on a bed of spinach.

Rosé, red or white wines: Tavel, Chusclan, Coteaux d'Aix-en-Provence.

CUISSES DE GRENOUILLES

FROGS' LEGS

THE FRENCH HAVE LONG BEEN ONE OF THE FEW NATIONS to appreciate the gastronomic qualities of the frog. Only the legs are used in cooking. The best season for frogs is autumn, and the most famed variety is the green frog, found in Dombes, Auvergne, Sologne and Alsace. However, it is now rare, and frogs are often imported from Central Europe these days. They can be fried or sautéed, made into brochettes, or served like young chicken. Frogs' legs are often highly flavoured with garlic, herbs, etc, and also make a tasty cream soup.

CUISSES DE GRENOUILLES FINES HERBES

——— FROGS' LEGS FINES HERBES ———

Preparation 45 minutes • Cooking 15 minutes

Soak the frogs' legs in cold salted milk, then drain and roll them in the flour. Sauté in the very hot butter, so that they fry very quickly. When cooked, sprinkle with parsley, finely chopped shallots and garlic. You may also add the juice of a lemon if liked.

Dry white wnes: Muscadet, Chablis.
Red wines: Bourgueil, Chinon, Beaujolais-Villages.
Rosé wine: Tavel.

US	Ingredients	Met/Imp
100	frogs' legs	100
	salt	
½ cup	milk	100 ml/4 fl oz
1½ cups	flour	200 g/7 oz
14 tbsp	butter	200 g/7 oz
1 tbsp	chopped parsley	15 ml/1 tbsp
2	shallots	2
1	sliver garlic	1
1	lemon, juice of (optional)	1

FRITURE DE GRENOUILLES AUX POMMES DE TERRES

— FRIED FROGS' LEGS WITH POTATOES —

Preparation 1 hour • Cooking 12 minutes'

Clean the frogs' legs and season with salt, pepper and lemon juice. Dust with the flour, dip in the beaten eggs and roll in breadcrumbs. Fry in oil and serve with a salad of hot potatoes diced and tossed in the mayonnaise and herbs.

Dry white wines: Menetou-Salon, Quincy.
Red wine: Beaujolais-Villages.

US	Ingredients	Met/Imp
100	frogs' legs	100
	salt and pepper	
2	lemons, juice of	2
1 cup	flour	150 g/5 oz
4	eggs	4
8 cups	fresh white breadcrumbs	500 g/1 lb
	oil for frying	
1 lb	potatoes	500 g/1 lb
½ cup	Mayonnaise (page 72)	100 ml/4 fl oz
1 tbsp	chopped fresh herbs (chives, chervil, shallots)	15 ml/1 tbsp

HUÎTRE

OYSTER

THERE ARE TWO TYPES OF OYSTER ON THE MARKET: THE flat oyster, of which there are several varieties, and the hollow kind, of which the original variety is the Portuguese oyster. The latter is the most abundant variety to be found, and is mainly reared in Marennes. Oyster consumption is very high in France, particularly at certain times throughout the winter, such as New Year. Normally, oysters are eaten raw, and each person is served with about a dozen. In Saintonge, Arcachon oysters are served with small grilled sausages.

Some oyster lovers prefer them cooked. In the old days, they were never eaten raw, and old-fashioned cookery books are full of recipes for oyster soups, cooked shelled oysters with vegetables, cream, butter, etc. Today, these dishes are enjoying a revival of popularity. Oysters should be very fresh, and should still contain all their juice. If served raw, they should be opened and presented on a bed of seaweed or crushed ice, together with half a lemon per person and freshly milled pepper, or alternatively with a vinaigrette made with shallots. Flat oysters are generally more suitable for cooking.

BARQUETTES AUX HUÎTRES
——— OYSTER BARQUETTES ———

Preparation 50 minutes • Cooking 35 minutes

US	Ingredients	Met/Imp
3 dozen	oysters	3 dozen
scant ½ lb	hake	200 g/7 oz
1	lemon, juice of	1
12	shortcrust (pie) pastry barquettes, made with 250 g/8 oz (1¾ cups) flour, 125 g/4½ oz (9 tbsp) butter, a pinch of salt, ½ glass of water	12
½ lb	Paris mushrooms	250 g/8 oz
4 tbsp	butter	50 g/2 oz
1	parsley sprig	1
a few	chives	a few
1 tbsp	flour	15 ml/1 tbsp
½ glass	white wine	½ glass
	salt and pepper	
2	egg yolks	2
½ cup	crème fraîche	100 ml/4 fl oz

Shell the oysters over a bowl, catching the juice. Put the shelled oysters into a sauté pan as each one is opened.

When all the oysters are ready, line a fine sieve with cheesecloth and strain the oyster juice into the sauté pan (this is essential, in order to ensure that no fragments of shell or grains of sand become mixed with the oysters).

Place the sauté pan over a brisk heat and watch it very carefully. As soon as it reaches boiling point, remove it from the heat. The oysters should only be lightly sealed, not cooked through. Leave them to cool in their own juice.

Rinse the hake and slash the skin in 2–3 places. Poach for 15 minutes in hot salted water with the lemon juice; cool in the cooking liquid.

When the oysters are cool, remove them from the pan with a slotted spoon and cut off the beards; chop the oysters up. Remove the bones and skin from the hake and chop the flesh, then mix with the chopped oysters.

If the barquettes have been made in advance, put them in the oven to warm. Trim off the ends of the mushroom stalks, wash them under running water, then wipe them dry and cut into very small pieces. Melt the butter in a saucepan, add the mushrooms and brown them.

Add the chopped parsley and chives, then sprinkle in the flour; stir well and leave to brown for a few minutes. Pour in the wine, then a glass of the juice from the oysters, stirring all the time. Reduce the mixture over a low heat.

Add the chopped oysters and hake, stir well and leave to cook for 2–3 minutes. Season with pepper and check that the sea water from the oysters has made the mixture sufficiently salty, adding a small pinch of salt if necessary.

Whisk the egg yolks vigorously with the cream, then pour over the simmering ingredients in the saucepan. Stir well and remove from the heat immediately, or turn the heat off under the pan.

Take the barquettes out of the oven and fill them with this mixture. Serve at once, allowing 2 barquettes per person.

White wines: Muscadet de Sèvre et Maine *sur lie*, Savennières, Vouvray, Sancerre.

BOUCHÉES FEUILLETÉES AUX HUÎTRES

OYSTER VOL-AU-VENTS

Preparation 1½ hours • Cooking 30 minutes

Shell the oysters, then poach them in their own juice (first filtered to remove any sand). Drain, reserving the cooking juices, then pat dry.

Trim the mushroom caps into olive shapes and cook them in half of the butter. Reserve the cooking juices.

Make a golden roux (*page 50*) with the remaining butter and the flour. Add the milk and the reserved cooking juices from the oysters and mushrooms. Leave to thicken, then add the cream, mushrooms and oysters. Season to taste. Fill the vol-au-vent cases with this mixture and serve hot, accompanied by lemon wedges.

White wines: Sauternes, Monbazillac, Jurançon.

US	Ingredients	Met/Imp
3 dozen	oysters	3 dozen
¼ lb	small white button mushrooms	125 g/4½ oz
1 stick	butter	100 g/4 oz
6 tbsp	flour	50 g/2 oz
½ cup	milk	100 ml/4 fl oz
¼ cup	double (heavy) cream	50 ml/2 fl oz
	salt and pepper	
8	small vol-au-vent cases	8
1	lemon, wedges of, to serve	1

US	Ingredients	Met/Imp
4 dozen	oysters	4 dozen
8	smoked bacon slices	8
8	slices white toast	8
1 cup	fresh white breadcrumbs	50 g/2 oz
1 pinch	pepper	1 pinch
14 tbsp	butter	200 g/7 oz

— BROCHETTES OF OYSTERS IN BACON —

Preparation 50 minutes • Cooking 10 minutes

Remove the oysters from their shells and pat dry. Wrap each oyster in a small piece of bacon, then thread 6 oysters on to each of 8 small skewers. Cook under the grill (broiler). Arrange on slices of toast and sprinkle with the breadcrumbs mixed with a little pepper. Serve with melted butter.

Dry white wines: Chablis, Mâcon-Villages, Gros Plant du Pays Nantais, Pouilly-Fumé.

US	Ingredients	Met/Imp
4 dozen	oysters	4 dozen
	pepper	
5 cups	fresh white breadcrumbs	300 g/10 oz
1½ sticks	butter	175 g/6 oz
1 cup	Gruyère cheese, grated	100 g/4 oz

HUÎTRES À L'AMÉRICAINE

OYSTERS AMÉRICAINE

Preparation 40 minutes • Cooking 7 minutes

Remove the oysters from their shells and pat dry. Drain away the juices from the shells. Place a little pepper and some of the breadcrumbs fried in butter in the bottom of the concave shells. Add the oysters and sprinkle with grated cheese and more breadcrumbs. Place a dot of butter on each one and brown in a hot oven.

Dry white wines: Hermitage, dry Graves.

US	Ingredients	Met/Imp
2	shallots	2
scant 1 cup	champagne	200 ml/7 fl oz
3 dozen	flat oysters	3 dozen
14 tbsp	butter	200 g/7 oz
1	lemon, juice of	1
	salt and pepper	

HUÎTRES AU BEURRE BLANC DE CHAMPAGNE

OYSTERS IN CHAMPAGNE BEURRE BLANC

Preparation 30 minutes • Cooking 15 minutes

Peel the shallots and chop them finely; place in a saucepan with most of the champagne. Turn up the heat and cook until reduced by half; leave to cool.

Shell the oysters and place them in a small saucepan, together with the filtered oyster juice and remaining champagne. Set the saucepan over a low heat. When the mixture begins to boil, remove the oysters and pour the liquid into the first saucepan containing the reduced shallots. Whisk this sauce, adding the diced butter (unpasteurized, from Charentes if possible) as you go along. Add the lemon juice, season with pepper and add salt if necessary.

Put the oysters back in pairs into the washed shells and pour over the sauce.

Wine: the same Champagne as the one used for cooking.

OYSTERS ON CROÛTONS
WITH NOISETTE BUTTER

Preparation 30 minutes • Cooking 5 minutes

US	Ingredients	Met/Imp
4 dozen	oysters	4 dozen
14 tbsp	butter	200 g/7 oz
8	croûtons	8
	pepper	

Remove the oysters from their shells and pat dry. Heat the butter until nut-coloured and fry the oysters briefly. Arrange them on small round croûtons fried in butter. Season with pepper and pour over the butter in which the oysters have been cooked.

Dry white wines: Pouilly-Fuissé, -Loché or -Vinzelles, Chablis.

HUÎTRES À LA DIABLE

DEVILLED OYSTERS*

Preparation 1 hour • Cooking 8 minutes

US	Ingredients	Met/Imp
4 dozen	oysters	4 dozen
1 stick	butter	100 g/4 oz
6 tbsp	flour	50 g/2 oz
scant ½ cup	milk	100 ml/4 fl oz
1 cup	crème fraîche	250 ml/9 fl oz
	salt and pepper	
	nutmeg	
1 tsp	paprika	5 ml/1 tsp
1 cup	fresh white breadcrumbs	50 g/2 oz

Shell the oysters, then poach them in their filtered juices. Drain, reserving the cooking juices, then remove the beards.

Prepare a Béchamel Sauce (*page 62*) using half of the butter, the flour, milk, reserved cooking juices from the oysters and the crème fraîche. Season the sauce with salt, a pinch of nutmeg and the paprika, then tip in the oysters. Line the concave shells with this mixture, then sprinkle with the breadcrumbs fried in the remaining butter. Arrange the oysters on a dish and heat through in a hot oven for a few minutes before serving. Try not to let the mixture boil.

Dry white wines: dry Graves, Arbois, Alsace Riesling.

HUÎTRES AU FOUR À L'ÉCHALOTE

BAKED OYSTERS WITH SHALLOTS

Preparation 40 minutes • Cooking 20 minutes

US	Ingredients	Met/Imp
4 dozen	large flat oysters	4 dozen
10 tbsp	butter	150 g/5 oz
3	shallots	3
	salt and pepper	
2½ cups	fresh white breadcrumbs	150 g/5 oz

Remove the oysters from their shells and pat dry. Place 6 oysters in each of 8 scallop shells and place them in an ovenproof dish greased with the butter, on a bed of chopped shallots, seasoned with a little salt and pepper. Sprinkle with the breadcrumbs, cook in a moderate oven for 20 minutes and serve hot.

Dry white wines: Hermitage, Alsace Riesling, Muscadet.

US	Ingredients	Met/Imp
4 dozen	oysters	4 dozen
2 cups	stock	500 ml/18 fl oz
6 tbsp	butter	75 g/3 oz
6 tbsp	flour	50 g/2 oz
2 cups	white wine	500 ml/18 fl oz
1 pinch	nutmeg	1 pinch
	cayenne	
1 pinch	ground ginger	1 pinch
scant ½ cup	crème fraîche	100 ml/4 fl oz

HUÎTRES FRANÇOIS VILLON

——— OYSTERS FRANÇOIS VILLON ———

Preparation 50 minutes • Cooking 5 minutes

Shell the oysters, then poach them in the stock. Drain, reserving the cooking liquid. Hold the oysters under cold running water to harden them, then leave to drain on a napkin.

Put the butter into a small saucepan, add the flour and brown it very slightly. Add the wine and a little of the reserved cooking liquid, then add the nutmeg, a hint of cayenne pepper, the ginger and the crème fraîche. Skim off any impurities from the surface of the sauce so that it is smooth, golden and creamy; it should have plenty of flavour.

When you are ready, add the oysters to the sauce and return to the heat. Warm the oysters through, but do not allow the mixture to boil. Serve very hot.

Dry white wines: Alsace Sylvaner or Pinot Blanc, Pouilly-Fuissé, dry Graves.

US	Ingredients	Met/Imp
4 dozen	oysters	4 dozen
10 tbsp	butter	150 g/5 oz
1	onion	1
1	carrot	1
1	bouquet·garni	1
2 cups	white wine	500 ml/18 fl oz
1 tbsp	flour	15 ml/1 tbsp
4	egg yolks	4
	pepper	
1 cup	fresh white breadcrumbs	50 g/2 oz

HUÎTRES EN SAUCE AU GRATIN

——— OYSTERS AU GRATIN ———

Preparation 1 hour • Cooking 8 minutes

Shell the oysters, then poach them in their filtered juice. Drain, reserving the cooking juices.

Make a stock with some of the butter, the chopped onion and carrot, the bouquet garni and wine. Melt a piece of the remaining butter in another pan and stir in the flour. Strain in the prepared stock, keeping the mixture fairly thick. Add the reserved cooking juices from the oysters, then add the egg yolks, season with pepper and cook for 2 minutes until thickened.

Arrange the oysters on a heated ovenproof dish and place a spoonful of sauce on each. Sprinkle with the breadcrumbs, moisten with the remaining butter, melted, and brown in a hot oven.

Alternatively, the oysters may be soaked in the sauce, then coated with batter and fried in very hot oil. In this case, serve on a folded napkin, garnished with fried parsley.

In both cases, you may also serve a tomato sauce separately, in a sauce boat.

Dry white wines: Sancerre, Mâcon-Villages, Alsace Sylvaner or Pinot Blanc.

MARINATED OYSTER SALAD WITH HARD-BOILED EGGS

Preparation 30 minutes • Marinade 1 hour

US	Ingredients	Met/Imp
8	shallots	8
1 bunch	herbs	1 bunch
4	eggs	4
4 dozen	Portuguese oysters	4 dozen
	salt and pepper	
3 tbsp	olive oil	45 ml/3 tbsp
1	lemon, juice of	1

Peel the shallots. Wash the herbs, which should consist of parsley, chives, chervil and tarragon, then chop them finely with the shallots.

Boil the eggs for 9 minutes. Remove the shells and chop the eggs roughly. Shell the oysters, put them into a bowl and place the chopped herbs, shallots and eggs on top. Season with salt and pepper and sprinkle with the oil and lemon juice. Leave in a cool place for 1 hour to marinate.

White wines: Muscadet de Sèvre et Maine *sur lie*, Gros Plant du Pays Nantais.

OYSTER SOUFFLÉ

Preparation 1 hour • Cooking 26 minutes

US	Ingredients	Met/Imp
3 dozen	oysters	3 dozen
10 tbsp	butter	150 g/5 oz
6 tbsp	flour	50 g/2 oz
2 cups	milk	500 ml/18 fl oz
1 pinch	nutmeg	1 pinch
	salt and pepper	
1 pinch	cayenne	1 pinch
3	egg yolks	3
6	egg whites	6

Shell the oysters, then poach them in their own filtered juice. Drain, reserving the cooking juices, then remove the beards. Cut the oysters into 2–3 pieces, according to their size.

Make a white roux (*page 50*), with one-third of the butter and the flour. Stir in the reserved cooking juices from the oysters and the milk and season with nutmeg, salt, pepper and a pinch of cayenne. Bring to the boil and cook for a few minutes, until the sauce reaches the consistency of a thick gruel. Add the remaining butter and the egg yolks, then stir in the oysters and fold in the stiffly beaten egg whites. Turn into a well-buttered soufflé dish and cook in a moderate oven for 20 minutes, until risen and golden.

Dry white wines: Muscadet, Quincy, Sancerre.

MOULE

MUSSEL

THIS ABUNDANT AND CHEAP BIVALVE MOLLUSC IS HIGHLY esteemed as an accompaniment to numerous recipes for fish in sauce. However, mussels above all make a dish in their own right, lending themselves to many popular and simple recipes. These are often in the Belgian tradition of 'mussels and fried potatoes'.

The common mussel, which is small, well-rounded and tender, is found in the Atlantic. There is also, however, the Toulon mussel. This is a larger and rarer variety, flatter in appearance and less delicate. Specially reared mussels are small, but tasty and fleshy. Only use mussels that are tightly closed and still alive; brush and scrub them well under running water before cooking.

BROCHETTES DE MOULES

MUSSEL BROCHETTES

Preparation 35 minutes • Cooking 10 minutes

US	Ingredients	Met/Imp
6 dozen	mussels	6 dozen
scant ½ lb	lean fresh belly (side) of pork	200 g/7 oz
2 cups	fresh white breadcrumbs	100 g/4 oz
2	eggs	2
	melted butter, to serve	

Cook the mussels as for Mussels 'Marinière' (*page 268*), and then remove them from their shells while still warm.

Dice the pork into 1 cm/½ inch cubes. Place the breadcrumbs on a flat plate. Beat the eggs.

Fill 8 small skewers, alternating 2 mussels with 1 cube of pork. Roll the brochettes first in the beaten egg, then in the breadcrumbs. Grill (broil) them under a fast heat for 5 minutes, turning them as they cook.

Serve with melted butter.

White wines: Muscadet, Gros Plant du Pays Nantais, Quincy, Jasnières.

MUSSELS WITH SNAIL BUTTER

Preparation 1 hour • Cooking 5 minutes

US	Ingredients	Met/Imp
8 dozen	mussels	8 dozen
1	onion	1
	salt and pepper	
2 sticks	butter	250 g/8 oz
2	garlic cloves	2
2 tbsp	chopped parsley	30 ml/2 tbsp

Cook the mussels as for Mussels 'Marinière' (*page 268*): place them in a saucepan, together with the chopped onion and some pepper. When just cooked, remove them from the heat and take away the empty half of the shell.

Take some good-quality butter, the crushed garlic and the parsley – exactly as for Snail Butter (*page 52*). Season with salt and pepper and mix all the ingredients together thoroughly.

Top the shells containing the mussels with this butter and heat in the oven for a few minutes, as for snails. Serve hot.

White wines: Chablis, Bourgogne-Aligoté.

BRETON MUSSELS

Preparation 20 minutes • Cooking 6 minutes

US	Ingredients	Met/Imp
8 dozen	mussels	8 dozen
1	onion	1
1	fennel stick	1
1	bouquet garni	1
1 cup	dry white wine	200 ml/7 fl oz
1½ cups	Fish Velouté (*page 57*)	300 ml/½ pint
1 stick	butter	100 g/4 oz
	cayenne	

Take some very fresh mussels; scrub and wash them several times. Place them in a sauté pan with the chopped onion and fennel, the bouquet garni and wine. Sauté over a brisk heat, so as to open the mussels, then tip them into a sieve. Pour the cooking liquid into another pan and reserve. Put the mussels back into the sauté pan, removing the empty half of the shells as you go; keep warm.

Reduce the velouté sauce, then gradually stir in a few spoonfuls of the cooking liquid from the mussels. Turn the heat down low and add the butter, then a pinch of cayenne.

Arrange the mussels on a heated deep serving dish; pour over the sauce and serve.

Wines: as a general rule, serve the same wine as the one used for cooking.

US	Ingredients	Met/Imp
4 dozen	mussels	4 dozen
½ cup	white wine	100 ml/4 fl oz
½ cup	olive oil	100 ml/4 fl oz
I tsp	saffron powder	5 ml/I tsp
I	onion	I
I	garlic clove	I
¾ cup	long-grain rice	150 g/5 oz
I	thyme sprig	I
I	bay leaf	I
I tbsp	chopped parsley and tarragon	15 ml/I tbsp
	pepper	

MOULES FARCIES AU RIZ

—— MUSSELS STUFFED WITH RICE ——

Preparation 1 hour • Cooking 25 minutes

Scrub and wash some large Toulon mussels; open them in a pan with the wine, most of the oil and the saffron, then drain and reserve the cooking liquid to cook the rice. Remove 1 shell from each mussel and leave them to cool. Put the chopped onion and garlic in a little oil; add the rice, thyme and bay leaf and most of the cooking liquid from the mussels. Cook until the rice is tender, then leave to cool. Add the remaining cooking liquid from the mussels if necessary to make sure the rice maintains a creamy consistency.

Using a spoon, fill up the mussel shells with rice, doming the tops. Serve on hors-d'œuvre dishes. (If any rice is left over, make a thin bed on which to arrange the mussels.) Season with pepper and sprinkle with the herbs.

This dish may also be made using curry powder instead of saffron.

White or rosé wines: Cassis, Tavel.

US	Ingredients	Met/Imp
4 quarts	mussels	4 litres/7 pints
scant I cup	white wine	200 ml/7 fl oz
4	shallots	4
2	celery stalks	2
¼ lb	mushrooms	125 g/4½ oz
I stick	butter	100 g/4 oz
	pepper	
	nutmeg	
2½ cups	fresh white breadcrumbs	150 g/5 oz

MOULES GRATINÉES À LA ROCHELAISE

MUSSELS AU GRATIN
—— FROM LA ROCHELLE* ——

Preparation 25 minutes • Cooking about 10 minutes

Open the mussels in a pan with the wine, chopped shallots, celery and mushrooms, the butter, pepper and a pinch of nutmeg. Arrange the mussels on a dish, having first removed the empty shell from each. Reduce the cooking liquid by three-quarters; stir in the breadcrumbs and use to coat the mussels. Brown in a hot oven just before serving.

White or rosé wines: Muscadet, Cabernet d'Anjou, Chablis.

US	Ingredients	Met/Imp
4 quarts	mussels	4 litres/7 pints
½ cup	white wine	100 ml/4 fl oz
I	onion	I
4	shallots	4
	pepper	
10 tbsp	butter	150 g/5 oz
I tbsp	chopped parsley	15 ml/I tbsp

MOULES MARINIÈRE

—— MUSSELS 'MARINIÈRE' ——

Preparation 30 minutes • Cooking 6 minutes

Open the mussels by sautéeing them in a pan with the wine, chopped onion and shallots, pepper and butter over a high heat. Sprinkle with parsley and serve.

Dry white wines: Muscadet, Pouilly-Fumé, Cassis.

MUSSELS WITH SORREL

Preparation 45 minutes • Cooking about 35 minutes

US	Ingredients	Met/Imp
6½ lb	sorrel, trimmed	3 kg/6½ lb
3	egg yolks	3
10 tbsp	butter	150 g/5 oz
6 tbsp	flour	50 g/2 oz
½ cup	double (heavy) cream	100 ml/4 fl oz
3 quarts	mussels	3 litres/5 pints
½ lb	fresh belly (side) of pork	250 g/8 oz

Prepare a nice sorrel purée, thickened with the egg yolks, about one-third of the butter mixed with the flour and the cream. Spread in a heated serving dish.

Steam open the mussels and remove them from their shells. Fry them lightly in the remaining butter, together with the chopped pork. Season with salt and pepper and turn on to the sorrel purée. Serve piping hot.

Dry white wines: Arbois, Alsace Riesling, Quincy, Sancerre.

MUSSELS WITH SAFFRON

Preparation 20 minutes • Cooking 5 minutes

US	Ingredients	Met/Imp
¼ cup	olive oil	50 ml/2 fl oz
1	onion	1
2	leeks, white part only	2
2	tomatoes	2
1	garlic clove	1
1	bouquet garni	1
1 tsp	saffron	5 ml/1 tsp
1 cup	white wine	200 ml/7 fl oz
2 quarts	small mussels	2 litres/3½ pints
	chopped parsley, to garnish	

Heat the oil in a sauté pan, add the chopped onion and sliced leeks and brown for a few minutes. Add the skinned, de-seeded and chopped tomatoes, the crushed garlic, bouquet garni, saffron and wine. Reduce the wine completely.

Add the well-scrubbed mussels; cover the pan and open the mussels, tossing them from time to time. Leave them over a low heat for 5 minutes, then remove the shells and beards. Strain the cooking liquid through a fine cloth and leave until almost cold. Put the mussels on to hors-d'oeuvre dishes and pour over the cooking liquid; sprinkle with a little parsley.

This dish should be served tepid or completely cold.

White wines: Saumur, Vouvray.

SAUTÉED MUSSELS NORMANDE

Preparation 30 minutes • Cooking 7 minutes

US	Ingredients	Met/Imp
4 quarts	mussels	4 litres/7 pints
½ cup	Fish Fumet (page 57)	100 ml/4 fl oz
3	shallots	3
1 tbsp	chopped parsley	15 ml/1 tbsp
	pepper	
1 cup	crème fraîche	200 ml/7 fl oz
4 tbsp	butter	50 g/2 oz
4 tsp	wine vinegar	20 ml/4 tsp

Scrub and wash the mussels very carefully and cook them in the fish fumet, together with the very finely chopped shallots and the parsley (there is no need for water, as the mussels give out a sufficient quantity during cooking). Season with pepper.

When the mussels are fully open, and covered by the cooking liquid, remove the empty shell from each and place them in a sauté pan with a few drops of the cooking liquid. Add enough crème fraîche to half-cover them, together with the butter and vinegar. Sauté, then serve very hot, in deep bowls.

Dry cider or dry white wines: Muscadet, Gros Plant du Pays Nantais, Jasnières.

OURSIN

SEA URCHIN

SEA URCHINS, ALSO KNOWN AS 'CHÂTAIGNES DE MER' (SEA chestnuts) or 'hérissons de mer' (sea hedgehogs), are mostly found in the Mediterranean. They are normally eaten raw. Inside a sea urchin you will find the coral, which looks like 5 tongues. If removed with a spoon, this provides a tasty morsel with a strong flavour of iodine. The coral is also excellent with scrambled eggs, as a pie or omelette filling, and in sauces and soups.

SOUFFLÉ AUX OURSINS

—— SEA URCHIN SOUFFLÉ ——

Preparation 45 minutes • Cooking 20 minutes

US	Ingredients	Met/Imp
4 tbsp	butter	50 g/2 oz
2 tbsp	flour	20 g/¾ oz
½ cup	milk	100 ml/4 fl oz
	salt and pepper	
24	sea urchins	24
2 tbsp	crème fraîche	30 ml/2 tbsp
	saffron	
2	egg whites	2

Melt half of the butter over a gentle heat and stir in the flour. Add the milk, still stirring, and cook for 10 minutes; season with salt and pepper.

Open the sea urchins and remove the coral. Wash and dry half of the shells and grease the insides with the remaining butter. Pound the coral with the crème fraîche and a pinch of saffron.

Beat the egg whites until stiff. Mix the puréed sea urchin with the contents of the saucepan and fold in the egg whites.

Divide the mixture among the sea urchin shells, half filling each one, then bake in a moderate oven for 10 minutes.

White wines: Chablis Grand Cru, Montrachet, Hermitage.

CLAM (CARPET SHELL AND WARTY VENUS)

PALOURDE (CARPET SHELL), PRAIRE (WARTY VENUS) AND clovisse (the Provençal term for carpet shell) are all different varieties of clams. They are bivalve shellfish, and among the best-known and most highly esteemed species of mollusc to be found in the Channel, the Atlantic and the Mediterranean. Before cooking, it is advisable to put them into sea water or salted water, in order to make them discharge their sand. Connoisseurs like to eat them raw. However, grilled (broiled) carpet shell with snail butter is a highly esteemed dish in Brittany and Saintonge.

The warty venus is often even more delicately flavoured than the carpet shell. It is eaten raw (by itself or with lemon) like the oyster, but can be cooked and stuffed like the carpet shell or mussel.

GRATIN DE PALOURDES AUX ÉPINARDS

— CLAMS AU GRATIN WITH SPINACH —

Preparation 50 minutes • Cooking 35 minutes

US	Ingredients	Met/Imp
2 lb	spinach	1 kg/2 lb
6 tbsp	butter	75 g/3 oz
2 quarts	clams	1 kg/2 lb
6 tbsp	flour	50 g/2 oz
	pepper	
1 cup	crème fraîche	250 ml/9 fl oz
2 tbsp	Parmesan cheese, grated	30 ml/2 tbsp
	croûtons, to garnish	

Wash the spinach thoroughly. Melt one-third of the butter over a gentle heat and leave the spinach to cook in it for 10 minutes, turning from time to time. Wash and scrub the clams. Place them in a saucepan and open them over brisk heat. Remove them from their shells and filter the juice.

Take another saucepan and mix the remaining butter with the flour over a gentle heat. Add the clam juice and cook for 10 minutes, stirring constantly; season with pepper. Remove from the heat and add the crème fraîche, spinach and clams. Pour the contents of the saucepan into a greased gratin dish. Sprinkle with grated cheese and bake in a hot oven for 10 minutes. Garnish with small fried croûtons.

White wines: Cassis, Bellet, Saint-Joseph, Chablis.

PALOURDES GRILLÉES AU BEURRE D'ESCARGOTS

—— CLAMS WITH SNAIL BUTTER ——

Preparation 30 minutes • Cooking 10 minutes

US	Ingredients	Met/Imp
60	clams	60
2 sticks	butter	250 g/8 oz
2	garlic cloves	2
1 tbsp	chopped parsley	15 ml/1 tbsp
	salt and pepper	
1 pinch	nutmeg	1 pinch

Open the clams using a sturdy round-bladed knife; detach the meat from each one and put it back into one half of the shell. Use the remaining ingredients to make a snail butter. Add a piece of this to each clam and cook in a very hot oven for 10 minutes.

Dry white wines: Mâcon-Villages, Saint-Péray, Cassis.

POULPE

OCTOPUS

THE OCTOPUS IS CHARACTERIZED BY ITS 8 TENTACLES WITH suckers. There are 2 edible types, and these are found in abundance off the coast of Provence. The flesh needs to be well beaten in order to tenderize it; however, it is quite delicate. Octopus recipes are usually quite highly seasoned.

COCOTTE DE POULPES AUX OIGNONS

— STEWED OCTOPUS WITH ONIONS* —

Preparation 1 hour • Cooking 2 hours

US	Ingredients	Met/Imp
4, each about 14 oz	octopus	4, each about 400 g/14 oz
2 cups	wine vinegar	500 ml/18 fl oz
scant ½ cup	olive oil	100 ml/4 fl oz
2 cups	water	500 ml/18 fl oz
4	large onions	4
2	cloves	2
3	garlic cloves	3
	pepper	

Clean, wash, skin and beat the octopus. Cut them into small pieces and place in a flameproof casserole with the vinegar, oil and water, the chopped onions, the cloves, garlic and pepper. Do not add any salt. Cover tightly and seal with a ring of flour and water paste. Cook over a very low heat for 2 hours. If the saucepan is not properly sealed, the octopus will be too hard to eat.

Dry white wines: Cassis, Côtes de Provence, Coteaux de Pierrevert, Vin du Pays des Sables du Golfe du Lion.

POULTRY
&
RABBIT

THE TERM 'POULTRY' INCLUDES ALL FARM-yard birds which are bred for eating – chicken, boiling fowl, cockerel, turkey, duck, goose, pigeon, guinea-fowl, capon – to which the domestic rabbit is added. The recipes in this chapter offer a wide choice: from simple and inexpensive dishes to great regional classics and the refined recipes of haute cuisine. The word 'poultry' is used as a general term for the meat of chicken or boiling fowl in basic recipes, or in recipes making use of leftovers (stock, consommé, a dish cooked au gratin, *en coquilles*, etc). Recipes in this chapter which are intended for a specific bird or animal mention it by name.

The most common poultry dishes in household cooking are casseroles, fricassées, pilaus, capilotades (pieces simmered in a sauce), blanquettes, poule-au-pot (stuffed chicken poached with vegetables), fritters, au gratin dishes and curries. In more elaborate cooking, we find aspic, ballotine (a meat loaf made with poultry), chaud-froid, medallions, suprêmes, bouchées and vol-au-vents.

The most popular poultry in France is chicken. Next comes turkey which has recently been greatly diversified with escalopes or boneless slices of breast, gigot (leg roasts) and rôtis (boneless roasts). Geese are mostly raised to make foie gras. As for ducks, their breeding has developed thanks largely to the fashion for duck breasts. The introduction of seals of 'guarantee of origin' has helped produce high-quality poultry.

CANARD

DUCK

IN HAUTE CUISINE, THIS DOMESTIC BIRD TRADITIONALLY GOES under the name of 'caneton' (duckling). Rouen duck has fine flesh which is tinged with red, because it is strangled, not bled. It is served rare. Vendée (or Nantes) duck, Muscovy duck and farmyard duck are bled and require longer cooking.

Since duck meat is often fairly fatty (apart from Muscovy duck, which tastes more musky and has relatively firm flesh), it is not barded and the amount of fat used to cook it is considerably reduced. This is also why it is often combined with vegetables such as turnips, or indeed fruit such as pineapple or orange, because they counterbalance the excess fat. When preparing duck, remember to remove the glands on each side of the parson's (pope's) nose. Duck may also be preserved in fat like goose, and its liver (fattened or not) is used in many delicious ways. Boneless duck breasts, which have recently been introduced into cooking are delicious grilled (broiled) and well sealed, served with potatoes in goose fat or another suitable vegetable.

*Editor's note: cooking times in many of the recipes for duck and duckling in this chapter are quite short so that the meat is served underdone. This is because generally the breast only is eaten; the legs being reserved for later cooking in other dishes. If preferred, cooking times may be increased according to individual preference.

CANARD À L'ALBIGEOISE

———— DUCK ALBIGEOISE ————

Preparation 1¼ hours • Cooking 45 minutes

First prepare a meatless stock with water and the listed ingredients.

Fry the diced pork in the oil in a flameproof casserole, add the onions and cook until lightly browned. Lower the heat, sprinkle in the flour and add the ducks. Cook until lightly browned, then pour in the stock. Add the sliced leeks, celery and fennel and the thyme sprig. Sprinkle in the sugar, cayenne and salt and pepper to taste. Cook for 45 minutes.

Cut 8 croûtons (4×8 cm/1½×3¼ inches) from the bread. Each croûton should be 1 cm/½ inch thick. Fry them in the butter. To serve, spread the croûtons with apple compote, marmalade or redcurrant jelly. Remove the trussing strings from the ducks and place on top of the croûtons. Continue cooking the sauce until well reduced, work through a fine sieve and pour over the ducks.

Wines: Saint-Émilion, Pomerol.

US	Ingredients	Met/Imp
½ lb	fresh fat belly (side) of pork	250 g/8 oz
½ cup	oil	100 ml/4 fl oz
30	small onions	30
1 tbsp	flour	10 g/½ oz
2	Nantes ducks	2
3	leeks	3
1	small head celery	1
1	small head fennel	1
1	thyme sprig	1
2½ tsp	sugar	10 g/½ oz
1 pinch	cayenne	1 pinch
	salt and pepper	
8	slices firm-textured bread	8
4 tbsp	butter	50 g/2 oz
	MEATLESS STOCK	
1	onion	1
1	clove	1
2	leeks	2
a few	spinach leaves	a few
a few	lettuce leaves	a few
2	carrots	2

US	Ingredients	Met/Imp
3, each about 2 lb	small Nantes ducks	3, each about 1 kg/2 lb
	or	
2, each about 3–4½ lb	large ducks	2, each about 1.5–2 kg/3–4½ lb
2	tarragon sprigs	2
4	lemon slices	4
	salt and pepper	
3 cups	good Veal Juice or White Stock (page 56)	750 ml/1¼ pints
36	small globe artichokes from Provence	36
	lemon juice or white wine vinegar	
5 tbsp	butter	60 g/2½ oz
2	fresh mint leaves	2
1	garlic clove	1
1 tsp	potato flour	5 ml/1 tsp
1 tsp	cold water	5 ml/1 tsp
	chopped fresh parsley	
	watercress sprigs	

ROAST DUCK WITH GLOBE ARTICHOKES

Preparation 1¾ hours • Cooking 45 minutes

Young and tender ducks, which have better quality flesh, producing pink, juicy meat when roasted, are not always easy to find. It is therefore advisable to order them in advance. If young ducks cannot be found, buy 2 larger birds.

Check that the gland under each duck's parson's (pope's) nose has been removed. If not, cut it out yourself. Remove the fat covering both sides of the natural orifice. Remove the wing tips and make sure that the neck has been cut off at the shoulders so that the skin can be folded under the duck's back. Put 1 tarragon sprig, 2 lemon slices and salt and pepper to taste in the cavity. Truss the ducks, remembering to push the parson's (pope's) nose up between the legs. Leave to one side at room temperature. Roast the giblets (wing tips, necks, gizzards, but not the livers which can be kept to make a small pâté) until they are golden brown.

Roast the ducks in the oven. For small ducks, roast in a preheated hot oven for 15–16 minutes per 500 g/1 lb. If using 2 larger birds, roast them in a low oven for 35 minutes per 500 g/1 lb. This will allow the fat to melt evenly. The flesh will be well cooked but very soft, and there will be plenty of cooking juices to make an excellent sauce. While the ducks are cooking, put the roasted giblets in a saucepan and add two-thirds of the veal juice or stock. Bring to the boil and simmer until reduced by half. When large ducks have been cooking for 30 minutes, pierce their sides with a trussing needle above the breast fillet to make it easier for the fat to run out while they are cooking.

Meanwhile, prepare the artichokes. Small artichokes from the south of France are about 5 cm/2 inches long and have a diameter of 4–5 cm/1½–2 inches. When they have been cleaned and pared, they are only 2.5 cm/1 inch long and 2 cm/¾ inch wide, and are completely edible – bottom, leaves and choke, the latter being hardly formed.

Fill a large bowl with water and add lemon juice or white wine vinegar. Remove the large leaves from each artichoke, trim the bottoms with a small knife (preferably with a stainless steel blade) and remove the tips of the leaves. As you prepare them, drop them straight into the acidulated water. When all the artichokes are ready, wash them in fresh water and drain well. Heat two-thirds of the butter in a large saucepan and add the mint leaves, which have been crushed in the hands, and the crushed garlic. Cover and sweat for a few minutes over a very low heat.

Take out the mint and garlic and add the artichokes, salt, pepper, 1 tarragon sprig, 2 lemon slices and the remaining veal juice or stock. Cover and cook gently until the artichokes are tender, shaking the pan at regular intervals. The artichokes are ready when a clean darning needle stuck into them comes out easily.

Put the ducks on a heated large serving dish. Sprinkle with salt and pepper and keep warm.

Remove all the fat from the duck cooking juices and mix with the reduced giblet juice. Bring to the boil and simmer. Add the potato flour dissolved in the cold water to thicken it. Remove from the heat and beat in half of the remaining butter.

In a small saucepan, mix the cooking juices from the artichokes with a little of the duck sauce. Boil rapidly until reduced to a good 'glaze'. Add the remaining butter and roll the artichokes in this glaze. Taste to check the seasoning. Serve the ducks surrounded with artichokes sprinkled with chopped parsley and sprigs of watercress. Strain the sauce into a warm sauce boat.

Wines: red or white Bellet, Champagne, Bourgueil, Cornas.

DODINE DE CANARD DE L'HOSTELLERIE DE LA POSTE D'AVALLON

BONED STUFFED DUCK AS PREPARED AT THE 'HOSTELLERIE DE LA POSTE' —————— IN AVALLON ——————

Preparation 2¾ hours • Marinating the day before • Cooking 2 hours

Bone the duck completely, removing all of the meat. Leave the feet intact. Thinly slice the meat. Season the inside of the duck casing with a little armagnac, spice and salt and leave to marinate overnight.

Prepare the stuffing. Mix the pork with the veal and poultry livers. Pour over the Chablis and leave to marinate overnight. Next day, mix the stuffing with the eggs and chopped truffles, and flavour with madeira or truffle juice and a little armagnac. Add the sliced duck meat.

Put the stuffing inside the duck casing. Sew up, truss carefully and roast in a low oven for about 2 hours, basting often.

Deglaze with the remaining armagnac and serve hot. Dodine of duck can also be served cold with port-flavoured jelly. In this case, use the scraps and bones of the duck to make a stock which, when added to the cooking juices, makes an excellent jelly.

Red wines: Côte de Beaune-Villages, Côte de Nuits-Villages, Châteauneuf-du-Pape, Côte Rôtie.
White wines: Meursault, Montrachet, Coteaux Champenois.

US	Ingredients	Met/Imp
1, about 3 lb	fine Rouen duck	1, about 1.5 kg/3 lb
½ cup	armagnac	100 ml/4 fl oz
1 pinch	quatre-épices	1 pinch
	salt and pepper	
1 lb	very finely minced (ground) pork	500 g/1 lb
1 lb	diced veal, cut from top of leg	500 g/1 lb
6	poultry livers (including 1 from the duck)	6
½ cup	Chablis wine	100 ml/4 fl oz
2	eggs	2
5 oz	truffles	150 g/5 oz
⅓ cup	madeira or truffle juice	75 ml/3 fl oz

US	Ingredients	Met/Imp
I	Rouen duck	I
I lb (about 2 cups)	very finely minced (ground) pork	500 g/I lb
I lb	foie gras 'au naturel'	500 g/I lb
7 oz	cooked ham	200 g/7 oz
10 oz	veal escalopes (cutlets)	300 g/10 oz
2	eggs	2
¼ lb	truffles	125 g/4½ oz
⅔ cup	port wine	150 ml/¼ pint
½ cup	cognac	100 ml/4 fl oz
	salt and pepper	
I	fairly large piece larding bacon (15 × 20 cm/6 × 8 inches)	I

- RABELAISIAN BONED STUFFED DUCK -

Preparation 2¼ hours • (To be prepared the day before) • Cooking 2½ hours

Bone the duck by cutting the skin along the back (stopping the cut in the centre of the backbone). Remove the bones and the wing tips from the carcass, leaving just the drumsticks. Mix the pork and foie gras with the diced ham and veal in a terrine and add the eggs, chopped truffles, port and cognac. Season to taste with salt and pepper.

Stuff the duck with this preparation, holding it by its stomach, then place it on its back in a roasting tin that has fairly high sides but is not much larger than the stuffed bird. There is no need to sew up the skin. Cover the duck with the bacon and cook in a low oven for 2½ hours.

Remove from the oven, remove the larding bacon and leave to cool overnight. Before serving, coat the duck with a little aspic jelly made by boiling up the scraps and bones from the carcass, and decorate the ends of the drumsticks with 2 cutlet frills. Serve the duck surrounded by the roasting juices, which will have set to a jelly.

Red wines: Médoc, Graves, Côte de Beaune-Villages.
White wines: Meursault, Montrachet, Hermitage.

DUCK LIVER WITH GREEN AND BLACK OLIVES*

US	Ingredients	Met/Imp
I, about 1½ lb	duck's liver	I, about 750 g/1½ lb
2 cups	chicken consommé	500 ml/18 fl oz
I glass	dry white wine (Jurançon sec)	I glass
I ladle	tomato sauce	I ladle
12	green olives	12
12	black olives	12
I small glass	madeira	I small glass

Preparation 45 minutes • Cooking 35 minutes

Skin the liver and remove the sinews and tendons. Brown the trimmings in a flameproof casserole and add the consommé and white wine. Boil gently for 10 minutes. Put the liver in this hot stock and cook gently for 10 minutes. Take out the liver and keep it warm on a serving dish.

Remove the fat from the cooking liquid. Add the tomato sauce and cook over a high heat for 10 minutes or until reduced. After reducing for 5 minutes, add the stoned and blanched green olives, the stoned black olives and the madeira. After cooking for a further 5 minutes, taste the sauce to check the seasoning, then pour on to the liver.

Wines: Pacherenc du Vic-Bilh or Madiran.

DUCK LIVER WITH GRAPES

US	Ingredients	Met/Imp
4½ lb	ducks' livers	2 kg/4½ lb
	salt and pepper	
I	onion	I
I	carrot	I
I	bouquet garni	I
4 tbsp	butter	50 g/2 oz
¼ lb	Bayonne ham	100 g/4 oz
5	shallots	5
10 oz	white muscat grapes	300 g/10 oz
scant ½ cup	muscat wine	100 ml/4 fl oz
3 cups	Veal Stock (page 56)	750 ml/1 ¼ pints
5 oz	cep stalks	150 g/5 oz

Preparation 45 minutes • Cooking 1 hour

Remove the sinews and tendons from the livers, then season the livers with salt and pepper to taste. Put the thinly sliced onion and carrot and the bouquet garni in the bottom of a casserole. Place the livers on top and cook in a low oven for 1 hour. Melt the butter in a frying pan and cook the very thinly sliced Bayonne ham, the chopped shallots and the blanched, peeled and seeded white muscat grapes until brown. Deglaze with muscat. Add the veal stock and cep stalks and cook slowly until reduced. Put the livers in a heated serving dish and coat with the sauce.

Medium dry or sweet white wines: Graves, Sauternes, Barsac, Jurançon.

MOUSSE DE CANARD ROUENNAIS

—— ROUEN DUCK MOUSSE IN ASPIC ——

Preparation 5 hours • (To be prepared several hours in advance) • Cooking 3½ hours • Serves 10–12

US	Ingredients	Met/Imp
4½ lb	crushed calf's bones	2 kg/4½ lb
1	large onion	1
3	carrots	3
2	leeks	2
1	celery stalk	1
a few	parsley sprigs	a few
a few	chervil sprigs	a few
2 quarts	water	2 litres/3½ pints
6–8	leaves gelatine	6–8
	or	
1½–2 tbsp	powdered gelatine	30 ml/1½–2 tbsp
1, about 2¾ lb	Rouen duck	1, about 1.25 kg/2¾ lb
1	piece of butter	1
	salt and pepper	
½ lb	foie gras	250 g/8 oz
⅔ cup	sherry	150 ml/¼ pint
2	egg whites	2
1	lemon, juice of	1
2 cups	crème fraîche	500 ml/18 fl oz

Prepare a *fumet*. Put the calf's bones, roughly chopped vegetables and herbs in a large saucepan, cover with the water, lightly salted, and bring to the boil.

Soak the sheets of gelatine, if using, in a bowl of cold water for at least 2 hours. Meanwhile, skin and bone the duck. Dice the duck meat. Add the duck bones and gizzard to the boiling fumet. Boil gently for 3 hours in all. Meanwhile, melt the butter in a frying pan and fry the duck's liver and heart. Season to taste with salt and pepper.

Pound the diced duck meat, the liver and the heart in a mortar and pestle. When it is reduced to a paste, add the foie gras, in small slices, and two-thirds of the sherry. Mix well together and set aside. When the fumet is cooked, sieve it through a filter paper (or cheesecloth), then carefully remove the fat.

Put the egg whites in a saucepan and beat them with a fork until very frothy. Stir in the almost cold duck fumet and the lemon juice. Heat this mixture slowly, stirring continuously, and add the drained sheets of gelatine (or the powdered gelatine dissolved in water). As soon as a little white froth appears, lower the heat and simmer: the fumet aspic has clarified. Remove from the heat and add the remaining sherry. Put a filter paper (or a piece of cheesecloth soaked in hot water) in a sieve over a bowl and sieve the aspic through it. Repeat this operation several times, as the pores of the filter become blocked with the coagulated egg white.

Work the duck and foie gras mixture through a fine sieve. Stir this stuffing in a bowl and mix in 2 tablespoons of the liquid aspic. Season to taste with salt and pepper. Whip the crème fraîche and add it to the stuffing. Fill a charlotte mould with the lukewarm aspic. Put the mould in a bowl of crushed ice and leave it until the aspic has set around the edge of the mould. Take the runny aspic out of the centre of the mould and reserve for the garnish.

Carefully fill the mould with the duck mousse. Leave it in the refrigerator for several hours, until set.

Just before serving, dip the mould briefly in hot water and turn out the mousse on to an appropriate serving dish garnished with chopped aspic. Serve the mousse with slices of hot toast.

Sweet white wines: Sauternes, Loupiac, Monbazillac.
Medium dry white wines: Coteaux du Layon, Bonnezeaux.
Dry white wines: dry Vouvray, Savennières, Sancerre, Pouilly-Fumé.

BRAISED DUCKLING WITH TURNIPS FROM POITOU

Preparation 2½ hours • Cooking 1¼ hours

US	Ingredients	Met/Imp
2	Nantes ducklings	2
5	poultry livers (including 2 from the ducklings)	5
¼ lb	pig's liver	100 g/4 oz
¼ lb	fresh fat belly (side) of pork	100 g/4 oz
2	shallots	2
1	sage sprig	1
1	basil sprig	1
1	rosemary sprig	1
1	thyme sprig	1
¼	bay leaf	¼
2	parsley sprigs	2
	salt and pepper	
10 tbsp	butter	150 g/5 oz
4	egg yolks	4
scant 1 cup	aged madeira	200 ml/7 fl oz
2 tbsp	tomato paste	30 ml/2 tbsp
48	small onions	48
48	turnips	48
2 tsp	caster (superfine) sugar	10 ml/2 tsp
½ cup	crème fraîche	100 ml/4 fl oz
⅓ cup	cognac	75 ml/3 fl oz
1 tbsp	chopped parsley	15 ml/1 tbsp

Take 2 plump young ducklings and stuff them with the following filling: trim and finely chop the ducks' giblets and livers, the poultry livers, pig's liver and pork, and mix together in a large bowl. Season with the chopped shallots, sage, basil, rosemary, thyme, bay leaf, parsley and salt and pepper. Add half of the melted butter and the egg yolks. Use this mixture to stuff the ducklings, then truss.

Put the ducklings in a saucepan with two-thirds of the remaining butter and cook until well browned on both sides. Deglaze them with the madeira and add the tomato paste. Remove the ducklings from the pan and keep warm. Reserve the cooking juices.

Using another saucepan, cook the small onions and turnips in the remaining butter. Sprinkle with the sugar and pour in some stock from the ducklings. While this is cooking, thicken it by stirring in the crème fraîche.

Put the ducklings on the bed of turnips and onions. Stir the cognac into the remaining duckling cooking liquid and pour over the ducklings. Cover and simmer until cooked. Just before serving, transfer to a heated serving dish and sprinkle with chopped parsley. Serve very hot.

Red wines: Médoc, Graves, Côte de Nuits-Villages, Châteauneuf-du-Pape.
White wines: Meursault, Montagny, Hermitage.

BRAISED DUCKLING WITH NEW PEAS

Preparation 30 minutes • Cooking 30 minutes

US	Ingredients	Met/Imp
2	medium ducklings	2
1 stick	butter	100 g/4 oz
2	carrots	2
2	onions	2
1	bouquet garni	1
1	savory sprig	1
6½ cups	shelled new peas	1 kg/2 lb
20	small onions	20
½ lb	fresh fat belly (side) of pork	250 g/8 oz
	salt and pepper	

Cook the ducklings in a large saucepan with two-thirds of the butter, on a bed of sliced carrots and onions, the bouquet garni and savory.

When the ducklings are only just cooked, take them out and keep them warm. Work the vegetables and cooking liquid through a sieve placed over a bowl.

Cook the shelled peas and small onions in plenty of boiling water. Drain, then add the remaining butter and the sieved vegetables.

Dice the pork, which has been previously fried, and mix with the peas and onions. Surround the duckling with the mixture, season to taste with salt and pepper and simmer over a low heat until completely cooked.

Dry white wines: Pouilly-Fumé, Chablis, Pouilly-Fuissé.
Red wines: Côte de Beaune-Villages, Bourgueil, Chinon.

DUCKLING WITH MONTMORENCY CHERRIES

Preparation 2 hours • Cooking 45 minutes

Put the sliced carrots and onion in a deep flameproof casserole, then add the ducklings and the bouquet garni. Add the butter, cover and cook in a moderate oven for 45 minutes, basting often. Remove the ducklings from the casserole, untruss them, cut them into pieces and keep them warm. Remove the vegetable garnish and the bouquet garni from the casserole. Deglaze the casserole with cherry brandy and cognac and pour in the stock. Boil until reduced, then strain. Poach the cherries in the wine. Surround the duckling with cherries and coat with the sauce.

Medium dry and sweet white wines: Graves, Sauternes, Barsac.

US	Ingredients	Met/Imp
2	carrots	2
1	onion	1
2	ducklings	2
1	bouquet garni	1
10 tbsp	butter	150 g/5 oz
⅓ cup	cherry brandy	75 ml/3 fl oz
¼ cup	cognac	50 ml/2 fl oz
1¼ cups	thickened Veal Stock (*page 56*)	300 ml/½ pint
1½ cups	Montmorency cherries, stoned	200 g/7 oz
2 cups	bordeaux wine	500 ml/18 fl oz

DUCKLING STUFFED WITH OYSTERS

Preparation 1½ hours • Cooking 30 minutes

Prepare the ducklings for stuffing by removing the breast bones.

Shell the oysters, then poach them in their own juice. Cool, then drain. Finely chop the oysters, the duckling livers and gizzards and the shallots. Stir the eggs into this stuffing and season.

Stuff the ducklings and place them in an ovenproof dish on a bed of thinly sliced onions and carrots with a sprig of thyme, a bay leaf, the crushed tomatoes and the butter. Cover and cook in a moderate oven for 30 minutes. Work the cooking vegetables and juices through a sieve and serve them very hot as an accompanying sauce.

Dry white wines: Muscadet, Gros Plant du Pays Nantais, Pouilly-Fumé, Chablis.
Red wines: Côte de Beaune-Villages.

US	Ingredients	Met/Imp
2	Nantes ducklings	2
6 dozen	oysters	6 dozen
2	shallots	2
2	eggs	2
	salt and pepper	
2	onions	2
2	carrots	2
1	thyme sprig	1
1	bay leaf	1
3	tomatoes	3
4 tbsp	butter	50 g/2 oz

STUFFED DUCKLING FROM SOLOGNE

Preparation 2 hours • Stuff the ducks the day before • Cooking 50 minutes

Pluck, singe and draw the ducklings, reserving the livers. Put the duckling livers — with the gall bladder removed — in a bowl and sprinkle with the breadcrumbs, herbs, garlic, armagnac and salt and pepper to taste. Leave to stand for 2 hours. Transfer the mixture to a mortar and grind everything together. Use to stuff the ducklings; leave overnight.

The next day, place the ducklings in a roasting tin with the onions and tomatoes and cook in a moderate oven until the ducklings are tender.

Just before serving, remove the ducklings from the pan and strain the cooking juices. Mix these juices with any stuffing that has oozed out of the ducklings, add freshly ground pepper and serve as a sauce.

Red wines: Médoc or Saint-Émilion, Graves, Côte de Beaune-Villages, Moulin-à-Vent, Côte Rôtie.

US	Ingredients	Met/Imp
2	ducklings	2
2 cups	brioche breadcrumbs	100 g/4 oz
1 pinch	chopped thyme	1 pinch
1 pinch	chopped savory	1 pinch
1 pinch	chopped rosemary	1 pinch
1 pinch	crushed garlic	1 pinch
½ cup	armagnac	100 ml/4 fl oz
	salt and pepper	
4	onions	4
6	tomatoes	6

US	Ingredients	Met/Imp
I, about 5½ lb	duckling	I, about 2.5 kg/5½ lb
¼ cup	green peppercorns	60 ml/4 tbsp
I tbsp	cognac	15 ml/1 tbsp
2 tbsp	dry white wine	30 ml/2 tbsp
2 cups	Veal Stock (page 56)	500 ml/18 fl oz
¼ cup	crème fraîche	60 ml/4 tbsp

DUCKLING MARCO POLO

Preparation 1¼ hours • Cooking 1 hour 20 minutes

Recipe created by Claude Terrail, Tour d'Argent, Paris

Roast a fine, tender duckling in a moderate oven for about 45 minutes.

Place half of the crushed green peppercorns in a saucepan with the cognac and dry white wine. Boil rapidly until reduced. Halfway through the reduction, add the remaining crushed green peppercorns. When completely reduced, add the veal stock and boil for 20 minutes, skimming off the impurities. Lower the heat, add the crème fraîche and cook, stirring, until smooth. Coat the duckling with this sauce.

Red wines: Graves, Médoc, Bergerac.

US	Ingredients	Met/Imp
8	reinettes grises or other eating apples	8
4 tbsp	clarified butter	50 g/2 oz
⅓ cup	curaçao	75 ml/3 fl oz
I	Nantes duckling (not totally bled)*	I
	salt and pepper	
8	oranges	8
¼ cup	cognac	50 ml/2 fl oz
8	sugar cubes	8
¼ cup	vinegar	50 ml/2 fl oz

DUCKLING WITH ORANGE

Preparation 1½ hours • Cooking 30 minutes

Peel the eating apples, cut them into quarters and core them. Fry them quickly in the clarified butter until golden brown but not soft. Drain them and sprinkle with a few drops of curaçao; leave to cool.

Return a few of the apple quarters to the pan and cook until tender, to be used for the garnish. Use the remainder to stuff the duckling. Season the duckling with salt and pepper and put it on a spit (rôtisserie). Roast in a moderate oven or under a grill (broiler) for 30 minutes or until golden brown and tender, basting frequently. Meanwhile, squeeze the juice from 5 of the oranges and cut the rind of 1 orange into *julienne* strips. Cut one of the remaining 3 into wedges and the remainder into slices. Blanch the julienne strips in boiling water, then drain.

A few minutes before the duckling is cooked, remove the fat from the dripping pan and sprinkle the duckling with all but 1 glass of the orange juice, the cognac and most of the remaining curaçao. Mix all the juices in the dripping pan to make the *fumet* to flavour the sauce.

Cook the sugar and vinegar to a light brown caramel. Add the glass of orange juice and orange julienne; cook for 15 minutes or until reduced by one-third. Strain, then add the fumet and the remaining few drops of curaçao.

Put the duckling on a heated serving dish and arrange the slices of orange and the apple quarters around the edge. Arrange the orange wedges in a line on top of the duckling. Coat with some of the very hot, but not boiling, sauce. Serve the rest in a sauce boat.

***Editor's note**: this classic recipe for Caneton à l'Orange calls for a red-fleshed duck which has not been totally bled, and cooking time is kept very short so that the flesh remains red (saignant). A conventional roasting duck may be used if preferred, and the cooking time increased.

Sweet or medium dry white wines: Graves, Sauternes, Barsac, Vouvray.
Red wines: Médoc, Côte de Beaune-Villages, Chinon or Bourgueil.

DUCKLING WITH PEACHES*

Preparation 2 hours • Cooking 45 minutes

US	Ingredients	Met/Imp
2	Nantes ducklings	2
2	carrots	2
2	onions	2
1	bouquet garni	1
1 stick	butter	100 g/4 oz
	salt and pepper	
1 cup	cointreau	200 ml/7 fl oz
½ cup	cognac	100 ml/3½ fl oz
1½ cups	Veal Stock (page 56)	300 ml/½ pint
	potato flour	
8	peaches	8

Pluck, singe and draw the ducklings, removing the heads and feet. Truss the ducklings.

Thinly slice the carrots and onions and put them in the bottom of a large, high-sided flameproof casserole. Add the bouquet garni and butter. Season the ducklings with salt and pepper and put them on top of the vegetables.

Cook in a moderate oven until the ducklings are brown, then cover and continue to cook for about 45 minutes or until the ducklings are tender, basting often.

When the ducklings are cooked, take them out, place them on a serving dish and keep them warm. Remove the vegetables and bouquet garni from the casserole and drain off the fat. Pour the cointreau and cognac into the casserole, followed immediately by the veal stock, slightly thickened with potato flour. Boil fairly rapidly, then work through a fine sieve.

Meanwhile, peel the peaches, halve them and remove the stones. Put the peach halves in a saucepan, pour the veal stock mixture on top and boil gently for 4–5 minutes. Check the seasoning. Drain and arrange the peach halves around the duckling. Pour the sauce over the duckling and peaches.

Sweet or medium dry white wines: Graves, Sauternes, Barsac, Montlouis, Vouvray. Banyuls may be tried, but remember to drink a few mouthfuls of mineral water afterwards.

ROUEN DUCKLING

Preparation 1 hour • Cooking 28 minutes

US	Ingredients	Met/Imp
1	Rouen duckling	1
4 tbsp	butter	50 g/2 oz
1 tbsp	chopped shallots	15 ml/1 tbsp
	salt and pepper	
¼ cup	cognac	50 ml/2 fl oz
¼ cup	good burgundy wine	50 ml/2 fl oz

Pluck, singe and draw the duckling, removing the head and feet. Take care not to lose all the blood. Reserve the liver.

Remove the breast bone from the duckling and remove the gall bladder from the liver. Replace the liver inside the duckling and truss the bird. Roast in a moderate oven for 18 minutes.

Grease an ovenproof serving dish with the butter. Put the shallots, a little salt and some freshly ground pepper in the dish.

Remove the legs and wing tips from the duckling and set aside. Cut the breast into thin slices and put them on the dish. Flambé with the cognac.

Crush the duckling carcass and the liver in a meat press. Rinse the bones with the burgundy and press once more to extract all the blood. Spoon this blood on to the duckling slices in the dish and put in a hot oven until it coagulates (do not let it boil).

Grill (broil) the legs and wing tips and arrange them around the dish before serving.

Red wines: Côte de Nuits-Villages.

DINDE ET DINDONNEAU

TURKEY

A WHOLE ROAST TURKEY MAKES A TRADITIONAL FESTIVE DISH; it may be stuffed in various ways (with fruit; with sage and onion as in England; or with chopped herbs and sausagemeat), sometimes garnished with truffles or indeed with chestnuts. A turkey for roasting should be young and plump, and all the sinews and tendons should be removed from the legs before it is prepared. Turkey meat is sometimes a little dry, but if it is braised, or cooked in a ragoût, it becomes softer and more moist. A turkey provides a particularly large amount of good quality giblets, and the leftovers are easy to use. Turkey escalopes (boneless slices from the breast) and legs are both commonly used.

DINDONNEAU AUX MARRONS

TURKEY WITH CHESTNUTS

Preparation 2 hours • Cooking 2 hours

US	Ingredients	Met/Imp
I	young cock turkey or young, plump hen turkey	I
2 quarts	chestnuts	2 litres/3½ pints
4	slices pork back fat (or bacon fat)	4
I stick	butter	100 g/4 oz
½ cup	goose fat	100 ml/4 fl oz
	salt	

Pluck, singe and draw the turkey, removing the head, neck and feet.

Cook the chestnuts in a frying pan until they are browned but not burnt. Peel them and use them to stuff the turkey until it is pleasantly rounded. Sew up the flap of skin to seal in the chestnuts. Generously bard the turkey with the pork or bacon fat.

Thoroughly grease an ovenproof dish with plenty of butter and goose fat. Put the turkey in the dish and cook in a hot oven for 5 minutes. Brush the turkey with melted butter and fat from the dish and continue cooking for 2 hours, basting frequently. This is the secret of success. Add some salt. The turkey is ready when it gives off its characteristic smoky aroma.

Red wines: Saint-Émilion, Côte de Beaune-Villages or Côte de Nuits-Villages, Châteauneuf-du-Pape, Côte Rôtie.

ROAST TURKEY 'BONHOMME NORMAND'

Preparation 3 hours • Cooking 2 hours

Pluck, singe and draw the turkey, removing the head, neck and feet. Lard the turkey with strips of the pork or bacon fat.

Make the stuffing. Finely chop the veal and pork fat, then mix with the chives, shallot and fines herbes. Add the spice and the finely chopped truffles, mix well and use to stuff the turkey. Roast in a hot oven for about 1½ hours or until the turkey is three-quarters cooked.

Meanwhile, cut the apples into quarters and sauté them in butter in an earthenware cocotte. Arrange the apples in the bottom of a casserole and place the turkey on top. Continue cooking for a further 30 minutes or until the turkey is tender.

When the turkey is cooked, coat it with a garnish prepared as follows: sauté the mushrooms, truffle slices, artichoke bottoms, small blanched onions and fines herbes in butter, then pour over some veal stock mixed with calvados.

Red wines: Saint-Émilion, Pomerol, Châteauneuf-du-Pape.

US	Ingredients	Met/Imp
I, about 5–6 lb	young cock turkey	I, about 2.3–2.7 kg/5–6 lb
5 oz	pork back fat or bacon fat	150 g/5 oz
8	*reinette* or other eating apples, peeled and cored	8
	butter	
½ lb	button mushrooms	250 g/8 oz
¼ lb	truffles, in thin slices	125 g/4 oz
8	small artichoke bottoms, thinly sliced and sweated in butter	8
20	small blanched onions	20
I tbsp	chopped *fines herbes*	15 ml/I tbsp
1¼ cups	Veal Stock (page 56)	300 ml/½ pint
⅓ cup	*vieux calvados*	75 ml/3 fl oz
	STUFFING	
I lb	boneles veal, cut from top of leg	500 g/I lb
½ lb	pork back fat	250 g/8 oz
3 tbsp	finely chopped chives, shallot and *fines herbes*	45 ml/3 tbsp
I pinch	*quatre-épices*	I pinch
2 oz	truffles	50 g/2 oz

SPIT-ROAST TURKEY VIVANDIÈRE

Preparation 1 hour • Cooking 1¼ hours

Pluck, singe and draw the turkey, reserving the liver. Remove the head, neck and feet.

Truss the turkey and bard it with the fat. Roast in a hot oven, preferably on a spit, for 45 minutes–1 hour, basting frequently with the turkey juices and the butter.

Serve the turkey with the cooking juices, from which the fat has been removed.

Accompany with a salad made from lettuce hearts and the finely crushed turkey liver, which has been sealed in butter. When dressing this salad, replace some of the oil with a little fat from the roast. Toss well before serving.

Red wines: Médoc, Côte de Beaune-Villages or Côte de Nuits-Villages, Châteauneuf-du-Pape.

US	Ingredients	Met/Imp
I	young cock turkey	I
3	slices pork back fat or bacon fat	3
I stick	butter	100 g/4 oz
3	lettuce hearts	3
	salt and pepper	

LAPIN

RABBIT

ALTHOUGH FOR A LONG TIME THE LARGE NUMBERS OF THIS rodent were considered to be disastrous because of the damage they caused, they were, in fact, being bred for the table at the same time. From the 17th century onwards, 'lapin de chou' (domestic rabbit) was cooked with mustard, prunes, jelly, etc, whereas wild rabbit was roasted or sautéed. 'Fauve de Bourgogne' (wild Burgundy rabbit), 'argenté des champs' (silvered field rabbit) and 'géant du Bouscat' (giant Bouscat rabbit) are the reared breeds available in the market today. The rabbit best suited for cooking is young, small and rather stocky, with tender pink flesh, a pale-coloured liver and a clearly visible kidney. Anjou rabbit is the tastiest. Real wild rabbit has become rare since myxomatosis in the Fifties. Rabbit may be sautéed, roasted or steamed, it may be used in stews or blanquettes, not to mention pâtés and terrines, and it is therefore a meat which chefs and gourmands make the best possible use of.

US	Ingredients	Met/Imp
2	young wild rabbits	2
	salt and pepper	
2 tbsp	butter	30 g/1 oz
¼ cup	olive oil	50 ml/2 fl oz
3 tbsp	flour	30 g/1 oz
2 cups	white wine	500 ml/18 fl oz
2½ cups	White Stock (page 56)	600 ml/1 pint
1	bouquet garni	1
2	garlic cloves	2
½ cup	puréed tomatoes	100 ml/4 fl oz
1 lb	field mushrooms	500 g/1 lb

LAPEREAU AUX CHAMPIGNONS

— WILD RABBIT WITH MUSHROOMS —

Preparation 30 minutes • Cooking 1¼ hours

Skin and gut the rabbits, removing the heads and feet. Cut the rabbits into 4 pieces each (the 4 legs with the maximum of meat attached, removing the bones from the ribcage). Season with salt and pepper. Heat half of the butter and the olive oil in a large saucepan with salt and pepper and cook the rabbit pieces until well browned. Sprinkle with the flour and pour in just enough white wine and stock to cover the rabbit. Add a strong bouquet garni (parsley, thyme, bay leaf) and the crushed garlic. Add the puréed tomatoes and cook for 25 minutes.

Meanwhile, lightly fry the thinly sliced field mushrooms in the remaining butter and add to the pan. Finish cooking in a moderate oven, uncovered, for a further 50 minutes.

Dry white wines: Muscadet, Saumur, Pouilly-sur-Loire.
Red wines: Bordeaux, Fronsac, Côtes-Canon-Fronsac.

POACHER'S WILD RABBIT

Preparation 50 minutes • Cooking 1 hour

A young rabbit can be recognised by testing to see if its ear cartilage tears like paper; if the animal is old, the ear is as tough as leather. If field mushrooms are unavailable, use fresh ceps. The latter should be very finely sliced and browned in oil before being added to the rabbit.

Skin and gut the rabbits, removing the heads and feet. Reserve the livers. The prepared weight of each rabbit should be about 700 g/1½ lb. Cut the rabbits into small pieces.

Melt the freshly grated fat in a flameproof casserole and add the rabbit pieces. Stir them over a high heat until well browned. Sprinkle with the finely chopped onion, brown for a few more minutes, then add the chopped shallots and cognac.

Finally, add the white wine, the chopped lean ham, the finely chopped mushrooms, the herbs and salt and pepper to taste. Bring to the boil, then cover and cook in a fairly hot oven for 25 minutes.

Scald the slices of belly (side) pork in boiling water for 5 minutes, then drain and wipe them. Grill (broil) or sauté them lightly in half of the butter in a frying pan until brown.

Remove the gall bladders from the rabbit livers, then finely chop the livers and mix with the crushed garlic. Three minutes before serving, mix the livers into the rabbit cooking liquid.

Finally, remove the rabbit pieces from the casserole and put in a serving dish. Boil the sauce rapidly for a few moments, then remove from the heat and add the remaining butter. Pour over the rabbit pieces and sprinkle with parsley. Surround with the slices of pork and the fried croûtons.

Dry white wines: Muscadet, Pouilly-sur-Loire, Sancerre.

US	Ingredients	Met/Imp
2	young wild rabbits	2
2 oz	pork back fat or bacon fat	50 g/2 oz
I	medium onion	I
2	shallots	2
¼ cup	cognac	50 ml/2 fl oz
1¼ cups	white wine	300 ml/½ pint
5 oz	raw country ham	150 g/5 oz
½ lb	field mushrooms	250 g/8 oz
I pinch	chopped wild thyme	I pinch
I pinch	chopped thyme	I pinch
	salt and pepper	
8	slices of fresh fat belly (side) of pork	8
4 tbsp	butter	50 g/2 oz
½	garlic clove	½
I tbsp	chopped fresh parsley	15 ml/1 tbsp
8	fried heart-shaped bread croûtons	8

WILD RABBIT WITH GARDEN VEGETABLES

Preparation 1 hour • Cooking 1¼ hours

Skin and gut the rabbits, removing the heads and feet. Cut each rabbit into 8 pieces. Put in a casserole and pour in the consommé. Add the roughly chopped carrots, turnips, onions, celery and leeks, the bouquet garni and spice. Cook in a fairly hot oven for 1¼ hours or until the rabbit is tender.

Remove the rabbits from the casserole and put in a heated serving dish. Tip the vegetables and cooking liquid into a sieve, remove the bouquet garni and work the vegetables through to form a purée. Collect in a bowl and stir in the butter. Pour over the rabbits and serve.

Dry white wines: Saumur, Sancerre, Chablis.
Red wine: Montagne-Saint-Émilion, Saint-Georges-Saint Émilion.

US	Ingredients	Met/Imp
2	young wild rabbits	2
I quart	highly flavoured consommé	I litre/2 pints
4	carrots	4
4	turnips	4
2	large onions	2
2	celery stalks	2
2	leeks, white part only	2
I	bouquet garni	I
I pinch	quatre-épices	I pinch
10 tbsp	butter	150 g/5 oz

US	Ingredients	Met/Imp
2	young wild rabbits	2
½ lb	pork back fat or bacon fat	250 g/8 oz
	salt and pepper	
4 tbsp	butter	50 g/2 oz
4	shallots	4

SPIT-ROAST WILD RABBIT

Preparation 1½ hours • Cooking 50 minutes

Skin and gut the rabbits, removing the heads and feet. Reserve the blood and livers. Cut the fat into small strips and use to lard the rabbits. Sprinkle with salt and pepper, put the rabbits on a spit (rôtisserie), then brush with the melted butter. Cook in a hot oven for 50 minutes or until tender.

Towards the end of the cooking time, spoon some of the juices from the dripping pan into a saucepan and add the chopped shallots. Chop the rabbit livers, mix them with the blood and work them through a sieve. Add to the shallots and cook together to make a sauce. Serve with the rabbits.

Red wines: Côte Rôtie, Hermitage, Châteauneuf-du-Pape, Saint-Émilion, Pomerol.

US	Ingredients	Met/Imp
I	rabbit	I
	vinegar	
I cup	milk	250 ml/8 fl oz
1⅓ cups	stale breadcrumbs	100 g/4 oz
4 tbsp	butter	50 g/2 oz
7 oz	sweet (or Spanish) onions	200 g/7 oz
7 oz	fresh fat belly (side) of pork, finely chopped	200 g/7 oz
⅓ cup	pistachios, shelled and roughly chopped	50 g/2 oz
5	eggs	5
I tsp	mixed dried herbs (oregano, thyme, savory), ground to a powder in a mortar and pestle	5 ml/I tsp
I tsp	finely chopped fresh marjoram leaves and flowers	5 ml/I tsp
	cayenne	
	ground allspice	
	salt and pepper	
	pig's intestines (sausage casings)	
	olive oil	

RABBIT AND MARJORAM SAUSAGES

Preparation 1 hour • Cooking 25 minutes

Skin and gut the rabbit, removing the head and feet. Reserve 75 ml/3 fl oz (⅓ cup) of the blood, the liver, heart and lungs. Add a little vinegar to the blood and beat together to prevent it coagulating. Remove the gall bladder from the liver. Bone the rabbit completely and mince (grind) the meat, liver, heart and lungs together. You need 500 g/1 lb of this minced (ground) mixture.

Bring the milk to the boil, add the breadcrumbs and stir with a wooden spoon until thick and smooth. Work through a sieve.

Melt the butter in a heavy-based saucepan and cook the finely chopped onions over a very low heat for 30 minutes–1 hour or until soft but not coloured, stirring from time to time. Finally, stir in the sieved rabbit blood and continue stirring gently for a further 5 minutes.

Put all the ingredients, except the intestines and olive oil in a large earthenware bowl, adding cayenne, allspice and salt and pepper to taste. Work all the ingredients together thoroughly with the hands until well mixed. Raw stuffing of this kind is not very nice to taste, but it is best to do it at this stage to check the seasoning (there is no need to swallow).

Soak the pig's intestines (sausage casing) in lukewarm water, with a little vinegar added, until it is supple. Drain, then blow into the intestine to make sure there are no holes. Amateurs will find it easier to use 4 intestines which are no longer than 60 cm/24 inches each. With relatively firm stuffing like this, there is no need to tie up the end of the intestines before filling them. To do this, use a large plastic funnel and push in the stuffing with the fingers. Do not stuff the intestine too full in case it bursts during cooking. Distribute the stuffing equally by putting the filled intestine on a work surface and pressing it with one hand. Leave enough of the intestine empty at each end to be able to tie up the

Duck Liver with Green and Black Olives
Simmered in a pan with white wine, this duck's liver is served with green and black olives, while the cooking liquid is blended with some tomato sauce and flavoured with madeira: an invention of A. Daguin. (Recipe on page 278.)

Duckling with Peaches
Turnips or olives, oranges, cherries or peas: duck is receptive to a great variety of accompaniments and flavours. The fragrance of peaches and the texture of their flesh forms a perfect partnership with this somewhat fatty bird, which is pot-roasted. Here the cooking liquid is enhanced with cognac and cointreau. (Recipe on page 283.)

Preserved Goose (or Duck) Pipérade
A fondue of sweet peppers, onions and tomatoes, which is often served with eggs, th
Basque pipérade also makes an aromatic accompaniment for preserved goose fried i
its own fat. (Recipe on page 298.)

Chicken Liver Mousse Curnonsky
Mousseline of Bresse chicken livers may be cooked in one large mould, or in several small moulds as here. Whichever you choose, garnish the plate with a sprig of parsley and a little tomato coulis. (Recipe on page 334.)

Guinea-Fowl Chasseur with Ceps
For its tender and succulent flesh to be appreciated, it is best to eat guinea-fowl young;
hence in cooking it is normally referred to as 'pintadeau' (young guinea-fowl). Here
it is flavoured with Provençal herbs, stuffed with chopped ceps, garlic and shallots,
then served with a separate dish of sliced ceps. (Recipe on page 306.)

Rabbit with Prunes
This recipe is very well-known, probably dating from the Middle Ages. It comes from the Loire Valley, where the famous Tours prunes come from, which were brought back from Damascus by the Crusaders. (Recipe on page 293.)

Saddle of Hare with Beetroot
Tenderized and made fragrant by a marinade, then roasted 'en cocotte' in a rich, cream-based sauce, the meat of this hare is served with a slightly sharp garnish of crisp pickled beetroot (beet). (Recipe on page 478.)

Pheasant with Pineapple
Fruit is often the best accompaniment for game: the sweetness counterbalances the strong taste of this meat very pleasantly. Autumn or winter fruits may be used, but so may exotic fruits like pineapple. The latter, already a classic garnish for chicken and pork, here provides a sunny garnish for a pheasant cooked 'en cocotte', and the accompanying sauce is served in a hollowed-out pineapple. (Recipe on page 466.)

PALOMBE ET PIGEON RAMIER

WOOD PIGEON

'PIGEON SAUVAGE' (WILD OR WOOD PIGEON) IS MUCH ESTEEMED for the delicacy and aroma of its meat. The female is hunted in the South West of France and can be used for all the usual pigeon recipes; it can be roasted, braised or cooked in a sauce, depending on its age. The male is only considered a delicacy when very young.

PALOMBES FARCIES À LA BIGOURDANE

STUFFED WOOD PIGEONS BIGOURDANE

Preparation 1 hour • Cooking 1½ hours

Bone the pigeons by removing the breast bone and fill with a stuffing made from bacon, sausagemeat or chopped pork, breadcrumbs, beaten eggs, chopped garlic, parsley and armagnac. Put the pigeons in a roasting pan with the goose fat, add salt and pepper and roast in a hot oven for about 1½ hours. Skim the fat from the cooking juices. (Keep the fat.) Flambé with armagnac, moisten with wine, allow to reduce slightly with the bouquet garni, then thin down with the veal stock. Fry the croûtons in the pigeon cooking fat and use to garnish the dish.

Red wines: Madiran, Côtes de Bourg, Corbières, Châteauneuf-du-Pape.

US	Ingredients	Met/Imp
4	female wood pigeons	4
½ lb	lean bacon	250 g/8 oz
½ lb	pure pork sausagemeat or finely chopped pork	250 g/8 oz
3½ cups	fresh breadcrumbs	200 g/7 oz
3	eggs	3
½	garlic clove	½
1 tbsp	chopped fresh parsley	15 ml/1 tbsp
¼ cup	armagnac	50 ml/2 fl oz
½ cup	goose fat	100 ml/4 fl oz
	salt and pepper	
1 bottle	good red wine	1 bottle
1	bouquet garni	1
1 cup	Veal Stock (page 56)	200 ml/7 fl oz
	bread croûtons or puff pastry *fleurons*	

SALMIS DE PALOMBES

SALMI OF WOOD PIGEON

Preparation 40 minutes • First cooking 20 minutes • Second cooking 30 minutes

Pluck, singe, draw (reserving the livers and blood) and bard the pigeons. Smear them with a small piece of butter and season with salt and pepper. Roast them in a hot oven for 20 minutes, then remove the legs and wings and set aside. Leave the pigeons in a dish on the side of the stove.

Cut up the pigeon carcasses and place them in a saucepan with a nut of butter and the chopped shallots. Brown lightly, then flambé with a generous glass of armagnac. Add salt and pepper and pour over the white wine. Cook for 20 minutes. Add the pigeon livers at the last moment. Sieve this sauce, then pour it into a flameproof casserole. Add the legs, wings and blood of the pigeons and leave to simmer for a few minutes. Add a dash of lemon juice. Serve piping hot, with croûtons.

Red wines: Saint-Émilion, Pomerol, Graves, Médoc.

US	Ingredients	Met/Imp
4	bacon slices for barding	4
4	female wood pigeons	4
4 tbsp	butter	60 g/2½ oz
	salt and pepper	
4	shallots	4
½ cup	armagnac	100 ml/4 fl oz
½ bottle	dry white wine	½ bottle
1	lemon, juice of	1
8	rectangular bread croûtons, fried in butter	8

PERDREAU ET PERDRIX

YOUNG PARTRIDGE AND ADULT PARTRIDGE

THE MOST HUNTED GAME BIRD IN FRANCE IS THE GREY partridge which lives north of the Loire. The red-legged partridge, on the other hand, is to be found in the south. Young partridges up to a year old are usually roasted and eaten with the flesh still pink. They are not hung. The flesh of the older partridge is firmer and may be served with cabbage, or made into stews, salmis, terrines or pâtés. It is customary to serve one young partridge per person, or one older, adult bird between two.

Both young and adult partridges are highly esteemed by gourmets, and there is a particularly wide range of recipes, using foie gras, fruits, mushrooms, *lardons*, cabbage or lentils with subtle flavourings, cognac, brandy and sherry.

CRÉPINETTES DE PERDREAUX À LA FORESTIÈRE

CRÉPINETTES OF YOUNG PARTRIDGE FORESTIÈRE

Preparation 3 hours • Cooking 18 minutes

US	Ingredients	Met/Imp
3	shallots	3
½ lb	bacon	200 g/8 oz
6	game livers, plus the livers from the partridge	6
	parsley	
1 stick	butter	100 g/4 oz
3 cups	Dry Duxelles (page 49)	300 g/10 oz
	salt and pepper	
1¾ cups	cognac	400 ml/14 fl oz
4	young partridges	4
2 lb	pig's caul	1 kg/2 lb
8 cups	fresh breadcrumbs	500 g/1 lb
2 lb	morels	1 kg/2 lb
1 lb	fresh belly (side) of pork, diced	500 g/1 lb

Chop the shallots finely and also chop the bacon, the partridge and game livers and the parsley. Brown the shallots in a little of the butter and mix all these ingredients together with the duxelles. Add salt and pepper and cognac.

Cut the partridges in half and remove the bones from the stomach and the wing tips. Use the bones to make a small amount of stock to serve with the birds.

Divide the stuffing into 8 equal portions. Put 1 portion in each partridge half. Wrap each bird in a piece of pig's caul. Dip the birds in melted butter and fresh breadcrumbs, then cook in butter.

Arrange the cooked morels and diced pork around the crépinettes and pour over some of the cooking juices. Serve the game stock in a sauce boat.

Red wine: light, fruity bordeaux.

PARTRIDGE CHARTREUSE

Preparation 1 hour • Cooking garnish 2 hours; partridges 15–16 minutes

US	Ingredients	Met/Imp
4	young partridges	4
	fresh belly (side) of pork, for larding	
3	cabbages	3
	salt and pepper	
2	fatty bacon slices	2
I	onion	I
I	clove	I
3	carrots	3
I	bouquet garni	I
I	roasted adult partridge	I
I, about 8–10 oz	small uncooked boiling sausage	I, about 250–300 g/8–10 oz
I	small piece lean bacon, blanched	I
2 quarts	fatty stock	2 litres/3½ pints
	Demi-Glaze (*page 56*)	
	madeira	
⅔ cup	Petits Pois 'Anglaise' (*page 542*)	100 g/4 oz

Draw the young partridges. Truss them with their feet close against their bodies, then lard them with belly (side) of pork. Roast the birds in a hot oven for about 15 minutes.

Remove the thick stalks and large outside leaves from the cabbages, then wash the cabbages and blanch them in boiling water for a few moments. Drain them and leave to cool, then lay them out on a clean tea (dish) towel. Season with salt and pepper, then put them in a fairly deep saucepan lined with slices of bacon. Add the onion spiked with the clove, the carrots, bouquet garni, adult partridge (previously roasted), the sausage and the small piece of blanched lean bacon. Pour in enough fatty stock to just cover, place a piece of buttered paper on top and cook for 1½–2 hours.

Meanwhile, prepare a good, well-reduced game stock with the reserved giblets. Moisten with a little demi-glaze and flavour subtly with madeira, keeping the aroma of game predominant.

When everything is cooked, remove the onion and the bouquet garni, then the carrots, bacon, sausage and the partridge. The latter may be used to make croquettes or a purée.

Butter a large *timbale* (deep round mould). Place a slice of sausage in the bottom and put a ring of cooked petits pois around it. Next, make alternate and overlapping rings of carrot and sausage, finishing with a ring of carrots. You may alternate these with small, thin squares of lean bacon.

Drain the braised cabbages and press them in order to remove the excess liquid and fat. Line the bottom and sides of the mould with some of the leaves and place the young roast partridges in the centre. Fill up the gaps with cabbage, packing it in tightly. Cook *au bain-marie* for 12–15 minutes.

To serve, turn the mould upside-down on to a heated round serving dish. Leave for a moment so that the contents remain compact, and in order to force out any liquid from the cabbages.

Remove the mould. Finish off by pouring around the edges a sauce made by deglazing and reducing the 2 lots of cooking juices and adding a small amount of demi-glaze made from game.

The remainder of the cabbage may be served separately with the sausage, bacon and even the older partridge arranged nicely on top.

Red wine: light, fruity bordeaux.

US	Ingredients	Met/Imp
1	large onion	1
1 stick	butter	100 g/4 oz
¼ lb	cep stalks	100 g/4 oz
2	shallots	2
4	young partridges	4
4	game livers	4
¼ lb	lean cooked ham	100 g/4 oz
1 cup	fresh breadcrumbs	50 g/2 oz
1	egg	1
	chopped fresh parsley	
	salt and pepper	
1 pinch	quatre-épices	1 pinch
½ lb	fresh belly (side) of pork	250 g/8 oz
1 lb	cep caps	500 g/1 lb
	oil	
¼ cup	Veal Stock (page 56)	50 ml/2 fl oz

PARTRIDGE CHÂTELAINE

Preparation 1 hour • Cooking 20–25 minutes

Brown the chopped onion in butter. Add the cep stalks and chopped shallots and cook for a few minutes over a high heat, stirring continuously. Leave to cool.

Draw and clean the partridges, reserving the livers. The partridges should have been hung for no longer than the time necessary to make them tender. Chop the partridge livers, together with the other 4 game livers. Add the chopped cep mixture, the lean cooked ham, chopped, the breadcrumbs, soaked and pressed, the beaten egg, and a pinch each of chopped parsley, salt, pepper and spice. Pound this mixture together well to form a stuffing, then fill the partridges and truss them.

Dice the belly (side) of pork, cook it in boiling water for 5 minutes, then drain and pat dry with paper towels. Heat 30 g/1 oz (2 tbsp) of the remaining butter in a large flameproof casserole, add the belly (side) of pork and cook until brown, then drain and set aside on a plate. Place the partridges in this same butter and brown all over. Meanwhile, peel the small fresh ceps and slice them thinly. Sauté them in smoking hot oil in a separate pan until brown. Taste and add salt and pepper.

Surround the partridges in the casserole with the cep caps and the pork. Cover and bake in a moderately hot oven for 20–25 minutes.

A few minutes before serving, place the pan on top of the stove and pour in the veal stock to make a sauce. Sprinkle a little chopped parsley over the ceps and pork. Cover the pan again, wipe it clean and serve.

Red wine: light, fruity bordeaux.

PARTRIDGE NORMANDE

Preparation 1 hour • Cooking 20 minutes

US	Ingredients	Met/Imp
10 tbsp	butter	150 g/5 oz
4	young partridges	4
4	bacon slices for barding	4
	salt and pepper	
8	reinette or other dessert apples	8
1 small pinch	ground cinnamon	1 small pinch
½ cup	crème fraîche	100 ml/4 fl oz
½ cup	calvados	100 ml/4 fl oz

Heat some butter in a flameproof earthenware casserole. Add 4 young partridges, trussed and barded with the bacon. Cook until browned all over. Season with salt and pepper. Peel and core the apples and slice into quarters. Fry lightly in butter for a few moments and season with cinnamon. Surround the birds with some of the apple quarters and cover with the remainder. Pour over a little of the hot butter the apples were cooked in. Cover the casserole and bake in a moderate oven for 20 minutes. Pour the crème fraîche and calvados over the partridges and apples. Reheat in the oven, then serve immediately.

Red wine: light, fruity bordeaux.

'ROAST' PARTRIDGE

Preparation 30 minutes • Cooking 15–18 minutes

US	Ingredients	Met/Imp
2 oz	bacon	50 g/2 oz
2 or 3	game livers	2 or 3
1	thyme sprig	1
¼	bay leaf	¼
5 tbsp	butter	60 g/2½ oz
4	partridges	4
4	vine (grape) leaves	4
4	bacon slices for barding	4
	salt and pepper	
4	croûtons, cut the same size as the birds	4
1	bunch watercress	1
	Straw Potatoes (page 552)	

Make a Gratin Stuffing (*page 54*), using the diced bacon, game livers, thyme and bay leaf. Cook all the ingredients in butter until firm, leave to cool, then pound together, and set aside.

Trim the partridges, reserving the giblets. Wrap each partridge in a vine (grape) leaf and a slice of bacon. Season with salt and pepper. Place them in a flameproof casserole with some butter, and 'roast' them over a high heat for 15–18 minutes or until tender but still slightly rare. Use the giblets to make a very thick stock. Do not skim the stock and use to deglaze the pan the partridges were cooked in. (If you are unable to make this stock, or prefer not to, add a dash of cognac to the pan instead, just before you remove the partridges.)

Fry the bread croûtons, in the same butter in which you have cooked the partridges, then spread with the gratin stuffing.

Place the partridges on the croûtons spread with stuffing on a heated serving dish and arrange a bunch of watercress on one side and some straw potatoes on the other. Pour the sauce into a sauce boat. The partridges and croûtons are cut in half to serve.

Red wine: light, fruity bordeaux.

SANGLIER

WILD BOAR

THIS 'BÊTE NOIR', AS IT IS KNOWN BY THOSE WHO HUNT IT, HAS a delicate flavour, which becomes stronger with age; it is very marked in an adult boar. Up to 6 months old, the animal is called 'marcassin', from 6 months to 2 years it is called 'bête rousse'; between 1 and 2 years old it is called 'bête de compagnie'. Animals over 2 years old, called 'ragot', 'tiers-an', 'quartenier', 'porc entier' and 'solitaire', are hardly used any more in cooking. The flesh of a boar 6 months old or younger does not need to be marinated, while that of an older boar should be marinated for 5–8 hours. All venison and pork recipes are suitable for wild boar, but only an animal 6 months old or younger can be roasted. Highly seasoned wild boar stews are particularly delicious. The smaller new world peccary can be used for wild boar in all these recipes.

FILET DE MARCASSIN

——— FILLET OF YOUNG WILD BOAR ———

Preparation 1 hour • Marinating 48 hours • Cooking 3½ hours

US	Ingredients	Met/Imp
3 lb	young wild boar fillet (tenderloin)	1.5 kg/3 lb
	good red wine	
	fresh herbs, to taste	
1 stick	butter	100 g/4 oz
2 tsp	salt	10 ml/2 tsp
4	peppercorns, crushed	4
2 glasses	blood (preferably calf's or pig's)	2 glasses
1 tbsp	redcurrant jelly	15 ml/1 tbsp
1 glass	cognac	1 glass

Carefully remove all the sinews from the wild boar meat, then put in a bowl and cover with the red wine. Add plenty of herbs and leave to marinate for at least 48 hours. Remove from the marinade, wipe dry with paper towels and place in a flameproof casserole with the butter. Cook until well browned, then add 3 glasses of the marinade. Add the salt and peppercorns, cover and cook gently for at least 3 hours.

Remove the meat from the pan and thicken the sauce by adding first the blood, then the redcurrant jelly. Cook for 3–4 minutes. Pour over the cognac and flambé. Return to the stove for 2 minutes.

Red wines: Côte de Nuits, Côte Rôtie, Hermitage, Châteauneuf-du-Pape.

LEG OF YOUNG WILD BOAR WITH GIN

Preparation 2 hours • Marinating 48 hours • Cooking 1¼ hours

US	Ingredients	Met/Imp
I	leg of young wild boar	I
	Marinade (*page 59*)	
7 oz	fatty bacon, cut into thin strips	200 g/7 oz
10–14 tbsp	butter	150–200 g/5–7 oz
½ cup	gin	100 ml/4 fl oz
a few	juniper berries	a few
¼ cup	double (heavy) cream	50 ml/2 fl oz
	salt and pepper	

Leave the meat in the marinade for 48 hours, wipe dry, then lard with the thin strips of bacon. Roast in butter, leaving the meat somewhat rare. Skim the fat from the cooking juices, add the gin and flambé. Add the juniper berries and cream and cook until reduced. Season with salt and pepper.

This dish may be accompanied by a slightly sweetened apple compote.

Red wines: Côte de Beaune, Côte Rôtie, Châteauneuf-du-Pape.

SADDLE OF YOUNG WILD BOAR BORDELAISE

Preparation 2 hours • Cooking sauce 5 minutes; Meat about 50 minutes

US	Ingredients	Met/Imp
2 quarts	Cooked Marinade (*page 59*)	2 litres/3½ pints
	salt and pepper	
I	saddle young wild boar	I
¼ lb	fatty bacon, cut into thin strips	100 g/4 oz
I stick	butter	100 g/4 oz
4	carrots	4
I	onion	I
I	garlic clove	I
½ cup	flour	70 g/3 oz
I bottle	red bordeaux wine	I bottle
I	bouquet garni	I
½ cup	olive oil	100 ml/4 fl oz
¼ cup	armagnac	50 ml/2 fl oz
I tbsp	raspberry or redcurrant jelly	15 ml/1 tbsp
2 lb	chestnuts	I kg/2 lb
	good-quality butter, to finish	

Prepare the marinade and season with salt and pepper and herbs. Leave to cool.

Trim the meat and remove the sinews. Lard with strips of bacon, threading them crossways – the opposite way to a fillet (tenderloin) of beef. Brush all over with the marinade, then leave to marinate for 48 hours, together with the bones and scraps from the meat.

Start to prepare the sauce the day before the meal. Using a few trimmings from the bacon and some butter, brown the sliced carrots and onion, the garlic and the scraps and bones from the meat. Sprinkle with flour and make a good brown roux. Moisten with the bottle of red bordeaux and half of the marinade; add the bouquet garni. Cook gently for about 5 hours, skimming frequently.

Roast the meat at a suitable time, first rinsing it and tying it into a neat shape. Roast in a very hot oven to begin with, then reduce the oven temperature to moderate and cook until tender but still a little bit rare – 50 minutes in all. Use olive oil for basting. Meanwhile, skim the surface of the sauce to remove the impurities and return to the heat.

When the meat is cooked, remove it from the pan and pour off the fat. Deglaze the pan with the armagnac and a ladleful of the marinade. Cook until reduced by half, then strain through a conical sieve and add to the sauce. Bring to the boil again and taste: it should be highly flavoured. Add plenty of freshly ground pepper and continue cooking until reduced to about 750 ml/1¼ pints (3 cups). The sauce should be very liquid and glossy. Strain it through a conical sieve again, then, off the heat, add the redcurrant or raspberry jelly, and some butter cut into small pieces. Arrange the chestnuts around the meat. Pour a little sauce over them but not over the meat. This should be coated in melted butter.

Red wines: Côte de Nuits, Côte Rôtie, Hermitage, Châteauneuf-du-Pape.

SARCELLE

TEAL

THE TEAL IS A BIRD BELONGING TO THE DUCK FAMILY. LIKE the scoter duck, it was permitted by the church during times of fasting. Its oily flesh, which is rather difficult to digest, is appreciated by some but not others. Shot in France between September and May, it is prepared in the same way as other wild duck, ie it is normally roasted or made into a *salmi*.

US	Ingredients	Met/Imp
2	oranges, zest of	2
2	bay leaves	2
2	teal	2
	salt and pepper	
11	garlic cloves	11
2	bacon slices, for barding	2
I tbsp	olive oil	15 ml/I tbsp
2	onions	2
	flour	
I glass	dry white wine	I glass
I	lemon	I
2	Seville oranges	2
I pinch	saffron	I pinch
I glass	hot stock	I glass

SARCELLES À LA CATALANE

TEAL CATALAN

Preparation 1¼ hours • Cooking 50 minutes

Place the zest of 1 orange and a bay leaf on the breast of each bird. Rub them with salt and pepper, and 1 of the garlic cloves, crushed. Bard with the bacon.

Heat the olive oil in a flameproof casserole and brown the teal all over. Add the chopped onions, sprinkle with flour and moisten with white wine.

Cut the lemon and Seville oranges into, thick round slices; plunge into boiling water. Drain and add to the casserole containing the teal, together with the remaining 10 garlic cloves, peeled, and the saffron diluted in some of the stock. Finally, add the remaining hot stock. Cover the pan and simmer for 40 minutes.

Red wines: Corbières, Costières du Gard.

VEGETABLES

&

GARNISHES

WE READ IN OLD BOOKS THAT AT ONE TIME people used to live on 'herbs and roots'. However, it is worth bearing in mind that all vegetables growing below ground used to be called roots and all those above ground were given the name of herb, and that there were considerably more roots and, particularly, herbs than today, even though the potato had not yet been cultivated in Europe. This tuber eventually acquired an almost excessive importance in cooking, at the expense of other vegetables which have more flavour and blend better with other ingredients.

Vegetables are often used simply as an accompaniment, which is a pity given the variety they offer throughout the year. This shows real lack of imagination, because all vegetables, from the modest leek to the delicate asparagus, and the essential and versatile carrot and cabbage, are so rich in surprises. Now, more and more chefs are rediscovering the virtues of vegetables and making best possible use of them. Vegetables that were once used merely as a garnish are now finding their true place in cooking, both as an appetizer and as part of a main course. The nutritional and therapeutic value of vegetables as important sources of vitamins, minerals, fibre and water has of course long been well known.

ARTICHAUT

GLOBE ARTICHOKE

THE SEASON FOR THIS SUPERIOR TYPE OF THISTLE LASTS FROM March to November. Only the bottom (*fond*), sometimes also called the heart, and a part of the leaves are eaten, and they are always cooked, unless they are the very small artichokes which are served raw just with salt (*à la croque au sel*) or with a vinaigrette dressing (*à la poivrade*). The main varieties are the large, flat type from Brittany, the Bordeaux 'macau', the small Provençal 'pepper' artichoke and the Rhône valley 'purple' artichoke. A good artichoke should be heavy; the leaves should be brittle and compact, and free of blemishes. To prevent artichoke bottoms from turning brown, rub them with lemon juice or put them into water with lemon juice added, but do not leave for long or their delicate flavour will be impaired.

ARTICHAUTS À LA BARIGOULE

———— ARTICHOKES BARIGOULE ————

Preparation, including resting, about 1 hour • Cooking about 45 minutes

US	Ingredients	Met/Imp
2 quarts	water	2 litres/3½ pints
2	lemons, juice of	2
12	small artichokes with pointed leaves	12
2	large slices cooked ham	2
1 cup	fresh white breadcrumbs	1 teacup
3	garlic cloves	3
3	shallots	3
1 good handful	parsley	1 good handful
	salt and pepper	
1 glass	olive oil	1 glass

Pour the water into a large bowl and add the lemon juice.

Trim the artichokes, discarding the coarse outer leaves. Cut away the tender leaves about 1 cm/½ inch from the bottom and carefully scrape out the choke. As each artichoke is ready, put it into the acidulated water to prevent discoloration.

Make the stuffing. Mince (grind) the ham and put it into a bowl. Add the breadcrumbs, finely chopped garlic, shallots and parsley. Season lightly with salt and a pinch of pepper and mix well. Remove the artichokes from the acidulated water one at a time. Drain and stuff, spreading the stuffing out as evenly as possible.

Pour the oil into a saucepan, add 1 glass water and bring to the boil. Put in the artichokes. Cover and cook over a high heat for about 15 minutes, then lower the heat and cook very gently for about 45 minutes or until the artichokes are tender, checking them from time to time. When most of the cooking liquid has evaporated, baste each artichoke with a little of the remaining liquid. Turn off the heat and leave the artichokes to rest for 30 minutes in the saucepan before serving.

US	Ingredients	Met/Imp
12	small 'pepper' artichokes	12
1	lemon, juice of	1
½ cup	olive oil	100 ml/4 fl oz
	salt and pepper	
1 quart	shelled freshly picked peas	1 litre/1¾ pints
2	lettuces, coarsely shredded	2

— PEPPER ARTICHOKES PROVENÇAL* —

Preparation 40 minutes • Cooking 1¼ hours

Trim the artichokes to the bottom, removing the leaves and choke. Slice the bottoms into rings if large. Sprinkle with the lemon juice, then wipe dry. Heat the olive oil in a saucepan, add the artichokes, season with salt and pepper and cook gently for 15 minutes. Add the peas and lettuce and cook for about another hour, covered, until tender. Do not add any water. Serve straight from the cooking pan.

FONDS D'ARTICHAUTS AU CÉLERI ET À LA CRÈME

ARTICHOKE BOTTOMS WITH CELERY AND CREAM

Preparation 1 hour • Cooking 20 minutes

US	Ingredients	Met/Imp
20	fresh artichoke bottoms	20
1½ sticks	butter	175 g/6 oz
2	onions	2
½ lb	celery	250 g/8 oz
2 tbsp	flour	20 g/¾ oz
scant 1 cup	milk, boiled	200 ml/7 fl oz
	salt and pepper	
1 pinch	nutmeg	1 pinch
scant 1 cup	crème fraîche	200 ml/7 fl oz
1 tbsp	chopped parsley	15 ml/1 tbsp

Blanch the artichoke bottoms in boiling water, then drain and fry lightly in 50 g/2 oz (4 tbsp) of the butter, until tender.

Meanwhile, chop the onions and celery very finely and fry gently in half of the remaining butter until the celery is very soft. Add the flour, the boiled milk, a pinch of salt, a very small pinch of pepper and the nutmeg. Bring to the boil, stirring, then cook gently for 20 minutes. Rub through a sieve or strain through a cloth. Put the purée into a saucepan, add the crème fraîche and boil for 1 minute.

Cut each artichoke bottom into 3 slices, stir into the purée and heat gently, but do not allow to boil. Remove the pan from the heat and add the remaining butter, diced, shaking the pan to mix in the butter. Pour into a warmed serving dish and sprinkle the parsley on top to serve.

GRATIN DE FONDS D'ARTICHAUTS AUX ASPERGES

ARTICHOKE BOTTOM AND ASPARAGUS GRATIN

Preparation 1 hour • Cooking about 1 hour

US	Ingredients	Met/Imp
8	large artichokes	8
10 tbsp	butter	150 g/5 oz
1¾ lb	green asparagus spears	800 g/1¾ lb
	salt and pepper	
1 pinch	nutmeg	1 pinch
2 cups	Mornay Sauce (page 73)	500 ml/18 fl oz
½ cup	Dry Duxelles (page 49)	100 ml/4 fl oz
¾ cup	Gruyère cheese, grated	75 g/3 oz

Boil the artichokes for about 35 minutes or until the leaves come away easily. Drain and rinse. Remove the leaves and chokes and trim the bottoms. Cut each bottom into 3 slices, arrange in a shallow pan and braise with 40 g/1½ oz (3 tbsp) of the butter for 10 minutes.

Cut the asparagus into pieces 3 cm/1¼ inches long. About 20 minutes before serving, cook them in boiling salted water until tender but still slightly crisp. When cooked, drain well and place over a high heat until all the water has evaporated. Season with a pinch each of salt, pepper and nutmeg. Remove the pan from the heat and toss carefully in 75 g/3 oz (6 tbsp) of the remaining butter.

Mix the Mornay sauce with the duxelles. Spread a little of this sauce in

the bottom of 4 individual gratin dishes. Arrange the artichoke bottoms in a circle on top and place the asparagus tips in the centre. Cover with the remaining sauce. Sprinkle with the grated cheese and the remaining butter, melted. Brown in a hot oven and serve at once.

PETITS ARTICHAUTS À LA GRECQUE

— SMALL ARTICHOKES À LA GRECQUE —

Preparation 15 minutes • Cooking 20 minutes

Cut the stems off the artichokes. Trim the leaves with kitchen scissors. Cut the artichokes into quarters and remove the chokes. Peel the onions.

Heat the oil in a saucepan, add the wine, water, spices, herbs, tomato paste, lemon juice and salt to taste. Add the artichokes and onions. Bring to the boil, then cook, uncovered, over a high heat for about 20 minutes or until some of the liquid has evaporated and the artichokes and onions are tender. Serve cold, garnished with black olives.

US	Ingredients	Met/Imp
6	small artichokes	6
6	button (pearl) onions	6
¼ cup	olive oil	50 ml/2 fl oz
½ cup	white wine	100 ml/4 fl oz
½ cup	water	100 ml/4 fl oz
8	coriander seeds	8
10	peppercorns	10
1	thyme sprig	1
1	bay leaf	1
1	fennel sprig	1
1 tsp	tomato paste	5 ml/1 tsp
1	lemon, juice of	1
	salt	
	GARNISH	
12	black olives	12

PURÉE D'ARTICHAUTS À LA BÉCHAMEL

PURÉED ARTICHOKES WITH BÉCHAMEL —

Preparation 1 hour • Cooking about 1¾ hours

Trim the artichokes to the bottom, removing the leaves and the choke. Toss the bottoms in the lemon juice. Blend the flour with a little cold water in a saucepan, add 1 litre/2 pints (1 quart) water, season with salt and bring to the boil. Add the artichoke bottoms and the bouquet garni and cook until tender. Drain and rinse under cold running water, then slice them thinly. Braise in the butter to finish.

Meanwhile, reduce the béchamel or velouté with the crème fraîche until very thick, then strain through cheesecloth.

Work the artichokes through a fine sieve, then mix with the sauce using a wooden spoon. Add the nutmeg and check the seasoning. Serve in a heated dish surrounded by a border of fleurons.

US	Ingredients	Met/Imp
8	large 'Brittany' artichokes	8
2	lemons, juice of	2
3 tbsp	flour	25 g/scant 1 oz
	salt	
1	bouquet garni	1
4 tbsp	butter	50 g/2 oz
1 cup	Béchamel Sauce (page 62) or Chicken Velouté (page 57)	200 ml/7 fl oz
½ cup	crème fraîche	100 ml/3½ fl oz
1 pinch	nutmeg	1 pinch
	GARNISH	
	puff pastry *fleurons*	

ASPARAGUS

OF ALL VEGETABLES, ASPARAGUS HAS THE MOST DISTINCT season: from March to the end of June in France. The main varieties available in France are white Argenteuil asparagus with purple tips; green Lauris asparagus (highly valued but rare); purple Italian asparagus; and white jumbo asparagus, which is tender but relatively tasteless. Green asparagus always has a better flavour and is more delicate than the white variety, with particularly delicious tips. Cooked, asparagus should be slightly crunchy, never soft. A warm Hollandaise or mousseline sauce goes beautifully with asparagus, but even when served with a cold sauce or French dressing, it should be served hot (but not too hot), as it has more flavour this way.

To cook asparagus, tie the stalks (which should preferably be the same size) in medium bundles and stand upright, if possible, in a large saucepan of water. The tips should be out of the water so that they cook in the steam: this keeps them crisp. Cooking time depends on the freshness, ripeness and size of the asparagus.

When choosing asparagus, look for smooth, brittle stalks; they should never be yellow. As asparagus is expensive, it deserves careful preparation, either as an appetizer or as a garnish for fish or mild-flavoured meat. The tips in particular are excellent in braised spring and early summer vegetable mixtures.

ASPERGES À LA FLAMANDE

ASPARAGUS FLAMANDE*

Preparation 1 hour • Cooking 22–25 minutes

US	Ingredients	Met/Imp
9 lb	asparagus, peeled and cut into short pieces	4 kg/9 lb
	salt and pepper	
½ lb (2 sticks)	butter, melted	225 g/8 oz
4	egg yolks, hard-boiled	4
8 tbsp	chopped parsley	120 ml/8 tbsp

Cook the asparagus in boiling salted water. Drain. Serve with a sauce boat of melted butter, allowing about 30 g/1 oz (2 tbsp) per person, half a warm hard-boiled egg yolk per person and a dish of chopped parsley.

Each guest makes up his own sauce of the butter, egg yolk, parsley and salt and pepper.

The egg yolks may also be mashed in a bowl and mixed with the melted butter, salt and pepper and served in a sauce boat. Sometimes the hard-boiled eggs are served whole, with both white and yolk.

ASPARAGUS WITH PARMESAN

Preparation 1 hour • Cooking about 40 minutes

US	Ingredients	Met/Imp
9 lb	asparagus, peeled and tied in 8 bundles	4 kg/9 lb
	salt	
14 tbsp	butter, diced	200 g/7 oz
1¾ cups	Parmesan cheese, grated	200 g/7 oz

Cook the asparagus in boiling salted water. Drain and discard all the tough parts. Arrange in an ovenproof dish, alternating with layers of butter and grated cheese. Finish with butter and cheese.

Brown in a very low oven.

ASPARAGUS SOUFFLÉ

Preparation 25 minutes • Cooking 25 minutes

US	Ingredients	Met/Imp
2 lb	white Argenteuil asparagus	1 kg/2 lb
	salt and pepper	
3	eggs, separated	3
	grated cheese	

Cook the asparagus in boiling salted water. Drain and discard the tough parts.

Put the egg yolks into a bowl and add the grated cheese, mixing until smooth. Season with salt and pepper. Beat the egg whites until stiff and gently fold into the cheese mixture

Put the asparagus into an ovenproof dish. Top with the soufflé mixture, bake in the oven and serve at once.

AUBERGINE

THERE IS NO RATATOUILLE WITHOUT AUBERGINE (EGGPLANT), which is of Indian origin with a Persian name. But this attractive purple vegetable, the colour of which varies in intensity, lends itself well to other recipes when it is often combined with tomato and garlic, and lamb. Sometimes it is also used for stuffings, or as a case for small birds such as pigeon.

Before cooking, aubergines (eggplants) are often sprinkled with salt and left to *dégorge* for about 20 minutes to draw out the moisture. Naturally low in calories, this vegetable becomes the reverse if fried or cooked in oil as it readily absorbs fat.

The principal varieties of aubergine (eggplant) in France are the long, oval 'barbentane', the violet but whiter-fleshed Toulouse variety (good for stuffing), the round, firm-fleshed Valence, the short round 'baluroi', the plump 'bonica' and the unusual, white 'dourga', which has a very delicate flavour.

AUBERGINES STUFFED WITH MUSHROOMS AND PARSLEY

Preparation 1 hour • Cooking about 15 minutes

US	Ingredients	Met/Imp
8	aubergines (eggplants)	8
	olive oil, for frying	
6	shallots	6
10 oz	cooked ham	300 g/10 oz
¼ lb	button mushrooms	100 g/4 oz
	salt and pepper	
2 cups	Demi-Glaze (page 56)	500 ml/18 fl oz
4 cups	fresh white breadcrumbs	250 g/8 oz
2 tbsp	chopped parsley	30 ml/2 tbsp
I stick	butter	100 g/4 oz

A little tomato sauce may be added to the stuffing mixture if liked.

Cut the aubergines (eggplants) in half lengthways and fry in oil for about 10 minutes, until tender. Scoop out the flesh, making sure the shells remain intact, and reserve most of it.

Finely chop the shallots and fry briefly, add the minced (ground) ham and a few minutes later the finely chopped mushrooms. Season with salt and pepper. Cook until the liquid from the mushrooms has evaporated, then add the demi-glaze and simmer.

Mash the reserved aubergine (eggplant) flesh and mix into the pan. Stir in 150 g/5 oz (2½ cups) of breadcrumbs. Add half of the parsley, then taste and adjust the seasoning.

Fill the aubergine (eggplant) shells with the stuffing and arrange in a buttered gratin dish. Sprinkle the remaining breadcrumbs on top, dot with butter and brown in a hot oven.

Sprinkle the remaining parsley on top before serving. If liked, pour some good meat juices around the base.

AUBERGINES SAUTÉED WITH BACON AND HAM

Preparation 3 hours including draining • Cooking about 1 hour 20 minutes

US	Ingredients	Met/Imp
16	large aubergines (eggplants)	16
	salt	
14 tbsp	butter	200 g/7 oz
¼ lb	cooked ham	100 g/4 oz
¼ lb	bacon	100 g/4 oz
3½ tbsp	onions, finely chopped	50 g/2 oz
6 cups	fresh breadcrumbs	350 g/12 oz
scant 1 cup	milk	200 ml/7 fl oz
1 tbsp	chopped parsley and garlic	15 ml/1 tbsp

Halve the aubergines (eggplants), remove the seeds, then chop the flesh finely. Sprinkle with salt and leave to *dégorge* for 3 hours, then rinse.

Cook the aubergines (eggplants) in boiling salted water for about 10 minutes until tender, then drain and mash or process to a purée. Melt 100 g/4 oz (8 tbsp) of the butter in a frying pan. Add the finely chopped ham, bacon and onions and fry until softened. Add the aubergine (eggplant) purée and 250 g/9 oz (4½ cups) of the breadcrumbs, soaked in the milk and well squeezed out. Stir in the chopped parsley and garlic. Sauté over a high heat for 10 minutes, stirring continuously.

Spread the purée in a buttered ovenproof dish, sprinkle the top with the remaining breadcrumbs and dot with the remaining butter. Brown in a hot oven.

SOUFFLÉED AUBERGINES

Preparation 35 minutes • Cooking 1 hour •Serves 4

US	Ingredients	Met/Imp
4	aubergines (eggplants)	4
	olive oil	
2 tbsp	butter	30 g/1 oz
3 tbsp	flour	30 g/1 oz
1 cup	milk	250 ml/9 fl oz
	salt and pepper	
	nutmeg	
½ cup	Comté cheese, grated	50 g/2 oz
2	eggs, separated	2

Remove the stalks from the aubergines (eggplants), wash them and slice them in half lengthways, working quickly to prevent discoloration of the flesh. Score a criss-cross pattern on the flesh with a sharp knife, to speed up the cooking. Put the aubergines (eggplants) cut sides down into the hot oil in a frying pan. Cook for 7–10 minutes, then turn and cook for a further 5 minutes. Cool slightly.

Make the sauce. Melt the butter, add the flour and cook over a low heat for 5 minutes, stirring, then pour in the milk. Simmer for 10 minutes, stirring continuously. Season with salt, pepper and a little nutmeg. Stir in three-quarters of the cheese.

Gently scoop out the aubergine (eggplant) flesh without tearing the skins and leaving a little flesh at the stalk end so that they retain their shape. Mash the flesh with a fork, working quickly so that the flesh does not turn brown.

Stir the cheese sauce into the mashed aubergine (eggplant). Add the egg yolks. Whisk the egg whites until stiff and fold in gently. Arrange the aubergine (eggplant) shells in an ovenproof dish and fill with the soufflé mixture. Sprinkle with the remaining cheese and cook in a moderate oven for 25 minutes until the filling is puffy and golden. Serve at once.

AUBERGINE CURRY

Preparation 1 hour • Cooking 40 minutes

US	Ingredients	Met/Imp
¼ lb	bacon	125 g/4½ oz
2	large onions	2
¼ cup	olive oil	50 ml/2 fl oz
2 lb	aubergines (eggplants)	1.2 kg/2 lb
2 tsp	curry powder	10 ml/2 tsp
	salt	
1¼ cups	stock	300 ml/½ pint

Chop the bacon. Finely chop the onions. Put the oil into a saucepan over a low heat and fry the bacon and onions for 10 minutes until translucent.

Remove the stalks from the aubergines (eggplants), wash them and dice them finely.

Add the curry powder, then the aubergines (eggplants), to the onions. Season with salt and mix well. Add about half of the stock, cover and braise for 30–40 minutes, stirring from time to time and adding a little more stock when necessary. Serve in a heated dish.

CARDON

CARDOON

A COUSIN OF THE ARTICHOKE, THIS VEGETABLE IS LITTLE known or appreciated today, except in the Lyons area of France where it used to be popular and is still cultivated. It deserves a renewal of favour.

Cardoons are usually served as a garnish for roasts or braised meat, but may also be cooked in a gratin, stock or sauce. Only the white inner stalks and the heart are edible. The outer stalks are discarded (they are generally hollow or too coarse), then the fibres of the remaining stalks must be carefully removed, along with any woody parts from the heart. Sprinkle the cardoons with lemon juice immediately after preparation, then put into fresh water with lemon juice added to it. This is essential to prevent discoloration, as the cardoons must stay white.

BRAISED CARDOONS AND CARDOONS AU GRATIN

Preparation 1 hour • Cooking 1½–2 hours

US	Ingredients	Met/Imp
I	head cardoons	I
6 tbsp	flour	50 g/2 oz
2 quarts	water	2 litres/3½ pints
2	lemons, juice of	2
scant ½ lb	veal kidney fat	200 g/7 oz
	salt	

Prepare the cardoons as described (*left*) and cut into pieces about 10 cm/4 inches long. Cook until barely tender in a *blanc* (blanching liquid) made by mixing the flour with the water and adding the juice of both lemons. Add the kidney fat and salt (the cardoon has watery flesh and needs to be cooked in a fairly rich and fatty stock).

For braised cardoons, prepare a stock base with vegetables. Drain the cardoons from the *blanc* (blanching liquid), pat dry and simmer in the stock.

For cardoons au gratin, drain and dry well. Lightly fry in butter with salt and pepper. Put a little butter and a spoonful of Mornay sauce in the bottom of an ovenproof dish. Arrange the cardoons on top and coat completely with more Mornay sauce. Sprinkle with grated cheese, breadcrumbs and melted butter and brown in the oven.

CARDONS À LA MOELLE

CARDOONS WITH BEEF MARROW

Preparation 1 hour • Cooking 1½–2 hours

US	Ingredients	Met/Imp
3 tbsp	flour	30 g/1 oz
3 quarts	water	3 litres/5¼ pints
2	lemons	2
	salt and pepper	
a few	peppercorns	a few
2	carrots	2
I	onion	I
	cloves	
I	bouquet garni	I
¼ cup	wine vinegar	50 ml/2 fl oz
I	head cardoons	I
¼ cup	oil	50 ml/2 fl oz
14 oz	beef marrow	400 g/14 oz
½ bottle	red wine	½ bottle
2 tbsp	chopped shallot	30 ml/2 tbsp
2 cups	Demi-Glaze (page 56)	500 ml/18 fl oz
scant I cup	Veal Stock (page 56)	200 ml/7 fl oz
I stick	butter	100 g/4 oz

Blend the flour with the cold water and the pared zest and juice of both lemons. Add salt, the peppercorns, carrots, the onion spiked with cloves, the bouquet garni and vinegar. Bring to the boil.

Prepare the cardoons as described (*left*) and add to the boiling flour and water liquid. Add the oil, which will float on the surface of the liquid and prevent air getting to the cardoons so that they do not turn black. (A cloth laid on the surface of the liquid can be used for the same purpose.)

Slice the marrow into rings and poach in a separate pan of salted water. Reduce the red wine with the shallots to 125 ml/4½ fl oz (½ cup). Add the demi-glaze and veal stock.

Drain the cardoons well and place in a large saucepan. Strain the red wine sauce over them and simmer until tender.

To serve, arrange the cardoon stalks in a heated serving dish. Arrange overlapping marrow rings and cardoon hearts on top. Strain the sauce again into another saucepan. Beat in the butter in small pieces and add a little pepper. Taste and adjust seasoning. The sauce should be a glossy, rich brown colour.

CAROTTE

CARROT

AFTER THE POTATO, THE CARROT IS UNDOUBTEDLY THE MOST commonly used vegetable. Either raw or cooked, it is irreplaceable both for its nutritional value and vitamins and its role in cooking: grated raw, braised, glazed as a garnish, added to stews and meat dishes, ingredient of the *brunoise* or *mirepoix*, not to mention its use in soups, ragoûts, purées and vegetable 'gâteaux'.

Its two main seasons are spring (delicious small 'grelots', the tops of which are used in soups) and winter (long, less sweet, larger and more woody). Particular mention must be made of the Créances carrot (in season from the end of August to the end of May), which is guaranteed by a special seal, and the Crécy carrot, named after the town of Crécy in the Île-de-France which is renowned for its carrots. The more orange a carrot is, the more sweet and tender. New carrots are scraped and not peeled, then washed and wiped dry immediately. Winter carrots are thinly peeled and the centre is discarded if it is coarse and rather yellow.

BRAISED CARROTS WITH ONIONS BOURGEOIS

Preparation 10 minutes • Cooking about 1 hour

US	Ingredients	Met/Imp
1 lb	carrots	500 g/1 lb
½ lb	onions	200 g/7 oz
5 tbsp	butter	60 g/2½ oz
	salt	
	sugar	
	flour	
scant 1 cup	milk	200 ml/7 fl oz
1¾ cups	stock	400 ml/14 fl oz
	pepper	
	nutmeg	
2	egg yolks	2
1 tbsp	chopped parsley	15 ml/1 tbsp

Peel, wash and cut the carrots into thin rings of uniform size. Finely slice the onions.

Put the carrots into a large saucepan and, add the butter cut into small pieces with a little salt and sugar. Braise, uncovered, over a low heat for 30 minutes, stirring frequently to prevent sticking. Do not allow to brown.

Sprinkle in a little flour, stirring carefully, and cook for 2 minutes, then add the milk and stock mixed together. Bring to the boil, stirring gently. Add pepper and nutmeg to taste and simmer, uncovered, over a very low heat for a further 15–20 minutes, until the sauce is thickened. Bind with the egg yolks 5 minutes before serving. Taste and adjust the seasoning, sprinkle with the parsley and serve very hot.

SUGAR-GLAZED NEW CARROTS

Preparation 40 minutes • Cooking about 1 hour

US	Ingredients	Met/Imp
14 tbsp	butter	200 g/7 oz
4½ lb	new carrots	2 kg/4½ lb
4	sugar cubes	4
	salt	
½ cup	cognac	100 ml/4 fl oz
1 tbsp	chopped parsley	15 ml/1 tbsp

Heat the butter in a saucepan, add the washed and diced carrots, the sugar and salt to taste. Cover with buttered paper and a lid and cook over a low heat until tender.

Add the cognac 10 minutes before the carrots are cooked. Serve sprinkled with chopped parsley. The carrots should be golden and shiny.

PETITS GÂTEAUX DE CAROTTES

LITTLE CARROT CUSTARDS

Preparation 1¼ hours • Cooking 1½ hours • Serves 6

US	Ingredients	Met/Imp
1	onion	1
3 tbsp	butter	40 g/1½ oz
13 oz	carrots	375 g/13 oz
2 cups	stock	500 ml/18 fl oz
	salt and pepper	
6	eggs	6
⅔ cup	milk	150 ml/¼ pint
2 tbsp	chopped parsley	30 ml/2 tbsp
1 large pinch	nutmeg	1 good pinch
1½ cups	fresh breadcrumbs	75 g/3 oz

Finely chop the onion and fry in half of the butter. Coarsely grate the carrots into strips about 5 mm/¼ inch wide. Add to the onion and stir well. Add the stock, salt and pepper and cook, uncovered, over a high heat until there is only scant 4 tbsp liquid left in the pan.

Meanwhile, beat the eggs with the milk and stir in the parsley and nutmeg.

Grease 6 ramekins with the remaining butter. Mix the beaten eggs with the carrots and the cooking liquid. This should be done gradually to prevent curdling. Stir in the breadcrumbs.

Fill the ramekins with the mixture. Stand them in a *bain-marie* and bring the water to the boil. Cook in a moderate oven for 35–40 minutes, or until a needle inserted into each one comes out clean.

PURÉE DE CAROTTES À LA BRIARDE

CARROT PURÉE FROM THE BRIE REGION

Preparation 45 minutes • Cooking 1 hour

US	Ingredients	Met/Imp
1	onion	1
14 tbsp	butter	200 g/7 oz
4½ lb	carrots, preferably Crécy	2 kg/4½ lb
1 quart	stock	1 litre/1¾ pints
	salt	
	sugar	
1	bouquet garni	1
1 cup	long-grain rice	200 g/7 oz

Sweat the chopped onion in 50 g/2 oz (4 tbsp) of the butter, add the finely chopped carrots, then some of the stock, the salt, sugar and bouquet garni. Cover with buttered paper and a lid and cook gently.

When half-cooked, stir in the well-washed rice. Add more stock, replace the buttered paper and finish cooking in a moderately hot oven. Check from time to time that there is enough liquid, but not too much (it is better to add more at the end).

Remove the bouquet garni, rub the mixture through a sieve and beat with a wooden spoon. Add the remaining butter and adjust the seasoning.

CÉLERI

CELERY

'CÉLERI' IS A GENERAL TERM USED TO DESCRIBE BOTH CELERY and celeriac. In fact, celeriac is a root, and stick celery is characterized by long, leafy stalks. However, these two vegetables with their distinctive taste belong to the same family. Celeriac is most often eaten raw and grated with a *rémoulade* or *fines herbes* sauce, although when braised or puréed it is superior to the potato and goes particularly well with game. Celery, valued for its qualities as a stimulant, enjoys a better reputation. Cooked, it goes well with meat, especially poultry; raw, it is used in salads and its flavour complements certain types of cheese, especially blue cheese. Its leaves may be used to flavour stocks.

CÉLERIS EN BRANCHES AU JUS LIÉ

BRAISED CELERY

Preparation 45 minutes • Cooking 2 hours

US	Ingredients	Met/Imp
4	heads celery	4
½	carrot	½
1	onion	1
1	bouquet garni	1
1 quart	stock	1 litre/1¾ pints
3 oz	bacon	75 g/3 oz
scant 1 cup	cold Veal Stock (*page 56*)	200 ml/7 fl oz
2 tsp	potato flour	10 ml/2 tsp
3 tbsp	butter	40 g/1½ oz

If there is no veal stock available, use light brown stock. Braised celery keeps very well and it does not take much longer to cook twice the amount needed for immediate use.

Discard the tough, outer stalks from the celery. Trim off the ends of the stalks level where the white part ends so that the celery is about 15 cm/6 inches long. With a potato peeler or sharp knife, trim the root end into an oval shape.

Wash the celery thoroughly and plunge it into a saucepan of boiling water. Bring back to the boil and cook for 12 minutes, then drain and rinse. Drain again and shake well. Tie around each head with string.

Put the carrot and the onion cut into rings into a saucepan just big enough to hold the celery. Add the bouquet garni. Place the celery in the pan, cover with very lightly salted stock and add the bacon, chopped. Bring to the boil. Place a sheet of buttered paper on top, cover and cook very gently for about 2 hours, then test the celery to see if it is tender.

When the celery is cooked, drain and remove the string. Cut the heads in half lengthways and put into another saucepan. Measure out 200 ml/7 fl oz (scant 1 cup) of the cooking liquid and reduce by half. Skim off all the fat, add all but 30 ml/2 tbsp of veal stock and bring to the boil. Thicken with potato flour blended with the reserved cold stock. Cover the celery with this liquid and simmer for 10–12 minutes.

Remove the pieces of celery from the cooking liquid and arrange overlapping in a heated serving dish. Finish the sauce off the heat by beating in the butter, then pour over the celery.

CÉLERI-RAVES AU JUS

BRAISED CELERIAC

Preparation 20 minutes • Cooking about 1 hour

US	Ingredients	Met/Imp
4	heads celeriac	4
	salt	
1 stick	butter	100 g/4 oz
2 cups	good Veal Stock (page 56)	500 ml/18 fl oz

Peel and wash the celeriac. Cut in half, then in quarters, like an orange. Blanch in boiling salted water, then cook in salted water until tender but still crisp. Drain. Fry in the butter until lightly browned, then add the stock. Simmer for 20 minutes, covered with buttered paper. Serve in a heated dish.

PIEDS DE CÉLERI-BRANCHES AU LARD ET À L'OIGNON

CELERY WITH BACON AND ONION

Preparation 45 minutes • Cooking 2 hours

US	Ingredients	Met/Imp
8	heads celery	8
4 tbsp	butter	50 g/2 oz
4	bacon slices	4
¼ lb	pork rind	100 g/4 oz
2	large onions	2
2	carrots	2
1	bouquet garni	1
a few	peppercorns	a few
1 quart	White Stock (page 56)	1 litre/1¾ pints
1 quart	Demi-Glaze (page 56)	1 litre/1¾ pints
	salt and pepper	

Blanch and rinse the celery, making sure it is well cleaned and drained. Tie the heads in pairs with string.

Prepare a Russian sauce with the butter, 2 bacon slices, the pork rind, finely chopped onions and carrots, bouquet garni and peppercorns. Add the celery and place the remaining bacon slices on top. Sweat gently for a few minutes. Gradually add the white stock until the celery is covered. Partly cook on top of the stove, then finish off in a moderately hot oven.

When the celery is cooked, drain, remove the string and trim. Cut the celery lengthways, then horizontally, and arrange the pieces in a flameproof dish. Strain the stock, skim off the fat and reduce it. Add the demi-glaze and season to taste. Pour over the celery and simmer for a few minutes, then serve.

CÈPE

CEP (BOLETUS)

THERE ARE MORE THAN 20 VARIETIES OF CEP (BOLETUS), BUT the most common are the ones from Bordeaux and the black head (*tête de nègre*), that have established the reputation of this tasty, aromatic mushroom, in season in September and October. Brantôme is one of the major areas of cultivation in France.

Boletus mushrooms are always best eaten young as they become spongy when old. Cooked as a garnish for omelettes, *confits*, stews and even certain kinds of fish, stuffed or grilled (or broiled), flavoured with garlic, or preserved in goose fat – they are a gourmet's delight. They can also be preserved in olive oil, bottled and dried.

CÈPES À LA BORDELAISE

CEPS BORDELAISE

Preparation 20 minutes • Cooking 25 minutes

US	Ingredients	Met/Imp
2 lb	very fresh ceps	1 kg/2 lb
3	shallots	3
scant 1 cup	olive oil	200 ml/7 fl oz
	salt and pepper	
1	lemon, juice of	1
2 tbsp	chopped parsley	30 ml/2 tbsp

Use small or medium ceps. Canned ceps may be used, but they must first be rinsed in hot water to remove their sticky coating, then dried in a cloth. They must be cooked quickly until golden brown and served very hot.

Peel the stalks; clean, but do not wash the caps, and slice diagonally. Set aside about 100 g/4 oz (1½ cups) of the chopped stalks, mixing them with a spoonful of finely chopped shallot.

Put about half of the oil into a saucepan and heat until smoking. Put in the sliced ceps and fry over a high heat until browned. Take the pan half off the heat and continue cooking the ceps. Drain off most of the oil. Season the ceps with salt and pepper and fry again over a high heat to make them crisp. Put into a heated serving dish.

Put the remaining oil into the pan and heat quickly until smoking. Toss in the reserved chopped stalks and shallot, fry over a high heat for a few seconds, then pour over the ceps. Add a dash of lemon juice and sprinkle with the parsley.

CÈPES À LA CÉVENOLE

CEPS FROM CÉVENNES

Preparation 30 minutes • Cooking 12–15 minutes

US	Ingredients	Met/Imp
4½ lb	very fresh ceps	2 kg/4½ lb
scant 1 cup	olive oil	200 ml/7 fl oz
	salt and pepper	
4 tbsp	butter	50 g/2 oz
2 cups	fresh breadcrumbs	100 g/4 oz
2	garlic cloves, crushed	2
2 tbsp	chopped parsley	30 ml/2 tbsp

Use small or medium ceps. Separate the caps from the stalks. Clean them if necessary. Cut off the ends of the stalks, which should be peeled if necessary. Set aside a few stalks and slice the remainder into large rings which will be fried with the caps.

Use 2 frying pans, 1 large and 1 small. Put about two-thirds of the oil into the large pan and heat until it begins to sizzle. Add the caps and sliced stalks, season and stir until cooked, then drain off a little of the oil.

Meanwhile, dice the reserved stalks (they should be the size of a pea), and toss them in oil in the small frying pan. Fry until browned and cooked, then pour off all the oil, replacing it with the butter. Heat until the butter is frothy, then add the breadcrumbs, garlic and parsley. Toss, then add to the ceps in the large pan. Serve hot.

CÈPES À LA GASCONNE

CEPS FROM GASCONY

Preparation 40 minutes • Cooking about 1 hour, 20 minutes

US	Ingredients	Met/Imp
16	very fresh medium ceps	16
½ cup	olive oil	100 ml/4 fl oz
10 oz	Parma ham	300 g/10 oz
1	garlic clove	1
1 tbsp	chopped parsley	15 ml/1 tbsp
2 tbsp	flour	20 g/¾ oz
½ cup	white wine	100 ml/4 fl oz
	salt and pepper	

Separate the cep caps from the stalks. Fry the caps in the oil for about 20 minutes. Remove from the pan and set aside.

Put the chopped ham and chopped stalks, garlic and parsley into the pan. Fry until just golden, then add the flour and wine. Bring to the boil. Stir in the caps and add a little water if necessary. Cover with a tight-fitting lid and cook very slowly for a long time to bring out the flavour. Season to taste before serving.

US	Ingredients	Met/Imp
2 lb	medium very fresh ceps	1 kg/2 lb
½ cup	olive oil	100 ml/4 fl oz
10 tbsp	butter	150 g/5 oz
1	small onion	1
1	garlic clove	1
	salt and pepper	
1¼ cups	Duxelles Sauce (page 68)	300 ml/½ pint
2 cups	fresh breadcrumbs	100 g/4 oz
1	lemon, juice of	1
1 tbsp	chopped parsley	15 ml/1 tbsp

CEPS AU GRATIN

Preparation 40 minutes • Cooking 6 minutes

Slice the cep caps and cut the stalks into rings. Fry in smoking hot oil until just tender, then remove from the pan and drain well. Replace the oil in the pan with 50 g/2 oz (4 tbsp) of the butter, and add the chopped onion and garlic and salt and pepper to taste. Mix the ceps into the fairly liquid duxelles sauce. Pour into a deep dish and sprinkle with the breadcrumbs and remaining butter, melted. Brown in a hot oven and serve sprinkled with lemon juice and parsley.

US	Ingredients	Met/Imp
16	fresh ceps	16
	salt and pepper	
¼ cup	olive oil	50 ml/2 fl oz
1 stick	butter	100 g/4 oz
2 tbsp	chopped parsley	30 ml/2 tbsp
3	garlic cloves	3
1½ cups	fresh breadcrumbs	75 g/3 oz

CÈPES À LA PROVENÇALE

CEPS PROVENÇAL

Preparation 40 minutes • Cooking 6 minutes

Sprinkle the cep caps with salt and pepper and fry in the oil and butter until golden brown. Remove from the pan and keep hot. Add the parsley, crushed garlic and breadcrumbs to the pan and fry until they have absorbed the butter and turned golden brown. If necessary, add more butter (ceps absorb a great deal of fat).

When frothy, pour over the caps. Serve very hot on warmed plates.

US	Ingredients	Met/Imp
	Shortcrust Pastry (page 577)	
½ lb	Puff Pastry (page 579)	250 g/8 oz
1	egg yolk	1
3–4 tbsp	cheese, grated or finely chopped	25 g/scant 1 oz
⅔ cup	blanched almonds	100 g/4 oz
3 lb	fresh ceps	1.5 kg/3 lb
1 stick	butter	100 g/4 oz
	salt and pepper	
½ cup	crème fraîche	100 ml/4 fl oz

TOURTE FEUILLETÉE AUX CÈPES ET AUX AMANDES

CEP AND ALMOND FEUILLETÉ*

Preparation 1 hour • Cooking about 30 minutes

Make a pie shell 20 cm/8 inches in diameter with the shortcrust pastry. Moisten the edge and cover with a strip of puff pastry. Glaze with egg yolk and bake blind. Make a pie lid with the remaining puff pastry on an 18 cm/7 inch pie dish. Prick the lid, sprinkle the grated cheese and half of the chopped almonds on top, then bake until golden brown.

Finely chop the ceps and toss in butter with salt and pepper. Simmer, then add the crème fraîche and reduce.

Crush the remaining almonds in a mortar and pestle and add the remaining butter. Pound until creamy. Rub through a sieve and add to the ceps. Season well.

Cut the puff pastry lid into 4 triangles. Put the shortcrust pastry case on to a round dish and pile the cep mixture inside it. Arrange the puff pastry triangles on top so that the filling is visible.

CHAMPIGNON

MUSHROOM

WILD MUSHROOMS ARE VERY DELICATE IN FLAVOUR AND make excellent dishes when they are in season, especially the girolle or chanterelle, the field mushroom, the lactary (which has a milky white juice) and the craterelle (the so-called 'trumpet of the dead'). There is also the button mushroom, the flavour of which cannot be compared to that if its wild cousins, but which has numerous uses in stocks, veloutés and other sauces, and as various garnishes. Mushrooms are also used extensively in soufflés, quiches and pies.

CHAMPIGNONS FARCIS

STUFFED MUSHROOMS

Preparation 40 minutes • Cooking 20 minutes • Serves 4

US	Ingredients	Met/Imp
1½ lb	mushrooms	750 g/1½ lb
	salt and pepper	
a little	olive oil	a little
I thin	slice bread, without crusts	20 g/¾ oz
I	garlic clove	I
I	onion	I
6 tbsp	butter	75 g/3 oz
¼ lb	cooked ham	100 g/4 oz
I	bunch parsley	I
I	egg	I

Trim off the base of the mushroom stalks. Wash the mushrooms in cold water, rubbing well to remove any dirt, and drain in a colander. Remove the stalks and set aside. Butter an ovenproof dish. Place the mushroom caps in it, gill side down. Season with salt and pepper and brush lightly with oil. Bake in a hot oven for 12–15 minutes, depending on the size of the mushrooms. When cooked, turn off the oven, but leave the mushrooms in it to keep hot.

Make the stuffing. Cut the bread into small pieces and soak in warm water. Finely chop the garlic and onion. Melt two-thirds of the butter in a frying pan and gently fry the chopped garlic and onion until just golden.

Chop the mushroom stalks and ham with the bread, which has had all of the liquid squeezed out of it. Add to the frying pan, stir and cook over a low heat. Wash the parsley and discard the stalks. Chop it and add half to the stuffing. Season lightly with salt and pepper. Beat the egg with a fork. Remove the pan from the heat and add the egg to the stuffing a little at a time, mixing well.

Turn the mushroom caps so that the gills are facing upwards. Fill generously with the stuffing, piling it well on top as it will not spread during cooking. Sprinkle the remaining parsley on top and place a pat of the remaining butter on each one. Place under the grill (broiler) for about 4 minutes to heat through and brown, then serve at once.

US	Ingredients	Met/Imp
scant ½ lb	very small button onions	200 g/7 oz
I	garlic clove	I
scant ½ cup	olive oil	100 ml/4 fl oz
1¾ cups	wine vinegar	400 ml/16 fl oz
I	thyme sprig	I
I	bay leaf	I
I pinch	fennel seeds	I pinch
	parsley stalks	
5	peppercorns	5
	salt	
2	coriander seeds	2
1½ lb	small chanterelle mushrooms	750 g/1½ lb

MARINATED CHANTERELLES

Preparation 40 minutes • Cooking 25 minutes

Peel the onions and garlic. Heat the oil and vinegar in a saucepan. Add the thyme, bay leaf, fennel, garlic, parsley stalks and salt to taste. Bring to the boil and put in the onions.

When the onions are three-quarters cooked, add the peppercorns and coriander seeds, then the mushrooms. Boil briskly until the mushrooms are cooked. Pour the mushrooms and liquid into a bowl and leave to marinate until cold. Serve with some of the marinade.

US	Ingredients	Met/Imp
1½ lb	button mushrooms	750 g/1½ lb
3 tbsp	butter	45 ml/3 tbsp
	salt and pepper	
I glass	ruby port wine	I glass
2 tbsp	double (heavy) cream	30 ml/2 tbsp
I	egg yolk	I

GRATIN DE CHAMPIGNONS AU PORTO

GRATIN OF MUSHROOMS WITH PORT

Preparation 30 minutes • Cooking 20 minutes

Discard the mushroom stalks. Wash, dry and slice the caps. Fry in the butter with salt and pepper for 10 minutes. Drain and keep hot in an ovenproof dish.

Add the port wine and cream to the juices in the pan and boil for a few minutes to reduce. Remove from the heat and add the egg yolk. Whisk well and pour over the mushrooms. Put into a very hot oven for 4 minutes, then serve.

US	Ingredients	Met/Imp
2 lb	craterelle mushrooms ('trumpets of the dead')	I kg/2 lb
¼ lb	onions	100 g/4 oz
3	shallots	3
¼ lb	smoked ham	100 g/4 oz
I stick	butter	125 g/4½ oz
	salt and pepper	
½ tsp	snipped chives	2.5 ml/½ tsp
½ tsp	chopped parsley	2.5 ml/½ tsp
½ tsp	chopped chervil	2.5 ml/½ tsp
½ tsp	chopped tarragon	2.5 ml/½ tsp
¼ cup	mirabelle (plum) liqueur	60 ml/4 tbsp
6 tbsp	crème fraîche	90 ml/6 tbsp
2 tbsp	fresh white breadcrumbs	30 ml/2 tbsp

TROMPETTES-DE-LA-MORT À LA SAVOYARDE

'TRUMPETS OF THE DEAD' FROM SAVOY

Preparation 30 minutes • Cooking 1¼ hours

Clean and trim the mushrooms. Cut half of them lengthways and half horizontally into 3 cm/1¼ inch pieces.

Chop the onions and shallots. Finely slice, then chop the ham. Fry the onions, shallots and ham in the butter until soft but not browned. Add the mushrooms and stir. Fry over a high heat for 10 minutes, stirring with a wooden spoon. Cover and simmer over a moderate heat for a further 8 minutes.

Season with salt and pepper and add the herbs. Stir in the liqueur. Cover with a very tight fitting lid and cook over a low heat for 40 minutes.

Stir in the crème fraîche and simmer over a very low heat for 10 minutes. Sprinkle the breadcrumbs on top, cover and simmer for 3 minutes, shaking the pan constantly. Serve at once.

MUSHROOM SOUFFLÉ

Preparation 30 minutes • Cooking 20 minutes

US	Ingredients	Met/Imp
1½ lb	mushrooms, preferably wild	750 g/1½ lb
3	shallots	3
4 tbsp	butter	50 g/2 oz
1 cup	Béchamel Sauce (*page 62*)	200 ml/7 fl oz
3	egg yolks	3
½ cup	*crème fraîche*	100 ml/3½ fl oz
	salt and pepper	
1 pinch	nutmeg	1 pinch
a little	potato flour	a little
8	egg whites	8

Chop the mushrooms and shallots very finely and sweat in half of the butter. Thicken the mixture with the béchamel, egg yolks, remaining butter and the crème fraîche. Season with salt, pepper and nutmeg. Butter a soufflé dish and dust with potato flour. Whisk the egg whites until stiff, then fold into the mushroom mixture and pour into the soufflé dish. Bake in a moderately hot oven at first, then lower the temperature after a while. Gently insert a fine skewer into the centre of the soufflé: if it comes out clean the soufflé is ready.

CHICORÉE

CURLY ENDIVE

THIS VEGETABLE WITH ITS EDIBLE LEAVES IS USUALLY EATEN raw, but can also be cooked, usually braised or au gratin. The main varieties used in cooking are Friar's beard (a cultivated type of wild endive), curly endive, escarole and the Italian 'Trevi's salad', which is a beautiful violet colour.

Editor's note: curly endive (chicorée frisée) and escarole (la scarole) are the only varieties mentioned here that are members of the *Cichorium endivia* family. The other varieties — Friar's beard and Trevi's salad – are in the *Cichorium intybus* family, but they look more like curly endive than chicory (in the US called French or Belgian endive) and therefore the French cook them as such.

BRAISED CURLY ENDIVE

Preparation 45 minutes • Cooking 2¼ hours

US	Ingredients	Met/Imp
9 lb	endive (curly endive or chicory) with plenty of pale heart	4 kg/9 lb
10 tbsp	butter	150 g/5 oz
¾ cup	flour	100 g/4 oz
	clear stock	
	salt and pepper	
1 pinch	sugar	1 pinch
	nutmeg	

Trim off the outer leaves of the endive, keeping only the pale parts in the centre. Cut off and discard the stalks. Wash well and blanch for 10–12 minutes. Rinse, drain and squeeze out all the water. Chop finely.
  Make a roux with the butter and flour. Add the endive and stir well. Add some good stock, salt, pepper, sugar and nutmeg. Bring to the boil, cover with buttered paper and a lid and braise for 2 hours. Add more stock or *crème fraîche* if liked. Braised endive should be well cooked and well seasoned.

CHOU, CHOU-FLEUR, CHOU DE BRUXELLES ET BROCOLI

CABBAGE, CAULIFLOWER, BRUSSELS SPROUTS AND BROCCOLI

THE BRASSICA FAMILY OF VEGETABLES IS PARTICULARLY RICH and varied and provides tasty recipes throughout the year: crisp, delicate broccoli served with fish; Brussels sprouts, with their distinctive flavour, delicious with game and pork; sweet, crunchy spring cauliflower; large, green 'Milan' cabbage with curly leaves; white cabbage for sauerkraut; red cabbage for marinating and braising. No winter stew or soup is complete without cabbage, but in summer crisp green cabbage cooked in butter, stuffed and rolled, etc, is also a treat.

These vegetables are sometimes criticized for being rather indigestible, but this can be remedied by changing the cooking water several times. Round cabbage and Brussels sprouts should be compact and tight, without any withered leaves. Broccoli is particularly fragile, and cauliflower florets should be very white, small and close together (if they are loose they will disintegrate when cooked).

ACHARDS DE LÉGUMES AU CHOU-FLEUR

PICKLED VEGETABLES WITH CAULIFLOWER

Preparation 3 hours

Cut all the vegetables into uniform pieces about 4×1 cm/1½×½ inch. Divide the cauliflower into florets. Finely chop the peppers and onions. Put all the vegetables into a salad bowl, cover with coarse salt and leave for 24 hours. Drain and dry in a cloth.

Prepare the marinade. Crush the garlic and onions in a mortar and pestle with the ginger and cayenne. Tie the saffron threads in a cheesecloth bag and infuse in the vinegar. Mix the spiced garlic paste with the infused vinegar, add the oil and pour over the vegetables in a jar. Serve with cold meat instead of pickles.

US	Ingredients	Met/Imp
½ lb	carrots	200 g/8 oz
¼ lb	cucumber	100 g/4 oz
½ lb	French (fine green) beans	200 g/8 oz
a few	white cabbage leaves	a few
¾ lb	cauliflower	300 g/10 oz
3	large sweet red peppers	3
½ lb	button (pearl) onions	200 g/8 oz
	coarse salt	
	MARINADE	
I	bulb garlic	I
2	onions	2
1½–2 tsp	ground ginger	7.5–10 ml/ 1½–2 tsp
I tsp	cayenne pepper	5 ml/1 tsp
2 tbsp	saffron threads	30 ml/2 tbsp
I cup	good-quality malt vinegar	200 ml/7 fl oz
½ cup	olive oil	100 ml/3½ fl oz

BROCOLIS À LA CRÈME

BROCCOLI WITH CREAM

Preparation 10 minutes • Cooking 35 minutes

US	Ingredients	Met/Imp
2 lb	broccoli	1 kg/2 lb
2 quarts	water	2 litres/3½ pints
	salt and white pepper	
2	garlic cloves	2
4 tbsp	butter	50 g/2 oz
scant 1 cup	crème fraîche	200 ml/7 fl oz

Wash the broccoli and discard the coarse stalks and the leaves. Bring the water to the boil in a large saucepan, add a little salt and put in the broccoli and garlic. Boil for 20–25 minutes until very tender. Drain and chop coarsely.

Heat the butter in a large, shallow pan and pour in the crème fraîche. When the mixture begins to brown, add the broccoli and season lightly with salt and pepper. Simmer for 5–6 minutes. Serve very hot, with roast meat or poached fish such as hake or cod.

BROCOLIS AUX FINES HERBES

BROCCOLI WITH HERBS

Preparation 10 minutes • Cooking 15 minutes

US	Ingredients	Met/Imp
2 lb	broccoli	1 kg/2 lb
	salt and white pepper	
1	egg	1
1	lemon	1
6 tbsp	olive oil	75 ml/3 fl oz
2 tbsp	finely snipped chives	30 ml/2 tbsp
2 tbsp	finely chopped parsley	30 ml/2 tbsp
1 tbsp	finely chopped chervil	15 ml/1 tbsp
1 tbsp	finely chopped tarragon	15 ml/1 tbsp

Wash the broccoli and discard the coarse stalks and the leaves. Cut a cross in the base of the remaining broccoli stalks. Cook gently in boiling salted water for 15 minutes, until the broccoli is still slightly tender but crisp.

Meanwhile, hard-boil the egg. Rinse it in cold water, remove the shell and separate the white and the yolk. Put the egg yolk in a blender (reserve the white for another dish), add the lemon juice and gradually trickle in the oil, with the motor running. Season with salt and pepper. When the sauce has emulsified, stir in all the herbs.

Drain the broccoli thoroughly, arrange in a warmed serving dish and pour over the sauce. Serve hot with poached fish, or serve cold as an appetizer.

CHOU FARCI AU CHOU

CABBAGE STUFFED WITH CABBAGE

Preparation 1 hour • Cooking 1½ hours

US	Ingredients	Met/Imp
2	cabbages	2
2 tbsp	butter	30 g/1 oz
2	onions	2
a few	parsley sprigs	a few
6	eggs	6
2 cups	fresh breadcrumbs	100 g/4 oz
½ cup	milk	100 ml/4 fl oz
	salt and pepper	
	TOPPING	
1 stick	butter	100 g/4 oz
1 cup	fresh breadcrumbs	50 g/2 oz

Remove 4 outer leaves from each cabbage. Arrange the leaves, upper side facing downwards, on a large napkin or tea towel in a bowl.

Chop the cabbage hearts very finely and fry lightly in the butter. Fry the onions chopped with the parsley until softened, then stir in the eggs and the breadcrumbs which have been soaked in milk and squeezed dry. Season to taste.

Arrange the stuffing on the leaves on the napkin. Knot the napkin very tightly and boil in salted water for 1½ hours until tender. Drain. To serve, remove the napkin and the cabbage should hold its original shape. Dot with butter, cover with breadcrumbs and brown in a hot oven.

US	Ingredients	Met/Imp
2	aubergines (eggplants)	2
2	sweet peppers	2
scant 1 cup	olive oil	200 ml/7 fl oz
1 cup	Pilau Rice (*page 563*)	150 g/5 oz
	salt and pepper	
1	head cabbage	1
	GREEK DRESSING	
scant ½ cup	white wine	100 ml/4 fl oz
scant ½ cup	water	100 ml/4 fl oz
2	lemons, juice of	2
3 cups	olive oil	750 ml/1¼ pints
a few	coriander seeds	a few
a few	peppercorns	a few
15	button (pearl) onions	15
1	bouquet garni	1

— STUFFED CABBAGE À LA GRECQUE —

Preparation 1 hour • Cooking 30 minutes

First prepare the dressing. Pour the wine, water, lemon juice and the oil into a pan. Add the coriander seeds and peppercorns tied in a cheesecloth bag, the onions and bouquet garni. Bring to the boil and cook until the onions are tender, then cool.

Peel and dice the aubergines (eggplants) and peppers. Fry lightly in oil and mix with the rice. Season. Detach the leaves from the cabbage, blanch, drain and rinse. Spread them out in 16 small piles, flattening them down neatly on top of each other. Put 15 ml/1 tbsp vegetable and rice mixture in the centre of each leaf. Using a clean, very strong cloth, shape them into tight round parcels the size of a small peach.

Lightly oil a large shallow pan. Arrange the stuffed cabbage leaves in it side by side, making sure there are no gaps. (The parcels must keep their shape during cooking; if necessary, fill any gaps with potatoes.) Pour over the dressing, cover the pan with paper and a lid and cook, checking there is plenty of liquid from time to time, until tender.

There is no absolute rule for making Greek-style stuffing. Cooked peas, even currants, may be added. Vine (grape) leaves can be used instead of cabbage, although these should be shaped into oblongs, not balls.

US	Ingredients	Met/Imp
2, each about 3½ lb	cauliflowers	2 each, about 1.5 kg/3½ lb
a little	wine vinegar (optional)	a little
	salt and pepper	
	nutmeg	
1 stick	butter	100 g/4 oz
1 quart	Béchamel Sauce (*page 62*)	1 litre/1¾ pints
1¼ cups	Comté, Gruyère or Parmesan cheese, or a mixture of the three, grated	150 g/5 oz
1 cup	fresh breadcrumbs	50 g/2 oz

——— CAULIFLOWER CHEESE ———

Preparation 40 minutes • Cooking about 30 minutes

Divide the cauliflowers into florets. Cut the stalks fairly short, but leave enough to support the florets. Immerse in cold water, adding a dash of vinegar if liked. Blanch the cauliflower in an uncovered saucepan of boiling salted water until just *al dente* (overcooking destroys the flavour). When cooked, drain and refresh by running cold water through a colander on to them. (Do not place the florets directly under the tap or they may disintegrate.) Drain well.

Lightly butter a pan and gently put in the florets. Season with salt, pepper and a very little nutmeg and add a few pieces of butter. Fry for a few minutes to allow the moisture to evaporate and the seasoning to penetrate.

Place a layer of florets, flower side down, in a bowl. Add a thin layer of béchamel and sprinkle with grated cheese. Repeat 2–3 times, reserving a good quantity of béchamel and a little grated cheese. When all the florets have been used, press down gently.

Lightly butter an ovenproof dish. Place it over the bowl with the cauliflower and quickly turn it upside down into the dish. Cover liberally with the remaining béchamel and grated cheese mixed with the breadcrumbs. Sprinkle the remaining butter, melted, on top, then brown in a hot oven.

Pepper Artichokes Provençal
Small 'pepper' artichokes are best for this summer dish. Cooking them in olive oil
adds to their fragrance, while peas and lettuce are added later on and gently braised.
(*Recipe on page 492.*)

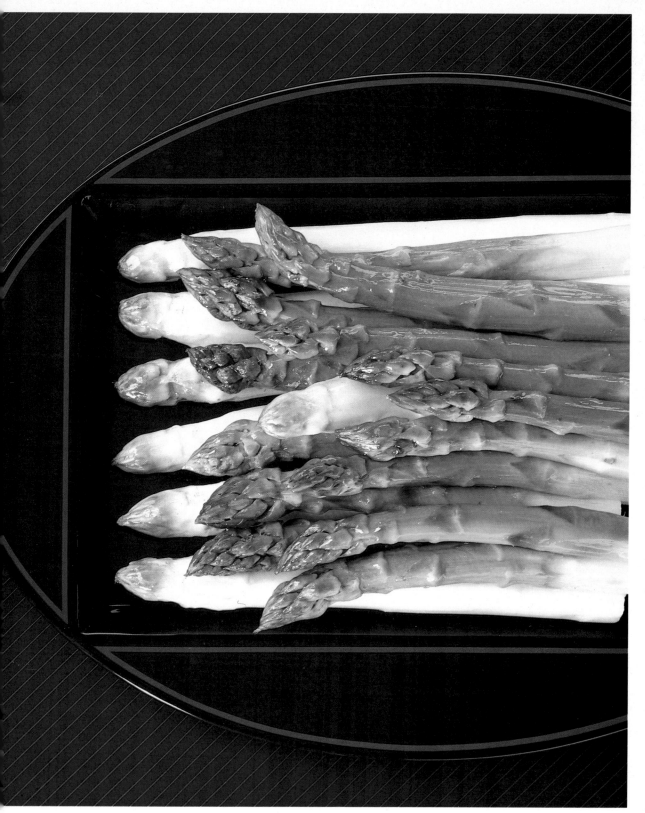

Asparagus Flamande

'À la flamande' is a classic preparation for this delicate vegetable, which is served lukewarm. It consists of melted butter, hard-boiled egg yolks and chopped parsley. This must be the flat-leaved parsley, carefully washed and dried, since the curly-leaved kind is not at all aromatic. Be sure to drain the asparagus thoroughly before serving. (Recipe on page 494.)

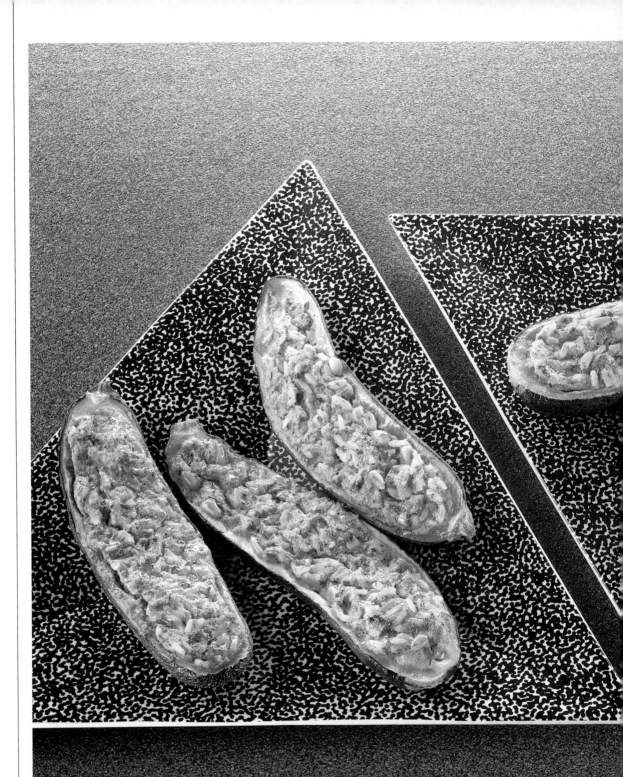

Oriental Courgettes
*This mixture of cooked rice, pine nuts and courgette (zucchini) flesh makes a
flavoursome stuffing with the addition of herbs, spices and garlic. The vegetables can
be served hot as a main course, but are better cold as a first course when the spices will
have had time to impregnate all the ingredients of the dish. (Recipe on page 517.)*

Warm Lentil Salad with Saveloy
Take care not to overcook lentils when they are to be served in a salad; here they are dressed with a highly-seasoned vinaigrette, which they absorb extremely well. The saveloy can be replaced with garlic sausage. (Recipe on page 533.)

Valencia-Style Rice
This dish, which combines rice, sweet peppers, petits pois and tomatoes, owes its character to the slices of chorizo. This sausage adds flavour and makes a good garnish for the 'paella'. (Recipe on page 564.)

Spinach and Green Vegetables Ancienne
*This delicate blend of spinach, watercress, dandelion leaves and curly endive, cooked
chopped and served with a béchamel makes an excellent accompaniment for white
meat. (Recipe on page 523.)*

— RED CABBAGE WITH CHESTNUTS —

Preparation 2½ hours • Cooking 2¼ hours

US	Ingredients	Met/Imp
I	head red cabbage	I
¼ cup	olive oil	50 ml/2 fl oz
I	large onion	I
2 lb	chestnuts	I kg/2 lb
	salt and pepper	

Wash the cabbage, cut it into quarters and put into a saucepan of boiling water. Cook for 5 minutes, then drain and shred finely.

Heat the oil in a saucepan and fry the finely chopped onion over a low heat for 5 minutes.

Meanwhile, make an incision in each chestnut, place them on a baking sheet and heat quickly in a hot oven to split the shells.

Add the shredded cabbage to the onion. Season with salt and pepper and mix well. Barely cover with water, bring to the boil and cover. Lower the heat and cook for 1 hour. Meanwhile, peel the chestnuts.

Add the peeled whole chestnuts to the pan with a little hot water if necessary. Bring back to the boil, then cover and lower the heat. Cook for 1 further hour.

Serve in a heated dish as an accompaniment to game.

GOURDS (PUMPKIN, MARROW AND SQUASH)

GENERALLY ONLY THE FLESH OF THESE WATER VEGETABLES IS eaten, usually cooked as a purée, au gratin or in soups. However, the 'brèdes' (young leaves and stalks) are highly appreciated in the French West Indies. As for pumpkin or squash pie, this is a speciality found in both Flanders and the United States.

BRÈDES DE CITROUILLE

PUMPKIN 'BRÈDES'

Preparation 1 hour • Cooking 1½ hours

US	Ingredients	Met/Imp
1¾ lb	young pumpkin brèdes	800 g/1¾ lb
¼ lb	bacon	100 g/4 oz
1	onion	1
¼ lb	pork fat	100 g/4 oz
5	garlic cloves	5
⅓ oz	fresh root ginger	10 g/⅓ oz
3	large tomatoes	3
	salt	

Carefully trim the brèdes. Wash in several changes of water, then leave to soak in fresh water.

Fry the diced bacon and chopped onion in the pork fat until golden-brown. Add the garlic crushed with the ginger, and the skinned, de-seeded and coarsely chopped tomatoes. Season to taste with salt. Cook over a low heat for 15 minutes.

Drain the brèdes and add to the pan. Cover and cook over a low heat for 1 hour, shaking the pan from time to time. Serve in a heated dish with Creole Rice (*page 563*).

GÂTEAU DE COURGE

GOURD CUSTARD

Preparation 40 minutes • Cooking 25 minutes

US	Ingredients	Met/Imp
4½ lb	gourds (pumpkin, marrow or squash)	2 kg/4½ lb
	salt	
1½ cups	sugar	300 g/10 oz
1 quart	boiling milk	1 litre/1¾ pints
6	eggs	6
1 small piece	vanilla pod (bean)	1 small piece

Coarsely dice the pumpkin, marrow or squash and cook in very lightly salted boiling water until tender. Drain, place in a cloth and squeeze well to extract all the water. Add the sugar to the boiling milk with the beaten eggs and the vanilla pod (bean) and mix with the pumpkin. Pour into an ovenproof dish and bake in a low oven for 25 minutes, cooking it like a custard in a *bain-marie*.

CONCOMBRE

CUCUMBER

FULL OF WATER, THIS REFRESHING VEGETABLE IS APPRECIATED for its lightness and delicacy of flavour. It is usually eaten raw, sometimes sprinkled with salt to remove the excess moisture, and sometimes cooked, for example as a garnish for white meat or fish. It can also be stuffed and served as a cold appetizer or as a vegetable accompaniment. When uncooked, serve with a cream, tarragon or dill sauce.

CONCOMBRES À LA CRÈME

—— CUCUMBER IN CREAM SAUCE ——

Preparation 40 minutes • Cooking 30 minutes

US	Ingredients	Met/Imp
6	cucumbers	6
½	lemon, juice of	½
	salt and pepper	
	sugar	
4 tbsp	butter	50 g/2 oz
2 cups	Velouté Sauce (page 57)	500 ml/18 fl oz
scant ½ cup	crème fraîche	100 ml/3½ fl oz

Peel the cucumbers and cut them in half lengthways. Scoop out the seeds. Cut the cucumber halves into pieces about 4 cm/1½ inches long, then cut each piece into 3, in the shape of a garlic clove. Blanch in boiling water with the lemon juice added, then drain very thoroughly.

Put the cucumber into a shallow pan and three-quarters cover with water. Add a little salt, a pinch of sugar and the butter. Cover with buttered paper and a lid. Place over a high heat, then lower it and cook until all the water has evaporated. Do not allow the cucumbers to turn brown.

Reduce the velouté with the crème fraîche and adjust the seasoning. Strain through cheesecloth, then mix with the cucumber.

US	Ingredients	Met/Imp
6	large cucumbers	6
	salt and pepper	
1 lb	good-quality pork, finely minced (ground)	500 g/1 lb
scant 1 cup	Dry Duxelles (page 49)	200 ml/7 fl oz
2	egg yolks	2
a little	Tomato Sauce (page 80), if necessary	a little
a few	bacon slices	a few
1½ quarts	stock	1.5 litres/2½ pints
1	bouquet garni	1
1 cup	fresh breadcrumbs	50 g/2 oz
scant 1 cup	strong Demi-Glaze (page 56)	200 ml/7 fl oz
	a little butter (optional)	

CONCOMBRES FARCIS

STUFFED CUCUMBER

Preparation 1 hour • Cooking about 40 minutes

Peel the cucumbers with a sharp knife and cut them into pieces about 4 cm/1½ inches long. Hollow out the centres. Blanch the pieces in boiling salted water, rinse and drain carefully. Butter a flameproof dish and sprinkle with salt and pepper. Arrange the cucumbers in it, laying them flat if possible, making sure there are no gaps.

Mix the pork with the duxelles and egg yolks. Season and soften with a little tomato sauce if necessary. Pipe the stuffing on to the cucumbers, using a forcing (pastry) bag fitted with a large plain nozzle (tube), then cover with the bacon, buttered paper and a lid. Allow to sweat for 1–2 minutes, then three-quarters cover with good stock and add the bouquet garni. Cook gently until tender.

Lift out the cucumbers very gently and put into an ovenproof dish. Sprinkle with breadcrumbs and glaze in a hot oven. Meanwhile, strain the cucumber cooking liquid, reduce by half and add the demi-glaze. Add a little butter if liked. Serve the sauce with the cucumbers.

US	Ingredients	Met/Imp
6	cucumbers	6
	salt and pepper	
2 tsp	sugar	10 ml/2 tsp
10 tbsp	butter	150 g/5 oz
1 tbsp	chopped parsley	15 ml/1 tbsp

CONCOMBRES PERSILLÉS

CUCUMBER WITH PARSLEY

Preparation 40 minutes • Cooking 30 minutes

Trim the cucumber ends. Cut the cucumbers into pieces 3 cm/1¼ inches long. Divide each piece into quarters, peel and cut in the shape of garlic cloves.

Put the cucumber into a fairly wide pan and add just enough water to cover them, a good pinch of salt, the sugar and 50 g/2 oz (4 tbsp) of the butter, diced. Bring to the boil, cover and cook over a very low heat.

When the cucumber is almost cooked, increase the heat, add the remaining butter and boil until the liquid has become a thick syrup. Add the parsley and toss well to coat.

COURGETTE

COURGETTE

A MEDITERRANEAN VEGETABLE LIKE THE TOMATO AND aubergine (eggplant), the courgette (zucchini) is used in similar recipes, of which ratatouille is the main example. Recipes for aubergines (eggplants), such as fritters, can be adapted to courgettes (zucchini), which are also prepared in spicy marinades and served as a salad. The small, very green courgette (zucchini) is generally considered the best.

COURGETTES À L'ORIENTALE

ORIENTAL COURGETTES*

Preparation 35 minutes • Cooking 50 minutes • Serves 4

Recipe supplied by Mademoiselle Decure, founder of the review 'Cuisine et Vins de France'

US	Ingredients	Met/Imp
4½ tbsp	long-grain rice	50 g/2 oz
	salt and pepper	
6–8	bay leaves	6–8
8	small, firm courgettes (zucchini)	8
4	parsley sprigs	4
4	garlic cloves	4
a few	chives	a few
	olive oil	
⅔ cup	pine nuts	50 g/2 oz
2	egg yolks	2
	ground cinnamon	
	nutmeg	

Wash the rice in cold water. Cook in plenty of boiling salted water with 1 bay leaf until tender, then drain.

Wash the courgettes (zucchini), cut off the stalks and cut in half lengthways. Scoop out the flesh, taking care not to tear the skin and leaving about 2 mm/⅛ inch of flesh at the stalk end, to help the shells keep their shape. Coarsely chop the parsley, garlic, chives and courgette (zucchini) flesh. Mix well.

Lightly oil a large shallow baking dish. Arrange the remaining bay leaves on it and place the courgette (zucchini) shells side by side on top. Sprinkle a little salt over each and brush lightly with olive oil. Place under the grill (broiler) until the shells are translucent.

Season the chopped courgette (zucchini) and herb mixture with salt and pepper and fry in olive oil for 10 minutes. Transfer to a bowl, then add the rice and pine nuts. Bind with the egg yolks, mixing very well. Adjust the seasoning and add a little cinnamon and nutmeg.

Spoon the mixture into the shells. Bake in a hot oven for 15–20 minutes, covering them with foil if they become too brown. Carefully transfer the courgettes (zucchini) to a serving dish and baste with the cooking oil. Serve hot, warm or cold.

COURGETTES FRIED IN BUTTER

Preparation 15 minutes • Cooking 20 minutes

US	Ingredients	Met/Imp
16	small courgettes (zucchini)	16
10 tbsp	butter	150 g/5 oz
1 tbsp	chopped parsley	15 ml/1 tbsp
	salt	

If the courgettes (zucchini) are very small, there is no need to peel them. Cut them into rings 2 cm/¾ inch thick. Melt two-thirds of the butter in a saucepan and gently fry the courgettes (zucchini), uncovered, until just beginning to turn brown. Toss in the remaining butter and parsley, and season with salt.

CROSNE

CHINESE ARTICHOKE

THIS SMALL, DELICATE TUBER WAS FIRST CULTIVATED IN THE nineteenth century in Essonne, at Crosnes, hence its name. This very light, delicate vegetable is cooked, unpeeled, in 10–12 minutes, but should be rubbed in a coarse cloth with salt to extract the excess water from the skin. Greatly appreciated between 1890 and 1920, the Chinese or Japanese artichoke deserves greater recognition today, for its succulence and slightly sweet flavour.

CHINESE ARTICHOKES WITH VELOUTÉ SAUCE

Preparation 30 minutes • Cooking 1¼ hours

US	Ingredients	Met/Imp
5 tbsp	butter	60 g/2½ oz
6 tbsp	flour	50 g/2 oz
1 quart	White Stock (page 56)	1 litre/1¾ pints
1	bouquet garni	1
2 lb	Chinese artichokes	1 kg/2 lb
	salt and pepper	
2	egg yolks	2
scant ½ cup	*crème fraîche*	100 ml/4 fl oz
	nutmeg	
2 tbsp	chopped parsley	30 ml/2 tbsp

Make a *roux* with the butter and flour. Add the stock and bouquet garni. Cook very gently for at least 1 hour.

Meanwhile, rub the artichokes in a large, strong cloth with a handful of coarse salt. Wash in several changes of water. Cook until tender in boiling salted water, then drain.

Strain the sauce through a cloth. Return to the heat, bind with the egg yolks and crème fraîche and reduce without boiling. Strain through a cloth again. Season with salt, pepper and nutmeg.

Coat the artichokes with the sauce and serve sprinkled with parsley.

ENDIVE

CHICORY

THIS VEGETABLE IS CALLED WITLOOF OR 'WHITE LEAVES' IN Belgium, its country of origin. It is an economical vegetable because there is practically no waste, although the base of the stalk has to be removed as it has a very bitter taste. Do not blanch it. Wash it quickly under running water and dry it immediately; do not leave in cold water or it will become bitter. This winter vegetable, which is eaten raw as often as cooked, has a delicate but distinct flavour which makes it suitable for adding to various dishes, for example mixed vegetable and fruit salads, gratins of ham and cheese, and for use as a garnish for fish, scallops, white meat, etc. Chicory (in the United States called Belgian endive) for use in cooking should be fairly small; medium and large ones are best finely chopped and used in salads.

CROQUETTES D'ENDIVES

CHICORY CROQUETTES

Preparation 20 minutes • Cooking 10–15 minutes • Makes 9

US	Ingredients	Met/Imp
½ lb (about 4)	chicory (Belgian endive), cooked	250 g/8 oz (about 4)
¾ cup	flour	100 g/4 oz
I	egg	I
	salt and pepper	
3 tbsp	groundnut (peanut) oil	45 ml/3 tbsp

Finely chop the chicory (Belgian endive) and mash with a fork. Add the flour, beaten egg, salt and pepper.

Heat the oil in a frying pan and drop in spoonfuls of the mixture, twisting the spoon a little so that the mixture drops in neat heaps. Fry for 10–15 minutes, turning once. Serve as a garnish for meat dishes.

US	Ingredients	Met/Imp
about 4½ lb	medium chicory (Belgian endive)	about 2 kg/4½ lb
	pepper	
	nutmeg	
1¾ cups	stock	400 ml/14 fl oz
4 tbsp	butter	50 g/2 oz
scant ½ lb	bacon	200 g/7 oz
½ lb	cooked ham	200 g/7 oz
	LIAISON	
5 tbsp	butter	60 g/2½ oz
1	lemon, juice of	1

CHICORY FROM THE ARDENNES

Preparation 40 minutes • Cooking 45–55 minutes

Trim the base of the chicory (Belgian endive), discard any withered leaves, wash quickly and shake well. Arrange head to tail in a well-buttered flameproof casserole. Season with a pinch each of pepper and nutmeg, add the very lightly salted stock (or half stock and half water) and the butter, diced. Bring to the boil, cover with buttered paper and a lid and simmer for 35 minutes.

Chop the bacon into 1 cm/½ inch pieces, then blanch for 5–6 minutes. Dice the ham. Add the bacon and ham to the casserole after 35 minutes. Cook for a further 15 minutes.

To serve, drain the chicory (Belgian endive) and place in a heated serving dish with the bacon and ham. Reduce the stock over a high heat to 200 ml/7 fl oz (scant 1 cup). Remove from the heat, add the butter and lemon juice and pour over the vegetable.

US	Ingredients	Met/Imp
3 per person	heads chicory (Belgian endive)	3 per person
	salt and pepper	
3–4 tbsp	water	45–60 ml/ 3–4 tbsp
½	lemon, juice of	½
1 stick	butter	100 g/4 oz
2 cups	Béchamel Sauce (*page 62*)	500 ml/18 fl oz
scant 1 cup	*crème fraîche*	200 ml/7 fl oz

CHICORY WITH CREAM

Preparation 40 minutes • Cooking about 1 hour

In principle, a vegetable served with a cream sauce should be covered with the cream when it is nearly cooked and the cream should first be reduced to half its volume. Béchamel sauce is used in this recipe for economy; it should be made with milk which has been substantially reduced.

Choose tight, compact chicory (Belgian endive) heads. Trim the base, discard any withered leaves, wash quickly, and shake well.

Arrange head to tail in a buttered flameproof casserole. Season lightly with salt, then add the water, lemon juice and the butter, diced. Bring to the boil, place a piece of buttered paper on top, cover and cook gently in the oven for 40 minutes. Add the béchamel and return to the oven for a further 20–25 minutes cooking.

Lift out the chicory (Belgian endive) with a fork and arrange in a heated serving dish. Cover with the sauce and hot crème fraîche.

GRATIN D'ENDIVES AU JAMBON

CHICORY AND HAM GRATIN

Preparation 15 minutes • Cooking 30 minutes • Serves 6

US	Ingredients	Met/Imp
6	large heads chicory (Belgian endive)	6
	salt and pepper	
I	bread crust	I
5 tbsp	butter	60 g/2½ oz
3 tbsp	flour	30 g/1oz
1¼ cups	milk	300 ml/½ pint
½ cup	Emmental cheese, grated	50 g/2 oz
½ cup	Comté cheese, grated	50 g/2 oz
2 tbsp	*crème fraîche* (optional)	30 ml/2 tbsp
6	slices cooked ham	6
	fresh white breadcrumbs	

Trim the base of the chicory (Belgian endive), discard any withered leaves, wash quickly and shake well. Cook in plenty of boiling salted water, with the crust of bread to remove the bitter taste, for about 20 minutes, until tender, but still crisp.

Meanwhile, to make the béchamel: melt 50 g/2 oz (4 tbsp) of the butter in a saucepan and stir in the flour. Cook for 10 minutes over a low heat, stirring continuously. Do not allow to brown. Gradually add the milk, bring to the boil, stirring, and cook for a few minutes. Add salt, pepper and both types of grated cheese, and the cream if a richer sauce is liked.

Discard the crust of bread and drain the vegetables well. Squeeze lightly to remove all the water. Roll each head of chicory (Belgian endive) in a slice of ham. Place in a buttered gratin dish and coat with the cheese sauce. Sprinkle with the breadcrumbs and dot with the remaining butter. Brown in a very hot oven for 5–10 minutes. Serve straight from the dish.

GRATIN D'ENDIVES À LA ROYALE

CHICORY GRATIN ROYALE

Preparation 30 minutes • Cooking 50 minutes

US	Ingredients	Met/Imp
6½ lb	chicory (Belgian endive), boiled and drained	3 kg/6½ lb
8	eggs	8
1¼ cups	*crème fraîche*	300 ml/½ pint
	salt and pepper	
I pinch	nutmeg	I pinch
I pinch	sugar	I pinch
4 tbsp	butter	50 g/2 oz

Butter the bottom of an ovenproof dish and put in the chicory (Belgian endive).

Beat the eggs in a bowl and add the crème fraîche. Season carefully with salt, pepper, nutmeg and sugar. Pour over the vegetables, dot with the butter and bake in a moderate oven. Serve straight from the dish.

ÉPINARD

SPINACH

THE YOUNG AND TENDER LEAVES OF SPINACH MAY BE EATEN raw, but more often than not this vegetable is served cooked. It is very delicate, and so should be cooked as soon as it is bought. Cooked, it is eaten in leaf form or puréed. It makes a welcome, light and fresh garnish for a great number of meat and fish recipes, and it may also be prepared au gratin, made into croquettes, used in soups, etc. All recipes described as 'à la florentine' contain spinach in one form or another. 'Tétragone' is a variety of New Zealand spinach which is prepared like spinach and is used as a substitute when spinach is unavailable because of dry weather conditions.

ÉPINARDS À LA CRÈME

SPINACH WITH CREAM

Preparation 50 minutes • Cooking 12–15 minutes

US	Ingredients	Met/Imp
6½ lb	spinach	3 kg/6½ lb
	salt and pepper	
½ lb (2 sticks)	butter	250 g/8 oz
	sugar	
	nutmeg	
2 tbsp	flour	30 ml/2 tbsp
1¼ cups	crème fraîche	300 ml/½ pint
	GARNISH	
	heart-shaped croûtons	

Trim the spinach, wash and shake dry. Put it into a large saucepan of boiling salted water – about 7.5 ml/1½ tsp salt per 1 litre/1¾ pints (1 quart) water. Cook over a high heat for 10 minutes if the spinach is young, a little longer if old, timing from when the water comes back to the boil.

Drain and rinse the spinach, squeezing out the water with your hands. Chop finely, then place in a cloth. Hold the cloth at both ends and twist to extract any remaining water.

Put the spinach into a saucepan with just over half of the butter and stir over a high heat for a few minutes until all the moisture has evaporated. Season with a good pinch of salt, a pinch of sugar, pepper and a little nutmeg. Sprinkle with the flour. Gradually stir in two-thirds of the crème fraîche, cover and simmer over a very low heat for 20 minutes.

Just before serving, remove from the heat and add the remaining butter. Turn the spinach into a heated serving dish. Heat the remaining crème fraîche, drizzle over the spinach and garnish with croûtons.

	US	Ingredients	Met/Imp

ÉPINARDS EN VERDURE À L'ANCIENNE

SPINACH AND
—— GREEN VEGETABLES ANCIENNE* ——

Preparation 1 hour • Cooking 20–25 minutes

	US	Ingredients	Met/Imp
	2 lb	spinach, trimmed and shredded	1 kg/2 lb
	3	bunches watercress, leaves only	3
	2 lb	dandelion leaves, trimmed	1 kg/2 lb
	2 lb	endive (curly endive or chicory) with plenty of pale heart	1 kg/2 lb
	1	small onion	1
	14 tbsp	butter	200 g/7 oz
	scant 1 cup	Béchamel Sauce (page 62)	200 ml/7 fl oz
		salt and pepper	

Blanch the spinach, watercress, dandelion leaves, endive and onion separately until tender (the dandelions and endive take longer).

Drain thoroughly, mix the vegetables together and chop very finely. Butter the bottom and sides of a gratin dish and put in the vegetables. Use plenty of butter as the dandelions, spinach and particularly the endive absorb it very easily. Cover with béchamel, season, then bake in a moderate oven for 15–20 minutes. Serve.

ÎLE VERTE

—————— GREEN ISLAND ——————

Preparation 20 minutes • Cooking 50 minutes • Serves 4

	US	Ingredients	Met/Imp
	2 lb	spinach	1 kg/2 lb
		salt and pepper	
	1 stick	butter	100 g/4 oz
	6½ tbsp	flour	60 g/2½ oz
	2½ cups	milk	600 ml/1 pint
	1½ cups	Comté cheese, grated	175 g/6 oz
	4	egg whites	4

This soufflé is sometimes enriched with a garnish of lightly fried bacon arranged around the spinach, which tastes as good as it looks.

Clean the spinach, cut off and discard the stalks, then wash the leaves in several changes of water. Put the spinach into a saucepan of boiling salted water, blanch for 5–10 minutes, then drain.

Make the béchamel sauce. Melt three-quarters of the butter in a saucepan. Sprinkle in the flour, then stir and cook until just beginning to turn colour. Gradually add the milk. Cook over a very low heat for about 10 minutes, stirring from time to time. Pour about one-quarter of the sauce into another pan and reduce until very thick. Set both pans of sauce aside.

Chop the spinach and purée it. (If liked, dry it in a non-stick saucepan.) Add about two-thirds of the grated cheese to the reduced béchamel, then mix with the puréed spinach. Gently fold in the stiffly beaten egg whites.

Pour into a soufflé dish which has been well greased with the remaining butter. Bake in a moderate oven for 30 minutes.

Add the remaining cheese to the unreduced béchamel. Pour into an ovenproof serving dish large enough to hold the spinach soufflé. Turn the soufflé into the centre and serve immediately.

US	Ingredients	Met/Imp
6½ lb	young spinach, washed and shredded	3 kg/6½ lb
	salt and pepper	
1 stick	butter	100 g/4 oz
1 tbsp	flour	15 ml/1 tbsp
	nutmeg	
½ cup	Béchamel Sauce (page 62)	100 ml/4 fl oz
½ cup	Gruyère cheese, grated	50 g/2 oz
½ lb	lean cooked ham	200 g/8 oz
4	eggs, separated	4

SPINACH SOUFFLÉ WITH HAM

Preparation 1 hour • Cooking about 20–25 minutes

Put the spinach into a saucepan of boiling salted water, using 7.5 ml/1½ tsp salt per 1 litre/1¾ pints (1 quart) water. (Always use a copper saucepan for blanching green vegetables, to retain their colour.)

Bring back to the boil and boil over a high heat for 8–10 minutes, then drain and rinse, squeezing out the water with your hands. Chop the spinach very finely or rub through a sieve.

Put the spinach into a saucepan with half of the butter. Stir over a high heat until the remaining water has evaporated, then stir in the flour, a pinch each of salt and pepper, a little nutmeg and the béchamel. Bring back to the boil, cover and simmer very gently for 20 minutes.

Remove from the heat and add three-quarters of the grated cheese, the diced ham, a small piece of butter and the egg yolks. Fold in the stiffly beaten egg whites.

Pour the mixture into a buttered soufflé dish, shape the top into a dome, sprinkle with the remaining cheese and the remaining butter, melted, and bake in a moderate oven for 20–22 minutes.

US	Ingredients	Met/Imp
1	calf's brain	1
	salt and pepper	
3 sticks	butter	350 g/12 oz
½ cup	olive oil	100 ml/4 fl oz
2 lb	spinach, trimmed	1 kg/2 lb
1 pinch	nutmeg	1 pinch
½ cup	thick Béchamel Sauce (page 62)	100 ml/4 fl oz
¼ cup	crème fraîche	50 ml/2 fl oz
½ cup	Parmesan cheese, grated	50 g/2 oz
2	eggs	2
2	egg yolks	2
	TO SERVE	
	Béchamel Sauce (page 62), with cream added	

ITALIAN SPINACH SUBRICS

Preparation 1 hour • Cooking 8 minutes

Season the calf's brain well with salt and pepper and cook *à la meunière* in some of the butter and the oil.

Cook the spinach in boiling salted water until tender. Drain, rinse and squeeze well between your hands, a little at a time. Chop finely, put into a cloth and wring out to extract the remaining water.

Put the spinach into a saucepan with 50 g/2 oz (4 tbsp) of the butter, a good pinch of salt, a pinch of pepper and the grated nutmeg. Stir over a high heat until all the moisture has evaporated. Add the thick béchamel sauce, stir and add the crème fraîche and the grated cheese.

Boil for a few minutes, then remove from the heat and add the calf's brain, mashed. Gradually whisk in the lightly beaten eggs and egg yolks.

Heat the remaining butter, clarified, in a large frying pan until smoking. Using 2 spoons, drop portions of the mixture into the pan leaving space between each to allow for spreading. After 1 minute, turn them with a fork and brown on the other side. Arrange on a heated dish and serve with béchamel sauce handed separately.

SPINACH TIAN

Preparation 30 minutes • Cooking 50 minutes

Wash and chop the spinach, then press to extract the water. Put it into a bowl with the flour, chopped garlic, salt and pepper. Stir in the milk and oil. Turn into an ovenproof dish and bake in a moderate oven for 45 minutes. Brown under the grill (broiler) for 5 minutes before serving.

US	Ingredients	Met/Imp
2 lb	spinach	1 kg/2 lb
2 tbsp	flour	30 ml/2 tbsp
2	garlic cloves	2
	salt and pepper	
1 cup	milk	250 ml/9 fl oz
2 tbsp	virgin olive oil	30 ml/2 tbsp

FENOUIL

FENNEL

THIS AROMATIC PLANT OF ITALIAN ORIGIN HAS AN ANISEED taste and its fleshy bulb is used as a vegetable: raw in salads and with cream; cooked as an accompaniment to meat; braised or sweated in butter; cooked au gratin; and braised with gravy or beef marrow. In sea bass with fennel, a classic combination, just a few sprigs of dried fennel are placed in the cavity of the fish to flavour the flesh.

US	Ingredients	Met/Imp
8–9, about 3 lb	fennel bulbs	8–9, about 1.5 kg/3 lb
1	lemon, finely grated rind and juice	1
	salt and white pepper	
1½ sticks	salted butter	175 g/6 oz
1	bunch parsley	1

FENNEL IN BUTTER

Preparation 10 minutes • Cooking about 1 hour

Carefully trim the fennel, discarding any withered outer parts. Cut off the stalks and trim the base. Add the lemon juice to a large saucepan of lightly salted water. Bring to the boil, put in the fennel and boil over a high heat for 20–25 minutes until tender but not over-cooked.

Drain thoroughly and cut each fennel bulb in half lengthways. Arrange in a gratin dish and dot with the butter, putting some between the bulbs and on the sides of the dish. Season lightly with salt and pepper and add the grated lemon rind. Cook in a slow oven for about 30 minutes, basting the fennel from time to time. Do not allow to brown. Sprinkle with chopped parsley and serve.

FÈVE

BROAD BEAN

EATEN IN MEDITERRANEAN COUNTRIES FOR CENTURIES, THE broad (or fava) bean is the most nutritious of all the leguminous plants, and it was the essential ingredient in cassoulet before dried beans were used. Fresh broad beans from the Midi region are available in summer and can be eaten raw while very young; older beans are shelled and boiled. Dried broad beans, which are even richer in protein than fresh broad beans, have to be soaked for about 12 hours before being cooked. New young broad beans make delicious salads, the older ones being used in stews or in purées, with savory as the most popular flavouring.

BROAD BEANS WITH CREAM

Preparation 1 hour • Cooking 35 minutes

US	Ingredients	Met/Imp
6½ lb	young broad (or fava beans	3 kg/6½ lb
I stick	butter	100 g/4 oz
2	savory sprigs	2
	salt and pepper	
I cup	boiling water	200 ml/7 fl oz
I cup	crème fraîche	200 ml/7 fl oz
2	egg yolks	2

Shell the beans and put them into a saucepan with the butter, savory and salt and pepper. Moisten with boiling water. Cook over a moderate heat for 35 minutes, until tender.

Just before serving, bind with the crème fraîche mixed with the egg yolks. Serve very hot.

RAGOÛT DE FÈVES AUX ARTICHAUTS

BROAD BEAN AND ARTICHOKE RAGOÛT

Preparation about 1½ hours • Cooking about 1 hour

US	Ingredients	Met/Imp
4½ lb	broad (or fava) beans	2 kg/4½ lb
3 quarts	water	2.8 litres/5 pints
9	globe artichokes	9
2	large onions	2
I glass	olive oil	I glass
	salt and pepper	
3	garlic cloves	3
I handful	parsley	I handful

Shell the beans. Bring half of the water to the boil in a saucepan, put in the beans and cook over a high heat for about 30 minutes, checking the volume of water which should be barely 500 ml/18 fl oz (2 cups) when the beans are cooked.

Meanwhile, prepare the artichokes. Remove all the coarse leaves, reserving only the most tender which should be cut into pieces of about 1 cm/½ inch. Carefully remove the chokes, then cut each bottom into 6–8 pieces. Bring the remaining water to the boil in another saucepan. Put in the artichokes and boil for about 15 minutes, then drain in a colander.

Peel the onions and cut into rings. Remove the beans and their liquid from the saucepan and pour in the oil. When hot, fry the onions until golden brown.

Add the beans with their liquid and the artichokes and season with salt and a good pinch of pepper. Simmer very gently for about 30 minutes. Add the finely chopped garlic and parsley 10 minutes before the end of cooking. Adjust seasoning. Allow to cool for about 20 minutes before serving.

HARICOT À ÉCOSSER

BEANS IN THE POD

WHETHER FRESH* OR DRIED, THESE BEANS ARE ALWAYS removed from their pods before cooking. They are distinguished by their size and colour, for example pale-green flageolets, are traditionally served with lamb; large white 'coco' beans and 'mogettes' from Poitou are used in ragoûts and cassoulets; large 'lingots' from the North are used for drying; and red kidney beans are simmered with bacon in red wine. Very nourishing and rich in protein, dried beans must be soaked for several hours before being cooked. Serve them with butter, cream, au gratin, with onion, as an accompaniment to salt cod or pork, or as warm, comforting winter meals.

*Editor's note: in France, these beans (haricots en grains) are sold fresh in the pod as well as semi-dried and dried, and many French recipes call for 'haricots blancs frais' (fresh white beans). These are not available in Great Britain and the United States, therefore dried white haricot beans (in the United States navy or Great Northern beans) may be substituted. Soaking and cooking times will depend on the freshness of the beans and recipes will have to be adapted accordingly.

ÉTUVÉE DE LÉGUMES NOUVEAUX AUX HARICOTS BLANCS

BRAISED NEW VEGETABLES WITH FRESH WHITE BEANS*

Preparation 50 minutes • Cooking 1 hour

US	Ingredients	Met/Imp
10 tbsp	butter	150 g/5 oz
4	heads lettuce, quartered	4
4	carrots, thinly sliced	4
4	turnips, thinly sliced	4
6	potatoes, thinly sliced	6
½ lb	French (fine green) beans, sliced diagonally into short lengths	250 g/8 oz
1 cup	fresh white beans	150 g/5 oz
2 cups	shelled freshly picked peas	500 ml/18 fl oz
	salt and pepper	

Liberally butter a flameproof earthenware casserole with a lid. Spread half of the lettuce over the bottom, then put half of each vegetable on top. Season with salt and pepper. Dot with half of the remaining butter, then add the remaining lettuce and vegetables. Season again with salt and pepper and dot with the remaining butter. Add 60 ml/4 tbsp cold water: this is enough liquid as the vegetables contain water. Cover the dish with a lid, sealing it with a ring of flour and water paste to prevent the steam from escaping. Bring to the boil, then cook in a moderate oven for 50 minutes. Remove the sealing paste and serve.

BORDEAUX-STYLE FRESH WHITE BEANS

Preparation 5 minutes • Cooking 1¼ hours

Bring the water to the boil in a saucepan. Put in the beans, half-cover and boil gently for 30 minutes.

Add the salt and pork fat. Cook for a further 30 minutes, making sure the beans do not stick to the pan when the water has been absorbed.

When the beans are nearly cooked, make the tomato sauce. Cut the tomatoes into quarters and remove the seeds. Heat the butter and fry the onion until soft. Add the tomatoes and stir over a moderate heat for 4 minutes. Add the herbs, clove, garlic, salt, pepper and nutmeg, then cover and cook over a low heat for 35–40 minutes, stirring from time to time, until the water from the tomatoes has evaporated. Rub through a sieve and set the purée aside.

Drain the beans thoroughly, reserving the cooking liquid for a stew. Put into a saucepan, add the tomato purée and heat through gently for 2 minutes. Serve sprinkled with parsley.

US	Ingredients	Met/Imp
2½ quarts	water	2.6 litres/4½ pints
2 lb (about 6 cups)	fresh white beans	1 kg/2 lb
1½ tsp	coarse sea salt	7.5 ml/1½ tsp
1 tbsp	pork fat	15 ml/1 tbsp
6	tomatoes	6
1 tbsp	butter	15 ml/1 tbsp
1 tbsp	chopped onion	15 ml/1 tbsp
3	parsley sprigs	3
1	thyme sprig	1
½	bay leaf	½
1	clove	1
2 tsp	crushed garlic	10 ml/2 tsp
	salt and pepper	
	nutmeg	
	chopped parsley	

RED KIDNEY BEANS WITH SALT PORK

Preparation 40 minutes • Cooking 2 hours

Wash the beans and soak them in cold water for 12 hours. Soak the pork in the same way.

The next day, drain the beans and pork and place in a large saucepan with the carrots, onion, garlic and bouquet garni. Cover with fresh cold water but do not add salt. Bring to the boil, skimming the scum from the surface, then cook until the beans are tender and neither too wet nor too dry. (If the pork is ready before the beans, take it out and set aside.)

Remove the bouquet garni and vegetable flavourings. Season to taste with salt, and cook for 1 further minute. Stir in the butter. Garnish with chopped parsley and serve with the salt pork.

US	Ingredients	Met/Imp
2 lb (about 5 cups)	dried red kidney beans	1 kg/2 lb
1 lb	salt pork	500 g/1 lb
2	carrots	2
1	onion, spiked with a clove	1
2	whole garlic cloves	2
1	bouquet garni	1
	salt and pepper	
4 tbsp	butter	50 g/2 oz
	parsley	

RED KIDNEY BEANS WITH RED WINE

Preparation 40 minutes • Cooking 2 hours

This recipe is made with the same ingredients as the previous one, but use 1 litre/1¾ pints (1 quart) full-bodied, strong red table wine instead of some of the water, allowing a little longer for cooking.

HARICOT VERT

FRENCH BEAN

THIS IS A LEGUMINOUS PLANT WITH A LONG, EDIBLE POD WHICH although called 'haricot vert' (green bean), comes in different colours according to its variety: string beans are long, thin and green and are available from May to September (very thin ones from Bagnols and the purple or 'triomphe' from Farcy); 'mange-tout' beans can be either green or yellow, the latter called 'beurre' being large and fleshy.

French beans must be used soon after picking or they begin to wither. Cook them in plenty of boiling water, adding salt at the same time as the beans. Boil, uncovered, over a high heat. Drain thoroughly, then dry out quickly at the front of the oven with the door open before using.

HARICOTS VERTS À L'ANGLAISE

FRENCH BEANS 'ANGLAISE'

Preparation 40 minutes • Cooking 20–25 minutes

US	Ingredients	Met/Imp
2¾ lb	French (fine green) beans	1.25 kg/2¾ lb
	coarse sea salt	
1 stick	butter	100 g/4 oz

For this recipe it is essential to choose very fine, fresh beans and to use them as soon as possible after picking.

Wash the beans in cold water, then plunge them into a saucepan of boiling water, adding salt at the same time as the beans, not before. Add a little more salt than usual (this is important). Cook uncovered until tender but still crisp, drain well, then return unrinsed, to the saucepan and allow the water to evaporate over the heat.

Put into a heated dish. Toss in diced butter to coat. The heat of the dish and the beans is sufficient to melt the butter. That is all, do not add anything more.

HARICOTS VERTS À LA LANDAISE

FRENCH BEANS FROM THE LANDES

Preparation 45 minutes • Cooking 25 minutes

US	Ingredients	Met/Imp
2¾ lb	French (fine green) beans	1.25 kg/2¾ lb
6 tbsp	butter	75 g/3 oz
1 cup	cheese, grated	100 g/4 oz
½ cup	crème fraîche	100 ml/4 fl oz
	salt and pepper	

Blanch the freshly picked beans. Drain. Toss in the butter in a saucepan. Sprinkle with grated cheese and stir in the crème fraîche. Season to taste and serve at once.

—— FRENCH BEANS WITH TOMATO ——

Preparation 1 hour • Cooking 55 minutes

US	Ingredients	Met/Imp
1½ lb	tomatoes	750 g/1½ lb
1	large onion	1
4	parsley sprigs	4
3 tbsp	olive oil	75 ml/3 tbsp
1¾–2 cups	vegetable stock	450 ml/¾ pint
	salt and pepper	
2¾ lb	French (fine green) beans	1.25 kg/2¾ lb

Wash the tomatoes, immerse them in boiling water for 1 minute, then peel.

Peel the onions, wash the parsley and chop both finely. Heat the oil in a saucepan and fry the onion and parsley. Add the chopped tomatoes and 200 ml/7 fl oz (scant 1 cup) of the stock. Cover and simmer 15 minutes.

Purée the tomatoes, then add a further 200 ml/7 fl oz (scant 1 cup) of the stock, and salt and pepper.

Trim and wash the beans. Add to the tomatoes. Cover, bring back to the boil, lower the heat and cook for 30–40 minutes, until tender. Add a little more stock if necessary. Turn into a heated dish and serve with meat.

LAITUE

LETTUCE

ALTHOUGH NORMALLY USED IN GREEN SALADS, LETTUCE MAY also be cooked: braised, puréed, with cream, even stuffed. Today the common varieties are: round (butterhead) lettuce, which is the most popular and looks like a loose cabbage with either smooth or curled leaves; batavia, with thicker, short, ridged leaves; cos (or romaine), with long leaves and thick veins and a long, loose heart. Lettuce is best in summer and spring, and must be washed very carefully. Round (butterhead) lettuce is used in Petits Pois 'Française' (*page 543*).

US	Ingredients	Met/Imp
16	large lettuces	16
¼ lb	bacon trimmings and rinds	100 g/4 oz
2	carrots	2
2	onions	2
1	bouquet garni	1
	salt and pepper	
	nutmeg	
8	long bacon slices	8
1¼ cups	White Stock (page 56)	300 ml/½ pint
8	croûtons, fried in butter	8
½ cup	Demi-Glaze (page 56)	100 ml/4 fl oz

BRAISED LETTUCE

Preparation 40 minutes • Cooking about 1 hour 10 minutes

This recipe should be well flavoured as lettuce is not a substantial vegetable. Do not discard the lettuce stalks until the end as they will prevent the leaves from disintegrating during blanching.

Wash the lettuces thoroughly, blanch, rinse, drain and gently squeeze out the water.

Line the bottom of a flameproof casserole with the bacon trimmings and rinds, and the chopped carrots and onions. Add the bouquet garni. Spread the drained lettuces out on a work surface and season with salt, pepper and a little nutmeg. Roll the lettuce in pairs in a bacon slice, then tie with string and place on top of the vegetables. Sweat, then add the stock and cover with buttered paper and a lid. Bring to the boil, then cook in a moderate oven until tender (about 1 hour).

Put the cooked lettuce rolls into a serving dish. Remove the string and bacon and discard the base of the stalks. Insert the croûtons between the lettuces.

Strain the cooking liquid and skim off the fat. Return to the pan and reduce, then add the demi-glaze. Pour over the lettuce and serve.

Prepare stuffed lettuce in the same way as braised lettuce. When braised and cooled, spread on a work surface. Trim the lettuces, removing some of the stalk and leaves damaged during cooking, cutting diagonally. Gently flatten the lettuces. Stuff them with the filling of your choice, fold over and return to a buttered pan. Moisten with a little good stock. Cover with buttered paper and simmer.

US	Ingredients	Met/Imp
heaping ½ cup	long-grain rice	100 g/4 oz
2½ cups	stock	600 ml/1 pint
¼ lb	cooked ham	100 g/4 oz
6 tbsp	butter	75 g/3 oz
8	heads lettuce	8
¼ lb	bacon rinds	100 g/4 oz
1	carrot, finely chopped	1
1	onion, finely chopped	1
1	bouquet garni	1
	salt and pepper	
scant 1 cup	Veal Stock (page 56)	200 ml/7 fl oz
2 tbsp	tomato paste	30 ml/2 tbsp

LETTUCE WITH RICE

Preparation 50 minutes • Cooking about 45 minutes

Blanch the rice for 6 minutes, then drain, rinse and cook in the stock until all the liquid has been absorbed. Mix the chopped ham with one-quarter of the butter. Put the lettuces into a saucepan of boiling salted water and boil for 8 minutes. Drain, rinse and squeeze well. Make a slit down 1 side of each lettuce and insert a good spoonful of rice and ham into it. Close up and tie with string.

Braise the lettuce parcels with the bacon rinds, carrot, onion, bouquet garni and salt and pepper. When cooked, remove the string, scrape the stuffed lettuce lightly on each side to remove any scum and arrange in a circle in a dish.

Skim the fat from the cooking liquid and reduce it to 100 ml/4 fl oz (½ cup). Add the veal stock and tomato paste and boil for a few minutes. Remove from the heat, add the remaining butter, pour over the lettuce and serve.

LENTILLE

LENTIL

CULTIVATED FROM TIME IMMEMORIAL, LENTILS ARE nourishing and full of protein. They are traditionally eaten with salt pork, but are also puréed, braised with meat juices, cooked with cream or even served either as a cold or warm salad with a well-seasoned vinaigrette dressing. The Puy variety of lentil is dark green with a strong flavour and is protected by an 'appellation', but there are also green, brown and white lentils of various origins. They are prepared like dried beans, although some say they should not be soaked.

PURÉE DE LENTILLES

LENTIL PURÉE

Preparation 10 minutes • Soaking 1–2 hours (optional) • Cooking about 40 minutes

US	Ingredients	Met/Imp
1¾ lb (about 4 cups)	green Puy lentils	800 g/1¾ lb
1½ tsp	coarse sea salt	7.5 ml/1½ tsp
a few	black peppercorns, crushed	a few
1	bouquet garni	1
1	large onion	1
2	cloves	2
1, about 2 oz	carrot	1, about 50 g/2 oz
4 tbsp	butter	50 g/2 oz

Pick over and wash the lentils. If liked, soak them for 1–2 hours in cold water. Drain and put into a large saucepan. Cover with water, bring to the boil and remove the scum from the surface. Add the salt, peppercorns, bouquet garni, the onion spiked with the cloves and the peeled and diced carrot.

Cover and boil very gently for 30–40 minutes until tender. (The cooking time depends on the freshness of the lentils.) Remove the bouquet garni and onion. Purée the lentils while still hot, adding a little of the cooking liquid if necessary. Reheat the purée gently, stirring constantly, then stir in the butter. Serve very hot.

SALADE DE LENTILLES TIÈDE AU CERVELAS

WARM LENTIL SALAD WITH SAVELOY*

Preparation 20 minutes • Cooking 30–40 minutes

US	Ingredients	Met/Imp
1¼ lb (about 3 cups)	lentils	600 g/1¼ lb
1	bouquet garni	1
1	onion	1
1	clove	1
1	small carrot	1
1	saveloy sausage	1
6 tbsp	corn oil	90 ml/6 tbsp
3 tbsp	red wine vinegar	45 ml/3 tbsp
1	shallot	1
	salt and pepper	
	parsley	

Cook the lentils as in the above recipe with the bouquet garni, the onion spiked with the clove and the peeled and diced carrot. Cook for a shorter time than above, so that the lentils are still slightly firm.

Meanwhile, poach the saveloy in water, then drain and slice diagonally. Make a vinaigrette dressing with the oil, vinegar, finely chopped shallot and salt and pepper.

Drain the lentils thoroughly and put into a serving dish. Fork the onion and carrot evenly through the lentils, then arrange the slices of saveloy on top. Pour the dressing over and leave to stand for a few minutes. Garnish with parsley and serve warm.

MAÏS

CORN

ORIGINALLY FROM MEXICO AND VERY POPULAR IN BOTH North and South American cooking, corn is a cereal which can be ground into flour or semolina to make porridge, bread, pancakes, cakes, etc, including the famous Italian polenta. From July until October fresh corn on the cob is available, which can be boiled or grilled. When the kernels are removed from the cob, they are served with butter or cream as an accompaniment to meat or poultry.

ÉPIS DE MAÏS AU BEURRE FONDU

CORN ON THE COB WITH MELTED BUTTER

Preparation 10 minutes • Cooking 6–8 minutes

US	Ingredients	Met/Imp
16	corn on the cob	16
2 cups	milk	500 ml/18 fl oz
	parsley sprigs	
10 tbsp	lightly salted butter, melted	150 g/5 oz
	lemons, to garnish (optional)	

Choose very tender ears of corn (best in August in France) with creamy kernels. Remove the outer husks, retaining the tender inner ones. Poach in boiling water with the milk added to it, for 6–8 minutes, or until tender.

Serve on individual plates, each garnished with a parsley sprig. Serve the melted butter separately. If liked, garnish each plate with a halved lemon. The kernels may also be scraped off with a fork and served in a dish. Corn on the cob may also be grilled.

POLENTA À L'ITALIENNE

ITALIAN-STYLE POLENTA

Preparation 3 hours • Cooking about 1 hour

US	Ingredients	Met/Imp
	olive oil	
	garlic	
	salt	
2 cups	cornmeal	250 g/8 oz
	butter and oil for shallow frying	
	Parmesan cheese, grated	

Put 1 litre/1¾ pints (1 quart) water into a saucepan with the olive oil, finely chopped garlic and a little salt. Bring to the boil.

Make a paste with the cornmeal and about 100 ml/4 fl oz (½ cup) cold water. Add the paste to the flavoured boiling water, stir and cook over a low heat for 40–50 minutes, stirring from time to time. Pour into a moistened dish and leave to cool completely.

Cut the polenta into slices, allowing one per person. Fry the slices in a mixture of half butter and half oil in a frying pan. Serve very hot, sprinkled with grated Parmesan.

MARRON

CHESTNUT

THE FRUIT OF THE CHESTNUT TREE IS ENCLOSED IN A THORNY husk. When there are several nuts inside the same husk the chestnuts are called 'châtaignes', and are grilled or used to make flour, as well as being traditional in some regional cooking. If there is just one nut in the husk, the chestnut is called 'marron' and is much better in quality. This type is cultivated in the Ardèche, the Dordogne, in Corsica and Lozère, and is used to make stuffings for large birds such as turkey or goose; it is also used with cabbage (green and red) and Brussels sprouts. Puréed, marrons are served with venison (stag, young wild boar, etc.)

Marrons also play an important role in pâtisserie and confectionery, particularly in sweet purées, preserves, marrons glacés, etc.

PURÉE DE MARRONS

CHESTNUT PURÉE

Preparation 1 hour • Cooking 40–50 minutes

US	Ingredients	Met/Imp
3 lb	chestnuts	1.5 kg/3 lb
1	celery stalk	1
3	sugar cubes	3
1 cup	stock	200 ml/7 fl oz
1 stick	butter	100 g/4 oz
½ cup	milk or single (light) cream	100 ml/3½ fl oz

Peel the chestnuts. There are 3 methods of doing this: 1) boil for 6 minutes; 2) place in a hot oven to break the husk without browning it; 3) immerse 7–8 chestnuts at a time in smoking hot oil. In each case, score the husks to prevent them from bursting open.

Put the peeled chestnuts into a high-sided narrow saucepan with the chopped celery, sugar and sufficient stock to cover them. Bring to the boil, cover and cook gently for about 45 minutes, until tender.

When cooked, rub the chestnuts quickly through a sieve while they are still hot. Put the purée into a shallow saucepan with 75–90 ml/5–6 tbsp stock and stir over a high heat for a few minutes until it thickens (it should be the same consistency as potato purée). Remove from the heat and stir in the diced butter, milk or cream. Heat through gently, but do not allow to boil.

MORILLE

MOREL

THIS TASTY SPRING MUSHROOM IS COMPARATIVELY RARE, BUT its delicate flavour makes it a luxury in cooking. It can be prepared with cream, stuffed, used as a garnish for chicken, as a pie filling, etc. As the morel caps are deeply pitted they must be very thoroughly cleaned to remove earth, grit and even small insects. Rinse the mushrooms in several changes of water and drain thoroughly. Morels have dark caps, ranging from white, which have the least flavour, through brown to almost black – which are the most prized.

MORILLES À L'ANDALOUSE

ANDALUSIAN-STYLE MORELS

Preparation 1 hour • Cooking 30–35 minutes

US	Ingredients	Met/Imp
½ lb	Bayonne ham	250 g/8 oz
½ cup	olive oil	100 ml/3½ fl oz
2 lb	morels	1 kg/2 lb
2	large onions	2
1 cup	dry sherry	200 ml/7 fl oz
½ cup	Veal Stock (*page 56*)	100 ml/3½ fl oz
½ cup	Demi-Glaze (*page 56*)	100 ml/3½ fl oz
2	sweet peppers	2
	pepper	

Fry the diced ham in the oil until golden brown, then drain on paper towels.

Wash and cut the morels in halves or quarters and put into the frying pan with the chopped onions. When the morels are lightly browned, pour off the oil. Return the ham to the frying pan and add the sherry. Reduce the liquid by half. Add the veal stock and demi-glaze, and finally the de-seeded, sliced peppers and a pinch of pepper. Simmer gently for just under 30 minutes, then serve in a vegetable dish.

MORILLES FARCIES

STUFFED MORELS

Preparation 2 hours • Cooking 30–40 minutes

US	Ingredients	Met/Imp
3 lb	large morels	1.5 kg/3 lb
	STUFFING	
1 lb (about 2 cups)	Forcemeat Stuffing (*page 54*)	500 g/1 lb
2 tbsp	chopped parsley	30 ml/2 tbsp
	salt and pepper	
1 pinch	quatre-épices	1 pinch
2	egg yolks	2
16	small bacon slices	16
8	croûtons	8
	butter	
¼ cup	good Veal Stock (*page 56*), if necessary	50 ml/2 fl oz

Wash the morels and blanch them for 2–3 minutes, then rinse and drain on a cloth. Dry well.

Fill the morels with the forcemeat stuffing combined with the parsley, salt, pepper, spice and egg yolks. Divide the stuffed morels into 8 equal portions and arrange each portion between the slices of bacon. Cover and cook in an ovenproof dish or shallow casserole in a slow oven for 30–40 minutes, until tender.

Meanwhile, cut 8 croûtons into the same size and shape as the morels and fry in butter.

Just before serving the morels, baste them with the cooking liquid, adding the veal stock if the morels seem rather dry. Serve garnished with the fried croûtons.

MORILLES FARCIES À LA FORESTIÈRE

—— STUFFED MORELS FORESTIÈRE ——

Preparation 1 hour • Cooking 20–25 minutes

US	Ingredients	Met/Imp
3 lb	large morels	1.5 kg/3 lb
1	large onion	1
6	shallots	6
1 lb	finely minced (ground) pork	500 g/1 lb
2 cups	fresh breadcrumbs	100 g/4 oz
1 tbsp	chopped parsley	15 ml/1 tbsp
1 pinch	crushed garlic	1 pinch
	salt and pepper	
2	eggs	2
10 tbsp	butter	150 g/5 oz

Trim off and chop the morel stalks. Put them into a bowl with the finely chopped onion and shallots, pork, three-quarters of the breadcrumbs, the parsley, garlic, salt, pepper and eggs. Mix very well. Blanch the morel caps and fill with the stuffing. Place the morels on a buttered baking sheet. Sprinkle with the remaining breadcrumbs and dot with the butter. Cook in a moderate oven for 20 minutes until browned. Serve hot.

MORILLES À LA NORMANDE

—— MORELS NORMANDE ——

Preparation 35 minutes • Cooking 15 minutes

US	Ingredients	Met/Imp
1 lb	morels	500 g/1 lb
	salt and pepper	
1 stick	butter	100 g/4 oz
1 cup	crème fraîche	200 ml/7 fl oz

Trim and soak the morels, changing the water to remove all the grit. Slice them in half and put them into a saucepan with 2 litres/3½ pints (2 quarts) cold salted water. Bring slowly to the boil, then boil for 2 minutes. Drain on a cloth.

Melt the butter in a frying pan. When it is hot but not brown, add the morels and cook over a low heat for 5 minutes. Season with salt and pepper. Add the crème fraîche and cook for a further 4 minutes. Serve at once.

— TIMBALE OF MORELS BEAUCAIRE —

Preparation 1½ hours • Cooking 1 hour

US	Ingredients	Met/Imp
1 lb (about 2 cups)	Forcemeat Stuffing (*page 54*)	500 g/1 lb
¼ lb	fresh truffles	100 g/4 oz
2 lb	morels	1 kg/2 lb
1 stick	butter	100 g/4 oz
	salt and pepper	
½	small lemon, juice of	½
2½ cups	Béchamel Sauce (*page 62*)	600 ml/1 pint
5	egg yolks	5
scant 1 cup	*crème fraîche*	200 ml/7 fl oz
	GARNISH	
2	hard-boiled eggs	2
1 tbsp	chopped parsley	15 ml/1 tbsp
2 cups	fresh white breadcrumbs	100 g/4 oz
1 stick	butter, melted	100 g/4 oz

If liked, this timbale can be served with a Cream Sauce (*page 67*), or with a sauce made from good stock flavoured with sherry.

Mix the forcemeat with the finely chopped truffles. Set aside.

Wash the morels in several changes of water, removing any grit from the caps. Set aside 10 of the best caps, and about 100 g/4 oz (1½ cups) of the stalks, chopped.

Put the remaining morels into a saucepan with 2 litres/3½ pints (2 quarts) water, the butter, a pinch each of salt and pepper and the lemon juice. Cover and bring to the boil, then keep on the edge of the heat for 6–7 minutes.

Remove the morels from the cooking liquid with a slotted spoon. If they are large, cut them in halves or quarters. Add their cooking liquid to the béchamel and work through a sieve into a saucepan. Bind with the egg yolks, stirring continuously over a high heat. Add the crème fraîche, a spoonful at a time, and cook until the sauce is reduced to 400 ml/14 fl oz (1¾ cups) and is very thick. Stir in the cooked morels and leave to cool.

Butter a wide charlotte mould and line the bottom and sides with about three-quarters of the forcemeat. Pour the morel sauce into the mould, cover with the remaining forcemeat, level the top and cover with buttered paper. Cook in a *bain-marie* in a moderate oven for 55 minutes.

Meanwhile, prepare the garnish. Make a Dry Duxelles according to the instructions on page 49, using the reserved chopped morel stalks. Mix in the chopped hard-boiled eggs and the parsley. Divide the reserved uncooked whole morels in half and fill each half with the duxelles. Arrange in a buttered dish and sprinkle with the breadcrumbs. Pour the melted butter over the top and brown in a hot oven for 20 minutes.

To serve. Remove the mould from the oven, leave to stand for 8–10 minutes, then turn out on to a round serving dish. Garnish with the stuffed morel halves.

NAVET

TURNIP

TRADITIONALLY USED IN SOUPS AND POT-AU-FEU, TURNIPS deserve to be more popular for their unique flavour and versatility. They can be cooked au gratin, puréed, in soufflés, stuffed, braised, glazed, etc. The main varieties are 'Milan', which is white and round with a purple ring around the top, 'Nantais', which is oblong, and the delicious 'boule d'or'. New turnips are delicate, but winter turnips benefit from blanching. They are traditionally served with fatty meats, especially duck and mutton.

CHOUCROUTE DE NAVETS

——— TURNIP SAUERKRAUT ———

Preparation 1 hour • Maceration 12 days • Cooking 5 minutes

US	Ingredients	Met/Imp
about 6½ lb	large turnips	about 3 kg/6½ lb
3 tbsp	coarse sea salt	50 g/2 oz
	black peppercorns	
	juniper berries	

Peel the turnips and discard any fibrous parts. Coarsely grate the flesh and place in 1–2 bowls. Add the salt and mix with your hands, then leave to stand for 5 minutes. (This softens the turnip and makes it easier to press down.)

Fill an earthenware dish with the salted turnip, pressing it down well. Sprinkle every second or third layer with peppercorns and juniper berries. Add the juice from the bowls and cover with a cloth. Put a plate on top and weight down. Refrigerate for at least 1 week.

Pour off all the fermented juice and rinse the turnip thoroughly. Blanch it in boiling water and serve in the same way as a real cabbage sauerkraut with meat and sausages, or else braise it in white wine and serve with pork.

NAVETS BRAISÉS À LA DANOISE

——— DANISH-STYLE BRAISED TURNIP ———

Preparation 6–8 minutes • Cooking about 30 minutes

US	Ingredients	Met/Imp
1¾ lb	young turnips	800 g/1¾ lb
3 tbsp	butter	40 g/1½ oz
1 cup	stock	200 ml/7 fl oz
	salt and white pepper	
1 tbsp	chopped fresh dill	15 ml/1 tbsp
1 tbsp	chopped fresh parsley	15 ml/1 tbsp

Peel, wash and dry the turnips. Cut them into medium dice. Melt the butter in a pan and fry the turnips over a moderate heat for a few minutes, then add the stock and cook for about 20 minutes, until tender. Season with salt and pepper and sprinkle with the dill and parsley. Cover and leave for 2 minutes to allow the vegetables to absorb the flavour of the herbs. Serve very hot with grilled (or broiled) mutton, fried sausages, etc.

OIGNON

ONION

ONIONS ARE A 'FOUNDATION VEGETABLE', A CONDIMENT AND A flavouring used in innumerable recipes, but they are also served in their own right, as in onion soup, all recipes described as 'soubise', flans, quiches and tarts, purées, garnishes for ragoûts and *matelotes*, in salads, etc. The main types of onion are differentiated by colour, size and season. There are white summer onions, which are crisp and full of flavour; spring onions (scallions) with their green tops (excellent for glazing, for making marinades *à la grecque*, etc); strong, yellow onions for use in soups and any cooked dish; and red or pink onions, which are best raw.

OIGNONS À LA CRÈME

ONIONS WITH CREAM

Preparation 1 hour • Soaking 5 hours • Cooking 30 minutes

US	Ingredients	Met/Imp
16	onions	16
½ cup	crème fraîche	100 ml/4 fl oz
	salt	
2 tbsp	chopped parsley	30 ml/2 tbsp

Some people find onions indigestible, but the following procedure makes them as easy to digest as boiled onions: peel the onions, then soak them in cold water for 4–5 hours, changing the water several times.

Leave the onions whole. Blanch them, being careful to keep them whole. Remove from the saucepan and immerse in cold water to cool. Drain. Arrange side by side in a dish and place in a very hot oven to dry out.

When dry, cover with the crème fraîche, season with a little salt and sprinkle with the parsley.

PAILLETTES D'OIGNONS FRITS

DEEP-FRIED ONION STRAWS

Preparation 1 hour • Cooking 5 minutes

US	Ingredients	Met/Imp
16	Spanish onions	16
½ cup	milk	100 ml/4 fl oz
¾ cup	flour	100 g/4 oz
	oil for deep frying	
	salt	

Slice the onions very finely. Dip in milk, then in flour. Deep-fry until golden and crisp. Arrange in a pyramid, sprinkle with salt and serve at once.

OSEILLE

SORREL

SORREL, WITH ITS VIVID GREEN LEAVES AND BITTER TASTE, IS prepared and used like spinach, ie puréed, cut into strips and cooked in butter, even raw in salads. Sometimes sweetened with *crème fraîche*, sorrel is a traditional accompaniment for veal, shad or pike, as well as eggs. Sorrel can have large or small leaves, smooth or ridged, which vary in colour from dark to fairly light green, and is available from March to August. Cooked sorrel usually weighs one-third of the weight of the raw leaves.

OSEILLE AU JUS

BRAISED SORREL

Preparation 1 hour • Cooking 2 hours 10 minutes

US	Ingredients	Met/Imp
9 lb	young sorrel	4 kg/9 lb
11 tbsp	butter	160 g/5½ oz
6 tbsp	flour	50 g/2 oz
2 cups	hot Veal Stock (page 56)	500 ml/18 fl oz
	salt	
	sugar	
4	egg yolks	4
scant ½ cup	crème fraîche	100 ml/3½ fl oz

Trim and wash the sorrel and put into a saucepan with 2 litres/3½ pints (2 quarts) water. Cook gently until tender, then drain thoroughly and rub through a sieve.

Make a white *roux* with 60 g/2½ oz (5 tbsp) of the butter and the flour in a flameproof casserole. Gradually add the sorrel purée and most of the stock. Season with about 10 ml/2 tsp salt and a good pinch of sugar. Bring to the boil, stirring. Cover with buttered paper and a lid and cook in a very moderate oven for 2 hours.

Lightly beat the egg yolks and crème fraîche and gradually blend in 60–75 ml/4–5 tbsp of the sorrel mixture (to heat the egg gradually without curdling). Stir in the remainder, place over a very low heat and simmer for 5–6 minutes. Blend in the remaining butter, pour into a serving dish and pour over the remaining veal stock.

PETIT POIS

PEA

THE SAINT-GERMAIN AND CLAMART VARIETIES OF PEA HAVE become so well known that they have given their names to certain special recipes. Fresh peas, which have to be shelled and are picked between May and July, are the most delicious and by far the best. The early peas known as 'lisses' have smooth pods, and the larger, sweeter ones known as 'ridés' have wrinkled pods. The sooner they are eaten after picking the better they are. Easily shelled, there is no need to wash them.

The *split pea* is small and pale green, the dried seeds of peas picked at full maturity. Rich in protein, they have to be soaked before cooking, and are particularly suitable for soups and purées.

As for *chick peas* (or garbanzos) which are frequently used in the south of France, they are also the seeds of a leguminous plant, and are beige, round and wrinkled. They are used as an accompanying vegetable, in soups and purées and in salads.

PETITS POIS 'ANGLAISE'

Preparation 30 minutes • Cooking 20 minutes

US	Ingredients	Met/Imp
2 quarts	shelled petits pois	2 litres/3½ pints
1 stick	butter	100 g/4 oz
	salt	
	sugar (optional)	

Blanch the peas in a copper saucepan (not tin-lined) or a cauldron. There should be a lot of water and a lot of salt. Throw the peas in when the water is boiling vigorously; do not allow the water to come off the boil. (By doing this you will get very green peas.)

Drain the peas and dry very thoroughly; it is absolutely essential that they do not retain a drop of water. Put the peas into a heated serving dish, just as they are. Just before serving, add the butter and toss the peas so that they are coated thoroughly in the softened butter. Season with a little salt, adding a little caster (superfine) sugar if liked.

PETITS POIS 'FRANÇAISE'

Preparation 40 minutes • Cooking 30–35 minutes

US	Ingredients	Met/Imp
2 quarts	shelled peas	2 litres/3½ pints
2	lettuce hearts, finely shredded	2
3½ tsp	salt	20 g/¾ oz
2½ tbsp	sugar	30 g/1 oz
10 tbsp	butter	150 g/5 oz
1	bunch parsley stalks (not the leaves)	1
20	button (pearl) onions	20

Put the peas, lettuce, salt, sugar, 100 g/4 oz (8 tbsp) of the butter, the parsley stalks and the onions into a high-sided saucepan and mix well.

Add a glass of water, cover with buttered paper and a tight-fitting lid and cook for about 30 minutes until tender. Remove from the heat and stir in the remaining butter. Adjust the seasoning if necessary. Turn into a dish, remove the parsley stalks and arrange the lettuce on top.

PURÉE DE POIS CASSÉS SAINT-GERMAIN

SAINT-GERMAIN SPLIT PEA PURÉE

Preparation 4 hours • Cooking 1½ hours

US	Ingredients	Met/Imp
5 cups	split peas	1 kg/2 lb
1	ham bone	1
scant 1 cup	Mirepoix (*page 50*)	200 g/8 oz
¼ lb	fatty bacon, blanched	100 g/4 oz
1	bouquet garni	1
1 stick	butter	100 g/4 oz

Soak the peas in cold water for 2 hours. Drain, cover with 2 litres/3½ pints (2 quarts) fresh cold water, then add the ham bone, mirepoix, bacon and bouquet garni. Cook gently for 1½ hours.

Drain the peas, reserving the liquid. Rub the peas through a fine sieve. Return to the rinsed-out pan and heat through, stirring with a wooden spoon. Dilute with a little of the reserved cooking liquid. Remove from the heat and stir in the butter before serving.

POIREAU

LEEK

NICKNAMED 'POOR MAN'S ASPARAGUS' AND USED IN NUMEROUS garnishes and for flavouring, this popular vegetable provides excellent vegetable dishes in its own right. Leeks are always cooked and can be served as an hors-d'œuvre, with vinaigrette dressing, or with béchamel, in flans, tarts and quiches, au gratin, in soup, braised in butter or as a garnish for fish. Young leeks and thin 'baguettes' are deliciously tender. Winter varieties also have a very good flavour and those with a thick, white root are also to be recommended. It is the white part that is most appreciated, but the green is also used in soups and purées.

FLAMICHE AUX POIREAUX

LEEK TART*

Preparation 15 minutes • Chilling 1 hour • Cooking 1 hour

US	Ingredients	Met/Imp
1½ cups	flour	200 g/7 oz
1 stick	butter	100 g/3½ oz
	salt	
1	small egg	1
	FILLING	
10 oz	leeks, white part only	300 g/10 oz
3 oz	bacon	75 g/3 oz
5 tbsp	butter	60 g/2½ oz
3 tbsp	flour	30 g/1 oz
1¾ cups	milk, boiled	400 ml/14 fl oz
	salt and pepper	
	nutmeg	

Make Shortcrust Pastry according to the instructions on page 577. Chill in the refrigerator for 1 hour.

Meanwhile make the filling. Cut the leeks into thin rings. Finely dice the bacon, then blanch it. Heat half of the butter in a saucepan and lightly fry the bacon. Add the leeks and fry for about 15 minutes until soft, stirring from time to time. Do not allow them to brown. Add the flour and cook for a few minutes. Gradually add the milk. Season with salt, pepper and nutmeg. Bring to the boil, increasing the heat slightly and stirring constantly, then lower the heat and simmer very gently for 20 minutes.

Roll out the pastry until 5 mm/¼ inch thick and use to line a 28 cm/11 inch flan dish (quiche or tart dish). Prick the base. Pour in the leek mixture, dot with the remaining butter and cook on the bottom shelf of a moderate oven for about 25 minutes. Serve very hot.

Braised New Vegetables with Fresh White Beans
This delicious 'jardinière' of spring vegetables shows off the fresh white beans to their best advantage: a mosaic of flavours and colours which goes very well with grilled (broiled) or roast lamb. (Recipe on page 528.)

Cep and Almond Feuilleté
Dedicated to the journalist and cookery writer Charles Monselet, who wrote the
Almanach gastronomique *in the 1860s, this 'tourte' is served hot as a first cour.*
(*Recipe on page 506.*)

Leek Tart
Called 'flamiche' in French, this leek tart used to be a flat cake made with bread dough; it was eaten hot with melted butter on top. Nowadays, it is usually a leek tart made with pastry, typical of Flemish cuisine. (Recipe on page 544.)

Tomatoes Filled with Eggs
The size of the tomatoes, their evenness and their firmness, play a decisive role in the success of this recipe of eggs 'au nid' (in a nest). The eggs must be softly set, not hard. You can also add a little crème fraîche or a pinch of grated cheese such as Emmenthal or, even better, Parmesan, if you like. The sprigs of chervil, added at the time of serving, add a contrasting note. (Recipe on page 557.)

Tagliatelle with Tomato and Aubergine Sauce
*A ribbon-shaped pasta which may be creamy-gold or green (flavoured with spinach),
tagliatelle is a speciality of Emilia-Romagna, here prepared as a simple vegetable
dish. Aromatics from the South of France are necessary to achieve the correct flavour.
Served as a hot first course in an Italian-style meal, it may be followed by small veal
escalopes (cutlets) cooked in marsala. (Recipe on page 561.)*

Turkish-Style Stuffed Peppers
A mixture of cooked lamb, sausagemeat, rice and olives flavoured with onions and garlic forms the stuffing of these sweet peppers, which should be served very hot. (Recipe on page 546.)

POIREAUX À LA CHAPELURE

LEEK GRATIN

Preparation 1½ hours • Cooking about 50 minutes

Boil the white part of the leeks with the potatoes. Put the leeks into the water first as they take longer to cook. Drain the leeks and place on a cloth to dry. Keep the potatoes hot.

Beat the eggs in a bowl with a little salt. Dip the leeks into the beaten egg, then roll in breadcrumbs. Dip again in the beaten egg. Place carefully in a generously buttered ovenproof dish and cook for about 20 minutes. Arrange the potatoes around and serve.

US	Ingredients	Met/Imp
4½ lb	leeks, white part only	2 kg/4½ lb
8	small new Dutch potatoes	8
3	eggs	3
	salt	
2½ cups	fresh white breadcrumbs	150 g/5 oz
1 stick	butter	100 g/3½ oz

POIREAUX À LA GRECQUE

LEEKS À LA GRECQUE

Preparation 15 minutes • Cooking 30 minutes

Trim the leeks, discarding the green leaves. Wash and chop the white part, then blanch in boiling water for 10 minutes. Meanwhile, pour the wine into a large saucepan and add the oil, the juice of 1½ lemons, the remaining ½ lemon sliced into thin rings, the bouquet garni, chopped fennel stalks, coriander seeds and peppercorns. Season with salt. Bring to the boil, adding a small ladleful of the leek cooking water. Simmer for about 8 minutes, then add the well-drained leeks. Cook for a further 10 minutes. When the leeks are very tender, drain them with the lemon rings. Arrange in a serving dish. Strain the cooking stock over the leeks, sprinkle with parsley and leave to cool completely. Serve cold as an hors-d'oeuvre, or as a garnish for cold meat.

US	Ingredients	Met/Imp
2 lb	small leeks	1 kg/2 lb
1 cup	dry white wine	200 ml/7 fl oz
½ cup	virgin olive oil	100 ml/3½ fl oz
2	lemons	2
1	bouquet garni	1
3	dried fennel stalks	3
1 tbsp	coriander seeds	15 ml/1 tbsp
1 tbsp	white peppercorns	15 ml/1 tbsp
	salt	
	chopped parsley, to garnish	

POIVRON

SWEET PEPPER

THIS VARIETY OF CAPSICUM CAN BE EATEN EITHER RAW OR cooked. Its colour (green, yellow or red) varies according to the degree of ripeness. The straight-sided 'carré' pepper is thick and very sweet, fleshier than that of Valence, whereas the Landes pepper is elongated. Always de-seeded before using, sometimes peeled and often stuffed, peppers are a summer vegetable with numerous applications in Mediterranean cooking, of which the Basque pipérade is one of the best examples.

US	Ingredients	Met/Imp
6	even-sized green sweet peppers	6
	salt and pepper	
3	garlic cloves	3
2	onions	2
½ cup	olive oil	100 ml/4 fl oz
½ lb	sausagemeat	250 g/8 oz
1½ cups	minced (ground) cooked lamb	300 g/10 oz
1 teacup	cooked rice	1 teacup
2 tbsp	chopped stoned black olives	30 ml/2 tbsp
2 tbsp	chopped parsley	30 ml/2 tbsp
1	egg, beaten	1
	cayenne	
14 oz	ripe tomatoes	400 g/14 oz
1	bouquet garni	1
1	lemon, juice of	1

— TURKISH-STYLE STUFFED PEPPERS* —

Preparation 45 minutes • Cooking 50 minutes • Serves 6

Wash and dry the peppers. Cut off the tops and set aside. De-seed and flatten the core with the back of a spoon. Lightly salt the inside and leave upside down on a cloth to drain. Peel and chop the garlic; peel and finely chop the onions and fry them with the garlic in 30 ml/2 tbsp of the oil until soft. Add the sausagemeat and lamb and fry gently, stirring. Remove from the heat and add the rice, olives, parsley and beaten egg. Season with salt, pepper and a pinch of cayenne. Mix well, stuff the peppers with the mixture and replace the tops.

Spread the skinned, de-seeded and chopped tomatoes over the base of an oiled ovenproof dish. Add the bouquet garni and stand the stuffed peppers on top. Sprinkle with the remaining oil and the lemon juice. Bake in a moderate oven for about 50 minutes. Serve hot, straight from the dish.

US	Ingredients	Met/Imp
2	large onions	2
1 cup	olive oil	200 ml/7 fl oz
3	garlic cloves	3
2	sweet peppers	2
8	tomatoes	8
6	aubergines (eggplant)	6
6	courgettes (zucchini)	6
	salt and pepper	
1	bouquet garni	1

—— RATATOUILLE FROM NICE ——

Preparation 1 hour • Cooking about 1 hour

Peel and finely chop the onions and put into a saucepan with 60 ml/4 tbsp of the oil. Fry until lightly coloured, then add the garlic and fry, stirring, for 5 minutes. Add the de-seeded and thinly sliced peppers and the skinned, de-seeded and coarsely chopped tomatoes.

Meanwhile, lightly fry the peeled and coarsely diced aubergines (eggplant) and courgettes (zucchini) in the remaining oil until golden-brown. Drain well in a colander, then mix with the other ingredients.

Season with salt and pepper and add the bouquet garni. Cover and simmer gently for a good hour until everything is very tender. Serve hot or cold.

US	Ingredients	Met/Imp
8	green sweet peppers	8
½ cup	Vinaigrette Dressing (*page 81*)	100 ml/4 fl oz
4	tomatoes	4
3	small spring onions (scallions)	3

—— GRILLED PEPPER SALAD ——

Preparation 45 minutes • Cooking 10 minutes

Place the peppers under a moderate grill (broiler) and turn on all sides to char and blister the skin so that it will be easy to remove. Cool slightly, then rub off the skins.

Remove the seeds, cut the pepper flesh into thin strips and season with a few spoonfuls of vinaigrette dressing. Add the skinned, de-seeded and thinly sliced or diced tomatoes.

Arrange the salad in small shallow bowls or hors-d'œuvre dishes and surround with very thinly sliced rings of spring onions (scallion).

POMME DE TERRE

POTATO

GIVEN THE VERSATILITY OF POTATOES IN COOKING, AS AN accompaniment to most meats, poultry, fish and even eggs (whole, sliced whole into rings, diced, cut into thin slices or sticks; puréed, boiled, steamed, sautéed, fried, deep-fried and baked in hot ashes, etc), it is essential to choose a variety which suits the recipe. There are 3 main varieties of potato. New potatoes called 'grenailles' have firm flesh and thin skin and do not keep for long; they are usually fried or deep-fried. Firm-fleshed waxy potatoes which retain their shape well during cooking and are suitable for steaming, frying, boiling in their skins and for use in salads and ragoûts are 'belle de Fontanay', 'B. F.15', 'ratte', 'roseval' and 'viola'. The most commonly used potatoes are the floury ones, which should be used for soups and purées. They are also good for French fries in that they remain soft in the centre when crisp on the outside. The main varieties are 'bintje', 'kerpondy', 'spunta' and 'urgenta'.

US	Ingredients	Met/Imp
2 lb	floury potatoes	1 kg/2 lb
1 tbsp	butter	15 g/½ oz
	salt and pepper	
	nutmeg	
2	eggs	2
3	egg yolks	3
2	slices cooked ham (optional)	2
1 cup	Comté cheese, grated (optional)	100 g/4 oz
	flour	
	fresh breadcrumbs	
	oil for deep-frying	

POTATO CROQUETTES

Preparation 1 hour • Cooking 40 minutes • Makes 30

Boil the potatoes in their skins. Drain, peel and purée. Place in a heavy saucepan over a high heat to dry out, stirring with a wooden spoon.

Add the butter cut into small pieces, stirring well. Season lightly with salt, pepper and nutmeg. If not using the cheese, add a little more salt.

Remove from the heat and add 1 whole egg, then the 3 yolks and mix well.

Finely chop the ham, if using, and add to the potatoes with the cheese, if used. Mix and allow to cool.

Put a few tablespoonfuls of flour on a plate. Break the remaining egg into a bowl and beat lightly with a little salt and pepper. Spread a few tablespoonfuls of breadcrumbs out on a separate plate. Take spoonfuls of the potato mixture and shape into cylinders in the flour. Dip in the beaten egg, then roll in the breadcrumbs. Heat the oil. Put a batch of croquettes into the basket and plunge into the hot oil. Fry for 3–5 minutes, depending on size, until golden-brown, then drain. Do not fry too many at a time. Keep hot while the remainder are being cooked.

The croquettes may be served on their own for a family main course, accompanied simply by a tomato and herb sauce. The ham and cheese may be replaced by the same quantity of minced (ground) prawns or chopped herbs, or mushrooms fried in butter and finely chopped. If no flavouring is used, serve the croquettes with meat, poultry or game.

US	Ingredients	Met/Imp
4½ lb	Dutch (waxy) potatoes	2 kg/4½ lb
	salt and pepper	
1 pinch	nutmeg (optional)	1 pinch
1	garlic clove	1
2 sticks	butter	250 g/8 oz
1¼ quarts	crème fleurette	1.5 litres/2½ pints

GRATIN DAUPHINOIS

Preparation 45 minutes • Cooking 1½–2 hours

Gratin dauphinois, which has nothing in common with its neighbour from Savoy, is a subject of continuous discussion, and cookery experts of both sexes never seem to come to any agreement about its true recipe.

One thing is certain: it is essential not to add eggs or cheese to gratin dauphinois. Eggs absorb all the moisture, leaving bits of egg in the potatoes, and cheese kills the true flavour.

Thinly slice waxy potatoes with yellow flesh (or red ones from Spain), then wash and dry them in a cloth. Season with salt and pepper, and a little nutmeg, if liked.

Rub a gratin dish with garlic and butter generously. Layer the potatoes in the dish to within 1 cm/½ inch of the top, then slowly pour in the cream so that it does not spill over the edge of the dish. Dot with the remaining butter.

Cook in a low oven for 1½–2 hours, depending on the size of the dish, until the potatoes are tender. Serve at once.

POTATO GRATIN FROM SAVOY

Preparation 45 minutes • Cooking 40–50 minutes

US	Ingredients	Met/Imp
4½ lb	Dutch (waxy) potatoes	2 kg/4½ lb
2 cups	Beaufort cheese, grated	200 g/8 oz
	salt and pepper	
	nutmeg	
2 quarts	White Stock (*page 56*) or consommé	2 litres/3½ pints
1	garlic clove	1
1 stick	butter	100 g/4 oz

Thinly slice the potatoes. Mix them in a large bowl with one-third of the grated cheese, salt, pepper and a pinch of nutmeg. Add the stock. Rub a flameproof gratin dish with the garlic and put in some chopped butter and half of the remaining grated cheese. Add the potatoes, dot with the remaining butter and sprinkle the remaining cheese on top. Partly cook over direct heat, then finish the cooking in a moderate oven, until the potatoes are tender.

POTATOES 'ANGLAISE'

Preparation 20 minutes • Cooking 50 minutes

US	Ingredients	Met/Imp
16	small Dutch (waxy) potatoes	16
	salt	

The potatoes should be cut into the shape of large olives. (There is a special utensil for doing this.) Cook them in boiling salted water or steam them, preferably keeping them whole. Dry them out at the front of the oven with the door open.

In principal, all boiled fish should be accompanied by 'pommes de terre à l'anglaise', which can be served as a garnish or in a separate vegetable dish.

DARPHIN POTATO CAKE

Preparation 20 minutes • Cooking 30 minutes

US	Ingredients	Met/Imp
2 lb	Dutch (waxy) potatoes	1 kg/2 lb
	salt and pepper	
3 tbsp	groundnut (peanut) oil	45 ml/3 tbsp
14 tbsp	butter	200 g/7 oz

Cut the potatoes into a fine *julienne*, then season lightly with salt and pepper. Once cut, do not wash them, but rub them between your hands. Heat the oil and butter in a frying pan. You can equally well use half butter and half groundnut (peanut) oil, which has no taste, this will prevent the butter going black. Put in the potatoes; do not have them too thick – the pan should be no more than half full. Cook over a high heat, turning once like a pancake, until browned on both sides and soft in the centre.

US	Ingredients	Met/Imp
4½ lb	floury potatoes	2 kg/4½ lb
	salt and pepper	
I pinch	nutmeg	I pinch
I stick	butter	100 g/4 oz
6	egg yolks	6
	Choux Pastry (page 578) made with 50 g/2 oz (4 tbsp) butter, 100 ml/4 fl oz (½ cup) water, 50 g/2 oz (6 tbsp) flour, 1 pinch of salt and 1½–2 small (US medium) eggs	
I cup	flour	150 g/5 oz
2	eggs, for coating	2
5 cups	fresh white breadcrumbs	300 g/10 oz
	oil for deep-frying	

DAUPHINE POTATOES

Preparation 1 hour • Cooking 30 minutes • Makes 24

Peel the potatoes and cut into quarters. Put into a saucepan of lightly salted cold water, bring to the boil and cook quickly until tender but not overcooked. Drain well. Put them into an ovenproof dish and dry out in the oven for a few minutes.

Rub the potatoes through a sieve and put the purée into a shallow saucepan. Add salt if necessary, pepper, nutmeg and the butter, cut into small pieces. Dry over a high heat, stirring with a wooden spoon.

When stiff, remove from the heat and add the egg yolks and choux pastry. Spread out on a buttered baking tray and allow to cool.

When cold, turn on to a floured surface and form into balls the size of an egg, then shape into ovals, making sure they are uniform in size.

Dip in beaten egg, then in breadcrumbs. Deep-fry in hot oil for 6 minutes, drain on paper towels, sprinkle with salt and serve.

DAUPHINOISE POTATOES

Preparation 30 minutes • Cooking 40–50 minutes

US	Ingredients	Met/Imp
3 lb	Dutch (waxy) potatoes	1.5 kg/3 lb
I½ quarts	milk, boiled	1.5 litres/2½ pints
I¾ cups	cheese, grated	200 g/8 oz
3	eggs, beaten	3
I pinch	nutmeg	I pinch
	salt and pepper	
I	garlic clove	I
I stick	butter	100 g/4 oz

Thinly slice the potatoes. Mix with the milk, half of the cheese, the eggs, nutmeg, salt and pepper.

Rub the inside of a flameproof earthenware dish with the garlic and put in the potato mixture. Sprinkle the remaining cheese on top and dot with the butter. Bring to the boil on top of the stove and boil for a few minutes, then cover with buttered paper and a lid and cook in a moderate oven. Depending on the heat of the oven, you may have to take the lid off the dish to ensure that the potatoes become well-cooked. Keep checking them; they should be neither too dry nor too wet.

Take care if you use earthenware dishes for cooking; they should be glazed. Unglazed earthenware is too porous, and will become impregnated with the flavours of the food.

DUCHESSE POTATOES

Preparation 1 hour • Cooking 6 minutes

US	Ingredients	Met/Imp
3 lb	Dutch (waxy) potatoes	1.5 kg/3 lb
	salt and white pepper	
	nutmeg	
4	egg yolks	4
14 tbsp	butter	200 g/7 oz
	flour, for coating	

Peel the potatoes and cut into quarters. Put into cold salted water and cook until tender, then drain. Turn on to a baking sheet and dry out in the oven, then rub through a fine sieve. Season. Dry the purée over a high heat. Remove and add the egg yolks and 50 g/2 oz (4 tbsp) of the butter. Spread out on the buttered baking sheet and allow to cool.

When ready to use, shape the purée into small cakes, roll in flour and fry in the remaining butter. Alternatively, brush with beaten egg and bake in a buttered dish.

When used as a garnish, this purée can be piped into rosette shapes.

ANNA POTATOES

Preparation 40 minutes • Cooking 35 minutes

US	Ingredients	Met/Imp
16	Dutch (waxy) potatoes	16
	salt and pepper	
2 sticks	butter	250 g/8 oz

This potato 'cake' is cooked in a 'bath' of butter, and in a fairly hot oven, rather than a moderate one. When cooked, the potatoes should be golden brown on the outside and soft on the inside.

Cut the potatoes into cylinder shapes. In large kitchens, there is a special gadget called a 'rabot' or mandolin for slicing the potatoes very thinly and with perfect regularity. Without this you have to cut the cylinders with a sharp knife into rings 2 mm/⅛ inch thick. Rinse in cold water, dry in a cloth, season with salt and sprinkle with a little pepper. Thickly butter the bottom and sides of a flameproof casserole. Arrange a layer of the potatoes in the casserole, overlapping the slices slightly in concentric circles like the scales of a fish. Spread butter over this first layer of potatoes. The butter should have been previously squeezed in a cloth to extract the whey or this would otherwise run to the bottom of the dish and coagulate there, making the potatoes stick to the bottom of the dish. Furthermore, so that the butter will spread easily, it should be melted and clarified.

Arrange a second layer of potatoes in the dish, reversing the direction of the circles in the first layer. Cover with another layer of butter, then repeat until all the potatoes are used up – there should be 5–6 layers in all.

Cover with a tight-fitting lid and bake in a hot oven for about 35 minutes, until tender and golden-brown. Turn out on to a plate and cut into 8 slices, then press together to re-form the potato cake. Slide on to a serving dish and serve at once.

US	Ingredients	Met/Imp
16	even-sized large Dutch (waxy) potatoes	16
I stick	butter	100 g/4 oz
½ lb	minced (ground) pork	250 g/9 oz
I cup	Dry Duxelles (page 49), made with plenty of shallots	250 ml/9 fl oz
4	large tomatoes	4
scant I cup	White Stock (page 56)	200 ml/7 fl oz
	salt and pepper	

STUFFED POTATOES

Preparation 1 hour • Cooking about 30 minutes

Cut off the ends of the potatoes, then trim the potatoes into barrel shapes. Scoop out the centres, leaving a shell 7–8 mm/⅓ inch thick.

Butter a flameproof dish and stand the potatoes side by side in it with the open ends facing upwards.

Mix together the pork and duxelles and stuff the potatoes. Press slices of de-seeded tomato in between the potatoes in the dish. Add the butter and stock. Season. Cover with buttered paper and a lid and half cook on top of the stove.

Remove the lid and transfer to the oven. Continue cooking until all the stock and butter have been absorbed and the potatoes are tender. Transfer carefully to a heated serving dish.

US	Ingredients	Met/Imp
10	Dutch (waxy) large potatoes	10
	oil for deep-frying	
	salt	

POMMES DE TERRE FRITES
(PAILLE, PONT-NEUF OU CHIPS)

DEEP-FRIED POTATOES (STRAW, 'PONT-NEUF' OR CHIPS)

Preparation 20 minutes • Cooking 4 minutes

The different names of these deep-fried potatoes come from the way in which they are cut. Straw potatoes are cut into very fine strips; French fries are cut into medium sticks; 'pont-neuf' are thicker sticks; wafer-thin slices are called chips.

Peel the potatoes, trim the sides straight and cut into slices about 2 mm/⅛ inch thick, then cut into the shape required. Wash in cold water, drain and dry thoroughly in a cloth. Put into a wire basket and plunge into hot oil to fry for 3 minutes, then drain.

After a few seconds, plunge the potatoes again into the oil, which should be smoking. Fry for 6–7 seconds until crisp and golden-brown, shaking the basket so that the potatoes spread evenly in the oil. Drain on a cloth and sprinkle with salt.

US	Ingredients	Met/Imp
¼ cup	Parmesan cheese, grated	30 g/l oz
I lb (about 2 cups)	Dauphine Potatoes (page 550)	500 g/l lb
6 tbsp	flour	50 g/2 oz
	oil for deep-frying	

POMMES DE TERRE LORETTE

LORETTE POTATOES

Preparation 2 hours • Cooking 6 minutes

Add the grated cheese to the dauphine potatoes. Divide into 10 portions and shape into crescents. Roll in flour and deep-fry in very hot oil.

— MASHED POTATO CAKE 'MACAIRE' —

Preparation 25 minutes • Cooking 55 minutes

US	Ingredients	Met/Imp
4½ lb	Dutch (waxy) potatoes	2 kg/4½ lb
2 sticks	butter	250 g/8 oz
	salt and pepper	

Bake the potatoes until tender, split them in half and scoop out the flesh. Mash with 200 g/7 oz (14 tbsp) of the butter, then season.

Melt the remaining butter in a frying pan. Add the mashed potato, spreading it over the bottom of the pan. Fry, turning once, until golden on both sides. Slide on to a heated serving dish.

——— MAÎTRE D'HÔTEL POTATOES ———

Preparation 20 minutes • Cooking 55 minutes

US	Ingredients	Met/Imp
4½ lb	floury potatoes	2 kg/4½ lb
1 stick	butter	100 g/4 oz
	salt and pepper	
	nutmeg	
1½ quarts	milk, boiling	1.5 litres/ 2½ pints
2 tsp	chopped parsley	10 ml/2 tsp

Steam the potatoes in their skins. Peel while still hot and mash in a saucepan with the butter. Season with salt, pepper and a pinch of nutmeg.

Add the boiling milk and allow the potatoes to absorb the milk and seasoning. Add a little extra milk if necessary. Serve sprinkled with parsley, in a vegetable dish.

——— SOUFFLÉ POTATOES ———

Preparation 20 minutes • Cooking 11 minutes

US	Ingredients	Met/Imp
16	Dutch (waxy) potatoes	16
	oil for deep-frying	
	salt	

One of the conditions for making beautiful soufflé potatoes is to use those Dutch potatoes which are long with yellow flesh. Trim the sides of the potatoes straight, then cut into uniform slices about 5 mm/¼ inch thick. Rinse in cold water, dry thoroughly in a cloth and put into smoking hot oil.

Let the potatoes fry for a few minutes until they have lost their moisture as a result of the heat, and until the flesh will give slightly under pressure, then increase the heat under the pan as much as possible so that the oil reaches its maximum heat quickly. Shake the potatoes in the oil by lightly moving the basket. By this simple action and the movement of the heat, the potatoes will swell up and become souffléed. Drain the potatoes in the basket and leave for 1 minute. Meanwhile, increase the heat of the oil to maximum again. Put the potatoes back in the oil, making sure they are completely immersed by pushing them down under the oil with a slotted spoon. Drain them as soon as they have puffed up and are crisp and dry. Sprinkle with salt. Serve as an accompaniment to grills (broiled meat), or separately on a paper napkin.

US	Ingredients	Met/Imp
4½ lb	floury potatoes	2 kg/4½ lb
	salt	
14 tbsp	butter	200 g/7 oz
2 cups	milk, boiling	500 ml/18 fl oz

POTATO PURÉE

Preparation 40 minutes • Cooking 30 minutes

Simple as potato purée is, there are still certain guidelines to follow when making it. In principal, it should be made quickly and started at such a time that it will be just ready at serving time. A purée that has been reheated, left to stand or kept hot in the oven tastes greasy and is quite disgusting.

Cut the potatoes into quarters, just cover with cold water, add 12.5 ml/2½ tsp salt per 1 litre/1¾ pints (1 quart) water and bring to the boil. Boil over a high heat until the potatoes are tender, but not overcooked.

Drain well and rub through a sieve into a heavy saucepan. Beat well with a wooden spoon or, better still, a whisk until white and slightly elastic. Add a pinch of salt and the butter, diced. Beat for a few minutes, then add the boiling milk 30–45 ml/2–3 tbsp at a time until the purée is creamy. Heat through, but do not allow to boil (this would spoil the flavour of the butter). Serve in a heated dish.

SALSIFIS ET SCORSONÈRE

SALSIFY AND SCORZONERA

TRUE SALSIFY HAS A LONG, TAPERING WHITE ROOT, AND IS different from scorzonera or 'black salsify' with its long, black, cylindrical root. Scorzonera is easier to peel than true salsify. Mainly used as an accompaniment (especially for white meats), and in sauces, salsify is deliciously tender when properly cooked, and is a good addition to the range of winter vegetables normally available.

SALSIFY WITH POULETTE SAUCE

Preparation 2 hours • Cooking 2 hours

US	Ingredients	Met/Imp
14 tbsp	butter	200 g/7 oz
½ cup	flour	75 g/3 oz
1 quart	White Stock (page 56)	1 litre/1 ¾ pints
4½ lb	salsify	2 kg/4½ lb
½ cup	wine vinegar	100 ml/4 fl oz
	White Court Bouillon (page 49) made with juice of 2 lemons	
	salt and pepper	
2	egg yolks	2
½ cup	crème fraîche	100 ml/4 fl oz
	parsley	

Make a velouté sauce (*page 57*) with 75 g/3 oz (6 tbsp) of the butter, the flour and the stock.

Scrape the salsify, putting them immediately into cold water to which the vinegar has been added. Drain, cut into 4 cm/1½ inch cubes, then bring to the boil in the court bouillon with salt and pepper. (As salsify is rather bland in flavour, you can improve it by adding to the water either a little kidney fat or 200 g/7 oz breast of lamb, or 250 g/8 oz pork rind, or even ½ glass olive oil.) When the salsify is cooked, drain off the court bouillon and put the salsify into a frying pan. Dry it out over the heat, then sweat it in some of the remaining butter.

Before serving, reduce the velouté sauce until it is very concentrated. Thicken with the egg yolks and crème fraîche, and the remaining butter, diced. Pour over the salsify and sprinkle with parsley to serve.

TOMATE

TOMATO

KNOWN AS THE 'LOVE APPLE' IN THE SOUTH OF FRANCE, THE tomato 'invaded' French cookery at the end of the eighteenth century. Although typical of the cuisine of southern France, where they are flavoured with garlic and herbs, used in sauces, with grilled (broiled) food or in ragoûts, tomatoes are an essential ingredient of many classic recipes, such as chicken Marengo and Choron sauce, and are used as an accompaniment for meat and poultry, not to mention their use in salads, and even jams, sorbets, vegetable 'loaves', soups and vegetable mixtures such as ratatouille. The best time for tomatoes is from July to October. Some of the best-known varieties are the ribbed, flattened, juicy 'marmande'; the small, 'tomate-cerise' or cherry tomato which is firm and fragrant; the large, round 'saint-pierre' which is smooth and juicy and ideal for stuffing; and the tiny 'olivette' which is long, melt-in-the-mouth and juicy. They are all preferable to hothouse or imported varieties, although these do provide a vegetable which is available throughout most the year.

US	Ingredients	Met/Imp
6	large even-sized tomatoes	6
	salt and pepper	
	STUFFING	
1 oz (about slice)	bread	25 g/scant 1 oz
	milk	
1	onion	1
1	garlic clove	1
4 tbsp	butter	50 g/2 oz
¼ lb	*Paris mushrooms*	100 g/4 oz
3 oz	fatty bacon	75 g/3 oz
3 oz	boneless veal shin or knuckle (shank)	75 g/3 oz
5 oz	boneless pork spare rib or chine (blade or Boston shoulder)	150 g/5 oz
2 tbsp	chopped parsley	30 ml/2 tbsp
1	egg	1

STUFFED TOMATOES

Preparation 30 minutes • Cooking 40 minutes • Serve 6

The stuffing can also be made with leftover chicken, veal or pork, or sausagemeat.

Wash and dry the tomatoes. Cut a 3 cm/1¼ inch circle from the top of each and set aside. Scoop out the seeds and juice. Strain and reserve the juice.

Place the tomatoes upside down on a wire rack to drain, then season lightly with salt and arrange in a buttered dish.

Make the stuffing. Dice the bread and soak in a little warm milk. Peel and finely chop the onion and garlic and fry gently in half of the butter until golden.

Peel and finely chop the mushrooms, then fry with the onion mixture. Squeeze the bread in your hands to extract the milk, then chop finely. Mince (grind) the bacon, veal and pork and mix together. Put into a bowl with the onion, garlic, mushrooms and parsley. Season and add the beaten egg. Mix thoroughly with a fork. Spoon the stuffing into the tomato cases; doming it up in the centre of each one. (If the stuffing is too dry, moisten with a little of the reserved tomato juice.)

Replace the tops on the tomatoes. Place a pat of the remaining butter in the centre of each and bake in a hot oven for 40 minutes. Serve straight from the dish.

US	Ingredients	Met/Imp
6	medium-sized tomatoes	6
1	onion	1
2 tbsp	butter	30 g/1 oz
1 lb	wild mushrooms	500 g/1 lb
	salt and pepper	
1	lemon, juice of	1
¼ cup	dry madeira	50 ml/2 fl oz
1 tsp	cornflour (cornstarch)	5 ml/1 tsp
⅔ cup	*crème fraîche*	150 ml/¼ pint
2 tbsp	grated Gruyère cheese	30 ml/2 tbsp

TOMATOES STUFFED WITH MUSHROOMS

Preparation 30 minutes • Cooking 25 minutes • Serves 6

Cut the tomatoes in half and scoop out the seeds, juice and core.

Fry the finely chopped onion in butter over a moderate heat for 5 minutes. Add the chopped mushrooms, salt, pepper and the lemon juice. Fry over a high heat until the liquid from the mushrooms has evaporated.

Blend together the madeira, cornflour (cornstarch) and crème fraîche. Add to the mushroom mixture, stirring until the sauce thickens. Fill the tomato halves with the mushroom mixture and sprinkle a good pinch of grated cheese over each. Bake in a hot oven for about 15 minutes.

—— TOMATOES FILLED WITH EGGS* ——

Preparation 20 minutes • Cooking 8–10 minutes

US	Ingredients	Met/Imp
8	tomatoes	8
I stick	butter	100 g/4 oz
8	eggs	8
	salt	
½ cup	cheese, grated (optional)	50 g/2 oz
½ cup	*crème fraîche* (optional)	100 ml/4 fl oz

Cut a circle from the stalk end of each tomato, with the help of a special gadget which will mark the 'hat' to be removed. Remove the 8 hats and carefully scoop out the seeds and juice. Arrange the tomatoes side by side in a buttered ovenproof dish. Place a piece of butter in the bottom of each tomato and break in an egg. Put another piece of butter on top and sprinkle with salt. Bake in a moderate oven until the eggs are set but not hard.

To be on the safe side, if the tomatoes are under-ripe, you can half cook them in advance (otherwise the cooking time for the tomatoes may be too long for the eggs). Take care, however, not to overcook the tomatoes before the eggs are added, or they will collapse.

An alternative method is to slow down the cooking of the eggs: put 5 ml/1 tsp crème fraîche in the bottom of each tomato, then add the egg and place a piece of butter and another 5 ml/1 tsp crème fraîche on top. Sprinkle with a small pinch of grated cheese and a pinch of salt.

—— FRIED TOMATOES ——

Preparation 25 minutes • Cooking 5 minutes

US	Ingredients	Met/Imp
16	medium-sized tomatoes	16
	salt and pepper	
	parsley	
	Fritter Batter (*page 580*)	
	oil for deep-frying	

Allow 2 firm tomatoes per person. Cut them into slices 7–8 mm/⅓ inch thick. Scoop out the juice and seeds, and sprinkle with salt, pepper and finely chopped parsley. Dip the tomato slices in the batter until thoroughly coated. Plunge into smoking hot oil so that the batter sets immediately. Deep-fry until crisp and golden-brown, then drain on a cloth and sprinkle with salt. Serve on a napkin garnished with a bright green sprig of fried parsley.

The tomatoes must be served at once before the steam inside the fritters makes the batter soggy.

TRUFFLE

KNOWN AS 'THE DIAMOND OF COOKERY' (BRILLAT-SAVARIN), 'the jewel of poor land' (Colette) and 'fairy apple' (Georges Sand), all gastronomes have sung the praises of this mysterious tuber which transforms countless recipes. The most prized is the black Périgord truffle, at its best in January and February after the first frosts, but it is also worth mentioning the white Piedmont truffle, recognized by enthusiasts. Truffles can be used both raw and cooked. They may be cut into strips, sliced, diced or shredded, and can be used to flavour stock, to improve sauces or to make meat and poultry more attractive. They add a subtle taste to salads, not to mention game, eggs, pâtés and terrines. And it is often worth adding them as much for the gastronomic bonus as for their decorative qualities.

TRUFFES AU CHAMPAGNE

TRUFFLES IN CHAMPAGNE SAUCE

Preparation 20 minutes • Cooking 25 minutes

US	Ingredients	Met/Imp
8, each about 3 oz	medium-sized fresh truffles	8, each about 75 g/3 oz
3½ sticks	butter	400 g/14 oz
	salt and pepper	
½ bottle	dry champagne	½ bottle
1 tbsp	concentrated Meat Glaze (*page 56*)	15 ml/1 tbsp

Scrub and rinse the truffles.

Put the butter into a saucepan. Arrange the truffles in the pan in a single layer, not overlapping, so they are half-immersed in the butter. Add salt and pepper. Cook for 10–15 minutes, stirring constantly.

Pour in enough champagne to come just to the top of the truffles, then add the meat glaze. Simmer for a further 10 minutes, stirring continuously until the sauce thickens.

TRUFFES EN PAPILLOTES

TRUFFLE PARCELS

Preparation 40 minutes • Cooking 30 minutes

US	Ingredients	Met/Imp
8, each 3–4 oz	truffles	8, each 75–100 g/ 3–4 oz
	salt	
8	slices bacon	8

Peel and salt the truffles, then roll a slice of bacon around each one. Sprinkle the bacon with salt, then wrap each truffle in a piece of foil.

These truffles should be cooked on an open fire in the country. Before cooking, make sure that the coals underneath are very hot and glowing red. Place the parcels on a *grillade* and cover them with hot ash and even some embers. When cooked, remove the foil and bacon and serve the truffles just as they are.

PÂTES ET RIZ

PASTA AND RICE

PASTA IS A FARINACEOUS PASTE WITH NUMEROUS CULINARY uses which comes in many different shapes. Made with durum or hard wheat semolina and water, or with flour and eggs, its appearance and use vary from pasta for soup, for boiling (ribbon pasta, spaghetti and macaroni), to baking (lasagne and large macaroni), and stuffed pasta (ravioli, cannelloni and tortelloni). It is the cooking of the pasta itself which is the biggest problem when making pasta dishes. It should be *al dente*, or just tender to the bite, having been cooked in lots of boiling salted water. The accompanying sauce also plays an important part, and Italian cuisine has an abundance of savoury pasta recipes. Alsace and Eastern Europe also offer high-quality pasta dishes.

There are two main types of rice: long-grain and short-grain. Only the former is suitable for savoury use and garnishes because the grains remain separate during cooking, whereas the grains of the latter become sticky. Short-grain rice is therefore mostly used for cooked milk puddings. Whether boiled, steamed or fried (for pilaus, risottos, paella or 'à la grecque', rice has numerous uses, as a garnish for fish and shellfish, as a dish in itself, in a timbale mould or as croquettes, as well as in mixed salads. In addition to white rice, there is also prefluffed or precooked rice, and brown rice, which retains the most vitamins and phosphorus.

CANNELLONI ROSSINI

———— CANNELLONI ROSSINI ————

Preparation 45 minutes • Cooking about 18 minutes

Melt 30 ml/2 tbsp of the butter in a saucepan and sweat the finely chopped onion. Add the finely chopped calf's and chicken livers and fry for a few minutes. Remove from the heat, sprinkle in the thyme flowers and stir in 60 ml/4 tbsp of the béchamel, the sieved foie gras and 15 ml/1 tbsp of the grated cheese. Add the egg yolks, salt and pepper and mix well. Keep warm.

Cook the cannelloni in boiling water for 10 minutes, drain, refresh under cold running water and drain well. Stuff the cannelloni, then arrange in a buttered shallow baking dish. Coat with the remaining béchamel and sprinkle with the remaining grated cheese. Brown under the grill (broiler) or in a hot oven for 5 minutes.

US	Ingredients	Met/Imp
6 tbsp	butter	75 g/3 oz
I	large onion	I
5 oz	calf's liver	150 g/5 oz
5 oz	chicken livers	150 g/5 oz
I pinch	thyme flowers	I pinch
2 cups	Béchamel Sauce (*page 62*)	500 ml/18 fl oz
2½ oz	foie gras	60 g/2½ oz
1¼ cups	Parmesan cheese, grated	150 g/5 oz
2	egg yolks	2
	salt and pepper	
16	dried cannelloni tubes or 7·5 cm/3 inch squares of fresh pasta	16

US	Ingredients	Met/Imp
2 cups	semolina (or 3 cups fine yellow cornmeal)	350 g/12 oz
1½ quarts	milk	1.5 litres/2½ pints
	salt and pepper	
1 pinch	nutmeg	1 pinch
10 tbsp	butter	150 g/5 oz
3	egg yolks	3
1¼ cups	Parmesan cheese, grated	150 g/5 oz
	Tomato Sauce (page 80), to serve	

ROMAN-STYLE GNOCCHI

Preparation 40 minutes • Cooking 25 minutes

Pour the semolina in a steady stream into the boiling milk in a casserole, stirring to prevent lumps forming. Season with a good pinch of salt, a little pepper and the nutmeg. Add one-third of the butter. Cover and bake in a moderate oven for 20 minutes, or until the semolina has absorbed the milk, without disturbing it during cooking.

Remove from the oven and break up the semolina with a fork. Beat in the egg yolks, then turn out on to a damp surface and spread out to a thickness of 1 cm/½ inch. Leave until completely cold.

Put the dough on to a damp cloth. Cut out shapes with a pastry cutter, leaving as few trimmings as possible. Butter an ovenproof dish and sprinkle the bottom with half of the grated Parmesan cheese. Put the gnocchi on top, either in a single layer or overlapping. Sprinkle the remaining grated cheese and butter over the top and brown in a hot oven.

Depending on the size, allow 2–3 gnocchi per person. Arrange them on a plate, then at the last moment, pour a ribbon of tomato sauce around them, or hand it separately if preferred.

US	Ingredients	Met/Imp
4½ lb	neck (chuck) of beef	2 kg/4½ lb
2 quarts	red wine	2 litres/3½ pints
	Mirepoix (page 50)	
¼ cup	pork fat	50 g/2 oz
1	bouquet garni	1
1 pinch	nutmeg	1 pinch
14 oz	long macaroni	400 g/14 oz
	salt and pepper	
1 stick	butter	100 g/4 oz
1¾ cups	Parmesan cheese, grated	200 g/8 oz

NEAPOLITAN MACARONI PIE

Preparation 1 hour • Cooking time for beef 8–10 hours • Cooking time for macaroni 26–28 minutes

Braise the beef in the wine with the mirepoix, pork fat, bouquet garni and nutmeg for 8–10 hours, until very tender. When cooked, mince (grind) it finely, reserving the cooking liquid.

Cook the macaroni in salted water until *al dente*. Drain and cut into pieces. Toss in the butter and three-quarters of the grated cheese.

Moisten the beef with some of its cooking liquid (or even a little tomato sauce). The macaroni will absorb the liquid during browning. Arrange the beef and macaroni in layers in an ovenproof dish, ending with macaroni. Sprinkle with the remaining grated cheese. Pour over a little more of the beef stock, well reduced, and brown gently in the oven. Serve straight from the dish.

ALSACE DUMPLINGS

Preparation 1 hour • Cooking 25 minutes

Cream the butter in a warm bowl with salt, pepper and nutmeg. Add the eggs one at a time, then the egg yolks, followed by the sifted flour. Finally fold in the stiffly beaten egg whites.

Divide the mixture into walnut-sized pieces, drop them into boiling salted water and poach until they puff up and rise to the surface.

Drain, arrange in a heated serving dish and serve sprinkled with the grated cheese and noisette butter.

These dumplings can also be served with a tomato, béchamel or romaine sauce, etc, or they can be browned in the oven.

US	Ingredients	Met/Imp
1 lb (4 sticks)	butter	500 g/1 lb
	salt and pepper	
1 pinch	nutmeg	1 pinch
4	eggs	4
4	egg yolks	4
2 cups	flour	300 g/10 oz
2	egg whites	2
	TO FINISH	
1¼ cups	cheese, grated	150 g/5 oz
⅔ cup	Noisette Butter (page 53)	150 g/5 oz

NOODLES WITH CREAM SAUCE

Preparation 10 minutes • Cooking 5–10 minutes

Boil the noodles in salted water until three-quarters cooked. Drain and dry in the saucepan over the heat until all of the water has evaporated. Add the boiling cream and simmer for 10 minutes. Add nutmeg and more salt if necessary. Serve in a heated dish.

US	Ingredients	Met/Imp
14 oz	fresh noodles	400 g/14 oz
	salt	
1¾ cups	double (heavy) cream	400 ml/14 fl oz
1 pinch	nutmeg	1 pinch

TAGLIATELLE WITH TOMATO AND AUBERGINE SAUCE*

Preparation 20 minutes • Cooking 50 minutes

Skin and de-seed the tomatoes and cut them into quarters. Heat 45 ml/3 tbsp of the oil in a saucepan. Add the chopped onions and garlic and the finely chopped celery and soften over a low heat, stirring. Add the tomatoes, basil, thyme and bay leaf. Cook for about 40 minutes over a low heat until most of the liquid has evaporated. Purée in a blender and keep hot.

While the sauce is cooking, cut the washed aubergines (eggplant) into rings, sprinkle with salt and leave for 30 minutes to *dégorge*. Dry them carefully, then fry them in the remaining oil. Drain well and arrange in an ovenproof dish, then cook in a moderate oven for about 10 minutes.

Cook the tagliatelle in plenty of lightly salted boiling water with 15 ml/1 tbsp oil. Drain thoroughly. Mix the tagliatelle with the aubergines (eggplant), then pour some of the tomato sauce on top. Serve at once, with the remaining tomato sauce and the grated cheese handed separately.

US	Ingredients	Met/Imp
2 lb	tomatoes	1 kg/2 lb
1 cup	olive oil	200 ml/7 fl oz
2	onions	2
2	garlic cloves	2
1	celery stalk	1
1	bunch basil	1
1	thyme sprig	1
½	bay leaf	½
1¼ lb	aubergines (eggplant)	600 g/1¼ lb
	salt and pepper	
1 lb	white and green tagliatelle (ribbon noodles)	500 g/1 lb
1 cup	Parmesan cheese, grated	100 g/4 oz

US	Ingredients	Met/Imp
10 tbsp	butter	150 g/5 oz
3	shallots	3
1	large onion	1
1¼ cups	risotto or short-grain rice	250 g/8 oz
1 quart	consommé	1 litre/1¾ pints
1	bouquet garni	1
	salt and pepper	
1 cup	Comté, Gruyère or Parmesan cheese, grated	100 g/4 oz

RISOTTO

Preparation 15 minutes • Cooking 20 minutes

Put the butter and finely chopped shallots into a large saucepan and fry gently until translucent. Rub through a sieve. Add the finely chopped onion to this flavoured butter in the saucepan and fry quickly. Add the rice and stir to coat all the grains.

After 3 minutes, sprinkle in 60 ml/4 tbsp of the boiling consommé and the bouquet garni. When all of the consommé has been absorbed, shake the saucepan to separate the grains of rice, then add a further 60 ml/4 tbsp consommé. Repeat this procedure for 20 minutes, then add salt and pepper to taste and gradually pour in a final glass of consommé until the rice is tender, moist and creamy and all the liquid has been absorbed. Remove from the heat and add the grated cheese. Serve at once.

RISOTTO AUX FONDS D'ARTICHAUTS ET AUX TOMATES

RISOTTO WITH ARTICHOKE BOTTOMS AND TOMATOES

US	Ingredients	Met/Imp
1	onion	1
1 stick	butter	100 g/4 oz
1¼ cups	risotto or short-grain rice	250 g/9 oz
1 quart	White Stock (*page 56*)	1 litre/1¾ pints
6	tomatoes	6
4	artichokes	4
1 cup	Parmesan cheese, grated	100 g/4 oz

Preparation 50 minutes • Cooking 20 minutes

Finely chop the onion and fry in half of the butter until translucent. Add the unwashed rice and stir continuously over a moderate heat until the grains are coated with butter and the rice turns translucent. Add the stock and bring to the boil, then cover and cook in the oven for 20 minutes.

Meanwhile, skin, de-seed and finely chop the tomatoes, then fry gently in a little butter.

Remove the leaves and chokes from the artichokes and discard. Thinly slice the artichoke bottoms and cook gently in a little butter until lightly browned.

When the rice has absorbed all of the liquid, separate the grains with a fork and stir in the remaining butter, diced, and half of the grated cheese. Stir in the fried tomatoes and artichoke bottoms, taking care not to break them up. Serve the risotto with the remaining grated cheese sprinkled on top.

Having been prepared as above, this risotto can be finished off in many different ways: either, simply, with tomatoes, or with a *julienne* of truffles, or with lean ham, or with mushrooms and truffles; it can also be flavoured with saffron.

RICE BERNOISE

Preparation 20 minutes • Cooking about 20 minutes

Remember that the volume of liquid should be twice that of the rice.

Finely chop the onion, carrot, celery and ham and fry in butter in a large saucepan. Wash the rice and add to the pan with the bouquet garni. Fry for 15 minutes, stirring constantly. Pour in the consommé or stock, one-third at a time, and season with salt and pepper. Add the grated cheese, saffron and tomato sauce. Serve hot, having removed the bouquet garni.

US	Ingredients	Met/Imp
I	onion	I
I	carrot	I
I	celery stalk	I
¼ lb	raw country ham	100 g/4 oz
4 tbsp	butter	50 g/2 oz
I cup	risotto or short-grain rice	250 g/9 oz
I	bouquet garni	I
2 cups	Consommé or White Stock (*page 56*)	500 ml/18 fl oz
	salt and pepper	
I cup	Gruyère cheese, grated	100 g/4 oz
I pinch	saffron	I pinch
½ cup	Tomato Sauce (*page 80*)	100 ml/3½ fl oz

CREOLE RICE

Preparation 30 minutes • Cooking about 30 minutes

US	Ingredients	Met/Imp
	salt	
1¾ cups	long-grain rice, preferably basmati	250 g/9 oz

If liked, a little lemon juice can be added to the cooking liquid, which will also make the rice very white. Do not forget to add more salt than usual to the water when boiling the rice.

Bring 2–3 litres/3½–5 pints (2–3 quarts) salted water to the boil in a large saucepan. Add the rice and cook for 12 minutes, then drain and put immediately into a sieve. Hold the sieve under very hot running water to remove the remaining starch without interrupting the cooking of the rice.

Line a baking sheet, or preferably a wire sieve, with a cloth. Place the rice in the cloth, then cover. Place just inside a fairly hot oven, with the door slightly open, until the rice is cooked, stirring with a fork from time to time. Remove the rice from the oven when cooked.

PILAU RICE

Preparation 15 minutes • Cooking about 20 minutes

US	Ingredients	Met/Imp
I	onion	I
10 tbsp	butter	150 g/5 oz
1¾ cups	long-grain rice	250 g/9 oz
2 cups	well-seasoned White Stock (*page 56*)	500 ml/18 fl oz
	salt and pepper	
	bouquet garni	I

Lightly fry the chopped onion in one-third of the butter in a large saucepan. Do not allow it to brown. Remove from the heat and add the rice, stirring with a wooden spoon until the rice has absorbed the butter. Gradually add twice the volume of stock as rice and bring to the boil. Add salt, pepper and the bouquet garni. Cover with buttered paper and a lid and cook over a low heat for 16–18 minutes until the rice is tender but not overcooked. Remove from the heat and carefully transfer to a heated dish (this prevents the rice from overcooking).

Add the remaining butter, diced. Stir the rice with a fork, turning it over very gently. Keep hot. Pilau rice must be made a little in advance and, if it is properly cooked, the grains should be separate.

US	Ingredients	Met/Imp
½ cup	olive oil	100 ml/3½ fl oz
1	large onion	1
1¼ cups	short-grain rice	250 g/9 oz
1	bouquet garni	1
3	tomatoes	3
1 cup	shelled petits pois	150 g/5 oz
2	sweet peppers	2
2 cups	Consommé or White Stock (page 56)	500 ml/18 fl oz
	salt and pepper	
½ lb	raw country ham	250 g/9 oz
2	chorizo sausages	2

VALENCIA-STYLE RICE*

Preparation 1 hour • Cooking 35 minutes

Put the oil into a flameproof casserole and sweat the finely chopped onion. Add the rice and stir with a wooden spoon, then add the bouquet garni. Fry for a few minutes, then add the skinned, de-seeded and coarsely chopped tomatoes, the blanched peas, the de-seeded and diced peppers, the consommé or stock and salt and pepper.

Dice the ham and cut the chorizos into rings 5 mm/¼ inch thick. Add to the rice. Season lightly, because of the saltiness of the ham and chorizos. Cover with buttered paper and a lid and bake in the oven for 20–25 minutes until tender. Add a little more stock if necessary during cooking to ensure the rice does not become too dry. Taste and adjust seasoning. Serve hot in a vegetable dish.

TURBAN DE RIZ AUX POIVRONS ET AU CHORIZO

SWEET PEPPER AND CHORIZO RICE RING

Preparation 25 minutes • Cooking 1¼ hours

US	Ingredients	Met/Imp
⅔ cup	green olives	100 g/4 oz
1¼ lb	red and green sweet peppers	800 g/1¼ lb
½ cup	olive oil	100 ml/4 fl oz
4	onions	4
2¾ cups	long-grain rice	400 g/14 oz
1 small can	tomato paste	1 small can
1	mild chorizo sausage	1
	salt	
1	small chilli pepper	1
scant ½ lb	smoked fatty bacon	200 g/7 oz

Blanch the stoned olives in boiling water for 2 minutes, then drain. Wash the sweet peppers and cut them in half; remove the seeds and slice the flesh thinly. Fry very gently in 45 ml/3 tbsp oil, stirring frequently. Peel and finely chop the onions and fry in 60 ml/4 tbsp oil. Place the rice in a sieve, wash and drain thoroughly.

When the onions are soft, add the rice. Stir and fry until the grains are translucent. Add the tomato paste dissolved in 100 ml/4 fl oz (½ cup) boiling water (the rice should be just covered). Add half of the blanched olives and half of the skinned and sliced chorizo. Next add salt and the finely chopped chilli pepper, then lower the heat. Cover and cook until all the water has been absorbed.

Meanwhile, blanch the bacon, pat dry and dice coarsely. Fry for a few minutes in its own fat until lightly browned, then line the bottom of a ring mould with it. Add the remaining chorizo cut into rings, and the remaining olives, coarsely chopped. Pour the rice mixture on top and press into the mould. Turn out on to a round serving dish and fill the centre with the drained fried peppers. Serve immediately.

CHEESE

THERE ARE SO MANY FRENCH CHEESES WITH such a variety of flavours that there is something to please everyone. Cheese is 'like the apotheosis of a good meal', as Curnonsky put it. In his 'Natural History', Pliny praised Roquefort and told us that Auvergne cheese was excellent roasted over an open fire. The poet Martial also mentioned the cheese of Toulouse, and it is known that the Romans valued the cheese of Nîmes and Mont Lozère. In fact, the history of cheese could fill several volumes.

Throughout history, local cheese-manufacturing techniques have given a great variety to cheese, particularly in terms of regional characteristics. For example one finds soft cheeses (usually made with cow's milk) in the west and north of France, goat's cheese in Touraine and Poitou, blue cheese in central France and the Auvergne, cooked-paste cheese in the Alps, etc.

Cheeses are primarily distinguished by the way in which they are made: cream or fresh cheeses (*petit-suisse*, *demi-sel*), soft cheeses with a white crust or rind (Camembert, Chaource, Brie), blue-veined cheeses (Gorgonzola, Fourme), pressed uncooked cheeses (Cantal, Cheddar, Tomme), pressed cooked cheeses (Comté, Beaufort, Emmental), goat's cheeses, sheep's milk cheeses, spun-curd cheeses which melt easily (mozzarella), and processed cheeses.

LES SAISONS DES FROMAGES

SEASONS FOR CHEESE

GOOD THROUGHOUT THE YEAR

Bel Paese, blue cheese made commercially, Brillat-Savarin, Caciocavallo, Camembert, Cantal, Carré de l'Est, Chabichou, Cheddar, Cheshire, Chester, Comté, Coulommiers, Derby, Edam, Emmental, Excelsior, Feta, Fontainebleau, Fourme, Gérardmer, Gloucester, Gorgonzola, Gouda, Mimolette, Mozzarella, Munster, Murol, Neufchâtel, Parmesan, Pecorino, Port-Salut, Provolone, Reblochon, Ricotta, Saint-Nectaire, Saint-Paulin, Sbrinz, Scamorza, Tilsit, Tomme.

BEST FROM 15 APRIL TO 15 NOVEMBER

Bagnes, Banon (goat's), farmhouse blue cheese, Bossons Macérés, Boulette, Broccio, Cabécou, Cachat, Cendré, Chevrotin, Coeur-de-Bray, Crottin de Chavignol, Dauphin, Époisses, Fontina, Laguiole, Livarot, Maroilles, Mont-d'Or, Niolo, Pavé d'Auge, Pélardon, blue-veined cheese, Picodon, Poivre-d'Âne, Pouligny-Saint-Pierre, Pourly, Rigotte, Roquefort, Sainte-Maure, Saint-Marcellin, Selles-sur-Cher.

BEST FROM 15 NOVEMBER TO 15 APRIL

Appenzell, Asiago, Baguette de Thiérarche, Banon (sheep's milk), Beaufort, Bouton-de-Culotte, Brie, Brousse, Feuille de Dreux, Fribourg, Gaperon, Géromé, Gris de Lille, Gruyère, Pithiviers, Pont-l'Évêque, Rollot, Saint-Florentin, Soumaintrain, Stilton, Vacherin.

Farmhouse cheeses made by traditional methods are always better than commercially produced cheeses. Of the latter, however, the best are those made with fresh untreated milk rather than pasteurized milk. It is also advisable to choose cheese according to its season and to ensure that it will complement the rest of the menu (depending on the main regional characteristics of the meal and the seasoning of the previous courses).

Cheese should be sealed well and kept in the bottom of the refrigerator. It should be taken out 1 hour before eating. Soft cheese improves by being stored in a cool place for a few days. Blue cheese should be slightly moist, and tradition has it that Gruyère ought to be stored in an airtight container with a lump of sugar.

In former times cheese was served as a dessert. In the nineteenth century it was regarded as a man's prerogative, and was served in the smoking room with spirits. Today its role, apart from its culinary importance (see the following cheese recipes on pages 568–572), is as an extension to a meal: it is served after the salad and before the dessert.

Cheese should be served on a glass, marble or ceramic platter, on wicker or a wooden board, with butter if necessary. As a general rule, there should be a choice of 3 cheeses: a cooked-paste cheese, a blue-veined one and a soft one with a white crust; nevertheless real cheese lovers like to have a selection of 5 or 6 (goat's, pressed cooked-paste, hard, blue-veined and soft with a white crust), although a single well-chosen cheese, such as farmhouse Camembert, Vacherin, Brie or Munster, is also acceptable. There are certain rules for cutting cheese: the serving plate should hold one or more special knives with 2 prongs for piercing the cheese, since cheese should never be touched with a fork.

VINS ET FROMAGES

WINE AND CHEESE

Cheese should, unquestionably, be accompanied by wine, and the wine should be a suitable one; this is a subject which has been never been open to debate in France. There are no hard and fast rules about it, however, and it is best to rely on individual taste. Differences in taste are illustrated by the following chart taken from the 'Dictionary of Cheese' by Robert J. Courtine, editor of Larousse, and based on two serious works, in which he shows that there is always room for two different opinions on how cheeses and wines are matched together.

Hard and cooked-paste cheeses	dry white wine, dry rosé	dry white wine, fruity red wine
Blue-veined cheeses	fruity, vigorous red wine	red or white light wine
Semi-hard cheeses	light, delicate and aromatic rosé and red wine dry white wine	any light, dry and fruity wine
Soft cheese	robust, powerful and velvety full-bodied red wine	robust, vigorous red wine
Cream cheese	light, dry rosé and white wine, champagne	light, fruity rosé and white wine
Melting cheese	honest table wine	any light, dry wine
Goat's cheese	'gulpable' white, rosé and red regional wine	any dry, light, fruity wine, especially *vins de pays*

SOME CHEESE RECIPES

(*TAKEN FROM* 'Larousse des Fromages')

ALIGOT DE MARINETTE

—— CHEESE AND POTATO PURÉE ——

Recipe from La Petite Tour restaurant in Paris

Make a purée with 1 kg/2 lb floury potatoes and add a little crushed garlic and some melted bacon fat. Dilute the purée with a little boiling milk.

Finely slice 600 g/1 ¼ lb fresh Laguiole cheese and add it to the purée (preferably in a *bain-marie*). Beat vigorously with a wooden spoon, using a figure-of-eight movement.

The mixture is ready when it is evenly mixed, smooth and elastic; do not over-cook it or it will lose its elasticity. Serve the whole thing from a spatula, using scissors to cut the 'strings'.

— ANGERS CREAM CHEESE MOULDS —

Whisk 125 ml/4½ fl oz (½ cup) *crème fraîche* with a fork. Whisk 1 egg white until stiff. Whisk the egg white into the cream and pour into moulds. Wrap in a cloth and leave to drain in a cool place. Serve turned out and covered with crème fraîche flavoured with vanilla sugar.

CROQUE-MONSIEUR CURNONSKY

— CURNONSKY'S CROQUE-MONSIEUR —

Spread 2 slices of bread with a mixture of butter and Roquefort cheese. Put a slice of cooked ham on 1 slice of bread, sandwich together and fry until golden-brown.

CRUMPETS AU ROQUEFORT

——— ROQUEFORT PINWHEELS ———

Pound 250 g/8 oz Roquefort cheese and the same amount of Cheddar in a mortar and pestle. Add 250 ml/9 fl oz (1 cup) of Béchamel Sauce (*page 62*) and season with salt, pepper and a little mustard. Melt gently in a *bain-marie*.

Slice a loaf of bread lengthways. Spread the cheese mixture over each slice. Roll up, bake in the oven until golden, then cut each roll into round 'pinwheel' slices.

FRIANDS SAVOYARDS

——— SAVOY FRITTERS ———

Make a Béchamel Sauce (*page 62*) with 80 g/3 oz (6 tbsp) butter, 60 g/2½ oz (6½ tbsp) flour and 1 litre/1¾ pints (1 quart) milk. Season with salt and nutmeg. Thicken with 4 egg yolks and ½ glass cream. Cook over a low heat.

Remove from the heat and add 150 g/5 oz (1¼ cups) grated Beaufort cheese, 100 g/4 oz (⅔ cup) diced cooked ham and 50 g/2 oz (½ cup) chopped ceps, previously steamed.

Spread the mixture out 1 cm/½ inch thick and allow to cool. Cut into rectangles. Coat with egg and breadcrumbs and deep-fry in hot oil. Drain and serve hot.

BRIE WAFERS

Mix 500 g/1 lb (3½ cups) flour with 100 g/4 oz (1 stick) softened butter, 150 g/5 oz runny Brie, rind removed, 2 egg yolks, salt and a little pepper and nutmeg. Leave to rest, then spread out to a thickness of 8 mm/⅓ inch, and cut into rounds with the rim of a bordeaux (red wine) glass. Brush the tops with milk, then draw a fork over to score. Bake in a moderate oven.

IMBRUCCIATE (GÂTEAUX AU BROCCIO)

BROCCIO FRITTER CAKES

Mix 500 g/1 lb (3½ cups) sifted flour with 3 eggs, a pinch of salt, 15 g/½ oz fresh (compressed) yeast and 30 ml/2 tbsp olive oil. Stir in 200–300 ml/⅓–½ pint (1–1¼ cups) cold water to make a smooth dough. Cover with a cloth and leave in a warm place for 3 hours.

Dice some fresh Broccio cheese. Wrap the cheese cubes in pieces of dough and shape into round cakes. Deep-fry in oil until golden-brown. Drain and dust with sugar before serving.

PÂTE DE FROMAGE DE CHÈVRE

GOAT'S CHEESE QUICHE

Make a white roux with 40 g/1½ oz (3 tbsp) butter and 40 g/1½ oz (4½ tbsp) flour. Add 500 ml/18 fl oz (2 cups) milk and boil for 10 minutes, stirring until the sauce thickens. Bind with 2 egg yolks.

Cut 5 small, very fresh goat's cheeses into thick slices and add to the sauce. Add 1 handful each of grated Beaufort cheese and minced (ground) cooked ham and mix everything together well.

Make some pastry with 500 g/1 lb (3½ cups) flour, 150 g/5 oz (¾ cup) caster sugar, a pinch of salt, 4 egg yolks and 125 g/4½ oz (½ cup) lard. Use to line a flan (quiche) dish and fill with the sauce. Glaze with egg yolk, sprinkle sugar on top and bake in a moderate oven for 45 minutes.

POIRE SAVARIN

PEAR SAVARIN

Recipe created by Curnonsky

Peel and core 12 pears. Fill the centres with Roquefort cheese mixed with a little butter. Mix 180 ml/12 tbsp fresh Roquefort cheese with some thick cream. Pour over the pears. Dust with paprika. Chill in the refrigerator.

—— BLUE CHEESE SOUFFLÉ ——

For 4 people. Make a fairly thick Béchamel Sauce (*page 62*) by mixing together 30 g/1 oz (2 tbsp) butter and 40 g/1½ oz (4½ tbsp) flour over the heat. When this mixture becomes foamy, pour in 250 ml/9 fl oz (1 cup) cold milk off the heat and all in one go. Season with salt, pepper and a little nutmeg, then return to the heat and simmer, stirring, until thickened. Remove from the heat and leave to cool. Meanwhile, whisk 2 egg whites until stiff. Add 2 egg yolks, one at a time, to the lukewarm sauce, then 100 g/4 oz blue cheese mashed with a fork. Whisk well with the fork, then fold in the egg whites. Butter 4 ramekins. Fill each one three-quarters full with the soufflé mixture, place on a baking sheet which has been preheated in the oven for 3–4 minutes, then bake in a moderate oven for 20 minutes. Serve immediately.

—— LAGUIOLE SOUP ——

Blanch some cabbage leaves in boiling water, drain, then finish cooking in chicken stock. Line a casserole with slices of country-style bread. Sprinkle some thin slices of Laguiole cheese (not too mature) on top, then a few cabbage leaves. Repeat the layering: bread, Laguiole, cabbage and stock, ending with a layer of bread and cheese. Sprinkle a little oil on top and brown in the oven.

—— SAINT-DENIS TARTLETS ——

Put 250 g/8 oz cream cheese into a bowl with the same quantity of Brie or Camembert, rind removed so that it is completely white. Add a little salt, 10 g/scant ½ oz (2½ tsp) sugar and 20 g/¾ oz (7 tsp) cornflour (cornstarch).

Add 2–3 whole eggs and 2 egg yolks.

Mix everything together well, first with a fork and then with a spatula. When a smooth dough is formed, whisk 2 egg whites until stiff, then fold into the dough. Use to fill tartlet cases made with shortcrust (pie) pastry (*page 577*) and bake in a hot oven.

—— CHEESE AND OLIVE QUICHE ——

Line a flan (quiche) dish with shortcrust (pie) pastry. Dot with butter, slivers of Gruyère cheese and stoned and blanched green olives. Mix 4 eggs with 350 ml/12 fl oz (1½ cups) milk and pour over. Dot the top with butter and cover with a layer of grated cheese. Bake in a hot oven.

'MACQUÉE' TART

Put 500 g/1 lb *fromage blanc* (called 'macquée') into a cloth and squeeze well to extract the liquid. Put it on to a plate and flatten slightly. Sprinkle with salt and leave in a warm place, like the kitchen, for example. Leave for about 1 week. By the end of this time a yellowish crust will have formed which indicates the cheese is ready. Put into a bowl and beat well with a wooden spoon, then add 6 egg yolks, one at a time. *Fines herbes* and pepper are sometimes added, but these are optional, and not authentic.

The cheese is ready. Roll out some risen bread dough about 5 mm/¼ inch thick and use to line a greased flan (quiche) dish. Prick the bottom all over with a fork and fill with the cheese. Brush the edge of the pastry with beaten egg and bake in a very moderate oven for 35 minutes.

Unmould the flan on to a wire rack and spread a layer of softened butter over the top. Prick with a fork to allow the butter to seep through. Serve hot.

GOAT'S CHEESE PIE

Make Shortcrust Pastry according to the instructions on page 577, leave to rest for 20 minutes, then use to line a 25 cm/10 inch flan (quiche) dish.

Bake blind in a moderate oven for 6 minutes. Mix 250 g/8 oz well-drained, fresh goat's cheese with 125 g/4½ oz (10 tbsp) sugar, a pinch of salt, 5 egg yolks and 50 g/2 oz (6 tbsp) potato flour. Add a dash of cognac.

Beat the egg whites until stiff and fold into the cheese mixture. Pour into the pastry case and bake in a moderate oven for 45 minutes.

POTATO AND CHEESE CAKE

Put about 20 pieces of diced bacon into a lightly oiled frying pan. Place over the heat until the fat runs. Remove the bacon and add 45 ml/3 tbsp olive oil to the pan.

Slice 6 potatoes, put into the frying pan and season with salt. Cover and fry for 15 minutes, uncovering and stirring frequently with a fork to break up the potatoes.

Cut 200 g/7 oz fresh Tomme cheese into slices. Mix into the potatoes over a high heat, then leave until golden-brown without stirring. Turn out on to a serving dish so that the golden, underneath part is on top.

DESSERTS

THE FINAL COURSE OF A MEAL IS BY NO MEANS the least important, as it should complement the menu and the balance of flavours. The word 'dessert' comes from the verb 'desservir', meaning to clear away what has been served, and therefore describes what is offered to guests at the end of a meal. It is a generic term encompassing all kinds of hot, cold or iced confections, all of which have sugar as their common ingredient, although cheese and plain fruit also count as desserts. There is an extensive range of hot and cold desserts: charlottes, soufflés, rice cakes, fritters, stewed fruit, crêpes, custards, 'œufs à la neige', sweet and soufflé omelettes, baked custards, meringues, 'puddings', various fruit desserts, ice creams, bombes and sorbets, fruit salads, petits fours and confectionery. In addition there are the equally numerous and varied applications of pâtisserie (pastry making) itself, using the basic pastry recipes: puff, shortcrust, rich shortcrust and sweet pastries, brioche and mousseline brioche doughs, sponge fingers (ladyfingers), choux pastry, and Genoese sponge. The great Parisian pastry cooks used regional dessert recipes and made them into classic creations, such as the baba and savarin, the Paris-Brest and St-Honoré, mille-feuille and religieuses, puits d'amour and mocha cake, vacherins, succès and progrès cakes, as well as the delicious range of seasonal fruit pies.

'There are five fine arts, namely, painting, sculpture, poetry, music, and architecture, and the principal branch of the latter is pastry cookery', said the great pastry cook Carême in an age when the 'pièce montée' (elaborate tiered pâtisserie) symbolized a well-laid table. Today desserts are less extravagant in appearance but their gourmet qualities are more apparent.

*Editor's note: the recipes in this chapter, particularly those for basic cakes and pastries, are often made in large quantities, as they would be in professional kitchens. Quantities will therefore have to be adapted for domestic use, and sizes of tins and moulds, etc, adjusted accordingly.

PÂTES

PASTRIES

— LEAVEN (YEAST 'STARTER' BATTER) —

Preparation 5 minutes

US	Ingredients	Met/Imp
½ pkg	fresh (compressed) yeast	10 g/⅓ oz
¾ cup	flour	100 g/4 oz

Crumble the yeast into a cup and blend with 45 ml/3 tbsp warm water. Put the flour into a bowl and pour in the yeast mixture. Mix well and add sufficient warm water to make a smooth, slightly soft dough. Dust with flour, cover with a cloth and leave in a warm, draught-free place.

The yeast dough may be left to rise in a bowl placed over a little warm water.

SUCRE

SUGAR

SUGAR TEMPERATURES AND THEIR USES IN COOKING

Name	Degrees Celsius/Fahrenheit	Degrees Baumé*	Description	Use
Coating	100°C/212°F	25°		
Small gloss	101°C/214°F	30°	2–3 mm/⅛ inch thread	almond paste, nougat
Large gloss	103°C/217°F	30°	5 mm/¼ inch thread	butter cream, icing
Small pearl	103–105°C/217–221°F	33°	small round bubbles	preserves
Large pearl	107°C/225°F	35°	large round bubbles; 2 cm/¾ inch thread	preserves, fondants glacé cherries, cake icing
Small ball	116°/241°F	37°	soft ball	Italian meringue, gâteau polonais
Large ball	121°C/250°F	38°	firm or hard ball	caramel
Crack	149–150°C/300–302°F	40°	hard crack; brittle but not sticky	cake icing, flowers, candy floss (cotton candy), pastilles, berlingots (small chocolate iced cakes)
Light caramel	150°C/302°F			caramelizing moulds, cake icing, nougatine, crème caramel
Dark caramel				colouring stock

*Editor's note: the Baumé scale is an old-fashioned method of measuring the density of sugar syrups by using a saccharometer. It is still used in the catering trade and sugar refining industry.

US	Ingredients	Met/Imp
16	eggs	16
2½ cups	caster (superfine) sugar	500 g/1 lb
¼ cup	rum or kirsch	50 ml/2 fl oz
2 cups	fine flour or potato flour	300 g/10 oz

SPONGE CAKE

Preparation 30 minutes • Cooking 40 minutes

Separate the eggs. Beat the yolks and sugar until the mixture is creamy and white and leaves a ribbon trail on its surface when the beater is lifted. Add the rum or kirsch and beat again. Fold in the flour and then the stiffly beaten egg whites. Bake at a low temperature.

3½ cups	flour	500 g/1 lb
½ pkg	fresh (compressed) yeast	10 g/⅓ oz
6	eggs	6
scant 1 tbsp	salt	15 g/½ oz
7 tsp	caster (granulated) sugar	30 g/1 oz
13 oz (26 tbsp)	good-quality unsalted butter	375 g/13 oz

BRIOCHE DOUGH

Preparation 24 hours

Blend 100 g/4 oz (¾ cup) of the flour with the yeast in a little warm water. Leave in a warm place for 30 minutes.

Break 3 eggs into the yeast mixture, add the remaining flour and mix well with a wooden spoon. It is not necessary to use your hands at this point. Beat the remaining 3 eggs with the salt and sugar and add gradually to the dough until it is well mixed and no longer sticks to the bowl or the wooden spoon. Beat well with the spoon until smooth and elastic.

Having first measured and kneaded the butter, place it in a warm room or near a source of heat so that it is soft but not melted. Remove the spoon from the dough, put a handful of dough (about one-fifth) on the baking table or in another bowl, and add the butter. Knead well until the mixture is smooth, then add some more of the dough. Continue until all of the butter and dough have been mixed and the mixture is no longer sticky. Scrape the hands clean with a knife. Put the dough in a bowl and dust it with flour. Cover with a cloth and leave in a cool place in summer or a warm one in winter. This kind of dough should be made the day before, or in the morning if to be used in the evening. After 2 or 3 hours the brioche dough should have increased in volume; beat it with a spoon until reduced to its original size. This is known as 'breaking' brioche dough. Cover and leave in a cool place overnight.

MOUSSELINE BRIOCHE DOUGH

Preparation 8–10 hours • Cooking 1 hour

US	Ingredients	Met/Imp
3½ cups	flour	500 g/1 lb
½ pkg	fresh (compressed) yeast	10 g/⅓ oz
13 oz (26 tbsp)	good-quality unsalted butter	375 g/13 oz
2 tsp	salt	12 g/2 tsp
7 tsp	caster (granulated) sugar	30 g/1 oz
6	eggs	6

Blend 125 g/4½ oz (¾ cup) of the flour with the yeast and a glass of warm water. Put into a bowl and leave in a warm place. Make a dough with the remaining flour, just under one-quarter of the butter, the salt, sugar and eggs. Knead, lifting the dough and alternately pulling it towards you and pushing it away, until it is very elastic. It is advisable, especially if you are inexperienced, not to add all of the eggs at once. Do take account of the absorbent qualities of the flour. Add the remaining butter, then the yeast mixture, but do not knead. Flour a bowl, put in the dough and sprinkle flour on top. Leave for 4–5 hours, then 'break' the dough. Leave for another few hours before baking.

  The proportion of butter may be varied to make a richer or plainer dough, from 300 g/10 oz (2 cups) to 425 g/15 oz (3 cups) per 500 g/1 lb (3½ cups) flour; the number of eggs may also be varied (from 6 to 10). Always use good-quality unsalted butter, which contains no water. This pastry works better in winter than summer, but it does need practice.

SHORTCRUST PASTRY FOR LINING

Preparation 2 hours

US	Ingredients	Met/Imp
1 tsp	salt	5 g/1 tsp
1 tbsp	caster (granulated) sugar	12 g/1 tbsp
1 stick	good-quality unsalted butter	100 g/3½ oz
1½ cups	flour, sifted	200 g/7 oz

Professional cooks work on a special pastry table called a 'tour', but it is much simpler to use a bowl and a wooden spoon (known as 'spatule' in French).

  Dissolve the salt and sugar in 100 ml/4 fl oz (½ cup) water. Soften the butter in advance by placing it near a source of heat in order to make it supple and to get rid of the water, air or whey it might contain.

  Place the butter, cut into small pieces, in a bowl with the flour. Mix with a wooden spoon, but do not try to make the flour absorb the butter. (You would not succeed, and if you did the pastry would be ruined, although there is no danger in prolonging this mixing.)

  From the moment the water is added, the various elements of the pastry should only be mixed enough to make a smooth ball which comes away from the sides of the bowl and the wooden spoon. So, when the salt and sugar have been dissolved in the water, pour it over the pastry all at once and incorporate it but do not overmix. Turn on to a lightly floured surface, fold it in two or three on itself, then wrap in a cloth and leave in a cool place. It can be kept for 2 days in summer or 3 in winter, if stored in a cool place.

  Note: there is no egg in this pastry. There used to be, but we no longer use it and the pastry is just as good, although a little less filling. The quality of flour often varies and therefore the quantity of water may vary accordingly by 100–200 ml/4–7 fl oz. If the dough is a little soft, add 15 ml/1 tbsp flour; if it is too stiff, add a little water, but this should be done as soon as it becomes hard to handle and not after the dough has been mixed.

CHOUX PASTRY AND PASTRY FOR ECLAIRS

Preparation 1 hour

US	Ingredients	Met/Imp
1¾ tsp	salt	10 g/⅓ oz
5 tsp	caster (granulated) sugar	20 g/¾ oz
1 tsp	orange-flower water	5 ml/1 tsp
1 lb (4 sticks)	good-quality unsalted butter	500 g/1 lb
3½ cups	flour	500 g/1 lb
16	eggs	16

Put 1 litre/1¾ pints (1 quart) water, the salt, sugar, orange-flower water and diced butter into a saucepan. Sift the flour on to a sheet of paper and break the eggs 2 at a time into cups. Stir the butter until it melts and the water boils.

Take the pan off the heat and pour in the flour all at once. Beat very well with a wooden spoon until the dough is thoroughly mixed. Replace the pan over a low heat to dry out the dough and stir constantly until it comes away from the sides of the pan and the spoon, and the butter begins to run out. This sometimes takes a long time, but it is essential to reach this stage.

Remove the pan from the heat and mix in the eggs, 2 at a time, until the dough is smooth. If the ingredients have been correctly measured and the dough properly dried out, it should absorb 16 medium eggs. The dough is ready when it slides off the spoon. Choux pastry is usually cooked as soon as it is made and does not need to be made the day before. If the dough is kept until the following day, add a beaten egg to it before using, but it will be less good.

CRÊPE BATTER

Preparation 45 minutes • Resting 2 hours • Cooking 3 minutes per crêpe

US	Ingredients	Met/Imp
2⅔ cups	flour, sifted	375 g/13 oz
¼ cup	caster (granulated) sugar	50 g/2 oz
1 pinch	salt	1 pinch
8	eggs	8
1 quart	cold boiled milk	1 litre/1¾ pints
4 tbsp	good-quality unsalted butter, melted	50 g/2 oz
	flavouring of your choice	
	icing (confectioners') sugar, for sweet crêpes	
	butter for frying	

Put the flour, sugar and salt into a bowl. Stir in the eggs, 2 at a time, but do not overbeat or the crêpes will be rubbery. Add the milk gradually, then the melted butter. Add optional flavouring (vanilla, finely grated lemon or orange rind, orange-flower water, rum or liqueur). If the batter is made carefully there is no need to strain it through a sieve, but if it needs to be strained, the butter should be added afterwards. Allow to rest for at least 2 hours.

Allow 3 crêpes per person. To make 24, served hot, you will need to use 2 or 3 frying pans. Choose small ones, ideally special crêpe pans which are very thick and heavy. Crêpes should be very thin and golden-brown. The pans must be very hot. Melt a small piece of butter in each pan before pouring in the batter.

For sweet crêpes, sprinkle icing (confectioners') sugar over each one.

To serve crêpes, either roll them up into cigar shapes or fold them into fans.

CRÊPE BATTER WITH COGNAC

Preparation 30 minutes • Resting 2 hours • Cooking 3 minutes per crêpe

US	Ingredients	Met/Imp
1¾ cups	flour, sifted	250 g/8 oz
1¾ tsp	salt	10 g/⅓ oz
4	eggs	4
1 tbsp	olive oil	15 ml/1 tbsp
3½ tbsp	cognac	50 ml/2 fl oz
2 cups	milk	500 ml/18 fl oz

Put the flour into a bowl. Add the salt, lightly beaten eggs, oil and cognac. Gradually stir in the milk. Add some water to make a smooth batter, free of lumps. Leave to rest for at least 2 hours before using.

Cook in a heavy, lightly greased frying pan.

PUFF PASTRY

Preparation 2 hours

US	Ingredients	Met/Imp
1¾ cups	flour, sifted	250 g/8 oz
1¾ tsp	salt	10 g/⅓ oz
10 tbsp	water	150 ml/¼ pint
½ lb (2 sticks)	good-quality unsalted butter	250 g/8 oz

Puff pastry is made in 2 stages. The first is mixing the dough, the second is buttering and turning the pastry. To make the dough, sift the flour, measure it and put into a bowl. Measure the salt and dissolve it in the water, then pour into the bowl all at once. Mix with a wooden spoon, just enough to combine the flour and water, then turn on to a floured surface. Fold in two or three, form into a roll, wrap in a cloth and leave in a cool place for 20 minutes.

The buttering and turning should be done in a cool place to prevent the butter becoming too soft. Certain kinds of butter, such as those from Poitou and Charentes, are more suitable than others, even of higher quality; unpasteurized butter is even better. Soften the butter by kneading it in a cloth several hours beforehand; this will make it supple and rid it of water. Return it to a cool place. (If the butter is very soft after kneading, put it in a large bowl of water as cool as possible and drain it just before using. This should only be a last resort.)

Put the dough on to a lightly floured surface to prevent it sticking. Fold it in 2 or 3 on itself, shape into a ball, then roll into a 22.5 cm/9 inch circle with a rolling pin or by hand. Shape the butter into a 20 cm/8 inch square and place it in the centre of the dough. Fold the dough over the butter, trimming the edges so there is no overlap.

Return to a cool place for 15 minutes, then give it 2 'turns'. To do this, lightly flour the surface and roll the dough out to a rectangle about 50 cm/20 inches long (on no account more). Fold in 3, give it a quarter 'turn' to the right, then roll it out to a rectangle again. Fold in 3 again, then give it another quarter 'turn'. Leave in a cool place for 15 minutes. Repeat this process to give a total of 6 'turns' before cutting and baking. The last 2 'turns' should be done quickly to prevent the dough losing its elasticity.

Preheat the oven because the pastry should be cooked in a hot oven. When ready, give the pastry the final 2 'turns' and roll out, but no longer than 50 cm/20 inches or the pastry will hardly rise and will look grey. For the same reason, do not overflour the surface.

When the pastry has been 'turned' 6 times, it is ready for use.

US	Ingredients	Met/Imp
4 tbsp	good-quality unsalted butter, melted	50 g/2 oz
scant 1 cup	flour, sifted	125 g/4½ oz
1 tsp	salt	5 g/1 tsp
1	egg	1
1 glass	beer	1 glass
4 tsp	eau-de-vie	20 ml/4 tsp
1	egg white	1

FRITTER BATTER

Preparation 1½ hours

Mix the butter, flour and salt together with a wooden spoon. Add the lightly beaten egg. Stir in the beer, then flavour with the eau-de-vie. The consistency of the batter should be such that it coats the spoon, and it should be free of lumps. Leave to rest for 1 hour. Just before using, fold in the stiffly whisked egg white.

US	Ingredients	Met/Imp
12	eggs	12
2½ cups	caster (superfine) sugar	500 g/1 lb
1 tsp	vanilla, lemon or orange sugar	5 ml/1 tsp
	or	
2 tsp	orange-flower water	10 ml/2 tsp
3½ cups	flour	500 g/1 lb
½ lb (2 stick)	good-quality unsalted butter, melted	250 g/8 oz

GENOESE SPONGE CAKE

Preparation 2 hours • Cooking 30 minutes

This cake, which is in fact just one of several types of sponge cake, is simple to make and has many applications. A variety of flavourings may be used, and even candied fruits or chopped almonds may be added.

Whisk the eggs and sugar in a round, unlined copper bowl (it is the most convenient receptacle). Place the bowl over a very low heat so that the mixture becomes lukewarm during whisking and continue whisking until it leaves a ribbon trail on its surface when the whisk is lifted.

Using a wooden spoon, stir in the chosen flavouring, sifted flour and melted butter and mix lightly. Pour immediately into moulds or buttered and floured cake tins, according to the required use, but do not fill more than two-thirds full. Bake in a low to moderate oven and turn out on to a wire rack or wicker trays to cool.

RICH SHORTCRUST PASTRY

Preparation 30 minutes • Resting 2 hours

US	Ingredients	Met/Imp
3½ cups	flour	500 g/1 lb
1 tsp	salt	5 ml/1 tsp
½ lb (2 sticks)	good-quality unsalted butter	250 g/8 oz

Sift the flour and salt into a bowl. Squeeze the butter in a cloth to extract the water and whey. Rub it into the flour with the tips of your fingers until evenly mixed; do not knead. Add sufficient cold water to make firm but not stiff dough. Shape into a ball and leave to rest for 2 hours before using.

SAVARIN DOUGH

Preparation 40 minutes • Resting a few hours • Cooking 30–40 minutes

US	Ingredients	Met/Imp
3½ cups	flour	500 g/1 lb
2–3 pkg	dried yeast	15–20 g/½–¾ oz
½ wine glass	milk	½ wine glass
8	eggs	8
2½ sticks	good-quality unsalted butter	300 g/10 oz
1 tbsp	salt	15 g/½ oz
2 tbsp	caster (granulated) sugar	25 g/scant 1 oz

Sift the flour into a skull-cap-shaped wooden bowl, or just a bowl. Make a well in the centre, add 15 g/½ oz (2 packages) yeast in summer and 20 g/¾ oz (3 packages) in winter and mix it with the lukewarm milk. Add the eggs (previously broken into a bowl); make into dough and knead well for a few minutes, scraping any dough from the sides of the bowl with a scraper or slice of potato and incorporating it back into the main bulk of the dough.

Soften the butter by kneading it in a cloth, then scatter small pieces on top of the dough. Cover and keep in a fairly warm place until the dough has doubled in size.

When the dough is ready, add the salt and knead by hand to ensure that the dough itself is well mixed and the butter incorporated in it. Work with the tips of your fingers to make a smooth, elastic dough. Add the sugar at this stage.

Divide the dough into pieces, butter some moulds and fill them one-third full. The remaining space will be filled by expansion of the dough caused by the fermentation of the yeast. If you want savarins which are taller than the moulds, fill them half full; but in this case it is necessary to surround the sides of the moulds with strips of white paper stuck together with beaten egg white to prevent the dough from overflowing.

Leave the moulds in a warm place until the dough has risen, then immediately put in a moderate oven. Bake for about 30 minutes, for normal-sized moulds.

This quantity is sufficient for 3 standard moulds. If liked, soak the savarins in a syrup flavoured with rum or kirsch while they are still hot.

Any kind of cake must always be placed on a wire rack or wicker tray as soon as it is removed from the oven so that air can circulate while it cools down.

US	Ingredients	Met/Imp
1 stick	good-quality unsalted butter	125 g/4 oz
10 tbsp	caster (granulated) sugar	125 g/4 oz
2	eggs	2
1¾ cups	flour, sifted	250 g/8 oz

SWEET PASTRY

Preparation 2 hours

This pastry is generally used as a case for almond mixtures which are too light to be cooked without a base. It is also used for desserts filled with confectioner's custard, butter cream or fruit.

With slight variations, it is also used to make sweet, crisp biscuits (cookies).

Put the butter into a bowl and cream with a wooden spoon, then beat in the sugar and gradually add the eggs. Mix well until smooth, pour in the flour all at once and blend with a wooden spoon just enough to incorporate the ingredients. During the first stage of the procedure, before the flour has been added, mixing and kneading can be carried out without risk; but once the flour has been added the beating must not be overdone or the consistency of the pastry will be spoilt, becoming hard and brittle.

Place on a floured surface and fold in 2 or 3, wrap in a clean cloth and keep in a cool place. The pastry will keep for 2 days in summer and 3 in winter.

US	Ingredients	Met/Imp
2 cups	boiled milk	500 ml/18 fl oz
3 cups	flour, sifted	400 g/14 oz
1 pinch	salt or caster (granulated) sugar	1 pinch

PÂTE À TARTE OU À CROUSTADES

TARTLET PASTRY

Preparation 10 minutes • (Collecting milk skin 1 week) • Cooking 20 minutes

Remove the skin (which many people do not like) from boiled milk with a skimmer. Place it in a bowl. Leave the milk to stand for 1 week, collecting the skin regularly until there is no milk left.

Using a wooden spoon, gently fold the flour into the creamy mass of skin, to make a thick dough. Add a little salt or sugar according to the required use. Do not overmix the dough or it will be too heavy.

Roll out this dough on a table and shape into small biscuits (cookies), 'croustades' (small, deep pastry cases) or 'barquettes' (small boat-shaped pastry cases), using small moulds in the latter two cases. When the moulds have been lined, put parchment paper in them, fill with lentils (to stop the bottoms rising) and bake in the oven. Unmould, let them dry out, and store until needed.

CRÈMES

CREAMS AND CUSTARDS

CRÈME ANGLAISE À LA VANILLE

——— VANILLA CUSTARD SAUCE ———

Preparation 30 minutes • Cooking 30 minutes

US	Ingredients	Met/Imp
10	egg yolks	10
I quart	milk	I litre/1¾ pints
I cup	caster (granulated) sugar	200 g/7 oz
I	vanilla pod (bean)	I

Whisk the egg yolks with a little cold milk in a saucepan. Bring the remaining milk to the boil with the sugar and the vanilla pod (bean). Leave to cool slightly, then strain on to the egg yolks. Cook in a *bain-marie*, whisking continuously, for about 30 minutes or until the custard thickens. Allow to become cold, whisking occasionally.

VARIATION
Substitute 15 ml/1 tbsp potato flour for 3 of the egg yolks.

CRÈME AU BEURRE

——— BUTTER CREAM ———

Preparation 1 hour • Cooking about 20 minutes

US	Ingredients	Met/Imp
½ lb (1¼ cups)	lump (or granulated) sugar	250 g/8 oz
scant I cup	water	200 ml/7 fl oz
10	egg yolks	10
I lb (4 sticks)	good-quality unsalted butter	500 g/1 lb

Boil the sugar and water until it reaches the 'small gloss' stage (see page 575). Pour slowly on to the egg yolks, beating continuously with a whisk until completely cold.

   Work the butter in to remove any excess water, then beat it in a bowl until soft. Gradually beat in the syrup.

VARIATIONS
To add a liquid flavouring to the cream (kirsch, coffee essence, etc) add this to the syrup. If using a solid flavouring (praline, chocolate, etc) mix it into the finished butter cream.

CRÈME FOUETTÉE ET CRÈME CHANTILLY

WHIPPED CREAM AND
CHANTILLY CREAM ———

Preparation 20 minutes

US	Ingredients	Met/Imp
2 cups	whipping cream	500 ml/18 fl oz
2 cups	double (heavy) cream	500 ml/18 fl oz
¾ cup	vanilla sugar	150 g/5 oz

Combine the 2 creams. Place over ice and whip until thick, taking care that the mixture does not turn to butter. Drain in a fine sieve and serve cold.

   Sweetened with the vanilla sugar, this whipped cream becomes Chantilly cream. To make it lighter, and give it more bulk, you can fold in 2–3 stiffly whisked egg whites.

US	Ingredients	Met/Imp
2 cups	milk	500 ml/18 fl oz
1	vanilla pod (bean)	1
7½ tbsp	flour	65 g/2½ oz
¾ cup	caster (granulated) sugar	150 g/5 oz
1 pinch	salt	1 pinch
6	egg yolks	6

CONFECTIONER'S CUSTARD OR PASTRY CREAM

Preparation 20 minutes • Cooking 20 minutes

Bring the milk to the boil, add the vanilla pod (bean), leave to infuse, then strain. Put the flour, sugar, salt and egg yolks in a saucepan. Mix together, beat for a moment, then gradually add the milk. Heat very gently until the custard thickens, stirring constantly with a wooden spoon to prevent the custard sticking to the bottom of the pan. Simmer for a few minutes, still stirring, then transfer to a bowl and leave to cool (taking care to stir it from time to time).

VARIATIONS

For coffee-flavoured custard, add strong coffee essence to taste just before use. In this case the vanilla is omitted.

For orange-flavoured custard, infuse the zest of an orange in the milk.

MISCELLANEOUS

FONDANT

US	Ingredients	Met/Imp
2 lb (5 cups)	lump (or granulated) sugar	1 kg/2 lb
¼ cup	glucose (light corn syrup)	75 g/3 oz
	liquid food colouring flavouring	

FONDANT

Preparation 1 hour • Cooking 30 minutes

Melt the sugar in a saucepan that has been rinsed out with water. As the sugar comes to the boil and bubbles, wipe around the inside of the saucepan with a damp cloth. Skim the surface of the sugar. When the sugar reaches the 'ball' stage (*page 575*), add the glucose (corn syrup). Remove from the heat and tip on to a damp marble slab. Work with a wooden spoon until the syrup starts to cool and becomes white and thick. Keep cool until ready to use, then heat gently and add colour and flavouring to taste. The fondant must never become more than lukewarm, or it will lose its shine.

FRANGIPANE

US	Ingredients	Met/Imp
1⅔ cups	shelled sweet almonds	250 g/8 oz
1 tbsp	shelled bitter almonds	10 g/½ oz
8	eggs	8
½ lb (2 sticks)	good-quality unsalted butter	250 g/8 oz
1½ cups	caster (granulated) sugar	300 g/10 oz
2 tsp	fine table salt	10 g/½ oz
1 tbsp	potato flour	15 ml/1 tbsp
3½ tbsp	kirsch	50 ml/2 oz

FRANGIPANE

Preparation 1½ hours

Skin the almonds and dry them in the oven. Crush them in a mortar and pestle and put them in a bowl. Mix in 4 of the eggs, adding them one by one, then mix in the softened butter, followed by the sugar and the salt. Beat until the paste becomes creamy, then mix in the potato flour, then the remaining 4 eggs, one by one. Add the kirsch and keep cold until ready to use.

ROYAL ICING

Preparation 25 minutes

US	Ingredients	Met/Imp
2½ cups	icing (confectioners') sugar	300 g/10 oz
2	egg whites	2
4 tsp	potato flour	20 ml/4 tsp
2 tbsp	kirsch	30 ml/2 tbsp

Work the sugar into the egg whites with a wooden spoon. Add the potato flour, then the kirsch and continue beating for at least 25 minutes.

This makes enough to coat just the top or the top and sides of a large cake.

ORDINARY (SWISS) MERINGUE

Preparation 40 minutes • Cooking 30 minutes

US	Ingredients	Met/Imp
8	egg whites	8
2½ cups	vanilla sugar	500 g/1 lb

Put the egg whites into a large round-bottomed bowl, preferably made of copper, and beat with a whisk until very stiff. Quickly add the sugar, folding it in with a spatula.

Bake in a very low oven so that the meringue dries out but does not colour.

COOKED MERINGUE

Preparation 30 minutes • Cooking 30 minutes

US	Ingredients	Met/Imp
8	egg whites	8
4 cups	vanilla icing (confectioners') sugar	500 g/1 lb

Put the ingredients in a bowl over a saucepan of gently simmering water. Whisk together until the mixture is hot, but not cooked, then bake in a very low oven.

ITALIAN MERINGUE

Preparation 40 minutes • Cooking 30 minutes

US	Ingredients	Met/Imp
1 lb (2½ cups)	lump (or granulated) sugar	500 g/1 lb
1	vanilla pod (bean)	1
scant 1 cup	water	200 ml/7 fl oz
6	egg whites	6

Put the sugar in a saucepan and add the vanilla pod (bean) and water. Bring to the boil and cook the syrup to the 'ball' stage (*page 575*), then put the saucepan in a *bain-marie*. Remove the vanilla pod (bean).

Beat the egg whites until very stiff. Pour the syrup on to the egg whites in a steady stream, beating with a whisk. This meringue is used as it is, without further cooking in the oven, except to give it a quick colouring.

US	Ingredients	Met/Imp
1⅔ cups	shelled almonds	250 g/8 oz
7 oz (about ⅓ quantity)	Fondant (page 584)	200 g/7 oz
1½ tbsp	powdered vanilla food colouring	10 g/½ oz

ALMOND PASTE

Preparation 20 minutes

Skin the almonds and dry out in the oven. Grind to a fine powder. Mix with the fondant by hand on a marble slab. Add the vanilla and, finally, the colouring.

US	Ingredients	Met/Imp
1⅔ cups	shelled almonds	250 g/8 oz
2 cups	shelled hazelnuts (filberts)	250 g/8 oz
2½ cups	caster (granulated) sugar	500 g/1 lb

PRALIN

PRALINE

Preparation 1 hour • Cooking 20 minutes

Praline can be used to flavour butter cream, or other creams and ice cream. It is often used in pastry-making as well as in confectionery. It is regarded as part of the 'stock-in-trade' of the pastry cook.

Brown the almonds in the oven, breaking one from time to time to see if they are ready and stirring them well so that they cook evenly. When they are golden, remove them from the oven. Brown the hazelnuts in the same way until they are golden. Take them from the oven and rub them in a sieve to remove their skins.

Melt the sugar in a saucepan without any water, stirring constantly until it is a light golden caramel. Mix in the almonds and hazelnuts, then pour on to a marble slab and leave to cool. Work the praline in a mortar and pestle, or put through a mincer (grinder), until finely crushed. Do not add anything at all, neither water, nor oil, nor anything else. Store in a jar covered with paper until required.

DESSERT RECIPES

ABRICOTS À LA CONDÉ

APRICOT CONDÉ

Preparation 1 hour • Cooking apricots 10–12 minutes; rice 25 minutes

US	Ingredients	Met/Imp
1¼–1½ cup	pudding or short-grain rice	250–300 g/ 8–10 oz
1 quart	milk	1 litre/1¾ pints
1 pinch	salt	1 pinch
½	vanilla pod (bean)	½
10 tbsp	caster (granulated) sugar	125 g/4½ oz
scant 1 cup	crème fraîche	200 ml/7 fl oz
4	egg yolks	4
12	firm apricots *or*	12
6	pears	6
scant 1 cup	sugar syrup: 28° Baumé (page 575)	200 ml/7 fl oz
½ lb	ripe apricots	250 g/8 oz
	glacé cherries	
	candied oranges	
½	candied angelica stalk	½
	pistachio nuts	
3½ tbsp	kirsch	50 ml/2 fl oz

Blanch the rice by putting it in a saucepan with a small quantity of water and bringing it to the boil. Drain, return to the rinsed-out pan and add the milk, salt and vanilla. Cook for about 25 minutes, then add the sugar and bring to the boil again. Discard the vanilla. Add the crème fraîche and bind with the egg yolks.

Halve the firm apricots or pears. Poach them in sugar syrup for 10–12 minutes or until cooked but still a little firm. Reserve the syrup. Halve and stone the remaining ripe apricots and poach them in the reserved syrup. Drain and reserve the syrup. Work the ripe apricots through a hair sieve to make a purée that is quite liquid.

Put the rice in a sufficiently large mould or, if preferred, in 2 smaller ring

moulds, bread tins or savarin moulds, while it is still hot. Keep it warm in a *bain-marie*. Keep the fruit and fruit purée warm too.

Just before serving, turn the mould or moulds out on to a round dish. Arrange the apricots or pears around the base like a crown and those left over in the centre of the ring. Decorate the fruit with halved glacé cherries, sliced candied Chinese oranges, angelica in shapes and pistachio halves. Flavour the apricot purée with kirsch. Heat a little of the purée with a little reserved sugar syrup and kirsch to make a glaze and brush over the fruit and rice mould. Serve the remaining purée separately in a sauce boat. Serve everything very hot.

ANANAS À LA MERINGUE SUR SON BISCUIT

PINEAPPLE MERINGUE
ON A SPONGE BASE

Preparation 2 hours • Cooking about 20 minutes

Make up the cake batter and bake it, if possible, in a 22 cm/8½ inch oval Genoese tin. Otherwise, bake in a 20 cm/8 inch round cake tin.

Cut the cake horizontally into 2 layers. Cover the lower layer with chopped candied pineapple mixed with half of the apricot marmelade and the rum. Cover it with the top layer. Roll out the pastry to a round 22 cm/8½ inches in diameter and 4 cm/1½ inches thick. Bake in a cool oven for 18–20 minutes. Leave to cool, then brush with the remaining marmelade, melted. Place the cake on the pastry base.

Make an Italian meringue (*page 585*) with the icing (confectioners') sugar, vanilla and egg whites. Spoon three-quarters of the meringue on to the cake, shaping it into an elongated dome. Smooth with a knife or thin card so that it is round at one end and pointed at the other, in imitation of a pineapple. It ought to be slightly elongated, even if a round cake has been used for the base.

Put the remaining meringue in a piping bag fitted with a 5 mm/¼ inch plain round nozzle. Pipe a line of meringue dots, working from the base of the meringue dome to the top, to resemble the 'eyes' on the pineapple skin.

Complete the gâteau in one of two ways. Either coat it with apricot marmelade or ice it with a light yellow fondant, to resemble a pineapple.

US	Ingredients	Met/Imp
⅙–⅛ recipe quantity	Savoy Sponge Cake batter (*page 627*) or Genoese Sponge Cake batter (*page 580*)	250 g/8 oz
1 lb	candied pineapple	500 g/1 lb
¼ cup	apricot *marmelade*	60 ml/4 tbsp
1 small glass	rum	1 small glass
¼ basic reci	Sweet Pastry (*page 582*)	150 g/5 oz
1 cup	icing (confectioners') sugar	125 g/4½ oz
1 pinch	powdered vanilla	1 pinch
2	egg whites	2
	TO FINISH	
6 tbsp	apricot *marmelade* or yellow Fondant (*page 584*)	100 g/4 oz

US	Ingredients	Met/Imp
8	bananas, from the Canaries	8
½ cup	caster (granulated) sugar	100 g/4 oz
3 tbsp	flour	25 g/scant 1 oz
scant 1 cup	milk	200 ml/7 fl oz
1 pinch	salt	1 pinch
2 tbsp	good-quality unsalted butter	25 g/scant 1 oz
3	whole eggs	3
1	egg white	1
	icing (confectioners') sugar, for dusting	

SOUFFLÉED BANANAS

Preparation 1 hour • Cooking 6 minutes

If possible, choose large bananas, just ripened and without any spots on the peel. Remove a strip of peel from the outside of each one, then take out the pulp from the inside. Emptied in this way, the skins are like little elongated cases.

Mix the sugar and flour in a sauté pan and pour in the boiled milk. Stir to dissolve. Add the salt and bring to the boil over a low heat, stirring continuously. Remove from the heat. Stir in the mashed banana, the butter and egg yolks. Finally, gently fold in the stiffly whisked egg whites.

Fill the banana skins with this mixture and arrange them in an ovenproof dish. Bake in a hot oven for 4 minutes, then dust the tops with icing (confectioners') sugar which will form a light coating of caramel when it melts. Serve 2 minutes later.

US	Ingredients	Met/Imp
12	gelatine leaves or	12
3½ envelopes (3½ tbsp)	powdered (unflavoured) gelatine	25 g/scant 1 oz
1¼ cups	milk	300 ml/½ pint
½	vanilla pod (bean)	½
6	egg yolks	6
2 cups	caster (granulated) sugar	400 g/14 oz
1¾ cups	*crème fraîche*	400 ml/14 fl oz
3½ tbsp	kirsch	50 ml/2 fl oz
1	Genoese Sponge Cake (*page 580*), made the same diameter as a savarin mould, or slightly smaller	1
12	glacé cherries	12
	chocolate vermicelli (sprinkles)	
	coloured sugar strands	
	whipped cream (optional)	

BAVARIAN CREAM WITH KIRSCH

Preparation 1 hour • Freezing 3 hours • Completion 15 minutes • Serves 6–8

Soften the gelatine in cold water. Bring the milk to the boil with the vanilla. When it boils, remove from the heat, discard the vanilla and add the gelatine.

Mix the egg yolks well with two-thirds of the sugar in an enamel saucepan. When the mixture is really pale and fluffy, carefully pour on the hot milk. Cook over a low heat, stirring continuously, until the custard coats the back of the spoon. Strain the custard through a sieve and leave to cool.

Beat the crème fraîche, add half of the remaining sugar to it and mix it with the cooled custard. Oil or butter a savarin mould and fill it with the custard mixture. Cover with foil and freeze for at least 3 hours.

Make a syrup with the remaining sugar, a little water and the kirsch. Soak the genoese cake with this syrup, put it on a serving plate and gently unmould the Bavarian cream on top of it. (To make this easier, run the hot blade of a knife between the sides of the mould and the cream, or dip the mould for a few moments in lukewarm water.) Decorate with glacé cherries, chocolate vermicelli (sprinkles), sugar strands and whipped cream, if liked.

ACACIA FLOWER FRITTERS

Preparation 1 hour • Macerating several hours • Cooking about 10 minutes

US	Ingredients	Met/Imp
1 lb	acacia flowers in clusters	500 g/1 lb
½ cup	cognac	100 ml/4 fl oz
	sugar	
1 quart	Fritter Batter (page 580)	1 litre/1¾ pints
	fat for deep frying	

Remove the stalks from the acacia clusters. Clean the flowers and macerate them for a few hours in cognac and sugar. Dip the acacia flowers in the batter and plunge them into hot deep fat.

Fry just 2 or 3 fritters at first to test the cooking temperature, then they may be fried in larger quantities. Drain and serve hot, sprinkled with sugar.

BANANA FRITTERS

Preparation 20 minutes • 1st Cooking 25 minutes • 2nd Cooking 5 minutes

US	Ingredients	Met/Imp
12	bananas	12
2 cups	Fritter Batter (page 580)	500 ml/18 fl oz
	fat for deep frying	
	sugar	

Put the unpeeled bananas (from the Canaries if possible) in an ovenproof dish and cook them in a hot oven for 25 minutes, turning them over once.

When the bananas are cooked, peel them and cut them in half. Dip them in the batter, then plunge them into very hot deep fat. Serve them piled high, dusted with sugar.

APPLE FRITTERS

Preparation 1 hour • Cooking 12 minutes

US	Ingredients	Met/Imp
6	medium *reinette* or other eating apples	6
¼ cup	caster (granulated) sugar	50 g/2 oz
3½ tbsp	calvados	50 ml/2 fl oz
1 pinch	ground cinnamon (optional)	1 pinch
	oil and lard for deep frying	
1 quart	Fritter Batter (page 580)	1 litre/1¾ pints
	icing (confectioners') sugar, for dusting	
1 cup	apricot sauce (optional)	200 ml/7 fl oz

Core the apples, peel them and cut them into thin slices. Put them in a deep dish with the sugar, calvados and cinnamon, if liked. Cover and leave to macerate for a few moments.

The cooking fat must be fresh and quite hot. When dipping the apple slices in the batter, it helps to put a small amount of the batter in a deep dish. Completely coat the slices and plunge them into the hot deep fat. Put in several slices at a time. Increase the heat of the cooking fat to maximum, as the apples will have cooled it. When the apples are cooked and have a good colour, remove them and drain them on a cloth. Keep them hot.

To add a little variety and extra flavour to the fritters, spread them on a (very clean) baking sheet and put them in a very hot oven after having dusted them with icing (confectioners') sugar. Through the heat of the oven, the sugar will form a very fine, slightly crisp glaze, which combines very well with the soft consistency of the apple and with the batter.

Serve the fritters with the apricot sauce or a good aromatic fruit syrup or *marmelade* in a sauce boat.

US	Ingredients	Met/Imp
	cooked rice mixture as for Rice Croquettes (page 597)	
I quart	Fritter Batter (page 580)	I litre/1¾ pints
	fat for deep frying	
½ jar	apricot jam	½ jar
½ cup	liqueur of your choice	100 ml/4 fl oz

BEIGNETS DE RIZ

RICE FRITTERS

Preparation 3 hours • Cooking 10 minutes

The rice mixture used for these fritters is very substantial, the batter should therefore be light.

Spread the cooked rice mixture on a baking sheet and leave to cool.

The rice mixture should be very soft. Cut it into small shapes and dip them in the batter. Plunge into hot deep fat.

These fritters need the accompaniment of a good apricot sauce made with the jam and liqueur.

US	Ingredients	Met/Imp
3½ cups	flour, sifted	500 g/1 lb
1½ pkg	fresh (compressed) yeast	25 g/scant 1 oz
I tsp	salt	5 g/1 tsp
¼ cup	caster (granulated) sugar	50 g/2 oz
4	eggs	4
scant ½ cup	water	100 ml/3½ fl oz
4 tbsp	good-quality unsalted butter	50 g/2 oz
	oil and lard for deep frying	
	icing (confectioners') sugar, for dusting	
I cup	apricot jam	200 ml/7 fl oz

BEIGNETS VIENNOIS

VIENNESE FRITTERS

Preparation 45 minutes • Proving 2 hours • Cooking 7–10 minutes

Sift 100 g/4 oz (¾ cup) of the flour into a bowl and make a little well in the centre. Add the yeast mixed with a little lukewarm water and leave in a moderately warm place sheltered from draughts.

Sift the remaining flour into a bowl and make a well in the centre. Add the salt, sugar and eggs and mix to a light dough (softening it with a little water). Gradually add the yeast mixture and the diced butter without kneading the dough too much. The dough should be a little lighter than for ordinary brioches. Let it rest for 2 hours in a moderately warm place.

Just before serving, prepare some sufficiently hot deep frying fat. Drop tablespoons of the dough into it and cook until golden. Drain on a cloth and dust them with icing (confectioners') sugar.

Serve the fritters as they are, accompanied by a sauce boat of melted apricot jam, or pierce them and fill them with jam using a piping bag.

US	Ingredients	Met/Imp
2 cups	shelled sweet almonds	300 g/10 oz
2 tbsp	shelled bitter almonds	15 g/½ oz
scant I cup	warm water	200 ml/7 fl oz
2 cups	whipping cream	500 ml/18 fl oz
17	gelatine leaves	17
	or	
5 envelopes	powdered (unflavoured) gelatine	35 g/1¼ oz
2 cups	milk	500 ml/18 fl oz
1¼ cups	caster (granulated) sugar	250 g/8 oz
3½ tbsp	orgeat cream or liqueur (made from almonds)	50 ml/2 fl oz

BLANC-MANGER

BLANCMANGE

Preparation 3 hours

Drop the almonds into boiling water for just a few minutes; drain them, then without letting them cool, spread them on a marble slab and carefully blanch them, that is to say, remove them from their skins, by pressing them between the thumb and forefinger. Put them in a mortar. Pound them vigorously with the pestle several times. Little by little, add the warm water and then the whipping cream. Squeeze this mixture in a cloth over a bowl in order to extract and collect all the almond-flavoured milk. Meanwhile, soak the gelatine in lukewarm water and bring the milk and sugar to the boil. Mix together the hot sweetened milk, the gelatine and the almond milk. Strain it all through a fine sieve and add the orgeat cream. Pour the mixture into a mould. Put the mould in

a large bowl and surround it with crushed ice. Leave for about 2 hours or until the mixture becomes set and firm. The mould could be put in the refrigerator but it would set less rapidly.

Just before serving, prepare to unmould the blancmange by laying a folded napkin on the serving plate to isolate the plate from the blancmange. Holding the mould with a cloth, very quickly plunge up to four-fifths of the mould into boiling water. Immediately wipe the mould and unmould the blancmange on to the napkin. Serve.

If you follow the quantities in this recipe, this blancmange will not be too firm, but it will be solid enough to unmould without breaking up.

BUGNES LYONNAISES

LYON FRITTERS*

Preparation 1 hour • Cooking 5–6 minutes

US	Ingredients	Met/Imp
about 1½ cups	flour	about 200 g/7 oz
1 tbsp	oil	15 ml/1 tbsp
2	eggs	2
2 tbsp	caster (granulated) sugar	30 ml/2 tbsp
1 pinch	salt	1 pinch
3½ tbsp	rum	50 ml/2 fl oz
	fat for deep frying	

Put the flour on a plate, make a well in the centre and add the oil, eggs, sugar, salt and rum.

Combine everything using a fork, mixing in the flour as necessary to make a ball of smooth dough. Roll it out with a rolling pin to make the thinnest possible layer and cut out of it little squares or rectangles. Drop these shapes into hot deep fat and deep fry until golden. Remove and dust with extra sugar.

These fritters are generally prepared the day before, since they are eaten cold.

CERISES FLAMBÉES

FLAMBÉED CHERRIES

Preparation 40 minutes • Cooking 15 minutes

US	Ingredients	Met/Imp
4 pints	cherries	1 kg/2 lb
½ cup	water	100 ml/4 fl oz
¾ cup	vanilla sugar	150 g/5 oz
1 tsp	potato flour	5 ml/1 tsp
½ cup	cherry brandy	100 ml/4 fl oz
½ cup	kirsch	100 ml/4 fl oz

Stone the cherries. Poach the fruit in the water with the vanilla sugar for about 15 minutes or until the cherries release their juice and are just tender. Remove from the heat and drain the cherries, reserving the syrup. Leave to cool.

Mix the potato flour with a little of the cooled fruit syrup, then stir back into the rest of the syrup. Bring to the boil and mix in the cherries and cherry brandy.

Just before serving, heat the cherries. Transfer them to a really hot serving bowl or, better still, to hot individual silver or porcelain goblets or pots, preferably made of silver or tin-lined copper. Dust the cherries with sugar, pour over a little kirsch and flambé. Serve immediately, placing the bowl or goblets on a folded napkin on a large dish.

Petits fours or flavoured sponge cake or sponge fingers (lady fingers) are good accompaniments for this dessert.

US	Ingredients	Met/Imp
10 oz	marron glacé pieces	300 g/10 oz
1¾ cups	vanilla-flavoured double (heavy) cream	400 ml/14 fl oz
	caster (superfine) sugar	
2 tsp	vanilla sugar	10 ml/2 tsp
2½ sticks	good-quality unsalted butter	300 g/10 oz
	Genoese or sponge finger (ladyfinger) crumbs	
1	glacé cherry	1
3	whole *marrons glacés*	3
	GEONESE SPONGE CAKE	
10 tbsp	caster (superfine) sugar	125 g/4½ oz
3	eggs	3
¾ cup	flour	100 g/4 oz
2 tbsp	vanilla sugar	1 sachet
4 tbsp	good-quality unsalted butter, melted	50 g/2 oz
8–10	shelled hazelnuts (filberts)	8–10
	SYRUP	
6 oz (14 tbsp)	lump (or granulated) sugar	175 g/6 oz
scant 1 cup	water	200 ml/7 fl oz

—— MARRON GLACÉ CHARLOTTE* ——

Preparation 24 hours in advance

As the Genoese Sponge Cake should be a little dry, make it at least 24 hours in advance. It may be replaced with about 20 sponge fingers (ladyfingers), but the charlotte will lose one of its main characteristics.

Make a Genoese Sponge Cake according to the instructions on page 580 with the caster (superfine) sugar, eggs, sifted flour, vanilla sugar, melted butter and toasted and finely chopped hazelnuts. Bake it in a buttered and floured square paper case. Turn out and leave to cool on a wire rack.

Make a syrup with the lump sugar and water and boil for 1 minute.

Put the marron glacé pieces in a bowl, sprinkle with some of the syrup and leave until they become very soft. Line the bottom and sides of a large charlotte mould with parchment paper. Cut the Genoese Sponge Cake into rectangles 2.5 cm/1 inch wide and 8 mm/⅓ inch thick. The length of the rectangles should be equal to the height of the sides of the mould, or even exceed it by 1 cm/½ inch. Line the sides of the mould with these rectangles, placing them upright and very close to one another. If using sponge fingers (ladyfingers), arrange these in the same way.

Whip the cream until thick. Put 60 ml/4 tbsp in a bowl and keep cold. Mix 30 ml/2 tbsp caster (superfine) sugar and the vanilla sugar into the remaining whipped cream.

Crush the marron glacé pieces in a mortar and add the unsalted butter. Mix by pounding with the pestle, then work the mixture rapidly through a sieve. Collect the purée in a bowl and thin it by stirring in the remaining syrup. This purée ought to have the consistency of a thick sauce. Quickly mix the vanilla-flavoured cream with the purée and spoon this mixture immediately into the mould. Strew the surface with Genoese crumbs or with coarsely crumbled sponge finger (ladyfinger) crumbs.

If the mould can be surrounded with ice, the mixture will set in 1 hour. If not, leave it in a cold place for 3 hours. (It should be clear that it is the solidifying butter which ensures that the charlotte sets firm.)

Add a little caster (superfine) sugar to the cream which has been set aside and put it into a piping bag fitted with a fluted nozzle. If unavailable, use a greaseproof (wax) paper cone.

Unmould the charlotte on to a plate covered with a cotton or paper lace doily. Remove the lining paper. Decorate the top of the charlotte with piped cream rosettes or dots. Place the glacé cherry in the centre and arrange the whole marrons glacés around it.

APPLE CHARLOTTE

Preparation 2 hours • Cooking 25–35 minutes

US	Ingredients	Met/Imp
6½ lb	reinette or other eating apples, if possible from Canada	3 kg/6½ lb
3¾ cups	caster (granulated) sugar	750 g/1½ lb
½ lb (2 sticks)	good-quality unsalted butter	250 g/8 oz
I	vanilla pod (bean) or cinnamon stick	I
	or	
I	lemon, pared rind of	I
I	firm-textured loaf	I
	extra caster (granulated) sugar, for dusting	
2	eggs	2
¾ cup	apricot *marmelade*	200 ml/7 fl oz

Peel the apples, cut them into quarters and remove the cores. Slice them thinly and put them in a sauté pan with the sugar and 150 g/5 oz (10 tbsp) butter. Cook over a high heat, stirring vigorously with a tinned copper spatula. Add the vanilla, cinnamon or lemon rind and cook until reduced to a concentrated purée.

Meanwhile, cut the crust off the loaf of bread and cut out 8 heart-shaped pieces to fit in the bottom of a 1 litre/1¾ pint (1 quart) charlotte mould in the shape of a rosette. Cut another 16 slices 4 cm/1½ inches wide and 5 mm/¼ inch thick and exactly as high as the mould. Brush the inside of the mould with melted butter and sprinkle lightly with sugar. This will give the bread a greater chance of being a good golden colour. Dip the 16 cut slices of bread in the remaining melted butter. Arrange the 8 heart shapes in the bottom of the mould in the shape of a rosette, and arrange the 16 slices (soaked in butter) overlapping one another around the sides of the mould.

To make unmoulding easier, beat the eggs well and brush all over the inner surfaces of the slices lining the sides of the mould. When cooked, this coating will give stability when the charlotte is unmoulded.

Thicken the well-reduced apple purée with apricot marmelade. Pour into the mould and cook in a hot oven for 25–35 minutes. Leave to rest for a few minutes before unmoulding. Serve hot.

CHARLOTTE RUSSE

Preparation 2 hours • Cooling 3–4 hours

US	Ingredients	Met/Imp
2 cups	milk	500 ml/18 fl oz
½	vanilla pod (bean)	½
9	egg yolks	9
10 tbsp	caster (superfine) sugar	125 g/4½ oz
4	gelatine leaves	4
	or	
I envelope	powdered (unflavoured) gelatine	15 ml/1 tbsp
scant I cup	Chantilly Cream (*page 583*)	200 ml/7 fl oz
3½ tbsp	kirsch, maraschino or other liqueur	50 ml/2 fl oz
20	sponge fingers (ladyfingers)	20

Bring the milk to the boil with the vanilla, then leave to infuse. Whisk the egg yolks and sugar until the mixture leaves a ribbon trail on its surface when the beater is lifted. Gradually pour the strained milk on to the eggs and sugar, whisking constantly. Pour the mixture back into the milk saucepan and cook very gently without boiling, stirring until the custard covers the spoon. Leave to cool, stirring often.

Dip and swirl the gelatine leaves in warm water, drain well and squeeze. Add to the custard, stir to dissolve, then strain through cheesecloth. Whisk the Chantilly cream. When the custard is cold, flavour with liqueur and mix with the cream.

Line a 1 litre/2 pint (1 quart) charlotte mould with parchment paper. Cut 4–5 sponge fingers (ladyfingers) into lozenges to make a rosette at the bottom of the mould with the rough side of the fingers facing down. Line the sides of the mould with the remaining sponge fingers (lady-fingers), trimmed slightly at both ends. Pour in the custard and cream mixture. Fill to the top. Put in the freezer or the refrigerator and leave until the mixture is resistant to touch. It needs at least 2 hours in a freezer or 3–4 hours in a refrigerator. Unmould on to a napkin on a serving plate.

US	Ingredients	Met/Imp
4 tsp	butter	20 g/¾ oz
½ cup	flour	75 g/3 oz
1½ pints	very ripe and juicy black cherries	400 g/14 oz
2	whole eggs	2
1	egg yolk	1
¼ cup	caster (granulated) sugar	50 g/2 oz
1 pinch	salt	1 pinch
1 small pinch	powdered vanilla	1 small pinch
1 tbsp	thick *crème fraîche*	15 ml/1 tbsp
scant 1 cup	milk	200 ml/7 fl oz
2 tbsp	kirsch	30 ml/2 tbsp
	icing (confectioners') sugar, for dusting	

CHERRY CLAFOUTIS

Preparation 30 minutes • Cooking 20 minutes

Soften the butter. When it is creamy, use to brush all over the inside of a round 22 cm/8½ inch flan tin (tart pan) or dish. Tip a spoonful of flour into the tin and shake the tin to distribute the flour over the buttered surface, then turn it upside-down and tap the base to remove any excess flour. Remove the cherry stalks, but leave in the stones which will give the clafoutis a very good flavour.

Break the 2 whole eggs into a bowl and add the extra yolk, the sugar, salt and flour. (If the cherries are not very juicy, 65 g/2½ oz (7 tbsp) flour will suffice.)

Beat with a whisk to obtain a smooth and creamy batter. Add the vanilla and mix, then add the cream, milk and kirsch. Mix well again, then add the cherries. Tip the mixture into the prepared tin and distribute the cherries evenly over the bottom. You can fill the tin up to within 5 mm/¼ inch of the top. Bake in a hot oven for 15–20 minutes. The clafoutis will rise beautifully above the tin. Leave to cool.

Turn out the clafoutis upside-down on to a wire rack, then quickly turn it the right way up on to a serving plate. To serve, dust lightly with icing (confectioners') sugar.

1	pineapple	1
2 tbsp	caster (granulated) sugar	25 g/scant 1 oz
½ cup	rum	100 ml/4 fl oz
3 pints	large, ripe cherries	750 g/1½ lb
1 bottle	burgundy	1 bottle
1 lb (2½ cups)	lump (or granulated) sugar	500 g/1 lb
½ cup	kirsch	100 ml/4 fl oz

CHERRY COMPOTE WITH PINEAPPLE

Preparation 6 hours • Cooking 7–8 minutes

This cherry compote can be served in two ways: chilled as here, or flambéed with kirsch.

Peel the pineapple thickly and remove the hard and fibrous core in the centre. Cut it into 5 mm/¼ inch thick slices. Arrange the slices on a plate and dust them with the caster (granulated) sugar, then sprinkle them with rum. Leave to macerate for several hours in a cold place, turning from time to time.

Stone the cherries, reserving the stones. Crack open about 20 stones and remove the kernels. Crush in a mortar. Put the burgundy wine and the lump sugar in an untinned copper saucepan (don't forget that tin gives red fruit a purple colour) and melt the sugar. Add the 20 or so crushed cherry kernels enclosed in a piece of cheesecloth tied with a knot. (This kind of infusion of the kernels gives the compote a light and agreeable flavour of bitter almonds.)

Boil until reduced to a wine syrup, then put in the cherries (and also any of their juice that has escaped). Cover and cook over a very low heat to keep the syrup barely simmering. It will only take 7–8 minutes to poach the cherries and make them very tender.

Remove the cherries with a small copper skimmer, put them in a bowl and leave until nearly cold. Surround the bowl with crushed ice and leave the cherries for 30–35 minutes. Meanwhile, reduce the syrup to

250 ml/8 fl oz (1 cup). Strain through a fine sieve. Let it cool, then mix in the kirsch. Chill.

Serve in a 'compotier' (shallow fruit dish on a low stand) or, better still, a crystal bowl: arrange the pineapple slices in a mound and put the cherries in the centre. Add a spoonful of water to the syrup in which the pineapple slices were macerated. Add this to the well-chilled wine syrup, and pour over the cherries. If the cherries are served in a glass bowl, place this on a dish and surround with finely crushed ice.

Serve wafer biscuits (cookies) with the compote.

COMPOTE DE FRUITS FRAIS AUX FROMAGES DE FONTAINEBLEAU

—— FRESH FRUIT COMPOTE WITH FONTAINEBLEAU CHEESES ——

Preparation 24 hours in advance

US	Ingredients	Met/Imp
5½ lb	assorted fruit	2½ kg/5½ lb
I small pinch	powdered vanilla	I small pinch
I cup	caster (granulated) sugar	200 g/7 oz
4	oranges, juice of	4
I–3	Fontainebleau cheeses	I–3

Prepare the fruit, eg pears, apples, bananas and clementines, cutting them into segments or slices. Arrange attractively in a fruit dish. Cover with a mixture of the vanilla and sugar, and sprinkle with the orange juice. Place one or several (depending on how substantial the compote is intended to be) Fontainebleau cheeses in the centre and serve cold.

CRÈME DE CALVILLES EN SUÉDOISE

—— CALVILLE APPLE SUÉDOISE ——

Preparation 3 hours • Cooking 30 minutes

US	Ingredients	Met/Imp
¾ cup	caster (granulated) sugar	150 g/5 oz
2 cups	water	500 ml/18 fl oz
I	vanilla pod (bean)	I
I lb	*calville* or other eating apples	500 g/I lb
a few drops	red food colouring	a few drops
6	gelatine leaves	6
	or	
2 envelopes	powdered (unflavoured) gelatine	12 g/⅓ oz
I	lemon, juice of	I
3½ tbsp	kirsch	50 ml/2 fl oz
½ cup	glacé cherries	100 g/4 oz

Make a syrup with the sugar, water and vanilla. Peel and core the apples and cut them into small, even segments. Poach them in the syrup. Remove half of the apple segments. Colour the syrup deep red with food colouring and bring to the boil once or twice so that the remaining apple segments turn red. Drain and allow to cool.

Dissolve the gelatine in a little water in a *bain-marie* and add to the syrup. Add the lemon juice and strain through cheesecloth. When cold, add the kirsch, then pour into a ring mould and put on ice.

As soon as the jelly starts to set, empty the mould into a bowl. Only an even layer of jelly 5 mm/¼ inch thick should remain on the sides of the mould. Decorate the bottom of the mould with cherries and apple segments, alternating the red segments with the white. Pour some jelly back into the mould, put on ice and leave until almost set. Repeat the process, alternating the layers of fruit and jelly. Leave to set completely.

To serve, dip the mould very quickly into boiling water, then un-mould on to a very cold plate. Surround with any leftover jelly, diced.

US	Ingredients	Met/Imp
1¾ cups	cocoa powder	150 g/5 oz
	or	
5 oz	plain (semisweet) chocolate	150 g/5 oz
1 quart	milk	1 litre/1¾ pints
1¼ cups	caster (granulated) sugar	250 g/8 oz
5	egg yolks	5
5	whole eggs	5

CHOCOLATE CREAM MOULD

Preparation 25–30 minutes • Cooking 35–40 minutes

Dissolve the cocoa, or melt the crushed or roughly chopped chocolate, in a glass of water. When it turns to a paste, pour on the milk and leave to simmer for a few minutes. (There is little point in adding vanilla, chocolate being already flavoured.)

Beat the sugar with the egg yolks and the whole eggs. Gradually pour the milk on to this mixture, adding only a little at a time to avoid cooking the eggs. Strain and skim, then pour into a charlotte mould. Cook gently in a *bain-marie* for 35–40 minutes, without boiling the water in the bain-marie. The cream must be well cooled before being turned out of the mould.

US	Ingredients	Met/Imp
15	red pralines	15
8	eggs	8
1 tsp	powdered gum tragacanth	5 ml/1 tsp
1½ cups	caster (superfine) sugar	300 g/10 oz
1 drop	red food colouring	1 drop
1 quart	milk	1 litre/1¾ pints

CRÈME RICHELIEU AUX PRALINES

RICHELIEU CREAM WITH PRALINES

Preparation 25 minutes • Cooking 50 minutes

Finely crush the pralines. Separate the eggs. Whisk the egg whites with the gum tragacanth and one-third of the sugar. Fold in the pralines. Add the food colouring.

Make a caramel with half of the remaining sugar and use it to coat the sides of a mould. Pour in the praline mixture and cook in a *bain-marie* for 50 minutes.

Make a Vanilla Custard Sauce (*page 583*) with the milk, egg yolks and remaining sugar. Just before serving, dip the mould in boiling water for 30 seconds and unmould on to a serving dish. Leave until cold, then pour over the custard sauce. Serve with wafer biscuits (cookies).

US	Ingredients	Met/Imp
10 tbsp	good-quality unsalted butter	150 g/5 oz
2 cups	thick *crème fraîche*	500 ml/18 fl oz
6	macaroons, preferably *macarons de Nancy*	6
scant ½ cup	crème de cacao liqueur	100 ml/4 fl oz
1 tbsp	cocoa powder	15 ml/1 tbsp
¼ cup	caster (granulated) sugar	50 g/2 oz
2 oz	candied orange peel	50 g/2 oz
	cognac	
	CRÊPE BATTER	
1¾ cups	chestnut flour	250 g/8 oz
1 pinch	salt	1 pinch
6	eggs	6
1 quart	milk	1 litre/1¾ pints

CRÊPES FLAMBÉES

FLAMBÉED CRÊPES

Preparation 2 hours • Cooking 10 minutes

Make up a crêpe batter in the usual way but replace the white flour with sifted chestnut flour. Cook the crêpes, using 100 g/4 oz (8 tbsp) butter, and keep hot.

Just before serving, mix together the crème fraîche, roughly chopped macaroons, crème de cacao, cocoa powder, half of the sugar and the chopped candied orange peel. Spread each crêpe with this mixture and fold into quarters (fan shapes). Lightly butter a silver dish and put the crêpes on it. Dust with the remaining sugar and heat in the oven. Flambé with cognac.

CRÊPES SUZETTE*

Preparation 30 minutes • Resting several hours • Cooking 15 minutes

US	Ingredients	Met/Imp
1¾ cups	flour	250 g/8 oz
3	eggs	3
2 glasses	milk	2 glasses
2	mandarin oranges	2
2 tbsp	curaçao	30 ml/2 tbsp
1 tbsp	oil	15 ml/1 tbsp
4 tbsp	good-quality unsalted butter	50 g/2 oz
¼ cup	caster (granulated) sugar	50 g/2 oz

This is the true recipe for Crêpes Suzette, which too many ignorant chefs or restaurateurs like to prepare with orange and serve flambéed.

Put the flour in a bowl and make a well in the centre. Break in the eggs, mix with a wooden spoon, then gradually add the milk. Finally, add the juice of 1 mandarin, half of the curaçao and the oil. Leave to rest for several hours.

Cream the butter with the juice and grated rind of the remaining mandarin, the remaining curaçao and the sugar.

To cook the crêpes, if possible use a heavy-based frying pan that is kept only for this purpose and is never washed, but wiped each time with paper towels. Beat the batter. Heat the pan and pour in a small ladleful of batter. Cook in the usual way and repeat until all the batter is used. Keep the crêpes warm on a plate.

Having finished the crêpes, return them, one by one, to the pan. Spread each one with a little of the mandarin butter and fold in four. Serve piping hot.

CROQUETTES DE RIZ

RICE CROQUETTES

Preparation 40 minutes • Cooking rice 35 minutes • Frying 6–7 minutes

US	Ingredients	Met/Imp
1¼ cups	pudding or short-grain rice	250 g/8 oz
1 quart	milk	1 litre/1¾ pints
1 pinch	salt	1 pinch
½ cup	caster (granulated) sugar	100 g/4 oz
1	lemon, pared rind of	1
4 tbsp	good-quality unsalted butter	50 g/2 oz
5	egg yolks	5
scant 1 cup	Confectioner's Custard (page 584)	200 ml/7 fl oz
3½ cups	fresh white breadcrumbs	200 g/7 oz
	oil for deep frying	
	icing (confectioners') sugar, for dusting	
scant 1 cup	rum-flavoured apricot sauce	200 ml/7 fl oz
	EGG WASH	
3	whole eggs	3
1 small pinch	salt	1 small pinch
¼ cup	oil	50 ml/2 fl oz

Blanch the washed rice by putting it in a saucepan with a small quantity of water and bringing it to the boil. Drain, return to the rinsed-out pan and add the milk, salt, sugar and lemon rind (cut into strips and tied with thread so that you can remove them after cooking the rice). Bring to the boil, cover and continue cooking in the oven for 35 minutes. Stir the rice from time to time with a fork. When cooked, thicken with the butter, egg yolks and confectioner's custard.

Pour the rice on to a buttered or oiled baking sheet to a thickness of about 2 cm/¾ inch. Cover with oiled paper and leave to cool. When cold, place the baking sheet over a high heat for several seconds, moving it so that it heats evenly. Turn the slab of rice on to a marble slab or floured cloth on the work surface. Cut the rice into lozenges or rectangles, or use a round or oval pastry cutter. To make the egg wash, beat together the eggs, salt and oil. Dip the shapes in this mixture, then coat with breadcrumbs.

Fry the croquettes in batches in deep hot oil, using a frying basket the same diameter as the pan. Deep fry until golden. Keep the croquettes hot and dust with icing (confectioners') sugar. Serve on a hot plate lined with a napkin. Serve hot rum-flavoured apricot sauce on the side.

US	Ingredients	Met/Imp
8	square slices from a firm-textured loaf	8
scant 1 cup	double (heavy) cream	200 ml/7 fl oz
½ cup	caster (granulated) sugar	100 g/4 oz
2 tbsp	vanilla sugar	1 sachet
2	eggs	2
1⅓ cups	dried white breadcrumbs	100 g/4 oz
1 stick	good-quality unsalted butter	100 g/4 oz
4	canned pineapple rings, with syrup	4
3½ tbsp	rum	50 ml/2 fl oz

CROÛTES À L'ANANAS

PINEAPPLE CROÛTES

Preparation 1 hour • Cooking 10 minutes

Put the bread slices on a plate. Pour over the cream, sweetened with the caster (granulated) sugar and flavoured with the vanilla sugar, and let them gently soak it up. Drain, then dip the slices in the beaten eggs and toss them in the dried white breadcrumbs. Fry gently on both sides in hot butter. Arrange the slices in a ring on a serving plate and fill the centre with the canned pineapple slices, cut into large chunks. Sprinkle with the pineapple syrup from the can, reduced over a high heat and cooled, to which a little rum has been added.

US	Ingredients	Met/Imp
8	*biscottes* or toasted slices of firm-textured bread	8
1 stick	good-quality unsalted butter	100 g/4 oz
¾ cup	currants	100 g/4 oz
1 cup	candied fruit	150 g/5 oz
scant ½ cup	liqueur of your choice	100 ml/4 fl oz
1 quart	sweetened milk	1 litre/1¾ pints
6	eggs	6
	apricot or redcurrant jam (optional)	

CROÛTE PUDDING 'OUAILLENOTT'

'WHY NOT' PUDDING

Preparation 1½ hours • Cooking 40 minutes

This recipe is from Mme Ettlinger, dedicated to Curnonsky. 'Ouaillenott' is the French phonetic spelling of the American 'Why not', a translation of the Latin 'Cur non'.

Butter the biscottes or toasted bread. Arrange in 1–2 layers in the bottom of a flameproof porcelain mould with the buttered sides against the mould. Sprinkle each layer with currants and candied fruit and moisten with the liqueur.

Bring the sweetened milk to the boil. Beat the eggs together and stir them gradually into the milk. Pour over the bread and leave to rest for 1 hour. Cook the pudding in a *bain-marie* in a low oven for 40 minutes. The rusks will rise to the surface and the custard should be just set.

Serve hot or cold. In the latter case, glaze the top with apricot or redcurrant jam.

US	Ingredients	Met/Imp
2 cups	white wine	500 ml/18 fl oz
1½ cups	semolina (farina)	250 g/8 oz
1 small pinch	salt	1 small pinch
1¼ cups	caster (granulated) sugar	250 g/8 oz
2	whole eggs	2
	water	
4	egg whites	4
2 pints	ripe raspberries	500 g/1 lb
1¼ cups	icing (confectioners') sugar	150 g/5 oz
2 cups	raspberry *eau-de-vie* from Alsace	500 ml/18 fl oz

FLAMRI À LA PURÉE DE FRAMBOISES

SEMOLINA PUDDING WITH RASPBERRY PURÉE

Preparation 1½ hours • Cooking 45 minutes

Bring the white wine to the boil with the same amount of water. Pour in the semolina (farina), stirring with a spoon. Cover and cook over a very low heat for 20 minutes. Once cooked, stir in the salt, caster (granulated) sugar, lightly beaten whole eggs, then the stiffly whisked egg whites. Put the mixture into a well-buttered ring mould. Do not fill it more than three-quarters full. Lightly knock the mould on a folded cloth on the work surface to settle the mixture. Poach in a covered *bain-marie* for 45 minutes. After poaching, take the mould out of the water

and leave it to cool completely. Work the raspberries through a sieve into a bowl and stir in the icing (confectioners') sugar. Stir with a spoon until the sugar has completely dissolved. Keep cool. Just before serving, complete the purée by stirring in the eau-de-vie.

Unmould the pudding on to a cold plate and cover it completely with the raspberry purée.

FLAN BRETON

BRETON 'FLAN'

Preparation 1½ hours • Cooking 50 minutes

US	Ingredients	Met/Imp
15	eggs	15
2½ cups	caster (granulated) sugar	500 g/1 lb
2 cups	flour	300 g/10 oz
1 pinch	salt	1 pinch
1 quart	milk	1 litre/1¾ pints
	powdered vanilla or orange-flower water	
1⅓ cups	Muscat raisins	200 g/7 oz

This 'flan' should be cooked in a Genoese mould, with smooth, sloping sides 4–5 cm/1½–2 inches in height, but it can also be made in Genoa cake moulds that are not quite as deep, or even in antique tart tins or in an ordinary cake tin with sloping sides. Although it is not made with pastry and is therefore simple, it uses a fair amount of eggs.

Beat together the eggs and sugar until pale, then add the flour and salt. Dilute with the milk and flavour with powdered vanilla or orange-flower water.

De-seed the raisins, if necessary. Butter the mould with melted butter and dust with flour. Put one-quarter of the mixture into the mould and cook in the bottom of a low oven for about 10 minutes or until the custard has thickened. Take the mould from the oven and stud the custard with the raisins. Return the mould to the open oven, pour in the rest of the mixture, then push the mould into the oven. Cook in a moderate oven for 45–50 minutes. When the flan is brown enough, turn down the heat and cover with greaseproof (parchment) paper. Continue cooking at a low heat.

FLAN GRILLÉ

LATTICED APPLE TART

Preparation 2 hours • Cooking 40 minutes

US	Ingredients	Met/Imp
about 1 recipe quantity	Shortcrust Pastry (*page 577*)	250 g/8 oz
1 cup	apple *marmelade*	250 ml/9 fl oz
¼ lb	Puff Pastry (*page 579*)	100 g/4 oz
1	egg	1
½ cup	icing (confectioners') sugar	50 g/2 oz

Place a flan ring on a baking sheet and line with shortcrust pastry. Fill to the height of the ring with apple marmelade. Let the pastry stand up above the rim of the ring like a crest, but do not pinch it. Fold the crest of pastry inwards at a 45° angle and moisten with water.

Cut the thinly rolled out puff pastry into long strips 3 mm/⅛ inch wide. Place half of the strips across the tart, parallel to one another and 3 mm/⅛ inch apart. Trim the ends of the strips by simply pressing with your thumbs against the flan ring, not against the pastry edge or it will be squashed. After the first row is finished, glaze with beaten egg, then make a second layer of strips crossing the first on the diagonal. Trim and glaze in the same way with beaten egg. Bake in a hot oven for 40 minutes. Towards the end of the cooking time, dust the tart with icing (confectioners') sugar, then return to the oven to glaze.

US	Ingredients	Met/Imp
about 1 recipe quantity	Shortcrust Pastry (page 577)	250 g/8 oz
1 cup	apple *marmelade*	250 g/8 oz
1 cup	caster (superfine) sugar	100 g/3½ oz
1 pinch	powdered vanilla	1 pinch
4	egg whites	4
½ cup	icing (confectioners') sugar	50 g/2 oz
2 cups	apricot *marmelade*	500 ml/18 fl oz
⅓ cup	redcurrant jelly	100 g/3½ oz

——— MERINGUE AND APPLE TART ———

Preparation 1 hour • Cooking 35 minutes

Place a flan ring on a baking sheet and line with the shortcrust pastry. Fill three-quarters full with apple marmelade. Bake in a hot oven for 35 minutes.

Flavour the caster (superfine) sugar with vanilla and fold into the stiffly whisked egg whites. Set aside an amount of meringue the size of an egg for decoration. Spread the remainder over the cooked tart and carefully smooth the top to make it level.

Put the reserved meringue into a paper piping cone and snip off the point. Pipe a series of parallel lines 2 cm/¾ inch apart on the tart, then another series across, diagonally to the first. Finally, pipe a line of little dots around the edge.

Dust the tart well with icing (confectioners') sugar and put it in a very cool oven for a few minutes in order to dry out the meringue without colouring it. Remove the tart from the oven.

Decorate the tart by piping apricot marmelade and redcurrant jelly into the diamond shapes formed by the meringue, alternating the colours.

——— RAISIN 'FLAN' ———

Preparation 1 hour • Macerating of raisins 48 hours • Cooking 30–35 minutes

Recipe from the Pierre Traiteur restaurant in Paris

US	Ingredients	Met/Imp
1⅔ cups	muscat raisins	250 g/8 oz
scant ½ cup	rum	100 ml/4 fl oz
3 tbsp	flour	45 ml/3 tbsp
1¼ cups	caster (granulated) sugar	250 g/8 oz
1 pinch	salt	1 pinch
6	eggs	6
1 quart	milk, boiled and cooled	1 litre/1¾ pints
2 tbsp	good-quality unsalted butter	25 g/scant 1 oz

It is important to de-seed muscat raisins and to macerate them in the rum, covered, for 48 hours. To seed them, you just need to soak them in lukewarm water for a few moments and to arm yourself with enough patience to extract every seed.

Blend together the flour, sugar, salt and 2 eggs. Continue to beat the mixture while adding the remaining eggs, one by one, until the batter forms ribbons and becomes bulky. Add the boiled milk, then the raisins and rum. Turn the mixture into a buttered charlotte mould and put a few small pieces of butter on top.

Cook in a moderately hot oven with or without a *bain-marie* for 30–35 minutes. As a precaution, cover the flan with greaseproof (parchment) paper to prevent the cream forming a crust.

CARROT CAKE

Preparation 45 minutes • Cooking 30 minutes

US	Ingredients	Met/Imp
6	eggs, separated	6
1¼ cups	caster (granulated) sugar	250 g/8 oz
3⅓ cups	ground almonds	250 g/8 oz
½ lb	carrots	250 g/8 oz
1 tbsp	kirsch	15 ml/1 tbsp
2 tsp	ground cinnamon	10 ml/2 tsp
1 tsp	finely grated lemon rind	5 ml/1 tsp
1 tbsp	lemon juice	15 ml/1 tbsp
3½ tbsp	potato flour	30 g/1 oz
1¼ cups	icing (confectioners') sugar	150 g/5 oz

If this cake is made well, it will rise to a truly amazing size, although it always sinks a little on being taken from the oven. It is important to put the completed cake batter immediately into a very hot oven, and it should be stirred constantly until it is placed in the oven.

With a wooden spoon, vigorously beat together the egg yolks, caster (granulated) sugar, almonds, grated carrots, kirsch, cinnamon, lemon rind, lemon juice and potato flour. Continue beating until the batter will make a ribbon trail on its surface when the beater is lifted.

Whisk the egg whites until very stiff, sweeten with the icing (confectioners') sugar, then fold gently into the carrot mixture. Pour into a buttered and floured Genoese mould or cake tin and bake immediately in a very hot oven for 30 minutes or until well risen.

Just before serving, dust with extra icing (confectioners') sugar.

CHESTNUT GÂTEAU

Preparation 3 hours • Cooking chestnuts about 45 minutes; Gâteau 30–40 minutes

US	Ingredients	Met/Imp
1 cup	flour	150 g/5 oz
7 tbsp	caster (granulated) sugar	90 g/3½ oz
6 tbsp	good-quality unsalted butter	75 g/3 oz
2 pinches	salt	2 pinches
2	egg yolks	2
¼ cup	milk	60 ml/4 tbsp
20	large chestnuts	20
1¾ cups	boiled milk	400 ml/14 fl oz
½	vanilla pod (bean)	½
¼ cup	crème fraîche	60 ml/4 tbsp
3	egg whites	3
	vanilla sugar, for dusting	

This genuine family cake is to be doubly recommended, because it is easy to make and will keep well for several days.

Sift the flour on to the work surface and make a well in the centre. Add 60 g/2½ oz (5 tbsp) of the sugar, the softened butter, 1 pinch of salt, the egg yolks and the cold milk. Mix to a dough, then knead lightly once or twice to form a smooth ball. Leave in a cool place for 2 hours.

Make an incision in the chestnut skins and drop them into a saucepan of boiling water. Leave them there for 5 minutes, then drain them and remove the shells and brown inner skins. Put the chestnuts in a saucepan with the boiled milk, vanilla pod (bean) and 1 pinch of salt. Cook gently for 45–50 minutes or until the chestnuts are soft.

As soon as the chestnuts are cooked, remove the vanilla and pound the chestnuts in the saucepan with a pestle, or work them through a sieve. (It is preferable to pound them, simply to preserve the original character of the cake.) Add the remaining sugar, the crème fraîche and stiffly whisked egg whites to the chestnut purée.

Thoroughly butter an 18–20 cm/7–8 inch flan ring with quite high sides, placed on a baking sheet. Roll out the pastry to a 5 mm/¼ inch thick circle, and use to line the flan ring, making sure the pastry falls inside and pressing it down with your fingertips. Trim off the excess pastry by rolling the rolling-pin across the flan ring, then form a raised edge by pinching the pastry with your fingertips. Prick the bottom of the pastry case to prevent blisters forming during baking. Pour in the chestnut mixture and bake in a low oven for 35–40 minutes.

To serve, dust the surface with vanilla sugar. Serve warm or cold.

US	Ingredients	Met/Imp
7 oz	Puff Pastry (page 579)	200 g/7 oz
⅓ recipe quantity	Frangipane (page 584)	200 g/7 oz
5	egg whites	5
1¼ cups	caster (superfine) sugar	250 g/8 oz
½ cup	toasted flaked (sliced) almonds	50 g/2 oz
	icing (confectioners') sugar, for dusting	

MARCH CAKE

Preparation 3 hours • Cooking Base 25 minutes; Meringue 15 minutes

Roll out the puff pastry to a rectangular strip about 50 cm/20 inches long, 9–10 cm/3½–4 inches wide and 5 mm/¼ inch thick. Put this strip on a baking sheet, lightly push up and pinch the sides all around, then spread with a layer of frangipane 1 cm/½ inch thick. Bake in a low oven for 25 minutes, then leave to cool.

Meanwhile, whisk the egg whites until very stiff, fold in the sugar and spread this meringue on the cooled strip, giving it an overall thickness of 2.5 cm/1 inch.

Sprinkle the meringue with the almonds, dust with icing (confectioners') sugar and divide the strip into pieces 5 cm/2 inches wide. Arrange these pieces on a baking sheet and bake in a very cool oven for 12–15 minutes to dry and lightly colour the meringue.

US	Ingredients	Met/Imp
1¾ cups plus 2 tbsp	caster (superfine) sugar	375 g/13 oz
1	whole egg	1
6	egg yolks	6
1⅔ cups	ground walnuts	125 g/4½ oz
1⅔ cups	ground almonds	125 g/4½ oz
¾ cup	potato flour	100 g/4 oz
1 tsp	*powdered vanilla*	5 ml/1 tsp
scant 1 cup	Chantilly Cream (page 583)	200 ml/7 fl oz
2 cups	coffee-flavoured Vanilla Custard Sauce (page 583)	500 ml/18 fl oz

WALNUT AND ALMOND CAKE

Preparation 1 hour • (To be prepared 24 hours in advance) • Cooking 35 minutes

In a bowl, vigorously beat together the sugar, the whole egg and the egg yolks until the batter leaves a ribbon trail on its surface when the beater is lifted. Add the ground walnuts, almonds, potato flour and powdered vanilla. Whisk the egg whites until they hold stiff peaks, then fold them carefully into the mixture.

Turn the mixture into a buttered and floured cake tin, filling it three-quarters full. Bake in a moderate oven for 35 minutes, then leave to cool. The cake must be made at least 24 hours in advance.

Cut the cake horizontally into thin layers and spread them thickly with Chantilly cream. Re-assemble the cake and coat generously with the coffee custard sauce. Serve on a cake stand.

JELLIED MARASCHINO MOULD

Preparation 5–6 hours • Cooking 15 minutes

US	Ingredients	Met/Imp
½ lb (1¼ cups)	lump or granulated sugar	250 g/8 oz
3 cups	lukewarm filtered water	750 ml/1¼ pints
20	gelatine leaves	20
	or	
6 envelopes	powdered (unflavoured) gelatine	40 g/1½ oz
2	egg whites	2
scant ½ cup	dry white wine	100 ml/4 fl oz
1	small lemon, pared rind and juice of	1
⅔ cup	maraschino liqueur	150 ml/¼ pint

Dissolve the sugar in the water, which can be lukewarm. Put the gelatine in cold water and leave to soak until well softened.

Put the egg whites in a saucepan with the white wine and beat until fluffy. Add the lemon juice and 2 slivers of lemon rind. Gradually add the sugar syrup, whisking vigorously in order to mix the liquid into the egg whites (which have clarifying properties). Whisk in the softened gelatine.

Bring the mixture to the boil over a moderate heat, whisking continuously, then simmer over a very low heat for 15 minutes. Soak a napkin in warm water, wring it out and attach it firmly to the 4 legs of an up-turned stool. Place a bowl underneath and pour the hot jelly into the napkin. Leave to strain through into the bowl.

Since the first batch of strained jelly is sometimes a little cloudy, it may be necessary to strain it a second time in order to get a completely clear liquid. After straining twice, leave the jelly until nearly cold, then mix the maraschino into it and pour it into a ring mould. If it is possible to surround the mould with ice (make sure you add some salt), 2½ hours will be sufficient time to set the jelly. Without ice, the jelly will need at least 5 hours in a very cold place to set.

Just before serving, dip the mould quickly into hot water and wipe dry. Turn the jelly out on to a serving plate covered with a napkin or doily.

VARIATIONS

The jelly may be flavoured with other liqueurs, such as kirsch, rum, etc. To flavour the jelly with an infusion (eg orange or lemon), the proportions are the same except that the citrus rinds should be boiled in the syrup in advance and left to infuse until the jelly is strained.

If a fortified wine, such as a madeira, port, etc, is used, it is necessary to add a larger quantity of this than of liqueur. The proportions are 600 ml/1 pint (2½ cups) water, the same quantity of sugar and gelatine and 200 ml/7 fl oz (scant 1 cup) of the chosen wine. Like a liqueur, wine should be added to the nearly cold jelly.

US	Ingredients	Met/Imp
8	small torpedo-shaped rolls made with milk-enriched dough	8
I cup	milk, sweetened and flavoured with vanilla	250 ml/9 fl oz
2	eggs, beaten	2
2 cups	fine soft breadcrumbs	100 g/4 oz
2 pints	cherries	500 g/1 lb
5 oz (¾ cup)	lump or granulated sugar	150 g/5 oz
I glass	red wine	I glass
I	small piece cinnamon stick	I
2	strips lemon rind	2
15	almonds	15
	candied angelica	
	oil or fat for deep frying	
I tsp	arrowroot	5 ml/1 tsp
¼ cup	kirsch	60 ml/4 tbsp

GRENADES WITH CHERRIES

Preparation 1 hour • Cooking about 10 minutes

As with all fruit desserts, this dish does not have to be served very hot. It just needs to be warm. The cherry compote can, therefore, be prepared in advance, the kirsch being added at the last moment.

Choose torpedo-shaped rolls with soft crusts. If these are not available, cut a very stale firm-textured loaf into 8 rectangles 7.5 cm/3 inches long, 4 cm/1½ inches wide and at least 1 cm/½ inch thick. Cut off the corners to give the pieces an oval shape.

Spread out the finger rolls or bread ovals on a plate and sprinkle them with sweetened, vanilla-flavoured milk. Turn them over and sprinkle the other side in the same way, but be careful not to sprinkle them too much. The bread simply has to be moistened, not soaked. Blot them gently, one by one, on a fine cloth or cheesecloth, then dip them in the beaten egg and roll them in the breadcrumbs. Press the crumbs on lightly with the blade of a knife. Lay the rolls or bread ovals in the basket of a deep frying pan and set aside.

Stone the cherries. In an unlined copper saucepan, dissolve the sugar in the red wine. Add the piece of cinnamon stick and the lemon rind, tied together with a thread. Bring to the boil, then add the cherries and cook for 2 minutes. Remove from the heat but keep hot. This will be enough cooking to make the cherries tender. Shell, blanch and skin the almonds. Split them in 2, then cut them into small slivers. Prepare the same quantity of small strips of angelica.

About 12 minutes before serving, plunge the rolls or bread ovals into very hot deep fat and cook for about 10 minutes or until golden. Drain on a cloth. Spike each one with about 10 almond slivers and 10 angelica strips. (To do this, spear the crust of each roll with the point of a skewer.) Pile the rolls in a circle on a round serving dish.

Drain the cherries in a colander and discard the lemon rind and cinnamon stick. Quickly reduce the syrup to 200 ml/7 fl oz (scant 1 cup) and thicken it with the arrowroot dissolved in a little cold water. Bring to the boil, then remove from the heat and add the cherries and kirsch. Pour on to the fried bread rolls and serve.

VARIATION
The syrup can be thickened with 30 ml/2 tbsp redcurrant jelly instead of the arrowroot.

MELON 'SOUVAROFF'*

Preparation 12 hours

US	Ingredients	Met/Imp
I	medium melon	I
I pint	wild strawberries	250 g/8 oz
¾ cup	icing (confectioners') sugar	100 g/3½ oz
¼ cup	eau-de-vie	50 ml/2 fl oz
2	mint sprigs	2

Choose a melon which is within a day of ripeness. Make an incision all round, 4 cm/1½ inches from the stem end, and cut through the width of the melon. (Cut in a zig-zig pattern, if liked.) Lift off the top, scoop out the seeds from the centre with the edge of a spoon and discard. Scoop out the flesh, then cut into dice. Hull the strawberries.

Generously dust the inside of the melon with icing (confectioners') sugar and fill the melon with alternating layers of wild strawberries and diced melon. Thickly dust each layer of fruit with sugar. Finish by pouring in the eau-de-vie. Close the melon by replacing the 'lid' and chill for up to 12 hours. If you want to make this more quickly, use a ripe melon; then you will need only 2 to 3 hours for the maceration of the strawberries and the melon flesh.

To serve, lift off the top segment of melon and decorate with mint sprigs inserted in small scoops of melon flesh. Serve with a spoon and offer wafer biscuits (cookies) at the same time.

MERINGUES AUX AMANDES SAUCE VANILLE

ALMOND MERINGUES WITH VANILLA SAUCE

Preparation 1 hour • Cooking 30 minutes • Drying 12 hours

US	Ingredients	Met/Imp
12	egg whites	12
I pinch	salt	I pinch
2½ cups	caster (superfine) sugar	500 g/1 lb
1⅔ cı	shelled sweet almonds	250 g/8 oz
	icing (confectioners') sugar, for dusting	

These meringues, well dried and served individually or in pairs, are preferable to a meringue moulded in a savarin mould.

Whisk the egg whites to a very stiff froth, add the salt and pour in the sugar. Fold in gently, then, before the mixing is completed, add the blanched, skinned, finely shredded toasted almonds.

With a piping bag and a large plain nozzle, pipe the meringue into shell shapes on a buttered and floured baking sheet. Dredge with icing (confectioners') sugar and cover with parchment paper. Bake in a low oven with the door open for about 30 minutes. Turn off the heat and leave in the oven to dry out for about 12 hours.

Serve the meringues with a plain Vanilla Custard Sauce (*page 583*), or with a custard sauce flavoured with coffee or chocolate, or with Chantilly Cream (*page 583*). They can also be served with ice cream.

US	Ingredients	Met/Imp
2 lb	apples	1 kg/2 lb
2 tbsp	good-quality unsalted butter	30 g/1 oz
½	vanilla pod (bean)	½
⅓ cup	honey	125 g/4½ oz
4 tsp	sugar syrup: 32° Baumé (page 575)	20 ml/4 tsp
1 cup	double (heavy) cream	250 ml/8 fl oz
2 tbsp	caster (granulated) sugar	30 g/1 oz
6	red pralines	6

APPLE MOUSSE GÂTINAISE

Preparation 6 hours • Cooking 40 minutes

The apple that is most suitable for this dish is the grey *reinette*; if unavailable, use the Canadian reinette, the winter *calville* or another eating apple.

Peel, core and thinly slice three-quarters of the apples. Put the slices in a sauté pan with the butter, vanilla and 45 ml/3 tbsp water. Cook over a very low heat, keeping the pan tightly covered, until the apple has reduced to a purée, then stir over a high heat until the purée becomes what might be called a thick pulp.

Add the honey to the apple pulp, cover the saucepan and remove from the heat. As soon as the honey has completely melted, mix it into the apple pulp. Remove the vanilla and tip the pulp into a china bowl. Leave to cool, stirring from time to time.

Make up the sugar syrup in a saucepan. Cut the remaining apples into segments, peel, core and slice them and throw them into the boiling syrup. As they must maintain their shape, do not leave them in the syrup for any longer than the time needed to soften the flesh. Remove the apple slices from the syrup and leave them to cool on a dish.

As soon as the honeyed apple purée is completely cool, mix it with the cream that has been whipped with the sugar until stiff. Tip this mixture into a crystal bowl (or a deep fruit dish on a low stand), smooth the top into a rounded shape and chill in the refrigerator for 2½–3 hours.

Just before serving, arrange the caramelized apple slices all around the mousse, piling them on top of each other. Strew the centre of this apple ring with the red pralines, crushed into coarse crumbs with a rolling pin.

US	Ingredients	Met/Imp
8 oz	plain (semisweet) chocolate	250 g/8 oz
1 quart	milk	1 litre/1¾ pints
4	egg yolks	4
3	whole eggs	3
¾ cup	caster (granulated) sugar	150 g/5 oz

BAKED CHOCOLATE CUSTARD

Preparation 30 minutes • Cooking 30–40 minutes

Roughly chop the chocolate and melt it in a saucepan with half a glass of water. Bring the milk to the boil. Meanwhile, blend the egg yolks, eggs and sugar with a spatula. Once the chocolate has melted, pour on the boiling milk, then gradually stir in the well-beaten egg and sugar mixture. Mix all together and strain through cheesecloth.

Pour the chocolate mixture into a deep dish of just the right capacity. Cook in a *bain-marie* in a moderately hot oven for 30–40 minutes. Leave to get cold and serve from the dish.

BAKED CUSTARD

Preparation 20 minutes • Cooking 30–40 minutes

US	Ingredients	Met/Imp
I quart	milk	I litre/1¾ pints
½	vanilla pod (bean)	½
4	egg yolks	4
4	whole eggs	4
1¼ cups	caster (granulated) sugar	250 g/8 oz

Bring the milk to the boil with the vanilla. Blend the egg yolks, the whole eggs and the sugar together in a bowl, using either a whisk or a spatula. When the milk is boiling, gradually pour it on to the egg and sugar mixture, stirring constantly. Strain through cheesecloth. Pour the custard into a dish of the right capacity and cook in a *bain-marie* in a moderately hot oven for 30–40 minutes. To make sure that the custard is cooked, insert a knife into the centre; the blade should come out clean.

VARIATIONS
For a coffee-flavoured baked custard, use the same ingredients but infuse 75 g/3 oz (¾ cup) coarsely ground or crushed coffee beans, tied in a cloth, in the milk. Make a fairly strong infusion. Finish as above.
For a chocolate baked custard, proceed in the same way, but use chocolate-flavoured milk instead of plain milk.

'SNOW EGGS'

Preparation and Cooking 20 minutes • Cooling 1 hour

US	Ingredients	Met/Imp
1–2	vanilla pods (beans)	1–2
I quart	milk	I litre/1¾ pints
7	medium eggs	7
¾ cup	vanilla sugar	160 g/5½ oz
I cup	caster (granulated) sugar	175 g/6 oz

Split the vanilla pods (beans) lengthways. Pour the milk into a large shallow pan and add the vanilla. Bring to the boil, cover and leave to simmer over a very low heat for 10 minutes.

Meanwhile, separate the eggs. Whisk the egg whites to a stiff froth, sprinkle them with the vanilla sugar and fold the sugar into the egg whites, cutting through them with a wooden spatula or metal spoon and turning them over in order to incorporate the sugar.

Remove any skin from the vanilla-flavoured milk. Keep it at a gentle boil and slide in 3–5 tablespoons of the sweetened egg whites. Cook for 1½–2 minutes, then turn them over with an egg slice (pancake turner) and let them cook for the same time on the second side. Do this several times, not putting in more than 3–5 portions of egg white each time, so that they have enough room in the pan. As the egg whites cook, remove them from the pan, put them on a napkin and leave them to drain.

Strain the milk and measure it. If necessary, add a little cold milk to make it up to 750 ml/1¼ pints (3 cups). Bring to the boil again.

Pour the caster (granulated) sugar on to the egg yolks and beat until the mixture becomes pale and leaves a ribbon trail on its surface when the beater is lifted. Pour the boiling milk in a stream on to the sugar and egg yolk mixture, stirring carefully. Return to the saucepan and cook very gently over a low heat, stirring constantly with a wooden spoon, until the custard thickens and will coat the back of the spoon. Strain through a fine sieve into a serving dish and leave to get cold.

Float the drained egg whites on the custard and keep cold. Serve with biscuits (cookies) such as almond tuiles.

US	Ingredients	Met/Imp
12	eggs	12
1 pinch	salt	1 pinch
1 tbsp	caster (granulated) sugar	15 ml/1 tbsp
scant 1 cup	jam, eg redcurrant jelly, strawberry, apricot, quince	200 ml/7 fl oz
3½ tbsp	eau-de-vie	50 ml/2 fl oz
1 stick	good-quality unsalted butter	100 g/4 oz
	icing (confectioners') sugar	

JAM OMELETTE

Preparation 15 minutes

For 8 people it is advisable to make 2 omelettes, each with 6 eggs; they will be much softer and better shaped. If you glaze them in a hot oven, they will be slightly better cooked.

Break 6 eggs into each of 2 separate wooden bowls. Add a small pinch of salt and half the caster (granulated) sugar to each. Flavour the jam (divided into 2) with eau-de-vie.

Melt a little butter in a frying pan. Beat the eggs with a fork, tip them into the foaming butter and sauté the omelette, as if making sauté potatoes, but without using a fork. When the omelette begins to form a skin but the centre is still soft, raise the side of the pan with the left hand and fold 2 opposite sides of the omelette towards the centre. With a spoon, fill the space in the centre with the jam. With the right hand, lightly shake the handle of the pan a few times to dislodge the omelette, then, with a brisk jerk, turn the omelette over on to a heated serving dish. Repeat the process and place the second omelette next to the first. Dust with icing (confectioners') sugar and serve immediately.

US	Ingredients	Met/Imp
6	Canadian *reinette*, *calville* or other eating apples	6
10 tbsp	good-quality unsalted butter	150 g/5 oz
½ cup	caster (granulated) sugar	100 g/4 oz
12	eggs	12
1 pinch	salt	1 pinch
	icing (confectioners') sugar, for dusting (optional)	

OMELETTE WITH CARAMELIZED APPLES

Preparation 40 minutes • Cooking 15 minutes

Peel the apples, cut them into small segments and cut out the cores. Put the apple segments in a sauté pan with several small pieces of butter and dust with sugar. Cook over a high heat, without stirring too much, until the apples are well cooked and lightly caramelized, without being too broken up.

Make 2 omelettes in the same way as for Jam Omelette (above). Break 6 eggs into each of 2 wooden bowls and add a little sugar and a little salt. Make the omelettes and fill them with the apples. If you wish, dust the finished omelettes with icing (confectioners') sugar and glaze them quickly under a hot grill (broiler) before serving.

US	Ingredients	Met/Imp
scant ½ cup	caster (granulated) sugar	90 g/3½ oz
6	eggs, separated	6
1 small pinch	salt	1 small pinch
4 tsp	good-quality unsalted butter	20 g/¾ oz
½ cup	rum	100 ml/4 fl oz

FLAMBÉED SOUFFLÉ OMELETTE

Preparation 30 minutes • Cooking 8–10 minutes • Serves 4

Recipe created by Guy Nouyrigat, the Pierre Traiteur restaurant in Paris

Over a gas flame or on an electric ring, slowly heat up the iron (a poker or a large metal skewer) which will be used to decorate the omelette.

Lyon Fritters
Squares or rectangles of pastry sealed in very hot oil, these 'bugnes' are a traditional delicacy at carnival time in Lyon. They are often prepared the day before as they are just as good cold as hot, sprinkled with sugar. (Recipe on page 591.)

Crêpes Suzette
It was Auguste Escoffier who produced the formula for this classic French dessert: curaçao and mandarin juice in the crêpe batter, as well as in the butter and sugar mixture used to fill them before they are folded in four and served piping hot. The use of orange instead of mandarin is considered heretical, while flambéeing them is a pointless adulteration. (Recipe on page 597.)

Melon 'Souvaroff'
*Melon may be either a first course or a dessert. Here, sprinkled with sugar and
decorated with strawberries (preferably wild ones), it makes an exquisitely scented
summer dessert. (Recipe on page 605.)*

Alsacienne Tart

When a tart is defined as 'alsacienne' it means that the fruit – apples, pears or prunes – has been coated with 'crème anglaise' (vanilla custard sauce) before cooking. Sometimes a pinch of cinnamon is added. (Recipe on page 639.)

Chocolate Nut Gâteau

This is a very rich sponge cake made with chocolate, sugar, butter, nuts and eggs, flavoured with orange and rum. It is coated with a shiny chocolate icing, decorated with walnut halves and served with a coffee-flavoured custard sauce. Crystallized violets are an optional extra. (Recipe on page 630.)

Strawberries Ginette
A delicate and refined dessert, Strawberries Ginette consists of strawberries soaked in champagne and curaçao on a layer of lemon ice cream, decorated with crystallized violets and whipped cream. (Recipe on page 642.)

Add 75 g/3 oz (6 tbsp) sugar to the egg yolks and beat with a whisk until the sugar is thoroughly dissolved and the mixture leaves a ribbon trail on its surface when the beater is lifted. Add the salt to the egg whites and whisk to a very stiff froth.

Tip the egg yolk and sugar mixture on to the stiffly whisked egg whites and fold in the egg whites with a metal spoon. Fold very gently so that they do not collapse.

Thoroughly heat an ovenproof pan or dish in a moderately hot oven and melt in it just enough butter to cover its surface. Pour the omelette mixture into the pan and cook in the oven for 7–8 minutes. Watch carefully. If, at the end of 5 minutes, the omelette is browning too much, cover with a sheet of buttered greaseproof (parchment) paper.

Turn out the cooked omelette on to a heated serving dish. The omelette should not have sunk and should be quite firm. Even so, the inside will remain light and fluffy. Dust with the remaining sugar and apply the very hot iron here and there to caramelize the sugar and decorate the omelette.

Heat the rum and pour it over the omelette. Flambé and serve immediately.

ORANGES SOUFLÉES

—————— SOUFLÉED ORANGES ——————

Preparation 40 minutes • Cooking 25 minutes • Serves 6

US	Ingredients	Met/Imp
6	perfect oranges, with thick skins	6
3	eggs	3
10 tbsp	caster (granulated) sugar	125 g/4½ oz
2 tbsp	cornflour (cornstarch)	30 ml/2 tbsp
1 tbsp	orange-flavoured liqueur	15 ml/1 tbsp

Slice a large round from the top of each orange. Make sure the oranges will sit firmly on their bases, cutting off a thin slice, if necessary, to make them balance.

Using a grapefruit spoon, completely hollow out each orange and save the pulp and the juice. Do not pierce the skin.

Tip the orange pulp and juice into a fine sieve and crush the pulp well to extract all the juices. Separate the eggs, put the yolks in a heavy-based saucepan and blend with the sugar and the cornflour (cornstarch) until very pale. (It is preferable to mix these directly in the saucepan, since you are working with small quantities; to transfer the mixture would cause wastage.)

Pour the orange juice through a fine sieve on to the egg and sugar mixture, making sure that all traces of orange pulp are removed. Heat gently, stirring constantly, and remove from the heat just before the mixture comes to the boil. When the mixture has thickened a little, add the liqueur. Tip this custard into a china bowl and leave to cool down a little. Carefully add the stiffly whisked egg whites and fill the orange shells with this mixture.

Stand the oranges in an ovenproof dish and bake in a hot oven for 20 minutes. Serve very hot, straight from the cooking dish or, preferably, lift the oranges with an egg slice (pancake turner) on to a heated serving dish.

US	Ingredients	Met/Imp
1½ cups	caster (granulated) sugar	300 g/10 oz
2½ cups	water	600 ml/1 pint
2	vanilla pods (beans)	2
10	gelatine leaves	10
	or	
3 envelopes	powdered (unflavoured) gelatine	20 g/¾ oz
24	small, very ripe apricots	24
1	blood orange, juice of	1
½	lemon, juice of	½
1 tsp	sweet almond oil	5 ml/1 tsp
12	large apricots	12
15	sweet almonds	15
2	bitter almonds	2

APRICOT MOULD WITH ALMOND MILK

Preparation 3 hours • Cooking about 25 minutes

Make a sugar syrup with 125 g/4½ oz (10 tbsp) of the sugar and 175 ml/6 fl oz (¾ cup) water. Boil for 2 minutes; add 1 vanilla pod (bean). Cover, remove from the heat and leave to infuse. Soak the gelatine in cold water until softened, then dissolve it in the syrup, stirring with a silver spoon. Strain the syrup through fine cheesecloth.

Work the small apricots through a fine sieve. Crack the stones without breaking the kernels. Plunge the kernels into boiling water for a few seconds, drain and peel. Split them in 2 and cut them into very fine flakes.

Stir the flaked apricot kernels into the apricot purée with the gelatine syrup (cold or just tepid) and the orange and lemon juices. From this moment onwards, stir the purée until it starts to set. Pour the purée into a dome-shaped mould (or any deep, narrow bowl), brushed on the inside with the sweet almond oil. Keep on ice or in a cold place until the purée is firmly set.

Make a fresh syrup with the remaining sugar, 300 ml/½ pint (1¼ cups) water and the remaining vanilla pod (bean). Keep at a simmer. Cut the large apricots in half and remove the stones. Poach the apricot halves in the syrup (6–7 halves at a time, the quantity of syrup not being sufficient to poach all the apricots at the same time) for a few minutes or until the apricots are tender but still intact. As soon as the apricot halves are ready, remove them from the syrup and leave them to drain and cool on a dish. Reduce the syrup to 100 ml/4 fl oz (scant ½ cup).

Shell, blanch, skin and very finely crush the sweet and bitter almonds, gradually adding the remaining water. Put this almond paste in the corner of a tea (dish) towel and twist tightly to extract the milk. Mix this almond milk into the reduced syrup, then strain through fine cheesecloth. Keep on ice or in a cold place until ready to serve.

Turn the apricot mould out on to a round serving dish. Surround it with the poached apricot halves and sprinkle with the almond milk syrup. This dessert should be served very cold.

12	apples	12
1½ sticks	good-quality unsalted butter	175 g/6 oz
1¼ cups	caster (granulated) sugar	250 g/8 oz
2	vanilla pods (beans)	2
1¼ cups	double (heavy) cream	300 ml/½ pint
3	large eggs	3
⅓ cup	raisins	50 g/2 oz

APPLE MOULD WITH CREAM

Preparation 3 hours • Cooking 40 minutes

Peel, quarter, core and finely slice 8 of the Normandy apples. Put them in a sauté pan with 30 ml/2 tbsp water, 125 g/4½ oz (1 stick) butter, half of the sugar and 1 vanilla pod (bean). Cover tightly and cook to a purée. (The vanilla can be replaced by a small spoonful of grated lemon rind, if preferred.)

Meanwhile, peel and core the remaining apples and cut each one into 8 small segments. Put them into a boiling syrup made with 300 ml/½ pint

(1¼ cups) water and the remaining sugar and vanilla (or lemon). Leave the apple pieces in the syrup for a few minutes only or until tender. Take out 16 of them and put them on a plate. Leave the rest to complete cooking to a purée.

As soon as the apple purée is ready, beat it for a moment with a whisk to make it smooth, then stir it over a high heat until it is the consistency of a paste. Remove the vanilla. Off the heat, mix in 45 ml/3 tbsp cream, the lightly beaten eggs, the 16 cooked apple segments and the raisins.

Tip the mixture into a buttered charlotte mould and poach in a *bain-marie* for 40 minutes or until moderately firm and elastic to the touch. Having taken it out of the water, leave the mould to rest for 15 minutes so the mixture can settle a little.

Strain the syrup through a conical sieve with the apple segments that were left to cook, forcing them through with a wooden spoon. Reduce this syrup to a scant 150 ml/¼ pint (⅔ cup). Add the remaining boiled cream and remove from the heat. Finish by stirring in the remaining butter.

Just before serving, unmould the dessert on to a round serving dish and completely cover it with the sauce.

PÊCHES FLAMBÉES

FLAMBÉED PEACHES

Preparation 1 hour

When serving dessert fruits, such as pears, peaches, etc, choose fruit of the best quality, just ripe and very sound.

Poach the peaches in the syrup with the vanilla, then skin and stone them and return them to the syrup immediately to avoid discoloration. Work the strawberries and the raspberries through a fine hair sieve and sweeten the purée with a little icing (confectioners') sugar.

Arrange the peaches in a fairly deep flameproof dish. There are 2 ways in which to serve them:

Heat them in a hot oven so that they are really hot, making them easier to flambé, pour over the kirsch and flambé them at the table, taking care to dust the peaches with icing (confectioners') sugar. The purée of strawberries and raspberries is served separately.

Heat the peaches in the oven and arrange them in a circle, on bases of Genoese or Savoy sponge cake. Pour the purée into the centre, pour over the kirsch and flambé at the table.

Accompany the dessert with slices of small, plain almond-flavoured cakes or Genoa cake.

US	Ingredients	Met/Imp
8	peaches	8
2 cups	sugar syrup: 24° Baumé (*page 575*)	500 ml/18 fl oz
¼	vanilla pod (bean)	¼
1 pint	wild strawberries	250 g/8 oz
1 cup	raspberries	125 g/4 oz
1¼ cups	icing (confectioners') sugar	150 g/5 oz
3½ tbsp	kirsch	50 ml/2 fl oz

US	Ingredients	Met/Imp
3 cups	water	700–750 ml/ 23–25 fl oz
1 pinch	salt	1 pinch
1 tbsp	caster (granulated) sugar	15 g/½ oz
10 tbsp	good-quality unsalted butter	150 g/5 oz
	flavouring of your choice (eg orange-flower water, rum, finely grated lemon rind or vanilla)	
2¾ cups	flour	400 g/14 oz
12	medium eggs	12
	fat for deep frying	
	icing (confectioners') sugar, for dusting	

NUN'S SIGHS

Preparation 2 hours • Cooking 8–10 minutes

Put the water, salt, sugar, butter and the flavouring of your choice in a large saucepan. Bring to the boil, then remove from the heat and pour in the flour. Mix with a spatula, then heat gently, beating the paste vigorously until dry. The drier the paste becomes, the better it will absorb the eggs, and the puffier the fritters will be. Do not remove from the heat until the paste no longer sticks to the pan.

Remove the pan from the heat and add the eggs, 1 by 1 (or 2 by 2), still whisking briskly. (Break the eggs into a bowl first, instead of breaking them directly into the paste, in case there is a bad one, and everything would be wasted.) The number of eggs used will vary according to their weight and size, but the paste should be dry and well beaten. Cover the paste with paper and a cloth and leave it to rest for a few moments.

In a fairly large pan, heat some fresh deep frying fat (oil with a little lard). It should be quite hot but not smoking.

With a tablespoon, pick up some paste, scraping the spoon lightly against the side of the pan. Going as near as possible to the surface of the fat, slide the paste off the spoon with your left forefinger into the fat. Quickly repeat this action 8–9 times. Increase the heat gradually under the pan of deep fat, until it is really hot. Swirl the hot fat around: this has the particular virtue of making the fritters swell. Cook the fritters for 8–10 minutes or until they are well risen, crisp and as brown as you wish them. Lift them out carefully with a slotted spoon (or tongs) and drain them on a board covered with a cloth. Keep them hot while cooking the remaining fritters. Serve very hot, dusted with icing (confectioners') sugar, on a hot dish covered by a doily, and on hot plates.

These fritters can be accompanied by an apricot sauce flavoured according to choice and served in a sauce boat, or they can be filled as follows: make an opening in the side of each fritter and fill with jam, using a paper piping bag.

US	Ingredients	Met/Imp
16	small juicy pears	16
1 cup	caster (granulated) sugar	200 g/7 oz
2 tsp	ground cinnamon	10 g/⅓ oz
1½ cups	water	350 ml/12 fl oz
	Vanilla Custard Sauce (page 583) or	
1 quart	Chantilly Cream (page 583)	1 litre/1¾ pints
1	Genoese Sponge Cake (page 580), to serve 8 people	1
	kirsch	
	apricot *marmelade*	
	flaked (sliced) almonds	

PEARS 'BELLE HÉLÈNE'

Preparation 2 hours • Cooking 25 minutes

Peel the pears and poach them whole with the sugar, cinnamon and water for 25 minutes. Drain them and leave them to cool, then cut them in half, core them and fill them with the custard or cream. Reshape the pears and arrange them on the Genoese sponge cake, which has been soaked in kirsch. Decorate with the apricot marmelade and almonds.

RUM PLUM PUDDING

Preparation 5 days in advance • Cooking 5 hours

Plum pudding served very hot with flaming rum, brandy butter or sabayon sauce, is a good dessert, although rather heavy.

Remove the filaments and sinews from the suet and pass it through a mincer (grinder), or chop it finely with a knife, dusting it with a little of the flour.

Put the suet, flour and all the remaining ingredients, except the eggs and rum, in a bowl. Stir and set aside for 4 days, stirring twice a day with a spatula. On the fifth day, add the eggs and leave for a further day. If the mixture seems a little dense or dry, add some rum, beer or milk.

For this quantity of mixture you will need 2 buttered and floured tea (dish) towels or large linen napkins. Divide the mixture into 2 equal portions, compress well and tie each one up in a cloth. Plunge the puddings into a copper pan full of boiling water, cover and cook continuously for 5 hours. Remove from the heat and leave to cool a little.

Meanwhile, make the Suzette butter. Rub the sugar lumps over the rinds of the mandarin and lemon so the zest or oil is absorbed. Crush the lumps of sugar with the rum and beat into the unsalted butter.

Serve the pudding on hot plates and flambé with the rum. Top each serving with a spoonful of Suzette butter.

US	Ingredients	Met/Imp
½ lb	fresh beef suet (kidney fat)	250 g/8 oz
1¼ cups	flour	175 g/6 oz
3 cups	fresh breadcrumbs	175 g/6 oz
⅔ cup	currants	100 g/3½ oz
⅔ cup	Muscat raisins	100 g/3½ oz
⅓ cup	dried figs	50 g/2 oz
¼ lb	peeled, cored and chopped apples	125 g/4 oz
⅓ cup	finely chopped candied citron peel	50 g/2 oz
⅓ cup	finely chopped candied orange peel	50 g/2 oz
½ cup	prunes, well cooked, stoned and puréed	125 g/4 oz
scant 1 cup	moist brown sugar	125 g/4 oz
1	orange, finely grated rind and juice of	1
1	lemon, finely grated rind and juice of	1
1 tsp	salt	5 ml/1 tsp
1 tsp	mixed spices (*quatre-épices*, ground cinnamon, freshly grated nutmeg and ground ginger)	5 ml/1 tsp
scant ½ cup	beer	100 ml/4 fl oz
3	eggs	3
scant ½ cup	rum	100 ml/4 fl oz
	SUZETTE BUTTER	
several	sugar lumps	several
1	mandarin orange	1
1	lemon	1
1 tbsp	rum	15 ml/1 tbsp
14 tbsp	unsalted butter	200 g/7 oz

PEARS DAME SIMONE

Preparation 2 hours • Cooking 35 minutes

Shell, blanch, skin and flake (slice) the almonds. Put them in a low oven with the door open to dry and brown gently.

Peel, quarter, core and finely slice the apples, put them in a sauté pan with the caster (granulated) sugar, 30 ml/2 tbsp water and the vanilla, cover and cook over a gentle heat until the apples form a purée. Remove the vanilla, then beat the apples with a small whisk until smooth. Cook over a high heat until very thick, stirring constantly. Mix the apple with the tomato jam and unsalted butter.

Meanwhile, halve the pears, peel and core them. Poach the pears in a copper saucepan with the lump sugar and red wine until they are tender but still quite firm. Drain.

Spread the apple purée in a fruit dish on a low stand and arrange the pear halves on top. Quickly reduce the cooked wine to a scant 200 ml/7 fl oz (scant 1 cup) and pour it over the pears. Strew the top with the toasted almonds. Heat the rum, sprinkle over the dessert and flambé at the table.

US	Ingredients	Met/Imp
12	almonds	12
5	sound *reinette grise* or other eating apples	5
3 tbsp	caster (granulated) sugar	45 ml/3 tbsp
½	vanilla pod (bean)	½
⅔ cup	tomato jam	150 g/5 oz
2 tbsp	good-quality unsalted butter	25 g/scant 1 oz
8	medium pears	8
7 oz (1 cup)	lump (or granulated) sugar	200 g/7 oz
2½ cups	red bordeaux wine	600 ml/1 pint
scant ½ cup	rum	100 ml/4 fl oz

US	Ingredients	Met/Imp
½ cup	caster sugar	100 g/4 oz
I cup	water	250 ml/8 fl oz
8	juicy pears	8
I heaping cup	long-grain rice, cooked and prepared as for Rice in Milk for Desserts (page 620)	200 g/8 oz
1¼ cups	Frangipane (page 584)	300 ml/½ pint
scant ½ lb	macaroons	200 g/8 oz
I stick	good-quality unsalted butter	100 g/4 oz

EMPRESS PEARS

Preparation 2 hours • Cooking 30 minutes

Put the sugar and water in a saucepan and heat gently until the sugar has dissolved. Peel the pears and, if large, cut them into halves or quarters. Drop them into the syrup and cook gently for 30 minutes.

Prepare the rice and stir in the frangipane, which will increase the quantity by one-third and make the rice creamier. Make a bed of half of the rice at the bottom of a buttered dish.

Drain the pears, arrange them on the rice and cover with another layer of rice. Sprinkle with crushed macaroons, dot with butter and brown in the oven.

VARIATION
If macaroons are not available, use toasted and chopped almonds mixed with their own weight of sugar (½ cup sugar to each cup of almonds).

US	Ingredients	Met/Imp
8	medium pears	8
4	sugar lumps	4
I	vanilla pod (bean)	I
I quart	Vanilla Custard Sauce (page 583)	I litre/1¾ pints
3½ tbsp	rum	50 ml/2 fl oz

PEARS DRESSED IN WHITE

Preparation 1 hour • Cooking about 25 minutes

Peel the whole pears and trim their stalks. Put them in a saucepan, cover them with water and add the sugar and vanilla. Cover and cook over a gentle heat for about 25 minutes or until the pears are so tender that the point of a knife goes into them as if into butter.

Take the pears out of their juice and drain them, then place them with their stalk upwards on a 'compotier' (fruit dish on a low stand). Cover with a fairly thick vanilla custard sauce into which the rum has been mixed.

US	Ingredients	Met/Imp
8	perfect William pears	8
1¼ cups	caster (granulated) sugar	250 g/8 oz
I pint	fresh or bottled raspberries	250 g/8 oz
⅔ cup	raspberry jelly	200 g/7 oz
½ cup	raspberry *eau-de-vie*	100 ml/4 fl oz

SUMMER SURPRISE PEARS

Preparation 1 hour • Cooking 35 minutes

Peel the pears, cut them in half and take out the cores, hollowing them out a little more than you normally would. Poach them in a sugar syrup for 35 minutes or until tender, then drain them and leave them to cool. Fill the cavities in the pear halves with fresh sugared raspberries, or raspberries preserved in syrup. Reshape the fruit and arrange in a serving dish.

Add the raspberry jelly and eau-de-vie to the sugar syrup in which the pears were cooked. Mix well and pour all over the pears, taking care that they are completely covered. Cool, but do not chill, and serve.

APPLES BONNE FEMME

Preparation 20 minutes • Cooking 35 minutes

Core the apples and arrange them in an ovenproof dish. Fill the insides with a mixture of the butter and sugars. Put a little water in the bottom of the dish and bake in a fairly hot oven for about 35 minutes or until tender. Arrange them on the croûtons.

US	Ingredients	Met/Imp
8	reinette or other eating apples	8
1 stick	good-quality unsalted butter	100 g/4 oz
½ cup	caster (granulated) sugar	100 g/4 oz
5 tbsp	vanilla sugar	20 g/¾ oz
8	croûtons, cut the same size as the apples, fried in butter	8

APPLES FIGARO

Preparation 2 hours • Cooking 50 minutes

Slit the skins of the chestnuts and put them in a saucepan of cold water. Bring to the boil and cook for 5 minutes. Take them out of the water, 5–6 at a time, peel them and remove the dark skin which sticks to the chestnuts. It is easier to skin them when they are hot than when they are cool. Put them in a deep, narrow saucepan, so that they are heaped on top of one another. Add the salt, vanilla pod (bean), and enough boiled milk to cover them, then cook very gently until very soft.

Shell, blanch and skin the almonds. Split them in half and cut them into small flakes. Spread them out on a baking sheet and leave them to dry and toast in a cool oven with the door open. Mix the coarsely chopped marron glacé pieces with these toasted almond flakes.

Remove the cores and pips (seeds) from the apples with an apple corer, peel thinly, then poach in a light sugar syrup which is strongly flavoured with vanilla, keeping them quite firm.

In a small saucepan, mix 125 g/4½ oz (10 tbsp) of the sugar and the egg yolks. Beat until the mixture leaves a ribbon trail on its surface when the beater is lifted, then add the flour. Gradually beat in the boiled milk in which the vanilla has been infused. Bring to the boil, stirring, then leave to simmer for 1 minute. Remove from the heat and stir in the butter. Do not let this custard sauce cook any longer.

Work the chestnuts quickly through a sieve, collecting the purée in a sauté pan. Mix in the remaining sugar and the crème fraîche. Cook this purée over a high heat for 2 minutes, stirring constantly, then tip it on to a serving dish.

Take the apples out of the syrup with a fork and drain them well. Arrange them in a circle on the chestnut purée, lightly embedding them.

Coat the apples with the vanilla custard sauce and sprinkle with the almonds and marron glacé pieces.

US	Ingredients	Met/Imp
1 quart	medium chestnuts	1 litre/1¾ pints
1 pinch	salt	1 pinch
1	vanilla pod (bean)	1
1½ quarts	boiled milk	1.5 litres/2½ pints
16	almonds	16
½ cup	marron glacé pieces	50 g/2 oz
8	reinette or other eating apples	8
1 quart	sugar syrup: 24° Baumé (page 575), strongly flavoured with vanilla	1 litre/1¾ pints
1 cup plus 2 tbsp	caster (granulated) sugar	225 g/7½ oz
4	egg yolks	4
6 tbsp	flour	50 g/2 oz
3 tbsp	good-quality unsalted butter	40 g/1½ oz
scant ½ cup	crème fraîche	100 ml/4 fl oz

US	Ingredients	Met/Imp
I cup	water	250 ml/8 fl oz
¼ lb (½ cup)	lump (or granulated) sugar	100 g/4 oz
½	vanilla pod (bean)	½
12	perfect *reinette* or other eating apples	12
4 tbsp	good-quality unsalted butter	50 g/2 oz
¼ cup	caster (granulated) sugar	50 g/2 oz
¾ cup	icing (confectioners') sugar	100 g/4 oz
I	egg white	I
⅔ cup	flaked (sliced) almonds	60 g/2½ oz

APPLES GRATINÉES

Preparation 2 hours • Cooking about 25 minutes

Make up a vanilla-flavoured sugar syrup (32° Baumé, see page 575), using the water, lump sugar and vanilla pod (bean).

Peel 8 of the apples, cut them into quarters, core them and poach them in the vanilla sugar syrup until tender but still whole shapes. Remove them from the syrup and place them on a cloth. Leave to cool and drain.

Peel, core and chop the remaining apples and put them in a sauté pan with the butter and caster (granulated) sugar. Cook over a high heat until reduced to a purée, stirring constantly. Gradually blend in the sugar syrup. When the mixture is firm, spread it on a flameproof dish.

In a small bowl, beat the icing (confectioners') sugar with the egg white until the mixture becomes light and thick. Mix in the almonds.

Lay the poached apple quarters neatly on the purée in the dish and spread the almond topping over them. Dust lightly with extra icing (confectioners') sugar and bake in a warm oven until heated through and the praline has turned golden.

US	Ingredients	Met/Imp
¾ cup	long-grain rice, preferably Carolina	125 g/4½ oz
2 cups	milk	500 ml/18 fl oz
2½ oz (5 tbsp)	lump (or granulated) sugar	60 g/2½ oz
½	vanilla pod (bean)	½
I pinch	salt	I pinch
4 tsp	good-quality unsalted butter	20 g/¾ oz
7	medium apples, preferably a firm orchard variety	7
I tbsp	caster (granulated) sugar	15 ml/I tbsp
¾ cup	redcurrant jelly	250 g/8 oz
7–8	hazelnuts (filberts)	7–8
I stick	good-quality unsalted butter, clarified	100 g/4 oz
3 tbsp	kirsch	45 ml/3 tbsp

APPLES MADELON

Preparation 1 hour • Cooking about 40 minutes

Blanch the rice in boiling water for 5 minutes, then drain. Bring the milk to the boil in a flameproof casserole with the lump sugar and vanilla pod (bean), then remove the vanilla and add the rice, salt and butter. Bring to the boil again, cover and cook in a warm oven for 28–30 minutes.

At the same time, cook, in a small sauté pan, 3 peeled, cored and finely sliced apples, one-third of the caster (granulated) sugar and 2 teaspoons water. As soon as the apples are cooked, mash them with a fork to reduce them to a thick purée. When the rice is ready, break it up with a fork and mix in the apple purée.

Peel and core the remaining apples and cut them in slices 1 cm/½ inch thick. Lay them on a dish and dust both sides with caster (granulated) sugar.

Melt the redcurrant jelly. Shell the nuts and brown them in a low oven with the door open. Rub them in a cloth to remove their skins, then chop them.

About 7–8 minutes before serving, heat the clarified butter in a large frying pan. Place the apple slices in the pan after having floured them, and turn them over 2–3 times. They must not cook too much, just enough to make them tender.

Spread the rice and apple mixture out on a dish, in the shape of a flat cake. Arrange the apple slices on top. Stir the kirsch into the redcurrant jelly and pour over the apple slices. Sprinkle the top with the nuts.

CHOCOLATE PROFITEROLES

Preparation 2 hours • Cooking about 25 minutes

US	Ingredients	Met/Imp
2 cups	water	500 ml/18 fl oz
I pinch	salt	I pinch
5 tbsp	good-quality unsalted butter	60 g/2½ oz
scant I cup	flour	125 g/4 oz
5	eggs	5
2 cups	crème fraîche	500 ml/18 fl oz
2 tsp	caster (granulated) sugar	25 g/scant I oz
3 cups	cocoa powder	250 g/8 oz

Bring the water, salt and butter to the boil and pour in the flour. Stir with a spatula over the heat until the paste is thoroughly dry. Remove from the heat and add the eggs one by one. Stir constantly until the paste is soft without being pale in colour. This depends above all on the quality of the flour and the size of the eggs.

Using a piping bag fitted with a small plain nozzle, pipe the profiteroles (little choux buns, the size of walnuts) on to a buttered baking sheet, 4 per person. Bake in a moderately hot oven for about 25 minutes. Reserve a thimbleful of crème fraîche for the chocolate sauce and whip the remainder with a whisk. Fold in the sugar to make a lightly sweetened Chantilly. Make a small incision in the side of each profiterole, or even make a hole with a pencil. Fill a second piping bag fitted with a small plain nozzle with the Chantilly cream and fill the profiteroles.

Dissolve the cocoa in a glass of water and add the thimbleful of crème fraîche. Arrange the profiteroles on a cake stand. Cover them with the chocolate sauce just before serving.

PRUNES IN BURGUNDY

Preparation 20 minutes • Macerating 48 hours

US	Ingredients	Met/Imp
I lb	prunes	500 g/I lb
2 cups	hot water (50°C/125°F)	500 ml/18 fl oz
I	vanilla pod (bean)	I
½ cup	caster (granulated) sugar	100 g/4 oz
3 cups	excellent burgundy wine (of good vintage)	750 ml/1¼ pints
	Genoa cake	

This is very simple to prepare, but calls for excellent ingredients.

Choose sound prunes of very good quality. Wash them, put them in a bowl and cover them with the hot water. Cover and leave to soak for 24 hours.

Drain the prunes, dry them and put them back in the bowl with the vanilla and sugar. Pour over the wine and leave in a warm place to macerate for a further 24 hours.

Take out the vanilla and serve the prunes in a crystal bowl, accompanied by Genoa cake.

US	Ingredients	Met/Imp
½ lb	Agen prunes	250 g/8 oz
5 oz (¾ cup)	lump (or granulated) sugar	150 g/5 oz
1	piece cinnamon stick	1
1	small strip orange rind	1
1 cup	very good red wine	250 ml/9 fl oz
8	medium apples	8
2 tbsp	good-quality unsalted butter	25 g/scant 1 oz
3 tbsp	caster (granulated) sugar	45 ml/3 tbsp
2–3 tbsp	greengage plum jam	30–45 ml/ 2–3 tbsp
8–10	walnuts	8–10
3	large eggs	3
1	small orange, with thick skin	1
	SUGAR SYRUP	
¼ cup	water	60 ml/4 tbsp
2 tsp	caster (granulated) sugar	10 ml/2 tsp

PRUNEAUX À LA MODE D'AGEN

PRUNES AGEN STYLE

Preparation 4 hours • Cooking 45 minutes

Put the prunes to soak in warm water. With Agen prunes of very good quality, 12–15 minutes will be enough. If they are ordinary prunes, however, the soaking time should be increased until they are swollen.

Put the prunes in an earthenware pot, or other narrow heatproof container, so that they are piled on top of one another. Add the lump sugar, cinnamon, strip of orange rind and enough red wine to cover them well. Bring to the boil and simmer very gently until the prunes are just cooked but retain their shape and are still slightly firm.

Cut into quarters, peel, core and slice the apples. Put them in a sauté pan with the butter and caster (granulated) sugar. Cover tightly and cook over a very low heat until they turn to a purée. Increase the heat and stir over a very high heat until the purée becomes very thick, then mix in the jam and the shelled, chopped and toasted walnuts. Lightly beat the eggs and gradually add to the mixture.

Put the apple purée in a buttered ring mould and poach in the oven in a *bain-marie* for 40–45 minutes. After poaching, remove the mould from the water and leave to rest for 10–12 minutes to allow the mixture to settle before unmoulding.

Remove the rind from the orange and cut it into fine strips. Make up the sugar syrup, then boil the orange rind strips in it for 5 minutes. Reduce the heat and simmer for 10 minutes.

Unmould the ring on to a round serving dish. Pick up the prunes with a fork and put them in the centre. Reduce their cooking syrup to about 200 ml/7 fl oz (scant 1 cup) and pour it over the prunes. Strew the well-drained orange strips over the top.

US	Ingredients	Met/Imp
3½ cups	shelled sweet almonds	500 g/1 lb
1 lb (4 sticks)	good-quality unsalted butter	500 g/1 lb
½ cup	crème fraîche	100 ml/4 fl oz
4	eggs	4
1 cup	caster (granulated) sugar	200 g/7 oz
½ cup	white wine	100 ml/4 fl oz
¼ cup	orange-flower water	50 ml/2 fl oz
2 tbsp	potato flour	30 ml/2 tbsp

PUDDING AUX AMANDES

ALMOND PUDDING

Preparation 1½ hours • Cooking 25 minutes

Plunge the almonds into boiling water, leave until the water comes to the boil again, then drain immediately. While the almonds are still hot, spread them on the table and skin them between your thumb and forefinger, by pressing them against the table.

Pound the almonds vigorously in a mortar and pestle, gradually adding the butter, cream (in spoonfuls), eggs (1 by 1), the sugar, white wine and orange-flower water. Finally, add the potato flour to form a paste.

Butter a charlotte mould, fill it with the almond mixture and cook in a low to moderate oven for 25 minutes.

CABINET PUDDING

Preparation 30 minutes • Macerating several hours • Cooking 35–45 minutes

US	Ingredients	Met/Imp
⅓ cup	sultanas (golden raisins) and raisins	50 g/2 oz
⅓ cup	mixed candied fruit	50 g/2 oz
scant ½ cup	rum, kirsch or maraschino	100 ml/4 fl oz
4 tsp	good-quality unsalted butter	20 g/¾ oz
8	sponge finger biscuits (ladyfingers)	8
1 tbsp	apricot jam	15 ml/1 tbsp
	CUSTARD CREAM	
5	egg yolks	5
5	whole eggs	5
1¼ cups	caster (granulated) sugar	250 g/8 oz
1	vanilla pod (bean)	1
1 quart	milk	1 litre/1¾ pints
	VANILLA CUSTARD SAUCE	
6	egg yolks	6
¾ cup	caster (granulated) sugar	150 g/5 oz
1	vanilla pod (bean)	1
2 cups	milk	500 ml/18 fl oz
	flavouring of your choice	

Rub, clean and rinse the sultanas (golden raisins) and raisins. Macerate them with the candied fruit for several hours in the desired flavouring: rum, kirsch or maraschino. If this pudding is made often, keep some of these fruits ready-macerated in a sealed preserving jar. They will then be well impregnated with the flavouring, and very juicy as a result.

Lightly butter a charlotte mould and arrange the candied fruit in the bottom. Coat the sponge fingers (ladyfingers) with the slightly melted jam. Arrange in the mould in alternating layers with the sultanas (golden raisins) and raisins.

Make the custard cream. Using either a whisk or a spatula, thoroughly beat the egg yolks, whole eggs and sugar together until the mixture leaves a ribbon trail on its surface when the beater is lifted. Gradually pour over the boiling vanilla-flavoured milk, mixing in small quantities only in order not to cook the eggs. Strain through a conical sieve, then skim. Gradually pour into the mould, waiting for the sponge fingers (ladyfingers) to soak up each addition before adding more. Fill the mould right to the brim. Cook in the oven, in a *bain-marie*, without allowing the water in the bain-marie to boil.

Make the vanilla custard sauce. Beat the egg yolks and sugar together, then very gently pour on the boiling vanilla-flavoured milk. Heat gently, stirring constantly, until the custard begins to coat the spatula. Do not allow the custard to boil or it will curdle. Remove from the heat and stir. Strain through a conical sieve and keep warm. Just before serving, flavour with the spirit or liqueur of your choice. Serve on the side.

BREAD PUDDING

Preparation 1 hour • Macerating the day before • Cooking about 40 minutes

US	Ingredients	Met/Imp
⅔ cup	sultanas (golden raisins) and raisins	100 g/4 oz
1 pinch	flour	1 pinch
3½ tbsp	rum	50 ml/2 fl oz
½ lb (8–10 slices)	firm-textured bread	250 g/8 oz
1¼ cups	caster (granulated) sugar	250 g/8 oz
8	eggs	8
1 quart	milk	1 litre/1¾ pints
⅓ cup	icing (confectioners') sugar	50 g/2 oz

The day before, put the sultanas (golden raisins) and raisins in a sieve with the flour. Shake and rub the fruit on the mesh of the sieve until clean, then transfer to a bowl. Add the rum, cover and leave to macerate overnight.

Cut the bread into even slices and dust them lightly with a little of the caster (granulated) sugar. Dry and lightly brown them in the oven.

Blend the eggs with the remaining caster (granulated) sugar in a bowl. Gradually beat in the boiling milk, as for a custard cream. Strain through a fine sieve or a cloth.

Lay the slices of bread on top of one another in a buttered deep baking dish or, preferably, an English pie dish. Strew the well-steeped raisins over the slices of bread, pour over the custard and cook in a *bain-marie* in a moderately hot oven for about 40 minutes.

Just before serving, dust the pudding with icing (confectioners') sugar. Serve cold.

US	Ingredients	Met/Imp
1¾ cups	long-grain rice, preferably Carolina	300 g/10 oz
1 quart	milk	1 litre/1¾ pints
1 pinch	salt	1 pinch
1	vanilla pod (bean)	1
10 tbsp	caster (granulated) sugar	125 g/4½ oz
scant ½ cup	crème fraîche	100 ml/4 fl oz
4	egg yolks	4
4 tbsp	butter (optional)	50 g/2 oz

RICE IN MILK FOR DESSERTS

Preparation 30 minutes • Cooking 35 minutes

Blanch the washed rice by putting it in a saucepan with a small quantity of water and bringing it to the boil. Drain, return to the rinsed-out pan and add the milk, salt and vanilla. Cook for 35 minutes or until the rice is tender. Remove the vanilla.

Add the sugar, then remove from the heat and add the cream and the egg yolks to bind it. If liked, add the butter during cooking, at the same time as the milk.

US	Ingredients	Met/Imp
¾ cup	long-grain rice, preferably Carolina	125 g/4½ oz
1 quart	sweetened, vanilla-flavoured milk	1 litre/1¾ pints
6	eggs	6
½ cup	caster (granulated) sugar	100 g/4 oz

MERINGUE RICE

Preparation 2 hours • Cooking Rice 40 minutes; Mould 30 minutes

Cook the well-washed rice in the sweetened, vanilla-flavoured milk for about 40 minutes, taking care to add the milk in small quantities as it is absorbed. Separate the eggs. When all the milk has been absorbed and the rice is swollen, remove the pan from the heat and mix in the egg yolks. Whisk the egg whites to a very stiff froth, and fold them into the mixture.

Use the sugar to make a caramel and brush round the inside of a mould. Leave to set. Fill the mould three-quarters full with the rice mixture and cook in a cool oven for 30 minutes.

VARIATION
This dessert can be made more special with toasted flaked (sliced) almonds sprinkled on to the hot caramel in the mould.

US	Ingredients	Met/Imp
8	egg yolks	8
1½ cups	caster (superfine) sugar	300 g/10 oz
3 glasses	wine (eg port, marsala, madeira, frontignan, champagne, etc)	3 glasses
	maraschino liqueur	
	CHILLED CUSTARD	
4	egg yolks	4

SABAYON SAUCE

Preparation 25 minutes • Cooking 35 minutes

This is usually served as a sauce to accompany puddings; however, it can be served as a dessert in champagne glasses, particularly in summer. It can be served hot or chilled.

Put the egg yolks and sugar in a saucepan and beat hard with a small whisk until the mixture is pale. Add the chosen wine. Place the saucepan in a *bain-marie* and beat by rolling the whisk between the hands, until increased in volume to a thick, foamy mousse. Flavour with maraschino and serve at once, if serving hot.

When the sabayon is to be served cold, add 4 extra egg yolks. When thickened, flavour with maraschino and put it on ice, whisking until it is completely cold.

FRUIT SAVARIN

Preparation about 2 hours • Cooking 45–50 minutes

This dessert can be made with a brioche dough.

Work one-quarter of the flour in a bowl with the yeast and warm milk or cream. Cover and leave in a fairly warm place.

Put the remaining flour in a bowl and make a well in the centre. Add half of the softened butter, then add the sugar, salt and enough beaten egg to knead the dough by hand to a soft dough. Add the yeast mixture and the remaining butter. Put in a savarin mould and leave to rise. Cook in a hot oven for 45–50 minutes. Cut the cooked savarin vertically into thin slices, allowing 2 per person.

Cut the pineapple into thin pieces that will fit between the savarin slices. Put them to one side and add any leftover pineapple to the prepared mixed fruit. Lay the slices of savarin on a baking sheet; dust them with icing (confectioners') sugar and put them in a hot oven until toasted a golden colour. Brush the slices with hot apricot marmalade and re-assemble them in the shape of the savarin on a round dish, inserting a thin piece of pineapple between each one. Decorate with glacé cherries, almonds and angelica.

Serve with mixed fresh fruit, or fruit preserved in its own juice or in syrup. If only cherries are used, the savarin is called 'croûte Montmorency'; with pineapple, it is 'croûte Singapore'. Mix the fruit with a sauce made of sieved redcurrant jelly or apricot marmalade thinned down with the fruit juice, fruit syrup or water and flavoured with liqueur.

US	Ingredients	Met/Imp
	SAVARIN	
3½ cups	flour	500 g/1 lb
1 pkg	fresh (compressed) yeast	15 g/½ oz
scant ½ cup	milk or whipping cream	100 ml/3½ fl oz
2 sticks plus 5 tbsp	good-quality unsalted butter	325 g/11 oz
1 pinch	caster (granulated) sugar	1 pinch
1 pinch	salt	1 pinch
6–7	eggs	6–7
	GARNISH	
	canned pineapple rings	
1 lb	mixed fresh (or bottled) fruit	500 g/1 lb
	icing (confectioners') sugar	
⅔ cup	apricot *marmalade*	150 g/5 oz
	glacé cherries	
⅔ cup	almonds	100 g/4 oz
	candied angelica	
scant 1 cup	liqueur of your choice	200 ml/7 fl oz
	redcurrant jelly (optional)	

SOUFFLÉ

Preparation 30 minutes • Cooking 15–20 minutes

Put the caster (granulated) sugar and sifted flour in a bowl, make a well in the centre and add the egg yolks, stirring them slowly with a whisk until the flour and sugar are incorporated.

Boil the milk with the vanilla pod (bean) and pour it very gently over the batter mixture, stirring with a whisk. Return everything to the saucepan in which the milk was boiled, and bring very slowly to the boil, beating constantly and scraping the bottom of the pan so that the mixture does not burn. Discard the vanilla. Transfer to a bowl and cover with buttered greaseproof (parchment) paper.

Make the soufflé. Put some of the batter mixture in a bowl and beat vigorously. Separate the whole eggs and add 1 egg yolk per person, then the desired flavouring (*eau-de-vie*, liqueur, fruit juice, chocolate, etc). Beat the egg whites to a very stiff froth and, with a wooden spatula, fold them very gently into the mixture, without breaking them down.

Put the mixture in a buttered soufflé dish dusted with sugar and bake in a fairly hot oven for 15–20 minutes. When the soufflé starts to brown, dust it with the icing (confectioners') sugar and finish cooking.

US	Ingredients	Met/Imp
1¼ cups	caster (granulated) sugar	250 g/8 oz
¾ cup	flour	100 g/3½ oz
8–10	egg yolks	8–10
1 quart	milk	1 litre/1¾ pints
1	vanilla pod (bean)	1
8	whole eggs	8
	flavouring of your choice	
2 tbsp	good-quality unsalted butter	30 g/1 oz
6 tbsp	icing (confectioners') sugar	50 g/2 oz

US	Ingredients	Met/Imp
6, total weight about 1¾ lb	medium bananas	6, total weight about 800 g/1¾ lb
¼ lb (½ cup)	lump or granulated sugar	100 g/4 oz
2 tbsp	good-quality unsalted butter	30 g/1 oz
¼ cup	icing (confectioners') sugar	60 ml/4 tbsp
5	eggs	5
⅓ cup	ground almonds	30 g/1 oz
2 tbsp	crème fraîche	30 ml/2 tbsp
3 tbsp	rum	45 ml/3 tbsp

BANANA SOUFFLÉ

Preparation 40 minutes • Cooking 25 minutes • Serves 4–6

Peel the bananas and cut them into slices about 3 mm/⅛ inch thick. Put them in a saucepan with the lump sugar and 30 ml/2 tbsp water, cover and cook over a very low heat, stirring frequently with a wooden spoon to stop the mixture sticking to the bottom of the saucepan.

Meanwhile, generously butter a 15 cm/6 inch soufflé dish and dust the inside with the icing (confectioners') sugar. To do this, pour the sugar into the bottom of the dish and move the dish around, tapping it with your hand to spread the sugar evenly. Tip out the sugar that does not stick to the dish and reserve it.

When the bananas are reduced to a purée, work them through a very fine mill (or through a fine hair sieve), using a pestle. Separate 2 of the eggs. Mix the almonds with the crème fraîche in a bowl. Add this mixture to the banana purée, then add the 2 egg yolks. Add the rum and mix well.

Separate the 3 remaining eggs and add the 3 whites to the 2 already reserved. (The 3 yolks will not be used.) Beat the egg whites to a very stiff froth. This is very important for the quality of the soufflé.

Add one-quarter of the stiffly beaten whites to the banana purée, folding them in gently so that they do not sink. Add the rest of the whites all at once and fold them in without beating, cutting them into the bulk of the purée and turning them over. Fill the prepared dish nearly to the top and smooth the surface into a rounded shape with the blade of a knife.

Bake the soufflé in a preheated moderately hot oven. After 20 minutes, gently open the door and, without removing the soufflé from the oven, quickly dust the surface of the soufflé with the reserved icing (confectioners') sugar. Increase the oven temperature to hot and continue cooking for 2–3 minutes in order to caramelize the top of the soufflé. Serve the soufflé as soon as it is taken from the oven.

CHOCOLATE SOUFFLÉ

Preparation 1 hour • Cooking 20–25 minutes

US	Ingredients	Met/Imp
8 oz	plain (semisweet) chocolate	250 g/8 oz
1 quart	milk	1 litre/1¾ pints
6 tbsp	potato flour	50 g/2 oz
8	egg yolks	8
12	egg whites	12

Dissolve the chocolate in the milk and bring to the boil. Add the potato flour and return to the boil. Transfer the chocolate mixture to a bowl and mix in the beaten egg yolks. Whisk the egg whites to a stiff froth and fold into the chocolate mixture. Turn into a buttered soufflé dish.

Bake the soufflé in a moderate oven for 10 minutes, then increase the temperature to moderately hot and continue baking for 15–20 minutes until the soufflé has risen well and is a good colour. This soufflé, just like a soufflé omelette, is served immediately, straight from the dish in which it is cooked.

LIQUEUR SOUFFLÉ

Preparation 30 minutes • Cooking 15–18 minutes

US	Ingredients	Met/Imp
1¼ cups	caster (granulated) sugar	250 g/8 oz
3 tbsp	flour	25 g/scant 1 oz
5	egg yolks	5
scant ½ cup	milk	100 ml/4 fl oz
10	egg whites	10
8	sponge finger biscuits (ladyfingers)	8
scant ½ cup	liqueur of your choice	100 ml/4 fl oz

Sponge finger biscuits (ladyfingers) are added to this soufflé because they retain the flavour of the liqueur or spirit. If only the custard is flavoured, during cooking the flavour will evaporate and the much-sought-after result will only partially be achieved.

Beat together the sugar, flour and egg yolks until the mixture leaves a ribbon trail on its surface when the beater is lifted. Gradually mix in the boiling milk. Whisk the egg whites to a stiff froth, gently to begin with, then more vigorously. Fold the whites carefully into the custard.

Soak the sponge finger biscuits (ladyfingers) in the chosen liqueur. Any leftover liqueur can be folded into the soufflé mixture.

To be served successfully, a soufflé should not exceed 3–4 servings, so butter 2 soufflé dishes and coat them with caster (superfine) sugar or potato flour. Put about one-quarter of the mixture in each dish and arrange the soaked sponge fingers (ladyfingers) on top. Fill the dishes only three-quarters full with the remaining mixture. Bake in a moderately hot oven, especially towards the end of the cooking time.

MARZIPAN SOUFFLÉ

Preparation 1 hour • Cooking 40 minutes

US	Ingredients	Met/Imp
1 quart	sweetened, vanilla-flavoured milk	1 litre/1¾ pints
½ cup	cornflour (cornstarch)	75 g/3 oz
4	Nancy marzipan biscuits (cookies) or macaroons	4
4	egg whites	4
½ cup	caster (superfine) sugar	100 g/4 oz
2 tbsp	good-quality unsalted butter	30 g/1 oz

Bring the sweetened milk to the boil and stir in the cornflour (cornstarch). Cook over a low heat for 5 minutes, stirring with a wooden spoon. Add the crushed marzipan biscuits (cookies) or macaroons, then fold in the egg whites which have been stiffly whisked with the sugar. Turn into a buttered soufflé dish and bake in a moderate oven for 40 minutes.

US	Ingredients	Met/Imp
2½ cups	milk	600 ml/1 pint
¼ lb (10 tbsp)	lump (or granulated) sugar	125 g/4½ oz
1	vanilla pod (bean)	1
¼ lb	praline (page 586) or nougat	100 g/4 oz
7 tbsp	potato flour or wheat flour	60 g/2½ oz
8	eggs, separated	8
4 tbsp	good-quality unsalted butter	50 g/2 oz
2	egg whites	2
10	red pralines	10
	icing (confectioners') sugar, for dusting	

PRALINE SOUFFLÉ

Preparation 2 hours • Cooking 18–20 minutes

Bring two-thirds of the milk to the boil and add the lump sugar, vanilla and praline, or hard nougat, crushed to a powder. Cover and leave to infuse for 10–12 minutes, making sure that the sugar dissolves. Remove the vanilla. Gradually stir the remaining cold milk into the potato flour or flour and mix to a smooth paste. Stir into the flavoured milk.

Bring the milk back to the boil, stirring, and simmer for several moments. Remove from the heat and add the egg yolks, butter and one-quarter of the 8 stiffly whisked egg whites. Mix thoroughly. (If the soufflé base is made a little in advance, the butter should be scattered on top and the final mixing not carried out until the moment when the egg whites are added, just before cooking.) Add the remaining egg whites and this time fold in lightly, cutting through and turning the mixture over with a spatula, in such a way that the egg whites keep their lightness. Put this mixture immediately into a round mould or china soufflé dish, which has been buttered and dusted with icing (confectioners') sugar or very fine caster (superfine) sugar.

With the blade of a knife, smooth the top of the mixture, giving it a cone shape. Insert the point of a knife deep into the mixture in several places (to make it easier for the heat to penetrate). Sprinkle the surface with crushed red pralines and bake the soufflé in a low to moderate oven for 18–20 minutes. Dust the soufflé with icing (confectioners') sugar and return to the oven. Watch over the glazing closely, ie the formation of a light coat of caramel resulting from the melting of the sugar on the surface. Serve immediately. A soufflé will not wait.

US	Ingredients	Met/Imp
1 heaping cup	rice	200 g/7 oz
1 quart	milk	1 litre/1¾ pints
1¼ cups	caster (granulated) sugar	250 g/8 oz
	vanilla, finely grated lemon or orange rind or coffee essence (extract)	
5 oz	macaroons or praline (page 586), crushed	150 g/5 oz
8	eggs, separated	8
	icing (confectioners') sugar, for dusting	

RICE SOUFFLÉ

Preparation 1 hour • Cooking 20–25 minutes

Cook the rice in the milk as for Rice in Milk for Desserts (*page 620*). When it is cooked, stir in the sugar and flavour with vanilla, lemon, orange or coffee and the crushed macaroons or praline. Bind with the egg yolks.

Beat the egg whites into a very stiff froth, preferably in a special copper bowl. Fold into the rice mixture and put into a buttered mould or soufflé dish, buttered and dusted with sugar. Bake in a fairly hot oven for 20–25 minutes. Dust with icing (confectioners') sugar just before serving.

SEMOLINA SUBRICS WITH REDCURRANT JELLY

Preparation 2 hours • Cooking 2–3 minutes

US	Ingredients	Met/Imp
I quart	milk	I litre/1¾ pints
¾ cup	caster (granulated) sugar	150 g/5 oz
I pinch	salt	I pinch
I	vanilla pod (bean)	I
	or	
I	strip pared lemon rind	I
1⅓ cups	semolina (farina)	250 g/8 oz
4 tbsp	good-quality unsalted butter	50 g/2 oz
5	egg yolks	5
½ cup	clarified butter	100 g/3½ oz
⅓ cup	redcurrant jelly	100 g/3½ oz

Bring the milk to the boil and add the sugar, salt and vanilla pod (bean) or lemon rind. Pour the semolina (farina) into the boiling milk, then add the butter. Cover the pan and cook over a very low heat or, preferably, in a low oven with the door open so that the mixture cooks gently.

When the milk has been absorbed and the mixture is dry, remove from the heat and discard the lemon rind or vanilla. Beat in the egg yolks. Turn this mixture out on to a buttered work surface and spread it out with a knife to an even thickness of 2 cm/¾ inch. Dab the surface lightly with a lump of butter, to prevent it drying out, and leave to get cold.

When the mixture is completely cold, turn it on to a cloth spread out on the work surface. Cut it into small discs with a 5 cm/2 inch pastry cutter, or into squares or diamond shapes (this avoids wasting any leftover pieces of paste). Lay each shape, as soon as you have cut it out, on a floured board.

About 10 minutes before serving, slide the shapes carefully into a large frying pan or sauté pan containing very hot clarified butter. Cook for 2–3 minutes or until brown on both sides, then take them out of the pan with a small palette knife and lay them on a plate. Decorate the centre of each subric with a spoonful of cold redcurrant jelly and serve immediately.

BAKED RICE PUDDING

Preparation 45 minutes • Cooking 8 hours

US	Ingredients	Met/Imp
1¼ cups	short-grain rice	250 g/8 oz
¾ cup	caster (granulated) sugar	150 g/5 oz
I pinch	ground cinnamon	I pinch
I pinch	salt	I pinch
1½ quarts	milk	1.5 litres/ 2½ pints

Blanch the rice by putting it in a saucepan with a small quantity of water and bringing it to the boil. Drain, place in a bowl and add the sugar, spice and salt. Pour over the cooled boiled milk, mix well and put in an ovenproof dish.

Cook in a low oven for 8 hours or until the rice is well browned. Serve cold, accompanied by small sablé, or shortbread, biscuits (cookies).

LYON TIMBALE

Preparation 1 hour • Cooking 40 minutes

US	Ingredients	Met/Imp
I	Vol-au-vent Case (*page 91*)	I
¾ lb	marrons glacés	350 g/12 oz
4	juicy pears	4
4	*reinette* or other eating apples	4
I cup	caster (granulated) sugar	200 g/7 oz
½ cup	kirsch	100 ml/4 fl oz
½ cup	glacé cherries	100 g/4 oz
⅔ cup	candied greengages	100 g/4 oz

Fill the pastry case with marrons glacés, segments of pears and apples cooked in a syrup made from the sugar and kirsch, glacé cherries and the candied greengages. They should all be mixed together with a kirsch-flavoured syrup, thickened with a purée of marrons glacés.

US	Ingredients	Met/Imp
	MOUSSELINE BRIOCHE DOUGH	
3½ cups	flour	500 g/1 lb
½ pkg	fresh (compressed) yeast	10 g/⅓ oz
3 sticks plus 1 tbsp	good-quality unsalted butter	375 g/13 oz
2 tsp	salt	10 g/⅓ oz
5 tsp	caster (granulated) sugar	20 g/¾ oz
6	eggs	6
	FRESH FRUIT SALAD	
¼ lb each	fresh seasonal fruits (eg strawberries, grapes, cherries)	125 g/4½ oz each
1 cup	sugar syrup: 18° Baumé (page 575)	200 ml/7 fl oz
½ cup	kirsch or rum	100 ml/3½ fl oz
1 cup	apricot marmelade	150 g/5 oz
8	apples	8
10 tbsp	good-quality unsalted butter	150 g/5 oz
½ cup	caster (superfine) sugar	100 g/4 oz
1	lemon, finely grated rind of	1
8	biscottes	8
1 cup	strawberries	150 g/5 oz
1	egg white	1
	Puff Pastry (page 579)	
	Royal Icing (page 585)	

PARISIAN TIMBALE

Preparation 48 hours • Cooking brioche 1 hour

The day before, make the mousseline brioche dough according to the instructions on page 577. Leave to rest in a cold place.

The next day, put the dough into a charlotte mould, leave it to rise in a warm place, then bake in a moderate oven for 1 hour. Leave to cool.

Prepare a *macédoine* of seasonal fresh fruits. Cut the fruit into pieces of equal size and sweeten with the sugar syrup. Flavour with the chosen liqueur or spirit then, at the last moment, thicken with the apricot marmelade.

Hollow out the brioche, fill it with the fruit salad and replace the top. Decorate the outside of the timbale with chopped almonds, sugar crystals, very green chopped pistachio nuts or candied angelica, if liked.

TOASTS AUX POMMES MERINGUÉES

MERINGUE APPLE 'TOASTS'

Preparation 1 hour • Cooking 15–20 minutes

Use sound medium apples of good quality. Peel and core them and cut them into pieces. Melt some butter in a frying pan and cook the apples, uncovered, for 5 minutes. Add sugar to taste and a little of the lemon rind. Butter the biscottes and spread them with the apple mixture. Place them in an ovenproof dish and arrange the strawberries on top. Beat the egg white to a stiff froth and sweeten with sugar. Spread over the strawberries. Cook in a very hot oven for 15–20 minutes. Eat hot.

PÂTISSERIES

CAKES AND PASTRIES

ALLUMETTES

'MATCHSTICKS'

Preparation 1 hour • Cooking 20–25 minutes

Cut the pastry, which has been 'turned' 6 times and rolled out, into long strips 10 cm/4 inches wide and 1 cm/½ inch thick. Brush off any flour remaining on top and trim neatly with a knife on all 4 sides of each strip, otherwise the pastry will not puff up on the side which has not been cut. Spread with a layer of royal icing, using a knife or palette knife. Divide the strips into 4 cm/1½ inch slices and arrange on a dry baking sheet. Bake in the oven with the door half open for 20–25 minutes.

SPONGE FINGER BISCUITS OR LADYFINGERS

Preparation 1 hour • Cooking 40 minutes

US	Ingredients	Met/Imp
2½ cups	caster (granulated) sugar	500 g/1 lb
16	eggs	16
1 tsp	orange-flower water	5 ml/1 tsp
scant 2 cups	flour, sifted	275 g/9 oz

Beat together the sugar and egg yolks until the mixture leaves a ribbon trail on its surface when the beater is lifted. Mix in the orange-flower water and flour, then fold in the stiffly whisked egg whites. Mix by cutting through and turning over the mixture with a spoon in such a way that you do not break down the egg whites too much. Put the mixture into a cloth piping (pastry) bag fitted with a plain 1 cm/½ inch nozzle. Fold the edges over to close the bag and pipe finger shapes on to sheets of strong parchment paper. Generously dust them with extra sugar then, after a few moments, lift the sheets of paper at both ends and allow the excess sugar to run off. Using a small brush, sprinkle a few drops of water on to the sugar which remains on the surface of the biscuits (cookies), to help make them sparkle.

Put the sheets of paper on to baking sheets and bake in a low oven for 40 minutes.

SAVOY SPONGE CAKE

Preparation 1 hour • Cooking 45 minutes

US	Ingredients	Met/Imp
2½ cups	caster (granulated) sugar	500 g/1 lb
14	eggs	14
2 tbsp	vanilla sugar	1 sachet
1½ cups	plain white flour, sifted	200 g/7 oz
¾ cup	potato flour	100 g/3½ oz
	clarified butter	
	icing (confectioners') sugar	

Beat together the sugar and egg yolks in a bowl until the mixture leaves a ribbon trail on its surface when the beater is lifted. Add the vanilla sugar and flours, then one-quarter of the stiffly whisked egg whites. Mix in thoroughly to increase the volume of the mixture, then add the remaining stiffly whisked egg whites and fold in lightly by cutting through the mixture, lifting it and turning it over.

Carefully coat the inside of the mould (or moulds) with clarified butter, then, just before filling, turn upside-down to let the excess butter drain off. Dust the bottom and sides with a thin layer of a half-and-half mixture of potato flour and icing (confectioners') sugar.

Fill the mould(s) with the mixture, but only two-thirds full as the cake will rise during cooking and fill the mould(s). Bake in a moderate oven for 45 minutes.

US	Ingredients	Met/Imp
scant ½ quantity	Brioche Dough (*page 576*) or Mousseline Brioche Dough (*page 577*)	500 g/1 lb
	SPONGE CAKE	
¾ cup	caster (granulated) sugar	150 g/5 oz
6	eggs	6
½ cup	flour	75 g/3 oz
1⅔ cups	ground almonds	150 g/5 oz
1 pinch	powdered vanilla	1 pinch
2 tbsp	Grand Marnier	30 ml/2 tbsp
	BUTTER CREAM FILLING	
14 tbsp	good-quality unsalted butter	200 g/7 oz
1 cup	caster (granulated) sugar	200 g/7 oz
¼ cup	water	50 ml/2 fl oz
3	egg yolks	3
3 tbsp	Grand Marnier	45 ml/3 tbsp
	JELLY FILLING	
½ cup	raspberry jelly	150 g/5 oz

NANTERRE BRIOCHE

Preparation 24 hours • Cooking 40 minutes

Nanterre brioche is traditionally baked in a rectangular or hexagonal cake tin. You can, in fact, bake a mousseline brioche more easily in a Nanterre brioche tin than in the classic tall and cylindrical brioche tin because domestic ovens are not very high and the top of a tall brioche comes close to the roof of the oven.

Butter a rectangular cake tin and line the sides with a strip of buttered paper which stands about 4 cm/1½ inches above the rim. Divide the dough into 6 or 8 equal portions and put them into the tin, laying them side by side.

Leave the brioche to rise to at least the height of the sides of the tin. Glaze with beaten egg and bake in a moderate oven for 40 minutes. Cover the brioche with buttered greaseproof (parchment) paper if it starts to brown too much and reduce the oven temperature to low after 30 minutes. Unmould the brioche on to a wire rack or wicker tray and leave to cool.

BÛCHE DE NOËL AU GRAND MARNIER

CHRISTMAS LOG WITH GRAND MARNIER

Preparation 1 hour 20 minutes • Cooking 5 minutes

Make the sponge cake. Put the sugar in a bowl placed in a warm *bain-marie*. Add the whole eggs and beat until the mixture leaves a ribbon trail on its surface when the beater is lifted.

Sift together the flour, ground almonds and powdered vanilla. Add to the sugar and egg mixture and combine gently with a wooden spoon. Using a piping (pastry) bag, pipe the mixture in strips close together on a rectangular baking sheet covered with a sheet of parchment paper. (While cooking, the mixture will spread out evenly.) Bake in a moderate oven for 5–6 minutes or until light golden, watching very carefully to see that the sponge does not cook too much.

Make up the Grand Marnier syrup, then make up the butter cream according to the instructions on page 583 and flavour it with the 45 ml/3 tbsp Grand Marnier.

Turn the cake face down on the work surface and moisten the lining paper with a brush dipped in water. The paper can then be removed very easily. Lightly drench the surface of the sponge with the Grand Marnier syrup and spread the raspberry jelly on the cake using a spatula. Spread half of the Grand Marnier butter cream over the jelly in the same way. Roll up the sponge, applying a little pressure with the fingertips in order to form a nice, even roll. Cover the cake with the rest of the butter cream and make decorative designs on it as desired, using a fork dipped in warm water.

APPLE TURNOVERS

Preparation 1 hour • Cooking 25 minutes

US	Ingredients	Met/Imp
I lb	Puff Pastry (*page 579*)	500 g/1 lb
about I cup	apple *marmelade*	200 ml/7 fl oz
I	egg	I

Roll out half of the pastry to a strip about 5 mm/¼ inch thick, 50–60 cm/20–25 inches long and about 7.5 cm/3 inches wide. Cut into 8 circles, using a fluted round pastry cutter. Put 15 ml/1 tbsp apple marmelade in the centre of each round and moisten the edges of the pastry with a brush dipped in water. Fold over one side of each round and press lightly to seal the edges.

Roll and cut out the second portion of pastry, fill and fold over in the same way, making a total of 16 turnovers. Place on a moistened baking sheet. Using a brush, glaze the turnovers with beaten egg thinned with a little water and bake in a moderately hot oven for 25 minutes.

VARIATION
The apple marmelade can also be mixed with the same amount of apricot marmelade and a little rum.

PUFF PASTRY COOKIES

Preparation 1 hour • Cooking 20–25 minutes

US	Ingredients	Met/Imp
	Puff Pastry (*page 579*)	
3 tbsp	caster (granulated) sugar	45 ml/3 tbsp

When making the puff pastry, 'turn' 6 times, then roll out until 1 cm/½ inch thick. With a fluted pastry cutter 7.5 cm/3 inches in diameter, cut out about 10 circles from the puff pastry. Sprinkle a little flour on the work surface, then a little sugar. Arrange the circles next to one another on top of the sugar. With one single movement, roll the pastry circles out to a length of 12–15 cm/5–6 inches each. Transfer them to a dry baking sheet with their sugared sides upwards and bake in a moderate oven for 20–25 minutes or until the sugar has melted and the cookies are golden and glossy.

ANISEED AND PISTACHIO GÂTEAU

Preparation 24 hours • Cooking 20 minutes

US	Ingredients	Met/Imp
⅓ basic recipe quantity	Butter Cream (*page 583*)	125 g/4½ oz
	aniseed liqueur	
	green food colouring	
	yellow food colouring	
	oval, square or round Genoese Sponge Cake (*page 580*), made with 250 g/8 oz (about ⅛ basic recipe quantity) batter	
⅓ cup	shelled pistachios	50 g/2 oz

Make up the butter cream, flavour it with aniseed liqueur and colour it very pale green, using a very little green colouring mixed with the same amount of yellow colouring.

Cut the sponge cake horizontally in half. Spread a layer of butter cream on the lower half, then cover with the other half. Cover the whole cake (top and sides) with more of the butter cream. Make a design on the top of the cake with the remaining butter cream, using a piping (pastry) bag fitted with a small fluted nozzle. Pipe the design lengthways on an oval base, diagonally on a square base. (The conventional motif is a ship's anchor.) Sprinkle the finely chopped pistachios around the edge.

US	Ingredients	Met/Imp
½ lb	plain (semisweet) chocolate	250 g/8 oz
3–4 tbsp	rum	3–4 tbsp
1 stick	good-quality unsalted butter	125 g/4 oz
1¾ cups	caster (granulated) sugar	350 g/12 oz
5	eggs	5
1¼ cups	flour	185 g/6½ oz
1 tsp	baking powder	5 ml/1 tsp
1 cup	walnut halves	100 g/4 oz
2	oranges, finely grated rind of	2
1 tbsp	Grand Marnier	15 ml/1 tbsp
1 pinch	salt	1 pinch
	TOPPING	
¼ cup	icing (confectioners') sugar	30 g/1 oz
⅓ cup	cocoa powder	30 g/1 oz
½ tsp	wine vinegar	2.5 ml/½ tsp
	walnut halves	

CHOCOLATE NUT GÂTEAU*

Preparation 35 minutes • Cooking 1 hour 10 minutes • Completion 15 minutes

Break the chocolate into pieces and put in a saucepan with the rum. Melt over a low heat, stirring with a wooden spoon to make a smooth mixture. Remove from the heat and add the diced butter. Mix well, then add the sugar and mix again.

Separate the eggs. Add the egg yolks, one by one, to the chocolate mixture, beating constantly. Add the flour and baking powder and continue stirring the mixture with a wooden spoon until it becomes very smooth. Cut the walnut halves in half and mix them in, then add the orange rind, followed by the Grand Marnier.

Add the salt to the egg whites, beat them to a snow, then fold them gently into the mixture. Thickly butter 2 rectangular cake tins and fill each one three-quarters full. Put each tin on a baking sheet in a low to moderate oven and bake for 1 hour 10 minutes.

Make the topping. Sift together the icing (confectioners') sugar and cocoa powder and mix with a very little cold water to make a fairly fluid cream (the consistency of a custard sauce). Add the vinegar to make the mixture glossy.

When the cake is cooked, dip each tin in cold water 2–3 times; this makes unmoulding very easy. Turn the cakes out on to a wire rack, brush the top of each one (hot or cold) with the prepared chocolate mixture and gently press in some walnuts to decorate.

This cake is excellent just as it is, or it can be accompanied by a coffee-flavoured custard sauce. It will keep very well for several days in an airtight tin.

US	Ingredients	Met/Imp
1 cup plus 2 tbsp	caster (granulated) sugar	225 g/8½ oz
scant ½ cup	water	100 ml/4 fl oz
3 tbsp	Grand Marnier	45 ml/3 tbsp
2 pints	strawberries	500 g/1 lb
2 cups	crème fraîche	500 ml/18 fl oz
2 tbsp	vanilla sugar (optional)	25 g/scant 1 oz
1	Genoese Sponge Cake, 20 cm/8 inches in diameter (page 580)	1
	raspberry jelly	
⅔ cup	blanched almonds (optional)	100 g/4 oz

STRAWBERRY GÂTEAU*

Preparation 1¼ hours • Cooking 2 hours • Serves 6

Put 100 g/4 oz (½ cup) sugar and the water in a saucepan and boil for 2 minutes to form a syrup. Leave to cool, then add the Grand Marnier. Hull and wash the strawberries (quickly so that they do not lose their flavour), then drain.

If the cream is very thick, add 30–45 ml/2–3 tbsp fresh milk. Whisk until thick, then add the remaining sugar, or 100 g/4 oz (½ cup) sugar and 25 g/scant 1 oz (2 tbsp) vanilla sugar. Whisk again for a moment to mix well. (The cream can also be beaten with an electric beater.)

Using a knife with a serrated edge, cut the sponge cake horizontally into 3 layers of equally thickness. Place 1 layer on a plate and, using a brush or spoon, saturate the top evenly with syrup. Spread 15 ml/1 tbsp raspberry jelly on this sponge round, then cover it with a thick layer of whipped cream.

Cut some strawberries in 4 lengthways and arrange them over the cream. Spread a thin layer of cream on the second sponge round and place,

cream side down, on the strawberries on top of the first sponge round. Press gently so that they stick together. Saturate the top of the second round with syrup. Once again spread with a little raspberry jelly, a layer of cream and some strawberries, and cover with the last sponge round which has likewise been spread with cream. Cover all around the sides of the cake with cream, then saturate the top with the rest of the syrup.

Slide a cardboard disc of the same size (covered with foil) under the cake so that you can hold it in 1 hand. Press chopped toasted almonds two-thirds of the way up the side of the cake, if liked. Decorate the centre of the cake with strawberry halves, their tips towards the centre, and surround them with whipped cream. Press some strawberry slices all around the cake (they will stick easily to the cream) and lightly coat the strawberries on top with 1–2 spoonfuls of melted raspberry jelly.

This gâteau should be served very cold. Chill in the refrigerator for 1–2 hours before serving.

GÂTEAU RÉMOIS

RHEIMS CAKE

Preparation 4 hours • Cooking 45 minutes

US	Ingredients	Met/Imp
4 cups	superfine (cake) flour	500 g/1 lb
1 pkg	fresh (compressed) yeast	20 g/¾ oz
scant ½ cup	milk	100 ml/4 fl oz
8	eggs	8
3 sticks	good-quality unsalted butter	375 g/12 oz
1¾ tsp	salt	10 g/⅓ oz
3 tbsp	caster (granulated) sugar	30 g/1 oz

Mix 100 g/4 oz (şcant 1 cup) flour with the yeast in a bowl and pour in the warmed milk. Add the remaining flour and, without allowing the mixture to rise, stir in the eggs which have been warmed in their shells in hot, but not boiling, water. Once the dough is really smooth and soft, leave it in a warm place to rise.

While the dough is rising, half melt the butter, add the salt and sugar to it, mix to form a paste, and set aside. Butter a deep cake tin, such as a traditional deep Savoy cake tin.

Once the dough has doubled in volume, mix in the butter paste and knead the dough until it is perfectly smooth and elastic. Fill the prepared tin half full. Leave to rise until the dough reaches the top of the tin.

Bake the cake in a moderate oven for about 45 minutes. Check carefully that it is cooked before turning it out on to a wire rack or wicker tray.

US	Ingredients	Met/Imp
I	Genoese Sponge Cake (*page 580*), made with 250 g/8 oz (about ⅛ basic recipe quantity) batter	I
¼ lb	candied fruits	100 g/4 oz
	apricot *marmelade*	
I small glass	rum	I small glass
¼ lb	pale pink fondant icing	100 g/4 oz

— RUM AND CANDIED FRUIT GÂTEAU —

Preparation 3 hours

Divide the sponge cake horizontally in half. Spread the bottom half with the diced candied fruits bound together with some apricot marmelade and rum. Cover with the other sponge layer.

Spread the entire cake with apricot marmelade and cover with slightly warm pale pink fondant icing, flavoured with rum.

about ⅙ basic recipe quantity	Genoese Sponge Cake batter (*page 580*)	300 g/10 oz
¾ cup	apricot *marmelade*	150 g/5 oz
	toasted almonds	
	Praline (*page 586*)	

GÂTEAU ROULÉ

— GÂTEAU ROLL —

Preparation 1 hour • Cooking 20 minutes

Bake the sponge batter in a Swiss roll tin (jelly roll pan) for 20 minutes, then remove from the oven and turn out on to a damp, well wrung-out tea-towel (dish towel). Spread with marmelade and roll up immediately (otherwise it will crack). Sprinkle with almonds and crushed praline.

I quantity	Shortcrust Pastry (*page 577*)	250 g/8 oz
¼ lb	Choux Pastry (*page 578*)	100 g/3½ oz
I cup	light vanilla-flavoured Confectioner's Custard (*page 584*)	200 g/7 oz
1½ cups	toasted flaked (sliced) almonds	150 g/5 oz
2½ tbsp	icing (confectioners') sugar	25 g/scant I oz

HÉRISSONS

— 'HEDGEHOGS' —

Preparation 2 hours • Cooking 7–8 minutes

Roll out the shortcrust pastry until 3 mm/⅛ inch thick and cut into rounds 6.5 cm/2½ inches in diameter. Lay them on a dampened baking sheet and prick with a fork. Using a piping (pastry) bag fitted with a 5 mm/¼ inch plain nozzle, pipe a border of choux pastry on each round. Bake in a moderate oven.

Using a piping (pastry) bag fitted with a 2 cm/¾ inch plain nozzle, pipe confectioner's custard into each cake, mounding it up in the centre. Press the almonds into the custard, putting one at the top and the others all around and below, spacing them 1 cm/½ inch apart. Dust with icing (confectioners') sugar and return to a low oven until the custard just begins to colour.

½ lb	Puff Pastry (*page 579*)	250 g/8 oz
	flour	
¾ cup	apricot *marmelade*	150 g/5 oz
I	egg	I
¼ cup	medium sugar crystals	50 g/2 oz

JALOUSIES

— 'VENETIAN BLINDS' —

Preparation 2 hours • Cooking 20–25 minutes

Roll out the puff pastry and cut into 2 strips. Put 1 strip on to a dampened baking sheet and set aside. Put the other strip on the work surface and dust it lightly with flour, then fold it lengthways in half.

Spread the strip of pastry on the baking sheet with apricot marmelade, leaving a clear 4 cm/1½ inch border around the edges. Using the back of a knife blade, cut the other pastry strip every 3 mm/⅛ inch along its folded side, stopping at least 2.5 cm/1 inch from the other side of the strip where the 2 edges of pastry lie on top of one another. (Thus only the centre of the strip is cut.) Having done this, unfold the cut strip and transfer it, carefully so that it does not break, on to the strip which is spread with marmelade. Adjust it and press the pastry down well. Seal the edges of the 2 strips with water, and glaze the surface (but not the edges) with beaten egg. Bake in a moderate oven for 20–25 minutes. When it is taken from the oven, brush with warm apricot marmelade and cut into equal pieces. Sprinkle the pastries with sugar crystals.

MILLE-FEUILLES

MILLE-FEUILLES*

Preparation 2 hours • Cooking 28 minutes

US	Ingredients	Met/Imp
1½ lb	Puff Pastry (page 579)	750 g/1½ lb
2 cups	Confectioner's Custard (page 584)	500 ml/18 fl oz
½ cup	apricot jam or redcurrant jelly	100 ml/3½ fl oz
	icing (confectioners') sugar	

Roll out the puff pastry in a single piece at least 1 cm/½ inch thick. It should be the same size as a baking sheet, ie 40–42 cm/16–17 inches long and 35 cm/14 inches wide. Place the pastry on the baking sheet and prick all over with a fork. Bake in a hot oven for 28 minutes.

When the pastry is cooked, put it on a marble slab and cut it into 3 strips of equal length, each one 11–12 cm/4½–5 inches wide. Spread the first strip thickly with confectioners' custard and cover it completely with the second strip. Spread this with jam or jelly and cover with the third strip. Dust with icing (confectioners') sugar. Cut into 8 equal portions with a very sharp knife, making rectangles measuring 5 × 11–12 cm/ 2 × 4½–5 inches.

MOKAS

MOCHA SLICES

Preparation 24 hours • Cooking 35 minutes

US	Ingredients	Met/Imp
⅛ basic recipe quantity	Genoese Sponge Cake batter (page 580)	250 g/8 oz
⅓ basic recipe quantity	Butter Cream, various flavours (page 583)	250 g/8 oz
5 oz	fondant icing, various flavours	150 g/5 oz
¼ lb	mixed candied fruits, chopped	100 g/3½ oz
⅓ cup	shelled pistachios or chocolate vermicelli (sprinkles)	50 g/2 oz

Spread the sponge batter in a buttered and lined baking tray (jelly roll pan) with sides 4 cm/1½ inches high. Bake in a moderate oven for 30–35 minutes, then leave to cool.

The next day, cut the sponge cake horizontally in half, then cut each layer across into 4 strips. You will thus have 8 separate pieces. Spread the 4 pieces of the bottom sponge layer with butter cream, each with a different flavour, eg vanilla, coffee, chocolate, praline. Put the 4 pieces of the top layer on top and ice each pastry with the fondant icing corresponding to the butter cream. Decorate, as desired, with candied fruits and pistachios or chocolate vermicelli (sprinkles), or even cream.

VARIATION
The Genoese slices can also be filled with a mixture of half confectioner's custard and half softened unsalted butter. Flavour with liqueur.

US	Ingredients	Met/Imp
3½ tbsp	milk	50 ml/2 fl oz
1 pkg	fresh yeast	15 g/½ oz
1¾ cups	flour	250 g/8 oz
9 tbsp	good-quality unsalted butter	125 g/4 oz
4	eggs	4
10 tbsp	caster (granulated) sugar	125 g/4 oz
1⅓ cups	ground almonds	100 g/3½ oz
1 pinch	salt	1 pinch
1 tbsp	kirsch	15 ml/1 tbsp
⅔ cup	blanched whole almonds	100 g/3½ oz

ALMOND BREAD

Preparation 20 minutes, 5 hours in advance • Cooking 40 minutes • Serves 6–8

Warm the milk, pour it over the crumbled yeast and mix well. Put one-third of the flour in a bowl and mix in the milk. Knead by hand, to obtain an elastic dough, then roll into a ball and leave to rise in a warm place for about 1 hour or until doubled in volume. Meanwhile, dice 75 g/3 oz (6 tbsp) butter and work with a fork to soften to a cream.

Put the remaining flour in a large bowl, make a well in the centre and break in 2 eggs, adding 15 ml/1 tbsp warm water. Blend with a wooden spoon, then add 60 g/2½ oz (5 tbsp) sugar, followed by the creamed butter. Knead well with your hands. Put this dough on a floured work surface, make a well in the centre and put in the yeast mixture.

Knead the dough (ie break it into several pieces and combine them again by flattening them with the palm of the hand) several times with floured hands, until the dough acquires an even texture. Roll all the dough into a ball, put it in a bowl and leave it in a warm place for 4–5 hours.

Prepare the butter cream. Blend the remaining butter and sugar together, then add 1 egg, the ground almonds, salt and kirsch and mix well. Put a sheet of foil on a baking sheet and lay out the risen dough on it in an elongated shape. Tip the almond butter cream on top, fold over the dough and form into a loaf shape. Glaze with the remaining egg yolk, beaten with 15 ml/1 tbsp water, then press the whole almonds on to the bread. Bake in a hot oven for 40 minutes.

This almond bread can be eaten warm or cold, and is very good served with tea.

MECCA BUNS

Preparation 1 hour • Cooking 30–35 minutes

US	Ingredients	Met/Imp
2 cups	milk or water	500 ml/18 fl oz
1 pinch	salt	1 pinch
4 tsp	caster (granulated) sugar	15 g/½ oz
4 tbsp	good-quality unsalted butter	50 g/2 oz
1 cup less 1½ tbsp	flour, sifted	125 g/4½ oz
about 8	eggs	about 8
a little	icing (confectioners') sugar	a little
½ cup	sugar crystals	100 g/4 oz

Choux pastry is usually made with water but, for Mecca buns, milk can be used instead. As these buns have no filling, the milk helps to make the pastry more tasty and less dry.

Put the milk in a saucepan with the salt, sugar and butter. Bring to the boil and pour in the flour. Mix and beat over low heat to dry out the dough. Stir constantly until it comes away from the sides of the pan and the spoon. Remove the pan from the heat and immediately add the eggs, 2 at a time at first, then 1 at a time, adding enough to make a soft, smooth dough. Leave to rest for a moment.

Using a piping (pastry) bag fitted with a 7–8 mm/⅓ inch plain round nozzle, pipe the buns into large éclair shapes, ie like elongated choux buns, on to a buttered baking sheet. Dust with icing (confectioners') sugar. With the back of the blade of a kitchen knife dipped in water, make an incision down the length of each bun, then cover immediately with sugar crystals. Bake in a hot oven for 25–30 minutes.

PARIS-BREST

Preparation 1 hour • Cooking 20 minutes

Pipe the choux paste on to an unbuttered baking sheet in the shape of a ring. Sprinkle with almonds, dust with icing (confectioners') sugar and bake in a hot oven at first, then reduce the heat to moderate. Leave to cool, then cut horizontally in half and fill with praline-flavoured confectioner's custard.

US	Ingredients	Met/Imp
I quart	Choux Pastry (page 578)	I litre/1¾ pints
I cup	flaked (sliced) almonds	100 g/3½ oz
	icing (confectioners') sugar	
about ⅓ basic recipe quantity	praline-flavoured Confectioner's Custard (page 584)	250 g/8 oz

PITHIVIERS

Preparation 2 hours • Cooking 40 minutes

Put the sweet and bitter almonds, the butter, sugar, egg yolks and vanilla in a bowl and beat vigorously with a wooden spoon. After mixing, add the confectioner's custard, crème fraîche and the kirsch or rum. Roll out the puff pastry and cut into 4 rounds, 16–18 cm/6½–7 inches in diameter. (For 8 people, it is preferable to make 2 Pithiviers cakes.) Place 2 of the rounds on a baking sheet and brush the circumference of each one with water: Fill the centre of the rounds with the previously prepared almond cream and cover with the remaining pastry rounds. Seal them well together and scallop with a kitchen knife to make a fluted edge, thus strengthening the join.

Glaze the tops of the cakes by brushing with beaten egg and decorate the pastry with a kitchen knife or fork. Bake in a low oven for 40 minutes.

US	Ingredients	Met/Imp
1⅓ cups	ground sweet almonds	100 g/4 oz
I tbsp	ground bitter almonds	15 ml/1 tbsp
I stick	good-quality unsalted butter, softened	100 g/4 oz
½ cup	caster (granulated) sugar	100 g/4 oz
3	egg yolks	3
¼ tsp	powdered vanilla	¼ teaspoon
½ cup	Confectioner's Custard (page 584)	100 ml/4 fl oz
½ cup	crème fraîche	100 ml/4 fl oz
¼ cup	kirsch or rum	50 ml/2 fl oz
I lb	Puff Pastry (page 579)	500 g/1 lb
I	whole egg, beaten	I

PLUM CAKE

Preparation 1 hour • Soaking 48 hours • Cooking 1–1¼ hours

Shake the sultanas (golden raisins) and currants with a little flour in a cloth. Rub them well, then shake them in a large metal sieve to remove any impurities. When they are clean, put them in a bowl with the seeded muscat raisins, the candied fruit and the rum. Leave to soak for 48 hours.

Put the butter in a warm place to soften, then beat it in a bowl with a wooden spoon. Add the sugar and pour in the flour, beating continuously. Add the eggs, 2 by 2, beating well. When the paste is well blended, add the soaked fruits and raisins. From this moment on, only mix gently and do not beat the paste any more.

Butter a rectangular tin or tins and line the bottom and sides with strips of parchment paper, allowing the paper to stand 1–2 cm/½–¾ inch above the sides of the tin(s). Fill the tin(s) no more than three-quarters full with the mixture. Leave to rest for a few minutes before baking at a moderate heat for 1–1¼ hours.

US	Ingredients	Met/Imp
1⅔ cups	sultanas (golden raisins), currants and muscat raisins	250 g/8 oz
⅔ cup	finely diced candied fruit pieces, eg cherries, orange peel, angelica	125 g/4 oz
½ cup	rum	100 ml/4 fl oz
2 sticks	good-quality unsalted butter	250 g/8 oz
1¼ cups	caster (granulated) sugar	250 g/8 oz
1¾ cups	flour, sifted	250 g/8 oz
6–8	eggs	6–8

US	Ingredients	Met/Imp
½ lb	Puff Pastry (page 579)	250 g/8 oz
1	egg	1
½ lb	cherries, mirabelle plums or apricots	250 g/8 oz
scant 1 cup	icing (confectioners') sugar	100 g/3½ oz

'POLONAIS'

Preparation 1 hour • Cooking 8–10 minutes

The puff pastry should be 'turned' 6 times and rolled out 1 cm/½ inch thick. Cut out rounds about 7.5 cm/3 inches in diameter with a fluted pastry cutter and place them on a dampened baking sheet. Press each round firmly in the centre with your thumb to make a hollow. Glaze with beaten egg and score with a knife. Fill each hollowed round with 4 cherries, 3 mirabelle plums or half an apricot. Bake in a hot oven for 8–10 minutes. Dust with icing (confectioners') sugar, then return to the oven to glaze.

US	Ingredients	Met/Imp
½ basic recipe quantity	Sweet Pastry (page 582)	250 g/8 oz
1–1½ cups	Frangipane (page 584)	200 g/7 oz
16	small chocolate or coffee choux buns	16
about ⅛ basic recipe quantity	Butter Cream (page 583)	100 g/3½ oz

'RELIGIEUSES'

Preparation 1 hour • Cooking 15 minutes

Line 16 small round moulds with the pastry and crimp the edges. Fill them two-thirds full with frangipane and bake in a moderate oven for 15 minutes. Leave to cool.

Put a filled and iced chocolate or coffee choux bun on each pastry base. Pipe a line of butter cream dots all around the base and the choux bun, using a piping (pastry) bag with a fluted nozzle. Pipe a rosette of butter cream on the top.

US	Ingredients	Met/Imp
5	large eggs	5
about 3 sticks	good-quality unsalted butter	about 350 g/12 oz
about 1¾ cups	caster (granulated) sugar	about 350 g/12 oz
1	lemon, finely grated rind of	1
about 2⅓ cups	flour	about 350 g/12 oz
1 pinch	salt	1 pinch

POUND CAKE

Preparation 30 minutes • Cooking 50 minutes

The weight of the sugar, flour and butter should be exactly the same as the weight of the eggs.

Break the eggs one at a time into a cup to make sure they are perfectly fresh. Put them all together in a bowl. Put the butter in a small heavy-based saucepan over a very low heat until soft but not melted. When the butter is of a paste-like consistency, beat it well so that there are no lumps, then remove it from the heat and leave it to stand. Add the sugar and lemon rind to the eggs, mix, then beat with a whisk until pale, increased in volume and light and foamy.

Sift the flour and salt through a fine sieve to remove any lumps. Blend it into the egg and lemon mixture, then add the softened butter to obtain a thick mixture which holds its shape very well.

Thickly butter a square tin with fairly high sides. Line it with a sheet of parchment paper the same size as the bottom and butter the paper in the same way. Tip the mixture into the tin. It is better not to fill the tin completely, to allow the cake to rise slightly. Bake in a low to moderate

oven for about 50 minutes. Take the cake out of the oven, leave to cool in the tin for 15 minutes, then turn out on to a wire rack.

If you wish to keep this cake for several days, wrap it in foil as soon as it is cold.

VARIATIONS

This pound cake goes well with tea. To serve as part of a dessert, serve it with vanilla or chocolate custard sauce or a lemon mousse. The pound cake can also be flavoured with 30 ml/2 tbsp orange-flower water, kirsch or rum.

SAINT-HONORÉ

———— GÂTEAU SAINT-HONORÉ* ————

Preparation 2 hours • Cooking 30 minutes

US	Ingredients	Met/Imp
⅓ basic recipe quantity	Shortcrust Pastry (page 577)	100 g/4 oz
10 oz	Choux Pastry (page 578)	300 g/10 oz
I	beaten egg, for glazing	I
10 tbsp	sugar	125 g/4½ oz
1½ tbsp	honey	30 g/1 oz
I cup	Chantilly Cream (page 583) or Confectioner's Custard (page 584)	200 ml/7 fl oz

This is the 'king' of cream cakes. It is made in 3 stages: the pastry base, the choux crown and the cream filling.

Roll out the shortcrust pastry until it is 3 mm/⅛ inch thick and cut out a 20 cm/8 inch circle. Put on a baking sheet.

Using a cloth piping (pastry) bag fitted with a 2 cm/¾ inch plain round nozzle, and filled with choux pastry, pipe a border, the diameter of the nozzle, around the edge of the pastry base. Prick the base, so that it will not rise during cooking and pipe a choux pastry 'comma' in the centre of the shortcrust to help prevent burning. Glaze the choux border with beaten egg and bake in a moderate oven for about 30 minutes. Leave to cool.

Using a piping (pastry) bag fitted with a 1 cm/½ inch nozzle, pipe about 24 small dome-shaped choux buns, about the size of 2 large plums, on to a baking sheet. Glaze with beaten egg and bake in a hot oven. Leave to cool.

Cook the sugar with the honey to the hard crack stage (*page 575*). Holding a choux bun by its base, dip the top into the sugar syrup, then dab a little of this on to the choux ring. Stick the base of the choux bun on to the choux ring. Repeat with the remaining choux buns and syrup, arranging them immediately next to each other so that they stick together as a crown.

The Saint-Honoré can be filled with Chantilly cream, or with confectioner's custard made lighter with the addition of egg whites.

US	Ingredients	Met/Imp
	flaked (sliced) almonds	
⅓ basic recipe quantity	Savarin Dough (*page 581*)	500 g/1 lb
scant 1 cup	liqueur or *eau-de-vie*	200 ml/7 fl oz
1 cup	Chantilly Cream (*page 583*)	250 ml/9 fl oz
	SYRUP	
1½ cups	sugar	300 g/10 oz
	finely grated lemon rind, ground cinnamon or vanilla pod (bean), to flavour	

CHANTILLY CREAM SAVARIN

Preparation 3 hours • Cooking 30–40 minutes

Butter a plain ring mould, ie a savarin mould. Scatter a few almonds in the bottom, then fill the mould two-thirds full with the savarin dough. Leave it to rise to the height of the mould, then bake in a moderate oven for 30–40 minutes. Turn out on to a wire rack.

Prepare the syrup. Put the sugar in a heavy-based saucepan with 450 ml/¾ pint (2 cups) water, bring just to the boil and skim, then add the flavouring of your choice.

Put a dish underneath the wire rack and sprinkle the savarin with the hot syrup. Collect the syrup in the dish, reheat it and pour it over the savarin once again, until the cake is well saturated. You will be able to remove the cake without breaking it by holding the rack. Leave the soaked cake until completely cold before serving.

Just before serving, slide the savarin on to a round plate. Sprinkle liberally with liqueur or eau-de-vie and fill the centre with Chantilly cream. Put the remaining cream in a piping (pastry) bag fitted with a fluted nozzle and pipe a dome-shaped decoration on top of the savarin and a border of rosettes around the base.

SINGAPORE CAKE

Preparation 2 hours • Cooking Genoese sponge 30 minutes

US	Ingredients	Met/Imp
¼ basic rec quantity	Genoese Sponge Cake batter (*page 580*)	500 g/1 lb
4	canned pineapple slices	4
1	chinois (small candied Chinese orange)	1
3½ tbsp	kirsch	50 ml/2 fl oz
1 cup	apricot *marmelade*	200 ml/8 fl oz
⅔ cup	toasted almonds	100 g/4 oz
16	blanched almond halves	16

Put the sponge batter into a 22–25 cm/8½–10 inch round tin or, if unavailable, a square or rectangular tin. Bake for 30 minutes. Turn out and leave to cool.

Meanwhile, cut 2 slices of pineapple into 8 triangles 2.5 cm/1 inch wide at the bottom and 4 cm/1½ inches long. Set them aside.

Finely chop all the remaining pineapple and half of the Chinese orange, then soak the fruit in the kirsch. Thicken with 15–30 ml/ 1–2 tbsp apricot marmelade.

Slice the Genoese sponge horizontally in half. Spread the well-blended pineapple and orange mixture on the lower half and cover with the top half. Spread apricot marmelade thickly over the top and sides of the cake and press chopped or flaked (sliced) toasted almonds on to the sides to give a rough finish. Place the remaining half of the Chinese orange in the centre of the cake and surround it with 8 almond halves. Coat the 8 triangles of pineapple with apricot marmelade and place round the top edge of the cake, their points towards the centre. As a finishing touch, place the 8 remaining almond halves on or between the pineapple triangles.

APRICOT TART
WITH FRANGIPANE CREAM

Preparation 30 minutes • To be prepared about 2 hours in advance • Cooking 20 minutes • Finishing 10 minutes

US	Ingredients	Met/Imp
	SHORTCRUST PASTRY	
I tsp	salt	5 g/I tsp
about 6 tbsp	water	about 100 ml/ 6½ tbsp
I stick	good-quality unsalted butter	125 g/4 oz
1¾ cups	flour	250 g/8 oz
	FRANGIPANE CREAM	
¾ cup	flour, sifted	100 g/4 oz
½ cup	caster (granulated) sugar	100 g/4 oz
I pinch	salt	I pinch
I	whole egg	I
4	egg yolks	4
2 cups	milk	500 ml/18 fl oz
½ tsp	powdered vanilla	2.5 ml/½ tsp
4 tbsp	good-quality unsalted butter	50 g/2 oz
⅓ cup	ground almonds	30 g/I oz
	DECORATION	
2 lb	fresh apricots and sugar syrup	I kg/2 lb
	or	
I jar	apricots in syrup	I jar
¼ cup	sugar crystals	50 g/2 oz

Make the shortcrust pastry according to the instructions on page 577. Wrap the ball of pastry in parchment paper and keep it cold for about 2 hours.

Make the frangipane cream. Beat together the flour, sugar, salt, whole egg and egg yolks for 2–3 minutes. Pour in the boiled milk, flavoured with vanilla. Bring to the boil over a gentle heat and cook for 2 minutes, stirring constantly, as for a confectioner's custard (*page 584*). Remove from the heat and add the butter, then the ground almonds. Mix well. Pour the cream into a bowl and dot the surface with small pieces of butter to prevent a skin forming. Leave the cream to cool.

Cut fresh apricots in half and remove the stones. Poach them in sugar syrup. Alternatively, open a jar of apricots in syrup. Drain the apricots in a sieve and set them aside.

Butter a 30.5 cm/11 inch tart tin. Roll out the pastry on a lightly floured surface and use to line the tin. Prick the pastry with a fork in several places, then cover with a sheet of parchment paper, cut the same size as the tart tin. Put dried beans or rice on to the paper (to stop the pastry rising during cooking) and bake the pastry case in a hot oven for about 20 minutes. Take out of the oven and remove the paper and beans. Fill the tart with frangipane cream and smooth with the back of a spoon. Arrange the apricot halves on top. To serve, dust lightly with sugar crystals.

ALSACIENNE TART*

Preparation 2 hours • 1st Cooking 15 minutes • 2nd Cooking 10 minutes

US	Ingredients	Met/Imp
scant I quantity	Sweet Pastry (*page 582*)	400 g/14 oz
8	reinette or other eating apples, or pears sugar syrup: 24° Baumé (*page 575*)	8
2 cups	Vanilla Custard Sauce (*page 583*)	500 ml/18 fl oz
½	glacé cherry	½
scant I cup	fresh cream, to serve	200 ml/7 fl oz

Line a fairly high-sided flan ring placed on a baking sheet with the pastry and finish it off with a fluted edge. Line with paper and fill with dried beans or cherry stones so that the pastry base does not rise during cooking. Bake in a low to moderate oven for 15 minutes.

Peel, core and quarter the apples or pears and poach them in the syrup. Drain them on a cloth. Arrange them in a circle in the pastry case and top them with the vanilla custard sauce. Bake in a moderate oven for 10 minutes, then leave to cool. Top with half a glacé cherry and serve with a bowl of fresh cream on the side.

VARIATION

If you wish, the fruit may be cut into very neat slices and arranged so that the slices overlap one another, with no gaps in between.

US	Ingredients	Met/Imp
I quantity	Shortcrust Pastry (page 577)	250 g/8 oz
1–1½ cups	Frangipane (page 584)	250 g/8 oz
I	egg	I
scant ½ cup	icing (confectioners') sugar	50 g/2 oz

FRANGIPANE TART

Preparation 3 hours • Cooking 45 minutes

Line a tart tin with shortcrust pastry and fill with frangipane to the top of the tin. Smooth the top well.

Roll out remaining shortcrust pastry 3 mm/⅛ inch thick and cut out a strip 35–40 cm/14–16 inches long and 1–2 cm/½–¾ inch wide. Using a pastry wheel, make a series of diagonal cuts at 1 cm/½ inch intervals along one side and across half the width of the strip. Fold the strip over to make a double thickness, then hold it in your left hand and make a spiral out of it, starting from the centre with the cuts turned outwards, so that they form a crest. This motif is called a 'fleuron' (floret).

Brush the fleuron with beaten egg and bake the tart in a hot oven for 45 minutes. Shortly before the end of cooking, dust the tart with icing (confectioners') sugar and return to the oven to glaze.

ENGLISH APPLE TART

Preparation 1 hour • Cooking 35 minutes

US	Ingredients	Met/Imp
	SHORTCRUST PASTRY	
I pinch	salt	I pinch
2 sticks	good-quality unsalted butter	250 g/8 oz
1¾ cups	flour	250 g/8 oz
6	sound apples, eg *calvilles* or other eating apples	6
½ cup	caster (granulated) sugar	100 g/3½ oz
scant ½ cup	apricot *marmelade* or apple jelly	100 ml/4 fl oz
I	egg	I

Make the shortcrust pastry according to the instructions on page 577. Roll out and use to line a tart tin. Prick with a fork and fill with peeled and cored apple segments. Dust with sugar and spread with apricot marmelade or apple jelly. Make a lattice top with strips of rolled-out leftover pastry, spacing them evenly. Brush with beaten egg and bake in a moderate oven for 35 minutes.

POMPADOUR TART

Preparation 2 hours • Cooking 40 minutes

Recipe from Lucien Tibier, former chef to president Auriol, at the Élysée Palace

US	Ingredients	Met/Imp
I quantity	Sweet Pastry (page 582)	500 g/1 lb
I stick	good-quality unsalted butter	125 g/4½ oz
4½ oz	plain (semisweet) chocolate	125 g/4½ oz
1⅓ cups	ground almonds	125 g/4½ oz
10 tbsp	caster sugar	125 g/4½ oz
4	eggs	4
3 tbsp	flour	25 g/scant 1 oz
½ tsp	ground cinnamon	2.5 ml/½ tsp
⅓	clove	⅓
scant 1 cup	unwhipped *crème fraîche*	200 ml/7 fl oz

Line the bottom and sides of a deep 25–28 cm/10–11 inch flan ring placed on a baking sheet with the pastry. Prick with a fork and leave to rest.

In a bowl, beat together the softened butter, grated chocolate, ground almonds, sugar and egg yolks. Add the flour, cinnamon and crushed piece of clove and continue beating until the mixture leaves a ribbon trail on its surface when the beater is lifted.

Whisk the egg whites until stiff, then fold into the chocolate mixture. Use to fill the pastry case and bake in a moderately hot oven for 40 minutes. Serve with the half-whipped crème fraîche in a bowl or sauce boat on the side.

Mille-Feuilles
Showing the layers of puff pastry perfectly, this cake may be filled in several ways: usually with confectioner's custard, sometimes with jam. In this case it is filled with both. (Recipe on page 633.)

Marron Glacé Charlotte
The principle of the 'charlotte' consists of a filling in a mould lined with sponge
fingers (ladyfingers). There is a whole range of variations: here, the mould is lined
with slices of Genoese sponge cake made with hazelnuts (filberts), then filled with a
sumptuous cream made of marrons glacés, unsalted butter and vanilla-flavoured
whipped cream, making it a particularly rich dessert. (Recipe on page 592.)

Strawberry Gâteau

The preparation of this strawberry gâteau demands a precise succession of delicate operations: an undercrust of Genoese sponge cake is made and soaked in syrup, coa with raspberry jelly and whipped cream, then topped with strawberries. You can repeat these layers once more if you like, or simply finish the cake with a layer of pla

sponge cake, soaked in syrup. For the decoration, pink glacé icing looks most effective, topped with fresh strawberries coated with raspberry jelly. Alternatively, the cake can be covered with cream and decorated with nuts and strawberries, as in the recipe on page 630.

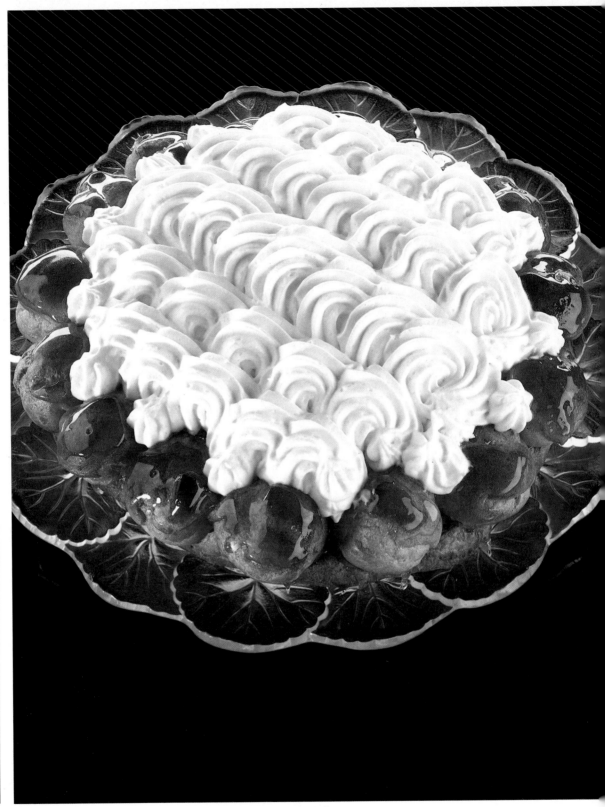

Gâteau Saint-Honoré
The 'Saint-Honoré' is said to owe its name to the patron saint of pastry makers, bu[t]
its crème pâtissière (confectioner's custard), made lighter with egg whites, was
actually created by Chiboust, established in the rue Saint-Honoré in Paris in the
19th century. (Recipe on page 637.)

Sugar-Coated and Marzipan Fruits
*Delicious dainties served at the end of a meal, these 'disguised' fruits owe their
attraction to their brilliant colours and wide range of flavours. (Recipe on page 662.)*

Neapolitan Slices
With its layers of three visually attractive flavours, this iced dessert recalls the pre-eminence of the Neapolitan ice cream makers in Paris at the beginning of the 19th century. (*Recipe on page 648.*)

	US	Ingredients	Met/Imp
# RICE TARTLETS	10 oz	Puff Pastry (page 577)	300 g/10 oz
	1 cup	short-grain rice, cooked and prepared as for Rice in Milk for Desserts (page 620)	200 g/7 oz
Preparation 1¼ hours • Cooking 30 minutes	3½ tbsp	rum	50 ml/2 fl oz
		apricot jam	
		glacé cherry, blanched almond or candied angelica, to decorate	

Line 8 well-buttered tartlet tins with puff pastry – the shape of the tins is unimportant. When lining the tins, take a walnut-sized piece of pastry, flour it and press it against the pastry inside the tins so that the pastry assumes their shape and contour. Fill with the rice, which should be very soft and well-flavoured with the rum. Bake in a moderate oven for 25–30 minutes, remove from the oven and leave to settle very briefly, but keep warm.

Both for the taste and the appearance of this kind of tartlet, it is preferable, when they have settled a little, to glaze them well with apricot jam and to put half a cherry, half a blanched almond or a lozenge of angelica on top. Serve on a napkin or paper doily.

GLACES ET ENTREMETS GLACÉS

ICES AND ICED DESSERTS

PÂTE À BOMBE GLACÉE

# BASIC ICED BOMBE MIXTURE	US	Ingredients	Met/Imp
		SYRUP	
Preparation 1 hour • Cooking 20 minutes	3¾ cups	sugar	750 g/1½ lb
		BOMBE	
	32	egg yolks	32

Make a syrup (30° Baumé – page 575) with the sugar and 1 litre/1¾ pints (1 quart) water. Boil until 1 litre/1¾ pints (1 quart) syrup is obtained. Beat the syrup into the egg yolks with 50 ml/2 fl oz (3½ tbsp) cold water.

Once the egg yolks and syrup are well mixed, strain the mixture through a sieve into a container, bowl or saucepan. Put in a *bain-marie* and cook gently for 20 minutes, stirring frequently. Alternatively, cook over a low heat, stirring constantly.

Once the mixture is cooked, place it over ice and beat until it has become light, foamy and completely cold.

If this dessert is stored chilled, over ice if possible, it will keep for 4 days in winter, 2 in summer.

US	Ingredients	Met/Imp
4 pints	strawberries, preferably wild	1 kg/2 lb
5 tbsp	caster (granulated) sugar	75 ml/5 tbsp
⅔ cup	curaçao	150 ml/¼ pint
1 small glass	champagne	1 small glass
1¾ cups	whipping cream	400 ml/14 fl oz
2 tbsp	vanilla sugar	1 sachet
1½ quarts	lemon ice cream	1.5 litres/ 2½ pints
1	candied orange	1
⅓ cup	crystallized violets	60 g/2½ oz
1	mint sprig	1

——— STRAWBERRIES GINETTE* ———

Preparation 3 hours

Put the strawberries in a bowl and dust them with 45 ml/3 tbsp sugar. Sprinkle with the curaçao and champagne and leave to soak for 30 minutes, turning them over from time to time so that they become impregnated with the alcohol.

Whip the cream and flavour with the remaining sugar and vanilla sugar.

Spread the lemon ice cream to an even thickness in a large crystal bowl. Put all but 1 of the strawberries on top and sprinkle with their syrup, strained through cheesecloth to remove any little seeds. Add the candied orange, sliced. Quickly spoon the whipped cream into the centre of the strawberries, then sprinkle with the lightly crushed violets. Finish with the reserved strawberry and a mint sprig.

1¼ lb	wild or 'four-seasons' strawberries	600 g/1¼ lb
1¾ cups	caster (granulated) sugar	350 g/12 oz
1¼ cups	water	300 ml/½ pint
2	oranges, juice of	2
1	lemon, juice of	1
	crushed ice	
	sea salt	
	saltpetre	

——— STRAWBERRY ICE ———

Preparation 3 hours

To prepare this ice, the following equipment will be needed: a sorbetière or electric or hand-cranked ice cream maker, an ice tub and a spatula. Nowadays, the coldest part of the refrigerator (freezing compartment) or freezer can be used instead.

Work the strawberries through a fine cloth sieve. Dissolve the sugar in the water and boil for 2 minutes to obtain a syrup (28° Baumé – page 575). Leave to cool, when the Baumé will increase to 32°, due to evaporation causing increased concentration.

When very cold, mix the syrup into the strawberry purée and add the orange and lemon juices. Check the degree of concentration using a saccharometer (an indispensable utensil), which should indicate 18° on the graduated scale. If the reading is higher, add a little water to correct it.

Surround a sorbetière with alternate layers of ice, sea salt and saltpetre at least 15 minutes beforehand, as follows: use a sorbetière with a 3 litre/5¼ pint (3 quart) capacity and place a layer of crushed ice in the bottom of the tub. Sprinkle a large handful of sea salt and a little pulverized saltpetre on top. Close the sorbetière with a round piece of paper under its lid and put it on the layer of ice in the tub. Surround with layers of crushed ice, salt and saltpetre up to the top of the tub. (To pack a standard sorbetière, 10–12 kg/22–26 lb ice, 2 kg/4½ lb salt and about 250 g/8 oz saltpetre are needed.) The salt and saltpetre will effect the freezing of the mixture, syrup or cream, contained in the sorbetière.

At least 15 minutes after packing the ice, pour the strawberry mixture into the sorbetière. Seal with a round of paper to secure the lid, then take hold of the handle and churn briskly from right to left for 5

minutes. Open the sorbetière and, using the spatula, scrape off the first layer of ice from the sides and let it fall back into the mass. Reseal the sorbetière and continue churning as before, scraping the ice off the sides every 5 minutes. Once the mixture has frozen and forms a solid mass, work it with the spatula to make it smooth. Prepared like this, strawberry ice, and every other kind of fruit ice as well, can be served 'en rocher', that is, piled up in spoonfuls on a dish covered with a napkin, in a little mound resembling a rough contoured rock. It can also be served in glass or porcelain shell-shaped dishes but, in this case, the ice should be kept hard.

If the sorbet remains for some time in the sorbetière, carefully drain off some of the melted water from the crushed ice, and replace it with more crushed ice, salt and saltpetre around the sorbetière.

The sorbet can also be moulded. Put the already-frozen mixture into the chosen mould, pressing it in with a spoon so that there are no cavities. Cover with a round piece of white paper, slightly larger than the diameter of the mould. Secure the cover which will fit tightly on the mould because of the paper folded over the edges. As a safety measure, the seam between the cover and the mould can also be smeared with butter or margarine which will become as hard as stone when in contact with the ice. Any infiltration of salty water into the mould can thus be prevented.

Pack the mould in a narrow tub with crushed ice, salt and saltpetre, as described previously. Cover it with ice and salt and leave like this, over the ice, for 1 hour.

However, if an ice mixture is put in a mould without having been frozen in advance, it will require at least 2 hours to freeze solid.

To unmould, remove the mould from the ice and rinse it with cold water. Dip it briskly in hot water and unmould on to a folded napkin or a doily.

To make an ice in an electric machine, fit the sorbetière on to the central axle and pack with crushed ice, salt and saltpetre as instructed previously. The proportions will naturally vary depending on the size of the tub. This packing of the ice should always be done 15 minutes in advance, to make sure that the inside of the container is thoroughly cold.

Pour in the mixture to be frozen, close the sorbetière tightly and start rotating it with the handle. There is no need to scrape off the mixture which sticks to the sides, as with the sorbetière worked by hand; this scraping is done automatically by the working of a paddle inside.

These ices with a fruit juice or acid base are known as 'thin ices'; the other kind are known as 'cream ices' or 'rich ices'.

US	Ingredients	Met/Imp
4	egg yolks	4
I cup	caster (granulated) sugar	200 g/7 oz
I cup	milk	250 ml/9 fl oz
I small cup	very strong coffee	I small cup
	or	
I tbsp	instant coffee powder	15 ml/I tbsp
	or	
2 tsp	coffee essence (extract)	10 ml/2 tsp
scant I cup	crème fraîche	200 ml/7 fl oz
½ cup	liqueur-filled coffee beans (optional)	100 g/4 oz

COFFEE ICE CREAM

Preparation and cooking 25 minutes • Freezing 5–6 hours • Serves 4–5

Beat the egg yolks and sugar together until the mixture leaves a ribbon trail on its surface when the beater is lifted. Boil the milk and pour on to the egg and sugar mixture, stirring constantly. Cook over a very low heat until the foam disappears from the surface and the custard coats the back of the spoon. Remove from the heat.

Strain the custard and mix in the coffee. (If it is in powder form, dilute it first in a very little water.) Lightly whisk the crème fraîche, add it to the cooled custard and mix well. Pour into a freezer container rinsed with cold water and put it into the freezer or freezing compartment of the refrigerator.

When half set, beat the frozen cream for some time with a fork in order to make it soft and pliable. Add the liqueur coffee beans, if liked, reserving some for the final decoration. Pack the ice cream in a mould, in an ice cube tray or in freezerproof glasses and refreeze. Serve in the glasses, or dip the mould or ice cube tray in cold or warm water for a few moments and then unmould. Decorate with the reserved liqueur coffee beans.

2 cups	Vanilla Custard Sauce (*page 583*), flavoured with chocolate	500 ml/18 fl oz
I quart	whipped cream	I litre/1¾ pints

ICED CHOCOLATE MOUSSE

Preparation 3 hours

Prepare a very strongly flavoured chocolate custard sauce. Half-freeze it, stirring occasionally, then mix it with the whipped cream. Put it into a mould and freeze.

I cup	fresh fruit pulp	250 ml/8 fl oz
1¼ cups	caster (granulated) sugar	250 g/8 oz
2	gelatine leaves	2
	or	
½ tbsp	powdered (unflavoured) gelatine	7.5 ml/½ tbsp
3½ tbsp	water	50 ml/2 fl oz
2½ cups	whipped cream	600 ml/I pint
I	lemon, juice of	I

ICED FRUIT MOUSSE

Preparation 3 hours

Mix the fresh fruit pulp with the sugar and stir with a silver spoon or spatula to help the sugar dissolve. Dissolve the gelatine in the water and stir into the fruit. Fold in the whipped cream and lemon juice. Freeze rapidly.

VARIATION
Whatever kind of fruit purée you use, the process is the same. You can use fruit preserved in its own juice or in syrup, or fruit that has been specially preserved for ice cream, that is, chilled, uncooked, and mixed with 1½ times its own weight in sugar. Always freeze it rapidly, and allow at least 2 hours in the freezer before unmoulding.

	US	Ingredients	Met/Imp

MOUSSE GLACÉE À LA VANILLE

ICED VANILLA MOUSSE

Preparation 3 hours

Make the sugar syrup, then infuse in it the vanilla pods (beans), split in half. Soak the gelatine, then melt in the syrup. Leave to cool.

Chill the mousse mould. Once the syrup is cool, remove the vanilla and gently fold in the whipped cream. When it is well mixed, pour into the mould, filling it as full as possible. Cover with a piece of paper, then with the lid, and pack ice tightly around the mould.

This mousse can be made without gelatine, but then it must be made very quickly otherwise the mixture will separate and the syrup will sink to the bottom and will not freeze; the cream will develop ice crystals.

US	Ingredients	Met/Imp
2 cups	sugar syrup: 30° Baumé (*page 575*)	500 ml/18 fl oz
1½	vanilla pods (beans)	1½
2	gelatine leaves	2
	or	
½ tbsp	powdered (unflavoured) gelatine	7.5 ml/½ tbsp
2 cups	whipped cream	500 ml/18 fl oz

MOUSSE À LA LIQUEUR À L'ANCIENNE

LIQUEUR MOUSSE 'ANCIENNE'

Preparation 40 minutes • Freezing 3 hours

Prepare a charlotte mould with a lid or, better silll, a Marie-Louise mould (a rectangular mould with a lid). Line the bottom and sides with paper.

Put the caster (granulated) sugar, egg yolks and whole egg in an egg bowl (an untinned copper bowl). Starting gently, beat with a whisk until the mixture becomes very frothy. Continue whisking, at the same time making the Chantilly by whipping the crème fraîche with an electric beater and adding the icing (confectioners') sugar to it. Combine the 2 mixtures very gently, using a whisk. Flavour with the spirit or liqueur of your choice.

Tip this very frothy mixture into the prepared mould. Cover with a sheet of parchment paper and put the lid on firmly. This should seal it sufficiently. As a precaution, however, you can cover the join between the lid and the mould with a thin layer of softened butter. When the mould is sealed, put it in a large stockpot or tub and cover it with crushed ice. Add a few handfuls of coarse salt and cover with a thick cloth or sack. Put in a cool place and leave to freeze for about 3 hours.

To serve, plunge the mould for a few seconds into very hot water, dry it with a cloth and turn the frozen mousse out on to a doily. Remove the lining paper. Serve with crisp sweet biscuits or petits fours. Take care to flavour this mousse strongly as cold, like heat, makes the flavour less strong.

US	Ingredients	Met/Imp
¾ cup	caster (granulated) sugar	150 g/5 oz
7	egg yolks	7
1	whole egg	1
3½ tbsp	spirit or liqueur	50 ml/2 fl oz
	CHANTILLY	
1¼ cups	*crème fraîche*	300 ml/½ pint
scant ¼ cup	vanilla-flavoured icing (confectioners') sugar	50 g/2 oz
	coarse salt	

US	Ingredients	Met/Imp
2 cups	coffee or vanilla Basic Iced Bombe Mixture (page 641)	500 ml/18 fl oz
2½ cups	vanilla-flavoured whipped cream	600 ml/1 pint
	butter or lard	

—— COFFEE OR VANILLA PARFAIT ——

Preparation 3 hours

A parfait must always be frozen immediately, as soon as it is put in the mould. Otherwise the cream can separate and form whey which would collect at the bottom of the mould.

Mix the iced bombe mixture with the whipped cream and turn into a plain, tall, conical mould, filling the mould to the top. Cover with a sheet of parchment paper, then with the lid. Trim off the extra paper and seal the mould and lid with butter or lard so that salt water from the freezing mixture in the sorbetière cannot get into the mould.

To make sure, take care that the salt water never comes up to the top of the mould. Remove surplus water and see that the freezing mixture is tightly packed.

US	Ingredients	Met/Imp
¾ cup	caster (granulated) sugar	150 g/5 oz
2 cups	water	500 ml/18 fl oz
1	vanilla pod (bean)	1
8	peaches	8
	vanilla ice cream	
¼ cup	raspberry purée	60 ml/4 tbsp
	flaked (sliced) almonds (optional)	

—————— PEACH MELBA ——————

Preparation 2 hours

Make a sugar syrup (30° Baumé – page 575) with the sugar, water and vanilla. Halve, stone and peel the peaches and poach in the syrup. Let them cool, then drain and arrange them on vanilla ice cream in a bowl. Spoon over the raspberry purée and sprinkle with almonds, if liked.

HOW TO 'PRESENT' ICE CREAM — —— THE OLD-FASHIONED WAY ——

Take a copper, or other kind of metal, bowl that is larger than the bowl in which the dessert is to be served.

Break up about 1 kg/2 lb ice from an ice block into very coarse pieces. Place in the bowl, fill the gaps with cold water and let the water rise at least 1 cm/½ inch above the chopped ice. Let 2–3 drops of red or green food colouring, or both colours, fall on to the chopped ice.

Fill another, larger container with crushed ice almost like snow. Add a few handfuls of coarse salt. Embed the bowl of coloured ice in this freezing mixture and leave for 4–5 hours or until frozen.

Just before serving, dip the bowl of coloured ice briefly into very hot water and unmould on to a folded napkin so that the water from the ice is absorbed. Use this as a pediment on which to present the bowl containing the ice cream.

SORBETS

Sorbets are very light ices made without milk or cream. As they are only half-frozen, they should be drunk rather than eaten. They come in various flavours, but the basic formula is always as follows:

Ingredients: juice of 1 lemon (or 1 small orange), 150 ml/¼ pint (⅔ cup) fruit juice, champagne, port or sauternes. Enough cold sugar syrup (22° Baumé – page 575) to give a saccharometer reading of 15° when added to the above ingredients. For liqueur-flavoured sorbets, you need 50 ml/2 fl oz (3½ tbsp) liqueur per 500 ml/18 fl oz (2 cups) sugar syrup (18° Baumé).

Freezing: do not stir the mixture while it freezes in the sorbetière. Simply scrape the ice off the sides, letting it fall back into the mixture. Serve in glass dishes.

Italian-style presentation: when the sorbet mixture is fairly firm, gently stir in some whipped cream or meringue mixture. Serve in very tall glasses.

Quantity: allow 1 litre/1¾ pints (1 quart) sorbet to serve 8 people.

SORBET AU MELON

MELON SORBET

Preparation 10 minutes • Freezing about 3 hours

US	Ingredients	Met/Imp
1	perfect melon	1
scant 1 cup	icing (confectioners') sugar	100 g/4 oz
1 tbsp	cream	15 ml/1 tbsp
2 tbsp	kirsch	30 ml/2 tbsp
a few drops	lemon juice	a few drops

Choose a well-ripened melon with a good flavour. Cut out the flesh, discarding the seeds, and reduce it to a purée, either in a blender or with a fine vegetable mill. Add the other ingredients. Whisk, then tip the sorbet into an ice tray or freezer container. Freeze for about 3 hours.

SORBET AUX FRUITS ROUGES

RED FRUIT SORBET

Preparation 30 minutes • Freezing 3 hours

US	Ingredients	Met/Imp
3 pints	strawberries	1 kg/2 lb
2 pints	raspberries	500 g/1 lb
2 pints	blackberries	500 g/1 lb
2¼ cups	caster (granulated) sugar	450 g/15 oz
½	lemon, juice of	½
½	orange, juice of	½

Wash and hull the strawberries. Mash them, then work them through a conical sieve. Collect all the juice. Do the same with the raspberries, then with the blackberries. Mix the 3 juices well together. Add the sugar and stir until dissolved. Finally, add the lemon and orange juices. Tip the mixture into a sorbetière and let it work for about 1 hour.

Tip the sorbet into a cake tin and freeze for another 2 hours. Alternatively, put the mixture directly into the tin and freeze for 3 hours, without using the sorbetière.

To serve, take out some scoops of sorbet with a big spoon and serve them in very cold glass dishes.

US	Ingredients	Met/Imp
2½ cups	caster (granulated) sugar	500 g/1 lb
10	egg whites	10
	kirsch or maraschino (optional)	
2 cups	fruit purée (strawberries, raspberries, etc)	500 ml/18 fl oz
2 cups	cream, very stiffly whipped	500 ml/18 fl oz
⅔ cup	toasted almonds	100 g/4 oz

ICED SOUFFLÉ

Preparation 1 hour • Freezing 2 hours

Dissolve the sugar in a heavy-based saucepan, then boil to the large pearl stage (*page 575*). Whisk the egg whites into a very stiff froth and add the sugar syrup. Transfer to a bowl and leave to cool. Flavour with kirsch or maraschino, if liked, before it has completely cooled. Add the fruit purée, then the whipped cream. Wrap a collar of strong paper around a timbale mould to come about 4 cm/1½ inches above the rim of the mould and attach it firmly by brushing the join with softened butter. Fill the mould with the mixture, pack ice around it and put it in a cold place.

Just before serving, gently remove the paper collar. The ice above the rim of the timbale will give a perfect illusion of a baked soufflé. Sprinkle over the toasted almonds and serve on a napkin.

US	Ingredients	Met/Imp
½ pint	vanilla ice cream	250 ml/9 fl oz
½ pint	strawberry ice cream	250 ml/9 fl oz
½ pint	chocolate ice cream	250 ml/9 fl oz

TRANCHES NAPOLITAINES

NEAPOLITAN SLICES*

Preparation 3 hours

These ice cream slices are generally made in rectangular moulds and are often made of 3 different flavoured ice creams. As the ice creams are frozen before going into the mould, they can simply be placed on top of one another. If you have only 2 flavours, you can put the ice cream into the mould in 4 layers (with alternate layers of each flavour). For example, for a Neapolitan vanilla-strawberry slice, 2 layers of vanilla and 2 layers of strawberry are alternated. This makes it a joy to behold. Neapolitans delight in offering temptation and giving pleasure!

US	Ingredients	Met/Imp
¼–⅓ basic recipe quantity	Italian Meringue mixture (*page 585*)	200 g/7 oz
¼ cup	cocoa powder	25 g/scant 1 oz
½ pint	vanilla ice cream	250 ml/9 fl oz
½ pint	seasonal fruit ice cream	250 ml/9 fl oz
½ pint	chocolate ice cream	250 ml/9 fl oz
scant ½ cup	Chantilly Cream (*page 583*)	100 g/3½ oz
4	peaches, poached in syrup	4
	or	
3½ tbsp	raspberry *eau-de-vie*	50 ml/2 fl oz

VACHERIN LYONNAIS

LYON MERINGUE CAKE

Recipe from M J Nandron, Restaurant Nandron, Lyon

Make some large meringue rings with the Italian meringue mixture. Using the same mixture, at the same time make a few small button-shaped meringues, lightly sprinkled with cocoa. Fill 1 meringue ring with vanilla ice cream and put another ring on top of it. Fill this with seasonal fruit ice cream, preferably strawberry or raspberry. Put a final ring on top and fill with chocolate ice cream.

When cut, the perfect combination of flavours and the 3 colours will be apparent.

Using a spatula, coat the sides with Chantilly cream. Pipe decorations on it, then top with half a peach or syrup flavoured with a little raspberry eau-de-vie, and the meringue buttons.

PETITS FOURS

PETITS FOURS

BISCUITS FOURRÉS

FILLED SPONGE FINGERS

Preparation 1 hour

US	Ingredients	Met/Imp
10 oz	Sponge Finger Biscuits or Ladyfingers (*page 627*)	300 g/10 oz
½ cup	redcurrant jelly or apricot jam	150 g/5 oz

Spread redcurrant jelly or apricot jam on the underside of half the sponge finger biscuits (ladyfingers) and stick them together in pairs.

BOUCHÉES DE DAMES

LADIES' KISSES

Preparation 1 hour • Cooking 10–15 minutes

US	Ingredients	Met/Imp
1 cup	caster (granulated) sugar	200 g/7 oz
6	eggs	6
1¾ cups	flour	250 g/8 oz
1 tsp	orange-flower water	5 ml/1 tsp
½ cup	apricot jam	150 g/5 oz
½ lb	fondant icing, flavoured as desired	250 g/8 oz

Prepare a sponge finger biscuit (ladyfinger) mixture according to the instructions on page 627 with the sugar, eggs, flour and orange-flower water. In exactly the same way as for sponge finger biscuits (ladyfingers), pipe 60 macaroon shapes (1 bouchée will be made from 2 of them) on to baking sheets covered with parchment paper. Dust with sugar and bake in a cool oven for 10–15 minutes.

After they have cooled, remove them from the paper. Spread their flat sides with apricot jam which has been worked through a sieve and boiled until reduced. Put them together in pairs and, using a little brush, lightly coat the tops with apricot jam. Then, half dip them in the chosen fondant icing, whether coffee, chocolate, vanilla or any other flavour. Put them on to a wire rack, leave to dry, then arrange on a dish.

As these bouchées have a rounded shape, trim the bottom ones slightly to ensure that they remain balanced.

CHARLOTTES

CHARLOTTES

Preparation 1 hour

US	Ingredients	Met/Imp
scant ½ basic recipe quantity	Sweet Pastry (*page 582*)	200 g/8 oz
¼ lb	Sponge Finger Biscuits (ladyfingers) (*page 627*)	100 g/3½ oz
½ cup	sugar syrup cooked to the crack stage (*page 575*)	100 ml/3½ fl oz
2 cups	Chantilly Cream (*page 583*)	500 ml/18 fl oz
scant 1 cup	liqueur of your choice	200 ml/7 fl oz
⅔ cup	glacé cherries	100 g/4 oz

Roll out the pastry 3 mm/⅛ inch thick and cut out some 5 cm/2 inch rounds. Bake in a moderate oven for 10 minutes.

Cut the sponge finger biscuits (ladyfingers) horizontally in half. Trim their sides straight and cut them all to the same length. Dip the straight end of each half biscuit (cookie) into the sugar syrup. Stick them vertically, side by side, on to the pastry bases to form crowns. With a knife, drop a little sugar syrup on the 4 joins in each crown. Cool, then fill with Chantilly cream flavoured with liqueur. Decorate with cherries.

US	Ingredients	Met/Imp
½ lb	Puff Pastry (page 579)	250 g/8 oz
⅔–1 cup	Frangipane (page 584)	150 g/5 oz
⅔–1 cup	almond cream (see method)	150 g/5 oz
½ cup	Royal Icing (page 585)	100 g/3½ oz

'CONVERSATION PIECES'

Preparation 1 hour • Cooking 25 minutes

Puff pastry trimmings can be used to line tartlet tins for these petits fours. Butter the tins and spread them out side by side on the work surface. Roll out the puff pastry and lay it on top of the tins. Press the pastry into the tins with a floured ball of pastry. Reserve excess pastry.

Fill the lined tartlet tins two-thirds full with a mixture of frangipane and almond cream (confectioner's custard with a mixture of equal amounts of crushed almonds, butter and sugar added to it).

Moisten the edges of the pastry and lay another rolled-out sheet of puff pastry over the tins. Press the pastry over them by hand or with the rolling pin and remove the excess. To finish, spread each little tart with a light coating of royal icing, using a knife. With the reserved pastry trimmings, make 2 thin parallel lines on top of each tartlet, and another 2 crossing diagonally. Bake in a low oven for 20–25 minutes.

US	Ingredients	Met/Imp
1 cup	icing (confectioners') sugar	125 g/4½ oz
1 cup less 1½ tbsp	flour, sifted	125 g/4½ oz
1	egg	1
3½ tbsp	milk	50 ml/2 fl oz

'COPEAUX'

Preparation 30 minutes • Cooking 10 minutes

Mix the sugar and flour together in a bowl with the egg and milk. Beat well to form a spreading consistency. Using a piping (pastry) bag fitted with a 3 mm/⅛ inch round nozzle, pipe the copeaux in the form of 20 cm/8 inch long sticks. Make 2 first as a test and bake in a low oven for 10 minutes. As soon as the edges turn golden, peel off the copeaux and roll them like tendrils around a 1 cm/½ inch round stick. If a copeau cracks when rolled while still very hot, it is because the dough is too thick and should be thinned with a little more milk.

US	Ingredients	Met/Imp
3½ cups	flour	500 g/1 lb
1 tbsp	baking powder	10 g/⅓ oz
1¼ cups	caster (granulated) sugar	250 g/8 oz
1 tbsp	orange-flower water	15 ml/1 tbsp
1¾ cups	shelled almonds	200 g/7 oz
4	eggs	4

'CROQUETS'

Preparation 2 hours • Cooking 10–12 minutes

Sift the flour on to the work surface. Make a well in the centre and add the baking powder, sugar, orange-flower water, unskinned almonds (picked over) and the eggs. Mix in the usual way, knead the dough once or twice to gather it together, then leave to rest for 1 hour.

Roll the dough into a sausage shape and slice finely to cut the almonds, then divide it in half. Roll out each piece 30.5 cm/12 inches long, maintaining the sausage shape. Flatten the pieces with the rolling pin to make them 10–12 cm/4–5 inches wide and 1 cm/½ inch thick. Straighten the sides and ends to give the strips of dough an even shape. Place them on a baking sheet and brush them with beaten egg. Score

with a fork and bake in a moderately hot oven for 10–12 minutes.

When they are taken out of the oven, cut the strips into small sticks 2 cm/¾ inch wide.

CROQUETS FONDANTS

─── ICED 'CROQUETS' ───

Preparation 2 hours • Cooking 25 minutes

Sift the flour on to the work surface and make a well in the centre. Add the butter, egg and baking powder. Mix together to form a dough, then leave to rest for a moment. Roll out and cut into a rectangular strip 40 cm/16 inches long and 10 cm/4 inches wide. Moisten with water and sprinkle with the almonds. Bake in a moderately hot oven for 25 minutes. Remove from the oven and brush with apricot marmelade.

Make the icing with the sugar and unbeaten egg whites. Beat, using a small wooden spoon, then flavour lightly with rum. Spread the rum icing over the pastry strip with a spoon and leave to set. Cut into 'croquets' (little matchsticks).

US	Ingredients	Met/Imp
1½ cups	flour	200 g/7 oz
6 tbsp	good-quality unsalted butter	75 g/3 oz
1	egg	1
1 pinch	baking powder	1 pinch
1 cup	shelled sweet almonds	150 g/5 oz
scant ½ cup	apricot *marmelade*	100 ml/4 fl oz
	RUM ICING	
1¼ cups	icing (confectioners') sugar	150 g/5 oz
3	egg whites	3
6 tbsp	rum	scant 100 ml/ 4 fl oz

DORIAS

─── 'DORIAS' ───

Preparation 1 hour • Cooking 2–3 minutes

Mix together the flour, butter, sugar and chocolate and knead to a dough. Roll out thinly, put on a baking sheet and bake in a moderate oven for 2–3 minutes. Cut into rounds with a pastry cutter. Glaze half of them and sprinkle almonds over the top. Spread with chocolate butter cream or jam and stick 2 together.

US	Ingredients	Met/Imp
1 cup	flour	150 g/5 oz
1 stick	good-quality unsalted butter	125 g/4½ oz
2 tbsp	caster (granulated) sugar	30 g/1 oz
1 oz	plain (semisweet) chocolate, grated	30 g/1 oz
1 cup	unblanched almonds, shredded (slivered)	100 g/4 oz
	FILLING	
about ½ cup	chocolate Butter Cream (*page 583*)	150 g/5 oz
	or	
	jam	

ÉCORCES D'ORANGES

─ ORANGE AND ALMOND PETITS FOURS ─

Preparation 1 hour • Cooking 12 minutes

Very finely chop or, better still, crush the candied orange peel. Mix into the almond paste followed by the flour. Roll out 3 mm/⅛ inch thick.

With an oval pastry cutter, cut out small 'tongue' shapes from the orange almond pastry. Mould these tongue shapes around a buttered and floured metal tube. Glaze 3 times with the beaten egg mixed with a little red food colouring. Bake in a hot oven for 12 minutes, leave to cool, then detach them from the tube.

Glaze the inside of the petits fours with a mixture of icing (confectioners') sugar and orange juice, thick enough not to run. Leave to dry naturally.

US	Ingredients	Met/Imp
2 oz	candied orange peel	50 g/2 oz
½ lb	Almond Paste (*page 586*)	250 g/8 oz
3 tbsp	flour	25 g/scant 1 oz
1	egg	1
	red food colouring	
1¼ cups	icing (confectioners') sugar	150 g/5 oz
2	oranges, juice of	2

US	Ingredients	Met/Imp
1⅓ cups	ground almonds	125 g/4½ oz
scant 2 cups	caster (granulated) sugar	375 g/13 oz
3 tbsp	flour	25 g/scant 1 oz
10	egg whites	10
10 tbsp	good-quality unsalted butter	150 g/5 oz
5 tsp	vanilla sugar	25 g/scant 1 oz

'DAINTIES'

Preparation 40 minutes • Cooking 20 minutes

Put the ground almonds, sugar and flour in a copper bowl. Moisten with the egg whites and beat the mixture well. Warm over a gentle heat, stirring constantly with a wooden spoon. Add the vanilla sugar and diced butter and mix thoroughly.

These petits fours are generally baked in small barquette or boat-shaped tins, but other tins may be used. Butter them generously, fill with the mixture and bake in a cool oven for 20 minutes or until golden.

US	Ingredients	Met/Imp
½ lb	Choux Pastry (page 578)	250 g/8 oz
6 tbsp	chopped blanched almonds	50 g/2 oz
¼ cup	sugar crystals	50 g/2 oz

FRISONS

'SMALL CURLS'

Preparation 1 hour • Cooking 15 minutes

These are dry choux buns, fairly flat in shape. They are made with a piping (pastry) bag fitted with a medium fluted nozzle. Fill the bag with choux pastry and pipe the buns on to a baking sheet. Make them 3 cm/1¼ inches wide in the centre and 8 cm/3¼ inches long. When piping the choux, make side to side movements with the nozzle touching the baking sheet, increasing the width towards the centre then decreasing it towards the end. Sprinkle a pinch of chopped almonds mixed with sugar crystals over each biscuit as soon as it is piped.

Bake in a moderate oven and serve plain.

US	Ingredients	Met/Imp
1½ cups	caster (granulated) sugar	300 g/10 oz
2 sticks	good-quality unsalted butter	250 g/8 oz
3	whole eggs	3
2 tsp	orange-flower water	10 ml/2 tsp
3½ cups	flour, sifted	500 g/1 lb
1	egg yolk	1
scant 1 oz	gum arabic	25 g/scant 1 oz

GÂTEAUX SECS (RECETTE DE BASE)

SWEET CRISP BISCUITS (BASIC RECIPE)

Preparation 1 hour • Resting mixture 2 hours • Cooking 12 minutes

Mix the sugar, butter, whole eggs and orange-flower water, then gradually blend in the flour and knead it all together. Gather the dough into 1 piece and knead it once or twice to make it smooth. Dust the work surface lightly with flour and roll the dough into a ball. Wrap in a cloth and leave to rest for 2 hours.

Roll out the dough 1 cm/½ inch thick and cut it into small rounds or other shapes with a pastry cutter. Roll what is left of the dough into a ball, then roll it out and cut it as before. Continue until all the dough is used up.

Arrange the shapes on lightly dampened baking sheets and brush with beaten egg yolk mixed with a few drops of water. Bake in a moderately hot oven for 12 minutes.

Remove the biscuits (cookies) from the oven and brush them with a little gum arabic, or simply with sweetened milk cooked to a thick syrup. This is to make them shine.

—— 'CATS' TONGUES' WITH CREAM ——

Preparation 30 minutes • Cooking 8–10 minutes

US	Ingredients	Met/Imp
1¼ cups	caster (granulated) sugar	250 g/8 oz
2½ tsp	vanilla sugar	10 g/⅓ oz
1½ cups	flour	200 g/7 oz
1 cup	cream	250 ml/9 fl oz
5	egg whites	5

Sift the sugars and flour together into a bowl. Stir in the cream, then fold in the stiffly whisked egg whites.

Using a piping (pastry) bag fitted with a 3 mm/⅛ inch plain round nozzle, pipe the mixture in diagonal strips on a baking sheet, making them 8–9 cm/3–3½ inches long and spacing them 4 cm/1½ inches apart. The baking sheet should look like a page of written strokes such as may be done at school, but the 'strokes' should be leaning to the left.

Bake towards the bottom of a low to moderate oven for 8–10 minutes until only the edges are brown. The centres should remain white. Remove with a palette knife and cool on a marble slab or cold baking sheet.

—— LUXEMBOURG PETITS FOURS ——

Preparation 6 hours • Drying 4–5 hours • Cooking 10–12 minutes

US	Ingredients	Met/Imp
¼ lb	crystallized pineapple	100 g/4 oz
10 oz	Almond Paste (page 586)	300 g/10 oz
4 tsp	kirsch	20 ml/4 tsp
scant 1 oz	gum arabic	25 g/scant 1 oz

Finely chop the crystallized pineapple and mix half into the almond paste together with the kirsch.

Using a piping (pastry) bag fitted with a large fluted nozzle, pipe the almond paste mixture in the shape of large rosettes on to a parchment paper-lined baking sheet. Put a small piece of crystallized pineapple in the centre of each one. Leave to dry for 4–5 hours.

Bake the petits fours in a low oven for 10–12 minutes or until lightly browned, then brush them lightly with gum arabic as soon as they are taken out of the oven. Detach them by moistening the back of the paper.

—————— 'MIRLITONS' ——————

Preparation 2 hours • Cooking 25–30 minutes

US	Ingredients	Met/Imp
½ lb	Puff Pastry (page 579) trimmings	250 g/8 oz
10 tbsp	caster (granulated) sugar	125 g/4 oz
2	eggs	2
13 tbsp	ground almonds	60 g/2½ oz
2 tbsp	cream	30 ml/2 tbsp
1 tsp	orange-flower water	5 ml/1 tsp
⅓ cup	unskinned almonds	50 g/2 oz
6½ tbsp	icing (confectioners') sugar	50 g/2 oz

Roll out the puff pastry trimmings 3 mm/⅛ inch thick and cut out rounds of a suitable size to line tartlet tins, using a fluted pastry cutter. Make the edges of the pastry stand well proud of the rims of the tins. Prick the pastry bases with a fork to stop them blistering during cooking.

Beat the caster (granulated) sugar and eggs together with a whisk until foamy, then add the ground almonds and beat a little more. Add the cream or, if unavailable, 30 ml/2 tbsp melted butter, and the orange-flower water.

Fill each tartlet with 15 ml/1 tbsp mixture and decorate the centre of each with 3 almond halves, arranged with their points towards the centre. Dust thickly with icing (confectioners') sugar and bake in a low to moderate oven for 25–30 minutes.

US	Ingredients	Met/Imp
scant ½ basic recipe quantity	Sweet Pastry (page 582)	250 g/8 oz
1	egg	1
⅔ cup	ground almonds	50 g/2 oz
¼ cup	caster (granulated) sugar	50 g/2 oz

'NANTES CAKES'

Preparation 1 hour • Cooking 20 minutes

Roll out the pastry 3 mm/⅛ inch thick and cut out pastry ovals, using a boat-shaped pastry cutter. Arrange them on a lightly buttered baking sheet and brush with beaten egg. Using a fork, score them twice diagonally across their width and put a pinch of ground almonds mixed with sugar in the middle. Bake in a low oven for about 20 minutes.

US	Ingredients	Met/Imp
¼ lb	candied angelica	100 g/4 oz
1 lb	Almond Paste (page 586)	500 g/1 lb
a few drops	green food colouring	a few drops
2 tbsp	rum	30 ml/2 tbsp
1	egg white	1
¾–1 cup	sugar crystals or finely chopped almonds	150 g/5 oz
scant 1 oz	gum arabic	25 g/scant 1 oz

'NIORTAIS'

Preparation 2½ hours • Drying 12 hours • Cooking 15–18 minutes

Mix the finely chopped angelica into the almond paste and colour it a soft green. Flavour it with the rum. Using your hands moistened with egg white, make a sausage of the paste and then cut it into pieces weighing about 25 g/scant 1 oz each. Roll them first into balls and then into olive shapes. Roll them in sugar crystals or finely chopped almonds until coated. Arrange them on a parchment paper-lined baking sheet and leave them to dry overnight.

Bake the cakes in a moderate oven for 15–18 minutes. As soon as they are removed from the oven, brush them with a solution of gum arabic and water.

US	Ingredients	Met/Imp
3½ cups	flour, sifted	500 g/1 lb
1¾ cups	light soft brown sugar	250 g/8 oz
2½ sticks	good-quality unsalted butter	300 g/10 oz
1¾ cups	unskinned almonds, coarsely crushed	250 g/8 oz
1½ tbsp	ground cinnamon	10 g/⅓ oz
1¼ tsp	bicarbonate of soda (baking soda)	5 ml/1 tsp
2	eggs	2
2 tbsp	milk	30 ml/2 tbsp

GHENT ALMOND SHORTBREAD

Preparation 6 hours • Drying 12 hours • Cooking 15 minutes

Mix all the ingredients together to make quite a firm paste which is just soft enough not to crumble. Roll on a lightly floured surface into one or several sausages, 5 cm/2 inches in diameter. Flatten them a little to make them oval. Leave to harden in a cold place for several hours.

Cut the rolls into 3 mm/⅛ inch thick slices and arrange them on a lightly buttered baking sheet 2 cm/¾ inch apart. Leave to dry out naturally for 5 hours or overnight.

Bake in a low oven for 15 minutes. Store in airtight tins or jars.

—— PINEAPPLE SHORTBREAD ——

Preparation 1 hour • Drying 3 hours • Cooking 12–15 minutes

US	Ingredients	Met/Imp
14 oz	Almond Paste (*page 586*)	400 g/14 oz
⅓ cup	candied pineapple, chopped	50 g/2 oz
4 tsp	kirsch	20 ml/4 tsp
½	beaten egg	½

Mix all the ingredients together, except the beaten egg, then shape by hand into a sausage on a dampened marble slab. Cut into walnut-sized pieces. Roll into olive shapes and arrange them 4 cm/2½ inches apart on a baking sheet lined with parchment paper. Using a fork dipped in beaten egg, slightly flatten the shapes by pressing the prongs of the fork into them twice, making a criss-cross pattern. Leave to dry for 3 hours.

Bake the biscuits (cookies) in a low oven for 12–15 minutes. Detach them from the paper by dampening the underside, then leave to dry and cool on a wire rack before arranging them on a serving plate.

—— ENGLISH SHORTBREAD ——

Preparation 1 hour • Cooking 15–18 minutes

US	Ingredients	Met/Imp
10 tbsp	good-quality unsalted butter	150 g/5 oz
1 cup	sugar	200 g/7 oz
2 cups	ground almonds	150 g/5 oz
3	whole eggs	3
1	egg yolk	1
1½ tsp	baking powder	6.25 ml/1¼ tsp
1½ cups	flour	200 g/7 oz
about 2 tbsp	rum	about 30 ml/2 tbsp

Beat together the butter, sugar, ground almonds, 2 whole eggs, the egg yolk and baking powder. Once all the ingredients are well blended, lightly mix in the flour and the rum, taking care not to overwork the mixture. Roll into a long sausage shape and cut into pieces weighing about 20 g/¾ oz each. Roll these pieces into balls, then extend them into 12 cm/4¾ inch long boat shapes, pointed at both ends. Arrange them on a buttered baking sheet.

Brush the biscuits (cookies) with the remaining beaten egg, wait 20 minutes, then brush them again. Press the flat side of a knife blade into them, to spread them out and give them a flat bread shape. Bake in a low oven for 15–18 minutes. Put the biscuits (cookies) on a wire rack or wicker tray to cool. Store in an airtight tin.

—— RUM AND RAISIN ROUNDS ——

Preparation 48 hours • Soaking raisins 48 hours • Cooking 12 minutes

US	Ingredients	Met/Imp
1 cup	seedless raisins	150 g/5 oz
3 tbsp	rum	45 ml/3 tbsp
1 stick	good-quality unsalted butter	125 g/4½ oz
10 tbsp	caster (granulated) sugar	125 g/4½ oz
2	eggs	2
1 cup less 1½ tbsp	flour, sifted	125 g/4½ oz

Coarsely chop the raisins and put in a bowl. Cover with the rum and leave to soak for at least 48 hours.

Cream the butter with a wooden spoon. Add the sugar, then the eggs, one at a time. Add the flour, then the raisins.

Fill a piping (pastry) bag fitted with a 1 cm/½ inch plain round nozzle with the mixture and pipe walnut-sized balls well spaced out on a baking sheet lined with parchment paper. Bake in a low oven for about 12 minutes. When they are cold, they can be taken off the paper easily.

US	Ingredients	Met/Imp
10 oz	Puff Pastry (page 579)	300 g/10 oz
¾ cup	caster (granulated) sugar	150 g/5 oz
¾ cup	icing (confectioners') sugar	100 g/4 oz

'BUTTERFLIES'

Preparation 1 hour • Cooking 12 minutes

After 'turning' the puff pastry 4 times, 'turn' it twice more in the caster (granulated) sugar. Roll out to 21–22 cm/8¼–8½ inches long. Cut into 4 strips, each 5 cm/2 inches wide. Put them one on top of the other. Place the rolling pin on them, lengthways in the middle, and press very hard so that the centre is no more than 1 cm/½ inch thick. Cut diagonally into 1 cm/½ inch pieces. Pick up each piece by both ends and give it a half-twist in the centre where it is thin. Arrange the 'butterflies' on a dry metal baking sheet, spacing them 4 cm/1½ inches apart. Dust them lightly with icing (confectioners') and sugar and bake in a hot oven for 12 minutes.

US	Ingredients	Met/Imp
1½ lb (6 sticks)	good-quality unsalted butter	700 g/1 lb 7 oz
4 cups	icing (confectioners') sugar	500 g/1 lb
6	egg yolks	6
7 cups	flour	1 kg/2 lb
1 pinch	salt	1 pinch
	powdered vanilla	
	or	
	lemon juice	
	DECORATION	
1	egg	1
	sugar crystals	
	raisins	
	Royal Icing (page 585)	
	cocoa powder	
	flaked (sliced) almonds	

RICH PETITS FOURS

Preparation 1¼ hours • Cooling dough overnight • Cooking 15 minutes

It is best to prepare these petits fours the day before. Soften the butter, then work it together with the sugar and the egg yolks by hand. Mix well, then add the flour and salt, and flavour with vanilla or lemon juice according to the type of petits fours you are making. Mix well again. Put the dough in a cool place until the next day.

Sugared sablés: roll out the dough with a floured rolling pin and cut into small rounds with a pastry cutter. Brush them with beaten egg yolk and dip them in a saucer of sugar (which will stick to the surface of the petits fours).

Raisin sablés: work a handful of raisins into the dough. Form into a very firm sausage-shape, then cut into slices about 1 cm/½ inch thick with a sharp knife.

Dominoes: roll out the dough and cut out a long strip, 5 cm/2 inches wide. Using a spatula, ice the strip with royal icing. Cut into rectangles about 2.5 cm/1 inch wide. Mix a little cocoa powder with 1 spoonful of royal icing, then pipe a domino pattern on them.

Chocolate-flavoured sablés: mix cocoa powder into the dough to give it a good colour.

Dutch sablés: interleave 4 rectangular strips of chocolate-flavoured dough with 3 rectangular strips of plain dough. Cut into slices just under 1 cm/½ inch thick.

Chequer-boards: make 4 small 1 cm/½ inch round 'sausages' with chocolate-flavoured dough and 4 more with plain dough. Pile them on top of one another, alternating the chocolate and plain doughs in a chequer-board pattern. Cut out a rectangle of plain dough, the length of the chequer-board and brush lightly with beaten egg yolk. Wrap it around the chequer-board. Cut slices 1 cm/½ inch thick.

Chocolate sablés: roll out chocolate-flavoured dough and brush with

beaten egg yolk. Sprinkle with some flaked (sliced) almonds and cut out small rounds with a pastry cutter.

All these sablés are cooked in a low oven for about 15 minutes. Take care not to let them brown too much.

LITTLE SABLÉS

Preparation 2 hours • Resting dough 2 hours • Cooking 20 minutes

US	Ingredients	Met/Imp
3⅓ cups	ground almonds	250 g/8 oz
1¾ cups	flour	250 g/8 oz
14 tbsp	good-quality unsalted butter	200 g/7 oz
1 tsp	salt	5 g/1 tsp
2½ tsp	vanilla sugar	10 g/⅓ oz
3½ tbsp	cream	50 ml/2 fl oz
¾ cup	icing (confectioners') sugar	100 g/3½ oz

Mix together all the ingredients to make a pastry like Sweet Pastry (*page 582*). Leave it to rest for 2 hours.

Roll out the pastry 3 mm/⅛ inch thick. Cut out rounds with a plain 10 cm/4 inch pastry cutter, then cut each round into 4. Put them on a lightly buttered baking sheet and bake in the lower part of a low oven for 20 minutes. Only the edges should turn a light golden colour, the centres remaining almost white.

ROCHERS AUX AMANDES

ALMOND ROCK CAKES

Preparation 45 minutes • Cooking 12–15 minutes

US	Ingredients	Met/Imp
2½ cups	icing (confectioners') sugar	300 g/10 oz
4	egg whites	4
3 cups	flaked (sliced) almonds	300 g/10 oz
2½ tsp	vanilla sugar	25 g/scant 1 oz
scant 1 oz	gum arabic	25 g/scant 1 oz

Put the icing (confectioners') sugar and egg whites in a saucepan. Spread the almonds on a baking sheet and put in a low oven with the door open. Heat the egg white and sugar mixture gently, stirring with a wooden spoon. When it starts to thicken, add the almonds and the vanilla sugar. Continue to stir the mixture as it heats up, but this time with a fork. When there is no more shrinkage of the mixture in the saucepan, set out little mounds of it on a paper-lined baking sheet. Bake in a low oven for 12–15 minutes or until the cakes are a good golden colour. Remove them from the oven and brush with a solution of gum arabic and water.

SANS-SOUCIS

SANS-SOUCIS

Preparation 1 hour • Cooking 20 minutes

US	Ingredients	Met/Imp
½ lb	Puff Pastry (*page 579*)	250 g/8 oz
½ lb	cherries, mirabelle plums or apricots	250 g/8 oz
¾ cup	icing (confectioners') sugar	100 g/3½ oz

The puff pastry should be 'turned' 6 times and rolled out 1 cm/½ inch thick. Cut into 7.5 cm/3 inch squares. Lift up the corners of the squares and fold them over on to the pastry. Place these squares on a dampened baking sheet and decorate them by placing some fruit (4 cherries, 3 mirabelle plums or half a small apricot) in the centre of each one.

Bake in a hot oven for 20 minutes, then dust with icing (confectioners') sugar and return to the oven to glaze.

US	Ingredients	Met/Imp
about ½ basic recipe quantity	Sweet Pastry (page 582)	250 g/8 oz
1 cup	Frangipane (page 584)	200 g/7 oz
about ⅕ basic recipe quantity	Italian Meringue mixture (page 585)	150 g/5 oz
5 oz	fondant icing, in various colours and flavours	150 g/5 oz
3½ tbsp	apricot *marmelade* or redcurrant jelly	50 ml/2 fl oz

'SIGHS'

Preparation 2 hours • Cooking 15 minutes

Roll out the pastry thinly and use to line tartlet tins. Do not crimp. Fill with frangipane and bake in a moderate oven for 15 minutes. Leave to cool.

Fill a cloth piping (pastry) bag fitted with a 1 cm/½ inch plain round nozzle with Italian meringue mixture. Pipe a meringue peak 7–8 cm/3–3½ inches high in each tartlet. Ice with light fondant icing in various colours and flavours, or coat with thick apricot marmelade or redcurrant jelly.

US	Ingredients	Met/Imp
7 oz	Choux Pastry (page 578)	200 g/7 oz
1 cup	currants	150 g/5 oz
scant ½ cup	icing (confectioners') sugar	50 g/2 oz

TORTILLONS

'ZIGZAGS'

Preparation 1 hour • Cooking 25 minutes

Fill a piping (pastry) bag fitted with a medium fluted nozzle with choux pastry. Pipe 12–15 cm/5–6 inch long zigzag lines on a baking sheet, holding the nozzle at an angle of 45° to the baking sheet. Sprinkle about 10 currants over each of these lines and dust lightly with icing (confectioners') sugar. Bake in a low oven for 20–25 minutes. Leave to cool slowly before serving.

CONFISERIES

CONFECTIONERY

US	Ingredients	Met/Imp
¾ cup	chopped blanched almonds	100 g/4 oz
¾ cup	icing (confectioners') sugar	100 g/4 oz
about 6½ tbsp	orange-flower water	about 100 ml/ 4 fl oz

AMANDES PRALINÉES

SUGARED ALMONDS

Preparation 1 hour

Put the chopped almonds and sugar in a bowl and sprinkle with 5 ml/1 tsp orange-flower water. Gradually add the remaining orange-flower water, stirring with a wooden spoon and adding only as much as is necessary to make all the sugar stick to the almonds. Do not let lumps form and break them up as they develop. Leave to dry naturally or in a low oven, and store in an airtight tin.

ANGÉLIQUE FOURRÉE GLACÉE

STUFFED ANGELICA

Preparation 1 hour

US	Ingredients	Met/Imp
12	12–15 cm/5–6 inch crystallized angelica stalks	12
½ lb	Almond Paste (*page 586*)	250 g/8 oz
¼ cup	vanilla sugar *or*	50 g/2 oz
1 pinch	powdered vanilla	1 pinch

Split open one stalk of crystallized angelica by making a cut in the side.
Prepare some soft almond paste. Work it by hand to make it elastic and blend in the vanilla sugar or powder. Roll one-twelfth of the paste into a sausage shape as long as 1 angelica stalk and thick enough to fill it. Put the almond paste into the stalk. Reshape the angelica stalk and cut it diagonally into 3 cm/1¼ inch long pieces. Repeat with the remaining angelica and almond paste. Spear each piece with a metal or wooden cocktail stick.

CARAMELS AU CHOCOLAT

CHOCOLATE CARAMELS

Preparation 1 hour • Cooking about 35 minutes

US	Ingredients	Met/Imp
scant 3 cups	cocoa powder	250 g/8 oz
1¼ cups	sugar	250 g/8 oz
2 cups	crème fraîche	500 ml/18 fl oz
4 tbsp	good-quality unsalted butter	50 g/2 oz
¾ oz (1 tbsp)	glucose (or light corn syrup)	20 g/¾ oz

Put everything into a heavy-based saucepan and cook to the large ball stage (*page 575*). Tip on to an oiled marble slab and cut when cold. Serve in fluted paper cases.

CASSIS DÉGUISÉS

SUGAR-COATED BLACKCURRANTS

Preparation 1 hour

US	Ingredients	Met/Imp
1 lb	blackcurrants in eau-de-vie	500 g/1 lb
½ lb	Fondant (*page 584*)	250 g/8 oz
a few drops	red food colouring	a few drops
1 glass	clear blackcurrant eau-de-vie	1 glass

Drain the spirit from the blackcurrants and leave them on a cloth to drain for several hours. You will need 3 blackcurrants to make each petit four.
Heat the fondant and colour it with several drops of food colouring. Flavour it with blackcurrant spirit. Use a special little 'ring utensil', like a brass skewer with a ring at the end, to fish out the fruit. This utensil comes in many sizes.
Once the fondant is warm, drop in a blackcurrant and leave it to become well coated. Drain and put on a board or paper. Try to make a loop on the top with the fondant which sticks to the ring. Dip a second one and attach it to the first, then dip a third, attaching it to the first 2. Keep repeating, using 3 blackcurrants for each petit four.
Serve in fluted paper cases.

US	Ingredients	Met/Imp
½ lb	sweetened cherries in eau-de-vie	250 g/8 oz
3½ oz	gum arabic	100 g/3½ oz
¾ cup	sugar	150 g/5 oz
a few drops	red food colouring	a few drops

PRESERVED CHERRIES ICED WITH CARAMEL

Preparation 12 hours

Drain the cherries preserved in eau-de-vie. Keep their long stalks to help dip them into the sugar syrup. Put the cherries on cheesecloth and leave in a warm place for at least 6 hours or until very dry.

The cherries should be coated at the last moment. As a safety measure, dip them in gum arabic, not in gum tragacanth as recommended by some cooks.

Cook the sugar to the hard crack stage (*page 575*) and colour it red by adding a few drops of food colouring. Boil it up 2 or 3 times. Take a cherry by its stalk and dip it in the sugar syrup. Take it out, let it drain over the saucepan, then put it on a lightly oiled baking sheet. Repeat with all the cherries. Leave to cool.

When completely cold, detach the cherries with a knife. Above all, do not pull them by the stalks. Serve in fluted paper cases.

US	Ingredients	Met/Imp
32	dates	32
5 oz	Almond Paste (*page 586*), coloured, or marzipan, coloured	150 g/5 oz
16	blanched almonds	16
	or	
	walnuts	

STUFFED DATES

Preparation 24 hours

Slit the dates lengthways and remove their stones. Fill each cavity with coloured almond paste or marzipan and add half an almond or walnut. Reshape the dates, leaving the contents visible. Leave in a cool place for 24 hours. Serve in paper cases.

US	Ingredients	Met/Imp
1¾ cups	flour	250 g/8 oz
10 tbsp	good-quality unsalted butter	150 g/5 oz
5 tbsp	caster (granulated) sugar	60 g/2½ oz
2	eggs	2
1 drop	bitter almond essence (extract)	1 drop
	or	
2	bitter almonds	2
	apricot *marmelade*	
	sugar, for coating	

SPANISH DELIGHTS

Preparation 1 hour • Baking 12 minutes

Sift the flour into a bowl and make a well in the centre. Add the butter, sugar, eggs and almond essence (extract), or bitter almonds, finely crushed with several drops of water. Mix them all together to form a paste, neither too firm, nor too soft. Roll out the paste thinly and cut into 2.5 cm/1 inch rounds. Place on a baking sheet and bake in a hot oven for 12 minutes. When they are baked, leave to cool, then spread one side of each with apricot marmelade. Stick the rounds together in pairs and roll the edges in sugar to coat.

DRAGÉES

Preparation 30 minutes • Cooking about 30 minutes

US	Ingredients	Met/Imp
3 oz	gum arabic	75 g/3 oz
¾ cup	sugar	150 g/5 oz
2¼ cups	shelled hazelnuts (filberts)	300 g/10 oz

Melt the gum arabic in a glass of water. Strain through a cloth, then mix it with 75 g/3 oz (6 tbsp) sugar cooked to the gloss stage.

Blanch the hazelnuts in boiling water, then skin and dry them well in a saucepan over a low heat. Put the hazelnuts in the syrup and stir so they become saturated with sugar. Heat the remaining sugar to the gloss stage and put the nuts in it. When they have absorbed all the sugar, take them out and leave them to dry.

FRAISES GLACÉES

ICED STRAWBERRIES

Preparation 1 hour

US	Ingredients	Met/Imp
1½ pints	strawberries	500 g/1 lb
1⅔ oz	powdered gum arabic	50 g/2 oz
¾ cup	sugar, cooked to the hard crack stage (*page 575*)	150 g/5 oz

Use very sound, firm strawberries, above all without any trace of moisture, ie not too ripe. They should be very clean, with no earth on them, so that they do not need washing. Leave their stalks on so they can be picked up easily. Roll them in powdered gum arabic.

Dip the strawberries, one by one, in the sugar syrup. Lay them on a baking sheet or an oiled marble slab. Remove them before they have cooled completely and put in fluted paper cases to serve.

FRUITS CRISTALLISÉS

CRYSTALLIZED FRUIT

Preparation 15 minutes

US	Ingredients	Met/Imp
1 lb	fruit	500 g/1 lb
3½ oz	gum arabic	100 g/3½ oz
	or	
1	egg white	1
1 cup	caster (superfine) or granulated sugar	200 g/7 oz

Any fruit, whether fresh, preserved in spirit or syrup, or iced with caramel or fondant, can be crystallized.

Dry the pieces of fruit, if necessary. Dip them in a weak solution of gum arabic or in the lightly, not stiffly, whisked egg white. Then coat them in fine- or coarse-grained sugar. Blackcurrants, cherries and grapes, fresh or preserved in spirit, can be dipped in fine sugar. Strawberries, raspberries and cubes of pineapple can be dipped either in fine- or coarse-grained sugar.

SUGAR-COATED ─────── AND MARZIPAN FRUITS*

(STUFFED PRUNES, CHOCOLATE WALNUTS AND CHESTNUTS, CHERRIES AND ALMONDS)

Preparation 2 hours • Cooking 3 minutes

US	Ingredients	Met/Imp
30	large Agen prunes	30
⅓ cup	walnut pieces	50 g/2 oz
¾ cup	shelled hazelnuts (filberts)	100 g/4 oz
	icing (confectioners') sugar	
1 lb	Almond Paste (*page 586*)	500 g/1 lb
½ glass	aniseed liqueur	½ glass
	sugar crystals	
1 lb	chestnut paste	500 g/1 lb
1 glass	rum	1 glass
1 lb	white Fondant (*page 584*)	500 g/1 lb
3 oz	plain (semisweet) chocolate	75 g/3 oz
5 tsp	butter (cocoa butter is preferable but difficult to find)	25 g/scant 1 oz
20	walnut halves	20
about 15	cherries in *eau-de-vie*	about 15
a few drops	red food colouring	a few drops
a few drops	green food colouring	a few drops
⅔ cup	perfect blanched almonds	100 g/4 oz

Put the prunes on a wire rack over a saucepan of boiling water. Invert a small bowl over them and leave them to steam for 10 minutes or until swollen. Remove the stones from the prunes with a little spoon, without damaging them too much. Set aside.

In a mortar, pound the walnut pieces and some of the hazelnuts, with any little pieces of prune that were left attached to the stones, add a little icing (confectioners') sugar to make a paste. Fill 10 prunes with this paste and reshape them. Flavour half of the almond paste with a little aniseed liqueur and roll it into a long sausage shape. Cut into sections and use to stuff 10 more prunes. Reshape them well. Roll these 20 prunes in sugar crystals and put them in fluted paper cases.

Flavour the chestnut paste with rum and mix well. Add a little icing (confectioners') sugar, if necessary, to obtain a very smooth paste. Fill the last 10 prunes but do not close them up completely. Press 2 hazelnuts into the chestnut purée in each prune.

Put a saucepan in a *bain-marie* and put half of the fondant and the diced chocolate in it. Once the mixture is melted and well blended, add the butter. Stir well to make it really smooth. Shape the remaining rum-flavoured paste to look like chestnuts and dip them into the warm chocolate without completely immersing them so that a circle of chestnut paste remains visible.

Dip the walnut halves, one after the other, into the warm chocolate icing. Put them on a lightly oiled surface to cool.

Let the cherries dry out well. Put the remaining white fondant in a *bain-marie* and add 2 drops of red food colouring. Stir well. Carefully dip each cherry in the fondant, holding it by its stalk. Leave to dry on an oiled plate.

Colour the rest of the almond paste with 2 drops of green food colouring. Roll balls of paste in your hands to form almond shell shapes. Make a slit in them with a knife and put a perfect almond in it, protruding slightly.

To present them, put all the sweets in little paper cases, if liked, and arrange so the colours alternate: prunes and chestnuts, walnuts, cherries and almonds.

ICED SUGAR-COATED APRICOTS

US	Ingredients	Met/Imp
I lb	candied apricots	500 g/I lb
I lb	Fondant (*page 584*)	500 g/I lb

First recipe

Preparation 1½ hours

Use small candied apricots. If they are too large, divide them in 2, 3 or 4 pieces.

Heat some fondant in a saucepan, stirring continuously. Above all, do not thin it until it feels warm, which is essential for this kind of icing. If you put your finger in it, it should feel quite hot. Carry out a test. Dip a piece of apricot into the fondant, completely immersing it. Take it out with a fork, wipe the bottom of the fruit on the edge of the saucepan and put it on to a piece of parchment paper or a baking sheet dusted with icing (confectioners') sugar. The fondant should not run and you should not be able to see the colour of the fruit through it. If the fondant seems a little thick, but only in this case, thin it with a little kirsch or rum. However, the fondant ought to be flavoured with kirsch or rum anyway. If you cannot do this without making it runny, it is because it is not cooked enough. To remedy this, add 15 ml/1 tbsp icing (confectioners') sugar to the fondant.

If liked, you can put a minute piece of candied fruit on top of the fondant while it is still hot, ie immediately the apricot has been put on the baking sheet.

Second recipe

Melt some sugar, moistened with a little water, until it boils. When a drop of sugar syrup solidifies into a thread in a glass of water, add a small spoonful of white vinegar for every 30 g/1 oz (7 tsp) sugar. Boil the syrup to a light caramel (*page 575*). Using a wooden skewer, spike the fruit, quickly dip them in the syrup and arrange them on an oiled baking sheet.

NANCY MACAROONS

US	Ingredients	Met/Imp
2 cups	blanched almonds	300 g/10 oz
I tsp	potato flour	5 ml/1 tsp
4 cups	icing (confectioners') sugar	500 g/I lb
6	small egg whites	6
I tsp	vanilla essence (extract)	5 ml/1 tsp

Preparation 1 hour • Cooking 12–15 minutes

Pound the almonds in a mortar with the potato flour. Gradually add the sugar, then the egg whites, a small amount at a time, and the vanilla, to obtain a paste that is soft but does not spread out. Spoon the paste on to pieces of parchment or rice paper, moisten lightly with water and dust with icing (confectioners') sugar. Bake in a low oven for 12–15 minutes. To remove the macaroons from the paper, put it on a damp surface.

US	Ingredients	Met/Imp
I per person	perfect mandarin oranges	I per person
½ lb	Fondant (page 584)	250 g/8 oz
a few drops	red food colouring	a few drops
	or	
2 per person	small mandarin oranges	2 per person
½ lb	Fondant (page 584)	250 g/8 oz
½ cup	sugar, cooked to the hard crack stage (page 575)	100 g/4 oz
a few drops	green food colouring	a few drops

—— SUGAR-COATED MANDARINS ——

Preparation 2 hours

Peel and segment the mandarin oranges and dry the segments. Using a fork, dip them in melted fondant coloured with red food colouring.

Alternatively, very small mandarins can be dipped whole into the fondant, using a special ring to fish them out. If whole mandarins are coated with fondant or caramel, you can make a small stalk and 2 small leaves out of sugar cooked to the hard crack stage and coloured pale green. Stick them on to the fruit.

US	Ingredients	Met/Imp
1¼ cups	granulated sugar	250 g/8 oz
I lb	Almond Paste (page 586)	500 g/1 lb
2	egg whites	2
2 tbsp	orange-flower water	30 ml/2 tbsp
¾ cup	caster (superfine) sugar	150 g/5 oz

—— 'MARZIPANS' ——

Preparation and Drying 24 hours • Cooking 12–15 minutes

Knead the granulated sugar into the almond paste. Soften with the egg whites and beat this paste well with a wooden spoon. Add the orange-flower water.

Using a piping (pastry) bag fitted with a 1 cm/½ inch plain nozzle, pipe walnut-sized mounds of the almond paste mixture on to parchment paper. Make a hole in the centre of each marzipan with the rounded end of a small stick, lightly moistened and dipped in caster (superfine) sugar. Leave the marzipans to dry overnight.

Bake the marzipans in a low oven for 12–15 minutes or until they become a nice golden colour. To detach the marzipans, lay the paper on a dampened marble slab. The marzipans can be stuck together in pairs.

These marzipans are not glazed with gum.

VARIATION
To make pink marzipans, add 25 g/scant 1 oz (2 tbsp) vanilla sugar and a little red food colouring to the mixture above.

US	Ingredients	Met/Imp
24	perfect shelled walnuts	24
5 oz	Almond Paste (page 586)	150 g/5 oz
⅔ cup	light caramel (page 575)	150 g/5 oz

—— CARAMELIZED WALNUTS ——

Preparation 1 hour • Cooking 35 minutes

Cut the walnuts in half lengthways and join the 2 halves together with the almond paste. Press together well to reshape the walnut.

Dip in the light caramel and take out with a fork. Dry on a wire rack and serve in paper cases.

NOUGAT

Preparation 24 hours • Cooking about 20 minutes

US	Ingredients	Met/Imp
1¾ cups	shelled almonds	250 g/8 oz
1¼ cups	caster (granulated) sugar	250 g/8 oz
a few drops	lemon juice	a few drops

The preparation of nougat does not present serious difficulties unless you are going to use it to make decorative pieces. These require skill and manual dexterity only gained after long experience of this kind of work.

Blanch and skin the almonds. Wash them in cold water and split each one lengthways in half. Cut each half into 5–6 shreds or slivers. Lay them on a paper-covered dish and leave to dry in a warm place for at least 12 hours.

Put 200 g/7 oz (1 cup) sugar in a small shallow copper bowl over the heat with the lemon juice. Melt it gently by pushing it bit by bit with a spatula towards the hottest part of the bowl. When it is melted, the sugar should be a deep gold, but not have become caramel brown. Add the almonds to the sugar, mix everything together well with a wooden spoon and put the bowl in a warm oven with the door open, to keep the nougat hot.

Tip half of the nougat on to a lightly oiled marble slab. Flatten it with an oiled pâtisserie rolling pin or the blade of a large knife, until it is 5 mm/¼ inch thick. Cut it immediately into squares, lozenges or rectangles, or with a plain or fluted pastry cutter. Roll the remaining nougat out in the same way and repeat. You can greatly vary the appearance of a dessert with these different shapes, which simply need to be cut out very quickly.

If, however, you prefer a moulded nougat, a 'decorative piece', proceed as follows: choose, for preference, a Savoy sponge cake tin, with well defined details (that is, one with designs that are not too complicated) and lightly oil the inside.

Roll out some of the nougat as explained above. Line the bottom and some way up the sides of the tin with the rolled-out nougat. Press firmly with a lemon to imprint the pattern of the tin on to it well. Then, roll out some more nougat and join it on to the first. Continue up the sides of the tin until it is completely lined. If, once the tin is completely lined, there are any spaces between the parts of nougat, it is easy to fill these by simply plugging the gaps with little bits of nougat which have been kept hot.

In any case, so that these pieces can be properly joined together, it is essential that the nougat already in the tin is still hot. Otherwise, it will inevitably break when the next piece is pressed on to it. This is why we strongly recommend that the work should be done extremely swiftly.

Afterwards, when the tin has been completely lined, leave it for several minutes before unmoulding. It can then be fixed with a little melted sugar on to a base of sweet shortcrust (pie) pastry and finished with some nougat cut into lozenges or crescent shapes, according to taste.

US	Ingredients	Met/Imp
	quince segments caster (superfine) sugar granulated sugar	

QUINCE PASTE

Preparation and Drying 48 hours • Cooking 30 minutes

After the juice has been extracted from quinces for jelly, the segments can be used to make the following quince paste.

Work the segments through a sieve, then weigh this purée and place in a bowl with the same weight of caster (superfine) sugar. Using a spatula, stir continuously over the heat until the paste becomes the consistency of a very thick potato purée. Pour it on to a lightly oiled baking sheet and spread it 1 cm/½ inch thick.

The next day, turn the slab of paste out on to a napkin. Divide it, as wished, into lozenges, squares or other shapes, then roll them in granulated sugar. Store in layers, interleaved with sheets of parchment paper, in airtight tins.

US	Ingredients	Met/Imp
1 lb	grapes	500 g/1 lb
½ lb	Fondant (*page 584*)	250 g/8 oz
3½ oz	gum arabic	100 g/3½ oz

CARAMEL GRAPES

Preparation 2 hours

These can be made either with grapes in *eau-de-vie* or with fresh grapes. When using fresh grapes, dip them into the melted fondant in clusters of 3 with tongs or even by hand. If using grapes in eau-de-vie, drain them and leave them a long time to dry. Roll them in powdered gum arabic and ice them in the same way as cherries in eau-de-vie (*page 660*).

Always detach them from the baking sheet or marble slab with a knife before they are completely cold.

US	Ingredients	Met/Imp
⅔ cup	apple jelly	200 g/7 oz
3 cups	sugar, cooked to the hard crack stage (*page 575*)	600 g/1¼ lb
½ cup	caster (granulated) sugar	100 g/3½ oz

SWEET APPLE PASTE

Preparation 3 hours • Cooking 20 minutes

Put the apple jelly in a saucepan and add the sugar syrup. Place over a low heat and stir to prevent the mixture sticking.

When it is well blended, tip the apple paste on to a lightly oiled marble slab and leave until cold. Cut the paste into sticks and roll in sugar.

WINE

The dream of many wine enthusiasts, or of those who entertain regularly, would be to have a complete list of dishes with the most appropriate wine for each dish shown opposite, and another list of wines, showing the ideal dish with which to serve them. These lists would be computerized, regularly updated, and capable of infinite expansion.

Such lists do not exist, and if some pseudo–expert were to take it into his head to compile them, they would be a sterile and lifeless achievement, like a rigid guide to the interpretation of dreams that leaves the dreamer confused and unsatisfied.

In any case, they would teach us nothing, and would keep us in ignorance of the deeper levels of the subject. It would be like claiming to be able to teach a foreign language using vocabulary alone, and completely ignoring grammar. When it comes to the proper enjoyment of wine, the 'syntax' is the most entrancing part of the learning process.

What follows is a brief discussion of some of the factors that condition the development and character of French wines. This will go some way towards showing why they are so well suited to French cuisine.

Wine is defined by law as the product of fermented grape juice, but this formula is too simple to have any real significance.

First of all, it should be pointed out that there are two kinds of grapes: table grapes and those for making wine. The first type are good for eating, but do not make good wine; while the second type are not so pleasing to eat fresh, but reveal hidden qualities when fermented and turned into wine. (There are, in fact, a few types of grape suitable for both purposes – Chasselas, for example.) In order to make good wine, you must have the right kind of grape, picked from a well–cultivated vine grown in suitable soil. The fruit must be healthy, and the juice should be carefully fermented and perfectly matured. This essential phase of winemaking depends to a large extent on the art or science of the winemaker himself, who will struggle to produce an authentic wine, one faithful to its soil and aspect, its climatic environment, and the characteristics of the particular vintage. To summarize, good wine comes from a combination of the following three equally important factors:
— the vine;

— the 'terroir' (soil, aspect and climatic environment);
— the winemaker.

Equilibrium between each of these factors will give a harmonious wine.

The vine

This means a vine which produces grapes suitable for winemaking, in other words one belonging to the family *Vitis vinifera*. In the same way that we distinguish between numerous types of apple (Golden Delicious, for example, or *reinette* or *calville*), there are also several thousand species of vine. Of the hundreds of vines that have been grown in France in the past, only about thirty or so are found in today's vineyards, and these have all been adapted and developed over centuries to suit the climate, the amount of sunshine and the growing conditions of their region. There is no doubt, however, that some of these vines are related to one another; they probably come from the same parent stock. The majority of French vines are of native origin, despite myths to the contrary, although a small minority do come from neighbouring countries.

In order to be able to understand wine, it is necessary to know about the principal types of vine, as it is the vine that determines the basic character of the wine. The 'terroir' on the other hand, gives the wine its individual personality; and the winemaker also has an influence, being able to develop or even alter a wine by the way in which he or she makes and matures it.

Wines made from aromatic grapes, such as the Muscat and Gewürztraminer produced in Alsace, provide extreme examples of the way in which the vine can influence the basic character of wine. Their powerful bouquet dominates the drinker's perception and enjoyment of the wine. It also harmonizes perfectly with numerous Alsace specialities, particularly Munster cheese.

The natural rapport between products from the same region is one of the foremost principles of French gastronomy, and one which the great Curnonsky never ceased to remind us of.

The terroir

It is a common error, within France, to understand the word 'terroir' as signifying no more than the varying suitability of different places and soils for winegrowing.

The 'terroir' is — in the broadest sense — the place where the vine grows, and is almost an equivalent of the term *cru*, or 'growth'. 'Terroir' should be taken to mean a combination of apparently dissimilar factors which form a coherent whole in respect of growing grapes for wine: climate, composition of the soil and subsoil, aspect, sunshine, rainfall, prevailing winds and so on.

The importance of 'terroir' can be highlighted by dividing French wines into two major categories: northern or 'septentrionale' wines, and southern or 'méridionale' wines.

The first type come from north of an imaginary and erratic line starting from the Vendée in the west of France, running south of the Loire, taking in upper Poitou, reaching Nevers and then going north as far as Auxerre before plunging right down to the south to include Burgundy and Beaujolais, following the Rhône as far south as Valence, then returning north towards Isère, Savoy, the Jura and Alsace.

Thus, all vineyards to the south of this line, including Bordeaux, the whole of the South West, Languedoc-Roussillon, the Rhône valley as far as Montélimar, Drôme, Haute–Provence and Provence are southern.

One of the major differences between these large zones is that in the north, a single grape variety will produce different kinds of wine (all of them well structured) depending on the region in which it is grown, while in the south, wines of similar styles will be produced from a number of different grape varieties.

The reason for this is simple. Red wine attains a satisfactory structural balance when there is a good relationship between alcohol, acidity and tannin, but for white wines, it is the relationship between alcohol, acidity and sweetness that is important. In the north, these balances are threatened by a deficit in alcohol due to insufficient sunlight. In 1984, for example, Touraine had a total of 1,465 hours of sunshine, as opposed to 1,633 hours in the more generous year of 1985. The action of the sun determines the natural sugar content of the grapes and consequently, the alcohol content of the wine — since this results from the conversion of sugar into alcohol (by yeast). It takes 17 g (just over ½ oz) of natural sugar per 1 litre (35 fl oz) of grape juice to obtain 1 per cent of alcohol. Bandol in the south, by way of contrast to Touraine, has 3,000 hours of sunlight a year, and the grapes are very rich in sugar, therefore they produce a powerful wine. On the other hand, southern wines tend to lack acidity, a shortcoming that is overcome by growing a number of different grape varieties with complementary qualities.

Another consequence of these climatic differences is that the idea of the vintage is much more important and significant in the north than in the south.

As a general rule, you can say that the wines of the north are naturally more acid than tannic and are low in alcohol, except when this is corrected, while the wines of the south are more tannic and alcoholic than acid.

This does not mean that the first type is without alcohol and tannin and the second type without acidity, but it does explain why more white wine is produced in the north and more red wine in the south. It also explains why, generally speaking, the red wines of the north have less colour than those of the south, since it is the alcohol, and the fermentation process itself, that dissolves the colouring matter from the grape skin into the wine. The actual juice of the grape is white, at least in the case of grape varieties producing French wines of guaranteed origin. The vineyards of Champagne, for example, are nearly three-quarters planted with dark red Pinot Noir and Pinot Meunier grapes, which are pressed as soon as they have been harvested, in order to obtain a white wine that is acid rather than tannic.

It is noticeable that, because of the nature of the leading grape varieties and prevailing climatic conditions, the wines of the north have floral and mineral fragrances that develop, with age, into complex animal aromas such as game or offal (variety meats) as with red burgundy. The wines of the south are more fruity than floral, and with age, develop fragrances resembling cooked fruit, jam, prunes, truffles or humus; complex fragrances reminiscent of leather or fur; or so-called empyreumatic (burnt matter) fragrances, such as wood smoke, resin, incense and tobacco.

You can guess some of the uses made of these differing characteristics in gastronomy, and we shall discuss relevant food and wine combinations later. First, we must take a look at the third major factor involved in the production of wine: man, the winemaker, *homo vinens* . . .

The winemaker

The role of the winegrower/winemaker is crucial, of course, for wine is very much a human

creation. It begins with the choice of grape variety and continues through the growing process, a particularly important part of which is annual pruning. Finally, the art (or science) of wine-making can be performed with varying degrees of skill, good sense or genius.

Different methods of winemaking are employed according to the 'terroir', the style of wine required, the grape variety and, sometimes, the quality of the harvest. For example, the grapes are fermented with their skins for a few hours for a rosé wine, a few days for a light red or carafe wine and up to three weeks for a good red keeping wine. The three types of wine thus obtained respond to varying needs. Rosé is a lively wine and goes well with light summer cuisine. Carafe wine is suitable for the kind of simple meal you would share with family or friends. A good keeping wine takes a number of years to reveal its full range of qualities. It is a wine for special occasions, and will leave its mark on them to such an extent that it may even be the very thing that you remember them by afterwards.

Wine is, in fact, the heart and soul of a meal. The same carefully prepared menu, served with indifferent wines or served with great wines, will create two totally different impressions. In the first case you will quickly forget the meal; in the second case it will leave you with a lingering and voluptuous memory.

Wine is also the heart and soul of a region, of a 'terroir' and of its winegrowers. It embodies the natural harmony that exists between things and people. This is why it is a good general rule to serve, as far as possible, foods and wines of the same region together. Finally, do not let yourself be misled by the idea that only expensive wines will be memorable. The greatest wines are, of course, usually authentic masterpieces of nature and human intervention, but many more modest wines can achieve real perfection within their own type.

Serving wines

A harmonious meal can be compared with a concerto: the food is the orchestra and the wine is the solo instrument — the violin, the piano, the trumpet. No-one has yet written a concerto for strings and penny whistle, though, and by the same token there are wines that are unsuitable for certain dishes. A dish with an average intensity of flavour, depending of course on what its main ingredient is, should be served with a light white or red wine. Interesting and highly seasoned haute cuisine dishes will require no less than a red or white wine of great vitality.

In general, it should be borne in mind that a white wine lightens and a red wine smothers. With careful selection, though, certain meals can be accompanied with either red or white wine. For example, take a simple light spring menu composed of herb quiche followed by cold roast chicken, salad and cream cheese. This would go well with a white wine such as an Alsace Sylvaner, a Bourgogne-Aligoté, a Mâcon-Villages, or perhaps a dry Vouvray or Graves, and so on. If the wines are of first-class quality, this meal can be extremely refined in its simplicity. However, it is also necessary to take into consideration the factor that some people do not like white wine. A red wine of the same weight and intensity, such as an Alsace Pinot Noir, Chinon, Bourgueil or Premières Côtes de Bordeaux would match the food well and lend the same note of refinement to it as would the white wines.

The season determines both the choice of menu and the choice of wines. In summer, marinated meat served with a highly seasoned sauce is as hard to enjoy as a powerful, tannic, youthful Châteauneuf-du-Pape. This is autumn or winter food, and autumn or winter wine.

A balanced and well-structured menu follows a certain progression of flavours, always going from the simplest to the most complex. The same rule should apply to wines. Therefore, in accordance with this simple rule, avoid serving sweet fortified wines or spirits as aperitifs: they are so full-bodied, heavy and high in alcohol that they deaden the taste buds, thus preventing you from appreciating the delicacy of the first wine. It is better, in fact, to serve the first wine as an aperitif or, better still, if possible, a Brut Champagne, preferably a Blanc de Blancs. If the meal has a regional note to it, you should not hesitate to serve an appropriate regional sparkling wine as an aperitif: Crémant from Alsace, Loire or Burgundy; Clairette de Die; Saint-Péray Mousseux; Blanquette de Limoux, and so on. The principle is always to ensure that this initial drink does not overwhelm the first table wine that you serve.

Always serve:
A light wine before a full-bodied wine.
A dry white wine before a sweet white wine.
A dry white wine before a red wine.

A red wine before a sweet white wine.

A simple wine before a complex wine.

A young wine before an old wine, unless the younger wine is of a superior vintage, in which case the preceding principle comes into operation and you should serve the simpler wine before the more complex one. A second wine should never make you hanker after the first wine. If you serve a sweet wine like a fine Sauternes as your first wine – together, say, with foie gras, a popular combination in the Bordeaux region – this does not pose any particular problems, since a meal that begins in this way can only continue with other equally refined courses, and with these you should serve a red wine with plenty of vitality, such as a fine Haut-Médoc, Graves, Saint-Émilion or Pomerol.

The classic tradition in France was always to serve wines in threes: a dry white, a red, then a medium dry or sweet white. This tradition was widely followed several decades ago, when the production of white wine far outweighed the production of red. Today, the most popular practice when serving three wines is to serve a white wine to begin with (this is often replaced by champagne), and then two red wines, the second being the better of the two and used to accompany the cheese which often takes the place of dessert. In some ways this is a pity, as cheese does not need to be treated with such respect, but economy may well be a factor here. When serving one white and two red wines, you should avoid at all costs serving two wines of the same colour but different origins: a Burgundy after a Bordeaux, for example, or vice versa. The two red wines should be from the same region or from closely neighbouring ones. For example, the first wine could well be Beaujolais and the second a Burgundy, or else you could have a red wine from the Côte Chalonnaise (such as Mercurey or Givry) followed by a Côte Rôtie or Hermitage. Each wine comes from within the eastern part of the northern zone. Other examples spring to mind: a Côtes de Provence followed by a Châteauneuf-du-Pape, or any one of the many Languedoc-Roussillon wines followed by an old Banyuls, especially if the cheese board includes a top-quality Roquefort.

It is best to respect, as far as possible, the natural harmony that exists between products from the same region. It is therefore a good idea to get to know the French regions, and their foods and wines, as well as possible. Cuisine that uses ingredients from one region alone is naturally harmonious, which is why, for example, 'tripes à la mode de Caen' is so well partnered by a top-quality cider, which in turn will do wonders for the Pont l'Évêque or Livarot cheese that follows it. A meal in which a Loire wine is served with an Alsace sauerkraut dish, or a fine Médoc with beef bourguignon, would be much less successful.

ALSACE

Situated on the eastern slopes of the Vosges mountains in the *départements* of Bas-Rhin (Lower Rhine) and Haut-Rhin (Upper Rhine) are the 12,600 hectares/31,134 acres of Alsatian vineyards. The region has varied soils, to which a number of different grape varieties have adapted very well. Alsace has its own *appellation contrôlée*, followed by the name of the grape variety from which the wine in question has been made. Alsace Grand Cru is a superior *appellation* from one of a number of named vineyards.

Alsace Gewürztraminer: aromatic, spicy and rich. Serve with strong cheeses such as Munster, Alsace desserts, tarts, kugelhopf, etc.

Alsace Pinot Blanc: a light, fruity wine. Serve as for Alsace Riesling and Alsace Sylvaner.

Alsace Pinot Gris or **Tokay:** a broad, rich white wine which ages particularly well. Serve with foie gras, roasts and small game birds.

Alsace Pinot Noir: the region's only red wine – light, elegant and fruity. Serve with red meats.

Alsace Riesling: the most complete of the region's wines and the pride of its winemakers. Serve with fish in sauce, shellfish dishes cooked in white wine, snails, pheasant, sauerkraut.

Alsace Sylvaner: light and fresh, with a slight prickle of bubbles in a good year. Serve with shellfish, grilled (or broiled) fish and charcuterie.

Muscat d'Alsace: extremely aromatic and very dry. Serve as an aperitif.

The life span of Alsace wines is several years for Edelzwicker (made from a blend of grape varieties), Pinot Blanc, Pinot Noir, Sylvaner and Muscat, about ten years for Gewürztraminer of a reasonably good vintage and from a good site and grower, and about twenty years or more for top-quality Riesling and Pinot Gris. The best wines of exceptional vintages (such as 1983 or 1985), wines from grapes picked late in the season (*vendange tardive*) or wines made from first-class *grand cru* sites will keep even longer. A 1922

Riesling tasted in 1987 had an extraordinarily expressive bouquet, and was ample and fresh on the palate.

CHAMPAGNE

Wine from Champagne conforms to special standards. Unlike many French wines, the finest champagne is the result of an expert blending of wines from different *crus* and grape varieties, and of different ages, all of which complement and balance one another, making a whole that is superior to the sum of its parts. Naturally, in a vintage champagne, this balance is achieved using wines from the same year, and in the case of a Blanc de Blancs, from a single grape variety – the Chardonnay. The idea of the *cru* is also very important in Champagne, despite the fact that champagne is a blended wine. Much of the vineyard area of the region is graded, and this hierarchy of *crus* governs the price of a kilo of grapes at harvest time. Seventeen *grands crus* fetch 100 per cent of the set price; about 40 *premiers crus* fetch from 99 to 90 per cent of the maximum price; and the other *crus*, which are classed from 90 to 80 per cent, will receive an according percentage price per kilo of grapes. As these figures suggest, a blend of wines produced from *grand cru* and *premier cru* grapes gives better results than a blend based on wines from those *crus* classed at 80 per cent. The leading Champagne houses consider that they produce the best wines, while the cooperatives think that they do just as well. Certain individual winegrowers, known as 'récoltants-manipulants', who also make their own champagne and then sell it directly to the public, are very proud of their product, sometimes justifiably so. The range of prices for champagne is enormous, and certain vintage champagnes and 'prestige' blends are among the most expensive of all the world's wines.

A Blanc de Blancs Champagne makes an excellent aperitif, and the Brut (vintage or otherwise) can serve as a table wine – there are many who love a meal served with champagne throughout. Rosé Champagne is a suitable accompaniment for meat dishes, and medium dry (Demi-Sec) for desserts.

BURGUNDY

The vineyards of Burgundy are considered to begin in Auxerre, with Chablis, and end almost as far south as Lyon, at the southern tip of Beaujolais. The range of wines produced in this region is enormous, with the most modest and the most prestigious wines both playing important roles.

Chablis is suitable for serving with various dishes according to its degree of quality. The most humble is Petit Chablis, which goes well with shellfish, fried dishes and charcuterie; then comes Chablis, which should be served with shellfish or grilled (or broiled) fish; then Chablis Premier Cru, which is a richer wine suitable for all sorts of fish in sauce; and finally, Chablis Grand Cru, which should be reserved for haute cuisine dishes.

Other wines from the Chablis area such as Sauvignon de Saint-Bris are modest in price alone, and will accompany most fish dishes very happily. (Because it is made from the Sauvignon Blanc grape rather than the Chardonnay, Sauvignon de Saint-Bris has more in common with Upper Loire white wines than with Chablis.) The red wines of Irancy are also produced near Chablis, as are some white Bourgogne-Aligoté and red and white Bourgogne wines.

Travelling south past Dijon brings us to the Côte de Nuits: the northern of the two stretches of vineyard that collectively make up the Côte d'Or. The wines of the Côte de Nuits can be served with the best red meats and with furred or feathered game. Whether you serve a simple Côtes de Nuits-Villages or a sublime Romanée-Conti depends largely on your pocket. The same thing applies to the Côte de Beaune, the southern half of the Côte d'Or, which offers the most attractive red and white wines to accompany the most delicate fare for special occasions.

South of the Côte d'Or lies the Côte Chalonnaise, where the villages of Mercurey, Rully, Givry and Montagny produce red and white wines that are very good value for money. The Mâconnais region, south of the Côte Chalonnaise, is best known for its white wines, of which the leading example is the famous Pouilly-Fuissé. Pouilly-Loché and Pouilly-Vinzelles produce similar wines, while Saint-Véran and, to an even greater extent, plain Mâcon-Villages, both offer white wines of great versatility for the table. With honest country food, there are few better accompaniments than light red Beaujolais-Villages, served slightly chilled. Better still will be one of the Beaujolais

'Sacred Vine, what does it matter! Beneath heaven's clear light, we will grow drunk on your precious blood! (. . .) The sacred stream of wine runs and dazzles, to the sound of divine song!' (Théodore de Banville, Cariatides)

(CAVES MALLARD-GAULIN, BEAUNE)

The wine of Burgundy 'was the most cheerful colour, just like the precious red carbuncle: not too hard, not too soft, but supple; neither warm nor cold, but rich and innocent', said Erasmus. He saluted this region with the following words: 'Happy Burgundy! You deserve the title of mother of men, since you gave them such milk!'

'*A few wines were fading – pale, but still fragrant, like a dying rose; they rested on tannic lees which stained the bottle, but most of them preserved their ardent distinction, their invigorating virtue . . . I have drunk the finest wine of my father's cellar, mug by mug, thoughtfully. . . . My mother re-corked the half-empty bottle, and gazed at the glory of French wine on my cheeks.*' (Colette, Prisons et Paradis)

'The amber hue of Sauternes and Barsac, the yellow straw tone of Yquem, the golden notes of Montrachet, Meursault and Chablis, the water green of Pouilly: all these are too precious to be turned blue or pink. Serve these wines in pure crystal glass. Before drinking, lift your glass to the light and you will see it filled with a brilliant ray of sunlight, for the greater joy of your eyes and palate.' (Maurice des Ombiaux, Traité de la Table)

'A bottle of champagne must always be left for a good minute to rest in its ice buck after it has been uncorked.' This valuable advice is from Fernand Point.

crus. These vary in style from the lighter Chiroubles and Fleurie to the richer Morgon or Moulin-à-Vent.

CÔTES DU RHÔNE

After many years of having been undervalued, prices for Rhône wines have now risen to the level that their quality merits. Nevertheless there are still many reasonably priced wines, even among the very best Rhône names like red Côte Rôtie, white Condrieu, red and white Saint-Joseph, the powerful red Cornas, Crozes-Hermitages and the fine red and white Hermitages; these are wines that should, at some moment or other, grace every high-quality table. They are all from the northern part of the region. The southern part of the Côtes du Rhône produces generous, sundrenched wines. The powerful Châteauneuf-du-Pape, for example, is quite at home with strongly flavoured game and marinated meats, and the same can be said of Gigondas or red Lirac. The rosé wine of the Rhône, and that of Gigondas in particular, is both elegant and powerful. It goes well with red meat in summer. Tavel is superb – a king among rosé wines. It is at its best with fillets of red mullet, and goes equally well with other fish or light meat. These are all rich, complex wines that will rarely disappoint. However, we should not overlook the various Côtes du Rhône-Villages: warm, harmonious wines suitable for accompanying roasts, grilled (or broiled) meat and small game birds. Of equal merit are the neighbouring *appellations* of Coteaux du Tricastin, the often impressive Côtes du Ventoux and Côtes du Luberon, all of which are reasonably priced and a faithful reflection of their herb-scented 'terroirs'.

You could create a memorable and harmonious meal using Rhône wines alone. Begin by offering a Clairette de Die or a Saint-Péray Mousseux as an aperitif, followed by one of the deep, sound red wines described above. The meal could end in grand gourmet style with a still, sweet *vin doux naturel*, such as Muscat de Beaumes de Venise, with dessert.

PROVENCE AND CORSICA

Provence and Corsica readily evoke visions of the lost paradise of Eden, since all the ingredients that go to make up happiness for most of us are to be found there: blue seas and skies, beaches and mountains, sunshine and, of course, those two most friendly plants, the olive tree and the grapevine. Both these areas offer tasty, simple and authentic regional cuisines that are perfectly matched by their respective wines. What better wine could there be to accompany a brochette flavoured with thyme than a rosé from Provence or Ajaccio? For a daube simmering away in the tiled shade of a Provençal kitchen, nothing could better than a sumptuous red Bandol, and to accompany freshly caught local fish, a white Cassis or Porto Vecchio is admirable.

Matching the right wine with the right food can improve your guests' enjoyment of a meal beyond recognition. For example, if you serve a bouillabaisse or bourride, grilled (or broiled) fish with fennel or ratatouille and accompany it with a rosé wine from the Loire, no one will complain. But if you offer them a rosé from Palette or Bellet, both rare and fine Provençal wines, everyone will be enchanted and the meal is sure to become one to remember! It is useless to go to a lot of trouble in the kitchen if the wines do not match in every way the quality and inspiration of the food. Every province in France has its own food and wine specialities, and these blend perfectly with one another, thanks to centuries of mutual evolution. Other excellent wines from Provence include Coteaux d'Aix-en-Provence, Coteaux des Baux-de-Provence, Côtes de Provence and Coteaux de Pierrevert.

LANGUEDOC-ROUSSILLON

Lozère is the only one of the five *départements* of Languedoc-Roussillon that is not a winegrowing area. The other four *départements* (Pyrénées-Orientales, Aude, Hérault and Gard) produce so much wine that they constitute the largest wine-producing area of France, and the second largest quality wine-producing area in France, after Bordeaux.

For all this, the wines of Languedoc-Roussillon are still under-appreciated, and few wine-lovers take the trouble to seek out the best among them. These are still very much overshadowed by the huge quantity of ordinary wine produced from the vineyards on the plains! One of the first surprises you might discover is Clairette de Bellegarde, a delicious and delicate fruity white wine, typical of the Clairette grape and characterized by an exceptional 'terroir'. A wine

close to it, although with a few shades of difference, is the Clairette du Languedoc. Both these dry white wines are very different from other dry white wines, particularly those of the Loire valley in northern France. Other good white wines worth looking out for are Picpoul de Pinet, a dry white wine that goes marvellously with Bouzigues oysters and other seafood; wines from La Clape and Corbières; and the white wines of the Côtes du Roussillon, made uniquely from the Macabeu grape. This can be vinified into either a dry or sweet wine, and the latter will surprise you wonderfully and tempt you to a second helping of dessert.

Among the red wines of Languedoc-Roussillon are so many of such rapidly improving quality that one is spoilt for choice. The best include Costières du Gard, La Clape, Montpeyroux, Saint-Chinian, Faugères, Fitou, Minervois and Corbières, each one warmer and more subtle than the next, and all of them reasonably priced. Languedoc-Roussillon has still to be discovered.

GAILLAC

The remains of jars found in the walls of houses in this part of France prove the existence of vineyards here in times of antiquity, particularly at Gaillac and Rabastens. The chalky slopes on the right bank of the Tarn river in the north of Gaillac are favourable for the production of dry white wines, while the granite alluvium of the left bank is better suited to red ones. There are about fifteen different red and white grape varieties in Gaillac. Some of the wines are the product of a single vine, such as the Gamay, which gives a fruity, easy-drinking red wine, or the Mauzac, which gives a most attractive sweet or dry white wine. There is even a rare wine produced by methods similar to those used for the *vin jaune* of the Jura region, being kept in a partly empty cask ('on ullage') for six years. The result is wonderful, half way between *vin jaune* and sherry.

The most unusual Gaillac wine is Gaillac Perlé, and this is obtained by a local method that involves bottling the wine so that it retains a very slight natural effervescence. It is a delicate wine with fine bubbles that give it extra bouquet and freshness, and it makes a perfect aperitif for a summer lunch.

Red Gaillac is deeply coloured wine with good keeping potential and a distinguished bouquet.

The rosé is unusual, being made from Gamay grapes among others, sometimes with a touch of Syrah that gives it a cherry-red tinge and enhances its finesse and longevity.

CÔTES DU FRONTONNAIS

The Frontonnais area straddles the *départements* of Haute-Garonne and Tarn-et-Garonne, half way between Toulouse and Montauban. Classic Côtes du Frontonnais is a French country wine like no other: the principal grape variety from which it is made, the Négrette, gives it a unique colour, smell and flavour. Legally, at least half of the *appellation* area must be planted with Négrette (which produces very black grapes, as its name suggests), but there is no minimum requirement for the proportion to be included in the wine. Consequently, a significant amount of wine of this *appellation* does not fulfil its admirers' expectations. Wine from the Négrette is also made into rosé, which is only fermented for a short time, thus diminishing the particular characteristics of the variety. Red Côtes du Frontonnais also contains wine made from other grape varieties such as Cabernet Sauvignon and Cabernet Franc, often in large proportions. This is a pity, and is most detrimental to the traditional wine, which has an unusual character that makes it one of the many gems among the great wines of France. The real Frontonnais has a very dark colour, but is nevertheless an elegant red wine, comparatively low in alcohol. It offers some unusual flavour-analogies such as iodine, cooked prunes, herbs, vanilla and even burnt wood. It first confuses and then seduces when served with roast pork and prunes, spiced red meats, special cheeses, pastries, plum tarts, and so on. It will prove a real revelation to lovers of eclectic wines.

CAHORS

This has been famous winegrowing country since the early Middle Ages. The vineyards were nearly destroyed by the phylloxera vine pest towards the end of the last century. They have only recently been replanted to any great extent; new vines have again taken over the stony slopes that once enabled the area to attain the heights of glory.

Cahors is a dark, lustrous wine which makes a wonderful and appropriate partner for the other

specialities of the area, such as truffles, foie gras, 'confits' (preserved meats) and other delicacies from the Quercy area.

It is exclusively a red wine, made mainly from Côt grapes (also known as Malbec, and locally called the Auxerrois), with the addition of wine made from Tannat and Jurançon Noir grapes. Whatever the exact blend, the resultant wine is dark, quite powerful and tannic. It keeps for a long time. Despite its appearance, it is not particularly high in alcohol, but it has a penetrating bouquet and powerful velvety taste.

CÔTES DE BUZET

This is a wine close, in every sense of the word, to those of Bordeaux; in fact, until the end of the last century, it was confused with Bordeaux and sold as such. It is, nevertheless, a quality wine in its own right. Nearly all of it is made by the Buzet wine cooperative, from grape varieties identical to those of Bordeaux. It is quite fleshy and full-bodied, and is suited to long bottle-maturation, depending on the vintage, of course. It is a wine that goes well with roasts, grilled (or broiled) meat or meat in sauce, and with refined cuisine in general.

JURANÇON-MADIRAN-IROULÉGUY

The geographical order in which we have named these three wines is not the order in which they should be served at table. It would be better to serve a fresh, almost gulpable Irouléguy with a first course (this is a Basque wine from the mountains and coast, with a spicy aroma and taste): it would be perfect with a pipérade, for example.

The Madiran should be reserved for red meat, marinated or otherwise, or for special game dishes. Madiran is a powerful, dark red wine, almost black. At least 40 per cent of the blend must be provided by the Tannat grape variety which, as its name suggests, gives tannic wines. However, after a year or more in cask and several more years in bottle, this once uncouth youngster mellows impressively. The odour of truffles suits it perfectly. It shares its *appellation* area (which is situated south-west of that of Armagnac) with a most agreeable white wine with the curious name of Pacherenc du Vic-Bilh. This wine can either be dry or sweet, but tends to be the former more often than the latter. It is

light, delicate and pleasantly fruity. It goes well with simple first courses such as seafood pastries and coquilles Saint-Jacques, etc.

Jurançon, a white wine which is made in dry, medium dry and sweet form, has been popular since the birth of Henry IV, whose father made him taste it the day he was born. The dry variety is extremely dry, almost tart, while the sweet kind is luscious, slightly spicy, with a citrus finish. Both are made from the same grape varieties (Gros and Petit Manseng, Courbu), but the latter comes from grapes gathered later in the year when the fruit has dried and rotted a little and the juice is thereby concentrated (see 'Bordeaux', overleaf). It is an admirable dessert wine and can be served with most pastries and fruit tarts.

BERGERAC

Bergerac is a vast region bordering the *département* of the Gironde, in the south-west corner of the *département* of the Dordogne. Its red and rosé wines, and its dry, medium dry and sweet white wines (such as the famous Monbazillac) are all of good quality and reasonably priced.

The red wines come from grape varieties identical to those of Bordeaux. While they can never match the quality of Bordeaux's best wines, they are nevertheless excellent wines in their own right, and of a quality to match many of Bordeaux's lesser wines. Those which come under the Pécharmant *appellation* are particularly good, thanks to the fact that the vineyards are situated on sloping ground (in the local dialect 'pé' has the same meaning as 'puy' or 'pech' ie a mountain or summit). Pécharmant is a powerful, well-structured wine with a delicate bouquet. It reaches its best after a few years in bottle.

A little-known *appellation* from this area is Rosette, a medium dry white wine which has intrigued many a curious traveller to the Dordogne. A delicate aperitif or dessert wine, it is as refined as it is rare.

Monbazillac, however, is the region's greatest white wine. It regained its true character about ten years ago, after some years of eclipse due to abuses in the period after the Second World War, when poverty and the consequent popularity of cheap, sugared wines poisoned the market. It is a powerful, oily, full-bodied wine that goes wonderfully with foie gras or Roquefort cheese, and equally well with rich desserts. You have to

be prepared to wait, though – like Sauternes, top-quality Monbazillac needs to be bottled for a number of years before reaching its best. The length of time varies according to vintage: most 1976 wines are ready for drinking now, while the finest wines of 1975 will not begin to show at their best until 1995.

BORDEAUX

1 Red Wines

In ascending order of quality, we begin with the general *appellation* Bordeaux, available to all the wines of the region. Next come the broad regional *appellations* such as Médoc or Entre-Deux-Mers; and then smaller regions such as the Haut-Médoc. Finally we come to the 'commune' or 'parish' *appellations* like Margaux, Listrac or Saint-Julien. Within these *appellations*, certain properties are classified hierarchically by their château name. 'Château' (castle or mansion) is a conventional term applied to all the winegrowing estates in Bordeaux. The scale of prices is an easy guide to the extremes of quality, but not necessarily to those many wines that occupy the middle ground, hence the difficulty of choice.

More than is the case with any other region, in Bordeaux there are no 'good' and 'bad' wines, only more complex and less complex wines which respond to different needs at different times.

The character of the wines depends upon the type of grape variety or varieties they are made from and the particularities of the different 'terroirs'. The red wines of the Médoc and Graves accompany leg of lamb and game birds superbly, while the warmer, earthier wines from Saint-Émilion and the other regions where the Merlot grape predominates are a better choice to serve with furred game and marinated red meats. Apart from these two very major regional divisions (between the predominantly Cabernet Sauvignon wines of the Médoc and the predominantly Merlot wines of Saint-Émilion) there are many other wines in between, each one in harmony with its soil and able, at the right time and place, to give as much pleasure as the most prestigious châteaux.

2 White Wines

There are three main categories of white wine in Bordeaux: dry, medium dry and sweet. All are made from the same pool of grape varieties: Sauvignon Blanc, Sémillon and Muscadelle. The latter is always used in very small quantities – between five and ten per cent of the final blend. Some dry wines are the product of the Sauvignon Blanc alone, particularly in the Entre-Deux-Mers region. They will be simple, fruity wines, often very good value for money. The name of the grape will sometimes be shown on the label. They make an excellent accompaniment to all seafoods, especially shellfish.

The most highly reputed white wines from the Graves sub-region are far more complex than this. They should be served with cooked dishes, good-quality fish dishes and crustaceans.

The medium dry and sweet wines, such as Graves Supérieures, Sauternes, Barsac, Cérons, Sainte-Croix-du-Mont, Cadillac and Premières Côtes de Bordeaux are made from very ripe grapes: the Sémillon, for example, after it has attained the famous 'noble rot'. This 'noble rot' is a fungus that concentrates the juice of the grape, increasing its sugar content so that when fermented the grapes produce a wine that is very high in alcohol, with differing proportions of natural residual sugar. These wines have a very rich and varied bouquet, with a complex, honeyed succulence on the palate. They are exceptional, as the rot does not occur every year; they can only be made when climatic conditions permit. They are also time consuming and labour intensive to harvest: pickers have to go through the vineyards several times in order to gather affected bunches at the right moment.

MUSCADET AND GROS PLANT DU PAYS NANTAIS

Muscadet and Gros Plant du Pays Nantais are readily associated with one another because they are both very dry white wines, and they are both produced in the same area near Nantes. The difference between them is important, however, as it concerns grape variety: in this part of France, near the mouth of the Loire, the Folle Blanche grape variety is known as Gros Plant, and the Melon de Bourgogne as Muscadet. The similarities that exist between the two wines have nothing whatsoever to do with the varieties, which are completely different from each other, but are rather to do with the fact that they share

the same 'terroir'. This proves (if there is any need to do so) just how important the concept of 'terroir' really is!

Gros Plant is an acid wine: drier and lower in alcohol than Muscadet. It goes perfectly with shellfish, especially oysters, and even more perfectly when these can be eaten by the sea.

Gros Plant *sur lie* ('on the lees') is superior in quality to the ordinary version. A wine described in this way must still be resting on its sediment when bottled. It should be bottled before 1 July in the year following the harvest, and the year of the harvest must be indicated on the label.

The practice of bottling wine directly from its lees is most widespread for Muscadet, especially Muscadet de Sèvre et Maine: this is the best-quality Muscadet and, fortunately, also the type that is produced in the greatest quantity. There are, in fact, three types of Muscadet: one — 'simple' Muscadet — is produced throughout the whole *appellation*; the second type is Muscadet des Coteaux de la Loire; and the third is Muscadet de Sèvre et Maine.

When bottled *sur lie*, the latter is suitable not only for shellfish and crustaceans, but also for fish in sauce or with beurre blanc — in fact for all the most refined seafood dishes.

ANJOU

The gentleness and sweetness of Anjou, birthplace of Maurice Edmond Sailland, known as Curnonsky, is reflected in its wines as much as in its soft river landscape and agreeable climate.

From Brittany, you approach Anjou via a small district on the right banks of the river Loire where a fine dry white wine called Savennières is produced. It is produced in small quantities (average annual production is about 1,800 hl), and it is dry, delicate and extremely refined. It should be served with sophisticated dishes, from the best-quality fish to white meats. Considering its fineness, it is very reasonably priced.

Anjou is particularly associated with delicate medium dry or sweet white wines, such as Coteaux du Layon, Quarts de Chaume and Bonnezeaux, all of which attain the very highest quality in good years (like 1985, 1983, 1982 and 1978). Coteaux de l'Aubance achieved distinction by producing medium dry wines which, for a long time, delighted the faithful clientèle of local bars and bistros, along with the two rosé wines of Anjou and Cabernet d'Anjou.

All these wines are now decreasing in production, while production of red wines is on the increase. The red wines of Anjou are well structured, generally made from the Cabernet Franc grape, sometimes with a little Cabernet Sauvignon or other grape varieties added. The quality is good, but does not match the magnitude of the best red wines of the Loire valley, like Chinon, Bourgueil or Saumur-Champigny. The red wines of Anjou complement and will be complemented by light dishes, roasts and grilled (or broiled) meats, spit-roasted fowl, and so on.

TOURAINE

Touraine, like Anjou, is one of those privileged provinces of France that can offer a very wide range of quality wines to the purchaser. There is a wine for every occasion, from the simplest to the most sophisticated meal.

Choose your aperitif from among the dry Vouvrays, either sparkling or still. The leading red wines are Chinon, Bourgueil and Saint-Nicolas de Bourgueil. Chinon comes in a range of styles, from dry white through rosé to a sturdy red. Among the reds, connoisseurs and local winemakers can distinguish between wines from different soils — for example, sandy deposits, gravel, or clay-chalk combinations. These varying soils affect the delicacy or firmness of the wine. (Such differences also exist in Bourgueil.) For dessert, choose a sweet white wine from Vouvray or Montlouis.

The range is not limited to these famous communes. The red wines of Touraine-Amboise and Touraine-Mesland, which are made from Gamay, Cabernet Franc and Côt grapes, are balanced and solid, if more rustic than the Chinons and Bourgueils. Among the lighter wines for ordinary occasions, Gamay de Touraine — produced throughout the *appellation* — has freshness and charm. Other reasonably priced wines include the red, white and rosé wines of Cheverny, Coteaux du Vendômois and Valençay. The alluring Gris Meunier from Orléans is fine, aromatic and unusual.

SANCERRE AND POUILLY

Although these two winegrowing areas are still within the Loire valley, they are a long way upstream from Touraine and Anjou. Their geo-

graphical situation is far inland, with no maritime influences at all, and consequently the wines have a different character to those from the Loire valley discussed so far. The gentleness of the Angevin and Touraine skies is faithfully and subtly reflected in their wines. The wines of Sancerre and Pouilly have none of these qualities: they are not delicate, and still less are they mellow; instead they are dry and virile. Nowhere else does the Sauvignon Blanc grape produce such overwhelmingly aromatic wines, with such a solid and imposing flavour. Different types of soil within the growing area influence the personality of the wine, as does the length of maturation it undergoes in cask and bottle.

When young, Sancerre and Pouilly-Fumé have a lively, herbaceous perfume, like that of blackcurrant leaves. After they have matured for a few years, the bouquet widens and begins to suggest the aroma of fruit such as redcurrants, blackcurrants and morello cherries. The flavour is always very dry, even tart, but concentrated and full of fruit. Sancerre and Pouilly-Fumé are wines to accompany the best fish cooked in sauce, poached fowl, and white meats of all sorts. The rosé and red wines of Sancerre, which are made from the Pinot Noir grape variety, are light and elegant, closer to a Rosé des Riceys (from Champagne) or an Alsace Pinot Noir than to a burgundy. They should be served cool.

Years	Red Bordeaux	White Bordeaux	Red Burgundy	White Burgundy	Rhône Valley	Alsace	South West France	Muscadet	Anjou (Sweet Wines)	Saumur	Chinon and Bourgueil	Vouvray	Sancerre and Pouilly-Fumé
1945	20	20	20	16	19	19			16	17	gcl	19	
1947	18	20	18	18	16	18			19	19	18	20	
1948	14		15	14	15	13				12	16	10	
1949	19	17	19	17	15	20			16	15	17	14	
1952	15	14	15	14	13	14			13	12	15	14	
1953	17	18	17	17	15	17			14	13	14	15	
1955	18	18	16	18	16	11			17	17	17	15	
1957	12	15	14	15	14	12			13	11	14	13	
1959	16	18	19	18	19	20			17	18	18	19	
1961	19	18	17	19	18	18			13	13	15	14	
1962	14	16	14	16	15	15			12	13	14	14	
1964	14	8	14	16	14	18			14	16	18	16	
1966	18	15	17	16	16	16			13	12	14	14	13
1967	13	16	17	16	13	15			11	10	12	11	
1969	10	8	18	13	13	14			15	15	16	15	
1970	19	18	10	15	16	13			13	14	16	15	
1971	14	16	16	15	14	19			14	11	15	16	
1972	8	10	13	12	14	8			10	13	14	9	
1973	8	10	10	10	11	15			11	12	13	12	16
1974	12	10	11	10	9	13			12	13	13	10	12
1975	18	18	8	11	9	14	18	15	15	15	14	12	10
1976	14	16	17	11	15	19	17	17	15	12	17	17	16
1978	19	14	18	17	17	11	16	14	16	15	15	12	16
1979	15	14	15	17	17	15	17	15	12	12	13	10	10
1980	10	9	13	16	13	10	12	11	11	12	12	10	8
1981	14	16	10	16	13	15	16	13	12	14	15	14	13
1982	18	10	13	16	15	14	14	15	12	12	17	13	13
1983	16	17	13	15	14	19	17	14	13	13	15	14	16
1984	10	12	13	12	14	12	12	15	12	11	11	10	8
1985	18	16	17	17	17	18	17	16	15	14	18	17	17
1986	16	16	14	15	14	15	16	17	17	16	16	15	18
1987	12	12	11	12	12	16	13	15	12	13	10	12	16

Evaluation of the vintages of the great wines of France from 1 to 20 according to quality

THE GREAT WINEGROWING REGIONS OF FRANCE

1 Alsace
2 Champagne
3 Bourgogne
4 Beaujolais
5 Côtes du Rhône
6 Provence and Corsica
7 Languedoc-Roussillon
8 South West
9 Bordeaux
10 Cognac
11 Muscadet region
12 Anjou
13 Touraine
14 Upper Loire

GLOSSARY

bain-marie: also called a water bath, this is a receptacle containing hot or just simmering water in which pans or dishes of food are cooked very gently or kept hot. A bain-marie is used for foods that are too delicate for contact with direct heat. Custards and creams are often cooked in a bain-marie on top of the stove, and some pâtés, mousses, PAINS, and delicate egg dishes are cooked in a bain-marie in the oven. In domestic kitchens, a roasting pan or wide shallow sauté pan can be used as a bain-marie.

ballotine: a boned piece of fish, meat, poultry or game bird, that is stuffed, rolled and tied up into a cylindrical shape (usually wrapped in cheesecloth), then braised or poached to be served hot or cold.

bard (barder): to cover roasts of lean meat and breasts of poultry or game birds with thin slices of bacon or pork fat (called 'bardes'). The fat prevents the meat from drying out during cooking, and is usually removed before serving. Pâté dishes and terrines are often lined with bardes as are pastry cases for pâtés.

barquette: small boat-shaped tartlet made from shortcrust (pie) pastry or puff pastry.

bavarois: also called Bavarian cream, this is a cold moulded dessert made from rich egg custard and whipped cream set with gelatine.

beignet: deep-fried pastry or fritter, which may be sweet or savoury.

beurre manié: also called kneaded butter, this is made from softened butter and flour worked together to a paste. Beurre manié is used to thicken stews and sauces towards the end of their cooking, and is added a little at a time while the liquid is whisked.

beurre noisette: butter (preferably clarified) heated gently until it turns golden brown and smells nutty. Usually served with sweetbreads, vegetables, eggs and fish.

bisque: rich soup based on a purée of shellfish such as crayfish and lobster, seasoned with wine, herbs and cognac, and enriched with cream.

blanc: white COURT BOUILLON made from salted water, a little flour and lemon juice. White offal (variety meats) and vegetables such as artichoke bottoms, salsify, cardoons and chard, that would otherwise be likely to darken, are cooked 'à blanc'.

blanch (blanchir): to immerse raw foods such as giblets, bacon and vegetables (cabbage and turnips, for example) in boiling water for some minutes, to remove excess salt or bitterness, to make them firmer, to purify them, and so on. The term is also used for a brief scalding of foods such as tomatoes, peaches and almonds to make skinning easy.

blanquette: stew of white meat such as veal and poultry cooked in white stock or water. The cooking liquid is thickened and enriched with egg yolks and cream.

au bleu: method of cooking freshly caught fish such as trout in a boiling vinegar COURT BOUILLON, which gives the skin of the fish a bluish tinge.

bombe: frozen dessert set in a cylindrical mould with a rounded top. Traditionally, two or more layers of ice cream and/or sorbet are used to line the mould, and the centre is filled with a rich custard cream.

bouchée: small, round puff pastry case filled with a savoury mixture and served hot.

bouquet garni: small bunch of herbs and aromatics used to flavour stocks, stews, soups and other dishes. Traditional ingredients in a bouquet garni are 2-3 parsley sprigs, 1 thyme sprig and 1-2 bay leaves, but other herbs, vegetables such as celery and leek, and spices may also be included. The bouquet is tied together with string to make it easy to remove before serving; it may also be enclosed in a cheesecloth bag.

en brochette: pieces of meat, poultry, fish and vegetables threaded on to a large skewer, to be cooked over charcoal or under the grill (broiler).

brunoise: very finely diced vegetables such as carrot, turnip, celery and leek, often braised in butter, used singly or mixed in the preparation of sauces, stuffings, SALPICONS and so on, as well as for garnishing.

canapé: slice of fried or buttered toasted bread, cut into various shapes, that is used as a base for pieces of food or as a garnish.

chantilly: fresh cream whipped to the consistency of a mousse, then often sweetened and flavoured with vanilla.

charlotte: name given to two different desserts. One consists of a thick fruit purée baked in a mould lined with buttered bread slices, and served hot. The other is a cold, uncooked dessert made from a bavarois or mousse set in a mould lined with sponge fingers (ladyfingers). There are also savoury charlottes made from vegetables or fish, cooked in unlined moulds. The traditional charlotte mould is round, with a slightly flared rim.

chartreuse: preparation of game birds, meat or fish with vegetables (particularly braised cabbage), arranged decoratively in layers in a domed mould, cooked in a BAIN-MARIE and turned out for serving hot.

chaud-froid: piece of meat, poultry, game or fish prepared as a hot dish but served cold, coated with a brown or white sauce and glazed with aspic.

chiffonnade: leaves of lettuce, sorrel or chicory (Belgian endive) cut into strips or shreds, to be used as a garnish. The chiffonnade may be braised in butter or used raw.

civet: rich stew, usually of game such as hare, wild rabbit, venison and wild boar cooked in red wine with small onions and bacon, thickened with blood. Fish and shellfish cooked in the same way (without the blood) may also be called a civet.

clarify (clarifier): to make clear a cloudy substance. Stock to be used for aspic is clarified with egg white then strained very carefully. Butter is clarified by heating it gently, skimming and then straining through cheesecloth, leaving milky sediments behind. Clarified butter is used to seal pâtés and other preserved meats, and for sautéeing at high temperatures.

cocotte: round or oval pan with two handles and a close-fitting lid, used for slow, gentle cooking.

compôte: dish of fresh or dried fruit cooked in a sugar syrup. The term may also be used for a dish of game birds, rabbit, onions or sweet peppers cooked very gently for a long time until reduced almost to a purée.

confit: preserve of meat or poultry that has been cooked in its own fat. The term can also be applied to fruit and vegetables preserved in alcohol.

consommé: clear soup made from clarified meat, poultry or fish stock, served hot or cold. A consommé may be thickened with egg yolks, cream or arrowroot, and may be garnished in many ways such as with bone marrow, poached eggs, tiny QUENELLES, pasta and vegetables.

en coquille: a preparation of fish, shellfish, brains, sweetbreads, chicken, etc, presented in a scallop shell.

coulis: liquid purée made from cooked seasoned vegetables (especially tomatoes), shellfish or raw or cooked fruit, used as an ingredient or as a sauce on its own.

court bouillon: aromatic liquid or stock, sometimes containing wine, vinegar or lemon juice, used mainly for cooking fish and shellfish, but also sometimes white offal (variety meats) and some white meats.

crépinette: small flat sausage, made from meat such as pork or poultry, wrapped in caul (*crépine*).

croquette: savoury preparation of meat, poultry, fish or vegetables bound with a thick sauce, shaped into corks, balls, sticks or rectangles, coated in breadcrumbs and deep fried until crisp and golden. Sweet croquettes are made with rice, semolina, etc, bound with confectioner's custard (pastry cream).

croustade: deep shell or case made from shortcrust (pie) pastry, puff pastry, bread, duchesse potato, rice or semolina, fried or baked and then filled with a sweet or savoury mixture.

croûte: round, oval or square slice of crustless bread hollowed out and filled, or used flat as a base for savoury or sweet preparations. Savoury croûtes are usually fried in butter; sweet croûtes (made from stale brioche, savarin and other enriched breads) are dried in the oven. Small shortcrust (pie) and puff pastry cases may also be called croûtes.

croûton: crustless piece of bread, of varying size, that is toasted, fried in butter or oil, or dried in the oven. Small diced croûtons are used to garnish soups, omelettes, purées and so on. Larger croûtons in decorative shapes (crescents, hearts, diamonds and so on) are used to garnish dishes in sauce. Even larger croûtons are used as a base for serving a game bird or piece of meat such as a TOURNEDOS steak, and are usually cut to the same size as the bird, etc.

daubière: tightly-lidded cooking vessel made of stoneware, earthenware or galvanized copper, used for daubes – dishes that require long, slow braising.

deglaze (déglacer): to dissolve the cooking juices and sediment left in the bottom of a pan after roasting or sautéeing, to made a sauce or gravy. Wine, vinegar, stock or another liquid is added and brought to the boil, stirring to mix in the juices and sediment.

dégorger: to remove impurities and traces of blood from offal (variety meats), white meats, poultry and fish by soaking in water. Also, to remove excess water from vegetables such as aubergines (eggplants) and cucumber by sprinkling with salt. Snails are also sprinkled with salt before being prepared.

al dente: Italian expression meaning 'to the tooth'. Used to describe correctly cooked pasta (tender but still slightly firm). The term is also used for green vegetables such as French (fine green) beans.

dents-de-loup: literally 'wolves' teeth', this is a garnish of triangular CROÛTONS or pieces of aspic arranged around the edge of a dish with their points outwards. The term is also used for a crisp biscuit (cookie) baked in a special long, pointed mould.

duxelles: preparation of finely chopped mushrooms and onions or shallots sautéed in butter, used as a stuffing, as an ingredient in a sauce, and as a garnish.

entrée: originally the third course of a full French menu, following the hors-d'œuvre or soup and the fish course, and preceding the roast. Nowadays in France, however, the fish course is often omitted and the 'entrée' is simply served after the hors-d'œuvre and before the main course. Today in English the term 'entrée' is mostly used for the main course of a meal.

entremets: originally this was the term used to describe all the dishes in a menu that came after the roast, ie the vegetables and desserts. Today in France it is generally used just for the dessert course, which comes after the cheese.

en escabèche: food, primarily cold cooked fish, preserved in a cold spicy marinade.

à la ficelle: literally 'on the string', this term is used for the method of tying up a piece of beef (usually fillet/tenderloin) with string before poaching.

flamber: to flame food by pouring a warmed spirit such as brandy, rum or whisky over it and setting it alight. This burns off the alcohol, leaving the aromatic flavour of the spirit.

flan: a shallow pastry case filled with a sweet or savoury mixture. The term is also applied to baked egg custard that is unmoulded for serving cold.

fleuron: small decorative puff pastry shape (often a crescent) used to garnish pie crusts or food in sauce.

fond: aromatic cooking liquid or stock, used in making a sauce or soup or to provide the moisture for a RAGOÛT or braised dish.

fricadelle: ball or patty of minced (ground) meat that is shallow or deep fried or cooked in a RAGOÛT.

fricassée: dish of white meat, usually chicken, or fish, cooked in a creamy sauce, garnished with small onions and mushrooms.

fumet: liquid with a concentrated flavour, obtained by reducing a fish or mushroom stock or cooking liquid.

galantine: cold dish made from boned and stuffed poultry, game, meat or fish, pressed into a symmetrical shape, cooked in stock and served glazed with aspic.

gâteau: literally 'cake', this term is applied to both sweet cakes (Genoese and whisked sponges, as well as pâtisserie made with puff pastry, choux pastry, meringue and so on) and savoury cakes or 'loaves' made from vegetable purées, cabbage, chicken livers, etc. **Gâteaux secs** are plain, sweet biscuits (cookies) and petits fours.

gratin: dish cooked or finished off in the oven or under the grill (broiler) so that it has a golden and crispy surface. The crust is usually made from grated cheese or breadcrumbs and melted butter.

grenadin: small round slice of boneless veal cut from the fillet (tenderloin) or loin. Grenadins are usually larded and then sautéed or grilled (broiled).

grillade: charcoal grill. The term is also applied to food that has been grilled over charcoal.

hors-d'œuvre: literally 'outside of the main work', meaning the first course served in a menu. The dishes may be hot or cold, and are generally light and in small portions.

jambonnière: large, deep, ham-shaped receptacle used for cooking a whole ham (or other large piece of fresh or cured pork).

jardinière: mixture of buttered vegetables – usually carrots, turnips, French (fine green) beans and peas – used as a garnish for meat dishes.

julienne: matchstick-like strips of vegetables, meat, citrus fruit peel and so on, to be used as a garnish or in an hors-d'œuvre.

lard (larder): to thread small strips of pork fat, lean bacon or sometimes ham (called 'lardons') here and there into a piece of lean meat or fish, using a larding needle. The lardons help keep the meat or fish moist during cooking, and add flavour.

liaison: ingredient(s) used to bind or thicken a soup, sauce, stew, etc. Liaisons include BEURRE MANIÉ, cornflour (cornstarch), arrowroot, potato starch, egg yolks, *crème fraîche*, blood and pounded liver.

macédoine: mixture of vegetables or fruit cut into regularly-shaped small strips or dice, used in hot or cold dishes.

marmite: large, deep pot made of metal or earthenware, with two handles and a lid, plus feet if it is to be used for cooking in a hearth.

matelote: stew of freshwater fish, red or white wine and aromatics, garnished with small onions, mushrooms, bacon and CROÛTONS. Dishes of brains, veal or eggs cooked and presented in the same way may also be called matelotes.

matignon: preparation of mixed vegetables cooked gently in butter, with or without bacon, until reduced to a pulp. Used as a stuffing and garnish.

medallion (médaillon): small round or oval piece of beef (also called a TOURNEDOS) or other meat, poultry, fish, shellfish or foie gras, cut in varying thicknesses.

mirepoix: mixture of diced vegetables – usually carrot, onion and celery – and sometimes ham or bacon, cooked gently in butter, and used to enhance the flavour of a dish of meat, game or fish being cooked. A mirepoix is also used in the preparation of some sauces, and as a garnish.

noisette: small round steak of lamb, mutton or pork, cut from the rib or loin.

pain: French word for bread or loaf. The term is also applied to a preparation of fish, shellfish, poultry, white meat, game or vegetables cooked in a mould in a bain-marie and turned out for serving. Some 'pains' are set in a mould lined with aspic and served chilled.

panada (panade): paste used to bind mixtures for QUENELLES and stuffings. The panada may be based on flour, potatoes, bread, rice or eggs. The term is also applied to a type of soup based on bread, bouillon and milk.

en papillote: food cooked and served in a parcel, usually of parchment paper. Foil may also be used, in which case the food is not served in the parcel.

parfait: frozen dessert made with fresh cream.

pâté: preparation of meat, poultry, game or fish cooked in a round, oval or rectangular dish or mould lined with bacon, and served cold. 'Pâté en croûte' is cooked in a pastry crust, and is served hot or cold.

paupiette: thin slice of fish or meat (mainly veal, beef or turkey) rolled up around a stuffing and secured with string or wooden cocktail sticks (toothpicks). Paupiettes can also be made with blanched cabbage leaves.

persillade: mixture of finely chopped parsley and garlic or shallots, added to various dishes at the end of cooking.

pommes gaufrettes: thin latticed slices of potato, deep fried until crisp and golden.

pommes noisettes: small balls of potato, fried in butter until golden brown.

pommes soufflées: thin slices of potato deep fried twice until puffed and golden brown.

potage: thickened soup. The term is used synonomously with 'soupe', although the latter is more commonly applied to everyday soups of unstrained vegetables, meat or fish, which often contain pasta, rice or bread.

purée: smooth preparation made by sieving foods (usually cooked) or by using a blender or food processor.

quenelle: oval or sausage-shaped dumpling, made from a very finely-textured mixture based on fish, white meat or poultry, usually poached in boiling water. Quenelles may be served in a sauce as an ENTRÉE in a French menu, or used as a garnish.

ragoût: stew made from even-sized pieces of meat, poultry, game, fish or vegetables cooked in a thickened liquid.

reduce (réduire): to boil a liquid to reduce its volume and concentrate its flavour.

refresh (rafraîchir): to plunge food that has been cooked or blanched into cold water, or to pour cold water over it, to stop the cooking process and to help set the colour.

roux: cooked mixture of flour and fat (usually butter) that forms the base and thickening of many sauces. The length of time the roux is cooked determines whether it will be white, blond or brown.

sabayon: light, foamy mixture of egg or egg yolk, sugar and wine served barely warm, as a sauce or as a dessert. The term is also used for a foamy sauce made with champagne and whipped cream, served with fish or shellfish.

salmis: game stew, usually made with woodcock, wild duck or pheasant, although domestic duck and other game birds can also be used. The bird is partially cooked by roasting, then it is cut up and the cooking is finished in a saucepan, with mushrooms and wine.

salpicon: preparation of diced ingredients such as vegetables, meat, poultry, fish, shellfish or eggs, bound with a sauce, or fruit bound in syrup or cream. Salpicons are used to fill sweet and savoury pastries, CROÛTES, brioches, crêpes and so on, and as a garnish.

subric: small croquette, made from leftover cooked meat, fish, chicken livers, rice, puréed vegetables and so on, bound with a sauce, sautéed in clarified butter. Sweet subrics are made from rice or semolina, and are served with jam or poached fruit.

suprême: piece of chicken or game consisting of the breast and wing. The term is also used for a fillet of fish.

sweat (suer): to cook vegetables in fat over low heat so that they soften and their juices run, to be concentrated in the cooking fat.

terrine: deep, straight-sided baking dish with two handles or grips and a close-fitting lid, made from glazed earthenware, porcelain, glass or enamelled cast iron. By extension, the food cooked in the dish is also called a terrine, and is most likely served in the dish or in slices taken from it. Mixed meats, fish, seafood and vegetables are used to make terrines, as is fruit set in a sweet jelly.

tian: shallow earthenware dish from Provence in which preparations similar to GRATINS are cooked. The preparations are also called tians.

timbale: a plain, deep, round mould and, by extension, the preparation cooked in the mould. The term is also applied to preparations set in dariole moulds, and to pastry cases with a sweet filling to be served as a dessert.

tournedos: small round slice of beef cut from the centre of the fillet (tenderloin).

tourte: round pie with a shortcrust (pie) pastry or puff pastry case and lid, and a sweet or savoury filling. Some sweet tourtes do not have lids, and are basically deep-sided tarts.

turbotière: fish kettle specially designed for cooking large flat fish.

turn (tourner): to trim vegetables into regular shapes. For example, carrots, potatoes, turnips and cucumbers are trimmed into balls, ovals or 'olive' shapes.

vol-au-vent: round puff pastry case, about 15-20 cm/6-8 inches in diameter, with a lid, filled with a moist savoury mixture and served hot. In the United States, vol-au-vents are also called patty cases and patty shells.

ENGLISH & FRENCH RECIPE INDEXES

ENGLISH
RECIPE INDEX

C

Cabbage stuffed with cabbage 511
Cabinet pudding 619
Caillettes from the Ardèche 88
Calf's liver Médéric 432
Calf's liver spiked with bacon 432
Calf's liver stew from the Brie
  region 431
Calville apple Suédoise 595
Cannelloni Rossini 559
Capon with sea salt 308
Caramel grapes 666
Caramelized walnuts 664
Cardinal sauce 65
Cardoons with beef marrow 499
Carp in the Jewish style 158
Carp loaf 158
Carrot cake 601
Carrot purée from the Brie region 501
'Cats' tongues' with cream 653
Cauliflower cheese 512
Celeriac soup with small croûtons 35
Celery with bacon and onion 503
Cep and almond feuilleté 506
Ceps Bordelaise 504
Ceps from Cévennes 505
Ceps from Gascony 505
Ceps au gratin 506
Ceps Provençal 506
Cévennes pie 103
Chantilly cream savarin 638
Char with cream and white Crépy
  wine 187
Char from the lake 'done my way' 187
Charlotte Russe 593
Charlottes 649
Chasseur sauce 66
Châteauroux-style veal kidneys 444
Cheese fondue croquettes 90
Cheese fritters 89
Cheese gougères 93
Cheese and olive quiche 571
Cheese and parsley ravioli 99
Cheese and potato purée 568
Cheese straws 85
Cheese tartlets 101
Cherry clafoutis 594
Cherry compote with pineapple 594
Chestnut gâteau 601
Chestnut purée 535
Chicken with aubergines 335
Chicken in Auvergne wine 312
Chicken in a bladder 325
Chicken blanquette 327
Chicken casserole Ancenis style 337
Chicken casserole in aspic 325
Chicken casserole cooked 'as in
  Hendaye' 314
Chicken casserole with truffles, apples
  and calvados 332
Chicken Célestine 336
Chicken with champagne 336
Chicken chaud-froid with tarragon 330
Chicken 'Churchill' 314
Chicken consommé with almonds 30
Chicken with cream 338
Chicken with cream and artichoke
  bottoms 308
Chicken with cucumber 315

Chicken curry 333
Chicken with field mushrooms 341
Chicken flambéed with five types of
  spirit 339
Chicken 'Française' 317
Chicken fricassée with Ripaille wine 333
Chicken galantine with truffles 326
Chicken 'Grand Palais' 315
Chicken gratin with mustard and
  cheese 341
Chicken gratin with straw potatoes 318
Chicken 'Henri IV' 318
Chicken in lemon sauce 345
Chicken liver mousse Curnonsky 334
Chicken liver terrine 352
Chicken liver terrine with cognac 334
Chicken livers en croûte 334
Chicken 'Maxim's' 319
Chicken meurette 340
Chicken with Moulin-à-Vent wine 319
Chicken with onion purée 344
Chicken parcels Provençal 342
Chicken 'Père Lathuile' 342
Chicken pie Bourbonnais 310
Chicken pie from the Foix region 310
Chicken pie 'Franc-Comtoise' 309
Chicken pie 'Française' 332
Chicken pilau 335
Chicken with port and tarragon 343
Chicken 'in the pot' Bourbonnaise 328
Chicken 'in the pot' fermière 321
Chicken poyaudine 321
Chicken with prunes 344
Chicken in red wine 311
Chicken 'à la reine' 344
Chicken roasted on a spit over a wood
  fire 322
Chicken soup with veal and beef
  marrow 35
Chicken stewed in Burgundy wine 337
Chicken stuffed with pig's trotters 316
Chicken with tarragon 338
Chicken Trianon 324
Chicken 'Vallée d'Auge' 350
Chicken velouté 57
Chicken in vermouth 340
Chicken with 'Viscount' sauce 346
Chicken vol-au-vent 352
Chicory from the Ardennes 520
Chicory with cream 520
Chicory croquettes 519
Chicory gratin royale 521
Chicory and ham gratin 521
Chilled cream of sorrel soup 37
Chinese artichokes with velouté
  sauce 518
Chitterling sausages 403
Chocolate caramels 659
Chocolate cream mould 596
Chocolate nut gâteau 630
Chocolate profiteroles 617
Chocolate soufflé 623
Choron sauce 67
Choux pastry and
  pastry for éclairs 578
Christmas log with Grand Marnier 628
Clams au gratin with spinach 271
Coffee ice cream 644
Coffee or vanilla parfait 646
Cold eggs Marinette 125

Cold hake with Tartare sauce 159
Cold halibut with tomato and Bresse
  Bleu sauce 167
Cold loin of pork with apple sauce 404
Cold poached red mullet with
  shallot 192
Cold ravigote sauce 77
Cold red mullet oriental style 191
Cold salmon mousse 202
'Cold' sauce 69
Cold tourteaux with mayonnaise 236
Confectioner's custard or pastry
  cream 584
'Conversation pieces' 650
Cooked marinade 59
Cooked meringue 585
Coopers' stew 436
'Copeaux' 650
Corn on the cob with melted
  butter 534
Cotriade of mackerel 177
Country chicken pie 104
Country foie gras pâté 94
Country-style roast pork 417
Courgettes fried in butter 518
Crab Escoffier au gratin with
  paprika 235
Crab omelette 131
Crab pêcheur 234
Crab pilau with mussels Pont-Aven 235
Crab soup 41
Crab toasts with paprika 235
Crawfish Biarrote 251
Crawfish with cream 252
Crawfish medallions in aspic
  Monégasque 255
Crawfish medallions with caviar 255
Crawfish with morels 253
Crawfish Parisienne 254
Crawfish soufflé gastronome 254
Crawfish stew 251
Crayfish bisque 29
Crayfish Bordelaise 239
Crayfish casserole with whisky 239
Crayfish with cream 240
Crayfish and dill salad 238
Crayfish flambéed in cognac 240
Crayfish flambéed in whisky 240
Crayfish au gratin 'Rouergate style' 241
Crayfish, lobster or crawfish butter 51
Crayfish Morvandelle 241
Crayfish tails au gratin Nantua 242
Crayfish with York ham 241
Cream of barley soup with crayfish
  butter 32
Cream of celery soup 30
Cream of cucumber soup 31
Cream of pumpkin soup 36
Cream sauce 67
Cream of tomato soup 41
Cream of white bean soup with
  young vegetables 31
Creole rice 563
Crêpe batter 578
Crêpe batter with cognac 579
Crêpes stuffed with prawns 237
Crêpes Suzette 597
Crépinettes of young partridge
  forestière 482
'Croquets' 650

693

FRENCH
RECIPE INDEX

ACKNOWLEDGEMENTS

Photographs illustrating The Art of the Table are by Pascal Hinous-Top, with the exception of the table setting 'Maison de Marie-Claire', which is a Pataut photo.

Photographs illustrating wine bottles, glasses and champagne are by Daniel Czap.

Photographs illustrating grapes and wine cellars are by Jean-Daniel Sudres-Scope.

ends, then twist the intestines at regular intervals to form sausages of the required length. Tie the sections with string.

Put the sausages in a large saucepan of hot, not boiling water, bring to the boil, then simmer gently to poach the sausages for 10 minutes. Transfer the sausages straight into cold water to cool, then leave them to drain on paper towels.

Brush the sausages with olive oil and cook them under a moderate grill (broiler) for about 10 minutes, turning frequently.

A good lentil purée (put through a vegetable mill and then through a fine sieve), with plenty of butter added, makes a perfect accompaniment to these sausages.

Wines: Beaujolais-Villages, Chinon, Bourgueil.

GALANTINE DE LAPIN EN GELÉE GRANDGOUSIER

RABBIT GALANTINE IN GRANDGOUSIER ASPIC

Preparation 30 minutes • Cooking 2 hours

US	Ingredients	Met/Imp
1	domestic rabbit	1
2	calf's feet	2
2 cups	consommé	500 ml/18 fl oz
scant ½ cup	vinegar	100 ml/3½ fl oz
2 cups	dry Vouvray wine	500 ml/18 fl oz
2	leeks	2
2	parsley sprigs	2
1	thyme sprig	1
½	bay leaf	½
1	onion	1
2	cloves	2
	salt and pepper	
2	carrots	2
2	shallots	2

Skin and gut the rabbit, removing the head and feet.

Cut the rabbit into even-sized pieces and put in a saucepan with the calf's feet. Pour in the consommé, vinegar and wine. Tie the leeks, parsley, thyme and bay leaf into a bouquet garni and spike the onion with the cloves. Add to the pan with salt and pepper, the sliced carrots and the shallots. Bring to the boil and cook gently for about 2 hours, or until the rabbit is tender. Add more liquid, if necessary, and check the seasoning from time to time during cooking.

When they are cooked, carefully remove the pieces of rabbit and place in a bowl. Remove the calf's feet. Taste the cooking liquid, adjust the seasoning if necessary, and sieve through a piece of cheesecloth. Pour over the rabbit. There should be enough liquid left just to cover the rabbit. Boil to reduce a little, if necessary.

Put the rabbit in the refrigerator or another very cool place and leave overnight. The next day, serve the rabbit very cold in its cooking liquid, which will have set to a jelly.

The calf's feet may be used for something else. They are only used here to provide the gelatine for setting the cooking liquid. They must be served hot, since they are inedible when cold.

White wines: Vouvray, Saumur.
Red wines: Beaujolais-Villages, Bourgueil, Chinon.

US	Ingredients	Met/Imp
1	domestic rabbit	1
2 tbsp	vinegar and red wine, mixed	30 ml/2 tbsp
7 oz	salt pork	200 g/7 oz
1 lb	pork back fat, or bacon fat or lard	500 g/1 lb
20	small onions	20
	salt and pepper	
¼ cup	flour	35 g/scant 1½ oz
3 cups	red wine	750 ml/1¼ pints
2 cups	stock	500 ml/18 fl oz
1	bouquet garni	1
1	garlic clove	1
8	Dutch or other waxy potatoes	8

GIBELOTTE OF RABBIT WITH RED WINE

Preparation 40 minutes • Cooking 1½ hours

There are many ways to prepare a gibelotte; the main thing is for the seasoning to be just right and for the gibelotte to be served very hot. A few days before it is slaughtered, mix some parsley, thyme and wild thyme with the rabbit's food.

Kill the rabbit, bleed it and collect the blood in a bowl. Immediately mix the vinegar and red wine with it to stop it coagulating. Keep it cool.

Skin and gut the rabbit, removing the head and feet. Cut into fairly small pieces. Reserve the liver, having removed the gall bladder and everything that has been contaminated by it. Cut the liver into thin slices.

Soak the salt pork in lukewarm water, then drain and cut into large cubes. Scald in boiling water for 5–6 minutes, then drain and wipe thoroughly. (If unavailable, some lean bacon, with the rind removed, can be used instead.)

Melt the grated fresh pork or bacon fat or lard in a saucepan and sauté the pork or bacon until lightly browned. Remove from the pan and drain on a plate. Put the small onions in the pan and cook until evenly browned. Drain on a plate. Add the rabbit pieces to the same fat in the pan, add salt and pepper and cook over a high heat, stirring, until they are lightly browned and the meat is well sealed. Sprinkle with flour, mix well and continue cooking, stirring, until browned. (Alternatively, transfer to a casserole and brown in the oven.) Pour in the red wine and stock, add salt and pepper and bring to the boil, stirring constantly. Add the fried pork or bacon, onions, bouquet garni (in which thyme is slightly dominant) and the crushed garlic. Cover and continue to cook for 15 minutes, boiling slowly and evenly. Cut the potatoes in half and make into olive shapes. Add to the pan, pushing them well into the sauce. Cook for a further 30 minutes. The total cooking time, from the start of boiling, should be 45 minutes.

About 10 minutes before serving, add the sliced liver to the pan. Gradually stir 4–5 spoonfuls of the hot sauce, 1 spoonful at a time, into the blood so as to heat it progressively, and pour into the pan. Shake the saucepan to mix and then simmer.

For a family dish such as this, there is no need for elaborate presentation; just pour the contents of the saucepan into a heated serving dish or bowl and serve very hot.

Wines: as a general rule, serve the same wine as the one used for cooking. A light and fruity red Bordeaux, Cahors, Minervois or Corbières would be a good choice.

—— RABBIT WITH CRÈME FRAÎCHE ——

Preparation 40 minutes • Cooking 1½ hours

US	Ingredients	Met/Imp
I	domestic rabbit	I
10 oz	fresh fat belly (side) of pork	300 g/10 oz
I stick	butter	100 g/4 oz
3 tbsp	flour	30 g/1 oz
I	bouquet garni	I
I	large onion	I
I	garlic clove	I
¼ cup	vinegar	50 ml/2 fl oz
	salt and pepper	
2	egg yolks	2
½ cup	crème fraîche	100 ml/4 fl oz

Skin and gut the rabbit, removing the head and feet. Cut the rabbit into fairly small, even-sized pieces. Dice the pork and blanch in boiling water, then drain well. Melt the butter in a saucepan and sauté the diced fat and rabbit pieces until brown. Drain off the fat, add the flour and cook until golden brown. Add the bouquet garni, chopped onion and crushed garlic. Pour in the vinegar and a very little water. Add salt and pepper. Bring to the boil and cook gently for 1½ hours.

Remove the rabbit, add the egg yolks and crème fraîche to the sauce and heat, stirring, until thick. Sieve, then pour over the rabbit.

White wines: Arbois, Côtes du Jura, Coteaux Champenois.
Red wine: Mercurey, Givry.

—— RABBIT WITH SHALLOTS ——

Preparation 40 minutes • Cooking 1½ hours

US	Ingredients	Met/Imp
I	domestic rabbit	I
10 tbsp	butter	150 g/5 oz
	salt and pepper	
25	shallots	25
I	bouquet garni	I
scant I cup	consommé	200 ml/7 fl oz
	chopped fresh parsley, to garnish	

Skin and gut the rabbit, removing the head and feet. Cut the rabbit into even-sized pieces. Melt the butter in a flameproof casserole and sauté the rabbit until browned. Add salt and pepper and half the chopped shallots, and cook for 1½ hours or until the rabbit is tender.

Add the remaining shallots and the bouquet garni and simmer for a few more minutes. Remove the rabbit from the casserole and deglaze with the consommé. Pour the sauce over the rabbit and garnish.

White wines: Arbois, Côtes du Jura, Coteaux Champenois.
Red wines: Cahors, Corbières, Minervois.

—— STUFFED RABBIT ALSACIENNE ——

Preparation 1¾ hours • Cooking 1¼ hours

US	Ingredients	Met/Imp
I, about 3½ lb	domestic rabbit	I, about 1.6 kg/3½ lb
	salt and pepper	
6 tbsp	strong mustard	90 ml/6 tbsp
I	cooked pig's trotter, (foot)	I
I	fairly large piece of pig's caul	I
	oil	
¼ lb	noodles	125 g/4½ oz

Skin and gut the rabbit. Cut off the head and the ends of the legs. Break the front legs at the joint so that the rabbit will fit into the roasting tin.

Add salt and pepper to the rabbit and coat the inside with mustard. Put mustard on the pig's trotter (foot) too, having first removed the small toes which protrude at the joint. Place the trotter (foot) inside the rabbit. Wrap the rabbit around, closing the stomach skin over. Sew up firmly, starting at the head end and finishing near the hind legs, which should be sewn together, so that they stay side by side.

Coat the rabbit completely with plenty of mustard and wrap the pig's caul several times around it. Place in an oiled roasting tin and roast in a hot oven for about 1¼ hours or until well cooked.

Boil the noodles in salted water for 2–3 minutes; drain. Place the rabbit on a dish and keep warm. Tip the noodles into the roasting tin, mix with the cooking juices, then arrange around the rabbit.

·Wines: red Pinot Noir from Alsace, white Arbois, red Chiroubles or Moulin-à-Vent.

US	Ingredients	Met/Imp
I, about 3¼ lb	domestic rabbit	I, about 1.6 kg/3¼ lb
7 oz	slightly salted lean belly of pork (slab bacon)	200 g/7 oz
3 tbsp	butter	40 g/1½ oz
2 tbsp	oil	30 ml/2 tbsp
12	small onions	12
	salt and pepper	
4½ tbsp	flour	40 g/1½ oz
I cup	stock	250 ml/9 fl oz
2 cups	dry white wine	500 ml/18 fl oz
I	bouquet garni	I
7 oz	small mushrooms	200 g/7 oz

LAPIN EN GIBELOTTE

— RABBIT GIBELOTTE IN WHITE WINE —

Preparation 40 minutes • Cooking 50 minutes • Serves 6

Skin and gut the rabbit, removing the head and feet. Reserve the liver, having removed the gall bladder and everything that has been contaminated by it. Cut the rabbit into medium-sized pieces. Dice the belly of pork (bacon) and blanch for a few minutes in boiling water. Drain and wipe with paper towels.

Melt the butter with the oil in a deep, heavy frying pan. Add the diced belly of pork (bacon) and the onions and cook until browned. Drain, put them on a plate and set aside.

Salt the pieces of rabbit. Add to the pan and brown on both sides. (It may be necessary to do this in several batches.) When all the pieces of rabbit are browned, put them all in the pan and sprinkle with flour. Mix well, then cook gently for 10 minutes, stirring from time to time. Add the pork (bacon) and onions, pour in the stock and all but 2 spoonfuls of the white wine and mix well.

Add the bouquet garni, and salt and pepper if necessary. Cover and cook gently for 30 minutes. Add the mushrooms, cut in half if they are too big, and cook for about 15 minutes. Add the sliced liver and cook gently for a further 5 minutes.

Arrange the pieces of rabbit on a heated serving dish, pour the sauce into a jug and set aside. Deglaze the pan with the remaining wine, boil for a moment, then return the sauce to the pan. Check the seasoning.

Coat the rabbit pieces with the sauce and serve. The dish may be garnished with a few shortcrust (pie) pastry croustades filled with mushrooms.

VARIATION
Potatoes, cut into large pieces, may be added to this dish. Cook them separately in boiling water, or in the rabbit sauce, for the last 20 minutes.

White wine: serve the same wine as the one used for cooking.
Light red wines: Beaujolais-Villages, Côtes du Ventoux, Côtes du Luberon, Côtes de Provence, Coteaux du Languedoc.

US	Ingredients	Met/Imp
½ lb	pork back fat or bacon fat	250 g/8 oz
3	rabbit saddles	3
	salt and pepper	
scant I cup	madeira	200 ml/7 fl oz
I	bouquet garni	I
scant ½ cup	mustard	100 ml/3½ fl oz
I stick	butter	100 g/4 oz
scant I cup	*crème fraîche*	200 ml/7 fl oz

LAPIN À LA MOUTARDE

RABBIT WITH MUSTARD

Preparation 1 hour • Marinating 12 hours • Cooking 1¼ hours

Cut the fat into strips and use to lard the rabbit saddles. Add salt and pepper and put in a bowl. Pour over the madeira, add the bouquet garni and leave to marinate for 12 hours, turning frequently.

Wipe the rabbit with paper towels and spread with plenty of mustard. Put in a roasting tin and pour melted butter on top. Roast in a hot oven for 1¼ hours or until tender.

Meanwhile, put the marinade in a saucepan and boil to reduce. Add the crème fraîche. When the rabbits are cooked, transfer them to a heated serving dish and use the marinade mixture to deglaze the roasting tin. Taste and adjust the seasoning and serve as a sauce with the rabbit.

Red wines: Cahors, Minervois, Corbières.

RABBIT WITH PRUNES*

Preparation 2 hours • Marinating 24 hours • Cooking 1¼ hours

US	Ingredients	Met/Imp
I, about 2½ lb	rabbit	I, about 1.1 kg/2½ lb
a little	wine vinegar	a little
I	thyme sprig	I
I	bay leaf	I
I	carrot	I
I	onion	I
I bottle	red wine	I bottle
2 tbsp	oil	30 ml/2 tbsp
I lb	prunes	500 g/I lb
6 tbsp	butter	75 g/3 oz
4	bacon slices	4
10	small white onions	10
I tbsp	flour	15 ml/I tbsp
	salt and pepper	
	redcurrant jelly	
	thyme, to garnish	

Skin and gut the rabbit, removing the head and feet. Reserve the blood and liver, removing the gall bladder from the liver and everything that has been contaminated by it. Mix the blood with the wine vinegar and chop the liver. Set aside and keep cool.

Cut the rabbit into pieces and put in a bowl with the thyme, bay leaf, sliced carrot and onion, 500 ml/18 fl oz (2 cups) of the red wine and half of the oil. Leave to marinate for 24 hours.

Stone the prunes and soak them in lukewarm water for several hours to plump them up. Put them in a saucepan with a generous glass of the remaining red wine and heat gently.

Heat the butter and remaining oil in a flameproof casserole and fry the bacon, which has been cut into small strips, and the small onions until lightly browned. Drain them and put them on a plate.

Drain the pieces of marinated rabbit and wipe them carefully with paper towels. Fry them in the casserole until evenly browned. Sprinkle with the flour, mix, then put the bacon and onions back in the casserole. Pour in the marinade juice through a fine sieve. Add salt and pepper, cover and simmer for 1½ hours. Just before the end of the cooking time, add the prunes.

When the rabbit is cooked, take the lid off the casserole and add the blood and vinegar mixture and the chopped liver. Also add the currant jelly. Boil rapidly for a few minutes and, as soon as everything is well mixed together, pour into a heated serving dish. Serve immediately, garnished with thyme.

Wines: as a general rule, serve the same wine as the one used for cooking. A Chinon would be a good choice.

SAUTÉED RABBIT WITH CREAM

Preparation 2 hours • Cooking 1¾ hours

US	Ingredients	Met/Imp
I, about 2½ lb	domestic rabbit	I, about 1.1 kg/2½ lb
	salt and pepper	
	butter	
	oil	
I liqueur glass	cognac	I liqueur glass
¼ lb	shallots	125 g/4½ oz
I glass	dry white wine	I glass
I	bay leaf	I
I	thyme sprig	I
scant I cup	*crème fraîche*	200 ml/7 fl oz

Skin and gut the rabbit, removing the head and feet.

Cut the rabbit into pieces and sprinkle each piece with salt and pepper. Heat some butter and oil in a flameproof casserole and sauté the rabbit pieces until just beginning to brown. Drain them and put them on a heatproof dish. Sprinkle with cognac and flambé.

Heat another piece of butter in the casserole and brown the chopped shallots in it. Return the rabbit to the casserole, along with the flambé juices, the white wine, bay leaf and thyme. Cover and cook for 1½ hours or until the rabbit is tender.

When the rabbit is well cooked, remove the pieces from the casserole and arrange on a heated serving dish. Keep warm. Take the bay leaf and thyme out of the casserole and put in the crème fraîche. Boil for a few minutes, then check the seasoning. When the sauce is creamy, pour it over the rabbit and serve immediately.

Wines: Cornas, Madiran, Côtes du Frontonnais, Côtes de Buzet, Côtes de Bourg.

US	Ingredients	Met/Imp
I, about 2 lb	domestic rabbit	I, about I kg/2 lb
	walnut oil	
	olive oil	
2 lb	ceps	I kg/2 lb
3	shallots	3
	salt and pepper	
I cup	dry white wine	250 ml/8 fl oz
4	garlic cloves	4
3 tbsp	chopped fresh parsley	45 ml/3 tbsp
2 cups	fresh breadcrumbs	100 g/4 oz

LAPIN SAUTÉ À LA MIE DE PAIN

SAUTÉED RABBIT WITH BREADCRUMBS

Preparation 1¼ hours • Cooking 55 minutes

Skin and gut the rabbit, removing the head and feet.

Cut the rabbit into pieces. Heat 60 ml/4 tbsp each of walnut oil and olive oil in a flameproof casserole and add the rabbit pieces. Sauté gently, turning the pieces constantly so that they brown evenly. When they are browned, cover the casserole and continue to cook gently for 30 minutes. Drain the rabbit pieces, put them on a plate and keep warm.

Peel and wipe the ceps and fry them in the casserole until golden brown. If necessary, add more oil (half olive oil, half walnut oil). When nearly cooked, add the chopped shallots and salt and pepper. Mix gently, taking care not to damage the ceps. Drain the mushrooms and shallots, put them on a plate and keep them warm.

Return the pieces of rabbit to the casserole and pour in the white wine. Add salt and pepper, cover and cook for 10 minutes. Add the chopped garlic and two-thirds of the parsley.

Arrange the pieces of rabbit on a heated serving dish and surround with the mushrooms. Heat a little more walnut oil in a frying pan and fry the breadcrumbs until golden brown. Spoon over the rabbit, then sprinkle with the remaining chopped parsley. Serve hot.

Wines: Médoc, Cahors, Madiran.

US	Ingredients	Met/Imp
I, about 3 lb	young domestic rabbit	I, about 1.4 kg/3 lb
scant ½ cup	strong mustard	100 ml/3½ fl oz
3 tbsp	olive oil	45 ml/3 tbsp
6 tbsp	butter	75 g/3 oz
a few	parsley, chervil, tarragon, thyme and rosemary sprigs	a few
I	bay leaf	I
a few	celery leaves	a few
I	onion	I
2	shallots	2
I	garlic clove	I
	salt and pepper	
a few spoonfuls	Veal Stock or Juice (page 56)	a few spoonfuls

LAPIN SAUTÉ À LA MOUTARDE

SAUTÉED RABBIT WITH MUSTARD

Preparation 30 minutes (3 hours in advance or the day before) • Cooking 1½ hours • Serves 4

Skin and gut the rabbit, removing the head and feet. Reserve the liver, removing the gall bladder and everything that has been contaminated by it.

At least 3 hours in advance (or the day before, if possible), cut the rabbit into pieces and spread them with plenty of mustard. Put the pieces in a bowl, cover and keep cool (not in the refrigerator).

Heat the oil and butter in a flameproof casserole until hot but not coloured. Add the whole herbs, celery leaves, chopped onion and shallots, the crushed garlic and salt and pepper and cook for 5–10 minutes, stirring from time to time.

Using a wooden spoon, remove the excess mustard from the rabbit pieces. (You will need to remove only 2–3 spoonfuls as most of it will have been absorbed by the meat.) Remove the herbs from the casserole with a slotted spoon and sauté the rabbit pieces, one at a time, in the flavoured oil. They will quickly go brown. Remove each piece from the casserole when brown and keep warm while browning the others.

When all the pieces of rabbit are brown, return them to the casserole, cover and cook over a low heat for 1 hour, stirring from time to time, so that the same pieces do not always stay at the bottom of the casserole.

Add the sliced liver to the casserole and cook for a further 5 minutes. Remove the rabbit pieces and liver from the casserole and arrange on a hot serving dish. Deglaze the casserole by pouring in a few spoonfuls of the veal stock or juice (having first removed the fat) or hot water. Stir to remove all the particles sticking to the sides of the casserole, and to form a good sauce. Bring to the boil for a moment. Adjust the seasoning, if necessary, the pour over the rabbit and serve.

Dry white wines: Saumur, Savennières, Sauvignon de Touraine.
Light red wines: Côtes de Provence, Coteaux du Languedoc, Côtes de Roussillon, Côtes de Duras, Bergerac, Côtes de Buzet, Minervois.

RÂBLES DE LAPIN À L'ESTRAGON

SADDLE OF RABBIT WITH TARRAGON*

Preparation 20 minutes • Cooking 1½ hours

Cut each saddle into 4 pieces (2 legs and the back cut in half). Heat half of the butter with the oil in a flameproof casserole and sauté the rabbit pieces until brown. Stir in the flour and continue cooking until golden brown.

Meanwhile, in a frying pan, melt the remaining butter and fry the thinly sliced shallots until soft. Blanch, peel, seed and crush the tomatoes.

Add the fried shallots and crushed tomatoes to the rabbit pieces with the tarragon, crushed garlic and bouquet garni. Pour in the vinegar, cognac and white wine, and enough water to moisten, then add salt and pepper. Simmer gently for about 1¼ hours or until the rabbit is tender.

Dry white wines: Muscadet, Quincy, Pouilly-sur-Loire, Sancerre.
Red wines: Chinon, Bourgueil.

US	Ingredients	Met/Imp
2	rabbit saddles	2
5 tbsp	butter	60 g/2½ oz
¼ cup	oil	50 ml/2 fl oz
3 tbsp	flour	30 g/1 oz
10	shallots	10
6	tomatoes	6
1 tbsp	chopped fresh tarragon	15 ml/1 tbsp
6	garlic cloves	6
1	bouquet garni	1
½ cup	vinegar	100 ml/4 fl oz
¼ cup	cognac	50 ml/2 fl oz
½ cup	white wine	100 ml/4 fl oz
	salt and pepper	

TERRINE DE LAPIN

RABBIT TERRINE

Preparation 3 hours • Cooking 1 hour

Skin, gut and bone the rabbit, removing the head and feet. Reserve the liver, removing the gall bladder and everything that has been contaminated by it. Cut the rabbit and the veal into strips. Chop the rabbit's liver and add to the sausagemeat with salt and pepper.

Place a piece of larding bacon, a bay leaf, a sprig of thyme, some salt, pepper and spice in the bottom of a terrine. Cover with a layer of sausagemeat, then with a layer of veal and rabbit meat. Cover with another layer of sausagemeat and continue layering the 2 meat mixtures until the terrine is full. Press firmly and top with the remaining larding bacon, thyme and bay leaf. Add salt and pepper and make some holes in the mixture with a skewer. Pour in the cognac and half a glass of water.

Put the lid on the terrine and seal with a paste made by mixing the flour with a little water so that it is airtight. Cook in a moderate oven for 1 hour.

White wines: Chablis, Saumur, Muscadet.
Red wines: Bourgueil, Chinon, Beaujolais-Villages.

US	Ingredients	Met/Imp
1	large domestic rabbit	1
½ lb	boneless veal	250 g/8 oz
¾ lb	sausagemeat	375 g/13 oz
	salt and pepper	
2	slices pork back fat or bacon fat	2
2	bay leaves	2
2	thyme sprigs	2
	quatre-épices	
1 wineglass	cognac	1 wineglass
a little	flour	a little

GOOSE

IT IS THE SMALL, FATTENED GOOSE (UP TO 6 kg/13 lb), WHICH IS best for serving at table, stuffed and roasted, casseroled or braised. Balzac used to call it the 'cooper's pheasant'. Large geese (called 'grey' or 'farmyard'), weighing from 10–12 kg/22–26 lb and very fatty, are used for preserves. It is livers of these large geese, when hypertrophied by methodical force-feeding, that are made into the excellent foie gras of Gers, Landes, Périgord or Alsace. The Romans were partial to the livers of geese, which they fattened with figs, wine and honey. The preparation of the livers requires great care, but gives remarkable results. Preserved goose (or duck) is kept in its own fat in stoneware pots. The gizzards, necks, giblets and hearts are used in tasty preparations in regions where preserves are made. According to Curnonsky, foie gras is a miracle of the culinary art in the eyes of the gourmet: it is the 'quintessence of aromas and flavours which epitomizes the superior quality of the good things in our country'. And the prince of gourmets added: 'It should be served at the start of the meal. Its very richness demands that it be approached with a keen and joyful appetite . . . '

ABATTIS DE VOLAILLE AUX CHAMPIGNONS

POULTRY GIBLETS WITH MUSHROOMS

Preparation 30 minutes • Cooking 1½ hours

US	Ingredients	Met/Imp
3 sets	poultry giblets (goose, turkey, etc)	3 sets
1 stick	butter	100 g/4 oz
6 tbsp	flour	50 g/2 oz
2	garlic cloves	2
2 cups	stock	500 ml/18 fl oz
	salt and pepper	
8	skinned tomatoes	8
1	bouquet garni	1
¼ lb	*Paris mushrooms*	100 g/4 oz
	chopped fresh parsley	

Cut the giblets into pieces. Melt the butter in a flameproof casserole and fry the giblets until brown. Sprinkle with the flour and add the crushed garlic. Pour in the stock and add salt and pepper. Add the tomatoes and the bouquet garni. Cover and cook in a moderate oven for 1 hour. Add the mushrooms, then continue cooking for a further 30 minutes or until the giblets are tender and the sauce thickened. Serve sprinkled with parsley.

Red wines: Médoc, Saint-Émilion, Côte de Beaune, Côte Rôtie, Châteauneuf-du-Pape.

GOOSE STEW

Preparation 40 minutes • Cooking 1½ hours

US	Ingredients	Met/Imp
1, about 5–6 lb	goose	1, about 2.3–2.7 kg/5–6 lb
½ lb	fresh fat belly (side) of pork	250 g/8 oz
2	large onions	2
½ cup	flour	75 g/3 oz
2 bottles	fairly full-bodied mature Côtes de Nuits wines	2 bottles
¼ cup	*marc* from Burgundy	50 ml/2 fl oz
1	bouquet garni (including 1 sprig wild thyme)	1
1 tbsp	chopped fresh parsley	15 ml/1 tbsp
1	bay leaf	1
1	garlic clove	1
4	shallots	4
	salt and pepper	
½ cup	goose blood	100 ml/4 fl oz
16	croûtons fried in butter	16

Cut the goose into pieces. Cut the pork into small cubes and heat in a flameproof casserole. Add the goose pieces and sliced onions and fry lightly, then sprinkle with the flour. Pour in the wine. Sprinkle with the marc and flambé. Add the bouquet garni, parsley, bay leaf, crushed garlic, chopped shallots and salt and pepper. Simmer for 1½ hours or until the goose is tender. Mix in the blood. Remove the pieces of goose from the casserole and keep them warm. Work the sauce through a fine sieve and return to the casserole with the pieces of goose. Reheat and serve very hot on the croûtons.

Red wine: Côte de Nuits.

PRESERVED GOOSE

Preparation 1–1½ hours • (To be prepared 24 hours in advance) • Cooking 2 hours

US	Ingredients	Met/Imp
1, about 6½ lb	goose (including gizzard and liver)	1, about 3 kg/6½ lb
	salt	
	lard	

Put the goose on its back. Cut open the stomach along the breast bone from the base of the neck to the parson's (pope's) nose. Detach the meat attached to the carcass on both sides of the breastbone. Break the wing and leg joints. Cut the backbone and bone the remaining meat.

Lift out the carcass, retaining just the wing and leg bones. Cut the neck off at the base. Cut the goose into 4 portions, separating the legs from the wings and taking care to avoid slicing the breast meat. Remove the fat from around the gizzard and the liver and reserve. Also reserve the fat from around the intestines for cooking. Sprinkle salt on each goose quarter and put them in a bowl. Set aside in a cool place for 24 hours.

The next day, melt some goose fat and lard in a flameproof casserole and cook the goose pieces over a low heat for 1½–2 hours, according to the age of the bird. Transfer the goose pieces to an earthenware pot and cover them with the cooking fat. Store until required.

Red wines: Cahors, Côtes du Frontonnais, Madiran, Bordeaux, Saint-Émilion, Graves.

US	Ingredients	Met/Imp
3	pieces preserved goose or duck (including 1 wing and 1 leg)	3
½ lb	fat from preserved goose	250 g/8 oz
2	onions	2
½ lb	small sweet green peppers	250 g/8 oz
8–10	tomatoes	8–10
½ cup	Veal Stock (page 56)	100 ml/4 fl oz
½ cup	double (heavy) cream (optional)	100 ml/4 fl oz

PRESERVED GOOSE (OR DUCK) PIPÉRADE*

Preparation 1 hour • Cooking 25 minutes

Put the goose pieces in a roasting tin with some of the fat from the preserved goose and heat through in a moderate oven. Pour off the fat. Melt some more of the fat in a frying pan and add the thinly sliced onions. Fry until brown, then add the green peppers, sliced lengthways, and the skinned, de-seeded and crushed tomatoes. Cook the mixture until it has a light consistency. Before serving, stir in the stock and the cream, if liked, which will make the flavour of the peppers milder. Check the seasoning. To serve, spoon the pipérade mixture into a heated serving dish and top with the preserved goose pieces, cut up if liked.

Red wines: Béarn, Irouléguy.

US	Ingredients	Met/Imp
4	goose necks	4
1¾ lb	finely minced (ground) pork	800 g/1¾ lb
	trimmings (wings and legs) from 4 geese	
¼ lb	truffle scraps	100 g/4 oz
¼ lb	foie gras scraps	100 g/4 oz
	salt and pepper	
	quatre-épices	
	goose or duck fat or lard	

COUS D'OIE FARCIS À LA GASCONNE

STUFFED GOOSE NECKS FROM GASCONY

Preparation 2 hours • Cooking 1½ hours

When making preserves (of goose or duck), keep the skin from the birds' necks. Clean the outsides of the skins thoroughly, leaving fat inside.

Mix together the pork, 200 g (7 oz) of the goose trimmings, the truffle scraps (there is no point in using whole truffles), foie gras scraps, salt, pepper and spice. Use to stuff the goose necks and sew up the ends. Melt the goose or duck fat or lard in a large saucepan, add the stuffed necks and the remaining goose trimmings and cook for 1½ hours. When cooked, put them in earthenware pots and cover with the cooking fat.

The stuffed necks may be served cold as an hors-d'œuvre or with a salad, but are especially good in vegetable soups. Do not cook them again in the soup, just warm them up in it for a few minutes.

Red wines: Béarn, Irouléguy, Madiran, Pacherenc du Vic-Bilh.

US	Ingredients	Met/Imp
1, about 2–2½ lb	goose liver	1, about 1–1.2 kg/2–2½ lb
2 tbsp	goose fat	30 ml/2 tbsp
4	shallots	4
3 tbsp	flour	30 g/1 oz
½ cup	Veal Stock (page 56)	100 ml/4 fl oz
¼ cup	mature marc	50 ml/2 fl oz
½ lb	truffles	250 g/8 oz
	salt and pepper	
1	orange, juice of	1
⅔ cup	capers	100 g/4 oz

FOIE GRAS D'OIE AUX TRUFFES ET À L'ORANGE

GOOSE FOIE GRAS WITH TRUFFLES AND ORANGE

Preparation 30 minutes • Cooking 18 minutes

Choose a fine goose liver from Valence-d'Albigeois, as hard as stone. Melt half of the fat in a saucepan and add the liver. Fry gently on each side for a few minutes or until browned, then remove from the heat. In another saucepan, melt the remaining fat and add the finely chopped shallots. Cook until brown, then stir in the flour. With a wooden spoon, gradually stir in the veal stock and marc until blended and smooth.

Place the thinly sliced truffles in the bottom of a saucepan and put the goose liver on top. Add the shallot sauce, bring to the boil and simmer for 18 minutes. Add salt and pepper. Just before serving, add the orange juice and capers. The marc and the orange go together very well.

Sweet white wines: Sauternes, Monbazillac, Coteaux du Layon.
Red wines: Côte de Nuits, Saint-Émilion, Pomerol.

FOIE D'OIE AUX RAISINS

——— GOOSE LIVER WITH GRAPES ———

Preparation 30 minutes • Cooking 8 minutes

Cut the goose liver into 8 slices 1 cm/½ inch thick and coat them with flour. Melt two-thirds of the butter in a frying pan and add the liver slices. Cook gently for 4–5 minutes, turning the slices over so that they brown on both sides. Meanwhile, melt the remaining butter in a pan and sweat the mushrooms for 5 minutes. Keep warm.

Remove the liver slices from the frying pan and keep them warm. Pour off two-thirds of the fat from the pan and add the peeled grapes. Fry quickly to seal, then flambé with the armagnac. Mix the veal stock with the crème fraîche and add to the pan with salt and pepper. Arrange the liver slices on a heated round serving dish and surround with the mushrooms. Coat with the sauce and serve.

Medium dry or sweet white wines: Graves, Sauternes, Barsac, Jurançon.

US	Ingredients	Met/Imp
I	goose liver	I
	flour	
6 tbsp	butter	75 g/3 oz
8	mushroom caps	8
I lb	seedless white grapes	500 g/I lb
½ cup	armagnac	100 ml/4 fl oz
½ cup	Veal Stock (*page 56*)	100 ml/4 fl oz
½ cup	crème fraîche	100 ml/4 fl oz
	salt and pepper	

MOUSSE DE FOIE GRAS TRUFFÉE

— FOIE GRAS MOUSSE WITH TRUFFLE —

Preparation about 2 hours • (To be prepared 48 hours in advance) • Cooking about 20 minutes

Put the liver in a bowl and add salt and pepper, spice, the truffle, cognac and port and leave to marinate for 24 hours.

The next day, put two-thirds of the aspic in a saucepan. Wrap the liver in a piece of cheesecloth and tie it up. Add it to the aspic and bring to the boil. Reduce the heat and simmer for about 20 minutes, then leave the liver to cool in the liquid until the fat solidifies on the surface.

The next day, take out the liver and set aside. Remove the fat from the aspic and clarify with the egg whites. Coat the sides and bottom of a charlotte mould with about 1 cm/½ inch aspic. Decorate with pieces of truffle and hard-boiled egg white and put in the refrigerator.

Unwrap the liver and dice, grind and sieve it, making it liquid by adding the remaining aspic. Taste and adjust the seasoning if necessary. Whip the cream and slowly fold it into the liver liquid. Turn immediately into the mould and put in the refrigerator for 2–3 hours to set.

Just before serving, dip the mould quickly into hot water, wipe it and tip the mousse out into a cold, round dish. Surround it with chopped aspic and garnish with a border of aspic triangles.

Medium dry or sweet white wines: Graves, Sauternes, Barsac, Alsace Gewürztraminer, Vouvray, Jurançon.

US	Ingredients	Met/Imp
I	goose liver	I
	salt and pepper	
I pinch	quatre-épices	I pinch
I	medium truffle	I
⅓ cup	cognac	80 ml/3 fl oz
⅓ cup	port wine	80 ml/3 fl oz
I ½ quarts	aspic jelly made with chicken	1.5 litres/2½ pints
3	egg whites	3
I	hard-boiled egg white	I
scant I cup	double (heavy) cream	200 ml/7 fl oz

US	Ingredients	Met/Imp
1, about 6–8 lb	plump young goose	1, about 2.7–3.6 kg/ 6–8 lb
2	onions	2
2	shallots	2
1	small garlic clove	1
1 oz	bread, without crusts	25 g/scant 1 oz
3 oz	cooked ham	75 g/3 oz
1 tsp	chopped fresh parsley	5 ml/1 tsp
1	egg	1
	salt and pepper	
3	sour (cooking) apples	3
½ cup	goose fat	100 ml/3½ fl oz
1	carrot	1
1	bouquet garni	1
scant 1 cup	clear Veal Stock (page 56)	200 ml/7 fl oz
1	small piece horseradish	1
½ cup	crème fraîche	100 ml/3½ fl oz
⅓ cup	fresh breadcrumbs	20 g/¾ oz
	GARNISH	
1 quart	chestnuts	1 litre/1¾ pints
¼ lb	raw country ham	125 g/4½ oz
6 tbsp	butter	75 g/3 oz
1½ cups	long-grain rice	250 g/8 oz
3 cups	stock	750 ml/1¼ pints

OIE FARCIE AUX MARRONS BRAISÉS

STUFFED GOOSE
WITH BRAISED CHESTNUTS

Preparation 2 hours • Cooking 1¾ hours

Draw and singe a small, plump one-year-old goose. Scald the feet and trim the webs. Reserve the liver.

Finely chop the goose liver (having removed all parts contaminated by the gall bladder) and put it in a bowl with 1 of the onions, chopped, the chopped shallots, crushed garlic, soaked and pressed bread, chopped ham, chopped parsley, egg, salt and pepper, and the cored and finely sliced or chopped apples. Work everything together with a wooden spoon, put it inside the goose and truss it so that the legs point upwards.

Put the goose in a roasting tin, brush it with some of the goose fat and cook over a high heat until browned on all sides. Meanwhile, heat some more goose fat in a frying pan and brown the finely sliced carrot and remaining onion, finely sliced. Spread these vegetables out under the goose. Add the bouquet garni and veal stock and continue cooking in a fairly hot oven for at least 1 hour, basting from time to time.

Make the garnish. Lightly grill (broil) or bake the chestnuts and peel them. Cut the ham into 5 mm/¼ inch cubes and brown lightly in one-third of the butter. Add the chestnuts, rice and stock and bring to the boil. Cover and cook in the oven for 20 minutes. After cooking, mix in the remaining butter in small pieces.

Untruss the goose and arrange it on a heated, long serving dish. Surround it with chestnuts. Strain the cooking juices from the goose through a fine sieve and remove most of the fat. Make a cold horseradish sauce: grate the horseradish and mix it with the crème fraîche and bread-crumbs. Serve the goose juice and horseradish sauce as accompaniments.

Red wines: Médoc, Saint-Émilion, Graves, Côte de Beaune or Côte de Nuits, Côte Rôtie, Châteauneuf-du-Pape.

—— GOOSE CASSEROLE FROM SEGRÉ ——

Preparation 2 hours • Cooking 1½ hours

Combine the breadcrumbs, grated bacon fat, chopped boned calf's foot, chopped livers, parsley, onion and shallots, crushed garlic, spice and salt and pepper. Mix thoroughly to form a stuffing.

At this point, add the beaten egg to the Vouvray wine, and stir in a *salpicon* of finely diced truffles. Add to the stuffing.

Cook the peeled chestnuts in the madeira until soft, then crush them, but not too finely. Mix them into the stuffing, in the proportion of one-quarter chestnuts to three-quarters stuffing. Add the madeira they were cooked in as well as some good-quality bacon, diced.

Put this stuffing inside the goose, sew it up and braise it slowly in a flameproof casserole for about 1½ hours, basting often with its own fat. When the goose is cooked, place it on a heated serving dish.

Pour the crème fraîche into the braising juices in the pan. Mix well, add the butter and cook this sauce over a low heat for a few minutes, stirring constantly. Pour on to the goose on the serving dish.

Garnish with thinly sliced artichoke bottoms, salsify *bâtons* and whole cultivated mushrooms, all lightly fried in butter.

Red wines: Médoc, Graves, Côte de Beaune or Côte de Nuits, Côte Rôtie, Châteauneuf-du-Pape.

US	Ingredients	Met/Imp
5 cups	crumbs made from stale firm-textured bread without crusts	300 g/10 oz
10 oz	pork back fat or bacon fat	300 g/10 oz
I	cooked calf's foot	I
5	poultry livers (including I from the goose)	5
	chopped fresh parsley	
I	onion	I
4	shallots	4
I	garlic clove	I
I pinch	*quatre-épices*	I pinch
	salt and pepper	
I	egg	I
½ cup	Vouvray wine	100 ml/4 fl oz
3 oz	truffles	75 g/3 oz
I quart	chestnuts	I litre/1¾ pints
scant I cup	madeira	200 ml/7 fl oz
	lean bacon	
I, about 6–8 lb	goose	I, about 2.7–3.6 kg/6–8 lb
I cup	crème fraîche	100 ml/4 fl oz
I stick	butter	100 g/4 oz
	GARNISH	
8	artichoke bottoms	8
I lb	salsify	500 g/I lb
I lb	mushrooms	500 g/I lb

ROAST GOSLING
—— STUFFED WITH SAGE AND APPLES ——

Preparation 2 hours • Cooking 1¼ hours

A 'gosling' is a bird from the first hatching of the year, which is still growing but is plump and weighs 1.8–2.3 kg/4–5 lb when drawn. The skin must be meticulously singed and cleaned.

Melt one-quarter of the butter in a frying pan and lightly fry the chopped onion and shallots. Leave to cool. Soak the bread in milk for a few minutes, then drain and press. Put the bread in a bowl and add the onions and shallots and the chopped livers. Also add the chopped bacon, the chopped parsley and sage leaves, the egg, salt, pepper and nutmeg. Peel, core and thinly slice the green apples, and sauté in one-third of the remaining butter for a few moments to soften them. Allow to cool, then add to the stuffing. Mix everything thoroughly together.

Put the stuffing inside the gosling. Sprinkle the bird with salt, brush it with plenty of melted butter and put it on a roasting rack fitted in the roasting tin. Cook in a moderate oven for about 1 hour.

During cooking, baste the gosling with butter, excluding any other liquid. When it is cooked, deglaze the tin with the stock and boil for a few minutes. Strain through a fine sieve and serve with the gosling.

Red wines: Graves, Côte de Nuits, Châteauneuf-du-Pape.

US	Ingredients	Met/Imp
I stick	butter	100 g/4 oz
I	onion	I
2	shallots	2
3 slices	firm-textured bread, without crusts	60 g/2½ oz
½ cup	milk	100 ml/4 fl oz
4	poultry livers (including I from the gosling)	4
2½ oz	unsmoked bacon	60 g/2½ oz
I tsp	chopped fresh parsley	5 ml/I tsp
2	sage leaves	2
I	egg	I
I pinch	salt	I pinch
I pinch	pepper	I pinch
I pinch	nutmeg	I pinch
3	green apples	3
I, about 4–5 lb	gosling	I, about 1.8–2.3 kg/4–5 lb
½ cup	White Stock (*page 56*) or stock made with a bouillon cube	100 ml/4 fl oz

PIGEON

YOUNG AND TENDER PIGEONS, OFTEN CALLED SQUABS, ARE appreciated by gourmets because they may be prepared in numerous subtle and attractive ways: roasted, grilled (broiled) or sautéed (braised or 'en compote' if they are a little older). The meat is a little heavy, but flavoursome and nutritious. Depending on where the pigeon comes from, the skin is pink or slightly bluish. Soft down, a plump rump and a flexible beak are signs of a good-quality bird. The liver is always left inside because it does not contain the gall bladder. (For wood pigeon, see page 481.)

CÔTELETTES DE PIGEONS EN COURONNE SUR MACARONI

CROWN OF PIGEON 'CHOPS' WITH MACARONI

Preparation 1¼ hours • Cooking 2 hours 40 minutes (including stock)

US	Ingredients	Met/Imp
4	large pigeons	4
2 sticks	butter	250 g/8 oz
6	shallots	6
I	bouquet garni (bay leaf, thyme, celery, parsley)	I
scant I cup	dry white wine	200 ml/7 fl oz
scant 3 cups	stock	700 ml/1¼ pints
3	parsley sprigs	3
	salt and pepper	
a little	flour	a little
2	eggs	2
3 tbsp	groundnut (peanut) oil	45 ml/3 tbsp
2¼ cups	fine dry breadcrumbs	200 g/7 oz
scant I cup	port wine	200 ml/7 fl oz
	GARNISH	
10 oz	macaroni	300 g/10 oz
	salt and pepper	
¼ lb	foie gras or butter	120 g/4¼ oz
¾ cup	Parmesan cheese, grated	80 g/3 oz

Singe the pigeons over a flame. Cut the skin on the back of each bird from the head to the parson's (pope's) nose and bone the birds, detaching the meat from the carcass with a knife. Cut off the wing tips at the first joint and the feet at the drumstick and reserve.

Remove the bones from the drumsticks and the wings. Draw the detached carcasses, throw away the intestines, cut the gizzards in half and empty them. Remove the skin covering the hearts.

Melt one-quarter of the butter in a sauté pan. Chop up the pigeon carcasses and the necks and brown them in the pan with the bones removed from the drumsticks and wings, the wing tips, the skinned and trimmed feet, the hearts, the livers and the gizzards.

When everything begins to brown, add the finely chopped shallots and the bouquet garni. Pour in the white wine and one-quarter of the stock, cover and cook until the liquid has reduced to about 60 ml/4 tbsp. At this point, pour in the remaining stock and bring to the boil, then cover and cook gently for 2 hours. Strain and reserve.

Skin the boned pigeon meat, removing the sinews. Put the meat in a saucepan with the strained cooking liquid from the carcasses. Bring to the boil, then lower the heat, cover and cook gently for 20 minutes.

Remove the meat from the liquid and mince (grind) it in a food processor or mincer (meat grinder) with the parsley sprigs which have been chopped and dried on paper towels. Put in a bowl, mix with two-thirds of the remaining butter and add salt and pepper.

Divide the minced (ground) pigeon mixture into 8 equal parts, make them into balls and roll them in flour. Make the balls into pear shapes, slightly curved where the stalk would be, and then flatten them on the

work surface to give them the shape of chops.

Beat the eggs in a bowl with one-third of the oil and salt and pepper. Dip both sides of the chops into this mixture and then in the breadcrumbs, making sure the chops are evenly covered. Use the flat side of a knife blade to make the breadcrumbs stick to both sides and all around the chops. Put the chops on a dish and keep cool.

Prepare the garnish. Cook the macaroni in boiling salted water for 10 minutes or until tender but still with a 'bite'. Drain, cool under running cold water and cut into small tubes no more than 1 cm/½ inch long.

If you are using foie gras, work it through a fine horsehair* sieve and collect everything that sticks underneath.

Put the macaroni in a saucepan over a high heat and evaporate off the excess moisture. Mix in the foie gras or, if unavailable, the same amount of butter, and the Parmesan. Add salt and pepper and keep warm in a boiling *bain-marie*.

Heat half of the remaining butter and the remaining oil in a frying pan. Cook the chops carefully until golden, then drain and keep warm.

Arrange the macaroni in a dome shape on a heated serving dish. Put the chops in a ring around the base of the dome, overlapping each other.

Strain off the fat from the juices in which the chops were cooked and scrape up the sediment from the bottom of the pan. Pour these juices and sediment into a saucepan, add the liquid in which the boned pigeon meat was cooked, the port and salt. Bring to the boil, remove from the heat and stir in the remaining butter until melted. Pour a border of sauce around the chops. Serve the rest in a heated sauce boat.

***Editor's note**: foie gras used to be sieved through horsehair to prevent discoloration of its creamy white flesh. Do not use a metal sieve as this would taint and discolour the foie gras; a fine nylon sieve would be the modern equivalent of horsehair.

Red wines: Richebourg, Romanée-Conti, fine Graves.

PIGEONNEAUX À LA BORDELAISE

PIGEONS BORDELAISE

Preparation 1 hour • Cooking 30 minutes

US	Ingredients	Met/Imp
8	pigeons	8
½ lb	pork back fat or bacon fat	250 g/8 oz
	salt and pepper	
4	garlic cloves	4
1 stick	butter	100 g/4 oz
8	slices firm-textured bread	8
	parsley	

Pluck, singe and draw the pigeons. Truss them securely. Heat the bacon in a frying pan until the fat runs, then add the pigeons. Add salt, pepper and 1 clove of chopped garlic and cook for 30 minutes. Drain the pigeons and keep them warm.

Heat the butter in a frying pan, add the livers and cook until browned. Work the livers through a sieve or purée in a blender or food processor. Toast the slices of bread and rub them with cut garlic cloves. Spread with the liver purée.

Arrange each pigeon on a slice of bread and garnish with very green parsley. Serve the sauce in a sauce boat, having removed the fat first.

VARIATION
This dish may also be served with a ring of aubergines (eggplants) sautéed in oil.

Red wines: Saint-Émilion, Pomerol, Graves.

US	Ingredients	Met/Imp
8	young, tender pigeons	8
	salt and pepper	
1 stick	butter	100 g/4 oz
¼ cup	oil	50 ml/2 fl oz
2	shallots	2
½ cup	white wine	100 ml/4 fl oz
½ cup	Veal Stock (page 56)	100 ml/4 fl oz
3⅓ cups	fresh breadcrumbs	200 g/7 oz
1	lemon, juice of	1
1 tbsp	chopped fresh parsley	15 ml/1 tbsp

PIGEONS CRAPAUDINE*

Preparation 1 hour • Cooking 15 minutes

Pluck, singe and draw the young pigeons. Truss the birds, tucking the feet up inside the cavities. Cut the pigeons open along the back, without separating them completely and flatten them slightly. Sprinkle them with salt and pepper. Heat the butter and oil in a frying pan, add the pigeons for 10 minutes on each side, without letting them change colour.

Remove the pigeons from the pan and leave them to cool. Add the chopped shallots to the fat remaining in the pan and stir for a few moments over a low heat, without letting them go yellow. Pour in the white wine and veal stock and cook until reduced.

When the pigeons are lukewarm, coat them with the breadcrumbs and cook them under a low grill (broiler). When they are cooked, arrange them on a heated serving dish. Finish the relish by adding the lemon juice and chopped parsley. Serve in a sauce boat.

Red wines: Médoc or Côte de Beaune.

US	Ingredients	Met/Imp
5 oz (about ⅔ cup)	Forcemeat Stuffing (page 54), made with veal	150 g/5 oz
½ cup	Dry Duxelles (page 49)	100 ml/4 fl oz
⅓ cup	minced (ground) pickled or salted tongue	30 g/1 oz
4	pigeons	4
14 tbsp	butter	200 g/7 oz
1 quart	Petits Pois 'Anglaise' (page 542)	1 litre/1¾ pints
6	carrots	6
24	small onions	24
8	pickled or salted tongue slices	8
8	fried bread croûtons	8
	Gratin Stuffing (page 54)	

STUFFED PIGEONS SAINT-CYR

Preparation 1 hour • Cooking 35 minutes

The most suitable young pigeons to use here are those that have left the nest for several weeks. They should first be plucked, singed and drawn.

Combine the forcemeat stuffing, duxelles and minced (ground) tongue and use to stuff the pigeons. Truss firmly.

Melt three-quarters of the butter in a flameproof casserole, add the pigeons and sauté until evenly browned. Transfer to a cool oven and cook for 35 minutes.

Meanwhile, prepare the ingredients for the garnish; cook the peas with thinly sliced lettuce but without onions; quarter the carrots, cut them into olive shapes and glaze them; cook the small onions (the size of hazelnuts) in butter until only slightly coloured; heat through the slices of tongue for a few minutes before serving.

When the pigeons are cooked, remove them from the casserole and cut them into pieces. Put the pieces in a pan, strain the cooking juices over them through a fine sieve, then simmer gently until heated through (do not boil).

Arrange the pigeon on a heated serving dish. Remove the sauce from the heat and stir in the remaining butter. Pour the sauce over the pigeon, arrange the garnish ingredients over and around, then surround with the croûtons spread with the gratin stuffing.

Dry white wines: Pouilly-Fumé, Pouilly-Fuissé, Chablis.
Red wines: Côte de Beaune or Médoc.

PIGEONS WITH PETITS POIS

Preparation 1½ hours • Cooking 30 minutes

US	Ingredients	Met/Imp
8	young pigeons	8
10 oz	fresh fat belly (side) of pork	300 g/10 oz
1 stick	butter	100 g/4 oz
20–30	small onions	20–30
3 tbsp	flour	25 g/scant 1 oz
1¾ cups	stock or White Stock (page 56)	400 ml/14 fl oz
1½ quarts	shelled petits pois	1.5 litres/2½ pints
1	bouquet garni	1
	salt	

Pluck, singe and draw the fine young pigeons, leaving the livers in place (there is no gall bladder in them). Truss the birds, tucking the feet up inside the stomachs (or simply lay them down flat).

Dice the pork (do not forget to remove the rind) and scald it in boiling water for 5 minutes. Drain and wipe it thoroughly. Melt the butter in a saucepan, add the pork and cook until lightly browned. Remove from the pan and drain on a plate. Brown the small onions (the size of hazelnuts) in the same butter and drain them on the plate next to the pork.

Next, put the pigeons into the same fat and cook until browned on all sides. Remove from the pan. Stir the flour into the same butter and cook, stirring, over a low heat until the mixture has turned a dark blond colour. Gradually add the stock and bring to the boil, stirring constantly.

Put the pigeons, onions and pork into this sauce. Add the petits pois, bouquet garni and salt. Cover, bring to the boil and then boil fairly rapidly for 30 minutes.

Arrange the pigeons on a heated round serving dish and remove the bouquet garni. Cook the sauce rapidly to reduce, if necessary, then cover the pigeons with it. Surround them with petits pois.

Red wines: Côte de Beaune, Moulin-à-Vent.
Dry white wines: Pouilly-Fumé, Pouilly-Fuissé, Chablis.

PINTADE ET PINTADEAU

GUINEA-FOWL

ORIGINATING IN WEST AFRICA AND APPRECIATED BY THE Romans who called it the 'chicken of Carthage', guinea-fowl have tender and succulent flesh which may be prepared in the same way as young pheasant or young partridge. Young birds are available in June, older birds in the autumn. Note that France is the leading producer of guinea-fowl in the world. Since guinea-fowl is usually eaten young, it is generally called 'pintadeau' or 'young guinea-fowl' in the catering trade. The Drôme is a traditional breeding region.

US	Ingredients	Met/Imp
3 or 4	young guinea-fowl, including the livers	3 or 4
a few	thyme, wild thyme, marjoram and savory sprigs	a few
1	sprig fennel (fresh or dried)	1
1 pinch	quatre-épices	1 pinch
	salt and pepper	
½ cup	olive oil	100 ml/4 fl oz
½ cup	cognac	100 ml/4 fl oz
2 lb	ceps	1 kg/2 lb
2	garlic cloves	2
4	shallots	4
1 stick	butter	100 g/4 oz
10 oz	fresh fat belly (side) of pork	300 g/10 oz
	cooking juices from roast meat or game	

GUINEA-FOWL CHASSEUR WITH CEPS*

Preparation 1 hour • (Birds to be hung the night before) • Cooking 35 minutes

Bring out the flavour of the guinea-fowl* by stuffing them the day before with the aromatic herbs, spice, salt and pepper, a trickle of olive oil and the cognac.

The next day, prepare the ceps. Thinly slice the caps and reserve. Chop the stems with the garlic and three-quarters of the shallots. Use this chopped mixture to stuff the insides of the guinea-fowl (with the herbs removed) along with their respective livers.

Put the guinea-fowl in a casserole with some butter and the diced pork. Roast in a moderate oven for 35 minutes or until brown. When they are almost cooked, add the reserved sliced cep caps which have been sautéed in olive oil with the remaining finely chopped shallots.

To serve, cut the guinea-fowl in half and present them with their stuffing inside. Serve the sliced ceps in a dish. Deglaze the cooking liquid with the juice from some roast meat or game, which has had some butter beaten into it. Sprinkle the guinea-fowl with this sauce.

Editor's note: The French term for hanging game birds is 'faisandage'. Instructions are given in the original French recipe for 'faisandage' or 'hanging' the guinea-fowl the night before required. Here the word is used as a *double entendre* – the guinea-fowl is not hung so that it will be high, but so that its flavour will resemble that of a 'faisan' (pheasant).

Red wines: Côte de Beaune, Côte de Nuits, Médoc, Saint-Émilion, Graves, Châteauneuf-du-Pape.

US	Ingredients	Met/Imp
4	young guinea-fowl	4
	olive oil	
	salt and pepper	
3	medium onions	3
2	carrots	2
2 bottles	red wine from Cassis	2 bottles
	Mirepoix (*page 50*)	
2	savory sprigs	2
2	sage sprigs	2
2	thyme sprigs	2
1 pinch	quatre-épices	1 pinch
1 pinch	nutmeg	1 pinch
½ cup	marc from Provence	100 ml/4 fl oz
½ cup	crème fraîche	100 ml/4 fl oz
1 lb	very small field mushrooms	500 g/1 lb
	butter	
8	croûtons fried in butter	8

GUINEA-FOWL WITH RED WINE

Preparation 1½ hours • Cooking 30 minutes

Roast the guinea-fowl in olive oil for about 30 minutes or until three-quarters cooked. Cut into pieces, removing the legs and wings and cutting the breast fillets off the bone. Reserve the juices which come out of the birds during cutting. Keep the pieces warm.

Roughly chop the carcass and brown in the oil in which the guinea-fowl were roasted. Add salt and pepper, 2 very roughly chopped onions and the chopped carrots and cook until these vegetables are browned, then press down hard and pour in the red wine. To this liquid, add the mirepoix with the herbs and spices. At this point, add the reserved juices from the roasted guinea-fowl and the remaining onion, finely chopped. Flambé the marc, pour it into the pan and cook for a few minutes until reduced. Work through a coarse-meshed sieve, then add the chopped raw guinea-fowl livers to flavour the sauce. Stir in the crème fraîche to thicken, then add the guinea-fowl pieces and cook through over a low heat. Meanwhile, sauté the whole mushrooms in butter, and add to the guinea-fowl. Arrange on the fried bread croûtons and serve at once.

Red wines: Cassis or Côtes de Provence.

POULE ET POULET, POULARDE, COQ ET CHAPON

BOILING FOWL AND CHICKEN, HEN, COCK AND CAPON

THIS VERY IMPORTANT FAMILY OF FARMYARD BIRDS IS sub-divided according to age: first of all there are 'poussins' (chicks or very young chickens) with delicate flesh, weighing from 250–300 g/8–10 oz) and sometimes sold as 'poussins de Hambourg'. Birds a little older and larger (but still less than 500 g/1 lb), are known as 'coquelets' (cockerels). They have tender flesh and are best for frying, roasting and serving with peas, etc (like pigeon). Next come 'poulets' (chickens): young two-pounders (about 1 kg) with somewhat soft flesh; 'poulets de grain' (free-range or corn-fed chickens) weighing 1.2–1.5 kg/2½–3¼ lb, which are better formed with firmer flesh; and free-range chickens with a 'seal of guarantee' (up to 2 kg/4½ lb), tender, firm and tasty. In this respect the bastion of quality is still the Bresse chicken, with its long tradition of providing both 'poulardes' (hens) and 'chapons' (capons or castrated cockbirds). These have been fattened and are therefore plump and rounded in shape; they can be roasted, braised or boiled. The true, mature 'poules' (boiling fowls/US stewing chickens) and 'coqs' (cockbirds), are becoming rare. However, the dishes requiring long cooking which were designed for them such as coq au vin and poule au pot, for example, should only really be made with these fairly old birds. As for young birds, they can be roasted, sautéed or grilled (broiled). It must be remembered, however, that a chicken which is to be roasted should be a little fatty, whereas if it is to be cooked in a casserole, it is better if it is plump and firm. For a fricassée, choose 2 or 3 small birds rather than 1 large one. More important than the age of the bird is where it came from and the fact that it was bred naturally and not in an industrial battery. Among the best available in France are the white chicken from the Auvergne, from Blois or from Loué; the Mayenne chicken; the black chicken from Challans or the south-west; the yellow Landes chicken (fattened with corn).

*Editor's note: Curnonsky's original recipes specify the exact type of bird for each dish, and French cooks would endeavour to select the correct one. Nowadays most birds are sold simply as 'chickens' in the UK and the US, with no indication of their age or gender. The type of bird has been specified in each of the recipes in this chapter, however, as much for culinary interest as for anything else.

US	Ingredients	Met/Imp
2	capons	2
3 quarts	consommé	3 litres/5¼ pints
	TO SERVE	
	coarse sea salt	
⅔ cup	cornichons	100 g/4 oz
I quart	Cream Sauce (page 67)	1 litre/1¾ pints
⅓ cup	capers	50 g/2 oz

CAPON WITH SEA SALT

Preparation 1 hour • Cooking 30 minutes

Singe the capons, then truss them with string using a large needle, so that the legs and wings are kept in the correct position. Put them in 2 large saucepans, cover with the consommé and cook for 30 minutes.

Transfer the capons to a serving dish. Continue cooking the consommé until reduced, then pour it over the capons. Serve with sea salt, either in a mill or mortar and pestle, the cornichons, and the cream sauce to which the capers have been added.

This dish may also be accompanied by carrots, turnips and leeks, cooked at the same time and in the same stock as the capons, but using only just enough liquid so that the stock is very concentrated. (Check the saltiness.) The vegetable stock may also be served as an accompaniment.

Dry white wines: Pouilly-Fumé, Alsace Riesling, Mâcon-Villages.
Red wines: Graves, Côte de Beaune, Beaujolais-Villages.

US	Ingredients	Met/Imp
2	chickens, preferably cockbirds	2
I bottle	dry white wine	I bottle
½ cup	wine vinegar	100 ml/3½ fl oz
I	bouquet garni	I
2	onions	2
4	shallots	4
¼ lb	mushroom trimmings	100 g/4 oz
¼	garlic clove	¼
	salt and pepper	
6	chervil, parsley and tarragon sprigs	6
I tbsp	Dijon mustard	15 ml/1 tbsp
2 cups	crème fraîche	500 ml/18 fl oz
4	egg yolks	4
½ cup	cognac	100 ml/3½ fl oz
14 tbsp	butter	200 g/7 oz
I tsp	paprika	5 ml/1 tsp
½ lb	cooked ham	250 g/8 oz
¼ lb	truffles	125 g/4 oz
8	artichoke bottoms	8
	White Court Bouillon (page 49)	
8	tomato slices	8

COQ À LA CRÈME AUX FONDS D'ARTICHAUTS

CHICKEN WITH CREAM AND ARTICHOKE BOTTOMS

Preparation 1¼ hours • Cooking the bird 25 minutes; the sauce 35 minutes

Poach the chickens in a *court bouillon* of the dry white wine, vinegar, bouquet garni, thinly sliced onions, half of the shallots, thinly sliced, the mushroom trimmings, crushed garlic and salt and pepper. Bring to the boil and cook for 25 minutes or until tender. Remove the birds from the pan, cut into quarters and keep them warm.

Boil the cooking juices until reduced by two-thirds, then work through a fine sieve, pressing the ingredients hard. Add the finely chopped chervil, parsley, tarragon and remaining shallots, and the Dijon mustard and cook over a low heat for 35 minutes.

Thicken the vegetable sauce with lightly whipped crème fraîche and with the egg yolks, lightly beaten with the cognac. Add the butter in small pieces and stir constantly over a low heat, taking care not to let it boil. Check the seasoning and add the paprika.

To this sauce, add the ham and truffles, cut in *julienne* strips, and the artichoke bottoms cooked in a white court-bouillon and cut into quarters. Pour the sauce on to the birds. Put a slice of tomato, which has been lightly fried in butter, on each piece of chicken and glaze in a hot oven before serving.

Dry white wines: Montrachet, Meursault, Pouilly-Fuissé.

— CHICKEN PIE 'FRANC-COMTOISE' —

Preparation 2 hours • First cooking 45 minutes • Second cooking 15 minutes

Choose cockbirds which have beautiful combs. Reserve the heads, which will be coated in breadcrumbs later on.

Truss the birds, season them with salt, pepper and spice and put them in a flameproof casserole with the giblets, sliced carrots, sliced onions and butter. Cook gently for about 45 minutes, then remove the birds from the pan and keep them warm.

Deglaze the saucepan with the brandy, port and crème fraîche to make a sauce.

Meanwhile, prepare a mixture of the mushrooms, morels, a few large cubes of ham and the braised veal sweetbreads. Strain the sauce over this mixture, simmer for a few moments, then thicken with the foie gras purée.

Cut the birds into quarters and place the pieces in a rectangular pie dish. Pour the sauce mixture over the top and sprinkle with chopped truffles. Cover the dish with puff pastry and cook in a low oven for about 15 minutes or until well risen and golden.

Meanwhile, coat the reserved cocks' heads with breadcrumbs and fry them. Just before serving the pie, push the heads through the pastry so that they stick up out of the pie crust.

Wines: red or white Arbois.

US	Ingredients	Met/Imp
2	fine chickens (cockbirds), including the giblets	2
	salt and pepper	
I pinch	quatre-épices	I pinch
3	carrots	3
2	onions	2
4 tbsp	butter	50 g/2 oz
½ cup	marc from the Jura	100 ml/3½ fl oz
½ cup	port wine	100 ml/3½ fl oz
2 cups	crème fraîche	500 ml/18 fl oz
I lb	small field mushrooms	500 g/I lb
10 oz	black morels from the Jura	300 g/10 oz
10 oz	cooked ham	300 g/10 oz
2 pairs	braised veal sweetbreads	2 pairs
½ lb	foie gras purée	250 g/8 oz
¼ lb	truffles	100 g/4 oz
10 oz	Puff Pastry (page 579)	300 g/10 oz
	breadcrumbs	

— BRAISED CHICKEN 'VIEUX PORT' —

Preparation 30 minutes • Cooking 35 minutes

Cut the chickens into quarters, then fry them in the olive oil and butter until well browned.

Drain off the oil, then flambé the birds with the marc. Deglaze with the wine, then add the skinned, de-seeded and crushed tomatoes, the peeled, cored and diced apples and the stoned and blanched green olives. Add salt and pepper, the curry powder, savory, thyme, bay leaf and a bouquet of parsley sprigs. Bring to the boil and simmer for 20–25 minutes or until the chicken is tender. Sprinkle with fines herbes just before serving.

Dry white wines: Côtes de Provence, Cassis, Bellet.
Red wines: Côtes du Rhône, Coteaux d'Aix-en-Provence, Cassis.

US	Ingredients	Met/Imp
2	fine chickens, preferably cockbirds	2
½ cup	olive oil	100 ml/4 fl oz
4 tbsp	butter	50 g/2 oz
¼ cup	marc from Provence	50 ml/2 fl oz
½ cup	very dry white wine	100 ml/4 fl oz
8	tomatoes	8
6	apples	6
I lb	green olives	500 g/I lb
	salt and pepper	
I tsp	curry powder	5 ml/I tsp
I	savory sprig	I
I	thyme sprig	I
¼	bay leaf	¼
a few	parsley sprigs	a few
I tbsp	fines herbes	15 ml/I tbsp

CHICKEN PIE BOURBONNAIS

Preparation 1½–2 hours • Marinating 2–3 hours • Cooking 1¼ hours

US	Ingredients	Met/Imp
I	chicken (cockbird)	I
	salt and pepper	
I pinch	*quatre-épices*	I pinch
½ cup	port wine	100 ml/4 fl oz
¼ lb	truffles	125 g/4 oz
2 sticks	butter	250 g/8 oz
I tbsp	tomato paste	15 ml/I tbsp
6 tbsp	flour	50 g/2 oz
I quart	White Stock (*page 56*) or chicken stock	I litre/1¾ pints
½ lb	lambs' sweetbreads	250 g/8 oz
½ lb	mushrooms	250 g/8 oz
½ lb	Forcemeat Stuffing (*page 54*), made into quenelles	250 g/8 oz
½ lb	cocks' combs and kidneys	250 g/8 oz
½ cup	madeira	100 ml/4 fl oz
	Shortcrust Pastry, for lining (*page 577*)	

Choose a fine cockbird which has a beautiful comb. Reserve the head, which will be coated in breadcrumbs later on.

Truss the bird, season it with salt, pepper and spice, then put it in a glazed earthenware dish or bowl with the port and the sliced truffles. Leave to marinate for 2–3 hours, basting often.

Make a velouté sauce. Make a good roux by melting the butter in a saucepan and stirring in the tomato paste and flour. Gradually stir in the stock, then mix in the port marinade, keeping back the truffles. Cook gently for 45 minutes.

Meanwhile, prepare the garnish. Sweat the sweetbreads, mushrooms, quenelles, cocks' combs and kidneys in a saucepan with the madeira, then drain well, reserving the madeira.

Cook the velouté sauce over a high heat to reduce, then thin it down with the reserved madeira. Boil to reduce once more.

When it is ready, pour the sauce into a pie dish with the chicken and slices of truffle. As a garnish, add the pieces of lamb sweetbread, the mushrooms, quenelles and cocks' combs and kidneys. Leave to cool.

Roll out the pastry and use to cover the pie. Bake in a low oven for at least 1 hour. Meanwhile, coat the cock's head (and comb) with breadcrumbs and fry. Just before serving the pie, push the head through the pastry so that it sticks up out of the pie crust.

Red wines: Saint-Émilion, Pomerol, Côte de Nuits, Côtes du Rhône.

CHICKEN PIE FROM THE FOIX REGION

Preparation 1½–2 hours • Marinating the day before • Cooking 1¼ hours; Velouté 1½ hours

US	Ingredients	Met/Imp
2	small chickens, preferably cockbirds	2
	salt and pepper	
I pinch	*quatre-épices*	I pinch
	foie gras scraps	
½ cup	aged madeira	100 ml/4 fl oz
¼ cup	armagnac	50 ml/2 fl oz
	truffle juice	
I, about 2 oz	truffle	I, about 50 g/2 oz
I	thyme sprig	I
I	bay leaf	I
I	parsley sprig	I
I	clove	I
½ lb	mushrooms	250 g/8 oz
I	calf's brain	I
	amourettes	
I lb	green olives, stoned	500 g/I lb
I stick	butter	100 g/4 oz
6 tbsp	flour	50 g/2 oz
20	small onions cooked in White Court Bouillon (*page 49*)	20
½ lb	cooked ham	250 g/8 oz
2	shallots	2
½ lb	foie gras	250 g/8 oz
I lb	Puff Pastry (*page 579*)	500 g/I lb

Cut the birds into pieces and season with salt, pepper and spice. Put in a bowl with the scraps of foie gras, the madeira, armagnac, truffle juice and truffle, sliced. Flavour with the thyme, bay leaf, parsley, clove and quartered mushrooms, and leave to marinate overnight, basting as often as possible.

The next day, remove the chicken pieces and strain the marinade. Reserve the marinade, foie gras, mushrooms and truffle. Blanch the calf's brain in boiling water with the amourettes and olives.

Prepare some chicken velouté: melt a large piece of butter and the same amount of reserved marinated foie gras in a saucepan. Add the flour and stir in some of the strained chicken marinade. Cook gently for 1 hour, then cook over a high heat until reduced. Add another piece of butter and the same amount of foie gras. Thin with a little marinade and cook to reduce once more. When this sauce is ready, put the chicken pieces in it, transfer to a pie dish and allow to cool.

Cut the calf's amourettes and brain into quenelle shapes and add to

the chicken with the reserved marinated mushroom quarters and the small onions. Meanwhile, brown the finely diced ham in a frying pan containing half butter and half foie gras. Remove the ham from the pan and fry the finely chopped shallots. Put in the rest of the reserved marinade and pour the mixture into the pie dish on top of the quartered poultry. Sprinkle lightly with the reserved marinated slices of truffle. Roll out the pastry and use to cover the pie dish. Bake in a low to moderate oven for at least another hour.

Red wines: Côte de Nuits, Côtes du Rhône, Saint-Émilion, Pomerol.

COQ AU VIN

CHICKEN IN RED WINE

Preparation 1 hour • Cooking 35 minutes

Singe and draw the birds, then cut them into pieces. Season the pieces with salt, pepper, thyme and bay.

Blanch the pork in boiling water, drain and dice. Place in a heavy sauté pan with the onions and the quartered ceps and sauté until brown.

In another pan, lightly brown the chicken pieces in the oil. Drain well. Put the sautéed vegetable mixture in the bottom of a large flameproof casserole, lay the pieces of chicken flat on top, then flambé with the cognac and pour in the wine. Bring to the boil, add the finely chopped garlic and check the seasoning. Cook for about 20 minutes per 1 kg/2 lb.

Strain the cooking liquid into another saucepan. Combine the butter with the flour to make *beurre manié* and use to thicken the cooking liquid. Bring to the boil, beating vigorously.

Arrange the chicken pieces in serving dishes with the vegetables. Remove the fat from the sauce and pour over the poultry. Serve with fried bread croûtons lightly rubbed with garlic.

Wines: as a general rule, serve the same wine as the one used for cooking.

US	Ingredients	Met/Imp
2, each about 2½ lb	fine chickens, preferably cockbirds	2, each about 1.2 kg/2½ lb
	salt and pepper	
I pinch	dried thyme	I pinch
I pinch	ground bay	I pinch
10 oz	fresh fat belly (side) of pork	300 g/10 oz
20	small onions	20
I lb	ceps	500 g/I lb
½ cup	oil	100 ml/4 fl oz
⅓ cup	cognac	80 ml/3 fl oz
2 bottles	red burgundy wine (Chambertin or Mercurey)	2 bottles
3	garlic cloves	3
1½ sticks	butter	175 g/6 oz
½ cup	flour	75 g/3 oz
16	heart-shaped croûtons fried in butter	16

US	Ingredients	Met/Imp
2	chickens, preferably cockbirds	2
6 tbsp	flour	50 g/2 oz
½ lb	fresh fat belly (side) of pork	250 g/8 oz
I stick	butter	100 g/4 oz
30	small onions, well glazed	30
⅓ cup	cognac	75 ml/3 fl oz
2 bottles	mature red wine from the Auvergne	2 bottles
	salt and pepper	
I	bouquet garni	I
4	shallots	4
2	carrots	2
½ cup	chicken blood*	100 ml/4 fl oz
16	fried triangular croûtons	16
I tbsp	chopped fresh parsley	15 ml/I tbsp

—— CHICKEN IN AUVERGNE WINE ——

Preparation 45 minutes • Cooking 50 minutes

Choose 2 plump cockbirds, 1–1½ years old. Cut them into pieces and coat with the flour.

Blanch the pork in boiling water, drain and cut into small rectangles. Melt the butter in a flameproof casserole, add the pork and cook until browned. Add the small onions and the chicken pieces and cook in the same butter until browned. When everything is golden brown, flambé with the cognac. Sprinkle with a heaped spoonful of flour, then pour in the wine. Add salt, pepper, the bouquet garni and the thinly sliced shallots and carrots. Cover and cook in a moderate oven for 50 minutes.

Remove the chicken pieces from the casserole and arrange on a heated serving dish. Keep warm. Stir the chicken blood into the sauce to thicken it, then strain through a fine sieve.

Check the seasoning and pour the sauce over the chicken. Put the small onions and pork pieces on top as a garnish, surround with the fried croûtons, sprinkle with parsley and serve.

***Editor's note**: in some rural areas of France, the blood is collected when the chicken's throat is cut; it is then used to enrich sauces. This stage will obviously have to be omitted with a chicken which has been bought.

Wines: as a general rule, serve the same wine as the one used for cooking.

I	garlic clove	I
6	chicken livers, preferably from Bresse hen birds	6
¼ lb	beef fillet (tenderloin)	100 g/4 oz
I glass	Veal Juice (page 56)	I glass
4	eggs	4
4	egg yolks	4
about 2 cups	milk	about 500 ml/18 fl oz
	salt and pepper	
¼ cup	oil	50 ml/2 fl oz
24	Crayfish Bordelaise (page 239)	24

—— BRESSE CHICKEN LIVER MOUSSE WITH CRAYFISH SAUCE ——

Preparation 3 hours • Cooking 1½ hours

This Bresse chicken liver mousse, coated with a sauce made with meaty crayfish tails, is a great delicacy. Do not use cream instead of milk because the ingredients which make up this dish often curdle and the mousse, which should have the consistency of a custard, breaks up, sinks down and goes watery.

Lightly rub the sides and bottom of a very large mortar with the cut garlic clove. Put the creamy white livers and the piece of beef in the mortar and crush with the pestle. Add the meat juice, the whole eggs and extra yolks and enough milk to form a very liquid purée. Mix together, add salt and pepper and work through a sieve.

Brush the entire inside of a decorative metal mould with oil, drain off the excess and put a piece of greased greaseproof or parchment paper in the bottom. Pour the liver mixture into the mould, without filling it completely, so that when the mousse rises, it will not overflow.

Put the mould in a cold *bain-marie*, making sure that the bottom of the mould does not touch the bottom of the saucepan containing the water. Heat gradually but do not allow the mixture to boil. If these directions are not followed, or if the eggs and the milk are not fresh, the

inside of the mousse will be veined instead of smooth and shiny; the ingredients will have separated and the mousse will be marbled.

Continue to heat gently for about 1½ hours, then remove the mould from the bain-marie and dry with a cloth. Invert a serving dish on top of the mould and turn the mousse out upside down. Coat with the crayfish and sauce.

Medium dry or sweet white wines: Sauternes, Monbazillac, Coteaux du Layon.

POULARDE DE BRESSE ÉTUVÉE AU CHAMPAGNE

BRESSE CHICKEN
BRAISED IN CHAMPAGNE

Preparation 45 minutes • Cooking 45 minutes

US	Ingredients	Met/Imp
2, each about 3 lb	chickens, preferably Bresse hen birds	2, each about 1.5 kg/3 lb
2 sticks	butter	250 g/8 oz
2	large onions	2
2	shallots	2
½ bottle	dry champagne	½ bottle
scant 1 cup	chicken stock	200 ml/7 fl oz
2 cups	double (heavy) cream	500 ml/18 fl oz
	salt and pepper	

Fry the chickens in the butter in a flameproof casserole until browned on all sides.

When the chickens are three-quarters cooked, add the thinly sliced onions and fry in the same butter until browned.

Add the thinly sliced shallots and brown them for a moment. Without draining off the butter, pour in the champagne. Cover the casserole and braise the chickens until they are tender and the wine has reduced.

Remove the chickens from the casserole and pour in the stock to deglaze. Finish by stirring in the cream. Add salt and pepper, then work the sauce through a fine sieve.

Cut up the chickens at the table and serve the sauce in a sauce boat.

Wines: serve the same champagne as the one used for cooking.

POULARDE DE BRESSE TRUFFÉE BRAISÉE AU PORTO

BRESSE CHICKEN
WITH TRUFFLES BRAISED IN PORT

Preparation 1½ hours • Cooking 50 minutes

US	Ingredients	Met/Imp
1, about 4–4½ lb	chicken, preferably a Bresse hen bird	1, about 1.8– 2 kg/4–4½ lb
1 lb	foie gras with truffles	500 g/1 lb
5 oz	mushrooms	150 g/5 oz
10 oz	truffles	300 g/10 oz
	quatre-épices	
	salt and pepper	
14 tbsp	butter	200 g/7 oz
½ cup	oil	100 ml/3½ fl oz
1	slice fatty bacon	1
1	onion	1
2	carrots	2
1	bouquet garni	1
½ cup	port wine	100 ml/3½ fl oz
6	very thin slices fresh truffle	6
about 1 cup	Veal Stock (page 56)	about 200 ml/ 7 fl oz

Stuff a very white Bresse chicken with the foie gras and the mushrooms, then stud the breast fillets and the legs with the truffles. Season the bird with spice and salt and pepper, then truss.

Heat the butter and oil in a flameproof casserole, add the chopped bacon, sliced onion and carrots and the bouquet garni and brown quickly for about 5 minutes. Add the chicken and cook for about 40 minutes, covering the casserole with a lid about halfway through.

Deglaze with the port, sprinkle with the fresh truffle slices and moisten with a little veal stock. Serve straight from the casserole.

Red wines: fine Haut-Médoc or Côte de Beaune.

CHICKEN CASSEROLE COOKED 'AS IN HENDAYE'

Preparation 30 minutes • Cooking 50 minutes

US	Ingredients	Met/Imp
1, about 1.6–1.8 kg/3½–4 lb	chicken, preferably a hen bird	1, about 1.6–1.8 kg/3½–4 lb
1 cup	olive oil	200 ml/7 fl oz
4	large onions	4
7 oz	Bayonne ham	200 g/7 oz
1	bouquet garni	1
1	garlic clove	1
	salt and pepper	
4	tomatoes	4
7 oz	sweet peppers	200 g/7 oz
½ cup	madeira	100 ml/3½ fl oz
6	courgettes (zucchini)	6
6	aubergines (eggplants)	6
1 tbsp	persillade	15 ml/1 tbsp

Fry the chicken in the oil with the onions, sliced into rings, the diced Bayonne ham, the bouquet garni, garlic, salt and pepper and a few skinned, de-seeded and crushed tomatoes. Add the sliced peppers. Pour in the madeira, cover and finish cooking. Meanwhile, sauté the round slices of courgette (zucchini) and aubergine (eggplant) in oil. Simmer them with the chicken and sprinkle with the persillade before serving.

Red wines: Saint-Émilion, Pomerol, Graves, Fronsac.

CHICKEN 'CHURCHILL'

Preparation 45 minutes • Cooking 55 minutes

Recipe created in honour of Churchill by Jacques Manière, chef of Le Pactole restaurant, Paris

US	Ingredients	Met/Imp
¼ lb	French (fine green) beans	100 g/4 oz
¼ lb	carrots	100 g/4 oz
¼ lb	celery heart	100 g/4 oz
¼ lb	truffles	100 g/4 oz
2	shallots	2
1, about 4½ lb	chicken, preferably a hen bird	1, about 2 kg/4½ lb
	salt and pepper	
	flour	
1½ tbsp	butter	20 g/¾ oz
1 tbsp	oil	15 ml/1 tbsp
½ bottle	brut champagne	½ bottle
1 cup	crème fraîche	250 ml/8 fl oz
4	egg yolks	4

Cut the beans in half. Cut the carrots, celery and truffles into a fine *julienne*. Chop the shallots separately.

Cut the raw chicken into 8 pieces. Add salt and pepper to these pieces and coat them in flour. Heat the butter and oil in a large sauté pan, add the chicken pieces and cook over a low heat for about 10 minutes or until browned. Drain, remove the excess fat from the pan and add the shallots. Fry for about 5 minutes or until golden. Put the pieces of chicken on top of the shallots, pour in the champagne, cover and cook slowly for 20 minutes.

Meanwhile, put the beans, carrots and celery in cold, salted water. Bring to the boil and blanch for 5 minutes, then drain.

Put the chicken pieces on a heated serving dish. Rapidly boil the liquid they were cooked in until reduced, then add the crème fraîche and simmer for 4 minutes. Pour a little of this hot cooking liquid into a separate small saucepan and beat in the egg yolks. Gradually whisk in the remaining liquid to obtain a frothy sauce. Spread the vegetables and the truffles over the chicken pieces. Coat with the sauce, having first checked the seasoning.

Wines: serve the same champagne as the one used for cooking.

——— CHICKEN WITH CUCUMBER * ———

Preparation 45 minutes • Cooking 35 minutes

US	Ingredients	Met/Imp
2, each about 2–2½ lb	chickens, preferably hen birds	2, each about 1–1.2 kg/2–2½ lb
	salt and pepper	
10 tbsp	butter	150 g/5 oz
¼ cup	oil	50 ml/2 fl oz
1 lb	medium white mushrooms	500 g/1 lb
16	young medium onions	16
6	tomatoes	6
scant 1 cup	crème fraîche	200 ml/7 fl oz
2	small cucumbers	2
1 pinch	dried thyme	1 pinch
1 tsp	chopped fresh tarragon	5 ml/1 tsp

Cut the chickens up in the usual way, then season with salt and pepper.

Heat the butter and oil in a large sauté pan, add the chicken pieces and fry them lightly and rapidly until golden. Remove them from the pan and keep warm. Add the quartered mushroom caps to the fat remaining in the pan and quickly fry them. Remove and keep warm.

Slice the onions very thinly and spread in the bottom of the pan. Put the pieces of chicken on top, followed by the mushrooms. Cover with a piece of buttered greaseproof or parchment paper, then the lid, so that the food will cook in steam and the onions will not become coloured. Continue to cook for about 35 minutes.

Meanwhile, prepare the tomatoes. De-seed them and cut each one into 8 pieces. Add them to the chicken after 15 minutes cooking. Adjust the seasoning if necessary. After a further 10–12 minutes cooking, add the crème fraîche. Remove the buttered paper and shake the pan over the heat to mix the ingredients. Cover again with the lid, but not the paper, and leave to simmer.

Peel the cucumbers. Cut them into sections, then into sticks which can be pared into olive shapes. Blanch them for quite a long time in boiling water, then drain thoroughly and add them to the chicken. Add the thyme and tarragon and simmer until the chicken is tender.

Dry white wines: Muscadet, Pouilly-Fumé, Chablis, Pouilly-Fuissé.
Red wines: Médoc, Côte de Beaune, Bourgueil, Chinon.

——— CHICKEN 'GRAND PALAIS' ———

Preparation 1 hour • Cooking 1 hour

Recipe created at the Laserre restaurant

US	Ingredients	Met/Imp
2	chickens, preferably hen birds	2
	salt and pepper	
2	slices fatty bacon	2
	butter	
½ cup	madeira	100 ml/3½ fl oz
1 cup	crème fraîche	200 ml/7 fl oz
½ cup	cognac	100 ml/3½ fl oz
8	thin truffle slices	8
8	very white Paris mushrooms	8
7 oz	foie gras	200 g/7 oz
	GRAND PALAIS RICE	
1 stick	butter	100 g/4 oz
2 tbsp	chopped onion	30 ml/2 tbsp
1½ cups	long-grain rice	250 g/8 oz
2½ cups	White Stock (page 56)	600 ml/1 pint

Sprinkle the chickens with salt and pepper and bard the breast of each bird with a slice of bacon, then fry in butter in a sauté pan until tender.

When they are cooked, remove them from the pan and keep them warm. Pour off the fat and deglaze with the madeira. Add the crème fraîche and cook until reduced. As soon as the sauce begins to stick slightly to the spoon, remove from the heat. Add the cognac and taste to check the seasoning. Put the chickens on a bed of Grand Palais rice (see below) on a long heated serving dish. Coat everything with sauce and garnish the chickens with a ring of truffle slices. Arrange the mushroom caps upside down around the chickens and fill them with the foie gras. Grand Palais rice. Melt half of the butter in a saucepan and fry the onion until golden. Add the unwashed rice and stir until it has a milky tinge. Pour in the stock and cook for 10 minutes or until the rice is tender. Stir in the remaining butter in small pieces.

Wines: vintage champagne.

US	Ingredients	Met/Imp
1, about 4–4½ lb	chicken, preferably a Bresse hen bird	1, about 1.8–2 kg/4–4½ lb
	salt and pepper	
1 tbsp	oil	15 ml/1 tbsp
4	pig's trotters (feet)	4
1	veal kidney	1
¾ lb	chicken livers	350 g/12 oz
about 1 stick	butter	about 100 g/4 oz
1	onion	1
1	thyme sprig	1
1	bay leaf	1
¼ cup	cognac	50 ml/2 fl oz
5 oz	lean boneless pork	150 g/5 oz
14 oz	pork back fat or bacon fat	400 g/14 oz
1	large (extra large) egg	1
½ tsp	chopped fresh parsley	2.5 ml/½ tsp
2	canned truffles	2
1	slice fatty bacon	1
1 cup	stock	200 ml/7 fl oz

CHICKEN STUFFED WITH PIG'S TROTTERS

Preparation 2 hours • Cooking 2 hours

Draw and singe the chicken, reserving the heart and liver. Cut off the feet and head. Sprinkle with salt, both inside and out.

Heat the oil in a frying pan and add the pig's trotters (feet). Cover and cook over a low heat for 30 minutes.

Meanwhile, skin and core the kidney and cut it into strips. Remove the gall bladders from all of the livers, taking care not to burst them because they would contaminate the livers and make them unusable.

Melt half of the butter in a pan and rapidly sauté the strips of kidney, livers and heart over a high heat, adding the finely chopped onion, the thyme and the bay leaf. Add salt and pepper and pour in the cognac. Lower the heat and boil for a few seconds until reduced. Remove the pan from the heat and leave to cool. Remove the thyme and the bay leaf and put the remainder through a mincer (meat grinder), using the finest blade, or work in a food processor. Mince (grind) the lean pork and the pork or bacon fat in the same way.

Put the minced (ground) mixture into a bowl, add salt and pepper and mix in the egg and parsley. Add the truffles, finely diced, and the juice from the can. Bone the pig's trotters (feet), finely dice them and mix them into the stuffing.

Put the stuffing inside the chicken and sew up the opening with white thread. Spread the remaining butter on the bottom of a roasting tin and add a drop of oil (to prevent the butter burning). Put the chicken in the dish and cover it with the slice of fatty bacon. Roast in a hot oven for about 2 hours.

Pour a little hot stock around the chicken after 15 minutes of cooking, then baste frequently as soon as the juice has formed. Add more hot stock if the liquid shows signs of reducing. Cut the chicken into serving pieces, place them on a heated serving dish and arrange the stuffing in a ring all around. Serve with the juice strained into a sauce boat and a dish of celery hearts.

Wines: Santenay, Mercurey, Cornas, Châteauneuf-du-Pape.

CHICKEN 'FRANÇAISE'

Preparation 4 hours • Cooking 1¼ hours

The sauce for this dish will be the liquid produced by the frying.

Prepare the bird for stuffing, reserving the trimmings and giblets. Melt some butter in a frying pan and add the breadcrumbs and a fine *julienne* of 1 carrot, the leeks, celery and fennel, together with 1 garlic clove, the thyme, bay leaf, salt, pepper and a pinch of sugar. Fry until lightly browned and completely dry. Stuff the bird, then truss.

Put the bird in a large flameproof casserole on a bed of the trimmings and giblets from the chicken, the remaining carrots, sliced, the sliced onions, the mushroom trimmings, remaining garlic, crushed, the tarragon and the tomatoes, skinned, de-seeded and chopped. Do not add liquid; the vegetables will produce enough liquid of their own. Cook for 1¼ hours or until the chicken is tender but only very lightly coloured. The vegetables will almost be reduced to a glaze. Remove the chicken from the pan and keep warm.

Deglaze the bottom of the pan with the champagne, without removing the vegetables. Remove any pieces of bone and work the sauce through a piece of cheesecloth. Return this purée to the heat, add the cream and season with a little cayenne.

Garnish: grease some dariole moulds with a little butter. Prepare a spinach *pain* (loaf) mixture composed of two-thirds puréed spinach and one-third forcemeat stuffing. Spoon into a piping (pastry) bag fitted with a medium nozzle. Pipe over the bottom and up the sides of the moulds. Fill the centres with a *salpicon* made from three-quarters of the tongue, the truffles and mushrooms bound together with the veal stock which has been reduced with the madeira. Cover the top with more of the spinach mixture. Cook in a *bain-marie*.

When it is time to serve, turn the moulds out and garnish with the remaining tongue, cut into tiny circles and coated with aspic.

Cook the artichoke bottoms in a white court bouillon. Sweat them in butter, then garnish them with nut-sized pieces of celeriac (or, if unavailable, cucumber), which have been blanched, drained and dipped in a little creamy velouté. Cut a small hole in the stalk end of each tomato, squeeze the tomatoes gently in a cloth to extract the seeds, then push them back into shape. Sweat the tomatoes in butter and season with salt and pepper, then place 1 tomato in the centre of each artichoke. Add a small pinch of sugar and a little chopped tarragon.

Sprinkle the mushroom caps with lemon juice. Season them with salt and pepper, then sweat them in butter. Fill them with small pearls of gnocchi made with Choux Pastry (*page 578*) to which a little of the grated Gruyère and a little nutmeg have been added, and which have then been rolled in the béchamel sauce with the remaining Gruyère added and cooked au gratin.

To assemble the dish, place the chicken on a large fried croûte in the centre of a long serving dish. If possible, use a skewer garnished with a tomato and a truffle to keep the chicken steady on the croûte. Pour a little sauce over the chicken and on the bottom of the dish, then put the garnishes in place. Serve the remaining sauce on the side in a sauce boat.

Red wines: fine Côte de Beaune, Haut-Médoc or Graves.

US	Ingredients	Met/Imp
1, about 3–4 lb	chicken, preferably a hen bird	1, about 1.5–1.8 kg
	butter	
8 cups	fresh breadcrumbs	500 g/1 lb
3	carrots	3
2	leeks, white part only	2
1	celery stalk	1
1	fennel sprig	1
2	garlic cloves	2
1	thyme sprig	1
¼	bay leaf	¼
	salt and pepper	
	sugar	
2	onions	2
	mushroom trimmings	
	tarragon sprigs	
4	medium tomatoes	4
1 bottle	*brut* champagne	1 bottle
1 cup	cream	200 ml/7 fl oz
	cayenne	
	GARNISH	
2 lb	spinach	1 kg/2 lb
1 cup	Forcemeat Stuffing (*second recipe – page 55*)	200 ml/7 fl oz
7 oz	pickled or salted tongue	200 g/7 oz
¼ lb	truffles	100 g/4 oz
5 oz	mushrooms	150 g/5 oz
½ cup	thickened Brown Veal Stock (*page 56*)	100 ml/3½ fl oz
½ cup	madeira	100 ml/3½ fl oz
	aspic jelly	
8	large artichoke bottoms	8
	White Court Bouillon (*page 49*)	
	butter	
2	heads celeriac	2
	Chicken Velouté (*page 57*)	
8	very small tomatoes	8
	chopped tarragon	
8	white mushroom caps	8
1	lemon, juice of	1
	gnocchi mixture (see method)	
1 cup	Gruyère cheese, grated	100 g/4 oz
	nutmeg	
½ cup	Béchamel Sauce (*page 62*)	100 ml/3½ fl oz
1	fried croûte	1
	1 tomato and 1 truffle speared on a skewer (optional)	

US	Ingredients	Met/Imp
2	small chickens, preferably hen birds	2
4	large onions	4
8	large mushrooms	8
I quart	Mornay Sauce (page 73)	I litre/1¾ pints
I lb	Straw Potatoes (page 552), cooked in 150 g/5 oz (10 tbsp) butter	500 g/1 lb
½ cup	cheese, grated	50 g/2 oz

CHICKEN GRATIN WITH STRAW POTATOES

Preparation 1¼ hours • Cooking 45 minutes

Braise the chickens with the onions and mushrooms in a large flameproof casserole without letting them colour.

When the chickens are cooked, remove them from the casserole, cut them into quarters and keep them warm.

Finely chop the onions and mushrooms that were cooked with the chickens, then add them to the Mornay sauce.

Make a base or 'nest' of the straw potatoes and put the quartered chickens on top. Coat with the Mornay sauce, sprinkle over the grated cheese and cook au gratin.

Red wines: Médoc, Côte de Beaune, Beaujolais-Villages.

US	Ingredients	Met/Imp
I, about 4½ lb	chicken, preferably a hen bird, including trimmings and liver	I, about 2 kg
	coarse sea salt	
	cornichons	
7 oz	vermicelli	200 g/7 oz
	POT-AU-FEU	
2 lb	knuckle (shank) of veal	I kg/2 lb
8	carrots	8
8	turnips	8
4	leeks, white part only	4
I	onion spiked with a clove	I
I	beef bone with marrow	I
	STUFFING	
2	chicken livers	2
¼ lb	lean bacon	100 g/4 oz
I tbsp	chopped fresh parsley	15 ml/1 tbsp
I pinch	dried tarragon	I pinch
I	garlic clove	I
4	shallots	4
¼ lb	*raw country ham*	100 g/4 oz
4 cups	fresh breadcrumbs	250 g/8 oz
2	eggs	2
	salt and pepper	

CHICKEN 'HENRI IV'

Preparation 1 hour • Cooking 3 hours

Put all the pot-au-feu ingredients in a large saucepan with the trimmings from the chicken. Cover with water and bring to the boil. Cover and leave to simmer for 2 hours.

Meanwhile, make the stuffing. Chop the 3 chicken livers, the bacon, parsley, tarragon, garlic, shallots and ham and mix with the breadcrumbs and eggs.

Season this stuffing with salt and pepper and put inside the chicken. Sew up the opening and truss the bird. Add it to the pot-au-feu and continue cooking for 1 hour. When the chicken is cooked, serve it with sea salt, cornichons and the vegetables from the cooking liquid. Make a pasta soup by adding the vermicelli to the cooking liquid.

Red wines: Madiran, Cahors, Bergerac, Vins de Marcillac.

POULARDE MAXIM'S

CHICKEN 'MAXIM'S'

Preparation 1¼ hours • Cooking 45 minutes

Truss the chicken with its feet inside its stomach, without forgetting to cut the joint tendon. Season with salt and pepper.

Put the chicken in a fairly high-sided casserole with the thinly sliced carrots and onions, a few mushroom stalks and a small bouquet garni. Add half of the butter and cook in a fairly hot oven until brown. Cover and continue cooking for about 45 minutes, basting often.

When the chicken is cooked, remove it from the pan, untruss it, put it in a casserole and keep it warm.

Remove the vegetables, bouquet garni and fat from the casserole and add the remaining butter. Heat until the butter is hot, then add the mushroom caps, quartered truffles and paprika. Pour in the cognac and port and boil fairly rapidly to deglaze. Add the crème fraîche and cook until reduced by half. Check and adjust the seasoning if necessary.

Pour everything over the chicken, then immediately put the lid on the casserole to conserve the heat. Serve very hot.

Red wines: Saint-Émilion, Pomerol, Côte de Nuits.

US	Ingredients	Met/Imp
1, about 4–4½ lb	chicken, preferably a Bresse hen bird	1, about 1.8–2 kg/4–4½ lb
	salt and pepper	
3	carrots	3
2	onions	2
7 oz	small mushrooms	200 g/7 oz
1	bouquet garni	1
2 sticks	butter	200 g/7 oz
½ lb	truffles	250 g/8 oz
1 tbsp	paprika	15 ml/1 tbsp
½ cup	cognac	100 ml/4 fl oz
½ cup	port wine	100 ml/4 fl oz
1 quart	crème fraîche	1 litre/1¾ pints

POULARDE AU MOULIN-À-VENT

CHICKEN WITH MOULIN-À-VENT WINE

Preparation 1 hour • Cooking 30 minutes

Recipe by Paul Blanc, Chapon Fin, Thoissey

Cut the chickens into serving pieces.

Blanch the pork in boiling water, then drain and dice. Heat two-thirds of the butter and the oil in a saucepan, and fry the onions and pork until brown. Add the pieces of chicken and sauté them until they are well browned. Add the shallots, garlic and parsley, and bouquet garni of thyme, bay leaf and celery. Pour in the wine and cook for about 30 minutes or until the chicken is tender.

Remove the chicken from the pan, arrange on a serving dish and keep warm. Remove the fat from the cooking liquid and strain the liquid through a fine sieve. Just before serving, thicken this sauce with *beurre manié* made by combining the flour and remaining butter. Bring to the boil, then add the blood mixed with the cognac. Coat the chicken pieces with the sauce and garnish with the small croûtons, rubbed with garlic and fried.

Wines: as a general rule, serve the same wine as the one used for cooking.

US	Ingredients	Met/Imp
2, each about 2–2½ lb	chickens, preferably Bresse hen birds	2, each about 1–1.2 kg/2–2½ lb
14 oz	fresh fat belly (side) of pork	400 g/14 oz
2½ sticks	butter	300 g/10 oz
¼ cup	oil	50 ml/2 fl oz
20	small onions	20
1 tbsp	chopped shallots	15 ml/1 tbsp
1 tbsp	chopped garlic	15 ml/1 tbsp
1 tbsp	chopped fresh parsley	15 ml/1 tbsp
1	thyme sprig	1
1	bay leaf	1
1	celery stalk	1
2 bottles	Moulin-à-Vent wine	2 bottles
6 tbsp	flour	50 g/2 oz
¼ cup	chicken or pig's blood	50 ml/2 fl oz
¼ cup	cognac	50 ml/2 fl oz
16	small heart-shaped croûtons	16

POACHED CHICKEN 'OLD MOTHER BRASIER'

Preparation 1¼ hours • Cooking about 40 minutes

US	Ingredients	Met/Imp
2, each about 2½–2¾ lb	chickens, preferably hen birds	2, each about 1.1–1.2 kg/ 2½–2¾ lb
¼ lb	truffles	100 g/4 oz
2 quarts	well-flavoured stock	2 litres/4½ pints
4	leeks, white parts only	4
4	small carrots	4
3	turnips	3
1	parsnip	1
2	celery stalks	2
10 oz	bacon	300 g/10 oz
10 tbsp	butter	150 g/5 oz
	salt	
scant 1 cup	Béarnaise Sauce (*page 61*)	200 ml/7 fl oz
2 tbsp	grated horseradish	30 ml/2 tbsp

Choose some good, succulent and tender 'Louhans' chickens. Cut the truffles into very thin strips and push under the skins of the chickens. Truss the birds and put them in a large saucepan. Cover with the stock and add the sliced leeks, carrots, turnips, parsnip, celery and diced bacon. Bring to the boil and cook for 35 minutes or until the chickens are tender. Remove all the vegetables from the pan, using a slotted spoon. Leave the chickens to stand in the cooking liquid for 20 minutes.

Meanwhile, melt half of the butter in another saucepan and add the vegetables which were cooked with the chicken. Cover and sweat for a few minutes, then serve them as an accompaniment to the chickens.

Remove the chickens from the cooking liquid, place on a serving dish and keep warm. Boil the cooking liquid until reduced, then beat in the remaining butter. Check the seasoning and sprinkle a little of the liquid over the chicken.

If liked, serve this dish with a little Béarnaise sauce to which the horseradish has been added.

White wines: Montrachet, Meursault, Graves, Barsac, Sauternes.
Red wines: Médoc, Côte de Beaune, Cornas.

FRIED CHICKEN FINANCIÈRE

Preparation 1¼ hours • Cooking 50 minutes

US	Ingredients	Met/Imp
1, about 3½–4 lb	fine chicken, preferably a hen bird	1, about 1.6– 1.8 kg/3½–4 lb
2	carrots	2
2	onions	2
1	bouquet garni	1
	salt and pepper	
10 tbsp	butter	150 g/5 oz
	SAUCE	
scant 1 cup	madeira	200 ml/7 fl oz
scant 1 cup	thickened Veal Juice (*page 56*)	200 ml/7 fl oz
2 cups	Demi-Glaze (*page 56*)	500 ml/18 fl oz
	FINANCIÈRE GARNISH	
	Forcemeat Stuffing (*page 54*), made into 16 quenelles	
½ lb	cocks' combs and kidneys (cooked in a White Court Bouillon – *page 49*)	250 g/8 oz
1⅓ cups	olives, stoned and blanched	250 g/8 oz
2 oz	*Paris mushrooms*	50 g/2 oz
½ lb	lamb sweetbreads	250 g/8 oz
8	thin truffle slices	8

Truss the chicken with its feet either inside its stomach or just lying flat, not forgetting to cut the joint tendon.

Put the chicken in a high-sided flameproof casserole with the sliced carrots and onions and the bouquet garni. Add salt and pepper. Put plenty of butter on the chicken and cook until browned on all sides. Cover and continue to cook for 45–50 minutes, basting with butter from time to time.

Remove the chicken from the pan and put it on a dish. Pour the madeira and veal juice into the pan. Boil fairly rapidly to deglaze and reduce the liquid by half. Strain this juice through a fine sieve, remove the fat and add it to the demi-glaze.

For a formal presentation, place the chicken on a fairly thick rectangular croûte of bread fried in oil. Surround it with the garnish ingredients, arranged in separate bouquets and coated with a little sauce. Serve the remaining sauce in a sauce boat on the side.

Alternatively, just place the chicken on the dish, surround it with a few spoonfuls of sauce and serve the garnish separately.

White wines: Montrachet, Meursault, Graves.
Red wines: Haut-Médoc, Côte de Beaune.

— CHICKEN 'IN THE POT' FERMIÈRE —

Preparation 1¼ hours • Cooking 1 hour

US	Ingredients	Met/Imp
1, about 5–5½ lb	chicken, preferably a hen bird	1, about 2.3–2.5 kg/5–5½ lb
2	very thin slices fatty bacon	2
1 quart	white wine	1 litre/1¾ pints
1 quart	stock or water	1 litre/1¾ pints
8	well-blanched large onions	8
6	parsley sprigs	6
1	clove	1
1	thyme sprig	1
6	carrots	6
1	basil sprig	1
2	lemon slices	2
5–6	chives	5–6
	salt and peppercorns	
	coarse sea salt	

Singe and draw the chicken, leaving the wings and feet on. Truss the bird and bard it with the bacon. Place in a large saucepan with the white wine, stock, sliced onions, parsley, clove, thyme, sliced carrots, basil, lemon slices, chives and salt and pepper. Cook over a low heat for 1 hour or until tender.

When the chicken is cooked, remove it from the pan and place it on a heated serving dish surrounded by the onions and carrots. Remove the fat from the cooking liquid and serve with the chicken. Serve some coarse sea salt on the side as a condiment.

Red wines: Beaujolais-Villages, Cornas, Côtes du Rhône-Villages.

———— CHICKEN POYAUDINE ————

Preparation 1 hour • Cooking 35 minutes

US	Ingredients	Met/Imp
2, each about 2½–2¾ lb	young chickens, preferably hen birds	2, each about 1.1–1.2 kg/ 2½–2¾ lb
3 sticks	butter	350 g/12 oz
	salt and pepper	
2	shallots	2
¼ cup	cognac	50 ml/2 fl oz
½ cup	dry white wine	100 ml/4 fl oz
1 cup	double (heavy) cream	200 ml/8 fl oz
¼ cup	cooking juices from mushrooms	50 ml/2 fl oz
6 tbsp	flour	50 g/2 oz
16	heart-shaped croûtons fried in butter	16
2 tbsp	Béarnaise Sauce (page 61)	30 ml/2 tbsp

Cut the chickens into quarters.

Melt half of the butter in a flameproof casserole, add the pieces of chicken and brown them without letting the butter burn. Add salt and pepper. Cook in a fairly hot oven for 35 minutes or until three-quarters cooked.

Remove the casserole from the oven and add the very finely chopped shallots. Flambé with the cognac. Add the dry white wine, the cream and the mushroom cooking juices (from mushrooms which have been cooked for 1 minute only). Continue cooking in a cool oven. Do not let the pieces become too coloured.

When the chicken pieces are cooked, take them out of the casserole and set aside. Thicken the sauce with *beurre manié* made by combining the remaining butter with the flour, and strain it through a piece of cheesecloth. Put the chicken pieces back in the sauce and leave in a *bain-marie* (the sauce must not boil) to keep warm.

Arrange the chicken pieces on the croûtons. Add the Béarnaise sauce to the sauce and coat the chicken pieces with it before serving.

White wines: Montrachet, Meursault, Graves, Barsac.

US	Ingredients	Met/Imp
2, each about 2½–3¾ lb	young chickens, preferably hen birds	2, each about 1.1–1.2 kg/ 2½–2¾ lb
	salt and pepper	
5 cups	fresh breadcrumbs	300 g/10 oz
1 pinch	quatre-épices	1 pinch
1 pinch	cayenne	1 pinch
14 tbsp	butter	200 g/7 oz
½ cup	oil	100 ml/4 fl oz
	Devil Sauce (page 68)	
½ cup	double (heavy) cream	100 ml/4 fl oz
24	small onions	24
10 oz	fresh fat belly (side) of pork, diced	300 g/10 oz
2	large onions	2
	flour	
1 tbsp	chopped fresh parsley	15 ml/1 tbsp

POULARDE RISSOLÉE À LA MANCELLE

SAUTÉED CHICKEN MANCELLE

Preparation 45 minutes • Cooking 30 minutes

Cut the chickens into quarters. Reserve the livers.

Season the chicken with salt and pepper. Season the breadcrumbs with spice and cayenne. Sprinkle the chicken with melted butter, then roll in the breadcrumbs until each piece is evenly coated. Heat the oil with some butter in a frying pan. Add the chicken pieces and sauté over a high heat for about 30 minutes or until they are a fine golden colour.

Prepare the devil sauce and thicken it with the reserved chicken livers, chopped, and the cream. Blanch the small onions and the diced pork and fry in butter. Add to the sauce.

Slice the large onions into rings, coat with flour and fry in butter until crisp and golden.

Arrange the chicken quarters on a heated serving dish and cover with fried onion rings. Sprinkle with chopped parsley. Serve with the devil sauce in a sauce boat on the side (the small onions and diced pork act as a garnish).

Dry white wines: Muscadet, Pouilly-Fumé, Chablis.
Red wines: Côte de Beaune, Côtes du Rhône.

POULARDE RÔTIE À LA BROCHE AU FEU DE BOIS

CHICKEN ROASTED ON A SPIT OVER A WOOD FIRE

Preparation 1½ hours • (Marinate the truffles in advance) • Cooking 1 hour

US	Ingredients	Met/Imp
1, about 5–5½ lb	chicken, preferably a Bresse hen bird	1, about 2.3–2.5 kg/5–5½ lb
5 oz	truffles	150 g/5 oz
½ lb	fat from *Bayonne ham*	250 g/8 oz
⅓ cup	armagnac	75 ml/3 fl oz
⅓ cup	madeira	75 ml/3 fl oz
	salt and pepper	
1 stick	butter	100 g/4 oz
½ cup	chicken *fumet*	100 ml/4 fl oz

Remove as much fat as possible from the chicken and reserve.

Cut the truffles into strips and place in a bowl with the fat from the Bayonne ham, the reserved chicken fat, the armagnac and madeira. Add salt and pepper and leave to marinate until required.

Transfer the marinated fats to a saucepan and heat gently until melted. Mix them together thoroughly, then leave to cool. When the fat is just about to set, dip in the strips of truffle so that they are thoroughly coated.

Push these strips between the skin and the flesh of the chicken. Be generous with the truffles, using about 8 strips in all.

Put the remaining solidified fat – about the size of an egg – inside the chicken, then truss the bird. Butter the outside of the bird as usual. Put it on a spit and cook it over a wood fire for about 1 hour, basting continually with the fat which runs off into the dripping pan. When the bird starts to colour, deglaze the dripping pan with a little very condensed chicken fumet and some of the juice from the marinade. Continue to baste the chicken generously until it is cooked. Remove some of the fat from the juice which collects at the bottom of the dripping pan, but the juice should still be fairly fatty. Serve with the chicken.

Red wines: Médoc, Graves, Côte de Beaune, Côte de Nuits, Côte Rôtie, Châteauneuf-du-Pape.

— SAUTÉED CHICKEN FROM ANJOU —

Preparation 1½ hours • Cooking chicken 30 minutes; vegetable garnish 50 minutes

US	Ingredients	Met/Imp
2, each about 2¾ lb	young 'Longué' chickens, preferably hen birds	2 each, about 1.2 kg/2¾ lb
	salt and pepper	
14 tbsp	butter	200 g/7 oz
6	small onions	6
2	garlic cloves	2
a few	parsley sprigs	a few
a few	thyme sprigs	a few
½ bottle	dry white Saumur wine	½ bottle
scant ½ cup	Tomato Sauce (page 80)	100 ml/3½ fl oz
scant ½ cup	Chicken Velouté (page 57)	100 ml/3½ fl oz
2 cups	double (heavy) cream	500 ml/18 fl oz
7 oz	mushrooms	200 g/7 oz
	GARNISH	
½ lb	new carrots, cut into garlic-clove shapes	250 g/8 oz
½ lb	turnips, cut into garlic-clove shapes	250 g/8 oz
½ lb	French (fine green) beans, diced	250 g/8 oz
1⅔ cups	shelled petits pois	250 g/8 oz

Cut the chickens into serving pieces, taking care to separate the suprêmes (breast and wing fillets). Season the pieces with salt and pepper. Seal all of the chicken pieces in some of the butter, without letting them colour, then simmer them gently for 15 minutes. Remove the suprêmes and keep warm.

Add the small onions to the chicken pieces remaining in the pan, then add the crushed garlic and a bouquet garni of parsley and thyme. Braise for 45 minutes.

Remove the chicken pieces from the casserole and keep warm. Drain off the butter and reserve. Deglaze the pan with the white wine, pour in the tomato sauce and chicken velouté and cook until heated through. Strain through a piece of cheesecloth. Finish by adding the cream and the reserved butter.

Quickly sweat the sliced mushrooms in butter and add them to the sauce. Coat the pieces of chicken with the sauce and serve the remainder in a sauce boat.

Garnish: prepare the new vegetables and toss in the remaining butter. Arrange them in separate bouquets '*à la bouquetière*' (flower girl style).

Wines: as a general rule, serve the same wine as the one used for cooking.

SAUTÉED CHICKEN WITH MORELS AND CREAM —

Preparation 1¼ hours • Cooking 45 minutes

US	Ingredients	Met/Imp
2, each about 2¾–3 lb	chickens, preferably hen birds	2, each about 1.2–1.4 kg/ 2¾–3 lb
	salt and pepper	
14 tbsp	butter	200 g/7 oz
½ cup	flour	70 g/2¾ oz
½ bottle	dry white wine	½ bottle
2 cups	crème fraîche	500 ml/18 fl oz
1½ lb	black morels	750 g/1½ lb
4	egg yolks	4
1	lemon, juice of	1
scant ½ cup	madeira	100 ml/3½ fl oz

Cut the chickens into serving pieces. Season the pieces with salt and pepper.

Melt half of the butter in a frying pan, add the chicken pieces and sauté until three-quarters cooked without letting them become too brown. Sprinkle with the flour and pour in the wine. Add the crème fraîche and finish cooking.

Meanwhile, melt the remaining butter in another frying pan and sauté the morels. Drain well.

Remove the chicken from the pan and keep it warm. Finish the sauce by beating in the egg yolks and lemon juice. Strain through a sieve.

Return the pieces of chicken to the sauce and add the sautéed morels. Finally, add the madeira.

Red wines: Médoc, Saint-Émilion or Pomerol.
White wines: Montrachet, Meursault, Coteaux Champenois.

US	Ingredients	Met/Imp
1, about 3½–4½ lb	chicken, preferably a hen bird	1, about 1.6–2 kg/3½–4½ lb
1	lemon, juice of	1
3	very thin slices fatty bacon	3
¼ lb	bacon rinds	100 g/4 oz
2	carrots	2
1	onion	1
1	bouquet garni	1
1 quart	light chicken consommé	1 litre/1¾ pints
½ bottle	Sauternes or Barsac wine	½ bottle
scant 2 cups	Forcemeat Stuffing (page 54)	450 g/15 oz
1½ oz	truffles	40 g/1½ oz
5½ oz	pickled or salted tongue	140 g/5½ oz
1 tbsp	Dry Duxelles (page 49)	15 ml/1 tbsp
1 tsp	chopped fresh parsley	5 ml/1 tsp
2½ sticks	butter	300 g/10 oz
	salt	
½ cup	flour	75 g/3 oz
1 pinch	white pepper	1 pinch
2 oz	mushroom trimmings	50 g/2 oz
1	bouquet parsley sprigs	1
5	egg yolks	5
scant 1 cup	crème fraîche	200 ml/7 fl oz
¼ lb	foie gras purée	100 g/4 oz
20	thin truffle slices	20
8	small whole truffles	8

POULARDE À LA TRIANON

CHICKEN TRIANON

Preparation 2½ hours • Cooking 50 minutes

Choose a plump bird. Draw and singe it, then truss it, tucking the feet inside the stomach. Rub the breast with lemon juice and bard it well with the bacon.

Put the chicken in a casserole (oval if possible), on a bed of bacon rind, sliced carrots and onion and the bouquet garni. Add enough consommé and wine – in the proportions of three-quarters consommé to one-quarter wine – to just cover the bird, bring to the boil, then lower the heat, cover and simmer gently for about 50 minutes.

Divide the forcemeat stuffing into three. Mix the chopped truffles with 1 portion. Chop 40 g/1½ oz of the tongue (from the pointed end) and mix with another portion. Mix the duxelles and chopped parsley with the third portion. Use a teaspoon to mould 10 *quenelles* from each of these stuffings, or simply place spoonfuls on a buttered tray, giving them the shape of small meringues. (The weight of stuffing in each quenelle should be about 18 g/scant ¾ oz.) Twenty minutes before serving, drop the quenelles into boiling salted water and poach.

Melt one-third of the butter in a saucepan and stir in the flour. Cook to a blond roux. Gradually stir in 1 litre/1¾ pints (1 quart) chicken cooking liquid which has been strained and had the fat removed. Bring to the boil, stirring constantly, then add the white pepper, the mushroom trimmings and the bouquet of parsley. Cook slowly for 30 minutes, remembering to skim off the grease and impurities. Beat together the egg yolks and crème fraîche. Stir over the heat until the volume has reduced to about 600 ml/1 pint (2½ cups). Strain through a piece of cheesecloth. Off the heat, add the foie gras purée and half of the remaining butter. Add the remaining tongue, cut into small diamond shapes, and the thin slices of truffle.

Remove the string and bacon from the chicken. Rub some butter over the breast to make it shiny, then place the bird on a rectangular croûton of bread which has been fried in oil. Surround it with the quenelles, arranged in 8 separate bouquets, then place a small whole truffle between each one. (If this truffle garnish, which is optional, is not used, put a spoonful of sauce between each bouquet of quenelles.) Serve the sauce in a sauce boat.

Medium dry or sweet white wines: Graves, Sauternes, Barsac, Alsace Gewürztraminer, Vouvray.

POULARDE EN VESSIE

CHICKEN IN A BLADDER

Preparation 2½ hours • Cooking 1½ hours

US	Ingredients	Met/Imp
1, about 4–4½ lb	chicken, preferably a Bresse hen bird	1, about 1.8–2 kg/4–4½ lb
3	chicken livers	3
¼ lb	truffles	100 g/4 oz
½ lb	foie gras	250 g/8 oz
4	thin truffle slices	4
1	pig's bladder	1
	salt and pepper	
1 pinch	quatre-épices	1 pinch
¼ cup	cognac	50 ml/2 fl oz
¼ cup	truffle juice	50 ml/2 fl oz
½ cup	white wine	100 ml/4 fl oz

Take a very white Bresse chicken, draw it carefully and remove the neck and head. Bone the legs, from the feet to the thigh bones, taking great care not to tear the flesh. Reshape the legs and feet.

Finely chop the livers, whole truffles and foie gras and use to stuff the chicken. Insert the thin slices of truffle under the skin of the breast and truss as usual.

Very carefully wash and dry the pig's bladder and put the stuffed chicken inside it. Tie up the opening of the bladder securely, making sure that no air remains inside. Sprinkle with salt and pepper, the spice, cognac, truffle juice and white wine.

Poach for 1½ hours, then serve just as it is.

White wines: Meursault, Coteaux Champenois, Arbois, Graves.
Red wines: Beaujolais-Villages, Chinon, Bourgueil.

DAUBE DE POULE EN GELÉE

CHICKEN CASSEROLE IN ASPIC

Preparation 40 minutes • (To be prepared the day before) • Cooking 3 hours • Serves 6

US	Ingredients	Met/Imp
1	chicken, preferably a 1–2 year old boiling fowl (stewing chicken)	1
1	calf's foot	1
4	large onions	4
10 oz	carrots	300 g/10 oz
7 oz	fresh lean belly (side) of pork	200 g/7 oz
2	garlic cloves	2
1	bouquet garni (thyme, bay leaf, celery, parsley, tarragon, etc)	1
	salt	
½ bottle	dry white wine	½ bottle
3 liqueur glasses	cognac	3 liqueur glasses
a few	black peppercorns	a few
1	clove (optional)	1
	quatre-épices	

This cold dish, in aspic, is prepared the day before.

Remove the legs from the chicken. Split the calf's foot in half. Put the chicken legs and the calf's foot in a large saucepan, cover with water and add the sliced onions and carrots, roughly chopped pork, the garlic and the bouquet garni. Add salt and bring to the boil. Simmer for 30 minutes, then add the chicken. Bring back to the boil and skim. Cover and boil gently for a further 30 minutes. Add the white wine, cover and bring back to the boil. It must boil slowly so that the aspic will be clear. Skim several times, if necessary (A small spoonful of meat extract gives more body and colour to the aspic).

Continue cooking for a further 1½ hours, then add the cognac, ground black peppercorns, the clove (if using) and the spice. Cover and continue cooking until the chicken is tender. Remove the chicken from the pan and drain well.

Remove the calf's foot and the vegetables from the stock with a skimmer. The calf's foot, boned and reheated in the stock, can be served with a vinaigrette dressing made with herbs. Cut the chicken into serving pieces, remove the skin, then put the pieces in a large dish with the pieces of pork. Strain the stock through a fine sieve into a bowl and leave to stand for 15 minutes, then remove the fat from the surface with a spoon. Taste the stock to check the seasoning (it should he highly seasoned), the put it over the chicken pieces to cover. (If there is any stock left, chill it in the refrigerator to make some aspic.) Cover the dish containing the chicken, then chill it in the refrigerator overnight.

The next day, separate the pieces of chicken coated in aspic and arrange them on a serving dish. Decorate with chopped aspic, if available.

Dry white wines: dry Vouvray, Savennières, Muscadet de Sèvre et Maine *sur lie.*
Rosé from the Loire.
Light red wines: Chinon, Bourgueil.

US	Ingredients	Met/Imp
1, about 4–4½ lb	chicken, preferably a 1 year old boiling fowl (stewing chicken)	1, about 1.8–2 kg/4–4½ lb
½	lemon, juice of	½
10 oz	boneless pork (fat and lean)	300 g/10 oz
10 oz	pure pork sausagemeat	300 g/10 oz
3 pinches	quatre-épices	3 pinches
3 pinches	nutmeg	3 pinches
	salt and pepper	
1 tbsp	flour	15 ml/1 tbsp
3	eggs	3
2 tbsp	madeira	30 ml/2 tbsp
1	truffle	1
2	onions	2
1	clove	1
1	bouquet garni	1
½ bottle	dry white wine	½
1–2 tbsp	powdered gelatine	15–30 ml/ 1–2 tbsp

CHICKEN GALANTINE WITH TRUFFLES

Preparation 1½ hours • (To be prepared the day before) • Cooking 2 hours • Serves 10

Pluck and singe the chicken. Cut off the wing tips and feet. Do not draw.

Put the chicken breast side down, on the work surface in front of you and slit the skin down the back as far as the parson's (pope's) nose.

Use a knife to detach the skin from one side and remove the wing. Continue to detach the skin and remove the leg. Turn the bird round and do the same on the other side. Take care not to pierce the skin. When you have taken it all off, spread it out and sprinkle it with lemon juice.

Draw the chicken, remove some of the fat and reserve the liver (not including the gall bladder) and the gizzard. Bone first the leg and then the wing on one side and do the same on the other side. Cut the breast fillets away from the bone. Reserve the head, bones and carcass.

Cut 6 or 7 long thin pieces of meat from the breast fillets. Slice the remainder of the meat and put it through a mincer (meat grinder) or in a food processor with the reserved gizzard and liver and the roughly chopped pork.

Put the sausagemeat, the minced (ground) meats, spice, nutmeg, pepper, flour and eggs in a large bowl. Add the madeira and mix thoroughly together, kneading by hand if necessary.

Stretch out a 60 cm/24 inch square of thin cloth on the work surface and put the chicken skin on top. Spread about one-third of the stuffing on it then add 3 or 4 strips of breast fillet and some of the sliced truffle. Cover with another layer of stuffing, then more breast fillet, etc, until all the ingredients are used up. Carefully close the skin around the stuffing, then wrap the parcel tightly in the cloth. Tie up with string like a boned and rolled joint of meat for roasting.

Put the reserved chicken bones in the bottom of a flameproof casserole and put the chicken galantine on top. Add the reserved carcass, head, liver and gizzard and put in the sliced onions, the clove, bouquet garni and some salt and pepper. Pour the wine over and add just enough water to cover. Cover and boil slowly for 2 hours.

When it is cooked, remove the hot galantine from the casserole and put it in a dish. Cut the strings and remove the cloth.

Sprinkle the gelatine over the cooking liquid and bring to the boil, then pour over the galantine through a sieve lined with cheesecloth. Replace the chicken's head on the galantine, securing it in position with a cocktail stick, if necessary.

Leave to cool for 24 hours and serve decorated with chopped aspic.

White wines: Alsace Riesling or Pinot Gris, Bourgogne, Graves.

CHICKEN BLANQUETTE

Preparation 1 hour • Cooking 35 minutes

US	Ingredients	Met/Imp
2, each about 2–2½ lb	small chickens, perferably boiling fowls (stewing chickens)	2, each about 900 g–1.1 kg/ 2–2½ lb
14 tbsp	butter	200 g/7 oz
	salt and pepper	
6 tbsp	flour	50 g/2 oz
1 quart	White Stock (page 56)	1 litre/1¾ pints
30	small onions	30
2	carrots	2
1	bouquet garni	1
4	egg yolks	4
2 cups	crème fraîche	500 ml/18 fl oz

Take some tender chickens and cut them into serving pieces. Melt the butter in a large flameproof casserole, add the chicken pieces and salt and pepper and sauté lightly, without letting the bird become coloured.

Sprinkle in the flour and coat the chicken with it. Pour in the stock and add the onions, sliced carrots and bouquet garni. Cover and cook for 35 minutes or until the chicken is tender.

When the cooking is finished, remove the carrots and the bouquet garni. Finish by thickening the sauce with the egg yolks and crème fraîche.

Medium dry or sweet white wines: Graves, Sauternes, Barsac, Alsace Gewürztraminer, Vouvray.

STUFFED CHICKEN CASSEROLE

Preparation 2 hours • Cooking 1½ hours

US	Ingredients	Met/Imp
2, each about 2 lb	young chickens, preferably boiling fowls (stewing chickens)	2, each about 1 kg/2 lb
14 oz	finely minced (ground) pork	400 g/14 oz
2 slices	fresh bread, without crusts	50 g/2 oz
1	onion	1
1	garlic clove	1
1 tbsp	chopped fresh parsley	15 ml/1 tbsp
	salt and pepper	
1 pinch	quatre-épices	1 pinch
⅓ cup	cognac	80 ml/3 fl oz
¼ lb	pork back fat or bacon fat	100 g/4 oz
½ cup	white wine	100 ml/4 fl oz
1 quart	stock	1 litre/1¾ pints
1	bouquet garni	1
4	calf's feet	4
10 oz	carrots	300 g/10 oz
24	small onions	24
1 stick	butter	100 g/4 oz
½ lb	fresh fat belly (side) of pork	250 g/8 oz
1¼ cups	long-grain rice	200 g/7 oz

Draw and singe the chickens. Reserve the fat and the livers (not including the gall bladders).

In a large bowl, mix together the pork; the reserved chicken fat and livers, chopped; the bread, soaked and pressed; the onion, chopped, cooked in butter and allowed to cool; the crushed garlic; the chopped parsley; salt, pepper, spice and one-third of the cognac. Knead well together and use to stuff the chickens. Truss, keeping the legs parallel to the body.

Heat the grated pork or bacon fat in a flameproof casserole, preferably oval in shape, put in the chickens and brown them lightly on all sides. Add the white wine, the remaining cognac, flambéed, and enough stock to come about one-third of the way up the chickens. Add the bouquet garni and the calf's feet, blanched for at least 1 hour in advance, then boned and cut into small cubes. Bring to the boil, cover and continue cooking in a moderate oven for 1 hour, keeping it at a gentle simmer throughout.

Put the following around the chickens: about 20 carrot quarters, trimmed into long olive shapes and blanched in boiling water for 15 minutes (unless the carrots are new, in which case there is no need to blanch them); the small onions sautéed in the butter in a frying pan until just coloured; the belly (side) of pork cut into large dice and scalded in boiling water for 5–6 minutes. Continue cooking for at least another 30 minutes or until the chickens are tender.

Serve the chickens straight from the casserole, not forgetting to untruss them and remove the bouquet garni.

Serve with a bowl of cooked rice, moistened with a little of the cooking juices from the casserole.

White wines: Arbois, Graves.
Red wines: Médoc, Côte de Beaune.

CHICKEN 'IN THE POT' BOURBONNAISE

Preparation 2 hours • Cooking 1 hour

US	Ingredients	Met/Imp
2	chickens, preferably young boiling (stewing) hens, including the livers	2
1¼ lb	boneless pork	600 g/1¼ lb
1	garlic clove	1
1 pinch	dried thyme	1 pinch
1 pinch	dried rosemary	1 pinch
1 tbsp	chopped fresh parsley	15 ml/1 tbsp
1 tbsp	chopped fresh chervil	15 ml/1 tbsp
5 oz	fresh fat belly (side) of pork	150 g/5 oz
1	onion	1
1	clove	1
8	small carrots	8
8	small turnips	8
4	leeks, white part only	4
1	parsnip	1
	salt and pepper	
	toasted bread slices	
	mustard	
	cornichons	

Mince (grind) the chicken livers in a mincer (meat grinder) or food processor.

Remove the sinews from the pork and mince (grind) it finely. Put it in a bowl and add the minced (ground) chicken livers, crushed garlic and herbs, making it quite highly seasoned. Knead everything thoroughly together and use to stuff the chickens. Truss the birds and tie them up so that the stuffing cannot escape during cooking.

Heat the diced belly (side) of pork in a frying pan with the chickens and fry for a few minutes until they are very lightly coloured.

Spike the onion with the clove and put all the vegetables in the bottom of a flameproof casserole. Put the chickens and fried pork on top, add some water and bring to the boil. Skim off the fat and impurities and add a moderate amount of salt. Poach, uncovered, over a low heat for about 1 hour or until the chickens and vegetables are cooked. The stock should remain clear. Take the chickens and vegetables out of the stock, using a slotted spoon. Cut up the chickens and divide into portions with the stuffing. Keep warm.

Serve the stock as a first course soup. Adjust the seasoning and pour the stock into a heated tureen on to slices of toasted bread. Serve the chickens after the soup, with mustard and cornichons or, if preferred, with a vinaigrette dressing made with plenty of herbs.

Wines: red or white Saint-Pourçain.

BOILED CHICKEN WITH STUFFED CABBAGE

Preparation 1½ hours • Cooking 2 hours • Serves 4

US	Ingredients	Met/Imp
1, about 4 lb	boiling fowl (stewing chicken)	1, about 1.8 kg/4 lb
1½ lb	whole cabbage	750 g/1½ lb
	salt and pepper	
	STUFFING	
1 cup	milk	250 ml/8 fl oz
8 cups	cubes of bread	250 g/8 oz
1	small piece onion	1
1	shallot	1
1	small garlic clove	1
1 cup	parsley	50 g/2 oz
¼ lb	raw country ham	100 g/4 oz
2	chicken livers (including 1 from the chicken)	2
2	eggs	2
	STOCK	
8	small carrots	8
4	turnips	4
8	leeks	8
1 lb	shin or knuckle (shank) of veal	500 g/1 lb
1 lb	slightly salted belly of pork (slab bacon)	500 g/1 lb
1	onion	1
1	clove	1

Draw and singe the chicken, reserving the neck and feet. Reserve the liver, removing the gall bladder and everything contaminated by it.

Put the whole cabbage in a large saucepan of boiling water. Bring to the boil and cook for 10 minutes, then drain and allow to cool.

Make the stuffing. Bring the milk to the boil and pour it on to the bread. Stir gently so that the bread soaks up the milk.

Finely chop the soaked bread, the onion, shallot, garlic, parsley, ham and chicken livers. It is quicker to put all the ingredients through a mincer (meat grinder) or to work it in a food processor, but the stuffing is tastier if it is not reduced to a purée.

Add the eggs and a pinch of pepper to the stuffing and mix thoroughly. Sprinkle the inside of the chicken with salt and pepper and stuff with 2 large tablespoonfuls of stuffing. Sew up the bird and truss it.

Detach 6 or 7 outer leaves from the cabbage. Spread out 1 leaf on the work surface and put a tablespoonful of stuffing in the centre. Roll up

the leaf, wrapping the stuffing in a small but long parcel.

Put a spoonful of stuffing on another leaf and spread it over the surface of the leaf. Put the first parcel in the centre of the second leaf (with the opening at the bottom, against the stuffing). Wrap the second leaf around the first parcel, forming a larger parcel. Continue in the same way with the third and fourth leaves, covering them with stuffing and wrapping them around. Finish by wrapping this re-formed cabbage in the fifth, sixth and seventh detached leaves, so that it is secure and solid. Tie it up carefully.

Prepare the stock. Put the carrots, turnips, leeks, cabbage heart, veal, pork (bacon), the stuffed cabbage and the chicken's neck and feet in a large saucepan and cover with cold water. Spike the onion with the clove and add to the stock.

Bring to the boil, skim, taste and add salt to taste. Simmer for 50 minutes, then add the stuffed chicken. Cook for about a further 50 minutes.

Serve the chicken surrounded by the meat and vegetables, and the stuffed cabbage cut into slices. The stock may be served separately as a soup, garnished with toasted or fried croûtons.

White wines: Jurançon sec, Pacherenc du Vic-Bilh, Graves.
Red wines: Médoc, Graves, Bergerac, Côtes de Buzet.

TOURTE DE GELINE DE TOURAINE

——— TOURAINE CHICKEN PIE ———

Preparation 1½ hours • First cooking 30 minutes • Second cooking 20 minutes

If possible use 'gélines de Touraine' hens. Draw and truss them.

Place the hens in a large saucepan and add the carrots, leeks, turnips and celery. Spike the onion with the clove and add to the pan. Add salt and peppercorns, cover with water and cook for 30 minutes or until the hens are well cooked. Remove them from the pan, leave to cool slightly then bone them completely. Cut the meat into nut-sized pieces and set aside. Strain the stock, discard the vegetables and reserve 1 litre/1¾ pints (1 quart) stock.

Melt the butter in a saucepan and stir in the flour. Cook, stirring, for a few minutes, then remove from the heat and gradually stir in the reserved stock. Bring to the boil and cook, stirring, until fairly thick. Add salt and pepper and mix in the egg yolks and crème fraîche. The sauce should have the consistency of mayonnaise. Mix the pieces of chicken with the sauce and leave to cool.

Meanwhile, prepare the puff pastry and use half to make a 30 cm/12 inch pastry base. Spread with the chicken mixture and cover with the remaining puff pastry. Moisten the edges of the pastry and press firmly all the way round to seal.

Bake in a fairly hot oven for about 20 minutes or until well risen and golden. Serve hot.

Medium dry or dry white wines: Anjou, Vouvray, Saumur.

US	Ingredients	Met/Imp
2, each about 2 lb	young chickens, preferably boiling fowls (stewing chickens)	2, each about 1 kg/2 lb
3	carrots	3
4	leeks	4
2	turnips	2
1	celery stalk	1
1	onion	1
1	clove	1
	salt and peppercorns	
10 tbsp	butter	150 g/5 oz
½ cup	flour	75 g/3 oz
4	egg yolks	3
½ cup	crème fraîche	100 ml/4 fl oz
1 lb	Puff Pastry (page 579)	500 g/1 lb

US	Ingredients	Met/Imp
a few	veal knuckle (shank) bones	a few
	poultry giblets, including those from the chicken	
1	leek	1
2	carrots	2
1	onion	1
1	small turnip	1
a few	parsley sprigs	a few
2	tarragon sprigs	2
1	small thyme sprig	1
1	bay leaf	1
	salt	
1, about 4 lb	chicken	1, about 1.8 kg/4 lb
½	lemon	½
4 tbsp	butter	50 g/2 oz
3 tbsp	flour	40 g/1½ oz
4 heaped tbsp	thick *crème fraîche*	4 heaped tbsp
1 pinch	cayenne	1 pinch
	GARNISH	
	tarragon leaves	
	aspic jelly (optional)	

CHICKEN CHAUD-FROID WITH TARRAGON*

Preparation 1 hour • (To be prepared several hours in advance) • Cooking 5¼ hours •
Serves 4–6

Prepare the stock. Roughly chop the veal bones and as many poultry giblets as possible, then place in a large saucepan. Cover with 2 litres/3½ pints (2 quarts) cold water and bring to the boil. Use a slotted spoon to skim off the scum and grease which rise to the surface. Cover and cook for about 3 hours, skimming often.

Add all the vegetables, roughly chopped, then the herbs. Bring to the boil and skim off the grease and scum again, then add salt and continue to cook for about 45 minutes, skimming often.

Meanwhile, draw, singe and truss the chicken, then rub it all over with the cut surface of the lemon half so that it stays white during cooking. Put it in a large saucepan and cover with cold salted water. Bring to the boil and boil for 2 minutes only. Add some cold water to the pan to stop it boiling.

Drain the chicken and put it in the stock. Return to the boil and cook at a slow, even boil for about 50 minutes. Continue to skim off the scum during cooking. Remove the pan from the heat, drain the chicken and leave it to cool.

Prepare a roux. Melt the butter in a saucepan and stir in the flour. Cook gently for about 10 minutes, stirring constantly with a wooden spoon, without letting it brown. Remove from the heat and leave to cool.

Strain the stock through a fine conical sieve and measure out 1 litre/1¾ pints (1 quart). Gradually beat the stock into the cold roux. Cook over a low heat, stirring constantly. Add the crème fraîche and continue to cook for about 15 minutes or until the sauce coats the back of the wooden spoon. Add salt and cayenne. Remove from the heat and stand the saucepan in a large bowl of ice. Leave to cool, stirring occasionally to prevent a skin forming. Meanwhile, blanch the tarragon leaves in boiling water, drain and reserve.

When the sauce is cold, strain it by pouring it through a piece of cheesecloth into a bowl. Lift the cloth and twist it to squeeze through as much sauce as possible (2 people may be needed for this).

Alternatively, work the sauce through a fine sieve.

Cut the chicken into pieces and remove the skin and bones, leaving just the drumstick bone and the small wing bone in place. Put the chicken pieces on a wire rack and coat them with the sauce. Leave to set, then decorate with the blanched tarragon leaves. To make the tarragon leaves stick, soak them first in a little stock or melted aspic. Complete the decoration, if liked, by brushing the chicken pieces all over with a little melted aspic. Transfer to a serving plate and garnish with small heaps of chopped aspic jelly.

White wines: Chablis, Bourgogne, Meursault, Graves, Hermitage.
Red wines: Médoc, Chinon, Bourgueil, Saumur-Champigny.

CHICKEN PIE 'ANGLAISE'

Preparation 2 hours • Cooking 1¼ hours

US	Ingredients	Met/Imp
1 stick	butter	100 g/4 oz
1	onion	1
1 tbsp	chopped shallot	15 ml/1 tbsp
½ lb	mushrooms, sweated in butter	250 g/8 oz
	salt and pepper	
1 pinch	nutmeg	1 pinch
½ lb	bacon *or* fresh fat belly (side) of pork	250 g/8 oz
8, each about ¼ lb	veal escalopes (cutlets)	8, each about 100 g/4 oz
2	chickens, preferably free range or corn-fed	2
4	eggs	4
1 tbsp	chopped fresh parsley	15 ml/1 tbsp
1 quart	stock or White Stock (*page 56*)	1 litre/1¾ pints
1 lb	Puff Pastry (*page 579*)	500 g/1 lb
1	beaten egg, to glaze	1

If preferred, use puff pastry made with only half the amount of butter specified on page 579. The pie should be served as soon as it comes out of the oven, otherwise the steam inside will make the crust go soft.

Melt the butter in a frying pan and fry the chopped onion for 5–10 minutes or until golden. Add the shallot and chopped mushrooms (firmly squeezed in the corner of a cloth to extract all the water). Add salt, pepper and nutmeg and cook over a high heat for a few minutes, stirring, then remove from the heat and set aside.

If using belly (side) of pork, scald it in boiling water for 5–6 minutes, then drain. Cut the bacon or pork into small rectangles.

Place the slices of veal between sheets of greaseproof (wax) paper and beat with a mallet or rolling pin until they are very thin.

Cut the chickens into pieces as for a fricassée, ie remove the legs and wings and cut the breast portions away from the carcass. Cut each breast fillet into 2 pieces and the carcass into three. Cook the eggs in boiling water for about 10 minutes or until hard-boiled; shell them and cut them in half. Remove the yolks.

Put the veal in a pie dish or long ovenproof earthenware or porcelain dish measuring about 22 cm/8½ inches long and 16 cm/6½ inches wide. Arrange the veal so that it covers the bottom and sides of the dish. Put the pieces of chicken on top and sprinkle with salt and pepper. Arrange the bacon pieces and egg yolks in between the pieces of chicken. Stir the parsley into the onion and mushroom mixture and sprinkle over the chicken. Add enough stock to come two-thirds of the way up the pieces of chicken.

Roll out the pastry on a floured surface until it is 1 cm/½ inch thick and 5 cm/2 inches larger than the pie dish. Cut a 2.5 cm/1 inch wide strip from the outer edge of pastry and place it on the dampened rim of the dish. Seal the join and brush with water. Lift the remaining piece of pastry and lay it over the dish. Press it lightly on to the ribbon of pastry to seal. Trim the pastry and brush with beaten egg mixed with a little water. Decorate the top and seal the edges with a fork. Make a slit in the centre of the pastry to allow steam to escape during cooking. Bake in a moderate oven for about 1¼ hours or until the pastry is well risen and golden. As soon as the pastry is sufficiently coloured, cover it with a slighty moistened piece of greaseproof or parchment paper for the remaining cooking time.

Dry white wines: Muscadet, Pouilly-Fumé, Chablis.
Red wines: Côte de Beaune, Chinon, Bourgueil.

US	Ingredients	Met/Imp
2	chickens, preferably free-range or corn-fed	2
	salt and pepper	
10 tbsp	butter	150 g/5 oz
½ bottle	Chablis wine	½ bottle
½ cup	highly flavoured Madeira Sauce (page 72)	100 ml/4 fl oz
1 tbsp	Worcestershire sauce	15 ml/1 tbsp
8	small slices ham or bacon	8
4	hard-boiled eggs	4
8	thin truffle slices	8
10 oz	Puff Pastry (page 579)	300 g/10 oz
	beaten egg, to glaze	

CHICKEN PIE 'FRANÇAISE'

Preparation 1 hour • First cooking 20 minutes • Second cooking 10 minutes

Cut the chickens into pieces. Season them with salt and pepper.

Melt the butter in a flameproof casserole and, when it is very hot, add the chicken pieces. Cook for 20 minutes or until browned and well sealed, turning occasionally. Alternatively, transfer the casserole to a moderate oven and cook until browned. Cook only in the butter; do not add any liquid. Drain off the butter and put the chicken in a shallow, oval pie dish.

Pour the Chablis into the casserole in which the chicken was cooked, bring to the boil and cook, uncovered, until reduced. Add the madeira sauce and the Worcestershire sauce.

Arrange the slices of ham or bacon over the chicken pieces, then the halved hard-boiled eggs and truffle slices. Add the juice from the truffles to the madeira sauce and pour it over the chicken and ham. The chicken should not be swimming in sauce – a good dish needs little sauce.

Roll out the pastry on a lightly floured surface until it is 2–3 mm/⅛ inch thick and 5 cm/2 inches larger than the pie dish. Cut a 2.5 cm/1 inch wide strip from the outer edge of pastry and place it on the dampened rim of the dish. Seal the join and brush with water. Lift the remaining piece of pastry and lay it over the dish. Press it lightly on to the ribbon of pastry to seal. Trim the pastry and brush with beaten egg mixed with a little water. Cook in a hot oven for 10 minutes or until golden.

Red wine: Beaujolais-Villages.
White wines: Chablis, Mâcon-Viré.

COCOTTE DE POULET TRUFFÉE AUX POMMES ET AU CALVADOS

CHICKEN CASSEROLE WITH TRUFFLES, APPLES AND CALVADOS

Preparation 2 hours • Cooking 45 minutes

US	Ingredients	Met/Imp
¼ lb	pork back fat or bacon fat, for larding	100 g/4 oz
2, each about 2 lb	chickens, preferably free-range or corn-fed	2, each about 1 kg/2 lb
7 oz	boneless veal, cut from top of leg	200 g/7 oz
¼ lb	fresh fat belly (side) of pork	100 g/4 oz
2	chives	2
2	parsley sprigs	2
2	shallots	2
1 pinch	*quatre-épices*	1 pinch
	salt and pepper	
5 oz	truffles	150 g/5 oz
8	*reinette* or other eating apples	8
10 tbsp	butter	150 g/5 oz
6	artichoke bottoms	6
16	small onions	16
	fines herbes	
2 cups	Veal Juice (page 56)	500 ml/18 fl oz
¼ cup	*vieux calvados*	60 ml/2½ fl oz

Cut the pork or bacon fat into small strips and use to lard the chickens.

Finely chop the veal, pork, chives, parsley and shallots. Add the spice, salt and pepper and mix well together. Put some of the truffles under the skin of the chickens, then put the stuffing inside. Roast the chickens in a fairly hot oven until they are three-quarters cooked.

Meanwhile, peel, core and quarter the apples and sauté them in a little of the butter. Drain and place in the bottom of an earthenware casserole. Place the chickens on top and return to the oven to finish cooking.

Meanwhile, prepare the garnish. Melt the remaining butter in a frying pan and sauté the remaining truffles, sliced into rounds, the artichoke bottoms, blanched small onions and the fines herbes. Moisten with some good veal juice, to which a liqueur glass of calvados has been added, and with some reduced veal juice, if extra flavour is required.

Red wines: Pomerol, Saint-Émilion, Côte de Beaune or Côte de Nuits.
White wines: Meursault, Montrachet.

CHICKEN CURRY

Preparation 25 minutes • Cooking 40 minutes • Serves 6–8

US	Ingredients	Met/Imp
I, about 3½ lb	chicken	I, about 1.6 kg/3½ lb
3 tbsp	oil	45 ml/3 tbsp
4 tbsp	butter	50 g/2 oz
	salt	
2 tbsp	curry powder	30 ml/2 tbsp
I	banana	I
I	apple	I
I cup	long-grain rice	200 g/7 oz
6 tbsp	cornflour (cornstarch)	50 g/2 oz

Cut the chicken into 8 pieces. Heat the oil and butter in a large saucepan and fry the chicken pieces for about 5 minutes or until lightly browned, turning frequently. (Do this in 2 batches if the pan is too small.) Add salt and sprinkle with curry powder.

Add the whole peeled banana and the whole washed apple. Cover with water (or with a white stock prepared in advance with the chicken giblets and some veal bones), bring to the boil and put on the lid. Cook for 30–40 minutes. Meanwhile, wash the rice and cook in the Creole way (*page 563*), in plenty of boiling salted water. Cover, bring to the boil and cook for 18–20 minutes.

When the chicken is cooked, drain and arrange the pieces on a heated serving dish. Mix the cornflour (cornstarch) to a paste with some of the cooking liquid. Strain the rest of the liquid, return it to the pan and reheat. When it is boiling, stir in the cornflour (cornstarch) paste. Bring to the boil again, stirring, then pour the sauce on to the chicken.

When the rice is cooked, drain it and rinse it with hot salted water. Place in a heated serving dish and serve with the chicken.

Dry white wines: Bourgogne, Meursault, Pouilly-Fuissé, Hermitage, Alsace Riesling.
Light red wines: Beaujolais-Villages, Chinon, Bourgueil.

CHICKEN FRICASSÉE WITH RIPAILLE WINE

Preparation 1 hour • Cooking 35 minutes

US	Ingredients	Met/Imp
2	chickens, preferably free-range or corn-fed	2
	salt and pepper	
10 tbsp	butter	150 g/5 oz
6	shallots	6
2 tsp	chopped fresh tarragon	10 ml/2 tsp
I	garlic clove	I
I	thyme sprig	I
I	parsley sprig	I
½ cup	cognac	100 ml/3½ fl oz
scant I cup	dry white wine, preferably Ripaille	200 ml/7 fl oz
6	egg yolks	6
½ cup	thick *crème fraîche*	100 ml/3½ fl oz
I	lemon, juice of	I
I oz	field or other wild mushrooms	30 g/I oz
30	small new onions	30

Draw and singe the chickens. Cut each one into 4 pieces and season with salt and pepper. Melt the butter in a flameproof casserole and fry the chicken pieces for about 5 minutes or until just golden. Add the finely chopped shallots, half of the tarragon, the crushed garlic and a bouquet of thyme and parsley in which neither herb dominates. Cook for about 5 minutes or until the shallot is golden, then flambé with cognac and pour in the dry white wine. Cover the chicken and cook for about 35 minutes or until the flesh is tender and the juices run clear when a piece is pierced in the thickest part.

When the chicken is cooked, remove it from the casserole, place on a heated serving dish and keep warm. Put the egg yolks in the casserole and heat gently, beating all the time, until thickened. Remove from the heat, add the crème fraîche and check the seasoning. Add the remaining tarragon and the lemon juice, then pour the sauce over the chicken. Garnish with mushrooms and small onions cooked in their own juices.

Dry white wine: Vin de Savoie (Ripaille).

US	Ingredients	Met/Imp
6	chicken livers from Bresse	6
5 oz	beef marrow	150 g/5 oz
6 tbsp	flour	50 g/2 oz
6	eggs	6
4	egg yolks	4
2 tbsp	crème fraîche	30 ml/2 tbsp
3 cups	milk	750 ml/1¼ pints
	salt and pepper	
	nutmeg	
1 large pinch	chopped fresh parsley	1 large pinch
½	garlic clove	½
	tomato coulis	
	butter	

CHICKEN LIVER MOUSSE
CURNONSKY*

Preparation 1¼ hours • Cooking 45 minutes

Recipe by Paul Blanc, le Chapon Fin, Thoissey.

Roughly chop the livers and beef marrow, then work them through a sieve into a bowl. Add the flour and, using a whisk, beat in the eggs, egg yolks, crème fraîche and milk. Season with salt, pepper and nutmeg, add the parsley and crushed garlic and mix well.

Transfer the mixture to a large buttered mould and cook in a *bain-marie* in a moderate oven for about 45 minutes or until browned and slightly risen. Remove from the mould and serve with a tomato coulis to which some butter has been added.

Dry white wines: Montrachet, Meursault, Pouilly-Fuissé.

US	Ingredients	Met/Imp
2 lb	chicken livers	1 kg/2 lb
2 pinches	salt	2 pinches
1 pinch	pepper	1 pinch
¼ cup	cognac	50 ml/2 fl oz
1 tbsp	oil	15 ml/1 tbsp
1½ lb (6 sticks)	butter	750 g/1½ lb

PARFAIT DE FOIES DE VOLAILLE AU COGNAC

CHICKEN LIVER TERRINE
WITH COGNAC

Preparation 1¼ hours • Soaking 2 hours • Marinating 2 hours • Cooking 40 minutes

Soak the livers in ice-cold water for about 2 hours to remove any excess blood and impurities. Drain and wipe them dry with paper towels.

Place the livers in an ovenproof dish and add the salt, pepper, cognac and oil. Leave to marinate for 2 hours.

Place the dish in a *bain-marie*, cover and cook in a cool oven for 40 minutes. Leave to cool, then turn into a sieve placed over a bowl. Select about 8 of the best-looking livers and set aside.

Work the remaining livers through the sieve into the bowl, then beat in the softened butter with a whisk. Beat the mixture until a cream is obtained. Adjust the seasoning, then transfer to a terrine and place the reserved livers in the centre. When the terrine is completely cold, put it in the refrigerator for 24 hours to set. Serve in slices, with toast.

Red wines: Beaujolais-Villages, Côtes du Rhône, Bourgueil.

US	Ingredients	Met/Imp
1 lb	chicken livers	500 g/1 lb
14 oz	pork fillet (tenderloin)	400 g/14 oz
¼ lb	fresh truffles	100 g/4 oz
	salt and pepper	
	quatre-épices	
¼ cup	cognac	50 ml/2 fl oz
scant 1 cup	double (heavy) cream	200 ml/7 fl oz
3	eggs	3
	butter or oil	
1½ lb	Puff Pastry (page 579)	750 g/1½ lb
a few	thin slices fatty bacon	a few
1	bay leaf	1

PÂTÉ DE FOIES DE VOLAILLE EN CROÛTE

CHICKEN LIVERS EN CROÛTE

Preparation 1 hour • Cooking 1 hour

We recommend chopping up the stuffing with a knife rather than with a machine, because mincers (grinders) cause meat to lose a large part of its flavour. It is advisable to use shortcrust (pie) rather than puff pastry; if the pie is not eaten immediately (when it is very hot), puff pastry becomes tasteless. Shortcrust pastry retains its flavour better.

Using a sharp knife, finely chop the livers, pork and truffles. Mix well

and add salt, pepper, spice, cognac, cream and the 3 eggs, beaten.

Grease a large patterned rectangular pâté mould with butter or oil. Roll out half of the pastry on a lightly floured surface to a thickness of 1 cm/½ inch and use to line the bottom and sides of the mould

Line this pastry with the bacon slices, then put in the filling. Place the bay leaf on top. Roll out the remaining pastry and use as a lid. Decorate the top of the pie with pastry trimmings and glaze. Make a hole in the centre of the pastry to allow steam to escape. Bake in a moderate oven for about 1 hour.

White wines: Montrachet, Meursault, white Graves, Barsac.

PILAW DE POULET

CHICKEN PILAU

Preparation 50 minutes • Cooking 35 minutes

Cut up the chickens as for a fricassée, ie remove the legs and wings and cut the breast portions away from the carcass. Cut each breast fillet into 2 pieces and the carcass into three.

Melt two-thirds of the butter in a large saucepan and add the chicken. Season with salt and pepper and cook over a fairly high heat for 5–10 minutes or until they are lightly coloured. Add the chopped onion and the rice and continue cooking, stirring constantly, until the rice has become lightly coloured. Add the tomato paste (or 2 large tomatoes, skinned, de-seeded and chopped), the stock and bouquet garni. Bring to the boil, then cover and cook in a hot oven for at least 30 minutes or until the rice has completely absorbed the liquid and is tender but still in separate grains. Cook the chicken in the oven at the same time.

Break up the pieces of chicken and the rice with a fork. Serve the pilau in a deep, round bowl that has been heated in advance.

White wines: Alsace Pinot Gris, Sylvaner or Riesling.
Red wines: Côte de Beaune.
Rosé wine: Tavel.

US	Ingredients	Met/Imp
2, each about 1¾–2 lb	chickens, preferably free-range or corn-fed	2, each about 800 g–1 kg/1¾–2 lb
10 tbsp	butter	150 g/5 oz
	salt and pepper	
1	large onion	1
1 cup	rice, preferably Carolina	200 g/7 oz
2 tbsp	tomato paste	30 ml/2 tbsp
3 cups	white stock (consommé)	750 ml/1¼ pints
1	bouquet garni	1

POULET AUX AUBERGINES

CHICKEN WITH AUBERGINES

Preparation 1 hour • Cooking 25 minutes

The aubergine (eggplant) skins may be left on or removed, as desired, and a touch of garlic may be added to the persillade.

Fry the chickens in butter and oil. Sauté the aubergine (eggplant) slices, which have been *dégorgé* and floured, in butter and oil until slightly dry and a little coloured.

After cooking, remove the legs and wings from the chickens and put them on top of the aubergines (eggplants) in a round serving dish. Pour on a good tomato *coulis*, then top with the cooking liquid and the chicken livers, which have been sealed in butter. Finish with a light persillade. Serve very hot with the remaining chicken, cut into pieces.

Rosé wines: Tavel, Bandol, Cassis.

US	Ingredients	Met/Imp
2, each about 2½ lb	young chickens, preferably Bresse free-range, including the livers	2, each about 1.1 kg/2½ lb
10 tbsp	butter	150 g/5 oz
½ cup	oil	100 ml/4 fl oz
4	aubergines (eggplants), cut diagonally into 2–3 mm/⅛ inch slices	4
6 tbsp	flour	50 g/2 oz
6	tomatoes, skinned, de-seeded and crushed	6
	persillade	

US	Ingredients	Met/Imp
2, each about 2 lb	chickens, preferably free-range or corn-fed	2, each about I kg/2 lb
I stick	butter	100 g/3½ oz
7 oz	mushrooms	200 g/7 oz
5	tomatoes	5
½ cup	dry white wine	100 ml/4 fl oz
½ cup	highly flavoured Veal Juice (page 56)	100 ml/4 fl oz
¼ cup	cognac	50 ml/2 fl oz
	salt and pepper	
I tbsp	chopped fresh parsley	15 ml/I tbsp
I	garlic clove	I

CHICKEN CÉLESTINE

Preparation 50 minutes • Cooking 30 minutes

Cut some young, tender, plump chickens into pieces.

Melt the butter in a large saucepan and stir. Cook until the butter starts to turn nut-brown, then add the chicken pieces and cook over a high heat for about 10 minutes or until golden brown.

Add the mushrooms and the skinned, de-seeded and chopped tomatoes. Sauté for 5 minutes, then pour in the wine, veal juice and cognac. Add salt and pepper and cook for a further 15 minutes or until the chicken is tender.

Transfer the chicken pieces to a heated serving dish. Skim the fat from the sauce then sprinkle the sauce with the chopped parsley and finely chopped garlic. Pour on to the chicken pieces and serve at once.

Dry white wines: Chablis, Pouilly-Fuissé.
Red wines: Côte de Beaune, Côte Rôtie.

US	Ingredients	Met/Imp
14 tbsp	butter	200 g/7 oz
2, each about 2½ lb	chickens, preferably free-range or corn-fed	2, each about 1.1 kg/2½ lb
½ cup	cognac	100 ml/3½ fl oz
	brut champagne	
I tbsp	tomato paste	15 ml/I tbsp
I cup	crème fraîche	200 ml/7 fl oz
I cup	highly flavoured chicken stock	200 ml/7 fl oz
	salt and pepper	
¾ cup	Creole Rice (page 563)	150 g/5 oz
8	spinach pains, to serve	8

CHICKEN WITH CHAMPAGNE

Preparation 1½ hours • Cooking 30 minutes

Recipe from the Nandron restaurant, Lyon

Melt half of the butter in a large saucepan, add the chickens, cut into serving pieces, and sauté gently, without allowing them to brown. When they are half cooked, cover the pan and braise the chickens so that they do not become coloured.

Flambé the chickens with the cognac, moisten with some champagne, then add the tomato paste, crème fraîche, stock and salt and pepper. Cover and heat through quickly.

Remove the chickens from the pan and arrange on a heated serving dish. Work the sauce through a piece of cheesecloth, add the remaining butter and pour over the chicken. The sauce, which is made slightly acid by the champagne, should shimmer and be very reduced Serve the chicken with Creole rice. Spinach *pains* made in baba moulds also go very well with this dish.

Wines: sparkling Champagne, still Coteaux Champenois.

POULET EN CIVET AU BOURGOGNE

CHICKEN STEWED IN BURGUNDY WINE

Preparation 1¼ hours • Cooking 40 minutes

Recipe from the Hôtel de la Poste, Avallon

Cut each chicken into quarters.

Melt the butter in a large saucepan and add the diced bacon and roughly chopped onion and carrots. Add the chicken pieces and fry for about 10 minutes or until brown. Flambé the chicken with the marc, then sprinkle in the flour. Continue frying until the flour is light golden then pour in the wine and a little stock.

Add salt and pepper, the bouquet garni and the crushed garlic, bring to the boil and boil rapidly for a few minutes. Reduce the heat and simmer for 30 minutes or until the chicken is tender.

Remove the pieces of chicken from the pan and arrange on a heated shallow serving dish. Adjust the seasoning of the sauce and strain it through a sieve. Just before serving, thicken the sauce with the chicken blood or, if unavailable, pig's blood. Coat the pieces of chicken with the sauce. Combine the small onions, belly (side) of pork and mushrooms and use to garnish the dish. Surround the chicken with fried bread croûtons and serve at once.

Wines: as a general rule, serve the same wine as the one used for cooking.

US	Ingredients	Met/Imp
2, each about 2 lb	chickens, preferably free-range or corn-fed	2, each about 1 kg/2 lb
2½ sticks	butter	300 g/10 oz
a few	pieces diced bacon	a few
1	onion	1
2	carrots	2
¼ cup	marc from Burgundy	50 ml/2 fl oz
½ cup	flour	75 g/3 oz
1 bottle	burgundy wine	1 bottle
	White Stock (page 56)	
	salt and pepper	
1	bouquet garni	1
2	garlic cloves	2
¼ cup	chicken or pig's blood (see Editor's note, page 312)	50 ml/2 fl oz
	GARNISH	
20	small onions, glazed	20
¼ lb	fat belly (side) of pork, diced and fried	125 g/4 oz
½ lb	Paris mushrooms, sweated in butter	250 g/8 oz
16	heart-shaped croûtons, rubbed with garlic and fried	16

POULET EN COCOTTE À LA MODE D'ANCENIS

– CHICKEN CASSEROLE ANCENIS STYLE –

Preparation 3 hours • Marinating several hours • Cooking 35 minutes

Sprinkle the chickens with salt and pepper and put them in the marinade for several hours.

Take the chickens out of the marinade, butter them thickly, then place them in a casserole with the diced bacon. Cook until the chickens are a nice golden-brown colour, basting them often. At this point, take them out of the casserole and keep them warm.

Put a nut of butter in the casserole and mix in the flour. When this starts to become coloured, add the liquid and sliced shallot from the marinade, the veal juice and the chicken livers, which have been previously pounded. Add the small onions, diced belly (side) of pork, mushrooms and artichoke bottoms for the garnish, all of which have been blanched and sweated in fresh butter. Put the chickens back in the casserole. Cover and simmer over a low heat for a few minutes. Sprinkle with chives and serve.

White wines: Muscadet, Pouilly-Fumé, Chablis, Pouilly-Fuissé.
Red wines: Bourgueil, Chinon.

US	Ingredients	Met/Imp
2, each about 2 lb	chickens, preferably free-range or corn-fed, including the livers	2, each about 1 kg/2 lb
	salt and pepper	
1 stick	butter	100 g/4 oz
a few	pieces diced lean bacon	a few
6 tbsp	flour	50 g/2 oz
½ cup	Veal Juice (page 56)	100 ml/4 fl oz
	MARINADE	
1 bottle	Muscadet	1 bottle
½ cup	madeira	100 ml/4 fl oz
1	bouquet garni	1
1	garlic clove	1
1	carrot	1
6	shallots, thinly sliced	6
	GARNISH	
30	small new onions	30
½ lb	fresh lean belly (side) of pork, diced	250 g/8 oz
7 oz	Paris mushrooms	200 g/7 oz
8	small artichoke bottoms	8
	butter	
1 tbsp	snipped fresh chives	15 ml/1 tbsp

US	Ingredients	Met/Imp
2	chickens, preferably free-range or corn-fed	2
10 tbsp	butter	150 g/5 oz
2	small onions	2
	salt and pepper	
3 tbsp	flour	30 g/1 oz
1 quart	crème fraîche	1 litre/1¾ pints
3	egg yolks	3
½	lemon, juice of	½

CHICKEN WITH CREAM

Preparation 45 minutes • Cooking 30 minutes

Use Bresse chickens, if possible, as they are whiter and more tender than others. Draw and singe them, then cut them into pieces.

Melt the butter in a large heavy-based saucepan and add the small onions and chicken pieces. Add salt and pepper, cover and cook for about 30 minutes or until the chicken is tender, turning frequently to prevent the chicken browning.

When the chicken is cooked, sprinkle with the flour and pour in the crème fraîche. Bring to the boil and cook for 5 minutes.

Remove the chicken pieces from the pan and arrange on a heated serving dish. Beat the egg yolks with the lemon juice and stir into the sauce to thicken it. Strain the sauce through a fine sieve on to the pieces of chicken.

When prepared in this way, the chicken should be served immediately, otherwise the sauce will curdle. It should not be reheated.

Sweet or medium dry white wines: Graves, Sauternes, Barsac, Alsace Gewürztraminer, Vouvray.
Red wines: Chinon, Bourgueil.

CHICKEN WITH TARRAGON

Preparation 45 minutes • Cooking 40 minutes

US	Ingredients	Met/Imp
2	chickens, preferably free-range or corn-fed	2
½ cup	oil	100 ml/3½ fl oz
1 stick	butter	100 g/3½ oz
8	garlic cloves	8
½ cup	cognac	100 ml/3½ fl oz
1 cup	Meursault wine	200 ml/7 fl oz
½ cup	wine vinegar	100 ml/3½ fl oz
½ cup	Veal Juice (page 56)	100 ml/3½ fl oz
1 tbsp	tomato paste	15 ml/1 tbsp
1	bouquet tarragon sprigs	1
	salt and pepper	
4	egg yolks	4
1 cup	crème fraîche	200 ml/7 fl oz
1 tbsp	mixed chopped fresh chervil, tarragon and parsley	15 ml/1 tbsp

Cut the chickens into serving pieces. Heat the oil and butter in a large flameproof casserole, add the unpeeled garlic cloves and the chicken pieces and sauté until the chicken is tender.

Flambé with the cognac, then add the wine, wine vinegar, veal juice and tomato paste. Add the bouquet of tarragon and salt and pepper.

Remove the chicken pieces and arrange on a heated serving dish. Press the contents of the pan through a sieve, then thicken with the egg yolks and crème fraîche.

Just before serving, coat the pieces of chicken with the sauce and sprinkle with chopped fresh chervil, tarragon and parsley.

White wines: Montrachet, Meursault, Graves, Hermitage.
Red wines: Côte de Beaune, Beaujolais-Villages, Cornas.

CHICKEN FLAMBÉED WITH ─── FIVE TYPES OF SPIRIT ───

Preparation 1 hour • Cooking 35 minutes

Cut the chickens into serving pieces, then sauté them in some butter with the chopped shallots for about 10 minutes. Flambé with a 'cocktail' of the 5 spirits. Pour in the wine. Cook slowly for about 30 minutes or until the chicken is tender.

Meanwhile, cook the rice in twice its volume of boiling stock for 17 minutes or until tender. Drain well.

When the chicken pieces are cooked, remove them from the pan and place them on a heated serving dish. Keep them warm. Make a roux with 30 g/1 oz (2 tbsp) butter and the flour. Remove from the heat and gradually stir in the chicken cooking liquid. Bring to the boil and cook, stirring, until thickened and smooth.

To serve, arrange the rice, with a handful of stoned cherries in it, in a ring around the chicken. Add the shrimps and crème fraîche to the sauce, season well and pour over the chicken and rice. Serve with the guava jam.

Rosé, red or sparkling wines: Tavel, Côtes du Rhône-Chusclan, Clairette de Die.

US	Ingredients	Met/Imp
2	chickens, preferably free-range or corn-fed	2
	butter	
6	shallots	6
¼ cup	cognac	50 ml/2 fl oz
¼ cup	whisky	50 ml/2 fl oz
¼	gin	50 ml/2 fl oz
¼ cup	calvados	50 ml/2 fl oz
¼ cup	cherry brandy	50 ml/2 fl oz
I bottle	dry white wine	I bottle
I cup	rice	200 g/7 oz
2 cups	boiling stock (see *Pilau Rice*, page 563)	500 ml/18 fl oz
3 tbsp	flour	30 g/1 oz
1¼ cups	cherries	150 g/5 oz
½ lb	peeled cooked shrimps	250 g/8 oz
½ cup	*crème fraîche*	100 ml/4 fl oz
	salt and pepper	
I jar	guava jam	I jar

─── GRILLED CHICKEN AMÉRICAINE ───

Preparation 1¼ hours • Cooking 35 minutes

Cut each chicken into quarters. Flatten each piece with a cutlet bat (meat mallet), coat with breadcrumbs, sprinkle with melted butter and oil and cook until browned and tender, turning frequently. (See Devilled Grilled Chicken overleaf.)

Meanwhile, prepare the mushroom duxelles and a *coulis* of the skinned and de-seeded tomatoes.

To serve, form the rice into a ring on a heated serving platter. Put the chicken pieces in the centre and garnish with the mushrooms and tomatoes. Serve very hot, sprinkled with parsley.

Red wines: Côte de Beaune, Beaujolais-Villages.

US	Ingredients	Met/Imp
2, each about 2 lb	chickens, preferably free-range or corn-fed	2, each about 1 kg/2 lb
4 cups	fresh breadcrumbs	250 g/8 oz
10 tbsp	butter	150 g/5 oz
½ cup	oil	100 ml/4 fl oz
2 cups	Dry Duxelles (page 49)	250 g/8 oz
12	tomatoes	12
1¼ cups	Pilau Rice (page 563)	250 g/8 oz
	chopped fresh parsley	

US	Ingredients	Met/Imp
2, each 1¾–2 lb	young chickens, preferably free-range or corn-fed	2, each 800 g–1 kg/1¾–2 lb
	salt and pepper	
1 stick	butter	100 g/4 oz
	oil	
2 tbsp	mustard	30 ml/2 tbsp
3½ cups	fresh breadcrumbs	200 g/7 oz
1 cup	Devil Sauce (*page 68*)	200 ml/7 fl oz

—— DEVILLED GRILLED CHICKEN* ——

Preparation 1 hour • Cooking 35 minutes

Draw and singe the chickens and remove the feet. Split each chicken completely down the middle of the back. Beat them with a cutlet bat (meat mallet), to break the bones, then stretch the bones out flat.

Place the chickens in a roasting tin, add salt and pepper and brush with melted butter and oil. Cook in a fairly hot oven for about 15 minutes or until they are sealed and have just started to cook.

Remove the chickens from the oven and wipe them with a cloth. Coat them with mustard and sprinkle with breadcrumbs, pressing them on with the blade of a knife so that they combine with the mustard. Sprinkle with melted butter and put them on the grill (broiler) pan under a preheated moderate grill (broiler). Cook for about 20 minutes or until the breadcrumbs are browned and the chickens are tender, turning them and sprinkling them with butter from time to time. Serve the chickens hot, with the sauce on the side.

Red wines: Saint-Émilion, Pomerol, Beaujolais-Villages, Côtes du Rhône, Côtes de Provence.
Dry white wines: Muscadet, Pouilly-Fumé, Chablis.

US	Ingredients	Met/Imp
2, each about 2 lb	chickens	2, each about 1 kg/2 lb
10 oz	fresh fat belly (side) of pork	300 g/10 oz
30	small onions	30
1	bouquet garni	1
3	garlic cloves	3
7 oz	*Paris mushrooms*	200 g/7 oz
	salt and pepper	
1 bottle	red wine	1 bottle
	Kneaded Butter (*page 49*)	
1 tbsp	chopped fresh parsley	15 ml/1 tbsp

—— CHICKEN MEURETTE* ——

Preparation 1 hour • Cooking 40 minutes

Cut the chickens into serving pieces.

Cut the pork into fairly large dice and blanch in boiling water. Drain and put in a large flameproof casserole with the onions, bouquet garni and garlic cloves. Add the chicken pieces, mushrooms, salt and pepper and pour in the red wine. Cook for 35–40 minutes or until the chicken is tender. Thicken with the kneaded butter and garnish with parsley.

This chicken may be cooked in the same way with white wine, in which case it is called Pauchouse de Poulet (Chicken Matelote).

Wines: as a general rule, serve the same wine as the one used for cooking.

US	Ingredients	Met/Imp
2, each 1¾ lb–2 lb	chickens, preferably free-range	2, each 800–900 g/1¾–2 lb
10 tbsp	butter	150 g/5 oz
¼ cup	oil	50 ml/2 fl oz
¼ cup	brandy	50 ml/2 fl oz
6	tomatoes	6
½ cup	vermouth	100 ml/4 fl oz
30	small onions	30
½ lb	belly (side) of pork	250 g/8 oz
	salt and pepper	
½ cup	*crème fraîche*	100 ml/4 fl oz
1 oz	truffles	30 g/1 oz
1 tbsp	mixed chopped fresh chervil and tarragon	15 ml/1 tbsp

—— CHICKEN IN VERMOUTH ——

Preparation 1 hour • Cooking 25 minutes

Cut the chickens into serving pieces and sauté in some of the butter and the oil until golden. Flambé with the brandy, then add the skinned, de-seeded and crushed tomatoes and pour in the vermouth. Add the small onions, the diced pork and salt and pepper.

Bring to the boil and simmer for about 25 minutes or until the chicken is tender. Finish by adding the remaining butter and the crème fraîche. Just before serving, sprinkle with chopped truffles, chervil and tarragon.

Red and white vins de Savoie: Crépy, Ripaille, Abymes, Montmélian.

POULET AUX MOUSSERONS

— CHICKEN WITH FIELD MUSHROOMS —

Preparation 1 hour • Cooking 35 minutes

US	Ingredients	Met/Imp
½ lb (2 sticks)	butter	250 g/8 oz
2	medium onions	2
4	shallots	4
2	chickens, preferably free-range or corn-fed	2
1¼ lb	field or other wild mushrooms	600 g/1¼ lb
2 tbsp	chopped fresh parsley	30 ml/2 tbsp
	salt and pepper	
½ cup	white wine	100 ml/3½ fl oz
1 cup	Veal Juice (*page 56*)	200 ml/7 fl oz
½ lb	fresh fat belly (side) of pork	250 g/8 oz
	KNEADED BUTTER	
2 tbsp	butter	25 g/scant 1 oz
3 tbsp	flour	25 g/scant 1 oz

Melt one-quarter of the butter in a saucepan and cook the chopped onions and shallots for 5–10 minutes or until soft but not brown. Leave to cool. Draw and clean the chickens. Reserve the livers and finely chop them after removing the gall bladders.

Mix one-third of the mushrooms with one-third of the remaining butter, the chopped chicken livers, the cooked onions and shallots, half of the chopped parsley and a pinch of salt and pepper. Put this stuffing inside the chickens and truss them, keeping the legs parallel with the bodies.

Put the stuffed chickens in a flameproof casserole with half of the remaining butter and cook until browned on all sides, then put them in a fairly hot oven and cook for 10 minutes. Pour the white wine into the casserole and boil rapidly until reduced to 60 ml/4 tbsp. Add the veal juice.

Meanwhile, dice the belly (side) of pork and scald it in boiling water for 5 minutes, then drain. Melt the remaining butter in a frying pan and sauté the remaining mushrooms and the pork for 5–10 minutes or until the mushrooms are soft and the pork browned.

Tip the pork and mushrooms into the casserole to surround the chickens. Cover with a tight-fitting lid and continue cooking in the oven for a further 20 minutes.

Transfer the chickens to a heated serving dish. Make the kneaded butter according to the instructions on page 49 and use to thicken the chicken cooking liquid. Pour this sauce over the chickens and sprinkle with the remaining parsley before serving.

Red wines: Pomerol, Côte de Beaune, Côtes du Rhône.

POULET À LA MOUTARDE GRATINÉ AU FROMAGE

CHICKEN GRATIN WITH MUSTARD AND CHEESE

Preparation 50 minutes • Cooking 30 minutes

US	Ingredients	Met/Imp
2, each about 2–2½ lb	young chickens, preferably free-range or corn-fed	2, each about 1.1 kg/2–2½ lb
10 tbsp	butter	150 g/5 oz
	salt and pepper	
1 tsp	paprika	5 ml/1 tsp
1 cup	Gruyère cheese, grated	100 g/4 oz
scant 1 cup	white wine	200 ml/7 fl oz
1 tbsp	Dijon mustard	15 ml/1 tbsp
2 cups	thick *crème fraîche*	500 ml/18 fl oz
scant 1 cup	breadcrumbs, preferably fresh	50 g/2 oz

Cut the chickens into serving pieces.

Melt the butter in a flameproof casserole and add the chicken pieces. Cook over a low heat for about 30 minutes or until tender, turning frequently to prevent the chicken browning. Add salt, pepper and paprika.

When the chicken is cooked, remove the pieces from the pan and arrange in an ovenproof serving dish. Stir three-quarters of the grated Gruyère cheese into the hot cooking juices until melted. Add the wine, mustard and crème fraîche and heat through. Pour over the chicken pieces. Sprinkle with the breadcrumbs and remaining grated cheese and put in a hot oven until lightly browned. Serve at once.

Red wines: Côte de Nuits, Saint-Émilion, Côtes du Rhône, Beaujolais-Villages.

US	Ingredients	Met/Imp
2	chickens	2
8	thin slices fatty bacon	8
8	thyme sprigs	8
1 cup	olive oil	200 ml/7 fl oz
2	onions	2
8	large tomatoes	8
4	garlic cloves	4
	salt and pepper	
1 cup	white wine	200 ml/7 fl oz
½ cup	stoned black olives	100 g/4 oz

CHICKEN PARCELS PROVENÇAL

Preparation 1 hour • Cooking 35 minutes

Cut each chicken into quarters. Wrap each quarter in a slice of bacon with a sprig of thyme and tie up.

Heat the olive oil in a large saucepan, add the chicken 'parcels' and cook over a high heat for about 10 minutes or until brown. Add the chopped onions, skinned, de-seeded and crushed tomatoes, the crushed garlic, salt and pepper and white wine. Cover and cook over a gentle heat for about 35 minutes or until the chicken is tender.

Just before serving, remove the chicken from the pan, untie the strings and put the parcels on a heated serving dish just as they are. Continue to cook the sauce until reduced, add the olives and pour over the parcels.

Red wines: Côte Rôtie, Châteauneuf-du-Pape, Bandol.

US	Ingredients	Met/Imp
1, about 2½ lb	chicken	1, about 1.1 kg/2½ lb
	salt and pepper	
3	artichoke bottoms	3
	butter	
	oil	
1	thyme sprig	1
1	bay leaf	1
5	large potatoes	5
1	large onion	1
3 tbsp	chopped shallots	45 ml/3 tbsp
1 glass	dry white wine	1 glass
	Veal Juice (*page 56*) or the juices from roasted meat	
1	parsley sprig	1

CHICKEN 'PÈRE LATHUILE'

Preparation 1½ hours • Cooking 1 hour

Recipe by Jacques Manière, le Pactole, Paris

Use a fairly small casserole for this dish so that the ingredients are tightly packed and form a sort of 'cake' that can be turned out.

Cut the chicken into 8 pieces. Sprinkle the pieces with salt and pepper. Blanch the artichoke bottoms in boiling water, drain and slice thinly.

Heat a little butter and oil in a fairly small flameproof casserole, add the thyme and crumble in the bay leaf. Add the pieces of chicken and fry for about 10 minutes or until golden brown.

Meanwhile, heat a little more butter and oil in a frying pan. Cut 2 of the potatoes into thin, even slices and sauté them in the hot butter and oil, with a little salt, for about 10 minutes or until well browned. Remove from the pan and drain thoroughly.

Heat some more butter and oil in the frying pan and add the 3 remaining raw, thinly sliced potatoes along with the sliced, blanched artichokes. Add salt and pepper and cook until lightly browned.

Remove the chicken pieces and herbs from the casserole and pour the cooking juices into a bowl. Set aside. Put a little butter in the casserole. Cover the bottom with the browned slices of the first 2 potatoes, arranging them so that they overlap slightly. Put half of the fried potatoes and artichoke mixture on top, then add the chicken pieces. Cover with the remaining potato and artichoke slices and sprinkle with the cooking juices from the chicken. Cover and cook in a hot oven for 25 minutes.

Remove the casserole from the oven and place over a low heat on top of the stove. Cook for a further 20 minutes so that the potatoes in the bottom of the casserole become well browned. Turn the chicken 'cake' out on to a heated serving dish and keep warm.

Meanwhile, thinly slice the onion and fry in some butter until soft but

not brown. Make a shallot sauce. Melt some butter and oil in another flameproof casserole, add the chopped shallots and cook for 5–10 minutes or until golden brown. Pour the white wine into the casserole in which the chicken was cooked, mix well and pour on to the shallots. Stir, then add a ladleful of the veal juice or meat juices. Simmer gently until reduced to a fairly thick sauce. Garnish the chicken 'cake' with the fried onion rings and parsley and serve with the shallot sauce.

Red wines: Bourgueil, Beaujolais-Villages, Madiran.

POULET POÊLÉ BASQUAISE

— 'OVEN-FRIED' CHICKEN BASQUAISE —

Preparation 1 hour • Cooking 25 minutes

US	Ingredients	Met/Imp
2, each about 1¾ lb	chickens, preferably free-range or corn-fed	2, each about 800 g–1 kg/ 1¾–2 lb
10 tbsp	butter	150 g/5 oz
2	carrots	2
1	large onion	1
	salt	
8	large tomatoes	8
1 lb	sweet green peppers	500 g/1 lb
10 oz	Bayonne ham	300 g/10 oz
½ cup	madeira	100 ml/4 fl oz
1 tbsp	chopped fresh parsley	15 ml/1 tbsp

Put the 2 whole chickens in an ovenproof sauté pan. Add some butter and the roughly chopped carrots and onion rings. Sprinkle with salt and cook in a moderate oven for 20–25 minutes or until tender.

Meanwhile, skin, de-seed and crush the tomatoes and put in a flameproof casserole with the de-seeded and thinly sliced green peppers and a *julienne* of Bayonne ham. Cook for about 10 minutes or until the peppers are soft.

When the chickens are cooked, remove them from the pan and cut each bird into 5 pieces: legs, wings and main body portions. Arrange them in a serving dish and keep warm. Deglaze the pan with the madeira and cook until reduced. Arrange the pepper and tomato mixture in a ring around the chicken on the serving dish.

Add the remaining piece of butter to the reduced madeira sauce and pour over the chicken. Sprinkle with the parsley just before serving.

Red wines: Béarn, Irouléguy, Madiran.

POULET AU PORTO ET À L'ESTRAGON

CHICKEN WITH PORT AND TARRAGON

Preparation 50 minutes • Cooking 35 minutes

US	Ingredients	Met/Imp
2, each about 2 lb	chickens, preferably free-range or corn-fed, including the livers	2, each about 1 kg/2 lb
	salt and pepper	
10 tbsp	butter	150 g/5 oz
scant ½ cup	ruby port wine	100 ml/3½ fl oz
2 cups	thickened Veal Juice (page 56)	500 ml/18 fl oz
1 lb	veal fillet (tenderloin)	500 g/1 lb
1 tbsp	chopped fresh tarragon	15 ml/1 tbsp

Choose plump chickens. Sprinkle the chickens with salt and pepper. Fry them in half of the butter for about 35 minutes or until brown and tender, turning and basting them often. When the chickens are three-quarters cooked, add the port, boil rapidly to reduce, then add the veal juice and finish cooking, watching carefully.

Melt the remaining butter in a separate pan and fry the quartered chicken livers over a high heat for about 5 minutes or until browned but still rare. Cut the veal into thin strips and add to the chicken livers. Fry together until tender, then add the chopped tarragon.

Put the liver and veal garnish on a heated serving dish and place the chickens on top. Serve hot.

Red wines: Médoc, Pomerol, Graves, Côte de Beaune or Côte de Nuits.
White wines: Meursault, Montrachet, Pouilly-Fuissé.

US	Ingredients	Met/Imp
2 lb	prunes	1 kg/2 lb
	salt	
2, each about 2 lb	chickens, preferably free-range or corn-fed	2, each about 1 kg/2 lb
10 tbsp	butter	150 g/5 oz
	salt	

—— CHICKEN WITH PRUNES ——

Preparation 1 hour • Soaking prunes 4 hours • Cooking 35 minutes

Put the prunes in a bowl, cover with cold water and leave to soak for 4 hours. Drain and stone them.

Sprinkle salt inside the chickens and stuff them with the prunes. Truss them securely and place in a large roasting tin. Brush with melted butter and roast in a fairly hot oven for about 35 minutes or until brown and tender.

White wines: Muscadet, Pouilly-Fumé, Chablis.
Red wines: Bourgueil, Chinon, Beaujolais-Villages.

US	Ingredients	Met/Imp
10 tbsp	butter	150 g/5 oz
4	large white onions	4
2, each about 2–2½ lb	chickens, preferably free range or corn-fed	2, each about 900 g–1.1 kg/ 2–2½ lb
	salt and pepper	
2	garlic cloves	2
1	thyme sprig	1
1 quart	crème fraîche	1 litre/1¾ pints
scant ½ cup	madeira	100 ml/4 fl oz
3½ tbsp	calvados	50 ml/2 fl oz

—— CHICKEN WITH ONION PURÉE ——

Preparation 50 minutes • Cooking 30 minutes

Put the butter in a large ovenproof sauté pan and add the finely chopped white onions. Put the chickens, which have been cut into pieces, on top and add salt, pepper, the chopped garlic and the thyme sprig. Cover the pan and cook in a moderate oven for 30 minutes or until the chicken is tender.

Gradually add the thick crème fraîche to the pan while the chicken is cooking. As the cream cooks, it will reduce.

When the chicken pieces are cooked, remove them from the pan and place them on a heated serving dish. Keep them warm. Work the onion and crème fraîche mixture through a sieve. Add the madeira and calvados and put in a saucepan. Cook until reduced to the required thickness and pour on to the chicken pieces. Serve at once.

Red wines: Médoc, Côte de Beaune, Chinon.
White wines: Meursault, Montrachet, Hermitage, Pouilly-Fumé.

US	Ingredients	Met/Imp
2, each about 2–2½ lb	chickens, preferably free-range or corn-fed	2, each about 1–1.1 kg/ 2–2½ lb
4	small onions	4
1	clove	1
14 tbsp	butter	200 g/7 oz
	salt and pepper	
6 tbsp	flour	50 g/2 oz
2 cups	white wine	500 ml/18 fl oz
1	bouquet garni	1
5 oz	truffles	150 g/5 oz
4	egg yolks	4
scant 1 cup	crème fraîche	200 ml/7 fl oz
16	triangular croûtons	16

—— CHICKEN 'À LA REINE' ——

Preparation 1 hour • Cooking 50 minutes

Cut the chickens into serving pieces. Spike 1 onion with the clove.

Melt some butter in a sauté pan just large enough to take the chicken pieces in a single layer. Cook the butter over a high heat until it has turned a nut-brown colour, then add the chicken pieces, skin-side down. Add salt and pepper and cook for 5–10 minutes or until lightly browned. Reduce the heat, add the 4 onions and continue to simmer for 15 minutes.

Stir in the flour, cook for 3 minutes, then pour in the white wine. Add the bouquet garni, cover the pan and cook over a low heat for a further 10 minutes or until the chicken pieces are tender. When they are

cooked, remove the pieces from the pan and put them in a dish. Strain the sauce on to the chicken through a fine conical sieve, then return everything to the pan. Finely slice the truffles, sprinkle over the chickens and cover the pan. Simmer for 10 minutes, then turn off the heat. Whisk together the egg yolks and crème fraîche and pour over the chicken. Mix well until evenly blended, then place the pan on the edge of the stove top so that the sauce does not become too hot and curdle. Cover the pan and let the chicken stand in the sauce for 30 minutes before serving.

To serve, place the chicken pieces in a round serving dish and coat them with the sauce. Garnish the edge of the dish with the croûtons, which have been buttered and lightly fried at the last minute.

Red wines: Côte de Beaune, Côte Rôtie.
White wines: Meursault, Coteaux Champenois.

POULET EN SAUCE AU CITRON

—— CHICKEN IN LEMON SAUCE ——

Preparation 40 minutes • Cooking time 1 hour 40 minutes • Serves 4

Put the trussed chicken in a large copper saucepan with the giblets, the roughly chopped leek, celery or celeriac, shallots, carrot, thyme, bay leaf, herbs, wine, salt and a moderate amount of pepper. Bring slowly to the boil, then cover and simmer for about 1 hour or until the chicken is tender.

Pour off half of the stock and strain it through a fine sieve. Keep the chicken warm in the remaining stock in the pan.

Remove the fat from the strained stock by quickly passing a piece of paper towel over the surface. Bring the stock to the boil and cook until reduced to 120–150 ml/4–5 fl oz.

Put the cream, egg yolks, reduced stock, lemon juice and a fine *julienne* of lemon peel in another copper saucepan and beat together.

Place the sugar in a heavy-based pan with a drop of water and heat until the sugar has caramelized, then add 15 ml/1 tbsp water to obtain a syrupy liquid. Add 30 ml/2 tbsp of this caramel to the cream, egg and lemon mixture and whisk vigorously over a high heat until it boils. Continue to whisk over a very low heat (or in a *bain-marie*) for about 20 minutes or until the sauce thickens. If the sauce curdles, add a little cold double (heavy) cream and whisk vigorously.

Blanch the asparagus tips in boiling water, then drain and place on an ovenproof dish. Sprinkle with small pieces of butter and heat in the oven until all the moisture has evaporated.

Remove the chicken from the stock and detach its wings and legs. Wipe all the pieces with paper towels and arrange on a heated serving dish. Coat with sauce. Put some sauce in the pastry boats, then top with asparagus tips. Complete the garnish with fluted lemon slices and puff pastry fleurons.

Medium dry white wines: Graves, Alsace Gewürztraminer, Jurançon.
Dry white wine: Mâcon-Villages.
Red wines: Beaujolais-Villages, Côtes du Rhône.

US	Ingredients	Met/Imp
1, about 3 lb	chicken, including the giblets	1, about 1.4 kg/3 lb
1	leek, white part only	1
a few	celery leaves	a few
	or	
	small piece celeriac	1
1–2	shallots	1–2
1	carrot	1
1	thyme sprig	1
1	bay leaf	1
1 pinch each	finely chopped rosemary, marjoram, basil, sage and savory	1 pinch each
1 bottle	sweet white wine (sweet Graves or Barsac)	1 bottle
	salt and pepper	
1¼ cups	double (heavy) cream	300 ml/½ pint
5–6	egg yolks	5–6
1	lemon, juice of	1
2	lemons, peel and pith of	2
4–5	sugar cubes	4–5
14 oz	asparagus tips	400 g/14 oz
4	pastry boats	4
a few	fluted lemon slices	a few
4	puff pastry *fleurons*	4

US	Ingredients	Met/Imp
2, each about 2½ lb	chickens	2, each about 1.1 kg/2½ lb
	salt and pepper	
½ cup	flour	75 g/3 oz
14 tbsp	butter	200 g/7 oz
4	shallots	4
scant ½ cup	madeira	100 ml/3½ fl oz
1 bottle	Muscadet white wine	1 bottle
scant 1 cup	consommé or Veal Juice (page 56)	200 ml/7 fl oz
2 cups	crème fraîche	500 ml/18 fl oz
8	artichoke bottoms	8
10 oz (about 2 cups)	blanched asparagus tips or cooked peas	300 g/10 oz

— CHICKEN WITH 'VISCOUNT' SAUCE —

Preparation 1½ hours • Cooking chickens 15 minutes; artichokes 40 minutes; asparagus tips 20 minutes

Cut each chicken into 5 pieces: 2 wings, 2 legs and the main body portion. Season with salt and pepper and coat with flour. Melt half of the butter in a saucepan, add the chicken pieces and cook gently for about 10 minutes or until browned.

Drain off the butter and sprinkle the chicken with the very finely chopped shallots. Deglaze with the madeira and some Muscadet wine, then moisten with a little consommé or veal juice. Cook for a further 15 minutes or until the chicken is tender.

When the chicken is cooked, remove the pieces from the pan and keep them warm. Add some crème fraîche to the cooking juices to make a reduced and well-flavoured sauce. Serve on the side, together with a sauce boat of hot crème fraîche.

Place the pieces of chicken in the centre of a heated serving dish. Surround with the artichoke bottoms, which have been sweated in the remaining butter and topped with the asparagus or peas tossed in butter.

White wines: Muscadet, Alsace Sylvaner or Riesling.
Red wines: Côte de Beaune.
Rosé wine: Tavel.

US	Ingredients	Met/Imp
1, about 2½ lb	chicken	1, about 1.1 kg/2½ lb
4 tbsp	butter	50 g/2 oz
2 tbsp	olive oil	30 ml/2 tbsp
	salt and pepper	
24	large garlic cloves (2–3 bulbs)	24
3½ tbsp	chopped fresh parsley	50 ml/3½ tbsp

SAUTÉED CHICKEN DAUPHINOIS —— WITH GARLIC AND PARSLEY ——

Preparation 30 minutes • Cooking 50 minutes • Serves 4–5

Cut the chicken into serving pieces: detach the legs and wings and cut the main body portion into 4 pieces. Cut off the feet and the wing tips and cut the legs and wings into 2 pieces each.

Heat the butter and oil in a flameproof casserole. Add the chicken pieces and cook over a high heat for about 10 minutes or until browned on all sides, without letting the fat burn. Add salt and pepper, cover and cook over a low heat for 15 minutes.

Meanwhile, separate the garlic cloves, making sure you do not remove the shiny, pink skin. Do not use any cloves with a broken skin because the garlic must cook in its covering; this is very important for the subtle flavour of the dish. When the chicken pieces have cooked for 15 minutes, stir in the garlic cloves and replace the lid. Continue cooking over a low heat for a further 20 minutes or until the chicken is tender.

Transfer the chicken pieces and garlic cloves to a heated serving dish and sprinkle with the chopped parsley. Guests peel the garlic cloves on their plates by pressing them with a fork. The garlic will have reduced to a purée, which, together with the parsley, provides a subtle flavour.

Red wines: Crozes-Hermitage, Saint-Joseph, Côtes du Rhône, Coteaux du Tricastin, Côtes de Provence, Coteaux du Languedoc, Minervois.

POULET SAUTÉ AUX MORILLES

— SAUTÉED CHICKEN WITH MORELS —

Preparation 50 minutes • Cooking 40 minutes

US	Ingredients	Met/Imp
2, each about 2 lb	chickens, preferably free-range or corn-fed	2, each about 1 kg/2 lb
	salt and pepper	
½ lb (2 sticks)	butter	250 g/8 oz
1 lb	fresh morels	500 g/1 lb
	white wine	
½ cup	Veal Juice (page 56)	100 ml/4 fl oz
1 lb	potatoes cut into julienne, as for Darphin Potato Cake (page 549)	500 g/1 lb
1 tbsp	chopped fresh parsley	15 ml/1 tbsp

Cut the chickens into serving pieces. Season them with salt and pepper. Melt some butter in a saucepan, add the morels, cover and sweat until soft.

Melt some more butter in another saucepan, add the chicken pieces and sauté for 10 minutes or until browned. Add the drained morels. Deglaze with some white wine, then add the veal juice. Cover and cook for 30–35 minutes or until the chicken is tender.

Meanwhile, melt the remaining butter in a fairly large frying pan, add the potato julienne and sauté for about 10 minutes or until the potatoes form a golden-brown cake (known as a 'paillasson'). Turn the cake and sauté the other side until brown.

When the potato cake is cooked, slide it on to a heated round serving dish and put the chicken pieces and morels on top. Sprinkle with chopped parsley. Serve the cooking liquid on the side.

Red or white wines from the Jura: Arbois, Côtes du Jura, l'Étoile.

POULET SAUTÉ À LA NANTAISE

—— SAUTÉED CHICKEN NANTAISE ——

Preparation 1 hour • Cooking 30 minutes

US	Ingredients	Met/Imp
2, each about 2 lb	young chickens	2, each about 1 kg/2 lb
2	onions	2
2	carrots	2
1	bouquet garni	1
	salt and pepper	
14 tbsp	butter	200 g/7 oz
1 cup	Muscadet white wine	200 ml/7 fl oz
¼ cup	white wine vinegar	50 ml/2 fl oz
6	shallots	6
5 oz	mushrooms, quartered	150 g/5 oz
24	small onions	24
½ lb	carrots	250 g/8 oz
6	artichoke bottoms	6
½ cup	crème fraîche	100 ml/4 fl oz
1 tsp	paprika	5 ml/1 tsp
2 tbsp	Tomato Sauce (page 80)	30 ml/2 tbsp

Cut the 2 chickens into serving pieces. Put the thinly sliced onions and carrots in a flameproof casserole with the bouquet garni, plenty of seasoning, some butter and the pieces of chicken.

Cook for a few minutes over a moderate heat, then add the Muscadet and the white wine vinegar and continue cooking for 30 minutes. Transfer the pieces of chicken to a round serving dish. With the cooking liquid and the chopped shallots, make a very strong, vinegary reduction. Add to this reduction, as a garnish, the mushroom quarters, the small onions, the carrots cut into garlic-clove shapes and the diced artichoke bottoms, all of them blanched. Add the crème fraîche.

Adjust the seasoning; sprinkle in the paprika and a little tomato sauce, in order to give the sauce a reddish tinge, then coat the chicken with this sauce and the garnishes contained in it.

White wines: Muscadet, Gros Plant du Pays Nantais, Pouilly-Fumé, Chablis.

US	Ingredients	Met/Imp
I	medium chicken, including the giblets	I
	salt and pepper	
¼ cup	olive oil	50 ml/2 fl oz
¼ lb	onion	100 g/4 oz
I	large sweet pepper, cored, seeded and cut into strips	I
1¾ cups	water or chicken stock	400 ml/14 fl oz
3	garlic cloves	3
1½ cups	rice, preferably untreated Madagascar	250 g/8 oz
I bouquet	oregano sprigs	I bouquet
I pinch	ground saffron	I pinch
I pinch	saffron threads	I pinch
I pinch	cayenne	I pinch
½ cup	olives from Nice	100 g/4 oz
I large pinch	sugar	I large pinch
3	ripe tomatoes	3
4 tsp	butter	20 g/¾ oz
	fresh basil or parsley	

SAUTÉED CHICKEN WITH RICE PROVENÇAL

Preparation 1¼ hours • Cooking 45 minutes

Recipe by Raymond Oliver, le Grand Véfour

Cut the chicken into serving pieces. Break the legs into 2 pieces each (drumsticks and thighs). Remove and reserve the lobes of meat from the gizzard and throw away the remainder. Cut the liver, gizzard meat and heart into small pieces and set aside.

Sprinkle the chicken pieces with salt. Heat the olive oil in a large sauté pan, preferably made of thick copper, and sauté the chicken pieces for about 15 minutes or until brown, turning them over frequently. Remove the pieces from the pan, cover them and keep them warm. Add the pieces of liver, gizzard and heart to the oil in the pan and sauté for about 30 seconds or until just sealed. Push to one side of the pan.

Add the chopped onion and the strips of pepper and cook over a moderate heat for 5–10 minutes or until lightly coloured, turning frequently with a wooden spoon. Add salt, if water is to be used instead of stock. Add the chopped garlic and the rice and continue cooking, until the rice becomes milky, stirring from time to time. Add the oregano (rolling the bouquet between your hands so that the flowers and leaves drop into the rice), the 2 types of saffron and the cayenne. Stir to mix everything well together and add the well-rinsed olives and the boiling water or stock.

Stir once, put the pieces of chicken and sautéed giblets on top, remembering to add all the juice they have produced, cover with a tight-fitting lid and adjust the heat so that the liquid is only just simmering. (Insert a heat diffusing mat beneath the pan, if necessary.) Cook for 15–20 minutes or until the rice has absorbed all the liquid.

Meanwhile, add salt, pepper and sugar to the skinned, de-seeded and crushed tomatoes and sweat them in the butter for 15–20 minutes. Pour the tomatoes over the chicken and rice in the pan so that they cover the entire surface and their liquid is evenly distributed. Do this without touching the rice. Cover the pan again with the lid and continue cooking for a further 15 minutes.

Sprinkle the surface with chopped basil or parsley and leave to stand, with the lid on, for another 6–7 minutes. Serve straight from the pan on to heated plates.

VARIATIONS
Small artichoke bottoms, which have been sweated in butter, may be added at the same time as the olives.

If this dish is served on a large dish, it may be garnished with slices of aubergine (eggplant) fried in olive oil, or slices of courgette (zucchini) sautéed for 8–10 minutes in olive oil, or both these garnishes together.

Wines: Cassis, red or white Coteaux d'Aix-en-Provence.

– SAUTÉED CHICKEN WITH TOMATOES –

Preparation 1 hour • Cooking 30 minutes

US	Ingredients	Met/Imp
2, each about 2–2½ lb	young chickens, preferably free range or corn-fed	2, each about 1–1.1 kg/ 2–2½ lb
2½ sticks	butter	300 g/10 oz
½ cup	oil	100 ml/4 fl oz
½ cup	cognac	100 ml/4 fl oz
½ cup	very dry white wine	100 ml/4 fl oz
5½ lb	tomatoes	2.5 kg/5½ lb
	salt and pepper	
1	garlic clove	1
1 tbsp	chopped fresh parsley	15 ml/1 tbsp
16	heart-shaped croûtons, fried in butter	16

Choose some chickens from Bresse, if possible, and cut each one into 7 pieces.

Heat one-third of the butter with the oil in a large sauté pan (preferably made of copper). Add the chicken pieces and arrange in a single layer on the bottom of the pan. Sauté for 10–15 minutes or until they are pale yellow, turning once.

Pour the cognac and the white wine on to the pieces of chicken and add the skinned, de-seeded and crushed tomatoes. Add salt and pepper, cover and cook for about 20 minutes or until the chicken is tender. Remove the chicken pieces from the pan and arrange in a shallow serving dish. Keep them warm.

Cook the tomato sauce over a high heat until reduced to the required consistency. Meanwhile, chop the garlic with a nut of butter. Remove the pan from the heat and stir in the remaining butter, the garlic and chopped parsley. Stir well to combine, adjust the seasoning, if necessary, and pour over the chicken. Serve with the fried bread croûtons.

Red wines: Côte Rôtie, Côtes du Rhône, Châteauneuf-du-Pape.

— SAUTÉED CHICKEN TOURANGELLE —

Preparation 50 minutes • Cooking 30 minutes

US	Ingredients	Met/Imp
2, each about 2 lb	chickens, preferably free-range or corn-fed	2, each about 1 kg/2 lb
2½ sticks	butter	300 g/10 oz
4	shallots	4
½ cup	cognac	100 ml/3½ fl oz
½ cup	white port wine	100 ml/3½ fl oz
2 cups	crème fraîche	400 ml/14 fl oz
4	egg yolks	4
	salt	

Cut the chickens into serving pieces.

Melt one-third of the butter in a large sauté pan, add the chicken pieces and arrange them carefully in the bottom of the pan. Sauté them for 15 minutes, turning them frequently to prevent them going brown. Add the finely chopped shallots and turn them in the pan so that they heat up quickly. Continue cooking for a further 15 minutes or until the chicken is tender.

When they are cooked, remove the pieces of chicken from the pan and arrange in a round serving dish. Keep them warm. Deglaze the pan with the cognac and flambé. Add the port and cook until reduced.

Beat the crème fraîche, egg yolks and some salt together in a small bowl. Pour into the pan and whisk over a low heat. As soon as it begins to boil, remove from the heat and strain through a very fine, conical sieve. Add the remaining butter and pour on to the pieces of chicken. Serve at once.

Red wines: Chinon, Bourgueil.
White wine: Vouvray.

US	Ingredients	Met/Imp

SAUTÉED CHICKEN 'WINEGROWER STYLE' TOURANGELLE

Preparation 1 hour • Cooking 30 minutes

US	Ingredients	Met/Imp
2, each about 2 lb	chickens, preferably free-range or corn-fed	2, each about 1 kg/2 lb
10 tbsp	butter	150 g/5 oz
30	small onions	30
4	very small leeks, white part only	4
½ lb	fresh fat belly (side) of pork	250 g/8 oz
5 oz	Paris mushrooms	150 g/5 oz
4	tomatoes	4
1 bottle	Vouvray wine	1 bottle
	crème fraîche	
	salt and pepper	
1 tbsp	persillade	15 ml/1 tbsp

Cut the chickens into quarters.

Melt half of the butter in a flameproof casserole and add the onions, a *julienne* of leeks, the finely diced pork, mushroom caps and the skinned, de-seeded and crushed tomatoes. Fry for about 10 minutes or until lightly coloured, then moisten with the bottle of Vouvray wine and a few spoonfuls of crème fraîche. Add salt and pepper.

Sauté the chicken quarters in the remaining butter until lightly coloured, then simmer them with the vegetable and cream mixture until tender. Adjust the liaison, if need be, with some crème fraîche.

Just before serving, sprinkle with the persillade. Serve very hot.

Dry white wines: dry Vouvray, dry Montlouis, Saumur, Quincy, Sancerre.

SAUTÉED CHICKEN WITH WHITE WINE

Preparation 1 hour • Cooking 30 minutes

US	Ingredients	Met/Imp
2, each about 2–2½ lb	young chickens, preferably free-range or corn-fed	2, each about 1–1.1 kg/ 2–2½ lb
2½ sticks	butter	300 g/10 oz
scant ½ cup	oil	100 ml/3½ fl oz
2	shallots	2
2 cups	white Bordeaux wine	500 ml/18 fl oz
2 tbsp	tomato paste	30 ml/2 tbsp
	salt and pepper	
1 lb	potatoes cut into *julienne*, as for Darphin Potato Cake (*page 549*)	500 g/1 lb

Cut the chickens into serving pieces.

Heat one-third of the butter and the oil in a sauté pan, add the chicken pieces and sauté for 10 minutes or until golden brown. Add the very finely chopped shallots and cook for 1 minute or until brown. Moisten with white Bordeaux wine, add the tomato paste and salt and pepper. Cover and cook over a low heat for 30 minutes or until the chicken is tender.

Meanwhile, melt the remaining butter in a fairly large frying pan, add the potato julienne and sauté for about 10 minutes or until the potatoes form a golden-brown cake (known as a 'paillasson'). Turn the cake and sauté the other side until brown. When the potato cake is cooked, slide it on to a heated round serving dish and put the chicken on top. Pour on plenty of sauce and serve very hot.

Wines: Médoc, red or white Graves, red or white Côte de Beaune, white Arbois, Bourgueil, Chinon.

CHICKEN 'VALLÉE D'AUGE'

Preparation 50 minutes • Cooking 35 minutes

US	Ingredients	Met/Imp
2 each about 2–2½ lb	young chickens, preferably free-range or corn-fed	2, each about 1–1.1 kg/ 2–2½ lb
	salt and pepper	
10 tbsp	butter	150 g/5 oz
scant ½ cup	vieux calvados	100 ml/3½ fl oz
2 cups	crème fraîche from Isigny	500 ml/18 fl oz

Choose plump, white chickens. Draw and truss them, then season with salt and pepper.

Cook the chickens until golden in pale-coloured Normandy butter. When they are cooked, flambé the chickens with the vieux calvados.

Deglaze with crème fraîche, then sauté for a few minutes. Remove the chickens from the pan, cut them into pieces and arrange on a heated serving dish.

Adjust the seasoning of the sauce, coat the chicken with it and serve.

Sweet or medium dry white wines: Sauternes, Barsac, Alsace Gewürztraminer, Vouvray.
Dry or medium dry cider.

SUPRÊMES DE VOLAILLE AUX POINTES D'ASPERGES

POULTRY SUPRÊMES WITH ASPARAGUS TIPS

Preparation 1½ hours • Cooking 15 minutes

US	Ingredients	Met/Imp
4	medium chickens	4
	or	
8	'suprêmes'	8
½ lb (2 sticks)	butter	250 g/8 oz
10	asparagus stems	10
1¼ lb	asparagus tips	600 g/1¼ lb
	salt and pepper	

This dish may seem extravagant, but remember that the remainder of the chickens need not be wasted and may be used in a variety of ways.

The word 'suprême' refers to the most delicate portions of chicken meat, including the fillets and the 'filets mignons', ie all the white meat or, more simply, the breast meat. Sometimes their preparation includes being larded with truffles: a very simple operation which involves making small cuts in the meat into which thin slices of truffle are inserted.

Take some young chickens, each weighing about 1 kg/2 lb after being drawn. Remove the wing tips. Detach the skin from the breast and make a cut down between the meat and the breast bone on each side of the chicken. Put the knife into the wing joints and lift out the fillets in 1 piece, including the extra pieces of meat from underneath each breast (the 'filets mignons').

Put these fillets, or 'suprêmes' in a buttered ovenproof dish and cover with a piece of buttered paper. Keep them cool, if they are not to be used immediately.

About 15 minutes before serving, trim the asparagus stems to about 4 cm/1½ inches long and tie them in a bunch. Cook them with the asparagus tips in boiling salted water for about 10 minutes or until cooked but still a little firm. Drain them thoroughly and set aside the stems. Put the tips in a clean pan and sauté over a high heat to evaporate the moisture. Add salt and pepper and, while they are frying, mix in 75 g/3 oz (6 tbsp) butter in small pieces. (Note that this must not be done until the last minute.)

While the asparagus is boiling, about 10 minutes before serving, season the suprêmes with salt and sprinkle them with 5–6 spoonfuls of melted butter. Cover with a tight-fitting lid and cook in a very hot oven for 8 minutes.

Transfer the cooked suprêmes to a heated round serving dish and arrange the asparagus tips in the centre. Garnish with the bunch of asparagus stems. Serve immediately.

Dry white wines: Pouilly-Fumé, Montrachet, Meursault.

US	Ingredients	Met/Imp
1¼ lb	chicken livers	600 g/1¼ lb
I large handful	fresh breadcrumbs	I large handful
	milk	
1¼ lb	boneless pork chine or spare rib (blade)	600 g/1¼ lb
10 oz	boneless veal, cut from top of leg	300 g/10 oz
6 tbsp	butter	75 g/3 oz
2	shallots	2
I	garlic clove	I
½ glass	cognac	½ glass
I	egg	I
¼ cup	thick cream	50 ml/2 fl oz
	chopped fresh thyme	
	chopped fresh rosemary	
I pinch	quatre-épices	I pinch
5½ tsp	salt and pepper	30 g/l oz
¼ lb	cooked ham	100 g/4 oz
10 oz	fatty bacon slices	300 g/10 oz
I	bay leaf	I

CHICKEN LIVER TERRINE

Preparation 1 hour • Start 24 hours in advance • Cooking 2 hours

Remove the sinews from the chicken livers and set the livers aside. Put the breadcrumbs in a small bowl, add a little milk and leave to soak.

Cut the pork and veal into pieces and put them through the large blade of a mincer (meat grinder), then put them through the mincer (grinder) once more, using the small blade this time. Put half of the chicken livers through the fine blade also.

Melt a nut of butter in a frying pan and fry the chopped shallots and garlic until golden. Add them to the minced (ground) meats.

Add the remaining livers to the same frying pan and fry for 3–4 minutes or until sealed. Remove the livers from the pan and set aside. Deglaze the pan with the cognac and reserve the juices.

Add the squeezed breadcrumbs, beaten egg, cream, thyme, rosemary, spices, salt and pepper to the minced (ground) meats. Grind everything in a mortar and pestle until a thick purée is obtained. Add the diced ham and the juices from the frying pan.

Cut the bacon into strips 5 cm/2 inches wide and use some to cover the bottom and sides of a terrine. Fill the bottom of the terrine with half of the meat mixture and push the fried whole livers into it. Add the remaining mixture and press down well into the terrine. Smooth the surface, cover with the remaining bacon and put the bay leaf on top.

Put the lid on the terrine and stand the terrine in a larger baking dish or roasting tin. Pour in enough boiling water to come halfway up the sides of the terrine. Cook in a hot oven for about 1¾ hours.

When the terrine is cooked, leave it to cool slightly to allow the fat on the surface to solidify a little, then place a board wrapped in foil on top. Put a 2 kg/4½ lb weight on the board and leave in a cool place for 24 hours. The terrine may be kept in the refrigerator for 1 week.

Dry white wines: Meursault, Pouilly-Fuissé.
Light red wines: Saint-Amour, Chiroubles, Bourgueil, Chinon.

US	Ingredients	Met/Imp
2, each about 2½ lb	young chickens, preferably free-range or corn-fed	2, each about 1.1 kg/2½ lb
14 tbsp	butter	200 g/7 oz
½ cup	flour	75 g/3 oz
40	small onions	40
I quart	consommé	I litre/1¾ pints
I	bouquet garni	I
	salt and pepper	
2 cups	crème fraîche	500 ml/18 fl oz
4	egg yolks	4
½	lemon, juice of	½
I	Vol-au-Vent Case (page 91)	I

CHICKEN VOL-AU-VENT

Preparation 50 minutes • Cooking 40 minutes

Cut the chickens into small pieces, removing all skin and bones. Melt the butter in a saucepan and stir in the flour. Add the chicken pieces and cook for 15 minutes, turning frequently.

Meanwhile, blanch the small onions in boiling water and drain. Pour the consommé into the chicken and add the bouquet garni and onions. Add salt and pepper, cover and simmer for about 25 minutes or until cooked. Beat together the crème fraîche, egg yolks and a trickle of lemon juice and add to the chicken mixture. Heat gently until thickened. Pour into the vol-au-vent case and serve immediately.

Red wines: Côte de Beaune.

Pigeons Crapaudine
Split open and flattened, the young pigeon is first coated in butter, then covered in breadcrumbs and cooked under the grill (broiler). It is served with a 'relish' of cooking juices enhanced with lemon juice and parsley, and a green salad. (Recipe on page 304.)

Saddle of Rabbit with Tarragon
Tarragon is a very fine and delicate herb, but its flavour is distinctive nevertheless. It is used in numerous dishes ranging from eggs to eels, and rabbit, too, benefits from its aroma. In this recipe it is combined with garlic and shallots, and enhanced with the addition of cognac and white wine. It must be cooked slowly so that the meat can absorb the flavours. (Recipe on page 295.)

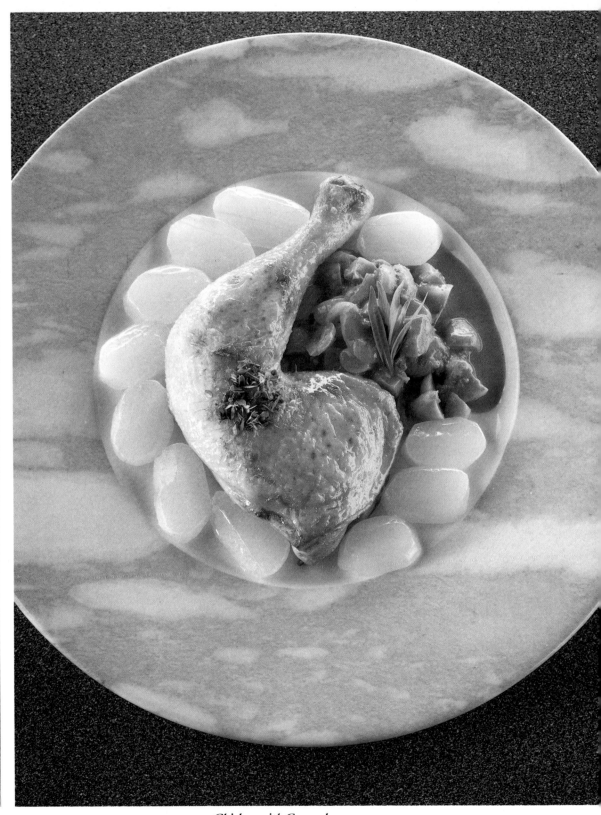

Chicken with Cucumber
After gentle braising with tomatoes and onions, chicken pieces are served garnished with mushrooms and pieces of cucumber trimmed into olive shapes. A sprinkling of fresh thyme completes the picture. (Recipe on page 315.)

Chicken Meurette
'Meurette' is a red-wine-based sauce from Burgundy, traditionally served with fish
'en matelote', but chicken may also be prepared in the same way. (Recipe on page 340.)

Devilled Grilled Chicken
Split open, flattened and well buttered, chicken is first cooked in the oven, then coated with mustard and breadcrumbs and finished off under the grill (broiler). The devil sauce which is served with it, based on white wine and vinegar, should be highly seasoned with pepper and shallots. Noisette and gaufrette potatoes make good accompaniments. (Recipe on page 340.)

Chicken Chaud-Froid with Tarragon
A characteristic way of preparing food for the cold buffet table, a chaud-froid is time consuming and requires particular attention to small detail. It can also be served a first course: chicken, white sauce and tarragon are its basic ingredients.
(Recipe on page 330.)

MEAT

FRESH BUTCHER'S MEAT – LAMB AND mutton, beef, veal, pork and offal (variety meat) – plays a fundamental role in the history of gastronomy. Cooks have always striven ingeniously to use every part of an animal; parts as different in taste and appearance as, say, calf's liver and leg of lamb, tournedos and *andouillette*, knuckle (shank) of veal and rib roast. For this reason, it is essential to know how to buy fresh meat, and how to distinguish one type from another. Above all, it is important not to confuse the 'category' of meat with the quality. The quality means the degree of excellence of the meat, and depends on the age and species of the animal, and the way in which it is fed. The 'category' denotes the way in which a particular cut is cooked. In the case of beef, veal and mutton, the 'first category' consists of cuts for roasting, frying or grilling (broiling); these are basically taken from the rear of the animal, and are nowadays the most expensive cuts. The 'second category' consists of cuts for braising or stewing (*ragoûts*, *daubes*, etc), which are usually taken from the forelegs and just behind. 'Third category' cuts are for lengthy boiling and braising and include neck, knuckle (shank), breast, tail, etc. Remember that a 'third category' cut of stewing beef can come from an animal of excellent quality, while a 'first category' fillet (tenderloin) of beef can come from an animal of mediocre quality.

Meat has a high nutritional value, being rich in body-building protein, and has traditionally been held to be the central ingredient of a well-balanced meal. However, because of its fat and cholesterol content, nutritionists warn against excessive meat consumption: 150–200 g/5–7 oz a day are considered ample for the needs of a normal, active adult. Nutritionists also advise alternating meat with fish, fowl or eggs as often as possible in order to achieve a properly balanced diet, both from a gastronomic and health point of view. Furthermore, contrary to popular belief, so-called white meats, such as veal, pork, rabbit and chicken, have more or less the same nutritional value as red meats, such as mutton, lamb and beef. A distinction is normally made between lean meats – veal and the offal (variety meats) of beef – semi-lean meats – certain cuts of beef and mutton – and fatty meats – beef, lamb and pork.

Remember that in order to attain optimum quality, meat should be hung in a cool place for two or three days after the animal has been slaughtered. There are different criteria for judging a good piece of meat in the butcher's. The most immediate indication is the colour, and this is linked with the diet, age and health of the animal. Beef and lamb should be bright red and veal and pork should be pink. Then there is the degrees of tenderness, that is the ease with which the meat can be cut or chewed, and the degree of succulence (or juiciness): a good meat gives out juice when chewed. Finally, there is the flavour and this depends on there being the right proportion of fat in the muscle fibres.

*Editor's note: in France, meat is butchered differently from in the UK and the US, therefore cuts of meat given in the recipes in this chapter are not English translations of French cuts but the nearest British and American equivalents. For further information on French, British and American cuts of meat, see pages 24–25.

AGNEAU ET MOUTON

LAMB AND MUTTON

LAMB, WHICH HAS LONG BEEN THE TRADITIONAL Easter dish, is the most widely cooked form of sheep's meat. A distinction is usually made between the three ages of lamb: 'agnelet' (baby or milk-fed lamb) comes from animals thirty to forty days old and has a tender and delicate but somewhat bland flavour. 'Laiton' or 'agneau blanc', available between Christmas and June, is a deep pink colour with markedly white fat; it is very tender when cooked. 'Agneau gris' or 'grey lamb' from older and larger animals, is firmer, and has a more marked flavour; it is much sought after by connoisseurs, and is often used in place of true mutton. French salt-meadow lamb from Pauillac or Mont-Saint-Michel is renowned for its quality, as is lamb from Limousin and Vienne. Lamb is cut up in the same way as mutton, and is mainly used for roasting. Grilled (broiled) cutlets or chops, leg steaks and best end of neck (rack) of lamb all provide succulent dishes, which are usually garnished with spring vegetables or with a *jardinière* of mixed vegetables.

Mutton is fattier than beef. It should be firm, dense, and dark red in colour with pearly white fat. The best time for mutton is late winter and spring, and the choicest type comes mainly from Pauillac, Sisteron or Bellac.

Lamb and mutton cuts:

Cuts for roasting are taken from the 'gigot' or hind leg, and can either be the whole leg, or the leg cut into two separate pieces – the fillet (sirloin) and the knuckle (shank) end; from the loin or saddle; and from the ribs and shoulder, boned or otherwise. The 'baron' (the saddle and both legs), is also a choice cut. The leg can also be boiled 'à l'anglaise' and served with mint sauce.

Cutlets and chops for grilling (broiling) come from the best end (rib), the middle neck (shoulder blade and arm), the chump (sirloin), the loin and the fillet end of the leg – called 'gigot chops' (US leg steaks). Lamb brochettes for grilling (broiling) come from pieces of shoulder, breast and neck. These cuts can also be **braised**, used for **sautés** or **boiled**. Mutton ragoût, Irish stew, 'navarin' and 'haricot de mouton' (mutton with beans), figure among the great classic recipes of French cuisine. As far as **sheep's and lamb's offal** (variety meats) are concerned, brains, kidneys, tongue and trotters (feet) are the most sought after.

US	Ingredients	Met/Imp
1, about 4 lb	baron of lamb	1, about 2 kg/4 lb
	salt	
14 tbsp	butter	200 g/7 oz
	GARNISH (optional)	
1 lb	cherry tomatoes	500 g/1 lb
4	truffles	4
	spinach *pain*	

— ROAST BARON OF MILK-FED LAMB —

Preparation 2 hours • Cooking about 40 minutes

The cut known as 'baron', consists of the 2 legs and the saddle in 1 piece. In milk-fed lamb, the baron is not very large.

Place the lamb on a rack in a roasting pan, season lightly with salt and brush copiously with melted butter. For this very tender, white meat, the heat of the oven should be moderate. Brush with more butter from time to time during the course of cooking, but do not add any other liquid. Allow 20 minutes per 1 kg/2 lb.

Garnish with grilled (broiled) tomatoes, whole truffles, spinach *pain*, or a garnish of your choice.

Red wines: Saint-Émilion, Saumur-Champigny, Bourgueil, Côte de Beaune, Beaujolais-Villages, Châteauneuf-du-Pape.

US	Ingredients	Met/Imp
4 lb	lambs' sweetbreads	2 kg/4 lb
	salt and pepper	
	raw white meat scraps	
10 tbsp	butter	150 g/5 oz
1 cup	*mirepoix*	200 g/7 oz
	sage, savory and rosemary sprigs	
scant 1 cup	dry white wine	200 ml/7 fl oz
2 cups	Demi-Glaze (*page 56*)	500 ml/18 fl oz
1 lb	mushrooms	500 g/1 lb
1 lb (2½ cups)	green olives	500 g/1 lb

— GOOD PRINCE 'CUR'S' CASSOLETTE —

Preparation 1 hour • Cooking 25 minutes

Soak the sweetbreads in salt water, then blanch them well; drain and trim thoroughly. Brown the trimmings and a few scraps of raw white meat in some butter, together with the mirepoix; add the herbs, then moisten with wine and demi-glaze. After cooking, strain through a conical sieve.

Cook the sweetbreads in butter in a flameproof dish and season with salt and pepper. Cover with a piece of buttered paper during cooking and baste the sweetbreads frequently with their cooking juices. When well-browned, deglaze with wine until almost completely reduced. Add the prepared stock, the mushrooms sweated in butter, and the stoned, blanched olives. Add butter to the sauce, which should be very thick and rich.

White wines: Graves, Chablis, Arbois, Alsace Riesling.
Rosé wine: Tavel.
Red wine: Bourgeuil.

MUTTON CASSOULET

Preparation 1½ hours • (Beans to be soaked the day before) • Cooking 2½ hours

US	Ingredients	Met/Imp
2 lb (5 cups)	dried white haricot beans (navy or Great Northern beans)	1 kg/2 lb
	salt and pepper	
2	carrots	2
3	large onions	3
1	clove	1
2	bouquets garnis	2
10 oz	very lean fresh belly (side) of pork	300 g/10 oz
5 oz	pork rind	150 g/5 oz
3	garlic cloves	3
2½ lb	mutton, two-thirds boned shoulder and one-third breast	1.25 kg/2½ lb
¼ cup	lard	60 ml/4 tbsp
2 tbsp	tomato paste	30 ml/2 tbsp
1, about 14 oz	raw garlic sausage	1, about 400 g/14 oz
8 cups	fresh white breadcrumbs	500 g/1 lb
scant 1 cup	goose or pork fat	200 g/7 oz

True cassoulet contains no mutton; it is made with beans, and locally made sausage. Stuffed goose necks or 'confit d'oie' (preserved goose) may also be added. The secret of a successful cassoulet lies in the final browning, during which the skin that forms on the surface should be pushed down into the middle several times.

Soak the beans in cold water for at least 6 hours. Drain, place in a saucepan and cover with plenty of cold water. Bring to the boil and add 7.5 ml/1½ tsp salt per 1 litre/1¾ pints (1 quart) water. Add the quartered carrots, 1 onion spiked with the clove and 1 bouquet garni and simmer gently for about 30 minutes or until the beans are about three-quarters cooked.

Meanwhile, cut the pork into large cubes and the pork rind into 2 cm/¾ inch squares. Blanch and set aside. Chop the remaining onions and crush 2 of the garlic cloves.

Season the mutton cut into 100 g/4 oz pieces with salt and pepper and place in a heavy sauté pan containing the smoking lard. Brown quickly on all sides. Using the lid to help you, tip the pan and drain away the fat. Add the onion and fry for a few moments more, then pour over some warm water or light stock, add the tomato paste (in the appropriate season, you can also add a few skinned and chopped tomatoes), the pork and pork rind, crushed garlic and remaining bouquet garni and boil gently for 1 hour. Add the well-drained beans and the garlic sausage. Cover with a piece of buttered paper, then seal hermetically and cook slowly in the oven for 1 further hour, removing the sausage after 40 minutes.

Rub the inside of 1 large earthenware dish (or 2 smaller ones) with a peeled clove of garlic, then pour in the cassoulet, taking care that the pieces of mutton are underneath the beans. Arrange slices of sausage over the surface.

Sprinkle with the breadcrumbs, dot with goose or pork fat and brown in a moderate oven, allowing the cassoulet to simmer.

Red wines: Bourgueil, Chinon, Madiran, Cornas.

US	Ingredients	Met/Imp
2 cups	Forcemeat Stuffing (page 54)	500 g/1 lb
2 cups	crème fraîche	500 ml/18 fl oz
2 lb	very white mushrooms for the purée	1 kg/2 lb
1	lemon, juice of	1
16	small lamb cutlets (rib chops)	16
	salt and pepper	
2 sticks	butter	250 g/8 oz

CUTLETS OF MILK-FED LAMB MONTROUGE

Preparation 1½ hours • Cooking 15 minutes

As these lamb cutlets are very small, allow 2 per person as a general rule.

Prepare in advance:

1 The forcemeat stuffing, adding the crème fraîche.

2 A mushroom purée, adding the lemon juice.

Trim the cutlets, flatten them slightly and season with salt and white pepper. Fry in butter for a few minutes only on each side. Wipe the cutlets with paper towels. Spread 1 side of each cutlet with forcemeat and smooth to form a slight dome. Arrange the cutlets in a buttered ovenproof dish.

Eight or 10 minutes before serving, put the cutlets at the front of the oven, to finish their cooking, and also that of the stuffing. Arrange them in a crown on a heated round serving dish, and pour the mushroom purée in the centre.

Alternatively, sauté the cutlets on 1 side only, spread the cooked side with the stuffing, then sauté the other side, basting with the cooking butter. A few minutes before they are ready, sprinkle them evenly with fresh breadcrumbs to give them a good colour. In this way, the cutlets and stuffing will finish cooking together. You could also serve the cutlets without any stuffing at all; simply baste with the cooking butter and place a handful of fried parsley in the centre. The mushroom purée should then be served separately in a bowl or sauceboat.

Red wines: Saint-Émilion, Pomerol, Graves, Médoc.

US	Ingredients	Met/Imp
8, each about 3½ oz	lamb loin chops	8, each about 90 g/3½ oz
1 lb	lean boneless veal fillet or topside (sirloin or rump)	500 g/1 lb
1 lb	pork fillet (tenderloin)	500 g/1 lb
2	egg yolks	2
1	lemon, juice of	1
14 oz	pig's caul	400 g/14 oz
2 cups	dry white wine	500 ml/18 fl oz
	salt and pepper	
1	thyme sprig	1
1 pinch	nutmeg	1 pinch
5 tbsp	butter	60 g/2½ oz
14 oz	sliced truffles	400 g/14 oz

LAMB CHOPS 'PÈRE LAURENT'

Preparation 1½ hours • (Marinating overnight) • Cooking 2 hours

Trim the chops of all excess fat so that just the meat and the bone remain. Pound the veal and pork very fine; add the egg yolks and the lemon juice.

Place a little of this stuffing on each of the chops, so as to double their thickness. Wrap them in the caul, then marinate overnight according to personal taste with white wine, salt and pepper, aromatics, etc.

The next day, remove the chops from the marinade and brown them well in the butter. Cover with the marinade, adding a little water if necessary, and cook gently for about 2 hours. Skim off the fat, add plenty of truffles and serve very hot.

Red wines: Saint-Émilion, Pomerol, Graves, Médoc, Bourgueil, Côte de Beaune.

MUTTON CRÉPINETTES

Preparation 1½ hours • Cooking 1 hour

US	Ingredients	Met/Imp
2 lb	breast of mutton, boned and trimmed of fat	900 g/2 lb
4	parsley sprigs	4
5–6	garlic cloves	5–6
1 tsp	ground cinnamon	5 ml/1 tsp
1 pinch	salt	1 pinch
	cayenne pepper	
1	pig's caul	1
2	onions	2
2	very ripe tomatoes	2
1	sweet pepper	1
2 tbsp	olive oil	30 ml/2 tbsp
1	bay leaf	1
2	thyme sprigs	2
1 cup	hot stock	200 ml/7 fl oz

Cut the meat into pieces and work in a mincer (grinder). Mix together the meat, washed and finely chopped parsley, the crushed garlic, cinnamon, salt and cayenne pepper.

Form this mixture into 6 balls of equal size and flatten them with the palm of the hand. Rinse the caul in cold water and dry it with a clean cloth. Smooth it out and cut it into 6 squares; wrap a portion of lamb in each square.

Peel and slice the onions. Scald the tomatoes, then skin and quarter them. Wash the sweet pepper and cut out the stalk, cut in half and remove the seeds, then chop the flesh.

Heat the oil in a sauté pan and fry the crépinettes quickly on both sides. Add the onions, bay leaf, thyme and sweet pepper. Turn the heat down and fry for 15–20 minutes, keeping an eye on the progress of the cooking. Next, add the tomatoes and 50 ml/2 fl oz (¼ cup) of the hot stock and season lightly with salt. Bring to the boil again, cover the pan, turn down the heat and cook for a further 40 minutes. Crush the tomatoes with a fork during the course of cooking and add more hot stock, as the cooking juices will tend to reduce. When cooking is complete, check the consistency of the cooking juices and thin them with the remaining hot stock if necessary. Remove the thyme and bay from the cooking juices and arrange the crépinettes in a heated deep dish. Spoon over the puréed vegetables and pour the strained cooking juices around them.

Red wines: Bergerac, Côtes du Frontonnais, Côtes d'Auvergne, Madiran.

SHOULDER OF MUTTON BOULANGÈRE

Preparation 30 minutes • Cooking 1 hour 5 minutes

US	Ingredients	Met/Imp
1	shoulder of mutton	1
	salt and pepper	
10 tbsp	butter	150 g/5 oz
3½ lb	potatoes	1.5 kg/3½ lb
2	large onions	2
1 tbsp	chopped parsley	15 ml/1 tbsp

Place the boned, rolled and seasoned shoulder of mutton in an earthenware dish. Cook in butter in a moderately hot oven for 25 minutes.

Slice the potatoes very thinly. Slice the onions and fry lightly in butter. Arrange the potatoes and onions around the mutton. Season with more salt and pepper, pour over the onion cooking butter and cook in a slow oven for 40 minutes.

Sprinkle the potatoes with chopped parsley and serve straight from the dish.

Red wines: Saint-Émilion, Bourgueil, Beaujolais-Villages, Côte de Beaune.

US	Ingredients	Met/Imp
1, about 3½ lb	boned shoulder of mutton	1, about 1.5 kg/3½ lb
1 cup	minced (ground) pork	200 g/7 oz
2	onions	2
1 stick	butter	100 g/4 oz
1 cup	fresh white breadcrumbs	50 g/2 oz
¼ cup	milk	50 ml/2 fl oz
1 tbsp	chopped parsley	15 ml/1 tbsp
1	garlic clove	1
	salt and pepper	
	quatre-épices	
1	egg	1
3	leeks, white part only	3
3	celery stalks	3
1	bouquet garni	1
1	clove	1
2	carrots	2
1 lb	celeriac	500 g/1 lb
4	large Dutch potatoes	4

SHOULDER OF MUTTON FROM BERRY

Preparation 2 hours • Cooking about 1 hour

Lay the mutton flat on a cloth and spread evenly with a stuffing mixture made with the pork mixed with 1 onion chopped and cooked in a little of the butter, then cooled, the breadcrumbs, soaked in the milk, then squeezed dry, the chopped parsley, crushed garlic, a pinch each of salt, pepper and spice and 1 egg. Roll up the shoulder so that the stuffing is well enclosed and tie securely.

If possible, choose an oval, fairly narrow casserole into which the mutton will fit snugly. Put the shoulder of mutton into it, cover well with water and add 10 ml/2 tsp salt per 1 litre/1¾ pints (1 quart). Bring to the boil and add the leek whites and the celery(all the tender parts, both white and green) tied up in a bundle, the bouquet garni, the remaining onion spiked with a clove and the quartered carrots. Cook for 1¼ hours. Arrange the celeriac cut into large pieces around the meat, and cook for a further 15 minutes, then add the large Dutch potatoes (these take less time to cook than the celeriac).

As soon as the vegetables are cooked (they should still be quite firm), lift them out with a slotted spoon and drain, including the carrots and the bundle of leeks and celery. Work through a sieve, then put this purée into a sauté pan and stir constantly over a brisk heat until very thick. Remove from the heat and finish off with the remaining butter, a pinch of salt and pepper and 5–6 spoonfuls of the mutton cooking liquid. The purée should be off the boil when the butter is added, and should be kept quite thick. Drain the mutton and untie it; arrange on a long heated dish and surround with the purée. Alternatively, carve the mutton into slices; arrange them in a crown on a round dish, and place the purée in the centre. Serve the strained cooking juices separately.

Red wines: Saint-Émilion, Pomerol, Bourgueil, Côte de Beaune.

LAMB GALANTINE

Preparation 3 hours • Cooking 4–5 hours

US	Ingredients	Met/Imp
1	small whole lamb	1
2 lb	fatty bacon	1 kg/2 lb
3½ lb	raw ham	1.5 kg/3½ lb
3½ lb (7 cups)	Forcemeat Stuffing (*page 54*), made with pork	1.5 kg/3½ lb
1 lb	truffles	500 g/1 lb
a few	lamb bones	a few
2	calf's feet	2
1	bouquet garni	1
2	carrots	2
2	onions	2
	salt and pepper	
1 pinch	quatre-épices	1 pinch
½ cup	white wine	100 ml/4 fl oz
2	thyme sprigs	2
1	lemon, juice of	1
2	egg whites	2

Bone a whole lamb and remove the meat from the legs, shoulders and loin. Cut this meat into large cubes. Cut the bacon and ham in the same way. Lay the lamb out flat on a work surface and spread it first with a layer of forcemeat stuffing, then add a layer of lamb cubes, followed by a layer of bacon, then ham, and lastly, a row of sliced truffles. Continue in this way, alternating the layers until all the ingredients are used up. Roll the lamb and wrap it up, like a galantine, in a strong cloth; tie at both ends.

Prepare a stock with the lamb bones, calf's feet, bouquet garni, the chopped carrots and onions and some salt, pepper and spice. Place the galantine in this stock and cover with water and the wine. Put it on top

of the stove to cook, preferably in a *daubière*, a braising pan, or even a *jambonnière*.

After 4–5 hours, take the galantine out of the pan and untie it. Transfer it carefully to a clean cloth and tie it up again; put it in an appropriate vessel, such as a fish kettle, and place a small board and a small weight on top, to give it an even shape.

While you have been doing this, the cooking liquid will have cooled slightly. Skim it thoroughly, add the thyme, the juice of the lemon and the egg whites; whisk juice until frothy. Mix well, then simmer for 30 minutes until reduced. Strain through a piece of cheesecloth and leave until jellied.

The galantine should be served cold, together with this aspic jelly.

Dry white wines: Graves, Chablis, Mâcon Viré, Arbois, Alsace Riesling, Cassis.
Red wines: Beaujolais-Villages, Bourgueil, Chinon.

GASCONNADE DE GIGOT AUX LÉGUMES NOUVEAUX

LEG OF LAMB GASCONNADE WITH NEW VEGETABLES

Preparation 2 hours • Cooking 40 minutes

Take a nice, meaty leg of lamb. Rub the outside with the cut garlic clove, then spread thickly with some of the butter.

Brown the finely diced belly of pork (slab bacon) in a roasting pan, add the lamb and roast in a low to moderate oven, basting often with white stock mixed with salt, sugar and butter.

Soften the chopped shallots and very finely chopped celery in a little butter in a saucepan. Cook the *turned* carrots and turnips, the button (pearl) onions and chopped lettuce hearts in butter, keeping each one separate. When this garnish is soft and browned, place it on a heated serving dish with the leg of lamb and the petits pois shortly before serving.

Deglaze the roasting pan with the madeira and reduced stock, then simmer for a few minutes.

Sprinkle with chopped parsley before serving. The lamb should be pink inside.

Red wines: Saint-Émilion, Pomerol, Bourgueil, Côte de Beaune.

US	Ingredients	Met/Imp
1, about 5½ lb	leg of lamb	1, about 2.5 kg/5½ lb
1	garlic clove	1
14 tbsp	butter	200 g/7 oz
10 oz	lightly smoked belly of pork (slab bacon)	300 g/10 oz
	White Stock (*page 56*)	
	salt	
1 pinch	sugar	1 pinch
1 egg-sized piece	butter	1 egg-sized piece
4	shallots	4
7 oz	celery	200 g/7 oz
1	bunch new carrots	1
2 lb	turnips	1 kg/2 lb
25–30	button (pearl) onions	25–30
a few	lettuce hearts	a few
1 quart	Petits Pois 'Française' (*page 543*)	1 litre/1¾ pints
½ cup	madeira	100 ml/4 fl oz
½ cup	reduced stock	100 ml/4 fl oz
2 tbsp	chopped parsley	30 ml/2 tbsp

US	Ingredients	Met/Imp
1	leg of Pauillac lamb, boned except for the knuckle (shank) bone at the end	1
14 tbsp	butter	200 g/7 oz
1½ lb	Shortcrust Pastry (page 577)	750 g/1½ lb
2 cups	finely minced (ground) fatty pork	500 g/1 lb
10 oz	fatty bacon	300 g/10 oz
7 oz	truffles	200 g/7 oz
1	bunch herbs	1
1 cup	Dry Duxelles (page 49)	250 ml/9 fl oz
¼ cup	cognac	50 ml/2 fl oz
	salt and pepper	
½ cup	madeira	100 ml/4 fl oz

LEG OF LAMB EN CHEMISE 'BERGERAC'

Preparation 2 hours • Cooking 55 minutes

Tie up the leg of lamb and roast in the butter until three-quarters cooked, but still very pink. Roll out the pastry to a large rectangle and cover the centre with a stuffing made from half of the pork, finely chopped bacon, finely diced truffles, chopped herbs, and duxelles mixed with half of the cognac. Place the leg of lamb on this stuffing and season with salt and pepper. Cover with another layer of stuffing, then fold over the edges of the pastry, so that the leg of lamb is completely enclosed.

Make an opening in the top, so that the steam can escape, and return to the oven until the pastry is golden. During cooking, pour small amounts of madeira through the hole in the top at regular intervals.

Red wines: Saint-Émilion, Pomerol, Graves, Bergerac.

US	Ingredients	Met/Imp
1, about 4½ lb	leg of salt-meadow lamb	1, about 2 kg/4½ lb
5 tbsp	butter	60 g/2½ oz
8	tomatoes	8
8	mushrooms	8
1¼ cups	Gratin Stuffing (page 54)	300 g/10 oz
16	puff pastry *fleurons*	16
	watercress sprigs	

LEG OF LAMB RICHELIEU

Preparation 1 hour • Cooking 35 minutes

Roast the lamb on a spit, basting it frequently with the butter. Carve it and put it back together again on a heated serving dish. Surround it with a Richelieu-style garnish consisting of tomatoes and mushrooms filled with gratin stuffing and grilled (broiled), the fleurons and watercress.

Red wines: Saint-Émilion, Pomerol, Côte Rôtie.

US	Ingredients	Met/Imp
1 handful	juniper berries	1 handful
1, about 5½ lb	leg of lamb, boned except for the knuckle (shank) bone at the end	1, about 2.5 kg/5½ lb
	salt	
½ cup	goose or pork fat	100 g/4 oz
a few	cubes bacon fat	a few

LEG OF LAMB WITH JUNIPER BERRIES

Preparation 2 hours • (To be prepared 3–4 days in advance) • Cooking 1½ hours

Place most of the juniper berries inside the boned part of the lamb, spreading them out evenly. Wrap up the lamb in a damp cloth and hang in a cool place with plenty of circulating air for at least 3–4 days.

Season the lamb with salt, spread with goose or pork fat and roast, preferably on a spit, basting well. Add the remaining juniper berries to the lightly salted cooking juices in the roasting pan.

The lamb must be flambéed at the last moment, and for this you will need a 'flamboir', a utensil common throughout Gascony and the Pyrenees, used to flambé wood pigeon, grouse and saddle of hare. It is a small upside-down cone with an opening at the top and a long handle. Put the bacon fat in the cone and hold over a flame. Let the blazing hot drops of fat trickle over the leg of lamb, making it sizzle under the

'shower of fire'. If you cannot get hold of a flamboir, use a strong iron ladle, heating it until red-hot before putting in the bacon fat. Serve the lamb with its brown, crispy skin, accompanied by the strained cooking juices.

Red wines: Saint-Émilion, Pomerol, Graves.

GIGOT À LA LANDAISE

————— LEG OF LAMB LANDAISE* —————

Preparation 2 hours • Cooking 50 minutes

Spike the lamb with 10 of the garlic cloves, cut into slivers, and smear thickly with a mixture of the butter and goose fat. Season with salt and pepper and roast on a spit, basting frequently. When cooked, skim the fat from the cooking juices, and deglaze with the wine and a little lemon juice. Reduce to a gravy to serve with the meat. Prepare the garnish of beans. Although served separately, it is this that gives the dish its special character. Proceed as follows:

Boil the beans in water, then drain thoroughly. Sauté them in oil in a frying pan, adding a little goose fat if necessary; stir in the ham cut into thin julienne strips. Thicken with a mixture of crème fraîche, tomato sauce, the chopped onion fried in goose fat, the remaining garlic cloves, crushed, the bouquet garni, salt, pepper, the egg yolks beaten in the cold reduced vinegar, and plenty of chopped herbs. This mixture will be fairly runny, and an attractive golden colour; it will taste strongly of vinegar. Mix most of it with the green beans, then coat with the remainder. Cook *au gratin* in a hot oven and serve as an accompaniment to the lamb.

Red wines: Saint-Émilion, Pomerol, Graves, Médoc.

US	Ingredients	Met/Imp
1, about 5½ lb	leg of salt-meadow lamb	1, about 2.5 kg/5½ lb
12	garlic cloves	12
10 tbsp	butter	150 g/5 oz
½ cup	preserved goose fat	100 g/4 oz
	salt and pepper	
½ cup	dry white wine	100 ml/3½ fl oz
1	lemon	1
4½ lb	French (fine green) beans	2 kg/4½ lb
2 tbsp	corn oil	30 ml/2 tbsp
½ lb	Bayonne ham	250 g/8 oz
1 cup	crème fraîche	200 ml/7 fl oz
½ cup	Tomato Sauce (*page 80*)	100 ml/3½ fl oz
1	onion	1
1	bouquet garni	1
3	egg yolks	3
½ cup	wine vinegar	100 ml/3½ fl oz
	fresh parsley, chervil and tarragon	

US	Ingredients	Met/Imp
1, about 5½ lb	leg of lamb	1, about 2.5 kg/5½ lb
	thin fatty bacon slices	
	salt and pepper	
	Cooked Marinade (page 59)	
14 tbsp	butter	200 g/7 oz
2 cups	Pepper Sauce for Game (page 76)	500 ml/18 fl oz
	GARNISH (optional)	
	purée of chestnuts or reinette or other dessert apples	
1 sauce boat	redcurrant jelly	1 sauce boat

LEG OF LAMB 'LIKE VENISON'

Preparation 1½ hours • Cooking about 35 minutes

Take a leg of lamb with a compact, even grain. Detach the bone at the knuckle (shank) end and remove the bone at the chump (sirloin) end, as this would make carving difficult. Remove the outside skin without piercing the meat, using a thin, sharp knife. Lard the surface of the lamb with 6 rows of bacon strips the thickness of a match, set as close together as possible. Put the lamb into an oval earthenware dish; season lightly with salt and pepper, then cover with 1.5 litres/2½ pints (1½ quarts) chilled marinade. The marinating time depends on the temperature: 4 days when the temperature is normal, 5 days in winter. Turn the leg of lamb quite frequently in the marinade, using kitchen tongs: do not touch it with your hands.

Remove the meat from the marinade, wipe it thoroughly with a cloth, and place it on a rack in a roasting pan. Brush with melted butter and sear in a hot oven to make sure that the moisture remaining in the meat evaporates quickly; otherwise it will be difficult to brown the outside of the meat. Once the outside is browned, pour 30–45 ml/2–3 tbsp marinade into the pan, to stop the bottom from burning, and turn the oven down to moderate. Roast the lamb, brushing with more butter from time to time during cooking, but do not add any liquid. In order to cook the joint to perfection, allow 13–15 minutes per 500 g/1 lb, depending on the size of the leg.

Reduce the marinade and add the pepper sauce. Place the leg of lamb on a heated, long serving dish, surround with a few spoonfuls of the sauce and serve the remainder separately. Garnish if liked.

Wines: Côtes du Rhône, Châteauneuf-du-Pape, Cahors, Saint-Émilion, Pomerol, Côte de Nuits.

LEG OF LAMB 'RENÉ LASSERRE'

Preparation 1 hour • Marinating 4 days • Cooking 45 minutes

US	Ingredients	Met/Imp
1	small leg of lamb	1
3 oz	fatty bacon	75 g/3 oz
	salt and pepper	
½ cup	red wine (Madiran)	100 ml/4 fl oz
½ cup	olive oil	100 ml/4 fl oz
2 tsp	vinegar	10 ml/2 tsp
2 tbsp	armagnac	30 ml/2 tbsp
3	shallots	3
1	garlic clove	1
1	bouquet garni	1
	beurre manié	

Lard the leg of lamb with the bacon cut into strips and seasoned with salt and pepper. Marinate the lamb for 4 days in a mixture of the red wine, oil, vinegar, armagnac, shallots sliced into rings, crushed garlic, bouquet garni and a little salt and pepper. Baste the meat 6 times a day.

Wipe the meat dry and roast on a spit, basting with the marinade. Skim the fat from the cooking juices and thicken with a small amount of beurre manié. Serve in a sauce boat. Garnish with a purée of celery, mushrooms, onions, red kidney beans or broad (fava) beans.

Red wines: Graves, Pomerol, Côte de Beaune, Madiran, Cahors.

—— 'SEVEN-HOUR' LEG OF LAMB ——

Preparation 1½ hours • Cooking 7 hours

Lard the leg of lamb with the bacon, as for Beef 'à la Mode' (*page 377*).

Brown the lamb with the carrots and bouquet garni in the oil in a *daubière* or braising pan. Drain away the fat and add the stock, tomato sauce and some of the cognac; arrange the onions around the lamb. Place the wine in a soup plate inside the pan and seal the lid of the pan tightly. Cook for 7 hours, adding more wine as it evaporates. When the lamb is well cooked (lamb prepared in this way is so tender that it is not carved, but served with a spoon), place it on a heated serving dish with the onions arranged around it. Strain the cooking liquid and reduce if necessary; taste for seasoning, then add the remaining cognac. The cooking liquid should be quite fluid, but thick.

Red wines: Côtes du Rhône, Châteauneuf-du-Pape, Cahors, Côte de Nuits.

US	Ingredients	Met/Imp
I, about 5½ lb	leg of lamb, boned except for the knuckle (shank) bone at the end	I, about 2.5 kg/5½ lb
7 oz	fatty bacon	200 g/7 oz
2	carrots	2
I	bouquet garni	I
scant ½ cup	oil	100 ml/4 fl oz
I quart	Brown Veal Stock (*page 56*)	I litre/1¾ pints
scant ½ cup	Tomato Sauce (*page 80*)	100 ml/4 fl oz
¼ cup	cognac	60 ml/4 tbsp
15	large onions	15
scant ½ cup	dry white wine	100 ml/4 fl oz
	salt and pepper	

—— LEG OF LAMB 'SOLOGNOTE' ——

Preparation 1 hour • Marinade 24 hours • Cooking 50 minutes

Leave the leg of lamb to marinate for 24 hours in a highly seasoned marinade consisting of the wine vinegar, the carrots sliced into rings, the sliced onions, the parsley, thyme and bay leaf, the crushed garlic, sliced shallots, salt, peppercorns, and cloves, and some very dry white wine. Add some long, rectangular strips of bacon.

When this length of time has passed, remove the lamb, wipe it thoroughly and lard copiously with the bacon strips from the marinade. Reduce the marinade to the consistency of a sauce and strain through a sieve, crushing the vegetables and other flavourings lightly. These vegetables must be well cooked.

Smear the lamb thickly with some of the butter, place in a roasting pan and roast in a hot oven in order to sear it well. When nearly cooked, deglaze the cooking juices lightly with a few spoonfuls of the strained reduced marinade. Continue cooking until done to your liking, basting the meat often. Garnish with the beans, blanched and sautéed in the remaining butter, moistened with the remaining marinade and sprinkled with the capers.

Red wines: Côtes du Jura, Côtes du Rhône, Châteauneuf-du-Pape, Cahors.

US	Ingredients	Met/Imp
I, about 5½ lb	leg of lamb	I, about 2.5 kg/5½ lb
½ cup	wine vinegar	100 ml/4 fl oz
4	carrots	4
2	onions	2
	parsley and thyme sprigs	
½	bay leaf	½
2	garlic cloves	2
2	shallots	2
	salt	
	peppercorns	
2	cloves	2
I bottle	very dry white wine	I bottle
10 oz	fatty bacon	300 g/10 oz
14 tbsp	butter	200 g/7 oz
3½ lb	French (fine green) beans	1.5 kg/3½ lb
⅔ cup	capers	100 g/4 oz

US	Ingredients	Met/Imp
2 lb	boned shoulder of mutton	1 kg/2 lb
2 lb	boned breast or neck of mutton	1 kg/2 lb
3	large onions	3
4	large very floury Dutch potatoes	4
3–4	leeks	3–4
1	large bouquet garni, containing a sprig of thyme, half a bay leaf, parsley stalks	1
	salt and pepper	
15	small new potatoes	15
15	small white onions	15
	parsley	

IRISH STEW

Preparation 1 hour • Cooking at least 2 hours

This is a *ragoût* prepared in a special way that is especially popular in Ireland. Unlike ordinary ragoûts, the meat is not browned, hence the name 'ragoût blanc' (white ragoût) which is often applied to it. No flour is used: the puréed potatoes are the only thickening, so it is important to use large floury potatoes that mash easily. The flavour of pepper should predominate.

Boned neck of mutton or lamb is particularly suitable for ragoûts, as it is soft and gelatinous.

Cut the mutton into pieces. In order to ensure that the ragoût is nice and white (which will not detract from its flavour in any way), soak the pieces of mutton for a few hours in advance in salt water, or blanch them just before you begin to prepare the ragoût. Put the pieces of mutton into a fairly large pan, add some water and bring to the boil, then, instead of skimming, sprinkle with more cold water. Drain the mutton.

Arrange layers of mutton, very thinly sliced large onions, sliced large potatoes and chopped leeks in a flameproof casserole and add the bouquet garni (you can add a celery stalk to this). Season with salt and pepper and cover with water. Cook for 1½ hours, on top of the stove, then take out the pieces of mutton and mash and whisk the vegetable purée left in the casserole. Put it back on top of the mutton in the casserole and add the new potatoes and blanched small onions; add a little more water if necessary and check the seasoning: there should be plenty of pepper. Cover with a piece of buttered paper and the lid and finish cooking. Sprinkle with a generous handful of chopped parsley just before serving.

White wines: Vouvray, Sancerre, Graves.
Red Wines: Beaujolais-Villages, Chinon, Bourgueil.

US	Ingredients	Met/Imp
8	small aubergines (eggplants)	8
	oil for frying	
1¾ lb (about 4 cups)	cooked mutton, finely chopped	800 g/1¾ lb
2	onions	2
4 tbsp	butter	50 g/2 oz
1	garlic clove	1
1 tbsp	chopped parsley	15 ml/1 tbsp
2	eggs	2
scant ½ cup	tomato paste	100 ml/3½ fl oz
	salt and pepper	
2 cups	Tomato Sauce (page 80), to serve	500 ml/18 fl oz

MOUSSAKA

Preparation 1 hour • Cooking 40 minutes

This is a good recipe if you have a large amount of cooked mutton or lamb leftover.

Split 4 of the aubergines (eggplants) in half lengthways and cook them in oil in a frying pan, then remove them and drain. Peel the remaining aubergines (eggplants), reserving the skin, and slice the flesh into rings; cook in oil.

Chop the flesh of the halved aubergines (eggplants) and mix with the lamb, chopped onions softened in butter, crushed garlic, chopped parsley, beaten eggs and tomato paste. Season well and mix together thoroughly.

Line a plain round mould with the (eggplant) aubergine skin, so that it protrudes just above the rim. Fill the mould with alternate layers of the lamb mixture and aubergine (eggplant) slices, packing them down well.

You can also insert some skinned, de-seeded and chopped tomatoes in between the aubergine (eggplant) slices. Bake in a *bain-marie* for 35–40 minutes, then turn out on to a heated round serving dish. Serve with the tomato sauce.

White wines: Chablis, Cassis.
Dry rosé wines: Côtes de Provence, Tavel.
Red wines: Beaujolais-Villages, Cassis, Coteaux d'Aix-en-Provence, Bellet.

NAVARIN

——— MUTTON STEW* ———

Preparation 20 minutes • Cooking 3 hours

US	Ingredients	Met/Imp
I, about 5 lb	shoulder of mutton	I, about 2.3 kg/5 lb
¼ cup	lard	50 g/2 oz
	salt and pepper	
I tsp	sugar	5 ml/I tsp
I tbsp	flour	15 ml/I tbsp
	stock	
I lb	small white onions	500 g/I lb
2 lb	small new potatoes	I kg/2 lb
	parsley	

Bone the mutton and trim off the fat, then cut into large cubes. Melt the lard in a stewpan and add the pieces of meat, sprinkled with salt, pepper and sugar. Brown them on all sides, then sprinkle with flour. Stir and brown slightly; add enough stock to just cover the meat. Bring to the boil, stirring all the time, then turn down the heat. Cover the pan and simmer for 1½ hours.

Add the onions, having first peeled and blanched them rapidly in boiling water, and also the potatoes, cut into pieces if necessary. Cook for a further 45 minutes.

Skim the fat from the sauce, pour the navarin into a heated deep serving dish and serve, garnished with parsley.

Red wines: Bourgueil, Beaujolais Nouveau.

NOISETTES DE PRÉ-SALÉ

— NOISETTES OF SALT-MEADOW LAMB —

Preparation 15 minutes • Cooking 15 minutes

US	Ingredients	Met/Imp
¼ lb	Paris mushrooms	100 g/4 oz
I stick	butter	100 g/4 oz
	salt and pepper	
8	best end of neck salt-meadow lamb cutlets (rib chops)	8
8	slices bread	8
½ cup	dry white wine	100 ml/4 fl oz

Trim the ends off the mushroom stalks, then wash and dry the mushrooms and cut into slices. Melt one-quarter of the butter in a saucepan and cook the mushrooms in it for about 10 minutes; season with salt and pepper.

Using a very sharp knife, remove the bone from the cutlets to make noisettes or, better still, ask the butcher to do this when you buy them.

Heat another quarter of the butter in a large frying pan and cook the noisettes for 4 minutes on each side; season with salt and pepper. Trim the bread slices the same size as the noisettes and brown them in the remaining butter. Arrange these croûtes on a heated serving dish, place a noisette on each and surround with the mushrooms. Deglaze the frying pan with the wine and 15 ml/1 tbsp hot water; boil this sauce for a moment, then serve in a sauce boat.

Red wines: Graves, Médoc.

US	Ingredients	Met/Imp
	Duchesse Potatoes (*page 551*), made into 8 oval croquettes	
3	eggs	3
3½ cups	fresh white breadcrumbs	200 g/7 oz
	fat for deep-frying	
	salt and pepper	
2 cups	Soubise (Onion) Sauce (*page 80*)	500 ml/18 fl oz
8, each about ¼ lb	lamb *noisettes*	8, each about 100 g/4 oz
10 tbsp	butter	150 g/5 oz
¼ cup	oil	50 ml/2 fl oz
½ cup	dry white wine	100 ml/4 fl oz
1	egg yolk	1

NOISETTES OF SALT-MEADOW LAMB 'BODELEY'

Preparation 1½ hours • Cooking 8 minutes

Recipe from Claude Terrail, Tour d'Argent, Paris

Dip the potato croquettes in the beaten eggs and coat with the breadcrumbs. Deep-fry the potato croquettes in the fat. Scoop out the centres, then fill each one with a little highly seasoned soubise sauce.

Sauté the lamb noisettes in a mixture of butter and oil, place 1 noisette in each croquette. Deglaze the pan with the wine and pour this sauce into the croquettes.

Cover the whole dish with the remaining soubise sauce, brush with the beaten egg yolk and glaze in the oven.

White wines: Saumur, Vouvray, Sancerre, Pouilly-Fumé.
Red wines: Bourgueil, Chinon, Beaujolais-Villages.

US	Ingredients	Met/Imp
1¼ lb	piece of boneless mutton, cut from fillet (sirloin) end of leg	600 g/1¼ lb
2	shallots	2
1	garlic clove	1
	parsley	
¼ lb	lean bacon	100 g/4 oz
2	slices *Bayonne ham*	2
1 tbsp	stale breadcrumbs	15 ml/1 tbsp
1	egg	1
	salt and pepper	
	olive oil	

PAUPIETTES DE MOUTON

MUTTON 'OLIVES'

Preparation 15 minutes • Cooking 20 minutes • Serves 4

Ask the butcher to cut the mutton into 4 rectangular slices and to flatten them.

Peel and chop the shallots and garlic. Trim and chop the parsley; chop the bacon and ham. Mix all these chopped ingredients together and add the breadcrumbs. Bind with the beaten egg, mixing well, and season with salt and pepper.

Spread one-quarter of this mixture on each of the slices of mutton and roll them up to form 'olive' shapes. Tie in several places with string.

Preheat the grill (broiler). Thread the mutton olives on to skewers and brush with olive oil. Grill (broil) for 10 minutes on each side under a moderate heat.

Serve on a heated serving dish, accompanied by a purée of potatoes, lentils or white beans.

Red wines: Beaujolais, Chinon, Bourgueil, Côtes-de-Provence.

SHEEP'S TROTTERS WITH POULETTE SAUCE*

Preparation 2 hours • Cooking 2½–3 hours

US	Ingredients	Met/Imp
24–25	sheep's trotters (feet)	24–25
½ lb	button mushrooms	250 g/8 oz
I	lemon, juice of	I
	chopped parsley	
	WHITE STOCK	
2 quarts	water	2 litres/4½ pints
6 tbsp	flour, mixed with a little water	50 g/2 oz
I	lemon, peeled and sliced	I
	salt	
2	carrots	2
I	bouquet garni	I
I	onion	I
I	clove	I
	POULETTE SAUCE	
I stick	butter	100 g/4 oz
½ cup	flour	65 g/2½ oz
2 cups	White Stock (page 56)	500 ml/18 fl oz
a few	mushroom trimmings	a few
I	bouquet garni, including leeks	I
2	egg yolks	2
½ cup	crème fraîche	100 ml/4 fl oz

In France, sheep's trotters (feet) are usually sold in bundles of 25, ready blanched. They can be bought singly, but since they keep so well in their cooking liquid, it is no problem to cook a larger amount.

In advance, prepare 2 litres/3½ pints (2 quarts) light white stock with the listed ingredients, spiking the onion with the clove.

Singe the trotters (feet) with alcohol or over a clear gas flame, in order to remove any remaining hairs, then take out the central bone, either by dislocating it (in order to do this twist it backwards and forwards) or by slitting the skin on the inside of the trotters (feet). Use the point of a sharp knife to remove the woolly plug between the 2 parts of the hoof.

Even though the feet will already have been blanched, it is a good idea to boil them again, for 8–10 minutes. Next, place them in the boiling white stock and simmer for about 2½ hours, until tender, depending on whether they are from young or old animals. As they are often sold mixed, you cannot be sure they will all take the same length of time.

Prepare a poulette sauce (*page 76*) with the ingredients listed here. A few minutes before serving, having added butter off the heat, add the mushrooms (which have been cooked *à blanc* with the lemon juice), then the trotters (feet). Sauté briefly to mix the ingredients thoroughly. Pour into a heated deep serving dish and sprinkle with parsley.

Dry white wines: Pouilly-Fumé, Côtes de Provence.
Rosé wines: Tavel, Arbois.
Red wines: Beaujolais-Villages, Bourgueil, Chinon.

SHEEP'S TROTTERS FROM MARSEILLE

Preparation 2 hours • Cooking about 4 hours

US	Ingredients	Met/Imp
8	sheep's trotters (feet)	8
2	whole sheep's stomachs	2
	salt and pepper	
3 cups	crushed garlic mixed with chopped parsley	200 g/7 oz
10 oz	lean bacon	300 g/10 oz
I quart	dry white wine	I litre/1¾ pints
1¼ cups	tomato paste	300 ml/½ pint

Bone the trotters (feet) and line a flameproof casserole with the bones. Wash the sheeps' stomachs and cut them into 15 cm/6 inch triangles; spread these out on a work surface and season with plenty of salt and pepper. Place on each one portion of mixed garlic and chopped parsley the size of a pigeon's egg, a strip of bacon and a boned trotter (foot); fold into a parcel and lay the parcels on top of the bones. Mix the white wine with the tomato paste and add this mixture to the ingredients in the casserole; cover the parcels with water and put a sheet of greaseproof (parchment) paper and a plate on top, to weight down. Cover, bring to the boil and cook for at least 4 hours on the edge of the stove (ie over a low heat), so that they do not colour.

Watch carefully during cooking, as the length of time required depends on the age of the sheep; prod the parcels in order to test them. The cooking liquid should have reduced by three-fifths. Taste and adjust the seasoning before serving.

Red, white or rosé wines from Provence.

US	Ingredients	Met/Imp
about 4 lb	breast of mutton, trimmed of as much fat as possible	about 1.8 kg/4 lb
	METHOD I	
4	carrots	4
4	baby turnips	4
4	leeks, chopped	4
a few	old potatoes, chopped	a few
I	small cabbage, shredded	I
	salt and pepper	
	METHOD 2	
8	small slices ham	8
8	thin slices bacon	8
4	carrots	4
I	bouquet garni	I
	sliced onions	
	salt	
	peppercorns	
2 cups	stock and water	500 ml/18 fl oz
3½ cups	fresh white breadcrumbs	200 g/7 oz

—— GRILLED BREAST OF MUTTON ——

Preparation 30 minutes • Cooking 2–3 hours

Put the mutton, halved carrots, turnips, leeks, potatoes and cabbage in water, season and cook for 3 hours. Take the meat out, bone it, then finish cooking under the grill (broiler). Serve on top of the vegetables.

An alternative way of preparing breast of mutton is to place the slices of ham and bacon together with the halved carrots, bouquet garni, onions, parsley, salt and peppercorns in a saucepan, then add the mutton and stock. Cook for 3 hours, then take out the meat and leave it to cool. Cut it into pieces, coat with the breadcrumbs and grill (broil). Serve on top of the vegetables.

Red wines: Cornas, Côtes du Rhône, Châteauneuf-du-Pape, Cahors, Corbières.

US	Ingredients	Met/Imp
2, each about 5½ lb	small trimmed legs of lamb, halved	2, each about 2.5 kg/5½ lb
10 tbsp	butter	150 g/5 oz
½ cup	flour	75 g/3 oz
2 quarts	White Stock (page 56)	2 litres/3½ pints
2	carrots, quartered	2
I	large onion	I
I	clove	I
I	bouquet garni	I
30	button (pearl) onions, cooked à blanc	30
I lb	small Paris mushrooms, cooked à blanc	500 g/I lb
I	lemon, juice of	I
2	egg yolks	2
1¼ cups	crème fraîche	300 ml/½ pint

LEG OF LAMB
—— WITH POULETTE SAUCE ——

Preparation 50 minutes • Cooking 2 hours

Blanch the legs of lamb, then drain and wipe dry. Immediately put them into a saucepan with the butter, cover and sweat for a few minutes but do not brown. Add the flour and turn the legs over.

Moisten with the stock; add the quartered carrots, onion spiked with the clove and the bouquet garni. Simmer until the lamb is tender, then take out of the liquid and keep warm.

Reduce the sauce and strain through a cloth. Return to the heat and add the cooking juice from the button (pearl) onions and mushrooms, together with the lemon juice. When the sauce is of the desired consistency, add the egg yolks mixed with the crème fraîche; let the sauce thicken until it is glossy and a nice yellow colour and coats the spoon. Taste and add more lemon juice if necessary. Strain again through a cloth, then add the small onions and mushrooms.

White wines: Sancerre, Graves, Chablis.
Red wines: Beaujolais-Villages, Chinon.

ROAST LAMB PÉRIGORD STYLE

Preparation 1 hour • Marinating 24 hours • Cooking 50 minutes

The 3 pieces of lamb should be separate, in order to make them easier to cook and prepare.

Marinate the pieces of lamb and the bacon for 24 hours in the wine, together with the carrots sliced into rings, the sliced onions, the bouquet garni, clove, peppercorns, lemon sliced into rings, the juniper berries and oil. The marinade should cover the meat.

Take the pieces of lamb out of the marinade, wipe them dry and lard them generously with the marinated bacon. Smear the pieces of lamb thickly with butter and cook in a hot oven until done to your liking.

Strain the marinade and reduce the liquid until it almost reaches the consistency of a sauce. A few minutes before the lamb is ready, use to deglaze the roasting pan, basting the meat with it frequently. Sprinkle the meat with a mixture of parsley and breadcrumbs, flavoured with the crushed garlic. Garnish with a mixture of sliced potatoes and truffles sautéed in butter. Serve the reduced sauce in a sauce boat to accompany the lamb.

Red wines: Saint-Émilion, Pomerol, Graves, Bourgueil, Chinon, Cahors.

US	Ingredients	Met/Imp
1	small leg of milk-fed lamb	1
1	saddle of lamb	1
1	piece of best end and middle neck (lamb square-cut shoulder roast)	1
¼ lb	fatty bacon	100 g/4 oz
1 quart	dry white wine	1 litre/1¾ pints
2	carrots	2
1	onion	1
1	bouquet garni	1
1	clove	1
a few	peppercorns	a few
1	lemon	1
a few	juniper berries	a few
½ cup	oil	100 ml/4 fl oz
14 tbsp	butter	200 g/7 oz
¼ cup	chopped parsley	60 ml/4 tbsp
2 cups	fresh white breadcrumbs	100 g/4 oz
1	garlic clove	1
3½ lb	waxy Dutch potatoes	1.5 kg/3½ lb
½ lb	truffles	250 g/8 oz

ROGNONS D'AGNEAU À LA VILLANDRY

LAMBS' KIDNEYS 'VILLANDRY'

Preparation 50 minutes • Cooking 10 minutes

Skin the kidneys and split them in half without separating them completely, as you will need to close them again when they have been stuffed. Mix the pork with the egg yolk and season well with salt, pepper and spice. Mix in the chopped truffles and foie gras, if using. Fill the kidneys with a layer of this mixture about 1 cm/½ inch thick.

Cut the bacon into strips about 15 cm/6 inches long. Wrap a bacon strip around each kidney to keep it together; tie with a piece of thread if necessary.

Place the kidneys on a baking tray. Put a nut of butter on top of each one and bake in a very hot oven for 10 minutes or until cooked through. Take them out of the oven and transfer to a heated serving dish. Flambé the cooking juices with the marc, thicken with the crème fraîche and pour over the kidneys.

Red wines: Bourgueil, Chinon.

US	Ingredients	Met/Imp
16	lambs' kidneys	16
1¼ cups	finely minced (ground) pork	300 g/10 oz
1	egg yolk	1
	salt and pepper	
1 pinch	*quatre-épices*	1 pinch
3 oz	truffles (optional)	75 g/3 oz
16	small cubes foie gras (optional)	16
16	slices bacon	16
4 tbsp	butter	50 g/2 oz
½ cup	*marc* from Touraine	100 ml/4 fl oz
½ cup	*crème fraîche*	100 ml/4 fl oz

US	Ingredients	Met/Imp
8	sheep's kidneys	8
10 tbsp	butter	150 g/5 oz
16	croûtons, cut the same shape as the kidneys and fried in butter	16
16	cooked mushroom caps	16
½ bottle	dry champagne	½ bottle
2 cups	Demi-Glaze (page 56)	500 ml/18 fl oz
	salt and pepper	
	chopped parsley	

—— SHEEP'S KIDNEYS IN CHAMPAGNE ——

Preparation 40 minutes • Cooking 8 minutes

Halve the kidneys and sauté rapidly in 100 g/4 oz (8 tbsp) of the butter. Arrange each half kidney on a croûton and place a mushroom cap on top. Drain off the cooking butter from the pan, deglaze the pan with champagne and reduce by two-thirds; add the demi-glaze and reduce a little more. Strain through a cloth and add the remaining butter. Season to taste. Sprinkle the kidneys with chopped parsley and pour over the sauce.

Rosé and white wines: Rosé des Riceys, Coteaux Champenois.

US	Ingredients	Met/Imp
16	button (pearl) onions	16
1 stick	butter	100 g/4 oz
16	mushroom caps	16
8	croûtons, fried in butter	8
16	chipolatas (small pork link sausages)	16
8	sheep's kidneys	8
	salt and pepper	
½ cup	dry white wine	100 ml/3½ fl oz
1 cup	Demi-Glaze (page 56)	200 ml/7 fl oz
2 tbsp	tomato paste	30 ml/2 tbsp
	chopped parsley	

ROGNONS DE MOUTON TURBIGO

———— SHEEP'S KIDNEYS TURBIGO ————

Preparation 50 minutes • Cooking 6 minutes

Take some small onions the size of hazelnuts and cook them in advance in butter. Cook the mushrooms and cut the croûtons into the shape of a cock's comb; grill (broil) the chipolatas.

Halve the kidneys. Season, then sauté quickly in butter. Remove them from the pan, pour off the cooking butter, then deglaze with the wine, demi-glaze and tomato paste. Cook this sauce until it is of the required consistency, then add the onions and mushrooms; simmer for 5–6 minutes. Put the kidneys into the sauce for just long enough to heat them through again; add some butter to the sauce. Arrange the kidneys in a crown on a heated round serving dish, alternately with the croûtons. Tip the garnish of onions and mushrooms into the centre, sprinkle with parsley, surround with the chipolatas and pour over the cooking butter.

Red wines: Pomerol, Côte Rôtie, Côtes du Rhône, Châteauneuf-du-Pape, Côtes de Provence, Cahors.

US	Ingredients	Met/Imp
1, about 3½ lb	saddle of lamb	1, about 1.5 kg/3½ lb
2 lb	French (fine green) beans	1 kg/2 lb
1 lb	tomatoes	500 g/1 lb
14 tbsp	butter	200 g/7 oz

SELLE D'AGNEAU À LA PORTUGAISE

—— SADDLE OF LAMB PORTUGAISE ——

Preparation 2 hours • Cooking 20 minutes

Roast the saddle of lamb in a very hot oven, so that the inside remains rare. Cook the beans until just tender. Sauté the beans and tomatoes separately in the butter. Place the lamb on a carving dish and garnish with the tomatoes and beans. Degrease the cooking juices and serve on the side, very hot.

Red wines: Saint-Émilion, Pomerol, Côte Rôtie, Hermitage, Corbières.

BŒUF

BEEF

IN BUTCHERY, THE TERM 'BEEF' IS APPLIED TO THE MEAT OF heifers, cows, oxen and baby steers as well as young bulls. The most popular beef cattle breeds in France are the Charolais and Limousin. Best-quality beef is a brilliant red colour, firm and elastic to the touch and with a light, sweet smell. The fat should be white or pale yellow in colour and compact, and should intersperse the meat. Meat well marbled with fat is especially full of flavour. Regarded as the aristocrat of meat par excellence, beef provides many different cuts, each one cooked according to its 'category'.

'FIRST CATEGORY' CUTS

Fillet (tenderloin) of beef, when trimmed, is a long roasting joint, barded and carefully interlarded, with one end a little wider than the other. The best cut of the fillet is the eye or centre, after the top and narrow end are cut away. As the fillet can sometimes be a little dry, it is a good idea to thread it with very thin, evenly spaced *lardons*. It is from the fillet that *tournedos* should be cut, in thick, even slices. Fillet of beef should never be coated with a sauce, however delicate: a little of the sauce should be poured around the beef and the bulk served separately in a sauce boat.

Sirloin and rump (or **top round**) are two succulent cuts which are served as roasts or steaks. For roasting, they should always be over 500 g/1 lb in weight, otherwise the meat will not be thick enough to retain all of its flavour during cooking. These cuts can also be sliced into thick steaks. Sirloin and rump (top round) steaks need a butcher's skill for the careful removal of the tendons and fat surrounding them. The proportion of waste is quite large.

Entrecôte literally means 'between the ribs', and in French butchery is a boneless gourmet cut taken from between the fore ribs – the rib eye.* It always looks speckled with fat, just enough of which should be left to give it the right degree of tenderness. Entrecôte steaks can be individually prepared, but preferably should be in just one piece to serve 2–4 people. Similarly, the meat should not only be of the very best quality, but also well hung.

***Editor's note**: British butchers often cut 'entrecôte' steaks from the sirloin; these are therefore not the entrecôtes specified in the recipes in this chapter.

Entrecôte can also be used as a roast, but the unboned **côte de bœuf (rib of beef)** is the favourite roasting cut for those who like their meat 'saignant' (rare) or 'à point' (medium rare).

'SECOND CATEGORY' CUTS

Topside (top round), **silverside (bottom round)**, and **thick flank** can be fashioned into roasting joints and steaks. They are more plentiful than the other cuts in this category and they are also less expensive. These are the grills (broiled meats) and roasts suitable for family meals and informal entertaining. They are made up into long roasting joints which the butcher cuts to order.

Skirt makes an excellent cut to pot-roast or grill (broil) and, with its long fibres, is full of flavour.

'THIRD CATEGORY' CUTS FOR BRAISING AND BOILING.

Clod or shoulder (chuck) and **neck** are suitable for dishes prepared by simmering or slow cooking such as a braise, *daube*, beef bourguignon, beef 'à la mode' and pot-au-feu, in which several cuts, lean such as clod (chuck), fatty such as brisket, flank, breast and ribs (short ribs), and gelatinous such as neck, shin (shank) and oxtail, are combined. Beef offal (variety meats) principally comprises heart, liver, tripe, tongue and kidneys.

Ox tongue is prepared fresh, salted or lightly salted. When fresh, it is always braised and accompanied by a madeira sauce, for example, or a purée of fresh or dried peas, celery or chestnuts.

A medium-sized tongue weighs about 2.5 kg/5½ lb. After removing the pharynx (or cornet) and the thymus gland (or sweetbread), leave the tongue to soak in cold water for several hours. Afterwards, put it in a saucepan, cover with plenty of cold water and boil for 15 minutes. Drain, rinse well, then remove the skin.

Ox kidney weighs about 500 g/1 lb. Preferably choose one which is a golden colour, a sign that it is from a young animal. If it is reddish-brown and gives off an alkaline smell, cut it up, place the pieces in a sieve and plunge it into boiling water. Drain and dry very carefully before cooking. To seal it in fat, it should be very dry. It also needs to be drained completely before being put in a sauce.

SPIT-ROASTED SIRLOIN

Preparation 1 hour • Marinating 12 hours • Cooking 40 minutes

Trim the sirloin, bard with the bacon and tie with string. Combine all the ingredients for the marinade and marinate the beef overnight. When the meat is well impregnated with the marinade, remove it and pat dry. Roast in the butter in a hot oven, preferably on a spit, until nicely browned but still pink inside. When the beef is cooked to your liking, remove it and keep hot.

Strain the marinade through a sieve and reduce by one-third. Deglaze the roasting pan with it, adding the chopped shallots. Adjust the seasoning and pour this sauce over the roast. It should be not much thicker than a gravy. Serve with well-browned sautéed potatoes, sprinkled with parsley.

Red wines: Saint-Émilion, Pomerol, Graves, Beaujolais-Villages, Côte Rôtie, Côtes du Rhône, Châteauneuf-du-Pape, Côtes de Provence, Cahors, Corbières.

US	Ingredients	Met/Imp
1, about 3½–4½ lb	boneless sirloin joint (roast)	1, about 1.5–2 kg/3½–4½ lb
3	slices fatty bacon	3
1 stick	butter	100 g/4 oz
4	shallots	4
2 lb	sautéed potatoes	1 kg/2 lb
	chopped parsley	
	MARINADE	
	salt and peppercorns	
	nutmeg	
2	carrots, sliced	2
1	onion, sliced	1
1	celery stalk, sliced	1
1	bouquet garni	1
1	garlic clove	1
2	cloves	2
2 cups	dry white wine	500 ml/18 fl oz
scant ½ cup	wine vinegar	100 ml/3½ fl oz
scant ½ cup	olive oil	100 ml/3½ fl oz

ALOYAU LARDÉ À LA BROCHE À LA LANDAISE

SPIT-ROASTED SIRLOIN
FROM THE LANDES

Preparation 1 hour • Marinating 6 hours • Cooking 35 minutes

Rapidly half cook the bacon cut into strips, then use to lard the surface of the sirloin. Marinate the meat for 6 hours in the wine and armagnac, with salt, peppercorns, the bouquet garni and nutmeg, turning frequently. Remove the sirloin from the marinade and pat dry. Roast it in a hot oven, preferably on a spit, basting it with its own juices and several spoonfuls of the marinade, until well browned but still pink inside. A very small quantity of spicy and aromatic stock should be left at the end of the cooking. Once the roast is done, keep it hot.

Meanwhile, prepare a thick *ragoût* by stewing the skinned, de-seeded and chopped tomatoes, the sliced aubergines (eggplants), courgettes (zucchini), sweet pepper and onion in half the butter until golden. Add 15–30 ml/1–2 tbsp of the reduced marinade and the finely chopped shallot and simmer until all the vegetables are tender, stirring frequently.

Fill a gratin dish with this ragoût. Arrange thick slices of potato here and there on the surface, and sprinkle with the breadcrumbs mixed with the parsley and crushed garlic. Dot with the remaining butter and brown in a hot oven. Serve with the sirloin of beef.

Red wines: Pomerol, Beaujolais-Villages, Côtes de Provence, Cahors.

US	Ingredients	Met/Imp
7 oz	fatty bacon, lightly smoked	200 g/7 oz
1, about 3 lb	well-hung boneless sirloin joint (roast)	1, about 1.4 kg/3 lb
2 cups	white wine	400 ml/14 fl oz
½ cup	armagnac	100 ml/3½ fl oz
	salt	
a few	peppercorns	a few
1	bouquet garni	1
1 pinch	nutmeg	1 pinch
5	tomatoes	5
2	aubergines (eggplants)	2
2	courgettes (zucchini)	2
1	sweet pepper	1
1	onion	1
4 tbsp	butter	50 g/2 oz
1	shallot	1
4	Dutch waxy potatoes	4
1 cup	fresh white breadcrumbs	50 g/2 oz
¼ cup	chopped parsley	60 ml/4 tbsp
1	garlic clove	1

US	Ingredients	Met/Imp
about 4½ lb	neck (chuck) of beef	about 2 kg/4½ lb
⅔ cup	pork fat	150 g/5 oz
½ cup	flour	75 g/3 oz
2	garlic cloves	2
	quatre-épices	
	salt and pepper	
2 bottles	red burgundy	2 bottles
1 tbsp	tomato paste	15 ml/1 tbsp
40	button (pearl) onions	40
4 tbsp	butter	50 g/2 oz
½ lb	bacon	250 g/8 oz
1 tbsp	chopped parsley	15 ml/1 tbsp

BEEF BOURGUIGNON

Preparation 1 hour • Cooking about 3 hours

Cut the beef into large chunks and brown in the fat; add the flour, crushed garlic and spice. Season with salt and pepper.

Moisten with half and half good burgundy and water. Stir in the tomato paste. Lightly brown the onions in butter with the bacon cut into small strips, and add. Leave to cook for 3–3½ hours, until the beef is very tender. Serve sprinkled with parsley.

Wines: as a general rule serve the same wine as the one used for cooking.

US	Ingredients	Met/Imp
1, about 2 lb	boneless piece of beef, eg fillet (tenderloin), rump (top round) or topside (rump roast)	1, about 1 kg/2 lb
	stock, chicken if possible	
	coarse sea salt	
	freshly ground pepper	
	CHOICE OF SAUCES TO SERVE	
	Béarnaise Sauce (*page 61*)	
	Madeira Sauce (*page 72*)	
	Périgueux Sauce (*page 75*)	

BEEF 'ON A STRING'

Preparation 10 minutes • Cooking 30 minutes

This piece of beef, usually a roasting cut, should be very carefully selected, tender and of excellent flavour. It should be thick cut, almost as wide as it is long. Have it tied carefully and ask the butcher to leave a long piece of string hanging from it. Above all, do not have it barded. A boned leg of lamb can be cooked in the same way.

Put sufficient stock to cover the beef in a 'marmite' (tall stock pot) and bring to a rolling boil. Put in the beef and tie the string to the handle of the stock pot so that the meat does not touch the bottom of the pot. Bring back to the boil, cover and leave like this for 25 minutes for very rare meat, 30 minutes for medium. The cooking time is crucial and depends upon the weight and shape of the meat. If it is long and narrow, reduce the cooking time to 15–20 minutes.

At the time of serving, untie the string and transfer the beef to a heated serving dish. Pay no attention to its slightly grey exterior. Carve it straightaway: the meat will be rare and very juicy. Each guest should season it to taste.

Hand the sauce of your choice separately in a sauce boat, or serve more simply with very fresh butter and parsley.

Red wines: Beaujolais-Villages, Chinon, Bourgueil.

BEEF 'À LA MODE'

Preparation 2 hours • Marinating 5 hours • Cooking about 4 hours

US	Ingredients	Met/Imp
7 oz	fatty unsmoked bacon	200 g/7 oz
	salt and pepper	
	quatre-épices	
scant ½ cup	cognac	100 ml/4 fl oz
1 tbsp	chopped parsley	15 ml/1 tbsp
1, about 5½ lb	piece beef top rump (sirloin tip roast)	1, about 2.5 kg/5½ lb
1 quart	dry white wine	1 litre/1¾ pints
2	calf's feet	2
4 tbsp	butter	50 g/2 oz
1 quart	Brown Veal Stock (page 56)	1 litre/1¾ pints
2	large carrots	2
2	large onions	2
12	shallots	12
1	bouquet garni	1
	beef bones	
7 oz	pork rind	200 g/7 oz
4½ lb	small carrots	2 kg/4½ lb
40–50	button (pearl) onions	40–50
1 tsp	potato flour (optional)	5 ml/1 tsp
1 tbsp	madeira (optional)	15 ml/1 tbsp

Beef 'à la mode' cannot be cooked conveniently except in a large quantity, but it is not uneconomical because it reheats well and also makes an excellent cold dish.

Cut the bacon into strips about 1 cm/½ inch wide. Season them with salt, pepper and a pinch of spice. Put them in a dish, sprinkle them with a little of the cognac and leave to marinate for 20 minutes. Just before using, dust them with a little chopped parsley. Using a special larding needle, thread the bacon strips right through the beef, spacing them out evenly. Season the beef lightly with salt and pepper. Put it in a bowl with 175 ml/6 fl oz (¾ cup) of the wine and the remaining cognac. Leave to marinate for at least 5 hours, turning the meat from time to time.

Bone the calf's feet. Boil them for 10 minutes, then rinse them and set aside.

Wipe the meat dry with a cloth and place in a flameproof casserole containing the smoking hot butter. The chosen casserole should be the right size for its contents, neither too big nor too small. This detail is important.

Brown the beef well on all sides, then drain off all the fat. Add the strained marinade and enough lightly salted brown stock to come almost two-thirds up the sides of the meat, the quartered large carrots, the sliced large onions, the sliced shallots, the bouquet garni, the calf's feet, the beef bones broken up small and the pork rind. It is these pieces of rind, together with the calf's feet, which make the stock gelatinous.

Bring to the boil, cover the casserole and simmer evenly and without interruption for 3 hours. Take out the beef and the calf's feet. Strain the stock through a conical sieve and skim off the fat. Return the beef, the stock and the calf's feet cut into small cubes, to the rinsed-out casserole. Add the small carrots cut into barrel shapes and blanched for 15 minutes (blanching is unnecessary if the carrots are new) and the small whole onions sautéed in butter to colour them lightly. Simmer as before for 1 further hour.

Place the beef on a heated serving dish. Surround with the carrots, the onions, the calf's feet and the requisite quantity of stock, which should have reduced by almost two-thirds. If necessary, thicken it with a little potato flour mixed with the madeira. Serve hot or cold. If cold, the beef is served in its jellied stock, decorated with the vegetables.

Red wines: Saint-Émilion, Pomerol, Graves, Médoc, Côtes de Bourg, Bourgueil, Beaujolais-Villages, Côte de Beaune.

US	Ingredients	Met/Imp
2	sets ox brains	2
scant ½ cup	wine vinegar	100 ml/3½ fl oz
	salt and pepper	
	court bouillon	
1	lemon	1
6 tbsp	flour	50 g/2 oz
1 stick	butter	100 g/4 oz
2 cups	Muscovite Sauce (page 74)	500 ml/18 fl oz

SAUTÉED OX BRAINS

Preparation 3 hours • Cooking about 15–20 minutes

Soak the brains in warm water to remove the membrane and filaments attached to them, then soak them for a further hour in fresh water with the vinegar and salt added. Cook them in the court bouillon for about 10–12 minutes, until firm.

Remove the brains from the pan, drain them and leave them to get cold. Cut them into slices and marinate them for 20 minutes in the lemon juice, salt and pepper. Drain and pat dry, flour them and sauté them quickly in the hot butter for about 5 minutes. Arrange the brains in a circle on a heated round serving dish with the Muscovite sauce in the centre.

Sheep's or calves' brains can be prepared in the same way.

Dry white wines: Muscadet, Saumur, Quincy, Pouilly-Fumé, Sancerre, Chablis, Mâcon, Cassis.
Dry rosé wines: Tavel, Arbois, Côtes de Provence.
Red wines: Beaujolais-Villages, Bourgueil, Chinon.

US	Ingredients	Met/Imp
1, about 4½ lb	rib joint (roast) of beef, boned	1, about 2 kg/4½ lb
	oil	
	salt and pepper	
1 lb	beef kidney fat	500 g/1 lb

CÔTE DE BŒUF À LA BROCHE

SPIT-ROAST RIB OF BEEF

Preparation 30 minutes • Cooking 30–40 minutes

Rub the beef with oil, salt and pepper. Cover with strips of well-flattened beef kidney fat and tie them on securely. The beef should be kept in a warm kitchen temperature for about 2 hours before being roasted. Put the beef on the spit and roast for about 9 minutes per 500 g/1 lb, basting well. It should not be cooked through nor browned all over. Take off the covering of barding fat and continue roasting until browned, basting constantly and taking care that the juices do not burn.

Remove from the spit and cook, covered, in a roasting pan in a slow oven until cooked through but still pink inside. Deglaze the roasting pan with a little water to make a gravy. Skim, add the beef cooking juices and serve in a gravy boat to accompany the beef.

Red wines: Côte de Beaune, Graves, Cahors.

PEPPERED RIB OF BEEF

Preparation 35 minutes • Cooking 25 minutes

Preheat the barbecue beforehand to prevent the meat sticking to it. Barbecue the rib for about 10 minutes on one side, then turn it over and dust the cooked side with crushed peppercorns. When the second side is cooked, put the beef in a heated, fairly deep dish, salt it lightly, sprinkle it with cognac and flambé. When the flames have died down, cover the beef with the crème fraîche. Invert a plate over the beef to keep it hot and leave to stand for 2–3 minutes before slicing.

Red wines: Beaujolais-Villages, Chinon.

US	Ingredients	Met/Imp
I	good-sized rib joint (roast), to serve 8 people	I
	crushed peppercorns	
	salt	
⅓ cup	cognac	75 ml/3 fl oz
½ cup	crème fraîche	100 ml/4 fl oz

BRAISED RUMP OF BEEF*

Preparation 1½ hours • Cooking 4 hours

Lard the beef with the strips of fatty bacon. Line a braising pan with the scraps of pork fat and the carrots and onions cut into rounds. Add the bouquet garni, put in the meat and season with salt and peppercorns. It is a good idea to add some beef or veal bones to the pan, to give extra body to the cooking juices. Moisten with the glass of stock and cook over a high heat to colour the beef. When this stock has reduced, add the wine and cognac. Cover the braising pan with a buttered paper and the lid. Cook over a slow heat for 4 hours, until the beef is very tender.

Strain off the cooking liquid. Reduce it and, if liked, thicken it with the potato flour mixed with the madeira. Place the beef on a heated serving dish and surround with vegetables such as glazed onions, carrots, petits pois, a *jardinière* of mixed vegetables, potato croquettes, fresh noodles, braised lettuce, various purées.

Red wines: Saint-Émilion, Beaujolais-Villages, Côtes du Rhône, Côtes de Provence, Cahors.

US	Ingredients	Met/Imp
I, about 5½ lb	piece beef top rump (sirloin tip roast)	I, about 2.5 kg/5½ lb
10 oz	fatty bacon, cut into long, rectangular strips	300 g/10 oz
	pork fat scraps	
4	carrots	4
2	large onions	2
I	bouquet garni	I
	salt	
	peppercorns	
	beef or veal bones (optional)	
I glass	beef stock	I glass
I quart	dry white wine	I litre/1¾ pints
3½ tbsp	cognac	50 ml/2 fl oz
I tbsp	potato flour (optional)	15 ml/1 tbsp
scant ½ cup	madeira (optional)	100 ml/4 fl oz

ENTRECÔTE STEAK BORDELAISE

Preparation 25 minutes • Cooking 12 minutes

Brush the steaks with oil or butter and cook over charcoal or, better still, on a bed of vine shoots, until done to your liking. Season with salt and pepper. When ready to serve, add a little nutmeg, the finely chopped shallots and the beef marrow. Sprinkle with parsley and serve on a heated serving dish, garnished with watercress and accompanied by the potatoes.

Red wines: Saint-Émilion, Pomerol, Graves, Médoc.

US	Ingredients	Met/Imp
4, each about 14 oz	entrecôte steaks (boneless rib steaks)	4, each about 400 g/14 oz
½ cup	oil or melted butter	100 ml/4 fl oz
	salt and pepper	
I pinch	nutmeg	I pinch
4	shallots	4
I lb	beef marrow, cut in round slices and poached	500 g/1 lb
I tbsp	chopped parsley	15 ml/1 tbsp
I	bunch watercress	I
3½ lb	'Pont-Neuf' Potatoes (page 552)	1.5 kg/3½ lb

ENTRECÔTE OR SIRLOIN STEAK ROUGEMONT

Preparation 1 hour • Marinating 1 hour • Cooking 10 minutes

US	Ingredients	Met/Imp
4, each about 14 oz	entrecôte or sirloin steaks (boneless rib or sirloin steaks)	4, each about 400 g/14 oz
	salt and pepper	
½ cup	olive oil	100 ml/3½ fl oz
1	onion	1
	parsley stalks	
	chopped thyme	
	ground bay	
20	tarragon leaves	20
10 tbsp	butter	150 g/5 oz
1 tbsp	Meat Glaze (*page 56*)	15 ml/1 tbsp
1 glass	white wine	1 glass
1 cup	Veal Stock (*page 56*)	200 ml/7 fl oz
1 tbsp	potato flour	15 ml/1 tbsp
1 tbsp	chopped tarragon	15 ml/1 tbsp

The steaks should be at least 2.5 cm/1 inch thick. Beat them with a meat mallet to break down the fibres and reduce them to a thickness of 2 cm/¾ inch, then season them with pepper. Put them on a plate and sprinkle them with some olive oil. Strew the top with finely sliced onion and a few stalks of parsley broken into pieces, a little thyme and ground bay. Do not salt the meat at this stage: it is only salted at the time of cooking in the sauté pan (this is very important). Leave to marinate in a cold place for 1 hour, turning the steaks from time to time.

Put the tarragon leaves in a sieve, dip them for a few moments in boiling water, drain and set aside. In a sauté pan, heat 45 ml/3 tbsp clarified butter or 25 g/scant 1 oz (2 tbsp) ordinary butter and 30 ml/2 tbsp oil until smoking. Add the steaks and fry them for 4 minutes, then sprinkle them with salt and turn them over. The steaks are 'à point' (medium rare) when droplets of pinkish blood are visible on the surface of the meat. Arrange the steaks on a heated long serving dish, lightly brush the surface with melted meat glaze and arrange the blanched tarrragon leaves on top.

Drain the fat from the pan and pour in the wine. Quickly reduce it right down, then add the veal stock. Boil for a few moments, then stir in the potato flour mixed with a little cold water, whisking to blend thoroughly. Let the sauce boil for a few minutes. Finish away from the heat with the remaining butter and the chopped tarragon. Serve with braised lettuce, celery in gravy, a purée of artichokes or fried salsify, as liked.

Red wines: Médoc, Côte Rôtie, Cahors.

'WINE MERCHANT'S' ENTRECÔTE STEAK*

Preparation 30 minutes • Cooking 15–20 minutes

US	Ingredients	Met/Imp
2, each about 1½ lb	entrecôte steaks (boneless rib steaks)	2, each about 750 g/1½ lb
	salt and pepper	
14 tbsp	butter	200 g/7 oz
2 oz	shallots	50 g/2 oz
½ bottle	good burgundy	½ bottle
½ cup	Veal Stock (*page 56*)	100 ml/4 fl oz
¼ cup	crème fraîche	50 ml/2 fl oz
	wine vinegar	
1 tbsp	chopped parsley	15 ml/1 tbsp

Season the steaks with pepper on both sides. Cook them to your liking in a sauté pan with a large piece of butter, then salt them. When the steaks are cooked, keep them warm on a plate. Put the chopped shallots into the pan. Deglaze with wine, then add the thickened veal stock, the crème fraîche, salt to taste and a dash of vinegar. Reduce. Surround the steaks with this sauce and serve sprinkled with parsley, accompanied by deep-fried potatoes.

Wines: in general, serve the same wine as the one used for cooking.

PROVENÇAL BEEF STEW

Preparation 1½ hours • Marinating 8 hours • Cooking 3½ hours

US	Ingredients	Met/Imp
about 4½ lb	neck (chuck) of beef	about 2 kg/4½ lb
3	carrots	3
2	large onions	2
2	leeks	2
1	celery stalk	1
	salt and pepper	
	quatre-épices	
1	bouquet garni	1
2 cups	red wine	500 ml/18 fl oz
2	cloves	2
	peppercorns	
a few	coriander seeds	a few
5 oz	fatty bacon	150 g/5 oz
1 lb	lean bacon	500 g/1 lb
3	pigs' trotters (feet)	3
1 tsp	potato flour	5 ml/1 tsp
6	tomatoes	6
1⅓ cups	green olives	250 g/8 oz

Cut up the beef into 75 g/3 oz pieces, as for a sauté, and marinate them for 8 hours or overnight with the sliced carrots, onions, leeks, celery, salt, pepper, spice and bouquet garni, all immersed in the red wine (Corbières, for example).

Take the meat out of the marinade and leave to drain in a sieve. Strain the marinade. Put the vegetables in a piece of cheesecloth with the cloves, peppercorns and coriander seeds. Tie to make a bag.

Fry the finely chopped fat bacon in a sauté pan until the fat runs. Put the pieces of beef into this smoking fat. Fry, turning, to seal the meat all over. Turn down the heat, cover and leave to simmer for 20 minutes.

Transfer the meat to an earthenware casserole and add the lean bacon, pigs' trotters (feet) and the bag of vegetables and spices. Pour the marinade into the sauté pan containing the beef juices. Bring to the boil and pour into the casserole, to cover the meat. Seal tightly with a double sheet of paper tied around with string. Put on the lid and leave to cook gently for 3 hours.

Take out the piece of lean bacon, the pigs' trotters (feet) and the spice bag, after squeezing it to extract the liquid. Strain the stock, thicken it with the potato flour, skim and adjust the seasoning.

Bone the pigs' trotters (feet). Dice them and also the lean bacon. Put them all back in with the pieces of beef, and add the skinned, de-seeded and roughly chopped tomatoes. Add the stoned green olives, blanched and lightly fried beforehand. Strain the stock over, simmer for a few minutes and the stew is ready.

Red wines: Côtes du Rhône, Châteauneuf-du-Pape, Côtes de Provence, Vin de Corse, or the wine used in the marinade.

FILLET OF BEEF IN PASTRY

Preparation 2 hours • Cooking about 45 minutes

US	Ingredients	Met/Imp
1, about 4 lb	eye of fillet of beef (beef tenderloin roast)	1, about 1.8 kg/4 lb
	salt and pepper	
½ cup	armagnac	100 ml/4 fl oz
1½ lb	foie gras	700 g/1½ lb
7 oz	truffles	200 g/7 oz
2 lb	Puff Pastry (page 579)	1 kg/2 lb
	Périgueux Sauce (page 75)	

Trim the beef and split it in half lengthways. Season with salt and pepper and sprinkle the cut surfaces with armagnac. Stuff it with the foie gras and truffles and tie securely. Roast for 15 minutes in a very hot oven, then leave it to rest for 10 minutes. Wrap it in the puff pastry and bake in the oven for a further 30 minutes or so, depending upon its size.

Serve separately with a very well-seasoned Périgueux sauce on the side.

Red wines: Saint-Émilion, Pomerol, Cahors, Madiran.

US	Ingredients	Met/Imp

FILLET OF BEEF IN PASTRY —— NIVERNAIS STYLE ——

Preparation 2½ hours • Marinating 24 hours • Cooking 1½ hours

US	Ingredients	Met/Imp
1, about 5½ lb	trimmed fillet of beef (beef tenderloin roast)	1, about 2.5 kg/5½ lb
10 oz	fat bacon strips for larding	300 g/10 oz
1½ quarts	white wine	1.5 litres/2½ pints
2	carrots	2
1	onion	1
14 tbsp	butter	200 g/7 oz
	parsley sprigs	
	bouquet garni	
	nutmeg	
	Dry Duxelles (page 49), made with fresh ceps	
10 oz	raw country ham	300 g/10 oz
	salt and pepper	
10 oz	chicken or goose livers	300 g/10 oz
7 oz	fat bacon	200 g/7 oz
4	eggs	4
scant ½ cup	cognac	100 ml/4 fl oz
2 lb	Puff Pastry (page 579)	1 kg/2 lb
scant ½ cup	madeira	100 ml/4 fl oz
8	lettuce hearts	8
8	tomatoes	8

Lard the beef well with the bacon strips. Marinate it for 24 hours in the wine with the sliced carrots and onion, tossed and stewed in the butter beforehand, with the parsley, bouquet garni and a little nutmeg.

Take out the beef and wipe it dry. To make the stuffing, mix the duxelles with the finely chopped ham, salt, pepper, a little nutmeg, the finely chopped chicken or goose livers and the finely chopped fat bacon; bind with the beaten eggs. Moisten this forcemeat with some of the marinade, reduced and cooled to the consistency of a sauce, then stir in the cognac. Spread the stuffing mixture over the beef and wrap completely in the pastry. Make 2 small vents in the top.

Cook in a hot oven, allowing 15 minutes per 500 g/1 lb for rare meat. Pour the madeira through the vents in the pastry shortly before the end of cooking. Let the beef rest for a good 15 minutes in a warm place before slicing. Serve accompanied by the lettuce hearts and tomatoes, braised in the remaining marinade.

Red wines: Saint-Émilion, Pomerol, Graves, Côte de Nuits.

—— FILLET OF BEEF FRASCATI ——

Preparation 1½ hours • Cooking 50 minutes

US	Ingredients	Met/Imp
1, about 4½ lb	eye of fillet of beef (beef tenderloin roast)	1, about 2 kg/4½ lb
7 oz	fat bacon for larding	200 g/7 oz
¼ lb	pork rinds	100 g/4 oz
2	carrots	2
1	large onion	1
1	bouquet garni	1
1 cup	Veal Stock (page 56)	200 ml/7 fl oz
½ cup	madeira	100 ml/3½ fl oz
8	slices fresh foie gras	8
	salt and pepper	
1½ cups	flour	200 g/7 oz
10 tbsp	butter	150 g/5 oz
4	small bundles asparagus tips	4
8, each about 1 oz	small fresh truffles	8, each about 30 g/1 oz
8	perfect *Paris mushroom* caps	8
½ cup	Demi-Glaze (page 56)	100 ml/3½ fl oz

Trim the beef thoroughly and thread it with the bacon cut into very thin *lardons*. Tie it in several places with string so that it keeps its shape, then put it in a long braising pan lined with the pork rind and the sliced carrots, onion and bouquet garni

Pour on half of the stock and let it reduce completely. Pour on half of the madeira and the remaining stock. Cover the beef with a buttered paper and cook in a hot oven, basting it very frequently, for 45–50 minutes, or a little longer, depending upon size. The beef should be pink inside. Eight minutes before the end of cooking, uncover it to brown the bacon and glaze the surface of the meat. Place the beef on a heated serving dish. On each side arrange the foie gras, sliced 1 cm/½ inch thick, seasoned with salt and pepper, dipped in flour and sautéed in clarified butter; the asparagus tips, cooked in boiling salted water and turned in butter; the peeled whole truffles; and the mushrooms

Strain the beef cooking liquid through a sieve and skim it. Reduce it by half and add just enough demi-glaze to thicken. Just before serving, add the remaining madeira.

Red wines: Saint-Émilion, Pomerol, Graves, Côte de Nuits, Côte Rôtie, Cornas, Côtes du Rhône, Côtes du Jura.

FILLET OF BEEF LUCULLUS

Preparation 3 hours • Cooking 1½ hours

Trim the beef and lard it with some strips of the fat bacon. Make an incision lengthways down 1 side, making a pocket in which to put the stuffing and the foie gras. The incision should stop 2 finger-widths from each end of the beef.

Take the foie gras, trim it and remove the veins and any parts which have dried up or been spoiled through contact with the gall bladder. Pound it and mix it with the egg whites. Season it well. Add the rum and cognac. Shape the mixture into a long sausage which will fit the pocket in the beef. Make incisions down the length of the foie gras and insert some large pieces of chopped truffle into them. Reshape the roll and coat it with a forcemeat made with the trimmings from the beef worked through a sieve, seasoned and mixed with the remaining chopped truffles. Place the roll of stuffing inside the beef, sew up the pocket, cover the seam with a bard of the fat bacon and tie it with string. Put the beef in a hot oven to brown.

Meanwhile, cook any remaining beef trimmings and the broken bones in some butter, with the sliced carrots and onions. These will be used as a base in the braising pan. Add the bouquet garni and put the browned beef on this base. Add two-thirds of the port and season with salt, pepper and spice. Cover the pan with a lid or buttered paper and cook in the oven for about 1 hour, basting frequently. Immediately the beef is done to your liking, remove it from the pan and leave it to rest for 20 minutes, tightly covered. Deglaze the braising pan with the stock, then strain through a conical sieve. Carefully skim off the fat, reduce and add the remaining port. Strain through a cheesecloth and put in a *bain-marie* (this stock should be slightly syrupy).

Slice the beef and arrange the slices on the croûtons of fried bread. Fill the pastry cases with the small truffles and asparagus tips, which have been sweated in butter, then place around the beef. Coat the beef with some of the sauce, pour a little around each serving and hand the rest separately in a sauce boat.

Red wines: Côte de Beaune, Côte de Nuits, Pomerol.

US	Ingredients	Met/Imp
1, about 4½ lb	fillet of beef (beef tenderloin roast)	1, about 2 kg/4½ lb
1 lb	fat bacon	500 g/1 lb
1½ lb	foie gras	700 g/1½ lb
2	egg whites	2
	salt and pepper	
3 tbsp	rum	50 ml/2 fl oz
3 tbsp	cognac	50 ml/2 fl oz
10 oz	chopped large truffles	300 g/10 oz
	butter	
a few	beef bones, broken	a few
2	carrots	2
2	onions	2
1	bouquet garni	1
1¼ cups	port	300 ml/½ pint
1 pinch	*quatre-épices*	1 pinch
2 cups	Veal Stock (*page 56*)	500 ml/18 fl oz
8	croûtons, cut the same size as the beef slices and fried in butter	8
16	small shortcrust (pie) or puff pastry cases	16
8, each about 1 oz	small whole truffles	8, each about 30 g/1 oz
8	small bundles asparagus tips	8

US	Ingredients	Met/Imp
1, about 4½ lb	fillet of beef (beef tenderloin roast)	1, about 2 kg/4½ lb
10 oz	fat bacon	300 g/10 oz
3 tbsp	butter	40 g/1½ oz
	salt and pepper	
	SAUCE	
1 stick	butter	100 g/4 oz
½ cup	flour	75 g/3 oz
3 cups	Clear or Brown Veal Stock (page 56)	750 ml/1¼ pints
1 tbsp	Meat Glaze (page 56)	15 ml/1 tbsp
3½ tbsp	madeira	50 ml/2 fl oz
scant ½ cup	white wine	100 ml/4 fl oz
1	bouquet garni	1
2 lb (5 cups)	green olives, stoned and blanched	1 kg/2 lb
	mushroom trimmings	

FILLET OF BEEF WITH OLIVES

Preparation 1½ hours • (Sauce prepared day before, 2–3 hours) • Cooking 30–40 minutes

Trim the beef and lard it with bacon. Tie it and put it in a roasting pan with the butter. Roast in a hot oven for 30–40 minutes. The beef should be well sealed to conserve all its juices. Season with salt and pepper at the time of serving.

To accompany a roast such as a fillet (tenderloin) of beef, a simple *roux* made quickly by adding stock, is not good enough. The sauce should be prepared the day before. It needs to be very carefully made, cooked for several hours and meticulously skimmed. Make a roux with the butter and flour, add the stock, reduce and stir in the meat glaze and madeira to strengthen the flavour. Add the white wine, bouquet garni, olives and mushroom trimmings and simmer very gently for 2–3 hours. All sauces containing olives should be very strong and highly flavoured, because far from enriching a dish, olives somehow absorb the richness of sauces and weaken their flavour. So you can safely increase the amount of madeira or substitute port wine or sherry.

Serve the beef carved into thin slices and reassembled in its original shape in a heated deep dish, surrounded by the olives and coated with the sauce. The serving dish and the plates should be very hot.

Wines: Saint-Émilion, Pomerol, Graves, Côte du Nuits, Côte Rôtie, Cornas, Côtes du Rhône, red wine from Côtes du Jura.

US	Ingredients	Met/Imp
1, about 4½ lb	trimmed fillet of beef (beef tenderloin roast)	1, about 2 kg/4½ lb
10 oz	fat bacon	300 g/10 oz
2 cups	dry white wine	500 ml/18 fl oz
2	shallots	2
6	peppercorns	6
scant 1 cup	*crème fraîche*	200 ml/7 fl oz
2 tbsp	butter	30 g/1 oz
1 tbsp	chopped tarragon	15 ml/1 tbsp
2 lb	field or other wild mushrooms	1 kg/2 lb
	MARINADE	
½ cup	wine vinegar	100 ml/3½ fl oz
½ cup	olive oil	100 ml/3½ fl oz
1	bouquet garni	1
3	cloves	3
	nutmeg	

ROAST FILLET OF BEEF 'CHARENTE DAIRYMEN'

Preparation 1 hour • Marinating 12 hours • Cooking 40 minutes

Marinate the beef overnight in a mixture of the vinegar, olive oil, bouquet garni, cloves and a little nutmeg. Remove the beef, lard it with the bacon and tie it. Roast in a very hot oven, basting it frequently with the marinade, until well-browned but still rare (about 40 minutes). Remove to a heated serving dish.

Pour the cooking juices into a saucepan. Add the wine, the finely chopped shallots and the crushed peppercorns. Season with a dash of vinegar. Skim and simmer for 10 minutes. Add the crème fraîche, strain through a conical sieve and, off the heat, add the butter and the tarragon. Coat the beef with this sauce and garnish with the mushrooms fried in butter.

Red wines: Saint-Émilion, Pomerol, Graves, Médoc, Bourgueil, Côte de Beaune.

Mutton Stew
*Garnished only with small white onions and new potatoes, the slowly braised
'navarin' of mutton or lamb makes a delicious spring dish. (Recipe on page 367.)*

Leg of Lamb Landaise
Spiked with garlic and coated with goose fat and butter to make a particularly sumptuous roast, this gigot deserves a special garnish, different from the usual sautéed potatoes. This consists of cooked beans sautéed in goose fat with a julienne of Bayonne ham, then thickened with crème fraîche, tomatoes, onions, garlic and egg yolks. (Recipe on page 363.)

Sheep's Trotters with Poulette Sauce
In the past, the sauce of this dish used to accompany chicken fricassées, hence the name 'poulette'. Nowadays, it is usually served with sheep's trotters (feet), or with calves' brains. (Recipe on page 369.)

'Wine Merchant's' Entrecôte Steak
When one speaks of 'entrecôte marchand de vin', it means a steak served with a sauce of shallots and red wine. The meat may be either fried or grilled (or broiled). The 'pommes frites' garnish is traditional. (Recipe on page 380.)

Braised Rump of Beef
Top rump (sirloin tip) roast is less tender than fillet (tenderloin) of beef, but it has more flavour. For braising, it must be larded in several places with fatty bacon. It may be accompanied by peas, onions and carrots, by fresh pasta or even braised lettuce. (Recipe on page 379.)

Tournedos Steaks 'on Toast'
The cooking juices of the steaks, deglazed with port wine and further enhanced by t
addition of cream and truffles, makes the delicate sauce which accompanies these
slices of beef served on toasted bread. (Recipe on page 397.)

— FILLET OF BEEF SAINT-FLORENTIN —

Preparation 2 hours • Cooking 25–30 minutes

US	Ingredients	Met/Imp
1	carrot	1
1	large onion	1
¼ lb	fatty bacon	100 g/4 oz
1	bouquet garni	1
10 tbsp	butter	150 g/5 oz
⅓ cup	white wine	75 ml/3 fl oz
1, about 3 lb	trimmed eye of fillet of beef (beef tenderloin roast)	1, about 1.4 kg/3 lb
5 oz	pork back fat or bacon fat	150 g/5 oz
	salt and pepper	
2 lb	ceps	1 kg/2 lb
¾ cup	oil	75 ml/3 fl oz
¼ lb	pickled or salted tongue	75 ml/3 fl oz
2 lb	Duchesse Potatoes (page 551)	1 kg/2 lb
2	eggs	2
½ lb	vermicelli	250 g/8 oz
2 cups	Bordelaise Sauce (page 63)	500 ml/18 fl oz
¼ lb	beef marrow	100 g/4 oz
1 tbsp	chopped parsley	15 ml/1 tbsp

Start by preparing a *mirepoix*: finely chop the carrot and onion. Add the finely diced fatty bacon and the bouquet garni. Put them all in a casserole with 25 g/scant 1 oz (2 tbsp) of the butter. Lightly brown over a brisk heat, then simmer over a gentle heat until completely cooked. Add the wine and reduce completely. Spread the mirepoix out on a dish and allow to cool (the purpose of this mirepoix is to allow the meat to be permeated with its flavours during cooking).

Lard the beef with the fat. Generously grease a large sheet of foil. Spread half of the cold mirepoix on it. On top of this, place the beef, seasoned with salt and pepper. Spread the remaining mirepoix over it. Wrap it in the foil, tie it up like a galantine and place it on a rack in an oval roasting dish. Put a few spoonfuls of water in the bottom of the dish. Cook in a very hot oven, allowing 10 minutes per 500 g/1 lb for rare meat and 12 minutes for medium rare. Ten minutes before the end of cooking, remove the covering foil and the mirepoix to ensure that the meat acquires a good colour and the fat is browned.

To prepare the garnish, cut the ceps into thick slices. Just before serving, season them with salt and pepper and sauté in smoking oil until well-browned. They should be piping hot when served.

For the potato croquettes, mix the finely diced tongue into the duchesse potato mixture. Divide this into 16 portions and form into large cork shapes. Dip them one after the other in the eggs beaten with salt, pepper and a dash of oil, then roll them in finely crumbled vermicelli and reshape (here, vermicelli replaces breadcrumbs which are usually used for croquettes). Deep-fry in very hot oil for 5 minutes before serving.

Immediately before serving, mix into the Bordelaise sauce the finely diced beef marrow, poached in salted water 3 minutes beforehand, and well drained with a slotted spoon.

Serve the beef on a heated long dish, surrounded by the ceps sprinkled with the parsley. Put small piles of the potato croquettes at each end of the dish. Serve the sauce on the side.

Red wines: Saint-Émilion, Pomerol, Graves, Médoc.

US	Ingredients	Met/Imp
about 9 lb	ox tripe	about 4 kg/9 lb
I	bouquet garni	I
4	carrots	4
2	onions	2
2	cloves	2
I	head garlic	I
10	peppercorns	10
	coarse sea salt	
I lb	Bayonne ham trimmings, fat and lean	500 g/I lb
2 lb	veal bones	I kg/2 lb
I lb	fat ham	500 g/I lb
¼ lb	pork fat	100 g/4 oz
½ cup	olive oil	100 ml/4 fl oz
I tbsp	chopped parsley	15 ml/I tbsp
I cup	flour	150 g/5 oz
I tbsp	saffron	15 ml/I tbsp
⅔ cup	capers	100 g/4 oz

GRAS-DOUBLE À L'ALBIGEOISE

OX TRIPE ALBIGEOISE

Preparation 3 hours • Cooking 13 hours

Wash the tripe thoroughly and press out the moisture. Cut it into large pieces and place them in a large casserole. Add the bouquet garni, sliced carrots, the onions sliced and spiked with the cloves, the garlic, peppercorns and salt. Add the ham trimmings and the veal bones. Pour on plenty of water to cover so that the tripe remains well covered during cooking and does not darken: it should remain as white as possible.

Bring to the boil, skim carefully, then cover and cook in a slow oven for 12 hours.

Drain the tripe and cut it into even squares. Strain the cooking liquid and reduce it. Coarsely dice the fat ham and fry lightly over a gentle heat in the pork fat and oil. Sprinkle in the parsley and before it can brown, add the flour, stirring briskly, without letting it colour. Stir in the reduced and finely strained cooking liquid. Cook this sauce over gentle heat, then put in the tripe. Cover tightly and simmer for 30 minutes. Add the saffron, stir well, cover again and simmer for a further 30 minutes. The sauce should have a good yellow colour and fully cover the tripe.

Serve in a very hot tureen, garnished with the capers.

Dry white wines: Tursan, dry Graves.
Red wines: Madiran, Côtes du Frontonnais, Côtes de Bourg.

US	Ingredients	Met/Imp
4½ lb	tripe	2 kg/4½ lb
2 lb	lard	I kg/2 lb
4	large onions	4
½ cup	wine vinegar	100 ml/4 fl oz
	salt and pepper	
	parsley and chervil	

GRAS-DOUBLE À LA LYONNAISE

TRIPE LYONNAISE

Preparation 24 hours • Cooking 30 minutes

Cut the tripe into strips. Fry it in some of the lard until it is a good colour. Take it out, drain it and put it in a flameproof casserole. Cover it with fresh lard and leave for 24 hours, to tenderize it. Heat gently, then drain off all the lard: reserve for another use. Lightly fry the sliced onions. Mix the tripe and the onions in a sauté pan. Add the vinegar shortly before serving, season with salt and pepper and sprinkle with chopped parsley and chervil.

Red wines: Beaujolais-Villages, Beaujolais Nouveau.

BASQUE TRIPE

Preparation 1 hour • Cooking 5 hours

Put the chopped tripe and the calf's feet cut in half (they can be boned) in a terrine and pour boiling water over them. Before it cools down too much, remove the tripe and drain it. Meanwhile, dice the belly (side) of pork, the carrots and 1 onion; spike the other onion with the cloves. Heat the fat in a flameproof casserole. Brown the pork, then the onions and the carrots. When they are all fried, add the tripe and calves' feet. Add the wine and season with salt and pepper. Add the sweet pepper, chopped with the garlic, parsley and tarragon. Boil quite briskly for 30 minutes, then cover tightly and simmer over a very gentle heat for 4–5 hours. Bind with the beaten egg yolks before serving.

Red wines: Saint-Émilion, Pomerol, Médoc, Madiran, Irouléguy.

US	Ingredients	Met/Imp
4½ lb	tripe	2 kg/4½ lb
2	calf's feet	2
1 lb	fresh belly (side) of pork	500 g/1 lb
1 lb	carrots	500 g/1 lb
2	large onions	2
2	cloves	2
½ cup	goose or pork fat	100 g/4 oz
1½ quarts	white wine	1.5 litres/2½ pints
	salt and pepper	
1	red sweet pepper	1
4	garlic cloves	4
	parsley and tarragon sprigs	
2	egg yolks	2

PICKLED OX TONGUE

Preparation and pickling 8 days in winter, 6 days in summer • Cooking 2½–3 hours

Trim the tongue, wash and dry it. Prick it all over with a trussing needle. Vigorously rub it all over with fine salt and a little saltpetre. Lay it flat in an earthenware container with more salt packed around it, cover and leave for 24 hours. Meanwhile, prepare the brine as follows:

Put 5 litres/9 pints (5 quarts) water, the coarse sea salt, saltpetre and sugar into a saucepan. Bring to a rolling boil. Remove from the heat and immediately add the peppercorns, juniper berries, coriander seeds, thyme, bay leaf, mint, garlic and basil. Cover and leave to infuse.

The next day, dry the tongue and immerse it completely in the prepared brine in a stoneware or earthenware receptacle. Weight down with a small board to stop the tongue from rising to the surface. Leave for several days, in a cool place, turning it every day without touching it with your hands.

When the tongue is pickled, wash it well and cook in fresh water in a large saucepan for 2½–3 hours until tender and thoroughly cooked. Let the tongue cool in its cooking liquid in a cold place. Remove it from the pan, skin it and wrap it in a cloth.

Red wines: Fitou, Corbières, Côtes du Frontonnais, Côtes du Roussillon, Coteaux du Languedoc, Cahors, Madiran.

US	Ingredients	Met/Imp
1	ox tongue	1
	fine salt and saltpetre mixed	
4½ lb	coarse sea salt	2 kg/4½ lb
¼ lb	saltpetre	100 g/4 oz
¾ cup	light soft brown sugar	150 g/5 oz
15	peppercorns	15
15	juniper berries	15
15	coriander seeds	15
	thyme sprigs	
1	bay leaf	1
1	mint sprig	1
1	head garlic	1
1	basil sprig	1

US	Ingredients	Met/Imp
I	ox tongue	I
7 oz	bacon rind and trimmings	200 g/7 oz
2	large onions	2
3	carrots	3
I	bouquet garni	I
	salt and pepper	
I glass	white wine	I glass
I quart	Brown Veal Stock (page 56)	I litre/1¾ pints
I tsp	tomato paste	5 ml/I tsp
I lb	noodles	500 g/I lb
I cup	Italian Sauce (see Duxelles Sauce, page 68)	200 ml/7 fl oz
2 cups	Parmesan cheese, grated	250 g/8 oz

OX TONGUE ITALIENNE

Preparation 1 hour • Cooking 3 hours

'Italian' sauce is Duxelles Sauce (*page 68*) to which chopped cooked ham has been added.

Put the tongue in a flameproof casserole, on the bottom of which you have put the bacon rind, onions sliced into rings, sliced carrots, bouquet garni and seasoning. Keep on the edge of the stove until the vegetables are lightly browned. Add the wine and let it reduce completely. Add the stock and tomato paste and bring to the boil, then cover with a piece of buttered paper and the lid. Cover and cook in a slow oven at a gentle simmer, taking care to turn the tongue over from time to time, for about 3 hours or until cooked through.

Arrange the whole or partly sliced tongue on a heated round serving dish surrounded by boiled noodles. Hand the Italian sauce and the reduced and skimmed braising juices from the tongue separately, together with a bowl of Parmesan.

Dry white wines: Muscadet, Pouilly-Fumé, dry Graves, Chablis.
Red wines: Beaujolais-Villages, Bourgueil, Chinon.

US	Ingredients	Met/Imp
8	large onions	8
¼ cup	lard	50 g/2 oz
6 tbsp	flour	50 g/2 oz
2 cups	clear stock	500 ml/18 fl oz
scant ½ cup	white wine	100 ml/3½ fl oz
I	bouquet garni	I
	salt and pepper	
2 lb	boiled beef from Pot-au-Feu (page 390)	I kg/2 lb
3½ tbsp	wine vinegar	50 ml/2 fl oz
6	cornichons	6
I tbsp	chopped parsley	15 ml/I tbsp

MIROTON BONNE FEMME

Preparation 1 hour • Cooking 10 minutes

In many French households, miroton is the usual way of using up boiled beef from the day before. Although you should not vary the basic recipe, you can vary the details.

Thinly slice the onions. Heat 2 spoonfuls of lard in a sauté pan. Put in the onions and brown them over a moderate heat, tossing them from time to time until they become a golden colour. (If they are very ripe onions, they should first be boiled for 7–8 minutes, to take away any sharpness and to make them tender. They should then be rinsed, drained well and dried in a cloth so there is no moisture left, otherwise it will be impossible to brown them.) Take out the onions and keep them hot.

Mix the flour with the lard in the sauté pan. Allow to brown for 7–8 minutes. Add the stock, wine, bouquet garni and a large pinch of pepper. Bring to the boil, stirring, and cook gently for 30 minutes. Mix in the browned onions. Add the leftover boiled beef, sliced as thinly and evenly as possible across the grain of the meat. Reheat the meat without letting it boil.

When ready to serve, stir in the vinegar. Tip the miroton into a heated serving dish and sprinkle with the cornichons, cut into thin rounds, and the parsley.

Red wines: Beaujolais-Villages, Beaujolais Nouveau, Bourgueil, young bordeaux.

TOP RUMP BOURGUIGNON

Preparation 1½ hours • Marinating 3 hours • Cooking 4–5 hours

US	Ingredients	Met/Imp
I, about 5½ lb	beef top rump (sirloin tip roast)	I, about 2.5 kg/5½ lb
10 oz	pork fat or bacon fat	300 g/10 oz
	salt and pepper	
	quatre-épices	
I tbsp	chopped parsley	15 ml/I tbsp
I quart	red wine	I litre/1¾ pints
3½ tbsp	cognac	50 ml/2 fl oz
3 tbsp	butter	40 g/1½ oz
40	button (pearl) onions	40
½ lb	fatty bacon	250 g/8 oz
½ cup	flour	75 g/3 oz
2 cups	Brown Veal Stock (page 56)	500 ml/18 fl oz
I	bouquet garni	I
¼ lb	mushrooms	100 g/4 oz

The authentic beef bourguignon is really a daube (a stew cooked in wine). However, a large piece of meat can be prepared by the same method.

Lard the beef as for Beef 'à la Mode' (*page 377*) with the fat cut into strips, seasoned with salt and spice and dusted with parsley. Season the beef with salt and pepper and leave to marinate for 3 hours in the red wine and cognac.

Heat the butter in a heavy flameproof casserole and put in the button (pearl) onions (they should be hazelnut size). Let them colour, take them out and drain them well on a dish. In the same fat, brown the fatty bacon, coarsely diced and boiled for 5–6 minutes beforehand. Drain and set aside with the onions.

Still using the same fat, heated until it is smoking, put in the beef, drained of the marinade and thoroughly dried with a cloth (if any moisture remains, it will be converted into steam and prevent the outside from browning). Fry the beef well on all sides so that it has a good brown coating, then set it aside on a plate.

Stir the flour into the fat. Cook the mixture until it turns a russet colour. Add the marinade and the stock and bring to the boil, stirring, then return the beef to this light sauce with a pinch of pepper, the bouquet garni and the mushrooms. (A small boned, scalded and tied calf's foot may be added too.) Bring to the boil, then put a piece of buttered paper directly over the beef. Cover and continue cooking in a slow oven at a regular simmer for at least 3 hours.

Take out the beef, strain the sauce and skim the fat from it. Put the beef, bacon, onions, mushrooms and sauce back into the rinsed-out casserole. Continue cooking very gently in the oven for at least another hour, until the beef is tender and the sauce reduced by half.

Wines: as a general rule, serve the same wine as the one used for cooking.

POT-AU-FEU

Preparation 30 minutes • Cooking 3 hours

US	Ingredients	Met/Imp
2 lb	flank of beef on the bone (flanken style ribs)	1 kg/2 lb
1¼ lb	clod (chuck blade) of beef	600 g/1¼ lb
14 oz	neck (chuck arm) of beef	400 g/14 oz
2	chopped pieces veal knuckle (shank)	2
	salt	
4–5	leeks	4–5
a few	celery stalks	a few
	or	
7 oz	celeriac	200 g/7 oz
2	onions	2
4	cloves	4
6	turnips or parsnips	6
8	carrots	8
1	bouquet garni	1
	peppercorns	
	toasted croûtons	
	Cheddar cheese, grated	

Pour about 4 litres/7 pints (4 quarts) cold water into a large flameproof casserole. Add all the meat and the bones, with 15 ml/1 tbsp salt. Bring to the boil, then skim, cover and simmer for about 1 hour.

Meanwhile, trim the leeks and tie them in bunches, likewise the celery stalks, if used. Spike the peeled onions with the cloves. Peel the turnips or parsnips and carrots. When the beef has been cooking for 1 hour, add the carrots, onions and bouquet garni to the casserole. Simmer for 30 minutes, then add the leeks, turnips, celery or celeriac and 15 ml/1 tbsp peppercorns. Add more water, if necessary, to cover the contents of the casserole. Continue simmering until all the ingredients are tender.

At the end of the cooking time, strain the cooking liquid through a fine sieve. Skim the fat off carefully. Serve the stock very hot in soup bowls, with small toasted croûtons and grated cheese. You can serve the marrow spread on toast to follow, then the pieces of meat, together with the vegetables. As accompaniments serve a selection of *cornichons*, coarse sea salt, pickles, mustard, small beetroot (beets), grated horseradish, etc.

Red wines: Beaujolais-Villages, Côtes du Rhône-Villages, Bandol, Bergerac, Cahors, Gaillac.

OXTAIL WITH CHIPOLATAS

Preparation 2 hours • Cooking 4½ hours

US	Ingredients	Met/Imp
2, each about 3½ lb	oxtails	2, each about 1.5 kg/3½ lb
5 oz	pork rind	150 g/5 oz
4	carrots	4
2	onions	2
1	celery stalk	1
1	bouquet garni	1
2 cups	Brown Veal Stock (page 56)	500 ml/18 fl oz
2 cups	white wine	500 ml/18 fl oz
	salt and pepper	
	GARNISH	
24	button (pearl) onions	24
12	chipolatas (small pork link sausages), fried	12
24	chestnuts, cooked in consommé	24
5 oz	lean bacon, blanched and browned	150 g/5 oz

Discard about one-third of each oxtail towards its tapering end and cut each into 16 sections of about the same thickness. The discarded pieces can be used in Pot-au-Feu (*above*). Cut the oxtails at the joints and saw the large sections at the root of the tail in half.

Soak the pieces of oxtail in plenty of cold water for 4 hours, or leave them under cold running water for 2 hours. This will dissolve the blood.

Put the oxtails into a large saucepan of cold water and boil them for 7–8 minutes, then drain and wipe them. Put them into a casserole, the base of which is covered with the pork rind, sliced carrots and onions, celery and bouquet garni.

Leave to sweat for 15 minutes in a fairly hot oven. Add 100 ml/4 fl oz (½ cup) of the stock and reduce completely, then add the wine and enough stock to cover the oxtail completely. Bring to the boil, cover and cook in a slow oven for 3½–4 hours, or until the meat comes away easily from the bones. Using a fork, remove the sections of oxtail and put them into a sauté pan. Add the glazed button (pearl) onions, the fried chipolatas, the cooked chestnuts and blanched and browned bacon. Simmer for 20 minutes, seasoning to taste with salt and pepper. To serve, simply tip the oxtail and the garnish into a heated deep serving dish or pile the oxtail on a platter and cover with the sauce and garnish.

Dry white wines: Pouilly-Fumé, Chablis.
Red wines: Beaujolais-Villages, Bourgueil, Chinon.

OXTAIL 'FRANÇAISE'

Preparation 2 hours • Cooking 5 hours

US	Ingredients	Met/Imp
8, each about 10 oz	pieces of oxtail	8, each about 300 g/10 oz
4	carrots	4
3	onions	3
2	garlic cloves	2
1	bouquet garni	1
1 lb	pork rinds	500 g/1 lb
2	calf's feet	2
2 bottles	white wine	2 bottles
	stock	
	salt and pepper	
1 pinch	*quatre-épices*	1 pinch
	TO SERVE	
1	bunch carrots	1
1	bunch turnips	1
1½ lb	potatoes, steamed	750 g/1½ lb
30	button (pearl) onions, sweated in butter and glazed	30

Arrange the pieces of oxtail in a flameproof casserole on a bed of chopped carrots and onions, crushed garlic, the bouquet garni, pork rinds and the boned calf's feet. Sweat these ingredients until they turn colour.

Pour on the wine and enough stock just to cover. Season with salt, pepper and spice. Cover and cook for 4 hours in a low oven.

Lift out the oxtail pieces, reduce the cooking liquid and strain through a fine sieve. Return the oxtail to the rinsed-out casserole. Adjust the seasoning of the liquid and skim off the fat. Pour the liquid back over the oxtail and finish cooking. Check the seasoning. Serve with boiled carrots, turnips and potatoes, and glazed onions.

Dry white wines: dry Graves, Chablis, Arbois, Alsace Riesling.
Red wines: Bourgueil, Chinon, Côte Rôtie, Châteauneuf-du-Pape.

OXTAIL HOTPOT

Preparation 1 hour • Cooking 8 hours

US	Ingredients	Met/Imp
1 lb	smoked belly of pork (slab bacon)	500 g/1 lb
16, each about ½ lb	pieces oxtail	16, each about 250 g/8 oz
4	large onions	4
2	garlic cloves	2
½ cup	cognac	100 ml/4 fl oz
3 quarts	stock	3 litres/5¼ pints
1	bouquet garni	1
2 bottles	red wine	2 bottles
½ cup	madeira	100 ml/4 fl oz
1 stick	butter	100 g/4 oz
¾ cup	flour	100 g/4 oz

Brown the diced belly of pork (bacon) slowly in a flameproof casserole. Remove and replace with the pieces of oxtail. Brown these thoroughly and add the chopped onions and garlic. Return the belly of pork (bacon) and flambé with the cognac. Pour in enough lightly salted stock to cover and cook for 30 minutes. Add the bouquet garni, the red wine and the madeira; continue cooking over a gentle heat for 3 hours.

Thicken the sauce with a *beurre manié* made with the butter and flour and finish cooking in a moderate oven for about 5 hours.

Red wines: Beaujolais-Villages, Bourgueil, Chinon.

US	Ingredients	Met/Imp
2 sticks	butter	225 g/8 oz
½ cup	oil	100 ml/4 fl oz
10 oz	button mushrooms	300 g/10 oz
4	shallots	4
6 tbsp	flour	50 g/2 oz
½ bottle	white wine	½ bottle
½ cup	Veal Stock (page 56)	100 ml/4 fl oz
	salt and pepper	
2	ox kidneys	2
1 tbsp	chopped parsley	15 ml/1 tbsp

ROGNONS DE BŒUF SAUTÉS AUX CHAMPIGNONS

SAUTÉED OX KIDNEYS WITH MUSHROOMS

Preparation 50 minutes • Cooking 50 minutes

Heat half of the butter and 30 ml/2 tbsp of the oil in a sauté pan. Add the thinly sliced mushrooms (caps and stalks) and sauté over a brisk heat until lightly browned. Add the chopped shallots and sauté for a few more minutes, then stir in the flour and brown in the oven. Next add the wine and stock. Season lightly with salt and pepper, bring to the boil and leave to simmer gently while preparing the kidneys.

After removing the skin surrounding the kidneys and cutting them in half lengthways, cut out the fat and gristle from the centres. Divide each part in half again lengthways, then cut into small slices about 5 mm/¼ inch thick. Season with salt and pepper. Put the kidneys in a frying pan with 50 g/2 oz (4 tbsp) of the remaining butter and the oil (this should be smoking) and sauté over a high flame, just to seal. Drain thoroughly.

Stir the kidneys into the sauce and, off the heat (boiling even momentarily will make the kidneys tough), strain the sauce, add the remaining butter and mix well. Turn into a heated deep serving dish and sprinkle with parsley.

Red wines: Saint-Émilion, Pomerol, Médoc, Bourgueil, Côte de Beaune.

US	Ingredients	Met/Imp
8	pieces oxtail, 2 joints in each	8
½ cup	lard	100 g/4 oz
¾ cup	flour	100 g/4 oz
2 bottles	red burgundy wine	2 bottles
	salt and pepper	
2	garlic cloves	2
2	large onions	2
1	bouquet garni	1
2 lb	neck (chuck) of beef	1 kg/2 lb
30	button (pearl) onions	30
10 oz	fresh fat belly (side) of pork	300 g/10 oz
5 oz	button mushrooms	150 g/5 oz

SAUTÉ DE BŒUF BOURGUIGNON

SAUTÉ OF BEEF BOURGUIGNON

Preparation 2 hours • Cooking about 7 hours

Brown the oxtail pieces in the lard. Put them into a flameproof casserole and sprinkle with the flour. Mix well in and then put in a hot oven for a few minutes. Pour in 1 bottle red wine and a little water, add salt and pepper, garlic, 1 chopped large onion and the bouquet garni. Cook gently for 4 hours.

Remove from the heat. Follow exactly the same process with the beef in another casserole but cook for just 2 hours.

Mix together the contents of the 2 casseroles then cook together for another 45 minutes. Add the glazed button (pearl) onions, the diced, blanched and browned belly (side) of pork and the mushrooms, browned in butter, and cook for a further 15 minutes.

If you start to prepare this dish the night before, the sauce will be smooth and even and a good colour; all the acidity from the wine will have gone, and, the meat will be done to a turn.

Wines: as a general rule, serve the same wine as the one used for cooking.

PEPPERED STEAKS

First recipe

Preparation 30 minutes • Cooking 10–12 minutes

US	Ingredients	Met/Imp
8, each about 6 oz	steaks	8, each about 175 g/6 oz
3 tbsp	freshly ground black pepper	40 g/1½ oz
	salt	
10 tbsp	butter	150 g/5 oz
½ cup	white wine	100 ml/4 fl oz

Roll each steak in pepper and season with salt. Sear them in a pan in about 75 g/3 oz (6 tbsp) very hot butter, then continue cooking slowly until done to your liking. Remove them from the pan and arrange on a heated serving dish.

Quickly deglaze the pan with the wine and stir in the remaining butter. Pour this sauce over the steaks.

Red wines: Beaujolais-Villages, Bourgueil, Chinon.

Second recipe

Preparation 30 minutes • Cooking 12 minutes

US	Ingredients	Met/Imp
8, each about 6 oz	steaks, eg sirloin, rib or, better still, well-hung rump	8, each about 175 g/6 oz
3 tbsp	freshly ground white pepper	40 g/1½ oz
	salt	
14 tbsp	butter	200 g/7 oz
3	shallots	3
½ cup	red burgundy wine	100 ml/4 fl oz

Roll the steaks in the pepper to coat thoroughly on both sides. Season them with salt and cook in about 75 g/3 oz (6 tbsp) of the butter until done to your liking, taking care that the pepper does not go black. Remove from the pan.

Sprinkle the finely chopped shallots into the pan and add the wine. Reduce, adding the remaining butter a little at a time, off the heat, stirring constantly.

Cover the steaks with this sauce and serve with Straw Potatoes (*page 552*).

Red wines: as a general rule, serve the same wine as the one used for cooking, or Beaujolais-Villages, Bourgueil or Chinon.

TOURNEDOS STEAKS BÉARNAISE

Preparation 1 hour • Cooking 15 minutes

US	Ingredients	Met/Imp
8, each about 7 oz	tournedos steaks (filet mignons)	8, each about 200 g/7 oz
14 tbsp	butter, melted	200 g/7 oz
¼ cup	oil	50 ml/2 fl oz
	salt and pepper	
2 lb	'Pont-Neuf' Potatoes (page 552)	1 kg/2 lb
1	bunch watercress	1
2 cups	Béarnaise Sauce (page 61)	200 ml/7 fl oz

In Béarn this dish is almost as popular as the famous 'poule-au-pot'.

Grill (broil) the steaks until fairly rare, basting with the butter and oil. Season with salt and pepper.

Arrange the steaks, accompanied by the potatoes, on a heated serving dish, garnished with watercress. Hand the Béarnaise sauce separately in a sauce boat.

Red wines: Saint-Émilion, Pomerol, Graves, Médoc, Haut-Médoc, Côtes de Bourg, Beaujolais-Villages, Bourgueil, Côte de Beaune.

US	Ingredients	Met/Imp
8, each about 5 oz	small tournedos steaks (filet mignons)	8, each about 150 g/5 oz
1 stick	butter	100 g/4 oz
8	croûtons, cut the same size as the steaks and fried in butter	8
5 oz	truffles	150 g/5 oz
½ cup	madeira	100 ml/3½ fl oz
1 cup	Demi-Glaze (page 56)	200 ml/7 fl oz
16	small chicken quenelles (page 54), shaped with a teaspoon	16
	salt and pepper	

— TOURNEDOS STEAKS ON CROÛTONS —

Preparation 1 hour • Cooking 12 minutes

Grill (broil) the steaks under a high heat, basting with about half of the butter, melted. Place each steak on a croûton.

Add the thinly sliced truffles and madeira to the demi-glaze, together with the quenelles.

Check the seasoning. Stir in the remaining butter just before serving, but do not let the sauce come to the boil.

Serve the steaks on a heated round serving plate, with the sauce poured over them.

Red wines: Saint-Émilion, Pomerol, Graves, Médoc.

US	Ingredients	Met/Imp
8, each about 5 oz	tournedos steaks (filet mignons)	8, each about 150 g/5 oz
	salt and pepper	
10 tbsp	butter	150 g/5 oz
8	small slices foie gras	8
8	croûtons, cut the same size as the steaks and fried in butter	8
½ cup	port wine	100 ml/4 fl oz
½ cup	thickened Veal Stock (page 56)	100 ml/4 fl oz
¼ lb	truffles	125 g/4½ oz
½ cup	double (heavy) cream	100 ml/4 fl oz

TOURNEDOS À LA CRÈME

TOURNEDOS STEAKS IN CREAM SAUCE

Preparation 1 hour • Cooking 10 minutes

Season the steaks on both sides and sauté in the butter until fairly rare. Place a slice of foie gras on each steak, then place each steak on a croûton.

Deglaze the sauté pan with the port. Add the stock, the shredded truffles and the cream. Bring to the boil and pour over the steaks. Serve very hot.

Red wines: Saint-Émilion, Pomerol, Graves, Médoc, Côte de Beaune.

— TOURNEDOS STEAKS CURNONSKY —

First recipe

Preparation 2 hours • Cooking 12–15 minutes

Sprinkle the steaks with oil, season with salt and put them, at the last possible moment, on a very hot charcoal grill. Turn them to grill on the other side. Keep them rare, or just cooked, according to the tastes of the guests.

Arrange the steaks on a heated serving dish. On each one put a piece of butter, a little chopped parsley, a little lemon juice and a pinch of freshly ground pepper. Top with a fairly thick onion ring, dipped in milk, then in flour and deep-fried until golden.

Garnish with the potatoes, grilled mushrooms, tomato halves cooked in butter and the watercress lightly salted and sprinkled with vinegar.

Red wines: Bourgueil, Côte de Beaune.

US	Ingredients	Met/Imp
8, each about 5 oz	tournedos steaks (filet mignons)	8, each about 150 g/5 oz
¼ cup	oil	50 ml/2 fl oz
	salt and pepper	
10 tbsp	butter	150 g/5 oz
	parsley	
1	lemon	1
2	large onions	2
½ cup	milk	100 ml/4 fl oz
¾ cup	flour	100 g/4 oz
	fat for deep-frying	
2 lb	Dauphine Potatoes (page 550)	1 kg/2 lb
8	mushroom caps	8
4	firm tomatoes	4
1	bunch watercress	1
1 tbsp	wine vinegar	15 ml/1 tbsp

Second recipe

Preparation 1 hour • Cooking 40 minutes • Serves 4

Drain the sweetcorn and warm it gently in butter. Add the béchamel sauce and a little salt and paprika, then bind the mixture with the egg yolks. Allow to cool. Shape into 12 croquettes and deep-fry in very hot fat just before serving.

Cut the potatoes into 12 small balls, with the scoop used for Parisienne potatoes. Cook them in butter. De-seed the tomatoes and sweat them in butter.

Poach the beef marrow in salted water. Keep everything hot. Cook the steaks in a sauté pan, until just done. Keep them hot on a heated serving dish.

Pour off the fat and deglaze the pan with the cognac and port. Add the chopped truffles. Reduce the mixture slightly, then add the stock. Complete the sauce by stirring in a nut of butter.

Arrange the sweetcorn croquettes and potatoes around the steaks. Put a cooked tomato on each steak and garnish with a slice of beef marrow.

Pour the sauce over the steaks and serve very hot.

Red wines: Côte de Beaune, Pomerol, Saint-Émilion.

US	Ingredients	Met/Imp
7 oz	canned sweetcorn	200 g/7 oz
4 tbsp	butter	50 g/2 oz
1 cup	Béchamel Sauce (page 62)	250 ml/9 fl oz
	salt and paprika	
2	egg yolks	2
	fat for deep-frying	
4–5	potatoes	4–5
4	small tomatoes	4
4	thin slices beef marrow	4
4, each about 5 oz	tournedos steaks (filet mignons)	4, each about 150 g/5 oz
2 tsp	cognac	10 ml/2 tsp
2 tbsp	port wine	30 ml/2 tbsp
½ oz	truffles	15 g/½ oz
1 cup	Veal Stock (page 56)	250 ml/9 fl oz

US	Ingredients	Met/Imp
I stick	butter	100 g/4 oz
8, each about 5 oz	tournedos steaks (filet mignon)	8, each about 150 g/5 oz
	salt and pepper	
½ cup	madeira	100 ml/4 fl oz
8	croûtons, cut the same size as the steaks and fried in butter	8
8	slices foie gras	8
¼ lb	truffles	100 g/4 oz
8	truffle slices, to garnish	8
8	croûtons	8
10 tbsp	butter	150 g/5 oz
I tbsp	Meat Glaze (page 56)	15 ml/1 tbsp
8	slices foie gras	8
	salt and pepper	
¾ cup	flour	100 g/4 oz
8, each about 5 oz	tournedos steaks (filet mignons)	8, each about 150 g/5 oz
32	truffle slices	32
½ cup	madeira	100 ml/3½ fl oz
I cup	Demi-Glaze (page 56)	200 ml/7 fl oz
¼ cup	truffle juice	50 ml/2 fl oz

TOURNEDOS STEAKS ROSSINI

First recipe

Preparation 30 minutes • Cooking 10 minutes

Place a heavy sauté pan over a high heat. When it is hot, grease the bottom with a little butter, put in the steaks and cook over a high heat for 5 minutes on each side. Season with salt and pepper. Deglaze the pan with the madeira.

Take out the steaks and arrange them on the croûtons on a heated serving dish. Put a round of foie gras on each steak and keep hot. Reduce the madeira in the pan. Off the heat, work in the remaining butter, cut into small pieces, and the chopped truffles. Work the butter so that it glazes the sauce. Pour the sauce over the steaks and garnish with the slices of truffle.

Red wines: Saint-Émilion, Pomerol, Graves.

Second recipe

Preparation 40 minutes • Cooking 10 minutes

Use a 6 cm/2¼ inch diameter pastry cutter to cut the 8 croûtons out of stale bread – they should be not quite 1 cm/½ inch thick. These will be fried in clarified butter while the steaks are being cooked, then covered on 1 side with the concentrated meat glaze, melted.

Cut 8 thin slices of raw foie gras just under 1 cm/½ inch thick, then trim them to the shape and size of the steaks. These foie gras slices will also be cooked in clarified butter, after being peppered and salted and rolled in flour, while the steaks are cooking.

Tie the steaks with string, about halfway down their sides. Season with salt and pepper and put them in a sauté pan containing 60 ml/4 tbsp clarified butter, smoking hot. (Clarified butter is required as it can reach the very high temperatures needed to sear the meat without burning; however, if absolutely necessary, it can be replaced by 30 g/1 oz [2 tbsp] butter and 30 ml/2 tbsp oil.) Cook the steaks over a high heat for 8–10 minutes, turning once, until rare or just done. As soon as they are cooked, put each steak on a croûte (on the part masked by the concentrated meat glaze) and arrange them in a circle on a heated round serving dish. Put a slice of foie gras on each steak and 4 thin slices of truffle on each slice of foie gras.

Thoroughly drain the fat from the pan, pour in the madeira and reduce quickly by one-third. Add the demi-glaze and truffle juice. Boil for 2 minutes, then strain over the steaks.

Red wines: Saint-Émilion, Pomerol, Graves.

TOURNEDOS SAUCE CHORON

TOURNEDOS STEAKS IN CHORON SAUCE

Preparation 50 minutes • Cooking 20 minutes

US	Ingredients	Met/Imp
8, each about 5 oz	tournedos steaks (filet mignons)	8 each about 150 g/5 oz
14 tbsp	butter	200 g/7 oz
	salt and pepper	
½ cup	Choron Sauce (page 67)	100 ml/4 fl oz
8	canapés or croûtons, cut the same size as the steaks and fried in butter (optional)	8
2 lb	Darphin Potatoes (page 549)	1 kg/2 lb
8	mushroom caps	8
8	tomatoes	8

Cook the steaks in very hot butter in a sauté pan, and season with salt and pepper.

Cover them with the choron sauce just before serving; canapé or croûtons fried in butter to go under the steaks are optional.

The garnish consists of: darphin potatoes (flat potato cakes), stuffed mushrooms, and tomatoes, de-seeded and grilled (broiled) whole.

To prepare the stuffed mushrooms, cook the caps in a saucepan with a nut of butter and the juice of 1 lemon. Remove when cooked and allow to cool, then stuff them with the following mixture:

Put a little butter or flavourless peanut oil in a saucepan. Add 1–2 very finely chopped shallots and cook until golden. Tip in 4 mushroom stalks, chopped, and cook, taking care to stir the mixture from time to time with a wooden spoon or spatula. As soon as the mixture is cooked and reduced, bind with the yolks of 2 eggs (or, more economically, with a little flour [cornstarch] or 15 ml/1 tbsp flour). Stir in 1 liqueur glass of sherry or port wine. Remove from the heat and add a little foie gras (or foie gras mousse), 30 ml/2 tbsp *crème fraîche* and a few pieces of truffle peel or very finely chopped morels. Mix everything together thoroughly, season with salt and pepper and allow to cool. Stuff the mushroom caps with the mixture. Bake the stuffed mushrooms in a hot oven while you cook the steaks.

Red wines: Saint-Émilion, Pomerol, Médoc, Bourgueil, Côte de Beaune.

TOURNEDOS SUR TOASTS

TOURNEDOS STEAKS 'ON TOAST' *

Preparation 30 minutes • Cooking 10 minutes

US	Ingredients	Met/Imp
8, each about 5 oz	tournedos steaks (filet mignons)	8, each about 150 g/5 oz
10 tbsp	butter	150 g/5 oz
½ cup	port wine	100 ml/4 fl oz
½ cup	Veal Stock (page 56)	100 ml/4 fl oz
8	croûtons, cut the same size as the steaks and toasted or fried in butter	8
½ cup	double (heavy) cream	100 ml/4 fl oz
½ lb	truffles	250 g/8 oz
	salt and pepper	
8	truffle slices, to garnish	8
2 lb	new potatoes	1 kg/2 lb
2 tbsp	chopped parsley	30 ml/2 tbsp

Sauté the steaks in butter.

Deglaze the pan with the port and reduce. Add the reduced stock. Arrange the steaks on the toasted or fried croûtons on a heated serving dish. Finish reducing the liquid in the pan with the remaining butter and the cream, to which the shredded truffles have been added. Season with salt and pepper. Serve with a thin slice of truffle on each steak accompanied by the boiled potatoes tossed in butter and chopped parsley.

Red wines: Saint-Émilion, Pomerol, Graves, Médoc.

US	Ingredients	Met/Imp
I, about 5½ lb	rib joint (roast) of beef	I, about 2.5 kg/5½ lb
I cup	dry white wine	200 ml/7 fl oz
¼ cup	cognac	50 ml/2 fl oz
2	shallots	2
½ cup	Brown Veal Stock (page 56)	100 ml/3½ fl oz
	parsley and tarragon sprigs	
I stick	butter	100 g/4 oz
	salt and pepper	
10 oz	fresh belly (side) of pork	300 g/10 oz
1½ lb	ceps	750 g/1½ lb
1½ lb	potatoes	750 g/1½ lb
8	lettuce hearts	8
I tbsp	chopped parsley and garlic	15 ml/I tbsp

TRAIN DE CÔTES À LA FAÇON DES CAUSSES

RIB OF BEEF FROM CAUSSES

Preparation 2 hours • Cooking 40 minutes plus 20 minutes standing

Roast the beef on a spit roast or in a roasting pan in the oven. Sear quickly but keep the meat rare, basting with its own fat while cooking.

When the beef is just done, remove from the spit or oven and keep hot, which allows it to rest. Deglaze the meat juices with half the wine and cognac. Cook the finely chopped shallots slowly in this liquid. Stir in the stock and reduce. Add the chopped parsley and tarragon, the butter and salt and pepper to taste.

Garnish the roast with the diced pork and the ceps, both blanched and then browned, the diced potatoes cooked in butter and the lettuce hearts braised in the remaining wine. Cover all with the sauce. Sprinkle with the chopped parsley and garlic mixture and serve.

To make carving easier, the rib roast should be stood upright.

Red wines: Saint-Émilion, Cahors, Côtes du Rhône, Corbières.

US	Ingredients	Met/Imp
I, about 5½ lb	rib joint (roast) of beef	I, about 2.5 kg/5½ lb
½ cup	dry white wine	100 ml/4 fl oz
½ cup	cognac	100 ml/4 fl oz
I	bouquet garni	I
I stick	butter	100 g/4 oz
½ cup	madeira	100 ml/4 fl oz
	salt and pepper	
8	lettuce hearts	8
8	tomatoes	8

TRAIN DE CÔTES DU LIMOUSIN À LA BROCHE À LA RABELAISIENNE

RABELAISIAN SPIT-ROAST RIB OF BEEF FROM LIMOUSIN

Preparation 2 hours • Marinating 3–4 hours • Cooking 50–60 minutes

Tie the beef loosely to keep its shape. Marinate it for a few hours in the wine and cognac, with the bouquet garni.

Lift the beef out of the marinade, drain thoroughly and dry. Spit-roast gently, basting with the marinade, allowing 12 minutes per 500 g/1 lb for rare meat.

Ten minutes before serving transfer the beef to a heated serving dish.

Strain and skim the cooking juices, then reduce. Add the butter and, at the last moment, pour in the madeira. Do not boil. The resulting sauce must be reduced, but not thickened. Season to taste.

Pour the sauce over the beef. Serve garnished with the lettuces braised in the marinade liquid and the tomatoes, skinned and stewed in their own juice.

Red wines: Beaujolais-Villages, Côte de Beaune, Bourgueil, Médoc.

TRIPE 'CAEN'

Preparation 1 hour • Cooking 8 hours

US	Ingredients	Met/Imp
1¼ lb	tripe	600 g/1¼ lb
3 tbsp	butter	40 g/1½ oz
¼ cup	oil	60 ml/4 tbsp
2	carrots	2
2	onions	2
¼ lb	fresh belly (side) of pork	100 g/4 oz
I	bouquet garni	I
2	garlic cloves	2
3	cloves	3
I	calf's foot	I
½ cup	dry white wine	100 ml/4 fl oz
4	thin slices of bacon	4
	a little cornflour (cornstarch)	

Thoroughly wash the tripe. Put the butter and oil in a flameproof casserole, lightly brown the thinly sliced carrots and onions, the diced pork, the bouquet garni, the crushed garlic, the cloves and the calf's foot, thoroughly cleaned and cut up.

Blanch the tripe and add to the casserole. Pour over the wine just to cover. Cover the tripe with the bacon slices, cover the casserole tightly and leave to cook gently for 7–8 hours. When the tripe is cooked, skim the fat from the gravy and remove the bouquet garni, then thicken with a little dissolved cornflour (cornstarch). Serve very hot.

Cider, or dry white wines: Muscadet, Jasnières, Quincy.

TRIPE 'PORTUGAISE'

Preparation 1 hour • Cooking 7 hours

US	Ingredients	Met/Imp
1¼ lb	tripe	600 g/1¼ lb
	salt	
2	lemons	2
¼ lb	fresh white beans	100 g/4 oz
3	onions	3
I	garlic clove	I
	oil	
	lard	
¼ lb	fat ham	100 g/4 oz
I, about 1¾ lb	chicken	I, about 800 g/1¾ lb
I	small cooked, smoked or dried sausage	I
I	black pudding (blood sausage)	I
2	carrots	2
⅔ cup	shelled peas	100 g/4 oz
20	olives	20
	parsley	

Wash the tripe in several changes of water, then rub with salt and lemon juice. Wash it once or twice more, then cut into small pieces.

Cook the tripe for 6 hours, covered, in a saucepan of salted water with slices of peeled lemon.

Cook the beans separately in salted boiling water. In a flameproof casserole brown the sliced onions and crushed garlic in oil and lard.

As soon as the onion has turned colour, add the sliced ham, the chicken cut up into pieces and boned, the sausage, black pudding (blood sausage), carrots and peas. Cover with boiling water. When everything is almost cooked, add the tripe and beans and simmer gently until completely cooked.

Serve garnished with the olives and chopped parsley.

Red wines: Saint-Émilion, Pomerol.

CHEVREAU

KID

BABY GOATS SLAUGHTERED FOR BUTCHERY ARE RELATIVELY rare and are always males from 6 weeks to about 4 months old. The season for kid (also called 'bicot' or 'cabri') extends from the end of April to the middle of June. Whatever way it is prepared, the accompaniment ought to have a very spicy, pronounced flavour because this young meat is somewhat tasteless and lacking in texture.

CUL DE CHEVREAU PERSILLÉ

——— PARSLEYED HAUNCH OF KID ———

Preparation 1 hour • Cooking 40 minutes

US	Ingredients	Met/Imp
I	haunch of kid (2 legs and the saddle in I piece)	I
	fat bacon, for barding	
I stick	butter	100 g/4 oz
4 cups	fresh white breadcrumbs	250 g/8 oz
	chives	
I	shallot	I
I tsp	chopped garlic and parsley	5 ml/I tsp
	salt and pepper	
	quatre-épices	
½ cup	white wine	100 ml/4 fl oz
½ cup	Veal Stock (page 56)	100 ml/4 fl oz

This recipe can be used for the hindquarters of kid, the leg, the fillets or the shoulders.

Cover the kid with thin slices of fat bacon. Roast the kid in the butter in an ovenproof dish, taking care to keep the butter nicely light in colour during cooking. At the last moment, dust the kid with the following mixture: fresh breadcrumbs, finely snipped chives and finely chopped shallot, the chopped garlic and parsley, salt, pepper and spice.

Return the kid to the oven for just long enough to colour lightly. Deglaze the roasting dish with the wine and veal stock. Let it reduce for a few moments to remove the acidity of the wine. The gravy will be lightly thickened by the sediment from the meat.

Red wines: Beaujolais-Villages, Côte de Beaune, Bourgeuil.

SAUTÉ DE CHEVREAU CHASSEUR

——— SAUTÉ OF KID CHASSEUR ———

Preparation 1 hour • Cooking 45 minutes

US	Ingredients	Met/Imp
about 5½ lb	kid	about 2.5 kg/5½ lb
	salt and pepper	
½ cup	olive oil	100 ml/4 fl oz
5 tbsp	butter	60 g/2½ oz
6	shallots	6
6½ tbsp	flour	60 g/2½ oz
I cup	white wine	200 ml/8 fl oz
¼ cup	cognac	50 ml/2 fl oz
3 cups	Brown Veal Stock (page 56)	600 ml/I pint
8	tomatoes	8
I	bouquet garni	I
I tbsp	chopped parsley and tarragon	15 ml/I tbsp
8	large croûtons, fried in butter	8

Cut the kid into 150 g/5 oz pieces, then season with salt and pepper. Put the pieces into a sauté pan containing the smoking hot oil and butter. Turn almost constantly over a high heat until browned all over. At this point, drain off all the fat. Sprinkle the kid with the finely chopped shallots and the flour. Mix well and leave over a gentle heat or cook in the oven for 7–8 minutes.

Add the wine and flambé with the cognac, then add the stock and skinned, de-seeded and chopped tomatoes and a good pinch of pepper. Bring to the boil, stirring constantly. Add the bouquet garni. Cover the

pan and continue cooking in the oven, until the kid is very tender. Turn into a heated deep serving dish. Sprinkle with the chopped herbs and garnish with the croûtons.

Red wines: Saint-Émilion, Pomerol, Beaujolais-Villages, Côte Rôtie, Cornas, Côtes du Jura, Côtes de Provence.

SAUTÉ DE CHEVREAU AUX POINTES D'ASPERGES

SAUTÉ OF KID WITH ASPARAGUS TIPS

Preparation 1 hour • Cooking 40 minutes

Baby lamb can also be prepared in this way.

Cut the kid into 150 g/5 oz pieces, then sauté in oil and butter to brown very lightly. Dust with the flour, stir for a moment and pour over the wine to cover. Add the tomato sauce, the bouquet garni, salt and pepper. Cook gently for 40 minutes. Add the chopped garlic, shallots and half of the parsley. Off the heat, bind with the egg yolks mixed with the crème fraîche.

Add the asparagus tips, blanched and cooked in butter. Arrange on a heated serving dish and sprinkle with the remaining parsley.

Red wines: Saint-Émilion, Pomerol, Côte de Beaune.

US	Ingredients	Met/Imp
about 5½ lb	kid, taken from the leg and saddle	about 2.5 kg/5½ lb
¼ cup	olive oil	50 ml/2 fl oz
5 tbsp	butter	60 g/2½ oz
scant ½ cup	flour	70 g/3 oz
1 quart	white wine	1 litre/1¾ pints
2 tbsp	Tomato Sauce (*page* 80)	30 ml/2 tbsp
1	bouquet garni	1
	salt and pepper	
a little	chopped garlic	a little
2	shallots	2
2 tbsp	chopped parsley	30 ml/2 tbsp
2	egg yolks	2
scant ½ cup	crème fraîche	100 ml/4 fl oz
2 lb	asparagus tips	1 kg/2 lb

PORK

THERE IS AN OLD SAYING 'EVERY PART OF A PIG CAN BE EATEN', and Grimod de La Reynière described the animal as a 'good all-rounder'. Butchers and pork butchers do in fact use almost all of the animal, even the ears and the blood (for black pudding or blood sausage). Ham is treated separately from fresh pork. Good-quality pork can be recognized by firm, pink flesh, not too red (this would indicate an old pig), and without a trace of moisture (this would indicate a factory-farmed pig).

Fresh pork cuts are as follows:

Spare rib or chine (blade or Boston roast) can be roasted or braised. It is used in potées (thick vegetable soups in which cabbage and potatoes are the main ingredients), in slices for grilling (broiling) or frying, cubed for *brochettes*, or minced (ground) or very finely chopped for sausagemeat and stuffings.

Fore loin (blade loin), hind loin (sirloin) and the **centre loin** itself make succulent roasts and also chops for grilling (broiling) and frying.

Fillet or tenderloin, when detached from the loin, gives exquisite, tender and tasty *tournedos*.

The **shoulder (arm or picnic)** is sometimes sold as lightly salted roast pork, as are the **loin, hock, blade bone** and **knuckle (shank)**, but can also be grilled (broiled).

Finally, pork is used for barding and larding, essential to almost all cooked dishes. We should also like to point out that whole roast **sucking pig** is a sumptuous dish, and the meat can be used for blanquettes and ragoûts as well.

Pork offal (variety meat) is such a vast subject that it should really have a chapter all to itself. There are so many succulent recipes for kidneys, liver, trotters (feet) covered in breadcrumbs and grilled (broiled), ears, various pâtés, not to mention the famous andouillettes (*right*).

CHITTERLING SAUSAGES

It was with our good prince Curnonsky in mind that Francis Amunategui, Henry Clos-Jouve, Jean D. Arnaboldi and Robert J. Courtine founded the most secret and exclusive of gourmet clubs, the AAAAA (Association Amicale des Amateurs d'Authentiques Andouillettes, The Brotherhood of True Andouillette Lovers). They knew how much Cur loved this product of the 'dear angel' of Monselet. But remember, no matter which type of andouillette you prefer, that of Troyes, Paris, Vouvray, Aubagne or elsewhere, it should be made in the traditional manner 'à la ficelle' – stuffed with strips of tripe, and it should be well grilled (or broiled) and soft but not greasy. It should *not* be served with 'pommes frites' as happens all too often.

After careful research, the AAAAA recommend, amongst others, the following accompaniments: pickled red cabbage, braised lettuce, fried onion, purée of celery, split peas, potatoes, apples, mushrooms, etc.

With andouillettes poached in white wine, drink a Mâconnais white wine (Mâcon-Villages), Saint-Véran, Bourgogne-Aligoté or Rully. With grilled andouillettes, drink the aforementioned white wines or a light rosé or red wine: Rosé des Riceys, Bourgogne Rosé Marsannay, Côtes Provence rosé, Bordeaux Clairet, Chinon or Bourgueil.

ATTRIAUX

FORCEMEAT BALLS

Preparation 50 minutes • Cooking 30 minutes

US	Ingredients	Met/Imp
1¼ lb	pig's liver	600 g/1¼ lb
10 oz	boneless veal	300 g/10 oz
	salt and pepper	
	tarragon, chives, sage and marjoram	
1	onion	1
2 oz	fatty bacon	50 g/2 oz
3	egg yolks	3
	pig's caul	
a little	butter and oil	a little

Chop the liver and veal very finely; place in a bowl with salt, pepper, chopped tarragon and chives, a little sage and marjoram, chopped onion and the minced (ground) bacon. Add 2 of the egg yolks and mix well to bind; shape into balls, each about 100 g/4 oz.

Cut out some rectangular pieces of pig's caul; soak them in the remaining egg yolk and place the forcemeat balls on them. Wrap them up, then flatten them slightly with your fist.

Butter a gratin dish and put in a small amount of oil. Arrange the forcemeat balls in the dish and simmer gently on top of the stove for 30 minutes.

Serve with leeks and potatoes.

Swiss wines: White Fendant or red Dôle.

US	Ingredients	Met/Imp
2 lb	onions	1 kg/2 lb
4 tbsp	butter	50 g/2 oz
7 oz (scant 1 cup)	lard	200 g/7 oz
scant ½ lb	chicken breast meat	200 g/7 oz
scant ½ lb	fatty bacon or pork fat	200 g/7 oz
3½ cups	fresh white breadcrumbs	200 g/7 oz
scant 1 cup	milk	200 ml/7 fl oz
4	egg yolks	4
¼ cup	double (heavy) cream	50 ml/2 fl oz
	salt and pepper	
1 pinch	nutmeg	1 pinch
1 pinch	dried thyme	1 pinch
1	bay leaf	1
	pig's intestines (sausage casings)	

WHITE PUDDING

Preparation 1½ hours • Cooking about 1 hour

Dice the onions finely; blanch in the butter, then cook in the lard.

Place the chicken, bacon or pork fat and the breadcrumbs soaked in milk in a mortar and pound to a smooth paste with a pestle. Add the egg yolks and cream, season with salt, pepper, nutmeg and thyme, then pour over the cooked onions and mix well. Add the bay leaf and gently cook for 15 minutes.

Remove the bay leaf and funnel the mixture into the pig's intestines (sausage casings), which should be well cleaned and scalded in advance. When the intestines have been filled, tie at each end and prick with a pin in several places to prevent them from bursting during cooking.

Have a saucepan of hot water ready and place the puddings in it at just below boiling point. Adjust the heat so that the water stays at this temperature. Do not allow to boil. Simmer the puddings for 45 minutes, then take them out, drain them and leave to cool. Score lightly and grill (broil) under a low heat for about 12 minutes before serving.

Dry white wines: Gaillac, Saumur, Quincy, Sancerre, Pouilly-Fumé, Muscadet.

CARRÉ DE PORC FROID SAUCE AUX POMMES

COLD LOIN OF PORK
WITH APPLE SAUCE

Preparation 20 minutes • Cooking the sauce 20 minutes

US	Ingredients	Met/Imp
1, each chop about ¼ lb	cooked loin of pork with 12 thin chops	1, each chop about 100 g/4 oz
5	cornichons	5
	SAUCE 1	
8–10	small cooking apples	8–10
1 glass	white wine	1 glass
1 tbsp	Dijon mustard	15 ml/1 tbsp
¼ cup	white wine vinegar	50 ml/2 fl oz
	salt and pepper	
	or	
	SAUCE 2	
8–10	reinette or other eating apples	8–10
½ cup	Mayonnaise (*page 72*)	100 ml/4 fl oz
1 tbsp	grated and finely chopped fresh horseradish	15 ml/1 tbsp
	salt and pepper	

This dish is served cold. Pickled red cabbage can be served with the pork instead of the apple sauce, if preferred.

Cut the cold cooked loin of pork into very thin chops. Arrange them into a crown on a serving dish and surround with cornichons. Serve with apple sauce prepared in one of the following ways:

1 Peel and core the apples, then slice thinly. Add the wine and cook quickly. Whisk to a pulp or work through a coarse sieve, then leave the purée in a bowl to cool. It should be quite thick. When cool, add the mustard, vinegar and a pinch of salt and pepper.

2 Make an apple purée as above; stir over a brisk heat to thicken slightly, then leave to cool. Add the mayonnaise, horseradish and season lightly with salt and pepper.

Dry white wine: Sancerre.
Dry rosé wine: Tavel.
Red wines: Beaujolais, Bourgeuil, Chinon.

ROAST LOIN OF PORK

Preparation 15 minutes • Cooking 1¼ hours

US	Ingredients	Met/Imp
1, about 3 lb	pork foreloin (loin blade roast), with 8–10 ribs	1, about 1.5 kg/3 lb
	salt and pepper	
5 tbsp	lard or butter	60 g/2½ oz

Trim the ends of the loin. Season with salt and pepper, brush with melted lard or butter and cook in a moderate oven, allowing 16–18 minutes per 500 g/1 lb, depending on the thickness of the roast. It is important that the pork is cooked through.

If served as a main course, the pork can be accompanied by a garnish such as sauerkraut, braised red or green cabbage, beans, etc, or with mashed potatoes, split peas, green celery or celeriac, or with apple purée. It is better not to serve it with a sauce; the cooking juices are sufficient.

Red wines: Beaujolais, Bourgueil, Chinon, Bordeaux, Bourgogne.

PORK STEW

Preparation 25 minutes • (To be prepared 48 hours in advance) • Cooking about 2 hours

US	Ingredients	Met/Imp
1, about 13 lb	leg of pork (fresh ham)	1, about 6 kg/13 lb
3	carrots	3
¼ lb	onions	100 g/4 oz
8	garlic cloves	25 g/scant 1 oz
1 handful	coarse salt	1 handful
1½ tsp	peppercorns	7.5 ml/1½ tsp
1	thyme sprig	1
1	bay leaf	1
7 tbsp	oil	105 ml/7 tbsp
½ glass	wine vinegar	½ glass
about 2 quarts	good red wine such as Beaujolais	(about 2 litres/3½ pints
½ glass	cognac	½ glass
½ cup	flour	75 g/3 oz
1 lb	Paris mushrooms	500 g/1 lb
1 stick	butter	100 g/4 oz
1	lemon, juice of	1
1 bowl	pig's blood	1 bowl
	GARNISH croûtons	

Remove any rind and surplus fat from the pork. Cut the leg into large pieces about 50–60 g/2–2½ oz each. Place in a stew pan. (We have given the amounts for a large piece of pork, but this recipe can also be made with a smaller piece or with a piece of shoulder pork.)

Add the sliced carrots and onions cut into rings, the roughly chopped garlic, salt, pepper, thyme, bay leaf, 60 ml/4 tbsp of the oil, the vinegar and sufficient wine to form a marinade. Leave the pan in a cool place for 48 hours without touching the pork.

Drain the pork, then fry in the remaining very hot oil until well-browned; keep warm in another stew pan. Pour the marinade juices and vegetables into the pan in which the pork was fried and bring to the boil. Pour the cognac over the pork and flambé.

Sprinkle the flour over the pork and turn each piece to coat thoroughly. Pour on the boiling marinade and cook over a gentle heat, uncovered, for at least 2 hours.

Trim the stalks from the mushrooms; wash the caps and then poach them in a little water with the butter and lemon juice added.

Just before serving, transfer the pieces of pork to a clean saucepan. Pour the sauce on to the pork through a conical sieve, add the poached mushrooms and pig's blood and mix well; heat gently but do not allow to boil.

Serve at once, garnished with croûtons fried in butter and accompanied by steamed potatoes.

Red wines: Côte Roannaise, Beaujolais, Beaujolais-Villages, Vins de Marcillac, Cahors, Côtes du Frontonnais, Vins de Lavilledieu, Vins d'Estaing.

US	Ingredients	Met/Imp
¼ lb	Parma ham	100 g/4 oz
¼ lb	Comté cheese	100 g/4 oz
4, each about ½ lb	thick pork loin chops with fillet (tenderloin)	4, each about 250 g/8 oz
4	small sage leaves, fresh if possible	4
	salt and pepper	
1 pat	butter	1 knob

STUFFED PORK CHOPS

Preparation 30 minutes • Cooking 25 minutes • Serves 4

Cut the ham and cheese into thin slices then cut into 2 cm/¾ inch pieces.

With a sharp, pointed knife, trim the fat from the chops, leaving only a very small border. Reserve the trimmings of fat. Insert the point of the knife horizontally into each chop, making a cut about 2 cm/¾ inch in diameter. Move the knife point backwards, forwards and around, cutting into the chop as far as the bone, but without cutting the circumference (apart from the original cut) and without perforating it. Thus you obtain a sort of pocket inside. Do the same with the fillet (tenderloin) meat on the other side of the bone (take great care as the meat is softer in this spot). Mix the ham and cheese together and place one-quarter of the mixture inside each chop, along with a sage leaf and some pepper.

Melt the butter in a large frying pan and render the fat trimmed from the chops without allowing it to brown. Add the chops, brown well on each side and season lightly with salt. Cover and cook gently for 25 minutes.

When cooked, season the chops with pepper and place on a serving dish with their cooking juices.

This dish is excellent hot or cold. If serving hot, accompany with cabbage or mashed potatoes. If cold, serve with a variety of salads.

If serving hot, light red wines: Arbois, Gamay de Savoie, Gamay de Touraine.
If serving cold, white wines: Arbois, Côtes du Jura, Mâcon-Villages, Rully.

US	Ingredients	Met/Imp
8, each about 5 oz	pork chops	8, each about 150 g/5 oz
	salt and pepper	
1 stick	butter	100 g/4 oz
15	reinette or other eating apples	15
1 pinch	ground cinnamon	1 pinch

FLEMISH PORK CHOPS*

Preparation 40 minutes • Cooking 25 minutes

Trim the chops, then pound the meat gently until thin. Season with salt and pepper. Brown well in the butter on both sides.

Cut the apples into fairly thin slices, bearing in mind how easily they disintegrate. Place the apple slices around the chops, or better still, put them in the bottom of a casserole and arrange the chops on top of them. Pour over the butter from the original cooking and add the cinnamon. Finish cooking in a slow oven (about 25 minutes).

Red wines: Beaujolais, Bourgueil, Chinon, Côtes du Rhône, Côtes de Provence.

NORMANDY PORK CHOPS*

Preparation 30 minutes • Cooking 20 minutes

US	Ingredients	Met/Imp
8, each about 5 oz	pork chops	8, each about 150 g/5 oz
I stick	butter	100 g/4 oz
	salt and pepper	
1¾ cups	cheese, grated	200 g/7 oz
1¼ cups	crème fraîche	300 ml/½ pint
scant I cup	cider vinegar	200 ml/7 fl oz
I tbsp	mustard	15 ml/I tbsp

Sauté the chops in the butter on one side. Season, turn them over and coat with the grated cheese mixed with 100 ml/4 fl oz (½ cup) of the crème fraîche. Bake in the oven for 20 minutes.

Remove the chops, which should be well glazed, from the oven and put the butter from the cooking to one side. Deglaze the dish with the cider vinegar, add the remaining crème fraîche and bind with the mustard and the butter from cooking.

Strain this sauce through a cloth into the bottom of a serving dish and arrange the well-browned chops on top of it in a crown. Garnish with *flageolet beans* in cream and fresh thyme sprigs.

Dry rosé wines: Tavel, Arbois, Côtes de Provence.

SAINT-VINCENT PORK CHOPS

Preparation 10 minutes • Cooking 40 minutes • Serves 2

US	Ingredients	Met/Imp
2, each about 7 oz	pork loin chops, with fillet (tenderloin)	2, each about 200 g/7 oz
	groundnut (peanut) oil or butter	
4	shallots	4
2 tsp	flour	10 ml/2 tsp
2 tsp	mustard	10 ml/2 tsp
scant I cup	dry Vouvray wine	200 ml/7 fl oz
	salt and pepper	
3 tbsp	water	45 ml/3 tbsp
	parsley	

Brown the chops on both sides in medium hot oil, or butter if preferred. Cook over a gentle heat for 15–20 minutes.

Remove the chops from the frying pan and keep warm. Reserve the cooking juices.

Peel the shallots and chop finely; add to the cooking juices and cook until golden-brown, stirring gently.

Remove from the heat, then add the flour and mustard. Whisk the mixture well and return the pan to a gentle heat.

Add the Vouvray; season with salt and pepper, then add the water. Simmer gently, uncovered, for 10–15 minutes, stirring from time to time to prevent sticking.

Place the chops in the sauce and cook gently for 5–10 minutes.

Place on a heated serving dish; coat with the sauce and sprinkle with chopped parsley.

White wines: Vouvray, Savennières, Sancerre, Pouilly-Fumé, Sauvignon de Touraine.
Light red wines: Touraine, Touraine-Mesland, Beaujolais-Villages.

US	Ingredients	Met/Imp
1, about 4½ lb	haunch of sucking pig	1, about 2 kg/4½ lb
1 stick	butter	100 g/4 oz
2 tbsp	tomato paste	30 ml/2 tbsp
2 cups	vinegar	500 ml/18 fl oz
10	peppercorns	10
⅔ cup	crème fraîche	150 ml/¼ pint
1	lemon, juice of	1
40	button (pearl) onions, cooked in a White Court Bouillon (page 49)	40
	MARINADE	
1¼ cups	white wine	300 ml/½ pint
1 glass	vinegar	1 glass
2	carrots	2
3	onions	3
2	garlic cloves	2
1	celery stalk	1
1	bouquet garni	1
1 pinch	salt	1 pinch
about 20	peppercorns	about 20
3	cloves	3

CUISSOT DE PORCELET À LA NISSARDE

PORK NISSARDE STYLE

Preparation 2 hours • Marinating 24 hours • Cooking about 1½ hours

Marinate the pork for 24 hours in the wine, vinegar, carrots cut into rings, sliced onions, crushed garlic, celery, bouquet garni, salt, peppercorns and cloves. Make sure the pork is well impregnated.

Take the pork out of the marinade, drain and dry. Place in a stew pan and bake in the butter mixed with the tomato paste plus the vegetables and a very small amount of liquid from the marinade. Leave uncovered and turn frequently.

When the pork is well-browned, reduce the remaining marinade by half and add to the stew pan. Continue cooking slowly, still uncovered, and baste frequently. Allow 20 minutes per 500 g/l lb. Remove the pork and keep warm. Pour the cooking liquid and vegetables into a jug.

Place the vinegar and peppercorns in the stew pan. Reduce by half. Skim the fat from the cooking juices and put back into the stew pan together with all the vegetables. Add the crème fraîche mixed with the lemon juice, then simmer for 20 minutes.

Work the sauce through a fine sieve, return to the rinsed-out pan and reheat. Add the onions.

Arrange the pork on a heated serving dish and coat with the sauce. Serve with ratatouille, braised fennel, spinach, Swiss chard au gratin, courgettes (zucchini) in butter, etc.

Wines: red or white Côtes de Provence.

US	Ingredients	Met/Imp
1 lb	sorrel leaves	500 g/1 lb
1 lb	spinach leaves	500 g/1 lb
1 lb	Swiss chard leaves	500 g/1 lb
1 lb	lettuce leaves	500 g/1 lb
1½ cups	flour	200 g/7 oz
6	eggs	6
1¼ lb	cured belly of pork (slab bacon)	600 g/1¼ lb
	salt and pepper	
1 pinch	nutmeg	1 pinch
1 lb	cabbage leaves	500 g/1 lb
	beef stock	

FARCI CHINONAIS

STUFFED CABBAGE LEAVES FROM CHINON

Preparation 2 hours • Cooking 3 hours

Chopped skylarks are sometimes added to the forcemeat.

Cut the sorrel, spinach, Swiss chard and lettuce leaves into *julienne*. Place in a bowl. Mix in the flour and then the eggs, one by one. Add the cured pork (bacon) cut into pieces; season with salt and pepper and add a little nutmeg. Make sure the forcemeat mixture is compact.

Blanch the cabbage leaves in boiling water, then lay out on a work surface. Wrap spoonfuls of the forcemeat in the leaves and shape into balls.

Place the cabbage parcels inside a piece of cheesecloth and close at the top. Simmer in beef stock for 3 hours.

Remove the cabbage parcels from the cheesecloth and place in a deep dish. Serve hot. The next day, the cabbage parcels can be eaten cold or cut into slices and fried in Noisette Butter (*page 53*).

White wines: Muscadet, Vouvray.
Red wines: Chinon, Bourgueil.

FILET DE PORC SAUCE POIVRADE À LA CRÈME

PORK IN PEPPER SAUCE WITH CREAM

Preparation and Marinating 24 hours • Cooking 2 hours

US	Ingredients	Met/Imp
1, about 3 lb	boned loin of pork, including the fillet (tenderloin)	1, about 1.5 kg/3 lb
1¼ cups	stock	300 ml/½ pint
	MARINADE	
1¾ cups	white wine	400 ml/14 fl oz
scant 1 cup	vinegar	200 ml/7 fl oz
¼ lb	onions, sliced	100 g/4 oz
¼ lb	carrots, cut into rings	100 g/4 oz
	bay leaf	
	thyme	
	celery	
	garlic	
	peppercorns	
	salt	
	SAUCE	
½ cup	vinegar	100 ml/3½ fl oz
	crushed peppercorns	
1¼ cups	double (heavy) cream	300 ml/½ pint
1 tsp	arrowroot	5 ml/1 tsp

Remove any excess fat from the pork; roll up tightly and tie. Place all the ingredients for the marinade in an earthenware pot; add the pork. Leave for 24 hours, turning the pork several times.

Place the pork in a large casserole, fatty side upwards, and surround with the drained vegetables from the marinade. Put the casserole in a hot oven, uncovered, so that the pork cooks in its own juice until the latter has evaporated and the vegetables are browned. Add the liquid from the marinade, complete with all its seasonings. Cook until the juices are reduced by one-quarter, basting from time to time. Add the stock; cover and leave until cooked (1½ hours cooking altogether). Take out the pork and keep very warm, on a heatproof dish, at the front of the oven.

Reduce the vinegar and pepper for the sauce over a brisk heat in a flameproof casserole. Skim the fat from the pork cooking juices and add to the reduced vinegar in the casserole. Add the cream and bring to the boil; cook slowly for 15 minutes. Work through a conical sieve and bind with the arrowroot. Adjust the seasoning. Cut the pork into slices and coat with the sauce; serve the remaining sauce in a sauce boat.

White wines: Alsace Riesling, Bourgogne, Mâcon-Villages, Côtes de Provence, Cassis, Gaillac, Jurançon sec, Vouvray, Anjou.

US	Ingredients	Met/Imp
1 lb	pig's liver	500 g/1 lb
1 lb	unsmoked fatty bacon	500 g/1 lb
5 tsp	salt	30 g/1 oz
1 pinch	ground mixed spice (apple pie spice)	1 pinch
10 oz	finely minced (ground) pork	300 g/10 oz
3	garlic cloves	3
1 tbsp	chopped parsley	15 ml/1 tbsp
1 lb	pig's caul	500 g/1 lb
1 stick (½ cup)	pork fat or butter	125 g/4 oz

——— GAYETTES FROM PROVENCE ———

Preparation 1 hour • Cooking 30 minutes • Makes 16

Chop the liver and bacon finely; place on a dish and sprinkle with the salt and spice mixed together. Leave for 20 minutes to allow the spice to penetrate. Place in an earthenware pot with the minced (ground) pork, crushed garlic and parsley and knead well to mix the ingredients thoroughly. Divide the pork caul, soaked in cold water in advance to make it pliable, into 16 rectangles about 15 × 10 cm/6 × 4 inches. Arrange these side by side on a cloth; place a portion of the mixture (about 75 g/3 oz) on each; wrap up into a sausage shape.

Arrange the gayettes on a buttered baking dish; brush generously with melted pork fat or butter and cook in a moderate oven for about 30 minutes.

Gayettes can be eaten hot or cold. If serving hot, accompany with a purée of lentils or split peas.

If served cold, they are accompanied by aspic and *cornichons*, and you may in this case make 8 large gayettes, which should be cooked for 50 minutes, served cut into slices like a galantine, with the slices arranged in the shape of a crown.

Provençal wines: white, rosé or red Côtes de Provence, Coteaux d'Aix-en-Provence or Coteaux des Baux-de-Provence.

US	Ingredients	Met/Imp
1, about 5½ lb	leg of pork (fresh ham)	1, about 2.5 kg/5½ lb
½ cup	good-quality brandy	100 ml/4 fl oz
scant 1 cup	Muscadet	200 ml/8 fl oz
scant 1 cup	*crème fraîche*	200 ml/8 fl oz
¼ cup	mustard	50 ml/2 fl oz
⅓ cup	capers	50 g/2 oz
3–4	*cornichons*	50 g/2 oz
½ lb	carrots	250 g/8 oz
½ lb	turnips	250 g/8 oz
½ lb	shelled petits pois	250 g/8 oz
½ lb	green beans	250 g/8 oz
½ lb (about 1½ cups)	*flageolet beans*, cooked	250 g/8 oz
10 tbsp	butter	150 g/5 oz

——— ROAST LEG OF PORK ———

Preparation 45 minutes • Cooking 2½ hours

Flambé the leg of pork in the brandy, then roast in a low oven for 2½ hours, until cooked. Transfer to a heated serving dish.

Pour the Muscadet into the cooking juices in the roasting pan. Stir in the crème fraîche, flavour with the mustard, then add the capers and sliced cornichons. Serve the pork with a macédoine of freshly cooked vegetables mixed with the sauce and butter.

Dry white wines: Muscadet, Chablis, Alsace Riesling.
Dry rosé wines: Cabernet d'Anjou, Tavel.
Red wines: Beaujolais-Villages, Bourgueil, Chinon.

MORVAN HAM
BRAISED IN BURGUNDY

Preparation 1 hour • Soaking 12 hours • Cooking about 2 hours

Soak the ham in cold water for 12 hours to remove the salt. Boil in plenty of water allowing 20 minutes per 500 g/1 lb. About 35 minutes before cooking is complete, remove the ham, trim it, then braise in the burgundy with the garlic and bouquet garni. When the ham is cooked, work the braising liquid through a conical strainer into a heavy-based saucepan.

Make the sauce. Add the demi-glaze to the cooking liquid, bring to the boil and reduce. Sauté the chopped mushrooms in the butter. Pour the sauce over them, add the diced truffles and the burgundy and season with pepper. Carve the ham, arrange the slices on a serving platter and cover with the sauce.

Wines: as a general rule, serve the same wine as the one used for cooking.

US	Ingredients	Met/Imp
1	small *Morvan* ham	1
2 bottles	good red burgundy	2 bottles
4	heads garlic	4
1	bouquet garni	1
	SAUCE	
1 quart	Demi-Glaze (*page 56*)	1 litre/1¾ pints
1 lb	*Paris* mushrooms	500 g/1 lb
1 stick	butter	125 g/4 oz
½ lb	truffles	250 g/8 oz
2 cups	good burgundy	500 ml/18 fl oz
	pepper	

HAM WITH HARD-BOILED EGGS
MORVAN STYLE

Preparation 30 minutes • Soaking 12 hours • Cooking about 3 hours

Cut the ham (preferably from a young pig) into 4 pieces, each piece weighing about 600 g/1¼ lb. Soak in cold water for 12 hours to remove the salt. Drain and cook in veal stock to cover for about 1 hour. Add the thyme, bay leaf, bouquet garni, onion spiked with the clove, leeks, peppercorns, juniper berries, carrots, and, in order to give the dish its principal flavour, a small bundle of rye straw. Continue cooking over a gentle heat for a further 1½ hours, until the ham is three-quarters done.

Add the hard-boiled eggs, shelled and pricked with a fork so that they become impregnated with the cooking juices. Cook for a further 30 minutes or until the ham is tender. Arrange the ham and eggs attractively in an earthenware pot, or in bowls.

Sprinkle with snipped chives and cover with the reduced cooking juices, strained through a conical sieve.

Chill and unmould when set to a jelly.

Dry white wines: Saumur, Sancerre, Quincy, Mâcon-Villages.
Red wines: Fleurie, Chiroubles, Saint-Nicolas de Bourgueil.

US	Ingredients	Met/Imp
1	small *Morvan* ham	1
3 quarts	unsalted Veal Stock (*page 56*)	3 litres/5¼ pints
1	wild thyme sprig	1
1	bay leaf	1
1	bouquet garni	1
1	onion	1
1	clove	1
2	leeks	2
a few	peppercorns	a few
a few	juniper berries	a few
2	carrots	2
1	small bundle rye straw	1
8	hard-boiled eggs	8
	chives	

HAM WITH PARSLEY BOURGUIGNON

Preparation 1 hour • Soaking 12 hours • Cooking 3 hours

US	Ingredients	Met/Imp
1, about 6½ lb	raw ham, boned	1, about 3 kg/6½ lb
1, about 4½ lb	shin or knuckle (shank) of veal	1, about 2 kg/4½ lb
2	calf's feet	2
1	bouquet garni with leeks, 5–6 chervil sprigs, tarragon and parsley stalks	1
6	shallots	6
2 bottles	white wine	2 bottles
	ASPIC	
6	egg whites	6
	parsley	
1 tsp	wine vinegar	5 ml/1 tsp
1 glass	white wine	1 glass

Soak the boned ham in cold water for 12 hours to remove the salt.

Boil the ham in fresh cold water for 1 hour, then rinse. Cook for 1 hour in a good stock made from the ham bone, the knuckle (shank) of veal and the calf's feet. Add the bouquet garni, chopped shallots and the wine, cook for 1 further hour until the ham is well done, then remove it from the stock. Crush the ham with a fork, mixing the fat with the lean as in *rillettes*. Place in a serving bowl, cover with a board and put weights on top.

Make the aspic. Strain the stock into a scrupulously clean saucepan and clarify it with the egg whites. Adjust the seasoning, cool and, when beginning to set, add plenty of chopped parsley, the wine vinegar and white wine. Pour over the ham. Chill until completely set, then serve from the bowl.

White wines: Chablis, Meursault, Montagny, Pouilly-Fuissé.
Red wines: Beaune, Volnay, Santenay.

HAM WITH MADEIRA SAUCE AND SPINACH

Preparation 45 minutes • Soaking 12 hours • Cooking 3 hours

US	Ingredients	Met/Imp
1	small *raw ham*	1
1	small bundle rye straw	1
2 cups	madeira	500 ml/18 fl oz
1¼ cups	Brown Veal Stock (page 56)	200 ml/½ pint
½ lb	*Paris mushrooms*	200 g/8 oz
1 stick	butter	100 g/4 oz
	salt and pepper	
	leaf spinach or spinach purée, to serve	

Soak the ham in cold water for 12 hours to remove the excess salt. Rinse and place in a fairly large saucepan of cold water; cook over a moderate heat for about 1½ hours, until half done, add the straw and cook for 1 further hour. Discard the straw and reserve the cooking liquid.

Remove the rind from the ham and place in an ovenproof dish with 200 ml/7 fl oz (scant 1 cup) of the madeira. Finish cooking in a moderately hot oven (about 30 minutes), basting frequently with madeira and a little of the brown stock. When cooked, take 200 ml/7 fl oz (scant 1 cup) of the original ham cooking liquid; reduce as much as possible; add the remaining brown stock, the mushrooms cooked in half of the butter, and the madeira sauce in which the ham was baked. Finish the sauce with the remaining madeira and butter and season well. It should be smooth, glossy and very tasty.

Serve garnished with leaf spinach or spinach purée.

Red wines: Côtes du Rhône, Côte Rôtie, Châteauneuf-du-Pape.

KNUCKLE OF HAM
AMALIA RODRIGUES

Preparation 1 hour • Soaking 12 hours • Cooking 1½ hours

US	Ingredients	Met/Imp
1	large knuckle joint of ham (ham roast, shank end)	1
1 cup	white port wine	250 ml/9 fl oz
	pepper	
1 glass	red port wine	1 glass
	PORT SAUCE	
1½ tbsp	butter	22.5 ml/1½ tbsp
1½ tbsp	flour	22.5 ml/1½ tbsp
	salt and pepper	
1 glass	stock	1 glass
½ glass	red port wine	½ glass

Soak the ham in cold water for 12 hours to remove the excess salt. Wrap up tightly in a napkin and boil for 1 hour in fresh water, with the white port and pepper.

Unwrap and place in an ovenproof dish with the red port; bake in a moderately hot oven for 30 minutes, basting frequently with the cooking liquid until cooked.

Make the sauce. Melt the butter in a saucepan. Add the flour and salt and pepper and stir over the heat until brown. Add the stock and bring to the boil. Add the port and the cooking liquid and juices from the ham. Adjust the seasoning, if necessary, then pour into a sauce boat. Serve with the ham.

Red wines: Graves or Médoc.

KNUCKLE OF HAM WITH PEARS*

Preparation 20 minutes • Cooking 3½ hours

US	Ingredients	Met/Imp
12	firm pears	12
3, each about 3 lb	knuckle joints of ham (ham roasts, shank end)	3, each about 1.5 kg/3 lb
	coarse salt and pepper	
2 lb	potatoes	1 kg/2 lb

Choose nice, regularly shaped, unmarked pears. Wash but do not peel; place whole in a large bowl of cold water and leave overnight.

Clean the ham thoroughly and place in a stew pan with cold, salted water. Bring to the boil, cover and cook for 2 hours. Drain the pears and put them in the pan with the ham. Cover and simmer for a further 1½ hours.

Boil the potatoes 30 minutes before cooking is complete.

When the ham is cooked, arrange with the whole pears and potatoes on a heated serving dish. Season the ham lightly with pepper.

Dutch beer, dry white wine or Beaujolais-Villages.

PORK NOISETTES WITH PRUNES FROM TOURS

Preparation 45 minutes • Cooking 30 minutes

US	Ingredients	Met/Imp
1 lb	prunes	500 g/1 lb
scant 1 cup	Vouvray wine	200 ml/7 fl oz
1, about 2½ lb	boned loin of pork	1, about 1.1 kg/2½ lb
	salt and pepper	
	flour for coating	
4 tbsp	butter	50 g/2 oz
½ cup	Tomato Sauce (*page 80*)	100 ml/3½ fl oz
scant 1 cup	crème fraîche	200 ml/7 fl oz

Leave the prunes to macerate in the Vouvray overnight, then cook for 30 minutes, until plump and very soft.

While the prunes are cooking, cut the pork into 8 slices, each about 1 cm/½ inch thick. Season on both sides with salt and pepper, then dip each slice in flour and fry in the very hot butter until cooked (about 15 minutes). Remove from the pan and arrange in a circle in a deep serving dish. Remove the prunes from the pan and place on the serving dish in the centre of the pork noisettes.

Deglaze the pan that has been used to cook the pork with the juice from the prunes; reduce by half and whisk in the tomato sauce. Finally, mix in the crème fraîche.

Pour this sauce over the pork and prunes and serve very hot.

White wines: Saumur, Vouvray, Sancerre, Quincy, Mâcon-Villages.
Red wine: Chinon.

STUFFED PIG'S TROTTERS*

Preparation 2 hours • Cooking about 3 hours • Serves 4

US	Ingredients	Met/Imp
4	lightly salted pig's trotters (feet)	4
1 quart	stock	1 litre/1¾ pints
1	bouquet garni	1
1	small chicken	1
	or	
2 lb	lean boneless veal	1 kg/2 lb
½ lb	truffles	200 g/7 oz
2 cups	good red wine	500 ml/18 fl oz
	salt and pepper	
1 pinch	ground mixed spice (apple pie spice)	1 pinch
14 oz	pig'caul	400 g/14 oz
4 tbsp	butter	50 g/2 oz
3½ cups	fresh white breadcrumbs	200 g/7 oz

These may also be made with the addition of a little Dry Duxelles (*page 49*) and chopped parsley.

Cut the pig's trotters (feet) in half and cook in the stock with the bouquet garni until tender (about 3 hours). Bone and cut into pieces. Have ready a stuffing made from the minced (ground) chicken meat or veal(*page 54*). Cook the finely sliced truffles in red wine and season with salt, pepper and spice.

Lay 4 pieces of pig's caul on a work surface; cover each with a layer of stuffing and arrange the pieces of pork on top. Continue layering, alternating meat, a little stuffing and a few pieces of truffle. Fold up the pieces of caul and shape into flat sausages; brush with the melted butter, then coat with breadcrumbs and grill (broil) under a low heat.

Dry white wines: Saumur, Sancerre, Quincy, Bourgogne-Aligoté.
Red wine: Côte de Brouilly, Juliénas.

PIGS' TROTTERS SAINTE-MENEHOULD

Preparation 2 hours • Cooking 4–6 hours

US	Ingredients	Met/Imp
8	pigs' trotters (feet)	8
1 quart	white wine	1 litre /1¾ pints
1 quart	red Saumur-Champigny	1 litre/1¾ pints
1	bouquet garni	1
3	carrots	3
2	onions	2
2	cloves	2
1	garlic clove	1
	pepper	
14 tbsp	butter	200 g/7 oz
8 cups	fresh breadcrumbs	500 g/1 lb
½ cup	oil	100 ml/4 fl oz

The front trotters (feet) are much more delicate than the hind ones. In order to keep them in 1 piece, tie them up with tape or thread.

Prepare a *court bouillon* using the white wine, Saumur, bouquet garni, carrots, the onions spiked with the cloves and the garlic. Boil the trotters (feet) in the court bouillon for 4–6 hours, topping up the liquid as necessary. Leave to cool in the cooking liquid.

Remove the trotters (feet); season with pepper and pour the melted butter over them. Dip in the breadcrumbs, then in the oil. Grill (broil) under a low heat until browned. The length of cooking depends on the quality of the pork, but it is better if they are over-cooked rather than under-cooked. If they have been properly seasoned, there is no need to serve them with a sauce. Serve simply with mashed or fried potatoes.

Red wines: Beaujolais-Villages, Chinon, Bourgueil, Saumur-Champigny.

ROAST SUCKING PIG

Preparation about 1 hour • Cooking about 3½ hours

US	Ingredients	Met/Imp
1	small sucking pig	1
8	white puddings (blood sausages)	8
16	cocktail sausages	16
8	small truffles	8
4 tbsp	butter	50 g/2 oz
½ cup	oil	100 ml/4 fl oz
8	*calville* apples	8

Clean the inside of the sucking pig thoroughly. Fry the white puddings, sausages and truffles in some of the butter without allowing them to brown. Fill the inside of the pig with these ingredients, then roast in a moderately hot oven for about 3½ hours, basting well with the melted butter and oil. Protect the ears with greaseproof paper or foil which should be removed after cooking.

Meanwhile, halve the apples and cook in the remaining butter. When the pig is cooked, reduce the cooking juices slightly, then skim off the fat and use the liquid to moisten the meat, which should be brown and crispy.

Sucking pig may also be stuffed with rice à la grecque, chestnuts, olives, truffles and even skylarks; or else in the English way, with breadcrumbs, smoked bacon and sage.

Red wines: Saint-Émilion, Pomerol, Haut-Médoc, Beaune Pommard, Volnay.

PORK STEW
WITH SPRING VEGETABLES*

Preparation 1½ hours • Cooking about 2½ hours

US	Ingredients	Met/Imp
2 lb	knuckle joint of ham (ham roast, shank end)	1 kg/2 lb
3 quarts	water	3 litres/5¼ pints
	salt and pepper	
1, about 3 lb	shin or knuckle (shank) of veal	1.5 kg/3 lb
1 lb	unsalted belly (side) of pork	500 g/1 lb
2	fresh pigs' tails	2
a few	spring onions (scallions)	a few
1	bunch new carrots	1
2	spring cabbages	2
1 lb	small turnips	500 g/1 lb
1 lb	fresh white haricot (or lima) beans	500 g/1 lb
1 lb	green beans	500 g/1 lb
2 lb	new potatoes	1 kg/2 lb

Place the knuckle (shank) of ham in a stew pan; cover with the water and add a suitable amount of salt. Bring to the boil and cook for 35 minutes, but do not allow to reduce. Next add the veal, the belly (side) of pork and the pigs' tails; make sure they are all well immersed and bring to the boil again; cover and leave to simmer for about 1¾ hours.

When the meats are three-quarters cooked, add the vegetables: first the onions (scallions), carrots and quartered cabbages, then, after 10 minutes, the turnips and white haricot beans, then the green beans and finally the potatoes, which only require 15 minutes cooking.

To serve, take out the meat and drain the vegetables. Place the pieces of meat on a heated serving dish and arrange the vegetables around; season the vegetables with pepper.

Red wines: Beaujolais-Villages, Saumur-Champigny, Chinon.

STUFFED PIGS' TAILS

Preparation 40 minutes • Cooking 2 hours • Serves 3

US	Ingredients	Met/Imp
6	pigs' tails	6
1	bouquet gàrni	1
1	garlic clove	1
1	onion	1
1	clove	1
	salt and pepper	
	STUFFING	
¼ lb	lean boneless veal	125 g/4½ oz
¼ lb	boneless pork, lean and fat	125 g/4½ oz
1	shallot	1
¼ lb	Paris mushrooms	100 g/4 oz
¼ cup	parsley	10 g/½ oz
1	egg	1
2 oz	pig's caul	50 g/2 oz
1 cup	fresh breadcrumbs	50 g/2 oz
	SAUCE	
¼ cup	parsley	10 g/¾ oz
1	shallot	1
¾ cup	dry white wine	100 ml/4 fl oz
1 tsp	mustard	5 ml/1 tsp

Place the pigs' tails in a flameproof casserole. Cover them amply with cold water and add the bouquet garni, garlic, onion spiked with the clove and salt and pepper. Bring to the boil, then skim and cook over a low heat for about 1½ hours. When the tails are cooked, drain and leave to cool.

Make the stuffing. Mix together the minced (ground) veal and pork, the finely chopped shallot, mushrooms and parsley. Add the egg and season with salt and pepper. Mix all together thoroughly. Bone the pigs' tails: cut them open lengthways, part the flesh to loosen the bone and lift it out. Fill each of the tails with a large spoonful of stuffing.

Join the tails together in pairs so as to form 3 large triangular sandwiches. Cut the pig's caul into 3 pieces and wrap around the tails. Sprinkle with the breadcrumbs.

Place the tails in a hot frying pan without any fat; the caul itself will provide plenty. Cook for about 10 minutes on each side; remove when nicely browned and place on a serving dish.

Drain the excess fat from the frying pan and put in the chopped parsley and shallot for the sauce; brown for a few moments over a moderate heat, then add the wine. Bring to the boil and reduce. Add the mustard, salt and pepper and stir; leave to boil for a few minutes. Pour this thick sauce over the tails and serve.

White wines: Alsace Riesling, Gewürztraminer or Pinot Gris.
Rosé wines: Bandol, Côtes de Provence.
Red wines: Côtes du Rhône, Côtes du Ventoux.

Stuffed Pig's Trotters
Cooked pig's trotters (feet) are boned, cut into small pieces and mixed with stuffing.
They are then shaped to make flat 'sausages', coated with breadcrumbs and grilled
(broiled). Always serve them piping hot. (Recipe on page 414.)

Flemish Pork Chops
The combination of apples and pork is traditional: choose 'reinette' or other crisp, juicy eating apples for this dish, and sprinkle them with cinnamon for extra flavou
(Recipe on page 406.)

Normandy Pork Chops
This pork chop has been sautéed, then lightly gratinéed with cheese and cream. The addition of mustard and cider vinegar adds piquancy to the sauce, and the dish is garnished with flageolet beans in cream. (Recipe on page 407.)

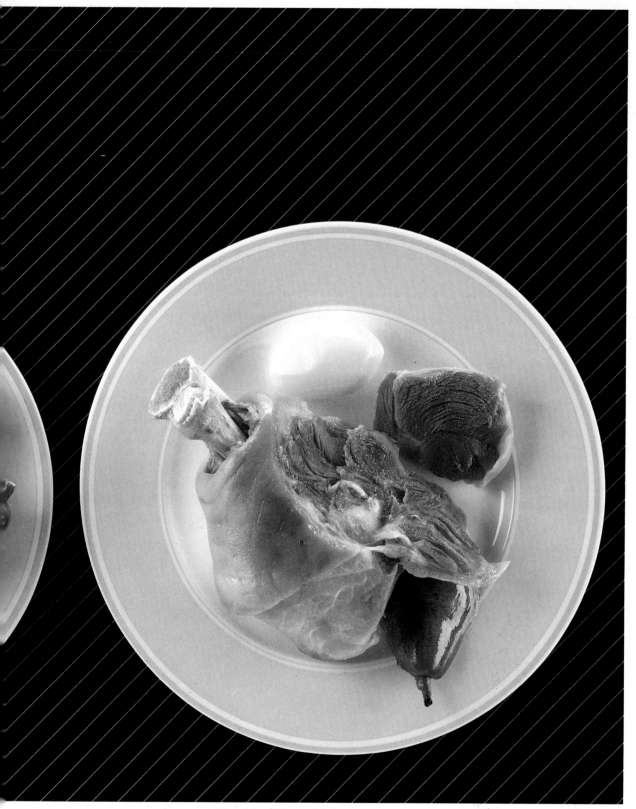

Knuckle of Ham with Pears

Commonly used for sauerkraut or 'potées', ham knuckle (hock) can also be boiled or braised. Here we have the unusual combination of cooking it with small firm pears known as 'poires de curé' (priest's pears), which only release their full flavour when cooked. Do not use dessert pears, which would 'melt' during cooking, Add pepper just before serving. (Recipe on page 413.)

Pork Stew with Spring Vegetables
As its name indicates, 'potée' refers to a mixture of meats and vegetables cooked together in a 'pot'. The main ingredients are always pork and cabbage, but the potée is not necessarily a warming winter dish. Here spring cabbages, little turnips, onions, small new vegetables and crisp green beans are used. (Recipe on page 416.)

Roast Pork Stuffed with Prunes
Prunes are a valuable accompaniment for pork (and also rabbit). Here they are stuffed into the roast before it is cooked 'en cocotte'. It is delicious whether eaten ho.. cold. (Recipe on page 417.)

PORK LOIN
STUFFED WITH PRUNES*

Preparation 20 minutes • Cooking 1 hour 40 minutes • Serves 6

US	Ingredients	Met/Imp
12	large Agen prunes	12
1, about 2½ lb	boned loin of pork with fillet (tenderloin), barded salt and pepper	1, about 1.1 kg/2½ lb
4 tbsp	butter	50 g/2 oz
1–2 tbsp	groundnut (peanut) oil	15–30 ml/ 1–2 tbsp
1 small glass	armagnac	1 small glass
¼ cup	crème fraîche	50 ml/2 fl oz

This is also excellent cold.

Stone the prunes and place them in very hot water for a few minutes to soften.

Using a sharp, pointed knife, make a hole in the centre of the pork. With a sharpening steel or very thick knitting needle, make a sort of canal in the centre, enlarging the cavity by moving the implement backwards and forwards.

Dry the prunes with kitchen towels and place them one by one inside the meat; use the handle of a wooden spoon to make sure the cavity is properly filled and the prunes are well packed in. Close the hole with your fingers. Sprinkle some salt and pepper on a plate and roll the pork in it, then tie with string to keep in shape.

Put the butter and oil into a pan and heat. When sizzling, add the pork and brown well on all sides; pour on the armagnac and flambé immediately; add the crème fraîche.

Cover and cook over a low heat for 1½ hours or until tender. Remove from the heat, remove the string and strain the sauce.

To serve, cut the pork into slices so that the prunes show in the centre. Serve the sauce separately.

Light, fruity red wines: Côtes du Frontonnais, Bergerac, Côtes de Duras.

COUNTRY-STYLE ROAST PORK

Preparation 10 minutes • Marinating at least 3 hours • Cooking about 1 hour

US	Ingredients	Met/Imp
1½ tbsp	coarse salt	30 g/1 oz
1 pinch	thyme flowers	1 pinch
1 pinch	bay leaf	1
12	peppercorns	12
1, about 2 lb	boned loin or shoulder of pork	1, about 1 kg/2 lb
3–4 tbsp	white wine	45–60 ml/ 3–4 tbsp

Combine the salt, thyme flowers, bay leaf and peppercorns. Crush with a rolling pin and mix together thoroughly. Rub the pork all over with this seasoning, making sure that it penetrates the meat. Place the pork in a dish and leave in a cool place to marinate for at least 3 hours (possibly as long as 1–2 days).

Transfer the pork to a roasting pan together with a few spoonfuls of water. Cook in a moderate oven for 1 hour, turning from time to time and adding a little extra water as necessary. When cooked, place on a heated serving dish and keep warm.

Skim the cooking juices and deglaze with the wine, scraping up the sediment. Boil for 1–2 minutes, then pour into a sauce boat and serve with the pork.

White wines: Alsace Sylvaner or Riesling, Coteaux Champenois, Bourgogne-Aligoté.
Red wines: Beaujolais-Villages, Côtes du Rhône, Côtes du Ventoux.

VEAL

VEAL IS CLASSED AS 'WHITE' MEAT, AND IS VERY HIGHLY regarded, being delicate and tender. Basically, the quality depends on how the animal is reared and fed. A calf fed exclusively on its mother's milk gives a pale pink meat which smells of milk, and has white, glossy fat. Some of the best areas in France for veal are Corrèze, Lot-et-Garonne, the Lyons district, the Upper Loire and Limousin. Rouergat veal, with its pink, firm, tasty flesh is particularly worth a mention. It is reared by a number of farmers in response to consumer demand for excellent-quality meat, free from all hormones and antibiotics.

Veal cuts and their uses:

Best end of neck cutlets (**rib chops**), often called **cotelettes**, and **loin chops** must be regular in shape and not cut too thinly. They can be shallow-fried, grilled (broiled) or baked *en papillote*. **Best end of neck joints** (**rib roasts**) are either chined and roasted on the bone, or boned and rolled for roasting, braising or stewing. **Middle neck** (**blade**) is a sinewy cut used for blanquettes.

Leg joints (**roasts**) of veal, with and without bone, are taken from the rump and top ends of the leg and are braised, stewed or sautéed. They can also be roasted, but should be larded with bacon as they need to be kept moist during cooking. Slices can be taken from the middle or lower part of the leg (round) to be used as **escalopes** (**scallopini**). The most tender escalopes, and the most expensive, are taken from the top of the leg (topside or rump). They are always flattened and trimmed into a regular shape. They can be fried, or stuffed and rolled up to form 'olives'.

Fricandeau is an old-fashioned bourgeois dish, mentioned as early as 1739 in *les Dons de Comus*. It consists of a large slice of veal, cut crossways from the top of the leg, usually no more than 4 cm/1½ inches thick. It should be larded with pieces of bacon before cooking.

Calf's liver should be pale in colour and absolutely fresh. It used to be larded, then roasted or braised whole, but nowadays, because of its high price, it is usually cut into slices, which can be sautéed.

Grenadins or medallions, are thick, round steaks of veal taken from the loin. They are barded, and sometimes larded with bacon, and can be fried or braised. Served cold in their own juices they make an excellent summer lunchtime dish.

Shin or knuckle (shank) of veal is very gelatinous, and is therefore mainly used for thickening cooking juices, stocks and aspic. However, it is also used to make ragoûts and braised meat dishes with vegetables and onions, along the lines of the Italian dish, *osso buco*.

The **loin** is still the favourite cut with veal enthusiasts. Normally it is boned and roasted, but it is also very tasty in a casserole, cooked on the bone. If the kidney is left attached to the meat, the resulting dish is known as a 'rognonnade'.

Breast of veal can be boned and stuffed, sautéed or used to make ragoût and blanquette.

Veal sweetbreads and kidneys are most highly esteemed. The former are first cleaned and trimmed, then blanched, cooled, chilled and pressed. After this, they can be fried, braised, roasted, grilled (or broiled), poached, cooked au gratin, made into brochettes or fritters, or used as a garnish for *timbales*. Veal kidneys are a great delicacy. First remove the skin, sinews and fat (unless they are being browned in their own fat), then grill, sauté or braise.

Shoulder is most often boned and used for making blanquettes, although it can also be boned, rolled and braised as a whole piece.

BLANQUETTE OF VEAL

First recipe

Preparation 1 hour • Cooking 2 hours

US	Ingredients	Met/Imp
4½ lb	boneless veal shoulder	2 kg/4½ lb
2 quarts	White Stock (*page 49*)	2 litres/3½ pints
	salt and pepper	
2	carrots	2
1	onion	1
2	cloves	2
1	bouquet garni (made with 1 leek, parsley stalks, thyme sprigs and ½ bay leaf)	1
1 stick	butter	125 g/4½ oz
¾ cup	flour	125 g/4½ oz
20	button mushrooms, cooked in salted water with a little lemon juice and flour	20
3	egg yolks	3
1	lemon, juice of	1
1 pinch	nutmeg	1 pinch
scant 1 cup	cream	200 ml/7 fl oz
	chopped parsley, to garnish	

Cut the veal into small pieces and place in a large saucepan with sufficient white stock to cover. Add a small pinch of salt and bring to the boil, stirring gently at regular intervals; skim with great care. Add the chopped carrots, the onion spiked with the cloves, and the bouquet garni. Cook gently for 1½ hours.

Make a velouté sauce. Prepare a white roux (*page 50*) with the butter and flour. Gradually stir in 2 litres/3½ pints (2 quarts) of the veal cooking liquid. Cook for 15 minutes; do not allow a skin to form.

Lift the pieces of veal out of the pan with a slotted spoon and drain thoroughly. Place in a clean pan with the mushrooms.

Complete the velouté at the last minute by adding the egg yolks, a dash of lemon juice, the nutmeg and cream. Season with salt and pepper. Strain through a conical sieve on to the veal and mushrooms; heat through but do not allow to boil. Transfer to a serving dish and garnish with chopped parsley.

White wines: Saumur, Vouvray, Quincy, Coteaux Champenois.
Red wines: Beaujolais-Villages, Côtes du Rhône.

Second recipe

Preparation 2 hours • Cooking 2 hours

US	Ingredients	Met/Imp
4½ lb	veal: two-thirds breast and middle neck (blade) and one-third shoulder	2 kg/4½ lb
	salt and pepper	
3	carrots	3
2	large onions	2
2	cloves	2
1	bouquet garni (including leek leaves and parsley stalks)	1
a few	peppercorns	a few
25	button (pearl) onions	25
2 sticks	butter	200 g/7 oz
scant ½ lb	button mushrooms	200 g/7 oz
1	lemon, juice of	1
½ cup	flour	70 g/2½ oz
3	egg yolks	3
	single (light) cream	
	puff pastry *fleurons*, to garnish	

Cut the veal into 125 g/4½ oz pieces. Soak the pieces overnight in cold water. Drain and place in a saucepan. Pour in water to just cover; add salt [7.5 ml/1½ tsp per litre/1¾ pints (1 quart)] and bring to the boil slowly. Add the quartered carrots, the large onions spiked with the cloves, the bouquet garni, and the peppercorns tied in a small piece of cheesecloth. Cover the pan and cook very gently for 1¼ hours. The meat should still be firm.

In another pan, cook the button (pearl) onions in several spoonfuls of the veal cooking liquid and 50 g/2 oz (4 tbsp) of the butter. (When the onions are mature, and especially in late autumn, they need to be blanched well before cooking.) Cook the peeled, sliced mushroom caps in 50 g/2 oz (4 tbsp) of the butter with a little lemon juice; the peelings and stalks can be used to flavour the sauce.

Make a velouté sauce. Prepare a white roux (*page 50*) with the remaining butter and the flour. Gradually stir in 750 ml/1¼ pints (3 cups) of the veal cooking liquid; add the mushroom peelings and stalks and cook gently for 40–45 minutes. Season carefully and cover with greaseproof (wax) paper to prevent the sauce from darkening.

Place the pieces of veal in a sauté pan. Add the onions and mushrooms and keep warm. Thicken the velouté sauce with the egg yolks mixed with the cream; strain through cheesecloth, then add the juice of ½

lemon. Heat through but do not allow to boil, then pour over the veal and vegetables.

Transfer to a serving dish, garnish with the fleurons and serve immediately.

White wines: Saumur, Vouvray, Sancerre, Coteaux Champenois.
Red wines: Beaujolais-Villages, Côtes du Rhône.

CARRÉ DE VEAU À LA PROVENÇALE

BEST END OF NECK OF VEAL PROVENÇAL

Preparation 45 minutes • Cooking about 1½ hours

US	Ingredients	Met/Imp
4 lb	best end of neck (rib roast) of veal	1.8 kg/4 lb
	salt and pepper	
½ cup	White Stock (page 49)	100 ml/4 fl oz
½ cup	white wine	100 ml/4 fl oz
	olive oil	
2 lb	button (pearl) onions	1 kg/2 lb
1	tomato	1
1	bouquet garni	1
2	basil sprigs	2
1⅓ cups	green olives	250 g/8 oz
1⅓ cups	black olives	250 g/8 oz

Trim the veal; season with salt and pepper, then braise gently in the stock and wine with a little olive oil added, for about 1½ hours until tender, basting often.

Cook the onions with the tomato, bouquet garni and basil in a little olive oil, then discard the bouquet garni and make into a purée.

Stone the green olives and blanch in a little water. Stone the black olives also.

The veal, when well browned, should be served on a heated dish, and the cooking juices skimmed and served in a sauce boat. Add plenty of butter to the onion purée and serve separately, garnished with the green and black olives.

Red wines: Côtes du Rhône, Châteauneuf-du-Pape, Côtes de Provence.

CÔTES DE VEAU AU CERFEUIL

VEAL CHOPS WITH CHERVIL*

Preparation 10 minutes • Cooking 25 minutes • Serves 4

US	Ingredients	Met/Imp
6 tbsp	butter	75 g/3 oz
4, each ab 7 oz	veal chops	4, each 200 g/7 oz
	salt and pepper	
1	large bunch chervil	1
1 tbsp	flour	15 ml/1 tbsp

Heat half of the butter in a deep frying pan and cook the veal chops over a moderate heat until tender (about 20 minutes). Season with salt and pepper.

While the veal is cooking, wash and trim the chervil; chop finely and mix with the flour and the remaining butter. Divide this mixture into 4 equal parts and place one-quarter on each chop during cooking.

The butter will melt and mix with the cooking juices to form a green, strongly flavoured sauce, which should be poured around the chops arranged on a heated serving dish.

White wines: Vouvray, Jasnières, Anjou, Cheverny.

US	Ingredients	Met/Imp
10 tbsp	butter	150 g/5 oz
8	veal chops	8
	salt and pepper	
1 lb	very white Paris mushrooms	500 g/1 lb
½ cup	white port wine	100 ml/3½ fl oz
½ bottle	very dry white wine	½ bottle
scant 1 cup	crème fraîche	200 ml/7 fl oz
a few drops	lemon juice	a few drops
1 tbsp	chopped parsley	15 ml/1 tbsp

CÔTES DE VEAU À LA CRÈME

————— VEAL CHOPS IN CREAM —————

Preparation 30 minutes • Cooking 20–30 minutes

Melt one-third of the butter in a large sauté pan. When it is clear but not yet browned, add the chops seasoned with salt and pepper. Cook, turning frequently to prevent them from becoming too brown, until tender (about 20 minutes). Remove from the pan, place on a heated serving dish and cover with a plate. Keep warm.

Quarter the mushrooms and place in the sauté pan. Shake the pan, then use a wooden spatula to stir the mushrooms thoroughly so that they become impregnated with the butter used to cook the veal. Season lightly with salt and pepper; moisten with the white port and wine. Cook over a brisk heat and reduce by two-thirds. When reduced and slightly glazed, add the crème fraîche and cook until the sauce will coat the back of a spoon.

Remove from the heat and add the remaining butter; stir constantly to perfect the emulsifying process. Taste the sauce and adjust the seasoning if necessary, then pour over the chops. Finish off this excellent dish with a few drops of lemon juice and a little very fresh parsley.

Red wines: Beaujolais-Villages, Bourgueil, Chinon, Côtes du Forez.

US	Ingredients	Met/Imp
1 stick	butter	100 g/3½ oz
8	veal chops	8
3½ cups	Comté cheese, grated	400 g/14 oz
2	eggs	2
¼ cup	crème fraîche	60 ml/4 tbsp
1 pinch	nutmeg	1 pinch
	pepper	
½ cup	Arbois wine	100 ml/4 fl oz

CÔTES DE VEAU À LA FRANC-COMTOISE

————— VEAL CHOPS FRANC-COMTOISF —————

Preparation 30 minutes • Cooking 20 minutes

Melt the butter in a large sauté pan; add the veal chops and three-quarters cook them (about 15 minutes). Place the cheese, eggs, crème fraîche, nutmeg and a little pepper in a casserole and mix well with a small wooden spatula. Remove the fat from the sauté pan before the chops have finished cooking and set it aside. Place equal amounts of the cheese mixture on each chop and moisten with the wine. Finish cooking in a hot oven, basting with the fat taken from the pan.

White Arbois wine.

VEAL CHOPS IN ASPIC

Preparation 1 hour • Cooking 30 minutes

US	Ingredients	Met/Imp
8	veal chops	8
	salt and pepper	
2 oz	salted tongue	50 g/2 oz
3 oz	truffles	75 g/3 oz
2 oz	lean bacon	50 g/2 oz
1 stick	butter	100 g/4 oz
½ cup	dry white wine	100 ml/3½ fl oz
2 cups	Plain Aspic (*page 58*)	500 ml/18 fl oz

You must choose prime-quality, identical looking veal chops for this recipe.

Season the veal chops with salt and pepper, then lard them generously and very carefully, alternating small strips of the tongue with the sliced truffles and bacon. Sauté in the butter, larded side upwards, then cook gently until golden and well-done (25–30 minutes). White meat served cold must be very well cooked.

When the veal is cooked, remove the fat from the pan and deglaze with the wine. Use some of the aspic jelly to coat the chops and save the remainder for the garnish.

In order to make this dish richer and more substantial, as well as more attractive, you can place a garnish in the centre or around the outside, or even serve a selection of cold garnishes separately – purées, mousses and aspic, for example.

White, rosé or red wines: Alsace Sylvaner or Gewürztraminer, Meursault, Tavel, Chinon.

CÔTES DE VEAU GRATINÉES AUX CHAMPIGNONS

VEAL CHOPS
WITH CHEESE AND MUSHROOMS

Preparation 30 minutes • Cooking 25 minutes

US	Ingredients	Met/Imp
2 cups	cheese, grated	250 g/8 oz
½ cup	crème fraîche	100 ml/4 fl oz
½ cup	Dry Duxelles (*page 49*)	100 ml/4 fl oz
	salt and pepper	
8	veal chops	8
2 sticks	butter	250 g/8 oz
½ cup	white port wine	100 ml/4 fl oz
½ cup	White Stock (*page 56*)	100 ml/4 fl oz
1 lb	noodles	500 g/1 lb
½ lb	*julienne* of lean cooked ham	250 g/8 oz

Place the cheese, crème fraîche and very dry duxelles in a bowl. Work together well with a wooden spatula until the mixture forms a smooth, fairly thick paste. Season carefully. Sauté the chops in some of the butter on one side only; turn them over and place a heaped tablespoonful of the cheese mixture on each one; moisten with a little of the cooking butter.

Cook in a hot oven for about 25 minutes or until tender, then arrange on a heated serving dish. Deglaze the cooking juices with the port and stock. Season and pour over the chops.

Serve with freshly cooked noodles tossed in the remaining butter with the ham julienne.

Dry white wines: Pouilly-Fumé, Alsace Sylvaner or Riesling.
Red wines: Bourgogne-Passetoutgrains; Givry, Mercurey.

US	Ingredients	Met/Imp
3, each about ½ lb	veal chops	3, each about 250 g/8 oz
	salt and pepper	
4 tbsp	butter	50 g/2 oz
6 tbsp	Comté cheese, grated	90 ml/6 tbsp
6 tbsp	crème fraîche	90 ml/6 tbsp
1 tbsp	armagnac	15 ml/1 tbsp

CÔTES DE VEAU DU MANOIR

MANOR HOUSE VEAL CHOPS

Preparation 10 minutes • Cooking 20 minutes • Serves 3

Season the chops on both sides with salt and pepper. Melt the butter in a frying pan and, when brown, put in the chops. Brown on one side over a moderate heat, but do not allow the butter to burn. Cook gently for about 10 minutes without turning.

Butter an ovenproof dish. Arrange the chops in it, browned side down. Cover with the cheese and bake in a hot oven for 8–10 minutes, until browned and bubbling. Add the crème fraîche to the butter in the frying pan. Mix, scraping the base of the pan with the back of a fork, then cook until the cream has been reduced to half its volume. Add salt and pepper.

Take the chops out of the oven. Add the juices to the cream sauce. Reduce again over a low heat, then stir in the armagnac.

Pour the sauce around the chops, but do not allow it to touch the browned cheese top.

Dry cider or dry white wines: Vin de Savoie, Sauvignon de Touraine.
Light red wines: Gamay de Touraine, Alsace Pinot Noir.

CÔTES DE VEAU PANÉES ET GRILLÉES

GRILLED VEAL CHOPS IN BREADCRUMBS

Preparation 30 minutes • Cooking 15 minutes

US	Ingredients	Met/Imp
8, each about 7 oz	veal chops	8, each about 200 g/7 oz
	salt and pepper	
¾ cup	flour	100 g/4 oz
1 stick	butter	100 g/4 oz
4 cups	fresh white breadcrumbs	200 g/8 oz
	Maître d'Hôtel Butter (page 52)	

Beat the meat of the chops until thin. Season, coat with the flour, dip in the melted butter, then coat with the breadcrumbs. Press the crumbs on with a palette knife or spatula. Sprinkle with more melted butter and grill (broil) until cooked (about 15 minutes), turning once. Serve the maître d'hôtel butter separately.

Red wines: Beaujolais-Villages, Côte Roannaise, Côtes d'Auvergne.

VEAL CHOP PARCELS

Preparation 1 hour • Cooking about 20 minutes

Season the veal chops with salt and pepper, then fry quickly in the butter to brown and seal on both sides. Cut 8 pieces of foil, each one large enough to enclose a chop. Butter the foil and place 1 slice of ham and 5 ml/1 tsp duxelles on each piece. Place 1 veal chop on top of each and cover with a little more duxelles and another slice of ham.

Fold over the foil and seal the edges tightly, but do not press down on the chops. Place the parcels on an oiled baking sheet and finish the cooking in the oven. Serve at once.

Red wines: Bordeaux, Côtes de Bergerac, Côtes de Buzet.

US	Ingredients	Met/Imp
8, each about 7 oz	veal chops	8, each about 200 g/7 oz
	salt and pepper	
1 stick	butter	100 g/4 oz
16	small slices York ham	16
scant 1 cup	Dry Duxelles (*page 49*) mixed with madeira-flavoured Veal Stock (*page 56*)	around 200 ml/7 fl oz
¼ cup	oil	50 ml/2 fl oz

VEAL CHOPS WITH PAPRIKA

Preparation 20 minutes • Cooking 25 minutes

Sprinkle the chops with paprika, salt and pepper. Fry gently in the butter until three-quarters cooked, then add the mushrooms. Finish cooking gently, then deglaze the pan with the crème fraîche. Serve at once.

White wines: Pouilly-Fumé, Alsace Pinot Blanc, Gewürztraminer or Riesling.
Red wines: Bourgueil, Chinon, Saumur-Champigny.

US	Ingredients	Met/Imp
8, each about 7 oz	veal chops	8, each about 200 g/7 oz
2 tbsp	sweet paprika	30 ml/2 tbsp
	salt and pepper	
10 tbsp	butter	150 g/5 oz
2 lb	wild mushrooms	1 kg/2 lb
2 cups	crème fraîche	500 ml/18 fl oz

VEAL CHOPS WITH PARMESAN

Preparation 10 minutes • Cooking 25 minutes • Serves 4

Ask the butcher to slice through each chop to the bone, to make a pocket.

Into this opening insert a slice of bacon and some cheese. Add a little salt and pepper (not too much salt because of the bacon). Press the open edges of the chop together to seal. Heat two-thirds of the butter in a large frying pan and brown the chops for 5 minutes on each side. Turn carefully, ensuring the stuffing does not escape. Sprinkle a little salt and pepper on each side and cook for 10 minutes over a low heat. Heat the grill (broiler).

When the chops are almost cooked, put them into a flameproof dish. Sprinkle the remaining cheese on top and dot with the remaining butter, then brown under the hot grill (broiler) for 5 minutes. Sprinkle with lemon juice and serve in the same dish.

Red wines: Morgon, Moulin-à-Vent, Côte de Brouilly.

US	Ingredients	Met/Imp
4, each 7 oz	veal chops	4, each 200 g/7 oz
4	thin slices lean bacon	4
¾ cup	Parmesan cheese, grated	75 g/3 oz
	salt and pepper	
6 tbsp	butter	75 g/3 oz
1	lemon, juice of	1

PAN-FRIED VEAL CHOPS JEANNE DE LASAS

Preparation about 30 minutes • Cooking 20 minutes

US	Ingredients	Met/Imp
8, each about ¼ lb	veal chops	8, each about 125 g/4½ oz
	salt and pepper	
¾ cup	flour	100 g/3½ oz
14 tbsp	butter	200 g/7 oz
scant 1 cup	white wine	200 ml/7 fl oz
4	shallots	4
	garlic	
8	tomatoes	8
scant 1 cup	Veal Stock (page 56)	200 ml/7 fl oz
¼ lb	mushrooms or mushroom trimmings	100 g/3½ oz
scant 1 cup	crème fraîche	200 ml/7 fl oz
	GARNISH	
8	small vol-au-vents	8
1 lb	white *Paris* mushrooms	500 g/1 lb
	a little *crème fraîche*	
4	celery stalks	4

Season the veal chops with salt and pepper, then coat in the flour and fry in about half of the butter in a heavy frying pan, over a low heat for 15–20 minutes. Take out the chops and keep hot on a serving dish. Deglaze the pan with the wine, then add the very finely chopped shallots, a little crushed garlic, the roughly chopped tomatoes and the veal stock. Add the mushrooms or mushroom trimmings.

Thicken the sauce with crème fraîche and half of the remaining butter, then rub through a sieve. Serve in a sauce boat. Pour the remaining butter, browned, over the chops.

For the garnish, fill small vol-au-vents with a purée of Paris mushrooms thickened with crème fraîche. Arrange fluted mushroom caps and diced braised celery around.

Red wines: Côtes de Bourg, Fronsac, Médoc.

VEAL CHOPS WITH SPAGHETTI

Preparation 1 hour • Cooking 25 minutes

US	Ingredients	Met/Imp
1 oz	lean bacon	30 g/1oz
¾ oz	salted tongue	20 g/¾ oz
½ cup	madeira	100 ml/4 fl oz
2 oz	truffles	50 g/2 oz
scant 1 cup	Veal Stock (page 56)	200 ml/7 fl oz
scant 1 cup	tomato paste	200 ml/7 fl oz
8, each about 5 oz	small veal chops	8, each about 150 g/5 oz
	salt and pepper	
¾ cup	flour	100 g/4 oz
2	eggs	2
2 cups	fresh white breadcrumbs	100 g/4 oz
10 tbsp	butter	150 g/5 oz
½ cup	olive oil	100 ml/4 fl oz
½ lb	spaghetti	200 g/7 oz
1 cup	Parmesan cheese, grated	100 g/4 oz
1 pinch	nutmeg	1 pinch

Shred the bacon and tongue and put into a saucepan with the madeira and sliced truffles. Cook until the liquid has evaporated. Thicken with the veal stock mixed with the tomato paste. Keep hot.

Beat the veal chops until thin, season, coat with the flour, dip in the beaten eggs, then coat with the breadcrumbs. Fry in two-thirds of the butter and the oil for about 20 minutes, until tender.

Meanwhile, cook the spaghetti in boiling salted water. Drain and dry over the heat. Add the remaining butter, the grated cheese and nutmeg.

Arrange the chops in the shape of a crown, surrounded by some of the tomato sauce. Sprinkle with the pan juices. Pour the remaining sauce over the spaghetti and serve.

Red wines: Beaujolais-Villages, Côtes du Ventoux, Fitou.

VEAL CHOPS FROM THE AUGE VALLEY

Preparation 50 minutes • Cooking 20 minutes

US	Ingredients	Met/Imp
8, each about ¼ lb	veal chops	8, each about 125 g/4 oz
	salt and pepper	
10 tbsp	butter	150 g/5 oz
1 lb	button mushrooms	500 g/1 lb
16	button (pearl) onions	16
4 tsp	crème fraîche	20 ml/4 tsp
¼ cup	calvados	50 ml/2 fl oz

Season the veal chops. Fry in the butter in a large heavy frying pan but do not allow to brown. While cooking, add the mushrooms and the blanched onions. Remove the veal when cooked.

Stir the crème fraîche into the meat juices in the pan. Adjust the

seasoning and add the calvados. Place the chops and vegetables in a heated serving dish and pour over the sauce.

Medium dry white wines: Anjou, Vouvray, Montlouis.
Red wines: Bourgueil, Chinon.

CUL DE VEAU À L'ANGEVINE

—— BRAISED VEAL ANJOU ——

Preparation 10 minutes • Cooking 2½ hours

Put the veal and butter into a large, heavy flameproof casserole and brown on all sides. Sprinkle with salt and pepper, then cook over a low heat for 1 hour, basting frequently.

Add the wine, the onions and whole carrots. Cover with greaseproof or parchment paper and the lid. Continue to cook, basting from time to time, for a further 1½ hours, or until tender.

Serve the veal on a heated serving dish surrounded by the vegetables.

Wines: as a general rule, serve the same wine as the one used for cooking.

US	Ingredients	Met/Imp
5 lb	joint (roast) of veal cut from top of leg, with bone	2.3 kg/5 lb
14 tbsp	butter	200 g/7 oz
	salt and pepper	
1 bottle	Anjou wine	1 bottle
40	button (pearl) onions	40
2	bunches new carrots	2

CUL DE VEAU AU MIEL

—— BRAISED VEAL WITH HONEY ——

Preparation 1 hour • Cooking 2¾ hours

Lightly brown the veal in butter in a large flameproof casserole. Deglaze with a glass of the wine and a glass of water (nothing must stick to the bottom of the casserole). Pour off the glaze and reserve. Line the bottom of the casserole with the pork rind cut into strips about 5 cm/2 inches wide. Finely chop and mix together the celery, carrots, onion and garlic and spread on top of the pork rind. Add salt and plenty of pepper and the leg of veal, then arrange the calf's feet, blanched and split in half lengthways, around it with the bouquet garni.

Coat the leg of veal with the honey and pour over the reserved glaze with the remaining wine. Pour in water or a very light white stock, to almost cover the veal, then cook over a high heat for 15 minutes. Cover and finish cooking in the oven for about 2½ hours, turning the meat over after 1 hour.

When the veal is cooked, take it out of the casserole. Skim off any fat and adjust the seasoning. Place the veal in a large heated serving dish. Coarsely dice the boned calf's feet and add to the dish. If necessary reduce the cooking liquid – remembering to remove the pork rind and vegetables – before pouring over the leg of veal.

Red wines: Corbières, Minervois, La Clape, Faugères.

US	Ingredients	Met/Imp
5½ lb	boned and rolled joint (roast) of veal, cut from top of leg, larded lengthways	2.5 kg/5½ lb
	butter	
1 bottle	Blanquette de Limoux	1 bottle
	fresh pork rind, cut into strips	
3	large heads celery	3
2½ lb	carrots	1.1 kg/2½ lb
3 lb	onions	1.5 kg/3 lb
2	garlic cloves	2
	salt and pepper	
2	calf's feet	2
1	bouquet garni	1
2 cups	rosemary honey	650 g/1¼ lb

US	Ingredients	Met/Imp
I	large onion	I
3 tbsp	groundnut (peanut) oil	45 ml/3 tbsp
I lb	calf's liver	500 g/I lb
2	veal kidneys	2
½ lb	button mushrooms	250 g/8 oz
	salt and pepper	
I cup	hot Veal Stock (page 56)	250 ml/8 fl oz
½ cup	madeira	100 ml/4 fl oz
I½ tsp	cornflour (cornstarch)	7.5 ml/I½ tsp
	Pilau Rice (page 563), to serve	

ÉMINCÉ DE FOIE ET DE ROGNONS DE VEAU

— SLICED CALF'S LIVER AND KIDNEYS —

Preparation 25 minutes • Cooking 15 minutes

Peel and finely slice the onion. Heat the oil in a pan and fry the onion over a low heat, until softened.

Finely slice the liver and set aside. Skin the kidneys, then slice them. Add to the onion, cover and cook gently for 10 minutes.

Meanwhile, peel the mushrooms, discarding the stalks, wash and slice them. Cook in salted water for 5 minutes, then drain.

Pour the hot stock over the kidneys, add the mushrooms, the madeira blended with the cornflour (cornstarch), salt and pepper. Stir.

Add the liver and return to the boil. Cover and simmer over a very low heat for 6–8 minutes until the liver is just cooked. Serve with pilau rice.

Wines: white or red Sancerre.

US	Ingredients	Met/Imp
4, each 5 oz	veal escalopes (cutlets)	4, each 150 g/5 oz
5 tbsp	butter	60 g/2½ oz
	salt and pepper	
I tbsp	hot water	15 ml/I tbsp
2	lemons	2
	parsley	

ESCALOPES DE VEAU AU CITRON

— VEAL ESCALOPES WITH LEMON —

Preparation 5 minutes • Cooking 20 minutes • Serves 4

Ask the butcher to cut the veal escalopes (cutlets) the same size.

Heat the butter in a frying pan and brown the veal over a high heat for 5 minutes on each side. Add salt and pepper and cook over a moderate heat for a further 10 minutes. Put on to a heated serving dish.

Deglaze the frying pan with the hot water and the juice of 1 lemon. Pour over the veal. Sprinkle with chopped parsley and surround with semi-circles of fluted lemon.

Wines: white Chablis or red Bourgogne-Irancy.

VEAL ESCALOPES WITH CREAM SAUCE

Preparation 10 minutes • Cooking 20 minutes • Serves 4

US	Ingredients	Met/Imp
3 tbsp	butter	40 g/1½ oz
2 tbsp	olive oil	30 ml/2 tbsp
4, each 5 oz	veal escalopes (cutlets)	4 each 150 g/5 oz
	salt and pepper	
1 tbsp	hot water	15 ml/1 tbsp
scant ½ lb	button mushrooms	200 g/7 oz
4 tsp	cognac	20 ml/4 tsp
½ cup	crème fraîche	100 ml/4 fl oz

Heat the butter and half of the oil in a frying pan. Brown the veal for 5 minutes on each side. Add salt and pepper and the hot water. Cover and cook over a moderate heat for a further 10 minutes.

Meanwhile, trim the stalks from the mushrooms, wash, drain and thinly slice the caps. Heat the remaining oil in a saucepan and fry the mushrooms, then add to the veal.

Heat the cognac in a small saucepan, pour over the veal, remove from the heat and flambé. Arrange the escalopes (cutlets) in a heated serving dish and surround with the mushrooms

Add the crème fraîche to the frying pan and stir well, but do not allow to boil. Pour over the veal and serve at once.

Cider or white or red wines: Vouvray, Jasnières, Saumur, Bourgueil, Chinon, Saumur-Champigny.

VEAL ESCALOPES WITH TARRAGON

Preparation 7 minutes • Cooking 20 minutes • Serves 4

US	Ingredients	Met/Imp
2 tbsp	butter	30 g/1 oz
1 tbsp	olive oil	15 ml/1 tbsp
4, each 5 oz	veal escalopes (cutlets)	4, each 150 g/5 oz
	flour	
½ cup	dry white wine	100 ml/4 fl oz
1 tbsp	tomato paste	15 ml/1 tbsp
	salt and pepper	
2	tarragon sprigs	2
	· paprika	

Heat the butter and oil in a large frying pan. Coat the escalopes (cutlets) in flour, shaking off the excess. Brown for 5 minutes on each side. Add the wine and tomato paste and scrape the bottom of the pan with a wooden spoon, but do not remove the veal. Add salt and pepper. Add all the leaves from 1 tarragon sprig. Cover and cook for a further 10 minutes.

Arrange the veal on a heated serving dish. Chop the remaining tarragon leaves and sprinkle over the meat with a pinch of paprika.

Wines: red or white Arbois, Côtes du Rhône, Côtes du Luberon.

US	Ingredients	Met/Imp
8, each about ¼ lb	veal escalopes (cutlets)	8, each about 100 g/4 oz
	salt and pepper	
¾ cup	flour	100 g/4 oz
2	eggs	2
¼ cup	oil	50 ml/2 fl oz
3½ cups	fresh white breadcrumbs	200 g/7 oz
10 tbsp	butter	150 g/5 oz
	GARNISH	
1	lemon, fluted and sliced into 8 rings	1
1 tbsp	chopped parsley	15 ml/1 tbsp
2	hard-boiled eggs (whites and yolks separated)	2

VIENNESE VEAL ESCALOPES

Preparation 50 minutes • Cooking 8–10 minutes

Season the veal with salt and pepper and coat in the flour. Dip in the eggs beaten with salt, pepper and a dash of oil, then coat in fine breadcrumbs, pressing the crumbs on well with the back of a large knife. Heat the butter and oil in a large frying pan until smoking. (Clarified butter can be used instead, which is preferable but a little more expensive.) Put the veal into the smoking fat and fry for 6 minutes, then turn and cook for a further 2–4 minutes until the meat is browned and the outside crisp.

Arrange the veal on a heated serving dish and pour over the pan juices. Place a slice of lemon on the centre of each and garnish with the parsley and chopped hard-boiled egg.

Red or white wines: Alsace Pinot Noir, Pinot Gris or Riesling.

US	Ingredients	Met/Imp
3	eggs	3
4	2 mm/⅛ inch slices lean *Bayonne* ham	4
2	sweet green or red peppers	2
2⅓ cups	green olives	400 g/14 oz
2, each 10 oz	large, thick veal escalopes (cutlets)	2, each 300 g/10 oz
¾ cup	flour	100 g/4 oz
	olive oil	
1 cup	dry white wine	250 ml/9 fl oz
1 cup	water	250 ml/9 fl oz
	salt and pepper	

SPANISH-STYLE STUFFED VEAL ESCALOPES

Preparation 40 minutes • Cooking 55 minutes • Serves 4–6

Hard-boil the eggs. Cut them into quarters.

Remove and discard the fat from the ham. Cut into 1 cm/½ inch pieces. Grill (broil) the peppers. Skin, de-seed and slice them.

Stone the olives and slice half of them lengthways (the others will be cooked whole in the sauce).

Cover each veal escalope (cutlet) with alternate layers of ham, sliced olives, hard-boiled egg and peppers. Roll up loosely, tie with string and coat with all but 15 ml/1 tbsp flour.

Heat some oil in a pan and brown the veal rolls on all sides. Sprinkle with the remaining flour. Add the reserved whole stoned olives. Add the wine, water and a little salt and pepper. Bring to the boil. Place a lid on top of the pan but do not cover it completely. Cook over a low heat for 30–45 minutes, until the veal is tender.

Remove the string. Cut the veal rolls into slices 1 cm/½ inch thick, surround with the olives and serve the sauce separately.

Rosé wines: Béarn, Irouléguy.
Light red wines from the south-west: Côtes du Brulhois, Côtes du Marmandais, Bergerac.

BREADED VEAL ESCALOPES ANDELYS STYLE

Preparation 1 hour • Cooking 20 minutes

US	Ingredients	Met/Imp
8, each about 5 oz	veal escalopes (cutlets)	8, each about 150 g/5 oz
	carrots	
	onions	
	bouquet garni	
10 tbsp	butter	150 g/5 oz
½ cup	consommé	100 ml/4 fl oz
3 cups	Mornay Sauce (page 73)	750 ml/1¼ pints
2	egg yolks	2
a few	truffles	a few
	fresh white breadcrumbs	
1 cup	Gruyère cheese, grated	100 g/4 oz
16	tomatoes	16

Braise the veal on a bed of chopped carrots and onions with the bouquet garni, basting frequently with melted butter and consommé (about 10 minutes). Remove the veal when cooked. Strain the cooking liquid and add it to the Mornay sauce with the beaten egg yolks. Reserve 8 truffle slices, chop the remainder and add to the sauce. Arrange the veal on a breadcrumb base, coat with the sauce and garnish with the reserved truffles. Sprinkle the cheese on top, garnish with small tomatoes and brown in the oven.

Cider, or white or red wines: Jasnières, Vouvray, Bourgueil, Chinon.

ESCALOPES DE VEAU AU JAMBON

VEAL ESCALOPES WITH HAM

Preparation 25 minutes • Cooking 10 minutes

US	Ingredients	Met/Imp
8, each about ¼ lb	veal escalopes (cutlets), preferably cut from leg	8, each about 100 g/4 oz
1 stick	butter	100 g/4 oz
½ cup	Tomato Sauce (page 80)	100 ml/3½ fl oz
8	very thin slices of Parma ham	8
1¾ cups	crème fraîche	400 ml/14 fl oz
	salt and pepper	

Fry the veal in the butter for about 10 minutes or until cooked. Deglaze the pan with the tomato sauce. Cover each escalope (cutlet) with a slice of ham. Add the crème fraîche to the cooking liquid, with salt and pepper. Reduce the sauce and coat the veal.

White wines: Vouvray, Chablis, Alsace Gewürztraminer.
Red wines: Graves, Pomerol, Saint-Émilion.

FOIE DE VEAU ÉTUVÉ À LA BRIARDE

CALF'S LIVER STEW FROM THE BRIE REGION

Preparation 50 minutes • Cooking 2½ hours

US	Ingredients	Met/Imp
¾ lb	fat bacon	350 g/12 oz
2 tbsp	cognac	30 ml/2 tbsp
1	whole calf's liver	1
	salt and pepper	
2 oz	pig's caul	50 g/2 oz
4 tbsp	butter	50 g/2 oz
8–10	carrots	8–10
2	onions	2
1	bouquet garni	1
½ cup	white wine	100 ml/4 fl oz
½ cup	White Stock (page 56)	100 ml/4 fl oz
1 pinch	quatre-épices	1 pinch
1 tbsp	chopped parsley	15 ml/1 tbsp

Soak 300 g/10 oz of the bacon, thinly sliced, in the cognac, then insert in the liver. Season with salt and pepper, wrap in the caul and brown in the butter with the remaining bacon, very finely chopped, turning several times. Skim off the excess fat. Add the carrots, cut into rings, and the finely chopped onions. Sweat for 1 minute. Add the bouquet garni, wine, stock and spice. Bring to the boil. Cover with a tight-fitting lid and simmer very gently, turning or basting frequently, for about 2½ hours or until cooked.

When cooked, put the liver on to a heated serving dish and keep hot. Drain the carrots and make into a thick purée. Skim the cooking liquid. Put the carrot purée into a vegetable dish. Pour some of the cooking liquid over the liver and sprinkle with parsley. Serve the remaining liquid separately in a sauce boat. A purée of celery or onions, or a mushroom sauce are also suitable accompaniments.

White wines: Pouilly-Fumé, Sancerre.
Red wines: Bourgogne-Hautes Côtes de Nuits, Bourgogne-Hautes Côtes de Beaune.

US	Ingredients	Met/Imp
¼ lb	fat bacon	100 g/4 oz
	parsley	
1¼–1½ lb	calf's liver, in one piece	700 g/1¼–1½ lb
1 bottle	red port wine	1 bottle
1	pig's caul	1
4	carrots	4
2	garlic cloves	2
1	onion	1
2 tbsp	butter	30 ml/2 tbsp
1	thyme sprig	1
1	bay leaf	1
a few	veal bones	a few
	salt and pepper	
½ cup	crème fraîche	100 ml/4 fl oz

FOIE DE VEAU MÉDÉRIC

CALF'S LIVER MÉDÉRIC

Preparation 1¼ hours • Marinating 1 hour • Cooking 1 hour

Cut the bacon into thin *lardons*. Roll in chopped parsley, then use to lard the liver with a larding needle.

Soak the liver in the port for a good hour, drain (reserving the port) and wrap in the caul. Finely chop the carrots, garlic and onion.

Heat the butter in a saucepan. Put in the chopped vegetables, thyme, bay leaf and a parsley sprig. Place the liver on top. Put the veal bones around. Add salt, pepper and the port from the marinade. Cover and simmer for about 1 hour or until the liver is cooked. Put it on to a heated serving dish, cut into thick slices and keep warm.

Strain the sauce. Return to the saucepan and boil, uncovered, until reduced to half its volume. Adjust the seasoning if necessary and add the crème fraîche. Pour over the liver.

Wines: Beaujolais-Villages, Vins de Marcillac, Bergerac, Côtes du Rhône.

US	Ingredients	Met/Imp
3 oz	fat bacon	75 g/3 oz
	salt and pepper	
1¾ lb	calf's liver	800 g/1¾ lb
1 tbsp	goose fat	15 ml/1 tbsp
¼ lb	*Bayonne ham*	100 g/4 oz
1	garlic clove	1
2	onions	2
	parsley	
1 tbsp	fresh white breadcrumbs	15 ml/1 tbsp
1 glass	dry white wine	1 glass
½ cup	stock	100 ml/4 fl oz
2 tbsp	armagnac	30 ml/2 tbsp

FOIE DE VEAU PIQUÉ DES POUSTERLES

CALF'S LIVER SPIKED WITH BACON

Preparation 15 minutes • Cooking 2 hours

Recipe created by André Daguin, Hôtel de France, Auch

Season the bacon with salt and pepper, cut it into thin *lardons*, then use to lard the liver. Put into a flameproof casserole with the goose fat. Add the diced ham and fry until golden. Mix together the crushed garlic, onions cut into rings, chopped parsley and breadcrumbs. Add to the liver, with the wine, stock and armagnac. Cook in a very moderate oven for about 2 hours, turning and basting from time to time.

Wines: Madiran, Vins de Marcillac, Vins d'Estaing, Minervois.

US	Ingredients	Met/Imp
10 tbsp	butter	150 g/5 oz
4	large onions	4
½ cup	white wine	100 ml/4 fl oz
¼ cup	oil	50 ml/2 fl oz
8, each about 3 oz	slices calf's liver, diced or thinly sliced	8, each about 75 g/3 oz
	salt and pepper	
4 tsp	cognac	20 ml/4 tsp
	parsley	
1	lemon, juice of	1

FOIE DE VEAU À LA VÉNITIENNE

VENETIAN-STYLE CALF'S LIVER*

Preparation 20 minutes • Cooking 5 minutes

Put about one-third of the butter into a shallow pan and add the thinly sliced onions. Cover and cook gently. When soft, add the wine. Reduce, making sure the onions do not brown. Put the oil and remaining butter into another saucepan. When it is very hot, toss in the liver seasoned with salt and pepper. Cook quickly, then mix in the onions. Do not allow to boil. Add the cognac, coarsely chopped parsley and lemon juice.

Red wines: Bourgueil, Chinon, Bordeaux.

VEAL FRICADELLES

Preparation 1 hour • Cooking 20 minutes

US	Ingredients	Met/Imp
14 oz	lean boneless veal	400 g/14 oz
½ lb	pork fillet (tenderloin)	250 g/8 oz
2 cups	fresh white breadcrumbs	125 g/4 oz
I	large onion	I
3	shallots	3
I stick	butter	125 g/4 oz
I tbsp	chopped parsley	15 ml/I tbsp
2	eggs, lightly beaten	2
I tbsp	salt	20 g/¾ oz
I large pinch	pepper	I large pinch
	nutmeg	
¾ cup	flour	100 g/4 oz
scant I cup	Demi-Glaze (*page 56*)	200 ml/7 fl oz
½ cup	white wine	100 ml/3½ fl oz

Mince (grind) the veal and pork, then place in a bowl with the breadcrumbs. Add the very finely chopped onion and shallots which have been fried in one-third of the butter and cooled, the chopped parsley, eggs, salt, pepper and nutmeg. Mix well with a wooden spoon.

Divide the mixture into 8 portions. Turn on to a floured surface and form into balls, then flatten and form into oval shapes.

Put the remaining butter into a large flameproof casserole. When it is very hot, put in the fricadelles, making sure that they do not touch each other. Brown on both sides, turning carefully. Transfer to a moderate oven and finish cooking for 20 minutes.

Deglaze the pan with the demi-glaze and white wine. Strain through cheesecloth into a heated serving dish and place the fricadelles on top. Serve with vegetables.

Red wine: Beaujolais-Villages.

VEAL FRICANDEAU BOURGEOIS

Preparation 1 hour • Cooking about 2½ hours

US	Ingredients	Met/Imp
5½ lb	boned and rolled joint (roast) of veal, cut crossways from top of leg	2.5 kg/5½ lb
¼ lb	fat bacon	100 g/4 oz
	salt and pepper	
2	carrots	2
2	large onions	2
I	bouquet garni	I
I stick	butter	100 g/4 oz
½ cup	dry white wine	100 ml/3½ fl oz
¾ lb	baby carrots	300 g/10 oz
½ lb	button (pearl) onions	200 g/7 oz
¼ lb	bacon collar (smoked pork shoulder)	125 g/4½ oz
I cup	Veal Stock (*page 56*)	200 ml/7 fl oz

Lard the veal with the bacon, cut into strips. Season. Put into a flameproof casserole on a bed of finely chopped carrots and onions, with the bouquet garni. Sweat in butter for about 30 minutes. Add the wine and reduce to half its volume. Strain, then return to the casserole. Add the baby carrots, the button (pearl) onions which have been lightly browned, and the diced and blanched collar of bacon (smoked pork shoulder). Pour in the stock. Cover with a piece of buttered paper, greaseproof or parchment and a lid. Transfer to a moderately hot oven and cook, basting frequently, for about 2 hours or until tender.

Dry white wines: Côtes du Rhône, Côtes de Provence.
Red wines: Bourgogne, Mercurey, Givry.

US	Ingredients	Met/Imp
5½ lb	joint (roast) of veal, cut crossways from top of leg	2.5 kg/5½ lb
½ lb	pork fat	250 g/8 oz
2	bacon slices	2
3	carrots	3
2	large onions	2
I	bouquet garni	I
	salt and pepper	
4½ lb	veal bones	2 kg/4½ lb
½ cup	white wine or madeira	100 ml/4 fl oz
	Veal Stock (page 56)	
	sorrel, to serve	

FRICANDEAU DE VEAU À L'OSEILLE

— VEAL FRICANDEAU WITH SORREL —

Preparation 45 minutes • Cooking 2 hours

Starting at the narrowest end, cut an opening along the length of the veal. Open the meat out like a book and beat until uniform in thickness (to ensure even cooking). Place on a cloth and lard with the pork fat.

Line the bottom of a flameproof casserole with the bacon slices, sliced carrots and onions and add the bouquet garni. Add a glass of water, but no stock. Season the veal and place on top of the vegetables with 2–3 crushed veal bones.

Roughly chop the remaining bones and spread on top of the veal. Cover with foil and a tight-fitting lid. Place over direct heat for about 5 minutes, then transfer to a moderately hot oven and cook for about 2 hours, or until the veal is tender. Do not baste, as the fat and water will turn to steam, keeping the veal moist.

When cooked, strain off the liquid and keep the veal hot. Return the bones and vegetables to the casserole and deglaze with the white wine or madeira. Reduce the liquid by half, then add a few ladlefuls of a lightly thickened veal stock. Strain through cheesecloth and skim off the fat.

Serve with sorrel, preferably, or with spinach, endive (chicory) in cream sauce, a *macédoine* of vegetables, Vichy carrots, carrots in cream sauce, or stuffed, braised lettuce.

White wines: Muscadet, Chablis.
Red wines: Beaujolais-Villages, Bourgueil, Chinon.

US	Ingredients	Met/Imp
3½ lb	slice veal, cut from centre of leg, 15–18 cm/6–7 inches thick, with bone	1.6 kg/3½ lb
	salt and pepper	
¼ lb	fat bacon, cut into small pieces, for larding	100 g/4 oz
	diced bacon for braising	
2	carrots	2
½ cup	*marc* from Provence	100 ml/3½ fl oz
	STUFFING	
I	large onion	I
3	shallots	3
I pinch	crushed garlic	I pinch
2 oz	pork fat	50 g/2 oz
¼ lb	lean collar bacon (smoked pork shoulder)	100 g/4 oz
I cup	Dry Duxelles (page 49)	250 ml/8 fl oz
2	parsley sprigs	2
I pinch	saffron	I pinch

FRICANDEAU DE VEAU À LA PROVENÇALE

—— VEAL FRICANDEAU PROVENÇAL ——

Preparation 1 hour • Cooking about 2 hours

Remove the centre bone from the veal and replace with the stuffing, made by frying the chopped onion, shallots and garlic in the pork fat with the finely diced bacon (smoked pork), then mixing with the duxelles, chopped parsley and saffron. Season the veal, lard it with the fat bacon, then tie to keep the stuffing in place.

Put the veal into a flameproof casserole on a bed of diced bacon and carrots.

Add the marc and simmer for a few minutes, basting. Cover with a tight-fitting lid and cook gently on top of the stove for at least 2 hours.

Serve with a ratatouille of tomatoes and aubergines (eggplant).

Wines: red or white Côtes de Provence.

	US	Ingredients	Met/Imp

VEAL GRENADINS WITH VEGETABLE MACÉDOINE

Preparation 50 minutes • Cooking 1¼ hours

Trim the grenadins into oval shapes and lard each one with 3 rows of bacon *lardons*. Arrange the grenadins in a casserole on a bed of pork rind, sliced carrots and onion rings and the bouquet garni. Season, cover the casserole and cook in a moderately hot oven for 15 minutes.

Pour in the wine and evaporate completely on top of the stove. Add 100 ml/4 fl oz (½ cup) of the stock and reduce until syrupy, then add the remaining stock. A stock (bouillon) cube may be used, in which case the quantity of pork rind must be doubled. Bring to the boil, cover with a piece of buttered greaseproof or parchment paper and the lid and cook in a moderate oven, basting frequently, for about 1 hour. Uncover the casserole about 8 minutes before the end of cooking, to glaze the top.

To serve, arrange the veal grenadins in a crown on a round serving dish. Place a *macédoine* of vegetables in the centre. Reduce the cooking liquid to 150 ml/¼ pint (⅔ cup) and serve separately.

Red wines: Côte de Beaune-Villages, Givry, Rully.

US	Ingredients	Met/Imp
8, each about 5 oz	veal grenadins or medallions	8, each about 150 g/5 oz
5 oz	fat bacon	150 g/5 oz
¼ lb	pork rind	100 g/4 oz
2	carrots	2
2	onions	2
l	bouquet garni	l
	salt and pepper	
½ cup	white wine	100 ml/3½ fl oz
2 cups	Veal Stock (*page 56*)	500 ml/18 fl oz

SHIN OF VEAL PROVENÇAL

Preparation 40 minutes • Cooking about 2 hours

Season the veal with salt and pepper. Coat with the flour.

Fry in the oil until brown. Prepare a Mirepoix (*page 50*) with the onions and carrots and add to the veal with the bouquet garni. Cover and stew gently for about 2 hours, until tender.

Remove the rind from the oranges, shred finely, then blanch and add to the stew.

Add the squeezed orange juice, wine and tomatoes to the stock and reduce it. Strain over the veal. Serve with pilau rice.

Red wines: Bandol, Coteaux d'Aix-en Provence, Coteaux des Baux-de-Provence.

US	Ingredients	Met/Imp
8, each about ¾ inch thick	meaty slices of veal shin or knuckle (shank cross-cuts)	8, each about 2 cm/¾ inch thick
	salt and pepper	
¾ cup	flour	100 g/4 oz
½ cup	olive oil	100 ml/3½ fl oz
2	large onions	2
3	carrots	3
l	bouquet garni	l
2	oranges	2
½ cup	white wine	100 ml/3½ fl oz
2	tomatoes, chopped	2
scant l cup	Veal Stock (*page 56*)	200 ml/7 fl oz
l cup	Pilau Rice (*page 563*), to serve	200 g/7 oz

US	Ingredients	Met/Imp
4½ lb	breast of veal, with a little fat	2 kg/4½ lb
10 tbsp	butter	150 g/5 oz
½ cup	flour	75 g/3 oz
2 bottles	good red wine	2 bottles
30	button (pearl) onions	30
8	carrots	8
	salt and pepper	
I	bouquet garni	I
	chopped parsley, to serve	

COOPERS' STEW

Preparation 45 minutes • Cooking about 1½ hours

Cut the veal into cubes weighing about 100 g/4 oz. In a *cocotte*, make a roux (*page 50*) with the butter and flour. Add the red wine.

Add the veal, onions and diced carrots, seasoning and bouquet garni. Cook gently for 1½ hours.

Take out the veal and reduce the cooking liquid. Pour over the veal and sprinkle with chopped parsley before serving.

Wines: as a general rule, serve the same wine as the one used for cooking.

US	Ingredients	Met/Imp
5½ lb	boned and rolled joint (roast) of veal, cut from top of leg	2.5 kg/5½ lb
½ lb	bacon	200 g/7 oz
10 tbsp	butter	150 g/5 oz
I cup	Veal Stock (page 56)	200 ml/7 fl oz
4	heads celery	4
8	onions	8
24	small carrots	24
12	small turnips	12
	salt and pepper	

NOIX DE VEAU À L'AIXOISE

AIX-STYLE POT ROAST VEAL

Preparation 1 hour• Cooking 2 hours

Lard the veal with the bacon cut into fingers. Put it into a flameproof casserole with the butter. Fry until golden-brown, then add the stock. Trim and blanch the celery, then place it around the veal with the whole onions, carrots and turnips. Season, then simmer for about 2 hours or until cooked.

Place the veal on a heated serving dish with the vegetables arranged in a crown around it. Serve the sauce separately.

Red wines: Saint-Émilion, Pomerol, Coteaux d'Aix-en-Provence.

US	Ingredients	Met/Imp
4½ lb	boned and rolled joint (roast) of veal, cut from top of leg	2 kg/4½ lb
I	calf's foot	I
a few	veal bones	a few
14 tbsp	butter	200 g/7 oz
	salt and pepper	
I pinch	*quatre-épices*	I pinch
scant I cup	water	200 ml/7 fl oz
6	medium onions	6
4	shallots	4
3	garlic cloves	3
2	carrots	2
I	bouquet garni (with sage, savory and tarragon sprigs)	I
½ cup	double (heavy) cream	100 ml/3½ fl oz
6	egg yolks	6
I	lemon, juice of	I

NOIX DE VEAU BRAISÉE À LA MARÉCHALE

'MARSHAL'S STYLE' BRAISED VEAL

Preparation 40 minutes • Cooking 1¾ hours

Brown the veal, roughly chopped calf's foot and bones in about half the butter in a flameproof casserole. Season with salt, pepper and spice. Add the water (not stock), with the chopped onions, shallots, garlic, carrots and the bouquet garni. Simmer for 1½ hours, basting frequently, to make a reduced veal stock.

Take out the veal and keep hot. Strain the stock, then leave to cool slightly. Make a liaison with the cream, egg yolks and stock. Whisk over a *bain-marie* as when making a *sabayon*, add the remaining butter and the lemon juice, then pour over the veal.

Do not serve on a very hot dish or the sauce will curdle.

Red wines: Bourgueil, Côte de Beaune-Villages.

NOIX DE VEAU À LA GELÉE

VEAL IN ASPIC

Preparation 2 hours • Cooking 1½ hours

US	Ingredients	Met/Imp
3½ lb	boned and rolled joint (roast) of veal, cut from top of leg	1.5 kg/3½ lb
½ lb	fat bacon	200 g/8 oz
¼ lb	pork rind	100 g/4 oz
	veal bones	
2	carrots	2
2	onions	2
	salt and pepper	
2	egg whites	2
1 ladleful	good liquid Plain Aspic (page 58)	1 ladleful
	GARNISH	
	asparagus tips	
	small carrots	
	young turnips	
	French (fine green) beans	
	cauliflower florets	
	peas	

Lard the veal with the bacon cut into matchstick strips. Put it into a large saucepan with the pork rind, chopped bones, finely chopped carrots and onions, and salt and pepper. Sweat and allow to brown slightly. Skim off the fat and half-cover with water. Cover with buttered greaseproof or parchment paper and a lid and cook gently, basting frequently, for about 1½ hours. When cooked, take out the veal and leave to cool completely. Strain the liquid through cheesecloth, clarify it with the egg whites and dilute with the aspic. When the veal is cold, slice it and reshape it on a serving dish. Glaze with some of the syrupy liquid. Chill the remaining liquid until set to a jelly, then chop finely to garnish, along with the vegetables, boiled and glazed.

Red wine: Beaujolais-Villages, Chinon.

NOIX OU ROUELLE DE VEAU AU JUS

POT ROAST VEAL

Preparation 1 hour • Cooking about 2 hours

US	Ingredients	Met/Imp
5½ lb	boned and rolled joint (roast) of veal, cut from top of leg	2.5 kg/5½ lb
½ lb	fat bacon	250 g/8 oz
2	carrots	2
1	large onion	1
6	bacon slices	6
1	bouquet garni	1
	salt and pepper	
1 quart	Brown Veal Stock (page 56)	1 litre/1¾ pints
1 tbsp	brandy	15 ml/1 tbsp

Trim the veal and lard it with the fat bacon cut into matchstick strips. Put it into a flameproof casserole on a bed of diced carrots, the onion cut into rings, 1 diced bacon slice and the bouquet garni. Season, then add the stock and brandy. Cover with the remaining bacon slices, then a sheet of buttered greaseproof or parchment paper. Cook over a low heat for 2 hours, basting frequently.

Transfer the veal to a roasting pan. Reduce the cooking liquid, strain it and skim off the fat. Pour it over the veal and glaze in a hot oven. Remove and serve on a hot serving dish.

Red wine: Saint-Émilion, Pomerol.

PAUPIETTES DE VEAU

VEAL OLIVES

Preparation 30 minutes • Cooking 20 minutes

US	Ingredients	Met/Imp
8	very thin veal escalopes (cutlets)	8
	parsley	
	tarragon	
	thyme	
a few	shallots	a few
	spring onions (scallions)	
8	slices York ham	8
4	hard-boiled eggs, shelled and halved	4
	salt and pepper	
	pig's caul	
10 tbsp	butter	150 g/5 oz
1 cup	white wine	200 ml/7 fl oz

Cover each escalope (cutlet) with mixed and finely chopped herbs, shallots and spring onions (scallions). Place a slice of ham on each one, then place a hard-boiled egg half in the centre. Roll and tie with string. Season. Place in a flameproof casserole and cover with a piece of pig's caul. Fry in half of the butter until golden, add a little thyme and cook, uncovered, over a very low heat for about 20 minutes.

Remove the veal rolls, deglaze the casserole with the wine, reduce the liquid and thicken with the remaining butter.

White wines: Sancerre, Pouilly-Fumé.
Red wines: Saint-Émilion, Pomerol, Côte de Beaune-Villages.

US	Ingredients	Met/Imp
8	veal escalopes (cutlets)	8
8	slices Parma ham	8
2	hard-boiled eggs	2
8	black olives	8
¼ cup	Anchovy Butter (page 51)	50 g/2 oz
a little	malt whisky	a little
8	bay leaves	8
8	sage leaves	8
8	bacon slices	8
2 oz	lean bacon	50 g/2 oz
I glass	white Rully wine	I glass
½ cup	Veal Stock (page 56)	100 ml/4 fl oz
2	onions	2
I	carrrot	I
I	garlic clove	I
2 lb	chanterelles	I kg/2 lb
	clarified butter	
8	green olives	8
I	fresh truffle	I
½ cup	crème fraîche	100 ml/4 fl oz

VEAL 'BIRDS'

Preparation 1¼ hours • Cooking 50 minutes

Choose large, thin escalopes (cutlets). Place a slice of ham on each. Over the ham spread a paste of hard-boiled eggs mashed with the stoned black olives and the anchovy butter. Roll up the escalopes (cutlets), pressing the edges together to seal. Sprinkle with malt whisky.

Put a bay leaf on one side of each roll and a sage leaf on the other. Wrap a slice of bacon around each, then tie with string. Fry the diced bacon in a flameproof casserole until brown, then add the veal rolls. Fry until golden-brown. Pour in the wine and stock. Add the finely chopped onions, carrot and garlic. Cook over a low heat for 40–50 minutes.

Meanwhile, in a separate pan, fry the chanterelles in clarified butter.

Fifteen minutes before the end of cooking, take the veal out of the pan and remove the bacon. Skim the fat off the cooking liquid and add a few stoned green olives and a whole truffle. Return the veal to the pan and finish cooking.

Take out the veal. Using a matchstick, place an olive at one end of each roll, to make a bird's head. At the other end, place a fan-shaped slice of truffle to make the tail. Place each veal 'bird' on a nest of chanterelles and keep hot.

Strain the stock through a fine sieve to give a smooth sauce. Add the crème fraîche and pour over the veal.

White wines: Pouilly-Fuissé, Rully, Mâcon-Viré.
Red wines: Santenay, Rully, Juliénas.

BREAST OF VEAL WITH PETITS POIS

Preparation 45 minutes • Cooking 1¾ hours

US	Ingredients	Met/Imp
4½ lb	breast of veal	2 kg/4½ lb
	salt and pepper	
12	button (pearl) onions	12
10 tbsp	butter	150 g/5 oz
¼ cup	olive oil	50 ml/2 fl oz
7 tbsp	flour	60 g/2½ oz
2 quarts	Veal Stock (page 56)	2 litres/3½ pints
I	bouquet garni	I
2 quarts	shelled petits pois	2 litres/3½ pints
1–2	lettuce hearts (optional)	1–2

Cut the veal into 100 g/4 oz pieces and season with salt and pepper. Fry with the onions in the butter and oil over a high heat until golden-brown. Skim off the fat. Sprinkle in the flour, stir with a wooden spoon and add the stock and bouquet garni. Cook in a moderately hot oven for 1 hour, then add the petits pois and lettuce hearts, if using. Adjust the seasoning and cook for a further 45 minutes. Before serving, remove the bouquet garni and lettuce hearts (if used).

Dry white wines: Saumur, Sancerre, Pouilly-Fumé.
Red wines: Beaujolais-Villages, Côte de Beaune-Villages, Saint-Nicolas de Bourgueil.

——— VEAL SWEETBREADS LASSERRE ———

Preparation 1 hour • Cooking 40 minutes

US	Ingredients	Met/Imp
8 (4 pairs)	veal sweetbreads	8
	butter, melted	
½ cup	consommé	100 ml/4 fl oz
3 cups	Mornay Sauce (page 73)	750 ml/1¼ pints
2	egg yolks	2
1	large slice Bayonne ham	1
4 cups	Dry Duxelles (page 49)	1 kg/2 lb
1 cup	Gruyère cheese, grated	100 g/4 oz
	FOR BRAISING	
	carrots	
	onions	
	garlic	
	bouquet garni	
	salt and pepper	

Blanch and trim the sweetbreads and braise on a bed of chopped carrots, onions and garlic, with the bouquet garni, salt and freshly ground pepper. Add some melted butter and the consommé. Cook in a moderately hot oven, basting frequently, for about 40 minutes. Cover with buttered greaseproof paper or parchment paper to prevent the dish from becoming too brown.

When cooked, put the sweetbreads on a plate, strain the cooking liquid and add it to the Mornay sauce with the egg yolks, beaten until frothy, and the minced ham.

Slice the sweetbreads in half horizontally. On one side of each put 30 ml/2 tbsp duxelles, slightly thickened with some of the Mornay sauce mixture. Cover with the other side of the sweetbread to make a sandwich.

Arrange on a lightly buttered serving dish. Coat with the remaining Mornay sauce, sprinkle the cheese on top and brown in the oven.

Red wines: Médoc or Graves.

RIS DE VEAU À LA BROCHE

——— SWEETBREADS ON SKEWERS* ———

Preparation 1 hour • Cooking 35–40 minutes

US	Ingredients	Met/Imp
4 pairs	veal sweetbreads	4 sets
	salt and pepper	
½ lb	fat bacon	200 g/7 oz
5 tbsp	butter	60 g/2½ oz

Season the sweetbreads with salt and pepper, then lard them with the bacon cut into matchstick strips. Wrap individually in squares of buttered foil. Put on to skewers and grill (broil) for 25 minutes. Remove the foil and grill (broil) for a further 10–12 minutes to brown, basting from time to time with the melted butter.

Remove the sweetbreads from the skewers. Skim the cooking liquid and serve it immediately.

The sweetbreads should be served with vegetables such as peas, French (fine green) beans, asparagus tips, spinach, artichoke hearts, stuffed mushrooms, stuffed lettuce.

White wines: Anjou, Vouvray, Quincy, Sancerre, Barsac.
Red wines: Chinon, Saumur-Champigny.

US	Ingredients	Met/Imp
I pair	veal sweetbreads	I set
2	bacon slices	2
	oil	
I	thyme sprig	I
	salt and pepper	
	bay leaves	
	parsley	

RIS DE VEAU EN BROCHETTES

—— VEAL SWEETBREAD KEBABS ——

Preparation 30 minutes • Marinating 10 minutes • Cooking 15 minutes • Serves 1

Blanch the sweetbreads and squeeze well to extract the water. Dice coarsely. Dice the bacon. Marinate the sweetbreads and bacon for 10 minutes in a bowl with the oil, thyme, salt and pepper. Drain.

Put a piece of bacon on a skewer, then a piece of sweetbread and a bay leaf. Repeat until the skewer is full, ending with a piece of bacon. Grill (broil) until browned on all sides. Serve garnished with a parsley sprig.

Wines: Chinon, Bourgueil, Saumur-Champigny, Beaujolais-Villages.

US	Ingredients	Met/Imp
10 tbsp	butter	150 g/5 oz
2 large pairs	veal sweetbreads	2 large sets
I	shallot	I
I pinch	nutmeg	I pinch
	salt and pepper	
½ cup	double (heavy) cream	100 ml/4 fl oz

RIS DE VEAU À LA CRÈME

— VEAL SWEETBREADS WITH CREAM —

Preparation 1 hour • Cooking 12 minutes

Heat the butter in a frying pan until browned. Add the cleaned, blanched, trimmed and diced sweetbreads and fry until golden-brown (about 8 minutes).

Add the chopped shallot, nutmeg, salt, pepper and cream. Simmer for 4 minutes (do not allow to boil).

White wines: Graves, Barsac, Anjou, Vouvray.
Red wines: Côte de Beaune-Villages, Médoc.

US	Ingredients	Met/Imp
4 pairs	veal sweetbreads	4 sets
8	lean bacon slices	8
I quart	White Stock (page 56)	I litre/1¾ pints
	salt and pepper	
I quart	Ivoire Sauce (see Chicken Velouté, page 57)	I litre/1¾ pints

RIS DE VEAU À L'IVOIRE

VEAL SWEETBREADS
—— WITH IVOIRE SAUCE ——

Preparation 40 minutes • Blanching 4–5 hours • Pressing 1 hour • Cooking 30–40 minutes

For this recipe the sweetbreads should be very white: place in a colander under running water for 4–5 hours. Put into a saucepan, cover with cold water and bring to the boil. Boil gently for 5 minutes, then drain and rinse well. Separate the 2 lobes, discard the membranes, tubes and gristle. Weight down lightly and leave for 1 hour.

Wrap each sweetbread in a bacon slice, put into a deep saucepan and cover with the stock. Season. Bring to the boil, cover and cook in a moderately hot oven for 30–40 minutes. The cooking liquid should be just simmering.

Drain the sweetbreads, pat dry and arrange on a serving dish. Coat with some of the ivoire sauce and serve the remainder on the side. If liked, reduce the cooking liquid and add to the sauce.

When in season, serve with asparagus tips.

White wines: Anjou, Saumur, Vouvray, Quincy, Sancerre, Chablis, Champagne.
Red wines: Graves, Médoc, Bourgueil, Chinon.

NORMANDY-STYLE VEAL SWEETBREADS

Preparation 45 minutes • Cooking 30 minutes

US	Ingredients	Met/Imp
4 pairs	veal sweetbreads	4 sets
1 stick	butter	100 g/4 oz
	salt and pepper	
8	russet (tart) apples	8
½ cup	calvados	100 ml/3½ fl oz
2 cups	crème fraîche	500 ml/18 fl oz
8	croûtons	8

Soak the sweetbreads in cold water, then sweat in half of the butter. Season well. Cover with buttered greaseproof or parchment paper and a lid. Cook without allowing to brown.

Cut the unpeeled apples into quarters, remove the seeds and sweat in butter in another saucepan.

Pour the calvados over the sweetbreads and flambé. Remove the sweetbreads and deglaze the pan with the crème fraîche.

Arrange the sweetbreads in a crown on top of the croûtons fried in butter, interleaving them with apple quarters, and coat with the sauce. Adjust the seasoning.

Red wines: Gamay de Touraine, Chinon, Médoc.

VEAL SWEETBREADS WITH GRAPES

Preparation 25 minutes • Soaking 2 hours • Cooking 15 minutes

US	Ingredients	Met/Imp
2 pairs	veal sweetbreads	2 sets
¼ lb	truffles	100 g/4 oz
¼ lb	pickled tongue	100 g/4 oz
	salt and pepper	
	flour	
	butter	
	oil	
1 glass	White Stock (page 56)	1 glass
	white grapes	
1 glass	fresh grape juice	1 glass
1 liqueur glass	madeira	1 liqueur glass
	Kneaded Butter (page 49)	

Soak the sweetbreads in cold water for 2 hours, then drain, blanch and rinse. Remove the membranes, tubes and gristle. Weight down lightly and leave to cool.

Spike the sweetbreads with small pieces of truffle and tongue. Season, toss in flour and brown in a flameproof casserole in a little butter and oil. Pour in the stock, cover and cook in a moderately hot oven for 10 minutes, basting and turning the sweetbreads from time to time.

Put the cooked sweetbreads on to a heated serving dish. Add the peeled and seeded grapes to the pan with the grape juice and madeira. Reduce over a high heat. Remove from the heat and add a little kneaded butter to thicken the sauce. Stir, shaking the pan until the butter has melted. Season, then pour over the sweetbreads and serve very hot.

White wines: Alsace Riesling, Vouvray, Sauternes.

US	Ingredients	Met/Imp
16	white grapes	16
16	black grapes	16
1 glass	white port wine	1 glass
16	green olives	16
16	black olives	16
3 pairs	veal sweetbreads	3 sets
	salt and pepper	
2 tbsp	flour	30 ml/2 tbsp
2 tbsp	butter	30 ml/2 tbsp
1 tbsp	Veal Stock (page 56) or double cream	15 ml/1 tbsp
	cayenne	

RIS DE VEAU ROBERT COURTINE

VEAL SWEETBREADS ROBERT COURTINE

Preparation 50 minutes • Soaking 2 hours • Cooking 40 minutes

Peel the grapes and macerate in the port for 2 hours. Meanwhile, stone the olives and soak the sweetbreads in cold water for 1 hour.

Drain the sweetbreads and put into a saucepan with fresh cold water to cover. Bring to the boil and boil gently for 5 minutes. Drain and rinse in cold water. Cut the sweetbreads in half. Season with salt and pepper and coat with the flour.

Heat the butter in a flameproof casserole, but do not allow to brown. Cook the sweetbreads for 30 minutes.

Add the grapes with the port and the olives. Cover and boil for about 10 minutes. Arrange the sweetbreads on a heated serving dish surrounded by the grapes and olives. Add the stock or cream to the cooking liquid, with a pinch of cayenne. Adjust the seasoning if necessary. Pour over the sweetbreads.

Wines: Vouvray, Sauternes, red or white Graves.

US	Ingredients	Met/Imp
1½ sticks	butter	175 g/6 oz
1	veal loin with kidney	1
5 oz	bacon	150 g/5 oz
½ lb	mushrooms	250 g/8 oz
30	button (pearl) onions	30
2	garlic cloves	2
1	bouquet garni, including 1 lettuce heart	1
1 lb	small new potatoes	500 g/1 lb
1	bunch baby carrots	1
1	bunch baby turnips	1
2	cloves	2
1 quart	shelled petits pois	1 litre/1¾ pints
½ cup	double (heavy) cream	100 ml/4 fl oz
	salt and pepper	

ROGNONNADE DE VEAU BRAISÉE À LA TOURANGELLE

TOURAINE-STYLE LOIN OF VEAL

Preparation 1 hour • Cooking 2 hours

Put 100 g/4 oz (1 stick) of the butter into a copper saucepan and fry the veal, diced bacon, mushrooms, 6 onions and the unpeeled garlic cloves, until browned. Cook for about 2 hours, until tender, taking care not to disturb the bottom of the pan. Remove from the heat and keep hot.

Heat half of the remaining butter in another saucepan and fry the bouquet garni and the diced potatoes, carrots and turnips. Add the cloves, then the petits pois, the flavour of which should dominate. Finally add the remaining onions, blanched. Do not add water, the vegetables should cook in their own juice.

When cooked, remove the bouquet garni and pour the vegetables over the veal. Simmer together for a few minutes. Add the remaining butter and the cream. Adjust the seasoning and serve very hot.

The characteristics of this recipe are the mixed vegetables in a concentrated stock.

White wines: Saumur, Vouvray, Quincy, Sauvignon de Touraine.
Red wines: Saint-Émilion, Pomerol, Gamay de Touraine.

LOIN OF VEAL 'AS IN BOURGES'

Preparation 1 hour • Cooking about 2 hours

Trim the veal and season. Line a saucepan with the bacon, chopped vegetables and veal bone. Put the veal on top. Sweat, then fry until browned and add the white wine and a little water. Cover with buttered greaseproof or parchment paper and a lid. Cook, basting continuously, for about 2 hours. When cooked, remove the veal, skim off the fat, reduce the cooking liquid and adjust the seasoning.

Make a quiche in the normal way, using the listed ingredients. Serve as an accompaniment to the veal.

White wines: Pouilly-Fumé, Sancerre.

US	Ingredients	Met/Imp
1	veal loin with kidney	1
	salt and pepper	
¼ lb	bacon slices	100 g/4 oz
2	onions	2
3	carrots	3
1	veal bone	1
1 bottle	white wine	1 bottle
	QUICHE	
1 lb	Puff Pastry (page 579)	500 g/1 lb
6	egg yolks	6
1¾ cups	double (heavy) cream	400 ml/14 fl oz
1 pinch	nutmeg	1 pinch
1 lb	French (fine green) beans	500 g/1 lb

VEAL KIDNEYS IN COGNAC*

Preparation 15 minutes • Cooking 8 minutes

Trim the fat from the kidneys, then split them in half lengthways. Put half of the butter into a heavy saucepan and fry the kidneys until golden-brown. Cook quickly, then keep hot.

Meanwhile, cream the remaining butter with the flour, to make a *beurre manié*. Skim the fat from the kidney cooking liquid and add the chopped shallots and wine. Reduce by one-third, gradually whisk in the beurre manié and thicken quickly. Remove from the heat. Pour the cognac over the kidneys and flambé. Put them into the sauce. Season with salt, pepper and sugar. Arrange on a serving dish, sprinkle with the parsley.

Dry white wines: Chablis, Mâcon-Viré, Saumur.
Red wines: Médoc, Bergerac, Bourgueil, Chinon.

US	Ingredients	Met/Imp
4	veal kidneys	4
1 stick	butter	100 g/4 oz
1 tbsp	flour	15 ml/1 tbsp
3	shallots	3
1¼ cups	white wine	300 ml/½ pint
scant 1 cup	cognac	200 ml/7 fl oz
	salt and pepper	
1 pinch	sugar	1 pinch
1 tbsp	chopped parsley	15 ml/1 tbsp

BOURBON VEAL KIDNEYS

Preparation 30 minutes • Cooking 40–60 minutes

Put the kidneys into a cast iron pan and fry whole with most of their fat. Add the butter, onions, carrots, seasoning and bouquet garni. Skim off some of the fat and add a little of the wine. Simmer, covered, turning the kidneys from time to time.

Serve the kidneys surrounded by the vegetables. Deglaze the pan with the remaining wine and the cognac, then pour over the kidneys.

Wines: as a general rule, serve the same wine as the one used for cooking.

US	Ingredients	Met/Imp
4	veal kidneys	4
1 stick	butter	100 g/4 oz
40	button (pearl) onions	40
2	bunches baby carrots	2
	salt and pepper	
1	bouquet garni, including savory and rosemary sprigs	1
½ bottle	white Saint-Pourçain wine	½ bottle
½ cup	cognac	100 ml/4 fl oz

CHÂTEAUROUX-STYLE VEAL KIDNEYS

Preparation 30 minutes • Cooking 15 minutes

US	Ingredients	Met/Imp
½ lb	smoked bacon	250 g/8 oz
½ lb	button mushrooms	250 g/8 oz
3	shallots	3
3, to serve 5 oz per person	large veal kidneys	3, to serve 150 g/5 oz per person
	salt and pepper	
3 glasses	red wine	3 glasses
5 tbsp	butter	60 g/2½ oz
1 tbsp	flour	15 ml/1 tbsp

Finely slice, then dice the bacon. Clean and wash the mushrooms. Finely chop the shallots.

Ask the butcher to trim the kidneys. Cut them into thin slices.

Put the bacon, mushrooms and kidneys into a frying pan over a high heat. Add salt and pepper after 2 minutes.

When the kidney and bacon are lightly browned, remove all the ingredients from the pan and keep hot on a heated serving dish. Add the shallots to the frying pan and pour in the wine. Bring to the boil and boil for 2–3 minutes to reduce.

Cream the butter with the flour, to make a *beurre manié*, and whisk gradually into the sauce, then boil gently for a few minutes. Check the seasoning. Pour the sauce over the kidneys and serve.

White wines: Sancerre, Pouilly-Fumé, Menetou-Salon.

FLAMBÉED VEAL KIDNEYS

Preparation 20 minutes • Cooking 8 minutes

US	Ingredients	Met/Imp
4	veal kidneys, trimmed	4
1 stick	butter	100 g/4 oz
	salt and pepper	
1 lb	button mushrooms	500 g/1 lb
¼ cup	brandy	50 ml/2 fl oz
½ cup	double (heavy) cream	100 ml/4 fl oz

Choose large kidneys with the fat removed. Slice thinly lengthways. Fry in the butter over a high heat to seal. Season with salt and pepper, then cook the kidneys for about 5 minutes, turning them once.

Add the thinly sliced mushrooms. Deglaze with the brandy, then flambé. Stir in the cream and adjust seasoning. Serve very hot.

Red wines: Saint-Émilion, Hermitage, Côte Rôtie.

VEAL KIDNEYS ÎLE-DE-FRANCE

Preparation 40 minutes • Cooking 6 minutes

US	Ingredients	Met/Imp
4	veal kidneys	4
10 tbsp	butter	150 g/5 oz
½ cup	calvados	100 ml/3½ fl oz
1 lb	button mushrooms	500 g/1 lb
10 oz	cooked ham	300 g/10 oz
½ cup	madeira	100 ml/3½ fl oz
2 cups	double (heavy) cream	500 ml/18 fl oz
	salt and pepper	
1 pinch	nutmeg	1 pinch
1 tbsp	chopped parsley	15 ml/1 tbsp
8	small artichoke bottoms	8

Trim the kidneys and cut them into pieces 5 mm/¼ inch thick. Fry in half of the butter over a high heat. Pour the calvados over and flambé.

In another frying pan brown the mushrooms and diced ham in the remaining butter. Deglaze with the madeira. Add the cream and reduce.

Add the kidneys and season with salt, pepper and nutmeg. Do not allow to boil.

Pour into a heated serving dish and sprinkle with the parsley. Garnish with the quartered artichoke bottoms, fried in butter.

Dry white wines: Saumur, Vouvray, Quincy, Sancerre.
Red wines: Bourgueil, Chinon, Saumur-Champigny.

ROGNONS DE VEAU À LA MAÎTRE D'HÔTEL

— VEAL KIDNEYS MAÎTRE D'HÔTEL —

Preparation 15 minutes • Cooking about 10 minutes

US	Ingredients	Met/Imp
8	small veal kidneys with some of their fat	8
	salt and pepper	
10 tbsp	butter	150 g/5 oz
4 cups	fresh white breadcrumbs	250 g/8 oz
	chopped parsley	
1	lemon, juice of	1
1	bunch watercress, to garnish	1

Slit the kidneys lengthways, but do not cut in half completely. Each kidney will need 2 skewers to keep its shape. Season the kidneys with salt and pepper, dip in 25 g/1 oz (2 tbsp) of the butter, melted, then coat with the breadcrumbs, pressing them on firmly. Sprinkle with a further 25 g/1 oz (2 tbsp) melted butter and cook under the grill (broiler) until very rare.

Make Maître d'Hôtel Butter (*page 52*) with the remaining butter, salt, pepper, parsley and lemon juice, beating well. Put 5 ml/1 tsp of the butter in the centre of each kidney and garnish with watercress.

Red wines: Crozes-Hermitage, Côtes du Ventoux, Coteaux de l'Ardèche.

ROGNONS DE VEAU À LA PARISIENNE

— PARISIAN-STYLE VEAL KIDNEYS —

Preparation 50 minutes • Cooking about 25 minutes

US	Ingredients	Met/Imp
1 lb	asparagus tips	500 g/1 lb
	salt and pepper	
2 sticks	butter	250 g/8 oz
½ lb	truffles	250 g/8 oz
4	small veal kidneys with some of their fat	4
½ cup	madeira	100 ml/4 fl oz
½ cup	Demi-Glaze (*page 56*)	100 ml/4 fl oz
½ cup	Veal Stock (*page 56*)	100 ml/4 fl oz
1	lemon, juice of	1

Clean and blanch the asparagus tips in a casserole or copper saucepan. The tips should be very green. Drain on a cloth, then heat without adding any liquid. Season with salt and add half of the butter at the last minute.

Cook the thinly sliced truffles in half of the remaining butter.

Cut each kidney into 6 rings and fry quickly in the remaining butter until rare. Arrange in a circle on a heated serving dish.

Deglaze the pan with the madeira, demi-glaze and veal stock diluted with the lemon juice, then add the truffles. Pour the sauce over the kidneys. Put the asparagus tips in the centre.

Dry white wines: Crozes-Hermitage, Châteauneuf-du-Pape, Hermitage.
Red wines: Saint-Émilion, Côte Rôtie.

US	Ingredients	Met/Imp
4	veal kidneys	4
1 stick	butter	100 g/4 oz
½ cup	brandy	100 ml/4 fl oz
½ cup	crème fraîche	100 ml/4 fl oz
6	tomatoes	6
1	lemon, juice of	1
	salt and pepper	

VEAL KIDNEYS POMPADOUR

Preparation 30 minutes • Cooking 12 minutes

Trim the kidneys, leaving some of their fat. Fry in the butter until very rare, then keep hot.

Deglaze the pan with the brandy. Add the crème fraîche, skinned, de-seeded and chopped tomatoes, fried in a little butter, and a few drops of lemon juice. Season.

Slice each kidney into 6 rings. Return to the pan and coat with the sauce.

White wines: Bâtard-Montrachet, Meursault, Graves, Hermitage.

US	Ingredients	Met/Imp
4	veal kidneys	4
	salt and pepper	
10 tbsp	butter	150 g/5 oz
½ cup	olive oil	100 ml/4 fl oz
½ lb	mushrooms, thinly sliced	200 g/7 oz
3	shallots	3
½ bottle	Chablis wine	½ bottle
½ cup	Dijon mustard	100 ml/4 fl oz
1	lemon, juice of	1
1 tbsp	chopped parsley	15 ml/1 tbsp

ROGNONS DE VEAU SAUTÉS AU CHABLIS

SAUTÉED VEAL KIDNEYS WITH CHABLIS

Preparation 20 minutes • Cooking 10 minutes

Trim and slice the kidneys. Season, then sauté in two-thirds of the butter and the oil over a high heat.

Put the kidneys into a sieve. Skim the fat from the cooking juices in the pan. Fry the mushrooms. Add the chopped shallots and the wine. Simmer until the shallot is cooked, then thicken with mustard and the remaining butter, but do not allow to boil.

Add the kidneys and a little lemon juice, adjust the seasoning and serve sprinkled with parsley.

Wine: Chablis.

US	Ingredients	Met/Imp
3	veal escalopes (cutlets), each about 18 × 7.5 cm/7 × 3 inches	3
	salt and pepper	
1	bunch parsley	1
5 oz	smoked bacon slices	150 g/5 oz
1	small onion	1
1	shallot	1
1	small celery stalk	1
4 tbsp	butter	50 g/2 oz

ROULADES ALSACIENNES

ALSACE ROULADES

Preparation 35 minutes • Cooking 1½ hours • Serves 3

Flatten the escalopes (cutlets) with the blade of a knife, or ask the butcher to do it. Trim them, reserving the trimmings, to make 3 rectangles about 5 mm/¼ inch thick. Season with salt and pepper. Finely chop the parsley, reserving the stalks. Sprinkle the parsley over the veal.

Remove the bacon rinds (if any) and set aside. Put a slice of bacon on each escalope (cutlet) to cover four-fifths of it (if necessary put 2 bacon slices on each). Roll each escalope (cutlet) up, starting from the end covered with bacon, which should be completely enclosed. Tie each roulade in 3–4 places with string.

Finely chop the onion, shallot and celery together with the veal and bacon trimmings and the parsley stalks. Fry gently in the butter in a flameproof casserole for a good 5 minutes to soften. Place the veal roulades on top and fry over a very low heat, but do not allow to brown.

Cover the casserole and cook over a very moderate, even heat for 1½ hours. Turn the roulades several times during cooking, especially towards the end, to brown them. When cooked, drain and cool on a wire rack. Remove the string. Serve whole or sliced in rings.

If liked, garnish the serving dish with lettuce leaves, tomato rings or sliced olives, cucumber, etc.

Red wines: Alsace Pinot Noir, Coteaux Champenois, Bourgogne-Irancy.

TERRINE DE BODY

VEAL TERRINE

Preparation 1 hour • Cooking 1½ hours

Finely chop the onions and mix with the chopped parsley (about two-thirds onion to one-third parsley). Add freshly ground white pepper and the bacon fat.

Remove the bacon rinds (if any) and discard. Line a 2.5 kg/5½ lb rectangular terrine with bacon slices. Place a layer of veal inside. Sprinkle a little of the onion and parsley mixture on top and a little pepper. Repeat until the terrine has been filled, ending with a layer of bacon. Add the wine, thyme sprig and bay leaf. Cover and bake in a moderate oven for about 1½ hours. Cool with a weight on top. Serve very cold so that the layers do not disintegrate when the terrine is sliced.

White wines: Pouilly-Fumé, Sancerre.
Red wines: Sancerre.

US	Ingredients	Met/Imp
2	large onions	2
a few	parsley sprigs	a few
	white pepper	
a few	pieces bacon fat	a few
2 lb	very thin bacon slices	1 kg/2 lb
2 lb	thin veal escalopes (cutlets), cut from leg	1 kg/2 lb
½ cup	white wine	100 ml/4 fl oz
1	thyme sprig	1
1	bay leaf	1

VEAL WITH PISTACHIOS

Preparation 35 minutes • Cooking 1 hour 10 minutes • Serves 6

US	Ingredients	Met/Imp
⅓ cup	stale breadcrumbs	30 g/1 oz
2 tbsp	milk	30 ml/2 tbsp
10 oz	boneless veal shoulder	300 g/10 oz
4	shallots	4
1	large bunch parsley	1
1	egg	1
1	egg yolk	1
¼ cup	cognac	50 ml/2 fl oz
1	firm *demi-sel* cheese	1
	salt and pepper	
4, each about 7 oz	veal escalopes (cutlets), cut from leg	4, each about 200 g/7 oz
30	shelled unsalted pistachio nuts	30
1	large piece (slab) bacon	1
6 tbsp	butter	75 g/3 oz
2	onions	2
1 tbsp	cornflour (cornstarch)	15 ml/1 tbsp
1 glass	dry white wine	1 glass

This dish may be eaten hot or cold, but it is easier to slice when cold.

Soak the breadcrumbs in the milk and press out the liquid with a fork. Mince (grind) the shoulder of veal with the peeled shallots and washed and dried parsley. Put into a bowl with the breadcrumbs, egg and egg yolk, 15 ml/1 tbsp cognac and the fromage frais, finely diced. Season with salt and pepper and mix very well. Put a veal escalope (cutlet) on to a cloth and season lightly with salt and pepper. Make a few incisions at the edges. Spread one-third of the forcemeat over the veal and sprinkle a few pistachios on top, having removed as much of the outer skin of the pistachios as possible. Cover with another veal escalope (cutlet). Repeat, ending with veal. Wrap the veal 'roast' in the bacon, cut into wide strips, and tie with string.

Melt the butter in a large saucepan and quickly fry the peeled and quartered onions. Add the veal and brown on all sides.

Pour in the remaining cognac and flambé. Cover and cook over a low heat for 1 hour, basting from time to time. Take out the veal and put on to a warmed serving dish.

Strain the cooking liquid into a saucepan. Blend the cornflour (cornstarch) with the wine. Place the pan over the heat and stir in the wine mixture. Bring to the boil, stirring constantly.

Remove the string and bacon from the veal. Pour the sauce over and serve sliced.

Dry white wines: Meursault, Montagny, Pouilly-Fuissé, Saint-Veran.
Light red wines: Saint-Amour, Fleurie, Côtes de Provence.

Veal Chops with Chervil
It is the chervil butter which gives this dish its scent and colour as it melts. Tarragon or sorrel can also be used in the same way. (Recipe on page 421.)

Sweetbreads on Skewers
Sweetbreads always require meticulous preparation but, simply basted with melte[
butter during cooking, they make an exquisite dish. Serve with fresh vegetables.
(Recipe on page 439.)

Veal Kidneys in Cognac
One of the best ways of preparing veal kidneys is to cook them whole: for example, with a sauce made of cognac and white wine as here. (Recipe on page 443.)

Venetian-Style Calf's Liver
*Sautéed quickly in butter, small 'scaloppine' of calf's liver are garnished with frie
onion rings. Finished off with cognac and lemon juice, this dish should be served i
hot. (Recipe on page 432.)*

GAME

GAME THAT CAN BE HUNTED LEGALLY in France for food provides choice, and sometimes prestigious, dishes which are often borne of long tradition: chartreuse of partridge, for example, woodcock salmi, hare royale and roast venison. There are two categories of game that only appear on the market and in restaurants during the hunting season: namely ground game and game birds. The former category is divided into large game (deer and wild boar) and small game (hare and wild rabbit). Small birds, such as larks, warblers, thrushes and buntings form a category apart, as do water game (teal and other wild duck, moorhen, etc).

Game meat is highly flavoured and has a powerful aroma. The older the animal, the more pronounced the aroma. Rich in protein, game is always healthier if the animal has been surprised rather than brought to bay (which causes the animal's system to become full of uric acid).

Game should always be allowed to hang for a certain time before cooking, as this makes it more tender and enhances the flavour. However, the traditional practice of allowing game to hang for long periods of time is now almost obsolete. The normal time for a hare, for example, is now 2 days, for a woodcock, 4 days, for large game, 6–8 days. Game is often marinated before cooking, but it is cut and prepared in the same way as poultry (in the case of feathered game) or any other butchered meat. In other words, it is cut into rump, saddle and ribs for roasting; shoulder and neck for ragoûts and stews; fillet and chops for sautéeing and grilling (broiling). Game can also be used in pâtés. It is often accompanied by sweet garnishes such as cranberries, apples and grapes, and by chestnuts, as these ingredients bring out the pronounced flavour of the meat.

ALOUETTE

LARK

IN FRANCE, SEVERAL KINDS OF LARK ARE SHOT FOR FOOD – THE crested lark, the skylark, and the common lark that nests in the fields and meadows in summer. In French cuisine, however, they are all classed under the general term 'mauviette'. They can be barded and roasted, and are sometimes used to make brochettes, particularly in Corsica and the south of France. You will find them most often, however, in pâtés: lark pâté from Pithiviers has been renowned since the time of Charles IX.

ALOUETTES EN CASSEROLE AUX CHAMPIGNONS

– BRAISED LARKS WITH MUSHROOMS –

Preparation 1 hour • Cooking 8–10 minutes

Blanch the pork (1–2 pieces per bird) in boiling water. Drain thoroughly, then brown in the butter in a large saucepan or flameproof casserole. Add the larks, trimmed and seasoned inside with salt and freshly ground pepper. Cover and cook over a high heat for 5 minutes, tossing from time to time. Add the mushrooms, cut into quarters, cover the pan again and continue cooking, still tossing from time to time, until the larks are lightly browned. Drain off the excess fat, add the cognac and flambé, then add the meat glaze. Cook over a very low heat, without boiling, until the liquid has evaporated.

Pour the contents of the pan into a heated serving dish and squeeze over a few drops of lemon juice. Sprinkle with chopped parsley and surround with fried bread croûtons.

Red wine: light, fruity bordeaux.

US	Ingredients	Met/Imp
10 oz	fresh belly (side) of pork, diced	300 g/10 oz
1 stick	butter	100 g/3½ oz
24	larks	24
	salt and pepper	
7 oz	Paris mushrooms	200 g/7 oz
¼ cup	cognac	50 ml/2 fl oz
½ cup	Meat Glaze (page 56)	100 ml/4 fl oz
a few drops	lemon juice	a few drops
1 tbsp	chopped fresh parsley	15 ml/1 tbsp
8	fried bread croûtons cut in the form of dents-de-loup	8

US	Ingredients	Met/Imp
½ cup	goose fat	100 ml/4 fl oz
24	larks, thoroughly cleaned and seasoned	24
	salt and pepper	
1 lb	raw country ham, thinly sliced	500 g/1 lb
8 cups	croûtons (bread cubes), fried in butter	250 g/8 oz
	cognac	

LARKS 'EN COCOTTE'

Preparation 1 hour • Cooking 6–7 minutes

For this recipe, be sure to use a flameproof earthenware casserole with a lid so that the food can be served from the casserole at the table.

Heat the goose fat in the casserole and, when very hot, add the larks, arranging them neatly. Add salt and pepper, cover and rotate the pan slightly from time to time to ensure that the larks cook evenly.

After 5–6 minutes, lift the lid from the pan and add the ham and croûtons. Shake the pan lightly, quickly add the cognac and cover again. Remove from the heat and serve at once, straight from the casserole.

VARIATIONS
Use lightly crisped slightly salted bacon instead of the ham, and 100 g/4 oz (1 stick) butter instead of goose fat if goose fat is not available.

Red wine: light, fruity bordeaux.

BROCHETTES OF SMALL BIRDS WITH COMTÉ CHEESE

Preparation 35 minutes • Cooking 35 minutes • Serves 4

US	Ingredients	Met/Imp
1	garlic clove	1
	butter	
1 lb	potatoes	500 g/1 lb
	salt and pepper	
½ cup	Comté cheese, grated	50 g/2 oz
1 teacup	milk	1 cup
2 tbsp	double (heavy) cream	30 ml/2 tbsp
12	small birds, barded	12
1 small glass	cognac	1 small glass

Rub a gratin dish with the cut clove of garlic, then grease generously with butter. Arrange the peeled and thinly sliced potatoes in the dish and add salt and pepper. Sprinkle with the grated cheese and pour over the milk and cream beaten together. Bake in a hot oven for 25 minutes.

Thread the small birds on to 3–4 skewers and place in a buttered ovenproof dish. Pour some melted butter over them and bake in a hot oven for 10 minutes.

When almost cooked, remove the brochettes from the dish and stir the cognac into the cooking juices. Arrange the brochettes on top of the potato and cheese mixture and pour over the cooking juices.

Red wines: Juliénas, Moulin-à-Vent, Châteauneuf-du-Pape.

– RABELAISIAN LARK PÂTÉ EN CROÛTE –

Preparation 3 hours • Cooking 1¼ hours

Bone the larks, keeping the bones for concentrated stock. Marinate the birds in half of the cognac, the truffle juice and salt and pepper.

Prepare separately a game forcemeat and a fine forcemeat. Mix together the ingredients for each forcemeat, pound separately, then work each one through a fine sieve. Mix the 2 forcemeats together and flavour with the remaining cognac and a little of the madeira.

Lay the larks out flat on the work surface and stuff each one with a small amount of stuffing, a cube of foie gras and a slice of truffle, then wrap up in a slice of bacon.

Make the pastry. Mix the flour and salt, rub in the lard, then stir in the beaten eggs. Roll out half to a large thin round to use as a base crust for the pie. Cover with a very thin slice of bacon, spread half of the remaining stuffing over the slice of bacon and arrange the stuffed larks on top. Cover with the remaining stuffing and another slice of bacon. Moisten the edges of the pastry crust with water. Roll out the remaining pastry and use to cover the larks. Place the pie in a pie dish; brush with egg yolk, then decorate delicately with pastry trimmings. Brush again with egg yolk. Cut 1–2 openings in the pastry top and bake in a fairly hot oven for about 1¼ hours.

Brown the bones and carcasses of the birds thoroughly, moisten with madeira and make a concentrated stock to be funnelled into the pie through the openings(s) in the top.

Dry white wines: dry Vouvray, dry Montlouis, Saumur, Quincy, Pouilly-sur-Loire, Sancerre.
Red wines: Chinon, Bourgueil, Saumur-Champigny.

US	Ingredients	Met/Imp
8	larks	8
½ cup	cognac	100 ml/4 fl oz
	truffle juice	
	salt and pepper	
¼ cup	madeira	50 ml/2 fl oz
8	cubes foie gras	8
8	truffle slices	8
10	very thin slices bacon	10
1	egg yolk, to glaze	1
	GAME FORCEMEAT	
5 oz	fatty bacon, diced	150 g/5 oz
½ lb	chicken and game livers	250 g/8 oz
	thyme	
1	bay leaf	1
1 pinch	quatre-épices	1 pinch
	FINE FORCEMEAT	
½ lb	boneless pork loin, fat and lean	250 g/8 oz
5 oz	foie gras	150 g/5 oz
3	eggs	3
	PASTRY	
7 cups	flour, sifted	1 kg/2.2 lb
2 tsp	salt	10 g/scant ½ oz
½ lb	lard	250 g/8 oz
3	eggs	3

STUFFED LARKS IN POTATOES

Preparation 2 hours • Cooking: Potatoes 45 minutes; Larks 5 minutes

Bone the larks completely, reserving the bones. Stuff each bird with a cube of foie gras, into which you have inserted a piece of fresh truffle. Wrap the birds in small slices of fatty bacon and tie. Roast in a hot oven for about 5 minutes, together with the diced bacon.

Bake the potatoes in a hot oven for about 45 minutes. When the potatoes are well done, cut off the tops to form lids. Scoop out the flesh and mash. Add nutmeg, spice, salt, pepper and a little butter.

Place some of the mashed potato mixture back in the bottom of each potato skin, followed by 2 larks. Surround with the remaining mashed potato mixed with the skimmed cooking juices from the larks. Put back in the oven briefly. Arrange the stuffed potatoes on a heated serving dish and deglaze the cooking dish with cognac, madeira and the cooking juices made by boiling up the bones of the larks. Serve very hot, putting the cooking juices in a separate sauce boat.

Red wines: Côte de Nuits, Côte Rôtie, Châteauneuf-du-Pape, Saint-Émilion, Pomerol.

US	Ingredients	Met/Imp
16	larks	16
16	cubes foie gras	16
16	pieces truffle	16
16	small, very thin slices fatty bacon for barding	16
1 oz	bacon, diced	25 g/scant 1 oz
8	large Dutch potatoes	8
1 pinch	nutmeg	1 pinch
	quatre-épices	
	salt and pepper	
	butter	
½ cup	cognac	100 ml/4 fl oz
¼ cup	madeira	50 ml/2 fl oz

BÉCASSE

WOODCOCK

MUCH SOUGHT AFTER BY GOURMETS AND HUNTERS, THE woodcock is particularly plump and tender in autumn. When it has been hung for a sufficiently long time, the tail feathers can be detached easily and the skin on the underside is glossy. Some people prefer to eat woodcock fresh, however, while others like to wait as long as eight days before eating it. In nouvelle cuisine, woodcock is usually roasted until just pink, and is therefore not hung. Simply remove the gizzard and roast just until the flesh is pink. Some consider the head to be the best part. Woodcock is often flambéed in alcohol, and there are two classic ways of preparing it: as a *salmi*, or roasted and served on fried bread. Do not confuse 'bécasseau' (young woodcock) with 'bécassine' (snipe), even though they are cooked in the same way.

—— WOODCOCK WITH ORANGE ——

Preparation 30 minutes • Cooking 15 minutes

US	Ingredients	Met/Imp
4	woodcock	4
	marc, to flambé	
	salt and pepper	
4	small very thin bacon slices for barding	4
10 tbsp	butter	150 g/5 oz
4	bread slices, cut the same size as the birds	4
4	oranges	4
1 glass	Banyuls Grand Cru	1 glass
1 tbsp	cornflour (cornstarch)	15 ml/1 tbsp

Pluck the birds just before use. Make a slit in the throat and remove the gizzard. (The intestines should be left in, but if you prefer to remove them do so in the same way as for other birds.)

Wipe the woodcock and flambé them quickly in the marc. Wipe again gently and season lightly with salt and pepper. (In order to flambé, pour 5 ml/1 tsp marc over each bird and set alight immediately.)

Wrap each woodcock in a slice of bacon and tie with strong thread. Melt about three-quarters of the butter in a large saucepan and cook the birds for 10–15 minutes or until brown. Check that the woodcock are cooked by pricking them gently; the flesh should not be bloody and the juices should be pink.

While the woodcock are cooking, fry the bread slices in the remaining butter and arrange on a heated serving dish. Squeeze the juice from 2 of the oranges and slice the other 2 thinly. Remove the peel and pith by laying the slices out flat on a plate and cutting round each one. Cut each slice in half. When the birds are cooked, remove them from the pan and place them on the fried bread. Keep warm.

Pour the Banyuls and the orange juice mixed with the cornflour (cornstarch) into the saucepan, bring to the boil and pour this sauce over the woodcock just before serving. Garnish with the orange slices.

Red wines: Corbières, Fitou, Châteauneuf-du-Pape.

STUFFED ROAST WOODCOCK 'ÉLYSÉES'

Preparation 1 hour • Marinade 2–3 days • Cooking 12–15 minutes

This recipe was created by Lucien Tibier, President Auriol's chef

US	Ingredients	Met/Imp
4	woodcock	4
½ lb	foie gras	250 g/8 oz
5 oz	truffles	150 g/5 oz
I pinch	nutmeg	I pinch
⅓ cup	cognac	75 ml/3 fl oz
4	thin bacon slices for barding	4
½ cup	white port wine	100 ml/4 fl oz
I handful	mushrooms	I handful
I	thyme sprig	I
1½ sticks	butter	175 g/6 oz
4	bread slices	4
a few drops	lemon juice	a few drops
	salt and pepper	

Remove the intestines and gizzards from the woodcock. Discard the gizzards. Pound the intestines together with a little foie gras and a fresh truffle. Add the nutmeg and cognac. Set aside enough of the stuffing to spread on the 4 slices of toast to be cooked at the last moment, then use the remainder to stuff the birds. Bard the birds with the bacon and leave for 2–3 days in a marinade of white port wine, sliced mushrooms and thyme.

Remove the woodcocks from the marinade and roast them with two-thirds of the butter in a hot oven for 12–15 minutes. Toast the slices of bread and spread with the reserved stuffing. Put a woodcock on each slice. Remove some of the fat from the roasting pan, pour in the marinade and a few drops of lemon juice. Strain these juices through cheesecloth, adjust the seasoning, then add the remaining butter. Pour over the woodcock and serve.

Red wines: Nuits-Saint-Georges, Richebourg, Clos de Vougeot.

STUFFED WOODCOCK BRAISED IN WHITE WINE

Preparation 2 hours • Cooking 16 minutes

US	Ingredients	Met/Imp
4	woodcock	4
4	egg yolks	4
7 oz	fatty bacon	200 g/7 oz
	salt and pepper	
	parsley	
I	spring onion (scallion)	I
	thin bacon slices	
½ cup	white wine	100 ml/4 fl oz
	lemon juice	
I tbsp	golden Meat Glaze (page 56)	15 ml/I tbsp

Draw the woodcock and place all their insides (with the exception of the gizzard which should be thrown away) in a mortar together with the egg yolks, finely chopped bacon, salt, pepper, finely chopped parsley and spring onion (scallion). Pound these ingredients together well with a pestle to form a stuffing and use to stuff the birds. Truss and arrange them in a flameproof earthenware casserole lined with bacon.

Place the pan on the heat. As everything begins to heat up (this is what is known as sweating), add the white wine, cover the pan and cook over a moderate heat for about 16 minutes.

When the woodcock are cooked, remove them from the pan. Skim the cooking juices, strain them and cook until reduced to a thicker consistency. Add a little lemon juice and pour on to a serving dish. Arrange the woodcock on top, glaze lightly with good meat jelly and serve at once.

Dry white wines: Quincy, Pouilly-Fuissé, Alsace Riesling.
Red wines: Pomerol, Côte de Nuits, Hermitage.

US	Ingredients	Met/Imp
			BÉCASSES RÔTIES

ROAST WOODCOCK

Preparation 30 minutes • Cooking 10–12 minutes

US	Ingredients	Met/Imp
4	woodcock	4
4	bacon slices for barding	4
4	croûtons, cut the same size as the woodcock	4
4 tbsp	butter	50 g/2 oz
½ lb	foie gras	250 g/8 oz

Wrap the woodcock in bacon, place them on a skewer and roast in a hot oven for 10–12 minutes depending on their size. The birds should be slightly rare inside as they suffer in quality if overcooked.

Place each woodcock on a croûton fried in clarified butter and spread with foie gras. Serve a small amount of the cooking juices separately.

Alternatively, serve as follows: cut up the cooked woodcock and place the intestines in a dish. Mash with a fork and moisten with a few spoonfuls of brandy, which has first been flambéed. Divide the croûtons into small pieces and arrange the woodcock and croûtons in a ring. Place the puréed intestines in the centre; they complement the game well.

Red wines: Côte de Nuits, Côte Rôtie, Hermitage, Châteauneuf-du-Pape, Pomerol.

BÉCASSES RÔTIES À LA FINE CHAMPAGNE

ROAST WOODCOCK IN COGNAC

Preparation 40 minutes • Cooking 12–15 minutes

US	Ingredients	Met/Imp
4	woodcock	4
1 stick	butter	100 g/4 oz
⅓ cup	cognac	75 ml/3 fl oz
1	lemon, juice of	1
	pepper	

Roast the woodcock in three-quarters of the butter in a hot oven for 12–15 minutes. Cut them into serving pieces and place in a heated serving dish. Deglaze the cooking juices with the cognac.

Chop up the carcasses and squeeze them in a press. Thicken the concentrated stock thus obtained with the finely chopped intestines mixed with the remaining butter.

Finally, add the lemon juice and freshly milled pepper. This dish should be quite highly seasoned.

Dry white wines: Chablis, Saumur, Coteaux Champenois

PÂTÉ CHAUD DE BÉCASSES GASTON GÉRARD

HOT WOODCOCK PÂTÉ GASTON GÉRARD

Preparation 3 hours • Marinade 24 hours • Cooking 1½ hours

US	Ingredients	Met/Imp
4	woodcock	4
	Marinade (*page 59*)	
1	foie gras	1
5 oz	fatty bacon	150 g/5 oz
	salt and pepper	
1 pinch	*quatre-épices*	1 pinch
triple quantity	Shortcrust Pastry (*page 577*)	triple quantity
8	truffles	8
½ cup	cognac	100 ml/4 fl oz
7 oz	Mirepoix (*page 50*)	200 g/7 oz

Bone the woodcock and marinate for 24 hours. Make a forcemeat using the foie gras, finely chopped fatty bacon, salt, pepper and spices and with the addition of the woodcock intestines.

Roll out two-thirds of the pastry and use to line a pâté mould. Cover with a thin layer of forcemeat. Place the woodcock and the truffles, cut into quarters, on top and finish by adding the remaining forcemeat and a little cognac. Roll out the remaining pastry and place on top. Decorate with pastry trimmings and cut an opening in the top. Cook in a hot oven for 1½ hours.

Make a rich game stock using the bones, carcass and trimmings of the

woodcock and the mirepoix. Add the skin from a few of the truffles. Cover with water and boil until reduced while the pie is in the oven. A few minutes before the end of the cooking time, remove the pie from the oven and pour the stock into it through the opening in the top, with the aid of a funnel, having first added the remaining cognac to give it extra flavour. Leave the pie to settle for a while before serving.

Red wines: Côte de Nuits, Côte Rôtie, Châteauneuf-du-Pape, Saint-Émilion, Pomerol, Corsican red wines.

SALMIS DE BÉCASSES

─── SALMI OF WOODCOCK ───

Preparation 1½ hours • First cooking 10 minutes • Second cooking (reducing) 20 minutes

US	Ingredients	Met/Imp
4	woodcock	4
10 tbsp	butter	150 g/5 oz
a few	peppercorns	a few
½ bottle	best red burgundy	½ bottle
1 cup	very good Demi-Glaze (*page 56*)	200 ml/8 fl oz
¼ cup	cognac	50 ml/2 fl oz
12	slices truffle	12
8	fried bread croûtons	8

Roast the woodcock in a hot oven with some butter for 8–10 minutes. Cut them into pieces, removing the bones and intestines, and keep warm. Crush the bones and carcasses and put in a saucepan with the butter in which the birds have been cooked and cook until browned. Add a few crushed peppercorns, then moisten with the red burgundy, which must be mature and of excellent quality or the dish will not succeed. Cook for about 20 minutes or until reduced by three-quarters, then add the demi-glaze. Leave to simmer. Meanwhile, chop the birds' intestines and mix with an equal volume of butter. Blend with the cognac.

When the stock is sufficiently reduced, leaving enough to coat the woodcock, strain it through a conical sieve, pressing the debris down hard so that as much juice as possible is extracted. Return to the stove until heated through. Just before serving, thicken the sauce with the purée of intestines mixed with butter. At the same time, add the slices of truffle and garnish with the croûtons.

Red wines: Côte de Nuits, Côte Rôtie, Châteauneuf-du-Pape, Saint-Émilion, Pomerol, Médoc, Corsican red wines.

TIMBALE DE BÉCASSES À LA MOUTARDE

─── WOODCOCK WITH MUSTARD ───

Preparation 1 hour • Cooking 12–15 minutes

US	Ingredients	Met/Imp
4	woodcock	4
1 stick	butter	100 g/4 oz
½ cup	oil	100 ml/4 fl oz
¼ cup	cognac	50 ml/2 fl oz
¼ cup	mustard	50 ml/2 fl oz
1	lemon, juice of	1
	salt and pepper	

Roast the woodcock in the butter, basting with the oil from time to time. Remove the birds from the oven while they are still rare. Cut the woodcock into pieces, removing the bones and intestines.

Make a concentrated stock by crushing the bones and intestines of the birds and adding the cognac. Put in a saucepan and leave to simmer. Arrange the pieces of woodcock meat in a round serving dish and coat them with a mixture of the mustard and lemon juice. Add salt and pepper. Pour the stock on to the meat through a conical sieve and rotate the dish so that the meat becomes well soaked. Place the thoroughly cleaned heads of the birds on top and serve at once.

Red wines: Côte de Nuits, Côte Rôtie, Châteauneuf-du-Pape, Saint-Émilion, Pomerol.

CAILLE

QUAIL

WILD QUAIL THAT FEED ON GRAIN FROM THE FIELDS ARE becoming increasingly rare. When young, they are plump and succulent. They should be eaten 'au bout du fusil' (no more than 24 hours after they have been killed), and can be roasted, sautéed, baked *en papillotes* in paper or foil, or made into a fricassée. They can be cooked with grapes, olives, cherries or mushrooms, among other things. Quail that have been specially reared never have as much flavour as their wild counterparts, but they are more readily available in poulterers' shops.

ASPIC DE CAILLES AU FOIE GRAS TRUFFÉ

QUAILS IN ASPIC —— WITH FOIE GRAS AND TRUFFLES ——

Preparation 1 hour • Cooking 15 minutes

US	Ingredients	Met/Imp
8	plump quails	8
½ lb	foie gras	250 g/8 oz
¼ lb	small truffles·	125 g/4 oz
2	carrots	2
1	onion	1
1	bouquet garni	1
2 tbsp	butter	30 g/1 oz
	salt and pepper	
1 cup	well-flavoured jellied Veal Juice (*page 56*)	200 ml/7 fl oz
32	chicken kidneys	32
½ cup	Alicante Moscatel wine (or Sauternes)	100 ml/3½ fl oz

Draw the quails and place a cube of foie gras and a quarter of a small truffle inside each one. Truss in the usual way. Place the thinly sliced carrots and onion and the bouquet garni in a sauté pan with the butter and lay the quails on top, squeezing them in tightly side by side. Add salt and pepper and cover them in the veal juice. Bring to the boil, cover tightly and simmer gently for 15 minutes. Leave the birds to cool in the cooking juices.

Arrange the birds in a star shape in a round dish. Garnish each one with a slice of truffle cut with a fluted cutter. In between them, arrange the chicken kidneys which have been cooked in a White Court Bouillon (*page 49*). Skim the cooking juices in the pan and strain through cheesecloth. Add a few spoonfuls of Alicante Moscatel or Sauternes wine and pour over the quails and chicken kidneys. Chill until the cooking juices have jelled lightly.

Red wine: light, fruity bordeaux.

SPIT-ROASTED QUAILS
WRAPPED IN VINE LEAVES*

Preparation 30 minutes • Cooking 12 minutes

US	Ingredients	Met/Imp
8	quails	8
¼ cup	cognac	50 ml/2 fl oz
24	vine (grape) leaves	24
8	thin bacon slices, for barding	8
4 tbsp	butter	50 g/2 oz
8	slices toast	8

Draw and singe the quails. Flambé them with the cognac, then wrap them in vine (grape) leaves and bard with very thin slices of bacon. Roast them on a spit for about 12 minutes, and serve on buttered toast.

Red wine: light, fruity bordeaux.

CAILLES AU JAMBON ET PURÉE DE PETITS POIS

QUAILS WITH HAM
AND PETITS POIS PURÉE

Preparation 40 minutes • Cooking 10 minutes

US	Ingredients	Met/Imp
1 quart	shelled petits pois	1 litre/1¾ pints
1 pinch	sugar	1 pinch
2	lettuces	2
½ cup (1 stick)	goose fat or butter	100 g/4 oz
	salt and pepper	
½ cup	cream	100 ml/4 fl oz
4	vine (grape) leaves	4
8	slices *raw mountain ham*	8
8	quails	8
4 tbsp	butter	50 g/2 oz

Cook the petits pois in boiling water with the sugar until just tender. Drain. Cut up the lettuces and put them in a pan with the goose fat or butter. Leave them to sweat until soft. Mix these ingredients together, then work them through a fine sieve. Add salt, pepper and the cream and keep warm.

Wrap half a vine (grape) leaf and a slice of ham around each plucked and drawn quail and tie. Brush with melted butter and bake in a very hot oven for 8 minutes. Untie the birds and remove the leaf, but put back the slice of ham.

Pour the petits pois purée into a deep serving dish and arrange the quails on top in a ring. Pour over the cooking juices.

Dry white wines: Quincy, Sancerre, Pouilly-Fuissé, Alsace Riesling.
Red wine: light, fruity bordeaux.

CAILLES AUX RAISINS

QUAILS WITH GRAPES

Preparation 40 minutes • Cooking 13–15 minutes

US	Ingredients	Met/Imp
8	quails	8
4 tbsp	butter	50 g/2 oz
	salt and pepper	
2	bunches muscat grapes	2
⅓ cup	armagnac	75 ml/3 fl oz
¼ cup	golden Meat or Chicken Glaze (*page 56*)	50 ml/2 fl oz

Draw and truss the quails. (It is not necessary to bard them as they are normally fatty enough not to need it.) Place the birds in a flameproof earthenware casserole with the melted butter. Add salt and pepper and cook in a hot oven for 10–12 minutes. Drain the quails, then untruss them and return them to the casserole. Place the grapes in a sieve and dip them twice in boiling water. Peel them and remove the pips. Add the grapes to the casserole and pour in the armagnac and the melted meat or chicken glaze. Heat through for 3 minutes more, without boiling. Serve straight from the casserole.

Red wine: light, fruity bordeaux.
White wines: Alsace Muscat or Gewürztraminer.

US	Ingredients	Met/Imp
I lb	large white grapes (8–10 per quail)	500 g/I lb
about ½ cup	Banyuls Grand Cru	100 ml/4 fl oz
8	quails	8
	salt and pepper	
8	bacon slices for barding	8
4 tbsp	butter	50 g/2 oz

QUAILS IN BANYULS WITH GRAPES

Preparation 1 hour • Cooking 20 minutes

Peel the grapes, put them in a saucepan with the Banyuls and leave to macerate for about 1 hour. The wine should more or less cover the grapes. If not, add a little more. If the grapes are very sweet, use a dry Banyuls, if they are a little sour, use a sweeter wine.

Draw and singe the quails, then season with salt and pepper and wrap each one in a slice of bacon. Tie up with string. Melt the butter in a large saucepan and cook the quails for a few minutes or until brown, turning from time to time.

Cover the pan, lower the heat and leave the birds to cook for 8–10 minutes. Meanwhile, cover the grapes and bring gently to the boil.

Remove the quails from the pan and remove the strings and bacon. Keep the birds warm until it is time to put them in the sauce to finish cooking. Drain the grapes, reserving the Banyuls, and add them to the quails.

Skim the fat from the pan in which the quails were cooked, leaving just the juices in the bottom. Deglaze the pan with the reserved Banyuls. The sauce should be quite thick, so you might not need to add all the wine. Bring the sauce to the boil and cook until reduced.

Place the quails and grapes in the sauce, cover and simmer over a low heat for 3–5 minutes. Adjust the seasoning, adding more salt and pepper if necessary. Serve piping hot.

Warm red wines: young Banyuls, Fitou, Cahors, Madiran, Côtes du Roussillon-Villages, Médoc, Saint-Émilion.

BRAISED STUFFED QUAILS WITH MUSHROOMS

Preparation 1 hour • Cooking 10–12 minutes

US	Ingredients	Met/Imp
I	carrot	I
I	onion	I
I	celery stalk, white part only	I
⅓ cup	mushroom trimmings	25 g/scant I oz
I oz	*raw country ham*	25 g/scant I oz
I small pinch	chopped thyme	I small pinch
I stick	butter	100 g/4 oz
I cup	white wine (Sauternes or Graves)	200 ml/7 fl oz
I cup	good-quality Veal Stock (*page 56*)	200 ml/7 fl oz
I cup	Gratin Stuffing (*page 54*)	250 g/8 oz
7 oz	truffles	200 g/7 oz
7 oz	foie gras	200 g/7 oz
8	quails	8
8	bread slices	8
	clarified butter	
I lb	mushrooms	500 g/I lb
	salt and pepper	

Finely chop the carrot, onion, celery, mushroom trimmings and ham. Place in a small saucepan together with the thyme and one-quarter of the butter. Cover and cook until almost tender, then add the white wine and continue cooking until reduced to about 2 spoonfuls. Add the veal stock and leave to simmer gently.

Place the gratin stuffing, truffles and foie gras in a mortar and pound together thoroughly with a pestle. Draw and clean the quails and stuff each one with half a spoonful of the pounded mixture. Truss the birds with their feet flat along their stomachs.

Heat two-thirds of the remaining butter in a sauté pan, add the quails and brown evenly all over. Cover the birds with the vegetable *mirepoix*, which was prepared at the beginning, cover the pan tightly and cook slowly for 12 minutes.

Meanwhile, cut out 8 rectangular croûtons the same size as the quails. Fry them in clarified butter, then spread thickly with the remaining

pounded stuffing mixture. Finely chop the mushrooms and sauté in the remaining butter.

Place 1 quail on each bread croûton and then arrange in a ring on a heated round serving dish. Pour the cooking juices on top through a conical sieve, pressing down well with a spoon so that as much as possible of the juice from the mirepoix goes through. Adjust the seasoning, adding salt and pepper, if necessary. Arrange the mushrooms in the centre and serve.

White wines: Montrachet, Pouilly-Fuissé, Alsace Riesling or Gewürztraminer, Sauternes, Barsac, Jurançon, Vouvray, Anjou.
Red wines: Graves, Cahors, Bourgueil.

COCOTTE DE CAILLES À LA SOUVAROFF

—— BRAISED QUAILS 'SOUVAROFF' ——

Preparation 30 minutes • First cooking 4 minutes; Second cooking 6 minutes

Stuff the quails with the cubes of foie gras and the truffle halves, then truss securely and season.

Melt the butter in a flameproof serving dish. When it is frothy, add the quails and arrange the 8 small truffles or 16 pieces around them. Cook briskly over a high heat. Drain off the butter, add the madeira and meat glaze and cover the pan. Mix the flour to a thick paste with a little water and use to seal the lid of the pan. Braise in the oven for 6 minutes.

Red wines: Côte de Nuits, Côte Rôtie, Châteauneuf-du-Pape.

US	Ingredients	Met/Imp
8	quails	8
5 oz	foie gras, cut into 8 cubes	150 g/5 oz
8, total weight about 5 oz	truffle halves	8, total weight about 150 g/5 oz
	salt and pepper	
2 tbsp	butter	30 g/1 oz
8	very small truffles	8
	or	
16	pieces truffle	16
½ cup	madeira	100 ml/4 fl oz
¼ cup	golden Meat Glaze (page 56)	50 ml/2 fl oz
6 tbsp	flour	50 g/2 oz

CANARD SAUVAGE

WILD DUCK

VARIOUS SPECIES OF WILD DUCK ARE HUNTED FROM JULY TO February. The best known of these is the mallard, but there are others, such as the pintail, spoonbill, sheldrake, and so on, not to mention the teal and the scoter, which come from the same family. The mallard is the favourite with gourmets on account of its firm, tasty flesh. Wild duck is traditionally coupled with orange or olives, but it also goes well with any of the ingredients used for domestic ducks. It can also, of course, be made into a salmi.

SALMIS DE CANARD SAUVAGE

SALMI OF WILD DUCK

Preparation 1½ hours • (Sauce to be prepared the night before) • Cooking 25–30 minutes

US	Ingredients	Met/Imp
½ cup	flour	70 g/3 oz
2	carrots	2
I	onion	I
I	bouquet garni	I
I stick	butter	100 g/4 oz
2	plump ducks, including the giblets	2
I bottle	wine	I bottle
I quart	Brown Veal Stock (page 56)	I litre/1¾ pints
10 oz	mushrooms, trimmings reserved	300 g/10 oz
¼ cup	cognac	50 ml/2 fl oz
	salt and pepper	
8	large croûtons, fried in butter	8
½ cup	Gratin Stuffing (page 54), made with fatty bacon and livers	100 g/4 oz
¼ lb	truffles	100 g/4 oz

The day before, make a fairly brown *roux* with the flour, a *mirepoix* of the carrots and onion, diced, a bouquet garni, a nut of butter and the duck giblets. Moisten with some of the red wine and add the stock and the mushroom trimmings to make a sauce. Skim.

The next day, roast the ducks in a hot oven for about 20 minutes or until three-quarters cooked. Remove from the oven and leave to cool. Cut the ducks into serving pieces and remove the skin from each piece. Trim the pieces and arrange in a buttered sauté pan. Cover and keep warm.

Crush the duck carcasses and meat trimmings in a mortar and pestle and add to the sauté pan. Deglaze the duck in the roasting pan with the cognac and 100 ml/4 fl oz (½ cup) wine. Boil until reduced, then add the sauce which was made the day before. Cook for a few minutes, then work through a fine sieve, pressing hard to extract all the juices. Return to the heat, then sieve again through a conical strainer. Add salt and pepper, if necessary, and some butter. Pour this sauce over the pieces of duck. Spread the croûtons with gratin stuffing and arrange around the dish with the mushrooms and truffles.

Red wines: Pomerol, Côte de Nuits, Hermitage.

CHEVREUIL

VENISON

THE BUCK (MALE), DOE (FEMALE), FAWN (YOUNG DEER OF LESS than 6 months) and chamois-buck (6–12 months) are still abundant in the Sologne and Alsace regions of France, but venison is also imported from Austria and Romania. The flesh of a young deer is, by its very definition, more tender and delicate, while that of an older animal is best marinated first. The most sought-after cuts are the saddle and haunch, for roasting, and chops for frying. Note that the best results are obtained by cooking in oil rather than butter.

CÔTELETTES DE CHEVREUIL SAUTÉES

—————— SAUTÉED VENISON CHOPS ——————

Preparation 30 minutes • Cooking 6–8 minutes

US	Ingredients	Met/Imp
16	venison chops	16
	salt and pepper	
½ cup	oil	100 ml/3½ fl oz
16	heart-shaped fried bread croûtons	16
1 cup	Pepper Sauce for Game (*page 76*)	200 ml/7 fl oz

Choose young meat if possible. Normally, only chops from the loin are used; those from the neck are used for stewing or other purposes.

Season the chops with salt and pepper. Heat the oil in a sauté pan until very hot and smoking, add the chops and sauté for 6–8 minutes or until tender.

Arrange the chops in a crown, alternating each one with a heart-shaped croûton. Fill the centre with your chosen garnish (see below). Venison chops are always accompanied by a light pepper sauce. Suitable garnishes are: chestnut, celeriac or Jerusalem artichoke purées, or stewed apple with little or no sugar.

Red wines: Côte de Nuits, Côte Rôtie, Châteauneuf-du-Pape, Corsican red wines.

US	Ingredients	Met/Imp
7 oz	fatty bacon slices	200 g/7 oz
I	haunch young venisc	I
	MARINADE	
I	lemon, juice of	I
	or	
½ cup	wine vinegar	100 ml/4 fl oz
½ cup	olive oil	100 ml/4 fl oz
	salt and pepper	
2	onions	2
I	shallot	I
a few	parsley sprigs	a few
a few	thyme sprigs	a few
I	bay leaf	I
I pinch	*quatre-épices*	I pinch

GIGUE DE CHEVREUIL MARINÉE ET RÔTIE

ROAST MARINATED HAUNCH OF VENISON

Preparation 40 minutes • Marinating 24 hours • Cooking 45 minutes

Cut the bacon into fine strips and use to bard the venison. Put the venison in a bowl with the lemon juice or vinegar, the oil, salt, sliced onions and shallot, parsley, thyme, bay leaf and spice. Leave to marinate for 24 hours.

Drain the venison, reserving the marinade, and roast on a spit, for about 45 minutes or until brown and tender, basting with the marinade during cooking. Serve the cooking juices and marinade separately.

This dish may be served with a Pepper Sauce for Game (*page 76*) made with the venison scraps and trimmings. It may also be garnished with chestnut or mushroom purée or with poached pears.

Red wines: Côte de Nuits, Côte Rôtie, Châteauneuf-du-Pape, Saint-Émilion, Pomerol.

US	Ingredients	Met/Imp
I	saddle venison	I
	oil	
	butter	
	salt and pepper	
	cognac	
8	avocados	8
	flour	
I	egg, beaten	I
	fresh breadcrumbs	
	chopped blanched almonds	
	Béarnaise Sauce (*page 61*)	
I pinch	chopped fresh tarragon	I pinch
16	croûtons, cut the same size as the noisettes	16
½ cup	Pouilly–Fuissé wine	100 ml/4 fl oz

NOISETTES DE CHEVREUIL AUX AVOCATS

NOISETTES OF VENISON WITH AVOCADOS

Preparation 45 minutes • Cooking 25 minutes

Cut 16 small round noisettes from the saddle of venison. Heat some oil and butter in a frying pan and fry the noisettes very quickly until brown. Add salt and pepper and drain off the fat. Pour in the cognac and flambé, then cover the pan and cook over a moderate heat for about 20 minutes.

Meanwhile, halve, stone and peel the avocados and cut them lengthways into six slices. Coat each slice in flour, beaten egg and breadcrumbs, then roll in the chopped almonds. Fry in clarified butter, drain and add salt and pepper.

Make the Béarnaise sauce, adding only a very small amount of tarragon.

Drain the noisettes and arrange on the croûtons on a heated serving platter. Deglaze the cooking juices with the Pouilly, then add the Béarnaise sauce. Pour some of this sauce over the meat and surround with the pieces of avocado. Serve the remaining sauce separately.

Fine red burgundy: Richebourg, Romanée-Conti, Close de Vougeot.

COQ DE BRUYÈRE

GROUSE

ALSO KNOWN AS 'GRAND TÉTRAS' (WOOD GROUSE), THE ADULT male sometimes grows to the size of a turkey. In France, grouse are to be found in the mountains (Ardennes, Vosges, Pyrenees), and have a characteristically resinous taste on account of their feeding habits. The small grouse, or 'tétras-lyre', is more delicate and is often preferred to the large wood grouse for cooking. It is prepared in the same way as pheasant.

COQ DE BRUYÈRE AUX RAISINS SECS

—————— GROUSE WITH RAISINS ——————

Preparation 45 minutes • Marinating 2–3 days • Cooking at least 1½ hours

Recipe from Raymond Oliver, Grand Véfour

US	Ingredients	Met/Imp
I	wood grouse	I
	salt and pepper	
a few	thyme sprigs	a few
a few	wild thyme sprigs	a few
a few	savory sprigs	a few
2 oz	ham	50 g/2 oz
I glass	red wine	I glass
I small glass	armagnac	I small glass
6–8	small onions	6–8
I	carrot	I
I	garlic clove	I
I bunch	parsley sprigs	I bunch
⅓ cup	raisins	50 g/2 oz
I glass	white or muscat wine	I glass
	fried bread croûtons (optional)	

Pluck and draw the grouse, reserving the liver and heart for another dish. Season the cavity well with salt and pepper and stuff with mountain herbs: thyme, wild thyme and savory.

Cut the ham, which should be more fat than lean and not too moist, into thin strips and use to lard the white meat of the grouse. Alternatively, cut the ham into pieces and set aside to be used later. Place the grouse in a bowl with the red wine and armagnac and leave in a cool place to marinate for 2–3 days.

Drain the bird, reserving the marinade. Remove the herbs, then place the bird in a cloth and pat dry. Brown in a flameproof casserole, then take the bird out of the pan and put in the pieces of ham (if not used for larding), the small whole onions, carrots, sliced into rings, the garlic and parsley. Brown these ingredients, then return the grouse to the pan. Work the reserved marinade through a fine sieve into the pan.

Add salt and pepper and cook for as long as necessary, which could take several hours. The cooking should be even but slow. Towards the end of cooking, add a handful of raisins, which have been soaked in advance in the white or muscat wine. Cook for a short while longer, then serve straight from the casserole, with or without fried bread croûtons.

Red wines: Châteauneuf-du-Pape, Côte de Nuits, Pomerol.

PHEASANT

THE PHEASANT ORIGINALLY CAME FROM ASIA AND IS considered the king of game birds. In France, it is hunted from September to January, but nowadays it is also reared intensively in a way which often violates the rules of hunting. You can recognize a young pheasant by its shiny feet with no spur and shiny, flexible beak. The hen pheasant is preferred for cooking as it is more tender and tasty. If a pheasant's stomach has been punctured by shot or a dog's teeth, the bird should be drawn and eaten quickly. Young pheasant can be roasted, whereas older pheasant are usually braised or stewed, or made into salmis, pâtés and pies.

FAISAN À L'ANANAS

—— PHEASANT WITH PINEAPPLE* ——

Preparation 2 hours • Cooking 1¼ hours

US	Ingredients	Met/Imp
I	pheasant	I
3	fatty bacon slices	3
I	carrot	I
I	onion	I
I	garlic clove	I
6 tbsp	butter	75 g/3 oz
	salt and pepper	
I	fresh pineapple from the Azores	I
	'sirop d'ananas' (canned sweetened pineapple syrup)	
	Veal Stock (page 56)	

Draw the pheasant and bard with the bacon slices. Put the sliced carrot and onion, crushed garlic clove and butter in the bottom of a large saucepan. Add salt and pepper and place the pheasant on top. Cook over a low heat for about 1 hour or until tender, basting frequently.

When cooked, remove the bird from the pan, increase the heat and brown the vegetables. Drain off the butter.

Poach the peeled and sliced Azores pineapple (this is the only pineapple of excellent quality) in the syrup. Drain, reserving the syrup. Place the pineapple pieces in a cool oven to dry.

Deglaze the pan in which the pheasant was cooked with a little of the pineapple syrup. Add the veal stock and bring to the boil in order to remove the skin from the sauce, then strain through a conical sieve.

Arrange the pheasant on a serving dish with the pineapple slices all around it. Pour over the sauce.

White wines: Château-Chalon, Anjou, Sauternes.

PHEASANT WITH CABBAGE

Preparation 1½ hours • Cooking 1¼ hours

US	Ingredients	Met/Imp
I	small fine head white cabbage	I
¼ lb	bacon slices	100 g/4 oz
I tbsp	lard	15 ml/I tbsp
	salt and pepper	
¼ cup	crème fraîche	50 ml/2 fl oz
I	pheasant, trussed and barded	I

Cut the cabbage into thin slices, then blanch in boiling water and rinse in cold water. Cook in a flameproof casserole with the bacon, lard, salt and pepper for 30 minutes. Remove from the pan.

Put the crème fraîche inside the trussed pheasant, then brown the bird in the fat remaining in the pan. Add the cabbage, cover and simmer over a low heat until cooking is complete.

Red wines: light, fruity bordeaux, Chiroubles, Cahors.

PHEASANT FLAMANDE

Preparation 1 hour • Cooking chicory 30 minutes • Pheasants 35 minutes

US	Ingredients	Met/Imp
2	hen pheasants	2
	salt and pepper	
2	fatty bacon slices	2
I stick	butter	100 g/4 oz
I	carrot	I
I	large onion	I
I	bouquet garni	I
4½ lb	chicory (Belgian endives)	2 kg/4½ lb
2	lemons, juice of	2
I pinch	sugar	I pinch

Truss 2 nice pheasants, pressing the feet tightly against the breast. Season inside and out with salt and pepper and bard each one with a slice of unsalted fatty bacon.

Heat up a large nut of butter in a high-sided flameproof casserole until it sizzles, then add the pheasants and surround with the roughly chopped carrot and onion. Add the bouquet garni, cover the saucepan, turn the heat up as high as possible to begin the cooking process, then leave to cook on a very low heat for about 30 minutes, remembering to turn the pheasants from time to time.

Meanwhile, prepare the chicory (Belgian endives). Trim and wash them, then make incisions, 2 cm/¾ inch long, in each head. Season with salt and pepper. Melt a piece of butter the size of an egg in a flameproof casserole, add the chicory (Belgian endives) with a few spoonfuls of water, the lemon juice and a pinch of sugar. Cook for about 30 minutes or until soft. All of the liquid should have evaporated.

When the pheasants are almost cooked, remove them from the pan and untruss. In order to extract the cooking juices from the pan, add a little warm water. Strain the juices through a sieve. Place the chicory (Belgian endives) in the bottom of this pan and arrange the pheasants on top. Moisten with the cooking juices, then cover the pan and simmer for 8 minutes.

Place the pheasants in a deep serving dish and surround with the chicory (Belgian endives).

Red wines: Beaujolais-Villages, Châteauneuf-du-Pape, Côtes de Provence.

US	Ingredients	Met/Imp
I	pheasant	I
3	bacon slices	3
I lb	reinette or other dessert apples	500 g/ I lb
½ cup	calvados	100 ml/3½ fl oz
I cup	crème fraîche	200 ml/7 fl oz
I	lemon, juice of	I
	salt and pepper	

FAISAN À LA NORMANDE

PHEASANT NORMANDE

Preparation 2 hours • Cooking 1¼ hours

Truss the pheasant and bard with bacon. Cook in a hot oven or on a spit until browned. Make a bed of cored and sliced apples in the bottom of an earthenware casserole. Untruss the browned pheasant and put on top of the apples. Moisten with the juices from the roasting pan deglazed with calvados. Add the crème fraîche, lemon juice and some salt and pepper and cover. Mix some flour to a thick paste with a little water and use to seal the casserole. Bake in a hot oven for at least 1 hour.

Normandy cider or white wines from Sauternes.

US	Ingredients	Met/Imp
I	hen pheasant	I
	salt and pepper	
I	fatty bacon slice	I
½ cup	goose fat	100 g/4 oz
2 lb	white grapes, peeled and seeded	I kg/2 lb
I	shallot	I
I glass	Lirac red wine	I glass
I glass	armagnac	I glass
½ cup	crème fraîche	100 ml/4 fl oz
I	sugar cube	I
a few drops	lemon juice	a few drops
I	large slice fried bread	I

FAISAN AUX RAISINS

PHEASANT WITH GRAPES

Preparation 1¼ hours • Cooking 50 minutes

Pluck, draw and singe the pheasant. Season the inside lightly with salt and then bard with the bacon. Melt half of the goose fat in a flameproof casserole, brown the pheasant, then cover and cook for 40 minutes.

Meanwhile, cook the grapes with the remainder of the goose fat, the chopped shallot and half of the wine for 10 minutes.

Remove the pheasant from the pan when cooked, then deglaze the pan with the remainder of the wine and the armagnac. Cook until reduced. Add the crème fraîche and cook until reduced again.

Remove the grapes and strain their sauce into the pheasant cooking pan. Mix well and add the grapes, salt, pepper, sugar and lemon juice. Cut the pheasant into pieces, arrange on croûtons and pour over the sauce.

Red wines: Pommard, Chambertin, Madiran.

US	Ingredients	Met/Imp
2	pheasants	2
2	bacon slices	2
2	carrots	2
I	onion	I
2	shallots	2
a little	butter	a little
I	bouquet garni	
2 cups	white wine	500 ml/18 fl oz
1¼ cups	Demi-Glaze (page 56)	300 ml/½ pint
5 oz	mushrooms, cooked	150 g/5 oz
5 oz	truffles	150 g/5 oz
scant ½ cup	cognac	100 ml/3½ fl oz
	mushroom trimmings	
	salt and pepper	
2	game livers	2
2 oz	fatty bacon	50 g/2 oz
8	medium croûtons, fried in butter	8

SALMIS DE FAISANS

SALMI OF PHEASANT

Preparation 1 hour • Cooking 25 minutes

Draw and truss the pheasants. Bard with the bacon slices, then roast in a hot oven until only about three-quarters cooked. Dice the carrots, onion, shallots and parsley and brown in the butter together with the thyme and a bay leaf. When golden brown, add the white wine and continue cooking until the mixture is reduced by two-thirds. Add the demi glaze and simmer.

Cut up the pheasants, remove the skin from the pieces and place the meat in a sauté pan with the vegetable *mirepoix*, mushrooms and thinly sliced truffles. Flambé in cognac, then remove the pheasant pieces from the pan, cover with a piece of buttered paper and keep warm. Add to the sauce the pounded pheasant skins and carcasses, the mushroom trimmings and some pepper. Cook slowly for 15 minutes.

Season the sliced livers with salt and pepper and fry with the finely chopped bacon. Add a little thyme and a bay leaf and fry until firm. Put through a sieve to form a purée and spread this on the fried bread croûtons. Work the sauce through a fine conical sieve, pressing down well; skim gently and sieve again.

Pour the sauce over the pieces of pheasant, then return to the heat for 7–8 minutes, but do not boil. Remove from the heat and add some butter. Arrange on a heated dish and surround with the croûtons.

Red wines: Côte de Nuits, Côte Rôtie, Châteauneuf-du-Pape, Pomerol, Corsican red wines.

GRIVE

THRUSH

THE THRUSH IS NOT A GAME BIRD IN THE TRUE SENSE OF THE word. In France it is shot at the time of the wine harvest in September and October, when it is as plump as you could wish for. It feeds on sorb-apples and grapes, and consequently the flesh is very tasty. The most common garnish for thrush is juniper berries.

GRIVES 'CUR. 1er' AU BEURRE D'ANCHOIS

THRUSHES 'CURNONSKY I' WITH ANCHOVY BUTTER

Preparation 30 minutes • Cooking 8 minutes

Recipe dedicated to Curnonsky by the chef Mennessier

US	Ingredients	Met/Imp
16	juniper berries	16
16	thrushes	16
16	small bacon slices, for barding	16
8	rectangular bread canapés (2 thrushes on each)	8
4 oz	canned anchovy fillets	100 g/4 oz
2½ sticks	butter	300 g/10 oz
6	poultry livers, preferably from duck or guinea fowl	6
1 bottle	marsala	1 bottle
1 pinch	nutmeg	1 pinch
	salt and pepper	
	Gratin Stuffing (page 54)	
⅔ cup	cognac	150 ml/¼ pint
3	oranges	3

Place a juniper berry inside each thrush, bard the birds with the bacon, then roast in a hot oven. Brown the bread canapés over charcoal.

Wash and pat dry the anchovy fillets, then pound together with 250 g/8 oz (2 sticks) of the butter. Work through a fine sieve to make a smooth paste.

Poach the poultry livers in marsala, together with nutmeg, salt and plenty of pepper. Use to make the gratin stuffing instead of the chicken livers. Deglaze the pan in which the livers were cooked with two-thirds of the cognac and the cooking juices from the livers. Cook until reduced, then strain through a cloth and add the remaining butter.

Spread the canapés generously with anchovy butter, then add a 5 mm/¼ inch layer of gratin stuffing. Place thin slices of orange on each one, then 2 roast thrushes on top.

Mix together the cooking juices from the thrushes with the reduced cooking liquid from the livers. Moisten with the remaining cognac. Serve very hot.

Red wines: Côte de Nuits, Côte Rôtie, Châteauneuf-du-Pape, Saint-Émilion, Pomerol, Corsican red wines.

US	Ingredients	Met/Imp
16	thrushes	16
1 stick	butter	100 g/4 oz
	salt and pepper	
30–35	juniper berries	30–35
16	small bread croûtons fried in butter	16
¼ cup	gin	100 ml/4 fl oz

GRIVES À LA LIÉGOISE

THRUSHES WITH GIN AND JUNIPER BERRIES

Preparation 1 hour • Cooking 6–7 minutes

Clean the thrushes, removing the gizzards. Remove the hard parts of the beak and the eyes. Next, fold the legs underneath the body and join the feet together one over the other. Insert the head into the opening in the stomach, beak first.

Put the butter in a large flameproof casserole with a lid. Add the thrushes and salt and pepper and begin cooking over high heat. Sprinkle with juniper berries and continue cooking for 6–7 minutes or until the thrushes are browned and tender. Remove from the heat and place a fried croûton under each thrush. Return to the heat, add the gin and cover immediately. This will ensure that the birds become impregnated with the butter and the vapours from the gin while still cooking. Serve immediately.

Dry white wines: Côtes de Provence, dry Vouvray, Saumur, Muscadet, Chablis, Coteaux Champenois.
Red wine: light, fruity bordeaux.

US	Ingredients	Met/Imp
16	thrushes	16
16	vine (grape) leaves	16
16	bacon slices	16
14 tbsp	butter	200 g/7 oz
60	grapes	60
4 tsp	cognac	20 ml/4 tsp
¼ cup	Brown Stock (page 56)	60 ml/4 tbsp
⅔ cup	Gratin Stuffing (page 54)	150 g/5 oz
	fried bread canapés	

GRIVES AUX RAISINS SUR CANAPÉ

THRUSHES ON CANAPÉS WITH GRAPES

Preparation 1 hour • Cooking 15 minutes

Singe the thrushes, then truss them and wrap each one in a vine (grape) leaf and a slice of bacon.

Heat the butter in a flameproof casserole and, when very hot, add the thrushes. Bake in a hot oven for 8 minutes.

Remove the thrushes from the casserole and untruss them, then return them to the casserole with the seeded and blanched grapes. Baste with the fat from the thrushes and place at the front of the oven without a lid. Cook for 5 minutes.

Remove the thrushes from the casserole and deglaze with cognac and brown stock. Spread the gratin stuffing on the canapés and arrange the birds on top on a heated serving platter. Surround with the grapes and serve at once.

Wines: light, fruity reds.

—————— THRUSH PIE 'FLEURIGNY' ——————

Preparation 3 hours • Marinating 4 hours • Cooking 40–50 minutes

US	Ingredients	Met/Imp
1¼ lb	Shortcrust Pastry (page 577) or Puff Pastry (page 579)	600 g/1¼ lb
8	thrushes	8
	salt and pepper	
1 pinch	dried thyme	1 pinch
1 pinch	ground bay	1 pinch
½ cup	cognac	100 ml/4 fl oz
1 tbsp	oil	15 ml/1 tbsp
½ lb	chicken livers	250 g/8 oz
	Gratin Stuffing (page 54)	
2	round and very thin slices fatty bacon	2
1	egg, beaten	1
	FINE FORCEMEAT	
½ lb	lean veal	250 g/8 oz
½ lb	pork fillet (tenderloin)	250 g/8 oz
½ lb	fatty bacon	250 g/8 oz
1 pinch	*quatre-épices*	1 pinch
2	egg whites	2
½ cup	Dry Duxelles (page 49)	100 ml/4 fl oz
6	juniper berries	6
	MADEIRA SAUCE	
½ cup	game stock	100 ml/4 fl oz
¼ cup	madeira	50 ml/2 fl oz
¼ cup	cognac	50 ml/2 fl oz

Prepare the shortcrust pastry or, better still, puff pastry, in advance.

Take some fresh plump thrushes, clean them well and make a slit in the back (having removed the feet); remove the gizzards. Put the intestines and livers to one side. Flatten the thrushes slightly, remove the bones as far as possible and lay the birds on a dish. Season with salt and pepper, then sprinkle with a pinch each of thyme and bay. Moisten with the cognac and oil and leave in a cool place to marinate for 4 hours, turning the birds from time to time.

Add the thrush intestines and the chicken livers to the gratin stuffing and pound together.

Make the fine forcemeat. Dice the veal, pork and fatty bacon and season with salt, pepper and spice. Pound together until very smooth. Add the egg whites, then work through a sieve. Mix in the duxelles and the ground juniper berries.

Drain the thrushes, reserving the marinade. Divide the gratin stuffing between them, placing a little inside each bird. Return the birds to their normal shape.

Add the cognac in which the birds have been marinated to the fine forcemeat.

Divide the pastry into 2 portions so that you have two-fifths in 1 piece and three-fifths in another. Roll out the smaller piece until it is about 22 cm/8½ inches in diameter and use it to line the bottom of a deep pie or baking dish with a rim. Place 1 round thin slice of bacon on top, leaving a 3 cm/1¼ inch border all round.

Spread half of the fine forcemeat on this slice of bacon, then arrange the thrushes on top. Cover them with the remaining forcemeat and then the remaining round of bacon.

Roll out the second piece of pastry to a slightly larger round than the first. Moisten the edges of the pie with water and place the second piece of pastry on top. Press together and raise the edges. Brush the top of the pie with beaten egg and decorate the edges with a fork. Make a slit in the centre to allow steam to escape. Bake in a moderate oven for 40–50 minutes.

Meanwhile, make the madeira sauce by combining the game stock, madeira and cognac. As soon as you take the pie out of the oven, pour the madeira sauce into the pie through the slit in the top. Slide the pie onto a heated serving dish.

Instead of raising the edges of the pie, you could improve the appearance by adding a strip of puff pastry all around the edge.

White wines: Meursault, Pouilly-sur-Loire.
Red wines: Saint-Émilion, Châteauneuf-du-Pape.

LIÈVRE

HARE

IN FRANCE, THE MALE (BUCK) HARE IS CALLED 'BOUQUIN' AND the female (doe) is called 'hase'. The best hares are hunted between September and January, in Beauce, Champagne, Normandy and Poitou, but also in Gascony and Périgord, the latter being the place of origin of the famous 'lièvre à la Royale' recipe. The way in which hare is cooked depends on its age: leverets from 2–4 months old, and weighing about 1.5 kg/3½ lb, are roasted; leverets called 'trois-quarts', which are from 6 to 12 months old and weighing 2.5–3 kg/5½–6½ lb, provide saddle for roasting and sautéeing; hares of 1 year or over called 'capucins', weighing 4–6 kg/9–13 lb are normally 'jugged'. 'Trois-quarts' are the most popular hares for cooking, but as a way of cooking older hares, daubes and terrines are equally to be recommended. Fillet, thigh and rump of hare provide choice dishes.

CIVET DE LIÈVRE

JUGGED HARE

Preparation 1 hour • Marinating at least 12 hours • Cooking about 1 hour

US	Ingredients	Met/Imp
I	hare	I
2½ cups	oil	600 ml/I pint
scant ½ cup	cognac	100 ml/3½ fl oz
	salt and pepper	
	usual flavourings (thyme and bay leaf)	
2 tbsp	lard	30 g/I oz
30	small onions	30
3 cups	mushrooms, thinly sliced	200 g/7 oz
½ lb	fresh belly (side) of pork, cut into large cubes	250 g/8 oz
¼ cup	grated or chopped bacon	60 g/2 oz
I tbsp	flour	10 g/⅓ oz
2 bottles	good red wine	2 bottles
I	garlic clove	I
I	bouquet garni	I
I	wild thyme sprig	I
	blood and liver of the hare	
a few	fried bread croûtons (optional)	a few

A good 'civet' requires good wine to the exclusion of all other liquids. If you have none, the best alternative is pure water. When making a civet, if you change saucepans or pass the sauce through a sieve, always rinse out the pan with a little wine and then add this to the sauce.

Cut the hare into pieces and leave to marinate in three-quarters of the oil, the cognac, salt and pepper for at least 12 hours.

Drain the hare pieces and pat dry with paper towels. Heat the lard and the remaining oil in a large flameproof casserole and brown the onions, mushrooms and belly (side) of pork. Remove from the pan and set aside. Add the grated or chopped bacon and the flour and brown lightly. Add the hare pieces and stir until they all become impregnated with the roux. Pour in enough red wine to cover the hare and add the garlic, bouquet garni and thyme. Cover and cook for about 45 minutes.

When the hare is three-quarters cooked, remove it from the pan and place on top of the onions, mushrooms and pork. Rinse out the pan, if need be, with a little red wine, then strain the sauce through a conical strainer. Bring to the boil again, adjust the seasoning, then thicken with the hare's blood and crushed liver. Return the hare pieces to the pan with the onions, mushrooms and pork and continue cooking for 15 minutes. Adjust the seasoning again, if necessary. Hare should be well cooked; it is better to cook it too much rather than too little. Garnish with fried bread croûtons, if liked.

Wines: as a general rule, serve the same wine as the one used for cooking.

JUGGED HARE 'AGENAISE' WITH PRUNES

Preparation 1 hour • Marinating 6–7 hours • Cooking 2 hours

Cut up the hare and leave to marinate for 6–7 hours in the red wine and cognac with the thyme, bay, parsley, garlic and chopped carrots, shallots and onions. Leave the prunes to soak in cold water at the same time.

Cut the belly (side) of pork into small pieces. Blanch the pieces in boiling water and drain them, then brown in the oil. Remove from the pan and replace with the small onions. Brown these, then remove them from the pan. Drain the hare reserving the marinade. Put the hare into the same pan and cook until browned. Add the flour and cook gently. Add the strained marinade, plus sufficient wine to cover the meat. Add salt and pepper and leave to cook slowly for about 2 hours.

Halfway through cooking, add the small onions, the pork, the mushrooms and the drained prunes.

When the hare is cooked, thin the blood with a few spoonfuls of the liquid from the civet and add the crème fraîche. Stir into the civet, together with the croûtons.

Red wines: Chinon, Bourgueil, Saumur-Champigny.

US	Ingredients	Met/Imp
1	young hare, including the blood	1
1 lb	prunes	500 g/1 lb
½ lb	fresh belly (side) of pork	250 g/8 oz
1 cup	oil	200 ml/7 fl oz
15	small onions	15
3 tbsp	flour	30 g/1 oz
1 bottle	good red wine	1 bottle
	salt and pepper	
7 oz	small *Paris* mushrooms	200 g/7 oz
3–4 tbsp	crème fraîche	45–60 ml/ 3–4 tbsp
	MARINADE	
1 bottle	good red wine	1 bottle
½ cup	cognac	100 ml/3½ fl oz
1	thyme sprig	1
1 pinch	ground bay	1 pinch
1 tbsp	chopped fresh parsley	15 ml/1 tbsp
1	garlic clove	1
	carrots	
	shallots	
	onions	

JUGGED HARE ARDENNAISE

Preparation 1 hour • Marinating 12 hours • Cooking about 2½ hours

Cut the hare into pieces, taking care to keep the blood and liver. Leave the pieces to marinate for at least 12 hours in flavourings (parsley, thyme, bay, chopped onions, chopped shallot, half a garlic clove, a few juniper berries, salt and peppercorns) and sufficient good red wine to cover.

Remove the pieces of meat from the marinade and drain them, reserving the marinade.

Heat the lard in a cast iron pan and add the chopped bacon. Cook until browned, then add the flour and cook until well coloured. Add the hare pieces and brown on a high heat, for about 20 minutes, stirring, until all the roux has been absorbed. Add the flavourings from the marinade, then the wine. Stir, cover the pan and cook over a low heat for about 2 hours.

About 15 minutes before serving, crush the hare's liver with a fork (first removing the gall bladder and sinews) and mix it with the blood. Add the crème fraîche, then stir into the civet, which should then be kept hot but not allowed to boil because of the crème fraîche. Serve in a warm dish.

Wines: as a general rule, serve the same wine as the one used for cooking.

US	Ingredients	Met/Imp
1	hare	1
	flavourings (see method)	
1 bottle	good full-bodied red wine	1 bottle
¼ cup	lard	50 g/2 oz
10 oz	lean smoked bacon	300 g/10 oz
3 tbsp	flour	30 g/1 oz
½ cup	crème fraîche	100 ml/4 fl oz

US	Ingredients	Met/Imp
1	hare	1
scant ½ cup	wine vinegar	100 ml/4 fl oz
3¼ cups	olive oil	800 ml/1¼ pints
	salt and pepper	
1 bunch	thyme sprigs	1 bunch
2	large onions	2
2 slices	fatty bacon	25 g/scant 1 oz
6 tbsp	butter	70 g/3 oz
3 tbsp	flour	30 g/1 oz
1 cup	beef stock	250 ml/9 fl oz
1 cup	good-quality red wine	250 ml/9 fl oz

JUGGED HARE
'DIANE CHÂTEAUMORAND'

Preparation 1½ hours • Marinating at least 12 hours • Cooking 1½ hours

This civet may be made the day before it is to be eaten; it is better reheated. Its succulence depends on the quality of the hare and the quantity of blood collected; the civet should be the colour of good-quality melted chocolate.

Skin and draw the hare, reserving the blood and liver. Place the hare in a large bowl and pour over a glass of wine vinegar and half a glass of the olive oil. Add salt and pepper, the thyme and one onion, sliced into rings, and leave to marinate for at least 12 hours, turning frequently. Drain the hare, reserving the marinade.

Chop the remaining onion and the bacon and mix together. Cut the hare into pieces. Place the onion, bacon and hare pieces in a flameproof casserole together with the butter and all but 1 spoonful of the remaining olive oil. Cook over a low heat for 20 minutes or until the meat is greyish white and all the moisture has been given off. Sprinkle with the flour and simmer for 25 minutes, stirring frequently. Pour the beef stock and red wine into the dish, season with salt and pepper and cook for another 35 minutes.

About 10 minutes before cooking is complete, pound the hare's liver (first removing the gall bladder and sinews) to a fine purée and thin with the strained marinade. Stir in the blood, then work the mixture through a sieve. Add to the stew 5 minutes before serving and bring to the boil. Taste the sauce, and if it is too bland, season with a dash of vinegar according to Martial's maxim: 'The dish is tasteless without a touch of vinegar'. Finally, add a spoonful of olive oil.

Red wines: Côte de Nuits, Côte Rôtie, Châteauneuf-du-Pape, Saint-Émilion, Pomerol.

HARE CABESSAL

Preparation 2 hours • Marinating 12 hours • Cooking 4 hours

Take a young skinned, drawn hare [keep the blood to thicken the sauce, or failing that, use 50 ml/2 fl oz (¼ cup) pig's blood].

Fill the hare with a stuffing made by pounding together the following ingredients: the hare's liver (first removing the gall bladder and sinews), the foie gras, veal, ham, pork fillet (tenderloin) (all these should be chopped) and eggs. Sew the flesh together again, put the hare in a large bowl and leave to marinate for 12 hours in the red wine and oil with salt, pepper, spice, thyme, bay leaf, chopped carrots and onion and sliced shallots.

Remove the hare from the marinade and pat dry with paper towels. Reserve the marinade. Wrap the hare completely in the thin bacon slices, taking special care to cover the underneath well. Heat half of the goose or pork fat until very hot, then brown the hare on all sides, together with the small onions and the diced belly (side) of pork. Place the hare, tightly curled, inside a large saucepan and moisten with the armagnac. Add half of the reserved marinade. Cover and cook for 3 hours.

In a separate saucepan, melt the remaining goose fat and stir in the flour. Cook until browned, then remove from the heat and gradually stir in the remaining marinade. Add the bouquet garni, return to the boil and cook for at least 1 hour.

When the hare is three-quarters cooked, remove it from the pan. Mix the sauce made with the roux into the hare cooking juices and add the hare's blood. Bring to the boil and add the wine vinegar. Adjust the thickness and the seasoning, then put through a fine sieve. Remove the hare's head, then remove the bacon slices and the threads holding the stuffing in. Put the hare back in the pan and pour over the sauce. Add the truffles, sliced into rings, and continue cooking.

In the last stages of cooking, make sure that there is sufficient sauce, but not too much. Add some fried bread croûtons.

Red wines: Côte de Nuits, Côte Rôtie, Châteauneuf-du-Pape, Saint-Émilion, Pomerol.

US	Ingredients	Met/Imp
1	young hare	1
5 oz	foie gras	150 g/5 oz
½ lb	lean boneless veal	250 g/8 oz
½ lb	raw ham	250 g/8 oz
½ lb	pork fillet (tenderloin)	250 g/8 oz
2	eggs	2
2 bottles	red wine	2 bottles
½ cup	oil	100 ml/4 fl oz
	salt and pepper	
1 pinch	quatre-épices	1 pinch
2	thyme sprigs	2
½	bay leaf	½
2	carrots	2
1	large onion	1
2	shallots	2
	thin bacon slices, for barding	
½ cup	goose or pork fat	100 ml/4 fl oz
20	small onions	20
7 oz	fresh fat belly (side) of pork, diced	200 g/7 oz
½ cup	armagnac	100 ml/4 fl oz
3 tbsp	flour	30 g/1 oz
1	bouquet garni	1
1 glass	wine vinegar	1 glass
10 oz	truffles	300 g/10 oz
a few	fried bread croûtons	a few

US	Ingredients	Met/Imp
I	young hare	I
I	lemon, juice of	I
½ cup	oil	100 ml/4 fl oz
	salt	
a few	peppercorns	a few
a few	thyme sprigs	a few
I	bay leaf	I
½ lb	fresh belly (side) of pork	250 g/8 oz
I stick	butter	100 g/4 oz
I lb	button mushrooms	500 g/I lb
2 bottles	red wine	2 bottles

——— HARE CHASSEUR ———

Preparation 40 minutes • Marinating overnight • Cooking 2–2½ hours

Marinate a hare or, better still, a leveret, for the appropriate length of time using lemon juice, oil, salt, peppercorns, thyme and bay.

Cut the belly (side) of pork into small pieces and brown in the butter in a large saucepan. Remove from the pan. Drain the hare, reserving the marinade, and brown in the same pan. Return the pork to the pan together with the mushrooms. Add the red wine and the strained marinade, cover and cook for 2–2½ hours or until tender. Skim the sauce and serve.

Red wines: Côte de Nuits, Côte Rôtie, Châteauneuf-du-Pape, Saint-Émilion, Pomerol.

— HARE ROYALE 'RAYMOND OLIVER' —

Marinating livers 8 days • Preparation 2 hours (to be prepared 18 hours in advance) • Cooking hare 1½ hours • Serves 6–8

US	Ingredients	Met/Imp
I or 2	large or small fresh foie gras	I or 2
a little	cognac	a little
½ bottle	port wine	150 g/5 oz
	quatre-épices	
	cayenne	
I, about 7 lb	hare	I, about 3.2 kg/7 lb
a little	vinegar	a little
	red wine	
	salt and pepper	
	nutmeg	
a few	thyme leaves	a few
	game bones	
2	carrots	2
2	onions	2
I	celery heart	I
	bacon fat	
	butter	
3 bottles	Pomerol wine	3 bottles
I bottle	Sauternes wine	I bottle
I	ham knuckle (hock)	I
2 half	chicken breasts	2
5 oz	air-dried ham, half fat and half lean	150 g/5 oz
5 oz	pork fillet (tenderloin)	150 g/5 oz
	goose fat	
3	cloves	3
	bacon slices or good-quality ham fat, for barding	
10 oz	fresh truffles	300 g/10 oz
I glass	madeira	I glass
a little	brandy	a little
7 oz	cooked foie gras	200 g/7 oz
I cup	crème fraîche	200 ml/7 fl oz
	fried bread croûtons	

Place the fresh foie gras in an earthenware pot with the cognac, port, spice and cayenne. Leave to marinate for 8 days, turning and basting every day. Do not remove the sinew first, or soak in salt water.

Skin and draw the hare, reserving the lungs, liver (first removing the gall bladder and sinews), heart and blood. Put the blood in a bowl with a little vinegar and set aside. Rinse the inside of the hare with red wine, then remove the head, tail and ends of the feet. Bone the hare with a thin knife so that the hare remains whole. First, carefully loosen the bones of the feet, then the rib cage, the shoulders, the spinal column and, finally, the whole carcass. Avoid piercing the skin and leave a little meat on the bones. Reserve the bones. Lay the hare out flat on its back on a board. If the skin has been pierced, stop up the holes with small pieces of meat. Season the hare with salt, pepper, nutmeg, a few leaves of thyme and a little cognac. Roll it up and leave it in a cool place for 12–18 hours.

Prepare a Pepper Sauce according to the instructions on page 76, using the bones of the hare, some game bones and the carrots, 1 onion and the celery heart browned gently in bacon fat and butter. Add 3 bottles of Pomerol and 1 bottle of Sauternes and the ham knuckle (hock) and cook for several hours, without seasoning.

Make the stuffing. Mince (grind) together very finely the skinned and boned chicken breasts, the air-dried ham and the pork fillet (tenderloin). Add salt and cayenne and just enough of the foie gras marinade to give the stuffing an oily texture. Place in an earthenware pot, cover and keep in a cool place.

On the day of the meal, melt a small amount of goose fat in a flameproof casserole. Add the remaining onion spiked with cloves and fry until browned, turning frequently. Add the foie gras and marinade, season with salt, cover and bake in a hot oven for 7–8 minutes or until the livers have expelled their surplus fat. Remove the pan from the oven, leave it

to cool, then skim the fat from the cooking juices as it begins to congeal.

Rinse out a fairly large linen cloth and spread it out on a board. Place a layer of bacon slices (or better still, ham fat that is not too moist) the same size as the hare in the centre and lay the hare on top. Place a few fresh, scrubbed truffles and the foie gras in the centre and cover with stuffing. Fold the cloth around the hare so that it forms a small parcel and tie the ends.

Put the hare in a saucepan and cover with the pepper sauce (having first removed the ham and the bones). If the sauce does not cover it adequately, add a sufficient quantity of very good quality consommé. Bring to the boil, then simmer for 1½ hours or until the hare is cooked. Drain the hare and leave it to cool, then unfold and remove the cloth. Rinse the cloth in warm water, spread it out again, place the hare on it and fold up in the same way as before. Place on a dish and cover with a board the same length as the hare. Place a 250 g/8 oz weight on top and leave to cool for 1–2 hours or until it is time to eat.

Strain the pepper sauce through a sieve, then through a conical strainer. Return the sauce to the saucepan and simmer until reduced. Adjust the seasoning if necessary. Thicken by adding the blood of the hare and the finely chopped liver and heart. Strain the sauce through a conical strainer once again, then through cheesecloth. Keep warm until ready to serve.

Just before serving, take the hare out of the cloth and heat it gently in the madeira and brandy.

Meanwhile, put the cooked foie gras through a sieve, add an equal quantity of crème fraîche and mix well. Pour into the boiling pepper sauce. Keep warm.

When the hare is warmed through, remove the bacon slices and place it in a deep gratin dish. Skim the fat from the juices in which the hare has just been heated, strain the juices and add to the sauce. Bring to the boil, stirring all the time, and then pour over the galantine.

Surround the dish with croûtons fried in fat from the goose livers. Serve, garnished with whole cooked chestnuts, braised celery, ceps, Soufflé Potatoes (*page 553*), or apples browned in goose fat. This dish may be presented on a bed of glowing embers (special containers are available). Cut the hare into fairly thick slices, using a knife with a thin, rigid blade. Serve 1 slice per person and cover thickly with sauce.

Fine red wines: Romanée-Conti, Richebourg, Corton, aged Cahors, Pomerol.

US	Ingredients	Met/Imp
2 oz	pork fat	50 g/2 oz
¼ lb	fresh fat belly (side) of pork, diced	100 g/4 oz
2	onions	2
1	garlic clove	1
1	bouquet garni	1
1	hare (head, liver, heart, scraps and blood reserved), larded, barded and roasted	1
scant ½ cup	red wine vinegar	100 ml/3½ fl oz
1 tbsp	flour	15 ml/1 tbsp
2 cups	good red wine	500 ml/18 fl oz
	salt and pepper	
1 pinch	cayenne	1 pinch
¼ cup	armagnac	50 ml/2 fl oz

HARE SAUPIQUET

Preparation 2 hours • Cooking 1¾ hours

Heat the pork fat in a saucepan and fry the diced belly (side) of pork, the sliced onions, the garlic and the bouquet garni with the head, liver, heart and scraps reserved from the hare. Cook until brown, then add the vinegar and cook until reduced. Stir in the flour, add the red wine, salt, pepper and cayenne and cook for at least 1 hour. Work the mixture through a sieve, then add the blood and cooking juices from the hare, which has been roasted separately. Flambé with the armagnac, then season well. Cut the hare into pieces and coat with the sauce.

Wines: Médoc, Pomerol, Côte de Nuits, Châteauneuf-du-Pape.

US	Ingredients	Met/Imp
1	saddle hare, plus 2 thighs, larded	1
1 cup	red wine vinegar	250 ml/8 fl oz
	herbs and seasonings, to taste	
¼ lb	fatty bacon slices	100 g/4 oz
	salt and pepper	
1 stick	butter	100 g/4 oz
⅔ cup	double (heavy) cream	150 ml/¼ pint
1 tbsp	flour	15 ml/1 tbsp
1	large pickled beetroot (beet)	1

RÂBLE DE LIÈVRE À LA BETTERAVE

SADDLE OF HARE WITH BEETROOT*

Preparation 1¼ hours • Marinating 2–3 days • Cooking 50 minutes

Marinate the hare, which has been previously larded, in the vinegar with herbs and seasonings to taste for 2–3 days, turning occasionally. When ready for cooking drain the hare, reserving the marinade, and wipe dry with paper towels. Bard with the bacon slices and place in an ovenproof earthenware dish. Add salt and pepper and three-quarters of the butter, then cook in a very hot oven for about 40 minutes, basting alternately with some of the cream and a little of the marinade. When cooking is complete, thicken the remaining cream with the flour and stir into the sauce. While the meat is cooking, take some finely chopped beetroot (beet) and fry it lightly in the remaining butter. Sprinkle with salt.

Slice the hare, garnish with a crown of beetroot (beet) and coat with some sauce. Serve the rest in a sauce boat.

Red wines: Alsace Pinot Noir, Arbois, Beaujolais-Villages.

US	Ingredients	Met/Imp
2	saddles hare	2
7 oz	unsmoked fatty bacon, cut into thin strips	200 g/7 oz
1 quart	Uncooked or Cooked Marinade (page 59)	1 litre/1¾ pints
½ cup	oil	100 ml/3½ fl oz
2	shallots	2
a little	garlic	a little
½ cup	cognac	100 ml/3½ fl oz
1 cup	cream	200 ml/7 fl oz
	fried bread croûtons	

RÂBLE DE LIÈVRE À LA CRÈME

SADDLE OF HARE WITH CREAM

Preparation 1 hour • Marinating 24–48 hours • Cooking 15 minutes

Lard the saddles of hare generously with strips of bacon, place in a large dish and cover with marinade. Leave to marinate (24 hours for cooked marinade; 48 hours for uncooked marinade).

Place the hare in the oven in very hot oil and sear, then continue cooking at a moderate heat, leaving the meat rare. Remove from the dish, then pour off the cooking fat. Put the shallots, garlic and cognac into the same pan and reduce by half. Add the cream, reduce further and taste. Serve the hare with 8 large croûtons, fried in oil.

Red wines: Cahors, Corbières, Fitou, Costières du Gard.

— SADDLE OF HARE TOURANGELLE —

Preparation 1 hour • Marinating 30 hours • Cooking 25 minutes

US	Ingredients	Met/Imp
2	saddles hare, trimmed and *larded*	2
I bottle	aged Chinon	I bottle
¼ cup	olive oil	50 ml/2 fl oz
¼ cup	wine vinegar	50 ml/2 fl oz
	usual herbs and seasoning	
½ cup	Dijon mustard	100 ml/4 fl oz
I lb	fine pig's caul	500 g/I lb

Marinate the saddles of hare for 30 hours in the Chinon, oil, vinegar, tarragon, thyme and other usual seasonings. Drain and pat dry with paper towels. Reserve the marinade.

Coat the hare pieces in a thin layer of Dijon mustard; wrap in fine caul and place in the oven, preferably in an earthenware pot. As they are cooking, baste the pieces frequently with the marinade (which should reduce by two-thirds), until cooking is complete. Season well with pepper. Surround the hare with the vegetables from the marinade and serve in the dish.

Red wines: Chinon, Bourgueil, Saumur-Champigny.

TERRINE DE LIÈVRE

—————— TERRINE OF HARE ——————

Preparation 2 hours • Marinating 24 hours • Cooking 1½ hours

US	Ingredients	Met/Imp
I	medium hare	I
	salt	
	peppercorns	
	quatre-épices	
2	thyme sprigs	2
½	bay leaf	½
½ cup	cognac	100 ml/4 fl oz
½ lb	finely chopped pork	250 g/8 oz
¾ lb	fatty bacon	350 g/12 oz
2	eggs	2
I	carrot	I
2	shallots	2
I	bouquet garni	I
½ bottle	red wine	½ bottle

Begin by boning the hare. Separate the fillets and the best parts of the thighs, remove all of the sinews from the meat, then cut into thin strips. Season with salt, peppercorns, spice, thyme and bay, then place in an earthenware pot and marinate in the cognac for 24 hours. Reserve the remaining meat and the bones.

Meanwhile, prepare the following forcemeat: take the 250 g/8 oz finely chopped pork, 250 g/8 oz of the fatty bacon, the reserved meat from the hare, 15 g/½ oz (1 tbsp) salt, a pinch of spice and the eggs. Finely chop or mince (grind) all the meats separately, then mix everything together and work through a fine sieve.

While the meat is marinating, make a small amount of very thick stock using the bones, trimmings and scraps from the hare, the sliced carrot and shallots, the bouquet garni and red wine. When cooked, you should have 100–200 ml/3½–7 fl oz (½–1 cup) very good stock. Leave to cool, then mix into the stuffing with the marinade from the hare.

Cut the remaining fatty bacon into very thin strips and use to line the bottom and sides of a large earthenware ovenproof terrine. Place a layer of forcemeat about 1 cm/½ inch deep in the bottom, cover with some well-drained strips of marinated hare, each one wrapped in a slice of bacon. Continue to fill the pot in this manner, alternating layers of hare strips and layers of stuffing and finishing with a layer of stuffing covered with a large slice of bacon.

Put the lid on the terrine and place in a large shallow dish containing warm water. Cook in a warm oven for about 1½–2 hours or until pale in colour. The cooking time for a terrine depends on the size of the pot and the nature of the ingredients used. If the terrine is not to be eaten at once, some aspic jelly may be added. In this case, place a 200 g/7 oz weight on top. When the terrine is cool, remove the fat and trim the top. Slice the terrine into serving portions and serve in the pot, or on a plate with the aspic jelly arranged all around.

Red wines: Côte de Nuits, Côte Rôtie, Saint-Émilion, Pomerol.

ORTOLAN

ORTOLAN OR BUNTING

THIS 'MOST DISTINGUISHED ROAST' AS IT WAS CALLED BY Grimod de la Reynière, is considered a great delicacy. A small bird, it is usually baked, or roasted on a spit, and cooked in nothing but its own fat. However, recipes for lark or thrush also suit it very well. Nowadays, it has become very rare, and is an officially protected species. However, a tolerant attitude exists in the Landes region, where it is still captured live and fattened. It is a luxury dish and a speciality (which is forbidden to be served in restaurants).

US	Ingredients	Met/Imp
24	ortolans	24
	salt and pepper	
24	bread slices from soft-textured loaf	24
	goose fat ·	
	Roquefort cheese	

ORTOLANS AU ROQUEFORT

—— ORTOLANS WITH ROQUEFORT ——

Preparation 45 minutes • Cooking 30 minutes

Season the ortolans with salt and pepper and place each one in a fluted paper bun (cup cake) case. Put these paper cases on a sheet of oiled paper and place in the oven on a baking sheet. Cook the birds for about 25 minutes or until their melted fat sizzles. Fry the bread slices in the goose fat and spread with Roquefort.

Pour the fat from the paper cases over the fried bread and serve with the birds.

Red wines: Médoc, Graves.

US	Ingredients	Met/Imp
24	ortolans	24
	salt	
4 tbsp	butter	50 g/2 oz
8	rectangular bread croûtons	8

ORTOLANS RÔTIS

—————— ROAST ORTOLANS ——————

Preparation 30 minutes • Cooking 4–5 minutes

Slit open the neck of each bird and remove the gizzard, then twist the neck and fix the beak into the skin of the stomach. Thread the birds on to skewers and sprinkle with salt. Roast in a moderately hot oven for 5 minutes, basting with a very small amount of lightly salted butter, or better still, the birds' own fat. Add the butter to the fat in the roasting pan and fry the bread slices in it.

Deglaze the roasting pan to make a sauce, which should be sieved, skimmed and served separately.

Red wines: Madiran, Graves, Médoc.

Spit-Roasted Quails Wrapped in Vine Leaves
Allow about 12 minutes to spit-roast these plump quails, drawn and flambéed, over a hot fire. They can be garnished with cress and lemon quarters. (Recipe on page 459.)